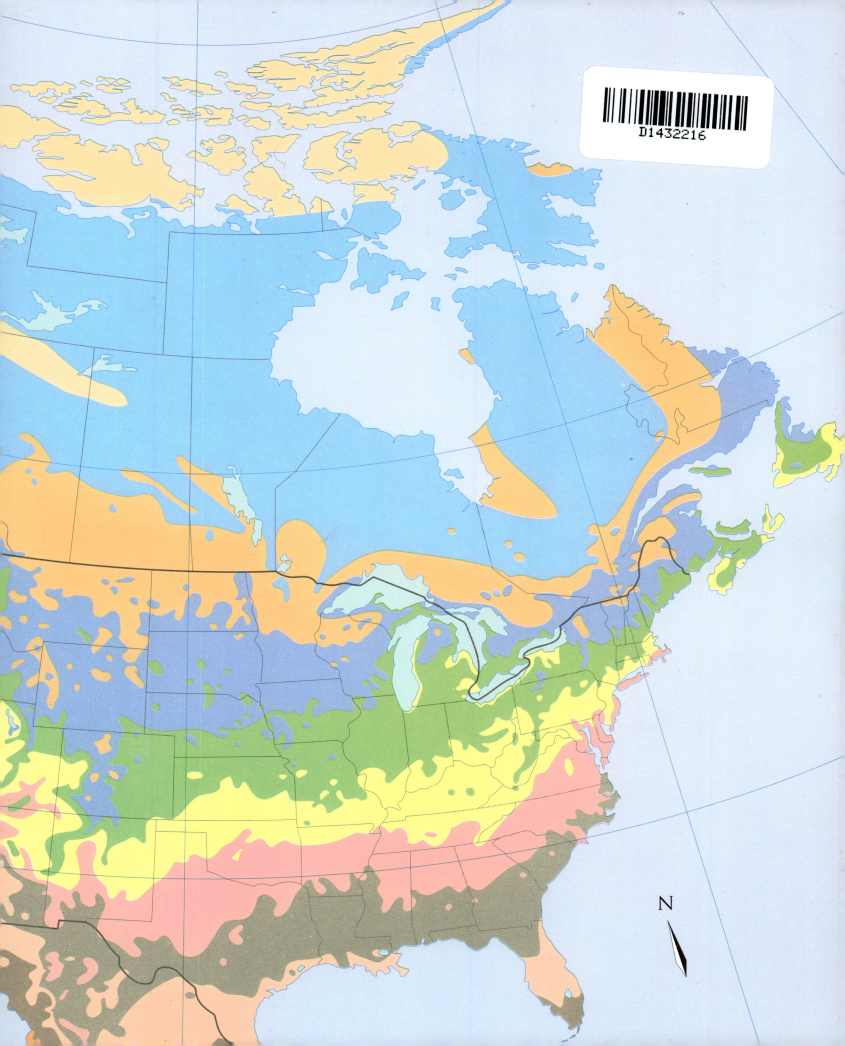

N

AMERICAN HORTICULTURAL SOCIETY

ENCYCLOPEDIA OF
PERENNIALS

AMERICAN
HORTICULTURAL
SOCIETY

AMERICAN HORTICULTURAL SOCIETY

ENCYCLOPEDIA OF
PERENNIALS

GRAHAM RICE
EDITOR-IN-CHIEF

KURT BLUEMEL, CONTRIBUTING EDITOR

LONDON, NEW YORK, MUNICH, MELBOURNE, DELHI

IMPORTANT NOTICE
This encyclopedia follows Royal Horticultural Society guidelines on potentially hazardous plants, although the properties of many garden plants have not yet been fully evaluated. Where a plant is known to have potentially harmful properties, a warning has been included in the appropriate alphabetical entry. However, any plant substance has the potential to cause an allergic reaction in some people, so caution should be exercised.

SENIOR PROJECT EDITOR Pippa Rubinstein
SENIOR ART EDITORS Joanne Doran, Sue Metcalfe-Megginson
US SENIOR EDITOR Jill Hamilton

EDITORS Louise Abbott, Helen Fewster, Caroline Reed, Diana Vowles, Kim Dennis-Bryan (proofreading), Katie Dock, Christine Heilman, Jane Perlmutter, Jenny Siklós, Jennifer Williams

DEVELOPMENT Pamela Brown, Ursula Dawson

DESIGNERS Alison Shackleton, Sue Storey, Elly King, Rachael Smith, Murdo Culver, Rebecca Johns

DTP Louise Waller, Pete Quinlan
DTP (DK DELHI) Ashwani Tyagi, Pankaj Sharma

PEARSON PICTURE LIBRARY Lucy Claxton, Richard Dabb

PHOTOGRAPHERS Peter Anderson, Claire Austin, Martin Page, Roger Smith

PICTURE RESEARCH Celia Dearing, Mel Watson, Liz Boyd

SENIOR JACKET DESIGNER Nicola Powling
JACKET EDITOR Anna Stewart

PRODUCTION Luca Frassinetti

MANAGING EDITOR Anna Kruger
MANAGING ART EDITOR Alison Donovan

First American Edition, 2006
06 07 08 09 10 9 8 7 6 5 4 3 2 1

Copyright © 2006 Dorling Kindersley, London

Published in the United States by DK Publishing, Inc.
375 Hudson Street, New York, New York 10014

DK books are available at special discounts for bulk purchases for sales promotions, premiums, fund-raising, or education use. For details, contact: DK Publishing Special Markets, 375 Hudson Street, New York, NY 10014 or SpecialSales@dk.com
A Cataloging-in-Publication record for this book is available from the Library of Congress.
ISBN-10: 0-7566-1343-4
ISBN-13: 9780756613433

Color reproduction by Colourscan, Singapore
Printed and bound in China by Toppan Printing Co.

Discover more at
www.dk.com

PAGE 1 *Kniphofia* 'Wrexham Buttercup' and *Agapanthus* 'Midnight Blue' PAGE 2 *Sanguisorba menziesii, Nepeta clarkei,* and *Astrantia major* 'Roma' PAGE 3 *Eryngium variifolium* PAGE 4–5 *Foeniculum vulgare,* hostas, and *Tellima grandiflora* PAGE 6–7 *Kniphofia rooperi* and *Cornus alba* 'Aurea'

CONTENTS

CONTRIBUTORS

DR. DENISE ADAMS
JAMES ARMITAGE
DAVID G. BARKER
PETER BARNES
DAVID BASSETT
KENNETH A. BECKETT
MASHA BENNETT
RICHARD BIRD
KURT BLUEMEL
C. COLSTON BURRELL
FREDERICK W. CASE, JR
PHILIP CLAYTON
TREVOR COLE
DR. JAMES COMPTON
IAN COOKE
DR. JANET J. CUBEY
DR. LAURA DEETER
DAVID ELLIS
MIKE L. GRANT
DR. CHRISTOPHER GREY-WILSON
MIKE HARDMAN
SARAH HIGGENS
DANIEL J. HINKLEY
DR. TIM INGRAM
ROD LEEDS
TONY LORD
MARGARET E. MCKENDRICK
TOVAH MARTIN
HENRY NOBLETT
DR. CHARLES G. OLIVER
DR. MARTIN PAGE
JOHN P. PEAT
TED L. PETIT
PAUL PICTON
GRAHAM RICE
PROF. JOHN RICHARDS
MARTIN RICKARD
GEOFF STEBBINGS
DR. STEVEN STILL
JOHN SUTTON
SIMON THORNTON-WOOD
MARY THORP
ALAN TOOGOOD
DR. JAMES W. WADDICK
TIMOTHY WALKER
JUDY WHITE
DR. CHRISTOPHER WHITEHOUSE
MARK R. ZILIS

RIGHT *This impressive summer planting features plants with noticeably contrasting habits of growth and coloring yet it hangs together as a satisfying whole.*

FOREWORD

Welcome to another milestone in garden reference publishing, this time focusing on perennials—the most popular single group of garden plants.

Featuring more than 5,000 different plants spread across almost 100 plant families, 450 genera, and 2,000 species, and accompanied by over 1,400 color pictures, this is the most comprehensive illustrated single volume on perennials ever published. It contains easy-to-follow descriptions of a vast range of old favorites, together with the latest new introductions from plant collectors and plant breeders around the world.

This book is more than just an illustrated A to Z of plant descriptions. Entries on many of the most popular plants feature suggestions for planting associations to encourage creative planting and to stimulate ideas for your own garden. Individual issues of special interest on a wide variety of topics are also highlighted: specific pest or disease problems, historical insights, identification confusions, propagation ideas, and other fascinating details add richness and depth to our coverage.

The "botanical" language is kept to a minimum as much as possible. Newcomers to growing perennials as well as avid enthusiasts without a botanical background will find the text easy to follow, while all readers, including more botanically minded enthusiasts and professionals, will discover all the information they need. This is a book designed to be as accessible as possible to gardeners—although the breadth of its detailed coverage will certainly appeal to horticulturists, too.

COMPREHENSIVE COVERAGE

The *AHS Encyclopedia of Perennials* covers only hardy perennial plants. There are no bulbs, no annuals or biennials, no seasonal flowers, no alpines except a few that are easily grown in "perennial" situations, no aquatic plants, and no shrubs or woody climbers. Instead, it concentrates on providing comprehensive coverage of hardy herbaceous perennial plants.

Included here are plants that are generally available, good or interesting plants that are not as easy to find but should be, new plants that I or my contributors expect to become popular, plants introduced long ago that deserve mention, and a few interesting but obscure plants that would continue to be unknown if they were omitted.

Special attention has been given to four groups. Gardeners have become increasingly fascinated by aroids—members of the arum family—which have a unique flower structure with its own special terminology (explained on *p. 74*). Ferns, too, are now more widely grown; they also have their own terminology and a method of reproduction unlike that of any other plants in this book (*see p. 197*). The enthusiasm for ornamental grasses is reflected in the breadth of their coverage throughout the book, while the potential of hardy orchids to be more widely grown is discussed on page 345.

A TRADITION OF EXCELLENCE

I have drawn on the expertise of over 40 contributors from both sides of the Atlantic, including leading authorities on individual plants who have grown them, studied them, and deduced from their experience what is most significant about each one. I have drawn on the expertise of the Royal Horticultural Society and the American Horticultural Society, for their authority on horticulture generally and horticultural plant names and plant hardiness in particular. Kurt Bluemel and his team have added their valuable North American expertise, and I have drawn on my own determination to combine in this book authority, clarity, and accessibility.

The *AHS Encyclopedia of Perennials* is a comprehensive volume that follows the long traditions of great books on perennials. *The English Flower Garden* by William Robinson (1883), *Hardy Herbaceous Perennials* by Leo Jelitto and Wilhelm Schacht (1955), *Hardy Perennials* by Alan Bloom (1957), *Border Plants* by Frances Perry (1957), *Perennial Garden Plants: Or the Modern Florilegium* by Graham Stuart Thomas (1976), and *Herbaceous Perennial Plants* by Allan Armitage (1989)—all made their mark in their day, bringing new knowledge and new wisdom to gardeners. I hope that this volume takes the tradition forward by providing contemporary enthusiasts for perennials with both knowledge and inspiration, and makes your own growing of perennials even more rewarding.

Graham Rice

Graham Rice
EDITOR-IN-CHIEF

RIGHT *Piet Oudolf's border at Pensthorpe in Norfolk looks both to natural meadow and prairie habitats as well as the flowing designs of Gertrude Jekyll.*

WHAT ARE PERENNIALS?

A simple question? Not so fast. A perennial is any plant that lives for more than two years and usually flowers every year; that seems simple enough. But this definition could be applied to a wide range of plants, including trees, succulents, and bulbs. In fact, gardeners appreciate perfectly well that woody plants such as trees and shrubs are usually excluded—this in spite of the fact that certain plants, like some salvias, may remain woody at the base, and some may become woody in mild climates and yet be cut to the ground in harsher regions. Climate has a dramatic influence; a plant that is perennial in its natural habitat may behave as an annual in an area with colder winters and hot summers.

BELOW *At Great Dixter in Sussex, England, Christopher Lloyd specialized in bringing vivid colors together in borders planned to bring a long succession of color and interest. Convention is turned upside down here by planting the tall* Verbena bonariensis *at the front and viewing the border through its open growth.*

ABOVE **1** *Most perennials are "herbaceous," like these peonies, which die back to the ground at the end of the season, then emerge again in spring.* **2** *Hellebores are evergreen and retain their leaves all winter, although they may become ratty and the plants often look better if the old leaves are removed.* **3** *A few plants, like this arum and some grasses, die back during the hottest summer months but retain their foliage all winter.*

IN AND OUT

Alpines are also excluded from our definition of perennial, although this can be hazy territory when an alpine proves sufficiently robust to be grown in different situations. Bulbs, too, are perennial, but gardeners, being commendably pragmatic in this respect, tend to separate them from perennials. Other plants with underground storage organs, like *Crocus* with their corms, are treated by gardeners as bulbs, but tubers occupy another hazy area… Arisaemas, for example, are usually classed as perennials, even though they grow from distinct tubers. Plants with fat rhizomes, like cannas or many irises, are also treated as perennials.

The phrase "herbaceous perennial" introduces a further anomaly. "Herbaceous" is a term used to describe a plant whose top-growth dies off completely in the fall and which sprouts anew from the base in spring. But many familiar perennials, like most hellebores, are determinedly evergreen, although it may be prudent to remove the foliage in the fall. And there are many other evergreen perennials that provide valuable foliage effect in winter.

So the plants in this book, and perennials generally, can conveniently be described as those that live for more than two years and have no, or perhaps a minimal amount of, woody growth above ground. Just to be clear, annuals pass through their life cycle in one season, biennials in two seasons. Plants that spend more than two years, even five or six years, building up their reserves before flowering are termed monocarpic (literally, "fruiting once"). These, in their way, are considered perennials, too.

WHY DO WE GROW PERENNIALS?

The obvious answer is for their beauty and variety. Every color is represented in the flowers, and every pairing of colors, often in intriguing patterns, and all in a tantalizing variety of flower shapes held in a wide range of flowering structures. Perennials provide impressive color from a distance and captivating detail at close quarters—and in every season of the year.

And there is more to their foliage than simply green leaves. Even within that single, most widespread color, in shape, size, texture, and even fragrance, the leaves of perennials present extraordinary opportunities. Add in the blues, the yellows, bronzes, reds, and even pinks, plus the increasing range of colorful variegations, and it becomes wonderfully clear that as foliage plants alone, the choice is extraordinary. The texture of foliage, the very touch of it, adds a whole new dimension, be it the fuzz of stachys, the spines of eryngiums, or the squeaky leatheriness of bergenias. And even plants grown primarily for their flowers, like meconopsis or verbascums, may surprise us with the appeal of their foliage rosettes.

Then there are fruits: berries in every color of the rainbow, often persisting through winter; fat pods, and seed heads of downy or silky fluffiness. It may also be the whole structure of the fruiting plant that appeals, rather than the fruits themselves.

Plant habit is becoming increasingly appreciated. From the tall and slender foxtail lilies (*Eremurus*) to absolutely prostrate lysimachia and, in between, upright kniphofias, foamy gypsophila, mounded geraniums, stately delphiniums, effervescent crambes, and climbing perennial sweet peas, form can be an architectural delight.

There are also unexpected and captivating details: the surprisingly red leaf stems of some hostas; the droplets of rain that collect on columbine leaves; the shining maroon shoots of emerging peonies; the intriguing swirl of an inula bud; the buttery fall leaf color of amsonia, and the delicate hairs on an alchemilla leaf.

MORE THAN MEETS THE EYE

Perennials enhance the garden in other ways: scent, for example. Fragrance seems to have the capacity to transform our mood and conjure up lost memories—and, of course, for gardeners whose eyesight is not what it was, fragrance becomes an even more significant feature. Scent is a characteristic of so many perennials, even though some scents may prove elusive to some gardeners. There are also plants for which the word "scent" is, perhaps, unrealistic; "stink" might be more appropriate, and these plants are generally better admired in other people's gardens.

Some perennials are underappreciated because their ornamental qualities are not the first to come to mind. Many culinary and medicinal herbs, for example, are available in impressive foliage forms, like the variegated mints, and although they may be considered primarily as herbs, they are also valuable ornamentals.

Even perennials sometimes considered primarily as weeds, like white dead-nettle, are worth their place—in the right situation where they can spread without causing problems and also attract wildlife. While unwelcome "wildlife" in the forms of aphids, slugs, and mildew may sometimes occupy our attention, the range of more colorful creatures that perennials attract is unexpectedly large. Bees, of course, but also butterflies, from the yellow brimstones of spring to the patterned tortoiseshells of fall, add color, unpredictability, and sheer charm to the garden; they feed on the nectar in the flowers of perennials, and their caterpillars may feed on the leaves—an imposition we can surely tolerate. Other welcome insect visitors include hoverflies and ladybugs, pretty in themselves and whose larvae eat so many aphids.

Birds, too, are welcome. Finches, and especially goldfinches, feed on the fall seed heads of thistles and other members of the

ABOVE *Many flowers attract insects like ladybugs or hoverflies, whose larvae eat pests, or less useful but far more attractive insects like butterflies.*

daisy family, and the fluffy down may also be used to line their nests; thrushes crack snails on convenient rocks, robins have a sharp eye for worms or, preferably, the dreaded vine weevil grubs as we divide our plants and work over the soil surface, while plants that provide nectar for hummingbirds are particularly sought out.

BELOW *Many plants originally grown mainly as herbs or for their aromatic foliage are now available in forms, like this* Agastache foeniculum *'Golden Jubilee', that are valuable purely as ornamentals.*

ADAPTABLE AND VERSATILE

While annuals and biennials are too fleeting for gardeners who prefer plants with more staying power, perennials reward for many years. Some, like peonies, can survive benign neglect for decades, although most are less long-lived without care and attention.

Most perennials are also relatively easy to grow. Witness the wide range thriving in gardens across the country that receive little special attention. Some require particular conditions—shade, free-draining soil—but few are so demanding as to be awkward in their requirements. Those that do present more of a challenge do so with the definite possibility of success.

Perennials are also, with a few exceptions, easy to propagate. At its simplest, you can dig up the plant in its dormant season, split it in two, and replant the pieces—giving you a 100 percent increase in your stock. Many will also spread by shedding seed that germinates nearby, or sometimes farther afield, and although the results can be overwhelming in numbers and disappointing in their unpredictable variation, for many garden perennials it certainly works.

Finally, perennials are so versatile. They look good as specimens or planted *en masse* with others of their kind. They integrate well with shrubs, bulbs, annuals, and biennials; they make such good garden escorts to a wide variety of plant types. As a tapestry of ground cover, scrambling through shrubs, or in close partnership with each other in formal or informal styles, perennials make an indispensable contribution. It is not surprising that they are consistently popular.

BELOW AND RIGHT *Throughout the year:* **1** *Oriental poppies bring an increasing range of brilliant and softer shades to the summer garden.* **2** *In the spring shade garden, bold emerging hosta foliage is surrounded by more delicate violas and epimediums.* **3** *The biscuit tones of grasses, like this miscanthus, bring a whole range of new shades as fall advances.* **4** *Postponing the fall cleanup allows the structure of phlomis to enhance the fall and winter garden, especially when touched by frost.*

THE ORIGINS OF GARDEN PERENNIALS

In every plant habitat on the planet are perennials that will settle amiably into our gardens if we give them the chance. For example, buttercups, goldenrods, and orchids color meadows and prairies; cool shaded woodlands are knitted with primroses, ferns, disporums, trilliums and more orchids into a companionable tapestry; and watersides are alive with irises, skunk cabbages and primulas. Sometimes these plants prove less specific in their needs when grown in gardens. Gravel beaches give us campion, eryngo, and sea kale, and from grazed grassland come pasque flowers, trefoil, cowslips, and, yes, more orchids. Many other habitats also provide us with perennial garden plants: grasses and sedges come from just about everywhere.

Even after centuries of botanical exploration—during which time plant-hunters, both well known and unheralded, brought us countless now-familiar garden plants from around the world, as well as in local fields and woods—discoveries are still being made, new plants are still arriving. But even before enthusiasts endured great hardships exploring for plants, they were being cherished closer to home.

FROM THE WILD TO THE GARDEN
The earliest gardeners noticed the plants around them. They noticed their beauty, discovered their virtues, and appreciated where they grew. In the transition from hunting and gathering into primitive agriculture and a more settled lifestyle, when they brought a comfrey plant nearer to home for convenience, these early gardeners learned to replant it in a situation similar to the one from which they had dug it up.

By an extension of exactly the same process, plants have been brought into our gardens from different parts of the world. As they explore for plants, plant hunters such as Jim Archibald, Chris Brickell, James Compton, Chris Grey-Wilson, Daniel Hinkley, Darrel Probst, and others notice species that are not grown in gardens, as well as forms of familiar species that have some unusual and distinctive feature. These dedicated people continue in the tradition of the great plant hunters, such as David Douglas and Frank Kingdon Ward, whose combination of dedication, knowledge, persistence, and a good eye have immeasurably enriched our gardens and our perennial plantings in particular. These observant horticulturists bring back not only the plants for gardeners to grow but also recommendations on how to grow them in situations that relate to their natural habitat.

There is, though, a danger. Gertrude Jekyll popularized the Japanese knotweed, now known as *Fallopia japonica*, as an imposing plant for borders, entirely unaware of the monster that was being set free in landscapes around the world as this highly invasive plant

ABOVE *Some perennials from warmer climates, like this ginger,* Zingiber zerumbet, *may need winter protection to allow them to give their best in more temperate gardens.*

established dominating monocultures, smothering native flora. Now, with an increasing number of such sad stories in mind, such as the invasiveness of purple loosestrife, *Lythrum salicaria*, in North America, horticulturists look at new introductions with the potential for this problem in mind.

RIGHT 1 *The humble yarrow, Achillea millefolium, is an attractive wild flower and lawn weed and it is the origin of a wide range of valuable garden plants in bright and pastel shades.* **2** *Occasionally, a plant like this blue campanula will produce a spontaneous mutation in a different color. If marked with a cane, the new form can be separated from its parent at the proper season and grown for further assessment.*

SELECTING THE BEST

Take a walk in the country, or even along a quiet road or in a country park, and look at the wildflowers. If you look carefully, you will often see that not all the individuals of one species are quite the same. Some primrose plants, for example, carry far more flowers than their neighbors; the variation in leaf patterns in lesser celandines can also be very surprising—and collectible. Plants showing especially gardenworthy variations (for example a dwarf habit, new color, or double flowers) have been collected from the wild for centuries to add to our garden flora. (Always ask the landowner's permission before you do any collecting yourself.)

In gardens and nurseries, where related plants are brought together and monitored, self-sown seedlings sometimes show a new combination of features. In such a situation they are more likely to be noticed, retained, evaluated, propagated, named, and distributed.

Some of these will be hybrids, but some new forms also arise as spontaneous mutations (often called "sports") of existing plants. Many variegated cultivars arise as spontaneous mutations, and it is surprising just how many occur in wild plants as well as in gardens. They also occur when plants are propagated in the laboratory, as so many now are, and a number of new hostas in particular have arisen in this way.

Finally, as perennials become more popular and thus more important in the economic life of nurseries, breeding programs are yielding more and more good plants. Best known for this approach was Alan Bloom at Bressingham in Norfolk, England, while more recently Dan Heims at Terra Nova Nurseries in Oregon has been working on a wide range of plants including heucheras and pulmonarias. Projects currently underway at nurseries around the world involve echinaceas, geraniums, hellebores, primulas, zantedeschias, and many more.

BELOW *Fields of familiar wild buttercups have occasionally yielded forms with double or pale-colored flowers that make good garden plants.*

PERENNIALS IN THE GARDEN

Perennials are extraordinarily rich in features that excite the artistic sensibility in gardeners. The vast range of form, color, and season in their flowers is immediately obvious, but there is also infinite variety in the greens and other colors of their foliage, along with an enticing range of leaf textures, from leathery to furry, and leaf shapes that range from broad, flat paddles to filamentous threads. In addition, growth habits vary from determinedly vertical to absolutely prostrate. These features not only make them supreme in their own individuality, but also allow the gardener to group them together in captivating plant pictures.

LEFT *The perhaps unexpected variety of coloring in the foliage of grasses and sedges has fostered their popularity and encouraged the planting of grass gardens.*

PLANTS ON DISPLAY

For centuries, plants were treated as individuals, rather than components of a more expansive visual picture. Whether brought into gardens as medicinal herbs

LEFT *At Adrian Bloom's garden at Foggy Bottom in Norfolk, England, perennials from Europe, Asia, Africa, and the Americas are brought together with conifers and other woody plants in a long season of color.*

or, later, added for their individual visual appeal or for their powerful fragrance (invaluable before basic ideas of hygiene were developed), they were planted with space between them, lined up like apothecaries' jars on a shelf. While a few historic gardens still demonstrate this formal approach, it is generally now only as plants for exhibition that perennials are still grown in this way—but the chrysanthemums or carnations planted formally in rows are intended to be admired, and judged, as cut blooms at a show and not in the garden. Those that grow them are the contemporary cultural descendants of the original "florists"—that is, gardeners who bred, grew, and exhibited choice flowers, not tradesmen who sold cut flowers in shops. Their highly structured craft was at its peak in the 19th century, when auriculas, carnations, chrysanthemums, dahlias, primroses, ranunculus, violas, and more were bred and

grown for their fascinating form, their singular symmetry, their captivating colors, and their exquisite patterning.

Enthusiasm for exhibiting is still alive and well in the world of perennials—especially in relation to chrysanthemums, primulas, and auriculas—and even thriving in the world of alpines. But the inclination to grow selected cultivars for the special beauty of their individual flowers has long been in decline, although there are signs of a revival—in hellebores, for example—and this can only be welcomed. And hostas are exhibited in North America and Japan as individual cut leaves; indeed, in Japan, what you might call the florists' movement has an independent life with its own exhibitions.

But on a less esoteric level, there are growing numbers of gardeners who fall under the spell of particular groups of perennials. Hardy geraniums, hostas, daylilies, grasses, irises, hellebores, and orchids all have their devotees, as well as smaller plants such as wood anemones, primroses, and heucheras, together with more disparate groups such as variegated or fall-flowering plants. Whether a collection is thoughtfully integrated into the garden as a whole or whether it is grown together in one area of the garden, the chance to appreciate, and study, a single group of plants can be very rewarding.

BELOW *Perennials are indispensable container plants, whether used as the only perennials in a tiny courtyard garden or for emphasis in a larger space. Here three very distinct hostas are gathered around the shiny deep green leaves of* Myosotidium hortensia.

BEDS AND BORDERS

It was in the cottage gardens that Gertrude Jekyll found inspiration in the 19th century, and in the grander gardens of those who employed the cottagers, that most modern styles of growing perennials originated. In cottage gardens, plants of all kinds—roses, fruit, and herbs as well as perennials—were planted more tightly together and intermingled. In the grander borders of country houses, the formal border featured perennials. Today, there is—or should be—nothing that is off the agenda. There is no single "right way" of planting perennials; gardeners grow them in the widest variety of ways. But the traditional herbaceous border is what often springs first to mind.

THE HERBACEOUS BORDER

What we now know as the traditional herbaceous border is one that features only hardy perennials. These dramatic plantings were historically grown in front of walls or hedges and were mostly at their peak in summer; the plants were, on the whole, organized with the tallest at the back and the shortest at the front; discrete clumps of three or five plants were grown adjoining

BELOW *A classic double herbaceous border in the traditional style at Arley Hall, Cheshire, England. Backed by a tall brick wall and divided by neatly clipped stepped hedges, perennials are the focus for the summer season, apart from the occasional climber on the wall.*

each other, inconspicuously supported, but rarely intermingled intimately. While Jekyll introduced a more flowing style into borders and a more highly attuned sense of color coordination, the space and labor required sent this style into decline in the 1950s. However, in the 1960s Alan Bloom's concept of the "island bed," featuring smaller, shorter perennials that did not require staking and

were planted in informally shaped beds cut out of the lawn, caused a noticeable revival.

CONTEMPORARY COTTAGE GARDENS

The other response to the decline of the formal herbaceous border was the modernizing of the cottage garden. The rural poor grew a medley of plants in a less formally organized way than those living

on large estates, or the more successful middle class. Apples, roses, delphiniums, marigolds, rosemary—plants of all kinds were grown in a rich profusion.

With increasing industrialization and a growth in more sophisticated tastes, the cottage garden also declined and changed. But in the 1950s it began to be reinvented by Margery Fish—who, paradoxically, was gardening at the relatively grand East Lambrook Manor in Somerset, England—as a style that largely focused on ornamentals, and on perennials in particular.

Her ideas were epitomized in two books, *A Flower for Every Day* and *An All Year Garden*, in which she expounds the belief that through the thoughtful integration of a wide range of plants, especially perennials, gardens can be attractive all year.

MIXED BORDERS

Taking a step up from the cottage garden, the mixed border, at its best, is an altogether more artful creation where, again, perennials feature strongly. The great borders created by Christopher Lloyd at Great Dixter, Sussex, England, and by Nori and Sandra Pope at Hadspen Garden, Somerset, England, for example, reveal the consistent level of inspired associations of color, form, and texture—not to mention sheer impact— that it is possible to create.

The other quality needed to create the best mixed borders is a sense of when to allow plants to spread and to self-sow and to intermingle, as many perennials do, and when to intervene to remove or restrict them. Sophisticated mixed borders reveal a greater sense of control and planning than do the less formal cottage gardens.

PUTTING PLANTS TOGETHER

But it does not require artistic—or indeed any other—training to create plantings of perennials in which the total is greater than the sum of the parts. It just needs an idea of what you like and the willingness to look and to learn, and for your tastes to develop. The multitude of ways in which perennials can be associated with each other and with other plants is limited only by your imagination. Perennials are often incredibly adaptable: not only are many surprisingly content with less than ideal conditions, but a choice of perennials is available for every

soil, every site, and every situation.

Throughout this book you will find included suggested planting associations that are illustrated and discussed. Use these as starting points for imaginative and effective plantings in your own garden—as the saying goes: Adopt, Adapt, and Improve. And Invent.

NATURALISTIC PLANTING STYLES

In recent years a new informality of planting has become popular as some gardeners turn away from plantings that are conspicuously horticultural and develop more naturalistic styles based on prairies and woodlands.

PRAIRIES AND MEADOWS

Meadow gardens, in which areas of grass are treated rather like hay meadows, mowed each summer and the cuttings removed, develop a rich native flora and are enhanced by the planting of carefully chosen garden perennials and bulbs. This annual cutting and removal of the debris reduces the vigor of forage and lawn grasses and encourages the spread of broad-leaved perennials, bulbs, and even orchids, creating a more interesting and varied balance. Meadows can work even in

very small areas. Prairie plantings are generally at their best in a more expansive setting, and feature the plants of the American prairies as well as perennials in a similar vein from Europe and elsewhere, often planted in broad and interlaced drifts that may need careful management to prevent a few species from taking over.

WILD AND NATIVE PLANT GARDENS

A reaction against highly bred bedding plants, and the non-native plants that are establishing themselves in our landscape, together with the belief that native plants are inherently more suitable than other plants in gardens in the areas in which they are native, has led some gardeners to give native plants more prominence or even to

grow them exclusively. The definition of a native plant varies according to whom you ask, but very effective enhanced natural habitats can be created in garden situations by choosing appropriate natives. Such plantings are enriched by the native wildlife that tends to be attracted to native plants.

WOODLAND GARDENS

Shade is often seen, especially by new gardeners, as a problem, whereas in truth some of the most exquisite perennials are shade-lovers; shade is an opportunity. And bringing together these typically spring jewels into moisture-retentive soil creates a tapestry of foliage and flowers, whose season can be extended year-round in mild climates through thoughtful planting. The first flowers of spring are especially captivating. Whether in suburbs or country gardens,

BELOW *Wild meadow gardens, mowed each summer like hay meadows, soon develop a rich natural flora that can be augmented by appropriate garden plants.*

areas under deciduous trees or shaded by neighboring buildings can be developed into delightful interminglings of the prettiest of flowers, with many new introductions from around the world.

The key to making any of these more naturalistic approaches work well is not only choosing the right plants for the soil and situation but also selecting plants that look natural. This does not necessarily imply a slavish dependence only on pure species, but also thoughtfully and creatively using garden cultivars and hybrids that look relatively unsophisticated.

RIGHT *An intriguing tapestry of pulmonaria and fern foliage creates fascinating effects in a cool shady corner.*
BELOW *This colorful but natural effect is the result of thoughtful interplanting of echinaceas with other perennials and alliums.*

USING THE A-Z DIRECTORY

The A-Z Directory of Perennials contains entries for 450 genera, arranged alphabetically. Each entry describes the plants, gives advice on how to grow them, and is accompanied by close-up color photographs revealing the huge variety of size, habit, and color and shape in both flowers and leaves that exists in this extraordinary group of plants. In addition, there are plant association boxes showing how to use plants in attractive combinations with perennials and other plants. We also explain the structure of individual flowers, provide galleries of cultivars for easy comparison and, in the green-tinted gardeners' notes panels, explore fascinating background to the plants and how to grow them.

Genus entry

Each genus has a general introduction that gives the range of plant types included in the genus (for example, some genera comprise only perennials, while others may include shrubs or annuals). This is followed by information on its distribution and native habitats, its broad unifying features, and popular garden uses. Alphabetically arranged subentries follow, giving more detailed information on the various species and hybrids contained within it.

Plant association box

Throughout the A–Z, popular perennials are shown in planting associations that suggest perfect plant partners.

Flower structure box

While in general the A–Z avoids specialized or botanical language, there are instances where an annotated explanation of particular flower parts greatly aids the appreciation of descriptions of individual plants and the differences between them.

Gallery

Galleries may distinguish types or groups within a genus, or flower shapes, or just display a range of popular cultivars of a particular species for comparison.

Gardeners' notes

These panels offer additional information on a range of topics, from the history of a plant's use in the garden to the story behind the breeding of colorful new cultivars.

KEY TO SYMBOLS

↕ Maximum height of the plant in normal cultivation, including any flowers

⚠ Potentially harmful plant (for a full listing *see p.493*)

Z1–12 Hardiness: guide to the minimum temperature usually tolerated by the plant (*see p.28–29*)

H1–12 AHS Heat zone guide to the maximum temperature usually tolerated by the plant (*see p.28–29*)

HARMFUL PLANTS ⚠

Most garden plants present no hazard to humans or animals, but some can cause digestive upset, while a very few are more dangerous. These are indicated by the symbol ⚠ throughout the book. Also highlighted are plants that may cause irritant, allergic, or other skin reactions in some people.

For gardeners who wish to minimize the number of potentially harmful plants in their garden as a whole (for example, those with young families), these plants are gathered together in a list on p.493.

Genus entry

Common name

Family name

Cultivation
Most perennials thrive in sunshine and good fertile soil that is neither waterlogged nor drains so quickly that it is often parched. Many, however, are shade-lovers or have other particular requirements, usually associated with their native habitats, and these are noted in the text. Perennials are also generally tolerant in relation to the acidity/alkalinity of the soil (the pH), but those with special preferences are marked in the text.

Propagation
Many perennials are among the easiest of plants to increase. Genus entries give the most common methods recommended for that group of plants with, usually, advice on timing where appropriate. Individual species entries may contain additional information on methods that are particularly recommended for that plant.

Problems
Most perennials are resilient plants that do not suffer from specific pest or disease problems, and these are marked "usually trouble-free." Where particular problems affect individual plants, these are noted.

Species entry
All species are listed alphabetically regardless of whether the name contains an x, indicating a hybrid species

ABOVE *Gaillardia* x *grandiflora* 'Dazzler'

G

GAILLARDIA
Blanket flower
ASTERACEAE

Brilliantly colorful, though often short-lived, sparklers for summer sun.

Thirty species of these annual, biennial, and perennial plants are all natives of the prairies and other open grasslands of the Americas. Their common name is derived from the plants' ability to cover the ground with a mass of colorful flowers. Each plant has a basal rosette of hairy leaves that may be entire, lobed, or toothed, and erect stems with alternate leaves. The daisylike flowers have brown, red, yellow, or purple centers and brightly colored petals. They produce their sometimes dazzling flowers throughout the summer and make good cut flowers. Best planted in groups of four to five in the middle or front of the herbaceous border.

CULTIVATION Grow in full sun, in any moderately fertile but well-drained soil. Deadhead regularly.

PROPAGATION By division or root cuttings, or from seed (which will produce variable offspring).

PROBLEMS Downy mildew, slugs. Roots may rot in wet soil.

G.* x *grandiflora An attractive but short-lived, hairy plant with a basal rosette of entire, toothed, or lobed, lance-shaped leaves. The flowers, from midsummer to late fall, are borne on erect stems and can measure up to 4 in (10 cm) across. Usually needs staking; cut back in fall to improve winter survival. A hybrid between the perennial species *G. aristata* and the annual *G. pulchella*, which rarely lives beyond its fourth year. The cultivars are very vigorous, usually with bright yellow, orange, or red flowers. Deadhead them regularly and cut down to a height of 6-in (15-cm) at the end of the summer to stimulate the development of new buds at the base and increase longevity. Often raised from seed, so some cultivars may prove variable. ↕ 14–30 in (35–75 cm). Z3–8 H8–1. **'Bijou'** Dwarf, with yellow tipped, orange-red petals. ↕ 18 in (45 cm). **'Bremen'** Bright scarlet petals with yellow tips. ↕ 30 in (75 cm). **'Burgunder'** Deep wine-red petals with yellow tips. ↕ 14 in (35 cm). **'Dazzler'** Deep mahogany-red flowers with yellow-tipped ray florets. ↕ 30 in (75 cm). **'Fanfare'** Deep reddish brown center and bright red, tube-shaped petals, with bright yellow tips. ↕ 24 in (60 cm). **'Goldkobold'** (**Golden Goblin, Yellow Goblin**) Free-flowering with relatively large golden yellow flowers with a slightly darker center. ↕ 14 in (35 cm). **'Kobold'** (**Goblin**) Red disk florets, red ray florets and yellow tips. ↕ 15 in (38 cm). **'St. Clements'** An important color break: the flowers have a peach and orange center with yellow petals tips, in late spring and early summer. Raised by Hardy's Cottage Garden Plants in Hampshire, England. ↕ 24 in (60 cm). **'Tokajer'** Rusty-orange flowers, flushed with purple toward base of the petals. ↕ 24 in (60 cm). **Yellow Goblin** see 'Goldkobold'.

AWARDS

The Perennial Plant Association (PPA) is a professional trade association dedicated to improving the perennial plant industry. The PPA provides education on selecting, maintaining, and planting perennials, and information on production, promotion, and the use of perennial plants.

Most notable among its activities, perhaps, is the organization's Perennial Plant of the Year Program, in which four perennials are selected by a committee from nominations made by PPA members. The members vote for one of the four. Attributes considered include suitability for a wide range of climates, ease of maintenance, ease of propagation (easily comes true from seed or vegetative propagation), and degree of multiple seasonal interest. Past winners include: *Dianthus gratianopolitanus* 'Feuerhexe' (Firewitch) (2006); *Helleborus* x *hybridus* (2005); *Athyrium niponicum* 'Pictum' (2004); *Leucanthemum* 'Becky' (2003); *Phlox* 'David' (2002); *Calamagrostis* x *acutiflora* 'Karl Foerster' (2001); *Scabiosa columbaria* 'Butterfly Blue' (2000).

Species distribution in the wild (or parentage/provenance of hybrids) is given when known

Height range for plants within the species

USDA hardiness and AHS heat zone ranges (see p.28)

Cultivars, subspecies, varieties and forms listed alphabetically

Trade designation or translated name

Height of individual cultivar

Cross reference

HOW PLANTS ARE NAMED

The agreed international standards for the naming of plants make this book possible. Without an agreed formal naming system, we would have no shorthand with which to refer to plants and we would have to revert to describing them in full detail whenever we discussed them—as was the case before Carolus Linnaeus invented the system we use today (*see* The Linnaean System).

Some gardeners prefer to use common names. Many of these are evocative and charming, with a familiarity that has grown up over hundreds of years, while other plants have had common names invented for them in more recent times simply as a way to help people avoid using botanical names.

However, the use of common names is fraught with problems, especially now that plants and plant information move around the world so freely. The name "bluebell," for example, has been applied to at least fifteen quite different plants and makes for a lot of confusion (*see* The Bluebell, *p.329*). Botanical names are much clearer and are understood all over the world.

WHY NAMES CHANGE

Sometimes, botanical names change— and gardeners find this annoying. Name changes are deemed necessary for a number of reasons. First, new information about a plant may come to light, and when the agreed international rules are applied, it is determined that a name must be changed

BLUEBELLS

The common name "bluebell" has been used around the world for at least fifteen different plants in a wide variety of plant families. In these days of easy international communication online and the international marketing of seeds and plants, only by using botanical names can we confidently refer to plants with accuracy and precision.

Campanula rotundifolia   *Hyacinthoides non-scripta*

Mertensia virginica   *Wahlenbergia gloriosa*

THE LINNAEAN SYSTEM

FAMILY

Flowering plants are grouped according to the structure of their flowers, so all plants with a basically similar flower structure are considered together: those with daisylike flowers in the Asteraceae (the daisy family) and so on. Within a family, plants with narrower similarities are grouped together into genera: there are about 1,100 in the Asteraceae, including *Anthemis*, *Helianthus*, and *Helenium* (above).

GENUS

Within a genus such as *Aster* (above), at the next level down is the basic unit of plant classification, the species; each genus contains anything from just one species to hundreds of individual species and hybrids. Plants within a species are all very similar, although not necessarily identical. Minor natural variations are given as subspecies (subsp.), variety (var.) and forma (f.). Cultivars are distinct plants grown in gardens; they may have arisen in cultivation or been found in the wild. Their names are always given in single quotation marks.

Some cultivars are of known or unknown hybrid origin, and their names are simply presented along with the generic name.

SPECIES

Aster tradescantii   *Aster pilosus* var. *demotus*   *Aster* 'Coombe Fishacre'   *Aster novae-angliae* 'Barrs Pink'

LEFT *Previously classified as a Cimicifuga, Actaea racemosa has now been brought together with the berried woodland plants we have long known as Actaea.*

in order to conform to the rules. The first name given to a newly identified plant is the one that usually must stand, so if it is found that a named plant is, in fact, the same as one with an earlier, different name, its name should be changed to that which was used first. Names can also change simply because a plant has been misidentified and, when the mistake is understood, the name must be changed to the correct one.

Names may also change for another reason. Scientific names reflect the botanical relationships between plants, so as understanding develops—perhaps as a result of the application of genetic studies, or simply following a detailed study of a group of plants that has not been thoroughly assessed for some time—it is possible that names will change. Some recent and pending changes affect familiar perennials:
• Plants previously known as *Cimicifuga* are now included in the genus *Actaea*.
• Plants previously known as *Smilacina* are now included in the genus *Maianthemum*.
• It is now thought that the two genera *Fragaria* and *Potentilla* may not be sufficiently distinct and they may be brought together into one genus.
• Many species in the genus *Aster* are now thought to be sufficiently distinct to be placed in their own genera, although this has not yet been universally accepted.

New names on the block
Many of the most popular perennials are cultivated varieties, bred from species for larger or double flowers, unusual foliage, or other special qualities, and most gardeners are familiar with the naming convention that

places these cultivar names within inverted commas—for example, *Hosta* 'Francee'. Less familiar, perhaps, are issues in relation to names that have arisen in recent years.

Series With international flower breeders applying their science to perennials in addition to annuals and seasonal bedding plants, some perennials are now seen in series. A series is a range of generally seed-raised plants that are more or less identical except in one ornamental feature, usually flower color. Bedding plants have been created in series for many years, and now perennials are being developed in this way. *Aquilegia* Swan Series and *Lobelia* Fan Series are popular examples.

Trade designations It sometimes happens that the correct cultivar name for a plant is not one that retailers feel is very appealing. This is increasingly the case when plant breeders give their potential introductions code names for use while they are being assessed and these codes are, technically, the cultivar names. When such a plant is chosen for introduction it is given a trade name, or selling name, which is more appealing. A good example is *Geranium* 'Gerwat', better known as *Geranium* Rozanne. The trade or selling name is presented in a different typeface and without the single quotation marks used for cultivar names.

Translations When a cultivar name is translated into another language, the translation is treated in the same way as a trade designation. This avoids the muddle that would be created if one plant were listed under a range of different translated cultivar names, as has been the case, for example, with *Achillea* 'Hoffnung' which has been translated as both Hope and Great Expectations. Plants carrying all three names have been sold, implying that they are all different plants.

Ensuring that plants you buy are true to name is not easy. Every nursery makes mistakes at times, but the general practices of the nursery and their overall reputation can be a good guide. Ideally, nurseries should continually update the perennial plant names on their stock as they become known, and many nurseries do demonstrate a conscientious effort to keep up-to-date. Thoughtful comments on—and explanation of—names, both in catalogs and in discussion, is also a good sign.

RIGHT *Lobelia 'Fan Zinnoberrosa' is one of a number of Lobelia hybrids in the Fan Series that differ only in color. Although translated into English as* Fan Cinnabar Rose, *the correct cultivar name is the original German.*

PLANTS RAISED FROM SEED

This is a very important issue. Some nurseries and gardeners find that many cultivars of perennials are slow to propagate by division or cuttings and they may not have enough stock to meet the demand. The result is that seed may be collected from these plants and the resulting plants sold under the name of the cultivar from which the seed was collected.

However, many cultivars are selected and named because of the new combination of distinctive features that they display. This is often the result of a unique genetic makeup, a unique combination of genes that leads to the exhibition of a unique combination of features. When such plants are raised from seed, they often exhibit different combinations of features—that is, they are different from their parent plant. This may be the result of cross-pollination with different but related cultivars or of the reorganization of the plant's genes (not all of which may be expressed in the chosen cultivar) that results from self-pollination.

The result is that plants raised from seed collected from a cultivar intended to be propagated by division or cuttings may be identical to the parent plant, show a range of slight differences, or exhibit significant, even dramatic, differences from the parent. But gardeners may distribute the seedlings under the cultivar name of the parent, leading to enormous confusion, and the devaluing of the system of plant names on which we all rely.

There are many such instances in this book—too many, unfortunately, for each to be discussed on a case-by-case basis—although some of the more common examples are mentioned.

This is not to say that we should ban raising plants from seed collected from cultivars intended to be propagated vegetatively. It is more a case of distributing them under an appropriate name, perhaps a Group name, as in the case of *Helleborus foetidus* Wester Flick Group and *Geranium clarkei* Purple-Flowered Group, to make it absolutely clear that the stock is quite different from stock derived from vegetative propagation of the same plant.

HARDINESS IN PERENNIALS

Some perennials are hardier than others. The origins of this variation in tolerance of winter weather are in the natural habitats of wild species and those of the parents of hybrid plants. Plants adapt to their natural circumstances and they have little evolutionary need to develop tolerance of climates significantly different from those to which they are accustomed. So one of the factors that determines both their physiology and their more obvious features is the climate in which they grow naturally. Because these factors interact with each other and with additional adaptations including seasonal growth patterns, it is often difficult to predict whether a given plant will be hardy simply by looking at it. Even different individuals of the same species that originate in different climates can sometimes vary in their hardiness. Our assumptions on the hardiness of specific groups can also lead us astray.

Orchids, for example, are sometimes assumed to be tropical plants, and many are, but some species are hardy in even

nontropical regions of the US. The hardiness of plant species can be a very useful clue, and in this book the hardiness of cultivars is assumed to be the same as that of the parent species unless stated otherwise.

WHAT CAN YOU GROW?

In the past, a number of different, largely unrelated and often incompatible systems were used to indicate hardiness. In this book a zone system devised by the United States Department of Agriculture (USDA) has been adopted to provide gardeners with a basic guide to plant hardiness. The USDA system, based on average minimum temperatures, is the most thoroughly researched and comprehensive system and has been used, or adapted by, some other countries. As the movement of plants, and plant information, around the world becomes more common, a uniform system for identifying plant hardiness will become increasingly valuable.

Within the United States and Canada, there is a wide variation in climate and, therefore, a correspondingly broad range of hardiness zones. The USDA hardiness zone system divides the United States and Canada into numbered zones based on lowest average winter temperatures. The current version of the USDA Plant Hardiness Zone Map, pictured on the front endpaper of this

book, is divided into 12 zones; the lower the zone number, the colder the average minimum temperatures in that region. However, large urban areas may have a warmer hardiness zone than the surrounding suburbs and countryside because of the urban heat island effect.

> **BELOW** *Perennials exposed to temperatures below those indicated by their hardiness zone may experience injury. For less frost-hardy plants, leaving the top growth in place all winter before cutting back in spring provides protection, and also adds to the enjoyment of the winter garden.*

AHS HEAT-ZONE MAP

Hot temperatures can also influence the success or failure of a plant. To complement the USDA's hardiness zone map, the American Horticultural Society developed the AHS Plant Heat-Zone Map (see back endpaper) in 1997, under the supervision of Dr. Marc Cathey.

The AHS Plant Heat-Zone Map divides the United States into 12 heat zones that are based on the average number of "heat days" in which temperatures reach or exceed 86°F (30°C). For example, Zone 1, in northern regions of the United States and at high altitudes, averages less than one heat day per year, while, in the most southern part of the United States, Zone 12 averages more than 210 heat days per year.

Each species or cultivar in this book is given a heat-zone range. The first number indicates the hottest zone in which the plant will successfully grow. The second number is the zone with the minimum amount of summer heat needed for the plant to grow and produce flowers or fruits.

As was the case with cold hardiness, considerations other than temperature factor into any given plant's tolerance for heat. For example, summer rainfall (or the lack of it), high humidity, cool nights, exposure to sun, and various characteristics of the soil also influence whether a plant will survive in a given heat zone.

WORLD HARDINESS ZONES

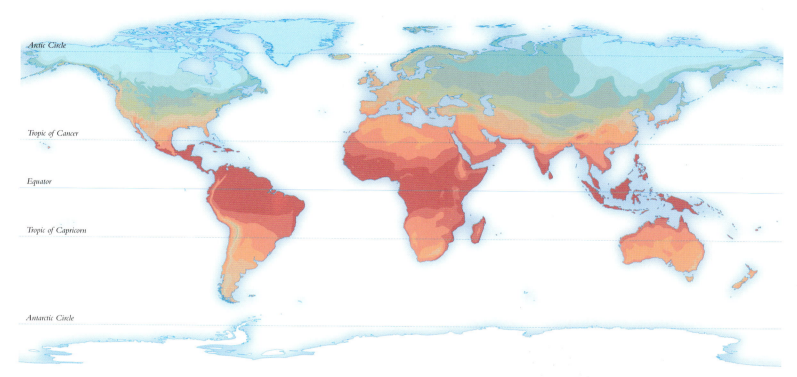

A hardiness zone range is provided in each plant description, because some plants require exposure to a certain degree of cold temperatures in order to break dormancy or successfully flower or produce fruit. The first number in the range indicates the coldest zone in which the plant will thrive. The second number indicates the warmest zone that satisfies a plant's cold requirements.

In areas that experience high summer temperatures, heat exposure can also be a limiting factor. For this reason, a range of heat tolerance zones is included in each plant description (*see panel, p.28*).

The world map reveals how the USDA zones would appear if applied to the entire globe. This map includes 12 hardiness zones to reflect subtropical and tropical regions, which do not exist in the continental United States and Canada.

WHAT CAN AFFECT HARDINESS

The hardiness zone system is a valuable tool for gardeners, but it is not a foolproof approach to selecting plants. A variety of other factors can influence the hardiness of a given plant in a given garden. These include soil type, drainage, snow cover, exposure to wind, winter rainfall (or the lack of it), and whether the low temperature is consistent or alternates with warmer spells.

RIGHT *Plants like these agapanthus growing wild in South Africa do not have a very high tolerance of cold, as they do not require it in their natural habitat, and so they will only be hardy in milder gardens.*

Two other factors are especially important: microclimates and protection. Plants growing in areas of the garden protected from the worst of the winter weather by walls, fences, partially overhanging evergreen trees, or nearby evergreen shrubs will often prove hardier than the same plants grown in open, unprotected places in the same garden.

Plants of borderline hardiness may also thrive by providing areas that are sheltered from winter winds and improving drainage; existing features like walls and established evergreen shrubs also provide warmth and shelter. Protection in the form of a mulch of bark chips, shredded leaves, pine branches, or other organic material serves as an insulating blanket to protect the crown and roots of the plants from the worst of the cold.

KEY

The zones shown on the map above represent approximate regions where the following average winter minimum temperatures apply:

Zone		°F	°C
	Z1	Below −50°	Below −46°
	Z2	−50° to −40°	−46° to −40°
	Z3	−40° to −30°	−40° to −34°
	Z4	−30° to −20°	−34° to −29°
	Z5	−20° to −10°	−29° to −23°
	Z6	−10° to 0°	−23° to −18°
	Z7	0° to 10°	−18° to −12°
	Z8	10° to 20°	−12° to −7°
	Z9	20° to 30°	−7° to −1°
	Z10	30° to 40°	−1° to 4°
	Z11	40° to 50°	−4° to 10°
	Z12	50° to 60°	−10° to 16°

A-Z

DIRECTORY

A

ACAENA
Sheep bur, Pirri pirri
ROSACEAE

Attractive evergreen carpeter offering a range of foliage colors with interesting spiky fruits in late summer.

A large group of about 100 species of evergreen perennials, some woody at the base, and native mainly to temperate regions of the Southern Hemisphere. Of the 17 or so species in cultivation, only a few are widely grown, most coming from grassland habitats in New Zealand and the southern tip of South America. Their trailing stems form low, creeping mats of soft, dainty foliage in bright green or blue-gray, which may be suffused with bronze or purple. Each leaf is divided into opposite pairs of toothed leaflets, fernlike in the ground-hugging dwarf species, but resembling the closely related salad burnet (*Sanguisorba minor*) in some larger species.

In summer, small spherical flowerheads, densely packed with inconspicuous flowers, rise like pompons on upright stalks above the leaves. These become far showier once they have gone to seed, when the burlike fruits bristle with slender, hooked spines. The burs latch onto passing animals and can be widely dispersed. In some places they are noxious weeds (*see* Coastal Invader).

Species are variable, making this a difficult group for botanists to classify and differing interpretations exist. The situation is complicated

LEFT *Acaena saccaticupula* 'Blue Haze'

by the fact that many of those grown in gardens look similar and sometimes circulate under the wrong names; some can hybridize.

CULTIVATION Grow in sun or part-shade in well-drained soil. Useful for ground cover and gaps in paving, and effective as a foliage mosaic of different species. Some acaenas root rapidly along their stems and can be invasive, but are generally poor competitors among other plants and are easily controlled by cutting back.

PROPAGATION By division or cuttings (stem tip or self-rooted), or from seed (not cultivars).

PROBLEMS Usually trouble-free.

A. anserinifolia see *A. novae-zelandiae*

A. buchananii A dwarf species that forms a neat mat, recognizable by its short-stemmed flowerheads hidden beneath fine, gray-green foliage. Pale brown or green stems, up to 12 in (30 cm) long, carry leaves ⅝–2¼ in (1.5–5.5 cm) long, oval in shape. On stems no taller than ½ in (11 mm), green flowerheads appear in summer, developing into large burs, about 1¼ in (3 cm) wide, with green-yellow spines. From New Zealand (South Island). ↕¾–2 in (2–5 cm). Z6–9 H9–6

A. caesiiglauca One of several species with blue-gray leaves, this vigorous plant is distinguished by its soft, hairy stems and foliage. Pale brown stems up to 24 in (60 cm) long bear leaves 1½–3 in (4–8 cm) long, with seven to nine oblong to egg-shaped leaflets. Pale green flowerheads with long white stamens are held on stems 4–5½ in (10–14 cm) high. The burs that follow are up to 1 in (2.5 cm) across, with green-brown spines. Leaves may take on a purple tint in fall. New Zealand. ↕4–5½ in (10–14 cm). Z6–9 H9–6

A. inermis Unusual among acaenas for its spineless burs—its name means "unarmed"—although, confusingly, in some forms, short, thick soft-tipped spines are present. The quick-rooting salmon pink to brownish blue stems, up to 12 in (30 cm) long, carry leaves that are usually ¾–1½ in (2–4 cm) long with fan-shaped to square leaflets with five

to ten teeth. The foliage is matte brownish or bluish gray, turning yellow-orange with age. In late summer, short stems of ½–2½ in (1–6 cm) bear fruit up to ½ in (1.5 cm) across. Similar in habit to *A. microphylla* but has grayer foliage and smaller burs, usually without spines. From New Zealand (South Island). ↕ 2–4 in (5–10 cm). Z6–9 H9–6. '**Purpurea**' Makes neat mats of dusky purple foliage. More popular than the species, though the validity of the name is in doubt.

A. microphylla The smallest species, with the largest burs. Forms a flat mat of foliage, varying from bronze-edged yellow-green to matte purple-brown, on quick-rooting, pale- or green-brown stems up to 12 in (30 cm) long. The leaves are no more than 1¼ in (3 cm) long, divided into diminutive leaflets edged with three to seven teeth. Short, ½–1½-in (1–4-cm) stalks hold the abundant flowerheads aloft in summer, followed by decorative 1¼-in (3-cm) burs. Covered with distinctive bright red, soft, barbless bristles, the burs almost mask the underlying leaves. Sometimes confused with *A. inermis*, which is of similar stature but has grayer foliage and smaller burs lacking spines. From New Zealand (North Island). ↕¾–2 in (2–5 cm). Z6–8 H8–6. '**Kupferteppich**' (**Copper Carpet**) Coppery foliage.

A. myriophylla Unmistakable among cultivated acaenas for its elongated or spike-shaped flowerheads and 13–23 (or more) narrow leaflets, which are not toothed but deeply cut into slender segments, giving the leaves a feathery outline. These yellow-green leaves are among the longest, reaching up to 5 in (12 cm) by 1¼ in (3 cm), on low-lying stems up to 30 in (75 cm). Tiny greenish flowers, clustered in cylindrical heads in late spring and early summer, held well above the foliage on leafy 8–12-in (20–30-cm) stalks. Fruit thickly covered in pale yellow spines. From central and southern Argentina. ↕8–12 in (20–30 cm). Z6–9 H9–6

A. novae-zelandiae One of the larger species, spreading strongly, with vivid green, glossy foliage on long, pink-flushed stems reaching 3¼ ft (1 m). Its leaves are 1¼–4 in (3–10 cm) long, composed of 9 to 13 narrow oblong leaflets with a slightly wrinkled surface. In summer, stems 4–10 in (10–25 cm) long hold the flowerheads well above

the leaves. The red-spined burs are up to 1¼ in (3 cm) wide. It is a commonly naturalized acaena. Sometimes sold as *A. anserinifolia*, causing confusion with this quite different, rarely seen species. From New Zealand, Australia, and Tasmania. ↕4–10 in (10–25 cm). Z6–8 H8–6

A. saccaticupula '**Blue Haze**' One of the best blue-gray acaenas, its steely foliage contrasts with the coppery stems and flowerheads. Stems up to 20 in (50 cm) in length bear lacy leaves ¾–2¾ in (2–7 cm) long, divided into small fan-shaped or oblong leaflets, which tend to be edged in bronze. Red stalks, 5–7½ in (13–19 cm) tall, hold the flowerheads well above the leaves. In late summer, the ½–¾-in (1.5–1.8-cm) burs bristle with pinkish red spines. When first introduced, this species was not identified and the plant was named 'Blue Haze', but it may not be distinct from the species. Other blue-leaved forms are also sometimes sold under this name. New Zealand. ↕5–7½ in (13–19 cm). Z7–9 H9–7

ACANTHUS
Bear's breeches
ACANTHACEAE

Handsome, vigorous, large-scale perennials, with architectural foliage and many weeks of imposing columns of flowers.

Of the 20 or so *Acanthus* species, ranging from herbaceous plants to shrubby trees, many are found in tropical Africa and two are even mangroves from Australia. There are around six European natives, from dry hillsides and scrub in the Mediterranean region; at least five are in cultivation.

Plants form bold mounds of handsome, long-stalked leaves, the clumps relentlessly expanding. The

THOSE ROOTS

Acanthus roots provide both a problem and an opportunity. They stretch so deep into the soil that when you dig up an acanthus to move it to another part of the garden, inevitably some roots are left behind; it is just impossible to remove them all. But while you are caring for the plant in its new home, the roots left behind will start to grow and emerge through its successor. The answer is either to be very thorough in removing these roots, or wait before putting a new plant in its place and treat any acanthus shoots with a systemic weedkiller.

At the same time, these roots provide an ideal method of propagation. In late winter or early spring, scrape the soil away from the roots and cut off pieces 2–3 in (5–8 cm) long. Insert them vertically in pots of sandy potting mix with their tops just covered, keep them at about 70°F (21°C), and do not let them dry out. Shoots will appear in about four weeks and plants can then be moved into individual pots to grow on before planting out.

species differ most in the size and shape of their foliage, which, at its most decorative, is dark green, jaggedly cut, and huge (all leaf measurements include the stalks). In summer, statuesque flower spikes rise high above the leaves on sturdy stems, and the closely packed hooded flowers last for many weeks. From beneath each stiff, curved hood in muted tones of purple or green, spreads a broad, liplike petal, and under this lies a spiny bract that makes the flower distinctly sharp to touch. The hood persists while the beadlike fruit develops, turning from green to dark brown. The dried flower stems are used in floral arrangements. Typical forms of the larger species (*A. hungaricus*, *A. mollis*, and *A. spinosus*), are clearly distinct, but they vary greatly in the wild and have also possibly given rise to accidental hybrids in cultivation, so plants may be hard to identify.

CULTIVATION Easy to grow in any well-drained soil and full sun. Some species also thrive in light shade, although they may produce fewer flower spikes. They dislike winter rain. The larger species need plenty of space, away from delicate plants they could smother. Useful as robust ground cover, for adding dramatic accents to a spacious border, or in more naturalistic plantings on rocky banks or a sunny woodland edge.

PROPAGATION By division or root cuttings (cultivars), or from seed (species).

PROBLEMS Slugs and snails. Powdery mildew.

A. balcanicus Nearly all plants grown under this name are *A. hungaricus*.

A. dioscoridis An attractive dwarf species and the only hardy acanthus with rich pink flowers. These appear in summer on short spikes above a low rosette of gray-green foliage that is not usually prickly. The smooth-edged leaves, up to 14 in (35 cm) long, are

DO NOT DISTURB

IF YOU HAVE ONE plant that is best left undisturbed in a sunny border, why not combine it with another sharing the same preference? Although *Acanthus mollis* will grow in shade, in sun it reaches its luxuriant best. The bold foliage and summer spikes rival the impact of the tree poppy, *Romneya coulteri*, while its foliage hides the latter's bare basal stems. The white lower lip of the acanthus flower makes a bright color connection with the frilly white petals of the romneya, and this holds the display together. Both plants are best cut back hard in winter, and both may need their roots restricted to prevent them from spreading too far, so let them mingle in a limited space. Do not move either plant, since new shoots will emerge from deep roots unavoidably left behind.

narrow, tapering, and without lobes. While the foliage is plainer than in other species, this pretty acanthus, suitable for smaller gardens, has the cachet of rosy-purple flowers, around 2 in (5 cm) long, peeping in succession from under green- or purple-tinged hoods. The noninvasive tufts increase gradually in size, although offshoots sometimes emerge up to 12 in (30 cm) away. Appreciates sharp drainage and a warm, sunny position. From eastern Turkey and northern Syria, into Armenia and northwestern Iran. ‡12–20 in (30–50 cm). Z6–9 H9–6. **var. perringii** Deeply toothed and slightly spiny leaves. From southern Turkey.

A. hirsutus Forming a rosette of jagged-toothed, prickly leaves, this small and unusual species has a distinctive covering of silky hairs on foliage, stems, and flower spikes. Its leaves are similar to those of *A. spinosus* but much narrower—3 in (8 cm) or less across—and shaped like a dandelion's, reaching up to 16 in (40 cm) in length. In summer, green-hooded, creamy-white flowers, 1½–2½ in (4–6 cm) long, are clustered on a short spike. Needs good drainage and sun. From the Balkans and Turkey. ‡10–18 in (25–45 cm). Z8–10 H10–5 **f. roseus** Pink flowers. **subsp. syriacus** syn. *A. syriacus* Stocky flowering spikes above very spiny leaves display white or greenish flowers with hoods and bracts heavily tinted with dark purple. Less densely hairy than the species. From southern Turkey to Israel, usually in limestone soil. ‡10–18 in (25–45 cm). Z9–11 H12–10

A. hungaricus syn. *A. longifolius* Reliably prolific, tall-stemmed columns of white to pale pink 2-in (5-cm) flowers beneath green or purplish hoods tower over a dense clump of giant matte-green leaves, up to 3¼ ft (1 m) long and 8 in (20 cm) wide. The leaves are not usually spiny and, although roughly oval in outline, are deeply dissected almost to the center of the leaf, into widely spaced, tooth-edged lobes, ¾–2½ in (2–6 cm) across. Unlike cut-leaved forms of *A. mollis*, with which it can be confused, each lobe narrows where it meets the body of the leaf, so the gap between adjacent lobes is shaped liked a flat-bottomed flask. Tolerates part-shade. From woods and open, scrubby places in the Balkans. ‡3¼–5 ft (1–1.5 m). Z6–9 H9–5

A. longifolius see *A. hungaricus*

A. mollis Glossy, ornate, and non-spiny foliage forms a substantial, robust, semi-evergreen clump of huge, fairly upright, dark green leaves to 3¼ ft (1 m) long, varying in size, shape, and depth of lobing. Some have long, narrow, deeply cut leaves and jagged teeth; at the other extreme are broad-leaved plants, with only shallow-lobed foliage. None is truly spiky. In summer, soaring stems carry magnificent flowering columns

RIGHT 1 *Acanthus dioscoridis* var. *perringii* **2** *A. hirsutus* **3** *A. mollis* (Latifolius Group) 'Rue Ledan'

LEFT **1** *Achillea filipendulina* 'Parker's Variety' **2** *A. millefolium* 'Credo' **3** *A. millefolium* 'Summerwine'

up to 28 in (70 cm) high, bearing white or pink-veined 2-in (5-cm) flowers with green-purple hoods. Cut-leaved forms resemble *A. hungaricus*, but in *A. mollis* the leaf lobes are closer together and never narrowed at the base. Needs plenty of space, prefers deep, well-drained soil, and thrives in light shade. From rocky woods and other shady places in southwestern to south central Europe and northwestern Africa. ‡5–6 ft (1.5–1.8 m). Z7–11 H12–7. **'Hollard's Gold'** Young foliage, produced in spring and fall, is golden-yellow, turning mid-green with age. Discovered in New Zealand. **'Jardin en Face'** *see* (Latifolius Group) 'Rue Ledan'. **Latifolius Group** These plants have the broadest leaves, oval to roundish in outline, shallow-lobed and up to 4 ft (1.2 m) long. **(Latifolius Group) 'Rue Ledan'** syn. 'Jardin en Face' Pure white flowers with green hoods. Found in a Brittany garden.

A. spinosus A vicious plant. Its arching leaves, exquisitely cut into slim lobes no more than 1 in (2.5 cm) wide, are deeply incised and make a dense mound. Prominent, rigid white veins run out to the leaf edges, where jagged teeth are tipped with fiercely sharp white spines that are painful to touch. The shiny leaves are roughly oval, up to 24 in (60 cm) long and 3–12 in (8–30 cm) wide. The white flowers have purplish hoods and clothe only the top 4–16 in (10–40 cm) of the spike. This species is less vigorous and invasive than *A. mollis*, and much more spiny. Wild plants vary in leaf shape and in the quantity of spines; some horticulturists suggest that most cultivated plants are not pure *A. spinosus*. Can be grown in light shade. From eastern Italy, the Balkans, and southwestern Turkey. ‡36–48 in (90–120 cm). Z5–9 H9–5. **'Lady Moore'** New leaves appear almost white, revealing creamy spots as they develop before turning dark green during summer. Named for the renowned 19th century Irish gardener, Phyllis Moore. **Spinosissimus Group** Forms a low mound of super-spiny leaves that have very narrow lobes. May not flower freely except during unusually hot summers.

A. **'Summer Beauty'** Resembles *A. mollis*, but withstands intense summer heat better. Possibly a hybrid between *A. mollis* and *A. spinosus*.

A. syriacus see *A. hirsutus* subsp. *syriacus*

ACERIPHYLLUM *see* MUKDENIA

ACHILLEA
Yarrow
ASTERACEAE

Easy to grow and invaluable in the summer border, with a range of flower colors including some that change spectacularly as they fade.

More than 100 species of often woody-based plants are distributed throughout the Northern Hemisphere and generally enjoy full sun and well-drained soil. Some are tightly clump-forming, others run at the root, and a few are disagreeably invasive. The alternate, aromatic, green or gray foliage may be smooth-edged, or more often repeatedly dissected, sometimes in more than one plane, to give a pretty, finely feathered, rather fernlike look; early in the year, in particular, the bold basal leaves of many species provide an attractive foliage effect.

The usually stiff, sometimes slightly ridged stems carry small daisylike flowers, often in large, flat-topped heads; the ray florets are generally relatively short, with only female flower parts, and come in white, pink, or yellow with a range of other colors in the garden cultivars; the disk florets in the

FIRE WITH FINESSE

THERE ARE OBVIOUS REASONS why a fiery summer grouping of crocosmia and *Achillea millefolium* 'Feuerland' works so well. The scarlet-orange crocosmia and the achillea flowers, in almost exactly the same shade, blend together perfectly—and the fact that the flat heads of the achillea are in such contrast to the arching spikes of the crocosmia emphasizes the color similarity. The difference in foliage, with the bright green swords of the crocosmia set against the feathery achillea leaves, has the same effect. The dark, even more finely cut bronze fennel (*Foeniculum vulgare* 'Purpureum') in the background and the delicate heads of *Stipa gigantea* add interesting variations in style. But a closer look reveals a more subtle match: each scarlet-orange crocosmia flower has a yellow-orange tube that almost exactly echoes the shade of the fading achillea flowers.

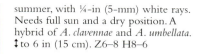

center are usually yellow and contain both male and female flower parts. It is the total mass of flowers that creates the effect.

This is a complex genus with a number of natural hybrids, and also an increasing range of complicated garden hybrids posing difficult identification problems, even for the specialist. The familiar *A. millefolium* has given rise, through a complex history of selection and hybridization, to a colorful group of border plants; particularly fine color forms have been achieved in crosses with *A. clypeolata*, although the plants can be rather short-lived.

CULTIVATION Thrives in light, sandy soil; some species are particularly demanding of sharp drainage and full sun but will grow well at the front of well-drained sunny borders. In general, species and hybrids with silvery gray leaves, including *A. clypeolata*, tend to be short-lived. Others, with green leaves, and more adapted to moist, nutrient-rich soil, will tolerate a wider range of conditions, but can be invasive.

PROPAGATION Divide every 3–5 years. Plants often seed freely, but the seedlings are seldom worth keeping and plants should be deadheaded before the seed ripens. Seed-raised selections are available, but do not offer the best performance.

PROBLEMS Powdery mildew.

A. aegyptiaca see *A.* 'Taygetea'

A. ageratum syn. *A. decolorans* Somewhat spreading, the rather small and hairless, gland-dotted green leaves, up to 2 in (5 cm) long, are shallowly toothed or divided. Numerous compact flowerheads of many flowers appear in summer, with 1/16-in (1-mm) yellow rays. A number of other *Achillea* species and hybrids are mistakenly grown under this name. From southwestern Europe. ‡ 32 in (80 cm). Z5–7 H7–5

A. aurea see *A. chrysocoma*

A. cartilaginea see *A. salicifolia*

A. chrysocoma syn. *A. aurea* Quite small but distinctive, with attractive, finely-divided leaves covered with silky hairs, the narrow segments angled to give the leaf a rounded appearance. The compact flowerheads have many flowers in late spring and early summer, with bright yellow 1/8-in (3-mm) rays. From the Balkan Peninsula. ‡ 16 in (40 cm). Z3–7 H8–1. **'Grandiflora'** Larger flowerheads.

A. clavennae A small and rather delicate plant, the 3 in (8 cm) basal leaves narrowing toward the base and with two to five pairs of simple leaf divisions. Loose flowerheads of five to twenty-five flowers, each have white 1/8-in (4-mm) rays. Dry, open, and sunny conditions are essential. From the southern and southeastern Alps. ‡ 10 in (25 cm). Z3–8 H8–1

ACHILLEA FLOWERS

Achillea flowerheads are composed of many daisylike flowers, loosely or tightly packed together. Each contains a few disk florets, surrounded by a single row of ray florets, all held tightly together within a cluster of bracts. In some yellow-flowering species, the rays can be difficult to detect; often, their shape and color are the most distinctive characteristics of the species or cultivar.

Disc floret

Ray floret

Achillea millefolium 'Lansdorferglut'

A. clypeolata Clump-forming, with flat, oval, or long and narrow, basal leaves, to 6 in (15 cm), which are deeply divided with 20–25 pairs of segments and grayish with densely felted hairs. Compact, usually flat-topped, 1¼–2¾-in (3–7-cm) flowerheads comprise 20 or more flowers, with 1/16-in (1-mm) golden-yellow rays. A number of hybrids are in cultivation that may be mistakenly grown under *A. clypeolata*. Found across the Balkan Peninsula. ‡ 20 in (50 cm). Z3–9 H9–1

A. **'Coronation Gold'** Greenish gray foliage topped with flat-topped heads of bright yellow flowers. Hybrid between *A. clypeolata* and *A. filipendulina*. 36 in (90 cm). Z3–9 H9–1

A. decolorans see *A. ageratum*

A. filipendulina A tall, upright, and distinctive species. The basal leaves are oblong or lance-shaped in general outline and deeply divided with 10–15 paired segments; the stem leaves are similar, less divided, and somewhat crowded toward the base. Dense, slightly domed flowerheads of 50–300 or more flowers open from midsummer to early fall, each floret having 1/16-in (1-mm) yellow rays. The cultivars are more vigorous, with larger flowering heads. All are excellent for cutting and drying. Found in the Caucasus, across to central Asia. ‡ to 3¼ ft (1 m). Z3–9 H9–1. **'Cloth of Gold'** Taller and unbranched. Sometimes incorrectly listed as 'Parkers Variety'. ‡ to 5½ ft (1.7 m). **'Gold Plate'** Taller, unbranched, and with a distinctly flat-topped flowerhead. ‡ to 5 ft (1.5 m). **'Parker's Variety'** Taller, usually unbranched, with a more rounded flowerhead. ‡ to 4½ ft (1.4 m).

A. grandifolia Tall and robust, the large and attractive oval, dark green leaves, up to 5 in (13 cm) long, are deeply

divided into 4–6 paired segments. Slightly domed flowerheads, to 4½ in (11 cm) across, are made up of 80 to 100 flowers with 1/8-in (3-mm) white rays that appear throughout the summer. *Tanacetum macrophyllum* is sometimes grown under this name. Found in the Balkan Peninsula and adjacent parts of Turkey. ‡ to 4 ft (1.2 m). Z4–8 H8–1

A. x **huteri** Low and mat-forming, with rounded, deeply divided and grayish green basal leaves. The flowerheads comprise ten to 15 flowers and appear in early summer with ¼-in (5-mm) white rays. Needs full sun and a dry position. A hybrid of *A. ageratifolia* and *A. rupestris*. ‡ 6 in (15 cm). Z3–7 H8–1

A. x **kolbiana** A striking, dwarf plant with distinctly silver-gray foliage, the 2-in (5-cm) basal leaves are rounded and deeply divided with 4–6 pairs of narrow segments. Loose flowerheads of six to 15 flowers develop in the

summer, with ¼-in (5-mm) white rays. Needs full sun and a dry position. A hybrid of *A. clavennae* and *A. umbellata*. ‡ to 6 in (15 cm). Z6–8 H8–6

A. macrophylla Tall and sturdy, the broadly triangular or oval leaves, to 2¾ in (7 cm) long, are deeply divided into four to seven paired, toothed segments. Loose flowerheads are made up of three to 40 flowers on slender stalks, with ¼-in (5-mm) white rays. A bold foliage plant early in the season. Found in the Alps. ‡ 12–40 in (30–100 cm). Z3–9 H9–1

A. millefolium (Yarrow, Milfoil) Very variable, and familiar as a tough, spreading invasive lawn and roadside weed. Many selections and hybrids have been named, and some recent introductions are outstanding. The basal leaves are long, narrow, and green, up to 8 in (20 cm) long, divided two to three times, with slender segments; the stem leaves are similar, though smaller. More or less flat-topped flowerheads are made up of 50 to 150 or more flowers, with white or occasionally pink 1/16-in (2-mm) rays. Cutting back the flowerheads will encourage repeat flowering through the summer, although this should not be undertaken hastily: the quality of fading in some selections and hybrids can be impressive, although some fade into unattractive shades (*see Achillea Flowers*). The grayish leaved cultivars are generally more short-lived, somewhat less hardy, and require a drier situation. Both cultivars of *A. millefolium* and its hybrids are listed here together for convenience. Widely naturalized around the world, including in all 50 states. Native to Europe and western Asia. ‡ to 4 ft (1.2 m). Z3–9 H9–1 **Anthea** (**'Anblo'**) Light yellow, fading to creamy yellow; grayish green foliage. Probably a hybrid with *A. clypeolata;* raised by Alan Bloom. ‡ 28 in (70 cm). **'Alabaster'** Pale yellow, fading to white. ‡ 28 in (70 cm).

RIGHT 1 *Achillea millefolium* Summer Pastels Group **2** *A. millefolium* 'Terracotta'

AGING GRACEFULLY

The flowers of most selections and hybrids of *Achillea millefolium* change color as they age. Some, like those of 'Forncett Fletton', age harmoniously, changing from rich brick orange-red to yellow. By contrast, each floret of 'Fanal' is bright scarlet with a yellow eye when at its peak, but slowly deteriorates, eventually becoming a very murky shade that has been likened to dirty dishwater. If you deadhead promptly, to prevent seed being shed, discoloration will not be a problem; but if, like most gardeners, you are unable to deadhead every day or two, choose *Achillea* cultivars that age well. These include 'Belle Epoque', 'Christine's Pink', 'Credo', 'Forncett Fletton', 'Heidi', 'Martina', and 'Terracotta'. However, be sure to deadhead these before too long or the garden may be swamped by seedlings.

'**Apfelblüte**' (**Appleblossom**) Rose pink, with compact, gray-green foliage. ‡36 in (90 cm). '**Apricot Beauty**' Pale apricot and yellow. ‡36 in (90 cm). '**Bahama**' Biscuit yellow. ‡36 in (90 cm). '**Belle Epoque**' Opening red with yellowish streaks, fading to lemon yellow and pink. ‡40 in (100 cm). '**Bloodstone**' Very deep red. ‡28 in (70 cm). '**Cassis**' Deep cherry red. From seed, sometimes variable. ‡24 in (60 cm). '**Cerise Queen**' Vigorous; dark pink. From seed, sometimes variable. ‡24 in (60 cm). '**Christine's Pink**' Opening pale pink, fading almost to white. ‡36 in (90 cm). **Colorado Group** Mixed red, pink, apricot, and white colors. From seed, so unpredictable in its color balance. ‡24 in (60 cm). '**Credo**' Opening yellow, fading creamy yellow; grayish foliage. Raised by Ernst Pagels. ‡4 ft (1.2 m). '**Fanal**' (**The Beacon**) Opening bright red, fading to a murky brownish yellow. ‡24 in (60 cm). '**Faust**' Long-lasting red; grayish foliage. ‡28 in (70 cm). '**Feuerland**' (**Fireland**) Opening bright reddish orange, fading unevenly but attractively to orange and yellow. Bred by Ernst Pagels. ‡24 in (60 cm). '**Forncett Beauty**' Lilac pink; fading pinkish white. ‡24 in (60 cm). '**Forncett Candy**' Pink to mauve. ‡32 in (80 cm). '**Forncett Citrus**' Lemon yellow, with grayish green foliage. ‡32 in (80 cm). '**Forncett**

Fletton' Bright brick orange, fading to golden yellow, with grayish green foliage. ‡24 in (60 cm). '**Forncett Ivory**' Ivory white. ‡32 in (80 cm). **Forncett Series** A series of six cultivars raised by John Metcalf of Four Seasons Nursery at Forncett St. Mary, Norfolk, England. **Galaxy Series** Series of German origin, with sturdy stems and a variety of colors from white and yellow to rosy pink. Cultivars include 'Apfelblüte', 'Lachschönheit', and 'Paprika'. ‡24 in (60 cm) **Great Expectations** *see* 'Hoffnung' '**Heidi**' Opening pink, fading almost to white with a pale pink flush. ‡24 in (60 cm). '**Helios**' Yellow. Probably a hybrid with *A. filipendulina*. ‡32–40 in (80–100 cm). '**Hella Glashoff**' Lemon yellow, fading slightly. ‡20 in (50 cm). '**Hoffnung**' (**Great Expectations, Hope**) Pale yellow. Probably a hybrid with *A. clypeolata*. ‡36 in (90 cm). '**Inca Gold**' Terra-cotta orange flowers, with grayish foliage. Perhaps a hybrid with *A. clypeolata*. ‡28 in (70 cm). '**Kelwayi**' ♀ Dark red. 24 in (60 cm). '**Lachsschönheit**' (**Salmon Beauty**) Opening salmon-orange, but fading to white with a pale pink flush. ‡32–42 in (80–110 cm). '**Landsdorferglut**' The rays open bright rosy pink, fading to grayed yellow; the disk flowers open yellow, darkening to orange. ‡36–42 in (90–110 cm). '**Lilac Beauty**' Pale lilac. ‡28 in (70 cm). '**Lucky Break**' Lemon yellow, fading yellowish white; grayish green foliage. Perhaps a seed-raised derivative of 'Taygetea'. Found in the garden at Great Dixter by Christopher Lloyd. ‡32–40 in (80–100 cm). '**Marie Ann**' Pale lemon yellow flowers; grayish foliage. Short. ‡16 in (40 cm). '**Marmalade**' Orange and yellow shades. ‡28 in (70 cm). '**Martina**' Yellow, fading to pale yellow; grayish green foliage. Perhaps a hybrid with *A. clypeolata*. ‡32 in (80 cm). '**McVities**' Biscuit yellow, fading to ivory. 36 in (90 cm). '**Mondpagode**' Creamy yellow with grayish foliage. Said to be a hybrid of *A. filipendulina*. ‡30–48 in (75–120 cm). '**Moonwalker**' Bright yellow; gray-green foliage. Hybrid with *A. ageratum*. ‡28 in (70 cm). Z3–8 H8–1. '**Old Brocade**' Yellow, golden yellow, and bronze. ‡32 in (80 cm). '**Paprika**' Deep red, fading with age; gray-green foliage. ‡28 in (70 cm). '**Prospero**' Creamy yellow; grayish foliage. ‡24 in (60 cm). '**Red Beauty**' Deep red. ‡24 in

(60 cm). '**Red Velvet**' Rosy red. ‡24 in (60 cm). '**Rose Madder**' Soft red; short. ‡14 in (35 cm). **Salmon Beauty** *see* 'Lachschönheit' '**Sammetriese**' Red to dark red. ‡32 in (80 cm). **Summer Pastels Group** A mixture of, not always pastel, colors from white, pink, and yellow to orange and red. From seed, and unpredictable in its height, flowering season, and color balance. ‡12–24 in (30–60 cm). '**Summerwine**' Opening deep red-purple, fading evenly pinkish purple and eventually yellowish brown. ‡28–36 in (70–90 cm). '**Taygetea**' Pale creamy yellow; grayish green foliage. A very variable, seed-raised hybrid, perhaps with *A. clypeolata*. '**Terracotta**' Opening deep orange-yellow, fading to cream; grayish green, feathered foliage. Bred by Ernst Pagels. ‡36–48 in (90–120 cm). **The Beacon** *see* 'Fanal' '**Walther Funcke**' Orange-red flowers, fading to creamy yellow; gray foliage. Short. Probably a hybrid with *A. filipendulina*, bred by Ernst Pagels. ‡12–24 in (30–60 cm). '**Wesersandstein**' Pinkish orange, fading to cream. ‡16–24 in (40–60 cm). '**White Queen**' White, but from seed so not uniformly clean. ‡20 in (50 cm).

A. '**Moonshine**' Greenish-gray foliage, forming a sturdy clump; wide flowerheads of 30 or more bright lemon yellow flowers. Probably a hybrid between *A. clypeolata* and *A. millefolium*. ‡24 in (60 cm). Z3–8 H8–1

A. nobilis Leaves oval in general outline and deeply divided, the segments themselves then regularly divided. Flowerheads of 50 to 150 or more flowers have 1/16-in (1-mm) white rays. Similar to *A. millefolium* but an altogether more dainty plant. From southern and central Europe. ‡28 in (70 cm). Z4–8 H8–2. **subsp.** *neilreichii* Creamy-yellow rays and grayish green foliage. Can be slightly invasive, but copes with some shade. From Austria, the Balkans, and the Caucasus.

A. ptarmica (Sneezewort) Large, vigorous, and spreading and noticeably lacking a basal leaf rosette, the 3½-in (9-cm) leaves are stalkless and narrowly lance-shaped. Loose flowerheads have three to 15 flowers with ¼-in (5-mm) white rays; the semidouble and double forms are common in gardens. Thrives in semishade, with moist ground. ‡ to 5 ft (1.5 m). Z3–8 H8–1. '**Ballerina**' Short, white, double-flowered form fading somewhat to gray. ‡16 in (40 cm). '**Boule de Neige**' syn. 'Schneeball' Double-flowered, but raised from seed so the degree of doubling is variable. ‡24–36 in (60–90 cm). '**Nana Compacta**' Short, compact, single-flowered, grayed white. ‡8 in (20 cm). '**Perry's White**' Double, taller, and less leafy than 'The Pearl'. ‡36 in (90 cm). '**Schneeball**' *see* 'Boule de Neige'. **The Pearl Group** A name loosely covering a range of more or less

LOST IN TRANSLATION

When the first of the new range of *Achillea* introductions emerged from Germany in 1986, they naturally carried names in the German language. In the English-speaking world, where the German language is often found unusually difficult, these names were immediately replaced by English translations. In some cases the translation was direct—for example, 'Apfelblüte' became Appleblossom. But at first 'Hoffnung' (literally "hope") became the more lyrical Great Expectations. Later 'Hoffnung' was translated more literally, and *Achillea*

Hope was listed by some nurseries. Finally, plants were imported with their original German-language name, so this meant that the plants were being grown in gardens and nurseries under three different names—'Hoffnung', Great Expectations, and Hope—but all were the same plant.

Obviously, this caused great confusion, so now the rules on the naming of plants do not allow the translation of cultivar names into other languages—the original name must be used. Translations are given in the entries here as cross-references.

RIGHT 1 *Achillea* 'Moonshine'
2 *A. ptarmica* 'Boule de Neige'
3 *A. ptarmica* 'The Pearl'

double forms, usually seed-raised, but often sold under one of the two common cultivar names, 'The Pearl', and 'Boule de Neige'. ↕20–36 in (50–90 cm). **'The Pearl'** The correct plant is dependably double, pure white, and somewhat shorter than doubles raised from seed. Expect impostors. Propagate by division. ↕16–24 in (40–60 cm).

A. salicifolia syn. *A. cartilaginea* Vigorous and aggressive, the unbranched stems are lined with usually doubly-toothed, lance-shaped leaves, 3½ in (9 cm) long and ⅝ in (1.4 cm) wide, and topped with loose heads of up to 15 flowers with ¼-in (5-mm) white rays. Similar to *A. ptarmica*, and similarly tolerant of a wide range of conditions. From western Europe to Central Asia. ↕To 5 ft (1.5 m). Z4–8 H8–2. **'Silver Spray'** Shorter and more prolific. ↕12–18 in (30–45 cm).

A. sibirica A more pleasing foliage effect than many other tall species; the leaves are stalkless, long, and narrow, regularly toothed and dark green, and borne on unbranched stems. Somewhat dense flowerheads of ten to 15 or more flowers, with white or pink-tinted rays. Most plants now grown are descended from a Japanese collection made by the Alpine Garden Society in 1988. From northern Asia. ↕to 30 in (75 cm). Z3–8 H8–1 **'Love Parade'** Pinkish white. **'Stephanie Cohen'** Pale pink. Named for the Pennsylvania garden writer.

A. umbellata A distinct, small plant, forming a clump with silver-gray, stalked lower leaves, to 1½ in (3.5 cm), elliptic in general outline, deeply divided with up to six segments. Flowerheads of usually three to seven flowers have ¼-in (5-mm) white rays. Needs an open, dry and sunny position. From southern and central Greece. ↕4 in (10 cm). Z6–8 H8–6

***A.* 'W. B. Childs'** A spreading, but not aggressive plant with dark green leaves, regularly divided with prominent, sawlike teeth. Loose flowerheads of ten or more flowers through the summer have ¼-in (5-mm) white rays and a darker center. Suited to moist soil and tolerant of slight shade. ↕20–28 in (50–70 cm). Z5–7 H7–5

ACHLYS
Deerfoot
BERBERIDACEAE

Hardy spring- and summer-flowering shade-lovers whose bold foliage contrasts dramatically with their wispy flowers.

From mountain forests or woods of Japan and western North America, three deciduous species thrive in cool, moist, shady places such as a woodland garden or shrub border. They spread widely by scaly, underground stems, and the overlapping leaves of established colonies make good ground cover. The plants have long-stalked leaves, each with three leaflets, and spikes of tiny, petal-less flowers that rise up through the leaves like wisps of white smoke in spring and summer.

CULTIVATION Best grown in steadily moist, humus-rich soil with dappled or unbroken shade and shelter from drying winds. Add leaf mold or well-rotted garden compost to the soil before planting.

PROPAGATION By rooting pieces of creeping stem in a cold frame, or dividing clumps, in early spring. From seed, sown freshly ripe in an open cold frame.

PROBLEMS Slugs and snails, caterpillars.

A. triphylla (Deerfoot, Vanilla leaf) The best-known species; a bold, clumping plant for woodland gardens. Long-stalked, fan-shaped, rich green leaves, each of three broad leaflets with wavy-toothed edges, are about 6 in (15 cm) across. They make a good background for the 2-in (5-cm) spikes of tiny, white flowers that appear on wiry stems from late spring to midsummer. From North America (British Columbia to California). ↕12–20 in (30–50 cm). Z6–9 H9–6

ACONITUM
Monkshood
RANUNCULACEAE

Easy, though virulently poisonous, plants for full sun or part-shade, including many that provide bold vertical accents.

About 300 species from northern temperate regions, mostly from Asia, but relatively few are widely grown. Many have tuberous rootstocks and the leaves are usually deep green, more or less round in outline and divided into three to seven lobes, each of which may be toothed or further divided into narrow lobes, giving a feathery effect in some. They are often withered on the lower part of the stem by flowering time, so selecting companion plants to hide the bare lower stems can improve the effect.

Flowers are most commonly blue or violet, occasionally white, pink, or soft yellow, and often borne in a spikelike inflorescence; some are produced as early as late spring, others continue until late fall. As with many other members of Ranunculaceae—the buttercup family—the sepals, provide the display, the uppermost one, called the helmet, having a characteristic hooded shape. The true petals within the flower are much reduced; the upper two are modified into nectaries that project up into the helmet. All parts of the plant are highly poisonous (*see* Deadly Monkshoods). ⚠

CULTIVATION All appreciate retentive soil with adequate moisture and moderate humus content. Upright types predominate and usually need no staking, though twining or more branching species benefit from brushwood support. Twiners can also be allowed to scramble over shrubs, into small trees, or among wall plants.

PROPAGATION Division in fall. Use gloves, since the plants are very poisonous. Tuberous species produce a few new tubers from each old tuber during the growing season; the largest of these should be replanted, discarding both old tubers and the smallest young tubers. Species can also be raised from seed.

PROBLEMS Disease problems are rare but include crown rot, verticillium wilt, bacterial spotting of the foliage, and powdery mildew.

DEADLY MONKSHOODS

Monkshoods, including the widely grown *Aconitum napellus*, contain some of the most dangerous poisons of any garden plants. They may even have been first brought into gardens for this very reason, perhaps for use as poison for arrowheads. John Gerard, in his famous *Herball* of 1597, was restrained, saying the flowers were "so beautifull, that a man woulde thinke they were of some excellent vertue, but" he concluded, *"non est semper fides habenda fronti"*—appearances can be deceptive. For gardeners, although roots have been accidentally eaten in place of horseradish, the chief danger is that the poison can be taken in through the skin. Consequently, when working with the plant in any way—from deadheading to splitting the roots—always wear gloves and cover exposed skin. Livestock—horses, for example—are also susceptible. There is no specific antidote. However, as Gerard mentioned, the monkshoods are beautiful plants and while care should clearly be taken while working with them, and they should be handled carefully when brought into the house as cut flowers, neither should they be banished from our borders.

A. anglicum see *A. napellus* subsp. *napellus* Anglicum Group

***A.* 'Blue Sceptre'** Tuberous plant with deeply lobed, deep green leaves and terminal and some subsidiary spikes of flowers in blue, merging to white in mid- and late summer. A hybrid of *A.* 'Newry Blue' and *A.* x *cammarum* 'Bicolor' raised by Alan Bloom. ↕28 in (70 cm). Z3–7 H8–3

***A.* 'Bressingham Spire'** Sturdy, tuberous, upright plant with dark green, deeply fingered leaves and noticeably tapering spikes of violet-blue flowers in late summer and early fall with plentiful secondary spikes. A hybrid of *A.* 'Newry Blue' and *A.* x *cammarum* 'Bicolor' raised by Alan Bloom. ↕3¼ ft (1 m). Z3–7 H8–3

A.* x *cammarum Rather varied, tuberous plants varying in habit from upright to more bushily branched, with green, deeply lobed leaves and flowers in a range of shades, sometimes two-toned, from early to late summer. A hybrid of the upright *A. napellus* and the well-branched, sometimes bicolored *A. variegatum*. ↕2–5 ft (60–150 cm). Z3–7 H8–3. **'Bicolor'** White flowers edged with violet-blue sparkle on a branched plant, early to midsummer. ↕4 ft (1.2 m). **'Eleanora'** White flowers in early and midsummer, lightly tinged blue at the edge of the sepals, on branched stems. Selected in Holland by Elly Geerlings from 'Bicolor'. ↕3¼ ft (1 m). **'Grandiflorum Album'** Flowers, spaced out along the stem on an upright plant, emerge pure white from green buds in mid- and late summer. ↕3½ ft (1.1 m). **'Pink Sensation'** Upright spikes of pale shell pink flowers in mid- and late summer, a little deeper at the edge of the sepals; black anthers at the center of each floret. Raised in Holland by Piet Oudolf; probably the best pink. ↕3¼ ft (1 m).

A. carmichaelii Tuberous species with deeply divided, leathery deep green leaves and varying considerably in height from 2 ft to 6½ ft (60 cm to 2 m), although usually about 4 ft (1.2 m). The unbranched 4-in (10-cm) flower spikes tend to be shorter than for *A. napellus*. Large, usually light lavender-blue flowers have a tall helmet, opening in late summer and early fall, taller selections flowering into mid-fall. Embraces the majority

RIGHT *Aconitum* 'Bressingham Spire'

of the more popular fall-flowering monkshoods. Found throughout most of China, also north Vietnam. ‡ 2–6½ ft (60–200 cm). Z3–8 H8–3. **'Arendsii'** Superlative for the richness of its lavender-blue flowers in early and mid-fall. The variable seedlings of this cultivar are often less impressively colored and are referred to as *A. carmichaelii* Arendsii Group. A hybrid between typical *A. carmichaelii* and *A. carmichaelii* Wilsonii Group. ‡ 4 ft (1.2 m). **'Royal Flush'** syn. *A. carmichaelii* 'Redleaf' Leaves deep red in spring, later becoming green, with deep blue flowers in early and mid-fall. ‡ 24 in (60 cm). **Wilsonii Group** (syn. *A. wilsonii*) Tall, flowering in early and mid-fall. ‡ 6 ft (1.8 m). **(Wilsonii Group) 'Barker's Variety'** Mid-lavender-blue flowers, reputed to breed true from seed. Raised by Edwin J. Barker of Kelmscott near Ipswich, Suffolk. ‡ 5 ft (1.5 m). **(Wilsonii Group) 'Kelmscott'** Deeper, richer lavender blue. From Edwin J. Barker of Kelmscott, Suffolk. ‡ 5 ft (1.5 m). **(Wilsonii Group) 'Spätlese'** Lighter lavender blue. ‡ 5 ft (1.5 m).

A. **hemsleyanum** Tuberous shade-tolerant twiner with vinelike leaves divided into three lobes a little beyond the middle; usually purplish stems and terminal clusters of two to six (more rarely up to 12) florets midsummer to mid-fall. Flower color varies—some have flowers as much gray or green as purple or blue, but the best, in lavender, rich violet-blue, or vinous purple, are extremely showy. The most common twining species in gardens, almost all plants offered as *A. volubile* belong here.

From woods in China and Burma. ‡ 6–15 ft (2–5 m). Z5–8 H8–5.

A. **henryi** 'Spark's Variety' see *A.* 'Spark's Variety'

A. **'Ivorine'** syn. *A. septentrionale* 'Ivorine' Fibrous-rooted monkshood with spires of creamy white, high-hooded, almost cylindrical, florets above plentiful dark green foliage in early and midsummer, sometimes earlier. Perhaps a variant of *A. lycoctonum* but with larger and more abundant flowers. One of the earliest monkshoods. ‡ 30 in (75 cm). Z3–8 H8–3

A. **lamarckii** see *A. lycoctonum* subsp. *neapolitanum*

A. **lasianthum** see *A. lycoctonum* subsp. *vulparia*

A. **lycoctonum** (Wolfsbane) Variable, fibrous-rooted species with leaves that can vary from saw-edged with three lobes, each divided into three more lobes, to deeply cut and toothed. The flowers, in early and late summer, may be violet, blue, yellowish, or creamy white with a tall helmet. Found in much of Europe, also North Africa and Asia. ‡ 2–6½ ft (60–200 cm). Z5–8 H8–5. **'Darkeyes'** Dark foliage, nearly black stems, and pale primrose-yellow flowers showing black stamens at the mouth. Selected by Bob Brown, of Cotswold Garden Flowers, Worcestershire, England. ‡ 30 in (75 cm). **subsp. lycoctonum** syn. *A. septentrionale*. Dark violet flowers and dark green leaves divided into four to six segments. From Norway eastward to Russia, Mongolia, and southwestern China. ‡ 2–5 ft (60–150 cm). **subsp. neapolitanum** syn. *A. lamarckii, A. neapolitanum,*

A. pyrenaicum, A. ranunculifolium Light green leaves with five to eight segments, divided several times to beyond the middle, and large, many-flowered spikes of soft yellow flowers. From the mountains of southern Europe (France and Spain east to Bulgaria, northern Greece and Romania) and Morocco. ‡ 16–48 in (40–120 cm). **subsp. vulparia** syn. *A. lasianthum, A. thyriacum, A. vulparia* Few-flowered spikes of rather small pale yellow flowers and dark green leaves divided as far as the middle. From France and Holland, eastward to Romania. ‡ 16–48 in (40–120 cm).

A. **napellus** (Common monkshood) Tuberous, the leaves divided to the base, with the narrow segments divided to halfway or more to the midrib. Stems may be branched or unbranched; flowers are usually violet or blue, with a wide range of flowering seasons, from late spring to late summer. Deadheading can give some reblooming from late summer onward. Many variants have been treated as species in their own right. From Europe, North America, and Asia. ‡ 3¼–6½ ft (10–300 cm). Z3–8 H8–3. **'Bergfürst'** Dusky dark blue flowers in mid- and late summer. ‡ 4 ft (1.2 m). **'Blue Valley'** Narrow spires of large dark blue florets in mid- and late summer. 3¼ ft (1 m). **subsp. napellus Anglicum Group** syn. *A. anglicum* Bright lavender blooms on a branched stem, the narrowly lobed dark green leaves tapering to a pointed tip. Valuable as one of the earliest monkshoods, flowering in late spring and early summer. Native to southwestern England and southern Wales. ‡ 36 in (90 cm). **'Rubellum'** A dubious name, best not used, for pinkish and reddish flowered forms of species including *A. x cammarum* and *A. napellus*. **subsp. vulgare** Flowers later, from midsummer to early fall, with narrow leaf lobes and a usually unbranched flower spike. ‡ 3¼–5½ ft (1–1.7 m). **subsp. vulgare 'Albidum'** Dense spires of white flowers in mid- and late summer but marred by grayish overtones except in cool and moist summers. ‡ 5 ft (1.5 m). **subsp. vulgare 'Carneum'** Flesh pink flowers with grayish shading in mid- and late summer but a clearer color in cooler areas. ‡ 5 ft (1.5 m).

A. **neapolitanum** see *A. lycoctonum* subsp. *neapolitanum*

A. **'Newry Blue'** Outstanding tall, narrow, tuberous monkshood with spikes of rich, deep blue flowers from midsummer to early fall, sometimes branching near the base. The very long flower spike, about 24 in (60 cm), makes it useful for vertical accents; it is especially effective contrasted with horizontal plates of yellow achillea. Originating from Daisy Hill Nursery, Northern Ireland, before 1954, and perhaps a variant of *A. napellus,* but the true plant is rarely seen. Midsummer to early fall. ‡ 5 ft (1.5 m). Z3–7 H8–3

A. **pyrenaicum** see *A. lycoctonum* subsp. *neapolitanum*

A. **ranunculifolium** see *A. lycoctonum* subsp. *neapolitanum*

A. **septentrionale** see *A. Ivorine, A. lycoctonum* subsp. *lycoctonum* syn. *A septentrionale*

A. **'Spark's Variety'** syn. *A. henryi* 'Spark's Variety' One of the most prolific and useful monkshoods, branched flower stems bear short, dense spikes of violet-blue florets from midsummer to early fall above finely cut, dark leaves. The parentage of this old tuberous hybrid from C. M. Prichard's Riverslea Nursery, England, *c.* 1898 is uncertain but does not involve, as is suggested, the twining *A. henryi.* ‡ 5 ft (1.5 m). Z5–8 H8–5

A. **'Stainless Steel'** Dense upright spikes of unusual silvery blue flowers from early summer to early fall over deeply cut, dark green foliage. Found by Aad and Elly Geerlings in Holland. ‡ 3¼ ft (1 m). Z4–8 H8–4

A. **thyriacum** see *A. lycoctonum* subsp. *vulparia*

A. **vulparia** see *A. lycoctonum* subsp. *vulparia*

A. **wilsonii** see *A. carmichaelii* Wilsonii Group

ACORUS
Sweet flag
ACORACEAE

Grassy moisture-lovers with aromatic foliage but insignificant flowers.

Two species are widespread in a variety of moist sites—from stream and pond edges to wet meadows—in subtropical to temperate areas of North America and Asia, and widely naturalized in Europe. Both species are cultivated, and there are many named cultivars. Rhizomes support mostly evergreen foliage, which varies enormously in length, and can be bold and irislike or more grassy. The crushed leaves have an anise or licorice scent that varies with the cultivars. The insignificant flowers appear in midsummer and, although long considered a member of the *Arum* family, Araceae, the details of its flower structure are sufficiently distinct for *Acorus* to usually be placed in its own family. Plants may spread uncomfortably quickly in the garden when growing well.

CULTIVATION Undemanding in most damp sites in sun or shade, and tolerant of a wide variety of sites.

PROPAGATION By division.

PROBLEMS Usually trouble-free.

A. **calamus** (Sweet flag) Large irislike perennial spreading by woody rhizomes. The dramatic, bright green foliage, to 5 ft (1.5 m), may be puckered along one edge as it emerges, and may be partially deciduous depending on the severity of winter conditions. Flowers, gathered into a 3–4-in (8–10-cm) yellow, hornlike growth, turning green, are held at a bold angle to the stem. Both rhizomes and foliage are tough and aromatic; the leaves were once used as a bedding herb, and spread as floor covering. Grows in any soil, in up to 8 in (20 cm) of still or slow-moving water, or in any damp border in full sun. Found in most northern temperate marshes. ↕5 ft (1.5 m). Z4–11 H12–2. **'Argenteostriatus'** ('Variegatus') Leaves clearly marked in creamy white.

A. gramineus (Dwarf sweet flag) Small grasslike perennial with tight rhizomes that support fans of slender pointed evergreen leaves, the whole fan often angled forward slightly. Small, unremarkable, hornlike, 1½–3-in (4–8-cm) flowers are produced on upright stems, more often on the wild form than on the variegated cultivars, many of which never flower. Plants may be divided at any time and kept damp. The smaller cultivars can tolerate submerged growth for extended periods but should not be planted permanently in such situations. Colored-leaved cultivars contrast well with other foliage textures. Often grouped with grasses by gardeners. From temperate East Asia. ↕12 in (30 cm). Z10–11 H12–2. **'Hakuro-nishiki'** Leaves striped golden-yellow and mid-green. ↕8 in (20 cm). **'Licorice'** Smaller all-green foliage, said to have stronger, more aromatic, licorice flavor when crushed. Has been used as herbal additive in Asia. ↕5 in (13 cm). **'Masamune'** Foliage striped cream to golden and pale green. Modest. ↕5 in (13 cm). **'Minimus Aureus'** Very short, with bright gold foliage in spring turning mid-green by summer. Small size requires careful placement. ↕3 in (7.5 cm). **'Oborozuki'** Golden foliage lightly striped in green. Quickly makes a decorative tuft. 'Ogon' may be mistakenly supplied under this name. Excellent. **'Ogon'** Golden yellow foliage, slightly greener in summer. **var. pusillus** Very dwarf, place thoughtfully. From Japan and China. ↕3 in (7 cm). **'Variegatus'** Slender, grasslike leaves striped in creamy white.

ACTAEA
Baneberry, Bugbane
RANUNCULACEAE

Long-lived, shade-loving, summer- and fall-flowering plants with attractive foliage, flowers, and berries.

Includes species formerly listed as *Cimicifuga*, making a total of 28 species of often rather tall herbaceous perennials, with wide-ranging origins in North America, Europe, and Asia. From a compact rootstock, most produce large basal leaves, some to 30 in (75 cm) across, each split either into many attractive

---

ACTAEA AND CIMICIFUGA

Many gardeners may be surprised to see the genus *Cimicifuga* disappearing from catalogs and books (including this one) but it has recently been appreciated that the two genera that were formerly familiar as *Actaea* and *Cimicifuga* are more alike than was realized.

The original five species of *Actaea*, mainly woodland garden plants and distinguished by fleshy red, black, or white berries, had previously been separated from the 23 species formerly known as *Cimicifuga*, which carry their seed in dry capsules.

However one species, now known as *A. racemosa*, has thickened fruits that are intermediate between a dry capsule and a fleshy berry. So in this case it seems that berries are only an evolutionary extension of one single natural group that contains all the species formerly separated into the two genera. Similar natural groups are found in other genera, such as *Hypericum*. In addition, the results of DNA analysis plus the many clear overall similarities between the two groups of species confirmed the impression that the two groups are not sufficiently distinct to remain separated and all are now classified as *Actaea*.

---

small leaflets or into fewer much larger ones. The flowering stems may be tall, upright, and tapering, or shorter and more branched, all bearing small stem leaves and many small but plentiful white, cream, yellow, or pinkish five-parted flowers. The flowerheads on some species are elongated into slender spikes, while on others they divide into many smaller side-branches.

The flowers are typical of the buttercup family, with white, cream, yellow, orange, or pink "petals," which are in fact, as they are in

hellebores, showy modified versions of the sepals. The true petals are often reduced to cup-shaped nectaries that may produce nectar to attract pollinating insects, or may remain more petal-like. The white, yellow, or pink stamens and ovaries protrude from the center of the flower. In the majority of species, the flowers develop into dry pods that split to release the seeds, although five species produce shiny black, red, or white berries.

Species can be distinguished from each other by the number and placement of very small leaflike bracts beneath each flower, by the shape of the cuplike nectaries, and by fruit type, number of fruits per flower, and seed shape.

There is much confusion between the species and many are grown under incorrect names—not because of the recent aggregation of *Cimicifuga* into *Actaea* (see panel), but because many look so much alike (hence the detail given here). Most species are harmful if eaten and can trigger skin irritations. ⚠

CULTIVATION All like a cool position in dappled shade with rich, deep, damp but not wet soil. Most species prefer acidic or neutral soil, although several will tolerate some alkalinity. Never let them dry out. A light mulch of rich leaf mold in winter is beneficial to all.

PROPAGATION Best propagated by division of established clumps during fall or early spring. Actaeas can also be grown from seed, but there are natural chemical inhibitors within the seed of many species that can delay germination for two to three years. Sowing seed as soon as it is ripe helps minimize this effect.

PROBLEMS Aphids, bacterial soft rots, slugs and snails.

A. alba see *A. pachypoda, A. rubra* f. *neglecta*

A. cordifolia syn. *Cimicifuga rubifolia* (Kearney's bugbane) Basal foliage is shiny green above and frequently with nine leaflets, each leaflet hand-shaped with five to seven heart-shaped, pointed lobes, 6 in (15 cm) across. The stems are upright and rather dark-stained, with several upright, lateral branches carrying, from mid- to late summer, long, 12–24-in (30–60-cm) flower spikes. The flowers are pale creamy white, without nectaries, and carried on short stalks. There are three short but broad pointed bracts under each flower stalk. One of the easiest species to grow, sometimes sold as *A. racemosa* var. *cordifolia*, to which this plant is not closely related. Enjoys dappled shade or a more or less shady position in a herbaceous border; tolerates more open and drier conditions than many other species. Found on wooded slopes of the central and southern Appalachian Mountains. ↕4–6½ ft (1.2–2 m). Z3–7 H7–3

A. dahurica (Dahurian bugbane) Basal leaves dull green above and frequently with nine to twenty-seven or more leaflets; each leaflet is diamond-shaped or oval and the apical leaflet on each leaf has three, rarely five, lobes. Stems are among the tallest, usually 3–5 ft (1–1.5 m) long, often carrying many hundreds of small white flowers on several horizontal, lateral branches from early to mid-fall. The only species with male and female flowers on separate plants; male plants have more flowers. Flowers are white with two to four small, cuplike nectaries; three very short pointed bracts under each flower stalk. Sometimes masquerades as *A. cimicifuga*. Enjoys woodland conditions: a cool, damp position in good rich loamy soil with plenty of organic matter. From Siberia, Korea, and China (Manchuria). ↕6½–10 ft (2–3 m). Z5–7 H7–5

A. heracleifolia (Hogweed-leaved bugbane) One of the finest species; smooth, almost leathery dark green leaves of nine or more leaflets. Each leaflet hand-shaped, 4–6 in (10–15 cm)

across, with five to seven pointed lobes. The upright green stems have several horizontal, lateral branches carrying flower spikes 12–36 in (30–90 cm) long. The white flowers, sweetly fragrant with two cup-shaped nectaries, borne on short flower stalks from early to mid-fall. Three short pointed bracts under each flower stalk. Best in a dappled border or woodland. From Korea, eastern Siberia, and China (Manchuria). ‡4–6½ ft (1.2–2 m). Z5–7 H7–5

A. japonica (Japanese bugbane) A relatively short species, its leaves are divided into three large smooth leaflets, each hand-shaped or maplelike, 4–6 in (10–15 cm) across, with five to seven pointed lobes. Each leaflet has a zone of fine hairs alongside the margin on the upper surface. The stems are upright, brown-stained, with a few shorter upright lateral branches, and carry white unstalked flowers, rarely flushed with pink, in 12–24-in (30–60-cm) spikes in early and mid-fall. There are three quite long and broad pointed bracts under each flower stalk. Best in a dappled border or woodland. Needs rich organic soil. From Japan, South Korea, and central China. ‡3¼–4 ft (1–1.2 m). Z5–7 H7–5

A. matsumurae syn. *A. simplex* var. *matsumurae* (Matsumuras bugbane) Basal foliage divided into 27 diamond-shaped leaflets, each apical leaflet having three lobes. The pale green stems are upright, with two or three very short, upright lateral branches. Flower spikes are long, usually 6–12 in (15–30 cm) and sometimes arching over at the apex. The white flowers are slightly fragrant and carried on flower stalks up to ½ in (1 cm) long from early through mid-fall, sometimes into late fall. There are three very short pointed bracts under each flower stalk. One of the easiest to grow; closely related to *A. simplex*, but shorter and flowering later. Best in a dappled border or woodland and can tolerate some alkalinity. From Japan (Kyushu, Shikoku, Honshu). ‡24–48 in (60–

DARK FOLIAGE

In recent years the most striking development in actaeas has been in what is now known as *Actaea simplex*. In 1970 Ernst Pagels, who has bred many fine plants from his nursery in Germany, introduced what was then called *Cimicifuga simplex* 'Braunlaub'—literally, "brown leaf"; in fact, the foliage was more a deep, purple-tinted shade of green. Over the years seedlings were selected for better leaf color and named, then even better seedlings named—'Braunlaub' all but disappeared, and now 'Brunette', 'Hillside Black Beauty' (introduced by Fred and Mary Ann McGourty in Connecticut), and 'James Compton' are the pick of this group, often with

wonderfully sultry, almost black foliage. Other unproven selections have been named including 'Bernard Mitchell' and 'Black Negligee'.

These dark-leaved plants are slow to propagate by division, so gardeners and nurseries have raised them from seed—but the seedlings vary in the color of their foliage. Unfortunately, these seedlings have been sold and passed around under the cultivar names of their parents—with the result that poor plants are glorified under the names of superb cultivars. However, the best cultivars are now being propagated by tissue culture so, before buying, ask the nursery how they propagate their dark-leaved actaeas.

120 cm). Z3–7 H7–3. **'Elstead'** Brown-stained stems, leaves, and flower buds; the flowers are white with dark-stained petals. ‡36–48 in (90–120 cm). **'Frau Herms'** Shorter, with smaller leaflets and white flowers with green petals. Sometimes listed under *A. simplex*. ‡32–36 in (80–90 cm). **'White Pearl'** Tall, with pale green stems, leaves, and flower buds. Sometimes listed under *A. simplex*. ‡3¼–4 ft (1–1.2 m).

A. pachypoda (Doll's eyes) Leaves composed of 27 diamond-shaped to oval leaflets, the apical leaflet on each leaf having three lobes. The pale green stems are upright, with one or rarely two very short, upright lateral branches and 2–6-in (5–15-cm) flower spikes. The flowers are white, lacking nectaries but with four to six nectary-like petals, and are carried on ½–1-in (1–2.5-cm) flower stalks in early and midsummer. The flower stalks thicken as the fruits ripen, giving the stems a heavy look. There is a single short pointed bract under each flower stalk. The oval, shining, stalkless elliptical white fruits have a purple tip and are produced from mid- to late summer. One of the tallest of the berried species. Sometimes incorrectly called *A. alba*. Lovely in a

dappled-shaded border or woodland garden, and can tolerate some alkalinity in the soil. From eastern Canada and the US (Appalachian Mountains at low elevations). ‡2–3 ft (60–90 cm). Z4–9 H9–1. **f. rubrocarpa** Oval berries shining red. Occasionally found among the usual white-fruited populations throughout the range of the species.

A. racemosa (Black cohosh) Leaves split into 27 lance-shaped or slightly broader leaflets, each apical leaflet having three lobes. The stems are upright, pale green, with one to several long, upright lateral branches topped with 12–36-in (30–90-cm) flower spikes. In midsummer, white or cream, fetid flowers carried on stalks ½–1 in (1–2.5 cm) long; they lack nectaries but have four nectary-like petals. A single short pointed bract is under each flower stalk. One of the easiest to cultivate, in a dappled border or woodland, and can tolerate some alkalinity. In recent years this species has been found to yield products that affect the human hormone system and can dramatically reduce the symptoms of menopause in women. As a result, wild populations have been seriously overcollected. From Canada (Ontario), and the central and eastern US. ‡3¼–6½ ft (1–2 m). Z3–7 H8–3

A. ramosa see *A. simplex*

A. rubra (American red baneberry) A variable species with leaves divided into 27 diamond- to oval-shaped leaflets, the apical leaflet on each leaf having three lobes. The stems, upright and pale green with one or rarely two very short, upright lateral branches, are topped with short, 2–6-in (5–15-cm) flower spikes, in early and midsummer, carrying white ½–1-in (1–2.5-cm) flowers; the flowers lack nectaries but have four to six nectary-like petals. The flower stalks remain thin during fruit ripening and a single short pointed bract is under each flower stalk. Round, shining red fruits, without individual stalks, are produced from mid- to late summer. Similar to a red-fruited version of the European *A. spicata*. A good woodland garden plant and can tolerate some alkalinity in the soil. Canada, the continental US. ‡24–36 in (60–90 cm). Z4–8 H8–1. **f. neglecta**

Sometimes incorrectly sold as *A. alba*. Shining white berries, occasionally found among red-fruited populations throughout the range of the species.

A. simplex syn. *A. ramosa* (Simple stemmed bugbane) Increasingly popular, with basal leaves split into 27 diamond shaped to oblong or lance-shaped leaflets, each apical leaflet having three lobes. The upright, pale green stems may have two or three very short, upright lateral branches. In early fall, the 24–36-in (60–90-cm) flower spikes, sometimes arching downward at the apex, carry strongly fragrant white flowers with two cup-shaped nectaries on flower stalks up to ¾ in (2 cm) long. There are three very short pointed bracts under each flower stalk. Closely related to *A. matsumurae*, but taller and flowering earlier. Good in partially shady borders or dappled woodland. From western to northeast China, northern Japan (Honshu, Hokkaido), Korea, and Russia (Kamchatka, Kurile Islands, Siberia). ‡4–7 ft (1.2–2.2 m). Z3–7 H7–3. **Atropurpurea Group** Covers any seed-raised plants that exhibit a flush of purple on the stems, leaves, and flowers. **(Atropurpurea Group) 'Brunette'** Purple-red stems, deep purple-red leaves, and purple-flushed pink flower buds opening to heavily fragrant flowers that are white flushed pink with purple-red petals. The flowering stems arch over strongly at the tips. Raised by Paul Petersen, Denmark. ‡4 ft (1.2 m). **(Atropurpurea Group) 'Hillside Black Beauty'** Tall, with purple-red stems and leaves and purple-flushed pink flower buds. The flowering stems are erect or slightly arching and carry heavily fragrant flowers, opening pale pink with purple-red sepals. Raised by Fred and Mary Ann McGourty, CT. ‡5–7 ft (1.5–2.2 m). **(Atropurpurea Group) 'James Compton'** Tall, purple-red stems with a bluish bloom emerge through broad, slightly paler purple-red basal leaves; purple-flushed pink flower buds open to white, heavily fragrant flowers with purple-red petals. Raised by Dutch horticulturist Piet Oudolf. ‡5–7 ft (1.5–2.2 m). **var. matsumurae** see *A. matsumurae*. **'Mountain Wave'** Slightly paler reddish purple stems, leaves, and floral parts. A selection from the Atropurpurea Group. **'Prichard's Giant'** Green-stemmed, green-leaved, and intensely fragrant; the unbranched erect stems carry white flowers in 24–36-in (60–90-cm) spikes. One of the best, raised by Maurice Prichard at Riverslea Nursery in Hampshire, England. ‡10 ft (3 m). **'Silver Axe'** syn. 'Scimitar' Green-stemmed and green-leaved, with powerfully fragrant white flowers. The unbranched erect stems curve strongly downward at the tips. Similar to 'Prichard's Giant' but shorter. Raised by Michael Wickenden at Cally Gardens, Scotland. ‡6 ft (1.8 m).

A. spicata (Black baneberry) Bold, dark green basal foliage; up to 27 oval, often three-lobed, toothed leaflets through which rise smooth, pale green, upright

ACTAEA FLOWERS

All acteas have the same general structure to their flowers and flowerheads. A central stem, with one to many side branches, carries the flowers on individual stalks that hold a single flower. Each flower is at first enclosed in five petal-like sepals, which soon fall to reveal the stamens surrounding and radiating from one to eight central female ovaries with their pointed styles. Below the junction of the flower stalk and the main stem, one or three small bracts may be found.

Flower buds enveloped in five sepals

Flower stalk

Bracts at junction of flower stalk and main stem

Stamens

Actaea racemosa

stems with occasional lateral branches. Short flower spikes, 2–6 in (5–15 cm) long, carry white ½–1-in (1–2.5-cm) stalked flowers, lacking nectaries but with four to six nectary-like petals, in early to midsummer. Single short pointed bract under each flower stalk. The flower stalks remain thin during fruit ripening and carry round, shining, black, individually stalkless fruits in mid- and late summer. Differs from the American *A. rubra* mainly in its black fruits. Superb woodland garden plant; can tolerate some alkalinity in the soil. From Europe (rare British native), and from Scandinavia through Asia to the Altai Mountains. ‡24–36 in (60–90 cm). Z4–8 H8–1. **var. rubra** see *A. rubra*

ADENOPHORA
Ladybells
CAMPANULACEAE

Showy, easy, summer-flowering plants with spires of blue bellflowers enhance a sunny border.

At least 40 species of clumping, deciduous plants of grasslands or open woodlands, in temperate Europe and in most of Asia east to China and Japan. Upright, leafy growth develops from a tight crown of fleshy roots; upper-stem leaves smaller and narrower than rounded, lower leaves. Nodding, bell-shaped, violet to light blue flowers carried in large, open, often branched clusters in summer. They differ from campanulas in small, botanical details. Several species are widely grown; others are becoming available and are well worth trying. *A. liliifolia, A. divaricata,* and some other species make long-lasting cut flowers.

CULTIVATION Moist, well-drained soil in full or part-sun.

BELOW *Adenophora tashiroi*

PROPAGATION From seed or by basal cuttings; avoid root disturbance.

PROBLEMS Slugs and snails, especially on young shoots; vine weevils.

A. aurita Compact plant with gray-green leaves and narrow, densely packed spikes of short, light mauve-blue bells, 1¼–1½ in (3–4 cm) long, from midsummer to early fall. Grows in open scrub on mountains in western China. ‡24–32 in (60–80 cm). Z3–7 H7–1

A. bulleyana Upright plant with rough hairy leaves to 3 in (8 cm) long; the pale blue, funnel-shaped flowers, ½ in (12 mm) long, are borne in branched spikes, often in clusters of three, in late summer and early fall. From mountain grasslands and woods in western China. ‡24–40 in (60–100 cm). Z4–8 H8–1

A. confusa Erect plant with smooth, oval, slightly toothed leaves and, in midsummer, dark blue ¾-in (2-cm) bells, in branched sprays, on sometimes slightly downy stems. From mountain grasslands in western China. ‡2–3 ft (60–90 cm). Z3–7 H7–1

A. divaricata Slender, underrated plant with oval leaves to 4 in (10 cm) long, in clusters of three or four up the stem. Funnel-shaped, light blue or white flowers borne in an open spray. Some forms have a pretty sheen of silvery hairs on the stems. From mountain grasslands and open woodlands in Japan, Korea, and northeastern China. ‡20–32 in (50–80 cm). Z3–7 H7–1

A. khasiana Tall, with lance-shaped leaves; in mid- and late summer, deep violet-blue, unusually broadly flared bells with a dark ring around the throat are borne on long, well-branched stems. Thrives in rich soil. From northern India. ‡3¼ ft (1 m). Z3–7 H7–1

A. liliifolia Has rounded basal leaves and narrow stem leaves. Numerous pale blue or white, open bells are carried in a broad spray in early and midsummer. Unusually, they are scented. From eastern Europe and Siberia. ‡20 in (50 cm). Z3–7 H7–1

A. nikoensis Compact plant with upright stems and toothed, narrowly lance-shaped leaves. The few pale blue flowers, ¾–1 in (2–3 cm) long in a loose spike, appear in late summer and early fall. From mountains in northern Japan. ‡12–18 in (30–45 cm). Z4–7 H7–1

A. pereskiifolia Variable plant with long-stalked basal leaves and narrower, clustered stem leaves, all coarsely toothed. Many ¾-in (2-cm) pale blue bells are carried in simple or branched spikes in mid- and late summer. From Mongolia and Siberia. ‡20–40 in (50–100 cm). Z3–7 H7–3

A. polyantha Narrow leaves are held in clusters or spiralled up the stem. Many sky blue bells, ½–¾ in (1.5–2 cm) long, are carried in a loose spray in mid- and late summer. From Korea and northern China. ‡2–3 ft (60–90 cm). Z3–7 H7–3

A. potaninii Upright or sprawling plant with lance-shaped leaves, slightly hairy on the veins and edges. Loose sprays of open, violet-blue bells, 1 in (2.5 cm) long, open in mid- and late summer. From western China. ‡2–3 ft (60–90 cm). Z3–7 H7–3

A. takedae var. *howozana* Slender, dwarf plant with smooth stems, oval lower leaves and narrower upper ones. Violet-blue flowers are carried in loose spikes in late summer and early fall. From high mountains in northern Japan. ‡4–6 in (10–15 cm). Z3–7 H7–3

A. tashiroi Differs from most species in being small and often having sprawling stems. Strongly toothed, oval leaves, to 3 in (8 cm) long, become smaller and narrower on the stems. Lax sprays of the few, violet flowers open in mid- or late summer. From open, grassy places in southern Japan and South Korea. ‡8–12 in (20–30 cm). Z4–7 H7–1

ADIANTUM
Maidenhair fern
ADIANTACEAE

Delicate-looking but remarkably tough ferns, and essential features of shade gardens.

About 200 species of unusually beautiful evergreen or deciduous ferns, found worldwide in moist shady places, of which only about ten are hardy in cool temperate regions. All these are well worth growing, but some are relatively undiscovered. They are mainly clump-forming plants, which develop a dense mass of growth; some have a creeping rhizome that eventually allows large colonies to develop. The wiry leaf stalks are a distinctive shiny black and support fronds that may be once, twice or three times divided, or may be fan-shaped. In some species the fronds are divided so they radiate from a central point like fingers on a hand. The surface of the leaves repels water. The spores are formed under the folded margin of the edge of each leaf segment. In temperate gardens, most species are deciduous; new fronds appear early in spring— sometimes contributing subtle pink or purplish coloring—and, although they may appear alarmingly early, significant frost damage is rare.

CULTIVATION Best in dappled shade in rich organic soil with good drainage and shelter from wind.

PROPAGATION By division in spring, or by sowing spores in summer.

PROBLEMS Usually trouble-free.

A. aleuticum (Aleutian maidenhair) Deciduous, fan-shaped, 8–12-in (20–30-cm) fronds on short rhizomes. Along each side of the midrib, each

RIGHT **1** *Adiantum aleuticum* **2** *A. pedatum* **3** *A. venustum*

radiating section of the fan is divided into a series of pale, slightly bluish green segments with delicately incised outer margins. Between the incisions the margin is rolled under to protect the developing spore-bearing structures. Often confused with *A. pedatum*, in which the leaf segments are larger and usually in the same plane as the frond; in *A. aleuticum* they are often slightly twisted. Native to northwestern US and Canada, and northeast Asia. ↕12–24 in (30–60 cm). Z3–8 H8–1. **'Imbricatum'** Dwarf, with leaf segments close to together on the midrib, often touching. ↕8 in (20 cm). **'Japonicum'** Foliage is a beautiful bright red in spring. ↕12–16 in (30–40 cm). **'Miss Sharples'** see *A. pedatum* 'Miss Sharples'. **'Subpumilum'** syn. 'Minimum' Dwarf form with leaf segments overlapping and very short fronds. ↕2 in (5 cm).

A. capillus-veneris (Maidenhair fern) Short, slowly spreading rhizomes carry deciduous, more or less triangular fronds to 28 in (70 cm) in length, divided two or three times into opposite pairs of pale green leaflets. Distinguished from most other species by the spore-bearing organ (sorus), seated under the outer edge of the leaf segments, being elongated rather than round. Less hardy than other species; enjoys alkaline soil and grows well on damp limestone walls. Native throughout the world in warm temperate regions, spreading into colder areas along coastal cliffs. ↕6–16 in (15–40 cm). Z8–11 H12–8

A. pedatum (Eastern maidenhair) Deciduous, broadly fan-shaped, rather spreading 8–14-in (20–35-cm) fronds are carried on short stout rhizomes; each radiating section of the fan is divided into a series of segments along each side of the midrib. The segments are pale green with the outer margin delicately incised. Between the incisions the margin of the leaflet is rolled under to protect the developing spores. Very similar to *A. aleuticum*, which is often sold under this name, but with slightly larger leaf segments, broader fronds, and more spreading habit. Northeastern US and Canada. ↕12–24 in (30–60 cm). Z3–8 H8–1. **'Miss Sharples'** Plants under this name are no different from the species. A plant with this name on its label was at first thought to be, and sold as, a cultivar when the name was only intended to indicate the source of the plant. Often, to add to the confusion, listed under *A. aleuticum*.

A. venustum (Himalayan maidenhair) From creeping rhizomes, pink croziers emerge in early to mid-spring, unfurling into distinctive, lance-shaped, slightly yellowish green 16 in (40 cm) fronds. These are twice divided into opposite pairs of fan-shaped segments that are rounded along the far margin with one or two rounded spore-bearing areas. The fronds tend to lie horizontally. Once established, it can withstand several hours of daily exposure to sun. Remove old fronds

in late winter before new growth emerges. A very attractive, tough, almost evergreen plant that spreads well and is easily divided. Native to the Himalaya up to around 13,000 ft (4,000 m). ↕6–8 in (15–20 cm). Z5–8 H8–5

ADONIS
RANUNCULACEAE

Showy, early-flowering, delicate-looking but hardy and long-lived plants for full or part-shade with beautiful, fernlike foliage.

About 20 species of clumping, deciduous perennials or annuals that grow in a range of habitats from Europe to northeast Asia, from light woodlands to open grasslands, in acidic or alkaline soil. Three perennial species grown in gardens. In late winter or spring, solitary buttercup yellow, white, or red flowers open at the same time as the finely dissected leaves. The foliage of most plants dies down in summer.

CULTIVATION Well-drained, retentive soil. Some adonis are shade-loving, while others prefer a more open situation.

PROPAGATION From fresh seed, which does not need chilling, although the resulting plants may take five years to flower, or by division.

PROBLEMS Slugs and snails, emerging shoots especially susceptible.

A. amurensis Slow-growing with a sturdy root, its triangular or oval leaves, to 6 in (15 cm) long, are attractively divided into narrow segments and are red-tinted as they emerge. Bright yellow, bowl-shaped flowers, 1¼–1½ in (3–4 cm) across with about 20 oblong petals, open in early and mid-spring—

BELOW **1** *Adonis amurensis*
2 *Aegopodium podagraria* 'Variegatum'

often earlier—and are surprisingly tolerant of very cold weather. Grows in well-drained, humus-rich, acidic to neutral soil, in full or part-shade; it can also be grown in pots in a cold greenhouse. Easily increased by division in early summer or early fall, or by fresh seed when available. It is native to China, Korea, eastern Siberia, and Japan, where it has long been cultivated; breeders have raised many striking forms, including a range of doubles and a bright orange, which are occasionally available. Some sold as *A. amurensis* may be the little-known *A. multiflora*, from southern Korea; the semidouble cultivar 'Fukujukai' is often sold as the wild species. Neither cultivar sets seed. ↕6–12 in (15–30 cm). Z4–7 H7–1. **'Fukujukai'** Larger, semidouble flowers. **'Pleniflora'** Fully double flowers with a greenish tinge, and narrower petals toothed at the tips. This plant may be a form of *A. multiflora*, 'Sandanzaki'.

A. brevistyla Ferny, deeply dissected leaves to 4 in (10 cm) long. Shallowly bowl-shaped flowers, 1¼–1½ in (3–4 cm) across, are white, tinged with blue on the backs of the petals, and have yellow stamens. They open in mid- or late spring. Best grown in part-shade, in humus-rich soil. Variable. Resents division; sow seed. From open hillsides in Tibet, Bhutan, and southwestern China. ↕8–16 in (20–40 cm). Z4–9 H–1.

A. vernalis Compact, tufted plant with bright green, broadly oval leaves finely divided into narrow segments. Solitary, bowl-shaped, bright yellow flowers, 1½–3 in (4–8 cm) across with between 10 and 20 petals, appear in mid- or late spring. Prefers full sun in well-drained soil, preferably neutral or alkaline. It resents being divided; seed is said to germinate better around the parent plant than in a pot, but even so, seedlings may take three or four years to emerge. From central, eastern, and southern Europe, usually growing in open places in rocky, alkaline soil, ↕15 in (38 cm). Z4–7 H7–1

AEGOPODIUM
Ground elder
APIACEAE

Extremely vigorous, spreading plants that thrive in shade; the variegated cultivars have attractive, carpeting foliage and can be used as weed-smothering ground-cover plants in selected situations.

Five to seven species of deciduous plants are usually found in light woodlands, particularly in moist soil, throughout much of Europe, except the far north, and into western Asia. The deep green leaves are divided into two or three broad-toothed, oval segments and closely resemble the leaves of the tree elder, hence the common name. Between early and late summer, white, flat-topped flowerheads (umbels) are held on branching stems above the foliage. Only one species, *Aegopodium podagraria*, is in cultivation.

CULTIVATION Grown in full or part-shade in any soil, but prefers heavier soil.

PROPAGATION Easily by division of rhizomes in spring or fall.

PROBLEMS Intolerant of extended drought.

A. podagraria (Bishopweed, Ground elder, Goutweed). A pernicious weed naturalized in many countries following its early use as a vegetable and cure for gout. Its specific name derives from the Latin word for "gout," *podagra*, while "bishopweed" refers to its frequent occurrence near ecclesiastical buildings. Gerard's *Herball* of 1597 describes it as "... so fruitful in its increase that where it hath once taken roote, it will hardly be gotten out againe, spoiling and getting every yeare more ground to the annoying of better herbes." This species is difficult to eradicate except by repeated applications of herbicide. The

variegated cultivars may be used in wilder, or self-contained, areas of the garden, especially where little else will grow, or in containers. They can also be invasive, moving out from borders along cracks in paving, so think carefully before planting—and if in doubt, don't. ↕ 1–2 ft (30–60 cm). Z4–9 H9–1. **'Dangerous'** Uncommon variegated form with leaves edged in pale yellow. **'Variegatum'** Pale gray-green leaves edged and splashed with ivory. Handsome grown in isolation in a large container if kept moist; when dry, the leaves may scorch. Occasionally reverts to the green-leaved weed; seedlings also revert. 'Variegatum' covers three slightly different forms; the one circulating in North America is said to be less likely to revert.

AGAPANTHUS
African lily
ALLIACEAE

Elegant and free-flowering plants for a sunny border or container that bring an ever-growing range of blue and white hues to the garden.

The ten species of evergreen or deciduous plants, native to open grasslands or rocky places in South Africa, are mostly represented in gardens by innumerable hybrid cultivars. Slowly spreading, they form a compact clump of many strappy, basal leaves and separate, upright flowering stems. The bell- or funnel-shaped flowers are usually blue and borne in a rounded cluster at the top of each leafless stem. The deciduous species are from cooler areas and are generally hardier than the evergreens from coastal localities at low altitudes. In gardens, plants are less easily grouped because of the effects of hybridization and the local climate.

In recent years, a huge number of cultivars have been introduced, many varying only slightly in color. Usually deciduous, they have funnel-shaped flowers borne for a month or two from early or midsummer. The many smaller cultivars are ideal for containers—especially since agapanthus flowers most freely when its roots are restricted. Differences between species are often indistinct—there may even be only one highly variable species. Most cultivars are of complicated hybrid origin, so are not listed here under individual species. Many have been raised from seed and names may sometimes not be correctly attributed.

CULTIVATION Plants thrive in full sun, and moist, fertile, but free-draining soil; best kept fairly dry in winter.

PROPAGATION By division from seed, but cultivars do not come true from seed and species may hybridize.

PROBLEMS Slugs and snails on young growth in spring.

Ardernei hybrid Flowers white, tinged

TOO MANY TO COUNT

Lewis Palmer raised and named many fine *Agapanthus* hybrids, although most are now hard to find (*see* Headbourne Hybrids, *p.44*). Since then, other gardeners and nurseries around the world have repeated the process; agapanthus are prolific seeders and easy to cultivate. Cultivars have been selected and introduced by the Crown Estate at Windsor in Berkshire, Lady Bacon at Raveningham Hall in Suffolk, Gary Dunlop at Ballyrogan Nursery Garden in Northern Ireland, Alan Bloom at Bressingham Gardens in Norfolk, and the NCCPG National Collection holder, Dick Fulcher in Devon. Recently, many have been raised in Holland, often for the cut-flower market.

The result is a huge number of worthy, but often very similar, cultivars that can be difficult to tell apart; often they arrive with a fanfare then disappear when the supplier ceases to list it. Cultivars included here are chosen for their quality and expected long-term availability.

It is easy to be impressed by the special qualities of an agapanthus seedling. However, it is likely that a similar, or even better, selection has already arisen. So check against an established collection before launching your treasure into the world under a new name—it may already have one.

purple toward the tip of the bud; dark anthers and pinkish leaf bases. Midsummer to late summer. ↕ 30 in (75 cm). Z8–11 H12–1

A. **'Ben Hope'** Dark blue flowers in mid- and late summer. ↕ 40–48 in (1–1.2 m). Z8–11 H12–1

A. **'Blue Companion'** Pale violet blue. Raised by Gary Dunlop in Northern Ireland. ↕ 40–48 in (1–1.2 m). Z8–11 H12–1

A. **'Blue Giant'** Rather open, bell-shaped, rich blue bells. ↕ 48 in (1.2 m). Z8–11 H12–1

A. **'Blue Globe'** Deep blue flowers borne in dense heads. ↕ 3¼ ft (1 m). Z8–11 H12–1

A. **'Blue Imp'** Compact plant with small clusters of dark blue flowers on slim stems in late summer. Raised in England by Lewis Palmer. ↕ 18 in (45 cm). Z8–11 H12–1

A. **'Blue Moon'** Pale grayish blue flowers in impressively massed heads. Raised in England by Eric Smith. ↕ 3–3¼ ft (90–100 cm). Z8–11 H12–1

A. **'Blue Triumphator'** Mid-blue, open, bell-shaped flowers. Variable, since

RIGHT **1** *Agapanthus* 'Blue Giant'
2 *A.* 'Bressingham White'
3 *A. campanulatus* subsp. *patens*
4 *A.* 'Gayle's Lilac'

LEFT 1 *Agapanthus* 'Jack's Blue'
2 *A.* 'Purple Cloud' **3** *A.* 'Snowcloud'

plants are often raised from seed. ‡ 3 ft (90 cm). Z8–11 H12–1

A. **'Bressingham Blue'** Robust plant with dense heads of rich, dark blue flowers in mid- and late summer. Selected by Alan Bloom of England from 2,000 seedlings. ‡ 3–3½ ft (90–110 cm). Z8–11 H12–1

A. **'Bressingham White'** Funnel-shaped, white flowers in mid- and late summer. Selected by Alan Bloom from the same batch of seedlings that produced 'Bressingham Blue'. ‡ 3 ft (90 cm). Z8–11 H12–1

A. **'Buckingham Palace'** Tall plant with deep blue flowers on waxy, relatively weak stems. Selected by the Crown Estate at Windsor, England. ‡ 5 ft (1.5 m). Z8–11 H12–1

A. **campanulatus** Deciduous plant with neat clump of narrow, strappy, dark gray-green leaves up to 16 in (40 cm) long. From early to late summer or later, it bears funnel- or bell-shaped, blue flowers that are ¾–1¼ in (2–3 cm) long. From eastern South Africa. ‡ 32–48 in (80–120 cm). Z7–11 H12–7. **var. albidus** White flowers midsummer to early fall. ‡ 24 in (60 cm). **'Albovittatus'** Slightly broader leaves, margined and striped creamy white. ‡ 24–32 in (60–80 cm). **'Isis'** Deep blue flowers in loose clusters. ‡ 30 in (75 cm). **'Meibont'** Leaves mottled with cream toward the tips; rich blue flowers from midsummer to early fall. ‡ 36 in (90 cm). **'Oxford Blue'** Deep indigo-blue flowers held above narrow, gray-green leaves. ‡ 30 in (75 cm). **subsp. patens** Smaller, more slender; shorter, more open, light blue flowers in late summer and early fall. ‡ 18 in (45 cm). **'Premier'** Deep green leaves and nodding, dark blue flowers. ‡ 24–32 in (60–80 cm). **'Profusion'** Abundant, dark-veined, light blue flowers. ‡ 36 in (90 cm). **variegated** Invalid name for a plant with cream-mottled leaves that green up in summer; flowers sparsely. ‡ 12–16 in (30–40 cm). **'Wedgwood Blue'** Loose clusters of nodding, pale gray-blue flowers and blue-green foliage. ‡ 36 in (90 cm).

A. **'Castle of Mey'** Large, deep blue flowers in loose clusters, in mid- and late summer. Selected by the Crown Estate at Windsor, England. ‡ 24–28 in (60–70 cm). Z8–11 H12–1

A. **'Doktor Brouwer'** Blue flowers with darker veins—darker in bud—in early and midsummer. ‡ 30 in (75 cm). Z8–11 H12–1

A. **'Donau'** Compact plant with light blue flowers on sturdy stems. ‡ 3–4 ft (90–120 cm). Z8–11 H12–1

A. **'Double Diamond'** Short stems carry pure white, double flowers, with ten to twelve lobes instead of the usual six. Raised in South Africa. ‡ 12–16 in (30–40 cm). Z8–11 H12–1

A. **'Gayle's Lilac'** Short, neat and late, with compact rounded clusters of pale lilac flowers in late summer and early fall. Raised in New Zealand. ‡ 16 in (40 cm). Z8–11 H12–1

A. **'Golden Rule'** Compact with yellow-edged leaves and light blue flowers in midsummer. ‡ 24 in (60 cm). Z8–11 H12–1

A. **Headbourne hybrids** Hardy plants with funnel-shaped flowers in shades of blue. (*see* Headbourne Hybrids) ‡ 24–36 in (60–90 cm). Z8–11 H12–1

A. **inapertus** Narrow, deciduous leaves; tall stems carry loose clusters of often nodding, tubular to narrowly funnel-shaped, mid- to deep blue, or rarely white, flowers from late summer to early fall. A variable species with five subspecies, four of them in cultivation. ‡ 4–6 ft (1.2–1.8 m). Z9–11 H12–7. **subsp. hollandii** Tall plant with upright, gray-green leaves. Slender stems, much taller than the leaves, bear a large cluster of nodding, narrowly tubular, dark blue flowers, 1¼–1½ in (3–4 cm) long. ‡ 5–6 ft (1.5–1.8 m). Z9–11 H12–7. **subsp. inapertus** Tall with 1 in (2.5 cm) wide leaves and deep blue flowers. ‡ 4–5 ft (1.2–1.5 m). Z9–11 H12–7. **subsp. intermedius** Usually deciduous (sometimes evergreen when young), with drooping clusters of tubular, blue flowers. ‡ 4–5 ft (1.2–1.5 m). 9–11 H12–7. **subsp. pendulus** Broader leaves, to 2 in (5 cm) wide, and deep violet-blue flowers. ‡ 5 ft (1.5 m).

A. **'Jack's Blue'** Deep violet-blue buds open to slightly paler flowers. Raised in New Zealand. ‡ 4–5 ft (1.2–1.5 m). Z8–11 H12–1

A. **'Lilliput'** Dwarf, with rich, dark blue flowers in rounded clusters. ‡ 18 in (45 cm). Z8–11 H12–1

A. **'Loch Hope'** Impressive, deep blue, broadly trumpet-shaped flowers in late summer and early fall. Selected at the Crown Estate at Windsor, England. ‡ 4 ft (1.2 m). Z8–11 H12–1

A. **'Midnight Blue'** Prolific dwarf plant with small, very deep blue flowers in mid- and late summer. ‡ 16 in (40 cm). Z8–11 H12–1

A. **'Midnight Star'** syn. 'Navy Blue' Very deep violet-blue flowers on strong stems, in mid- and late summer. From Raveningham Hall in Suffolk, England. ‡ 24–32 in (60–80 cm). Z8–11 H12–1

A. **'Mooreanus'** Originally, a dwarf with dark blue flowers. This name is now incorrectly associated with a similar plant that has pale blue flowers. ‡ 18 in (45 cm). Z8–11 H12–1

A. **'Peter Pan'** Very dwarf, with flared, light blue flowers in loose heads above glossy leaves in mid- and late summer. Raised in New Zealand. ‡ 12–18 in (30–45 cm). Z9–10 H12–1

A. **'Pinocchio'** Compact, with pale-centered, light blue flowers in mid- and

late summer. ‡ 24–32 in (60–80 cm). Z8–11 H12–1

A. **'Polar Ice'** Large clusters of pure white flowers in early and midsummer, above narrow leaves. Raised in Holland. ‡ 30 in (75 cm). Z8–11 H12–1

A. **praecox** Frost-tender, rather variable plant with broadly strappy, evergreen leaves. The open, funnel-shaped, blue flowers are 2–2½ in (5–6 cm) long and open in late summer and early fall. ‡ 16–39 in (40–100 cm). Z11 H12–7. **'Flore Pleno'** Double, mid-blue flowers. **subsp. orientalis** Compact plant with a dense clusters of slightly smaller, rich blue flowers. ‡ 24–36 in (60–90 cm). Z11 H12–7. **subsp. orientalis var. albiflorus** White flowers.

A. **'Purple Cloud'** Compact; very large clusters of nodding, violet-blue flowers in mid- and late summer, and broad leaves. Raised in New Zealand. ‡ 3¼–4 ft (1–1.2 m). Z9–11 H12–7

A. **'Rosewarne'** Large but tender evergreen; sky-blue flowers open in midsummer and late summer. Seed strain, slightly variable. ‡ 36 in (90 cm). Z8–11 H12–1

A. **'Royal Blue'** Open, rich blue bells on a compact plant; well suited to a container. Selected at the Crown Estate at Windsor, England. ‡ 24 in (60 cm). Z8–11 H12–1

A. **'Sandringham'** Very dark blue flowers in mid- and late summer; compact. Selected at the Crown Estate at Windsor, England. ‡ 24 in (60 cm). Z8–11 H12–1

A. **'Sea Coral'** Rather compact, with narrow leaves and white flowers that are tinged with pink. Raised in New Zealand. ‡ 24 in (60 cm). Z8–11 H12–1

HEADBOURNE HYBRIDS

The best known agapanthus by far are the Headbourne hybrids, named after the Hampshire garden of Lewis Palmer. He distributed the plants from this garden in the 1950s and 1960s. Palmer originally received seed from the *Agapanthus* bed at Kirstenbosch National Botanical Garden in Cape Town, South Africa. All the species were grown side by side in this bed, and Palmer raised hundreds of seedlings, which, understandably, proved to be hybrids in various colors from indigo, through every shade of blue, to white. Generally, they were similar to *A. campanulatus*, but with larger flowers, and were hardy. He gave away many seedlings and named only the best, but these were slow to increase, so seed from named and unnamed forms was distributed under the name Headbourne hybrids. In spite of their variability, these are generally good garden plants, but if a particular shade or feature is required, a named cultivar would be a better choice.

A. 'Sea Foam' Robust, hardy plant with broad leaves and pure white flowers. Raised in New Zealand. ↕ 36 in (90 cm). Z8–11 H12–1

A. Silver Moon ('Notfred') Vigorous, with white-margined leaves and blue flowers from midsummer to early fall. Introduced in England by Notcutts Nurseries. ↕ 24 in (60 cm). Z8–11 H12–1

A. 'Snowball' Pure white flowers in mid- and late summer, above partially evergreen foliage. Raised in New Zealand. ↕ 16–24 in (40–60 cm). Z8–11 H12–1

A. 'Snowcloud' Large clusters crowded with quantities of small, narrow, white flowers from midsummer to early fall. Raised in New Zealand. ↕ 4 ft (1.2 m). Z8–11 H12–1

A. 'Snowdrops' Dwarf plant with tiny, white flowers from midsummer to early fall. ↕ 14 in (35 cm). Z8–11 H12–1

A. 'Storm Cloud' Has nodding, narrowly trumpet-shaped, intense deep blue flowers. ↕ 4 ft (1.2 m). Z8–11 H12–1

A. 'Streamline' Nodding, gray-blue flowers; each petal has a darker central stripe. Raised in New Zealand. ↕ 18 in (45 cm). Z8–11 H12–1

A. 'Sunfield' Vigorous, with broad, glossy leaves and dark-veined, pale blue flowers from midsummer to early fall. ↕ 4 ft (1.2 m). Z8–11 H12–1

A. 'Timaru' Free-flowering; abundant clusters of rich blue flowers from midsummer to mid-fall. Raised in New Zealand. ↕ 30 in (75 cm). Z8–11 H12–1

A. 'Tinkerbell' Narrow, evergreen leaves striped with creamy white; the blue flowers are produced sparingly in mid- and late summer. Best in a container. Variegated form of 'Peter Pan'. ↕ 16–24 in (40–60 cm). Z8–11 H12–1

A. 'Torbay' Free-flowering; loose, sky-blue flowerheads from early to late summer and grayish green leaves. Raised in England by Eric Smith. ↕ 24–32 in (60–80 cm). Z8–11 H12–1

A. 'White Superior' Dense clusters on dark stems of large, white flowers with dark stamens, appear from early to late summer. ↕ 28 in (70 cm). Z8–11 H12–1

A. 'Windsor Grey' Curious, soft gray-blue flowers in large clusters, in mid- and late summer. Selected at the Crown Estate at Windsor, England. ↕ 3¼ ft (1 m). Z8–11 H12–1

AGASTACHE
Giant hyssop, Mexican hyssop
LAMIACEAE

Two contrasting types of aromatic plants, some with short, violet-blue flowers in dense spikes, and some larger flowers in fierier shades (*see* Two Very Different Groups).

Of the 22 perennial species, most are native to open, dry, rocky areas in the US and Mexico, but one comes from grassy, streamside habitats in East Asia. The aromatic, opposite leaves range from egg-shaped and deeply toothed to linear and untoothed, and the tubular or funnel-shaped flowers are held in dense spikes or elongated clusters. As often happens with a flurry of new introductions, and many are seed-raised, the names become confused. In the taller group especially, blue- and white-flowered cultivars have not always been assigned to the correct species. In fact, *Agastache foeniculum*, *A. rugosa*, and *A. urticifolia* can be identified by several features.

CULTIVATION Prefers well-drained, fertile soil in full sun, although *A. rugosa* tolerates damper, heavier soil. *A. mexicana* and related species are short-lived perennials; they flower in their first year from seed and can be grown as annuals. Species from southern North America flower for longer if the spent flower stems are removed, but they often lose much of their foliage by late summer. These are reasonably hardy in well-drained soil, although spring frosts may kill new shoots and plants. Cut stems back by half in late fall to reduce wind-rock.

PROPAGATION From seed sown in spring at 68°F (20°C) or by division in spring. Root semihard cuttings in late summer for overwintering in a frost-free place.

PROBLEMS Sometimes affected by powdery mildew.

A. 'Apricot Sunrise' Grayish green, triangular leaves with scalloped margins set off tubular, orange flowers, to 1½ in (3.5 cm) long, which open from darker buds. A hybrid of *A. aurantiaca* and *A. coccinea*. ↕ 16–28 in (40–70 cm). Z7–10 H10–7

A. aurantiaca Woody-based, deciduous perennial with narrowly lance- to egg-shaped leaves, 1½ in (4 cm) long, with white, hairy undersides and scalloped margins. Yellowish orange flowers, to 1¼ in (3 cm) long, in loose, interrupted, elongated clusters, appear from midsummer to early fall. Native to rocky outcrops in hills and open woodlands in Mexico. ↕ 20–36 in (50–90 cm). Z7–10 H10–7. **'Apricot Sprite'** Shorter, with a longer flowering season. Seed-raised. Selected by Thompson & Morgan Seeds. ↕ 16 in (40 cm).

A. 'Blue Fortune' Triangular to broadly lance-shaped leaves and compact flowerheads, with violet-blue flowers in distinct tiers, from midsummer to early fall. Sterile. A hybrid of *A. foeniculum* and *A. rugosa*. ↕ 40 in (100 cm). Z5–9 H9–5

A. cana (Mosquito hyssop) Woody-based, deciduous perennial with egg- to lance-shaped leaves that are gray

beneath, untoothed or scalloped, and 1½ in (4 cm) long. Flowers in shades of pinkish red, to 1¼ in (3 cm) long, are borne in mainly uninterrupted elongated clusters from midsummer to early fall. Native to rocky scrub zones in the southwestern US. ↕ 1–3 ft (30–90 cm). Z6–11 H12–1

A. 'Firebird' Mint-scented, grayish green, broadly lance-shaped leaves; pinkish orange flowers, up to 1 in (2.5 cm) in length. A hybrid of *A. coccinea* and *A. rupestris*. ↕ 32 in (80 cm). Z5–11 H12–5

A. foeniculum (Anise hyssop, Blue giant hyssop) Clump-forming, deciduous perennial with erect, sparsely branched stems. The licorice- or anise-scented, egg-shaped, toothed leaves, to 3 in (8 cm) long, are white beneath with minute, dense hairs. Small, tubular, blue flowers are borne in dense spikes from mid- to late summer. More rarely seen than its frequent appearance in catalogs would indicate; cultivars of the more common *A. rugosa* are often offered in its place—but the white undersides and

ABOVE **1** *Agastache foeniculum*
2 *A. rupestris*

pronounced scent of the leaves distinguish *A. foeniculum* from *A. rugosa*. Distinct from *A. urticifolia* by its flowers, which are less than ¼ in (7 mm) long, and its flower spikes being less than ¾ in (2 cm) in diameter. From fields, dry scrub, and hills in north-central regions of North America. ↕ 32–60 in (80–150 cm). Z5–11 H12–5

A. 'Fragrant Delight' Seed sold under this name is a mixture of species with flowers in blue, yellow, red, pink, and white, with a corresponding variety of foliage fragrances.

A. 'Glowing Embers' Leaves are broadly elliptical, flowers dusky orange and to 1½ in (4 cm) long. Possibly a hybrid of *A. coccinea* and *A. rupestris*. ↕ 12 in (30 cm). Z6–11 H12–1

A. 'Heather Queen' Triangular leaves; large tiers of pinkish purple flowers, to ¾ in (2 cm) long, that open from purple

TWO VERY DIFFERENT GROUPS

In recent years, the two very distinct groups of agastaches have enjoyed a boom in popularity. The taller group includes bold, bushy plants that form clumps with erect stems and broad, highly aromatic foliage. The flowers are mainly blue or white, or in one species yellowish, held in dense spikes, and are favored by bees. These have very much the look of a traditional border perennial, but have a tendency to self-seed too freely, and even be a nuisance, if not deadheaded. These four species—*A. foeniculum*, *A. nepetoides*, *A. rugosa*, and *A. urticifolia*—originate in relatively cool climates in Korea, China, and northern parts of North America. The shorter, sparser species with rather

twiggy, branched stems and somewhat woody bases come from hotter, drier climates farther south, from California to Mexico. Their larger flowers come in many hues of orange, pink, or red. These are arranged in a series of whorls, or clusters—each composed of several flowers all joined to the stem at the same point—and the whorls are spaced out on a long, open spike. The long flowers attract hummingbirds and flower over a longer period. This group includes some popular species—including *A. aurantiaca*, *A. cana*, *A. mexicana*, and *A. rupestris*—from which impressive hybrids have been, and continue to be, created. Hybrids between the two groups have not yet appeared.

buds with matching calyces. A hybrid of *A. cana* and *A. mexicana* or *A. pallida*. ↕32 in (80 cm). Z7–10 H10–7

A. mexicana (Mexican giant hyssop) Variable, deciduous perennial with creeping, woody stems and narrowly triangular, lemon-scented, toothed leaves to 3½ in (9 cm) long. Tiers of orange-pink, pink, magenta, red, or white flowers, 1–1¼ in (2.5–3 cm) long, are borne in an interrupted, elongated cluster from midsummer to early fall. Native to open conifer woods and volcanic slopes in Mexico. ↕24–40 in (60–100 cm). Z7–11 H12–7. **'Champagne'** Pale orange buds open to white flowers that are faintly flushed with salmon. Seed-raised. ↕3 ft (90 cm). **'Mauve Beauty'** Pinkish mauve flowers. ↕28 in (70 cm). **'Red Fortune' PBR** Cherry-red flowers, highly prolific. ↕28 in (70 cm). **'Toronjil Morado'** A form with pink flowers and a more intense, lemon scent. The name is invalid, since it is merely a Spanish vernacular name for the species, and so needs replacing. ↕6½ ft (2 m).

A. nepetoides (Yellow giant hyssop) Deciduous, clumping perennial with sturdy, erect stems and egg-shaped leaves up to 6 in (15 cm) long with scalloped margins. Dense, cylindrical spikes, to 4 in (10 cm) long, of small, yellowish green flowers, each about ¼ in (6 mm) long, borne from mid- to late summer. Found in fields and scrub in southern Canada and the eastern US. ↕3¼–8 ft (1–2.5 m). Z5–10 H10–5

***A.* 'Painted Lady'** Mint-scented, grayish green, broadly lance-shaped leaves and 1 in (2.5 cm) long flowers that are pink verging on coral. A spontaneous mutation of 'Firebird'. ↕32 in (80 cm). Z5–11 H12–5

***A.* 'Pink Panther'** Purplish green leaves, darker beneath, and deep rose-pink flowers. A hybrid of *A. coccinea* and *A. mexicana* 'Toronjil Morado'. ↕28 in (70 cm). Z7–10 H12–7

A. pringlei (Pringle's giant hyssop) Woody-based, deciduous perennial with erect, branched, tightly clustered stems and triangular, toothed leaves to 1½ in (4 cm) long. Elongated clusters of pink to pinkish purple flowers, to ½ in (1.5 cm) long, appear from midsummer to early fall. Native to rocky areas and open woodlands in Mexico. ↕8–32 in (20–80 cm). Z7–10 H12–7

A. rugosa (Korean mint) Clumping, deciduous perennial with erect stems and coarsely toothed, egg-shaped, mint-scented leaves, to 3 in (8 cm). It is distinguished from the rarely grown *A. foeniculum* by the gray undersides to its leaves and its softer fragrance. Violet-blue flowers, ¼–½ in (7–10 mm) long, are borne in dense, 4 in (10 cm) long spikes from mid- to late summer. Found in grassy places in mountains and along streams in east Asia. ↕32–60 in (80–150 cm). Z7–11 H12–7. ***f. albiflora*** syn. 'Alba' Includes seed-raised, all white-flowered cultivars, most of which are selected for their uniform height. ***f. albiflora* 'Alabaster'** ↕3 ft (90 cm). ***f. albiflora* 'Honey Bee White'** ↕2 ft (60 cm). ***f. albiflora* 'Liquorice White'** ↕4 ft (1.2 m). **'Golden Jubilee'** syn. 'Golden Anniversary' Violet-blue flowers and yellow leaves; the emerging foliage is particularly striking in early summer. but can look rather anemic. Seed-raised. **'Honey Bee Blue'** Violet-blue flowers. Seed-raised. ↕2 ft (60 cm). **'Liquorice Blue'** Violet-blue flowers. Seed-raised. ↕4 ft (1.2 m).

A. rupestris (Threadleaf giant hyssop) Woody-based, deciduous perennial with slender, branched, wiry stems and linear to lance-shaped, gray leaves to 2 in (5 cm) long. Orange-pink flowers, 1 in (2.5 cm) long, in tiers on interrupted, elongated clusters open from midsummer to early fall. Native to open forests and rocky and sandy slopes in southwestern US. ↕2 ft (60 cm). Z4–9 H9–4

***A.* 'Tangerine Dreams'** Triangular to lance-shaped leaves and large tiers of numerous orange flowers, which are 4 cm long with a contrasting, dark reddish brown calyx. Possibly a hybrid of *A. aurantiaca* and *A. coccinea*. ↕3 ft (90 cm). Z7–9 H9–7

***A.* 'Tutti-frutti'** Triangular to egg-shaped, prominently toothed leaves, which are scented lemon and mint. Flowers are 1¼ in (3 cm) long and pinkish purple with dusky, reddish brown calyces. A hybrid of *A. mexicana* 'Toronjil Morado' and *A. pallida*. ↕42 in (110 cm). Z6–10 H10–6

A. urticifolia (Nettle-leaf giant hyssop) Deciduous, clumping perennial with stout, erect stems and egg-shaped, 3 in (8 cm) long leaves, with coarsely toothed margins. Dense, cylindrical spikes, to 6 in (15 cm) long, of small, pink, violet, or white flowers, each about ⅜ in (8 mm) long, open from mid- to late summer. It is distinguished from *A. rugosa* by its powerful fragrance, and from *A. foeniculum* by the longer flowers and fatter flower spikes, which are more than ¾ in (2 cm) in diameter. Found in fields and scrub in western North America. ↕4–6 ft (1–2 m). Z5–10 H10–5

***A.* Western hybrids** A group of excellent hybrids of various parentages, including 'Apricot Sunrise', 'Firebird', 'Pink Panther', and 'Tutti-frutti'. They were raised by Richard Dufresne of North Carolina in the 1990s.

AGERATINA *see* EUPATORIUM

AGRIMONIA

Agrimony

ROSACEAE

Interesting plants that are best used to add color to a wildflower garden and other informal areas.

Most of the 15 or so species of mainly deciduous perennials are native to the northern temperate zone. They form clumps of arching, dissected leaves from which arise erect, wiry stems with smaller leaves. The stems are topped by slender spikes of small, five-petaled, yellow flowers. When the flowers fade, small, conical, woody seedpods develop, each one with a crown of tiny hooks to aid dispersal on the coats of wild animals—and on walkers' socks and pants.

CULTIVATION Grows well in ordinary, well-drained soil that is ideally, but not essentially, alkaline; best in a moderately to fully sunny site.

PROPAGATION From seed when ripe or by careful division in spring.

PROBLEMS Usually trouble-free.

A. eupatoria The best known agrimony. In spring, each hairy basal leaf is formed of several pairs of large and small, elliptic, coarsely toothed leaflets. These are deep green and lighter beneath. Erect, rarely branched, leafy stems terminating in slender spikes of ¼–¾ in (5–8 mm) wide, slightly scented, golden-yellow flowers arise in summer. The flowers have been widely used in herbal medicine; once they were combined with lemon, ginger, and sugar as a cold remedy. Familiar by roadsides in Europe and extending to western Asia and North Africa. ↕32–40 in (80–100 cm). Z5–9 H9–5. **var. *alba*** Rare white-flowered form.

AGROPYRON *see* ELYMUS

AGROSTIS

POACEAE

Tufted grasses, familiar in lawn mixes, but increasingly used for their delicate flowers.

About 220 species are found in open countryside and light woodlands throughout temperate regions. The fine, pointed leaves form a tufted base from which grow slender stems. These bear purplish or brownish flowerheads, which are sometimes loose and airy, sometimes compact and feathery. Of the many species, only one cultivar of one species is widely grown as an ornamental perennial.

CULTIVATION Grows well in an open but cool position in any fertile, well-drained soil; benefits from a light pruning in early spring.

PROPAGATION By division in spring or from seed.

PROBLEMS Usually trouble-free.

A. canina (Velvet bent) Slowly spreading from short, rooting runners, this species eventually forms a thick, evergreen, tufted carpet of narrow, flat leaves that are ¹⁄₁₆ in (1–2 mm) wide. Sleek, brown to purple, feathery flowerheads, ¼–⅛ in (3–5 mm) long, appear in early to late summer. In the garden, it is a delicate addition to wildflower meadows and lawns, and is also useful as a path edging. Best in sun or part-shade. From grasslands and open woodlands throughout Europe, Asia, and northeastern America. ↕2½ in (6 cm). Z4–8 H8–4. **'Silver Needles'** One of the best dwarf foliage grasses, with white margins on the needlelike leaves and purplish flowers. Occasional clipping promotes good color.

AJANIA

ASTERACEAE

Sun-loving, fall-flowering plants whose buttonlike flowerheads are complemented by arresting foliage.

The 30 species of these evergreen plants spread slowly by creeping underground stems in rocky, often coastal locations in Central and East Asia. Just one is commonly grown in gardens. The bushy growth is well clothed by neatly lobed leaves, often white-felted on the undersides. Bright yellow flowerheads open in fall. *Ajania* was formerly included in *Chrysanthemum*.

CULTIVATION Thrives in rather poor, well-drained soil in full sun.

PROPAGATION By division or cuttings.

PROBLEMS Usually trouble-free.

A. pacifica syn. *Chrysanthemum pacificum* Spreading bushy growth, wider than tall, with rather thick, shallow-lobed, mid-green, oval leaves, 1¼–2½ in (3–6 cm) long, the white felt beneath showing on top as a fine silvery outline. The foliage is attractive all year. Small, deep yellow flowerheads, ¾ in (2 cm) across, open in mid- and late fall, in loose clusters, making a useful contribution to the late fall garden. Good for the front of a sunny border, and useful in containers, but its habit and foliage develop best in poorer soil. Silver and Gold and Silver Edge are simply marketing names for the species. Hybrids with florists' chrysanthemums are being developed. From rocky cliffs on the Pacific coast of southern Japan. ↕12 in (30 cm). Z5–9 H9–1

AJUGA

Bugle, bugleweed

LAMIACEAE

Hardy shade-lovers that flower in spring or early summer, in a growing range of forms with colored or variegated foliage.

About 40 species of annuals and spreading or clump-forming evergreen or partially evergreen perennials, only three of which are generally grown, make attractive ground cover in a woodland garden or among border shrubs. From moist, shady places—especially open woodlands—throughout temperate Europe and Asia. Plants often spread vigorously, by creeping stems above or just below ground. The pairs of oval or spoon-shaped leaves form

ground-hugging rosettes. Two-lipped, tubular, mainly blue flowers are carried in tiers up leafy stems in spring or early summer. Expect to see new forms, including some from relatively neglected species.

CULTIVATION Best grown in steadily moist, rich soil. Part- or dappled shade cast by deciduous trees or shrubs is ideal. Some sun is needed for the best leaf color, but very strong sun may scorch some forms, particularly variegated cultivars. In full shade, purple-leaved cultivars become greener; cultivars with multicolored foliage may also vary in color according to available light.

PROPAGATION By dividing into hand-sized portions or removing rooted plantlets in spring or early fall.

PROBLEMS Powdery mildew.

A. genevensis (Blue bugle, Upright bugle) Clumping evergreen with no creeping stems; makes good, well-behaved ground cover. Medium- or light-green, basal leaves are long stalked, 5 in (12 cm) long, and oval but broadest at the tops, with shallow lobes or toothed edges. In mid-spring, ¾-in (2-cm) long flowers appear on upright, leafy stems; they are dark but bright blue, or sometimes pink or white. From southern Europe. ↕8–16 in (20–40 cm). Z3–9 H9–1. **'Tottenham'** Green leaves, slightly flushed purple, and lilac-pink flowers in dense spikes, sometimes until late summer; slow-spreading.

A. metallica see *A. pyramidalis*

A. pyramidalis syn. *A. metallica* (Pyramid bugle) Evergreen or partially evergreen, clumping plant without creeping stems is good ground cover. The hairy, deep green, oval leaves are broadest at the tops and 4½ in (11 cm) long with slightly toothed edges. Flowers appear in dense, leafy, pyramid-shaped spikes from mid-spring to early summer, and are up to ¾ in (2 cm) long. Their color varies from dark blue to light violet-blue, but may be white or pink. From northern and central Europe, including the Alps. ↕6–12 in (15–30 cm). Z3–9 H9–1 **'Metallica Crispa'** Metallic green-purple, crinkle-edged leaves ↕6 in (15 cm).

A. reptans (Bugle, bugleweed) Carpeting evergreen that makes excellent ground cover; spreads by creeping stems from which root new plantlets. The deep green leaves, 3½ in (9 cm) long, are somewhat spoon- or egg-shaped. The ½-in- (1.5-cm-) long, deep blue flowers are carried in 4¾-in- (12-cm-) long spikes in late spring and early summer; some cultivars have a later, second flush. Cultivars, especially those with colored or variegated foliage, are usually grown in gardens

rather than wild species; they tolerate poor (but not dry) soil and even full shade. Useful for controlling soil erosion on shady banks. Self-sown seedlings of dark-leaved forms may prove to be green, or intermediate in color. New forms continue to be selected in gardens and from the wild. Many of the purple-leaved forms listed here are thought to be hybrids with *A. pyramidalis* 'Metallica Crispa'. From Europe, the Caucasus, and Iran. ↕6 in (15 cm). Z3–9 H9–1. **f.** *albiflora* **'Alba'** White flowers, deep green foliage. Forms vary in height, and may have orange-tinted stems or slightly spotted flowers. **'Arctic Fox'** Leaves mostly cream with dark green edges, prone to reversion; bright blue flowers. Arose at the Gardenview Horticultural Park, Strongsville, OH. **'Argentea'** *see* 'Variegata'. **'Atropurpurea'** Leaves shiny, uniform dark purple with bronze tint. Very similar to 'Braunherz' and often confused with it. **'Braunherz'** Glossy, very deep purple leaves. Very similar to 'Atropurpurea' but darkening in summer. **'Burgundy Glow'** Leaves silver-green, flushed red; becoming darker toward fall. **'Carol'** *see* 'Burgundy Glow'. **'Catlin's Giant'** Deep bronze-purple leaves 6 in (15 cm) long; vigorous habit. ↕8 in (20 cm). **'Chocolate Chip'** *see* 'Valfredda'. **'Delight'** Bronze leaves variegated pink and yellow; tends to revert. **'Ebony'** Mildew-resistant spontaneous mutation of 'Braunherz'. **'Ermine'** White leaves with deep green, wavy edges. ↕5 in (12 cm). **'Grey Lady'** Small, shiny gray leaves that are marbled purple, with pale blue flowers. **'Jumbo'** *see* 'Jungle Beauty'. **'Jungle Beauty'** Larger flowers and leaves than the species; bronzed in winter. Originally from Holbrook Farms in North Carolina. 'Jungle Beauty Improved', introduced in England by Beth Chatto, has richer color and has mostly supplanted the

LEFT 1 *Ajania pacifica* **2** *Ajuga reptans* 'Atropurpurea' **3** *A. reptans* 'Braunherz' **4** *A. reptans* 'Burgundy Glow' **5** *A. reptans* 'Multicolor'

NOT QUITE UP TO THE MARK?

Bugles, especially those with colored or variegated foliage, are popular plants. Surprisingly, when the Royal Horticultural Society organized a trial of nearly 40 different cultivars from 1998 to 2001, no new awards for plants "of outstanding excellence" were given, although many cultivars were admired by the judging panel. There were a number of reasons for the lack of awards. The plants needed regular attention to keep them vigorous and in flower. Also, plants had to be cut back to stop them from invading their less robust neighbors; this pruning of vigorous new growth left weak, and rather sparse, older growth and seriously detracted from the display. Some of the handsome foliage forms also tended to revert, while some cultivars did not flower at all. Finally, there was confusion over the names. Even so, all agreed that bugles are useful garden plants with particular value as ground cover below deciduous shrubs.

original stock. **'Macrophylla'** *see* 'Catlin's Giant'. **'Multicolor'** Leaves variegated bronze-green, cream, and pink. ↕5 in (12 cm). **'Palisander'** Purple-bronze leaves, ↕8 in (20 cm). **'Pink Elf'** Compact habit, pink flowers, deep green leaves. ↕2 in (5 cm). **'Pink Surprise'** Deep purple leaves and deep pink flowers. **'Purple Brocade'** Dark purple leaves, vigorous growth. Introduced by the Coastal Gardens Nursery, SC. **'Purple Torch'** Pink flowers (not purple), deep green leaves flushed purple, ↕8 in (20 cm). **'Purpurea'** *see* 'Atropurpurea'. **'Rainbow'** *see* 'Multicolor'. **'Tricolor'** *see* 'Multicolor'. **'Valfredda'** Small, rich chocolate brown leaves, compact habit. Discovered in Italy. **'Vanilla Chip'** Small, green leaves with creamy-white edges, dwarf habit. Introduced by Terra Nova Nurseries, OR. ↕2 in (5 cm). **'Variegata'** Leaves gray-green, variegated cream; neat habit. ↕4 in (10 cm).

ALCHEMILLA
ROSACEAE

Good-looking workhorses of the garden, with pretty foliage and a long flowering season, combine well with almost any other plant.

Over 300 bewilderingly similar species come from upland meadows and woodland clearings in Europe and Asia. Even specialists can find them difficult to distinguish. The rounded or kidney-shaped leaves, which spring from tight, woody rhizomes, have up to 11 lobes, or sometimes separate leaflets, which are often covered in silky hairs. The stems carry smaller, simpler leaves and rather crowded clusters of small, yellowish or green, nectar-rich flowers. Most species are unusual in being able to produce seed without fertilization (apomictic), as are many brambles (*Rubus*) and dandelions (*Taraxacum*). Lady's mantle, *Alchemilla mollis*, is the most distinct species and so ubiquitous that other alchemillas are often described in terms of how they differ from it. Many are difficult to tell apart and nurseries may confuse them, so plants you buy, and the seed offered in seed lists, may be incorrectly labeled. In this case, if you like the plant and it does what you need, don't worry about the name. Almost any perennial can be combined with their chartreuse flowers.

CULTIVATION Generally easy to grow in sun, part-shade, or in some cases darker conditions. Some species suffer in heavy rains. Most are tolerant of heavy clay soil and just about any other insult. Remove flowers after blooming (they dry beautifully) and cut back older leaves shortly thereafter; fresh foliage, and often more flowers, will be on their way.

PROPAGATION By division or from seed.

AN ELEGANT COVER UP

LADY'S MANTLE, *Alchemilla mollis*, is an invaluable plant, hence its ubiquity in gardens. It has two exceptionally useful characteristics: its yellowish green color, both in foliage and flowers, works well with almost any other shade—it's impossible to create a color clash with alchemilla. It also has the practical quality of being dense enough to smother weeds, while not being so dense that strong plants cannot surge through.

Here the starry purple footballs of *Allium christophii* are opening just above the alchemilla foliage and among its flowers. The expanding foliage of the alchemilla not only provides a fine background to set off the allium flowerheads but will also hide the ragged allium leaves, which deteriorate rapidly once the flowers open, a service it can provide for other plants with similar deficiencies.

PROBLEMS Usually trouble-free.

A. alpina Neat, but rather slow, ground cover, the pale pea green, 1½-in-(3.5-cm-) long, shiny leaves have five or seven, pronounced fingers; sparkling hairs on the undersides extend from the edges to create a silvery rim. In mid- and late summer, the rather sparse, chartreuse flowers are intriguing but not dramatic. Cut back in midsummer for a denser mat. Prefers gravelly soil with good drainage. Best in sun but dislikes heat; shade can make it patchy. From the mountains of Europe. ↕4–6 in (10–15 cm). Z3–7 H8–1

A. conjuncta The steadily spreading rhizome carries blue-green leaves that are 1½–1¾ in (3.5–4.5 cm) long, deeply cut into seven or nine lobes, toothed at the tips, and covered with silvery hairs below. The greenish yellow flowers appear from midsummer to early fall. Often confused with *A. alpina*, but taller and usually with more lobes to its bluer leaves. From the Alps. ↕12 in (30 cm). Z3–7 H7–1

A. ellenbeckii A miniature, spreading, but ground-hugging rendition of the familiar *A. mollis*. Equally stoic, but with scalloped, deep green, five-lobed leaves, 1 in (2.5 cm) long, that are set on wine-red stems to form a dense mat. The chartreuse flowers are spindly, rather sparse, and may be hidden by the leaves, so they are not its shining feature. Grows best in moist, but well-drained soil; less tolerant of drought than *A. mollis*. East Africa. ↕2–4 in (5–10 cm). Z5–7 H7–5

A. erythropoda Adaptable, neat, clumping plant with rounded, slightly blue-green leaves, each 2¾–3½ in (7–9 cm) across and shallowly divided into seven or nine lobes that are edged with prominent, sharp teeth. The leaves are blush red in full sun. The yellowish green flowers, which age to pleasing reddish tones, appear from late spring to late summer. Somewhat similar to a miniature version of *A. mollis*. From the Balkans, western Carpathians, and Caucasus. ↕6–9 in (15–23 cm). Z3–7 H7–1

A. mollis (Lady's mantle) Invaluable, perhaps overused, clumping perennial, its densely packed, neat, rounded, 6-in (15-cm) leaves are indented into nine or eleven, lightly felted, deep green lobes, with serrated edges. The leaves cradle dew drops and display them like jewels. From early summer to early fall, the foliage is almost hidden by familiar clouds of tiny, chartreuse flowers that *en masse* make a strong statement. The foliage remains neat through most of the season, especially if cut back after blooming, but in rainy climates the display may flop before flowering is over. Thrives in clay soil as well as the fertile, moist, well-drained soil that it prefers; tolerates drought. Best in sun, but fine in shade, especially under a high canopy. Self-sows, often annoyingly, so cut back before the seed is shed. ↕12–24 in (30–60 cm). Z4–7 H7–1. **'Auslese'** A more pleated, gray-green, beefed-up plant with denser clouds of flowers. Requires cool, moist soil and light shade. **'Robusta'** syn. 'Select' Taller, more upright, and does not flop after flowering; often said to be less

The widely grown *Alchemilla mollis* is
undeniably a lovely plant and, under
the proper conditions, it can be used
as a ground cover under roses and
shrubs, along a pathway, or in the
front of a herbaceous border. It is
an excellent choice for the informal
garden, such as that created in a
cottage garden. Its self-sown seeds
germinate readily in a cool, moist,
well-draining site, making it an easy
plant to grow.

If too many seedlings become a
problem, regular deadheading will
control the population. After the
flowers have lost their fresh coloring,
the entire plant can be cut back to
the basal growth with either shears
or clippers. New fresh foliage should
then develop, creating a more beautiful
plant. Water the plants if cutting back
is followed by a hot, dry spell.

likely to self-seed. Good cut flower.
Tolerates denser shade and longer
drought. Sometimes listed, incorrectly,
as 'Robustica'. ↕24–30 in (60–75 cm).
'Senior' More gray-green foliage.
'Thriller' Even more prolific, with
flowers held in a more spreading
plume. **'Variegata'** Foliage randomly
accented with yellow markings.

A. xanthochlora Effervescent, clump-
former with rounded or kidney-shaped
2-in (5-cm) leaves, divided into nine or
eleven evenly toothed lobes, thickly
hairy beneath and often a yellowish
green. Tiny, yellowish green flowers on
sturdy stems in abundant clouds from
early summer to late summer. Like a
small version of *A. mollis,* but with hairs
on the undersides of the leaves only.

BELOW 1 *Alchemilla erythropoda*
2 *A. mollis* **3** *Allium schoenoprasum*
'Forescate' **4** *A. senescens*

Adaptable, but best in good soil in sun
or light shade. From northwestern and
central Europe. ↕18–24 in (45–60 cm).
Z4–7 H8–1

ALLIUM
Onion
ALLIACEAE

Hardy sun-lovers of variable
habit with showy flowers in
late spring or summer. Don't be
put off by the pungent smell.

About 700 species of deciduous
plants that grow mostly in dry,
scrubby places and on mountains
in the Northern Hemisphere. Taller
kinds are ideal for mixed borders
and gravel gardens, while smaller
species are suitable for the front of
borders. Most grow from bulbs, and
are not covered here, whereas those
that behave like perennials—
spreading to form clumps and not
adapted to drying off—are featured.
Leaves may be grassy or strap-
shaped, upright or spreading, and,
when crushed or bruised, give off
an onion smell. Sometimes they
die down before the flowers appear.
Flowering times range from the end
of spring, through summer, to early
fall. Starry to bell- or cup-shaped
flowers are carried in rounded heads
on upright stems.

CULTIVATION Sunny spot with well-
drained and reasonably fertile soil.
Plant just below the soil surface.

PROPAGATION Divide clumps in early
spring. Sow seed as soon as ripe, or
in spring, in a cold frame.

PROBLEMS Usually trouble-free.

A. amabile see *A. mairei* var. *amabile*

A. beesianum Most plants in gardens
are *A. cyaneum*

A. cyaneum A small species, ideal for
the front of the border where it makes
tight clumps of thin, grassy deep green
leaves up to 6 in (15 cm) long. The
tight, nodding ¾-in (2-cm) clusters of
six to eight brilliant blue bell-shaped
flowers are especially welcome in late
summer and early fall. Sometimes sold
as *A. beesianum.* China. ↕4–10 in (10–
25 cm). Z5–9 H9–5

A. glaucum see *A. senescens* subsp.
montanum var. *glaucum*

A. insubricum An indispensable, elegant,
large-flowered plant for the front of
the border, with narrow, strap-shaped
medium green leaves up to 8 in
(20 cm) long. The 1-in- (2.5-cm-)
wide heads of three to five nodding
bell-shaped pink-purple flowers appear
from early summer onward. This
species is often confused with, and sold
as, the much less frequently seen
A. narcissiflorum, which has more
flowers—between five and eight—in
each head, and upright rather than
nodding seed heads. From northern
Italy. ↕6–10 in (15–25 cm). Z4–9 H9–1

A. kansuense see *A. sikkimense*

A. macranthum An excellent front-of-
the-border plant with narrow medium
green leaves up to 18 in (45 cm) long.
From early summer onward, triangular
stems carry large loose flowerheads, up
to 4 in (10 cm) across, which contain
many dangling bell-shaped dark purple
flowers. Usually 5 to 12 flowers are
carried in each head, but 50 have
been seen. Slow to increase, but seed
germinates easily. From Sikkim in the
Himalaya, and western China. ↕8–12 in
(20–30 cm). Z4–10 H10–4

A. mairei A delightful little species for
border edging, with slender, medium-
green leaves up to 10 in (25 cm) long.
Loose heads, 1 in (2.5 cm) across, of
upright, bell-shaped pale or bright

pink, red-spotted flowers appear
from late summer onward. From
southwestern China. ↕6–10 in (15–
25 cm). Z4-10 H10–4. **var. *amabile***
syn. *A. amabile* Deep pink to magenta
flowers with darker spots. ↕4–8 in
(10–20 cm).

A. murrayanum see *A. unifolium*

A. narcissiflorum syn. *A. pedemontanum*
Ideal for the front of a border, the
strap-shaped dark green leaves growing
to 7 in (18 cm) long. Nodding heads,
about 1 in (2.5 cm) across, of up to
eight large bell-shaped pinkish purple
flowers appear from early summer
onward. Seed heads are held erect.
Described by Reginald Farrer as "the
glory of its race" but often confused
with the much more widely grown
A. insubricum. From Portugal and
northern Italy. ↕6–14 in (15–35 cm).
Z5–8 H8–5

A. obliquum A good border plant with
grassy gray-green leaves, up to 14 in
(35 cm) long, that sheathe the stems
to about half their height. Heads up
to 1½ in (4 cm) across are crowded
with cup-shaped pale yellow flowers in
early and midsummer. Sometimes said,
incorrectly, to smell unpleasant. From
Romania, Central Asia, and Siberia.
↕24–40 in (60–100 cm). Z3–8 H8–1

A. pedemontanum see *A. narcissiflorum*

A. schoenoprasum (Chives) Usually
grown for the edible leaves, its flowers
and those of its cultivars are decorative
as border plants. Hollow, cylindrical
deep green leaves grow up to 14 in
(35 cm) long, occasionally to 18 in
(45 cm), and form congested clumps.
Dense heads, about 1 in (2.5 cm) across,
of many bell-shaped light purple or
white honey-scented flowers appear
from early summer onward. Best grown
in moist soil. Deadhead to prevent self-
seeding and encourage further flowers.

The flowers are also edible and make an attractive addition to salads. Around a dozen cultivars have been named, but many are rarely seen. From Europe, Asia, and North America. ↕ 12–24 in (30-60 cm). Z5–11 H12–1. **'Corsican White'** Good clear white flowers, clumps up well, does not appear to self-seed. ↕ 12 in (30 cm). **'Forescate'** Purplish pink flowers. 24 in (60 cm). **'Polyphant'** Rose-pink flowers freely produced, robust habit. ↕ 12 in (30 cm). **'Schnittlauch'** Very dwarf form. ↕ 8 in (20 cm). **'Shepherds' Crook'** Foliage dramatically twisted. **var. *sibiricum*** Deep rose flowers, turning violet. ↕ 16 in (40 cm). **'Silver Chimes'** White flowers from late spring onward, finer leaves than species. ↕ 6 in (15 cm). **'Wallington White'** Ivory flowers, robust habit. ↕ 12 in (30 cm).

A. senescens A vigorous and highly variable border perennial with mid-green strap-shaped leaves 1½–12 in (4–30 cm) long, and dense ¾–2-in- (2–5-cm-) wide heads of many cup-shaped lilac flowers in mid- and late summer. From Europe and northern Asia. ↕ 3–24 in (8–60 cm). Z4–10 H10–1. **subsp. *montanum*** syn. 'Summer Beauty' Gray-green twisted foliage, pink flowers. ↕ 18 in (45 cm). **subsp. *montanum* var. *glaucum*** syn. *A. glaucum* Gray twisted leaves, pink flowers. ↕ 6 in (15 cm).

A. sikkimense syn. *A. kansuense, A. tibeticum* A somewhat slim plant for the front of borders, with thin grassy medium-green leaves up to 12 in (30 cm) long, and heads, 1 in (2.5 cm) wide, of small nodding bell-shaped, brilliant blue flowers, occasionally purple or white, from early summer onward. From western China and the Himalaya—Tibet, Nepal, and Sikkim. ↕ 6–10 in (15–25 cm). Z6–10 H10–6

***A.* 'Summer Beauty'** see *A. senescens* subsp. *montanum*

A. tibeticum see *A. sikkimense*

A. tuberosum (Chinese chives) A vigorous border perennial with fat roots, flat, ridged, solid medium-green edible leaves, up to 14 in (35 cm) long, and domed heads, 2 in (5 cm) wide, of sweetly fragrant, white star-shaped flowers in late summer and early fall. The leaves have a mild onion-garlic flavor and can be chopped and added to salads or stir-fries. From Southeast Asia. Prefers moist soil. ↕ 10–20 in (25–50 cm). Z4–8 H8–1

A. unifolium syn. *A. murrayanum* A lovely species for the front of the border. Narrow gray-green leaves, up to 8 in (20 cm) long, die down by the time the flowers appear. The domed flowerheads, 2 in (5 cm) wide, consist of up to 20 large bell-shaped flowers that are deep pink and appear from late spring onward. In spite of the name, each plant has two or three leaves. Prefers hot, dry conditions, reminiscent of its native habitat. From western North America (Oregon and California). ↕ 12 in (30 cm). Z4–9 H9–1

A. wallichii Useful and vigorous border plant. Medium green leaves have a central ridge and grow up to 36 in (90 cm) in length. Star-shaped purple flowers with a papery texture are carried in loose heads up to 2¾ in (7 cm) across in late summer and early fall. From monsoon areas, Nepal to western China. ↕ 12–36 in (30–90 cm). Z2–8 H8–1

ALOPECURUS

Foxtail grass

POACEAE

A tough, yet handsome grass for many different situations, which is available in forms with beautifully colored foliage.

The 36 species of annuals and perennials grow throughout northern temperate parts of the world, and parts of South America, in habitats ranging from damp meadows to rocky mountainsides. Flat, rather long, triangular leaves form loose tufts from which grow the flower stems, which are often bent, as if they had knees, near the bases. The dense, velvety flowerheads are cylindrical to oval in shape.

CULTIVATION Grows well in part-sun in moist, well-drained soil.

PROPAGATION By division in spring, or from seed.

PROBLEMS Usually trouble-free.

A. alpinus syn. *A. borealis* (Alpine foxtail, Alpine cattail) Slowly creeping, forming loose tufts of gray-green or gray, flat, lance-shaped leaves that are 1–2½ in (2.5–6 cm) wide and slightly rough. Foliage dies back in winter. In early to late summer, slender, smooth, often bent stems, bearing a few smaller leaves, carry silky, gray-green to purplish, oval flowerheads ⅛ in (3–4.5 mm) long. This rare alpine grass grows on wet mountainsides, moist rocks, and stream margins in Scotland, northern England, and over the Arctic. It prefers an open position. ↕ 14–18 in (36–45 cm). Z5–8 H8–5. **subsp. *glaucus*** (Blue foxtail) Leaves and flowerheads are a more intense blue-purple.

A. borealis see *A. alpinus*

A. pratensis (Meadow foxtail, Common foxtail) Slowly creeping grass that dies back in winter. Forms loose to dense tufts of finely pointed, green leaves, ⅛–½ in (3–10 mm) wide and 2½–16 in (6–40 cm) long. From mid-spring to early summer, smooth, slender, bent stems with smaller leaves up the stem appear, topped by poker-shaped, pale green to purplish flowerheads, ⅙–¼ in (4–6 mm) long and hung with conspicuous purple or orange stamens. A common grass throughout temperate parts of the world, in wet meadows and rough pasture. Prefers cooler conditions in sun or part-shade and fertile, well-drained soil. It is one of the earliest grasses to flower and makes a good addition to wildflower meadows and lawns. Forms with colored foliage are best clipped back in early summer to stop flowering and intensify the foliage color—they are particularly effective as ground cover or path edging. Division every three years ensures foliage vigor. Propagate variegated forms by division only. ↕ 1–4 ft (30–120 cm). Z5–8 H8–5. **'Aureovariegatus'** syn. 'Variegatus' (Golden foxtail) Leaves have vertical stripes of pale yellow and green with deeper gold margins. In poor soil, makes good, spreading ground cover up to 2–3 in (5–7.5 cm) tall. In richer soil, forms clumps up to 12 in (30 cm) tall. **'Aureus'** Gold leaves with pale green midveins. **'No Overtaking'** Gold leaves with a continuous, central silver stripe. **'Variegatus'** *see* 'Aureovariegatus'.

ALSTROEMERIA

Peruvian lily

ALSTROEMERIACEAE

Ubiquitous as long-lasting cut flowers and now transformed by modern developments from fleeting, weedy, and invasive to spectacular, well-behaved, and long-flowering border plants.

Fifty species, all from South America, have fleshy roots and upright stems with narrow, twisted leaves and terminal clusters of lilylike flowers with six petals, usually on several short branches. The outer three petals are broader than the inner, and may end in a narrow tip or be heart-shaped, especially in modern hybrids. The inner petals are usually narrower, the upper two erect and often at least partly yellow and usually marked with short, dark lines. Some modern hybrids show this streaking on the outer petals and have contrasting stripes and blotches of color. Mauve and purple shades are uncommon in cultivars but present in many species and are now being developed in hybrids. Flowers vary in width from 1½ in (4 cm) in some species, to 2¾–3 in (7–8 cm) in most hybrids, and 4 in (10 cm) in the largest.

Most species, including the common *A. aurea* and the *ligtu* hybrids, have a short flowering period, but modern hybrids are not only far less aggressive in their habits but flower for many months from midsummer onward. They are ideal cut flowers, lasting several weeks in a vase. However, since the sap is a skin irritant, care should be taken when handling the stems. Heights vary from 6 in to 48 in (15 cm to 120 cm).

In this era of many new cultivars being created for the cut-flower market by plant breeders worldwide, in addition to nurseries introducing their own selections, the availability of cultivars is constantly changing (*see* Keeping Up, *p.53*). What is more, many of the modern hybrid alstroemerias have both true cultivar names (which are usually apparently meaningless breeders' code names) and catchier selling names. To add to the confusion, not all cultivars may be released in all countries, and the names under which they are sold may vary around the world. ⚠

CULTIVATION Most prefer a sunny site in light soil and adequate moisture in summer; they dislike waterlogged conditions in winter and wet, heavy soil. The roots resent disturbance; plant from pots and do not purchase as bare roots. In cold areas, plant deeply in spring or summer and gradually refill over the summer so the crown is at least 6 in (15 cm) deep to protect them from frost. If new spring growth is frosted, shoots

LEFT *Alopecurus pratensis* 'Aureovariegatus'

LITTLE PRINCESS SERIES

In recent years breeding of alstroemerias has advanced significantly and one important development has been the arrival of short cultivars which are ideal for containers and for the front of the border. The Little Princess Series is becoming known around the world for its neat habit and prolific flowering in a good range of colors.

Alstroemeria Princess Angela

Alstroemeria Princess Marilene

Alstroemeria Princess Paola

Alstroemeria Princess Susana

usually regrow and flower normally. Dwarf cultivars are ideal for containers but must be protected from damaging frost in winter.

PROPAGATION The *ligtu* hybrids, Doctor Salter's hybrids, and species are easily raised from seed, although the results are unpredictable. Soak the seeds for several days in warm water, changing it daily, and then sow two or three seeds per small pot. Plant out the seedlings without disturbing the roots. If plants have to be divided, chop out sections in spring and plant intact, with the soil.

PROBLEMS Slugs and snails, aphids, virus.

A. **'Aimi'** Cream flowers flushed pink with gold zones on the upper petals and maroon streaks on all three inner petals. ‡26 in (65 cm). Z7–10 H10–7

A. **'Apollo'** White outer petals with yellow at the base, all three inner petals are deep yellow with white tips. ‡36 in (90 cm). Z7–10 H10–7

A. aurea Tuberous roots support upright stems with up to seven branches, each with one to three orange or yellow flowers; the two upper petals are darker and streaked with red. The resulting large seedpods crack open to disperse seeds over a wide area. This vigorous, even invasive, plant rapidly spreads into wide clumps—especially in light soil—sometimes flowers poorly, and is often more trouble than it's worth. Thrives in sun or light shade and the flowers are good for cutting. Although showy when in flower, the display only lasts a few weeks. Native to Chile. ‡40 in

(100 cm). Z7–10 H10–7. **'Dover Orange'** Bright orange flowers with paler inner petals. **'Lutea'** Yellow. **'Orange King'** Orange.

A. **'Blushing Bride'** Pale pink flowers have a deep pink flare through the center of the outer petals, and a greenish tip; the inner petals have a golden band. ‡18–24 in (45–60 cm). Z7–10 H10–7

A. brasiliensis Deep red, tubular flowers in clusters of about ten per stem; tip of each petal green, striped, and paler inside the blooms. Flowers for several months in late summer but requires moist soil. From São Paulo, Brazil, and introduced into Britain in 1825. ‡26 in (65 cm). Z7–10 H10–7

A. **'Coronet'** Pink flowers have dark pink outer petals, paler edges; upper petals are largely golden yellow, pink tips. ‡40 in (100 cm). Z7–10 H10–7

A. **'Dayspring Delight'** Early summer-flowering with neat, cream edges to the leaves, but the markings fade by the time the bright orange flowers open. ‡30 in (75 cm). Z7–10 H10–7

A. **Diana, Princess of Wales** (Princess Series) Pale flowers, white outer petals, flushed pink at the base, and green tips, and yellow-flushed upper petals. ‡40 in (100 cm). Z7–10 H10–7

A. **Doctor Salter's hybrids** Seed-raised strain with flowers in many bright and pastel shades. Similar to the *Ligtu*

RIGHT 1 *Alstroemeria* 'Apollo' **2** *A. aurea*
3 *A. aurea* 'Lutea' **4** *A.* 'Blushing Bride'
5 *A.* 'Coronet' **6** *A.* 'Evening Song'

HEALTHY COMPETITION

ALSTROEMERIA AUREA MAY BE a little too vigorous at times but it is impressively colorful and with crocosmia in an almost scarlet orange alongside makes a fiery combination. Both plants, in fact, have a tendency to spread and eventually mingle together so that their stems are completely mixed. And both are good for cutting. They will need a rich mulch to sustain good growth in the face of mutual competition. Overhead, arching from a tighter clump at a safe distance, the dancing showers of watered gold from *Stipa gigantea* flutter into the more flamboyant flowers.

hybrids but neater and slightly shorter. ‡28 in (70 cm). Z7–10 H10–7

A. 'Dusty Rose' Vigorous American selection with dark to light pink, salmon, coral, or rose florets—the exact shade depends on the summer climate. Retains its vigor in all climates, in full sun or part-shade. ‡32 in (80 cm). Z7–10 H10–7

A. 'Evening Song' Unusually small, burgundy-red flowers with a tiny pale yellow area on the upper petals. The lower inner petal is streaked. ‡24 in (60 cm). Z7–10 H10–7

A. 'Flaming Star' Bright orange with paler upper petals. The rounded flowers open from bronze buds and have pinkish shading at the ends of the outer petals. ‡28 in (70 cm). Z7–10 H10–7

A. 'Friendship' Palest yellow with some pink tinges on the outer petals, and green tips. The inner petals are brighter yellow with dark streaks. ‡36 in (90 cm). Z7–10 H10–7

A. 'Golden Delight' Golden flowers with large upper petals of deep gold. ‡36 in (90 cm). Z7–10 H10–7

A. Golden Jubilee Lily (Little Princess Series) Bright, coral-orange flowers with yellow upper petals with orange tips and neat dark streaks. ‡12 in (30 cm). Z7–10 H10–7

A. 'Inca Adore' (Inca Series) Rather open flowers of intense red with narrow petals. There is a yellow zone on the upper inner petals and streaks and yellow splashes on the outer petals. ‡18 in (45 cm). Z7–10 H10–7

A. 'Inca Exotica' (Inca Series) Yellow flowers with deep orange "thumbprints" on the outer petals; inner petals with short, broad streaks. ‡18 in (45 cm). Z7–10 H10–7

A. 'Inca Glow' (Inca Series) Mauve-pink with distinctly bilobed outer petals and inner petals with a pale yellow zone and a few streaks. ‡18 in (45 cm). Z7–10 H10–7

A. 'Inca Ice' (Inca Series) Palest pink or white flowers with a few dark streaks, shaded yellow and pink at the center. ‡18 in (45 cm). Z7–10 H10–7

A. 'Inca Moonlight' (Inca Series) Rather narrow petals in shades of cream and orange, deeper at the center. ‡18 in (45 cm). Z7–10 H10–7

A. 'Inca Obsession' (Inca Series) Outer petals deep rose pink with dark pink "thumbprints"; inner petals narrow, upper two with a central pale yellow zone. ‡18 in (45 cm). Z7–10 H10–7

A. Inca Series These mid-height alstroemerias, bred by Könst Alstroemeria of Holland, often have exotic-looking, almost bizarre flowers with unusual markings, showing signs of a wide variety of species in their breeding. While most series have been selected for their broad petals and dwarf height, these offer a wide range of flower shapes and patterns.

A. 'Inca Serin' (Inca Series) Pale apricot-pink and yellow with a few streaks on the upper petals. ‡18 in (45 cm). Z7–10 H10–7

A. 'Inca Tropic' (Inca Series) Outer petals are orange, with yellow and red blotches; inner petals are bright yellow, streaked with maroon and tipped with orange. ‡18 in (45 cm). Z7–10 H10–7

A. Ligtu hybrids Seed-raised plants produce pastel flowers in shades of pink, coral, and orange in early summer; often the color balance is poor and unpredictable. The flowers do not last long but are freely produced and are very showy. Easy to grow from seed, flowering in their second season. Despite their popularity, they have not been used in modern breeding, which was initially aimed at producing cut flowers, because of their short season of bloom and brittle foliage. Bred from *A. ligtu* and *A. haemantha*. ‡36–48 in (90–120 cm). Z7–10 H10–7

A. 'Little Eleanor' Pale yellow with some pink on the outer petals, the inner petals are deep yellow. ‡8 in (20 cm). Z7–10 H10–7

A. 'Little Miss Christina' (Little Miss Series) Pink buds open to creamy-white flowers tinged with pink and yellow on the upper petals. ‡6 in (15 cm). Z7–10 H10–7

A. 'Little Miss Gloria' (Little Miss Series) Deep red; yellow at base of the upper petals. ‡8 in (20 cm). Z7–10 H10–7

A. 'Little Miss Isabel' (Little Miss Series) Crimson-red; yellow base to the inner petals, edges of the broad outer petals are marked with streaks around the edge. ‡8 in (20 cm). Z7–10 H10–7

A. 'Little Miss Matilda' (Little Miss Series) White flowers with large inner petals, mostly yellow with streaks and white tips. Some streaks on the outer petals. ‡8 in (20 cm). Z7–10 H10–7

A. 'Little Miss Natalie' (Little Miss Series) Pale cream with pink blotches. ‡8 in (20 cm). Z7–10 H10–7

A. 'Little Miss Rosanna' (Little Miss Series) Violet-pink; dark streaks on all inner petals, yellow zone on the upper two. ‡8 in (20 cm). Z7–10 H10–7

A. 'Little Miss Roselind' (Little Miss Series) Deep bright pink; yellow blotches and dark streaks on all inner petals. ‡6 in (15 cm). Z7–10 H10–7

A. Little Miss Series Unusually short plants with large, rounded flowers from midsummer onward. Varying in height from 4 in to 10 in (10–25 cm), their neat dwarf habit makes them ideal for containers. Many have contrasting blotches on the inner petals and dark streaks on the outer petals.

A. 'Little Miss Sophie' (Little Miss Series) Pink buds open to pink and white flowers, pale yellow at the base of the upper petals. ‡6 in (15 cm). Z7–10 H10–7

A. 'Little Miss Tara' (Little Miss Series) Very large flowers of reddish pink; yellow at the base of the upper petals. ‡6 in (15 cm). Z7–10 H10–7

A. 'Little Miss Veronica' (Little Miss Series) Flowering earlier than most, blooms vary from cream to white with a pink flush, especially at the center of the flowers, with yellow on the inner petals. ‡10 in (25 cm). Z7–10 H10–7

A. Little Princess Series Neat, compact partners to the Princess Series in an increasing range of colors and color combinations, and becoming increasingly prolific as new introductions appear. Ideal for the front of the border and for containers, but container-grown plants may suffer in cold winters without protection. (*see Little Princess Series, p.51*) ‡4–12 in (10–30 cm). Z7–10 H10–7

A. 'Orange Gem' Rounded orange flowers; paler upper petals opening from bronze buds. H 28 in (70 cm). Z7–10 H10–7

A. 'Orange Glory' Deep orange flowers; bright yellow marks on upper petals. ↕ 36 in (90 cm). Z7–10 H10–7

A. 'Pacific Sunset' Unusually vigorous, with flowers in red, rose, and yellow with dark streaks on the upper petals. Has given its name to unpredictable seed-raised plants in various shades and heights. ↕ 28 in (70 cm). Z7–10 H10–7

A. 'Phoenix' Deep red flowers with variegated foliage edged with white, often flushed with pink. Probably a spontaneous muation of 'Evening Song'. ↕ 26 in (65 cm). Z7–10 H10–7

A. Princess Aiko ('Zabriko') (Little Princess Series) Bright pink with paler edges and yellow at the base of the upper petals. Bred specifically for Japan and now popular worldwide. ↕ 8 in (20 cm). Z7–10 H10–7

A. Princess Angela ('Staprilan') (Little Princess Series) Apricot-yellow with paler outer petals, with a lilac and white flare and streaks on all petals. ↕ 12 in (30 cm). Z7–10 H10–7

A. Princess Daniela ('Stapridani') (Little Princess Series) Cream and pale yellow flowers with pretty streaks on the inner petals. ↕ 8 in (20 cm). Z7–10 H10–7

A. Princess Isabella (Little Princess Series) Unusually large, rich orange flowers from darker buds with a yellow base to the upper petals. ↕ 12 in (30 cm). Z7–10 H10–7

A. Princess Ivana ('Stapriravane') (Little Princess Series) Early-flowering, deep purple-pink flowers; a yellow base to the upper petals. ↕ 12 in (30 cm). Z7–10 H10–7

A. Princess Leyla ('Stapriley') (Little Princess Series) Deep plum-red flowers with a yellow base to the upper petals. ↕ 10 in (25 cm). Z7–10 H10–7

A. Princess Marie-Louise ('Zelanon') (Princess Series) Pinkish lavender flowers; dark stripes on the outer and inner petals and little yellow coloring. ↕ 24 in (60 cm). Z7–10 H10–7

A. Princess Marilene ('Staprilene') (Little Princess Series) Creamy white flowers, flushed with cream at the center; yellow base on upper petals, few dark streaks. ↕ 10 in (25 cm). Z7–10 H10–7

A. Princess Monica ('Staprimon') (Little Princess Series) Creamy yellow flowers. with golden flushes and dark streaks on all of the inner petals. Outer petals flushed with purple. ↕ 8 in (20 cm). Z7–10 H10–7

A. Princess Paola ('Stapripal') (Little Princess Series) Vibrant bicolored flowers. The white outer petals have a deep pink central bar and yellow upper petals. ↕ 10 in (25 cm). Z7–10 H10–7

A. Princess Phoebe ('Stayelor') (Princess Series) Bicolored flower; yellow outer petals, tipped burnt orange and with a yellow base to the upper petals. ↕ 36 in (90 cm). Z7–10 H10–7

A. Princess Sara ('Staprisara') (Little Princess Series) Bicolored flowers in gold with a pink stripe through outer petals. ↕ 8 in (20 cm). Z7–10 H10–7

A. Princess Sarah ('Stalicamp') (Princess Series) Bright lemon-yellow flowers; dark streaks on the inner petals. ↕ 40 in (100 cm). Z7–10 H10–7

A. Princess Series Bred as cut flowers by Van Staaveren in Holland but excellent in garden borders, featuring improved vigor and an extended flowering period, often beginning in early summer and continuing to late fall, or longer in mild climates. ↕ 30–40 in (75–100 cm).

A. Princess Sissi ('Staprisis') (Little Princess Series) Bright pink flowers; the outer petals have paler edges in addition to a yellow band, edged white, on the upper petals. ↕ 8 in (20 cm). Z7–10 H10–7

A. Princess Stephanie ('Stapirag') (Little Princess Series) Bold flowers; pale pink outer petals, deep pink "thumbprints" plus a yellow base to the upper petals. ↕ 12 in (30 cm). Z7–10 H10–7

A. Princess Susana ('Staprisusa') (Little Princess Series) Ivory-white flowers with pale pink "thumbprints" on the outer petals and pale yellow flushes on all three inner petals. ↕ 10 in (25 cm). Z7–10 H10–7

A. Princess Victoria ('Regina') (Princess Series) Deep pink flowers that have darker "thumbprints" on the outer petals and show a yellow base to the upper petals. ↕ 40 in (100 cm). Z7–10 H10–7

A. Princess Zavina ('Staprivina') (Little Princess Series) Glowing blend of pink and orange; yellow flare on upper petals. ↕ 9 in (22 cm). Z7–10 H10–7

A. psittacina syn. *A. pulchella* Stems spotted in purple with branched clusters of 6–15 dark red flowers with green and white-striped petal tips, giving an unusual mix of green and red. Blooming from mid- to late summer, it prefers moist conditions and tolerates a little shade. Prone to virus infection. From Brazil. ↕ 36 in (90 cm). Z6–10 H10–6. **'Mona Lisa'** Crimson flowers have green and white at the petal tips and dark streaks on the shorter stems. ↕ 26 in (65 cm). **'Royal Star'** Leaves with irregular cream edges. ↕ 32 in (80 cm). **'Variegata'** see 'Royal Star'.

A. 'Purple Rain' Very large flowers of purplish red with pale yellow at the base of the upper petals. ↕ 28 in (70 cm). Z7–10 H10–7

A. Queen Elizabeth, The Queen Mother ('Stamoli') (Little Princess Series)

RIGHT **1** *Alstroemeria* 'Friendship' **2** *A.* 'Golden Delight' **3** *A.* 'Orange Glory'

White flowers flushed with pink, opening from bronzed pink buds. ↕ 14 in (35 cm). Z7–10 H10–7

A. 'Red Beauty' Shades of deep red and orange; yellow zone on lower part of upper inner petals and bold dark streaks. ↕ 36 in (90 cm). Z7–10 H10–7

A. 'Red Elf' Compact plants, red flowers. ↕ 26 in (65 cm). Z7–10 H10–7

A. 'Selina' Pale pink flowers, deeper flush at the tips of the outer petals. Inner petals have pale yellow zone, dark streaks. ↕ 26 in (65 cm). Z7–10 H10–7

A. 'Spitfire' Deep orange flowers and foliage; a pale yellow leaf edge. Variegated spontaneous mutation of 'Red Beauty'. ↕ 36 in (90 cm). Z7–10 H10–7

A. 'Spring Delight' Apricot-pink flowers in early summer plus cream-edged leaves. Grows best in light shade. ↕ 24 in (60 cm). Z7–10 H10–7

A. 'Sweet Laura' Bright yellow flowers; inner petals with dark streaks. Noted for hardiness, sweet scent. Slow-spreading hybrid of *A. caryophyllacea* raised at the University of Connecticut. ↕ 30 in (75 cm). Z7–10 H10–7

A. 'Tessa' Ruby-red flowers; golden orange zone on the upper inner petals. ↕ 36 in (90 cm). Z7–10 H10–7

A. 'White Apollo' Large white flowers; yellow-marked upper petals. ↕ 32 in (80 cm). Z7–10 H10–7

A. 'Yellow Friendship' Large, pale yellow; white tips. Inner petals deeper yellow, dark streaks. ↕ 36 in (90 cm). Z7–10 H10–7

KEEPING UP

You have to be nimble to keep up with the rapid introduction of *Alstroemeria* cultivars, as each year new ones appear and older ones are supplanted. This is driven primarily by competition between breeders, for whom taller cut-flower types and shorter container types are the main focus—although both groups make good plants for beds and borders in warmer climates.

Most new introductions are patented so they have restrictions on general propagation. Almost all are good garden plants but, as improved introductions appear featuring new colors or color combinations, more prolific flowering, or better lasting qualities as cut flowers, existing ones are withdrawn. So plants catalogued one year may be replaced by newcomers the next.

However, after a few years in limbo as their period of protection lapses, some, like the superb 'Yellow Friendship', may enjoy a new, royalty-free lease on life in a wider range of nurseries—and gardens.

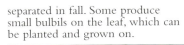

ALTHAEA
MALVACEAE

Tough, reliable, very colorful, and generally trouble-free plants for the herbaceous or cottage border.

Three of the 12 species are hardy perennials. Closely related to the more showy hollyhocks (*Alcea*), they have smaller flowers, usually on distinct stalks. All althaeas are vigorous with stiff, rather woody stems rising from a woody crown and oval or egg-shaped, lobed leaves in a rich dark green. Open clusters of five-petaled flowers appear in all the leaf joints toward the stem tops to create tall, airy flowerheads. The flowers open in succession for many months during summer and fall. Originally native to arable land, waste ground, seashores, and brackish marshes, from western Europe to Central Asia.

CULTIVATION Best in a sunny position and moist, well-drained soil. Cut back to ground level in the fall.

PROPAGATION Species from seed: sow in a seedbed early to midsummer and transplant to final positions in fall. Cultivars by division.

PROBLEMS Rust, capsid bugs.

A. armeniaca Erect with strong, slightly downy, self-supporting stems and 6-in-(15-cm-) long, triangular leaves with three to five, coarsely toothed, lance- or inverse egg–shaped lobes. Rich pink flowers open in succession midsummer to early fall. From southeastern Russia, and central and southwestern Asia. ‡4 ft (1.2 m). Z3–9 H9–1

A. cannabina Vigorous, erect perennial with hairy, reddish, speckled stems and large, rounded, 14-in (35-cm) leaves

that are hairy on both sides, but paler below, and often divided into three to five coarsely toothed, lance-shaped lobes. A succession of cup-shaped, deep pink or lilac flowers from midsummer to early fall. From northwestern Africa and southeastern and central Europe. ‡6 ft (1.8 m). Z3–9 H9–1

A. officinalis (Marsh mallow) Vigorous, erect perennial with simple or slightly branched stems and dark or bluish green, triangular or egg-shaped leaves that are undivided or have three to five shallow, toothed lobes. Both stems and leaves are covered in soft, gray hairs. Clusters of pink or lilac flowers, 1–2 in (2.5–5 cm) long, open at the shoot tips and in the leaf joints, from midsummer to early fall. The roots produce mucilage, which was originally used to make candy. Grows in moist habitats, brackish marshes, and beside streams and ditches in southern Europe and eastern Mediterranean; it has also naturalized in the eastern US. ‡6 ft (1.8 m). Z3–9 H9–1. **alba** Pure white flowers. ‡3–4 ft (90–120 cm). **'Romney Marsh'** Dwarf with pink-centered, white flowers from late spring to early fall. ‡16 in (40 cm).

AMORPHOPHALLUS
Voodoo lily
ARACEAE

Astonishing tuberous perennials with fantastic flowers, sometimes overpowering smells, and near-mythical qualities.

About 170 species of tuberous perennials from a range of habitats primarily in tropical Africa, and temperate Asia south through northern Australia. Some are grown

commercially for food. Only a few species are hardy enough for temperate gardens, where they are admired for their curious forms and flowers. From a tuberous root, which may be up to 10 lb (4.5 kg) in weight, usually a single large leaf appears and a curious, sometimes very striking, recognizably arumlike flowerhead that may have an unpleasant smell. Individuals of most species will not set seed unless pollinated by another plant, and the whole plant dies back in winter. Some species have flowers that are oddly colored or patterned and smell of dead animals to attract carrion flies; others have more pleasant aromas. The size, variety, rarity, and strangeness of some species make them much sought-after by collectors of the unusual—but few would be described as attractive garden flowers.

This is a very large genus, with only a few species suited to the open garden in milder climates, although in recent years more species have been tried and made available. The rare tropical *A. titanum* has the largest flowerhead in the world, over 6 ft (1.8 m) tall and wide. (*See also* The Arum Family, *p. 74*)

CULTIVATION Grows in light shade to sun in rich, moist, woodland soil. Mulch in winter when foliage is dormant. Some species are best grown in large pots and stored dry in their pots all winter; they can then be repotted in fresh potting mix in spring. Fertilize plants regularly with organic fertilizers when in active growth.

PROPAGATION Most produce offsets on the tubers, and these can be

ABOVE **1** *Althaea cannabina* **2** *A. officinalis*

separated in fall. Some produce small bulbils on the leaf, which can be planted and grown on.

PROBLEMS Usually trouble-free—except, perhaps, for the unpleasant smell of some species.

A. bulbifer A modest-sized tuberous plant, its single leaf, about 36 in (90 cm) tall, is deeply divided into 8-in (20-cm) lance-shaped or reverse egg–shaped divisions and held on a green stem patterned in brown or pink. The attractive, 12-in (30-cm) white flower, often flushed pale pink, is reminiscent of a porcelain seashell. The scent, however, is like that of some long-dead creature. Small bulbils that form on the leaf at intersections of the main veins can be removed when ripe and used to start new plants. Best in woodland to semiopen sites in rich well-drained soil. From northern India to Nepal. ‡36 in (90 cm). Z7–10 H10–7

A. kiusianus A small, relatively hardy species with a single leaf, about 24 in (60 cm) long, with multiple leaflets arranged into an umbrella–like structure on a 24–36-in (60–88-cm) fleshy stem. This is preceded by a pale green flower, the spathe spotted in white like a floral vase from which the black spadix emerges. One of the few self-fertile species, the flower may be followed by a stalk of berries, turning from green to red to lilac and, when ripe, to deep blue. From southern Japan. ‡24 in (60 cm). Z7–10 H10–7

A. konjac syn. *A. rivieri* (Konjak, Konjaku) The most widely grown, and hardiest, species. A single, much-divided leaf, sometimes reaching 6 ft (1.8 m) high and 5 ft (1.5 m) across, develops an umbrella-like shape; its stem is attractively blotched and rather reptilian-looking. The spathe is a shiny, deep red-purple and up to 24 in (60 cm) long with a large vertical

BELOW **1** *Amorphophallus konjac* **2** *Amsonia tabernaemontana*

purple spadix protruding. Widely grown in Southeast Asia and Japan for its edible tuber and the starch derived from it. From southern China. ↕6 ft (1.8 m). Z7–11 H12–10

A. paeoniifolius (Elephant yam) Spectacular in flower or foliage, with one of the most bizarre and widely cultivated flowers in the genus. The spadix is a broad, coarsely ruffled, inverted bell, colored a reddish purple brown with pale speckles and spots. This sits in a brown-maroon, 24-in (60-cm), broadly ruffled and reflexed spathe with spots and splashes and a paler center. The single dissected leaf is divided into many elongate segments and reaches 6 ft (1.8 m) high and 10 ft (3 m) across. The tubers may reach 12 in (30 cm) or more across, and are an important food source in many tropical regions. From India to China, and northern Australia. ↕6 ft (1.8 m). Z7–10 H10–7

A. rivierei see A. konjac

AMSONIA
Blue star
APOCYNACEAE

Easy and adaptable, the dainty summer flowers may be outshone by brilliant fall color.

Most of the 20 deciduous species are native to North America, with a few found in Japan and Europe. While some inhabit woods, others originate from damp grassland or drier, rockier places. Two species are well established as garden plants and more are becoming available.

Upright stems, from a defined crown, gradually increase in number as the plant matures to form a neat, bushy clump. Dark blue buds at the top of the stems open in late spring and summer, developing into clusters of light blue flowers, typically ⅝ in (1.5 cm) across. Periwinkle-like, the starry flowers have five pointed petals, which are joined behind into a short tube; some have a light fragrance. Slender, upward-pointing seedpods appear in pairs, in some species reaching up to 4¾ in (12 cm). In all species, the leaves alternate up the stems, but they vary in size and shape from very narrow and needlelike to lance-shaped or almost oval. Foliage turns attractively yellow, extending the plant's performance into fall.

CULTIVATION Most species thrive in full sun or part-shade. Stems contain a milky sap, so dip stems in boiling water or sear in a flame to use as a cut flower.

PROPAGATION From seed or cuttings; division is also possible, but splitting the mass of deep, woody roots found on mature plants can be challenging. Plants left standing over winter may self-seed.

PROBLEMS Usually trouble-free.

A. ciliata Finely textured foliage, either needlelike, or broader, especially lower down the stems, and rather variable in size, ranging up to ½ in (1 cm) across and 1½–3 in (4–8 cm) long. Fine hairs usually rim the leaves and the stems may also be softly downy. Powder-blue stars, among the showiest, are borne in crowded clusters held well above the leaves. Good fall color. Suits full sun or light shade, and amply drained soil, not too rich in organic matter. Heat- and drought-tolerant. From limestone glades and open woodlands in the southeastern US. ↕24–36 in (60–90 cm). Z6–10 H10–6

A. hubrichtii Outstanding among the blue stars, and worth growing for its foliage alone. Forms billowy mounds, with stems clothed in many fine, threadlike leaves, less than ⅟₁₆ in (2 mm) wide and up to 3 in (8 cm) long, giving the plant an alluringly soft, feathery texture. Summer color, from clusters of pretty light blue to almost white flowers, is followed by the vibrant golden yellow of the foliage in fall. Has great impact when planted in swaths. Tolerates drought once established but adapts to a wide range of soils. Fall color may be best when in full sun but also grows well in light shade. Discovered in 1942 and native only to Arkansas and Oklahoma, where it is found on dry, rocky outcrops. ↕24–36 in (60–90 cm). Z6–8 H8–5

A. illustris Tapering foliage, up to ¾ in (2 cm) across and 2¾–4¾ in (7–12 cm) long, with a glossy surface and an almost leathery feel. Flowerheads with a more or less pyramidal outline, and up to 6 in (15 cm) high, carry a profusion of light purple-blue flowers. Caramel fall color. Grow in full sun or part-shade in moist, well-drained soil. From rocky banks, streamsides, and prairies in central and southern US. ↕28–40 in (70–100 cm). Z5–9 H9–5

A. orientalis syn. *Rhazya orientalis* The only species from Europe and a lower-growing version of its close American relative, A. tabernaemontana. Thin-textured, matte leaves are slender or sometimes more oval in shape, 1¼–2¾ in (3–7 cm) long and up to ¾ in (2 cm) across, with a pale central vein and edged in fine hairs. Blooms from late spring to late summer, with broad heads carrying many softly gray-blue flowers. Performs best in full sun and free-draining soil. From damp, grassy habitats—generally close to the sea—in Greece and Turkey, where it is a protected species. ↕18–24 in (45–60 cm). Z5–8 H8–5

A. tabernaemontana One of the broader-leaved blue stars, with matte foliage that usually has a thin, papery texture. Leaves have a conspicuous pale green central vein and are typically oval but vary in size from ¾ to 2 in (2 to 5 cm) across and 2½ to 5½ in (6 to 14 cm) long. Steel-blue flowers are held in loose, slightly drooping clusters about 3 in (8 cm) high. In fall, the leaves turn pale yellow. Thrives in sun or part-shade. Tough, but best in

moderately fertile, moist yet free-draining soil. Some authorities recognize different varieties based on leaf shape, size, and hairs. Widely distributed in the eastern US, it grows in open woodlands, damp roadside ditches, and riverbanks. ↕28–40 in (70–100 cm). Z3–9 H9–1. **var. salicifolia** Slim, tapering, willowlike leaves, up to 1 in (2.5 cm) across, without hairs.

ANACYCLUS
Atlas Daisy
ASTERACEAE

Neat daisy flowers that are held above low mounds of feathery leaves characterize this slightly tricky sun-lover.

About nine species of deciduous or partly evergreen plants—some annuals—found in dry, sandy, and rocky habitats throughout the Mediterranean region—of which one is quite commonly grown. Spreading stems bear rosettes of finely divided leaves and provide an effective background to the relatively large daisylike flowers, with petal-like ray florets that are often a boldly contrasting color beneath. The smaller species are particularly fine plants for pot cultivation in an alpine house or unheated greenhouse.

CULTIVATION Dislikes winter rain, and grows best in rather poor, well-drained gritty soil in full sun.

PROPAGATION From seed, or by cuttings taken in early summer.

PROBLEMS Usually trouble-free, but dislikes wet winter conditions.

BELOW *Anacyclus pyrethrum* var. *depressus*

A. pyrethrum Loosely mat-forming, this more or less evergreen plant has rosettes of silvery leaves, 4¾ in (12 cm) long, that are much dissected into fine lobes, and with smaller stem-leaves. Handsome, yellow-centered white daisies 1½–2 in (4–5 cm) across, with broad ray florets, open from late spring to midsummer. The purple undersides of the petals are noticeable when the flowerheads close in cloudy weather. Although frost-hardy, this species is often short-lived and is best given some protection from winter rain. From rocky places in southeastern Spain and North Africa. ↕4 in (10 cm). Z3–8 H8–1. **var. depressus** More compact, with crimson backs to the ray florets. From the Atlas Mountains in Morocco. ↕2 in (5 cm). **var. depressus 'Garden Gnome'** Free-flowering and compact selection.

ANAPHALIS
ASTERACEAE

Easy and attractive plants that are grown for their clusters of papery white everlasting flowers and gray foliage.

About 100 herbaceous species—ranging from tall erect plants to smaller clump-forming ones—that grow in grasslands, alpine pastures, rocky places, dry woodlands, and scree in the Northern Hemisphere. Their leaves range in shape from narrowly lance-shaped to elliptical, or oval and broader at toward the tip. They are distinctively covered with white woolly hairs. Numerous daisylike flowers have yellow fertile florets surrounded by papery bracts. Good for planting in silver or white borders, they can also be used for cutting and drying. These are one of the few groups of plants with silvery leaves that will thrive in moist soil.

CULTIVATION Plant in a sunny position, in well-drained soil that does not dry out during the summer. Can also be grown in the shade of a wall and in moist soil; however, it will not tolerate heavy shade.

PROPAGATION By division in early spring, or cuttings in spring or early summer.

PROBLEMS Usually trouble-free.

A. margaritacea (Pearly everlasting) Spreads by rhizomes to form a large clump; the erect, woolly stems may only reach 8 in (20 cm) in the wild but are much taller in gardens. The leaves, 6 in (15 cm) long, are linear or narrowly lance-shaped—usually with three veins and with the margins curved downward—and green above but white and woolly beneath. Clusters of white flowers, the color coming from papery outer bracts, appear from midsummer to early fall. Flowers with only male parts, or with mostly female parts, occur on separate plants. Plant in a sunny position, in well-drained soil

ABOVE 1 *Anaphalis triplinervis*
2 *Anchusa azurea* 'Loddon Royalist'

that does not dry out in the summer. Plants may become untidy toward the end of the season and may need support. From sand dunes, lakeshores, dry meadows, and mountain slopes in northern North America, to central and eastern Europe, and the Himalaya. ‡24–36 in (60–90 cm). Z4–8 H8–1. **var. *cinnamomea*** Leaves densely covered underneath with woolly grayish white or cinnamon hairs. From India and Myanmar. ‡24 in (60 cm). **'Neuschnee' (New Snow)** Silvery white flowers. Short. ‡16 in (40 cm). **var. *yedoensis*** Leaves shorter, to 2½ in (6 cm), covered with woolly hairs; one vein. Bracts pearly white, but yellow-brown toward the base. From Japan.

A. triplinervis An attractive and much-used plant; the woolly stems are clasped by the bases of the leaves, which are dark green, spoon- or lance-shaped, densely woolly beneath and less so above, and up to 4 in (10 cm) long with three to five veins. The flowers, about ½ in (1 cm) across, are carried in dome-shaped clusters and have white, papery bracts. Will not tolerate drought and best in a sunny position or part-shade, in well-drained soil that does not dry out in summer. Good for cutting. From meadows and forest clearings, Afghanistan to southwestern China. ‡36 in (90 cm). Z3–8 H8–1. **'Sommerschnee' (Summersnow)** Smaller, with bright silvery white bracts. ‡20 in (50 cm).

A. yedoensis see *A. margaritacea* var. *yedoensis*

ANCHUSA
Alkanet
BORAGINACEAE

Coarse but useful sun-lovers with flowers in a sparkling range of blues.

About 35 species of deciduous plants—many annual or biennial, with a few perennials, which are often short-lived; they grow in dry, sunny places, including roadsides, hills, cliffs, and grasslands, in Europe, western Asia, and Africa. Mostly upright, bristly plants with basal rosettes of narrowly lance-shaped to elliptical, coarsely hairy leaves and bristly stems with alternate leaves. The stems are topped with clusters of tubular to funnel-shaped flowers, each with five spreading lobes, coiled at first, then uncoiling like forget-me-nots. The flowers are usually a shade of blue, are a magnet to bees, and light up herbaceous or mixed borders. Plants contain the toxic alkaloid cynoglossin. ⚠

CULTIVATION Best in full sun and well-drained, moderately fertile soil; does not tolerate waterlogging or shade and dislikes root disturbance. Tall species and cultivars, such as *A. azurea*, require staking, and benefit from division every few years. Deadhead to encourage a second flush of flowers. Cut stems back after flowering to promote the development of basal leaf rosettes.

PROPAGATION From seed in spring, or by division (for plants that form more than one basal rosette) or root cuttings in winter; or, for some, by basal stem cuttings in spring.

PROBLEMS Mildew, cucumber mosaic virus. Some species can self-seed excessively.

A. angustissima see *A. leptophylla* subsp. *incana*

A. azurea syn. *A. italica* (Large blue alkanet) Robust, clump-forming, roughly bristly plant with upright, branched stems and rosettes of long, coarse, lance-shaped or narrow elliptical leaves, 4–16 in (10–40 cm) long, covered with stiff hairs. Slender, branching heads of deep gentian blue flowers, aging to blue-purple, each ½ in (1.5 cm) across, are produced in summer. A popular border plant that is attractive to bees. Best in full sun in any reasonably fertile, well-drained soil. Tall forms need staking. Plants are fairly short-lived and benefit from division every few years. The wild species, and 'Feltham Pride', may be propagated from seed; other cultivars will not come true from seed and should be multiplied by root cuttings or division. Once grown as a fodder plant. Grows wild in southern Europe, western Asia, the Caucasus, and North Africa. ‡36–60 in (90–150 cm). Z3–8 H8–1. **'Dropmore'** Rich deep blue flowers. Oldest known cultivar, introduced in 1905. ‡5–6 ft (1.5–1.8 m). **'Feltham Pride'** Clear, bright blue flowers, compact plant; can be grown from seed, and may be treated as a biennial. ‡36 in (90 cm). **'Little John'** Deep blue flowers, long-lived dwarf form, ‡to 18 in (45 cm). **'Loddon Royalist'** Bright gentian blue flowers, sturdy plants. ‡36 in (90 cm). **'Opal'** Light blue flowers. ‡36–48 in (90–120 cm).

A. italica see *A. azurea*.

A. leptophylla subsp. *incana* syn. *A. angustissima* Tufted, softly hairy plant with tough, branching stems and rosettes of long, narrowly lance-shaped dark green leaves, to 4½ in (11 cm) long. Salver-shaped, gentian blue flowers with a white throat, each to ½ in (1.2 cm) across, are carried in one-sided dense clusters from late spring to midsummer, and occasionally again in fall. Sometimes incorrectly sold as *A. caespitosa*. Requires full sun, and any fertile well-drained soil. Good for a large rock garden as well as front of the border. Can be increased by basal stem cuttings in spring or from seed sown in a gritty mix. Endemic to Turkey. ‡12–16 in (30–40 cm), occasionally to 28 in (70 cm). Z6–8 H8–6

A. sempervirens see *Pentaglottis sempervirens*

ANDROPOGON
Beard Grass
POACEAE

Stately and robust grasses, dying back in winter, with colorful fall and winter foliage.

Over 150 species are found on the tropical savanna, temperate highlands, and the North American prairies, though few are grown in gardens. In late summer, tall stems grow from the lush vegetation, bearing unusual fingerlike flowerheads of usually two digits bearded with protruding silky white hairs. Resistant to drought, it becomes tall and uncomfortably vigorous in wetter conditions.

CULTIVATION Grow in a hot dry position in infertile soil for a more manageable plant, it will reward with beautifully colored foliage in the fall. Cut back dead foliage in the early spring.

PROPAGATION By division in late spring or from seed.

PROBLEMS Usually trouble-free, but it can be invasive.

A. gerardii (Big bluestem, Turkey-foot) A handsome, long-lived grass called "the King of Grasses" in its native prairies, with colorful foliage and unusual flowerheads. Tall and upright, from an extensive, slowly creeping root system, the leaves, ⅜ in (9 mm) wide, rise vertically to fall fountainlike at their tips. Blue-gray stems, suffused with purple, grow above the leaves, bearing three-fingered flowerheads with protruding silky white hairs in late summer. In hot, moist conditions it can grow "as high as a man on a horse"; in cooler climates it is more likely to reach 4 ft (1.2 m). Grown mainly for its lush blue-green foliage, which turns rich red, orange, and bronze in fall, it looks good as a specimen plant or in a prairie-style border. Grow in infertile, dry, sunny conditions to prevent floppy, untidy foliage. From the North American prairies, except the extreme western states. ‡3¼–10 ft (1–3 m). Z2–7 H7–1

ANEMANTHELE
POACEAE

A handsome grass with beautifully colored foliage and airy fountains of flowers.

This genus contains just one species—a plant that was a puzzle to botanists. Previously it had been classified in various genera, such as *Calamagrostis*, *Oryzopsis*, and *Stipa*, but there were enough small differences in the flowers of this species to justify creating a new genus, *Anemanthele*, in 1985. This grass is found from sea level up to mountain heights in forest and scrub, as well as in damp clefts on cliffs and rocky bluffs in New Zealand.

CULTIVATION Well-drained, but fertile, moisture-retentive soil, in sun or part-shade. Comb out dead leaves in spring and summer.

PROPAGATION By division or from seed in late spring.

PROBLEMS Usually trouble-free.

A. lessoniana syn. *Stipa arundinacea* (Pheasant's-tail grass, New Zealand wind grass) Semievergreen, slowly spreading clumps of arching, flat, green leaves, 2½ in (6 mm) wide, are transformed into fountains of orange-, yellow-, and red-tinted foliage from late summer and lasting through winter into spring. The beauty of the foliage is augmented in late summer by airy flowerheads, which bear tiny, glossy, purple-brown beads hanging at the ends of thread-thin, wiry stems that float among the foliage in soft clouds. Lovely planted in drifts to fringe a shady area, where the foliage can flow over rocks or steps, or down the sides of a tall container. From New Zealand. ‡20 in (50 cm). Z7–10 H10–7

ANEMONE
Windflower
RANUNCULACEAE

Delightful plants for a variety of situations, but sometimes uncomfortably vigorous.

Hugely variable, the 120 or so species are widely distributed over a range of habitats throughout the Northern Hemisphere; just a few species originate farther south. Their roots may be fibrous, tuberous, twiglike and brittle, or tough and woody. The leaves are a feature of many species, sometimes being patterned or suffused with a paler color. They spring from the base and are usually rounded or oval and may be split into three to seven segments, which may also be toothed, lobed, or divided, smooth or slightly hairy. Some species also carry leaves on the stems, often in a cluster just beneath the flower.

Flower stems vary in height from 3 to 60 in (7.5 to 150 cm). The flowers, ½–2¾ in (1.5–7 cm) in diameter, are solitary or occur in open clusters, and may be saucer- or cup-shaped, with five to 20, occasionally more, petals in a huge variety of bright and pastel colors.

The word "tepal" is sometimes used for what most of us would call the petals of an anemone. This is because it is unclear if they are in fact true petals or colored sepals (sepals sheath petals in the bud), or a mix of the two. Here, "petal" is used for simplicity. The petals surround a central cluster of stamens and so may superficially resemble a daisy. There are some double-flowered cultivars and a few oddly anomalous types. As the flowers fade, a mass of small fruits develops, sometimes with feathery outgrowths that form ornamental seed heads.

Most anemones are hardy, easily cultivated, and can easily and conveniently be split into four groups. Anemones with tubers from Mediterranean climates, flowering in spring, are usually found in hot, dry habitats and they need a hot, dry dormant period in summer; they are not covered here, being more akin, horticulturally, to bulbs. Anemones with more fibrous roots, often from low, alpine meadows, usually require some sun and good drainage. Woodland anemones have brittle rhizomes (underground creeping stems) and prefer damp, woodland sites. Tall fall-flowerers, sometimes called Japanese anemones, are stalwarts of the perennial border.

This is an unusually uncertain group. There are a number of similar species, which are not always correctly named in gardens and seed lists, and there is also much confusion among cultivars. The Chinese species, and also to some extent the American species, are still not fully understood, although current research should clarify their status. Research continues into the confused naming of fall anemones. The best advice is to trust a dependable nursery to supply the correct plant.

IDENTIFYING FALL-FLOWERING ANEMONES

Cultivars of tall, fall-flowering types, especially *Anemone hupehensis* and *A. x hybrida*, can be difficult to identify correctly and to distinguish one from another, for a number of reasons.

Some have been grown in gardens for over 150 years and in that time may have spontaneously mutated to different forms, still tagged with the original name. Some cultivars have been raised from seed and the variable offspring all given the parent's name. Slightly different forms of the same species have been introduced from the wild on a number of occasions. These can be very long-lived and survive in neglected gardens for decades; they may then be "discovered" and given a new name, when they already have a valid name.

Another difficulty is that the number of petals can vary on different flowers of the same cultivar. The size of individual petals also can vary unpredictably even on the same plant in the same season.

To help clarify some of the identification problems of these plants, pollen from many cultivars has been tested for viability. It is known that the cross between *A. vitifolia* and *A. hupehensis* var. *japonica* (i.e. *A. x hybrida*) results in a greatly reduced quantity of fertile pollen in the flowers of the hybrid. This provided an additional test for use when comparing similar plants and, when used alongside traditional methods of comparing vegetative and floral characters, helped reveal that 'Albert Schweitzer' and 'Max Vogel' are the same as *A. x hybrida* 'Elegans'; that plants grown as 'Bodnant Burgundy' are simply *A. hupehensis* var. *japonica*; that 'Bressingham Glow' is the same as 'Prinz Heinrich'; that plants sold as 'Luise Uhink' are either 'Honorine Jobert' or 'Whirlwind'; and that 'Terry's Pink' is the same as 'Monterosa'. 'Monterosa' has often been listed as 'Lady Gilmour' – which is a different plant altogether!

CULTIVATION While few are especially demanding, it is important to match species to the local conditions. Those in the fibrous-rooted group usually prefer some sun and good drainage. Woodland anemones grow best in well-drained, humus-rich soil that is never waterlogged in winter, and in woodland gardens or among shrubs. They thrive in part-shade but tolerate the soil drying out in summer. Fall-flowering types are best in light shade and prefer alkaline soil, but grow anywhere except in soil that is waterlogged in winter. Newly planted anemones may remain small until they become established and grow naturally.

PROPAGATION By division where possible. Plants with creeping underground stems, especially woodland species, often form large colonies: lift with a border fork, tease apart, and replant immediately in enriched soil. Take pieces from the edges of fall-flowering anemones in fall, or divide their rootstocks in spring. Most species set seed, but there are many cultivars, which do not come true from seed; also, species may hybridize.

PROBLEMS Slugs and snails, occasional aphids, and powdery mildew. Stem and leaf nematode may attack fall-flowering anemones. Leaves may yellow on plants grown in strongly alkaline soil.

A. apennina Steady-spreading, the long-stalked, basal leaves are divided into three parts, which in turn are much divided and toothed and lightly hairy beneath. Blue to white flowers, 1¼ in (3 cm) across and consisting of up to 14 oblong petals, open in early and mid-spring. Taller than the closely related, but more distinctly tuberous, *A. blanda* (which can be dried off for sale when dormant); eventually develops a large, elongated, nearly black tuber. Best in sunny or partly shaded positions in well-drained soil, where it will colonize an area quite quickly. Raise from seed or divide, with care, when dormant. Native from Corsica eastward to Greece; first found in the wild in 1724. ‡8 in (20 cm). Z5–9 H9–3. **var.** *albiflora* White.

A. baldensis Clump-forming plant that grows from a fibrous rootstock; there are three basal leaves, rather like parsley, with a similar cluster just below the solitary, summer flowers. These have eight to ten petals, are 1½ in (4 cm) across, and white—often with a blue flush on the reverse. The seed head is woolly. Best in a sunny site in moist, well-drained soil. The much taller, and less fussy, *A. sylvestris* is often supplied in error. Seed sown in fall, and exposed to winter weather, germinates well in the next spring. From northern Italy, Republic of Bosnia & Herzegovina,

RIGHT 1 *Anemone apennina* var. *albiflora* **2** *A. multifida* **3** *A. nemorosa* 'Robinsoniana'

Croatia, Macedonia, Slovenia, and Serbia & Montenegro. ↕ 4¾ in (12 cm). Z3–7 H7–1

A. barbulata This charming species has fibrous roots, long leaf stems, and dissected foliage. Each branched flower stem carries glistening white, blue-backed, many-petaled flowers, 1¼–1½ in (3–4 cm) long and held well above the foliage, in late spring and early summer. Reminiscent of the more widely grown *A. rivularis*, of which it has been treated as a variety, it is increasing in popularity. Easy in a well-drained, moisture-retentive, sunny site. Raise from seed. Originates from China. ↕ 24 in (60 cm). Z4–8 H8–1

A. canadensis Tough and easy, fibrous-rooted woodlander. Its long-stalked leaves have three to five lobes, which are in turn divided into smaller lobes; the stem leaves are similar but they are unstalked. All leaves are hairy beneath. The oblong, 1½-in (3.5-cm), five-petaled, white flowers are borne on branched stems. Ideal in a moist woodland border or wild garden, in sun or part-shade, but can be invasive. Raise from seed. North America (Labrador to Colorado). ↕ 24 in (60 cm). Z3–7 H7–1

A. cylindrica The fibrous rootstock gives rise to leaves with silky hairs; the five lobes of each leaf are divided into narrower divisions and the stem leaves are similar with short stalks. Clusters of two to six whitish green flowers, up to ¾ in (2 cm) across, appear in summer and are followed by ¾–1½-in (2–4-cm-) long, densely woolly seed heads. Differs from the similar, and more often seen, *A. canadensis* in the narrower divisions to its shorter-stalked leaves and the green tint to the flowers. Best in well-drained soil in sun or part-shade; raise from seed. From western North America. ↕ 24 in (60 cm). Z3–7 H7–1

A. drummondii Very variable, clump-forming species, with fibrous roots and finely divided, green leaves with a silver sheen. The solitary flower, on a coarsely hairy stem, is white, but it is often tinged with blue or lavender. The seed head is rounded, with woolly seed casings. Very similar to the European *A. baldensis*, of which it is has been considered an American variant; some forms seem similar to *A. multifida*. Needs a sunny site and moist, well-drained soil; raise from seed. From western North America. ↕ 4–8 in (10–20 cm). Z3–7 H7–1

A. flaccida From a black rhizome, forms a mound of dense foliage: the bronzed-green leaves soon turn green with pale marks at the bases of the lobed and toothed leaflets. Creamy white, 1¼-in (3-cm), solitary flowers with five to seven petals emerge in late spring, but rarely produce seed. Needs part-shade in humus-rich soil; hates spring droughts. Increase by division of rhizomes when the plants are dormant. Grows wild in mountain forests of Japan, China, and eastern Russia. ↕ 8 in (20 cm). Z4–8 H8–1

***A.* 'Guernica'** see *A. multifida* 'Guernica'

A. hupehensis A stout, woody, suckering rootstock produces large, dark, generally rounded leaves, 4–8 in (10–20 cm) long on long stems; each leaf is divided into three lobes, which are jagged-toothed. Upright stems carry smaller leaves and a succession of up to 15 flowers between late summer and mid-fall. Each 2–2½-in (5–6-cm) flower has five almost circular petals in various shades of pink or white, three of which may be larger than the other two. The plant thrives in any reasonable soil that is neither parched nor waterlogged, preferably in light shade. From western and central China. ↕ 20–40 in (50–100 cm). Z5–7 H7–5. ***f. alba*** Each flower has five white petals, their backs flushed with purple. From Yunnan province, southwestern China. ↕ 20–48 in (50–120 cm). **'Bowles' Pink'** Flowers are 2½ in (6 cm) across, with five petals, which are crimped at the tips and slightly twisted and taper toward the flower center. Three petals are dark purple-pink, while the two smaller petals are bright purple. Raised by E. A. Bowles, England. ↕ 24–36 in (60–90 cm). **'Crispa'** see *A.* x *hybrida* 'Lady Gilmour'. **'Eugenie'** Twenty-four slightly quilled and rolled, red-purple petals form each 2½-in (6-cm) flower. Very similar to *A.* x *hybrida* 'Bodnant Burgundy'. ↕ 24–36 in (60–90 cm). **'Hadspen Abundance'** Flowers are 2 in (5 cm) across with five medium-sized, purple-pink petals, three of which are noticeably smaller and darker, creating an intriguing, bicolored effect. Similar to 'Bowles' Pink', but with more rounded petals. Raised by Eric Smith, England. ↕ 24–32 in (60–80 cm). **var. *japonica*** (Japanese anemone) This variety of *A. hupehensis* was originally introduced by Robert Fortune in 1843 after he found it growing on graves around Shanghai, and it has since given rise to a large group of very popular garden cultivars. The original variety has flowers that are 2½ in (6.5 cm) long, with up to 25 deep reddish purple, rather narrow petals; these may be flattened, or quilled and twisted, into an irregular shape. A few outer petals may be green. The leaves are smaller than those of other species, with long, sharply pointed, terminal leaflets. This variety has naturalized widely in Japan. ↕ 20–40 in (50–100 cm). Z5–7 H7–5. **var. *japonica* 'Bodnant Burgundy'** Often listed, but it is doubtful if the correct form of this cultivar now exists. It should have about ten, narrow, flattened, deep pink petals. Plants sold under this name almost always prove to be 'Prinz Heinrich' or occasionally 'Rotkäppchen'. 'Eugenie' is similar but has more petals. **var. *japonica* 'Bressingham Glow'** Described by its breeder, veteran horticulturist Alan Bloom, as more vigorous and a deeper color than 'Prinz Heinrich', but even plants obtained from the original source cannot be distinguished from 'Prinz Heinrich'. **var. *japonica* 'Pamina'** Noticeably prolific form with regular, reddish purple flowers, just 2 in (5 cm) across, with about 40 flattened petals. Similar to 'Margarete', but with a more open flower. Often placed under *A.* x *hybrida*. ↕ 24–32 in (60–80 cm). **var. *japonica* 'Prinz Heinrich'** (**Prince Henry**) Flowers are semi-double with up to 26, deep rose-purple petals that fade as the flower ages and are usually rolled or quilled and variable in length. There are often two or three rounded, green and purple petals backing the 2½-in (6-cm) flower. Sometimes quoted as a dwarf form—this may be the only feature distinguishing it from *A. hupehensis* var. *japonica*, but in good conditions it will be as tall. ↕ 26–40 in (65–100 cm). **var. *japonica* 'Rotkäppchen'** About 25 rose-purple petals in a 2¾-in (6.5-cm) flower. This is another cultivar that is virtually indistinguishable from 'Prinz Heinrich'; the flowers are slightly larger and, in similar conditions, the plants will be slightly taller. ↕ 32–48 in (80–120 cm). **'Praecox'** Five (occasionally up to eight) rounded, medium-sized, pink petals narrow at their bases to form a flower 2½ in (6 cm) across. One of the earliest to flower. ↕ 24–32 in (60–80 cm). **'September Charm'** Flowers are 2½–3 in (6–8 cm) across, with five rounded petals in pale pink flushed with a darker color; two petals are slightly smaller and darker pink. The leaves are very hairy underneath. Some plants under this name feature rounded petals of a more uniform pale pink. Introduced by Bristol Nurseries, CT, which also introduced the Korean chrysanthemums. ↕ 32–40 in (80–100 cm). **'Splendens'** Five bright purple-pink petals, two of which are slightly smaller and darker than the others, form a flower about 2½ in (6 cm) across. Probably the form from which 'Bowles' Pink' and 'Hadspen Abundance' were selected, but pale and with more uniformly sized petals. ↕ 24–32 in (60–80 cm). **'Superba'** Five rounded petals in a uniform, pale purple-pink. At 2¾ in (6.5 cm), this plant has the largest flowers of any *A. hupehensis* cultivar, but it is less prolific than most. ↕ 24–32 in (60–80 cm).

A.* x *hybrida Vigorous, sometimes annoyingly so, with bold three-lobed leaves with a few soft hairs underneath. From late summer to mid-fall, the airy stems carry up to about 20 usually sterile flowers, up to 3 in (8 cm) across, with anything from six to fifteen petals in various pinks and white. Generally similar to *A. hupehensis*, but inheriting its white hairs from *A. vitifolia*, many cultivars of *A.* x *hybrida* have at various times been placed in both species. This plant is believed to be a seedling raised in the RHS garden in Chiswick, London, in 1848, from a cross between *A. hupehensis* var. *japonica* and *A. vitifolia*—see 'Elegans'. Easy in any good soil that is not waterlogged, in sun or light shade. ↕ 4–5 ft (1.2–1.5 m). Z4–8 H8–5. **'Alba'** Name wrongly used for 'Honorine Jobert'. **'Andrea Atkinson'** Flowers about 2¾ in (6.5 cm) across, the ten white petals are flushed with pink and green on their outer side. It does not seem possible to distinguish this from 'Honorine Jobert', and it is no improvement. ↕ 20–48 in (50–120 cm). **'Crispa'** *see* 'Lady Gilmour'. **'Elegans'** From six to fifteen light purple-pink petals—the outer ones broad and overlapping, the inner ring much narrower and often twisted and distorted—make up a flower about 2¾ in (7 cm) across. Produces very little pollen. This is the accepted version of the original cross, and what most people recognize as a Japanese anemone. ↕ 30–48 in (75–120 cm). **'Géante des Blanches'** syn. 'White Queen' A controversial plant with up to 24 broad, pure white petals, slightly frilled at the edges, making a flower about 2¾ in (7 cm) across, and with broad leaves in which two basal leaflets overlap. Very similar to 'Königin Charlotte' and 'Loreley' in leaf and flower form, but pure white in color. Unfortunately, the true plant is rarely sold under this name; those supplied are usually semidouble whites similar to 'Honorine Jobert' or have more numerous narrow, twisted petals like 'Whirlwind'. The name may, correctly, be 'Géante Blanche'. ↕ 40–54 in (100–130 cm). **'Honorine Jobert'** Up to 11 pure white petals, making a flower about 2¾ in (7 cm) across, with the outer petals broad and overlapping and inner petals narrower and often twisted and distorted. Identical to 'Elegans', of which it is said to be a spontaneous mutation, except in flower color. Often sold as 'Alba'. ↕ 20–48 in (50–120 cm). **'Königin Charlotte'** (**Queen Charlotte**) syn. 'Königin Charlotte of Wurtemburg'. Large flowers, 3 in (8 cm), with up to 20 broad, overlapping petals of a bright, clear pink. The lower leaflets on the large leaves have overlapping bases. One of the better forms, but the plant may need staking because of its heavy flowers. ↕ 32–50 in (80–125 cm).

PROPAGATING FALL ANEMONES

Anemone hupehensis, *A. tomentosa*, and *A. vitifolia* produce fertile seed, but since they are cross-pollinated freely by insects, their seedlings are unlikely to come true. It is not worth raising seedlings, even from seed offered in catalogs. Cultivars derived from *A.* x *hybrida* have only small amounts of fertile pollen, but still produce seed, which yields very variable seedlings due to their hybrid origins and cross-pollination.

Fall anemones are best propagated from cuttings taken in fall from the horizontal, underground stems found at the edges of a clump. Pieces 2–3 in (5–8 cm) long, with buds or small plantlets along their length, should be placed in pots of sandy potting mix until they are well grown. It is possible to divide the main rootstock in spring, but large, woody divisions are often difficult to handle, are very slow to establish, and should be discarded—use only non-woody material. The roots are also deep: it is not uncommon to lift and divide a plant, for replanting elsewhere, and find shoots growing from pieces of root left deep in the soil at the original site.

'Lady Gilmour' syn. *A. hupensis* 'Crispa' Uniquely, leaves on younger growth are heavily crested and fringed around the edges, creating a "love-it-or-hate-it" foliage plant. The pink flowers have about 12 petals, which tend to be narrow and slightly twisted, and form an irregular 2½ in (6.5 cm) flower. ‡ 24–40 in (60–100 cm).
'Loreley' Twenty broad, overlapping, pale rose petals, fringed at their tips, fade as the 3-in (7.5-cm) flower ages. Very similar to 'Königin Charlotte', with overlapping leaflet bases. A number of impostors are sold under this name: some are white, with twisted petals; some are like a pink form of 'Whirlwind'. ‡ 24–48 in (60–120 cm).
'Luise Uhink' A confusing cultivar. It should have over 20, pure white, slightly frilly-edged petals, but plants supplied under this name are either 'Honorine Jobert' or 'Whirlwind'. Introduced in 1919, it may now be lost, or this may be the correct name for the plant now grown as 'Géante des Blanches'. ‡ 3¼–4¼ ft (1–1.3 m).
'Margarete' Up to 50, deep pink, flattened petals form a regular, almost double, flower that is about 2¼ in (5.5 cm) across. Until recently, most plants supplied under this name were actually 'Monterosa', a better plant with larger flowers, but the correct plant is now sometimes available. ‡ 28–36 in (70–90 cm). **'Monterosa'** One of the best forms with one of the largest flowers in this group; they are about 3 in (8 cm) across, with up to 40 quilled and twisted, soft rose-pink petals. The two lower leaflets on the basal leaves overlap at the base. May need staking due to the weight of the large flowers. ‡ 32–50 in (80–125 cm).
'Richard Ahrens' Early flowering with five, very pale creamy pink petals in a 2¾-in (7-cm) flower. The two side leaflets on the main leaves tend to overlap at the bases. ‡ 32–40 in (80–100 cm). **'Robustissima'** The dark pink, 2-in (5-cm) flowers have five petals and are borne on reddish stems. The leaves are only slightly hairy below and are strongly lobed. Very similar to *A. tomentosa*, of which this sometimes considered a cultivar. There are many poorly colored forms, probably seedlings, with smaller flowers. ‡ 32–48 in (80–120 cm). **'Rosenschale'** Irregularly shaped flowers, with up to seven unevenly sized petals of rose pink. The petals are broad and fringed at the tips, narrowing to the bases. Plants with flowers in a paler pink, flaked with the darker color, are sometimes seen under this name. ‡ 24–38 in (60–100 cm). **'Serenade'** Semidouble flower, about 2¼ in (5.5 cm) across, with about 14 narrow, soft rose-pink petals that become narrower toward the flower center. ‡ 3¼ ft (1 m). **'Whirlwind'** (Tourbillon) Up to 25 white, narrow, quilled petals form an irregular 2½-in (6-cm) flower; several petals of the outer ring are green. There seem to be two different stocks of 'Whirlwind', one more

---

LEFT 1 *Anemone obtusiloba*
2 *A. ranunculoides* **3** *A. trullifolia*

vigorous than the other. Most cultivars listed as having double white flowers are likely to be this, whatever name they are given. ‡ 24–36 in (60–90 cm) or 4¼ ft (1.3 m). **'White Queen'** *see* 'Géante des Blanches'.

A. x *lesseri* An easy and attractive, but variable, fertile hybrid with three to five shiny green, hairy, basal leaves that have long stalks and deeply divided, toothed lobes. The stem leaves are similar, but fused at the bases. The glossy flowers are usually solitary, but occasionally up to three occur per stem. They are 1 in (2.5 cm) across and rose pink, or sometimes yellow, whitish, or purple; they have five to eight oval petals and yellow anthers. Named cultivars are expected on the market soon. This species thrives in any well-drained, sunny site. Divide the rootstock in spring. Hybrid of *A. multifida* and *A. sylvestris*. ‡ 8 in (20 cm). Z3–7 H7–1

A. leveillei Kidney-shaped, hairy, three-lobed leaves, each deeply divided and toothed, arise from a fibrous rootstock. The 1½-in (4-cm) flowers are white with a pink exterior and quite hairy, with prettily contrasting, purple anthers. Best in a damp, sunny position. Similar to *A. rivularis*, into which it is sometimes subsumed, but with larger, pink-flushed, usually eight-petaled flowers. From central China. ‡ 24 in (60 cm). Z5–9 H9–5

A. x *lipsiensis* syn. *A.* x *seemannii* A delightful hybrid of *A. nemorosa* and *A. ranunculoides* with a brittle, brown rhizome that produces quite dark, deeply lobed leaves up to 3 in (8 cm) long. The flowers, up to ¾ in (2 cm) across, are pale, creamy yellow and

composed of five to eight oval petals. A charming, slightly variable plant, with a pleasing contrast between flower and leaf. This is a natural hybrid found wherever the two parents grow in close proximity. Enjoys woodland sites that can dry out in summer. Propagate by separating dormant rhizomes. From Europe. ‡ 4–4¾ in (10–12 cm). Z5–8 H8–5. **'Pallida'** Pale cream.

A. magellanica see *A. multifida*

A. multifida syn. *A. magellanica* An attractive species with numerous, quite hairy, basal leaves, which have three lobes that are also narrowly divided. Stem leaves are similar with short stalks.

Each stem carries one to three flowers, up to 1 in (2.5 cm) across and composed of five to ten petals, which are usually cream, but may be white, pink, pale yellow, even greenish, or in shades of purple. The seed heads are woolly and rounded. The widely grown cream form, often sold as *A. magellanica*, is usually the South American selection of this essentially North American species. Native American peoples used this plant medicinally—for example, as a cold remedy. An easy plant for a sunny position. Tends to be short-lived, but self-seeds. From North and South America. ‡ 12 in (30 cm). Z2–6 H7–1. **'Guernica'** syn. *A.* 'Guernica' Cream flowers; the stems branch repeatedly to create a prolific display. **'Major'** Robust form with creamy yellow flowers. **'Rubra'** Dark purplish flowers.

A. narcissiflora Large, very variable, fibrous-rooted plant, with 16-in (40-cm) basal leaves divided into five-pointed, toothed lobes. The tiered stem leaves are unstalked. Heads of three to eight flowers, each ¾–1½ in (2–4 cm) with five or six petals, are white and often flushed with pink on the outsides. Best in well-drained soil in sun or semi-shade; not easy, but worth the effort. Raise from seed. From central and southern Europe. ‡ 16 in (40 cm). Z5–8 H8–5

A. nemorosa (Wood anemone) A vigorous plant, spreading by slender, brown, rather brittle rhizomes that carry long-stalked leaves divided into three, and three again. These toothed, quite narrow leaflets often do not appear until after flowering. The flowers are held well above the foliage and all face the same direction. They are 1¼ in (3 cm) with five to 12 petals and white flushed with purple or pink, which intensifies with age. Many excellent named selections exist, including forms with purple and blue flowers, and some doubles. The large-flowered white cultivars are being studied and may all prove to be the same. Despite their short flowering season, these are invaluable shade-lovers for early spring and are increasingly collected. Easy in well-drained soil in semi-shade, and ideal among deciduous shrubs or in woodland gardens. Divide

dormant rhizomes. From Europe. ‡ 6 in (15 cm). Z4–8 H8–1. **'Alba Plena'** Double white with an irregular center. **'Allenii'** Deep lavender-blue flowers, shaded pinkish on the reverse. An old selection and still one of the best. ‡ 1½ in (4 cm). **'Atrocaerulea'** Deep blue. **'Blue Beauty'** Pale blue flowers and a dark tinge to the foliage. **'Blue Bonnet'** Late-flowering, deep blue. **'Blue Eyes'** Whitish double with blue center. From Ireland. **'Bowles' Purple'** Late-flowering, purple with dark edging to the foliage. **'Bracteata'** Loose double white with some green petals. **'Bracteata Pleniflora'** Semidouble white and green flower framed by a jagged ruff of leaves. **'Buckland'** Early-flowering lilac-lavender. **'Cedric's Pink'** Pink, darkening with age. **'Dee Day'** Good blue. **'Flore Pleno'** Small, white double flower. **'Green Fingers'** Central boss of green petals within a pure white flower. **'Hannah Gubbay'** Late-blooming, single lilac flower. **'Hilda'** Neat, semidouble white. **'Knightshayes Vestal'** Pure white flowers and a buttonlike center; similar to 'Vestal', but with a visible ring of yellow anthers. **'Lady Doneraile'** Large, single white. ‡ 2 in (5 cm). **'Leeds' Variety'** Single white, very similar to 'Lady Doneraile'. ‡ 2 in (5 cm). **'Lychette'** Large, early-flowering, single white. **'Monstrosa'** Green-and-white-centered, semidouble flowers with jagged petals. ‡ 1½ in (4 cm). **'Parlez Vous'** Single, soft blue. **'Pentre Pink'** Single pink, darkening considerably with age. **'Robinsoniana'** Dark stem with a deep blue-mauve flower and a gray exterior. ‡ 1½ in (4 cm). **'Rosea'** Pink buds open white, then turn pink, especially on the exterior. **'Royal Blue'** Rich blue flowers; needs regular division to flower well. **'Vestal'** Very neat flower with pure white outer petals and buttonlike center. ‡ ¾ in (2 cm). **'Virescens'** The flower is replaced by a mound of deeply cut, green bracts, infertile and long-lasting. ‡ 2 in (5 cm). **'Viridiflora'** Probably the same as 'Virescens'. **'Westwell Pink'** Very dark pink. **'Wyatt's Pink'** Nodding flowers open pink, gradually fading to a paler shade.

A. obtusiloba Undeservedly neglected, variable species, with a compact

WOODLAND ANEMONES

A. apennina, an attractive blue-flowered species, will take more sun than other woodland anemones and, as well as this blue, it comes in shades through to pure white and may, rarely, have pinkish tints.

A. nemorosa 'Alba Plena' is this double white flowered form with a slightly messy center, but other double whites, such as 'Flore Pleno' and 'Vestal', may sometimes, incorrectly, be seen under this name.

A. nemorosa 'Cedric's Pink' is one of a number of valuable pink-flowered forms of *A. nemorosa*; it has narrower petals, which are paler on the backs, and the flowers are held on maroon stems.

A. ranunculoides with its bright buttery yellow flowers is a valuable ground-covering carpeter between shrubs; it is also the parent, with *A. nemorosa*, of the excellent hybrid *A. x lipsiensis*.

rhizome that produces softly hairy, mid-green leaves with three shallowly indented lobes. In late spring, heads of two to three flowers appear; they may be blue, white, or more rarely yellow. The flowers may be ¾–2 in (2–5 cm) across, composed of four to six rounded petals, and have an attractive boss of stamens. Enjoys a moist, humus-rich position in semi-shade. Raise from seed. From southwestern China. ‡ 4 in (10 cm). Z5–8 H8–5

A. italica see *Pulsatilla vulgaris*

A. ranunculoides Like a dainty, yellow-flowered form of *A. nemorosa*, this species has thin, light brown rhizomes and deeply divided, three-lobed, dark green basal leaves. These contrast well with the solitary, buttercup-like, spring flowers, which are ¾–1¼ in (2–3 cm) deep with five to seven yellow petals, on 6-in (15-cm) stems. The plant soon forms a colony in light shade in humus-rich soil. Divide dormant rhizomes. From Europe. ‡ 6 in (15 cm). Z4–8 H8–1. **f.** *laciniata* Leaves strikingly dissected. **'Pleniflora'** Slightly later flowering with semidouble, yellow flowers. **subsp.** *wockeana* Smaller form, with bronze juvenile foliage that soon fades to green.

A. rivularis Strongly growing, fibrous-rooted plant with three-lobed, highly toothed, and slightly hairy leaves on long stalks. Generous clusters of up to 20 flowers, 1¼ in (3 cm) wide, which are white with a violet to blue reverse and purple anthers. Very variable, but the best forms are handsome plants. For a damp, sunny, or part-shaded position; can self-seed prolifically. From northern India and southwestern China. ‡ 36 in (90 cm). Z6–8 H8–6

A. rupicola A long, woody rootstock produces stalked, three-lobed leaves with wedge-shaped, sharp-toothed, shiny green leaflets, which are sometimes purple beneath. The large, white, solitary flowers, with five quite substantial oval petals, are 2¾ in (7 cm) across in good forms and often pink-

CANDIDATES FOR A COLLECTION

Almost any group that includes many small and attractive plant forms is collected by enthusiasts. *Anemone nemorosa* has well over 50 forms and is a collector's plant.

These are plants to grow with other shade-lovers: with hellebores, trilliums, and ferns as well as pulmonarias, and with small woodland shrubs such as daphnes. While many are vigorous enough to hold their own among deciduous shrubs like viburnums, it makes sense not to risk the more choice forms in a shrub border.

The many blue-flowered anemones are easily confused, so they should be widely separated; be sure always to set other plants between, so that the dormant rhizomes never intermingle when being lifted; they spread into each other, if given the chance. Self-sown seedlings can be a problem: seedlings germinate among different clumps, and may not come true and so cause confusion. If you have a collection of different forms, new hybrids will undoubtedly appear. It is up to you to decide whether to cut off the dead flowers and keep your collection pure—or take a chance and invite the possibility of intriguing new hybrids.

WOODLAND ANEMONES

Dormant rhizomes of species such as *Anemone nemorosa*, *A. ranunculoides*, and *A. apennina* should be planted immediately after they are received from nurseries because they cannot tolerate drying out excessively. Buy them in flower, in pots, for a smooth transition from nursery to garden and to help confirm the name. When setting in an anemone rhizome, sift a little sharp sand around the plant to ensure that there are no air pockets, and water in well even if it is not in growth. When cleaning up foliage in fall, work some slow-release fertilizer around the colony.

These species often grow quite strongly, their brittle rhizomes forming colonies of delightful plants in just a few

years. In fall, these can be lifted carefully, teased apart, and immediately replanted.

It is inadvisable to grow most woodland anemones from seed because the results can be so variable, but seed of some species is worth trying. Collect it promptly before it blows or rolls away. Seed of *A. apennina* is ripe when it is barely yellow; collect the whole seed head quickly and dry in a paper bag. Sow the seed fresh, no later than early fall. Grow seedling plants for two growing seasons in the same pots, giving regular applications of liquid fertilizer and protecting them from severe weather. The next summer, the rhizomes will be easier to find and large enough to handle.

or violet-backed, and give way to rounded, woolly seed heads. Likes a sunny and moist, well-drained situation. Raise from seed. From Afghanistan to southwestern China. ‡6 in (15 cm). Z4–7 H7–4

A. x *seemannii* see *A.* x *lipsiensis*

A. sylvestris (Snowdrop anemone) Dark green, maplelike leaves, strongly lobed and lightly hairy beneath, arise from a woody rootstock that colonizes by root suckers. The fragrant, open cup-shaped, white, slightly nodding flowers, up to 2¾ in (7 cm) across, appear in late spring and have lovely, golden yellow anthers; they are followed by woolly seed heads. A beautiful flower produced in sparse numbers. Best in well-drained, alkaline soil in sun or part-shade. Propagate from seed or by division in early spring. From central Europe, to the Caucasus. ‡12–20 in (30–50 cm). Z3–9 H9–1. **'Elise Fellmann'** Semidouble form. **'Macrantha'** Larger flowers.

A. tomentosa A woody, spreading rootstock carries large, coarse leaves that have up to seven noticeably veined lobes, and lower surfaces thickly covered with white hairs. The 2½-in (6-cm) flowers have five pale pink, rounded petals surrounding a central boss of yellow stamens; they are carried in open, airy heads of 12 or more in late summer and early fall. The most vigorous of the three fall *Anemone* species, this variable plant can be extremely invasive and occasionally reaches 5 ft (1.5 m) when growing well. Inferior plants, lacking white hairs on lower leaf surfaces, sometimes occur. Thrives in most reasonable soils in sun or light shade. Remove and grow on plantlets in fall or divide rootstock in spring. Introduced by Reginald Farrer in 1914. From the high mountains of northern China. ‡32–48 in (80–120 cm). Z5–9 H9–3. **'Robustissima'** see *A.* x *hybrida* 'Robustissima'.

A. trifolia Superficially similar to *A. nemorosa*, with thin rhizomes but no basal leaves, so the stem leaves are enlarged in compensation and resemble three bright-green, broad-toothed spearheads joined at the bases. The solitary, usually white flowers are held well above the foliage and are composed of five to eight petals with a central boss of white or blue anthers. Very attractive ground cover, for early spring. Distinct from *A. nemorosa* in its absence of basal leaves. Best in well-drained soil in semi-shade. Divide rhizomes when dormant. From southern Europe. ‡6 in (15 cm). Z6–8 H8–6. **'Semiplena'** Semidouble white.

A. trullifolia Compact, fibrous-rooted plant, with three lobed, wedge-shaped leaves held on long stems. The ¾-in (2-cm) solitary flowers are carried above the foliage on pale brown stems, usually composed of five petals, and can be blue, white, or more rarely yellow, pinkish, or purplish. Relatively recently

introduced but increasing in popularity and very amenable to cultivation, even in drier climates. Best in well-drained soil in sun, or in part-shade in dry climates. Propagate from seed. From the eastern Himalaya and southwestern China. ‡6 in (15 cm). Z5–8 H8–5

A. virginiana Strong, bold, fibrous-rooted perennial, with long leaf stalks and broadly rounded, deeply toothed leaves, divided into three or five leaflets. The stem branches each hold two or three 1-in (2.5-cm) flowers, which are white tinged green. Pure white, green- and red-flowered forms occur in the wild. Best in well-drained soil in sun; raise from seed. From central and eastern regions of North America. ‡18 in (45 cm). Z5–8 H8–5. **var.** *alba* White.

A. vitifolia Bold, undivided, heart-shaped leaves, each indented to create five lobes, resembling vine leaves, with lower surfaces covered in thick layers of white hairs. Loose heads of up to seven 2½-in (6.5-cm) flowers appear in late summer and early fall; the five white petals are well rounded, with outsides shaded in pink and green. Thrives in any reasonable soil that is neither parched nor waterlogged, preferably in light shade. Can suffer in winter in cold gardens in some soils, especially if wet. From temperate mountains of northern India into Yunnan province, China. ‡20–40 in (50–100 cm). Z5–8 H8–3

ANEMONELLA
Rue anemone
RANUNCULACEAE

Dainty but tough shade-lover grown for delicate anemone-like flowers in spring and early summer, in a varied and increasing range of forms.

A single species of deciduous plant that is suitable for a woodland garden, or a choice, shady corner of a border. From eastern North

America, where it is found in open woodlands with moist, fertile soil, this tight clump–forming perennial grows from clusters of small tubers and takes time to settle down, but eventually forms a colony about 12 in (30 cm) across. Saucer-shaped flowers up to ¾ in (2 cm) across, either white or pink, with five petals or sometimes a few more, appear above *Thalictrum*-like leaves in spring and early summer. The plant becomes dormant once seeds have ripened in summer. Some botanists classify this as *Thalictrum thalictroides*: literally, the *Thalictrum* that looks like a *Thalictrum*— especially bizarre since most botanists see it as so different that they place it in its own genus.

CULTIVATION Needs moist soil containing abundant humus, and part-shade, but avoid soil that stays wet because this will cause the tubers to rot. Water in summer if the soil starts to dry out. Give shelter from strong winds. Plant with similarly restrained plants— small ferns, hardy cyclamen, and trilliums make good neighbors.

PROPAGATION Divide established colonies in early fall or very early spring, although plants resent disturbance. Simplest to remove a few tubers from the outside of a colony without disturbing the entire patch, although this will eventually lead to deterioration of the main plant. Nurseries lift choice forms, divide the crown using a scalpel, and pamper the divisions until growing well. Sow seed in a cold frame as soon as ripe; a thriving colony will self-seed.

PROBLEMS Slugs and snails. Powdery mildew. Can be overwhelmed by larger neighbors.

A. thalictroides syn. *Thalictrum thalictroides* Pretty, fragile-looking deep

blue-green leaves, 4–6-in (10–15-cm) long, resemble those of some *Thalictrum* species (hence the specific name, *thalictroides*). Anemone-like flowers ¾ in (2 cm) wide with five to ten petals, mainly white (but cultivars in others colors) appear on slender stems between mid-spring and early summer. Creates delightful little colonies with other small woodland plants and bulbs. Wild populations often show obvious variation in the number of petals and size of flowers. Widespread throughout eastern North America. ‡4–6 in (10–15 cm). Z4–7 H7–1. **'Amelia'** Single pale pink flowers. **'Cameo'** Double pale pink flowers, almost white in hot climates. **'Double Green'** Self-explanatory. Originates in Japan. **'Full Double White'** Very double off-white flowers. **f.** *rosea* Pale pink flowers. **f.** *rosea* **'Oscar Schoaf'** Double buttonlike pale pink flowers. Also known as 'Schoaf's Double', 'Schoaf's Double Pink' and 'Schoaf's Pink'. **semidouble white** From ten to many petals, but not fully double. **'Snowflakes'** Double pure white flowers.

ANEMONOPSIS
RANUNCULACEAE

A classically elegant early summer-flowering woodlander for cool, moist shade.

A choice, clumping plant with fresh, glossy foliage; the leaves are divided into three leaflets, which are themselves split once or twice into three toothed or lobed leaflets. Airy sprays of nodding, purple or lilac flowers open from late summer to mid-fall.

CULTIVATION Constantly moist but well-drained, humus–rich soil in shade. Needs a very sheltered spot to protect it from drying winds that

BELOW 1 *Anemonella thalictroides*
2 *A. thalictroides* f. *rosea*

may damage foliage and cause plants to die down prematurely, although they usually emerge again the following spring.

PROPAGATION By division, or from fresh seed sown in late summer.

PROBLEMS Slugs and snails may attack emerging shoots in spring.

A. macrophylla Desirable plant for the sheltered woodland garden, producing dainty, broadly ferny foliage of a rich green, from a thick, creeping rootstock. Leaves are divided into nine or 27 leaflets that are 1½–3 in (4–8 cm) long. In summer, lavender or purple, cup-shaped blooms, about 1¼ in (3 cm) across, appear well above the foliage on dark, slender stems in groups of up to ten, sometimes more. They superficially resemble aquilegia flowers (*see* Aquilegia Flower Structure, *p. 63*), but with a rather waxy, almost crystalline quality. The outer petals are paler than the inner ones, giving them a two-toned look. Best in cool shade in acidic soil; plants must not dry out. Rather scarce in its wild habitat—cool mountain woodlands in Honshu, Japan. ‡20–32 in (50–80 cm). Z5–8 H8–5

ANTHEMIS

ASTERACEAE

Showy, daisylike flowerheads and divided aromatic leaves mark these long-flowering sun-lovers.

One hundred or more species, some annuals or shrubs, that grow in dry, sunny habitats in poor rocky soil in Europe, western Asia, and North Africa. Only five perennial species are commonly grown: the larger suitable for a sunny border, the smaller best in a rock garden. Clumps or mats of strongly scented, usually divided leaves arise from a fibrous or woody rootstock. Over a long period, from late spring to summer, solitary daisies, with yellow disklike centers and white or yellow ray florets ("petals"), open on long stalks held well above the leaves.

CULTIVATION The plants are best in fairly poor, well-drained soil in full sun. Taller plants benefit from being cut back hard immediately after flowering.

PROPAGATION By division of clump-forming plants, by basal cuttings, or from seed (garden seed may not come true).

PROBLEMS Slugs and snails, aphids, and powdery mildew.

A. **'Beauty of Grallagh'** Upright growth, with golden-orange flowers, occasionally closer to yellow in some soils; the petals and the disk are almost exactly the same shade. Often included under *A. tinctoria* but, in fact, it is a hybrid with *A. sancti-johannis*. Not, as sometimes thought, the same as 'Grallagh Gold'. ‡36 in (90 cm). Z3–8 H8–3

GRALLAGH

'Grallagh Gold', 'Grallagh Glory', 'Beauty of Grallagh'—the name Grallagh (often misspelled "Grallach") appears in several cultivars and hybrids of *Anthemis tinctoria*, inviting curiosity as to its origin and significance.

Grallagh was the home of Miss Blanche Poë, in whose garden both 'Grallagh Glory' and 'Grallagh Gold' arose as chance seedlings. The hamlet is close to the town of Nenagh, near Lough Derg in County Tipperary, Ireland.

'Grallagh Gold' was introduced about 1940, and was first catalogued by Perry's Hardy Plant Farm at Enfield, Middlesex, England, in 1948. 'Grallagh Glory' was named a few years later, and was introduced by a local nursery in 1950, and by Perry's the next year, although it appears not to have survived to the present day. More recently, some nurseries have listed a plant under the name 'Beauty of Grallagh' or 'Pride of Grallagh', but this has no proven connection with Miss Poë. It seems that no other plants are associated with Miss Poë's garden. Her father introduced the double snowdrop 'Hill Poë'.

A. **'Blomit'** see *A.* Susanna Mitchell

A. **'Grallagh Gold'** Deep bright golden-yellow; tends to be short-lived. Often included under *A. tinctoria* but, in fact, a hybrid with *A. sancti-johannis* which arose at the garden of Miss Blanche Poë (*see* Grallagh). ‡30 in (75 cm). Z3–8 H8–3

A. **nobilis** see *Chamaemelum nobile*

A. **punctata** subsp. *cupaniana* (Sicilian chamomile) Mat-forming plant with a woody rootstock and lax spreading stems bearing finely dissected, grayish leaves to 4¾ in (12 cm) long. From mid-spring to midsummer, sometimes later, fine white daisies, up to 2½ in (6 cm) wide, open on long stalks well above the leaves. Free-flowering plant with good foliage, but best given some protection from winter rains in wet climates. Very successful in coastal gardens. From Sicily, in open rocky places. ‡12 in (30 cm). Z6–9 H6–9. **'Nana'** More compact. Up to ‡8 in (20 cm).

A. **sancti-johannis** Tufted plant with sparsely branched stems that bear oblong, deeply cut leaves to 2 in (5 cm) long. From early to late summer, bears flowerheads 1¼–2 in (3–5 cm) across, with ruffle-like, short, deep orange ray florets and a deep yellow central disk. Hybridizes with *A. tinctoria*, and many plants sold under the name are not true to type. Valued for striking flower color, but often short-lived.

From woodland clearings in southern Bulgaria. ‡24–36 in (60–90 cm). Z3–8 H8–3

A. **Susanna Mitchell** (*A.* 'Blomit') Pale creamy yellow flowers with petals slightly more yellow at the base, around a yellow eye and all set above attractive lacy gray foliage from late spring to early fall. A hybrid between *A. tinctoria* and *A. punctata* subsp. *cupaniana*. ‡18 in (45 cm). Z3–7 H7–3

A. **'Tetworth'** Semidouble, yellow-eyed white flowers from late spring to early fall, sometimes earlier or later, above dissected gray foliage. A hybrid between *A. tinctoria* and *A. punctata* subsp. *cupaniana*, and perhaps hardier than others of this parentage. ‡18–24 in (45–60 cm). Z3–7 H7–3

A. **tinctoria** (Dyer's chamomile, Yellow chamomile, Golden marguerite) Makes a clump of rather sprawling, branched stems bearing mid-green leaves divided into narrow, coarsely toothed lobes. From early to late summer or early fall, daisylike flowers 1¼ in (3 cm) across, with bright yellow to cream rays around a yellow disk, open in succession. Short-lived, and benefits from a hard cutting-back just after flowering. Formerly a valuable dye plant, and the flowers last well when cut. Several of the cultivars listed under this species are hybrids, usually with *A. sancti-johannis*; all have yellow central

CONTRAST AND HARMONY

THE COMBINATION SHOWN HERE sets a fine example for many plant associations in that it features harmony in one element and contrast in another, in this case flower color and plant habit. The two tones of yellow harmonize well: the bright buttery-lemon, almost piercing yellow of *Anthemis* 'E. C. Buxton' and above that the softer, pale primrose bells of *Digitalis grandiflora*.

However, in form the flowers contrast with each other and the foliage and stems, too, are distinct, the paler green of the foxglove emerging above the richer green of the anthemis. But it is the habits of the two that make the strongest contrast, with the slim, upright spikes of the foxglove emerging behind much flatter outline of the daisylike anthemis flowerheads.

1

2

3

4

ABOVE **1** *Anthemis punctata* subsp. *cupaniana* **2** *A. tinctoria* 'Kelwayi' **3** *Anthericum liliago* var. *major* **4** *Anthoxanthum odoratum*

disks. From dry, sunny places in much of Europe, North Africa, and the Caucasus, and occasionally naturalized elsewhere. ‡ 20–32 in (50–80 cm). Z3–8 H8–3. **Dwarf form** (which is sometimes grown as 'Compacta') Much more compact. ‡ 12 in (30 cm). **'Alba'** Flowers opening creamy white, fading to white. ‡ 18–24 in (45–60 cm). **'E. C. Buxton'** Lemon-yellow ray florets—an unusual color, good for picking. ‡ 24 in (60 cm). **'Eva'** Compact plant with rich yellow flowers. ‡ 16 in (40 cm). **'Kelwayi'** Bright yellow flowers above finely divided leaves. ‡ 16 in (40 cm). **'Sauce Hollandaise'** Very pale yellow, aging to creamy white. ‡ 24 in (60 cm). **'Wargrave Variety'** Light yellow, deeper than 'E. C. Buxton'. ‡ 36 in (90 cm).

ANTHERICUM
ANTHERICACEAE

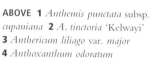

Easy-going and elegant plants with airy sprays of starry white flowers in summer.

About 50 species of deciduous perennials growing in open grassland in Europe, Africa, and tropical America. Two species are commonly grown; both form clumps of narrow, grasslike leaves. In spring or summer, slender stems arise just above the tufts of foliage, bearing spikes or loose sprays of small, starry white flowers.

CULTIVATION Grows best in full sun, in any moderately moist but well-drained soil.

PROPAGATION From seed or by division.

PROBLEMS Young growth may be damaged by slugs and snails.

A. liliago (St. Bernard's lily) Robust plant with narrow leaves and, in late spring and early summer, upright spikes of white flowers ¾–1¼ in (2–3 cm) across, with conspicuous yellow stamens. From mountain meadows in central and southern Europe. ‡ 28–40 in (70–100 cm). Z7–9 H9–7. **var.** *major* Star-shaped, wide-open flowers up to 1½ in (4 cm) across.

A. ramosum A more slender plant that forms a clump of grasslike, gray-green leaves, with branched, open sprays of starry white flowers ½ in (1.5 cm) wide, in early and mid-summer. From scrub or grassland in central and southern Europe and Turkey. ‡ 16–24 in (40–60 cm). Z5–8 H8–5

ANTHOXANTHUM
POACEAE

Spring-flowering grasses that, when dried or crushed, release a vanilla-like scent of hay fields.

Eighteen annual and perennial species growing in meadows and dry grassland throughout temperate Europe, Asia, tropical African mountainsides, and parts of Central America. All contain a chemical, coumarin, which is responsible for the vanilla-like scent. From tufted basal leaves, in mid-spring and through the summer, grow stems bearing spiky, lance-shaped flowerheads.

CULTIVATION Grows well in dry, open positions in any reasonably fertile, well-drained soil. Trim back in early spring.

PROPAGATION By division in spring, or from seed.

PROBLEMS Usually trouble-free.

A. odoratum (Sweet vernal grass) A tufted evergreen grass with bright green leaf-blades that are flat, soft, and finely pointed, 4¾–12 in (12–30 cm) long and 2–3½ in (5–9 cm) wide— becoming larger in damp situations. From mid-spring to early summer, erect, sometimes spreading, stems appear, most bearing lance-shaped, spiky flowerheads ½ in (1 cm) long. Green or purplish green, and hung with prominent purple or yellow stamens, the flowerheads turn yellow as they mature. Found throughout Britain, Europe, Asia—and introduced into North America—growing on hill pastures, heathland, and open woodland in a wide range of soils. The sweet smell is released when the leaves are dried or crushed, which makes it a welcome addition to wildflower lawns and meadows, or used to edge paths, where being mowed or walked upon will release its sweet scent. ‡ 12–40 in (30–100 cm). Z5–9 H9–5

AQUILEGIA
Columbine
RANUNCULACEAE

Elegant, bright, and cheerful flowers that bring glamour and charm to the early summer garden.

There are about 70 species of *Aquilegia*, all from the Northern Hemisphere. The stiff, upright, self-supporting stems may be smooth or slightly hairy, and emerge through a basal mound of attractively lobed, smooth foliage. The long-stalked leaves feature three lobes that are usually each themselves lobed to give nine leaflets; each of these lobes may again be divided in three, giving 27 leaflets in all.

The flowers appear mainly in early summer and typically have five colorful sepals that cover the nodding buds. When the flowers open, the sepals usually flare almost

AQUILEGIA FLOWER STRUCTURE

Typically, an aquilegia flower has five flat outer sepals (sometimes referred to as petals) flared around five petals. The petals, sometimes collectively called a skirt, each have a broad blade and a long, usually curved, nectar-secreting spur that protrudes between the sepals behind the flower. In the center of the flower a boss of golden (male) stamens surrounds the usually five carpels (the female parts). In most species the flowers are nodding, or face outward, but in a few species and hybrids they may face upward.

Spur

Sepal

Petals

Aquilegia fragrans

LEFT 1 *Aquilegia* 'Bluebird'
2 *A. canadensis* **3** *A.* 'Cardinal'
4 *A.* 'Dove' **5** *A. formosa*
6 *A.* McKana Group

horizontally and the blades of the five petals are revealed. These blades may be the same color as the sepals, but are often a contrasting color. At their base are nectar-loaded spurs that usually extend backward between the sepals; typically, they are the same color as the sepals. The cluster of golden stamens often protrudes attractively. This flower shape gives the plants their name "columbine," from the Latin *columba*—dove—because the flowers of *A. vulgaris*, in its normal form, look like five doves.

Species from Asia and Europe tend to have blue, purple, white, or pink flowers, with short spurs to enable pollination by insects, while the North American species have longer spurs to attract pollinating hummingbirds and are often red and yellow.

The flowers are usually nodding, but hybridizers have bred strains with upward-facing flowers, a characteristic of *A. coerulea*. Most work has been concentrated on the North American species, which have the largest flowers and widest color range. The McKana Group and the Mrs. Scott-Elliot hybrids were the first of these but have been superseded by F1 hybrid series with greater uniformity and large blooms, often on shorter plants. In recent years, developments have been made in forms of *A. vulgaris* with variegated leaves, new flower shapes, and even some fragrance.

CULTIVATION Generally short-lived and at their peak in their second year; most decline in vigor thereafter but are easily grown from seed. Species and cultivars hybridize very freely (*see* Promiscuity, *p. 66*), making it difficult to keep plants true to type over the years. With the exception of some alpine, Mexican, and desert species, aquilegias will thrive in average, well-drained soil. They prefer a sunny spot. Remove faded flowers to prevent seed production unless needed. Replace plants every 2–3 years.

PROPAGATION From seed sown in summer, as soon as it is ripe, or in spring. Most aquilegias require a cold period to initiate the flower buds, so even early spring sowings will not bloom until the following year. Division is not worth attempting in aquilegias.

PROBLEMS Aphids, sawfly, leaf miner.

A. **'Adonis Blue'** (Butterfly Series) Pale blue sepals, white blades, pale blue spurs. ↕14–16 in (35–40 cm). Z4–7 H7–1

A. **'Alaska'** (Swan Series) White sepals, blades, and spurs, with an occasional hint of pink. ↕24 in (60 cm). Z4–7 H7–1

A. alpina This small, very pretty aquilegia grows in alkaline soil in high open meadows and sometimes in open woods and among shrubs. The stems are hairy low down, less so higher up, and the basal leaves are split into nine leaflets. The nodding blue flowers have 1¼–1¾-in (3–4.5-cm) petals and long, straight spurs, to 1 in (2.5 cm) long. Many plants sold under this name are hybrids with *A. vulgaris*; these can be identified by their hooked spurs. From southwestern Switzerland, Austria, southeastern France, and northwestern Italy. ↕6–24 in (15–60 cm). Z4–7 H7–1. **'Alba'** White flowers.

A. atrata The leaves are split into three, with each lobe again split into three. The stems are smooth low down and densely hairy toward the top. The nodding flowers, which are deep purple or almost black, have ½–1 in (1.5–2.5 cm) long pointed petals and strongly hooked spurs, ½–⅝ in (1–1.5 cm) long. This plant is similar to *A. vulgaris* but its flowers are noticeably smaller. Found wild in open woodlands in southern Germany, Austria, Slovenia, Italy, France, and Switzerland. ↕24 in (60 cm). Z4–8 H7–1

A. **Biedermeier Group** Dwarf plants with inelegant, upward-facing flowers in shades including white, rose, purple, and blue, including bicolors. ↕20 in (50 cm). Z4–7 H7–1

A. **'Blue Jay'** (Songbird Series) Flowers have pale blue sepals, white blades, and pale blue spurs. ↕14–18 in (35–45 cm). Z4–7 H7–1

DOUBLE COLUMBINES

One of the most intriguing features of aquilegias developed from *Aquilegia vulgaris* is the variety of flower forms available. The wild flower form, also seen in garden selections such as 'Nivea', has been developed into three distinct double-flowered types.

The so-called clematis-flowered type, var. *stellata* (often incorrectly known as var. *clematiflora*) is a form without petals, blade, or spur, but with a mass of small, pointed sepals arranged like those of a double-flowered clematis.

It was described by John Parkinson in his *Paradisi in Sole Paradisus Terrestris* of 1629 as "rose columbine." A familiar example is 'Ruby Port'. The well known 'Nora Barlow' is similar, but sufficiently distinct in the relatively large number of its sepals, and their relative narrowness, to be placed in a separate group.

The third style of doubles is another old form, described by John Gerard in his famous *Herball* of 1597 as having one flower "thrust into the belly of another." Known as var. *flore-pleno*, or simply double, this name covers the so-called one-inside-the-other flowers with two or more layers of petals and includes cultivars such as 'Double Pleat' and the Bonnet Series.

VIGILANCE REWARDED

BY RIGOROUSLY REMOVING variants, it is not difficult to keep an aquilegia true to type and so maintain this lovely *A. vulgaris* var. *stellata* 'Ruby Port' as it should be. The introduction of other shades would ruin the color combination with the prettily dissected foliage of the biennial *Anthriscus sylvestris* 'Ravenswing' and its pink-tinted, white lace flowers. This will sometimes produce green-leaved, pure white-flowered seedlings, which should also be removed. The grayish red leaves of seedlings of the annual red orach, *Atriplex hortensis* var. *rubra*, will develop later in the season, from simply filling in the background to dominating this area—and when they produce poorly colored self-sown seedlings, these too should be pulled out.

A. **'Blue Star'** (Star Series) Blue sepals, white blades, and blue spurs. ↕ 24 in (60 cm). Z4–7 H7–1

A. **'Bluebird'** (Songbird Series) Blue sepals with white tips, white blades, and blue spurs. ↕ 14–18 in (35–45 cm). Z4–7 H7–1

A. **'Brimstone Yellow'** (Butterfly Series) Pale yellow sepals, blades, and spurs. ↕ 14–16 in (35–40 cm). Z4–7 H7–1

A. buergeriana This variable Japanese species has slightly downy, sometimes branched stems and noticeably thick leaves. The flowers have yellow or brownish purple sepals and petals, with yellow blades and purple spurs. Flower color varies; those with purple sepals are more common. From Honshu, Shikoku, and Kyushu, Japan. ↕ 20–32 in (50–80 cm). Z5–7 H7–1. **'Calimero'** Very pretty purple sepals and spurs, and yellow blades. ↕ 8 in (20 cm).

A. **'Bunting'** (Songbird Series) Light blue sepals, white blades, and pale blue spurs. 16 in (40 cm). Z3–9 H8–1

A. **'Burnished Rose'** Deep rose double flowers over burnished gold foliage. Not a form of *A. buergeriana* as sometimes, mysteriously, listed. ↕ 30 in (75 cm). Z3–9 H8–1

A. **Butterfly Series** (Origami Series in North America) Specifically developed not to need a cold period to trigger flowering, plants in this series from Goldsmith Seeds can be grown from a spring sowing to flower the same summer without special treatment, requiring only a few weeks at about 46°F (8°C) to initiate flowering. The flowers are medium to large, and held mostly 45° above horizontal. Height is usually 14–16 in (35–40 cm); in rich soil 18–24 in (45–60 cm) is more likely. Origami is the correct name but in Britain, Butterfly, a later synonym, is used. The series includes 'Adonis Blue' (blue and white), 'Brimstone Yellow' (all yellow), 'Crenise Rosa' (dark pink and white), 'Painted Lady' (pink and white), 'Red Admiral' (red and white), and 'White Admiral' (all white). Z3–9 H8–1

A. caerulea A beautiful but variable species, the large, 3-in (7.5-cm) flowers have sky blue sepals and white petals on stems growing 8–36 in (20–90 cm) tall in the wild, sometimes dwarfed by harsh habitat; in the garden they are usually around 20 in (50 cm) high. Unlike most species, the flowers face upward. It hybridizes readily and has given its upward flower stance to many hybrids that are often listed under this name. Best in well-drained soil. Used by American Indians to relieve abdominal pain. Native to Colorado,

where it is the only protected plant, and neighboring states. ↕ 20 in (50 cm). Z3–8 H8–1

A. canadensis An easily grown, very pretty plant with nodding flowers with red sepals and yellow blades with red spurs. These spurs are the most conspicuous parts of the flower because the sepals spread less than in most other species. The only species native to the eastern US, where it is often seen on roadside banks and in dappled shade. ↕ 28 in (70 cm). Z3–8 H8–1. **'Canyon Vista'** Bright flowers on red stems. ↕ 12 in (30 cm). **'Corbett'** Uniformly pale yellow. Discovered near the town of Corbett, Maryland. ↕ 12–24 in (30–60 cm). **'Little Lanterns'** ↕ 10 in (25 cm). **'Nana'** 10 in (25 cm).

A. **'Cardinal'** (Songbird Series) ('Redwing' in US) Vivid scarlet sepals, white blades, and scarlet spurs. ↕ 16 in (40 cm). Z3–8 H8–1

A. chrysantha One of the most beautiful of all aquilegias with all-yellow flowers on tall stems. The flowers face horizontally or upward at first and are among the largest of all, with sepals up to 1½ in (3.5 cm) long. But it is the spurs, which can be 2¾ in (7 cm) long, that make this plant exceptional. The leaves are usually divided into 27 leaflets. Easy to grow

and can live several years. Many plants in cultivation are actually 'Yellow Queen'. From the southwestern US. ↕ 32 in (80 cm). Z3–8 H8–1. **'Yellow Queen'** More vigorous, larger clumps with more flowers.

A. **'Clematiflora'** see *A. vulgaris* var. *stellata*

A. **'Colorado'** (Swan Series) Deep purple sepals, sometimes with white tips; white blades and purple spurs. ↕ 24 in (60 cm). Z3–8 H8–1

A. **'Crenise Rosa'** (Butterfly Series) Vivid pink sepals, white blades, and vivid pink spurs. ↕ 14–16 in (35–40 cm). Z3–8 H8–1

A. **'Crimson Star'** (Star Series) Horizontal or upward-facing flowers with deep red sepals, white blades, and red spurs. ↕ 20 in (50 cm). Z3–8 H8–1

A. **'Danish Star'** see *A.* 'Red Hobbit'

A. **'Dove'** (Songbird Series) All-white flowers, sometimes with a hint of blush pink at the tips of sepals and spurs. ↕ 16 in (40 cm). Z3–8 H8–1

A. **'Dragonfly'** Variable mixture of colors, resembling the McKana Group but shorter. Needs daytime temperature below 59°F (15°C) to initiate flower buds. ↕ 20 in (50 cm). Z4–7 H7–1

A. ecalcarata see *Semiaquilegia ecalcarata*

A. flabellata This alpine species has nodding, neat, compact flowers with rounded sepals and short, hooked spurs. Typically, the whole flower is blue or light purple but the blades may be paler and/or white at the tips. The foliage is divided into three leaflets, which may again be split in three. Usually better in a container than in the border. From northern Japan. ↕ 24 in (60 cm). Z4–9 H9–1. **f. *alba*** White flowers. **Cameo Series** Dwarf series in blue and white, light red and white, pink and white, pure white, soft pink, and a mix. ↕ 6 in (10 cm). **Jewel Series** Medium-height series in pure blue, deep purple, pink, purple, and white, plus a mix. ↕ 16 in (40 cm). **'Ministar'** Blue sepals, white blades. ↕ 6 in (15 cm). **var. *pumila*** syn. *A. japonica* Dwarf. ↕ 12 in (30 cm). **var. *pumila* f. *alba*** White flowers. ↕ 12 in (30 cm).

A. **'Florida'** (Swan Series) Pale yellow sepals and spurs, bright yellow blades. ↕ 24–30 in (60–75 cm). Z4–9 H9–1

A. formosa This widespread, variable species has nodding blooms on tall stems that are slightly downy toward the top. The leaves are divided into nine lobes, and the flowers are small for the size of the plant, with red sepals, ¾-in (2-cm) red spurs, and yellow blades. From the western states and provinces of North America. ↕ 20–40 in (50–100 cm). Z4–7 H7–1

A. fragrans A distinctive species with scented pale pink or creamy white flowers. The 1¼-in- (3-cm-) long sepals

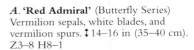

ABOVE 1 *Aquilegia* 'Robin'
2 *A. vulgaris* 'Nora Barlow'
3 *A. vulgaris* 'William Guiness'

are usually deeper in color than the blades; the spurs are ⅝ in (1.5 cm) long. The leaves are divided into 27 lobes. The sweet fragrance of the flowers, unusual in aquilegias, breeders have found difficult to transfer into more colorful hybrids. Best in moist soil, it tolerates part-shade. From northern India. ‡ 32 in (80 cm). Z4–8 H8–1

***A.* 'Georgia'** (Swan Series) Scarlet sepals, white blades, and scarlet spurs. ‡ 24 in (60 cm). Z4–8 H8–1

***A.* 'Goldfinch'** (Songbird Series) Pale yellow sepals, blades, and spurs, sometimes with a pale pink flush. ‡ 16 in (40 cm). Z4–8 H8–1

***A.* 'Hensol Harebell'** Wedgwood blue sepals, blades, and spurs; true form rare. A hybrid of *A. alpina* and *A. vulgaris*, raised in Scotland in the early 20th century. ‡ 30 in (75 cm). Z4–7 H7–1

A. japonica see *A. flabellata* var. *pumila*

***A.* 'Kansas'** (Swan Series) Bright red sepals, yellow blades stained red at the base, and red spurs. ‡ 24 in (60 cm). Z4–8 H8–1

A. longissima Named for its exceptionally long spurs, which it has passed to some hybrids, this species is superficially similar to *A. chrysantha*, although the flowers are smaller and the spurs shorter. The leaves are split into 27 leaflets; the yellow flowers have pale 1¼-in (3-cm) sepals and darker 1¼-in (3-cm) blades with spurs 3½–6 in (9–15 cm) long. From northern Mexico. ‡ 20–40 in (50–100 cm). Z4–9 H9–1

***A.* 'Louisiana'** (Swan Series) Deep red sepals, white blades, and deep red spurs. ‡ 24 in (60 cm). Z4–8 H8–1

***A.* 'Magpie'** see *A. vulgaris* 'William Guiness'

***A.* McKana Group** syn. McKana Hybrids, McKana's Giants Strong-growing, unpredictable mixture of large self-colored (plain) and bicolored flowers, with spurs up to 4 in (10 cm) long, held horizontally or facing slightly upward. Now this group is generally outclassed by the shorter Songbird and Swan Series. ‡ 3¼ ft (1 m). Z4–7 H7–1

***A.* 'Mellow Yellow'** Bright gold foliage and white or very pale blue flowers. Good as a summer foliage plant for containers, from a spring sowing. ‡ 30 in (75 cm). Z3–8 H8–1

***A.* 'Milk and Honey'** Large white, fragrant flowers. Derived from *A. fragrans* and *A. vulgaris*. ‡ 24–30 in (60–75 cm). Z3–8 H8–1

***A.* 'Montana'** (Swan Series) Rich rose pink sepals, white blades, and rose pink spurs. ‡ 24 in (60 cm). Z3–8 H8–1

***A.* Mrs. Scott-Elliot Hybrids** Strong-growing, unpredictable mixture of large self-colored and bicolored flowers; spurs up to 4 in (10 cm) long in a wide range of soft shades. Shorter, and in more pastel shades than the McKana Group. ‡ 24–36 in (60–90 cm). Z3–8 H8–1

***A.* Music Series** (syn. Musik Series) Mix of medium-sized plants with large, long-spurred flowers with spreading sepals. Individual colors are also available: blue-white, yellow, white, pink-white, red-gold, and red-white. ‡ 18 in (45 cm). Z3–8 H8–1

***A.* 'Nuthatch'** (Songbird Series) Purple sepals, white blades, and purple spurs. ‡ 16 in (40 cm). Z3–8 H8–1

***A.* 'Painted Lady'** (Butterfly Series) Pale pink sepals and spurs, white blades. ‡ 14–16 in (35–40 cm). Z3–8 H8–1

***A.* 'Red Admiral'** (Butterfly Series) Vermilion sepals, white blades, and vermilion spurs. ‡ 14–16 in (35–40 cm). Z3–8 H8–1

***A.* 'Red Hobbit'** (syn. 'Danish Star') Long-spurred flowers, scarlet sepals, white blades. ‡ 16 in (40 cm). Z3–8 H8–1

***A.* 'Red Star'** (Star Series) Red sepals, white blades, and red spurs. ‡ 24 in (60 cm). Z3–8 H8–1

***A.* 'Redwing'** (Songbird Series) see 'Cardinal'

***A.* 'Robin'** (Songbird Series) Deep rose sepals, white blades, and rose spurs. ‡ 16 in (40 cm). Z3–8 H8–1

***A.* 'Roman Bronze'** see *A. vulgaris* 'Roman Bronze'

A. skinneri This long-flowering Mexican species has nodding flowers with green sepals up to 1 in (2.5 cm) in length, ½-in (1-cm) green blades, and straight pale red spurs up to 2 in (5 cm) long. The leaves are repeatedly divided into 27 lobes. ‡ 3½ ft (1 m). Z3–9 H8–1. **'Tequila Sunrise'** Orange flowers, hardier than the species. Z3–8 H8–1

***A.* Songbird Series** Stocky plants covered in medium to large, long-spurred, mostly upward-facing flowers in a range of single colors and a mix. Bred by Charlie Weddle of Colorado Native Plants and derived from the Mrs. Scott-Elliot hybrids, the McKana Group, and various North American species. Will not flower reliably from a spring sowing—plants need a period of lower night temperatures and a move from short to long days to initiate flowering—nor when night temperatures exceed 59°F (15°C). Height is usually 14–18 in (35–45 cm); in rich soil 26–32 in (65–80 cm) is more likely. Includes 'Bluebird' (blue and white), 'Blue Jay' (dark blue and

white), 'Bunting' (pale blue and white), 'Cardinal' (red and white), 'Dove' (all white), 'Goldfinch' (all yellow), and 'Robin' (red and white). ‡ 14–32 in (35–80 cm). Z3–8 H8–1

***A.* Spring Magic Series** Medium-height series in blue and white, light red and white, pink and white, pure white, and a mix. ‡ 14 in (35 cm). Z3–8 H8–1

PROMISCUITY

In the course of their evolution, wild *Aquilegia* species have tended to develop in geographic isolation from each other and without any genetic or biochemical barriers to hybridization. Remove the geographic barriers by bringing them together in the garden and they often hybridize freely. Add to this the complex genetic makeup of many cultivars, and even when they self-pollinate, which they have a natural tendency to do, variation occurs in flower color, flower form, and height: purples might develop pink hues, doubles might develop into singles, and height become increasingly variable. The blue flower color of *A. vulgaris* also tends to be the most dominant.

Seed producers have the same difficulty in keeping their cultivars true as do gardeners. Many new introductions show an unwelcome variability in flower color or form, and even those that begin as high-quality selections can deteriorate rapidly. The most reliable modern introductions—the Butterfly, Songbird, State, and Winky series—are hybrids whose parents are carefully controlled by the seed producer. They are F1 hybrids, like many bedding plants, and thus are almost guaranteed to vary when they self-sow or are raised from home-saved seed. The result is both frustration and surprise: good forms may deteriorate in the garden as they self-sow, but some intriguing surprises may turn up.

A. **Star Series** Large, upward-facing flowers, all with white blades. A mix is often seen as well as 'Blue Star', 'Red Star', 'White Star', and 'Yellow Star'. ‡ 20–24 in (50–60 cm). Z3–8 H8–1

A. **'Sunburst Ruby'** Bright golden foliage and deep, ruby red flowers. ‡ 30 in (75 cm). Z3–8 H8–1

A. **Swan Series** Very large, upward-facing flowers in a range of bright colors, mostly 45° above horizontal with long spurs. The series was bred by PanAmerican Seeds from the Songbird Series. Will not flower reliably from a spring sowing. Height is usually 20–24 in (50–60 cm); in rich soil 30–32 in (75–80 cm) is more likely. It includes 'Alaska' (all white), 'Colorado' (violet and white), 'Florida' (all yellow), 'Georgia' (red and white), 'Kansas' (red and yellow), 'Louisiana' (maroon and white), and 'Montana' (pink and white). ‡ 24 in (60 cm). Z3–8 H8–1

A. **'Sweet Lemon Drops'** Cream sepals, bright yellow blades, and cream spurs. Lemon-scented. ‡ 18 in (45 cm). Z3–8 H8–1

A. triternata Easy, pretty species with red sepals to ¾ in (2 cm) long, short yellowish blades, sometimes tinged with red and pale red, and 1-in (2.5-cm) spurs. The leaves are subdivided in threes to make 27 leaflets in all. From Arizona, New Mexico, and Mexico. ‡ 24 in (60 cm). Z3–9 H8–1

A. viridiflora A unique, relatively long-lived species, easily recognizable by the flowers' circular "skirts" of chocolate-brown blades; the sepals are green and the long spurs are also brown. Although only this one form is usually grown in gardens, in the wild the blades may be yellowish green through dark purple to the typical rich brown. Basal leaves have nine leaflets. From forests, meadows, and wet places in China, Japan, Mongolia, and Serbia. ‡ 12 in (30 cm). Z3–9 H8–1 **'Chocolate Soldier'** An invalid cultivar name; plants are no different from the form of the species usually seen.

A. vulgaris The most familiar of all *Aquilegia* species and, because of its widespread distribution throughout Europe, extremely variable. Long cultivation in gardens in Europe and North America, where it is naturalized, has led to many variations being found and treasured. The wild plant, which is rarely found in gardens, has stems that are increasingly hairy higher up the stem and a basal mass of leaves divided into nine lobes. Its nodding flowers are blue-violet with 1-in (2.5-cm) sepals, ½-in (1-cm) blades and spurs up to 1 in (2.5 cm) long; the spurs are usually hooked and never straight. Many seed strains have been produced that differ in height, foliage color, and flower form, with flower color ranging from white through pinks and purple to almost black, plus many bicolors. The yellow and scarlet flower colors of New World species are uncommon. Easy to grow in most situations, including clay and

NORA BARLOW

'Nora Barlow' is one of the most popular of aquilegias. Named for the granddaughter of Charles Darwin, who discovered it in her garden in Cambridge, England, in the early 1980s, and first introduced by horticulturist Alan Bloom, it soon became widely grown.

However, as was to be expected, it soon hybridized with other forms, and the result was that seed and plants sold under the name often proved disappointing. More recently seed companies have produced large crops of 'Nora Barlow' but these plants seem to differ from the plants seen in the 1980s.

Veteran gardeners will remember that the nodding flowers of the original plant featured equal parts of rose pink, white, and green. Modern plants are shorter, the flowers are more outward-facing, and they have lost most of their green tints. Both forms are found under this name, so the best advice is to see the plants in flower before buying them.

alkaline soil. Easy to raise from seed, it self-sows widely, but is promiscuous (*see* Promiscuity, *p. 66*) and difficult to keep true to type. ‡ 12–36 in (30–90 cm); cultivars usually ‡ 24–30 in (60–75 cm). Z3–8 H8–1. **'Adelaide Addison'** Deep blue flowers with a ruff of double-spurred petals that are the same deep blue, edged with white. **var. *alba*** White flowers. **var. *flore-pleno*** Double flowers with many rows of petals. **var. *flore-pleno* Bonnet Series** Double flowers with many rows of spurred petals with white blades. **'Blue Bonnet'** (mid-blue) and **'Pink Bonnet'** (mauve-pink) are the most often seen. **var. *flore-pleno* 'Double Pleat'** Profusely doubled, spurred flowers of violet and white. **'Magpie'** *see* 'Willaim Guiness'. **'Michael Stromminger'** Deep rose pink single flowers. **'Nivea'** (**Munstead White**) Pure white single flowers on pale green stems above grayish leaves. A favorite of Gertrude Jekyll. **'Roman Bronze'** Yellow foliage flushed with bronze, and deep violet clematis-type flowers. Not a form of the alpine *A. rockii*, nor a hybrid between *Aquilegia* and *Semiaquilegia*, as sometimes suggested. **var. *stellata*** Spurless flowers comprising a mass of sepals (*see* Double Columbines, *p. 64*). **var. *stellata* Barlow Series** Bred from 'Nora Barlow', extending the range of colors in its distinctive, pompon flower shape. Available as a mix, it is also sold as separate colors including **'Black Barlow'** (dark purple) **'Blue Barlow'** (violet-blue), **'Christa Barlow'** (dark blue, edged white). **'Nora Barlow'** Pompon flowers with many rows of narrow sepals that overlay each other in ranks and are greenish pink at first, becoming pink, tipped with white (*see* Nora Barlow), and **'Rose Barlow'** (pale pink). **var. *stellata* 'Firewheel'** Bright, pink-red flowers. **var. *stellata* 'Greenapples'** Double flowers, crowded with sepals that are pale green at first, aging to cream. **var. *stellata* 'Royal Purple'** Deep purple. **var.**

stellata **'Ruby Port'** Deep maroon. **Vervaeneana Group** Foliage mostly yellow and more or less finely mottled with green. Forms with all-yellow foliage not included in the Vervaeneana Group. Z3–8 H8–1. **Vervaeneana Group 'Woodside Blue'** Mottled, golden foliage and deep, blue-violet flowers. Z3–8 H8–1. **Vervaeneana Group 'Woodside White'** Mottled, golden foliage and white or palest blue flowers. Developed by Mervyn Feesey at Woodside in Devon. Z3–8 H8–1. **'William Guiness'** syn. 'Magpie' Dark black-currant-purple sepals and blades with a white edge.

A. **'White Admiral'** (Butterfly Series) White sepals with a hint of a blush, palest yellow blades, and a blushed white spur. ‡ 14–16 in (35–40 cm). Z3–8 H8–1

A. **'White Star'** (Star Series) White sepals, blades, and spurs. ‡ 20 in (50 cm). Z3–8 H8–1

A. **Winky Series** Crowded stems of upward-facing flowers on compact plants, making them suitable for containers and the edge of borders. Ugly or entrancing, depending on your taste. Available as a mixture or as separate colors, including 'Winky Red and White', 'Winky Blue and White', 'Winky Purple and White', and 'Winky Rose and White'. ‡ 18 in (45 cm).

A. **'Yellow Star'** (Star Series) Yellow sepals, blades, and spurs. ‡ 20 in (50 cm). Z3–8 H8–1

ARALIA
Spikenard
ARALIACEAE

Bold plants reaching shrublike proportions that lend a tropical air to temperate gardens.

Though perhaps best known as dramatic shrubs, there are 40 herbaceous and woody species native to temperate and subtropical regions of the Americas and Asia. Most species are deciduous, and bear huge leaves divided into opposite pairs of 21–27 heart-shaped leaflets on stout, hairy or spiny stems. Large terminal flower clusters are composed of many smaller clusters of spherical heads, each packed with green flowers. In late summer, the fleshy berries ripen to deep purple and are very attractive to wildlife, especially birds.

Aralias have a long medicinal history. A poultice for curing wounds, ulcers, and sores was made by chewing or steeping the bark of the root—it sounds worse than castor oil, although not poisonous. A cordial of the berries was good for gout, and aralia-berry wine, like elderberry wine, was consumed for the fun of it. The emerging shoots of *Aralia cordata* are still eaten in Japan as a tonic, although today aralias sooth the soul with their beauty, more than heal the body.

CULTIVATION Aralias are woodland or meadow plants that thrive in light to full shade, although in cool gardens they will tolerate full sun. All perform best in humus-rich, evenly moist soil. Mature plants have massive root systems, making them difficult to transplant; the fleshy roots are easily damaged, so plants take up to three years to recover. Cut plants to the ground after a frost, since the berries are long gone. In spring, thin mature clumps to remove weak or inferior shoots to produce a full, even crown.

PROPAGATION Although propagation from root cuttings taken in spring or fall is possible, sowing ripe seed indoors after four weeks of cold, moist stratification, or outdoors in the fall, works well. Self-sown seedlings are often abundant.

BELOW 1 *Aralia cachemirica*
2 *A. racemosa*

PROBLEMS Usually trouble-free.

A. cachemirica (Himalayan spikenard, Kashmir spikenard) The most refined aralia, with huge horizontal to ascending leaves reaching up to 4 ft (1.2 m) bearing 27 narrow, oval, tightly packed leaflets with slender tips. Stout, spiny stems are crowned by elongated heads sporting well-spaced spherical flower clusters. Perhaps more curious than beautiful, this architectural gem is valued for its large size, eccentric look, and unusual creamy chartreuse flower color. The fall display of purple berries can be spectacular. Plant in a sunny to lightly shaded site with rich, well-drained soil. From open woods and meadows in Kashmir and Nepal. ↕4–10 ft (1.2–3 m). Z7–9 H8–7

A. californica (Elk clover, California spikenard) A sturdy plant with erect stems exuding a milky sap and carrying medium green, oval, sparsely toothed leaflets held flat. Densely clustered, rather variable heads of up to 70 white flowers, or pink flowers on darker pink stems, followed by deep purple berries, droop attractively from the ends of the arching stems. Grow in full sun to full shade in evenly moist, humus-rich soil. May be more sensitive to sun than other species and burns readily in hot, sunny, or dry sites. Found along streams and in rock outcroppings in dense conifer forests and other woodlands of northern California and Oregon. ↕4–6 ft (1.2–1.8 m). Z8–10 H10–8

A. continentalis (Korean spikenard) One of the more delicate and refined species, with 4–6-in (10–15-cm) elongated, heart-shaped leaflets on

slightly hairy stems. Creamy white to chartreuse flowers are carried in elongated flowerheads with short side branches, giving the appearance of a long terminal spike. Purple berries on pink-tinted stems follow the flowers, adding subtly but perceptively to the fall display. Similar in most respects to the Japanese *A. cordata*, but overall a less formidable, more genteel plant. Full sun to part-shade in moist, humus-rich soil. From woodlands and forest edges in Korea. ↕3–6 ft (90–180 cm). Z8–10 H10–8

A. cordata (Japanese spikenard) This gargantuan species can reach 10 ft (3 m) tall and wide, with stout stems holding massive 4–6-ft (1.2–1.8-m) leaves. The broadly heart-shaped leaflets are held horizontally in the intricate infrastructure of the compound leaves. Erect to drooping clusters of greenish white or pink flowers, held well above the leaves, top each cane of this extraordinary multistemmed species. A stout clump grows outside many Japanese houses, as the young shoots, called udo, are eaten as a vegetable and tonic. Best in full sun to part-shade in humus-rich, well-drained soil. From woodlands and along roadsides in Japan and China. ↕4¼–10 ft (1.3–3 m). Z7–9 H9–7

A. racemosa (American spikenard) This species has nothing short of a commanding presence. Though totally herbaceous, mature plants are often mistaken for shrubs. The enormous, tropical-looking leaves are layered in overlapping tiers, and may reach 3¼ ft (1 m) or more in length. In early to midsummer, numerous small spherical clusters of up to 20 pale green flowers are collected into dense terminal clusters 12–36 in (30–90 cm) long. In late summer, fleshy berries turn deep purple, almost black. Although attractive in the garden as long as they last, they are quickly devoured by birds. Thrives in light to dense shade in humus-rich, acidic, or alkaline soil. Found in deciduous and coniferous woodlands, from the northern Rocky Mountains east to the Atlantic coast. ↕4–6 ft (1.2–1.8 m). Z5–9 H9–1

ARISAEMA
Cobra lily
ARACEAE

Intriguing and sometimes spectacular flowers, with wide variation in both foliage and flower.

Around 170 species of spring- and summer-flowering, seasonally dormant, tuberous perennials found growing in many environments from temperate North America to tropical Africa and temperate and tropical Asia south through Malaysia but absent from Europe, South America, and Australia. Most cultivated species are from the Himalaya, China, and Japan and have attracted a fanatical cult following of collectors.

They vary in height from 8 in (20 cm) to almost 6½ ft (2 m) and

the one to three leaves may be simple and undivided, or they may be lobed, or even split into as many as 20 or more divisions. The spathe can be green, white, pink, purple, brown, or pale orange and may be solid, striped, or blotched. The hood may be neat and proportionate, striking, or even almost flamboyant, and have an array of extensions from "ears" to "tails" in seemingly endless variety. The flowers are followed by crowded heads of red berries.

But arisaemas have a strange feature. Some produce bisexual flowers, while others, although genetically bisexual, produce male or female or bisexual flowers in different years. This can be related to species and to age and vigor: young, stressed or weak plants are often male, while healthier more robust plants are female.

Although the most familiar are temperate in origin, a wide range of lesser-known tropical species are only suitable for greenhouse cultivation. This is a large and varied genus with at least a few species suited to most garden sites, and many deserve a place due to their unique flower and foliage forms (*see* The Arum Family, *p. 74*). ⚠

CULTIVATION The species considered here are generally suited to woodland conditions, some preferring brighter exposure. Outdoors they require good drainage, but should never dry out. They can also be grown in deep pots. Feed and water when in active growth. Some growers suggest that slow-release fertilizers should not be used on *Arisaema*.

PROPAGATION Most tubers produce tuberlets (tiny new tubers that are attached to the main tuber) annually and will form small colonies. The plants may be dug in the fall and the tubers separated and replanted. Seed is produced in often colorful heads in fall; if planted in spring, seedlings will bloom in three to five years.

PROBLEMS Some are susceptible to rusts and other fungi. Dormant tubers are prone to rot in sites with poor drainage. May be infected by virus, for which there is no cure—plants should be destroyed.

A. amurense Two leaves are divided into five, occasionally three, smooth to lightly toothed, reverse egg-shaped 5–6-in- (13–16-cm-) long green leaflets with red spots beneath. The flowerhead, which may be male or female, is held below the foliage and the green spathe, which may be purple-striped, is similar to the more familiar *A. triphyllum*. One of the hardiest species and easy to grow. From northeastern China and adjacent Korea and Russia. ↕10 in (25 cm). Z5–9 H9–5

RIGHT 2 *Arisaema consanguineum*
1 *A. flavum* **3** *A. jacquemontii*

CONSERVATION

Cultivation of arisaemas was for a long time largely confined to the showy and relatively easy to grow *Arisaema candidissimum* and *A. sikokianum*, but in recent years there has been an explosion of interest in these fascinating and often strange plants. In spite of (and partly because of) the fact that the less common species can be difficult to obtain and expensive to buy, and that they frequently take three or four years from seed sowing to flowering, arisaemas have become fashionable.

This is a treat for lovers of the weird and wonderful, rather than the flashy and flamboyant, and splendid for gardeners who like to intrigue their less horticulturally knowledgeable visitors. However, it has also led to an increase in the collecting of plants from the wild for sale to gardeners.

It is true that gardeners can add to conservation efforts by growing, propagating, and distributing threatened species, and often they are studied more closely in gardens than in the remote wild habitats where some grow naturally. However, if the plants grown in gardens are themselves taken from the wild, then clearly this can have an impact on native populations; even relatively widespread species can be significantly reduced in numbers by collection for commercial sale.

Seasoned growers are well aware of this problem, but if you find large numbers of uncommon species offered, perhaps at unexpectedly reasonable prices, then ask the supplier some pertinent questions about the origin of the plants.

A. candidissimum A single leaf, carried on a stem up to 24 in (60 cm) long, is split into three, broadly oval, slightly bluish green leaflets with cream margins, the central one the largest. The flowerhead (which may be male, female or, occasionally, bisexual) emerges in mid- to late spring. It is tubular and hooded and comes in varying shades from pure white to pale green; pink and rose forms are also known. All may be solid in color or striped. Unexpectedly, it is pleasantly scented, although the scent is fleeting. One of the most attractive species, discovered by the renowned plant collector George Forrest in 1914 and now also the most widely grown. From southwestern China. ‡12 in (30 cm). Z7–9 H9–7

A. ciliatum A single leaf is split into up to 20, more or less lance-shaped, 2–4½ in (5–11 cm), green leaflets that radiate in a nearly full circle and may have slender tails. The flowerhead, generally purple-tinged, which may be male or female, emerges as the leaf opens, and the spathe may be faintly or boldly striped in white, its tip extended up to 8 in (20 cm). The fruiting head turns downward as it develops. Similar to *A. consanguineum* but spreading at the root with short hairs around the mouth of the spathe. Recently

introduced and gaining in popularity. From southwestern China. ‡36 in (90 cm). Z6–9 H9–6

A. concinnum An impressive plant with a single large, long-stemmed leaf with 8–13, oval, slightly ruffled, 6–12-in (15–30-cm) leaflets with noticeably sunken veins and long pointed tips. The flowerhead, which may be either male or female, appears with the newly emerging spring leaf and the spathe forms a narrow tube in pale green or with a purple lip or edge. The spathe tip is up to 6 in (15 cm) long. Relatively new in gardens and less hardy than most. From the Himalaya to western China. ‡5 ft (1.5 m). Z6–8 H8–6

A. consanguineum This is a common species that reaches an impressive 6 ft (1.8 m) high and 24 in (60 cm) across. The single leaf has a circle of up to 22 lance-shaped, mid-green leaflets that may show a range of beautiful silver-centered patterns. Flowerheads may be male, female or occasionally bisexual; the spathe is up to 14 in (35 cm) long, colored green to brown and has an extended tip. One of the most readily available, easy to grow, and hardy species. Look for cultivars with especially good foliage that are being developed. From the Himalaya to western China. ‡6 ft (1.8 m). Z5–9 H9–7

A. costatum The single, often purple-flushed leaf up to 24 in (60 cm) wide has three green leaflets edged in red with striking red marked veins and distinctive parallel raised veins on the undersides. The broad, central, 16–18-in- (40–45-cm-) long leaflet is egg-shaped, the two outer leaflets being slightly shorter and asymmetrical. The spathe of the male or female flowerhead features a narrow hooded tube of deep red-brown, curved at the end and with a short, 2¾-in (7-cm), tip. From the Himalaya. ‡24 in (60 cm). Z6–8 H8–6

A. dracontium (Green dragon) The single medium-green leaf has around a dozen, elliptical to reverse lance-shaped leaflets, the central one shorter than its neighbors and the remaining leaflets decreasing in size in matched pairs. The leaf hides the nearly tubular green spathe from which emerges the male or bisexual spadix, which is up to 12 in (30 cm) long and can rise up through the leaflets. A woodland species fond of damp locations in light to medium shade. From North America. ‡24–48 in (60–120 cm). Z8–9 H9–8

A. fargesii A striking species with a single three-part leaf. The large, broadly egg-shaped central leaflet reaches 12 in (30 cm) in length and width, while the more narrowly egg-shaped side leaflets are smaller. The whole leaf turns yellow in fall. Red-brown, tubular spathes are produced in midsummer, curving over to an inverted U-shape with a short, pointed 1¼–1½-in (3–4-cm) tip and almost completely hiding the male or female spadix. From western China. ‡24 in (60 cm). Z6–8 H8–6

ARISAEMA FLOWER STRUCTURE

The "flower" of arisaemas, and of other members of the Arum family, is actually a unique and distinctive complex structure containing many small individual flowers. The large hood is known as the spathe, the "pulpit" in the "Jack-in-the-pulpit," and is often the most colorful and striking part of the flower. Within the tube of the spathe, sometimes emerging (the "jack" in the pulpit), perhaps up to 12in (30cm) or more, and sometimes hidden, is the spadix, which carries the male and female flowers hidden by the tube of the spathe. Colorful fruits often follow.

Spathe

Spadix

Arisaema sikokianum

A. flavum A rather variable, widely distributed smaller species. The one or two, seven- to nine-part leaves have more or less lance-shaped leaflets, the central one 2–6 in (5–16 cm) and the others decreasing in size outward. The small spathes, produced in midsummer, form a short cup, sometimes purple at the base on the inside, and with a bright yellow triangular flap covering the top. The spadix may be male, female, or bisexual. Best in bright shade. From East Africa sporadically to Tibet. ‡18–30 in (45–75 cm). Z6–7 H7–1

A. franchetianum syn. *A. purpureogaleatum* A striking and easy-to-grow species with a single, three-part, rather bluish leaf with egg-shaped leaflets, the central 8–20-in- (20–50-cm-) long leaflet being about twice the size of the smaller side leaflets. Red-brown, tubular, white-striped spathes are produced in midsummer, curving over to an inverted U-shape with a long, pointed 6–8 in (15–20 cm) tip. The spadix is male or female. Similar to *A. fargesii*, but with a smaller leaf, larger size, and longer spathe tip. From southwestern China. ‡36 in (90 cm). Z7–9 H9–7

A. galeatum A single three-part deep green leaf is divided into more or less egg-shaped, rough-textured, 8–12 in (15–20 cm) leaflets with a white central vein and a fine red margin. The hooded, helmetlike spathes are held on short stems just above the ground in spring when the leaf emerges and are somewhat obscured by the foliage. From India to western China. ‡36 in (90 cm). Z7–9 H9–7

A. griffithii A decidedly strange-looking plant, with two leaves made up of three, essentially equal-sized, egg-shaped to almost rhombus-shaped 4–16 in (10–40 cm) long leaflets that are green, blotched in purple. The hooded spathe is the strangest and most spectacular in the genus, the top being rolled over on itself like an exaggerated cobra hood. Heavily lined and veined

in purple and green, it is certainly reptilian and hides the male or female spadix. Its slender tail may be 24 in (60 cm) long. Foreboding and beautiful but variable, so look for a well-marked form. From India and the Himalaya. ‡24 in (60 cm). Z7–9 H9–7

A. helleborifolium see *A. tortuosum*

A. jacquemontii One or two leaves comprise five to seven, egg-shaped, plain green leaflets, the central one 2–7 in (5–18 cm) long, the others decreasing in size outward. The white-striped, green spathe, shaped like a simple tube with a wide flap partially covering the opening, appears later and overtops the leaves. The male or female spadix has a ¾–3-in (2–8-cm) purple or green tail. From open sunny spots from Pakistan to China. ‡24–36 in (60–90 cm). Z7–9 H9–7

A. nepenthoides The two or three, five-part leaves are deep glossy green above and purple-veined or entirely purple underneath, with wavy-edged, reverse-lance-shaped, 6–10-in (15–25-cm) leaflets. The spathe, appearing in late spring, has a very snakelike hood and two flat earlike appendages that look like the flattened cup of the insect-eating plant *Nepenthes*. May be male, female, or, rarely, bisexual. From the Himalaya to China. ‡24–36 in (60–90 cm). Z7–9 H9–7

A. propinquum The two or three, three-part leaves are approximately 6 in (15 cm) long and wide, each shiny green, broadly egg-shaped, 3–8-in (8–20-cm) leaflet with a short pointed tip. The male or female flowerhead opens close to the ground, well below the level of the leaves, and its green and purple striped spathe has a wide, slightly arched hood and an extended 1½–2-in (4–5-cm) tip. From the Himalaya: Pakistan and India. ‡32 in (80 cm). Z7–9 H9–7

A. purpureogaleatum see *A. franchetianum*

JACK-IN-THE-PULPIT

This familiar plant, *Arisaema triphyllum*, is found over a wide swathe of eastern North America from Canada right down to Florida. Such widespread plants often show a degree of variation across their range but, in this case, there can be a surprising degree of variability in individual populations. This has led to much confusion in the naming but not, as yet, to nurseries offering a proliferation of named cultivars—although some named forms circulate among enthusiasts.

So, in a single population, the spathes may be entirely green, almost entirely black, or an indeterminate in-between shade; they may be striped in white to varying degrees. The inside may be a different color from the outside, and it may—more rarely—be the same. The spadix too can vary in color from green to black or green speckled with black. The leaf and stem color can also vary and some forms have leaves veined in white. Consequently, there is plenty of scope for the selection and naming of outstanding forms, but all are intriguing plants for fairly wet conditions and a mature group of plants can also be spectacular in fruit.

A. serratum Very variable—the two leaves may have 7–17, more or less oval or egg-shaped leaflets, sometimes veined or marked in cream, the central leaflet 4–8 in (10–20 cm), the outer rapidly decreasing in size and the edges lightly toothed or wavy. The male or female flowers emerge and bloom very early; the spathe may be green or purple with white stripes and has a sharply pointed tip. Sold under various names, including *A. angustatum*, *A. mayebarae*, and *A. takedae*. From dense forests in Japan, and part of Korea and eastern China. ‡5 ft (1.5 m). Z5–9 H9–5

A. sikokianum Well known for its colorful foliage and distinctive spadix, the two leaves with three to five broadly lance-shaped or reverse egg-shaped plain green leaflets may be erratically marked in silver or white streaks or dots. The spathe appears with the foliage in early spring and ranges from deep rich chocolate brown to dark purple in color, with an open hood displaying a pure white button-shaped, male or female spadix in a brilliant-white lined tube. The effect is startling. Needs humus-rich soil with good drainage, and will produce abundant seed. Can be short-lived, so seeds should be started regularly. From Shikoku, Japan. ‡12–20 in (30–50 cm). Z4–9 H9–3

A. speciosum Tuberous plant spreading by rhizomes; both flower and foliage appear in spring. The single green leaf is split into three parts, each with a 1½–2-in (4–5-cm) stem; the central 12-in (30-cm) leaflet is oval, while the two outer 14-in (35-cm) leaflets are sickle-shaped. The funnel-shaped spathe is red-purple with white stripes and an extended tip. The interior is white with a white male or female spadix extending out up to 32 in (80 cm), becoming deep red-brown and threadlike at the end. From the Himalaya, India to China. ‡24 in (60 cm). Z8–9 H9–8

A. tortuosum syn. *A. helleborifolium* Long established in gardens, and highly variable, the two leaves each have up to 20 or more narrow lance-shaped leaflets, the central one the longest at 2–12 in (5–30 cm), the outer leaflets steadily decreasing in size outward. The spathe, appearing just at leaf height, is dull green outside, darker purple inside and blunt tipped. The male or bisexual spadix extends upward 12 in (30 cm) or more. Plants vary significantly in hardiness, so choose for your climate. From India to China and south. ‡24–72 in (60–180 cm). Z8–9 H9–8

A. triphyllum (Jack-in-the-pulpit) Highly variable both in foliage and flower, the two three-part leaves are usually medium green, the 6-in (15-cm) oval leaflets may have silver veins or red coloration. The spathe is typically green, but may be deep purple, red, or with white stripes; the male, female, or bisexual spadix may be green or white. Does best in moist shade. A number of forms have been given cultivar names, but the plants are rarely seen. Self-sown seedlings often give rise to a variety of forms. From woodlands and streamsides in eastern North America. (*see* Jack-in-the-Pulpit). ‡9–36 in (23–90 cm). Z4–9 H9–1

ARISARUM
Mouse plant, Mousetail plant
ARACEAE

Small, intriguing woodland plants grown for their foliage and their unique flowers.

Of three species of summer-dormant tuberous plants from the Mediterranean, only one is widely grown. More or less arrowhead-shaped leaves are held on long stems, making an attractive mound of growth. The foliage emerges early and dies away by midsummer. The spathe, which is tubular at the base, then opens into a forward-pointing hood that encloses the slender spadix. More intriguing than beautiful, but worth growing (*see* The Arum Family, *p. 74*).

CULTIVATION Best in light shade in damp woodland soil. Prefers good drainage and may form a colony if it is flourishing. Mark the location of clumps to avoid damage from cultivation when dormant.

PROPAGATION By division of tubers when dormant; replant promptly to prevent drying out.

PROBLEMS Usually trouble-free.

A. proboscideum Small tuberous perennial forming a short mat of foliage in light shade, the deep, glossy green arrowhead-shaped leaves are up to 6 in (15 cm) tall and long. The flower, produced in spring, are mostly hidden in foliage. At the base, the rounded spathes are white, perhaps with a few vertical purple streaks merging into solid purple and hooded above, then extended into a long, purplish brown tail protruding above the foliage. It looks like a family of mice disappearing among the leaves with only their tails to be seen. The slender, spongy spadix fits into the spathe and has a mushroomlike texture and smell to attract fungus gnats as pollinators. Definitely a conversation piece in bloom, but totally dormant by mid-summer. Best where summers are dry. From the Mediterranean. ‡6–10 in (15–25 cm). Z7–9 H9–7

ARISTOLOCHIA
ARISTOLOCHIACEAE

Several perennials among many climbers can be grown to add interest to the wild garden.

Aristolochias are widely distributed in both hemispheres, mainly in the tropics but also in

BELOW 1 *Arisaema sikokianum*
2 *A. triphyllum* **3** *Arisarum probiscideum*
4 *Aristolochia clematitis*

temperate regions; only one perennial is usually seen. Their flowers form traps for pollinating insects in much the same way as those of arums. There are no recognizable petals, these being replaced by a curved tube that is inflated at the base and expanded at the mouth to form a lip, funnel, or dish-shaped structure. Within the tube are many downward-pointing hairs that help flies to enter, but prevent them from leaving until the pollen is shed. The hairs then wither, allowing the flies to escape and carry pollen to another flower.

CULTIVATION Can be grown in a variety of soils, but is best in those of moderate fertility in a sunny site.

PROPAGATION By division or by basal shoot cuttings.

PROBLEMS Usually trouble-free.

A. clematitis (Birthwort) Deciduous plant spreading steadily underground, in time forming colonies. Branching, erect stems bear roughly heart-shaped, smooth leaves to 4 in (10 cm) long or more. The ¾–1¼-in- (2–3-cm-) long, soft yellow flowers have brown-veined, oval, pointed lips and appear in small clusters from the upper leaf joints during summer and fall. Once used to help conception, facilitate delivery, and in other gynecological and obstetric situations. Probably native to eastern and southeastern Europe, but following widespread cultivation it is now found across much of Europe, including parts of England. ‡ 28–36 in (70–90 cm). Z6–9 H9–6

ARNEBIA
BORAGINACEAE

Choice but neglected plants for frontal positions where they repay close inspection.

About 25 species of hardy deciduous perennials and annuals, native to woodlands, rocky places, and grassy slopes from North Africa to Central Asia. The roots of some species contain a purple dye, and a few are important as medicinal plants. Funnel-shaped, five-lobed flowers are borne in leafy clusters, and are often yellow, sometimes purple. The unusual dark spots marking the flowers of some species act as a signal to bees, and fade once the flower is fertilized.

CULTIVATION Good in a rock garden or mixed border, part-shaded wall crevice, or light woodland, requiring well-drained soil enriched with organic matter such as leafmold. The only species common in cultivation, *A. pulchra*, needs a cool, lightly shaded position, though many others grow in full sun in the wild.

PROPAGATION From seed in spring, by stem cuttings in winter, by division in spring, or, after flowering, by root cuttings in winter.

PROBLEMS Usually trouble-free.

A. echinoides see *A. pulchra*

A. longiflorum see *A. pulchra*

A. pulchra syn. *A. echioides*, *A. longiflorum* (Prophet flower) A hairy, clump-forming plant with rosettes of light green, lance-shaped to oblong leaves, to 6 in (15 cm) long, and unbranched, sprawling stems. Clear yellow, widely funnel-shaped flowers, to 1 in (2.5 cm) across, in compact clusters in summer, have unusual markings: five dark brown spots on the petals, which fade gradually and are said to symbolize the "prophet's fingerprints." A choice plant for the front of the border, it needs a sheltered, cool position in light shade, although it will tolerate full sun in cooler climates. Gritty soil with leaf mold is ideal. Propagate from seed or by careful division for plants that form more than one rosette. From northern Caucasus, northern Iran, and northeastern Turkey. ‡ 6–18 in (15–45 cm). Z6–8 H8–6

ARNICA
ASTERACEAE

Summer-flowering yellow daisies associated with mountain meadows also known for their medicinal properties.

Thirty-two species of deciduous plants, favoring pastures and open woodlands in northern temperate and arctic regions. Some have been used medicinally, but all parts are toxic if eaten and sap may irritate skin. Clump-forming or slowly spreading, the opposite leaves may be stalked or stalkless, sometimes mainly basal. The yellow to orange daisy flowers are borne on upright stems, which usually bear several pairs of stem-clasping leaves. ⚠

CULTIVATION Need full sun and humus-rich soil with good drainage.

PROPAGATION By division after flowering, or from seed sown in spring at 50°F (10°C).

PROBLEMS Usually trouble-free.

A. chamissonis (Chamisso arnica) Slowly spreading, forming seasonal ground cover, leaves are lance-shaped, softly hairy, to 8 in (20 cm) long, the basal ones stalked, those on the stems stalkless. Yellow daisylike flowers, up to 2 in (5 cm) across with 10–16 ray florets, borne in loose clusters from early summer to early fall. Deadheading prolongs the season. Needs full sun and well-drained soil; suitable for rough, grassy areas with poor fertility, or richer sites that can accommodate its potential spread. Native to western North America. ‡ 24 in (60 cm). Z3–8 H6–1

A. montana (Mountain tobacco) Clump-forming species with broad lance-shaped, softly hairy, basal stalkless leaves to 8 in (20 cm) long. From early summer to early fall, the upright stems bear few-flowered clusters of yellow daises, to 3 in (8 cm) wide with 11–15 ray florets, and two to three pairs of stem-clasping leaves. It is widely used medicinally (the philosopher Goethe is said to have taken arnica for his angina) but it should not be used without expert advice. From mountainous areas of Europe and western Asia, it prefers humus-rich, acidic soil in full sun. ‡ 24 in (60 cm). Z5–8 H8–5

ARRHENATHERUM
Oat grass
POACEAE

Coarse grasses of weedy places and dry grasslands, with only one redeeming foliage form.

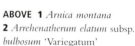

ABOVE 1 *Arnica montana*
2 *Arrehenatherum elatum* subsp. *bulbosum* 'Variegatum'

Six perennial species, native to Europe, the Mediterranean region, and the Middle East and introduced to other parts of the world, grow wild in many habitats from hedgerows to wasteland. Tufted grasses have swollen bases, some in the form of round corms; their long straight stems bear loose, feathery flowerheads. *Arrenatherum elatum* subsp. *bulbosum* (onion couch) is a troublesome weed, having pear-shaped basal corms up to ⅓ in (1 cm) across that become detached and rapidly spread on arable land; however, the variegated form is far less invasive and more attractive.

CULTIVATION Drought-resistant; suits most soils in sun and part-shade.

PROPAGATION From seed or by division in spring, or by separating basal corms.

PROBLEMS Usually trouble-free.

A. elatum subsp. *bulbosum* 'Variegatum' (Striped bulbous oat grass) Forms slowly spreading, dazzling, nearly white carpets of soft, fine, upright leaves to 12 in (30 cm) high, blue-gray with bold white vertical stripes and margins. Feathery flowerheads appear in early summer but are best cut back to improve the foliage and prevent seeding. The whole plant dies back in summer, then regrows in fall. Best grown in light shade, this drought-tolerant grass prefers well-drained, neutral to acidic soil. It needs frequent division to preserve foliage vigor. Seedlings have either all-green or all-white foliage. ‡ 12–24 in (30–60 cm). Z5–8 H8–5

growth is lush. Leaf miner can be a problem except in those with very narrow lobes.

A. absinthium (Wormwood) A relatively easy, though rather variable species, used to flavor vermouth and absinthe. It produces upright stems from a woody rootstock. The intricately lobed leaves, up to 4 in (10 cm) long and across and triple-cut along the main axis, are grayish and downy. Grayish yellow flowers in graceful sprays appear in mid- and late summer. Usually rather weedy in appearance, though there are a few choice cultivars selected for silvery foliage. Cut back to about 6 in (15 cm) in mid-spring. Cut off flower stems, either before flowering if a compact mound is required, or after blooming to encourage production of fresh leaves. This reduces the height of the plant considerably: plants should be set farther forward in beds and borders than the flowering height suggests. Temperate Eurasia and North Africa. ↕24–60 in (60–150 cm), less if prevented from flowering. Z4–8 H9–1. **'Lambrook Mist'** Vigorous, fast-growing, and tolerant of winter rain and clipping, with silvery foliage, though less pale and less finely divided than 'Lambrook Silver'. Selected by Andrew Norton at Margery Fish's garden at East Lambrook Manor, Somerset. ↕3¼ ft (1 m). **'Lambrook Silver'** An especially silvery selection championed by Margery Fish as perhaps the whitest selection, though slightly less hardy and less tolerant of winter rain. ↕3¼ ft (1 m). Z4–8 H9–1

A. alba A very variable, more or less evergreen, woody-based plant, with leaves that can be hairless and green to densely downy and white, deeply lobed along the axis and lobed again, or sometimes reduced to narrow threads. The fragrance is also variable but can be like camphor. Yellowish flowers are borne on spirelike stems from midsummer to early fall. Prefers sun and well-drained soil. Propagate from cuttings. From North Africa, southern and south central Europe. ↕Up to 3¼ ft (1 m). Z4–8 H8–1. **'Canescens'** syn. *A. canescens* Over a basal mound of filigree silvery foliage the flowers are not especially decorative, but the tall stems are, and can be left rather than pinched out to produce more leaves. Deadheading after the first flush encourages production of fresh leaves and more spires of flowers in fall. A choice plant for the front of a sunny border. Sometimes called, incorrectly, *A. splendens*. ↕18 in (45 cm) (flowers).

A. caucasica syn. *A. lanata, A. pedemontana* An evergreen, spreading, woody-based plant with glistening feathery silver foliage, cut along the main axis and cut again into linear lobes. Spires of yellowish flowers that appear in midsummer may be cut off to encourage production of fresh foliage. Recommended in extended plantings as a firebreak for hot, dry climates and a superlative plant for carpeting at the front of the border or in the rock garden. Often confused

with the herbaceous, rhizomatous *A. schmidtiana* 'Nana'—both are often referred to loosely as "Silver Mound." Enjoys sun and good drainage; resents excess nitrogen and winter rain. Propagate by cuttings or layering. Scattered across southern Europe from central Spain to Ukraine. ↕6–12 in (15–30 cm) (flowers). Z5–9 H9–1

A. lactiflora The odd one out among commonly cultivated artemisias, this clump-forming, herbaceous plant has dark green leaves deeply cut along the axis and again lobed. Until recent decades, this variable species was represented in western gardens only by plants with plumes of creamy flowers in late summer; recent introductions have had more diffuse flowerheads. Prefers rich, moist soil and fall planting; tolerates some shade. Tends to die from fungal disease if under stress from drought, waterlogging, or starvation. From India, southern Asia, and China. ↕5 ft (1.5 m). Z5–8 H8–5. **Guizhou Group** Seed introduction from the joint Kew/Chinese Academy of Sciences expedition to Guizhou in 1985. Variable, with mahogany stems, leaves more or less flushed purple, and loose sprays of white flowers from mid- to late summer: avoid plants with little or no dark coloring. ↕5 ft (1.5 m). **'Jim Russell'** Purple-flushed leaves and very spreading sprays of white flowers on arching stems. ↕5 ft (1.5 m). **'Rosenschleier'** Airy clouds of grayish-pink flowers in mid- to late summer. ↕5 ft (1.5 m). Z4–9 H9–1

A. lanata see *A. caucasica*

A. ludoviciana (White wormwood, white sagebrush) A tough, variable, rather invasive herbaceous plant, and one of the easiest of artemisias. The leaves are up to 4½ in (11 cm) long, the lower ones toothed or divided, white hairy beneath and green to silver above. The flowers, similar in color to the foliage and not showy, are borne in summer and fall in an open head that

ARTEMISIA

ASTERACEAE

Herbs and fragrant foliage plants, some with attractive silvery foliage.

There are about 350 species of aromatic evergreen or deciduous shrubs, herbaceous perennials that are either clump-forming or spreading by rhizomes, and annuals, mostly from north temperate areas. Several have traditional culinary or medicinal uses. Most have fibrous roots, although the rhizomes of a few can prove invasive. Their leaves are alternate, often grayish, jagged-edged or deeply cut, often divided twice or three times into narrow lobes. The flowers are generally insignificant, lacking the ray florets seen in most members of the daisy family and differing little in color from the leaves. They are usually borne on a much-branched

ABOVE 1 *Artemisia absinthium* 'Lambrook Mist' 2 *A. alba* 'Canescens' 3 *A. lactiflora* Guizhou Group 4 *A. vulgaris* Oriental Limelight

flowerhead. Pleasantly scented species can be planted beside a path, so that brushing past them releases their fragrance.

CULTIVATION Most prefer nutrient-poor, well-drained soil in sun, making them ideal for the gravel garden. Some benefit from cutting back by about one-third of their height in late spring to encourage bushier growth. The laxer species benefit from staking.

PROPAGATION By cuttings or division.

PROBLEMS The most compact silvery types are generally intolerant of hot, humid climates, where mildews destroy the foliage, especially if

may be broad or narrow. For well-drained soil in sun; avoid excess nitrogen. Cut back the flower stems by about half at about two-thirds its final height to make plants shorter and less floppy and keep the foliage brightly silver. Otherwise, stake the plant with brushwood, worked throughout the clump. From North America. ‡24–39 in (60–100 cm). Z4–9 H9–1. **subsp. albula** Invasive with small, almost white leaves, the lower ones ½–¾ in (1–2 cm) long, the upper ones tiny, giving an airy effect. Flowers midsummer to early fall. Often sold, mistakenly and confusingly, as Silver King. From the southwestern US. ‡36 in (90 cm). **subsp. candicans** syn. var. *latiloba* Lower leaves 2–4 in (5–10 cm) long, silvery and deeply divided. From western North America. ‡30 in (75 cm). **subsp. ludoviciana** syn. 'Latiloba' The typical subspecies with silvery leaves 1¼–4½ in (3–11 cm) long and more than ½ in (1 cm) wide, occasionally with a few teeth or small lobes near the tip. Flowers from midsummer to early fall. Found throughout most of North America. ‡24–39 in (60–100 cm). **'Silver Queen'** Near-white leaves, the lower ones 6 in (15 cm) long by 2½ in (6 cm) wide and deeply divided into narrow lobes; flowering in mid- and late summer, less freely than other cultivars Perhaps a selection of subsp. *candicans*. ‡30 in (75 cm). **'Valerie Finnis'** Shorter, and very silvery with broad lower leaves with a few lobes but with unlobed upper leaves. In hot, humid climates its foliage is killed by mildew in summer, though it regrows well by fall if cut back. ‡24 in (60 cm).

A. pedemontana see *A. caucasia*

A. pontica Aromatic, rather invasive herbaceous plant making a dome of upright stems clad with filigree gray-green leaves 1¼–1½ in (3–4 cm) long and producing heads of grayish yellow flowers ¾–3 in (2–8 cm) long in early summer. Prefers good drainage and is more attractive, grayer, shorter and less invasive in poorer, fairly dry soil. Can make good ground cover. From central and eastern Europe. ‡16–32 in (40–80 cm). Z4–8 H8–1

A. stelleriana (Beach wormwood) A densely downy, near-white perennial spreading by rhizomes, this is almost evergreen in mild regions. The leaves are deeply divided into fingerlike lobes; heads of insignificant yellowish flowers appear in late summer to early fall. Propagate from cuttings. From southeastern Asia and northeastern US. ‡Up to 24 in (60 cm). Z3–7 H7–1. **'Boughton Silver'** syn. 'Mori', 'Prostrata', 'Silver Brocade'. Very short and spreading, superlative silvery foliage makes it useful for ground cover and the front of the border. Especially good when underplanted with bulbs such as *Allium cristophii*. 'Boughton Silver' is the correct name, although it is widely marketed under its various synonyms. ‡16 in (40 cm), less, however, if it is prevented from flowering. **'Nana'** Probably, although not undoubtedly, identical to 'Boughton Silver'.

A. vallesiaca syn. *Seriphidium vallesiacum* Densely gray to white, sometimes woolly, woody-based perennial strongly scented of camphor. The feathery leaves are divided up to four times into tiny filaments. The lower part of the plant is furnished with short, non-flowering shoots that retain their foliage through the flowering season. The ascending, near-white, narrow sprays of flowers appear in July and August and usually arch gracefully toward the top with upright side branches a couple of inches long. Unlike other artemisias, all the florets are bisexual; in other species the outer florets in each flower are female and the inner ones are bisexual or male. This distinction has encouraged botanists to split this, and about 130 similar species, into a new genus *Seriphidium*. Best in sun and with good drainage. From southwestern Switzerland, southwestern France, and northeastern Italy. ‡16in (40cm). Z6–9 H9–6

A. vulgaris (Mugwort, Common wormwood) Variable tufted perennial with leaves that are cut along the main axis and further lobed, green above and whitish below with plumes of grayish green flowers from midsummer to early fall. The species is weedy and not used as a garden ornamental, but the variegated forms are useful. Although the species likes sunny, well-drained, rather dry conditions, variegated cultivars produce brighter variegation if given adequate moisture and will tolerate some shade; they will also keep better foliage if prevented from flowering. Stems reverting to a less bright variegation should be removed. Propagate by cuttings. From Eurasia and North America. ‡12 in–8 ft (30 cm–2.5 m). Z4–8 H8–1. **'Cragg-Barber Eye'** Bright, yellow-green foliage with occasional flecks of dark green. From Martin Cragg-Barber, an enthusiast for novel forms of British native plants. ‡36 in (90 cm). **Oriental Limelight ('Janlim')** Foliage heavily splashed and striped yellowish cream. ‡4 ft (1.2 m). **'Variegata'** Foliage lightly splashed and striped cream. ‡4 ft (1.2 m).

ARTHROPODIUM
ANTHERICACEAE

Pretty sun-lovers, with distinctive grassy foliage and airy heads of summer flowers.

Twelve species of both deciduous and evergreen plants, from varied open, sunny habitats such as scrub or rocky areas in New Zealand and southern Australia, do best in a sunny, well-drained situation or at the base of a warm, sunny wall. Tufted plants, slowly spreading by creeping stems, they have grassy or strappy foliage, and upright or lax stems carrying airy sprays of small, starry or rounded, six-petaled flowers in summer.

CULTIVATION Best in soil with that elusive combination of good

drainage and moisture retention, in a sheltered position in full sun.

PROPAGATION By division in spring, or (species only) from seed sown in spring at 50°F (10°C).

PROBLEMS Slugs and snails love the new growth.

A. candidum Deciduous plant shooting from small, cone-shaped tubers, grown mainly for its foliage. From among grassy, mid-green leaves, up to 12 in (30 cm) long, open sprays of rounded white flowers, ½ in (1 cm) across, appear in early and midsummer. Plants with foliage spotted with, or entirely in, copper or bronze may also be seen under this name. Grows well in shade, but flowers poorly. From New Zealand. ‡12 in (30 cm). Z8–9 H9–8. **var. purpureum** Attractive bronze foliage.

A. cirratum (Rengarenga, Rock lily) An evergreen perennial spreading by creeping stems, grown mainly for its foliage. The wide, strap-shaped leaves, up to 24 in (60 cm) long, are green above and white or grayish below, forming attractive clumps. Branched sprays of nodding, starry white flowers flecked with yellow and purple, up to 1 in (2.5 cm) across (sometimes more), rise above the foliage from early summer onward. Grows well in shade with dry soil. From New Zealand. ‡36 in (90 cm). Z8–9 H9–8. **'Matapouri Bay'** Broader leaves and large flowerheads.

ARUM
ARACEAE

Intriguing tuberous perennials with attractive foliage and showy flowers and fruits.

There are 25 species, all seasonally dormant, growing in open temperate to warm woods and open stony areas in shade to full sun depending on species. They occur from temperate Europe to the Middle East and western China, with the exception of most of the Arabian Peninsula and India. The foliage is usually arrowhead-shaped or heart-shaped, often attractively marked. Some produce foliage in the fall, dying away for the summer, while others produce foliage in spring. Most bloom in spring to early summer, often with large and intriguing spathes, and the flowers are followed by decorative stalks of red to orange berries. Some may have an unpleasant scent to the flowers. Favorites of collectors; a few are more widely grown in gardens, but the plant is poisonous and the sap can cause irritation to skin and eyes. (*see* The Arum Family, *p.74*). ⚠

CULTIVATION All prefer good light, but usually not full sun. The moisture needs vary with the species; plants usually appreciate ample water in growth, but less as dormancy approaches. Fertilize only when actively growing.

AROIDS

Amorphophallus The most widely grown of a spectacular group of aroids, *A. konjac* (see p.54) is also one of the hardiest.

Arisaema The most instantly attractive and elegant hardy aroid, *A. candidissimum* (see p.69) is unusual in being sweetly scented.

Dracunculus The smell from the dramatic Mediterranean *D. vulgaris* (see p.172) is as intense as its coloring.

Lysichiton A very hardy bog plant from the wilds of eastern Russia, *L. camtschatcensis* (see p.318) will also grow in a damp border.

Sauromatum Making bizarre colonies in the garden, *S. venustum* (see p.421) tubers will also flower if grown in a saucer on the windowsill.

Zantedeschia 'Green Goddess' (see p.486) is a striking form of *Z. aethiopica* and makes an impressive container plant.

THE ARUM FAMILY

Members of the Arum family, *Araceae*, often familiarly called aroids, are noticeably distinct from all other flowering plants. Encompassing houseplants like the Swiss cheese plant (*Monstera deliciosa*), and cut flowers like the flamingo flower (*Anthurium andraeanum*), the family also includes a number of hardy perennials that are covered in this book, including two common woodland flowers: the European lords-and-ladies (*Arum maculatum*), and the North American jack-in-the-pulpit (*Arisaema triphyllum*). They grow in all parts of the world—though mostly in tropical climates—in many habitats, and include climbers and floating aquatics, as well as deciduous perennials with corms or tubers. The foliage covers a surprising range, from slender and grasslike to large bold, broad, and divided. Some are edible, some toxic.

All the 3,000 species have in common their unique flower structure. Just to be picky, although the whole structure is often referred to as a flower by gardeners, it is in fact an aggregation of flowers and related parts and is technically an inflorescence. It can vary in size from less than ½ in (1 cm) to more than 6½ ft (2 m).

The two main parts of the inflorescence are usually quite obvious: a broad, cowl-like, sometimes tubular and hooded structure, called the spathe, which is the colorful part, and surrounds or stands alongside a narrow protruding structure, called the spadix, on which the small individual flowers are actually carried. The spathe is basically a modified leaf, and in some species even becomes green and photo-synthesizes like a leaf after flowering. It serves to protect the spadix as it develops and may be modified to trap insects around the flowers and so encourage pollination. The spadix is usually stick- or club-shaped and, toward the base, it is encircled by a mass of tiny flowers that may be hard to distinguish without magnification.

The individual flowers may be male, female, or bisexual (hermaphrodite) but, if not bisexual, the male and female flowers are gathered into distinct zones with the female flowers below the male flowers, sometimes with sterile flowers in between. The female flowers on any given plant open before the male flowers to encourage cross-pollination. In addition—in *Arisaema*, for example—some plants produce bisexual flowers, while others produce male or female or bisexual flowers in different years. The spadix may develop a long appendage, often generating an unpleasant smell to attract pollinating insects and, as the flowers fade, fleshy and attractive fruits often develop and are dispersed by birds or small mammals.

Ten aroids are covered in this book: *Alocasia, Amorphophallus, Arisaema, Arisarum, Arum, Colocasia, Dracunculus, Lysichiton, Sauromatum,* and *Zantedeschia*.

PROPAGATION Divide when dormant. Seed is produced in midsummer and germinates in fall or spring.

PROBLEMS None of significance, but some species may self-sow vigorously.

A. **'Chameleon'** Large, arrowhead-shaped but broadly rounded foliage marked in silver and white over various shades of green, emerges in fall. Broad, pale green spathes. Seedlings variable; almost always marked. Sometimes said to be a form of *A. italicum* but probably a hybrid with *A. maculatum*. ‡ 16 in (40 cm). Z6–9 H9–6

A. **concinnatum** One of the largest species of arum and spreading by rhizomes, the large, arrowhead-shaped, glossy dark green leaves are up to 20 in (50 cm) long and 12 in (30 cm) across and blotched with silvery gray. They emerge in the fall. The spring flowers have a spathe in pale greenish white with a purple-flushed edge, up to 10 in (25 cm) long, which is approximately the same height as the dull yellow spadix. Sometimes confused with *A. italicum* but with a longer spadix and an unpleasant smell. From southern Greece and eastern Turkey. ‡ 3¼ ft (1 m). Z7–9 H9–7

A. **dioscoridis** Dramatic but variable plant with roundly triangular, unspotted foliage, 5–18 in (13–45 cm) long and 3½–11 in (9–27 cm) wide, and emerging in the fall. The 4–16-in (10–40-cm) spathe may be pale green to deep brownish purple or patterned in both colors with a stout, 4¾–11 in (12–28 cm) dark purple spadix. The flowers emerge in spring and have a very unpleasant smell. From coastal Turkey to Israel. ‡ 15 in (35 cm). Z7–9 H9–7

A. **dracunculus** see *Dracunculus vulgaris*

A. **italicum** The most popular species, spreading by rhizomes; the variable,

triangular, 6–10-in- (15–25-cm-) long foliage, on stems up to 16 in (40 cm) long, may be plain green to silver-veined or marked with a spectacular network of silver and white. The foliage appears in the fall and stays evergreen even in harsh climates, but withers in mid-spring. The large, pale green spathe, wrapped around the large, club-shaped spadix about half its length, appears without foliage in midsummer, followed by stalks of bright red berries that may last until the foliage reappears in fall. Forms continue to be introduced, including one with black leaf stems and another with spotted spathes, but they can be hard to find. Thrives in light shade or full sun. From most of temperate Europe, the Caucasus and the Canary Islands. ‡ 14 in (35 cm). Z7–9 H9–3. **subsp. albispathum** Smaller, plain green, unmarked leaves, large, white 16-in (40-cm) spathes. From the Crimea and the Caucasus. Z7–9 H9–3. **'Cyclops'** Larger, dark green foliage marked and marbled in cream. Said to be hardier. **subsp. italicum** Leaves marked along the major veins in silver-white to cream, but sometimes all green. Spathe pale green to cream. Much of Europe, North Africa, and Turkey. **subsp. italicum 'Ghost'** Boldly green-edged leaves with gray-gold marbling between the silvery white veins. From Ellen Hornig at Seneca Hill Perennials, Oswego, NY. **subsp. italicum 'Marmoratum'** Major veins colored silver or cream. Variable. **subsp. italicum 'Pictum'** *see* subsp. *italicum* 'Marmoratum'. **subsp. italicum 'Sparkler'** Random cream variegation on dark foliage. **subsp. italicum 'Spotted Jack'** Leaves irregularly dotted with small black spots. **subsp. italicum 'Tiny'** A smaller form, flowering infrequently. ‡ 4 in (10 cm). **subsp. italicum 'White Winter'** A smaller form, heavily marked in white. Said to bloom prolifically. ‡ 6–8 in (15–20 cm). **'Nancy Lindsay'** Foliage starts yellow, then fades to green with creamy veins and edges.

A. **maculatum** (Lords-and-ladies, Cuckoo pint) Compact and very variable plant, with roundly triangular leaves, 2¾–11 in (7–27 cm) long and 1½–7½ in (3.5–19 cm) wide, which emerge in spring and may be plain green or variably spotted in black as the name indicates. These are followed by variable pale green to spotted 2½–11-in (6–27-cm) spathes. The plant dies down to dormancy by midsummer. Underappreciated for garden use. A common plant of hedgerows and woods in most of temperate Europe to the Caucasus. ‡ 24 in (60 cm). Z6–9 H9–6

A. **orientale** Handsome, rather variable plant. The deep green, broadly arrowhead-shaped leaves, 3–7 in (8–25 cm) long and 2–6½ in (5–17 cm) wide, emerge in fall and are usually stained purple toward the base of their long stem. The deep brown-purple to pale purple, 5½–12-in (14–30-cm) spathe emerges in spring and may be strongly, though variably, scented. Similar to *A. maculatum*, but slightly smaller, with a richer spathe color and fall-emerging foliage. Thrives in cold, wet winters. Native to rich woodlands from the former Yugoslavia to Austria and the Caucasus. Z6–9 H9–6

A. **pictum** (Black arum) Attractive lustrous deep green foliage, 3½–10 in (9–25 cm) long and 2½–7 in (6–18 cm) wide, tinged purple when emerging in fall and later developing silver veins and retaining a purple edge. The deep velvety purple, 4½–8-in (11–21-cm) spathe is slightly longer than the deep purple-black spadix. Uniquely, flowers emerge in fall before or as foliage emerges. From central Mediterranean islands and the west coast of Italy. ‡ 10 in (25 cm). Z6–9 H9–6

A. **'Streaked Spectre'** Broadly arrowhead-shaped leaves, which are unpredictably patterned in greens and white with bold black spots. Selected by Jerry Flintoff, and one of a number of hybrids between *A. italicum* and *A. maculatum*, originating over some years at the University of Washington, Seattle, WA. ‡ 16 in (40 cm). Z6–9 H9–6

ARUNCUS
Goatsbeard
ROSACEAE

Elegant, summer-blooming plants with feathery flower spikes for moist, shady locations.

The four species of these plants, all deciduous, are native to damp woods and streamsides in eastern North America, Europe, and Asia. *Aruncus* is closely related to *Filipendula* and *Spiraea*. Slowly spreading into dense clumps, the wiry stems carry the large, long-stemmed, alternate leaves, each of which is divided into pairs of

LEFT *Arum italicum* subsp. *italicum* 'Marmoratum' **1** in flower **2** fruiting

toothed leaflets with noticeable veining. Showy sprays of creamy blooms provide the summer display, male and female flowers usually on different plants.

CULTIVATION Moist, fertile soil in part- or full shade.

PROPAGATION From seed sown in fall or spring; named forms by division.

PROBLEMS Usually trouble-free.

A. aethusifolius A low-growing species that spreads slowly by underground runners, making an effective ground cover. The finely cut, bright green foliage is tinged bronze when it emerges in spring, remains attractive all summer, and turns yellow in fall. Branching sprays of tiny individual yellowish white flowers open in early summer. Grows well in clay soil and is good for shaded rock gardens. From Korea. ‡ 16 in (40 cm). Z3–9 H9–3. **'Little Gem'** Smaller, with more finely divided foliage. Collected by Bleddyn and Sue Wynn-Jones in South Korea in 2001. ‡ 8 in (20 cm). Z3–9 H9–3

ABOVE 1 *Aruncus aethusifolius* **2** *A. dioicus* 'Kneiffii' **3** *Asarum canadense* **4** *A. europaeum*

A. dioicus syn. *A. sylvester, Spiraea aruncus* An imposing, upright plant reaching 6½ ft (2 m) in dense shade, with bright green, fernlike leaves up to 3¼ ft (1 m) long. Male and female flowers appear on separate plants in early summer, on much-branched stalks. Male flowers are a creamy white and are the more showy. Female ones are usually greenish white, and slightly drooping, but give brown seed capsules that are attractive in fall and may be cut and dried for winter arrangements. However, they can also self-sow irritatingly. A reliable, easy plant that seldom requires staking. Grows well in full sun if the soil retains moisture but is well-drained. From eastern North America, and western and central Europe. ‡ 5–6½ ft (1.5–2 m). Z3–7 H7–1. **Child of Two Worlds** *see* 'Zweiweltenkind'. **'Glasnevin'** Smaller, with larger flower trusses. ‡ 5 ft (1.5 m). **var.** *kamtschaticus* Very dwarf, and less showy. ‡ 24–36 in (60–90 cm). **'Kneiffii'** Fine, intricately divided

foliage; may be a selection of var. *kamtschaticus*, being the same height but with larger sprays of flowers. **'Zweiweltenkind'** (**Child of Two Worlds**) More upright, with bronze-tinged leaves. May be a hybrid between *A. dioicus* and the rare *A. sinensis.* Often raised from seed, so plants may be male or female. ‡ 5 ft (1.5 m).

A. **'Horatio'** Large sprays of creamy flowers on self-supporting stems, and exciting red fall foliage color. A German hybrid between *A. aethusifolius* and *A. dioicus.* ‡ 3¼ ft (1 m). Z3–9 H9–3

A. sylvester see *A. dioicus*

ASARINA *see* LOPHOSPERMUM *and* MAURANDYA

ASARUM
Hardy ginger, Wild ginger
ARISTOLOCHIACEAE

Durable and desirable shade-loving ground-cover plants offering sensational effects in foliage.

About 75 species of low, spreading, deciduous or evergreen perennials from woodlands of both the New and Old World. The roots of all species are pungently scented and inspire the plants' common name while serving as a reliable identification tool. Grown for both their foliage and their curious flowers, the leaves are generally rounded to heart-shaped, with populations of many species exhibiting markedly diverse leaf markings. Exotic-looking flowers of purple-black, sometimes white, are produced in spring or fall and, though in some cases strangely beautiful, they are generally hidden beneath the foliage or sometimes even under the leaf litter. Although perfectly hardy, they particularly enjoy warm summers. It is only in recent years that the value and potential of these beautiful and fascinating plants is being appreciated and more forms are slowly becoming available. A few are sometimes separated out into a separate genus, *Hexastylis.*

CULTIVATION Best grown in shaded or part-shaded sites in cool, humus-rich soil with even moisture. Many species perform best under humid conditions in summer warm climates and will be slow to establish and fail to thrive in cooler conditions.

PROPAGATION By division in early spring as growth resumes. Propagation from seed is also possible; however, even freshly sown seed requires two years for germination to occur. Success with tissue culture has allowed the recent introduction of selected forms of several species.

PROBLEMS Very prone to slug and snail damage in early spring.

A. arifolium syn. *Hexastylis arifolium* Very durable clump-forming plant with handsome mounds of large, arrow-shaped, aniseed-scented leaves and enormous variation in foliage forms in native populations. Flowers, mottled black-purple, emerge in early spring. Best in warm, summer climates. Used by American Indians as a medicinal herb. From southeastern North America. ‡ 6 in (15 cm). Z4–8 H8–1. **'Beaver Creek'** Spreads by runners, making dense ground cover. From Tennessee's Beaver Creek Nursery.

A. canadense A vigorous, deciduous species forming large colonies of heart-shaped, matte-green leaves, coated in fine silky hair as they emerge in spring. Small, brown, urn-shaped flowers are produced beneath the foliage in early spring. A utilitarian ground-covering species for difficult woodland sites. From eastern North America. ‡ 6 in (15 cm). Z2–8 H8–1

A. caudatum A handsome and useful species with semi-evergreen foliage, coated with silky hair when emerging, later becoming glossy green. Some wild populations feature attractive silver leaf-veining. Spidery flowers of dark red-purple, occasionally white, are produced in spring. Will form substantial colonies over time in evenly moist soil, and tolerates cooler summer temperatures better than most species. From western North America. ‡ 3 in (7.5 cm). Z7–9 H9–7

A. caulescens A sensational deciduous species that emerges in spring with bright green, deeply impressed foliage hiding purple flowers beneath. Spreading vigorously by runners, it provides a terrific, highly textural ground cover in both cool and humid summer climates, although the leaves are especially prone to slug damage when emerging. ↕ 4 in (10 cm). Z6–8 H8–6

A. delavayi Enormous, evergreen, heart-shaped leaves in glistening black-green form impressive mounds, while in late spring large cup-shaped flowers of black velvet are produced in quantity near the ground. Thrives in both cool summer and warmer climates. Among the most dramatic species in foliage and flower. From China. ↕ 18 in (45 cm). Z6–8 H8–6

A. europaeum A popular, widely grown species forming spreading colonies of glossy rounded leaves, beneath which are red-purple flowers during spring. Probably one of the most commonly cultivated of all *Asarum* species, performing well under diverse climates although it is more vigorous in warm summer regions. In Britain, where the plant is naturalized but declining, it has been grown as a medicinal herb since at least the 13th century. ↕ 6 in (15 cm). Z4–8 H8–1

A. hartwegii A very diverse evergreen or semievergreen species offering a huge degree of variation in leaf patterning, often similar to the foliage of hardy cyclamen. Often seen growing in full sun and well-drained soil in its natural habitat. Difficult to grow in the moist, woodland conditions that are more generally suited to asarums, and probably the best species for dry gardens. From southern Oregon and northern California. ↕ 4 in (10 cm). Z2–8 H8–1

A. magnificum This aptly named species forms magnificent mounds of glossy, evergreen foliage with a pattern reminiscent of a pulmonaria—boldly silver with silver spots scattered through a green edging—and bears tubular purple flowers in spring. It performs best in warm, humid summer regions where it is quick to build into impressive clumps. From China. ↕ 8 in (20 cm). Z7–9 H9–7

A. maximum (Panda ginger) Sought-after species with delicately patterned, arrow-shaped, glossy green leaves forming low mounds, and enormous, 2 in (5 cm) flowers of black-purple, centered with a pandalike white "face." A superb plant that performs best in warm summer regions. From China. ↕ 8 in (20 cm). Z7–9 H9–7

A. shuttleworthii Highly patterned rounded leaves, to 3 in (7.5 cm) across, slowly develop into substantial mounds. Large purple flowers are borne at ground level in spring. This handsome species has a loyal following among gardeners in warm summer regions but is slow in areas with cool summers.

↕ 4 in (10 cm). Z5–9 H9–1. **'Calloway'** Slightly shorter, silver-veined spreading form from Calloway Gardens, GA. ↕ 3 in (7.5 cm).

ASCLEPIAS
Milkweed
ASCLEPIDACEAE

Sun-loving and drought-tolerant, leathery-leaved plants with exciting summer flowers—starry, fragrant, and brightly colored.

There are over 100 species, mainly perennials, with tuberous roots; most are clump-forming, although a few spread by suckers. The generally rather stout, upright stems exude a milky sap when bruised, which can irritate the skin; it is also poisonous to livestock. They carry undivided leaves, varying from slender and elliptical to broadly oval; these may be opposite, alternate, or even spirally arranged on the stems. Individual flowers, 1 in (2.5 cm) at the largest but usually smaller, are held in rounded, flat-topped, or drooping clusters, each round flower starlike with its five lobes thrown back (the hood) to reveal a crown of upturned lobes (the horn), emerging from the center. A generous nectar supply attracts bees, and also butterflies (*see* Milkweeds). The pairs of fat green pods that follow each flower (much prized by flower arrangers) swell, become brown, then burst to reveal seeds attached to a mass of silky hairs that aid distribution. ⚠

CULTIVATION Best in well-drained but fertile soil in full sun; some will take damp conditions. The more aggressive spreaders are better in wilder situations. Late risers in

MILKWEEDS

The milkweeds, in particular *Asclepias tuberosa*, have two valuable uses. They make excellent, long-lasting cut flowers, and *in situ*, they also attract butterflies.

For the house, cut the stems when half to two-thirds of the flowers are open, as the buds do not open well once the stems are cut. There is no need to sear the stems, as is sometimes suggested; put them straight into water after cutting, then into warm water, then into cooler water straight from the faucet. This will eliminate what little latex this species produces. Recut the stems immediately before arranging, and the flowers should last up to 10 days in average room temperature. The pods are also decorative: cut them when they are still green and before they burst.

Butterfly species that are attracted to these plants include painted ladies, red admirals, fritillaries, monarchs, swallowtails, and hairstreaks, which come for the generous supplies of nectar. Some of their caterpillars also feed on the plants.

spring, frequently to the point that gardeners give up hope—don't do so, even though after a ferocious, freeze-and-thaw winter your fears may be justified.

PROPAGATION From seed, or by short spring cuttings.

PROBLEMS Aphids, often in disgraceful numbers.

A. incarnata (Swamp milkweed) Stout, densely branched plant with plenty of milky sap and handsome, long, thin, willowlike leaves, to 6 in (15 cm) long, densely placed along the stems in opposite pairs. In fall, the leaves turn yellow and gold. Clusters of gorgeous, brilliant pink vanilla-scented flowers from midsummer to early fall have paler horns in the center. Prefers full sun; fond of moist soil but can also endure drought. From the eastern US. ↕ 3¼–4 ft (1–1.2 m). Z3–9 H9–2. **'Alba'** White flowers in heads resembling snowballs. **'Cinderella'** Similar in size and habit, but with denser heads of larger flowers in a rosier shade of pink. Blooms first year from seed. ↕ 3¼–4 ft (1–1.2 m). **'Ice Ballet'** Long-stemmed, long-lasting white flowers in larger flowerheads than other whites. A superb cut flower. **'Soulmate'** Taller, with rich, deep rose-purple blooms. Long-flowering. ↕ 3¼–4 ft (1–1.2 m).

A. speciosa Erect, downy stems carry attractive, oppositely arranged, oval leaves, 3 in (8 cm) long and felted in gray both above and below. The pink flower clusters are looser than in other species and appear in the leaf joints as well as at stem tips. They are followed by large, hairy, rather drooping, sometimes spiny seedpods. Good in dry conditions, tolerates part-shade amid a family of sun-lovers, and is restrained at the root. From dry areas in western North America. ↕ 3¼–4 ft (1–1.2 m). Z3–9 H9–1

A. syriaca Familiar North American roadside plant with upright stems arising from often aggressive fleshy roots. The rather fat, oval, oppositely arranged leaves, up to 10 in (25 cm) long, are bluish on their undersides. The handsome, loose, nodding, rounded heads of cream and pink scented flowers are carried in the upper leaf joints, and the fat, horned, softly spiny, 3–4 in (8–10 cm) seedpods with their silky contents are always striking. Not from Syria, but from eastern North America. ↕ 3¼–5 ft (1–1.5 m). Z3–9 H9–2

A. tuberosa (Butterfly weed) A tuberous, altogether hairy plant with many stout, upright, unbranched stems and long, slender, pale leaves arranged spirally. The eye-catching flowers, from midsummer to early fall, are in a truly shocking shade of pumpkin orange (or sometimes red or yellow) and carried in generous clusters in the leaf joints along the upper portion of the stems. These are followed by pods up to 5 in (13 cm) long. Excellent as both garden

ABOVE *Asclepias tuberosa*

accents and cut flowers; the milky sap can be messy when stems are cut, but cutting encourages further flower production, extending the show by a month or more. Prefers dry, sandy soil, but does not object to relatively fertile soil. Grows poorly in clay. From the eastern and southern US. ↕ 24–36 in (60–90 cm). Z4–9 H9–2. **Gay Butterflies Group** These expand the color realm into golds, scarlet, pink, and bicolor yellow and orange flowers, on more compact plants. ↕ 24–36 in (60–90 cm). **'Hello Yellow'** Yellow verging on gold, and earlier to flower. Tolerant of poor, dry soil.

ASPERULA
RUBIACEAE

A trouble-free, summer-flowering perennial good for moderately dry, alkaline soil. Alpine enthusiasts value those species that develop tight cushions.

This genus, which comprises a large group of approximately 90 species of annuals, perennials, and alpines, is closely related to *Galium* (Bedstraw). Most come from the Mediterranean and southwestern Asia. The Latin name *Asperula* refers to the characteristically rough leaves, which are arranged like a ruff, in tiers of four to eight leaflets around the square stems. Small but pretty flowers in pink, white, or yellow are usually held in branching heads above the foliage. When dry, the leaves and stems are often aromatic.

CULTIVATION Of the 15 or so cultivated species, many are dwarf plants suited to the rock garden or alpine house, with just one widely grown as a perennial. Most species need sun or light shade and well-drained soil, disliking winter dampness on their crowns.

PROPAGATION By cuttings, division, and from seed.

PROBLEMS Usually trouble-free.

A. tinctoria (Dyer's woodruff) Forms a bushy mat, spreading by horizontal orange roots that are a source of red dye. Upright or semi-trailing stems are have clusters of four to six very narrow, rough-edged leaves about 1½ in (4 cm) long. Airy, branching flowerheads of tiny white three-lobed flowers, about ⅛ in (4 mm) across, open above the foliage in early and midsummer. Flowers most freely and growth is densest in a sunny spot in well-drained and preferably alkaline soil, but will grow in bright shade and average soil. Propagate by division. From woodland edges, grassland and rocky slopes in central and southern Europe. ↕12–24 in (30–60 cm). Z4–8 H8–1

ASPHODELINE
Jacob's rod
ASPHODELACEAE

Striking, upright plants with spikes of showy yellow or white flowers above clumps of grassy foliage in early summer.

About 15 deciduous biennial and perennial species grow in dry, sunny meadows and scrub in the Mediterranean region, Turkey, and the Caucasus; three are worth trying but only one is widely grown. Fleshy root systems support dense tufts of gray–green, grasslike leaves. In late spring, leafy stems appear, terminating in dense spikes of starry yellow flowers, giving a strong architectural quality. Ideal for a gravel garden.

BELOW 1 *Asphodeline lutea*
2 *Asphodelus albus*

CULTIVATION Any well-drained soil in full sun.

PROPAGATION From seed or by division.

PROBLEMS Usually trouble-free.

A. liburnica Clump-forming plant with very narrow bluish green leaves to 8 in (20 cm) long. Pale yellow flowers, 2 in (5 cm) across, striped green on the back of each petal, are borne in spikes in early and midsummer. From sunny meadows in Austria and Italy to the eastern Mediterranean region. ↕3¼ ft (1 m). Z6–9 H9–6

A. lutea (Yellow asphodel) Tufted plant; many linear gray-green leaves to 12 in (30 cm) long. In late spring and early summer, erect leafy stems bear many fragrant, star-shaped, yellow flowers, 1¼ in (3 cm) across, in a dense spike. Each petal has a brownish line along the midrib on the back. The asphodel of Greek mythology; from the Balkan peninsula and the Aegean. ↕3¼–5 ft (1–1.5 m). Z6–9 H9–6. **'Gelbkerze'** syn. 'Yellow Candle' Seed-raised selection with slightly longer flower spikes. .

A. taurica Compact plant with very narrow leaves to 8 in (20 cm) long and dense spikes of white flowers to 1 in (2.5 cm) across, each petal with a buff central vein. From dry, open places in Greece, the Caucasus, and western Asia. ↕12–24 in (30–60 cm). Z6–9 H9–6

ASPHODELUS
Asphodel
ASPHODELACEAE

Tall, sun-loving plants from the Mediterranean with striking spikes of flowers in early summer.

Twelve annual and deciduous or evergreen perennial species are found growing in dry, rocky places in the Mediterranean region, from southwestern and southern Europe to North Africa and western Asia. Two species are commonly grown, others are worth trying. The stout

rootstock produces a clump of narrow grasslike leaves. Star-shaped white or soft pink flowers, often with a brown midvein on each petal, open in early summer in dense spikes or branched, airy sprays.

CULTIVATION Grow in moderately fertile, well-drained soil in full sun. Mulch for winter protection.

PROPAGATION From seed or by careful division.

PROBLEMS Usually trouble-free.

A. aestivus Imposing evergreen plant with strap-shaped, leathery leaves to 16 in (40 cm) long. From mid-spring to early summer, tall branched stems carry many brown-veined, white or pale pink flowers 2–2¾ in (5–7 cm) across. From dry, stony places in southern Europe and western Turkey. ↕3¼–6½ ft (1–2 m). Z7–10 H10–7

A. albus Deciduous; forms clump of grassy leaves to 24 in (60 cm) long. Unbranched, leafless stem bears a spike of starry white flowers 1¼–1½ in (3–4 cm) across, opening from mid-spring to early summer. A brown vein on each petal gives the flowers an off-white tinge. From southern Europe and North Africa. ↕3¼ ft (1 m). Z7–11 H12–7

ASPLENIUM
Spleenwort
ASPLENIACEAE

Startlingly varied and widespread ferns, that include some fine garden plants.

About 700 species are scattered across temperate and tropical regions; although the majority come from the warmer areas of the world, several are hardy in colder climates. Compact, occasionally creeping, rhizomes carry usually evergreen fronds that vary enormously in shape from undivided to repeatedly dissected. The fronds of most have a slightly leathery texture. Aspleniums

are defined by their elongated spore-bearing areas, which, in most species, are formed individually along the frond segments. Species hybridize with each other, and sometimes with species in other fern genera. In recent years, species from warm-temperate regions of the Southern Hemisphere have been introduced, but their value and hardiness is still being assessed.

CULTIVATION All species like shade and good drainage. In many cases, gritty soil is ideal, and most prefer alkaline conditions.

PROPAGATION By division or from spores; leaf-base propagation for *A. scolopendrium* (see panel).

PROBLEMS Slugs and snails (see Problems with Asplenium, p. 78).

A. dareoides Creeping rhizomes eventually form a small patch; support evergreen, lance-shaped, somewhat leathery, bright green, more or less triangular fronds twice divided into opposite pairs of rounded segments. Very hardy; needs good drainage but does well in north-facing borders with dappled shade. From South America, often growing as an epiphyte on trees in Chile. ↕6 in (15 cm). Z6–8 H8–6.

A. scolopendrium syn. *Phyllitis scolopendrium* (Hart's tongue fern) Erect, non-creeping rhizome carrying usually evergreen, upright or arching, undivided, strap-shaped, usually mid-green fronds to 24 in (60 cm) long and about 2 in (5 cm) wide. Spores are produced on the underside of the frond in long thin brown structures arranged in herringbone fashion in opposite pairs. An asset in a fern border, as the simple, glossy fronds give an attractive contrast to the more delicately divided species. Best in dappled shade in neutral to alkaline soil and with good drainage. Mature plants will recover from extreme drought. A huge number of cultivars have been named: in 1890, 445 from Britain alone were listed, but

LEFT *Asplenium scolopendrium*

walls at the nursery of fern pioneer Reginald Kaye in Lancashire, England. ↕8–12 in (20–30 cm). **Marginatum Group** Narrow fronds with a saw-edged margin differ from Angustatum Group in having a narrow ridge of tissue running the length of the underside of the frond just inside the margin. ↕12 in (30 cm). **Muricatum Group** Upper surface of the frond speckled with pimples. ↕12 in (30 cm). **Ramomarginatum Group** Narrow, irregularly forked fronds with a saw-edged margin and a narrow ridge of tissue running the length of the underside. ↕12 in (30 cm). **Ramosum Group** Fronds split into crests in the lower half of their length. ↕12–16 in (30–40 cm). **Undulatum Group** syn. 'Crispum Fertile'. Similar to the Crispum Group but fertile. The spore-bearing structures on the underside stiffens the frond a little and causes the undulations to be shallower and more irregular. ↕12–16 in (30–40 cm).

A. trichomanes (Maidenhair spleenwort) A charming small, usually evergreen, tuft-forming fern with short, slowly creeping or upright rhizomes. Narrowly lance-shaped fronds, 2–8 in (5–20 cm) long, are composed of many opposite pairs of rounded dark green leaflets borne on a shiny black midrib. Best in dappled shade in well-drained, acidic or alkaline soil, but can stand full sun. Propagate from spores—division is difficult. There are many hard-to-distinguish subspecies. Usually found growing on walls or rocks and widely distributed around the world including northwestern Europe. ↕4–8 in (10–20 cm). Z5–8 H8–3. **Incisum Group** Pretty form with deeply incised leaflets.

ASTER

Michaelmas daisy

ASTERACEAE

Classic fall flowers for gardens large and small.

More than 250 species are native to Europe, Asia, and North America, with the greatest numbers in the latter. They are mostly late summer- and fall-flowering, with a few blooming in spring and early

summer. The common name arises from the flowering time of late September, which coincides with Michaelmas Day in Britain (September 29). Many cultivars have been introduced since the end of the 19th century, and these form an important part of the display in fall gardens throughout the temperate regions of the world. Historically, asters have always been valued as cut flowers, and huge numbers are produced by the worldwide cut-flower industry.

Most asters form woody clumps with new shoots rising from the bases of previous years' flowering stems. Some have a central clump formed in this way from which shoots spread outward each spring. The size of clumps and the speed of growth varies greatly between different species and cultivars. Leaves are pale to dark green or gray-green, typically long and narrow, often lance-shaped but sometimes oval or heart-shaped. Leaves at the base of flowering stems and rising directly from the root clumps can often be larger than those higher up.

Flowering stems rise to heights between 6 in and 8 ft (15 cm and 2.5 m) with many being around 4 ft (1.2 m) in height. Flowering sprays can branch into bushy mounds, pyramids, graceful spires, or stiff stems bearing a flat-topped head of short sprays. Individual flowers can be as small as ½ in (1 cm) across or up to a comparatively massive 2 in (5 cm) in diameter. The petals, more correctly called ray florets, can be as few as five in some wild plants or as many as 250 in a modern double-flowered cultivar. Wild plants mostly have rays in white or pale shades of violet, lavender, purple, and pink, with deeper colors occurring more rarely. Cultivars offer a wider range of colors, including many rich and deep shades, but excluding yellow and orange rays. The central zones of the flowers comprise as many as 300 tiny disk florets. The overall color of this central disk is usually yellow, but, purple, orange, and brown are also seen.

CULTIVATION Most asters need a sunny position, although a few grow

many are impossible to distinguish and the names of even the more distinct and widely grown cultivars have become confused. Scattered through the northern temperate regions of Asia and North America and common in northwestern Europe. ↕6–24 in (15–60 cm). Z6–8 H8–6. **Angustatum Group** syn. Fimbriatum Group Narrow fronds with a saw-edged margin. ↕12–15 in (30–40 cm). **Crispum Group** Sterile fronds are deeply crisped. The leafy part is much longer than the midrib and since the midrib remains straight, the leafy section has to ripple and fold on itself to fit. The usually sterile fronds are less leathery. There are many cultivars of this type, most of which are difficult to distinguish. ↕12–21 in (30–60 cm). **'Crispum Bolton's Nobile'** Beautifully crisped fronds up to 4 in (10 cm) broad. ↕12–24 in (30–50 cm). **Cristatum Group** Tips of fronds split into neat crests to no more than halfway to the base. ↕12–16 in (30–40 cm). **Furcatum Group** Frond tips split once or a few times only. Less impressive than Cristatum Group. ↕12 in (30 cm). **'Kaye's Lacerated'** Fronds leathery, broad and deeply cut along the margins. A chance find on

DAISY CHAINS

COMBINING DAISIES will give you a variety of cheerful effects. Choose two cultivars of different genera but with an identical shape from the daisy family—in this case, *Aster amellus* 'King George' and *Rudbeckia fulgida* var. *deamii*—and plant them so that they mingle together. Here the cultivars are selected so the ray florets are entirely different in color. However, the yellow of the rudbeckia rays harmonizes with the yellow eyes of the aster, and so holds the grouping together in another way.

THE NAME ASTER

In recent years, botanical science has seen significant advances in genetic and molecular studies, and such work is now being used increasingly in the classification of plants. One of the results of using these techniques is that researchers in North America have discovered that the plants grown for so long under the name *Aster* are members of a number of distinctly different groups rather than one unified group.

The most significant implication of this research is the proposition that there are no true asters native to North America. In other words, the *Aster* species from North America are so distinctly different, in genetic structure, to those native to Europe and Asia that they do not belong in the genus *Aster* at all. This has resulted in the proposal to rename many North America Aster species *Symphyotrichum*, with others treated as *Eurybia*, *Seriocarpus*, or placed in a number of other smaller genera.

In the light of the unfortunate transfer of garden chrysanthemums to the genus *Dendranthema*, and then back to *Chrysanthemum*, much to the annoyance of gardeners around the world, here all species are retained in *Aster*. However, gardeners will find the new names are increasingly being used, especially in North America.

naturally at the edges of woods and are tolerant of dappled shade. While most thrive in a wide range of soil conditions, some asters demand good winter drainage and others will grow where the ground is moist year-round. The best results come from plants growing in well-textured, fertile soil, capable of retaining summer moisture. Alkaline soil is preferred, and essential for some species, although many will grow acceptably in slightly acidic soil. In the wild, asters find fresh soil by spreading their seeds or sending out creeping shoots to occupy new ground. This need for new soil to promote consistent vigor must be met in gardens by regular division of mature clumps, an operation best done in the early months of spring. It is in the nature of asters to produce huge quantities of fertile seed, and it is important to be constantly on guard against the danger of the (usually inferior), offspring engulfing the parent or neighboring plants. In formal garden plantings asters over about 3¼ ft (1 m) tall, will need support against wind and rain damage.

PROPAGATION By division, softwood cuttings, and from seed. Division is simple and best carried out in early spring. Young rooted pieces can also be detached from the outside of the plant and replanted, although only a few pieces should be taken or the main plant will be seriously weakened. Cuttings can be taken from the tips of new growth in spring; overwinter the resulting plants in a frame or unheated greenhouse and plant them in the garden the following spring. Raising asters from seed is best avoided since seedlings rarely come true.

PROBLEMS The many cultivars of *A. novi-belgii* are the most susceptible to problems. They must be sprayed regularly through spring and summer with a suitable fungicide to prevent powdery mildew. Tarsonemid mite, sometimes called Michaelmas daisy mite, can prevent the development of flower buds but is difficult to control (*see* Mildew and Mites *p. 83*). Most other asters are either less susceptible or entirely resistant to mildew attack and damage from mites. Aster wilt can sometimes attack shoots within a clump and rust may be a problem.

A. amellus (Italian starwort) Neat, very woody but sometimes short-lived clumps produce sturdy stems carrying mildew-resistant, green to gray-green, lance-shaped to broadly oval leaves that are slightly hairy. Branched sprays of comparatively large violet-blue, yellow-eyed flowers are clustered toward the tops from late summer into mid-fall. Flowers of cultivars come in lavender-blue, violet-blue, and purple-pink, and are 2–2½ in (5–6 cm) across. Probably the first aster to be cultivated, it was grown in England in the 16th century by John Gerard. Plants grow best in full sun in alkaline, fertile soil with excellent winter drainage but will also grow in lightly dappled or part-shade. Several of the compact cultivars can be grown as container plants. All are very attractive to butterflies. A parent of the longer-lived *A. x frikartii*. Now rare in central and southeastern Europe, Siberia, the Caucasus, Armenia, and Anatolia. ‡12–36 in (30–90 cm). Z5–8 H8–1. **‘Brilliant’** Bright, purple-pink, 2–2½ in (5–6 cm) flowers in erect sprays on reasonably strong growth. ‡24 in (60 cm). **‘Framfieldii’** Small 2 in (5 cm) lavender-blue flowers, late in the season. Neat, bushy growth. ‡20 in (50 cm). **‘Jacqueline Genebrier’** Small, 2-in (5-cm), rich purple-pink flowers in mid-fall in tall, upstanding sprays. ‡30 in (75 cm). **‘King George’** Large, rich, purple-blue flowers at least 2½ in (6 cm) across in late summer, in lax sprays on strong growth. The best-known cultivar, introduced by Amos Perry in 1914. ‡24 in (60 cm). **‘Lac de Genève’** Small, 2 in (5 cm), pale lavender-blue flowers carried on well-branched sprays. Strong growth. ‡24 in (60 cm). **‘Rosa Erfüllung’** (Pink Zenith) Bright purple-pink, 2–2½ in (5–6 cm) flowers, in early and mid-fall in bushy sprays from strong growth. ‡20 in (50 cm). **‘Rudolf Goethe’** Medium-sized, 2–2½ in (5–6 cm), lavender-blue flowers on strong growth. One of the

RIGHT **1** *Aster amellus* ‘Brilliant’
2 *A. amellus* ‘Rosa Erfüllung’
3 *A.* ‘Coombe Fishacre’
4 *A. cordifolius* ‘Silver Spray’
5 *A. cordifolius* ‘Sweet Lavender’

ASTER 'CLIMAX'

Two slightly different plants are grown under this classic name. The original plant was raised around 1906 by Edwin Beckett, head gardener to the Hon. Vicary Gibbs (see *Aster* 'Hon. Vicary Gibbs').

Features shared by both plants are broad, healthy foliage with good resistance to mildew when properly grown, and vigorous rootstocks producing growth to a height of at least 4½ ft (1.3 m). The flowering sprays of both are in the form of well-shaped spires, bearing perfectly formed flowerheads of 1¾ in (4 cm) diameter in mid-fall. However, one plant has clear lavender-blue rays that are moderately broad and somewhat rounded at the apex. The total number does not normally exceed 50. The other plant has rays of lavender-blue slightly shaded with purple, creating the effect of a less clean color, and can feature dark stems when grown in some soils. The flowers of this plant also have twice as many rays, about 100, and they are quite narrow and pointed at the apex.

It is unlikely that a plant raised as early as 1906 would have a ray count of 100, and all available descriptions mention the clarity of the shade of blue in the ray color of 'Climax' but do not mention dark stems. So it seems clear which is the true plant; the other may be a seedling for which a name is still lacking.

most reliable for less than ideal conditions. ↕ 30 in (75 cm). **'Sonia'** Small, often weak clumps with neat gray-green leaves and pale purple-pink flowers 2 in (5 cm) in mid-fall. The true plant is now difficult to find. ↕ 18 in (45 cm). **'Sonora'** Large, purple-blue flowers at least 2½ in (6 cm) across in upright sprays from neat, strong-growing clumps. One of the best recent cultivars, raised by Karl Foerster in 1966. ↕ 24 in (60 cm). **'Veilchenkönigen'** (**Violet Queen**) Small clumps with bushy sprays of small, 2-in (5-cm), deep violet flowers in mid-fall. Free-flowering. ↕ 16 in (40 cm).

A. **'Climax'** A tall, stately, vigorous plant with broad green, mildew-resistant leaves. Flowering sprays in the form of elegant spires. Large flowers, of excellent shape, 1½ in (4 cm) or more across, have clear, lavender-blue rays and appear from mid-fall. They are lovely at the back of a border and as cut flowers. Raised by Edwin Beckett around 1906 and probably a hybrid of *A. laevis*. There are now two plants being grown under this name (*see* Aster 'Climax') ↕ 4½ ft (1.4 m). Z4–8 H8–1.

A. x *commixtus* see *A.* x *herveyi*

A. **'Coombe Fishacre'** Compact but vigorous clumps carry green leaves and, in early and mid-fall, large numbers of flowers on strong, bushy sprays that branch sideways. The ¾-in (2-cm) flowers have light purple-pink rays and pale yellow disks that soon turn purple-red. Probably a hybrid between *A. lateriflorus* and *A. novi-belgii*, raised around 1920 and named after a South Devonshire hamlet in England. ↕ 36 in (90 cm). Z4–8 H8–1

A. **cordifolius** (Blue wood-aster, Bee-weed) Sturdy, woody clumps of distinctive, mildew-resistant, heart-shaped leaves each spring, some of which are maintained low down on the flowering stems through the growing season. The flowering sprays, opening in early and mid-fall, are erect and much-branched into graceful spires, the individual heads being around ½ in (1 cm) in diameter with 10–15 rays in pale violet, pale lavender, or white. Creates a wonderful misty effect in borders, good for cutting and among the few later-flowering species to grow well in lightly dappled shade. From clearings of woods and thickets in southern Canada and the northern US. ↕ 5 ft (1.5 m). Z5–8 H8–1. **'Chieftain'** Basal leaves large and unusually hairy; good spires of lavender-blue flowerheads. The giant of the group. ↕ 5 ft (1.5 m). **'Elegans'** Dense sprays of white flowerheads suffused with pale violet in mid-fall. 4 ft (1.2 m) **'Silver Spray'** Pale lavender flowerheads on wiry, slightly arching sprays. ↕ 4 ft (1.2 m). **'Sweet Lavender'** Upright stems carry arching branches of lavender-blue flowers in mid-fall. ↕ 4 ft (1.2 m).

A. **divaricatus** (White wood aster) Dense clumps support wiry branched stems that droop to the ground and carry deep green, oval to triangular leaves, up to 2½ in (6 cm) wide. Small, white, starry flowers 1 in (2.5 cm) in diameter with just six to nine petals appear in late summer to early fall. Best in good soil in part-shade, useful as ground cover with shrubs and trees. From open woodlands in eastern North America. ↕ 16 in (40 cm). Z4–8 H8–1. **'Eastern Star'** (syn. 'Raiche Form') Taller, with larger flowers. ↕ 24 in (60 cm).

A. **dumosus** see *A. novii-belgii*

A. **ericoides** (White-heath aster, Frost-weed aster) Neat clumps develop into graceful, arching mounds of flowering stems bearing long, narrow or lance-shaped leaves up to 2½ in (6 cm) and large numbers of flowers that bring gentle colors to brighten up the later days of fall. The flowerheads are ½ in (1 cm) in diameter with 15–25 white rays, sometimes violet, lavender, or purple-pink. Among the most easily

LEFT 1 *Aster ericoides* 'Erlkönig'
2 *A. ericoides* 'Pink Cloud' **3** *A.* x *frikartii* 'Wunder von Stäfa' **4** *A. lateriflorus* 'Horizontalis' **5** *A. novae-angliae* 'Andenken an Alma Pötschke' **6** *A. novae-angliae* 'Harrington's Pink' **7** *A. novae-angliae* 'Herbstschnee' **8** *A. novae-angliae* 'Purple Dome'

grown of fall asters, they do not need frequent division and will tolerate fairly dry summer growing conditions. Also good for cutting. Mildew is not usually a problem unless plants are under stress. From North America, Maine to Ontario, Canada, Minnesota, Missouri, and Florida. ‡12–48 in (30–120 cm). Z5–8 H8–1. **'Blue Star'** Lavender-blue. ‡36 in (90 cm). **'Brimstone'** Yellow buds open to good white flowers; erect growth. ‡48 in (120 cm). **'Erlkönig'** Pale lavender, strong growth. ‡48 in (120 cm). **'Esther'** Lovely purple-pink sprays and very compact, but weak, clumps. ‡20 in (50 cm). **'Golden Spray'** Dense sprays of flowers with narrow white rays and prominent golden-yellow disks. ‡36 in (90 cm). **'Pink Cloud'** Arching sprays of pale purple-pink flowerheads on strong growth. ‡36 in (90 cm). **f. prostratus 'Snow Flurry'** Fine, needlelike foliage forms wide carpets of pale green leaves, covered by tiny snow-white flowerheads in mid-fall and sometimes into late fall. Grow over dry stone walls, rocks, or gravel. A unique, lovely, and useful plant. ‡8 in (20 cm). **'White Heather'** Spirelike sprays of white flowers. ‡48 in (120 cm).

A. x frikartii Renowned for its vigor and long flowering season, coupled with complete resistance to mildew. The much-branched stems carry dark green, slightly rough, oblong foliage. The flowerheads, from midsummer to mid-fall, are 1½–3 in (4–8 cm) across, and have up to 50 narrow rays in lavender-blue or violet. A small and desirable group of plants, most suited to lighter alkaline loams where good winter drainage can be assured. Always plant young stock in the spring and remember to divide mature clumps in the same season. Taller sorts will sometimes need some support. A hybrid between the European

A. amellus and the Himalayan A. thomsonii (see The Problem of Aster x frikartii). ‡18–36 in (45–90 cm). Z5–8 H8–1. **'Eiger'** Slender, arching branches carry broad, green, lance-shaped leaves and 2-in (5-cm) flowers with violet rays. Intermediate in height between 'Jungfrau' and 'Mönch', with flowers similar to those of 'Jungfrau'. The least-often seen. ‡32 in (80 cm). **'Flora's Delight'** Compact, bushy growth with broadly lance-shaped, gray-green leaves and 1½ in (4 cm) flowerheads with pale violet rays, slightly tinged with pink. ‡18 in (45 cm). **'Jungfrau'** Bushy, with broad green lance-shaped leaves. The flowerheads are 2 in (5 cm) in diameter and the rays are colored violet. Later-flowering. ‡24 in (60 cm). **'Mönch'** Vigorous with thin, well-branched stems, oblong green leaves, and 3 in (8 cm) flowerheads with narrow rays in light violet-blue to lavender-blue according to soil conditions. Justifiably, one of the most popular asters ever raised, combining hybrid vigor with disease resistance and a long flowering season. ‡36 in (90 cm). **'Wunder von Stäfa'** Similar in all respects to 'Mönch'; but shorter-growing. ‡30 in (75 cm). (See The Problem of Aster x frikartii.)

A. 'Herfstweelde'. Compact yet prolific clumps carry 1¼-in (3-cm) flowerheads with lavender-blue rays and pale centers in mid-fall. Similar to cultivars of A. ericoides but with more robust flowering sprays and suitable for borders or naturalized planting where winter hardiness is good. Also an excellent cut flower. Raised by Piet Oudolf in Holland. ‡4 ft (1.2 m). Z4–8 H8–1

A. x herveyi syn. Aster x commixtus 'Twilight', A. macrophyllus 'Twilight' Valuable plant for late-summer color.

From vigorous, spreading clumps arise stiff, erect stems carrying mildew-resistant, deep green oval leaves up to 6 in (15 cm) long which, in late summer, branch at the top into sprays bearing 1¼-in (3-cm) flowerheads with rays in violet-blue. A hybrid between A. macrophyllus and A. spectabilis, it was previously thought to be a selection of A. macrophyllus. From the northeastern US. ‡36 in (90 cm). Z4–8 H8–1

A. 'Hon. Vicary Gibbs' Tall and vigorous but with elegant sprays of clear, light lavender-blue flowerheads, each about ¾ in (2 cm) across, in mid-fall. Needs support. A hybrid of A. ericoides, probably with A. cordifolius, raised by British aster breeder Edwin Beckett and named for his employer, the merchant banker, historian, politician, and editor of The Complete Peerage or A History of the House of Lords & All Its Members from the Earliest Time. ‡5 ft (1.5 m). Z4–8 H8–1

A. 'Kylie' Lax, arching sprays bearing clouds of ½ in (1 cm) wide flowerheads with pale pink rays. Resistant to mildew. A hybrid of A. novae-angliae 'Andenken an Alma Pötschke' and A. ericoides 'White Heather', raised by British aster enthusiastern Ron Watts. ‡4 ft (1.2 m). Z4–8 H8–1

A. laevis (Smooth aster) Variable in the wild, making strong clumps with mildew-resistant leaves up to 5 in (13 cm) long and broadly lance-shaped, thick, smooth and bright green. The flowering sprays are strong, with open branches, and often have noticeably purple stems supporting 1-in (2.5-cm) flowerheads with 15–30 lavender or violet rays. An important contributor to the vast race of hybrid plants we know as A. novi-belgii (see panel, p.82). Some cultivars reach 6½ ft (2 m). From North America. ‡4 ft (1.2 m). Z4–8 H8–1. **'Arcturus'** Flowering stems nearly black, open-branched sprays supporting deep rosy lilac flowerheads in early fall. ‡4 ft (1.2 m). **'Bluebird'** Violet-blue, 1-in (2.5-cm) flowers over disease-free foliage. **'Calliope'** Flowerheads are lilac-purple, at their best in mid-fall. Often mistakenly sold as 'Arcturus'. ‡6½ ft (2 m).

A. lanceolatus A tough plant with vigorous, spreading growth, pale green lance-shaped leaves and flowering stems that form graceful spires. The flowerheads, ¾ in (2 cm) across, are white or pale violet in mid-fall. Best in heavy, moisture-retentive soil. From the northeastern US. ‡6 ft (1.8 m). Z4–8 H8–1. **'Edwin Beckett'** Slightly larger flowerheads, 1 in (2.5 cm) wide, with pale violet-blue rays. Good in a wild garden and for cut flowers.

A. lateriflorus (Calico aster) Among the best asters for general planting, clumps are compact yet vigorous and the slightly arching flowering stems form a dense thicket. Light, bronze-purple spring shoots rise from strong clumps that may remain undivided for several years; they carry lance-shaped to oval

ORIGINS OF THE MICHAELMAS DAISY

Due to its inclination to hybridize readily in the wild and in gardens with many other North American species of Aster, the huge number of cultivars which, over the years, have appeared under the name of A. novi-belgii are in fact a very varied group that are mostly hybrids. The principal species that have found their way into this group, along with A. novi-belgii, under which they are listed, are: A. cordifolius, A. dumosus, A. ericoides, A. laevis, A. lateriflorus, A. lanceolatus, A. paniculatus, A. pilosus, and A. puniceus. They continue to be listed under A. novi-belgii mainly because their hybrid parentage is so uncertain.

These asters have been especially popular in the UK and Europe since the end of the 19th century. There is great diversity in the height and spread of plants and in the shape of the flowering sprays and colors of the flowers. The flowering season extends from late summer into mid-fall, according to cultivar, and the flowers can be from 1 in (2.5 cm) up to 2 in (5 cm) across. Flowers are classed as single or double depending on the number of rays; those referred to as double will have several rows of petals. Overall growth varies from low, compact mounds to tall, graceful sprays. Specially developed cultivars are extensively used in the commercial cut flower industry.

The path to fall border domination is, unfortunately, strewn with obstacles—in particular, susceptibility to powdery mildew and attack from tarsonemid mite (see Mildew and Mites, p.83). If these problems could be solved, even more cultivars would doubtless be introduced.

THE PROBLEM OF ASTER x FRIKARTII

Aster x frikartii is a hybrid between A. thomsonii from the Himalaya and A. amellus, from Europe. The cross was first made by the Reverend Wolley-Dod, who exhibited his flowers in 1892, but nothing more was heard of his plant.

Then, in about 1918, Karl Frikart introduced three forms through his Stäfa Nursery in Switzerland and named them for the three alpine peaks 'Eiger', 'Junfrau', and 'Mönch'. He followed them, in 1924, with 'Wunder von Stäfa' which we can assume must have been an improvement—or at least different. For nearly 50 years there was no more development until Alan Bloom introduced 'Flora's Delight', named after his wife, in 1964. This plant, from a cross made in 1954, used specific cultivars—the dwarf A. thomsonii 'Nanus' and the pink A. amellus 'Sonia'.

All five forms of A. x frikartii are fine garden plants, but there has been great confusion between the two best known, 'Mönch' and 'Wunder von Stäfa'. They seem very similar, but many people have claimed to know the distinctions between the two. However, it now

seems likely that the stocks have become thoroughly mixed and that, perhaps, there was less difference than we might assume in the first place.

There are two other complicating factors. Seed of A. x frikartii has sometimes been offered by seed companies. The plants often turn out to be forms of A. amellus or, if true hybrids, are bound to be variable. The final problem is that the original four A. x frikartii cultivars show tremendous variation in height, vigor, and ray color according to their growing conditions. Divisions from a single plant, grown in six locations around the same garden, have varied so much that they would seem to be six different cultivars.

Plants obtained in 2002 as 'Wunder von Stäfa' for the National Collection in Colwall have been grown for three years in a trial alongside 'Mönch' and have remained consistently shorter. But the breeder's records do not tell us which of his two popular cultivars is the taller. All are superb, mildew-resistant plants—buy from a specialist and be sure you are not sold a seedling.

leaves. Flowering sprays are usually wiry and bushy, often with horizontal side branches, and carry flowerheads between ½ in (1 cm) and ¾ in (2 cm) across with narrow, white rays numbering only nine–fifteen. A distinctive feature is the pale yellow disk that quickly ages to purple-pink, creating the "calico" effect. Flowering is in early and mid-fall, even into late fall. Thrives in sun or dappled shade, although bronze-leaved cultivars are best in sun. Fairly resistant to mildew but not totally reliable. From southern Canada, through the northeastern US to Texas. ‡4¼ ft (1.3 m). Z4–8 H8–1. **'Horizontalis'** Compact bushy growth, the leaves purple-tinted in spring, with horizontal, spreading branches hidden by myriad ½ in (1 cm) white-rayed flowerheads with rich purple-pink disks. ‡20 in (50 cm). **'Jan'** Bushy plant with unusually large flowerheads, up to 1¼ in (3 cm). Probably a hybrid with A. novi-belgii. ‡32 in (80 cm). **'Lady in Black'** Bright, bronze-purple spring foliage, fading only slightly in summer, with tall, graceful flowering sprays holding flowerheads with white rays and yellow disks. ‡4½ ft (1.3 m). **'Prince'** Rich bronze-purple spring

ASTER FLOWER STRUCTURE

Aster flowers have the same basic structure as so many members of the daisy family (Asteraceae). In the center of each flower is a central disk of tiny fertile flowers, the disk florets, which are usually yellow or orange, but sometimes in shades of brown, purple, or white. In one or two rings around these, the ray flowers, which may or may not be fertile, have one long colored ray (the ligule). Protecting the flower in bud is the involucre of bracts.

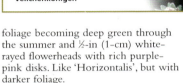

Ray florets

Disc florets

Involucre

Aster amellus
'Veilchenkönigen'

foliage becoming deep green through the summer and ½-in (1-cm) white-rayed flowerheads with rich purple-pink disks. Like 'Horizontalis', but with darker foliage.

A. 'Little Carlow' Generous, dense, woody clumps produce broad, lance-shaped, deep green leaves and masses of sturdy upright flowering sprays branching into plumed heads in early and mid-fall. The generous flowerheads are 1 in (2.5 cm) across, with bright lavender-blue rays. A hybrid between *A. cordifolius* and *A. novi-belgii*, it should be in every garden. Partially resistant to mildew. ‡4 ft (1.2 m). Z4–9 H9–1

A. 'Little Dorrit' Strong-growing clumps with lance-shaped, deep green leaves and sturdy flowering sprays with short branches, forming a spire of bright purple-pink 1-in (2.5-cm) flowerheads in mid-fall. A hybrid between *A. novi-belgii* and *A. cordifolius* raised by Isabel Allen, who formed the largest 20th-century collection of asters, near Bristol, England, between 1940 and 1970. Unfortunately, prone to mildew. ‡4 ft (1.2 m). Z4–8 H8–1

A. macrophyllus (Large-leaved aster) Woody, spreading clumps support rather handsome, broad, oval leaves. Stout, branched flowering stems bear flattened heads of branched sprays, the flowerheads 1 in (2.5 cm) across with 10–16 palest lavender rays in late summer, followed by attractive seed heads. Resistant to mildew. From eastern North America. ‡36 in (90 cm). Z4–8 H8–1. **'Albus'** White petals. **'Twilight'** see *A.* x *herveyi*.

A. novae-angliae (New England aster) Tough, vigorous, woody clumps, tightly packed with shoots, support erect, flowering stems carrying lance-shaped, green to gray-green foliage with coarse hairs, making them rough to touch. Between late summer and mid-fall the stems branch at the top into broad, flattened heads with many flowers, each up to 1½ in (4 cm) in diameter and

with up to 50 narrow rays, which are typically violet-purple but can be pink, reddish, or white and with up to 90 rays in some cultivars. They are followed by a generous seed crop producing mostly purple-flowered plants. The flowering sprays and retention of foliage on the stems deteriorates if the clumps are not lifted and split every two to four years. Most require support. Well suited to prairie-style planting and wild gardens. Relatively mildew-free. From North America, Quebec to Saskatchewan, South Carolina, Alabama, Kansas, and Colorado. ‡4–8 ft (1.2–2.4 m). Z4–8 H8–1. **'Andenken an Alma Pötschke'** Bright cerise-pink flowers about 1¾ in (4.5 cm) on compact growth. ‡36 in (90 cm). **'Barr's Blue'** Purple-blue flowers about 1¾ in (4.5 cm) across on strong growth. ‡4 ft (1.2 m). **'Barr's Pink'** Large rosy pink flowers more than 2 in (5 cm) across on robust growth. ‡5 ft (1.5 m). **'Barr's Violet'** Violet-blue flowers, about 1¾ in (4.5 cm) across; a deeper shade than 'Barr's Blue'. ‡4 ft (1.2 m). **'Harrington's Pink'** Small 1–1½-in (2.5–3.5-cm) flowers in pale rose-pink. Discovered in the wild in Canada by Millard Harrington, a farmer, and introduced by Perry's Nurseries in 1943. ‡5 ft (1.5 m). **'Hella Lacy'** Large, light violet-blue flowers more than 2 in (5 cm) across. A strong grower, similar to 'Mrs. S. T. Wright'. Found in a few New Jersey gardens by the American garden writer Allen Lacy. Especially attractive to butterflies. ‡4 ft (1.2 m). **'Herbstschnee'** White flowers about 1¾ in (4.5 cm) across. The only white cultivar now available. ‡4 ft (1.2 m). **'Lye End Beauty'** Bright purple-pink 2-in (5-cm) flowers on strong sprays. ‡4½ ft (1.4 m). **'Mrs. S. T. Wright'** Large, pale violet-blue flowers more than 2 in (5 cm) across. Similar to 'Hella Lacey', this robust plant dates from before 1907. ‡5 ft (1.5 m). **'Purple Cloud'** Purple-blue flowers more than 2 in (5 cm) across on vigorous growth. ‡6 ft (1.8 m). **'Purple Dome'** Violet-purple, 1–1½-in (2.5–

3.5-cm) flowers late in season on compact mounded growth. Found on a Pennsylvania roadside. ‡24 in (60 cm). **'Rosa Sieger'** Large rose pink flowers more than 2 in (5 cm) across. ‡4 ft (1.2 m). **'Sayer's Croft'** Purple-pink flowers more than 2 in (5 cm) across. ‡3¼ ft (1 m). **'Septemberrubin'** (**September Ruby**) Purple-red flowers more than 2 in (5 cm). ‡4¼ ft (1.3 m).

A. novi-belgii syn. *A. dumosus* (New York aster) Strong-growing, erect but very variable plant bearing smooth, oval or lance-shaped leaves, sometimes slightly toothed, 2–6 in (5–15 cm) in length. From late summer to mid-fall, flowerheads up to 2 in (5 cm) diameter are carried on well-branched sprays and are usually violet-blue, though other colors are quite common. These are followed by copious quantities of fertile seed that often produces many self-sown seedlings. Grow in a sunny location in fertile soil that will retain moisture in the summer months. The best flower production comes from plants that are divided every year or grown from single offsets. Taller varieties are best supported. Regular spraying to prevent powdery mildew is essential in most areas. Tarsonemid mite can ruin the buds but is, unfortunately, impossible for home gardeners to control (*see* Mildew and Mites, p.83). Many cultivars are hybrids with other species, in particular *A. laevis* (*see* Origins of the Michaelmas Daisy, p.81). Widespread in eastern North America and cultivated in gardens since 1710. ‡4 ft (1.2 m). Z4–8 H8–1. **'Alice Haslam'** Pale red, single, 1-in (2.5-cm) flowers in late summer. Neat, mounding growth. ‡10 in (25 cm). **'Albanian'** Clear white, double flowers about 2 in (5 cm) across in sturdy, open sprays. Useful cut flower. ‡3¼ ft (1 m). **'Alert'** Bushy and erect with rich reddish purple, double, 1–2-in (2–

ASTER NOVI-BELGII

Translated, *novi-belgii* means New Belgium but there is, of course, no such place and never was. It came about because Paul Hermann, the German botanist who coined the name in 1687, was attempting to name the plant for New Holland, at that time the name for the region of eastern North America between the 40th and 45th parallel—from Philadelphia north to the coastal border with Canada. This area, which had been colonized by the Dutch in the early 17th century, is the center of distribution for this species, although it can be found as far south as Florida.

The name is curious not only because of its clumsy rendition of New Holland as *novi-belgii*, but because more than 20 years earlier the British had renamed the area New York. So Paul Hermann was doubly mistaken—and when Carl Linnaeus formalized the name in his *Species Plantarum* of 1753 he failed to notice the mistake.

5-cm) flowers. Short and neat, so good for containers. ‡12 in (30 cm). **'Audrey'** Mauve-blue, 1-in (2.5-cm) flowers on strong dwarf clumps. ‡12 in (30 cm). **'Blue Eyes'** Rich lavender-blue, 1¾-in (4.5-cm), single flowers carried generously on strong sprays. Vigorous clumps that need not be divided frequently. ‡4½ ft (1.4 m). **'Blue Gown'** Spires of 2-in (5-cm), single, lavender-blue flowers on strong clumps. Very late, rather like a late, slightly ragged version of 'Climax'. ‡3¼ ft (1 m). **'Blue Lagoon'** Violet-blue, single flowers about 2 in (5 cm) across on strong mounding clumps.

BELOW 1 *Aster novi-belgii* 'Kristina'
2 *A. novi-belgii* 'Patricia Ballard'

‡20 in (50 cm). **'Blue Radiance'** Superb, light lavender-blue, 2-in (5-cm) single flowers. Modest to weak growth, so in most soils needs careful cultivation. Wonderful when well grown. ‡36 in (90 cm). **'Cantonese Queen'** Purple-blue flowers about 2 in (5 cm) across. Foliage is, uniquely, suffused with yellow during the growing season. ‡24 in (60 cm). **'Chatterbox'** Pale pink flowers about 2 in (5 cm) across. Good mounding growth and strong clumps for borders and containers. ‡14 in (35 cm). **'Chequers'** Deep violet, 1¾-in (4.5-cm) flowers on bushy plants from modest clumps. One of the richest colors at this height. ‡24 in (60 cm). **'Coombe Rosemary'** Double, heather-purple, 1¾-in (4.5-cm) flowers in sturdy sprays. Good as cut flowers. ‡36 in (90 cm). **'Dietgard'** Bright purple-pink, single, 1-in (2.5-cm) flowers late in the season on neat mounds that are lovely in containers as well as edging borders. ‡14 in (35 cm). **'Eventide'** Double, deep lavender-blue flowers about 2 in (5 cm) across early in the season. ‡3¼ ft (1 m). **'Fair Lady'** Bright lilac-blue, 1-in (2.5-cm) double flowers on bushy, compact growth. Good cut flower. ‡36 in (90 cm). **'Fellowship'** Double, pale pink flowers about 2 in (5 cm) across on strong, open sprays late in the season. ‡3¼ ft (1 m). **'Freda Ballard'** Double, bright purple-red, 2-in (5-cm) flowers early in the season. ‡36 in (90 cm). **'Freya'** Double, rich purple-pink flowers about 2 in (5 cm) across on strong growth. ‡3¼ ft (1 m). **'Gayborder Royal'** Double, pale lilac-blue, 1-in (2.5-cm) flowers late in the season on compact growth. ‡28 in (70 cm). **'Harrison's Blue'** Double, deep violet-blue, 1¾-in (4.5-cm) flowers late in the season. ‡3¼ ft (1 m). **'Heinz Richard'** Bright purple-pink double flowers about 2 in (5 cm) across on neat mounds. ‡12 in (30 cm). **'Jenny'** Bright purple-red, double flowers about 2 in (5 cm) across on compact growth. Good in both containers and borders. ‡16 in (40 cm). **'Kristina'** White flowers about 1¾ in (4.5 cm) across, late in the season. Probably the most reliable dwarf cultivar of this color. ‡12 in (30 cm). **'Lady in Blue'** Lavender-blue. Good mounds from strong clumps and suitable for containers and borders. ‡12 in (30 cm). **'Lisa Dawn'** Dusky, purple-red, single flowers early in the season on bushy growth. ‡18 in (45 cm). **'Little Pink Beauty'** Bright mauve-pink flowers about 2 in (5 cm) across on strong growth. ‡14 in (35 cm). **'Marie Ballard'** Clear lavender-blue, perfectly formed double flowers about 2 in (5 cm) across. Considered by many to be the ultimate Michaelmas daisy. ‡3¼ ft (1 m). **'Mary Deane'** Bright purple-pink, double, late-season flowers about 2 in (5 cm) across. ‡4 ft (1.2 m). **'Melbourne Magnet'** Pale violet-blue, double, superbly formal flowers about 2 in (5 cm) across late in the season. ‡36 in (90 cm). **'Mount Everest'** Graceful pyramids of single, white flowers about 2 in (5 cm) across. Indispensable at the

MILDEW AND MITES

They may be tough, colorful, and easy to grow but there are two reasons why asters are still not cultivated as widely as they should be—mildew and mites. Powdery mildew attacks the foliage of *Aster novi-belgii* in the wild and this species and its many cultivars almost always suffer in gardens. *A. divaricatus* growing wild near *A. novi-belgii* does not seem to become infected, so either the disease is very specific in its host or *A. divaricatus,* as well as some other species, has some natural resistance.

The problem is at its most severe in hot, dry seasons, but while plants can be seriously disfigured vigor is rarely reduced significantly. Damage is also usually most severe on the lower foliage, but ugly bare basal growth can be disguised by planting other shorter plants in front or cutting back stems at the front of the clump in early summer. These will regrow and the shorter fresh young growth will hide the bare stems. If spraying, it is important to spray regularly, starting before mildew is seen, and to continue into the fall, not neglecting young shoots emerging at the very edge of the clump late in the season.

Tarsonemid mites, sometimes known as Michaelmas daisy mites, at less than 0.25mm in length, are less obvious—except in the results of their attack. Damage is most clearly seen in the flowers, whose petals fail to open in the usual way but, after the mites have fed in the unopened buds, produce a ragged little rosette of leaves. Plants are also often stunted and may have brown streaks on the stems.

The same mite also attacks strawberries and a wide range of other perennials together with annuals and greenhouse plants. For the home gardener, there is no cure for these mites but they are most common when large numbers of plants are grown together. Treatments are available to commercial growers so infection tends to come with plants bought from poorly managed nurseries. For gardeners, it is largely a case of 'buyer beware'—and the bonfire.

back of a border and as a cut flower. ‡5½ ft (1.6 m). **'Patricia Ballard'** Bright mauve-pink, double flowers about 2 in (5 cm) across early in the season on robust growth. ‡36 in (90 cm). **'Peter Chiswell'** Bright purple-red, double flowers early in the season. Compact and reliable. Good for borders, containers, and cutting. ‡30 in (75 cm). **'Pride of Colwall'** Double, 1-in (2.5-cm) heather-purple flowers in neat, erect sprays. ‡36 in (90 cm). **'Professor Anton Kippenberg'** Lavender-blue, 1¾-in (4.5-cm) flowers on short, strong growth. Very reliable. ‡12 in (30 cm). **'Remembrance'** Lavender-blue, late-season flowers about 2 in (5 cm) across on strong, bushy growth. ‡20 in (50 cm). **'Rosenwitchel'** Deep pink, 1¾-in (4.5-cm) flowers late in the season on strong growth. ‡10 in (25 cm). **'Sandford's White Swan'** Very prolific,

double white, 1¾-in (4.5-cm), early-season flowers. ‡3¼ ft (1 m). **'Schneekissen'** Single, white, 1-in (2.5-cm) flowers late in the season on compact, low mounds. ‡10 in (25 cm). **'Snowsprite'** Double, white, 1¾-in (4.5-cm) flowers on low mounds of modest growth. ‡12 in (30 cm). **'Starlight'** Single, purple-red, flowers about 1¾ in (4.5 cm) across. ‡12 in (30 cm). **'Terry's Pride'** Double, deep purple-pink, 2-in (5-cm) flowers late in the season. Suitable for borders, containers, and cut flowers. ‡18 in (45 cm). **'Trudi Ann'** Deep heather-purple flowers about 2 in (5 cm) across on showy mounds. ‡16 in (40 cm). **'Twinkle'** Bright purple-pink, 1-in (2.5-cm) flowers on strong sprays late in the season. Suitable for cutting. ‡36 in (90 cm). **'Winston S. Churchill'** Single, bright purple-red, 1¾-in (4.5-cm) flowers in bushy sprays. ‡32 in (80 cm). **'Wood's Light Blue'** Single, clear blue flowers on relatively mildew-resistant plants. Good in containers. ‡15 in (38 cm). **'Wood's Pink'** Single, pure pink flowers over dark green, relatively mildew-resistant foliage. Good in containers. ‡15 in (38 cm). **'Wood's Purple'** Clear purple, single flowers. Good in containers. ‡15 in (38 cm).

A. oblongifolius (Aromatic aster) A variable species with woody, rather weak, branching growth from compact clumps. The 1–2-in (2–5-cm) lance-shaped to oblong leaves are aromatic and the stems are topped with prolific ¾-in (2-cm) flowerheads with 15–40 violet rays through early and mid-fall. Similar in general appearance to *A. novae-angliae*, which is without the foliage fragrance. Best in well-drained, alkaline soil in full sun, and unusually tolerant of drought and poor soil. Needs protection from winter rain in many areas, but resistant to mildew. From most of the US except the west. ‡to 3¼ ft (1 m). Z4–8 H8–1. **'Fanny's Aster'** Compact, very bushy, branched sprays. Very late. ‡20 in (50 cm). **'October Skies'** Purple-blue; short but creating wide clumps. Found in southwestern Pennsylvania by *Heuchera* breeder Charles Oliver. ‡18 in (45 cm). **'Raydon's Favorite'** Blue-purple flowers 1½ in (3.5 cm) across over a long season. Much used for roadside plantings. Found on Lookout Mountain in Tennessee. ‡36 in (90 cm).

A. **'Ochtendgloren'** syn. *A.* 'Pink Star'. Compact yet strong clumps have long, narrow, deep green leaves and sturdy, upright sprays with open branches. The 1-in (2.5-cm) flowerheads are medium purple-pink in color and produced prolifically in mid-fall right down to soil level. A superb garden plant, though originally bred as a cut flower. Probably a hybrid between *A. novi-belgii* and *A. pilosus* var. *pringlei*. Selected by Piet Oudolf in Holland. ‡4 ft (1.2 m). Z4–8 H8–1

RIGHT 1 *Aster novi-belgii* 'Professor Anton Kippenberg' **2** *A.* 'Ochtend-gloren' **3** *A. pilosus* var. *pringlei* 'Monte Cassino' **4** *A. sedifolius* 'Nanus'

A. **'Photograph'** Compact, woody clumps carry bold, heart-shaped foliage setting off the graceful, arching, well-branched sprays, creating clouds of flowerheads, each ½ in (15 mm) across, with clear, lavender-blue rays. A pre-1920 cross between *A. cordifolius* and *A. ericoides* and sadly lacking in vigor. ‡3¼ ft (1 m). Z4–8 H8–1

A. *pilosus* (Frost-weed aster) Robust clumps produce strong, erect stems with long, narrow, pale green leaves pointed at the tips and flowering sprays that branch into broad spires in mid-fall. The flowerheads have 15–20 white rays, and are about ⅝ in (1.5 cm) across. From the northeastern US. ‡3¼ ft (1 m). Z4–8 H8–1. **var. demotus** Free-flowering form, wonderful for mass planting. ‡5 ft (1.5 m). **var. pringlei** **'Monte Cassino'** Starry white flowers and very slender foliage, this is the "September flower" of the cut flower trade. Needs excellent drainage.

A. **'Pink Star'** see *A.* 'Ochtendgloren'

A. *pyrenaeus* Robust yet compact clumps support upright stems carrying oblong leaves with pointed tips and producing sprays that develop many spreading branches. The 1½-in (4-cm) flowerheads with 20–30 lilac rays are from late summer to mid-fall.

ASTERS AT COLWALL

It is said that in the 1950s Michaelmas daisies were, after roses, the most popular flowers in the UK. Ernest Ballard, father-in-law of hellebore breeder Helen Ballard and also a chemist in the vinegar industry, was the foremost specialist and introduced a long succession of new cultivars at Colwall Nursery in Herefordshire. His 'Beauty of Colwall' was the first recognizable double.

For many years the nursery manager was Percy Picton, whose eye for a good plant resulted in a wide range of new introductions, and he continued to introduce new asters after Ernest Ballard's death. But in the 1960s interest in asters declined, partly because they did not show themselves off well in the containers used by the rapidly expanding garden center industry and also because a new pest, tarsonemid mite, was proving so troublesome.

Then, from the 1980s, interest in asters increased, fostered by Percy Picton's son Paul, who holds the Aster National Plant Collection at his Old Court Nurseries in Colwall. New breeding programs have been set up in Holland, Israel, New Zealand, South Africa, and the US, mainly with the cut-flower trade in mind, but also for garden plants. Both in these programs and in gardens a wider range of species is being grown, or hybridized with familiar types, and the results are appearing more and more in the fall plantings which are becoming so popular. The garden and nursery at Colwall are again crowded with enthusiasts.

Completely resistant to mildew. From the eastern and western Pyrenees. ‡36 in (90 cm). Z4–8 H8–1. **'Lutetia'** Palest of lilac-blue flowers borne in great abundance on sprays that can branch out to nearly 36 in (90 cm) across. A superb, easy plant. Probably a hybrid with *A. amellus* ‡24 in (60 cm).

A. **'Ringdove'** Strong, compact clumps carry long, narrow foliage and flowering sprays that grow upright and bear arching branches. Flowerheads are ¾ in (2 cm) across with pale lavender rays and prominent, cream-yellow disks. Soft colors for the border or cutting in mid-fall. ‡3¼ ft (1 m). Z4–8 H8–1

A. *schreberi* Strong, spreading clumps are generously covered with attractive pale green, broad, slightly heart-shaped leaves. The arching flowering sprays have smaller, oval leaves with pointed tips. In late summer and early fall, short branches bear large numbers of well-spaced flowerheads, 1¼ in (3 cm) across, with about 10 white rays. Good in shade and perhaps better than the similar *A. divaricatus*. From the eastern US. ‡36 in (90 cm). Z4–8 H8–1

A. *sedifolius* Neat clumps produce narrow, gray-green, mildew-resistant, grassy foliage up to 3 in (8 cm) long. The sturdy flowering sprays branch at the top into broad heads, the massed 1½-in (3.5-cm) flowerheads each having eight–twelve, openly spaced, lavender-blue rays in late summer and early early fall. An easily grown and invaluable plant for sunny borders that associates well with sedums and the shorter rudbeckias. From southern and east-central Europe to northern Asia. ‡32 in (80 cm). Z4–8 H8–1. **'Nanus'** Compact form. ‡18 in (45 cm).

A. *thomsonii* Wiry stems rise from small clumps and carry hairy stems with 4-in (10-cm) oval, pale green leaves that are rough to the touch. Flowerheads 2 in (5 cm) across with about 20 thin, clear lavender-blue rays appear on slender branches from midsummer to mid-fall. Less easy to grow than most; best in well-drained, even gritty, alkaline soil, with spring and summer moisture and in sun or very lightly cast shade. Resistant to mildew. For an open position where other plants will not encroach. Rarely seen but important as a parent of the invaluable *A.* x *frikartii*. From the Himalaya. ‡36 in (90 cm). Z4–8 H8–1. **'Nanus'** Charming, compact, much more widely grown version; lovely in containers. ‡12 in (30 cm).

A. *tongolensis* Smallish, spreading plant with 3½-in (9-cm), slightly hairy, oblong leaves, pointed at the tips, carried on wiry stems that in early and midsummer bear solitary 1½–2-in (4–5-cm) flowerheads with lavender-blue rays and orange disks. Best in free-draining soil with spring moisture. Resistant to mildew. Cultivars can be prolific and showy. From western China to India. ‡20 in (50 cm). Z5–8 H8–1. **'Berggarten'** Bright violet-blue. ‡8 in (20 cm). **'Napsbury'** Deep violet.

‡12 in (30 cm). **'Wartburgstern'** Violet-blue. ‡16 in (40 cm).

A. *tradescantii* (Tradescant's aster) Vigorous, spreading, sometimes invasive clumps feature narrow, bright green leaves, pointed at the tips and up to 6 in (15 cm) long. The long, erect sprays branch into plumed heads, each with white-rayed ⅝-in (1.5-cm) flowerheads in mid-fall. Useful in wilder areas. From eastern North America. ‡5 ft (1.5 m). Z4–8 H8–1

A. *turbinellus* Strong clumps and graceful sprays, with wiry stems tinted purple-brown. The deep green leaves are long, thin and pointed at the tips; the 1½-in (3-cm) flowerheads have 20–30 bright violet-blue rays in mid-fall. An attractive plant in spite of its tendency to lose its lower leaves. Needs support and can be prone to mildew. Probably a more vigorous hybrid that has usurped the true, rarely grown species. ‡1.5m (5ft). Z4–8 H8–1

A. *umbellatus* (Flat-topped white aster) Strong, spreading clumps send up a thicket of stout shoots that develop into stiff, self-supporting, flowering stems, with broad, lance-shaped, green leaves, up to 6 in (16 cm) long. In late summer the sprays branch into wide, prolific, flat-topped heads carrying large numbers of ¾-in (2-cm) flowers with up to 15 dull white rays. Resistant to mildew. An impressive, stately plant and equally sensational in early and mid-fall when the silvery, fluffy seed heads are at their best. From northeastern North America. ‡5 ft (1.5 m). Z4–8 H8–1

ASTEROMOEA see KALIMERIS

ASTILBE
SAXIFRAGACEAE

Graceful, colorful, and hardy midsummer flowers for bold plantings in moist situations.

About 14 species of deciduous plants that grow in damp, grassy places and open woods in East Asia and eastern North America—four or five of which are grown in gardens. Woody rhizomes give rise to a mound of toothed leaves that may be simply lobed, or divided into many oval leaflets. The leaves are often attractively bronze-tinged, especially when young. In summer and early fall, small white, pink, red, or purple flowers open in foamy sprays on erect stems. Each tiny flower has five spoon-shaped or narrower petals, ten stamens (male parts), and two tiny seed capsules but in male plants the capsules may be rudimentary and nonfunctional. (The similar but unrelated goat's-beard, *Aruncus*, differs in having about 25 stamens and three seedpods.) Aging flower sprays turn rust-colored and often persist into early winter. Astilbes are elegant plants for open situations in moist soil, and are most effective when they are massed. Their airy sprays of

ORGANIZING ASTILBES

Astilbes hybridize quite freely, and there are now some 200 cultivars in cultivation. It is these hybrid cultivars that predominate in gardens, because of their wider range of colors and longer flowering season. Various hybrid groups have been named, based on their presumed parentage, but this is not an exact science. The main groups are:

Astilbe x arendsii Complex hybrids involving *A. chinensis* and *A. chinensis* var. *davidii*, *A. thunbergii*, *A. grandis*, and *A. japonica*. Most are tall plants with erect, tapering conical plumes of flowers (sometimes more lax) in mid- to late summer. Not surprisingly, with such a mix of parents, this has become something of a catch-all group for *Astilbe* hybrids, with the whole gamut of colors from white to pink and deep crimson. Originally developed by Georg Arends early in the 20th century, many more recent hybrids are also placed in this group.

Chinensis hybrids Plants derived from *A. chinensis*, and generally inheriting that species' stiffly erect, narrow sprays of flowers, ranging from rose-pink to white. Usually flowering in late summer.

Japonica hybrids Flowering in early summer, with rather loose sprays above glossy leaves, these are derived primarily from *A. japonica*. Also forced for sale as a potted plant.

Simplicifolia hybrids Small, late-flowering plants developed from *A. simplicifolia* but with glossy, smooth-edged leaves. These are hybrids with *A. japonica* or various cultivars. Most are less than 24 in (60 cm) tall and some are very dwarf.

Thunbergii hybrids Characterized by the arching branches of the flower sprays, which open in midsummer and are generally white to mid-pink, these are hybrids of *A. thunbergii*.

flowers and their dissected leaves contrast well with large-leaved moisture-loving perennials such as *Ligularia* and *Rodgersia*.

Although astilbes only came into cultivation in the West in the mid-19th century, nurserymen quickly saw their potential as garden plants, and the turn of that century saw much deliberate hybridization and selection. European nurseries were most active, and names such as Lemoine, Ruys, and Georg Arends (*see* Georg Arends, *p.87*), were responsible for many of the plants we still grow today. Alan Bloom then also introduced some good forms from the 1960s to the 1980s.

The interbreeding of astilbe species is so extensive that it is impossible to allocate all cultivars to specific hybrids with complete certainty. It is more practical to list them in alphabetical order, as below, with their presumed group (*see* Organizing Astilbes, *p.84*).

CULTIVATION Grow in well-drained but moist soil in dappled shade. Soil fertility and moisture have a marked effect on size and vigor. Most are intolerant of drought in spring and summer. They may be seriously damaged by late spring frosts.

PROPAGATION By division, discarding any old and weak growth.

PROBLEMS Vine weevil can be troublesome, the larvae attacking the roots and the adult weevils eating semicircular notches out of the edges of the leaves.

A. **'Amethyst'** (x *arendsii*) Strong purple flowers in large, slightly arching plumes to 14 in (35 cm) long in midsummer, held well above dark, matte green foliage. Excellent at the back of a border or in a woodland setting. Introduced by Georg Arends in 1920. ↕ 3¼ ft (1 m). Z4–8 H8–2

A. **'Aphrodite'** (*simplicifolia* hybrid) Red stems with broad, dark green leaves, 6 in (15 cm) long, carry slightly drooping, oval plumes of light reddish purple flowers, 8 in (20 cm) long, in midsummer. Not vigorous, requiring good conditions to thrive. Selected by Ernst Pagels in Germany. ↕ 20–24 in (50–60 cm). Z3–8 H8–1

A. **'Betsy Cuperus'** (*thunbergii* hybrid) Pale purplish pink flowers carried in arching plumes to 22 in (55 cm) long, above large, pale green leaves. Raised by Ruys in 1917 in Holland. ↕ 3½ ft (1.1 m). Z3–8 H8–1

A. **'Brautschleier'** (**Bridal Veil**) (x *arendsii*) Conical plumes, 10 in (25 cm) long, of white flowers in midsummer above glossy foliage. Of moderate vigor and particularly suitable for the smaller garden. Introduced by Georg Arends in 1929. ↕ 28 in (70 cm). Z3–8 H8–2

A. **'Bressingham Beauty'** (x *arendsii*) Deep purplish pink flowers in arching, conical plumes 8 in (20 cm) long, from midsummer; leaves are neat, dark green, and glossy. Excellent for display and cutting. Selected by Alan Bloom in 1967. ↕ 3¼ ft (1 m). Z3–8 H8–2

A. **'Bronce Elegans'** (*simplicifolia* hybrid) Compact plant with strong purplish pink flowers in late summer, borne loosely in pyramidal, drooping plumes, 10 in (25 cm) long, above leaves that change from dark green to red-purple as the season advances. To encourage the attractive red-purple foliage, unwanted green leaves should be removed. Not vigorous, it requires good conditions. Introduced by Arends in 1956. ↕ 20 in (50 cm). Z4–8 H8–2

A. **'Bumalda'** (x *arendsii*) Very striking *en masse*, with brilliant white flowers in long, loose, conical plumes, to 12 in

RIGHT **1** *Astilbe chinensis* var. *pumila*
2 *A.* 'Deutschland' **3** *A.* 'Irrlicht'
4 *A.* 'Professor van der Wielen'
5 *A.* 'Sprite' **6** *A.* 'Straussenfelder'

(30 cm) long, in midsummer. The sharply toothed leaves are bronze with deep red tints, contrast well with the flowers. ‡30 in (75 cm). Z4–8 H8–2

A. 'Cattleya' (x *arendsii*) Bold plant for the back of a border, with deep purplish pink flowers in large, loose plumes, to 16 in (40 cm) long, in late summer. Large, glossy, bright green leaves. Raised by Georg Arends. ‡4 ft (1.2 m). Z3–8 H8–1

A. chinensis Variable species spreading by runners, with brown-haired stems bearing dull green, divided leaves. In late summer, rose pink or white flowers open in characteristic narrow sprays with erect side branches, the petals narrow. Useful in being later-flowering than most astilbes, and much used in hybridizing. In good conditions, makes an imposing plant. From moist mountain woods in China, Mongolia, Korea, and Russia. ‡24 in (60 cm). Z4–8 H8–2. **'Finale'** Not to be confused with the red-flowered 'Fanal'; purplish pink flowers in narrow plumes to 10 in (25 cm) long; leaves dull dark green and rather coarse. Suitable for a pond-side position. Raised by Georg Arends in 1952. ‡28 in (70 cm). **var. pumila** Compact, with light rosy purple flowers in stiffly erect plumes, to 10 in (25 cm) long, in late summer and early fall, above a neat mound of often red-tinted foliage. Tolerates relatively dry conditions and more sun than most astilbes. Popular for its neat habit. From Tibet. ‡12–18 in (30–45 cm). **var. taquetii** Very tall astilbe of imposing presence, with narrow sprays of reddish purple flowers, to 18 in (45 cm) long, opening in late summer. Glossy, divided leaves grow to 16 in (40 cm) long. Spreads by runners and may be invasive in favorable conditions. A parent of many good hybrids, from Korea. ‡4–6 ft (1.2–2 m). **var. taquetii 'Purpurlanze'** (**Purple Lance**) Taller, with rich reddish purple flowers in narrow sprays. ‡5½ ft (1.7 m). **var. taquetii 'Superba'** Strong magenta-purple flowers densely arranged in narrow plumes to 20 in (50 cm) long, in late summer. Rounded leaflets are dark green and glossy. ‡4¼ ft (1.3 m). **'Visions'** Low-growing, sturdy plant with faintly fragrant, strong purple flowers in rather short, narrow spikes, 7 in (18 cm) long, above dark, glossy foliage. ‡22 in (55 cm). The first of a series that also includes: **'Vision in Pink'** Pink flowers. **'Vision in Red'** Red flowers. Raised by Van Veen.

A. x crispa Dwarf plants with glossy foliage of several sharply toothed leaflets, and short conical spikes of pale to deep pink flowers opening in midsummer. ‡8–10 in (20–30 cm). Z4–8 H8–2. **'Perkeo'** syn. *A.* 'Perko' Leaves dark bronze-green; spikes of purplish pink flowers, to 8 in (20 cm) long, open in midsummer. ‡8–10 in (20–30 cm).

A. 'Darwin's Snow Sprite' Profuse white flowers in midsummer; glossy foliage has many narrow, toothed leaflets. ‡22 in (55 cm). Z4–8 H8–2

CONTRAST IN COLOR AND HABIT

IN THIS MOIST SITUATION, the wonderful waved and white-variegated *Hosta undulata* foliage is impressive in itself but also contrasts appealingly with the darker, more prettily divided leaves of *Astilbe* 'Fanal'. The vertical, wiry, red astilbe stems strike up between the horizontal hosta leaves and carry brilliant scarlet plumes. These make a striking contrast with the white and fresh green of the hosta foliage. Of course, the effect is spoiled if slugs make holes in the hostas, of which they are notoriously fond. Both plants can be cut down in fall or winter and wood anemones planted among them to occupy the space in spring. A white astilbe would provide a cooler picture, while a pink cultivar would create a more pastel theme.

A. 'Deutschland' (*japonica* hybrid) Popular early-flowering astilbe with slightly arching, conical white plumes to 7 in (18 cm) long, displayed above moderately glossy leaves. An excellent plant for both garden display and forcing as a potted indoor plant. Raised by Arends in 1920. ‡26 in (65 cm). Z4–9 H8–2

A. 'Diamant' (x *arendsii*) Much grown in Europe as a cut flower, but it is also a fine border plant that flowers in midsummer, with dense, white, oval sprays up to 11 in (28 cm) long. The foliage is tinged bronze in spring, later mid-green. ‡36 in (90 cm). Z3–8 H8–1

A. Elizabeth Bloom (**'Eliblo'**) (x *arendsii*) Glossy, dark green leaves, to 12 in (30 cm) long and rather dense, with oval sprays, to 12 in (30 cm) long, of pale purplish pink flowers opening in midsummer. Raised by Alan Bloom and introduced in 1991. ‡32 in (80 cm). Z4–8 H8–2

A. 'Ellie' (x *arendsii*) Striking plant with red stems and dark green leaves that contrast with the oval-shaped plumes of brilliant white flowers, up to 10 in (25 cm) long. This is thought by some to be the best white, but is not vigorous and may be difficult to establish. ‡28 in (70 cm). Z4–8 H8–2

A. 'Erika' (x *arendsii*) Tall plant with glossy dark foliage, rich reddish bronze in spring. Light purplish pink flowers open in midsummer in large, loose trusses to 14 in (35 cm) long. Much grown as a cut flower but also a good border plant. A spontaneous mutation from 'Rosa Perle' raised by Georg Arends. ‡3¼ ft (1 m). Z3–8 H8–1

A. 'Etna' (x *arendsii*) Early-season, very reliable plant with deep red flowers in long, narrow upright plumes to 12 in (30 cm) long, opening in midsummer above glossy dark green foliage. The flowers fade to a rather bluish red. ‡24 in (60 cm). Z3–8 H8–1

A. 'Europa' (*japonica* hybrid) Very pale purple-pink flowers arranged in dense sprays, to 6 in (15 cm) long, above glossy, mid-green leaves. The flowers are small, but the unusually broad petals give the flowers particular impact. The earliest to flower, in early summer; much used for forcing as a potted plant. ‡20 in (50 cm). Z3–8 H8–1

A. 'Fanal' (x *arendsii*) The most popular red-flowered astilbe. Flowering in midsummer, it freely produces narrow plumes, to 10 in (25 cm) long, of long-lasting deep red flowers. The glossy leaves are dark reddish green and deeply toothed. An Arends selection. ‡24 in (60 cm). Z3–8 H8–2

A. 'Federsee' (x *arendsii*) Clump-forming plant with matte, mid-green leaves and deep rosy pink flowers in dense conical sprays to 14 in (35 cm) long, opening in midsummer. An attractive garden plant and also popular for forcing as a potted plant. ‡28 in (70 cm). Z3–8 H8–1

GEORG ARENDS (1863–1952)

The son of a German nurseryman, Georg Arends decided by the age of 16 to become a gardener. After training at a horticultural college near Wiesbaden, he gained experience at the botanic garden of Breslau, then in Thomas Ware's nursery in Tottenham, London—one of the first to specialize in herbaceous perennials—and in Trieste, Italy.

By 1888 he started his own nursery, and opened on a 2½-acre (1-ha) site at Wuppertal-Ronsdorf, in partnership with a friend. The nursery thrived and, although the partnership was dissolved in 1902, Georg continued to develop his interest in hardy perennials and alpine plants. By 1914, the nursery covered 32 acres (13 ha).

This period saw great activity in breeding new plants. Arends had wide tastes and made significant contributions to many genera, including rhododendrons and fruit trees. However, he is especially well known for his astilbe hybrids, and is commemorated in the name *A. x arendsii*, as well as in fine cultivars of *Aster, Bergenia, Eryngium, Phlox, Sedum*, and other perennials that remain among the mainstays of our 21st-century gardens.

The nursery remains in the family, and continues today under the guidance of Arends' great-granddaughter.

A. **'Feuer'** (**Fire**) (x *arendsii*) Rich purplish red flowers in conical plumes, to 14 in (35 cm) long, open in midsummer. Leaves are bright green and glossy, about 14 in (35 cm) long and wide. Raised by Georg Arends in 1940. ‡ 3¼ ft (1 m). Z3–8 H8–1

A. **'Flamingo'** (x *arendsii*) Compact clump of neat leaves with many small leaflets. Light purple flowers open in midsummer, in loose, conical 10-in (25-cm) sprays on arching branches. ‡ 20 in (50 cm). Z3–8 H8–1

A. glaberrima var. *saxatilis* Dwarf plant forming a low mound of glossy, deeply toothed, dark green leaves, to 4 in (10 cm) long, on contrasting red stems. In late summer, pink-tinged flowers with white petals open in small sprays, to 5½ in (14 cm) long. Also suitable for a rock garden or container. Native solely to Yakushima, a small island in southern Japan with many endemic plants. ‡ 4–8 in (10–20 cm). Z3–8 H8–1

A. **'Gloria'** (x *arendsii*) Clump of neat, slightly glossy, mid-green leaves, 6 in (15 cm) long. In midsummer, light purple flowers in dense conical sprays to 10 in (25 cm) long. An early Arends hybrid. ‡ 32 in (80 cm). Z3–8 H8–1

A. **'Gloria Purpurea'** (x *arendsii*) Clump-forming plant with short, dense, oval, 6½-in (17-cm) plumes of purplish pink flowers in midsummer. Glossy, very dark green leaves, about 8 in (20 cm) long, are a striking contrast to the flowers. Raised by B. Ruys in 1916. ‡ 32 in (80 cm). Z3–8 H8–1

A. **'Glut'** (**Glow**) (x *arendsii*) A tall plant for the back of the border, with a loose clump of neat, slightly glossy, rich green leaves to 12 in (30 cm) long. The beadlike flowers are deep red but have no petals, and form fairly broad plumes, to 12 in (30 cm) long, in midsummer. A spontaneous mutation from 'Feuer', raised by Arends. ‡ 3½ ft (1.1 m). Z3–8 H8–1

A. **'Granat'** (x *arendsii*) Glossy, dark green 10 in (25 cm) leaves; midsummer purplish red flowers in conical plumes to 18 in (45 cm) long. Long-established but still a useful garden plant. ‡ 24–36 in (60–100 cm). Z4–8 H8–2

A. **'Hennie Graafland'** (*simplicifolia* hybrid) Compact but vigorous and upright; small, sharply toothed, dark glossy green leaves. Light, purplish pink flowers in midsummer in loose, conical 7-in (18-cm) plumes. ‡ 26 in (65 cm). Z3–8 H8–1

A. **'Hyazinth'** (**Hyacinth**) (x *arendsii*) Tall plant making a good clump of slightly glossy, mid-green leaves with profuse light purple flowers opening in midsummer in dense conical sprays to 10 in (25 cm) long. An early Arends hybrid. ‡ 3¼ ft (1 m). Z3–8 H8–1

A. **'Inshriach Pink'** (*simplicifolia* hybrid) Dwarf plant forming a dense, low mound of small, sharply serrated, dark green leaves. In late summer, pale purplish pink flowers borne in oval sprays to 6½ in (17 cm) long. Good for moist corners of rock gardens. ‡ 14 in (35 cm). Z5–8 H8–2

A. **'Irrlicht'** (x *arendsii*) Clump-forming plant with olive-green leaves divided into numerous narrow, toothed leaflets. Reddish stems bear white flowers in early and midsummer in loose conical plumes up to 8 in (20 cm) long. ‡ 20–28 in (50–70 cm). Z4–9 H8–2

A. japonica Clump-forming plant with dark green leaves that are composed of about nine sharply toothed, diamond-shaped leaflets to 2¾ in (7 cm) long. White flowers with narrowly spoon-shaped petals are borne in dense to loose plumes up to 8 in (20 cm) long, in early summer. Earlier-flowering than other species, it has been important in the breeding of astilbes, and was formerly much used for conservatory decoration. Grows among damp rocks in mountain ravines in southern Japan. ‡ 20–32 in (50–80 cm). Z4–8 H8–2

A. **'Jo Ophorst'** (*davidii* hybrid) Upright plant with stout rhizomes and rather large, mid-green leaves, 14 in (35 cm) long. Purplish pink flowers open in late summer in slender sprays, to 20 in (50 cm) long. ‡ 4½ ft (1.4 m). Z4–8 H8–2

RIGHT *Astilbe* 'Willie Buchanan'

A. **'Key West'** Recently introduced, attractive and prolific dwarf form with feathery, deep magenta summer plumes set off by foliage that is dark green and burgundy red. Grouping uncertain. ‡ 15–18 in (38–45 cm). Z4–8 H8–2

A. **'Key Largo'** Another new, attractive and prolific dwarf form with full, feathery summer plumes opening rose pink and fading paler above glossy green foliage. Grouping uncertain. ‡ 15–18 in (38–45 cm). Z4–8 H8–2

A. **'Montgomery'** (*japonica* hybrid) Compact plant with attractive, finely cut, glossy dark green or reddish green foliage. Deep red flowers open in early and midsummer, forming tapering sprays to 6 in (15 cm) long. ‡ 20–28 in (50–70 cm). Z4–8 H8–2

A. **'Peaches and Cream'** (x *arendsii*) Clump-forming plant of compact habit, with mid-green leaves and slender sprays of white flowers that take on pink tints as they age. ‡ 24 in (60 cm). Z4–8 H8–2

A. **'Perkeo'** see *A.* x *crispa* 'Perkeo'

A. **'Professor van der Wielen'** (*thunbergii* hybrid) Forms a tall clump of divided, mid-green 12-in (30-cm) leaves. In midsummer, white flowers in graceful, arching sprays up to 16 in (40 cm) long. An early Dutch hybrid raised in 1917 but still a good strong plant. ‡ 4¼ ft (1.3 m). Z4–8 H8–2

A. **'Red Sentinel'** (*japonica* hybrid) Dark, glossy green leaves form compact clumps beneath deep red flowers that are borne in dense plumes to 12 in (30 cm) long. Similar to, but slightly taller than, 'Montgomery', and considered one of the best deep red cultivars, although the flower sprays may bend under heavy rain. ‡ 28 in (70 cm). Z3–8 H8–1

A. **'Rheinland'** (*japonica* hybrid) Clump-forming plant with mid-green, much-divided leaves and deep purplish pink flowers in compact, conical, 8-in (20-cm) sprays in early and midsummer. An early Arends hybrid. ‡ 20–28 in (50–70 cm). Z4–8 H8–2

A. x *rosea* **'Peach Blossom'** Clump-forming plant with attractive mid-green foliage; pale lilac-pink flowers in compact 6-in (15-cm) sprays, arching at the tips. One of the first pink-flowered hybrids, between *A. chinensis* and *A. japonica*, raised by Arends in about 1900. ‡ 20 in (50 cm). Z3–8 H8–1

A. **'Rotlicht'** syn. 'Spartan' (x *arendsii*) Compact, upright plant with mid-green leaves, tinged red in spring. Deep red flowers are carried in loose, conical 10 in (25 cm) plumes in midsummer. ‡ 24–32 in (60–80 cm). Z4–8 H8–2

A. simplicifolia Dwarf and compact plant with oval leaves 2–3 in (5–8 cm) long, sharply toothed and lobed but not further divided. Tiny, starry white flowers with narrow petals are borne in loose, arching sprays in late summer. A dainty, late-flowering plant, unusual in its simple leaves, thrives in open woodland conditions. A parent of many good dwarf cultivars, from mountain woods in southern Japan. ‡ 10–12 in (20–30 cm). Z4–8 H8–2

A. **'Snowdrift'** (x *arendsii*) Tall plant with glossy, mid-green leaves and long, loose sprays of white flowers in midsummer. Introduced by Alan Bloom in 1975. ↕ 36 in (90 cm). Z3–8 H8–1

A. **'Spartan'** see *A.* 'Rotlicht'

A. **'Sprite'** (*simplicifolia* hybrid) Slowly spreading clump of glossy, dark green leaves divided into sharply toothed leaflets. In midsummer, pale pink flowers open in loose, arching sprays to 14 in (35 cm) long. A seedling selected by Alan Bloom in 1969, and 1994 Perennial Plant of the Year. ↕ 18 in (45 cm). Z4–8 H8–1

A. **'Straussenfeder'** (*thunbergii* hybrid) Tall, clump-forming plant with slightly glossy mid-green leaves, tinged bronze in spring. Light rosy pink flowers are carried on slender, arching branches in distinctive open sprays in midsummer. ↕ 3¼ ft (1 m). Z3–8 H8–2

A. **thunbergii** Smooth stems and rather large leaves, composed of several oval, toothed leaflets to 4¾ in (12 cm) long, emerge from spreading rhizomes. White flowers with very narrow petals are carried in loose sprays with characteristic arching branches in early summer. Notable for its early flowering season—it may be damaged by late frosts. From sunny, grassy slopes in the mountains of central and southern Japan. ↕ 36 in (90 cm). Z3–8 H8–2

A. **'Venus'** (x *arendsii*) Tall plant forming a large clump, with dull green leaves and light pink flowers in loose, conical sprays up to 12 in (30 cm) long in midsummer. Well suited to a moist site with plenty of room. One of the earliest hybrids from Georg Arends; newer, more compact cultivars are more popular in most small gardens today. ↕ 3½ ft (1.1 m). Z3–8 H8–2

A. **'Vesuvius'** (*japonica* hybrid) Forms a clump of glossy, dark reddish green leaves to 6 in (15 cm) long, with, in midsummer, purplish red flowers in broadly conical, 9-in (22-cm) plumes. ↕ 24 in (60 cm). Z3–8 H8–2

A. **'W.E. Gladstone'** (*japonica* hybrid) Clump-forming plant with leaves divided into many narrow, mid-green leaflets. White flowers open in midsummer in broad conical sprays. ↕ 18 in (45 cm). Z3–8 H8–2

A. **'Weisse Gloria'** (x *arendsii*) Tall and vigorous; glossy green leaves; in mid- and late summer, creamy white flowers in dense sprays 9 in (22 cm) long. ↕ 28–40 in (70–100 cm). Z3–8 H8–1

A. **'Willie Buchanan'** (*simplicifolia* hybrid) Compact plant forming a neat mound of glossy, deeply toothed, dark green leaves. Pale pink flowers with narrow white petals open in midsummer and late summer in loose conical sprays. ↕ 8–12 in (20–30 cm). Z4–8 H8–1

A. **'Zuster Therese'** Forms a compact clump of glossy, dark green foliage. Pale lilac-pink flowers are carried in dense or irregular sprays in midsummer. ↕ 20 in (50 cm). Z4–8 H8–2

ASTILBOIDES
SAXIFRAGACEAE

This hardy shade- and moisture-lover is of great value as an accent plant in both wild and formal gardens.

A bold architectural plant, it has large parasol-like leaves and striking plumes of white flowers in summer. It is clearly distinguished from its close relatives *Astilbe* and *Rodgersia* by its distinctive rounded foliage, supported by its stem in the center. The only species is suited to cool, moist, shady places such as a woodland garden, or a more formal area shaded by tall buildings, where it makes an imposing specimen plant. A superb waterside plant if it is grown above water level. From moist woodland areas and the banks of lakes and streams in East Asia.

CULTIVATION Grows well in cool, moist soil, rich in humus, and part-shade. Avoid soil prone to waterlogging or drying out.

PROPAGATION By division in early spring as growth is starting. From seed sown in fall in a cold frame.

PROBLEMS Slugs and snails.

A. **tabularis** syn. *Rodgersia tabularis* Deciduous clump-forming plant with rounded, jagged-lobed, pale green leaves, up to 36 in (90 cm) long, carried on long stalks that join the leaf blade in the center. Plumes of tiny, creamy white flowers (like those of *Astilbe*) rise above foliage in early and midsummer. From northeastern China and North Korea. ↕ 5 ft (1.5 m). Z5–7 H7–5

ASTRANTIA
Masterwort
APIACEAE

Among the most popular and widely grown of herbaceous perennials, astrantias are particularly well-suited to shady corners and naturalistic gardens.

Ten species of these deciduous plants occur naturally in moist alpine meadows and woods from Europe to Asia, although only four or five are grown in gardens. Strongly clump-forming in habit, with basal leaves divided into characteristic lobes arising from a common center—like palm leaves—they are typified by their tight posies (technically umbels) of tiny, white to pink to blood-red flowers, held on erect wiry stems in elegant sprays. The central flowerhead of each umbel is characteristically larger than those around it. Each umbel is surrounded by a ruff of long-lasting bracts—modified leaves that resemble petals, and give the impression that the individual flowerheads last for many weeks until seed is ripe. All astrantias have a long season, flowering at varying intensity from early summer to early fall, and are becoming increasingly popular as cut flowers. Many deep red cultivars have recently been introduced. Some may be hybrids; these are easily confused and when raised from seed produce variable offspring.

CULTIVATION Best in fertile, moisture-retentive soil, in sun or part-shade. Deadheading will extend the flowering season significantly and prevent the nuisance of self-sown seedlings (*see* Self-seeding, *p. 90*).

PROPAGATION From seed sown fresh in fall (germination will occur the following spring) or by division, either in spring or after flowering in late summer to fall. The named forms rarely come true from seed and therefore should be propagated by division.

PROBLEMS Usually trouble-free, though can be vulnerable to leaf miner and fungal leaf spot.

RED AND BRONZE TINTS

IN THIS PREDOMINANTLY RED grouping, there are five plants present. The two most prominent—the small domed heads of *Astrantia major* 'Claret' and the paler, larger-domed heads of *Centranthus ruber*, which has self-sown among the astrantia—themselves make a pretty pairing. In addition, the astrantia foliage has a tendency to take on bronze tints, which is taken a stage further by the darker tones in the foliage of *Actaea simplex* Atropurpurea Group. There are blue lights from a dainty little viola in the front, and the slim spikes of the salvia behind—both set among, or against, slightly bronzed leaves, taking the border on to new color themes.

LEFT **1** *Astrantia* 'Buckland'
2 *A. carniolica* **3** *A.* 'Hadspen Blood'
4 *A. major* **5** *A. major* 'Primadonna'
6 *A. major* 'Rosensinfonie'

A. bavarica Small-flowered, slender species, rarely seen except in the gardens of enthusiasts, with deeply cleft, five-lobed lower leaves. Green-tipped white, strap-shaped bracts, 1 in (2.5 cm) across, surround the central umbel of white flowers to create a ruff slightly wider than the flowerhead. Differs from the closely related *A. carniolica* in its narrower leaf segments and its bracts, which exceed the width of the umbel of flowers. From the eastern Alps. ‡ 16 in (40 cm). Z4–7 H8–2

A. 'Bloody Mary' Silvery-centered, deep blood red flowers on dark, red-tinted stems over dark green foliage. Variable seed strain, at its best similar to *A.* 'Hadspen Blood' and *A. major* 'Ruby Wedding'. ‡ 20 in (50 cm). Z4–7 H8–2

A. 'Buckland' Distinctive soft pink flowers set off by broad white bracts tipped with green. Unlike most cultivars, the flowers are sterile, ensuring that 'Buckland' remains true in cultivation and is never invasive. Excellent combined with blue campanulas and geraniums in the garden. A fine hybrid, possibly between *A. major* and *A. maxima*, raised by Keith Wiley at the Garden House, Buckland Monachorum in Devon, England. ‡ 30 in (75 cm). Z4–7 H8–2

A. carniolica Rather slender plant, with long-stemmed basal leaves split into five-toothed, or slightly lobed, oval segments that are not fully divided to the base. The usual wiry stems branch at the top to carry open heads of rounded, white to pinkish flowerheads in late summer, with strap-shaped floral bracts that do not exceed the width of the umbel of flowers. Easily grown in good soil in sun or part-shade. More

WHICH IS WHICH?

To gardeners, the four taller species can all look rather similar and are often confused. They can, however, be easily distinguished and fall into two pairs of species. *Astrantia bavarica* and *A. carniolica* have smaller flowerheads, and grow up to 16–18 in (40–45 cm) tall, while *A. major* and *A. maxima* have larger heads and reach 24–36 in (60–90 cm).

A. bavarica Small flowerheads to 1 in (2.5 cm) across. Rare in cultivation.

A. carniolica Similar to *A. bavarica* but with broader, less divided leaves.

A. major The most common species, with many selected forms. Flowerheads usually wider than 1 in (2.5 cm) across, sometimes reaching 3½ in (9 cm), with strap-shaped bracts.

A. maxima At about 1½ in (4 cm), the flowerheads are usually smaller than those of *A. major,* and plants have less toothed leaves and fewer and broader, triangular-shaped bracts.

commonly found in cultivation than the rather similar *A. bavarica*, from which it differs in its leaf segments not being divided to the base and the bracts being less wide than the umbel of flowers. Native to the southeastern Alps. ↕12–18 in (30–45 cm). Z5–7 H7–5. **'Rubra'** Deep pink flowers; sometimes confused with pink forms of *A. major* but distinct in its compact habit and more globular flowerheads.

A. **'Hadspen Blood'** Flowers reddish purple, as are the bracts, especially at the tips. Effective in rich color schemes. Raised by Nori and Sandra Pope at Hadspen Garden in Somerset, England. ↕36 in (90 cm). Z5–7 H7–5

A. major A valuable but variable tough and robust species, plants forming steadily increasing clumps of three- to five- or occasionally seven-lobed basal leaves, characteristically coarsely toothed. The white flowerheads vary widely from 1 to 3½ in (2.5 cm to 9 cm) in diameter, the strap-shaped bracts often tipped in pink. Best in moist and fertile soil in part-shade; a stalwart of the cottage garden style, it will seed around freely and combine effectively with many other plants. Native to Europe, from northwestern Spain across the Pyrenees and Alps into Germany, Bulgaria, and east to western Russia; naturalized in Britain and parts of Scandinavia. ↕24–36 in (60–90 cm). Z5–7 H7–5. *alba* Pure white, green-tipped bracts with no color in the center of the flowerheads. **'Berendian Stam'** Free-flowering in very pale rose pink, similar to 'Buckland' but taller and with paler and whiter flowers. Raised in Holland, perhaps a hybrid between *A. major* and *A. maxima*. subsp. *biebersteinii* Small, with short-stemmed white flowers tinted pale pink, and with more divided leaves. ↕12–18 in (30–45 cm). **'Celtic Star'** Very large, pristine white flowerheads to 3½ in (9 cm) wide with the bracts tipped green. **'Claret'** Dark reddish purple flowers. Not dependable in color, obtained by growing seedlings of 'Ruby Wedding'. subsp. *involucrata* Very distinctive form; floral bracts up to twice as wide as the cluster of flowers, give a strong presence in the garden. Several forms have been selected and are best propagated vegetatively. subsp. *involucrata* **'Barrister'** Compact cultivar with large white flowerheads veined with green, and white-veined leaves. ↕12 in (30 cm). subsp. *involucrata* **'Canneman'** Unusually long season of green-tipped bracts and red-stained flowers in spring, turning to green in summer. Seed-raised, from Holland; similar to 'Shaggy' but with broader bracts. subsp. *involucrata* **'Margery Fish'** see subsp. *involucrata* 'Shaggy'. subsp. *involucrata* **'Moira Reid'** Striking cultivar with silver-tinted, green-veined, and green-tipped white flowers. subsp. *involucrata* **'Shaggy'** syn. 'Margery Fish' Famous

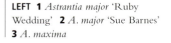
LEFT **1** *Astrantia major* 'Ruby Wedding' **2** *A. major* 'Sue Barnes' **3** *A. maxima*

ABOVE *Astrantia major* 'Sunningdale Variegated'

variety originally selected by Margery Fish at East Lambrook Manor in Somerset. The true plant has exceptionally large flowerheads with long pointed white bracts tipped green, though many inferior plants propagated from seed may be found under this name. **'Lars'** Named after Paul Petersen's grandson. Large plum-pink flowers produced on tall wiry stems from early summer to early fall. Good repeat-flowering cultivar from Denmark. **'Primadonna'** Shades of lilac-pink. A true-breeding seed strain if kept isolated from other forms, otherwise variable. **'Roma'** Flowers

SELF-SEEDING

When growing well, and especially with a less diligent gardener, *Astrantia major* in particular can become a nuisance. If the dead flowers are not cut off, it can self-seed aggressively, as it did at Margery Fish's unique cottage garden at East Lambrook Manor in Somerset after her death.

With selected forms in particular, it can be tempting to allow a few self-sown seedlings to grow around the parent plants, or to collect some seed to grow on, but the best *Astrantia* cultivars are intended to be raised from division and rarely come true.

Although the colored bracts can prolong the display of many cultivars, it pays, therefore, to snip back the first flowers as they fade, cutting to the secondary buds lower down the stem; then, when these too are past their best, cut the whole stem out at ground level. If the foliage is also looking shabby by this time, perhaps after a dry spell, cut back the whole plant hard—but be sure it does not dry out or the growth of fresh new foliage will be restricted and the plant weakened.

and bracts a warm rich pink, fading slowly to green. An excellent free-flowering sterile cultivar raised by Dutch horticulturist Piet Oudolf. ↕24 in (60 cm). **var. *rosea*** Rose-pink flowers. **'Rosensinfonie'** Variable red- and pink-flowered seed strain. **'Rubra'** Deep red flowerheads. Now largely superseded by 'Hadspen Blood' and 'Ruby Wedding'. **'Ruby Cloud'** Flowers red-purple, an improved version of 'Rosensinfonie'. **'Ruby Wedding'** In its true form, propagated by division, probably the best and darkest of all cultivars. The flowers and bracts are deepest ruby red; leaves and stems also strongly flushed with reddish purple. Long-flowering. **'Sue Barnes'** Variegated, with faint white speckling around the edge of the leaves. Good pink flowerheads. **'Sunningdale Variegated'** Leaves strongly margined with cream and yellow in the spring, fading during the summer; cutting back the foliage will encourage bright new variegated growth. Pale pink flowers only sparsely produced. The best variegation is seen in open sunny sites in moist soil.

A. maxima Arguably the finest species, and a more vigorously spreading plant with rounded leaves split into just three leaflets. The 1½-in (4-cm) flowerheads, with their broad, triangular floral bracts, are a delightful soft rose pink with a striking emerald-green underside. Much less tolerant of hot and dry weather than the more widely grown *A. major*, it needs rich, moist soil to thrive and good light to encourage prolific flowering. Found in woods and damp meadows throughout the Caucasus, and into Turkey and Iran. ↕24–36 in (60–90 cm). Z5–8 H8–1. **'Mark Fenwick'** Deep pink flowers. ***rosea*** Slightly stronger pink flowers.

A. minor The smallest species, and much more demanding than its relatives in cultivation. Its leaves are deeply cut, usually into seven narrow lobes, in contrast to the broader-lobed leaves of most of its relatives, and the very small white to pale-pink flowerheads are only ½ in (1.5 cm) across. Requires well-drained, neutral to acidic soil. Grows naturally on dry alpine screes in the Apennines, Alps, and Pyrenees. ↕6–16 in (15–40 cm). Z5–7 H7–5

***A.* 'Snow Star'** Large, very pale greenish white flowers with a faint aniseed fragrance. Raised by Piet Oudolf and similar to *A. major* 'Celtic Star'. ↕32 in (80 cm). Z4–8 H8–2

ATHYRIUM

Lady fern

WOODSIACEAE

Delightful deciduous ferns of graceful bearing that are easy to grow.

A large genus of 170–200 species of moist woodlands worldwide, especially in East Asia. Many are likely to be hardy, but relatively few are in cultivation. Most species are deciduous with thin-textured, arching fronds, hence "lady fern." The spores are produced in short, straight or J-shaped structures on the underside of the frond. All species are deciduous in cool temperate zones.

CULTIVATION Best in moist, neutral or acidic soil, in part- or full shade.

PROPAGATION By division or from spores (not cultivars).

PROBLEMS Aborted fronds may be caused by a small fly whose larva feeds within the developing frond. Thrips can cause some frond blotching late in the season.

***A. angustatum* 'Lady in Red'** A very handsome, medium-sized fern; finely divided, lance-shaped fronds have deep red frond stem and midrib. A similar, but inferior form, 'Rotstiel', appears in *A. filix-femina*. *A. angustatum* is a rarely seen North American species, often considered a subspecies of *A. filix-femina*. ↕24 in (60 cm). Z4–9 H9–1

***A.* 'Branford Beauty'** Clumps of upright, silver gray fronds on red stems, and altogether less colorful, but hardier, than *A. niponicum* var. *pictum* of which it is a hybrid; one of the tougher North American lady ferns. (*see* Athyrium Hybrids). ↕12 in (30 cm). Z4–8 H9–1

***A.* 'Branford Rambler'** Creeping rhizomes support red-stemmed, yellowish green fronds. Less colorful than *A. niponicum* var. *pictum* and 'Branford Beauty'—hardier than the former, but with more of its creeping tendencies. ↕12 in (30 cm). Z4–8 H9–1

A. filix-femina (Lady fern) A large elegant fern with lance-shaped, mid-green fronds, with green or occasionally dull red stems, deeply divided and somewhat feathery. In luxuriant specimens, frond segments can themselves be divided up to two times, making the ultimate segments very small and delicate. A characteristic fern of damp, shady places, disliking wind or sunshine. The appearance of the new fronds in spring is a wonderful sight, occurring before those of most other ferns; their season is, however, short, and by late summer most look rather tired. Cultivars should be increased by division. Native to Europe and western Asia ↕to 5 ft (1.5 m). Z4–9 H9–1. **Cristatum Group** Top of frond and tips of main frond divisions crested in two dimensions. ↕4 ft (1.2 m). **Cruciatum Group** All main divisions fork at their point of attachment to the midrib, giving the effect of a series of crosses running along the length of the frond. ↕20 in (50 cm). **'Frizelliae'** Delightful dwarf fern; the main frond segments are reduced to small circular structures along the midrib. Fronds of the true 'Frizelliae' are rarely more than 6 in (15 cm) tall by ⅝ in (1.5 cm) wide and never branch. Propagate by division; plants raised from spores often have crested fronds. More tolerant of exposure than most cultivars. **'Minutissimum'** A miniature of the species, tending to form a dense clump. Propagate by division; plants raised from spores are often larger. ↕12 in (30 cm). **Plumosum Group** Frond very finely and repeatedly divided, creating a very feathery effect. Much sought-after. Seldom comes true from spores. ↕3¼ ft (1 m). **'Rotstiel'** Stems red, but less showy than *A. angustatum* 'Lady in Red' though larger. ↕4 ft (1.2 m). **'Vernoniae'** The smallest frond segments (pinnules) are divided into fan-shaped ultimate divisions. This is one of the few *A. filix-femina* cultivars to come largely true from spores. ↕16–20 in (40–50 cm).

***A.* 'Ghost'** A striking fern with broad, largely gray fronds. A chance hybrid of the much smaller *A. niponicum* var. *pictum* with an unknown lady fern that occurred in a West Virginia garden. ↕36 in (90 cm). Z4–8 H9–1

A. niponicum* var. *pictum syn. *A. niponicum* 'Pictum', *A. goeringianum* 'Pictum' (Japanese painted fern) 2004 Perennial Plant of the Year. Pretty fern with a slowly creeping rhizome. The fronds are lance-shaped, arching, and light green, but a proportion of plants in the wild have grayish fronds with a purple midrib: the origin of var. *pictum*, which is not a single clone. Good selections are among the most colorful of the readily available garden ferns: the rich purple midrib and side-veins are complemented by the silvery gray fronds. Easily cultivated as long as it has a plentiful supply of moisture and some shade. Propagation from spores or by division of large plants; from spores, some of the progeny will lack the most colorful fronds. From woodlands in northeastern Asia. ↕8–12 in (20–30 cm). Z5–8 H8–1. **'Cristatoflabellatum'** Fan-shaped crests on the tips of the fronds and frond segments; sometimes the main frond stem branches. ↕8 in (20 cm). **'Silver Falls'** A vigorous selection in which the gray areas of the fronds are a vivid silvery shade. ↕12 in (30 cm). **'Ursula's Red'** Fronds with a larger, deep red zone along the center of the frond. As the season progresses, the red area contracts. ↕12 in (30 cm). **'Wildwood Twist'** Fronds more erect, slightly twisted, and mostly gray with some purple in the midribs. More curious than beautiful. ↕12 in (30 cm).

A. otophorum (Eared lady fern) Fronds lance-shaped, twice divided, and light green with a reddish purple stalk, midrib, and side-veins. In spring the leafy areas are almost cream. In mild winters it may retain its fronds much later than other lady ferns. Like all lady ferns, it needs plentiful moisture and shade, and is easily raised from spores. This and var. *okanum* may be supplied under either name. Native to Japan, China, and Korea. ↕18 in (45 cm). Z5–8 H8–1. **var. *okanum*** Main leaflets distinctly stalked.

ATHYRIUM HYBRIDS

Hybrids between different species are relatively uncommon in ferns—except among the aspleniums—perhaps because there are no flowers for gardeners or nursery workers to pollinate in a few seconds with the touch of a brush. With ferns, it all takes place on a microscopic level.

However, some of the finest recently introduced garden ferns have been hybrids between the native North American lady fern and the Japanese painted fern, *A. niponicum* var. *pictum*.

Bringing together the relative toughness of the compactly crowned native species and the more creeping habit and delightful foliage coloring of *A. niponicum* var. *pictum*, *A.* 'Ghost' was the first to make an impact.

ABOVE 1 *Athyrium* 'Ghost'
2 *A. niponicum* var. *pictum*

ABOVE 1 *Ballota acetabulosa*
2 *B.* 'All Hallow's Green'

B

BALLOTA
LAMIACEAE

Foliage forms of these otherwise unremarkable plants show promise, nevertheless, as easy-to-grow accent plants.

There are up to 35 perennial species, some of which are compact and others spreading, often woody at the base, from dry habitats in the Mediterranean and into Asia. Only a handful are cultivated, but interest is on the rise since they are drought-tolerant. The leaves are opposite, with notches or a series of small, rounded, scalloplike lobes, and are occasionally noticeably aromatic, sometimes unpleasantly so. Clusters of tiny, lilac-colored, dragonlike flowers, typical of the family, sit in clusters at the leaf joints but are insufficiently colorful or intriguing to excite. Instead, the woolly-textured or variegated foliage and stems have gained them recognition.

CULTIVATION Easy to grow in full sun, but need extremely good drainage. Thrives on alkaline soil.

PROPAGATION From seed and by division and cuttings.

PROBLEMS Sensitive to overwatering.

B. acetabulosa All parts of this attractive plant, including the stems and the small rounded leaves, are covered with its characteristic woolly white felt. The tiny pinkish lavender flowers are not particularly exciting, but more interesting are the open-faced flower bracts that form at the leaf joints and persist after the blooms have come and gone. Thrives in poor, sandy, well-drained soil; sitting in moisture is death to the roots. From Greece. ↕12–24 in (30–60 cm). Z8–9 H9–8

B. 'All Hallow's Green' Leaves low, spreading, woody-based, pungent, evergreen, densely stacked with heart-shaped, rough-textured, lime green with a noticeable golden cast. Small clusters of tiny green flowers crowd the leaf joints hardly enhance the display of this handsome foliage plant. Needs sun. Tolerant of poor soil and drought conditions but not wet roots. Introduced by veteran horticulturist Valerie Finnis, but now considered a form of *Marrubium bourgaei*. ↕12–24 in (30–60 cm). Z7–9 H9–7

B. nigra (Black horehound) Totally unimpressive without some sort of gimmick (such as variegation), this floppy, low-growing herb has deeply textured, toothed, oval leaves that smell rather noxious and lack sufficient distinction to warrant growing. The clusters of small pink flowers in the leaf joints do not compensate, but at least the plant is largely problem- and maintenance-free. Sun is a must. From Europe, Asia, and North Africa. ↕12–18 in (30–45 cm). Z7–9 H9–7. **'Archer's Variegated'** Redeemed by distinct snow-white random mottling and streaking of the foliage; the variegation makes the lilac-colored blossoms much more distinct. **'Prancing Jester'** Variegated, and taller. ↕20 in (50 cm). **'Zanzibar'** Variegated, and larger still. ↕36 in (88 cm).

BALSAMITA *see* TANACETUM

BAPTISIA
False indigo
FABACEAE

Adaptable plants with attractive, gray-green foliage, which were once an important source for dyes.

RIGHT 1 *Baptisia australis* **2** *Begonia grandis* subsp. *evansiana* var. *alba*

Of about 20 species of upright or spreading deciduous perennials, only a few are grown in gardens. Stout stems up to 6½ ft (2 m) tall carry alternately arranged foliage, each leaf is usually divided into three leaflets, these often broadest toward the tip. Yellow, white, or purple pealike flowers are carried in attractive spikes, and these are followed by inflated seedpods, useful for dried arrangements. One species of unremarkable appearance, *B. tinctoria*, is still grown commercially as a dye source; the genus name *Baptisia* comes from the Greek *bapto*, "to dye." All *Baptismia* are native to the eastern or southern US and found either in poor gravelly soil or in moist woodlands.

CULTIVATION Best in deep, rich, moist soil that is slightly acidic, but tolerant of poorer soil.

PROPAGATION From seed in fall, or by division in spring or fall. Seed germinates best when fresh, or stratify for 40 days at 41°F (5°C).

PROBLEMS Powdery mildew.

B. alba (White false indigo) Emerges early in spring with a purple tinge to the new growth. The stems are slightly swollen where the leaves arise, making this species easy to identify when not in flower. In late spring, 12-in (30-cm) sprays of about 20 pea- or lupinelike white flowers, often blotched with purple, are carried on tall stems and are followed by cylindrical yellow-brown seedpods about 2 in (5 cm) long. The sturdy, upright growth seldom needs staking. Grows best in full sun but will tolerate part-shade. A good candidate for the wildflower garden. A US native, from Virginia to Florida. ↕4–5 ft (1.2–1.5 m). Z3–9 H9–2. **var. macrophylla** Larger leaves, and taller. ↕6½ ft (2 m).

B. australis (Blue false indigo, Plains false indigo) Upright to spreading, early into growth, the gray-green leaves quickly expanding to make a dense bush. In spring, 10–12-in (25–30-cm) spikes of pale blue to mauve flowers open and last for 2–4 weeks, depending on the temperature. The flowers are followed by persistent 2-in (5-cm) swollen pods that turn black as they mature; the seeds inside rattle when ripe. The plant spreads by underground runners and can become very large. Offshoots can be dug up and replanted, or removed, but the parent plant has a deep taproot, so it is best left untouched. Plants raised from seed will vary in color intensity; grow enough to be able to select the darker colors for the best display. Generally needs some support, especially when grown in part-shade. Native to the eastern US. ↕5 ft (1.5 m). Z3–9 H9–1. **'Exaltata'** Deep blue flowers, in longer, denser flower spikes, on a shorter plant. ↕4 ft (1.2 m).

BEGONIA
BEGONIACEAE

Mostly perennial, fibrous- or tuberous-rooted plants, originating from tropics or subtropics, mainly grown for either their flamboyant flowers or their bold, dramatically patterned foliage.

There are a few hardy tuberous species; *B. grandis* is the species that is most often cultivated in cooler, temperate regions. It makes a fine foliage plant, adding a luxuriant, exotic effect to moist, shaded parts

of the garden, and produces attractive flowers usefully late in the season. New introductions of other species may also prove to be good hardy garden plants.

CULTIVATION Plants grow best in moist, fertile but well-drained soil in part-shade.

PROPAGATION From bulbils or by division of clumps.

PROBLEMS Vine weevil.

B. grandis subsp. *evansiana* An essential plant for the exotic or woodland garden, with large, slightly shiny, bronze-green, oval, rather fleshy leaves that are reddish and heavily veined beneath. The amount of red in the foliage is variable; some plants are greener than others. Leaves are held on slender, branched stems, and grow up to 6 in (15 cm) long and 4 in (10 cm) across. In cultivation, plants emerge rather late in spring from tuberous roots. Sprays of drooping flowers in shades of pink, up to 4 in (10 cm) long and lightly scented, appear in late summer and continue until the first frost, when plants die down to the ground. This begonia spreads quickly, increasing by bulbils that develop in the leaf joints after flowering and can be used for propagation. They drop off and grow the following spring around the original plant, effectively forming small clumps that quickly reach flowering size. Best in moist, but well-drained, rich soil in light shade, but will stand some sun in moist conditions. Protect the tubers from winter cold with mulch. Grows on shaded banks or in woodlands at quite high altitude in China, Malaysia, and Japan. ↕16–28 in (40–70 cm). Z6–9 H9–5. **var.** *alba* White flowers with paler green and less reddish tinted leaves. The white flowers show up well, especially in the shade. **var.** *alba* **'Claret Jug'** Strongly red-tinted foliage, especially the leaf undersides. **'Heron's Pirouette'** Large sprays of flowers twice as long as in the species and bright pink. A fine cultivar, selected at Heronswood Nurseries, WA, from seed collected in Japan. **'Sapporo'** Rich shell pink flowers and dark green red-backed foliage. The hardiest form. ↕36 in (90 cm).

BELLIS
Daisy
ASTERACEAE

The familiar lawn daisy has given rise to many showy, easily grown plants for sunny places.

Seven species of these low, tufted plants are found in a variety of grassy habitats—from lowlands to mountains—in Europe and the Mediterranean region, two of which are grown in gardens. They form neat rosettes of evergreen leaves which, in some species, spread by runners. From late spring to late summer, short, leafless stems bear solitary flowerheads with white, pink, or pale blue ray florets ("petals") surrounding a yellow disk.

CULTIVATION Grow in any soil in sun or light shade; deadhead regularly to prolong flowering and prevent seeding.

PROPAGATION From seed or by division.

PROBLEMS Usually trouble-free.

B. perennis (Lawn daisy, Common daisy) Forms a rosette of dark green spoon-shaped leaves 1¼–2½ in (3–6 cm) long, above which flowers open from early or mid-spring to late summer on a leafless stalk. In the wild form, many narrow, white, often red-backed, ray-florets surround a dull yellow central disk. Most cultivars have pomponlike, fully double flowerheads up to 2½ in (6 cm) across, which are red, pink, or white. The large-flowered, seed-raised, double daisy cultivars are widely used as spring-flowering bedding plants and although perennial, their flowers may deteriorate after the first year. ↕4–6 in (10–15 cm). Z4–8 H8–1. **'Alba Plena'** Double flowered; white ray florets are sometimes tinged pink. Flowerheads are 1¼–1½ in (3–3.5 cm) across. **'Dresden China'** Clear pink double flowerheads, 1¼ in (3 cm) across, with quilled ray florets; sterile, so propagation is by division after flowering. **Pomponette series** Relatively small, densely double flowerheads in shades of pink, red, or white, up to 1½ in (4 cm) across.

B. rotundifolia Neat rosette of shiny, rounded or kidney-shaped leaves to 2¾ in (7 cm) long, above which yellow-centered white flowers tinged with deep red, 1¼–1½ in (3–4 cm) across, open from mid-spring to early or midsummer. From damp, shaded places in southern Spain and northwestern Africa. Needs a moist, but well-drained, sheltered position. ↕8 in (20 cm). Z4–8 H8–1. **'Caerulescens'** Pale blue ray florets. The form usually seen.

BERGENIA
Elephant's ears
SAXIFRAGACEAE

These low-growing, clump-forming, usually evergreen plants are popular for both their bold foliage and their attractive sprays of spring flowers.

There are seven or eight species, native to damp woodlands, rocky areas, and open slopes, mostly in Central and eastern Asia. Developing fleshy, rather woody rhizomes that spread slowly over, or just below, the soil surface, they eventually form large, long-lived clumps. The loose rosettes of broad, rounded leaves, up to 14 in (35 cm) long, sometimes with bluntly toothed edges, are held alternately on short stems and are usually shiny and rich green in color. In winter, some develop attractive foliage tints. The five-petaled flowers, carried in branched sprays on short stems, are usually bell-shaped and about ¾ in (2 cm) across. Usually produced in spring and early summer; they may be damaged by frost.

Although their spring flowers are especially welcome after winter, the cold-season foliage is a longer-lasting and more dependable attraction, being more frost-resistant than the flowers, and comes in various dark and bright red, ruby, bronze, and purplish shades.

Bergenias have long been regarded as useful garden plants, making excellent ground cover, rarely reaching over 20 in (50 cm) high, but spreading well; some even grow in dry shade under established trees or shrubs. Many named selections and cultivars have been developed with improved flowers or foliage. Superb for providing contrast with strappy or delicate leaves, or repeated along the front of borders, they have found favor in recent years for use in gravel gardens, where they are particularly effective, especially those cultivars that develop burnished, coppery winter tints to their leaves.

CULTIVATION Most bergenias are easy to grow and will even succeed in demanding areas of dry shade. Indeed, those selections grown for winter foliage effect color up best if

RIGHT **1** *Bellis perennis* 'Alba Plena' **2** *Bergenia* 'Morgenröte' **3** *B. purpurascens*

ADD SPRING BULBS

BERGENIAS, WHICH HAVE A SLIGHTLY open habit and develop good winter leaf color, such as this 'Bressingham Ruby' and also 'Abenglut', particularly lend themselves to associations with a variety of early bulbs. Here, the palest ice-blue flowers of the delightful *Scilla mischtschenkoana*, with the lobes of each flower streaked with a single dark blue stripe, emerge over many weeks among the dark bergenia foliage. *Crocus tommasinianus* is another good candidate for this approach, as are vigorous snowdrops such as *Galanthus* 'Atkinsii'. In this case the bergenia and bulbs were initially planted together in the same hole, but bulbs could also be slipped in among roots of a maturing bergenia, when a slim bulb planting trowel would be helpful.

they are grown in poor soil in rather open, exposed positions. However, many bergenias also make fine flowering plants with lush elegant foliage when grown in good, fertile conditions; they relish rich, moist, but well-drained soil in sun or shade. Keep clumps tidy by removing dying leaves that turn an unsightly black, and mulch regularly to encourage good growth. Flowers may be spoiled by late frosts, turning blooms brown, so some shelter is recommended for those that bloom early. Clumps may eventually become open in the center, exposing the unsightly rhizomes, and stop flowering freely. To remedy this, divide the clumps after flowering, split up and shorten rhizomes, and replant in enriched soil, keeping divisions well watered.

PROPAGATION Divide established clumps, or cut off sections of rhizome with rosettes of leaves attached. Rhizome "cuttings" are also possible (*see* Making More, p.95). Some seed strains, such as *B.* 'Rotblum' and *B. cordifolia* 'Winterglut', as well as the species, may also be raised from seed.

PROBLEMS Slugs and snails, vine weevil, leaf spot.

B. 'Abendglocken' (**Evening Bells**) Open heads of rich reddish purple flowers on robust stems and large, 8-in (20-cm) red-tinted leaves. Raised in Germany in 1971 by Georg Arends Nursery (*see* p.87). ‡16 in (40 cm). Z4–8 H8–1

B. 'Abendglut' (**Evening Glow**) Short stems carry heads of usually semi-double, deep magenta blooms. The oval and slightly wrinkled leaves, claret on the reverse, no more than 6 in (15 cm) long and generally neater than in many selections. In open situations the foliage turns dark purple in winter. Raised by Georg Arends in Germany; introduced in 1950. ‡12 in (30 cm). Z6–9 H9–6

B. 'Baby Doll' Large, rather floppy, apple-green foliage with leaves about 4 in (10 cm) in length. Large, open flowers in rounded flowerheads. Individual blooms are a delicate shade of pink that becomes more intense as they age; they have reddish pink sepals. No winter leaf color, but neat, compact growth. ‡12 in (30 cm). Z4–8 H8–1

B. 'Ballawley' Large, leafy hybrid bearing dramatic sprays of bright reddish pink flowers on red stems in spring. The large, glossy leaves, dark green and up to 12 in (30 cm) in length, usually turn bronze-red in winter, but often damaged in exposed positions. Spectacular ground cover in good soil, although some find it rather crass. Raised in Ballawley Park, Dublin, Ireland, in 1950. ‡24 in (60 cm). Z6–9 H9–6

B. 'Ballawley Guardsman' Dark red flowers in mid-spring, and large glossy green leaves that turn bronze in winter. ‡24 in (60 cm). Z6–9 H9–6

B. Ballawley hybrids Rather variable seed strain, often simply raised from seed collected from 'Ballawley', with crimson flowers that are carried on red stems. The glossy mid-green leaves turn red in winter. ‡24 in (60 cm). Z6–9 H9–6

B. 'Beethoven' Superb—perhaps the best—white-flowered cultivar with only the faintest pink blush as the flowers age and a coral pink calyx. Particularly free-flowering, the early and mid-spring blooms held above large green leaves up to 10 in (25 cm) long that show little winter color. Raised by Eric Smith of England in 1971. ‡16 in (40 cm). Z4–8 H8–1

B. 'Bressingham Ruby' Especially neat, compact form with leaves that turn rich dark ruby red in winter, followed by strong red-pink flowers in spring. One of the most desirable for winter color. From Blooms of Bressingham, England. ‡12 in (30 cm). Z4–8 H8–1

B. 'Bressingham Salmon' Distinctive salmon pink flowers in early summer. The leaves become pink-tinged in winter. From Blooms of Bressingham. ‡12 in (30 cm). Z4–8 H8–1

B. 'Bressingham White' An excellent selection, producing an abundance of white flowers in late spring, blushing pink with age. The rich green leaves, up to 8 in (20 cm) long, have little winter color. From Blooms of Bressingham. ‡16 in (40 cm). Z3–8 H9–1

B. ciliata Distinctive in its luxuriant, softly hairy, almost furry leaves, up to 14 in (35 cm) long; the foliage is frost-sensitive and often deciduous in cold areas. Pale pink or white flowers appear in early spring, the color deepening with age, but are usually damaged by frost. A sheltered pocket near a house wall will help protect both foliage and flowers. From India and Nepal. ‡12 in (30 cm). Z7–8 H8–1. **f. ligulata** see *B. pacumbis*.

B. cordifolia Tough and reliable, one of the largest species, and among the most often seen in gardens. The green, rippled leaves are 12 in (30 cm) long, and oval or sometimes heart-shaped; in winter they may develop purplish tints. Flowerheads of rich pink blooms appear in early spring on tall reddish stems. From Siberia and Mongolia. ‡16–24 in (40–60 cm). Z3–8 H8–1. **'Flore Pleno'** Double flowers; rare. Z4–8 H8–1 **'Purpurea'** Rich purplish red flowers on tall red stems and large, rather more succulent, reddish leaves that turn purple in winter. Popularized by Gertrude Jekyll. Z4–8 H8–1. **'Tubby Andrews'** Leaves irregularly splashed and striped with gold and pale green on a mid-green background. A spectacular winter foliage plant, but needs good, fertile conditions; dramatic in a container. Flowers are bright pink, in early spring and sometimes again in fall. ‡12 in (30 cm). Z4–8 H8–1. **'Winterglut'** (**Winter Glow**) Seed-raised form for winter effect, leaves turn rich glossy red. The spring blooms too are red, carried on purplish stems; a second showing occasionally appears in fall. ‡14 in (35 cm). Z4–8 H8–1

B. crassifolia Bears slightly elongated, rounded, vaguely toothed green leaves up to 7 in (18 cm) across, which often become red-tinged during winter, especially in exposed situations and in poor soil. In late winter, greenish red flower stems carry nodding, pinkish purple flowers, all tending to hang to one side. From Siberia and Mongolia. ‡18 in (45 cm). Z3–8 H8–1

B. emeiensis Charming, less hardy species. Most spectacular in bloom; its elegant open sprays of large, pure white, bell-shaped flowers on pink stalks appear in late winter and flare to five-pointed stars as they age. The leaves are large, shiny, with a slight bronze tinge, and rather elongated. Best in a very sheltered, well-drained position in some sun; flowers are often destroyed by frost. A splendid container plant for the cool glasshouse, blooming in winter. First described in 1988 from Sichuan province, China. ‡12 in (30 cm) outside, 24 in (60 cm) under glass. Z7–10 H10–7

B. 'Eric Smith' Impressive winter foliage selection: in some seasons the upright leaves are almost scarlet, but

MAKING MORE

Dividing the fat clumps or breaking up the woody rhizomes into pieces with both leaves and roots works well for propagating bergenias, but should you need to make more than just a few, there is another way: by making "cuttings" from small pieces of rhizome. Near the end of the winter, cut off a length of woody rhizome and carefully remove the leaves and their stalks. Cut the stem into pieces about 1 in (2.5 cm) long, making sure there is a dormant "eye" in each piece. Fill a deep seed tray with potting compost to half of its depth. Fill the remaining volume with sand. Dust the rhizome pieces with fungicide and stick them into the sand on their sides as they grow in the garden. Cover with coarse sand, water well, and place in a warm area with a temperature of about 59°F (15°C). New shoots and roots should soon appear. Transfer each rooted piece to an individual 3½-in (9-cm) pot to grow on before planting in the garden. On a nursery scale, as with so many other plants, bergenias are sometimes now propagated in the laboratory by tissue culture.

may also be bronzy above and red beneath. Rich coral pink flowers follow, held on erect flower stems. ‡ 12–16 in (30–40 cm). Z4–8 H8–1

B. 'Eroica' Tall, especially in flower, with unusually long-lasting pink blooms held well above the foliage on branched stalks that are red-tinged, and vibrant reddish purple leaves. ‡ 16 in (40 cm). Z4–8 H8–1

B. Evening Bells see *B.* 'Abendglocken'

B. Evening Glow see *B.* 'Abendglut'

BELOW 1 *Bergenia ciliata*
2 *B.* x *schmidtii* **3** *Berkheya purpurea*

B. 'Morgenröte' Notable for its repeat-flowering habit, a second display of rich pink blooms held on red flower stems appear in midsummer if conditions are not too hot. The foliage is deep green and wrinkled, with little winter color, the small leaves up to 6 in (15 cm) long. ‡ 16 in (40 cm). Z4–9 H9–2

B. 'Overture' Fine compact selection with purplish green foliage that becomes more intensely purple-red in winter. The flowers are particularly attractive; claret red in color, bell-shaped and nodding, and carried on red-flushed stems. ‡ 12 in (30 cm). Z4–8 H8–1

B. pacumbis syn. *B. ciliata* f. *ligulata* Compact species; smooth green leaves, 4–6 in (10–15 cm) long, may be round, oval, or slightly broader toward the tip, topped in summer by pink or white flowers with almost round petals. From shaded woods in China, Afghanistan, Bhutan, northeastern India, Kashmir, Nepal, Pakistan, and Sikkim, usually at some altitude, often in rock crevices. ‡ 8 in (20 cm). Z4–8 H8–1

B. 'Perfect' Lilac-red flowers topping foliage that becomes purplish in winter. ‡ 14 in (35 cm). Z4–8 H8–1

B. 'Pugsley's Pink' Green leaves, tinged pink below and up to 6 in (15 cm) long, show off the clear pink late-spring flowers. Little winter foliage color. ‡ 16 in (40 cm). Z4–8 H8–1

B. purpurascens Fine deep green leaves, 4–6 in (10–15 cm) long, are fairly narrow and upright, and in fall turn rich red, the reverses almost mahogany. In mid-spring, reddish flower stems carry nodding purple red flowers. From the eastern Himalaya. ‡ 12 in (30 cm). Z3–8 H8–1. **var. delavayi** Sometimes grown purely as a foliage plant, its glossy evergreen leaves turning deepest beet red in winter. In spring, rich pink flowers appear as an added bonus. Choice and desirable.

B. 'Rosi Klose' Good, reliable cultivar well worth growing for its rose pink flowers on erect flower spikes. The leaves are large and the plant makes good ground cover, even in dry shade. ‡ 14 in (35 cm). Z4–8 H8–1

B. 'Rotblum' syn. 'Redstart' Bronze-tinted leaves, especially in winter, and rosy red flowers. Seed-raised form. ‡ 16–20 in (40–50 cm) Z4–8 H8–1.

B. x schmidtii Tough, vigorous garden plant with large, oval, rich green leaves up to 10 in (25 cm) long, with toothed margins and distinctively long stems. The flowers are bright rose pink and appear in dense heads up to 12 in (30 cm) tall in early spring, but they may be hidden by the leaves. A hybrid between *B. pacumbis* and *B. crassifolia* introduced in 1878. ‡ 12 in (30 cm). Z4–8 H8–1

B. 'Schneekissen' (Snow Cushion) Unusually tall; flowers pink or white tinged pink. The leaves are slightly puckered but have no obvious winter color. Raised by Karl Foerster of Germany. ‡ 20 in (50 cm). Z4–8 H8–1.

B. 'Schneekönigin' (Snow Queen) Unusually large and prolific pale pink flowers in spring that turn a darker shade as they age. The leaves are large and green, up to 8 in (20 cm) long, with slightly curled margins. ‡ 16 in (40 cm). Z4–8 H8–1

B. 'Silberlicht' (Silverlight) Perhaps the most popular of the white-flowered cultivars. Early spring blooms become pinkish with age. The foliage is mid-green, the leaves growing up to 8 in (20 cm) long, but no winter color. Raised by Georg Arends. ‡ 12 in (30 cm). Z3–8 H8–1

B. Silverlight see *B.* 'Silberlicht'

B. Snow Cushion see *B.* 'Schneekissen'

B. Snow Queen see *B.* 'Schneekönigin'

B. stracheyi The oval green leaves, up to 8 in (20 cm) long and dark red in winter; the nodding flowers are rich pink on short stems and are unusual in having a slight fragrance. From a wide area including Pakistan, Tibet, and Russia. ‡ 8 in (20 cm). Z4–8 H8–1 **Alba Group** Dense heads of pure white flowers above tidy foliage rosettes.

B. 'Sunningdale' A desirable cultivar with rounded green leaves up to 7 in (18 cm) long that turn bronze-red in fall; the flowers are rich mauve, and carried on deep red flower stems. Better suited to sunny open positions than many others in this genus, it makes excellent ground cover and is a fine garden plant. Selected by Graham Stuart Thomas of England in 1964. ‡ 16 in (40 cm). Z3–8 H8–1

B. 'Wintermärchen' (Winter Fairy Tales) Deep green, rather thick, 6 in (15 cm) leaves have dark red undersides, then the whole leaf becomes reliably reddish in winter. The flowers are deep pink and appear on high stems in early spring. Partly derived from *B. cordifolia*, but the long leaves are slightly narrower. ‡ 16 in (40 cm). Z4–8 H8–1

BERKHEYA

ASTERACEAE

Showy, rather thistlelike, sun-loving plants with bright yellow flowerheads.

Berkheya comprises about 80 species of spiny-leaved plants, some shrubby, found in dry grassland and rocky places in southern Africa, only one of which is generally grown. Handsome basal rosettes of large, spiny, lobed or divided leaves support stiffly erect, branched and leafy flower stems. Daisylike flowers, bright yellow in most species, open in summer, from spiny buds. Striking plants when in flower, but need a sheltered position, for example against a sunny wall.

CULTIVATION Full sun in any fertile well-drained soil, ideally with some protection from winter rains.

PROPAGATION From seed.

PROBLEMS Usually trouble-free.

B. purpurea Prickly winged stems, covered with cobweblike filaments, carry spiny, mid-green basal leaves up to 18 in (45 cm) long, more or less hairy above and white-woolly beneath. The stems branch to carry few-flowered inflorescences, with flowerheads 3 in (8 cm) across; petal-like ray florets, varying in color from pale mauve to purple, or near-white, surround a darker central disk. The most widely grown species, best given some shelter. From open grassy places in mountains in South Africa. ‡30 in (75 cm). Z9–10 H10–9

BERLANDIERA
Greeneyes
ASTERACEAE

Yellow-flowered and drought-tolerant daisies; *B. lyrata* is noted for its chocolate scent.

Four species of these herbaceous or slightly woody perennials are found on dry plains and rocky slopes in the southern US and Mexico. From their basal clumps of spoon-shaped, usually deeply lobed leaves with silver hairs below arise wiry, sparsely branched stems bearing few leaves and solitary yellow flowerheads, like small sunflowers with yellow or red centers. "Greeneyes" refers to the flowers' appearance after the petals have dropped.

CULTIVATION Full sun and good drainage. Intolerant of wet winters.

PROPAGATION From seed sown in spring at 68°F (20°C). Multi-crowned plants may be divided in spring if rooted portions of taproot are retained.

PROBLEMS Usually trouble-free.

B. lyrata (Lyreleaf greeneyes) Basal clump of dark green, lobed, spoon-shaped leaves, to 6 in (15 cm) long, silvery beneath. From late spring to mid-fall, sparsely branched stems have few leaves and a solitary flowerhead, up to 1½ in (4 cm) across, with 7–9 broad yellow ray florets, striped in red underneath, around a reddish brown eye. The flowers are chocolate-scented, especially at night. Native to southwest US and western Mexico. ‡4–20 in (10–50 cm). Z7–9 H9–7

BESCHORNERIA
AGAVACEAEAE

Bold architectural qualities combine with an exotic appearance and spectacular blooms.
Around 10 species of evergreen perennials, which bear a superficial

resemblance to *Yucca*, originate in Mexico where they inhabit cliffs, usually in areas of some altitude, even cloud forests. Usually grown for their dramatic appearance, they are impressive in bloom, with greenish tubular flowers on tall, often brightly colored stems. None is particularly hardy; they require a sunny, well drained, sheltered position in a warm garden to thrive. The hardiest species is *B. yuccoides*, and this is most often grown. Recent collections by American enthusiasts from high altitudes bring some promise of hardier selections.

CULTIVATION Best in a choice position, in the open in mild maritime gardens, or in sheltered city gardens, but elsewhere will usually need the protection of a warm, sunny wall. Plant in well-drained soil; add extra grit if required. Mulch the crown well with grit to avoid rotting over winter, and provide extra protection in particularly cold conditions. Plants bulk up slowly, forming clumps of individual rosettes that die off after flowering, new rosettes appearing from the base. Remove faded spikes after flowering. In unfavorable areas, plants grow well in large containers, which can be moved inside in the coldest weather.

PROPAGATION From seed, or by division in spring.

PROBLEMS Usually trouble-free.

B. 'Ding Dong' Large plant that forms rosettes of rough-textured greenish leaves about 3 ft (1 m) in diameter. The towering, pinkish red branching flowering spike bears red and green bell-shaped flowers. An American hybrid between *B. decosteriana* and *B. septentrionalis.* ‡6–10 ft (2–3 m). Z7–10 H10–7

B. septentrionalis Forms a large glossy rosette about 28–40 in (70–100 cm) in diameter, with apple green leaves that curl gently downward. Well-established plants produce a rich glossy red-stemmed flowering spike from which hang red and green flowers. As with most species, the flower spike grows out at a curious angle, rather than directly upward. A recent introduction, named in 1987, from shady areas in the Mexican mountains. ‡5 ft (1.5 m). Z7–10 H10–7

B. yuccoides The most familiar species, the 24-in (60-cm) long, swordlike leaves form a basal rosette and are usually gray-green and rather floppy. New leaves are held erect in the center, then as they mature fall outward. Individual rosettes measure up to 32 in (80 cm) across and about 24 in (60 cm) high. The rich pinkish red flowering stalk is arching and appears in summer on mature plants. It features large

RIGHT 1 *Blechnum penna-marina*
2 *B. spicant*

attractive coral pink bracts with green, pendent flowers, and remains attractive for several weeks. Mexico. ‡4 ft (1.2 m). Z12–13 H12–10.
'Quicksilver' Features particularly silvery foliage.

BETONICA *see* STACHYS
BISTORTA *see* PERSICARIA

BLECHNUM
Hard fern
BLECHNACEAE

Varied, mainly evergreen ferns, the largest species making magnificent specimens.
About 200 mostly evergreen species occur worldwide, mainly in the tropics but with several species of garden interest found in the temperate regions of both the Northern and Southern hemispheres. Growing from either short and erect or longer and creeping rhizomes, the fronds are usually lance-shaped, with a simple arrangement of undivided segments down each side of the frond. In most species, the fronds that produce spores differ from the normal, vegetative fronds by being much narrower. Spore-bearing structures are arranged in a line along each side of the segments' midribs. A number of species are enhanced by reddish young growth in spring.

CULTIVATION Grow in neutral or preferably acidic soil in a moist, shady position. Avoid alkaline or waterlogged soil.

PROPAGATION From spores; species with creeping rhizomes can be divided easily. Those with upright rhizomes can be divided if there are at least two distinct crowns.

PROBLEMS Usually trouble-free.

B. chilense A magnificent, large, evergreen fern with erect, long-stalked, leathery, dark green fronds with slightly

wavy segments. Rhizomes are erect and each crown forms a short trunk. The plant also spreads at the root to form colonies: new crowns may appear a little distance from the established plant. In moist, acidic soil with plenty of leaf mold, it may develop into the tallest of the evergreen, fully hardy ferns. For cool temperate gardens; it is best given space to develop, although excess growth is easily removed. Best increased by removing good-sized pieces from an established clump. From low altitudes in temperate Chile. ‡6 ft (180 cm). Z10–11 H12–10

B. discolor Deciduous fern with narrow, pale green fronds borne on an erect rhizome which, in very humid environments, can eventually form a short, narrow trunk. The undersides of the fronds are almost white. Fertile fronds appear late in the season in the center of the crown of vegetative fronds. In cold gardens, needs a site sheltered from extreme cold, but is well suited to moist city gardens and coastal areas. Straw in the crown or around the trunk over winter would be a wise precaution. From coastal and mountain woodlands in New Zealand. ‡16–20 in (40–50 cm). Z7–10 H10–7

B. nudum (Fishbone water fern) Usually evergreen plant with a short, upright rhizome, sometimes forming a short trunk, to 12 in (30 cm) tall, bearing narrow, once-divided, dark green fronds. The spore-bearing fronds appear late in the season and are more upright, with narrower segments. Very handsome, and can form multiple trunks. Best grown in sheltered, warmer gardens—in urban areas or coastal regions, for example. After severe winters, the main crown may die, especially if it has developed a trunk, but new crowns usually appear around the base. Grows in damp forests in southern and eastern Australia. ‡12–24 in (30–60 cm). Z8–10 H10–8

B. penna-marina Small, rather variable, evergreen fern with a creeping rhizome, capable of forming a large

ABOVE **1** *Bletilla striata* **2** *Boltonia asteroides*

colony of narrow, glossy dark green fronds. Spore-bearing fronds are taller and more erect, with narrower segments. Native to grassland and bogs in both lowland and alpine regions in Australia, New Zealand, and Chile. ‡4–8 in (10–20 cm). Z10–13 H12–10. **subsp. *alpinum*** Smaller fronds that are red in spring and dull dark green when mature. ‡2–6 in (5–15 cm). **subsp. *alpinum* 'Cristatum'** The tips of fronds are neatly crested.

B. spicant (Hard fern) Evergreen fern with a short, erect rhizome bearing a rosette of spreading, narrowly lance-shaped, dark green fronds. Fertile fronds arise from the center of the crown and are stiffly upright, with much narrower segments. Needs moist, acidic soil with plenty of leaf mold. Native to damp, acidic woodlands in Europe (including the British Isles), western Asia, and North America. ‡12–18 in (30–45 cm). Z10–11 H12–10. **'Cristatum'** Tips of all fronds are crested. ‡8 in (20 cm).

BLETILLA
ORCHIDACEAE

Garden orchids for a lightly shaded spot, with flowers like pink or yellow hummingbirds and lovely, pleated foliage.

Some nine species are native to woodland margins under the dripline of trees in temperate areas of eastern Asia. The small underground bulbous corms, technically called pseudobulbs, produce arching paper-thin foliage like 8–10-in (20–30-cm) swords but with parallel ribs. A slender flower spike arising from the center of the sometimes variegated, deciduous leaves bears a succession of nicely spaced, ½–2-in (1–5-cm) nodding

blooms with ridged lips, opening from the bottom upward. The show can last for more than a month.

Ranging from magenta to rose to yellow to white, the often half-open flowers are becoming increasingly popular in gardens as more hybrids appear, including some involving newly rediscovered species. The results are variable in color, form, and the degree of openness of the flowers, and the range of tone and combination is sometimes surprising. *Bletilla* is an ancient orchid, mentioned by the Chinese emperor in 280 BC, and still used medicinally to control bleeding and tuberculosis. *See Orchids, p. 345.*

CULTIVATION Easy to grow. Plant 2 in (5 cm) deep (4–6 in/10–15 cm in zones 5–6) in humus-rich, loamy soil in light shade, or in full sun if protected from afternoon heat. Growth is fastest in moist to waterlogged soil. Plants are best left undisturbed to spread into large clumps. Mulch well with compost where winter temperatures fall below 5°F (–15°C) and to prevent early emergence of shoots susceptible to early spring frosts. Needs several months near or below freezing to flower well. Thrives in containers.

PROPAGATION By division of cormlike pseudobulbs, removal of offsets; easy to propagate from seed (seedlings should bloom three years after pollination).

PROBLEMS Virtually trouble-free, although slugs can be a problem. Can get stressed if very dry.

B. hyacintha see *B. striata*

B. ochracea (Yellow hardy orchid) Gaining in popularity, this species flowers in yellow, with a showy deep

yellow or white lip strongly marked with red, orange, or lavender. Bears three to ten blooms in early to midsummer on a sometimes branched stem, about three weeks later than the more commonly grown *B. striata*. Some so-called *B. ochracea* plants available, particularly the rosier-toned ones, may be natural hybrids with the rarely grown *B. szetchuanica*. Growth is slow, and it prefers wet soil. In full sun, grows less tall and more branched, often with red-tinged flowers. In shade, blooms are more mustard in color. Excellent with ferns. Native to China's Yunnan and Sichuan provinces. ‡12–20 in (30–50 cm). Z7–8 H8–7

B. **Penway** Prefix given to a range of slightly variable hybrids created by English breeder Richard Evenden. ‡12–24 in (30–60 cm). Z7–9 H9–7. Includes **Penway Dragon**, generally purplish pink with a white lip, **Penway Rainbow**, in combinations of primrose and rose, **Penway Starshine**, light rosy purple with a strikingly marked yellow and red lip, and **Penway Sunset**, pale yellow flowers flushed peach.

B. striata (syn. *B. hyacintha*) (Hyacinth orchid) This best-known, widely available hardy species, from elevations as high as 12,000 ft (3,600 m), boasts bright magenta to pale pink or white flowers with striped, ruffled or ridged lips generally marked with deeper tones. Blooms for a month or more from mid-spring to early summer with up to a dozen successive 1–2-in (2.5–5-cm) flowers per spike; usually, 2–4 are open at once. The 4–6 beautifully pleated leaves can reach 18 in (45 cm). All forms have a slight, sweet scent. Takes more cold if well mulched. Looks good with *Aquilegia*, ferns, *Trillium,* and hostas. Found in China, Japan, and Tibet. ‡16–24 in (40–60 cm). Z5–8 H8–5 **var. *alba*** see *B. striata* var. *japonica* f. *gebina*. **'Albostriata'** Variegated leaf with narrow white

edges. An unnamed yellow-striped form is also sometimes available. **'Murasaki Shikibu'** Unexpectedly blue-toned. Z6–10 H10–6. **var. *japonica* f. *gebina*** syn. *B. striata* var. *alba*) White flowers, sometimes flushed pink, with red-streaked yellow lip. **var. *japonica* f. *gebina* 'Variegata'** White flowers and a highly prized white-edged leaf. Z6–10 H10–6

BOCCONIA *see* MACLEAYA

BOLTONIA
Doll's daisy, False chamomile
ASTERACEAE

Like a tall Michaelmas daisy, but with smaller flowers in billowing clusters.

Five species are native to moist, open situations in North America. All are tall, hairless perennials with erect stems and alternate linear or lance-shaped leaves. The stems branch readily toward the apex, where they bear large, open heads of small, daisylike flowerheads in attractive clouds. Best suited to the back of a border, these plants also excel in larger areas of naturalistic planting where other plants can lend support.

CULTIVATION Prefer fertile soil in sun or part-shade. All except 'Nana' need staking. Shorter self-supporting plants can be developed by chopping growth back by one-third in late spring. Divide every 2–3 years to maintain vigor.

PROPAGATION Sow seed in spring at 59°F (15°C), or divide.

PROBLEMS Powdery mildew.

B. asteroides (White doll's daisy) Deciduous, clump-forming or slowly creeping perennial with upright stems. The linear to lance-shaped leaves, to 4¾ in (12 cm) long, are grayish green, aging to green. Flowerheads to ¾ in (2 cm) across, with yellow centers and slender white to pinkish purple rays, are produced from midsummer to mid-fall. Found in waterside habitats and damp meadows in central and eastern North America. ‡6½–8 ft (2–2.5 m). Z4–8 H9–1. **var. *latisquama*** Flowerheads over ¾ in (2 cm) across, rays white to lilac. ‡6 ft (1.8 m). **var. *latisquama* 'Nana'** Short, rays white to lilac. ‡30–36 in (75–90 cm). **'Snowbank'** Rays white. ‡5 ft (1.5 m). **'Pink Beauty'** Rays pink, white at the base. Flowers larger, foliage more blue, and the season longer than 'Snowbank'. Introduced by Montrose Nursery in North Carolina. ‡5 ft (1.5 m).

B. *cantonensis* see *Kalimeris pinnatifida*

B. *incisa* see *Kalimeris incisa*

B. *indica* see *Kalimeris pinnatifida*

BORAGO
Borage
BORAGINACEAE

Rather coarse but attractive blue-flowered plants, with one perennial species commonly found in gardens.

Three species of these hardy deciduous perennial or annual plants hail from a variety of habitats in western, central, and eastern Europe and the Mediterranean. All have hairy alternate leaves, and bear loose branching clusters of nodding star- or bell-shaped flowers, usually blue, with five spreading lobes. *Borago officinalis*, an annual and so not included here, is one of the most popular garden herbs.

CULTIVATION Easy to grow and thrives best in light shade in moist soil. Tolerant of poor, gravelly soil. Remove flowered stems to prevent self-seeding. Grows well in gravel, and good in a mixed or informal perennial border.

PROPAGATION From seed or by division in spring, or cuttings of young shoots in late spring or summer. Self-seeds copiously, which can be a nuisance.

PROBLEMS Usually trouble-free, but can self-seed excessively.

B. *laxiflora* see *B. pygmaea*.

B. *pygmaea* syn. *B. laxiflora* (Slender borage, Dwarf borage) A short-lived, somewhat sprawling, branched perennial with large rosettes of coarse, hairy, elongated leaves to 8 in (20 cm). Clear, pale azure blue flowers are bell-shaped, nodding, to ¹⁄₁₆ in (1.5 mm) across, and carried in loose, branching sprays in summer. Very pretty, but tends to smother less robust neighbors that may not survive to reassert themselves at the end of its short life. Found wild on Corsica, Sardinia, and Capri. ‡6–24 in (15–60 cm). Z5–9 H9–5

BOTHRIOCHLOA
POACEAE

Drought-tolerant grasses with interesting, often aromatic foliage and unusual flowerheads.

Some 35 perennial species are found in tropical and warm temperate regions throughout the world, on rocky and sandy slopes and in dry places. Usually clump-forming, with leaves that die back over winter after developing attractive fall colors. The tall flower stems carry flowerheads that are made up of separate tassels carrying spiky little flowers that arch over from a central axis like fingers, or a bird's foot. These warm-season plants grow rapidly late in the spring and flower in late summer and early fall. Good in drifts in gravel gardens.

BELOW *Borago pygmaea*

CULTIVATION Grow in well-drained, light, sandy soil in full sun; protect from rain and cold in the winter. Transplant or divide in late spring.

PROPAGATION From seed or by division.

PROBLEMS Can rot at the base in wet or humid conditions.

B. *ischaemum* syn. *Andropogon ischaemum* (Yellow bluestem) Clump-forming, with conspicuous gray-green leaves turning purplish in fall. In mid-to late summer, slender purple stems bear graceful fans of 3–15 reddish purple, fingerlike spikes. Attractive fall color with purple foliage, stems turning yellow, and bronze flowerheads—plant in large drifts to appreciate fully. Best in a hot, sunny position. Divide in late spring. From dry rocky hillsides and sparse forests in the Caucasus to Japan. ‡32 in (80 cm). Z5–8 H8–5

BOUTELOUA
Grama grass
POACEAE

Drought-tolerant, turf-forming grasses with fascinating one-sided flowers.

About 24 annual and deciduous perennial species are found from Canada to Argentina but mainly in Mexico, on rocky hillsides and in open desert and grasslands. Usually forming low-growing clumps, they are predominant among the so-called "bunch-grasses" of the Great Plains of North America, and several species are important forage grasses. The flower stems carry distinctive one-sided flowerheads with up to 80 single spiky flowers hanging from short branches, sometimes held at an angle from the main stem. Warm-season grasses, sometimes flowering late in summer and into fall, they need high humidity and an open area protected from winter rain and cold. Grama grass is best grown where the flowers can be seen close-up.

CULTIVATION Prefer good well-drained soil in full sun, but with some protection from the intrusion of other plants.

PROPAGATION From seed or by division in late spring.

PROBLEMS Usually trouble-free.

B. *curtipendula* syn. *B. racemosa* (Sideoats grama) Blue-gray leaves, ⅛ in (3–4 mm) wide, form loose, low-growing tussocks that turn red-bronze in fall. Numerous slightly arching stems appear from midsummer, hung on one side like flags on a pole, with purplish oatlike flowers, 1¼–2½ in (3–6 cm) long, turning red-brown to gold. Drought-tolerant and very effective in gravel gardens, but may suffer in cold, wet winters. Grows on dry prairies and deserts from Ontario to Argentina. ‡3 ft (1 m). Z5–9 H9–5

B. *gracilis* syn. *B. oligostachys* (Mosquito grass, Blue grama) Very slow-growing rhizomes, carrying upright blue-green leaves ¼ in (6 mm) wide, form thick low-growing clumps. In mid- and late summer, numerous stems appear, bearing curious 2-in (5-cm) flowerheads, which are shaped like small inverted toothbrushes, reddish brown to straw-colored and attached almost horizontally to the tips of the stems. Plant this grass at path edges or in containers, where the unusual flowers can be appreciated. They prefer slightly acidic, sandy soil and appreciate protection in wet, cold winters. Found on dry prairies, from the Great Plains south into Mexico and through Central America to South America. One of the most common short grasses of the Great Plains; used as a food grain by American Indians. ‡8–15 in (20–38 cm). Z5–9 H9–5

BOYKINIA
SAXIFRAGACEAE

Delicately attractive, hardy shade-lovers for woodland gardens that flower in spring or summer and have attractive foliage.

Ten species of deciduous plants, related to *Heuchera*, are found in moist woodlands and on mountains in Japan and North America; only about half of these are grown in gardens. Spreading from short rhizomes, the plants create attractive ground cover with their long-stalked, basal, kidney-shaped or rounded leaves, bronze-tinted when young in some species. Somewhat dome-shaped branching heads of white, or more rarely red, five-petaled flowers on leafy stems.

CULTIVATION Ideal for cool, nonalkaline soil that is rich in humus, in a part-shade spot.

PROPAGATION By division in spring, or from seed sown as soon as ripe in a cold frame.

PROBLEMS Usually trouble-free.

B. *aconitifolia* Clump-forming, with hairy, medium green, five- to seven-lobed, tooth-edged leaves up to 6 in (15 cm) long. Rather shallow, bell-shaped white flowers with yellowish centers, ½ in (1 cm) across, are produced in early and midsummer. From the eastern US. ‡6–24 in (15–60 cm). Z6–8 H8–6

B. *elata* see *B. occidentalis*

B. *heucheriformis* see *B. jamesii*

B. *jamesii* syn. *B. heucheriformis*, *Telesonix jamesii* Forms a mound of growth with rosettes of slightly lobed, tooth-edged, kidney-shaped leaves up to 1¼ in (3 cm) long, medium green and leathery in texture. Open, bell-shaped flowers with frilled edges, ¾ in (2 cm) across, are carried in loose heads during mid- and late spring. The petals are spoon-shaped and pink-red with a

ABOVE **1** *Boykinia aconitifolia*
2 *Briza media*

green eye. Although this species likes acidic, humus-rich, moist soil, conditions must be well drained. Rarely sets seed in gardens. Previously sometimes listed as *Telesonix jamesii,* since it has twice the number of stamens as other *Boykinia* species. From mountainous habitats in the northwest US. ‡ 6 in (15 cm). Z5–9 H9–6

B. occidentalis syn. *B. elata* A tough patch-forming plant that makes excellent ground cover. The shiny, lobed, deeply toothed leaves, up to 4 in (10 cm) across, are almost circular or heart-shaped, but occasionally kidney-shaped. Small white flowers, with petals ¼ in (6–7 mm) long, are produced over most of the summer. From Vancouver Island to southern California. ‡ 24–36 in (60–90 cm). Z6–8 H8–6

B. rotundifolia Patch-forming, making effective ground cover. The shiny leaves, with shallow lobes and toothed edges—almost circular to heart-shaped, and sometimes kidney-shaped—can be as long or as wide as 6 in (16 cm). Branching heads of brilliant white flowers, ⅜–½ in (9–12 mm) wide, are produced during summer. From southern California. ‡ 24 in (60 cm). Z7–8 H8–7

BRIZA
Quaking grass
POACEAE

Delicate ornamental grasses with trembling flowerheads, hence the common name.

Twenty perennial and annual clump-forming species are found throughout temperate regions of Europe, Asia, and parts of South America, in both dry and moist soil on open grasslands. Loose or more compact, wiry stems are hung with small, rounded, nodding flowers like flattened oats or lockets. A few species are grown in gardens for their beauty and for drying.

CULTIVATION Easy to grow in an open area in fertile, well-drained soil.

PROPAGATION From seed or by division in spring.

PROBLEMS Usually trouble-free.

B. media (Common quaking grass, Trembling grass) Slowly forms a creeping mat of soft, purplish, pointed evergreen leaves 6 in (15 cm) long and ⅛ in (3 mm) wide. From early to late summer, slender stems with wiry branches growing out at right angles are hung with quivering, locket-shaped, green-purple flowers, ⅙–½ in (4–12 mm) long, which become buff later in the season. Best in poor soil, otherwise plants can become rather coarse and scruffy. Trim back the flowerheads in late summer to encourage a flush of new growth during the winter. Cultivated in gardens since medieval times, and lovely in wildflower meadows, this grass is lovely in lawns, and in mass plantings at path edges and in dry areas, and is excellent for drying. From Britain, Europe, and northern and western Asia, on dry grasslands and ancient, moist pasture. ‡ 6–30 in (15–75 cm). Z4–11 H12–1. **'Limouzi'** Deep purple-green leaves; larger flowerheads on purple stems. ‡ 18–24 in (45–60 cm). Z4–11 H12–1

B. subaristata syn. *Chasolytrum subaristatum* (Chilean quaking grass) Evergreen, forming a handsome clump. In early and midsummer, the dense sprays of arching stems bear nodding, silver-green, pearl-like flowers that hang from one side of the stem; these eventually turn buff. Best grown in loamy soil in sun or part shade, and lovely in drifts at the edge of wildflower meadows. Found on grassy hillsides in Chile. ‡ 16–24 in (40–60 cm). Z4–11 H12–1

BROMUS
POACEAE

Handsome nodding grasses for many situations that flower from early spring onward.

About 150 perennial and annual species are found in the temperate regions of the world, in woodlands, meadows, and wasteland. Stately, loosely branched or more compact and plume-shaped flowerheads, with spike- or wedge-shaped green flowers, sometimes tinged purple or pink, and often with stiff, occasionally longish hairs.

CULTIVATION Thrives in any well-drained—often alkaline—soil in sun to part-shade.

PROPAGATION By division in spring, or from seed; some can self-sow invasively.

PROBLEMS Usually trouble-free.

B. inermis 'Skinner's Gold' A steadily creeping rootstock carries clumps of vertically striped leaves with green margins and broad asymmetrical vertical light yellow bands. The yellow stems bear large, gold, drooping spike-shaped flowers in early summer and fall. Less invasive than the green-leaved *B. inermis,* and best grown in well-drained infertile soil in an open situation to create a neat plant. Cut back untidy growth and divide in spring. The green-leaved species has been used as a hay crop, and it has naturalized on rocky wasteland. ‡ 3 ft (1 m). Z4–9 H9–4

BRUNNERA
BORAGINACEAE

Tough yet quietly elegant, spring-flowering shade-lovers in an increasing range of attractive foliage forms.

Three species of these deciduous plants grow in forests and glades from the eastern Mediterranean into Turkey and Russia. Dense, slow-spreading growth, from black, thonglike roots, supports the basal leaves and flowers on separate, roughly hairy, upright stems. The slightly raspy foliage is broad and heart-shaped, and the sprays of blue flowers open just above the leaves in typical forget-me-not style.

CULTIVATION Grows well in dry shade, or in more open situations if the soil is moist.

PROPAGATION From seed (not cultivars) or by division.

PROBLEMS Usually trouble-free.

RIGHT **1** *Brunnera macrophylla* 'Dawson's White' **2** *B. macrophylla* 'Gordano Gold' **3** *B. macrophylla* 'Jack Frost'

A BRIGHT SPRING PARTNERSHIP

BLUE AND YELLOW IS A much-loved spring color combination, often seen in the form of forget-me-nots planted with yellow tulips. Here, in a part-shaded corner, the same two colors are showcased by two tough perennials. The compact dome of bright, almost daffodil-yellow flowerheads is provided by *Euphorbia polychroma*, which opens its first flowers in early spring, shortly after the shoots emerge, and continues the display for months. The airy blue sprays of *Brunnera macrophylla*, a relative of forget-me-not (*Myosotis*), are followed by broad heart-shaped foliage that contrasts with the much smaller and narrower euphorbia leaves. The brunnera will slowly but steadily spread itself around the euphorbia, providing a pretty bright blue mist to enhance the sunny face of the euphorbia flowers each spring.

B. macrophylla Slowly but relentlessly spreads to make an effective ground cover, with rough, hairy, boldly heart-shaped leaves, up to 6 in (15 cm) across, developing into a striking assemblage as the season progresses. Its typical forget-me-not sprays of sparkling blue flowers, about ¼ in (6 mm) across, open in mid- and late spring. Useful in dry shade, but the variegated forms are best in richer, moister conditions in shade. Thrives in sun if the soil is not dry; otherwise, the foliage, especially of variegated forms, may scorch. Variegated cultivars may also revert to green, so remove any shoots that are green rather than variegated. Propagate by division. Broken roots of variegated forms left in the soil usually produce green shoots. From Turkey and the Caucasus, but naturalized in Britain. ‡ 12–18 in (30–45 cm). Z3–7 H7–1. **'Aluminum Spot'** *see* 'Langtrees'. **'Betty Bowring'** White flowers, some seedlings come blue. **'Dawson's White'** Foliage irregularly patterned or edged in cream or white, some leaves almost completely white. **'Gordano Gold'** Foliage develops yellow patches as it matures. Introduced by Simon Wills, a former officer of the British Hardy Plant Society. **'Hadspen Cream'** Leaves broadly edged in cream. Raised by Eric Smith of England. **'Jack Frost'** Spectacular foliage entirely silvered with green veins and border. A superb container plant, a spontaneous mutation of 'Langtrees' selected at Walter's Gardens, MI. **'Langtrees'** Leaves spotted silver, especially toward the edge. Introduced by Dr. Rogersen and named for his Devon, England garden. **'Looking Glass'** Silver foliage with green veins at first, then becoming almost entirely silver. A spontaneous mutation of 'Jack Frost' also from Walter's Gardens, Michigan. **'Variegata'** *see* 'Dawson's White'.

BUGLOSSOIDES
Gromwell
BORAGINACEAE

One commonly grown, purple- to blue-flowered species is extremely useful as ground cover under trees and shrubs.

About 15 species of hardy annuals, perennials, and more-or-less evergreen subshrubs that are native to western and southern Europe and Asia. They are found in a variety of habitats, from arable fields to scrub and woodlands, often in the mountains. Hairy plants of varied habit, they have upright or sprawling stems that in some species may root at the tip when in contact with soil. The leaves of gromwells are variable in shape, hairy, and mid- to dark green. Flowers are funnel- or salver-shaped, five-lobed, often blue, and carried in terminal clusters. The one species common in cultivation was previously included within the genus *Lithospermum*.

CULTIVATION Best in well-drained, ideally neutral to alkaline soil.

PROPAGATION By division in spring, or from seed in spring or fall.

PROBLEMS Usually trouble-free.

B. purpurocaerulea syn. *Lithospermum purpurocaeruleum* (Purple gromwell, Blue gromwell) Deciduous ground-cover plant that spreads rapidly and can become invasive. Sprawling stems up to 24 in (60 cm) long, with dark green, lance-shaped to narrowly elliptical, pointed leaves to 3 in (8 cm) long, arise from creeping underground stems. The shorter, upright flowering stems bear clusters of velvety-textured flowers to ¾ in (2 cm) across. Buds purple-red; flowers turn an intense gentian blue. Excellent for wilder parts of the garden, and makes good ground cover under trees and shrubs, since it competes well with their roots. Tolerates sun and shade, with lightly shaded conditions being ideal. Does best in well-drained but moisture-retentive soil, neutral to alkaline, but will tolerate a degree of acidity. Easy to propagate by division of rooted stems, or from cuttings. Found throughout Europe, ‡ 6–12 in (15–30 cm). Z6–8 H8–6

BULBINELLA
ASPHODELACEAE

Neat, yellow-flowered plants with the appeal of small, red-hot pokers add a distinctive touch to the front of a bed or border.

Twenty species of evergreen and deciduous plants from South Africa and New Zealand; only the New Zealand species described here are hardy and easily obtainable. Clump-forming, deciduous perennials with fleshy roots, grassy foliage, and dense spikes of yellow, six-petaled, starry

RIGHT *Buglossoides purpurocaerulea*

flowers, they are much confused, and may be sold under each other's names, but can be distinguished by their seedpods.

CULTIVATION Easy to grow in moisture-retentive soil, particularly if neutral to acidic.

PROPAGATION Either from seed or by division.

PROBLEMS Usually trouble-free.

B. angustifolia Tufted clump-forming plant with erect, rich green leaves, 24 in (60 cm) long and up to 1.5 cm (⅝ in) wide, with their margins rolled inward. The dense flower spikes are 5–8 in (13–20 cm) long and just overtop the leaves. They are formed by numerous ½-in- (1-cm-) wide, bright yellow flowers in early summer, followed by long, stalkless seedpods. Thrives best in a sunny, preferably open site. From New Zealand. ‡16–24 in (40–60 cm). Z8–9 H9–8

B. hookeri In effect, this plant is a slightly more substantial version of *B. angustifolia*. The 30-in (75-cm) blunt-tipped leaves are ⅝–1¼ in (1.5–3 cm) wide, and erect to spreading. The slightly darker flowers, ½–⅝ in (1–1.4 cm) across, are followed by short-stalked, broadly oval seedpods. Native to New Zealand. ‡16–24 in (40–60 cm). Z8–9 H9–8

BUPHTHALMUM
Oxeye
ASTERACEAE

Modest but reliable daisies with a conveniently long flowering period.

Two species of these bright but unsophisticated deciduous plants grow in open habitats in Europe and western Asia. Form clumps or spread slowly, their erect stems bearing alternate, usually narrow leaves and yellow daisylike flowerheads. One of a number of plants with the common name, oxeye; *Leucanthemum vulgare*, with its dark-centered white flowers, is the more familiar oxeye.

CULTIVATION Best in poor, sharply drained soil in full sun.

PROPAGATION From seed sown in spring at 50°F (10°C), or by division in spring.

PROBLEMS Usually trouble-free.

B. salicifolium (Willow-leaf oxeye, Yellow oxeye) Clump-forming deciduous perennial with lance-shaped to reverse egg-shaped, toothed or untoothed leaves to 4 in (10 cm) long. The flowerheads, borne at the apex of the leafy stems from early summer to early fall, are usually solitary, to 2½ in (6.5 cm) across, and have yellow centers and yellow, blunt-tipped rays. Graham Stuart Thomas recommends that it is "far more beautiful when allowed to flop." Native to central and southern Europe. ‡24 in (60 cm). Z5–8 H8–5. **'Alpengold'** Flowerheads larger than the species. Seed-raised. **'Sunwheel'** Doubtfully distinct from the species, said to be slightly shorter. Seed-raised. ‡20 in (50 cm).

B. speciosum see *Telekia speciosa*

BUPLEURUM
APIACEAE

Distinctive plants featuring attractive species that are especially well adapted to relatively dry and poor soil.

Of approximately 100 species in this genus, only a few are grown, perhaps the best known being one of the few shrubby members of the family, *Bupleurum fruticosum*. Widely distributed through Eurasia, the Canary Isles, the northern US, and South Africa, bupleurums are characterized by their simple undivided leaves, often with parallel veins. Many feature attractive, leathery, blue-green foliage color. The flowerheads vary: in some species, the flowers are condensed into tight heads surrounded by green or yellow petal-like modified leaves (bracts), giving the look of single flowers; in others, the flowers form more open, typically cow-parsley-like heads. The flowers are yellow or greenish yellow, sometimes coppery, and often rich in nectar, attracting a wide range of insects.

CULTIVATION Grows well in any reasonably fertile but well-drained soil in a sunny position.

PROPAGATION From seed sown fresh in the fall; germination occurs in the following winter to early spring. Some may self-sow. Clump-forming species can also be divided as growth begins in the spring.

PROBLEMS Usually trouble-free.

B. angulosum A choice and very slow-growing species forming clumps of narrow, blue-green grassy leaves that form rosettes. An effective and useful plant for dry and sunny situations, where it will self-seed freely, flowering continuously for many weeks from midsummer onward. This species is native to England and is widely distributed in central and southern Europe eastward into Asia. ‡24–36 in (60–90 cm). Z4–9 H9–1

B. falcatum (Sickle-leaved hare's ear) Airy sprays of small, greenish yellow flowers, in umbels ¾–2 in (2–5 cm) across, are held on wiry stems clothed with narrow, sickle-shaped leaves, arising from broader-leaved basal rosettes. An effective and useful plant for dry and sunny situations, where it will self-seed freely, flowering for many weeks from midsummer onward. Best used in wildflower meadows in hot, rocky situations. This species is widely distributed in central and southern Europe eastward into Asia. ‡24–36 in (60–90 cm). Z5–9 H9–1

B. longifolium An upright plant, its basal leaves long and narrow, the leaf stalk characteristically winged and sheathing the stem at the base. The upper leaves are oval to heart-shaped, clasping the stem. The small, yellow, often red-tinged flowers are held in tight umbels surrounded by oval pointed bracts that can vary from green to yellowish or copper, giving a striking appearance in the summer garden. Individual plants are relatively short-lived and should be renewed by sowing fresh seed regularly. From central Europe into Siberia. ‡28–36 in (70–90 cm). Z4–9 H9–1

B. rotundifolium A short-lived species with characteristic silver-gray elliptical or rounded leaves, the upper leaves encircling the stem, the lower ones short stalked. The small umbels, to 1 in (2.5 cm) in diameter, of yellow-green—occasionally pure yellow—flowers are surrounded by oval pointed yellow-green, coppery gold, or light green bracts. Often found as a weed of arable land and grows naturally in open dry habitats, where it maintains itself by freely self-seeding. Found throughout Europe to Russia and naturalized in Britain and Holland. ‡18–24 in (45–60 cm). Z3–7 H7–1

ABOVE 1 *Bulbinella hookeri*
2 *Buphthalmum salicifolium*
3 *Bupleurum falcatum*

C

CALAMAGROSTIS
Reed grass
POACEAE

Handsome reedlike grasses, native to damp woodlands, that are adaptable to many garden situations.

About 270 perennial species from northern temperate regions and tropical mountains, growing mainly in damp areas, woods, heaths, and mountain grasslands. Slowly spreading clump- formers, they produce airy, feathery flowerheads that ripen to narrow bronze spikes. These hold well through the winter, thereby making them some of the most sought-after ornamental grasses, both for the summer garden and as handsome architectural features in winter.

CULTIVATION Fertile, moist soil, in sun and part-shade. Cut back old growth in early spring to about 5 in (13 cm).

PROPAGATION. By division, or from seed of species plants.

PROBLEMS Leaves can suffer from rust in wet summers or when densely planted.

C. x **acutiflora** syn. *C. epigejos* 'Hortorum' Forms slowly spreading, dense, deciduous clumps of narrow dark green leaves, up to 30 in (75 cm) long, that die back over winter. They support, in early summer, straight, sturdy stems topped with graceful arching blue-green plumes that open into light, feathery flowerheads tinged with purple. The heads mature to a narrow buff spike holding through the winter, making it a useful focal plant in the fall and winter garden. Best grown in full sun; in shadier condition, stems can become lax and topple over. Lovely grown with tall herbaceous perennials, as a container or specimen plant, or in drifts, where movement through this graceful grass can be appreciated. A hybrid, occasionally occurring naturally in the wild, between *C. epigejos* and *C. arundinacea*, both native grasses of Europe. Unappreciated as a hybrid at first, which has caused some name changes. ‡ 24–60 in (60–150 cm). Z5–9 H9–5. **'Karl Foerster'** The typical form, originally known as *C. epigejos* 'Hortorum', then named *C.* x *acutiflora* 'Stricta' and then renamed again, with the now-settled name of *C.* x *acutiflora* 'Karl Foerster' after the distinguished horticulturist and breeder who first recognized the hybrid nature of this grass. *C.* 'Karl Foerster', the 2001 Perennial Plant of the Year, is shorter and softer than other selections. ‡ 6½ ft (2 m). Z5–9 H9–5. **'Overdam'** Leaves with vertical cream stripes; flowerheads pinkish. Best in cool conditions with low humidity. ‡ 36 in (90 cm). Z5–9 H9–5. **'Stricta'** *see* 'Karl Foerster'—although some say 'Stricta' is shorter, with narrower, earlier flowerheads.

C. argentea *see Stipa argentea*

C. arundinacea (Rough reed grass) A rather coarse grass forming slowly spreading clumps of narrow leaves up to 20 in (50 cm) long, developing good fall color. In mid- and late summer, sturdy stems bear narrow, purple-brown, feathery flowerheads. It can be invasive, spreading at the root and prolifically self-seeding, but it is pleasing grown in drifts in woods or bog gardens. A parent of the more widely grown *C.* x *acutiflora*. Found wild in Europe and into Asia in moist, open woodlands. ‡ 5–5½ ft (1.5–1.7 m). Z5–9 H9–5

C. brachytricha syn. *C. varia*, *Stipa brachytricha* (Foxtail grass) Dense clumps of glossy gray-green leaves up to 24 in (60 cm) long turn yellow in fall; form a fountain of gently arching foliage. In late summer and early fall, tall stems carry narrow flowerheads opening into airy, silver-gray plumes tinged pinkish purple that remain fluffy throughout the winter. Tolerant of a variety of situations if given adequate moisture. Especially effective grown in drifts or as a specimen plant in a container. Good for drying. From moist woodlands and woodland edges in eastern Asia. ‡ 3–5 ft (90–150 cm). Z5–9 H9–5

LEFT *Calamagrostis* x *acutiflora* 'Karl Foerster'

C. epigejos (Feather reed grass) Dense, slowly spreading clumps carry rather lax foliage up to about 30 in (75 cm) long and appealing, slightly fluffy flowers with a somewhat loose seedhead 6–12 in (15–30 cm) long. It is most effective if allowed to spread in drifts by lakesides and in bog gardens; can be invasive through prolific self-seeding and spreading roots. Wild parent of *C.* x *acutiflora* found throughout Europe and into Asia in open woodland in moist, heavy soil. ‡ 2–6½ ft (60 cm–2 m). Z5–9 H9–5. **'Hortorum'** see *C.* x *acutiflora*.

C. varia see *C. brachytricha*

CALAMINTHA
Calamint
LAMIACEAE

Sweetly aromatic perennials bearing blue, pink, or white flowers over a long period in summer and fall.

About eight species of herbaceous perennials, some of them becoming woody at the base, found in woodland, open grassland, and rocky sites from western Europe to Central Asia and North America. Rarely the star attraction, calamints nevertheless earn their keep with a reliable and generous display of flowers; their name means "beautiful mint." The habit of growth may be ground-hugging, upright and spreading, or bushy; the leaves are hairy and smell wonderfully minty when crushed. A profusion of two-lipped flowers is carried in loose clusters over the summer months and into fall. *Calamintha* is sometimes included in the genus *Clinopodium* or *Satureja*.

CULTIVATION Excellent for alkaline soil, some in shady sites and some in sunny, well-drained conditions.

PROPAGATION By division of established clumps in early spring. Seed sown in a cold frame in spring germinates easily, and self-sown seedlings may also be potted up. Cultivars are often raised from seed and may be variable.

PROBLEMS Usually trouble-free, but may be prone to powdery mildew.

C. grandiflora (Large-flowered calamint) A bushy perennial with stems growing from a thin, slowly creeping rootstock. The egg-shaped leaves are jaggedly toothed, slightly hairy, and pleasingly aromatic when crushed; they grow to 3 in (8 cm) long. The sagelike flowers, about 1½ in (3 cm) long, are an eye-catching pink and borne in sprays from early summer to mid-fall. Tolerates more shade than most and will appreciate humus-rich soil. From damp woodlands and scrub, mostly in alkaline soil, in Iran, Turkey, and southern and central Europe. ‡ 8–24 in (20–60 cm). Z5–9 H9–3. **'Variegata'** Shorter, with foliage strongly speckled creamy white; ‡ 12 in (30 cm).

C. nepeta syn. *C. nepetoides* (Lesser calamint) Probably the finest species, this bushy, floriferous perennial grows from a short, creeping rootstock and is suitable for dry soil. The leaves are variably hairy, about ¾ in (2 cm) long, usually toothed on the edges, and smell delightfully of spearmint when crushed. The ½-in (1-cm) two-lipped flowers are usually lilac and borne in loose clusters that, in suitable conditions, can smother the plant from midsummer to mid-fall. Prefers well-drained soil and will flower most profusely in a warm, open position in full sun. Grows in dry, exposed sites in alkaline soil in North Africa, western Asia, and much of southern and central Europe as far north as eastern England. ‡ 12–32 in (30–80 cm). Z5–9 H9–5. **subsp. glandulosa 'White Cloud'** Makes a neat dome of dainty foliage and white flowers, pale blue in some seed-raised plants. ‡ 18 in (45 cm). **subsp. nepeta** Larger, more toothed leaves and more flowers per spray. **subsp. nepeta 'Blue Cloud'** Soft lilac-blue flowers, sometimes darker or pinker.

C. nepetoides see *C. nepeta*

CALANTHE
ORCHIDACEAE

Scented and showy spring or summer flowers like flying butterflies with beautifully pleated evergreen leaves.

Many handsome examples within the 120 to 150 species make these leafy plants testament to their Greek name, meaning "beautiful flower." These medium- to large-sized plants with bulbous stems and short

CHOOSING CALANTHE

Because *Calanthe* are a perennial favorite as garden plants, a wealth of new hybrids is becoming available, and, as a result of the sheer numbers, some of them have slightly confusing names. A number of natural hybrids exist, but those available for sale have been recreated using seed sown in laboratory conditions. These natural hybrids are often marketed under enticing names with descriptions that suggest particular colors or combinations of colors.

In reality, *Calanthe* come in many natural variations, even within a species, so that what you see in pictures or read in authoritative literature may be vastly different from the flowers that actually bloom in the garden; even the hybridizer can't know what surprises lie in store. Unexpected and beautiful leaf variegations are even possible. Whatever the result, however, the garden calanthes are well worth trying. Keep an eye out for hybrids with the exceptionally cold-hardy species *C. tricarinata* (Z6–9 H9–6), which are much prettier than the less distinguished (and justifiably rarely grown) parent (see Orchids, p.345).

underground tubers grow on the forest floors of tropical and temperate woodlands in Asia, Africa, Madagascar, the tropical Americas, and Australia. Arching or erect spikes bear from a few to many well-held flowers of almost every imaginable color and combination, including bicolors. With its large, flaring, markedly vivid lip, the bloom resembles a butterfly carrying a painted fiddle.

Some five to ten species from Japan and the mountains of Asia, and their hybrids, are increasingly widely grown in the outdoor garden. Evergreen to about 16°F (–9°C), their highly ornamental, ribbed oblong leaves taper into a sheathing stalk. The first gardening book in Japan, published in 1681, mentions the two species that are still the most widely available for outdoor use today. *Calanthe* has now become part of the cut-flower industry, due to the profusion of lovely, long-lasting, exceptionally well-presented blooms with their strong, sweet fragrance.

CULTIVATION Grow in a sheltered, partially sunny to lightly shady spot in slightly damp but well-drained, coarse but rich garden loam. The plants are in fact less fussy than this indicates. They appreciate protection from excessive rain, wind, and heat and could perhaps be grown near shrubs such as rhododendrons or under deciduous trees. Plant them so that the roots are ¾ in (2 cm) deep.

PROPAGATION By division when growth begins, or removal of offsets; from seed only in sterile laboratory conditions.

PROBLEMS Leaves susceptible to water spotting, leading to fungal disease, so water at ground level and protect from excessive rain or overhead drips. Buds may wither when opening in unusually hot weather (bud blast); wind can also damage fragile leaves. Also prone to virus: sterilize cutting tools and destroy infected plants.

C. discolor (Ebine, Shrimp root) The most widely available species is an elegantly reserved bicolor combination of mahogany or deep violet-rose (although variable from almost black to apple green) with a three-winged white lip; pink lips with red to yellow veins are not uncommon. From mid-spring to early summer, 15–30 fragrant flowers, 1¼ in (3 cm) wide, seem to soar off a tall, bright green stem 8–20 in (20–50 cm) long. A fibrous rootstock, shaped like a shrimp, produces two to three heavily pleated and interestingly textured oblong leaves, 8 in (20 cm) long and 2½ in (6 cm) wide. Durable, tolerant, and easy to grow. Prefers damp, grassy areas and likes a leaf mold mulch; it can form thick clumps over time. Evergreen to 16°F (–9°C). A great companion for ferns, hostas, and dicentras. From China, Japan, and Korea. ↕8–16 in (20–40 cm). Z6–9 H9–6. **var. *sieboldii*** see *C. sieboldii*.

C. Kozu syn. Kozu Spice A natural Asian hybrid producing up to 30 long-lasting, clove-scented, spring flowers, 1¼ in (3 cm) wide, per stem. More vigorous than either parent, with many bicolor combinations of purple, red, brown, pink, and white. If choosing only one *Calanthe*, make it this mid- to late-spring bloomer. With sufficient winter snow cover, it can be hardy to Z6–9 H9–6. A hybrid of *C. discolor* and *C. izu-insularis,* introduced from Japan by Barry Yinger. ↕8–16 in (20–40 cm).

C. reflexa (Back-bent calanthe, Natsu-ebine, Summer shrimp root) Unusual for its late-summer to early-fall blooming, with flowers featuring uplifted, reflexed petals that look like purplish pterodactyls. This oddly graceful species has up to 30 lavender and cream flowers with a three-cleft lip on a 8–20-in (20–50-cm) upright stem held well above the three to five pleated leaves, 8 in (20 cm) long. Appreciates shade in very warm summers to prevent flower bud blast. From swamps or cool, moist woodlands to 8,775 ft (2,700 m) in the Himalaya, Taiwan, and Japan. ↕8–16 in (20–40 cm). Z6–9 H9–6

C. sieboldii syn. *C. striata, C. discolor* var. *sieboldii, C. striata* 'Sieboldii' (Ki-ebine, Yellow shrimp root) The second most popular garden species is one of the showiest and earliest-blooming, with large bright yellow flowers with a trilobed lip. These are carried on 15-in (38-cm) stems erectly held above a clump of bold, deeply pleated, dark green foliage up to 15 in (38 cm) across. Usually blooms mid-spring to early summer, but after severe winters it can be later. Evergreen to 50°F (10°C). From East Asia. ↕10–24 in (25–60 cm). Z6–9 H9–6

C. striata see *C. sieboldii*

C. Takane Common, and very variable from seed, often with unusually large flowers in mid- and late spring. It is available in a wide range of colors, including red, brown, orange, yellow with yellow lips, cream, and various combinations. There are also some beautiful creamy leaf variations. May be grown even in zone 6 with persistent snow cover. Also known as *C. x takane*, this is a natural hybrid of *C. discolor* and *C. sieboldii*; it is proving a good parent. From Asia. ↕8–22 in (20–55 cm). Z7–9 H9–7

CALLIRHOE
Poppy mallow, Winecups
MALVACEAE

Floriferous blooming machines from the arid regions of North America with brilliant flowers resembling teacups.

LEFT 1 *Calamintha nepeta*
2 *Calanthe discolor* **3** *C. sieboldii*

Nine species are drought-tolerant plants native to the prairies and plains of southern US and northern Mexico. Three or four species are popular garden plants that are noted for their long flowering period, sturdy constitution, and drought tolerance. Growing up from fleshy, branched taproots, the leaves are deeply divided into five to seven lobed segments and the brilliant magenta- to burgundy-colored flowers are carried upright above the creeping stems. The plants begin blooming in spring, and continue for several months as the trailing stems spread outward.

Winecups are excellent weavers, best used to knit front-of-the-border plantings together. The trailing stems creep between or over clumps of plants and the flowers pop up here and there. In fertile soil, plants form denser clumps, best used at the edge of a bed or along a path.

CULTIVATION Plant in average, well-drained loamy or sandy soil in full sun or light shade. Set out young plants in their final positions, because they do not transplant well due to their deep taproots. Plants may form wide clumps by midsummer. If blooming wanes, cut the stems back by half to encourage branching and more flowers.

PROPAGATION From seed sown in winter; a cold, moist period is needed to spark germination, so place covered pots in the refrigerator for four to six weeks. Seedlings will be ready for planting out by fall or the following spring. Taking root cuttings in late summer works for some species.

PROBLEMS Rabbits will eat the roots if exposed; powdery mildew.

C. digitata (Standing winecups) Lax stems are sparsely clothed with deeply dissected, decorative leaves bearing five to seven narrow, linear lobes like slender fingers. The 1–2-in (2.5–5-cm) flowers are carried singly or in sparsely blooming clusters above the foliage. The color varies from white to light rose and wine red. The plants will grow up through large perennials or shrubs for support. From meadows and roadsides in Indiana and Nebraska, south to Louisiana and Oklahoma. ‡12–54 in (30–140 cm). Z5–8 H8–5

C. involucrata (Purple poppy mallow, Buffalo rose) A sprawling to creeping plant whose deeply dissected leaves have five to seven toothed lobes. The 2½-in (6-cm) deep wine red flowers are carried singly above the foliage. Plants begin blooming in mid- to late spring and flower for several months on new growth. This is the most adaptable species and can be raised from root cuttings. From open woods, meadows, and prairies in Michigan, North Dakota, and Colorado, south to Texas and New Mexico; also Mexico. ‡6–12 in (15–30 cm). Z4–6 H7–1. **var.** *lineariloba* **'Logan Calhoun'** Frilly, dissected leaves and pure white flowers. Plants may go dormant in summer. **var.** *tenuissima* Very narrow leaf segments, lending a lacy appearance to the clumps, with lavender-pink flowers that are carried singly. From northern Mexico. ‡4–6 in (10–15 cm). Z4–9 H9–4

C. triangulata (Clustered poppy mallow) The undivided leaves of this colorful species are broadly triangular to heart-shaped, although some leaves are shallowly lobed and others have no lobes. The 2-in (5-cm), deep purple-red flowers are carried in open clusters in the leaf joints at the ends of the 12–24-in (30–60-cm) stems. From meadows and along roadsides in Wisconsin and Nebraska, south to Georgia and Alabama; protected in Iowa, extinct in Indiana. ‡12–24 in (30–60 cm). Z4–9 H9–4

CALTHA
Kingcup, Marsh marigold, May blobs
RANUNCULACEAE

Much loved spring-flowering plants with sunny flowers and bold foliage, most loving a permanently wet situation.

Ten species of steadily creeping perennials from temperate regions of both the Northern and Southern hemispheres, of which one is widely grown, although most are garden-worthy. They form slowly spreading clumps of simple, oblong or rounded leaves, usually heart-shaped or lobed at the base. In spring or early summer, as the new leaves are expanding, loose clusters of buttercup-like, bowl-shaped, deep yellow or white flowers appear. A weaker second flush may come later. The flowers have no petals, but the sepals, the green parts that normally enclose the flower in bud, have become enlarged and petal-like and are usually referred to as petals—by gardeners if not by botanists. Toxic if ingested in large quantities. Many plants listed by nurseries, and labeled in public gardens, are misnamed. ⚠

CULTIVATION Most thrive in permanently moist sites (*C. palustris* will even grow in shallow water), in full sun or part-shade. Away from their natural watery habitat, they should have fertile, retentive soil and must be watered freely in dry summer weather.

PROPAGATION By division in late summer, or sow seed in moist soil in light shade.

PROBLEMS Usually trouble-free.

C. leptosepala Compact plant forming a clump of broadly oval leaves to 2 in (5 cm) long, flowering from mid-spring to early summer. Leafless stems each carry a single starry white flower 1 in (2.5 cm) across, the 6–12 oval petals often tinged with green or blue. Good for a moist spot in a rock garden or by a small pool. Western North America. ‡12–16 in (30–40 cm). Z5–8 H8–5

C. palustris (Kingcup, Marsh marigold) Vigorous plant forming a large clump of rich green, rounded or kidney-shaped, bluntly toothed leaves that may grow to 10 in (25 cm) across when mature. From early spring to mid-spring or early summer, vivid deep yellow, bowl-shaped flowers with five, sometimes more, oval petals are borne on leafy, upright or trailing stems. Invaluable for pond margins and similarly wet places and grows well in full sun if the soil is permanently wet. Propagate by division immediately after flowering or in late summer. Usually trouble-free, but the leaves may get powdery mildew in hot, dry summers. In Ireland, bunches of flowers were

BELOW 1 *Callirhoe involucrata*
2 *Caltha palustris* **3** *Caltha palustris*
'Flore Pleno' **4** *Caltha polypetala*

ABOVE *Calystegia hederacea* 'Flore Pleno'

hung over doors to protect the fertility of cattle. Widely distributed in the northern temperate region from Europe, including the British Isles, to Asia and North America. ‡6–18 in (15–45 cm). Z3–7 H7–1. **var. *alba*** Compact plant, the flowers milk-white with yellow stamens. ‡8 in (20 cm). Z3–7 H7–1. **'Flore Pleno'** More spreading, with long-lasting, fully double, deep yellow flowers. ‡6 in (25 cm). **'Multiplex'** Dark green leaves and fully double yellow flowers. ‡12 in (30 cm). **var. *palustris*** Vigorous plant with creeping rhizomes and leaves 4 in (10 cm) or more across; flowers 2½ in (6 cm) across. Demands wet conditions. Often sold, incorrectly, as *C. polypetala*. ‡24 in (60 cm). Z3–7 H7–1. **var. *palustris* 'Plena'** Strong-growing plant with fully double, deep yellow flowers. **var. *polypetala*** (see *C. palustris* var. *palustris*) Recently named, but probably not yet grown in gardens; plants found under this name are usually, in fact, *C. palustris* subsp. *palustris* but are also incorrectly listed as *C. polypetala*. **var. *radicans* 'Flore Pleno'** Long creeping stems rooting at the joints; fully double flowers in mid- and late spring. ‡10 in (25 cm). Z3–7 H7–1. **'Semiplena'** Semidouble flowers, with two rows of light yellow petals.

C. polypetala Golden yellow flowers similar to those of *C. palustris*, but with seven to ten narrower petals. Grows well in the mud by a pond or stream margins. Many plants that are grown under this name are, in fact, *C. palustris* subsp. *palustris*. From Bulgaria, Turkey, and Iran. ‡18 in (45 cm). Z3–7 H7–1

C. sagittata Forms a slowly spreading clump of blunt, broadly arrow-shaped leaves to 1½ in (4 cm) long; the narrow, elongated lobes at the base of the leaf fold up over the leaf. In late spring and early summer bears solitary flowers, 1¼–1½ in (3–4 cm) across, each with five to eight narrowly oblong, cream or pale yellow petals. Suited to the margins of a small pool or boggy area. From southern South America. ‡12 in (30 cm). Z5–8 H8–5

CALYSTEGIA
Bellbine, Bindweed
CONVOLVULACEAE

Rampant twining plants with beautiful flowers in summer and fall; unfortunately, they are inclined to be invasive but can be restricted to a container.

Twenty-five species of climbing plants from around the world, often growing in scrub or hedgerows, two of which are sometimes grown in gardens. Slender, often rapidly spreading underground stems support twining wiry shoots with triangular or heart-shaped leaves. The funnel-shaped flowers are borne in the leaf joints. Related to a number of unpleasant weeds, but more appealing.

CULTIVATION Grow in any soil in full sun, against a fence or other suitable support. In areas where they thrive, grow them in containers.

PROPAGATION By division.

PROBLEMS Aphids.

C. hederacea **'Flore Pleno'** Vigorous climbing plant with long-stalked, hairy, narrow arrow-shaped leaves up to 4 in (10 cm) long. The bright rose pink double flowers, 1½–2 in (4–5 cm) across, open from midsummer through early fall or later. The single-flowered wild form grows in open meadows and thickets in East Asia. ‡15 ft (5 m). Z5–9 H9–5

C. silvatica **'Incarnata'** Fast-growing climber with twining stems and arrow-shaped leaves. The funnel-shaped pale pink flowers 2–3½ in (5–9 cm) across, bloom from midsummer through early fall. The white-flowered wild form grows in scrubland in southern Europe and North Africa. ‡6½–10 ft (2–3 m). Z5–9 H9–5

SINGIN' THE BLUES

DIFFERENT SHADES OF BLUE and purple are always good companions, and in this bright and rich border one of the boldest of campanulas, *Campanula glomerata* 'Superba' with its clustered violet-purple heads, is backed by an old-fashioned bearded iris in two tones of blue, darker and paler than the campanula, to create a harmonious combination. In the border, *Iris* 'Braithwaite' shows off its coloring so much better than some of the modern introductions in which the petals are held closer to the horizontal and show off less color when viewed from a distance. Here, the deep blue and pale blue flowers rise above the campanula— which may, over time, need restricting, since it can prove to be too vigorous.

CAMPANULA
Bellflower
CAMPANULACEAE

A large and diverse group of showy, spring- and summer-flowering plants for a sunny or shady border in an ever-increasing range of forms.

Over 300 species of mainly deciduous plants, most perennial but some annual and a few evergreen, growing in a wide range of habitats from high mountains and moors to meadows and woodlands throughout the northern temperate region. This variety of habitats indicates the range of garden uses to which they can be put. The characteristic bell-shaped, tubular or star-shaped flowers with five lobes or divisions are mostly blue or violet, less often white, reddish, or yellow. The foliage is never divided, though it may be heart-shaped or toothed, and the basal leaves are usually larger and more boldly shaped than the smaller, simpler, alternately arranged stem leaves. Their habit varies from tightly compact to vigorously invasive; they may be neat and tufted or tall and almost aristocratic. All

described here are deciduous unless stated otherwise.

Experts on this family have recently decided that the plants formerly classified as *Symphyandra* should now be included in *Campanula*. They had been treated as a separate genus mainly because of a small difference in the structure of their flowers (in *Symphyandra* the anthers were fused together into a tube, while in *Campanula* they were not). Since 1830, when the name *Symphyandra* was first used, this distinction was seen as sufficiently important to justify their separation. Less weight is now given to this feature, and all species will be found under *Campanula*.

Many campanulas are fine garden plants, most are easy to grow, and some have been further developed by hybridization. They are valuable in many garden situations. Some make good, easy-to-manage clumps for the traditional formal herbaceous border. Those with a more relaxed habit of growth are ideal in mixed and informal borders were they will intermingle well with their neighbors, including partnering shrub roses. Several of the more vigorous species are better in wilder, more naturalistic situations, while the intricate flower structure of some repays close inspection and these are best planted where they can easily be seen.

Some of the smaller campanulas are suitable for containers, and new introductions have been made with this in mind. A few make good, long-lasting cut flowers. Many small bellflowers are excellent rock garden plants as well as container plants; the biennials can be spectacular.

CULTIVATION Most campanulas are hardy and easy to please, growing well in any fertile, well-drained soil in full sun or part-shade.

PROPAGATION Most by division in spring or fall. Some can also be propagated by detaching rosettes of foliage, with their attached roots, for immediate replanting in spring. Taking cuttings of new basal shoots in spring works well for many. A few will self-sow, and many can be raised from seed, although the cultivars will not come true.

PROBLEMS Slugs and snails may cause trouble and rust can be a serious problem (*see* Campanula Rust, *p.107*).

C. alliariifolia A reliable and very hardy clump-forming plant with nodding creamy white flowers above hairy, grayish basal leaves. The long-stalked, heart-shaped lower leaves grow to 3 in (8 cm) long. Erect spires of ¾-in (2-cm) bell-shaped flowers from early summer to early fall. Use as an upright accent to a border; good for a wild garden, where it may self-sow. From scrub and forest margins, often on cliffs or banks, in Turkey and Central Asia. ↕ 24 in (60 cm). Z3–7 H7–1

C. armena syn. *Symphyandra armena* Slowly spreading clumps of deciduous velvety foliage support upright stems bearing loose sprays of small flowers in summer. Softly hairy, heart-shaped leaves grow to 10 in (25 cm) long, with open clusters of white or blue-tinged ¾-in (2-cm) flowers in early and mid-

summer. May be short-lived. From woodland in Turkey, the Caucasus, and Iran. ↕ 18 in (45 cm). Z7–9 H9–7

C. **'Birch Hybrid'** Vigorous but compact plant forming a neatly spreading clump of rounded, toothed basal leaves. From early to late summer, these are covered with a succession of upward-facing, bell-shaped ¾-in (2-cm) violet-blue flowers with spreading lobes. An excellent front-of-the-border plant. A hybrid of *C. portenschlagiana* and *C. poscharskyana*, raised by Walter Ingwersen and named for his Birch Farm Nursery in England. ↕ 4 in (10 cm). Z4–7 H7–1

C. **'Burghaltii'** Tough, compact plant forming a mound of deciduous, heart-shaped lower leaves, and narrower stem-leaves. Strikingly large, tubular, grayish blue bellflowers to 4 in (10 cm) long open from bluish purple buds, hanging along the many upright stems in early summer and midsummer. As they fade, the flowers take on their original blue tones. Hardy and long-lived in partly shaded, cool soil. Does not set seed, so must be divided. A long-established hybrid of *C. punctata* and *C. latifolia*. ↕ 24 in (60 cm). Z4–8 H8–1

C. carpatica A rather variable, but always compact, clump-forming plant with bright green, toothed, rounded leaves to 1½ in (4 cm) long. In early summer and midsummer, upturned, broadly bell-shaped or bowl-shaped violet-blue flowers, 1¼–1½ in (3–4 cm) across, are carried singly on slender stems just above the foliage. A showy, sun-loving plant suitable for fronting a well-drained border, it should be clipped back after flowering to encourage a second bloom. Many forms have been introduced over the years, but most have disappeared, to

RIGHT 1 *Campanula* 'Birch Hybrid' **2** *C.* 'Burghaltii' **3** *C. garganica* 'Dickson's Gold' **4** *C.* 'Kent Belle' **5** *C. lactiflora* 'Loddon Anna' **6** *C. lactiflora* 'Prichard's Variety'

HYBRIDS OLD AND NEW

One of the features of new perennial plant introductions in recent years has been the number of hybrids between different species being discovered for the first time—or being created by gardeners and plant breeders. This is especially striking among campanulas.

Some such hybrids have been around for many years. 'Van-Houttei' (*C. latifolia* x *C. punctata*) has been grown since at least 1878, 'Burghaltii' (*C. punctata* x *C. latifolia*) may be of a similar vintage, and 'Birch Hybrid' (*C. portenschlagiana* x *C. poscharskyana*) has been grown since at least the 1950s.

'Kent Belle' (*C. takesimana* x *C. latifolia*) was probably the first of the more modern hybrids, a chance seedling whose parentage was deduced once it proved such a good garden plant. We have since seen 'Puff of Smoke' (*C. punctata* x *C. latifolia* var. macrantha)

and 'Sarastro' (*C. punctata* x *C. trachelium*). It is also possible that some of the plants listed as cultivars of *C. punctata* or *C. takesimana*—'Elizabeth' for example—are hybrids between the two.

Furthermore, there are hybrids with what used to be the genus *Symphyandra*. 'Swannables' is a pale lilac-blue hybrid between *C. punctata* and what was formerly *Symphyandra ossetica* (now *C. ossetica*). For some years, pretty but unnamed hybrid seedlings of this parentage in soft shades of pink, misty blue, and lilac were distributed; these may still be grown, unnamed, and this cross will doubtless be made again. And with the great range of plant habits and flower forms available among campanulas, plant breeders are constantly working to create more new hybrids.

be replaced by more modern, usually dwarfer, forms. Those intended to be raised from seed have been a modern preoccupation, often with the container-plant trade in mind. Most have a tendency to self-sow in the garden—but do not come true. From mountains in central Europe. ‡ 10–18 in (25–45 cm). Z4–7 H07–1. **f. alba** White flowers. **f. alba 'Weisse Clips'** White flowers; comes largely true from seed. ‡ 10 in (25 cm). **'Blaue Clips'** Light blue flowers; largely true from seed. ‡ 10 in (25 cm). **'Blue Moonlight'** Flowers bowl-shaped, palest blue. ‡ 8 in (20 cm). **'Chewton Joy'** Light violet-blue, shading to white in the center. ‡ 8 in (20 cm). **Clips Series** Seed-raised plants with cup-shaped flowers in white or shades of blue. ‡ 10 in (25 cm). **var. turbinata** Dwarf, with open, funnel-shaped light blue flowers. ‡ 4–6 in (10–15 cm). **var. turbinata 'Karl Foerster'** Deep violet-blue flowers from late spring to midsummer; compact. ‡ 8 in (20 cm).

C. collina Slowly spreading plant making a mat of long-stalked, oval leaves that are finely downy. In early summer, erect stems carry a few well-spaced, nodding flowers in a loose, one-sided spire. The bell-shaped, rich violet-purple flowers are 1½ in (4 cm) long and borne on slender stalks. Needs well-drained but moist soil, and sun or part-shade. From rocky meadows in acidic soil in the Caucasus. ‡ 8–12 in (20–30 cm). Z5–9 H9–5

C. cretica syn. *Symphyandra cretica* Upright plant making a clump of long-stalked, kidney-shaped lower leaves to 6 in (15 cm) long. In early summer and midsummer, nodding white, rarely pale blue, flowers to 1¼ in (3 cm) long open in a loose, one-sided cluster on the erect stems. Grows well in a sunny, well-drained, border. From open rocky places in Crete and elsewhere in Greece. ‡ 12–18 in (30–45 cm). Z5–9 H9–5

C. **'E. K. Toogood'** Bright green, heart-shaped leaves in a loose rosette, which becomes reddish in cold weather. These underlie the long leafy stems, bearing star-shaped, violet-blue, white-eyed flowers that open in early summer and midsummer. Effective planted to trail over a wall, and also makes a good basket plant. If trimmed immediately after flowering, it will usually produce a second flush of blooms. Probably a hybrid between *C. garganica* and *C. poscharskyana*. ‡ 8 in (20 cm). Z4–7 H7–1

C. **'Faichem Lilac'** Upright plant with nettlelike, jaggedly toothed mid-green basal leaves to 4¾ in (12 cm) long. The well-spaced, upward-facing, narrowly bell-shaped flowers, 2 in (5 cm) long, are pale lilac-pink with a darker center, borne in early and mid-summer. Probably a hybrid of *C. trachelium*. ‡ 36 in (90 cm). Z4–7 H7–1

C. garganica Neat plant with a clump of kidney-shaped, more or less evergreen leaves ¾–1¼ in (2–3 cm) wide. Short sprays of star-shaped, light or deep

purplish blue flowers ¾ in (2 cm) across appear in mid- and late summer. Often recommended for sunny crevices in a wall, or for a container, but usually more adaptable. From shaded rocks in southern Italy and Greece. ‡ 2–4 in (5–10 cm). Z4–7 H7–1. **'Blue Diamond'** Bright blue flowers with a pale ring in the center. **'Dickson's Gold'** Leaves bright yellow; flowers pale lavender-blue. **'Major'** More robust. ‡ 6 in (15 cm). **'W. H. Paine'** Deep violet-blue flowers with a pale center.

C. glomerata This vigorously spreading plant forms a wide clump of upright stems with toothed, oblong, dark green leaves, the lower ones with long stalks. In early and midsummer, ¾–1½-in (2–3.5-cm) violet-blue, bell-shaped flowers open in dense clusters toward the top of each stem. A very variable species, both in size and in flower color, but most forms tend to be rather invasive, especially in rich soil. From grassy places and scrub in much of Europe and Asia, east to China and Japan. ‡ 12–30 in (30–75 cm). Z3–8 H8–1. **var. acaulis** Very short stems carry violet flowers. ‡ 4–6 in (10–15 cm). **var. alba** White flowers; variable in height. **var. alba 'Schneekrone'** White flowers in dense clusters up the full length of the stems (not only at the top). ‡ 20 in (50 cm). **'Caroline'** Compact, with mauve-pink flowers; not vigorous. ‡ 8–12 in (20–30 cm). **var. dahurica** Vigorous plant with broader, deep purple flowers. From northeastern Asia. ‡ 30 in (75 cm). **'Joan Elliott'** Large violet flowers in early summer and midsummer. ‡ 16 in (40 cm). **'Superba'** Vigorous and rather invasive, with deep violet-purple flowers. ‡ 24 in (60 cm).

C. grossekii An evergreen rosette of long-stalked, heart-shaped leaves supports an upright, simple, or branched, bristly stem. From mid- to late summer or early fall, the stems carry loose clusters of nodding, bell-shaped, violet-blue flowers 1¼ in (3 cm) long. Grows best in sun, but tolerates part- or even full shade. From rocky woodlands and scrub in Hungary. ‡ 32–40 in (80–100 cm). Z4–7 H8–1

C. hofmannii syn. *Symphyandra hofmannii* Upright plant with deeply toothed, oval or lance-shaped leaves to 6 in (15 cm) long, including the flattened stalk. Nodding, creamy white ¾–1¼-in (2–3-cm) flowers open from pale yellow buds along the erect flowering stems between early summer and early fall. A short-lived perennial, sometimes biennial, lovely in flower but usually dying after flowering and setting seed. Prefers a cool, partly shaded situation. From open, rocky places in Bosnia and Herzegovina. ‡ 24 in (60 cm). Z4–7 H8–1

C. **'Kent Belle'** syn. 'Kent Blue' Dramatic and impressive upright plant with a creeping rootstock, making a compact mat of glossy, heart-shaped leaves. From early to late summer, leafy stems carry loose clusters of nodding, shiny, violet-blue bells 2–2½ in (5–6 cm) long. If cut back immediately

after flowering, it may produce a second flush of flowers. A chance hybrid between *C. latifolia* and *C. takesimana* found at Washfield Nursery, in Kent, England. ‡ 30 in (75 cm). Z5–8 H8–5

C. lactiflora One of the best and most effective perennials, although not currently fashionable. This robust plant with a branched rootstock forms a clump of erect, leafy, slightly bristly stems carrying thin, toothed, oval leaves and ending in broad clusters of upward-facing, widely bell-shaped flowers. The white-centered, pale milky blue flowers are about 1 in (2.5 cm) wide, with spreading lobes, and open from midsummer to early fall. Tolerates full sun, provided the soil is moist and fertile, but also grows well in light shade. From open forests, scrub, and mountain meadows in the Caucasus and western Asia. ‡ 3¼–5 ft (1–1.5 m). Z5–7 H7–5. **'Alba'** Pure white flowers. **'Blue Cross'** Mid-blue flowers. **'Loddon Anna'** Pale lilac-pink flowers.

‡ 36 in (90 cm). **'Pouffe'** Compact plant forming a close hummock of light blue flowers. A seedling of the much taller 'Prichard's Variety', introduced by prolific plant breeder Alan Bloom in 1935. ‡ 10–18 in (25–45 cm). **'Prichard's Variety'** Tall, with violet-purple flowers. ‡ 30 in (75 cm). **'Superba'** Slightly larger violet-blue flowers. **'White Pouffe'** White flowers on a compact plant; less prolific than 'Pouffe'. ‡ 10–18 in (25–45 cm).

C. latifolia A compact, fleshy rootstock produces a clump of oval, neatly toothed leaves with heart-shaped bases to 4¾ in (12 cm) long; through these emerge slightly hairy, upright stems bearing smaller, simple oval leaves. From early to late summer, the upper part of each stem bears a loose cluster of outward-facing, bell-shaped blue or

BELOW 1 *Campanula latifolia* 'Brantwood' **2** *C. latiloba* 'Hidcote Amethyst'

white flowers 1½–2 in (4–5 cm) long, with pointed, recurved petals. A lovely, resilient plant for the back of a border, preferably in part-shade, or for a wild garden, where it can be allowed to self-sow. From much of Europe, including the British Isles, growing in woodland or meadows, most often in limestone soil. ‡36–48 in (90–120 cm). Z3–7 H7–5. **var. alba** Flowers white, very striking when grown among the blue form. **'Amethyst'** Light amethyst-purple flowers. ‡36 in (90 cm). **'Brantwood'** Flowers deep violet-blue. ‡30 in (75 cm). **'Gloaming'** Flowers an attractive pale lilac-blue. ‡24 in (60 cm). **var. macrantha** Sparse foliage and longer, rather crowded, rich violet-blue flowers. ‡36 in (90 cm). **var. macrantha 'Alba'** Flowers white, narrowly bell-shaped. ‡36 in (90 cm).

C. latiloba syn. *C. persicifolia* subsp. *sessiliflora* From a rosette of narrow, toothed, evergreen lance-shaped leaves, up to 10 in (25 cm), the upright stems arise, clad in narrow, dark green leaves slightly clasping the stems. From early to late summer, bowl-shaped purplish blue, pale blue or white flowers, 1¼–2 in (3–5 cm) wide, open in dense spires up the stems. A showy but rather coarse plant, well-suited to a wild garden or the back of a border. Less refined but more robust than *C. persicifolia*, with more flared flowers and a substantial impact. From open meadows in northern Turkey. ‡30–36 in (75–90 cm). Z5–7 H7–5. **'Alba'** White flowers. **'Hidcote Amethyst'** Amethyst-blue flowers with purple tints. **'Highcliffe Variety'** Violet-blue flowers. **'Percy Piper'** Flowers rich lavender purple; not very different from 'Highcliffe Variety' (an opinion supported by Alan Bloom, who first introduced it). **'Splash'** Pale violet-blue flowers with deeper violet mottling; dwarf. ‡20 in (50 cm).

C. makaschvillii Forms a compact clump of erect or spreading stems bearing neat, heart-shaped leaves, in late summer and early fall. The upper parts of the stems carry several nodding white or pale pink ¾–1¼-in (2–3-cm) bell-shaped flowers, the lobes slightly recurved and suffused with pink. With its slightly two-toned flowers, this is one of the more striking recent introductions. From scrub and open woodlands in the Caucasus. ‡18–24 in (45–60 cm). Z4–7 H7–1

C. muralis see *C. portenschlagiana*

C. ochroleuca Rosette of long-stalked, rich green, broadly triangular or heart-shaped leaves. In early summer and midsummer, narrow bell-shaped, creamy white ¾-in (2-cm) flowers open up the stem, forming a narrow spike. Variable in height; taller forms good in a sunny border. Similar to *C. alliariifolia*, but flowers have conspicuous long style. From open woodlands and rocky places in the Caucasus. ‡12–28 in (30–70 cm). Z4–7 H7–1

C. ossetica syn. *Symphyandra ossetica* Branching, upright plant with rounded,

NEW FLOWER FORMS

A completely new flower form has recently appeared in campanulas. Doubles (*C. trachelium* 'Bernice'), hose-in-hose, sometimes called cup-in-cup types (*C. punctata* 'Pantaloons'), and cup-and-saucer types (*C. persicifolia* 'Hampstead White') have already been around for some time. But now two different species have produced cultivars in which the usual bell-shaped flower has been split into a number of narrow threads. In *C. takesimana* 'Beautiful Trust' the pure white flowers are split into five segments, each about 2 in (5 cm) wide. The result is reminiscent of the flowers of the related biennial, *Michauxia*. The original plant was found by Song Kihuan, of the Chollipo Arboretum in South Korea, and he gave the plant his daughter's name—which translates as 'Beautiful Truth'. Unfortunately, it was incorrectly submitted and registered for Plant Variety Rights as 'Beautiful Trust', and this name cannot now legally be changed to the name originally chosen.

A similar mutation has been found in Holland in the biennial *C. medium*, not covered in this book. 'Mystery' has five slender petals arranged in an open star, each one rose-pink fading to white at the base; 'Mystery Blue' is deep violet-blue at the tips fading to white; 'Mystery White' is pure white. If this kind of mutation can occur in two species, it can probably occur in more; two similar mutations have also been found in the biennial foxglove, *Digitalis purpurea*.

strongly toothed leaves to 2½ in (6 cm) long. Nodding, pale blue, bell-shaped 2-in (5-cm) flowers are carried in branched sprays in late summer and early fall. Good in sun or part-shade. From rocky places and woodland margins in the northern Caucasus. ‡16 in (40 cm). Z4–7 H7–1

C. 'Paul Furse' syn. *Symphyandra* 'Paul Furse' Loosely clump-forming plant with strongly toothed oval leaves to 6 in (15 cm) long. Bell-shaped, dusky light blue 1½–2-in (4–5-cm) flowers open in branched sprays from early summer to mid-fall. A compact plant, happy in sun or part-shade. Origin uncertain, but close to *C. pendula*. ‡14 in (35 cm). Z4–7 H7–1

C. pendula syn. *Symphyandra pendula* A neat clump of upright or arching stems bears hairy, narrowly heart-shaped leaves to 6 in (15 cm) long. From midsummer to early fall or later, a succession of narrowly bell-shaped, creamy white flowers to 2 in (5 cm) long, with deeply cut lobes opening in branched sprays. From rocky places in part-shade in the Caucasus. ‡20 in (50 cm). Z4–7 H7–1

C. persicifolia Lovely, erect plant, forming evergreen rosettes of narrowly lance-shaped, dark green leaves to 4 in (10 cm) long over a fibrous root system. The stiff stems are usually unbranched, with a few short slender leaves, and in mid- and late summer they carry short-stemmed, open bell-shaped flowers 1½–2 in (4–5 cm) across, which may be white or in various shades of blue. Similar in effect to *C. latiloba*, but more elegant. The plant may lean from the base of the stems after windy or wet weather but is difficult to stake unobtrusively. May self-sow, usually reverting to blue eventually. Weak and poorly grown plants are susceptible to rust (*see* Campanula Rust, *p.107*). From meadows and woodland margins in much of Europe, western Asia, and North Africa; it is also naturalized in parts of Britain. ‡24–32 in (60–80 cm). Z3–8 H8–1. **var. alba** White flowers. **'Alba Coronata'** Semidouble white flowers. ‡18 in (45 cm). **'Beau Belle'** Neat, rosettelike, double light blue

flowers. **'Bennett's Blue'** Fully double, pale blue flowers. ‡30 in (75 cm). **'Blue Bloomers'** Large, violet-blue, hose-in-hose flowers from early to late summer. ‡28 in (70 cm). **'Boule de Neige'** Fully double white flowers, creamy in the center. ‡24 in (60 cm). **'Chettle Charm'** Flowers white, tinged with pale violet-blue on the margins. Delightful. ‡24 in (60 cm). **'Coronata'** Neat, semidouble violet-blue flowers. **'Fleur de Neige'** Semidouble, pure white flowers with petal-like stamens. ‡28 in (70 cm). **'Frances'** Flowers double, white, tinged with violet-blue on the edges of the petals. ‡32 in (80 cm). **'Hampstead White'** Exquisite cup-and-saucer white flowers. ‡28 in (70 cm). **'Kelly's Gold'** Golden-yellow foliage becoming yellowish green in summer; flowers white, tinged blue on margins. ‡28 in (70 cm). **'La Belle'** Fully double, roselike mid-blue flowers. ‡24 in (60 cm). **'Moerheimii'** Slender

plant with semidouble white flowers. ‡24 in (60 cm). **var. planiflora** Surprisingly dwarf, some say ugly, with very dark green foliage and open 1¼–1½-in (3–4-cm) bowl-shaped flowers. ‡6 in (15 cm). **var. planiflora f. alba** Pure white, bowl-shaped flowers above dark foliage. ‡6 in (15 cm). **'Pride of Exmouth'** Pale blue, hose-in-hose flowers, in midsummer and again later. ‡24 in (60 cm). **subsp. sessiliflora** see *C. latiloba*. **'Telham Beauty'** Very large pale lavender-blue flowers to 2¾ in (7 cm) wide. ‡36 in (90 cm).

C. portenschlagiana syn. *C. muralis* A vigorous plant, its fleshy roots spreading beneath the soil, sometimes invasively. Forms a large mat of small, rounded or heart-shaped leaves to 1½ in (4 cm) long. From early to late summer, sprawling, leafy stems carry loose sprays of 1¾-in (2-cm), deeply cut, bell-shaped, violet-blue flowers. From rocky places in the mountains of Croatia. ‡6 in (15 cm). Z4–7 H7–1. **'Lieselotte'** Flowers pale lavender-blue, narrowly bell-shaped. **'Resholdt's Variety'** Vivid deep violet-blue flowers to 1 in (2.5 cm) long.

C. poscharskyana Tough and easy-going plant for sun or shade, making a compact mound of neatly toothed, rounded light green leaves ¾–1¼ in (2–3 cm) long. From early summer to early fall, spreading leafy stems to 12 in (30 cm) long, bear sprays of light blue, star-shaped flowers ¾–1 in (2–2.5 cm) across, paler in the center. Grows well in a wide range of situations; often self-sows freely; can be a nuisance. Cut back after flowering to promote a second season of bloom. From rocky, open

---

BELOW 1 *Campanula persicifolia* 'Chettle Charm' **2** *C. portenschlagiana*

places in Croatia. ‡8 in (20 cm). Z3–9 H9–1. **'Blauranke'** Violet-blue flowers with a conspicuous white center. **'Blue Waterfall'** Extra vigorous plant with clear blue flowers until mid-fall. Ideal cascading over the top of a wall. **'E. H. Frost'** Palest blue flowers above light green foliage. **'Lisduggan Variety'** Mauve-pink flowers on reddish stems. **'Stella'** Vigorous plant with bright violet-blue flowers on long trailing stems.

C. primulifolia Neat plant forming a rosette of leaves to 6 in (15 cm) long, shaped like those of a primrose. Erect, leafy stems develop in early summer, bearing small clusters of broadly bell-shaped flowers in the angle of each of the upper leaves. The 1¼–2-in (3–5-cm) flowers, which open in early summer and midsummer, are bluish purple with a paler center. Needs moist but well-drained, fertile soil in light shade. Short-lived; cut back promptly after flowering to extend its life. From damp, shady places in southern Portugal. ‡28–36 in (70–90 cm). Z4–8 H8–1. **'Blue Oasis'** Compact plant with dark-eyed, pale violet-blue flowers from early to late summer. ‡14–18 in (35–45 cm).

C. **'Puff of Smoke'** Upright plant with oval, finely toothed leaves to 4 in (10 cm) long. From early to late summer, the leafy stems bear dusky pale grayish blue buds that open to white flowers. A hybrid of *C. punctata* and *C. latifolia* var. *macrantha*. ‡24 in (60 cm). Z4–8 H8–1

C. punctata Sometimes unpredictable, although generally rather vigorous plant. Forms a colony of soft, slightly hairy, long-stemmed, heart-shaped leaves through which grow coarsely hairy, upright stems bearing light green, oval leaves on short or no stalks. From early summer to mid- or late summer, stems carry loose sprays of impressive tubular flowers to 2 in (5 cm) long. Variable in color, usually creamy white, more or less flushed with pink or red, and speckled with crimson inside. Can be invasive. Most forms produce later flowers if cut back immediately after flowering. The reddish single-flowered forms can be difficult to distinguish from each other. Similar to the Korean *C. takesimana*, but most obviously distinct in its hairy leaves. Many of the recent cultivars have been raised and introduced by Dan Heims of Terra Nova Nurseries, OR. From open grassy mountain meadows in Japan and Siberia. ‡12–16 in (30–40 cm). Z4–8 H8–1. **f. albiflora** Creamy white flowers speckled with reddish purple inside; variable in size. **f. albiflora 'Nana Alba'** Dwarf form with cream flowers lightly speckled inside with dull red. ‡8 in (20 cm). **'Alina's Double'** Large dusky rose pink, hose-in-hose double flowers from early to late summer. **'Flashing Lights'** Creamy white mottling and splashing on the leaves, with mauve bells. ‡16 in (40 cm). **var. hondoensis** Taller plant with long, deep rosy pink flowers, tending to be rather wiry and untidy in habit. ‡20 in (50 cm). **'Hot Lips'** Useful compact plant with dark

foliage and white flowers speckled with crimson toward the mouth. ‡8–12 in (20–30 cm). **'Milly'** Purplish pink flowers, the leaves mottled with cream. ‡12 in (30 cm). **'Pantaloons'** Chubby hose-in-hose double, light purplish pink flowers with the outer skirt half the length of the inner, from late spring to midsummer. ‡8–12 in (20–30 cm). **'Pink Chimes'** Compact plant with purplish rose flowers. ‡16 in (40 cm). **'Reifrock'** Flowers creamy white outside, heavily speckled with dark red within. ‡16 in (40 cm). **'Rosea'** Flowers mid-pink. **f. rubriflora** Flowers strongly flushed and speckled with reddish purple, overall rosy purple in effect. **f. rubriflora 'Beetroot'** Taller; striking purple young foliage and wine-red flowers. ‡16–20 in (40–50 cm). **f. rubriflora 'Bowl of Cherries'** Good compact habit, with deep purplish red flowers. ‡12 in (30 cm). **f. rubriflora 'Cherry Bells'** Long, deep rosy pink flowers tipped with cream; vigorous and self-supporting. ‡18 in (45 cm). **f. rubriflora 'Wine 'n' Rubies'** Dark reddish purple speckled flowers above deep green foliage. ‡12 in (30 cm). **'Wedding Bells'** Pale pink-flushed, creamy white, hose-in-hose double flowers. ‡18 in (45 cm). **White hose-in-hose** Double, creamy white flowers; one flower is within the other.

C. raddeana Compact plant, forming a cluster of rosettes of neat, dark, glossy, heart-shaped leaves. Slender, erect stems, sometimes red-tinted, carry several nodding, deep violet, broadly bell-shaped, lobed ¾-in (2-cm) flowers opening in mid- and late summer. The pollen is noticeably orange in color. Spreads gently by runners, which gives an easy means of propagation. From the Caucasus. ‡12 in (30 cm). Z5–8 H8–5

C. rapunculoides A pleasing species but liable to become a rampant weed, spreading by seed as well as by its creeping fleshy roots. Broadly heart-shaped lower leaves grow to 6 in (15 cm) long, but start to wither as the nodding, bell-shaped violet-blue flowers open in early summer. The flowers are ¾–1¼ in (2–3 cm) long, and continue into early fall. Most suitable for a truly wild, grassy area, as it is too invasive for most borders. From forest glades, meadows, and rocky places in most of Europe and Central Asia; also naturalized in many other countries including Britain. ‡36 in (90 cm). Z5–8 H8–5. **'Afterglow'** Compact, with grayish lilac flowers. ‡16 in (40 cm). **'Alba'** Shorter and less invasive, with pure white flowers. ‡24 in (60 cm).

C. rotundifolia (Harebell, Bluebell) Slender plant forming a neat clump; rounded basal leaves, long-stalked and about ½–¾ in (1–2 cm) across, wither as the flower stems develop. In mid- and late summer, nodding, violet-blue, bell-shaped flowers open on delicate stems bearing slim, dark green leaves. Variable in size, flower color, and other botanical characteristics, with many named local variants. From dry grassy banks in much of Europe, Britain, North America, North Africa, western Asia.

‡4–16 in (10–40 cm). Z5–7 H7–3. **'Olympica'** Strongly toothed, dark green leaves and more open flowers than the typical form. A good container plant. From the Olympic Mountains in the northwestern US. ‡8 in (20 cm).

C. **'Samantha'** Neat, scented plant for the front of a border, with small rounded leaves. In early summer and midsummer, the 8 in (20 cm) stems are covered by the upturned, bowl-shaped 1-in (2.5-cm) flowers, paling to near-white in the centers, with a slender, dark ring around the base. Unusually for campanulas, the flowers are fragrant. A chance seedling found on the rock garden at the fascinating Collectors' Nursery, WA. ‡18 in (45 cm). Z5–9 H9–5

C. **'Sarastro'** Compact plant, forming a clump of large downy leaves, with nodding, deep violet-blue tubular-bell-shaped flowers, 2 in (5 cm) long, in mid- and late summer. Like a shorter version of the better known 'Kent Belle'. A hybrid between *C. punctata* and, probably, *C. trachelium*. ‡18–24 in (45–60 cm). Z4–9 H8–1

C. sarmatica Upright plant forming a loose rosette of rather coarse, grayish, hairy, oval or triangular leaves to 3 in (8 cm) long. Downy stems carry small, oval leaves and spikes of slightly nodding, bell-shaped, light violet-blue flowers 1¼–2 in (3–5 cm) long. They open earlier than many bellflowers, from late spring to midsummer. Rather unrefined-looking, but colorful, early-flowering, and less attractive to slugs than most. Cannot be divided because the crown is too tight, but seed is generously produced. From rocky places in the Caucasus Mountains. ‡16–20 in (40–50 cm). Z5–9 H9–5

C. **'Swannables'** Steadily spreading, forming a colony of erect, leafy stems. Pale lilac-blue, bell-shaped flowers from early summer to early fall. Relatively untested; seems to spread vigorously, but also susceptible to slug or snail damage. Formerly listed as a hybrid between *C. punctata* and *Symphyandra ossetica*. ‡16 in (40 cm). Z5–8 H8–5

C. takesimana Vigorous spreader forms a large clump, with branched stems bearing glossy, heart-shaped leaves to 3 in (8 cm) long. From midsummer to early fall, arching sprays of tubular-bell-shaped creamy white flowers appear, tinged pink and finely speckled inside with dark red. The drooping flowers are 2–2½ in (5–6 cm) long, the lobes hardly flared. Valued for its long flowering season; several good selections have already been made. Similar to *C. punctata* but with glossy, rather than hairy, foliage. From open woodlands in South Korea. ‡20–30 in (50–75 cm). Z5–7 H7–5. **var. alba** More compact, with creamy white flowers. ‡14 in (35 cm). **'Beautiful Trust'** Curious form in which the bells are divided to

RIGHT 1 *Campanula punctata* **2** *C. punctata* **'Wedding Bells'** **3** *C. trachelium*

the base into long, narrow, ¼-in (5-mm) white segments. Very distinctive and rather appealing (*see* New Flower Forms, *p.108*). early to late summer. ↕14 in (35 cm). **'Elizabeth'** Large, narrow, pale pink bells. ↕20 in (50 cm). **'Elizabeth II'** Similar to 'Elizabeth' but with double flowers.

C. thyrsoides An unusual bellflower in habit and flower color. An upright, short-lived perennial or biennial forming a rosette of wavy, lance-shaped leaves to 4¾ in (12 cm) long. In early summer, bristly stems develop, bearing a dense, fat spike of slightly fragrant, cup-shaped, creamy yellow flowers up to 1 in (2.5 cm) long. One of the few campanulas with no blue forms; best in well-drained soil. From mountain meadows in the European Alps. ↕12–20 in (30–50 cm). Z5–8 H8–5

C. trachelium (Nettle-leaved bellflower, Bats-in-the-belfry) Robust plant forming clumps of coarsely hairy, upright stems bearing deeply toothed, nettlelike leaves to 6 in (15 cm) long. In mid- and late summer, ¾–1¼ in (2–3 cm), bell-shaped, light violet-blue flowers open on short side-branches up the stem to form a loose spray. Rather leafy, but tough enough to naturalize well in grass or other wild setting. The double-flowered forms are good border plants with shapely flowers. From much of Europe, western Asia, and North Africa, growing in open woodlands. ↕32–36 in (80–90 cm). Z5–8 H8–5. **var.** *alba* White flowers. **'Alba Flore Pleno'** Double white flowers; lovely. **'Bernice'** Double, violet-blue flowers. **'Snowball'** Double white; probably identical to 'Alba Flore Pleno'.

C. **'Van-Houttei'** Forming a compact clump of heavily veined, oval leaves to 4 in (10 cm) long, in early summer and midsummer; the upright stems carry nodding, tubular-bell-shaped, violet-purple flowers 2½ in (6 cm) long. A hybrid raised in Belgium, from at least 1878, probably of *C. latifolia* and *C. punctata*—which is the reverse of the cross that produced 'Burghaltii' (that is, with *C. latifolia* as the seed parent). ↕12–20 in (30–50 cm). Z4–7 H7–1

C. wanneri syn. *Symphyandra wanneri* Clump-forming plant with branched stems carrying oval leaves to 4 in (10 cm) long, which taper to the base. Loose clusters of nodding, violet-blue ¾–1¼-in (2–3-cm) flowers open in late summer and early fall to form a broad spray. Needs gritty, well-drained soil in full sun. From shady, rocky places in the mountains of southeastern Europe, from the Balkans to Bulgaria. ↕12–16 in (30–40 cm). Z4–8 H8–5

C. zangezura syn. *Symphyandra zangezura* Forms neat clumps of small, round, toothed leaves ¾–1½ in (2–4 cm) across. Slender, arching dark stems carry pale violet-blue, broadly bell-shaped, nodding 1¼–2-in (3–5-cm) flowers, from early summer to early fall. Similar to *C. wanneri*, but more compact. From Armenia. ↕10 in (25 cm). Z5–8 H8–5

CANNA
Indian shot plant
CANNACEAE

Exotic plants with brilliant flowers and huge leaves, hardy in mild situations but often grown as summer bedding.

With probably no more than ten true wild species, most originating in South America with one from Florida, cannas are loosely related to bananas (*Musa*) and *Strelitzia*. All are herbaceous perennials, growing from an underground rootstock that resembles a bearded iris rhizome.

Growing from 2 to 10 ft (60 cm to 3 m) tall, each stem produces six to nine leaves that are broad and large, generally oblong to broadly elliptical, and spirally arranged; the leaf sheath encloses the stem. The leaves, green, blue-green, purple, bronze, or multicolored, contribute considerably to the plant's value.

Canna flowers are usually large and showy, although the species and a few hybrids are small-flowered. The flowers are irregular, and better complimented on their size and color than their form; they have three united petals and most of the anthers also developed as petals. Blooms are carried in bold heads that, in some cultivars, are branched and provide a longer display.

Under tropical conditions cannas grow continuously, with new stems replacing old after flowering, but in cooler climates they die down to the ground in winter. The foliage is not frost-hardy but the rhizomes will survive underground in mild

CANNAS FROM SEED

In recent years, breeders have worked on cannas with a view to introducing cultivars that may be raised from seed. A number have appeared, including the Tropical Series, with tightly clustered flowers in yellow and three shades of pink, which reach no more than 24 in (60 cm).

It is only fair to say that, being so short, these seed-raised cultivars are entirely without the luxuriant tropical splendor of the taller cultivars, propagated by division. None of the seed-raised types, so far, feature the richly colored or variegated foliage of Tropicanna or 'Striata'. Good foliage color will come, however, and when this is brought together with less congested flowerheads, these seed-raised types will be worth trying. Plants that are raised from seed taken from the cultivars mentioned here will not come true.

Canna seed has a hard coat, and it pays to soften it before sowing. There are two ways to do this. File the seed gently to break the hard seed coat, soak it 24 hours, then sow the seed in the normal way in winter at about 70°F (21°C). Alternatively, wrap the seeds between moist paper towels for two to three days to soften the seed coat before sowing.

areas if well mulched. Cannas were widely grown and hybridized in the 19th century but they then fell from favor. They have recently become popular again with the current interest in exotic styles of planting and, as a result, new cultivars appear regularly.

CULTIVATION Cannas are not fussy plants, although they require a sunny situation and ample water and nutrients. They grow best in well-cultivated soil, generously enriched with organic matter and enhanced with a general fertilizer before planting. Plant them in growth when danger of frost has passed, spacing the plants 18–36 in (45–90 cm) apart, according to vigor. Water and fertilize generously during the growing season; mulching helps retain moisture. While deadheading will prolong the display and keep the plants looking neat, take care not to trim the stem too far down or future flower-bearing sideshoots may be accidentally removed. In some, so-called self-cleaning cultivars, petals drop off as they fade; in others they are retained and must be removed to enhance the display.

In fall, as soon as frost blackens the foliage, plants should be cut back to ground level and given a 4-in (10-cm) mulch as protection against frost. Dormant rhizomes will withstand occasional light frost down to 30°F (−1°C), so deep planting and a thick mulch provide protection if plants are overwintered in the ground in cool climates. Alternatively, dig them up and store them in frost-free conditions such as a dry basement or garage. In cool climates, they would normally be grown outside in the summer and given some protection in winter. For the best garden perennials, choose those rated as Z7–10 H10–7

PROPAGATION By division of the fleshy rhizomes. This is normally done in spring, before growth begins, or when the dormant rhizomes come out of winter storage. Wash or shake off excess soil, then pull them apart or cut them into sections with three to five growing points on each. If using a knife to cut, sterilize the blade in a flame between the division of clumps to avoid the transmission of viruses. Divisions should be potted in 6- or 8-in (15- or 21-cm) pots, using a well-aerated potting mix. After potting, water sparingly and keep warm at around 61°F (16°C). This is the ideal, although they will tolerate lower temperatures as long as they do not get frosted. Increase the watering as growth occurs. Cannas can also be raised from seed (*see* Cannas From Seed).

PROBLEMS Generally trouble-free,

RIGHT 1 *Canna* x *ehemanii*
2 *C.* 'Picasso' **3** *C.* 'Rosemond Coles'

except for virus diseases. Infected plants show stunted growth, twisted, spotted, and pale-streaked leaves, and streaking in the flowers. They should be destroyed—there is no cure and the disease spreads quickly.

C. 'Annaeei' Old very tall cultivar, mainly grown for the lush blue-green pointed foliage. Small, insignificant, pale orange flowers in late summer. ‡ 10 ft (3 m). Z7–10 H10–7

C. 'Aphrodite' Large well-shaped flowers in damask pink. Green foliage with a hint of bronze, especially in the midrib. ‡ 5 ft (1.5 m). Z7–10 H10–7

C. 'Apricot Dream' Large buff-salmon blooms with touches of gold and deep pink in the throat. Free-flowering, self-cleaning. ‡ 4 ft (1.2 m). Z7–10 H10–7

C. 'Assaut' Large red flowers over rich, bluish bronze foliage. An older cultivar that is reliable and readily available; a good specimen or background plant. ‡ 6 ft (1.8 m). Z7–10 H10–7

C. 'Bankok' see 'Striped Beauty'

C. 'Bengal Tiger' see 'Striata'

C. 'Bethany' Large, bright, yellow and orange flowers, like those of 'Florence Vaughan'; golden-striped foliage like 'Striata'. A choice recent introduction. ‡ 5½ ft (1.6 m). Z7–10 H10–7

C. 'Black Knight' Large, floppy, deep crimson flowers with reflexed petals. Foliage is deep bluish purple with an attractive white coating. ‡ 6 ft (2 m). Z7–10 H10–7

C. 'City of Portland' syn. 'Orchid' Gaudy, rich salmon pink flowers with yellow flushing and penciling. Reliable and free-flowering. Old flowers do not fall, giving an untidy appearance. A familiar, widely available old cultivar, superseded by modern introductions. ‡ 5 ft (1.5 m). Z7–10 H10–7

C. 'Cleopatra' syn. 'Yellow Humbert' An oddity, producing a random mixture of yellow and red flowers over foliage that can be green, bronze, or striped. Curious rather than beautiful. ‡ 5 ft (1.5 m). Z7–10 H10–7

C. 'Durban' One of the most brightly colored of all cannas. Large red flowers sit above spectacular foliage in a vivid mix of purple with pink veins fading to orange. Probably derived from 'Wyoming'. A little less dramatic than Tropicanna as well as less vigorous. (see Durban, Phasion, and Tropicanna). ‡ 5½ ft (1.6 m). Z7–10 H10–7

C. x ehemanii syn. *C. iridiflora* 'Ehemanii' Tall, with broad, paddle-shaped leaves and an overall goblet shape. Elegant, nodding, deep pink trumpet-shaped flowers on arching stems are produced in late summer. Also makes a good conservatory plant. A hybrid of *C. iridiflora* and 'Warszewiczii', often incorrectly sold as *C. iridiflora*. ‡ 6 ft (2 m). Z7–10 H10–7

DURBAN, PHASION, AND TROPICANNA

In 1989 Gary Hammer of Desert to Jungle Nursery in Los Angeles imported a dramatic red-flowered canna from South Africa. Named 'Durban' by Herb Kelly of Kelly's Plant World, another California nursery, it featured foliage striped in purple, pink, and orange, but its initial high price restricted its circulation.

At about the same time Ian Cooke, then a nurseryman specializing in tender perennials in Britain, heard of this plant and asked a friend on a visit to South Africa to bring back a piece—which he did, digging it up from a fencerow on a nursery where it was clearly unappreciated. But this plant had orange flowers, and even more dramatic leaves.

A short time before Ian Cooke's plant arrived in Britain, the same orange-flowered cultivar was imported to Britain by Brian Hiley, another nurseryman with a special interest in tender perennials. It featured the same extraordinary foliage, and orange flowers. He named it 'Durban' and showed it at the 1995 Chelsea Flower Show.

So within a very short time there were two similar plants circulating under the same name, 'Durban', with different-colored flowers; the orange-flowered version had the better foliage.

In 1997 the situation became even more complicated when a plant named 'Phasion' started to be sold in Britain under the marketing name of Tropicanna. Featuring the same spectacular foliage and orange flowers, it was reputed to be a spontaneous mutation of the orange-flowered 'Wyoming'. It had recently been given the protection of plant breeders' rights (PBR) and was the subject of a large marketing campaign. But it had its plant breeders' rights removed when evidence came to light that it was not a novel plant and had already been in circulation for many years. There was even evidence that it had been seen in a garden in Bulawayo, Zimbabwe, as long ago as 1955.

The result of all this is that in North America, 'Durban' is the red-flowered form—but it does not grow well in Britain, so it is very rarely seen there. By the time Brian Hiley named his orange-flowered plant 'Durban', the name had already been confirmed for the red-flowered plant. So, although there may have been earlier names for the orange-flowered plant, names established under PBR legislation take precedence.

To summarize: the correct, worldwide, cultivar name for the red-flowered plant is 'Durban', while the correct name for the orange-flowered plant, sometimes sold as 'Durban' in Britain and often marketed as Tropicanna, is 'Phasion'.

C. 'Erebus' Pale salmon flowers over blue-green, pale edged foliage. Raised at Longwood Gardens, PA. ‡ 5½ ft (1.6 m). Z7–10 H10–7

C. glauca Tall and willowy, with narrow, blue-green leaves. It naturally grows in wet places, often by streams or pools, therefore ample moisture should be provided if grown in the garden. Flowers are pale lemon yellow and a little more delicate than most hybrid cannas. Tropical America. ‡ 8 ft (2.4 m). Z7–10 H10–7

C. indica Medium-sized plant; green leaves and small flowers in cherry red with some yellow on the lip, which are freely produced from early summer on. This species, originally introduced in the UK in 1956, was the parent of many early crosses. Botanists now lump together a wide range of other cannas under this name, so plants available from nurseries can vary enormously. Tropical America. ‡ 4–6 ft (1.2–1.8 m). Z7–10 H10–7. **'Purpurea'** Rich purple foliage and small orange flowers with the foliage held in an upright habit. This widely grown cultivar makes an excellent specimen or background plant. ‡ 6 ft (1.8 m). Z7–10 H10–7. **'Russian Red'** Similar to 'Purpurea' but with larger leaves held at a wider angle and small orange flowers. ‡ 6 ft (1.8 m). Z7–10 H10–7

C. 'Ingeborg' Apricot orange flowers over wavy, shiny bronze foliage, especially dark in the main vein. ‡ 4½ ft (1.4 m). Z7–10 H10–7

C. iridiflora 'Ehemanii' see *C. x ehemanii*

C. King Humbert see 'Roi Humbert'

C. 'King Midas' see 'Richard Wallace'

C. 'Louis Cayeux' Sturdy cultivar with many spikes of rich salmon flowers over green leaves. Old, but reliable. ‡ 5 ft (1.5 m). Z7–10 H10–7

C. 'Lucifer' Old, very short cultivar with masses of smallish red and yellow flowers. 'Rosemond Coles' is sometimes sold under this name. ‡ 36 in (90 cm). Z7–10 H10–7

C. 'Minerva' see 'Striped Beauty'

C. 'Musifolia' Impressive foliage with huge, waving, banana-like leaves up to 36 in (90 cm) long with dark edges and red-tinted midribs. Occasional small orange flowers late in the season. Very early hybrid of unknown parentage, sometimes misspelled 'Musafolia'. ‡ 10 ft (3 m). Z7–10 H10–7

C. 'Mystique' Narrow pointed leaves in a rich iridescent mix of purple, blue, and pewter. Grown mainly as a foliage plant, although the small cherry red flowers make an excellent contrast. ‡ 7½ ft (2.3 m). Z7–10 H10–7

C. 'Nirvana' see 'Striped Beauty'

C. 'Orange Punch' Large orange flowers with yellow throats over green foliage. Long flowering season; self-cleaning. ‡ 4 ft (1.2 m). Z7–10 H10–7

C. 'Orchid' see 'City of Portland'

C. 'Panache' Quite distinct from most other cannas. Large open trusses of small delicate pale apricot flowers, shaded strawberry pink, give a delicate spidery effect. Large upright bluish leaves. ‡ 6 ft (1.8 m). Z7–10 H10–7

C. 'Phasion' see Tropicanna; (see Durban, Phasion, and Tropicanna)

C. 'Picasso' Large yellow flowers copiously spotted and blotched with red; green foliage. Although this is the most common spotted canna, stocks vary considerably, so beware of inferior forms. ‡ 5 ft (1.5 m). Z7–10 H10–7

C. 'Pink Sunburst' syn. 'Pringle Bay' Deep bottle green leaves overlaid with yellow and pink stripes with mid-pink flowers often hidden among the foliage. Less impressive than Tropicanna but still a good, much shorter foliage plant. ‡ 36 in (90 cm). Z7–10 H10–7

C. 'President' Well-known classic canna with huge scarlet flowers marked with yellow in the center. Wide green leaves. Very reliable, although a little coarse by modern standards. ‡ 5 ft (1.5 m). Z7–10 H10–7

C. 'Pretoria' see 'Striata'

C. 'Pringle Bay' see 'Pink Sunburst'

C. 'Ra' Lemon yellow flowers held high over narrow bluish foliage on an open, vigorous clump. Larger, darker flowers than its parent, *C. glauca*. Raised at Longwood Gardens, PA. ‡ 6½ ft (2 m). Z7–10 H10–7

C. 'Red Futurity' Intense, medium-sized, crimson flowers over rich, "dark chocolate" foliage. Perhaps the darkest canna; partially self-cleaning. The best of an American series of dwarf cannas. ‡ 36 in (90 cm). Z7–10 H10–7

C. 'Richard Wallace' syn. 'King Midas' Large clear yellow flowers with a few light spots in the throat and lightly frilled petals. The leaves are apple green and the habit is sturdy. A classic cultivar that is available under various names. ‡ 5 ft (1.5 m). Z7–10 H10–7

C. 'Roi Humbert' (**King Humbert**) An old name that is often used for any red-flowered canna with dark foliage. It is impossible to give a precise description for the real thing. ‡ 5–6 ft (1.5–1.8 m). Z7–10 H10–7

C. 'Roi Soleil' Shapely, large, and frilly, vivid red flowers with a prominent gold splash in the throat and carried over green leaves held on soft purple stems. ‡ 6 ft (1.8 m). Z7–10 H10–7

C. 'Rosemond Coles' Bright red and yellow flowers over green foliage. The flowerheads do not fall cleanly, and dead flowers tend to go mushy. By modern standards, a coarse plant with poor qualities, but a classic canna, widely grown and mistakenly sold as 'Lucifer'. ‡ 5 ft (1.5 m). Z7–10 H10–7

C. 'Strasbourg' Bright cherry red, iris-shaped flowers over compact plants with narrow green foliage, neatly

ABOVE *Canna* 'Striata'

ribboned in maroon. Readily available and always reliable. ‡ 36 in (90 cm). Z7–10 H10–7

C. 'Striata' syn. 'Bengal Tiger', 'Pretoria' The most familiar of the colored-leaved cannas, with pale green leaves conspicuously striped with gold. Stems and leaf edges have a plum coloring and the flowers are large and strident orange. Readily available and reliable. ‡ 5 ft (1.5 m). Z7–10 H10–7

C. 'Striped Beauty' syn. 'Bankok', 'Minerva', 'Nirvana' Buttercup yellow flowers open from red buds over bright, white-striped green foliage. Stocks vary in the intensity of their leaf markings. ‡ 5 ft (1.5 m). Z7–10 H10–7

C. Tropicanna ('Phasion') Probably the most brightly colored of all the cannas, the spectacular foliage is a psychedelic mix of purple with pink veins, fading to orange. Flowers are large and rich orange. Similar to, but more vigorous than, the red-flowered 'Durban'. Probably derived from 'Wyoming'. ‡ 5½ ft (1.6 m). Z7–10 H10–7. (see Durban, Phasion, and Tropicanna, p.111).

C. 'Verdi' Vivid, bright tangerine, iris-shaped blooms with yellow throats on shapely plants with deep bronze foliage. ‡ 5 ft (1.5 m). Z7–10 H10–7

C. 'Wyoming' Huge, soft orange flowers on vigorous plants, bearing massive bronze leaves. Excellent as a statement or at the back of the border. Possibly the most familiar canna of all time; readily available and totally reliable. ‡ 7 1/4 ft (2.3 m). Z7–10 H10–7

C. 'Yellow Humbert' see 'Cleopatra'

CARDAMINE
BRASSICACEAE

Delightful, underrated, and easy-going spring-flowering plants for moist positions in part-shade.

About 130 species of deciduous, or less often evergreen, perennials and annuals (including a few weeds). Most grow in the damp grasslands or streamsides of the temperate regions of the world, especially in the Northern Hemisphere; 36 in Europe. Perennial species usually have a fibrous rootstock or creeping underground stem (rhizome) bearing simple or divided leaves, and upright stems ending in a cluster of four-petaled white, yellow, pink, or purple flowers. All described here are deciduous unless stated otherwise. Invaluable for woodland gardens or a shady, damp border; good companions for hardy ferns. Some can be vigorous, making effective ground cover, but different forms of the same species may vary in vigor. Perhaps some gardeners find their relationship to a few nasty annual weeds (see Hairy Bitter Cress) alarming, but these spring woodlanders deserve to be more widely grown.

CULTIVATION Grow in full or part-shade, in any moist soil that is not waterlogged.

PROPAGATION By division, but can also be raised from seed. *C. pratensis* produces plantlets on its leaves in damp conditions.

PROBLEMS Aphids.

C. californica syn. *C. integrifolia, Dentaria integrifolia* (Milkmaids) From a short, fleshy rhizome emerges a loose rosette of leaves, mostly divided into three oval leaflets to 2 in (5 cm) wide. Erect stems carry a few narrower leaves and end in a spike of many ½–¾-in (1–2-cm) light pink flowers, sometimes white, opening in late spring and early summer. The leaves are quite varied in the wild, with a number of varieties named. From Oregon and California, growing in shady woods and canyons. ‡ 16 in (40 cm). Z5–7 H7–5

C. diphylla syn. *Dentaria diphylla* (Crinkleroot) The creeping rhizome throws up dark green basal leaves divided into three leaflets with bluntly toothed margins. In late spring, several white flowers, ⅝ in (1.5 cm) across, open on erect stems, each bearing two similar but smaller leaves, showing off the flowers. Lovely among ferns in a shady border. From damp woodlands and meadows in eastern North America. ‡ 12 in (30 cm). Z3–7 H7–1

C. enneaphylla syn. *Dentaria enneaphylla, D. enneaphyllos* Spreading clump of dark, sometimes purple-tinted leaves to 4¾ in (12 cm) long, divided into three or more toothed, lance-shaped leaflets, also carried in threes on the upright stems. In late spring and

early summer, nodding, creamy white flowers, about ¾ in (2 cm) across, open in loose clusters at the tips of the stems. Forms vary noticeably in their vigor. From damp forest habitats in the eastern European Alps, the Carpathian Mountains, and the northern Balkans. ‡ 12 in (30 cm). Z5–8 H8–5

C. glanduligera syn. *Dentaria glandulosa* Plant with a slender, scaly rhizome from which arise the stems, each with a group of three leaves below the flowers. Each leaf is composed of three narrow lance-shaped leaflets, sharply toothed on the edges. Bright purple ¾-in (2-cm) flowers open in late spring and early summer. Similar in effect to the white-flowered *C. enneaphylla*. From woodlands in the Carpathian Mountains of eastern Europe. ‡ 12 in (30 cm). Z5–7 H7–5

C. heptaphylla Relentlessly spreading rhizomatous plant forms a clump, with upright stems bearing three or more pairs of leaves divided, ladderlike, into several lance-shaped leaflets. Up to 20 showy ¾-in (2-cm) flowers open in late spring and early summer, and may be white, pink, or rosy purple. Note which color is offered before buying. From woodlands in the mountains of western and central Europe; lovely in woodland gardens. ‡ 24 in (60 cm). Z5–7 H7–5

C. integrifolia see *C. californica*

C. kitaibelii syn. *C. polyphylla, Dentaria polyphylla* Loosely clump-forming plant growing from a slender, scaly rhizome. Ladderlike leaves divided into seven or nine toothed, lance-shaped leaflets are borne in a cluster on upright stems. In late spring and early summer they carry several ⅝–¾-in (1.5–2-cm) flowers

HAIRY BITTER CRESS

While some cardamines are among the most appealing of woodland perennials and never create a nuisance by self-seeding, there are other species that are quite the opposite. Hairy bitter cress (*Cardamine hirsuta*) is one of the most irritating and widespread of weeds. In dry habitats, like gravel paths, it can flower and fruit when only 1 in (2.5 cm) high, yet an isolated plant in good soil may produce 50,000 seeds. Its explosive capsules can fling the seeds as far as 30 in (80 cm) away from the parent plant.

Hairy bitter cress spreads into new gardens mainly as a weed in the soil of newly purchased plants and has found its way from its native northern Europe to most other temperate parts of the world. In moist areas the slightly stouter *C. flexuosa*, with a wavy stem, is seen, and other, similar species are native to North America. Complete elimination is possible but difficult: once you have removed and burned large specimens (they will seed on the compost pile), carry a plastic bag in your pocket whenever you are in the garden and pull up every specimen you see, then bag it at once. Destroy the whole bag.

in a rarely seen shade of pale creamy yellow. From damp woodlands in the Swiss Alps, Italy, and the northwest Balkans. ‡ 12 in (30 cm). Z5–7 H7–5

C. macrophylla A bold, spreading plant with a slender, creeping rhizome. The main leaves are up to 10 in (25 cm) long, occasionally bronze-tinted, with a large, rounded terminal segment and smaller side leaflets. Erect stems bear several similar leaves with narrower leaflets, and numerous ½-in (1-cm) pale pink or purple flowers in early summer. Best suited to a moist, shaded, semiwild area where it can spread freely. From wet woodlands in northeastern Russia. ‡ 24–36 in (60–90 cm). Z5–7 H7–5

C. pentaphylla syn. *Dentaria pentaphylla, D. digitata* A slender rhizome forms a compact clump of dark green leaves divided into narrow, toothed, fingerlike leaflets. Loose clusters of rosy purple, pink, or white ¾-in (2-cm) flowers open in late spring and early summer. Excellent for underplanting shrubs or for open damp woods. From mountain woodlands in western and central Europe. ‡ 24 in (60 cm). Z5–7 H7–5

C. polyphylla see *C. kitaibelii*

C. pratensis (Lady's smock, Cuckoo flower) Compact plant with a short rhizome, forming a rosette of leaves composed of several rounded segments. Erect stems bear a few similar leaves with narrower leaflets, and a loose cluster of pale pink, white, or purplish pink ½-in (1-cm) flowers, opening in late spring and early summer. Double forms turn up in the wild from time

BELOW *Cardamine pratensis* 'Flore Pleno'

to time. A familiar sight in meadows and good for naturalizing in damp grasslands or around a pool. Will stand full sun if the soil is permanently moist. From damp grasslands in Europe, and the British Isles. ‡18 in (45 cm). Z5–8 H8–5. **'Edith'** Compact; double pale pink or white flowers from pink buds. ‡8 in (20 cm). **'Flore Pleno'** Flowers loosely double, pale pink. **'William'** Flowers double, deep lilac-pink.

C. quinquefolia syn. *Dentaria quinquefolia* Clump-forming plant; scaly rhizome bears upright stems. Each stem has a group of three leaves, divided into toothed, lance-shaped leaflets. Deep purple ¾–1-in (2–2.5-cm) flowers open in a cluster at the tip of each stem in late spring and early summer. From mountain woodlands in Eastern Europe, from Bulgaria to southern Russia and Turkey. ‡16 in (40 cm). Z5–8 H8–5

C. raphanifolia Spreading clumps of dark green leaves to 6 in (15 cm) long are borne by this slowly increasing rhizomatous plant. Each leaf is composed of several pairs of oval leaflets and a single large terminal one. In early summer and midsummer, ½–⅝-in (1–1.5-cm) reddish purple flowers open in loose sprays. From damp mountain meadows and stream banks in southern Europe—from France and Spain eastward to Bulgaria and Greece. ‡20–28 in (50–70 cm). Z3–9 H9–1

C. trifolia syn. *Dentaria trifolia* Mat-forming plant with bluntly toothed evergreen leaves composed of three rounded leaflets, usually purple beneath. In late spring and early summer, ½-in (1-cm) white flowers with prominent yellow stamens open in dense clusters on upright, almost leafless stems. Best in constantly moist conditions. Grows in mountain woods, usually on limestone, in central and southern Europe. ‡12 in (30 cm). Z5–7 H7–5

C. waldsteinii Neat, compact, clump-forming plant; stout rhizome bears upright stems. Leaves, usually three on each stem, composed of three lance-shaped leaflets. Pure white flowers, ½–⅝ in (1–1.5 cm) across, with violet stamens. Thrives in full sun if the soil does not dry out. From mountain woodlands in Austria and Slovenia. ‡8–16 in (20–40 cm). Z5–7 H7–5

CARDIANDRA
HYDRANGEACEAE

Unusual shade-loving plants with hydrangea-like flowerheads in late summer and fall.

Four or five species of deciduous plants growing in open woodlands in low mountains of China, Japan, and Taiwan; two species are occasionally cultivated but deserve to be grown more widely. Erect stems becoming woody at the base bear alternate shiny, oval, toothed leaves to 8 in (20 cm) long. In late summer, loose pink or white flower clusters open, consisting of many tiny fertile flowers interspersed with

a few larger, sterile flowers. Similar in overall effect to a demure, herbaceous lacecap hydrangea.

CULTIVATION Grow in part-shade in fertile, moist soil.

PROPAGATION From seed.

PROBLEMS Slugs and snails.

C. alternifolia Upright plant with several stems bearing toothed, elliptical leaves to 8 in (20 cm) long. The domed flowerheads open between late summer and mid-fall and comprise many small, pink or white fertile flowers and fewer, showy sterile ones, each with three rounded or oval, white or pink lobes. A quietly attractive and unusual plant for woodland gardens. From woods in low mountains in southwestern Japan. ‡16–32 in (40–80 cm). Z-10 H10–8

C. formosana Several upright stems bear up to eight elliptical, toothed leaves to 6 in (15 cm) long, clustered toward the top of the stems. A dome-shaped head of flowers opens at the stem tips in late summer, early fall, and even mid-fall. The showy sterile flowers are ¾–1½ in (2–4 cm) across, and have two unequal white, pinkish, or purple lobes. Relatively untried in gardens and its hardiness is not yet fully proven. From forests in low mountains in Taiwan and the Zhejiang province in southeastern China. ‡12–28 in (30–70 cm). Z8–10 H10–8

CAREX
Sedge
CYPERACEAE

Grasslike plants growing in damp, often shady places with decorative and sometimes unusually colored foliage.

About 2,000 species are found worldwide, usually in damp soil in woods, meadows, stony places, and often in bogs. Either densely tufted or with creeping roots, the often sharp-edged leaves generally form a basal rosette. Flower stems are solid and usually triangular. Male and female flowers are separate but on the same stem; male flowers are insignificant, usually at the top of the stem and very slender, female flowers often resemble little brown cones. *Carex* are grown primarily for their foliage, which has led to some confusion, especially with the New Zealand "bronze" sedges (*see* Bronze New Zealand Sedges, *p.114*), and the Japanese variegated sedges have been sold under several incorrect names.

The emergence of sedges as valuable garden plants would have stunned the gardeners of a hundred years ago: most sedge flowers are insignificant, and the foliage of many of the most popular is, well… brown. But for today's gardeners, with a subtle sense of style, color, and artistry, sedges are invaluable. With new and familiar variegated forms, with bluish foliage or bronze,

these apparently unlikely perennials have added a new dimension to our borders. Integrated with other foliage and flowering plants, their unusual colors and textures make them rewarding plants for modern urban settings.

CULTIVATION Generally preferring moisture-retentive soil with good drainage, some can be grown as marginal water plants, in sun or part-shade. The bronze sedges tend to need sun for more interesting colors; they also require some protection over winter.

PROPAGATION From seed or by division in spring.

PROBLEMS May be affected by rust.

C. albida (White sedge) Evergreen clumps of hair-thin leaves are whitish green, becoming nearly white in winter. The stems carry small spike-shaped flowers ⅝ in (1.5 cm) long; the lower part of some of the female flowers is white with a green midrib,

ripening to a white fruit with a tiny green beak. Often confused with *C. comans* 'Frosted Curls', but *C. albida* is a smaller plant preferring wetter conditions. Now reduced to just one population of plants in California. ‡6 in (15 cm). Z5–8 H8–5

C. atrata (Dark sedge) Slowly creeping, forming loose tufts of evergreen, pale blue-green to gray-blue leaves ½ in (1 cm) wide, looking a little like iris clumps. Sharply triangular stems support clusters of fat, blue-black, bullet-shaped 1¼-in (3-cm) flowerheads in mid- and late summer, followed by green or brownish yellow seedheads. Good for damp clefts in rock gardens or at the edges of bog gardens, but likes plenty of sun. From damp rocky or grassy places on mountains from northern Europe to Japan. ‡8–24 in (20–60 cm). Z5–8 H8–5

C. baccans (Crimson-seeded sedge) Evergreen clumps made up of arching, somewhat coarse, dark green leaves ⅝ in (1.5 cm) wide with purple-brown leaf bases. From early summer on, stems emerge carrying flowers like clusters of small berries, green at first, turning purplish red in late fall and keeping their color through winter. Best grown in a pot so it can be brought indoors and enjoyed in winter. Grows in damp soil near streams in part-shade from India to southern China. ↕24–72 in (60–180 cm). Z9–10 H10–9

C. berggrenii Flat, blunt-ended, metallic gray-brown hair-thin leaves with orange-green tints make very small, dense, slowly spreading tufts. Through the summer, stems carry three to four flowerheads, the top flower spike nodding above a cluster of bullet-shaped yellowish flower spikes 2–3 in (5–8 cm) long. Needs sun and moisture-retentive, well-drained soil to ensure the best leaf color. Native to exposed bogs, river flats, and lakeshores in low alpine areas of New Zealand. ↕4 in (10 cm). Z6–9 H9–6

C. brunnea Dense clumps feature long, thin, bronze-green leaves ¼ in (6 mm)

wide; from late spring to midsummer the flower stems carry loose heads of brownish flowers 1¼ in (3 cm) long that hang above the foliage. Grows in dry, open woods, near the sea and on grassland in the Himalaya, Japan, and Australia; the wild form is rarely grown. ↕24 in (60 cm). Z9–10 H10–9. **'Jenneke'** Compact clump of thinner, light green leaves with narrow creamy yellow borders. ↕18 in (45 cm). **'Variegata'** Leaves edged with a broad band of gold, sometimes confused with *C. morrowii* 'Variegata' but has more cream in the leaves. Often best grown under glass as a specimen plant in a pot that can be brought outside into sun or part-shade in summer.

C. buchananii (Buchanan's sedge, Silver spiked sedge) Upright clumps of hair-thin, wiry, flat leaves ending in distinctive wispy and curly pigtail tips; reddish brown, with orange tints in the winter, they remain upright as the plant matures. From early to late summer threadlike stems the same length as the

leaves carry five to six silver-gray flower spikes 2 in (5 cm) long. Needs sun and prefers moisture-retentive, well-drained soil but will tolerate dry conditions. Lovely in drifts next to plants with silver, blue, gold, or even black foliage. Self-seeds readily. From streamsides, grasslands, seashores, and low mountains in New Zealand. ↕32 in (80 cm). Z6–9 H9–5. **'Viridis'** Silvery green undersides to leaves; less upright habit. ↕20–24 in (50–60 cm).

C. caryphyllea **'The Beatles'** Pointed, dark green, very slim evergreen mop head leaves make up loose tufts. 'The Beatles' has shaggy green flowers in mid- and late spring, with the top male flower hung with yellow stamens. Best in moisture-retentive but well-drained soil as an evergreen ground cover or underplanting in contrast to blue or gold grasses and sedges. The wild species is native to short dry grassland in alkaline soil and mountainsides over a wide area from England to Siberia. ↕6 in (15 cm). Z5–9 H9–5

C. chathamica Stout clumps of rigid, pale green, ¼–⅜ in (6–8 mm) wide, pointed leaves with serrated edges and purple bases, throw up stems carrying light brown bullet-shaped flowers that stand erect on sturdy stalks. Best protected over winter, so grow in containers or sink the pots into bog gardens in the summer. Similar to *C. trifida* but a smaller plant. From open peaty and swampy areas, threatened in its native Chatham Island, New Zealand. ↕12 in (30 cm). Z9–10 H10–9

C. comans Dense evergreen clumps of very slender reddish brown or yellow-green leaves; the upper surfaces are matte and the lower surfaces shiny and more deeply colored. The flower stems,

shorter than the leaves and tending to be hidden by the foliage, are threadlike with small, light brown, oblong flower spikes. Unlike *C. buchananii*, the leaves flow down and have no pigtail curls at the tips. Grow in a sheltered area in a moist cleft in a rock garden where the foliage can tumble downward or in a contrasting-colored or metal container. Native to damp grasslands, river flats, or the sides of forest tracks in New Zealand. ↕18 in (45 cm). Z7–9 H9–7. **Bronze form** Bronze-colored foliage with red tints, smaller and finer textured than *C. flagellifera* but female flowers have three stigmas. **'Dancing Flame'** Hints of red-bronze in the leaves. **'Frosted Curls'** Silver-green foliage flowing down with slightly curled ends. **'Taranki'** syn. 'Small Red' Compact with bronze leaves flecked pink and red. ↕8 in (25 cm).

C. conica **'Snowline'** syn. 'Kiku-sakura', 'Marginata', 'Variegata' Variegated Japanese sedge; the wild form, which is not grown, has dense, evergreen tufts of glossy dark green leaves ⅛ in (4 mm) wide. 'Snowline' has conspicuous white edges on the foliage. From mid-spring to early summer, the stems, which are the same length as the leaves, carry three to five erect spiky flowers 1 in (2.5 cm) long; the upper flowers are light brown, the lower, purple to pale green. Prefers light shade and moisture-retentive soil, and stays evergreen if not too cold, making it a good edging for winter in woodland or spring borders. Cut back dead foliage in late winter for best variegation. From mountainsides and hillsides in open woodland in Japan and Korea. ↕6 in (15 cm). Z5–9 H9–5

C. dipsacea Dense evergreen clumps of harsh, light to dark olive green, hairlike leaves with unusual orange, yellow, and

GOING FOR BRONZE

THE BRONZE FORM of *Carex comans* presents many opportunities for unusual plant combinations: with winter snowdrops, for example, or fall sedums—and here, in a sunny summer association, with *Persicaria affinis*. The creeping persicaria sneaks in among the tight carex clumps and sometimes, harmlessly, right into them; the result is dense ground cover. In summer, the rose pink spikes stand out well against the dense cascades of lax, brown-bronze foliage before fading to match it almost exactly. It is important to prevent the carex leaves from growing too long, because in stiff winds they will swirl around and may damage even the sturdy persicaria stems.

BRONZE NEW ZEALAND SEDGES

The bronze New Zealand sedges are unique in their coloring, which may be a defense against powerful ultraviolet rays in the Southern Hemisphere. So unusual are the bronze colors that it is easy to confuse the different species, and all the main bronze-leaved species have been mistakenly offered under the wrong names. But they come from different habitats and need to be grown in slightly different conditions, so it is important to know which is which. *Carex comans*, *C. flagellifera*, *C. buchananii*, and their cultivars seem to cause most problems.

Carex comans
Pale green to bronze foliage, sometimes with red tints
Leaves very thin, even thinner than *C. flagellifera*, and feel slightly less rough
Flower stems a little shorter than the leaves; trail less around the base of the plant than in *C. flagellifera*
Flowers rusty brown; female flowers have three stigmas
Overall effect a dense cascade of lax foliage with a dull metallic sheen
Bronze form is the color of dull rust (but the plant offered under that name is all too often *C. flagellifera*)
Dislikes winter cold and rain

Carex flagellifera
Foliage a glossy buff shade with darker brown and sometimes hints of olive green and red
Stiff, rough leaves
Floppy flower stems trail on the ground
Flowers rusty brown; female flowers have two stigmas
Makes a more upright clump with leaves that feel slightly stiffer
Hardier than *C. comans* and more adaptable in the garden

Carex buchananii
Leaf colors very similar to *C. flagellifera*
Makes the most upright clump
The ends of the very thin leaves are wispy little pigtail curls
Flower stems do not trail but hide in the midst of the foliage
Flowers silvery white; female flowers have two stigmas

If in doubt, remember that *C. buchananii* has silvery white flowers and leaves tipped in curls, while *C. comans* and *C. flagellifera* have brown flowers and leaves with straight tips. *C. comans* is lax, and its female flowers have three stigmas; *C. flagellifera* is more upright and its female flowers have two stigmas.

bronze winter tints. Flower stems, shorter than the leaves, carry four to eight jet-black flower spikes 1 in (2.5 cm) long in midsummer. Needs a protected spot in moist conditions in sun or part-shade to ensure the most interesting leaf color. Grow for contrast with blue sedges or irises in bog or rock gardens. From the edges of swamps, boggy river flats, tussocky grasslands, and damp forests in New Zealand. ‡ 30 in (75 cm). Z7–10 H10–7

C. dolichostachya **'Kaga-nishiki'** (Golden fountains, Kaga brocade sedge) Variegated form of a Japanese sedge whose wild form, not grown, makes slowly creeping clumps of thin, arching, bright green evergreen leaves (deciduous in cool areas). Through these the flower stems emerge from late spring to midsummer with three to five widely spaced flower spikes 2½ in (6 cm) long. 'Kaga-nishiki' foliage is widely edged with gold, giving a lovely lacy effect. Grow in drifts in damp soil, though it is reasonably drought-tolerant, on woodland margins with other colored sedges. From mountain woods, Japan to Taiwan. ‡ 24 in (60 cm). Z5–9 H9–5

C. elata (Tufted sedge) Arching, sharp-edged thin leaves make evergreen clumps through which flower stems appear in late spring to early summer bearing three to five dark brown spikes 1 in (2.5 cm) long; the male flowers are hung with yellow stamens. Grows well in damp soil or with its roots in the water; the colored varieties look striking grown with blue water iris and other blue and variegated water plants. From swamps and still freshwater in northern Europe. ‡ 16 in (40 cm). Z5–9 H9–3. **'Aurea'** (Bowles' golden sedge) Bright yellow leaves with a narrow light green edge. **'Knightshayes'** Bright yellow leaves.

C. firma **'Variegata'** Variegated form of a tiny tufted European sedge with rigid, sharply pointed, slim dark green leaves; a short flower stem carries reddish brown spikes. The wild species is not grown; 'Variegata' foliage is edged creamy yellow. Grow the tiny clumps in choice spots in semishade, in moisture-retentive but well-drained soil. From rocky mountains, grassland, and rocky places on alkaline soil in central Europe. ‡ 4 in (10 cm). Z4–8 H8–1

C. flacca syn. *C. glauca* Slowly creeping, forming carpets of loose evergreen tufts with stiff hair-thin leaves, green on top and bluish underneath. Slender arching stems carry purple-brown flower spikes 1½ in (4 cm) long in mid- and late spring. Makes good, drought-tolerant ground cover but can become invasive, so best confined to small spaces or grown in a container in moisture-retentive, neutral to alkaline soil. Sometimes confused with *C. panicea*, a smaller, noninvasive sedge, and *C. nigra*, which grows in acidic soil and is less invasive. Grows in chalky soil on grasslands, dunes, and fens in Europe and North Africa. ‡ 18 in (45 cm). Z5–9 H9–5. **'Bias'** White margin on one edge of each leaf.

C. flagellifera (Mania sedge, Silver sedge) Dense evergreen tufts of weeping, shiny green to reddish brown, hairlike leaves with sharp edges; red colors more pronounced at higher altitudes. The flower stems are slightly wider than the leaves, elongating as the tiny brown flower spikes appear, trailing down below the foliage when the seeds ripen. Grow where it has some shelter, in a tall container where the weeping foliage can be admired, or use to soften hard landscaping. Courser than *C. comans* Bronze form, but *C. flagellifera* has longer, trailing triangular flower stems. Grows in damp open ground or forest margins in New Zealand. ‡ 14–30 in (35–75 cm). Z7–9 H9–7. **'Auburn Cascade'** Ginger, slightly wider leaves. ‡ 20 in (50 cm). **'Coca Cola'** More upright dark brown foliage with bronze-yellow tints. **'Milk Chocolate'** Slightly more upright, buff at base becoming darker brown toward ends of leaves. **'Rapunzel'** Slender, hairlike leaves. ‡ 12 in (30 cm).

C. glauca see *C. flacca*

C. grayi syn. *C. greyi* (Gray's sedge, Mace sedge, Morning star sedge) Evergreen clumps of bright green, pleated arching leaves ½ in (1 cm) wide. In midsummer to early fall, shorter flower stems carry conspicuous flowers—fat, exploding, pale green stars ¾–1½ in (2–4 cm) long, ripening to light brown seedheads. Best near the edge of streams and bogs where the flowers can be seen from a path. Makes an unusual cut flower. Native to moist woodlands of eastern North America. ‡ 30 in (75 cm). Z3–8 H8–1

C. greyi see *C. grayi*

C. hachijoensis **'Evergold'** see *C. oshimensis* 'Evergold'

C. **'Ice Dance'** see *C. morrowii* 'Ice Dance'

C. lurida Graceful evergreen clumps of bright green, pleated leaves ¼ in (7 mm) wide. From early summer to early fall, flower stems bear handsome nodding pale green flowers, like prickly cylinders 2¾ in (7 cm) long, hanging from thread-thin stems. Best in wet conditions by the edges of bogs and streams where they can be seen. Makes an unusual and long-lasting cut flower. Grows in wet woods and swamps in eastern North America to eastern Mexico. ‡ 30 in (75 cm). Z5–9 H9–5

C. morrowii A slow creeper, gradually forming a carpet of glossy, leathery, deep green leaves up to ½ in (1 cm) wide, which taper to a fine point. The flower stems appear in mid- and late spring with four to six greenish yellow flowers 1½ in (4 cm) long. Makes excellent ground cover in shady areas either in woods or as underplanting for

RIGHT 1 *Carex conica* 'Snowline'
2 *C. dipsacea* **3** *C. dolichostachya* 'Kaga-nishiki' **4** *C. elata* 'Aurea' **5** *C. grayi*

other grasses. Thrives in most soils, but can become invasive. There has been a confusing tendency to assign most variegated sedges to *C. morrowii*, but many are forms of other species and require different growing conditions. From low mountains in Japan. ↕16 in (40 cm). Z5–9 H12–1. **'Ice Dance'** Creamy white margins; can be invasive. **'Fisher's Form'** Edges and lines yellow, becoming whiter. **'Silver Sceptre'** Finer leaves, with narrow pale green and white variegation. **'Variegata'** A cover-all name for many of the other variegated forms of *C. morrowii*, and sometimes other species, most having leaves striped greenish white.

C. muskingumensis (Palm sedge) Slowly spreading evergreen clumps of pointed, pale green leaves ¼ in (7 mm) wide, becoming yellow after frost; they radiate palmlike from the tops of the stems. Pale green, spindle-shaped flowers hang in bunches among the foliage from early to late summer. Allow to colonize pond margins where the sun can filter through the delicate yellow foliage in fall; also thrives in any reasonably moist soil. Native to moist woods, scrub, and wet meadows in eastern and central North America. ↕24 in (60 cm). Z3–8 H8–1. **'Oehme'** Gold-edged leaves, the color becoming more pronounced through summer. **'Little Midge'** Dwarf. ↕9 in (23 cm).

C. nigra (Black or Common sedge) A noticeably variable deciduous sedge, slowly spreading or forming tussocks. The blue-green leaves are very fine; the flower stems appear in late spring and carry slender green to dark brown male flowers and plump spiky female flowers 2 in (5 cm) long; these look black as they ripen into seedheads from early to late summer. Lovely with yellow water iris (*Iris pseudacorus*). Found in bogs and damp grasslands in acidic to neutral soil throughout Europe and eastern North America. ↕28 in (70 cm). Z4–8 H8–1. **'On Line'** Gray-green foliage with yellow margins. ↕12 in (30 cm).

C. ornithopoda **'Variegata'** (Variegated bird's-foot sedge) Variegated form of a European sedge making tufts of thin dark green leaves; the flower stems carry small pale green to dark brown beady flowers in late spring to early summer. The wild species is not grown; 'Variegata' foliage has a broad central cream stripe. Makes good edging along paths and paving in alkaline soil. Often confused with *C. oshimensis* 'Evergold' but is much smaller and dies back in winter. From limestone banks and dry chalk grassland throughout Europe. ↕2–6 in (5–15 cm). Z4–8 H8–1

C. oshimensis **'Evergold'** syn. *C. hachijoensis* 'Evergold'; *C. oshimensis* 'Aureo-variegata', 'Old Gold', or 'Variegata' Variegated form of Japanese sedge, with stiff, glossy, deep green leaves ¼ in (6 mm) wide making dense evergreen clumps. The erect flower

stems appear in early summer with pale to dark brown flower spikes 1 in (2.5 cm) long; they are insignificant compared to the foliage. The wild species is rarely grown; 'Evergold' has a broad central stripe of cream to yellowish white. One of the most striking of the variegated sedges and used as edging or underplanting for spring bulbs or summer bedding. Needs a cool position in light shade for the best variegation. Originally from dry and rocky slopes in Japan. ↕20 in (50 cm). Z5–8 H8–5

C. panicea (Carnation sedge) Slowly spreading, with short rhizomes carrying semievergreen tufts of hair-thin blue-green leaves. The flower stems rise above the foliage in late spring and early summer, with a slender male flower above the purple-brown beady female flowers and seeds. Before flowering this sedge looks similar to a carnation; it is pretty in a damp border. Sometimes confused with *C. flacca* but is smaller and less invasive. A native of neutral grassland, marsh, and fen in Europe. ↕10 in (25 cm). Z5–9 H9–5

C. pendula (Weeping sedge) Distinctive evergreen sedge making substantial clumps of mid-green, rough-edged leaves up to ¾ in (2 cm) wide. The decorative flowers swing above the foliage, the long, thin, gray-green tassels up to 6 in (16 cm) long becoming brown. Best in large areas of wild garden or by big ponds, it is a vigorous self-seeder and will quickly monopolize a small garden—beware. Found in deciduous woods and streamsides throughout Europe, Asia, and North Africa. ↕24–54 in (60–140 cm). Z5–9 H9–5. **'Moonraker'** syn. 'Variegata' Leaves striped in white, but fading through the summer.

C. petriei (Dark brown New Zealand sedge) Dense evergreen upright or loosely spreading tufts of pink or greenish red hair-thin leaves have distinctive broad sheaths at the leaf base and twisted straw-colored points to the tips. Flower stems are usually shorter and thinner than leaves with three to six dark red-brown flower spikes ½–1¼ in (1–3 cm) long. Best in drifts in sheltered, moist, but well-drained soil; also good in containers. Similar to *C. buchananii* but much smaller. Native to streambanks, river flats, and tussocky grasslands in New Zealand. ↕12 in (30 cm). Z7–10 H10–7

C. phyllocephala An unusual Chinese sedge that looks like a *Cyperus*. Evergreen clumps of leafless stems with dark purple bases are topped by rosettes of arching, pointed leaves 8 in (20 cm) long and ½ in (1.3 cm) wide. The short flower stems grow out of the middle of the leaf rosettes, with chunky brown flower spikes ¾ in (2 cm) long adding a nice finishing touch. Best grown in a container in moist, fertile soil in a shady position and brought inside over winter. Native to China, introduced into Japan for medical uses. ↕20 in (50 cm). Z7–10 H10–7. **'Sparkler'** Dark green leaves with broad white

margins; a spectacular container plant. ↕16 in (40 cm). Z7–10 H10–7

C. pilulifera **'Tinney's Princess'** (Variegated pill sedge) Variegated semi-green variety of a European sedge; its arching, hair-thin, rough-edged dark green leaves make dense tufts and, when crushed, produce a distinct smell of turpentine. The threadlike flower stems grow straight above the foliage, carrying clusters of tiny brown egg-shaped flowers in late spring and early summer. 'Tinney's Princess' has leaves with a wide white midrib. Grow it as edging or in troughs or small depressions in moisture-retentive soil in sun or shade. The wild species, not grown in gardens, is found on dry grassland heaths and moors in acidic soil in Europe and into Russia. ↕4 in (10 cm). Z7–9 H9–7

C. plantaginea (Broad-leafed sedge, Plantain sedge) Evergreen clumps of unusually broad, pleated leaves 1 in (2.5 cm) wide, like those of ribwort-plantain, are tinged red at the base. In early spring tall flower stems carry many brown flower spikes; the male flowers are fluffy with yellow stamens. Effective in drifts in woodland gardens with spring bulbs or by stream edges with hostas and ferns. Found in moist forests in central and eastern North America. ↕24 in (60 cm). Z5–7 H7–5

C. pseudocyperus (Cyperus sedge, Hop sedge) Slowly spreading loose upright tufts of bright green-yellow leaves ¼–½ in (5–12 mm) wide; the rough-edged flower stems are shorter than the foliage and in early summer to midsummer carry three to five decorative, fat, bristly finger-shaped flowers 2–2½ in (5–6 cm) in length that dangle from long thin stalks and ripen to polished green seed heads. Makes a good marginal plant for ponds and bog gardens where the light can filter through the leaves and flowers. Sometimes confused with *C. lurida*, but is a bigger plant with foliage taller than the flowers. Found in swamps, slow-moving water, and lake edges throughout northern temperate regions. ↕4 ft (1.2 m). Z5–9 H9–5

C. remota (Remote sedge) Very thin, long, arching, pale green hair-thin leaves make dense semievergreen mounds. In early summer the long drooping flower stems carry small pale green flowers, ⅛–½ in (3–10 mm) long, with a wide space between each flower. Makes good ground cover. Found in damp woods and other moist places throughout Europe, including Britain. ↕28 in (70 cm). Z5–9 H9–5

C. riparia (Greater pond sedge) Vigorous creeping rhizomes carry large stands of arching, sharp edged, blue-green leaves ¼–⅝ in (6–15 mm) wide. The flower stalks carry handsome flower spikes up to 6 in (15 cm) long in late spring to early summer; the upper male spikes are golden with stamens, the female green-brown spikes below hang down from thin stems into the foliage. Very invasive, especially in wet soil; not recommended anywhere except where it will not overrun desirable plants. Found at the edges of ponds and ditches in up to 18 in (45 cm) of water throughout temperate regions. ‡24–54 in (60–130 cm). Z4–8 H8–4. **'Variegata'** Decorative foliage with bold white stripes. Less aggressive and looks good in a container but sometimes reverts to the green form. ‡16–24 in (40–60 cm). Z4–8 H8–4

C. secta Evergreen tussocks of arching, bright green, rough-edged leaves up to ¼ in (7 mm) wide, often forming thick trunks of matted rhizomes, roots, and old stem bases up to 36 in (90 cm) high and 20 in (50 cm) wide. Brown flower spikes appear in summer on drooping, sharp-edged stems usually a bit shorter than the leaves. Decorative in bog gardens, especially when grown with colored-stem deciduous shrubs. Native to swamps in New Zealand. ‡36 in (90 cm). Z7–10 H10–7. **var. tenuiculmis** Shorter; orange highlights on browner leaves. ‡20 in (50 cm).

C. siderosticha Creeping slowly to form dense, deciduous masses of broad, pleated, bright green leaves up to 1 in (2.5 cm) wide. In early spring, before new leaves unfurl, flower stems emerge carrying four to eight small flower spikes. Long-lived ground cover in moist woods, especially effective with early small spring bulbs. Native to mountain woods in China, Korea, and Japan. ‡8 in (20 cm). Z6–9 H9–6. **'Shima-nishiki'** syn. 'Island Brocade' Leaves yellow with cream central stripe. Z6–9 H9–6. **'Variegata'** Striking, pale green and bold white stripes, flushed pink on new leaves. Z6–9 H9–6

C. solandri Dense tufts of hard yellow-green arching leaves up to ¼ in (6 mm) wide; the flower stems, dark red at their base, carry five to ten brown to almost black small flowers that nod above the foliage on long thin stalks. Makes good ground cover in well-drained soil in damp shady parts of the garden; needs protection in cold areas. From damp forests and river flats in New Zealand. ‡12–32 in (30–80 cm). Z8–10 H10–8

C. sylvatica (Wood sedge) Slowly creeping to form dense evergreen clumps of shiny, soft olive green leaves ⅛–¼ in (3–6 mm) wide that turn yellow in fall and winter. In late spring to midsummer the tall flower stems are topped with male flowers covered with pale-colored stamens; the lower female flowers are thin tassels of pale yellow to brown up to 2¾ in (7 cm) long, hanging above the foliage on long threadlike stalks. A graceful addition to damp, shady areas of the garden. Found in heavy soil in damp woodlands throughout Europe and into Asia. ‡6–24 in (15–60 cm). Z3–7 H7–1

C. testacea (Slender sedge) Rough-edged, hair-thin leaves make dense evergreen mounds; each leaf is olive green at the base, with rusty orange tints farther up the blades if grown in full sun, the coloration increasing through winter. Very long, thread-thin flower stems grow up to 24 in (60 cm)

high above the foliage, then flop over to the ground as the seeds ripen; the female flowers are pale brown, ¼ in (5 mm) long, and hang from fine threads. For best color, grow in moist but well-drained soil in full sun. Sometimes confused with *C. dipsacacea* but distinct in its black flowers. Native to forest, tussocky grassland, and sand dunes in New Zealand. ‡16 in (40 cm). Z8–9 H9–8. **'Old Gold'** Leaves soft golden yellow, especially in winter.

C. trifida Light green, ½ in (1.2 cm) wide, evergreen leaves, blue-green on the undersides, make robust tussocks. The flower stems, shorter than the foliage, appear in mid- and late spring carrying clusters of three upright, furry, fat brown bullet-shaped flowers 4 in (10 cm) long. A handsome addition to sheltered, moist, well-drained beds and especially colorful in winter. Found on coastal cliffs and rocky outcrops in the Falkland Islands, New Zealand, and southwestern Chile. ‡6–36 in (15–90 cm). Z6–10 H10–6. **'Chatham Blue'** Leaves blue-green on both sides. ‡24 in (60 cm).

CARLINA
Weather thistle
ASTERACEAE

Thistlelike plants with handsome spiny leaves and striking flowerheads in summer.

About 30 species of spiny plants, some annuals, growing in dry places in Europe, Macaronesia, and the Mediterranean region, two of which are sometimes grown in gardens. Rosettes of boldly cut, spiny leaves

BELOW 1 *Carlina acaulis*
2 *Catananche caerulea*

provide a good foil to the thistlelike flowerheads, the most showy part of which is the spiny bracts behind the flower that close up in cloudy or wet weather. Good plants for a sunny rock or gravel garden. Low soil fertility will help keep the plants' natural character.

CULTIVATION Grow in well-drained, nutrient-poor soil in full sun.

PROPAGATION From seed; seedlings dislike root disturbance.

PROBLEMS Usually trouble-free.

C. acaulis Flat rosettes of spiny, lobed, gray-green leaves to 12 in (30 cm) long feature a solitary, usually stemless central flowerhead, 2–4 in (5–10 cm) across, from midsummer to early fall. The middle of the flowerhead is composed of purple-tinged or silvery florets, surrounded by a ruff of long-lasting, papery white bracts. There is also an unnamed bronze-leaved selection. From dry, sunny places in alkaline soil in southern Europe. ‡4 in (10 cm). Z5–7 H7–5. **Bronze form** Leaves purple-tinted with red midribs. **subsp.** *simplex* Up to six flowerheads borne on a tall stem; a long-lasting dried flower. ‡24 in (60 cm).

CATANANCHE
Blue cupidone, Cupid's dart
ASTERACEAE

Easily grown daisies for any sunny situation. Fine cornflower-like flowers in summer and early fall.

Five species of perennials and annuals from dry, grassy places in the Mediterranean region, one of which is commonly grown. From clumps of narrow, almost grasslike

basal leaves arise simple or branched stems ending in delicate flowerheads composed of strap-shaped ray florets with papery bracts beneath.

CULTIVATION Grow in full sun in any well-drained soil.

PROPAGATION From seed sown in spring, or from root cuttings.

PROBLEMS Powdery mildew.

C. caerulea Makes a clump of narrow, grassy, gray-green leaves to 12 in (30 cm) long. Solitary, dark-centered, violet-blue flowerheads, 1¼–1½ in (3–4 cm) across, surrounded by silvery, papery bracts, open from early summer to early fall. Short-lived, especially in heavy soil, where it is often treated as an annual or biennial. Makes a good cut flower, either fresh or dried. From dry meadows in southwestern Europe. ‡24–36 in (60–90 cm). Z3–8 H8–1. **'Alba'** Flowers white with a creamy center; comes true from seed. **'Bicolor'** syn. 'Stargazer' Flowers white with a conspicuous dark purple center; comes only partly true from seed. **'Major'** Deep lavender-blue flowers about 2 in (5 cm) across; propagated from root cuttings. **'Stargazer'** *see* 'Bicolor'.

CATHCARTIA SEE MECONOPSIS

CAULOPHYLLUM
Blue cohosh
BERBERIDACEAE

Hardy shade-lover whose fall display of blue berries is more striking than the spring flowers.

Two species of deciduous plants from mountain woods and forests of eastern North America and East

Asia, growing best in moist, shady places such as a woodland garden or shrub border. They spread slowly, by stout underground creeping stems. The sea green leaves, divided into up to 27 leaflets, are produced with the flowers, or soon after the blooms open. Tiny, mundane, yellow, purple, red, brown, or green, six-petaled star-shaped flowers, carried in open spikes, appear in spring; they are followed by attractive berries. American Indians used the rhizomatous roots medicinally. The berries are toxic if eaten. ⚠

CULTIVATION Best grown in steadily moist, humus-rich, acidic or neutral soil and part- or full shade. Add leaf mold or well-rotted garden compost before planting and mulch annually in fall with either one of these.

PROPAGATION By division of clumps in early fall or in spring before plants start into growth, or take cuttings from the creeping stems in early spring and place in a cold frame. Increase is slow with either method. Seed, with its pulp, can be sown as soon as it is ripe in an open cold frame, but be prepared for slow and erratic germination.

PROBLEMS Vine weevil, with possibility of fungal leaf spot.

C. thalictroides (Blue cohosh) A dense, clump-forming plant for late-season interest in a woodland garden. The sea-green leaves, with a white coating in spring, are divided into 1–3-in- (2.5–8-cm-) long, somewhat egg-shaped, lobed leaflets, each with conspicuous veins. The foliage is similar to that of meadow rue (*Thalictrum*), hence the species name. Starry, ½-in (1-cm) flowers, in a mix of chartreuse and antique-bronze, are produced in short, fat spikes during mid- and late spring; they are followed in early fall by deep blue berries, sometimes covered with a whitish bloom. From eastern North America. ‡30 in (75 cm). Z3–7 H7–1. **subsp.** *robustum* A variable, somewhat stronger grower; leaves are divided into many leaflets and flowers are yellow-green, otherwise very similar to the species. From East Asia. ‡32 in (80 cm).

CAUTLEYA
ZINGIBERACEAE

Exotic-looking clump-formers with delightful foliage and showy flower spikes in late summer.

A small but botanically confused group of about five species from the Himalayan foothills, in particular parts of China and India, including Sikkim, where they grow in cool, shaded valleys, sometimes epiphytically on trees. Fleshy shoots appear in late spring and bear rich green, lance-shaped leaves, up to 12 in (30 cm) long. Plants are quick-growing and reach 24 in

RIGHT *Cautleya spicata* 'Robusta'

(60 cm) in height once the terminal spikes of flowers, composed of a lip and a hood, appear. These flowers, generally yellow, emerge from red bracts in late summer over about two weeks, and may be followed by fleshy fruit capsules. Plants die down in winter after the first frosts but, with some protection, make reliably hardy plants in many frost-prone gardens in both borders and woodland areas.

CULTIVATION Cautleyas like moist but well-drained soil in dappled shade, although they will take some sun provided they are not allowed to dry out. Water plants well in dry periods. Make sure the rhizomes are planted about 6 in (15 cm) below the soil surface, especially in cooler areas, to help protect the roots from frost damage. After the shoots have been frosted, apply a thick mulch of leaf mold or well-rotted manure.

PROPAGATION By division of established clumps as growth begins in late spring or early summer. Alternatively, sow seed in early spring at about 59°F (15°C).

PROBLEMS Usually trouble-free, but slugs and snails can damage emerging shoots.

C. gracilis Slender plant with narrow leaves up to 8 in (20 cm) long, often with purplish undersides, which are rather sparsely held on the stems in late summer. These are topped by flower spikes bearing a succession of fairly small, pale yellow or sometimes orange flowers. Moist valleys from Kashmir to southwestern China, up to 10,000 ft (3,000 m). ‡16 in (40 cm). Z7–9 H9–7

C. spicata Fleshy, reddish stems carry broad, rich green leaves and are topped with numerous bright yellow flowers produced from vivid red bracts. From forests in Guizou, Sichuan, and Yunnan provinces in China. ‡3¼ ft (1 m). Z7–9 H9–7. **'Robusta'** syn. 'Autumn Beauty' A fine selection and perhaps the most widely cultivated. The flower spikes are generally longer than the species and the dark yellow flowers are produced from maroon bracts, to striking effect.

CENTAUREA
Knapweed
ASTERACEAE

Plants for poor and well-drained soil in meadows and borders, which are attractive to bees and butterflies.

About 500 species, mostly herbaceous perennials, some woody based, but including some annuals and biennials, the majority of which are from the Mediterranean area and western Asia. They derive their common name from their hard, round bud—the knap—from which the florets emerge. Some knapweeds are inclined to weediness, although, where they are native, selections can be made for neater habit, more flowers, or better foliage.

Many have hoary, even silvery, foliage, often broadly lance-shaped in outline but deeply lobed along the main axis—and in some cases lobed again—sometimes producing a feathery effect. Silvery-leaved species also tend to have white-downy stems.

The flowers are often thistlelike in appearance, sometimes with a cushion of brightly colored florets emerging from the buds. Species with the outer florets longer and trumpetlike, as in the common cornflower or bluebottle, *Centaurea cyanus*, are commonly called cornflowers. The roots are usually fibrous, though a few species spread by rhizomes; some can be moderately invasive.

CULTIVATION Most prefer sun, good drainage and nutrient-poor soil, often being tolerant of alkaline conditions. Deadhead any long-flowering plants to encourage prolonged bloom.

PROPAGATION From seed, by division or, for woody based species, basal cuttings; cultivars should always be propagated vegetatively. Silver-leaved plants are best divided in spring. The most dramatic, silver, intricately cut leaved species can often be grown as annual foliage plants from a late-winter sowing under glass.

PROBLEMS Aphids, rust, and powdery mildew are sometimes a problem.

C. bella Spreading by rhizomes, rosettes of grayish leaves, white beneath, have oval or lance-shaped lobes on either side of the midrib; larger terminal

lobe. Mauve-pink cornflowers appear from late spring to midsummer. Tolerant of most soils in sun. Grow from seed, or divide in the fall. From the Caucasus. ‡12 in (30 cm). Z4–8 H8–1

C. benoistii Tall, with gray-green leaves, broad at the base, becoming more finely divided up the stem. The plant usually seen—originating from Chelsea Physic Garden, London—has rich crimson button flowers from early summer to early fall. This species may actually be a hybrid with *C. atropurpurea*. For well-drained soil in sun, although it will tolerate some shade; divide in fall. From Morocco. ‡5 ft (1.5 m). Z4–8 H8–1

C. cheiranthifolia syn. *C. ochroleuca*, *C. montana* var. *citrina* Spreading by rhizomes, the basal leaves are lance-shaped and undivided, or with one or two (rarely three) pairs of lobes or coarse teeth. The stem leaves may also be undivided or may have a few coarse teeth. The bracts around the buds have dark borders edged with silvery "eyelashes," as opposed to dark brown to black ones for *C. montana*, from which it also differs in being less vigorous and with rather larger creamy white to pale yellow flowers. Tolerant of any soil but prefers sun; best divided. From Turkey. ‡18 in (45 cm). Z4–8 H8–1. **var.** *purpurascens* Flowers more or less overlaid with mauve pink to purple over the yellowish base, creating a curious mix of tints.

C. cineraria syn. *C. gymnocarpa* A variable, woody-based perennial, usually downy and near white, upright and with a few branches. **subsp.** *cineraria* The most widely seen form, the foliage is very brightly silver, intricately cut along the axis of the leaf and further divided into narrow lobes; the gracefully arched fronds resemble those of a small palm tree. Mauve cornflowers appear in mid- and late summer. Traditionally raised from seed as a bedding plant, it blends perfectly well in mixed planting toward the front of beds or borders; removing the untidy flower stems encourages yet more handsome leaves. Can prove unexpectedly hardy in well-drained soil, but overwintered plants become gawky. Sow seed in late winter or take basal cuttings. From Italy. ‡32 in (80 cm) in flower; basal foliage ‡18 in (45 cm). Z7–11 H12–1. **'Colchester White'** Unusually hardy, but uncommon, selection. Z7–11 H12–1

C. dealbata Leaves are light green above, white below, and lobed along the axis of the leaf—or, rarely, unlobed. Its upright flower stems, inclined to flop unless staked, carry mauve-pink, white-centered cornflowers from early to late summer. Staking is usually necessary. Divide in spring. From Turkey and the Caucasus. ‡36 in (90 cm). Z3–9 H9–1. **'Steenbergii'** A running rootstock and deep carmine pink, almost magenta, flowers on a shorter plant suggest this might be a hybrid. ‡24 in (60 cm).

C. gymnocarpa see *C. cineraria*

C. hypoleuca Clump-forming perennial with leaves that are light green above, white below, and of variable shape but usually divided into lobes toward the base and with a large terminal leaflet. Mauve-pink cornflowers are produced in early summer and midsummer. Rarely seen, but daintier than its more familiar cultivar. From Turkey and northern Iran. ‡ 18 in (45 cm). Z3–9 H9–1. **'John Coutts'** Bigger, brighter and coarser with flowers of a richer mauve-pink, reblooming into early fall. Perhaps a hybrid with *C. dealbata*. Selected by John "Jock" Coutts, one time Curator of the Royal Botanic Gardens, Kew, named by Graham Stuart Thomas and introduced by Sunningdale Nurseries, Berkshire, England. ‡ 24 in (60 cm).

C. jacea (Brown knapweed) A variable plant with more or less branched stems bearing mauve-pink, occasionally lilac or purple, rarely white, cornflowers—often paler at the center—above toothed or lobed green leaves in early to late summer. Suitable for wildflower meadows, especially in alkaline soil, and attractive to bees and butterflies. Can be raised from seed, though selected forms should be propagated by division. From Europe and adjacent Asia. ‡ to 5 ft (1.5 m). Z4–8 H8–1

C. macrocephala Green, unlobed leaves show off golden yellow flowers on unbranched stems from early to late summer; the bracts surrounding the buds are hidden by light brown, papery appendages that grow out from their edges. From Turkey and the Caucasus. ‡ 36–48 in (90–120 cm). Z3–7 H7–1

C. montana (Perennial cornflower, Mountain bluet) Spreading slowly and relentlessly, but not invasively, to make moderate sized clumps of downy, slightly grayish, lance-shaped leaves. The broadly winged stems carry

elegant cornflowers, typically with spreading, royal blue outer florets surrounding reddish purple inner ones. The buds are covered with tightly fitting scales dramatically fringed with dark brown to black bristles, a characteristic that separates it from its close relatives *C. cheiranthifolia* and *C. triumfettii*. A traditional cottage-garden plant—popular for cutting—that flowers in late spring and early summer and is a useful plant for bridging the "June gap" between spring and summer flowers. Likes sun, good drainage, and alkaline soil but is relatively tolerant of poor drainage, acidic soil, and a little shade. Benefits from pea-staking to prevent it from flopping. Cutting back after flowering encourages fresh foliage and a little reblooming in late summer and fall. Propagate by division. From the mountains of southern Europe. ‡ 18 in (45 cm). Z3–9 H9–1. **'Alba'** A name used for a number of white-flowered variants, sometimes with pinkish disk florets. **'Carnea'** Mauve-pink flowers. **var. citrina** see *C. cheiranthifolia*. **'Gold Bullion'** Leaves yellow-green, very bright in sun, tending more to lime green in part-shade. ‡ 16 in (40 cm). **'Lady Flora Hastings'** White flowers with longer, more deeply cut ray florets and slate-blue stamens above pale pink disk florets. **'Ochroleuca'** Creamy yellow flowers and gray leaves on a vigorous, spreading, rhizomatous plant. Perhaps a form of *C. cheiranthifolia*. ‡ 10 in (25 cm). **'Parham'** Larger, and with rather deeper lavender-blue flowers. ‡ 24 in (60 cm). **'Violetta'** Large, but with deep red-violet flowers. A number of quite different plants are grown under this name. ‡ 24 in (60 cm).

C. ochroleuca see *C. cheiranthifolia*

C. orientalis Stiffly upright and sparingly branched with dark green, leathery, unlobed basal leaves, which are divided into narrow lobes on the lower part of the flower stems. Straw-yellow

flowers emerge from buds covered with papery bracts in mid- and late summer. For well-drained soil in sun. From southeastern Europe and the Orient. ‡ 32–48 in (80–120 cm). Z6–10 H10–6

C. phrygia (Wig knapweed.) Upright, branched or unbranched stems, carry green to grayish downy smooth-edged or toothed leaves and mauve-pink to purple cornflowers in early summer and midsummer. Stalks are thickened beneath the flowerheads and bristling brownish outgrowths from the edge of the bud scales cover the bud, earning it its common name. For well-drained soil in sun, though it will tolerate light shade. From northern, central, and eastern Europe, extending to the northern part of the Baltic Peninsula. ‡ 12–48 in (30–120 cm). Z5–8 H8–5

C. pulcherrima A woody-based perennial with several basal rosettes of leaves that are downy gray to white beneath, sometimes slightly downy above, and variable in shape though generally lobed with a large terminal lobe. From the rosettes rise unbranched (or rarely branched) stems with mauve-pink cornflowers in midsummer. Best given sun and good drainage; propagate from seed or by basal cuttings. From the Caucasus and Asia Minor. ‡ 12–16 in (30–40 cm). Z4–8 H8–1

C. **'Pulchra Major'** Clump-forming, the basal leaves are about 12in (30cm) long, grayish above and near white below, toothed and more or less cut to the midrib into long lobes (sometimes all along the leaf, sometimes only in the lower part) while other leaves have unlobed margins—all on the same plant. From early to late summer deep mauve-pink flowers emerge from a bulbous structure, the knop, covered in papery outgrowths making a glistening quilt of palest brown that remains attractive after the flower has faded. They are carried on upright white-downy stems, with smaller leaves only

ABOVE **1** *Centaurea dealbata* **2** *C. hypoleuca* 'John Coutts' **3** *C. macrocephala* **4** *C. montana*

toward the base. Best in sun and with good drainage. Does not set seed in cool climates, but can be divided. Of uncertain origin, it is now understood not to be a *Centaurea* but more likely a *Rhaponticum* or *Stemmacantha*. ‡ 30 in (75 cm). Z6–9 H9–6

C. rupestris Slightly woolly to almost smooth leaves are divided into narrow lobes and, in mid- and late summer, unbranched stems bear yellow flowers from buds whose scales are usually tipped with outward-pointing spines. Best in sun, with good drainage and a nutrient-poor alkaline soil, but can look untidy, especially if grown in nitrogen-rich soil. From Italy and the Balkan Peninsula. ‡ 8–24 in (20–60 cm). Z5–8 H8–5

C. ruthenica A woody rhizome produces normally unbranched stems with finely divided leaves, with lance-shaped lobes, that are dark green above and woolly below. The pale yellow flowers appear in mid- and late summer. Thrives in most well-drained soils in sun and best raised from seed. Generally considered the choicest and most elegant of yellow-flowered knapweeds. From Romania to southern Russia. ‡ 3¼ ft (1 m). Z5–8 H8–5

C. scabiosa (Greater knapweed) A very variable upright perennial with deeply lobed (or, rarely, unlobed) leaves. The mauve to reddish purple cornflowers, their outer florets reflexed, appear in midsummer to early fall. A good plant for bees and butterflies, though inclined to be coarse; shorter, more floriferous selections would be valuable. Suited to grassland including meadows, and to poor, alkaline soil in sun; best raised from seed. From Europe, including the British Isles. ‡ 6 in–6½ ft (15 cm–2m).

Z3–8 H8–1. **f. albiflora** White flowers, and as variable as the species.

C. simplicicaulis An attractive, neat, relatively low-growing, clump-forming perennial, for the gravel garden or the front of the border. Its finely divided leaves are slightly downy above, usually enough to seem grayish or silvery, and downy white below. Mauve-pink cornflowers are borne on slender, usually unbranched stems from late spring to midsummer. Well-drained soil in sun. From the Caucasus. ‡ 8–12 in (20–30 cm). Z3–8 H8–1

CENTRANTHUS
Valerian
VALERIANACEAE

A long-blooming plant, popular with butterflies, for borders, walls, and rocky locations.

Approximately 12 species of perennials, annuals, and small shrubs found in the Mediterranean region in poor and gravelly, often alkaline, soil in open sunny sites. They are mostly erect-growing, with simple, opposite leaves and small flowers held in dense clusters above the foliage. Only one species is generally grown in gardens.

CULTIVATION Best in poor, alkaline, dry soil. Rich soil gives excessive growth and poor flowering.

PROPAGATION From seed or by division in early spring.

PROBLEMS Usually trouble-free.

C. ruber (Jupiter's beard, Keys of heaven, Red valerian) A free-flowering, sweetly scented plant forming an

BELOW **1** Centranthus ruber 'Alba'
2 Cephalaria gigantea

upright, many-branched clump that rarely needs staking. The rather fleshy, lance-shaped, blue-green leaves are 3 in (7.5 cm) long and on very short stalks. They are held on slightly woody stems topped with fragrant ⅝-in (1.5-cm) red to scarlet flowers in tall, branched heads. The flowers open for a long season in late spring, are good for cutting, and attract bees and butterflies. If cut back hard after flowering, a second flush open in summer. Self-seeds readily, can be invasive in a rock garden, and will pop up in crevices of walls or rock faces; it can be difficult to weed out because the stems snap just above the root. It grows taller, flops, and flowers less well in fertile soil. A number of shades are often found growing together. ‡ 3 ft (1 m). Z5–8 H8–5. **'Albus'** Off-white flowers with pinkish tinge; shorter. **'Atrococcineus'** Carmine-red, the darkest form. **var. coccineus** Deep red flowers but paler than 'Atrococcineus'. **'Snowcloud'** Pure white flowers without the pink tinge; foliage is fresh green.

CEPHALARIA
DIPSACACEAE

L ong-flowering, upright plants that are good for the back of a mixed border or for cutting.

Some 65 species of perennials, annuals, and shrubs native to Europe, Africa, and Central Asia. They are closely related to *Scabiosa* (the flower structure differs), with similar round heads of small individual flowers carried on thin stems, well above the foliage. Showy outer florets around a pincushion-like center are produced from midsummer into fall. The long leaves, composed of several toothed leaflets in opposite pairs, are mainly toward the base of the stems, with smaller versions where the flowering stems branch.

CULTIVATION Well-drained soil in sun or part shade.

PROPAGATION From seed (stratify for six weeks at 41°F (5°C) or by division in spring.

PROBLEMS Usually trouble-free.

C. dipsacoides Upright with dark green, divided and toothed leaves. Clumps of stout, sparsely branched stems topped by 2-in (5-cm) creamy yellow flowers, with a hint of green, speckled with dark spots (the mauve stamens). Seed heads are good winter decorations. From eastern Mediterranean. ‡ 5¼ ft (1.8 m). Z7–9 H9–7

C. gigantea syn. *C. tatarica* (Giant scabious, Yellow scabious) The most widely grown species and most effective if planted through tall, late-flowering grasses or against a dark hedge at the back of the border. The foliage, divided into opposite pairs of toothed, lance-shaped leaflets, is light green and the stout, openly branched stems are topped with an airy dance of primrose yellow flowerheads with greenish centers of unopened buds. The color comes mainly from the large outer florets. Some giant scabiosa have escaped from the garden and become naturalized. Siberia to northern Turkey. ‡ 6½ ft (2 m). Z3–7 H7–1

C. leucantha (White scabious) A long-blooming species, flowering from late spring to fall. The woody base produces wiry stems carrying foliage divided into linear or lance-shaped, toothed or lobed, oppositely arranged leaflets topped with freely produced creamy white, occasionally pure white or yellow, flowers. Dry, rocky places from Portugal to the Balkans. ‡ 6½ ft (2 m). Z8–10 H10–8

C. tatarica see *C. gigantea*

CERATOSTIGMA
Leadwort
PLUMBAGINACEAE

S un-loving, semiwoody plants bringing vibrant blue to the garden in late summer and fall.

Eight species of deciduous, woody-based plants from dry, open places in Asia, from the Himalaya to China, and in tropical Africa; three are common garden plants. The rounded or spreading bushy plants, sometimes running underground, have simple leaves that often color well in fall. Striking blue flowers, shaped like plumbago, in clusters at the ends of the shoots. In cooler areas, stems die back to ground level, to reemerge in late spring.

CULTIVATION Grow in any light soil in full sun.

PROPAGATION By cuttings, division, or detaching rooted layers.

PROBLEMS Usually trouble-free.

C. griffithii A twiggy, rounded plant with gray-green leaves on reddish brown stems; leaves turn red in late fall and early winter. In late summer and early fall, bright blue flowers 1–1¼ in (2–3 cm) across open in succession in clusters at the stem tips. Needs a warm, sheltered position. From dry, open places in the Himalaya and western China. ‡ 36 in (90 cm). Z7–10 H10–7

C. plumbaginoides Spreading plant with reddish stems bearing dark green leaves that turn bright red in fall and early winter. Low, upright stems end with a bristly cluster of vivid blue flowers ¾ in (2 cm) wide in early and mid-fall. From northern and central China. ‡ 12–16 in (30–40 cm). Z6–9 H9–4

C. willmottianum The dark green leaves of this rounded shrubby plant are often edged with purple and turn red in fall. Clusters of light sky blue flowers, 1 in (2.5 cm) across, open from late summer to mid-fall. Although more or less woody, this species may die back to soil level in cold areas. From China and Tibet. ‡ 36 in (90 cm). Z6–7 H9–6. **Desert Skies** (**'Palmgold'**) Yellow foliage, turning red in fall, contrasts well with sky blue flowers in late summer and early fall, but this form is less robust. **Forest Blue** (**'Lice'**) Mid-blue flowers are borne freely from late summer to mid-fall, above green leaves that turn red in fall.

CHAEROPHYLLUM
Chervil
APIACEAE

A delightful foliage and flowering plant whose generic name aptly means "pleasing leaf."

About 35 species grow wild in fencerows, open woodlands, and meadows across the north temperate zone; only a few are in cultivation. The leaves are finely cut several times into feathery segments, resembling ferns, and provide lovely backing to the clusters of white, pinkish, or yellow flowers.

CULTIVATION Best in moist, fertile soil in sun or part-shade.

PROPAGATION From fresh seed or by division of established plants in spring.

PROBLEMS Usually trouble-free.

C. hirsutum (Hairy chervil) Appealing species with heads of white, sometimes pink, flowers borne in late spring to early summer. The strong clumps of soft ferny foliage, produced from a deep branching rootstock, are delicately apple-scented. Grows in moist soil in shady sites and meadows in the mountains of central and southern Europe to southern Russia and the Caucasus. ‡ 24–36 in (60–90 cm). Z6–9 H9–6. **'Roseum'** A charming soft pink, one of the loveliest members of the family and very effective grown in combination with *Brunnera macrophylla* and *Tellima grandiflora*.

LEFT 1 *Ceratostigma plumbaginoides* **2** *C. willmottianum* **3** *Chaerophyllum hirsutum* 'Roseum' **4** *Chamaemelum nobile* 'Flore Pleno'

CHAMAEMELUM
Chamomile
ASTERACEAE

Neat, carpeting, sun-loving plants with feathery, aromatic foliage and a profusion of white daisylike blossoms.

Four species of these aromatic perennials and annuals are native to grassland and open places in Europe and the Mediterranean region, of which one species is commonly cultivated in gardens. Its spreading stems carry bright green leaves, finely dissected into threadlike segments, and small white daisies with yellow centers are borne freely in summer. Contact with the foliage may exacerbate skin allergies. ⚠

CULTIVATION Grow in any well-drained soil in full sun.

PROPAGATION By division or from seed sown in spring.

PROBLEMS Usually trouble-free.

C. nobile syn. *Anthemis nobilis* (Roman chamomile) Mat-forming plant with spreading stems that become more erect at the growing tips, with finely dissected bright green leaves to 2 in (5 cm) long. Yellow-centered white daisies, ⅜–1 in (1.5–2.5 cm) across, open over a long period from early to late summer. From western Europe, including the British Isles. The dried flowerheads are used to make chamomile tea, which is used by many to aid sleep. ↕10 in (25 cm). Z6–9 H9–6. **'Flore Pleno'** Pomponlike, fully double white flowerheads, tinged green in the center. **'Treneague'** Non-flowering cultivar forming a neat, low mat of foliage; ideal for use in paving as well as for making a chamomile lawn.

CHAMERION
ONAGRACEAE

Attractive but often invasive plants for the border, wildflower garden—or to admire from afar.

About 15 vigorous and often invasive perennial species from arctic and temperate zones of the Northern Hemisphere. Some suggest they should not be grown in gardens at all because of their invasive habits. Clumps or colonies of stout erect stems are clad in numerous simple, spirally arranged leaves and topped by spikes of four-petaled flowers. Sometimes placed in *Epilobium* (the true willowherbs), but *Epilobium* is distinct in its leaves being in opposite pairs and the flowers having noticeably long stamens that curve down.

CULTIVATION Thrives in practically all garden soils, in sun or part-shade.

PROPAGATION Either by division when dormant or by basal cuttings in spring.

PROBLEMS Usually trouble-free but may be invasive.

C. angustifolium syn. *Epilobium angustifolium* (Rosebay willowherb) Rapidly colony-forming plant best admired from a distance, its decorative, tapered spires of bright pink flowers, ¾–1¼ in (2–3 cm) wide, light up roadsides, woodland margins, and disturbed ground. The densely borne leaves are willowlike and 4–8 in (10–20 cm) long. In the garden its root system should be confined and seed heads promptly removed to prevent rapid spread. Once known as fireweed from its tendency to colonize burned ground. Found throughout the northern temperate zone. ↕5–6½ ft (1.5–2 m). Z3–7 H8–1. **'Album'** Pure white. **'Isobel'** Paler pink flowers with darker sepals. **'Stahl Rose'** A pleasing shade of magenta.

C. dodonaei syn. *C. rosmarinifolium*

HERBS AS ORNAMENTALS

In the earliest American gardens, herbs were included in the kitchen garden. Gardeners cultivated these plants for a specific use, whether for medicinal, culinary, fragrance, or dyes. Herbs were grown in rows, borders, or enclosed plots along with fruits, flowers, and vegetables. The herb garden as a separate garden did not become popular in the US until the 20th century.

Native Americans also used plants to enhance their lives. Culinary and medicinal herbs were integral to their survival and their use of indigenous plants continue among herbalists today.

As the years passed, many herbs were cherished for their appearance as well as their practicality. Plants such as lavender, thyme, and chamomile found their way into ornamental flowerbeds, where they could be appreciated more fully. Nursery seed catalogs, which formerly had segregated the herbs in separate lists, now included them in the lists of plants offered for primarily visual pleasure.

Among the decorative plants that have herbal backgrounds are *Achillea, Acorus, Actaea, Adiantum, Agastache, Agrimonia, Alchemilla, Allium, Anchusa, Anthemis, Aralia, Arnica, Artemisia, Asarum, Asperula, Baptisia, Caulophyllum, Chamaemelum, Dianthus, Echinacea, Eupatorium, Foeniculum, Geranium, Gillenia, Glycyrrhiza, Hepatica, Inula, Iris, Leonurus, Linum, Melissa, Mentha, Monarda, Myrrhis, Nepeta, Oenothera, Origanum, Pelargonium, Plantago, Podophyllum, Salvia, Solidago, Stachys, Symphytum, Tanacetum, Thalictrum, Tradescantia, Valeriana,* and *Zingiber.*

Clump-forming with rich, rose-purple flowers, 1–1½ in (2.5–4 cm) wide, at the tops of stems above slenderly strap-shaped, closely set, ¾–1¼ in (2–5 cm) long leaves. More modest and garden worthy, and also less invasive, than *C. angustifolium*. Primarily a mountain-dweller from central and south Europe, and eastward to western Ukraine. ‡30–36 ft (75–90 cm). Z6–8 H8–6

C. rosmarinifolium see *C. dodonaei*

CHASMANTHIUM
POACEAE

Woodland grasses closely related to bamboos with attractive, long-lasting oatlike flowers.

Six species are found in woodland and semiarid scrubland in the eastern US and Mexico. The foliage grows in deciduous clumps with smooth glossy bamboolike leaves, usually quite wide and pointed, and turning bronze in fall. In late summer, branched flower stems carry the sometimes flattened, green, oatlike flowers that hang from the tops of the stems and down among the foliage turning bronze as they mature. A warm-season grass coming into growth late in the spring. Grow in part-shade in large drifts in moist woods at the edges of woodland paths, or at the front of shady herbaceous borders.

CULTIVATION Best in moist, fertile soil with plenty of well-rotted compost or leaf mold in light shade,

PROPAGATION From seed, or by division in late spring.

PROBLEMS Usually trouble-free.

C. latifolium syn. *Uniola latifolia* (Wild oats, Northern sea oats, Spangle grass)

Clumps of bright green, bamboolike leaves, up to 8 in (20 cm) long and ¾ in (2 cm) wide, are upright in sun but more lax in the shade. They turn gold in fall. In mid- and late summer arching stems bear flattened, oatlike 1½-in (4-cm) flowers in olive green, becoming bronze, which dangle gracefully above the foliage looking delicately beautiful throughout winter. Grows well in moist or dry shade and attractive in drifts by shady pathways. Plants may need protection from cold winds. Excellent for drying. Native to moist fertile woodlands in southeastern US. ‡4 ft (1.2 m). Z5–9 H9–5

CHELIDONIUM
Greater celandine
PAPAVERACEAE

Tough but short-lived plant for light shade, with showy golden flowers in summer.

A single species of deciduous plant growing in woodlands, the bottoms of hedges, and waste places almost throughout Europe and western Asia, and sometimes grown in gardens. Rather fleshy roots bear erect stems with pleasingly lobed, blue-green leaves that release an orange sap when damaged. Golden-yellow flowers with four rounded petals open in loose clusters during the summer. △

CULTIVATION Thrives in almost any soil in sun or shade.

PROPAGATION From seed.

PROBLEMS Usually trouble-free.

C. japonicum see *Hylomecon japonicum*

C. majus (Greater celandine) An upright plant with deeply lobed, pale blue-green leaves, scalloped on the

margin, and growing to 10 in (25 cm) long. The brittle stems bear loose clusters of short-lived, bright yellow flowers about 1 in (2.5 cm) across in early summer and midsummer. This is a good plant for a wild garden or neglected corner, where it may seed itself; even the double-flowered cultivars seed about freely. According to the herbalist John Gerard, "The juice is good to sharpen the sight." However, the sap may irritate the skin. ‡18–24 in (45–60 cm). Z5–8 H8–5. △ **'Flore Pleno'** Flowers fully double and longer lasting. **var. *laciniatum*** Leaves much more deeply dissected; petals also deeply cut. **'Laciniatum Flore Pleno'** The prettiest form, with double flowers above deeply incised leaves.

CHELONE
Turtlehead
SCROPHULARIACEAE

Ideal contenders for moist soil in part-shade, the common name comes from the shape of the flowers.

Six species of North American plants from moist woodlands and mountains, three of which are readily available. The long-lasting, weatherproof summer flowers are similar to snapdragons, with a beard inside the lower lip; they are produced in dense terminal spikes in purple, pink, or white and followed by pretty seed heads. The shiny green leaves are toothed and in opposite pairs. Avoid contact with the seeds, because they may be a skin irritant. △

CULTIVATION Should be grown in part-shade to sun and moist to wet soil; the wetter the soil, the more sun is permissible. Pinching out the shoot tips in spring gives a bushier plant.

PROPAGATION From seed or by division in spring, or by softwood cuttings in spring and early summer.

PROBLEMS Occasionally mildew, rust, and a fungal leaf spot.

C. barbata see *Penstemon barbatus*

C. glabra syn. *C. obliqua* var. *alba* (White turtlehead, Snakeshead) Upright, square stems carry lance-shaped leaves up to 8 in (20 cm) long and are topped with compact heads of 1-in (2.5-cm) white flowers, sometimes tinged pink in bud, in late summer. A useful border plant provided the soil is never allowed to dry out, but better still in a bog garden. From Newfoundland to Georgia and west to Minnesota. Protected species in New York. ‡24–36 in (60–90 cm). Z3–8 H8–1

C. lyonii (Pink turtlehead) This upright, square-stemmed plant is distinguished by the long stalks on its oval or elliptical toothed foliage. The pink flowers have a yellow beard and last for about four weeks. Although this species prefers moist soil, it will take more sun than the others. Scattered through the eastern US. ‡4 ft (1.2 m). Z3–9 H9–3

C. obliqua (Rose turtlehead) The short-stalked, dark green, sometimes sharply toothed leaves have prominent veins; the dark pink to purple flowers open in late summer and have a yellow beard. It makes a good companion for dwarf fall asters. From wetlands in the eastern US. Protected species in Maryland and Michigan. ‡24 in (60 cm). Z3–9 H9–3. **var. *alba*** see *C. glabra*.

CHELONOPSIS
LAMIACEAE

Valuable, though undeservedly neglected, fall Orientals for rich and moist conditions.

About 16 herbaceous perennials and shrubs—named for their similarity to the genus *Chelone*, the turtleheads—growing wild from the Himalaya to Japan, but with the majority of species occurring in China. Oppositely arranged, toothed or scalloped leaves are topped by clusters of two to ten flowers borne in the leaf joints. The long-tubed flowers have two lips, the upper notched and the lower with three lobes, the middle of which is much longer than the others; colors range through white, to yellow and purplish red. *Chelonopsis* are undeservedly neglected, as they are valuable for late fall color, and useful for the herbaceous border.

CULTIVATION Best planted in fertile, moist soil.

PROPAGATION Grow from seed or divide in the spring.

LEFT **1** *Chasmanthium latifolium*
2 *Chelidonium majus* 'Flore Pleno'
3 *Chelone glabra*

PROBLEMS Usually trouble-free.

C. moschata Spreading by rhizomes. The slender stems carry narrow, reverse egg-shaped or broadly lance-shaped leaves. Clusters of one to three tubular rose-pink flowers, each one 1¼–1¾ in (3–4.5 cm) long, appear in the leaf joints from midsummer to early fall. This species is becoming popular, having been introduced to gardens by botanist Martyn Rix of England. Best in a shady position and moist, fertile soil. Grows in shady situations beside streams in Japan. ‡3 ft (1 m). Z5–9 H9–5.

C. yagiharana Tuft-forming plant with erect stems carrying slightly hairy, oblong or egg-shaped, sharply toothed leaves. The dark pinkish purple tubular flowers, 1¼–1½ in (3–3.5 cm) long, are borne singly in the joints of the upper leaves from late summer to late fall. Best in full sun or part-shade in poor, well-drained soil. *C. moschata* is often sold under this name, but is larger and requires different conditions. Found among rocks in Japan. ‡8–12 in (20–30 cm). Z5–9 H9–5.

CHIASTOPHYLLUM
CRASSULACEAE

Hardy plant that makes a mat of bright green leaves, heightened by sprays of tiny yellow flowers.

A single evergreen species that is found growing in rocky crevices in mountain woodlands in the Caucasus. Branching, creeping stems form a mat of leafy rosettes, with arching sprays of small, bell-shaped, bright yellow flowers held well above the foliage. The fleshy leaves are oval with rounded teeth and sometimes become suffused with red in late summer. Good at the front of a border of rich soil and also ideal for a partly shaded crevice in a damp wall.

CULTIVATION Grow in any open but moisture-retentive soil in sun or part-shade.

PROPAGATION By division after flowering or by cuttings.

PROBLEMS Usually trouble-free.

C. oppositifolium syn. *C. simplicifolium* A compact, mat-forming plant, with smooth, fleshy oval leaves to 4 in (10 cm) long, sometimes turning red in late summer; the leaves are borne in rosettes that arise from a branching rhizome. In late spring and early summer, arching stems bear dense sprays of bell-shaped, bright yellow flowers ¼ in (5 mm) long. Although succulent, it prefers a cool, moderately moist root run, such as under a gravel mulch. ‡6 in (15 cm). Z6–9 H9–6. '**Jim's Pride**' syn. 'Frosted Jade' Leaves boldly margined with creamy white; flowers lighter yellow.

C. simplicifolium see *C. oppositifolium*

ABOVE *Chiastophyllum oppositifolium* 'Jim's Pride'

CHIONOCHLOA
Snow grass, Tussock grass
POACEAE

Handsome tussock-forming grasses from New Zealand.

Some 20 species hail from New Zealand, and one from southeast Australia, mainly occurring in alpine grassland, where they grow in exposed situations in moist soil. Dense evergreen tussocks are formed by the leaves and woody leaf bases; the pointed leaves are often tough and sharp-edged. The flowers vary greatly, either appearing in impressive plumes or being very delicate but not very noticeable. Some species look particularly beautiful in fall, when the foliage can turn nearly white or a variety of bronze and red shades. There has been confusion with their names because some species appear very similar to the pampas grasses (*Cortaderia*).

CULTIVATION Fertile, well-drained soil, but not heavy clay, in an open situation protected from cold winds.

PROPAGATION By division in late spring, keeping the divisions quite big, or from seed.

PROBLEMS Usually trouble-free.

C. conspicua (Hunangamago, Plumed tussock grass) Dense tussocks of flat leaves with a distinctive orange midrib up to 5 ft (1.5 m) long and ½ in (1 cm) wide. From late spring to late summer, tall sturdy stems bear one-sided, feathery pale green to white plumes up to 18 in (45 cm) long. These ripen to fluffy brown with dropletlike seeds that are good for cutting or drying. In the wild they are often found near streams in open positions, and they look impressive grown in drifts near water

RIGHT *Chionochloa conspicua*

or as specimen plants in a sheltered area. From New Zealand. ‡6½ ft (2 m). Z7–10 H10–7. '**Rubra**' see *C. rubra*

C. flavicans (Green-leaved tussock grass) The rich green, stiff, straplike leaves with an orange woody base form dense tussocks. Robust, slightly arching stems appear in late spring to late summer bearing large, creamy yellow to green feathery plumes up to 30 in (75 cm) long; they last for many months and are good for drying. Can be slow to settle and flower. From high alpine regions, this grass looks good near hard landscaping in a position where it is protected from winter cold and can bake through the summer. From New Zealand. ‡5¼ ft (1.6 m). Z7–10 H10–7.

C. rubra syn. *C. conspicua* 'Rubra' (Red tussock grass) Dense clumps of foxy red, in-rolled, quill-like leaves with a blue-gray reverse. The flowers appear in late spring to early summer in delicate spikes on threadlike stems that float among the leaves; though not dramatic, they add to the graceful appearance of this grass. From lowlands to alpine grasslands in poorly drained, peaty valleys, it needs plenty of water; without it the foliage will turn a dingy gray. Beautiful in a container or as a specimen grass. From New Zealand. ‡30 in (75 cm). Z7–10 H10–7.

CHRYSANTHEMOPSIS *see* **RHODANTHEMUM**

CHRYSANTHEMUM
ASTERACEAE

The hardy chrysanthemums are valued for their dense habit and profuse flowers in great variety produced late in the season.

About 20 perennial species are found in a wide range of habitats and are native to Europe and Central and East Asia. Most are somewhat woody at the base and either clump-forming or with slowly spreading rhizomes; the stems can be upright or prostrate and carry alternate, lobed leaves. The daisylike flowerheads take many forms: single, semidouble, fully double, or pomponlike; they are held singly or in few-flowered clusters above the foliage. The disk florets, where visible, are usually yellow and the ray florets are flat, boat-shaped, quilled or, in a few cultivars, spoon-shaped.

The early types flower from late summer to early fall, while the latest flower from mid- to late fall or even early winter, but may disappoint in a cold, wet fall; they all make good cut flowers.

Only those cultivars that are good garden plants are included here; the vast variety bred as cut flowers or for exhibition are not covered. Many plants previously classified in

CHRYSANTHEMUM OR DENDRANTHEMA?

There was an uproar when the botanical name of the familiar garden chrysanthemum was changed from *Chrysanthemum* to *Dendranthema*. It was widely cited as an example of botanists being out of touch with gardeners, and jokes were made about the National Dendranthema Society and going to the florist for a bunch of dendranthemas.

This change initially came about as a result of the rigid application of the nomenclatural rules, set out in the International Code for Botanical Nomenclature and followed around the world. In particular, the rule of priority

was applied, whereby the first name for a plant that was published with a recognizable description is the one that should apply—and this was *Dendranthema*. Later, it was the application of another rule that in fact saved the day. The rule of conservation allows a familiar and commonly used name, especially one that has a wide commercial use and would otherwise be lost by the application of the rule of priority, to be retained—even when the rule of priority would indicate the need for a change. So the genus name, much to the relief of us all, then reverted to *Chrysanthemum*.

the genus *Chrysanthemum* are now considered sufficiently distinct to be treated separately and will be found under *Ajania, Leucanthemum, Leucanthemella, Nipponanthemum, Rhodanthemum,* and *Tanacetum* (*see also* Chrysanthemum or Dendranthema?). There are so many different forms of chrysanthemum that the National Chrysanthemum Society has created a system of classification as a simple guide to the different types (*see* And there's more…, *p.125*).

All parts of the plant may cause mild stomach upset if ingested in large quantities, and contact with the foliage can cause dermatitis or an allergic response in susceptible individuals. ⚠

CULTIVATION Fully hardy in most areas, these border chrysanthemums prefer a well-drained site in full sun, doing slightly better in alkaline, moderately fertile soil. Those exceeding 30 in (75 cm) in height benefit from discreet support. Divide every three years in spring. Cut down to 4 in (10 cm) after flowering and, in very cold areas, provide a dry mulch or dig up and overwinter in cold frame.

PROPAGATION By division in spring or by basal stem cuttings at the same time.

PROBLEMS Susceptible to chrysanthemum white rust.

C. **'Anastasia'** (28b) Dark purplish pink pompon, 1½-in (4-cm) wide flowerheads with yellow disks are carried on bushy plants from early to late fall. A pre-1939 cultivar, opinion varies on whether this cultivar is slightly earlier and darker than 'Mei-kyo', or identical to it. Also, the plant now grown under this name may not be identical to the original! ↕28 in (70 cm). Z5–9 H9–5

C. **'Apollo'** (29K) Single to semidouble 2-in (5-cm) flowerheads with yellow, orange-tipped ray florets, from mid- to late fall. One of the first Koreans to be introduced. ↕48 in (120 cm). Z5–9 H9–5

C. **'Apricot'** (29Rub) Rubellum producing single 2½-in (6-cm)

flowerheads with relatively broad, orange-red rays and yellow centers, from mid- to late fall; but see 'Hillside Sheffield'. ↕24 in (60 cm). Z5–9 H9–5

C. **'Bronze Elegance'** (28b) Orange-brown, 1¼-in (3-cm) Japanese semi-pompon flowerheads with yellow disks, from early fall. A spontaneous mutation of 'Mei-kyo', introduced by Will Ingwersen of England in 1973. ↕28 in (70 cm). Z5–9 H9–5

C. **'Carmine Blush'** (29Rub) Single pink 2½-in (6-cm) flowerheads with yellow centers from mid- to late fall; Rubellum. ↕28 in (70 cm). Z5–9 H9–5

C. **'Clara Curtis'** (29Rub) Rubellum producing single pink flowerheads, 2½ in (6 cm) across, from early to mid-fall. The yellow centers start off greenish yellow. Raised by Perry's Hardy Plant Farm, Middlesex, England, and introduced in 1937. ↕24 in (60 cm). Z4–8 H8–4

C. **'Color Echo'** (28) Reddish purple, single 1½-in (3.5-cm) flowerheads with yellow centers, from early to late fall. A spontaneous mutation of 'Mei-kyo' selected by Pamela Harper of Virginia in the late 20th century. ↕24 in (60 cm). Z5–9 H9–5

C. **'Doctor Tom Parr'** (28b) Reddish orange Japanese semi-pompon, 1¼ in (3 cm) across, from mid- to late fall. ↕24 in (60 cm). Z5–9 H9–5

C. **'Duchess of Edinburgh'** (29Rub) A lax Rubellum with deep red, semidouble 2¾-in (7-cm) flowerheads from early to late fall. The reverse of the ray florets is cream with streaks of red and there are often a few stray ones in the center of the yellow disk. Raised by Perry's Hardy Plant Farm, Middlesex, England, and introduced in 1948. ↕28 in (70 cm). Z4–8 H8–4

C. **'Edelweiss'** (29K) Korean, with semidouble, slightly ragged 2¾-in

RIGHT 1 *Chrysanthemum* 'Apricot'
2 *C.* 'Duchess of Edinburgh'
3 *C.* 'Mei-kyo' **4** *C.* 'Nantyderry Sunshine' **5** *C.* 'Pennine Polo'
6 *C.* 'Tapestry Rose'

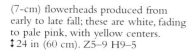
(7-cm) flowerheads produced from early to late fall; these are white, fading to pale pink, with yellow centers. ‡24 in (60 cm). Z5–9 H9–5

C. **'Emperor of China'** (29Rub) Old cultivar of rather lax habit resembling the later Rubellums. Double 2½-in (6-cm) flowerheads consist of deep pink quilled florets with a slightly silvery sheen. The leaves flush red at flowering time from late fall to early winter. ‡48 in (120 cm). Z5–9 H9–5

C. **'Hillside Sheffield'** (29Rub) Large flowers, 3 in (7.5 cm) across, are produced in mid-fall, with a single row of glowing apricot pointed petals surrounding a yellow eye; the flowers cover the dark green foliage on naturally mounded plants. A tough, reliable American favorite, found in a garden in Sheffield, Connecticut, and introduced by Fred McGourty of Hillside Gardens. 'Single Apricot', 'Sheffield Pink', 'Sheffield Apricot', and 'Hillside Sheffield Pink' are probably the same plant, and perhaps 'Apricot', too. ‡24–36 in (60–90 cm). Z5–9 H9–5

C. **'Innocence'** (29Rub) This name was originally applied to a white single Korean raised by Cumming (*see* And there's more…). Plants now grown under this name are Rubellums and have pale pink, single 2½-in (6-cm) flowerheads with an inner ring formed from the white bases of the ray florets, surrounding greenish yellow disks; they are produced from mid- to late fall. ‡32 in (80 cm). Z5–9 H9–5

C. **'Mary Stoker'** (29Rub) Rubellum with single 2-in (5-cm) flowerheads with yellow rays taking on orange hues as they age, eventually becoming apricot. The flowers appear from early to late fall and the yellow centers start greenish yellow. Raised by Perry's Hardy Plant Farm, Middlesex, England, and introduced in 1942. ‡28 in (70 cm). Z4–8 H8–4

C. **'Mei-kyo'** (28b) A bushy plant with pale purplish pink, Japanese semi-pompon 1½-in (4-cm) flowerheads, from early to late fall. Received in England by Will Ingwersen from Japan in the late 1950s. Sometimes said to be the same as 'Anastasia' but with paler semi-pompon flowerheads. ‡24 in (60 cm). Z5–9 H9–5

C. **'Mrs. Jessie Cooper'** (29Rub) Deep pink, single 3-in (7-cm) flowerheads with yellow disks, from mid-fall to early winter. Rubellum raised by Perry's Hardy Plant Farm, Middlesex, England, and introduced in 1940. ‡32 in (80 cm). Z5–9 H9–5

C. **'Nancy Perry'** (29Rub) Pink, semidouble 3 in (8 cm) flowerheads; ray florets unfurl irregularly from mid- to late fall. Raised by Perry's Hardy Plant Farm, Middlesex, England; introduced in 1945. ‡28 in (70 cm). Z5–9 H9–5

C. **'Nantyderry Sunshine'** (28b) Yellow, Japanese semi-pompon, 1¼-in

(3-cm) flowerheads with deeper yellow disks, opening from orange buds, from mid- to late fall. Introduced by Ingwersen's Nursery in 1991, a spontaneous mutation of 'Bronze Elegance' occurring in the Welsh garden of Rose Clay, 1989. ‡28 in (70 cm). Z5–9 H9–5

C. **Pennine Series** (29) A range of relatively hardy border chrysanthemums raised by Rileys of Alfreton, Derbyshire, England; virtually every color is represented in the series. ‡36–48 in (90–120 cm). Z5–9 H9–5

C. **'Pennine Polo'** (29d) Single 3-in (8-cm) flowerheads with white ray florets and yellow disks; blossoms from the end of summer to mid-fall. ‡36 in (90 cm). Z5–9 H9–5

C. **'Peter Sare'** (29Rub) Pink Rubellum with semidouble 3 in (8 cm) flowerheads. Perhaps a renaming of 'Nancy Perry'. ‡28 in (70 cm). Z5–9 H9–5

C. **'Purleigh White'** (28b) Japanese semi-pompon flowerheads 1¼ in (3 cm) with white ray florets bearing a faint pink tinge, from early to late fall. Introduced by Ingwersen's Nursery in 1990, a spontaneous mutation of 'Mei-kyo'. ‡28 in (70 cm). Z5–9 H9–5

C. **'Royal Command'** (29Rub) Dark red, single 3-in (8-cm) flowerheads, the ray florets quilled before fully opening in early to late fall. Rubellum raised by Perry's Hardy Plant Farm, Middlesex, England, and introduced in 1949. ‡32 in (80 cm). Z5–9 H9–5

C. **'Ruby Mound'** (29K) Maroon red, double 2¾-in (7-cm) flowerheads, mid- to late fall. ‡30 in (75 cm). Z5–9 H9–5

C. **'Sheffield Apricot'**, **'Sheffield Pink'** see 'Hillside Sheffield'

C. **'Single Apricot'** see 'Hillside Sheffield'

C. **'Tapestry Rose'** (29K) Deep pink Korean, single, 2¾-in (7-cm) flowerheads with green centers; mid- to late fall. ‡32 in (80 cm). Z5–9 H9–5

C. **'Venus'** (29K) Korean with mid-pink, single 2¾-in (7-cm) flowerheads; inner ring formed from the white base of the ray florets, surrounding yellow disks. ‡36 in (90 cm). Z4–9 H9–4

C. **'Wedding Day'** (29K) A lax Korean producing semidouble 2¾-in (7-cm) flowerheads from mid-fall to early winter. Creamy white ray florets, fading to apricot, surround a greenish yellow disk. Raised by Olive Murrell of Orpington Nurseries, Kent, England. ‡42 in (110 cm). Z4–9 H9–4

C. **'Winning's Red'** (29Rub) Rubellum with single 2¾-in (7-cm) flowerheads with narrow red ray florets around yellow disks; early to mid-fall. ‡30 in (75 cm). Z5–9 H9–5

CHRYSANTHEMUM

A STERS AND C HRYSANTHEMUMS are the two great classic fall perennials, grouped together here to colorful effect. To the rear, a pretty form of *A. novae-angliae* in a rich purple-blue, the rounded flowers appearing steadily for weeks, backs a group of chrysanthemums in colorful contrast. Years ago, in gardens on large estates, a display of this kind was created for a short and concentrated display by moving the plants into place in bud and then removing them at the end of the season to be replaced, perhaps, by spring flowers. Now, we interplant with daffodils or other vigorous spring bulbs, which are left to multiply and provide sparkling spring color.

AND THERE'S MORE...

The breeding of chrysanthemums is a vast industry, focused mainly on cultivars for commercial cut-flower growers and the "pot mum" trade. Exhibitors concentrate on cultivars in entirely different styles, yet all can be grown in the garden in suitable conditions. However, the more commercial types are often difficult for the home gardener to obtain; cut flowers and "pot mums" are rarely even listed by retail nurseries. Cultivars come and go quickly, and their propagation is often protected. Most exhibition cultivars tend to circulate in a relatively closed world and, while they may grow perfectly well in the garden, keeping the large and intricately formed flowers looking good is often difficult in ordinary conditions. The plants included here are those specifically intended for general garden use: the Koreans, the Rubellums, the Japanese pompons, and others generally available that perform well without special attention.

There are so many different forms that the National Chrysanthemum Society has created a system of classification as a simple guide to the different types.

Although the classification codes are rarely used by enthusiasts for garden perennials, and most apply only to exhibition cultivars of various kinds, they are worth noting. Most of the hardy garden cultivars (28 and 29) are selections of *C.* x *grandiflorum* (*C. indicum* x *C. japonicum*).

28 Early-flowering outdoor pompon.
28b Semi-pompon, sometimes called Japanese semi-pompon, with a yellow eye. Those in cultivation mostly originate from the import of 'Mei-kyo' from Japan, and were introduced in 1960.
29 Early-flowering outdoor spray
29d Single
29K Korean. Reputedly derived from a cross between *C. coreanum* and *C.* x *grandiflorum* 'Ruth Hatton', first raised by Alexander Cumming at Bristol Nurseries, Connecticut, in 1937. Bristol Nurseries is in Z4, so these are quite hardy.
29Rub Rubellum. Probably hybrids between *C. zawadskii* and *C.* x *grandiflorum*, a cross first recorded from Wales in 1929; they often have a slightly running habit.

CHRYSOGONUM
Golden knee, Golden star
ASTERACEAE

Quietly pleasing, mat-forming plant producing its starry yellow flowers over a long season.

One species of creeping plant growing in damp woodlands in the eastern US. Makes a neat mat of simple, bright green leaves, above which the star-shaped, deep yellow flowers open in spring and summer. A useful ground-cover plant, bringing a distinctive character to the front of a border.

CULTIVATION Thrives in full sun, given moisture-retentive soil, but also satisfactory in part-shade.

PROPAGATION By division or from seed.

PROBLEMS Usually trouble-free.

C. virginianum Leafy, low-growing, more or less evergreen plant spreading by rhizomes; the long-stalked oval leaves, 1–4 in (2.5–10 cm) long, have shallowly toothed margins. Golden-yellow flowers, 1½ in (4 cm) across with five oval, petal-like ray florets, open from mid-spring to late summer or early fall. ‡ 12 in (30 cm). Z5–9 H9–2

CHRYSOSPLENIUM
SAXIFRAGACEAE

Shade-tolerant, mat-forming plants for moist places, enlivened in early spring by small, bright flowers.

About 55 species of moisture-loving, creeping plants growing in damp, shady places, especially stream banks, in Europe, Asia, and North and South America. Just one species is widely grown in gardens, but others have been introduced and are being assessed. The prostrate stems root as they spread, and carry rounded, toothed leaves. The effect of the tiny white or yellowish flowers is enhanced in many species by the larger, brightly colored leaflike bracts in which they sit.

CULTIVATION Grow in permanently moist but free-draining soil in part-shade.

PROPAGATION By division.

PROBLEMS Usually trouble-free.

C. davidianum Evergreen or deciduous plant makes a steadily spreading mat of fleshy, rooting stems with rounded, bluntly toothed, dull green hairy leaves. From early to late spring or early summer, clusters of small yellow flowers appear at the tips of reddish shoots, surrounded by vivid yellow leaflike bracts. An excellent ground-cover plant bringing color in spring to constantly damp, shady places. May prefer acidic soil. The foliage may scorch in dry weather. From damp woodlands in western China. ‡ 2 in (5 cm). Z6–8 H8–6

CICHORIUM
Chicory
ASTERACEAE

Chicory, when not grown as a vegetable, is valued for its stiffly erect stems with blue daisies.

Eight species of perennials and annuals native to open, dry habitats in Europe, particularly the Mediterranean, southwestern Asia, and Ethiopia; all chicory have milky sap. The perennial species form clumps, often making conspicuous rosettes with deeply lobed leaves. The branched stems, with small, alternate leaves, bear blue flowerheads that consist only of ray florets, held in the leaf joints. The genus includes both edible chicory and endive. Contact with all parts of *Chicorium* plants may irritate the skin or aggravate skin allergies. ⚠

CULTIVATION Needs full sun and poor to moderately fertile soil with good drainage.

PROPAGATION From seed that is sown in fall or spring at 50°F (10°C). Pink and white forms may not come true from seed; the plant can be more reliably propagated by removing offsets.

PROBLEMS May suffer from slugs and snails, mildew, rust, and lettuce ringspot virus.

ABOVE **1** *Chrysogonum virginianum* **2** *Chrysosplenium davidianum* **3** *Cichorium intybus* 'Roseum'

C. intybus (Chicory, Wild succory) Rosette-forming perennial with substantial taproot. Leaves are deeply lobed to toothed and are roughly lance-shaped, up to 12 in (30 cm) long. Each of the stiff, erect, branched stems have only a few small leaves and bear short-stalked, blue flowerheads to 1½ in (4 cm) across. The flowers, which close by noon, open rather sporadically in a long succession from midsummer to mid-fall. Tolerant of most soil types but grows best in alkaline conditions. Native to Mediterranean area, and to southern and possibly western Europe. Widely naturalized, and often considered noxious or invasive in parts of the US. ‡ 4 ft (1.2 m). Z4–8 H8–1. **f.** *album* White flowers. '**Roseum**' Pink flowers.

CIMICIFUGA *see* ACTAEA

EDIBLE CHICORY

Native to much of southern Europe, chicory has long been cultivated for an unexpected variety of uses—culinary, medicinal, and agricultural. Chicory, some forms of which are known as radicchio, is grown to provide salad leaves with a nutty taste and crunchy texture. Traditional local forms were grown in Europe for many centuries, and plant breeders have now also created modern cultivars. Grown in the light in the same way as lettuce, the leaves have a bitter taste. Often, they are blanched or forced, by growing them in darkness, to produce paler, more delicately flavored leaves. This is done either in forcing houses or, outside in the garden, by tying the leaves together and covering the plant with a clay flowerpot to exclude light.

The fleshy roots of chicory have also long been dried, roasted, and ground for use as an additive to and, in hard times, a substitute for, coffee. It is still possible to buy coffee/chicory blends, and some people say that the chicory enhances the flavor. Well into the 19th century, the leafy growth of chicory was considered valuable animal fodder, being said to greatly increase the milk yield of cattle.

LEFT *Cirsium rivulare* 'Atropurpureum'

CIRSIUM
Thistle
ASTERACEAE

Tall, branching border perennial with spiny leaves sending up thistle flowerheads in summer.

About 200 species of perennials and biennials, growing in diverse habitats ranging from lowlands and mountain meadows to the banks of streams. Most are upright plants with simple or deeply lobed spiny leaves and characteristic red, purple, yellow, or white thistlelike flowerheads consisting of a tuft of small tubular florets, opening in summer. Many are invasive weeds, spreading by rhizome or by wind-blown seeds, but a few are better behaved and make handsome border plants.

CULTIVATION Thrives in any fertile soil in full sun. Deadhead after flowering to prevent seeding.

PROPAGATION From seed or by division.

PROBLEMS Susceptible to mildew.

C. helenoides syn. *C. heterophyllum*

C. heterophyllum syn. *C. helenoides* (Melancholy thistle) Robust plant spreading underground to form an extensive colony of undivided, toothed, lance-shaped leaves to 16 in (40 cm) long, the undersides covered with white felt. Purple flowerheads up to 2 in (5 cm) across and usually solitary open in mid- and late summer on cottony white stems. From damp grasslands in much of northern Europe, including the British Isles. ‡ 3–5 ft (1–1.5 m). Z5–9 H9–5

C. japonicum Slender, upright plant with mostly basal, deeply lobed, spiny dark green leaves up to 12 in (30 cm) long. From mid- to late summer or early fall, rose pink to lilac flowerheads 2 in (5 cm) across open on the branched, sparsely leafy stems. A good border plant, and useful for cutting, although short-lived. Cultivars are seed-raised and may be variable. From grassland at low altitudes in Japan. ‡ 3–5 ft (1–1.5 m). Z5–9 H9–5. **'Pink Beauty'** Soft pink flowers. **'Rose Beauty'** Rich carmine pink flowers.

C. rivulare Clump-forming plant with simple or divided, prickly-edged leaves to 18 in (45 cm) long, dark green above and grayish hairy beneath. In early and midsummer, rosy purple flowerheads, 1¼–1½ in (3–4 cm) across, on branched, sparingly leafy stems, singly or in clusters of two or three. From damp places in acidic soil in central and southwestern Europe. ‡ 3–5 ft (1–1.5 m). Z4–8 H8–1. **'Atropurpureum'** Flowers bright crimson-purple. The most common form in gardens, but beware paler-hued imposters.

CLEMATIS
RANUNCULACEAE

In a family known for its colorful climbers, many diverse perennial clematis make ideal border plants.

About 200 species of woody climbers and perennials, both evergreen and deciduous, from Europe, the Himalaya, China, Australasia, and both North and South America. The herbaceous perennial species are mostly woody-based but do not generally cling by their twisting leaf stalks as many familiar clematis do; most need some form of support.

The slender stems, usually woody at the base, carry pairs of leaves that can be somewhat leathery or more frail; in shape they vary greatly from simple lance- or heart-shaped to being divided into three or five lance-shaped or oval, sometimes toothed, leaflets. Flowers are often nodding, bell- or saucer-shaped, with four to ten petals; they may be borne singly or in sprays. Like other members of this family, the sepals, rather than the true petals, provide the color, the true petals being so small as to be insignificant. In many species, the flowers are followed by decorative, fluffy seed- heads. There is an ever-increasing number of named forms, including some pleasing hybrids between woody climbers and perennials (*see* Woody or Herbaceous?, *p.128*).

Botanists have been looking closely at many of the clematis species in recent years and some new cultivars have been reassigned to species, or left unassigned. While the situation is under review, the arrangement adopted here is neither conservative nor revolutionary.

Where improved classification is in the air, suggestions are made as to other species under which some cultivars may be found.

CULTIVATION Grow in well-drained, humus-rich soil in full sun and cut back almost to ground level in late fall or early spring. Some can be grown through bushy shrubs, where they support themselves on the branches. Others can be allowed to trail over a bank or through other perennials, or be staked and tied upright or supported in an obelisk.

PROPAGATION From seed of species as soon as they are ripe (remove the fluffy "tail" before sowing); by division in spring; by softwood cuttings in spring.

PROBLEMS Leaf spot, whitefly, scale insect. Perennial species are usually less susceptible to clematis wilt than the large-flowered climbers.

C. addisonii Upright at first, the stems later grow along the ground unless supported. The early blue-green leaves are simple and oval but later ones are divided into four to six oval leaflets of different sizes. The early summer flowers, ⅝–1¼ in (1.5–3 cm) long, are carried at both the tips of the shoots and in the leaf joints; they are urn-shaped, with four petals, curving back at the tips, purple outside with a cream edging, and cream inside. In good forms, the result is a bright purple, white-lipped flower with four vertical white stripes. Known only from dry, alkaline woods in a small area of western Virginia. ‡ 12–18 in (30–45 cm). Z4–9 H8–1

C. 'Alionushka' Tall but non-climbing, it can either be allowed to sprawl through surrounding plants or be supported on brushwood to form an

COMING UP ROSES

TWO PLANTS WITH famous connections make a lovely summer combination. Here the rose is 'Graham Thomas', a modern English rose named for the late popularizer of old roses and champion of perennials. Scrambling into it is *Clematis* Petit Faucon introduced by famed clematis breeder Raymond Evison, which although woody at the base is best treated as a perennial and cut back to the ground when the rose is pruned. More clematis of this type are being introduced, and they are ideal companions for English roses or other small shrubs. The lack of complication in the pruning combined with vigor and a long flowering season especially recommend them. On a smaller scale, *C. integrifolia* and its cultivars can perform the same task with low-growing shrubby plants, such as cultivars of *Potentilla fruticosa*.

WOODY OR HERBACEOUS?

The division between herbaceous perennial clematis and woody clematis is not simply a matter of genetic control of the plant's habit. The ferocity of the winter also has a significant influence: the colder the winter, the more likely some plants are to die back completely to ground level rather than retain a woody structure.

So in warmer climates, *C. viticella*, for example, maintains a woody structure over the winter, although it is usually cut back hard in spring to promote generous flowering. But in cold climates, (Z4–5), it dies back to the ground naturally and behaves as an herbaceous perennial, shooting again strongly in spring.

The distinction between woody climbers and herbaceous climbers is also blurred by the fact that types that are undeniably woody have been crossed with others that are clearly herbaceous. For example, *C. integrifolia* was crossed with *C.* 'Jackmanii' to give *C.* x *durandii*. Even more unlikely, *C. tubulosa* was crossed with *C. vitalba* to create the prolific and long-flowering *C.* x *jouiniana*. More recently, the superb 'Arabella' came from crossing 'Mrs. James Mason' with *C. integrifolia*, while Petit Faucon is a hybrid between 'Daniel Deronda' and *C. integrifolia*.

The hybrids with *C. integrifolia* have two invaluable features in common: they are neat in growth, not usually reaching more than 6½ ft (2 m), and they are also long-flowering and prolific. This makes them especially useful in small gardens, where they can be trained into mature shrubs and easily cut down each fall.

Just consider the possibilities. With the vast color range found in the large-flowered hybrids, together with the double flowers of many and the range of color in *C. integrifolia* (blue, white, pink, and almost red)—not to mention the many American and Asian species of which few hybrids have yet appeared—there is still enormous potential.

upright pillar. The 2¾-in (7-cm), pendulous, bell-shaped flowers are a rich rose color with a slight flare to the petal tips and are borne from early summer to mid-fall. The name is sometimes seen misspelled as 'Aljenushka', 'Aljonushka', and 'Alyonushka'; 'Alionushka', in Russian, is the affectionate form of a girl's name. A hybrid between the purple 'Nezhdannyi' and *C. integrifolia*, it was raised at the State Nikitsky Botanic Gardens, Crimea, Ukraine in 1961. ‡6½ ft (2 m). Z4–9 H8–1

C. **'Arabella'** A superb hybrid, with 3-in (7.5-cm) flowers borne prolifically over a long period, from early summer to mid-fall. The individual blooms have four or eight petals, violet-blue with a redder stripe down the middle of each petal as the flowers age, and a central boss of creamy stamens. Grow these plants through a shrub with an open growth habit, or trained on a trellis. Introduced in 1990, it is a cross between *C. integrifolia* and the large-flowered hybrid 'James Mason'. Raised by British clematis breeder Barry Fretwell. ‡6 ft (1.8 m). Z4–9 H8–1

C. x **aromatica** A plant with a delicate fragrance described as hawthorn, vanilla, or heliotrope but hardly overpowering. The deep green leaves have three or more leaflets on stems that die back to a woody base. The four-petaled flowers are dark violet, about 1½ in (4 cm) across, with the edges rolled under so that they appear narrow; carried in sprays on the shoot ends, they open in late summer. In great clouds from midsummer to early fall or later, their profusion compensates for their small size and poor form. A cross between the climbing *C. flammula* and the herbaceous *C. integrifolia*, first mentioned in 1855. ‡4–6½ ft (1.2–2 m). Z4–9 H8–1

C. x **bonstedtii** A relatively shrubby species with bold, slightly rough foliage

that is divided into several leaflets. The pale blue tubular flowers, clustered at the tips of the shoots, are only ¾–1 in (2–2.5 cm) long, with four petals that are curved back at the tips; they appear from midsummer onward. The flowers and foliage are closer to *C. tubulosa* than to the other parent, *C. stans*; the two cultivars may be listed in catalogs under *C. heracleifolia*. ‡5 ft (1.5 m). Z4–9 H8–1. **'Campanile'** Narrow, pale blue tubular flowers with very reflexed petals carried in small sprays from the leaf joints. **'Crepuscule'** Pale lilac and sweetly scented, with smoother foliage; ‡4 ft (1.2 m).

C. **'Cote d'Azur'** see *C.* x *jouiniana*

C. **crispa** A dainty, rather variable climbing species dying back close to the ground each winter, it is ideal for growing through shrubs. The foliage is divided into two to five leaflets, each with up to three lobes, and the nodding, ½–⅝-in (1–1.5-cm) flowers are carried individually on 3-in (7.5-cm) purplish stems. They are violet-red, sometimes pink, bell-shaped, flared at the mouth, and smell of oranges. A variety of other, generally similar plants are mistakenly sold under this name. Native to wet woodlands and swamps of the southeastern US. ‡6½ ft (2 m). Z5–11 H9–6

C. x **diversifolia** syn. *C.* x *eriostemon* Woody at the base, and more like a woody climber in mild areas. The foliage is divided into opposite pairs of lance-shaped leaflets, some of which will twist to clasp supports in the familiar manner. The flowers are bell- or lanternlike, becoming flatter and 1½–2½ in (4–6 cm) across, with four petals curving backward at the tips in various shades of blue and mauve, plus pink.

RIGHT 1 *Clematis* 'Alionoushka' **2** *C.* x *durandii* **3** *C. integrifolia* 'Hendersonii'

Resembles one parent, *C. viticella*, more than the other, *C. integrifolia*; cultivars may be listed under *C. integrifolia*. ‡10 ft (3 m). Z4–9 H9–1. **'Blue Boy'** Mid-blue flowers, paler at the edges. A cross made in Dropmore, Manitoba, Canada in 1947 and often sold simply as *C.* 'Blue Boy'. Z4–9 H8–1. **'Floris V'** Fragrant, burgundy red flowers. **'Heather Herschell'** Very distinctive deep pink with twisted and backward-curving petals. Raised by Barry Fretwell of Peveril Nursery, in Devon, England. **'Hendersonii'** Dusky purple flowers. This is the correct name for the original cross, made at Pineapple Nurseries in North London, 1835. **'Olgae'** Fragrant, noticeably open, violet-blue flowers.

C. x *durandii* A woody-based climber sprawling through shrubs if left to grow unsupported. The usual twiggy stems support pairs of 4–6-in (10–15-cm) dark green, oval, slightly toothed leaves almost enclosing the stem. The four- to six-petaled flowers, 4–5 in (10–13 cm) across, are a rich deep blue, with usually three pleats creating a prominent midrib; they are produced from midsummer to mid-fall. This species can be allowed to colonize its neighbors or be contained within a circle of stakes or an obelisk. A hybrid between the large-flowered *C.* 'Jackmanii' and *C. integrifolia*, it is similar to *C.* 'Arabella', which pales as the flowers ages and develops pinkish veining. Once widely used as a cut flower, it was raised in France in 1870. ‡6½ ft (2 m). Z4–9 H8–1

C. **'Edward Pritchard'** A tough, very free-flowering plant, it can nevertheless be overwhelmed by more vigorous neighbors. The 6–8-in (15–20-cm) leaves are divided into five lobed leaflets that may be smooth or slightly jagged. Masses of small, 1½-in (4-cm), cross-shaped, sweetly scented flowers with very narrow petals appear from midsummer onward; they are pale blue, shading to pink at the petal tips, and last well as cut flowers. A hybrid between *C. recta* and *C. tubulosa*, from Australia. ‡5 ft (1.5 m). Z4–9 H8–1

C. x *eriostemon* see *C.* x *diversifolia*

C. heracleifolia (Tube clematis) A sprawling species, and a rampant grower once established, it can either be allowed to sprawl through other perennials or be staked and tied to produce a column of flowers. The 8-in (20-cm) foliage is rather rough and dull green, the leaves split into three, with the central leaflet much larger than the other two. Crowded clusters of small, tubular ½-in (1-cm) flowers have four to six petals that curve back, almost touching the tube. These come in shades of blue, sometimes white, with prominent whitish stamens that give the entire plant a cloudlike appearance when in bloom in late summer. Male and female flowers are held in separate sprays on the same plant, growing from the leaf joints; they are sometimes scented. Native to scrub and forest edges in eastern China. ‡3–5 ft (1–

1.5 m). Z4–9 H8–1. **'Cassandra'** Violet-blue. **'China Purple'** Dark purple blooms on a slightly smaller plant; ‡4 ft (1.2 m). **var. *davidiana*** see *C. tubulosa*. **'Roundway Blue Bird'** Dark blue, fragrant flowers on short plants; ‡36 in (90 cm).

C. integrifolia (Solitary clematis) Slender stems arise from a tight crown carrying almost stalkless, oval, mid-green leaves; the leaf edges blacken if grown in too dry a soil. Solitary, or occasionally two or three nodding blue flowers open at the tip of each stem from midsummer onward; they are bell-like, with spreading, twisted petals and a central prominent mass of white stamens. The shade of blue varies from plant to plant and can have a decidedly mauve or pink tone. A good border plant, seen at its best when carefully supported; the beauty is lost if it is allowed to sprawl. This species has been much used by plant breeders to produce many of the hybrids listed here; plants with more extensively branched flowerheads are usually hybrids. See also *C.* x *diversifolia*. Some cultivars may be listed independently as hybrids. Native to southeastern Europe and western Asia. ‡3¼ ft (1 m). Z4–11 H7–1. **'Alba'** White flowers. **'Hendersonii'** Unusually large, very dark blue flowers. Named after the same nurseryman who first raised *C.* x *diversifolia*, but this is a different plant. **'Pangbourne Pink'** syn. *C.* 'Pangbourne Pink' Bright pink flowers, an improvement on 'Rosea'. **'Pastel Blue'** syn. *C.* 'Pastel Blue' Powder blue. **'Pastel Pink'** syn. *C.* 'Pastel Pink' Very pale pink. **'Rosea'** syn. *C.* 'Rosea' Fragrant, sugar pink flowers with a darker reverse. **'Tapestry'** syn. *C.* 'Tapestry' The largest flowers, in a rich purple-red.

C. x *jouiniana* This dramatic plant develops a tough woody framework from which long shoots carry large, rather coarse leaves divided into three to five leaflets 4 in (10 cm) long. From midsummer to mid-fall, the plants are covered with masses of small white, open, faintly scented, starlike flowers tinted with purple on the outside, although early frost may curtail the display. Not self-clinging, it tends to develop into a vast mass of foamy flowers. It can sprawl through large, stout shrubs, be trained to a trellis, or be used as effervescent ground cover. This vigorous plant is a hybrid of *C. tubulosa*, from which it gains its large foliage, while its profusion of flowers comes from both parents and is aided by their open display, inherited from *C. vitalba*; this is the only hybrid featuring old man's beard (*C. vitalba*). ‡10 ft (3 m). Z4–9 H8–1. **'Cote d'Azur'** syn. *C.* 'Cote d'Azur' Pale blue with more reflexed petals. Sometimes sold under *C. heracleifolia*. **'Praecox'** syn. *C.* 'Praecox' Blooms early, in midsummer, so avoids frost damage.

C. **'Mrs. Robert Brydon'** Combines a woody base with upper stems that die back for the winter. The large, dull green foliage is rough and divided into

three leaflets, similar to that of *C. tubulosa*. Masses of fragrant off-white flowers with a light blue tinge appear in late summer and early fall. Not vigorous, so does best in rich, moist soil. A hybrid of *C. tubulosa* and *C. virginiana*; sometimes listed under *C. heracleifolia* or *C.* x *jouiniana*. ‡6½ ft (2 m). Z4–9 H8–1

C. **'New Love'** A neat, bushy hybrid of *C. tubulosa* with bold, rough, saw-toothed foliage dying back to a woody base. The 1½-in (4-cm) flowers are violet blue, darker on the outside than the inside; they are very fragrant and are carried prolifically from midsummer to early fall. Good in containers. Raised by Dutch clematis breeder John Fopma. ‡24–36 in (60–90 cm). Z4–9 H8–1

C. **'Pangbourne Pink'** see *C. integrifolia*

C. **'Pastel Blue'** see *C. integrifolia*

C. **'Pastel Pink'** see *C. integrifolia*

C. **Petit Faucon ('Evisix')** Deep green foliage, sometimes tinted purple, backs a profusion of small purple flowers with shadowy tints from midsummer to early fall, the petals prettily waved and rolled. The central creamy yellow fluffy stamens add to the attraction. Looks good scrambling through small shrubs, as ground cover, or tumbling from large urns. A hybrid of 'Daniel Deronda' and *C. integrifolia* from the Guernsey nursery of renowned clematis breeder Raymond Evison. ‡5 ft (1.5 m). Z4–9 H8–1

C. **'Praecox'** see *C.* x *jouiniana*

C. **'Rosea'** see *C. integrifolia*

C. recta (Ground clematis) The common name comes from its habit of sprawling across the ground; it can be allowed to sprawl, guided into a stout shrub, or supported discreetly with brushwood. The pairs of opposite leaves, themselves split into three or four pairs of dark green, sometimes

ABOVE *Clematis recta*

blue-flushed, oval or lance-shaped leaflets, back large clouds of small, white, scented flowers appearing from early to late summer. Often grown from seed, resulting in an unpredictable quantity of flower and strength of scent. From southern Europe. ‡6½ ft (2 m). Z4–11 H7–1. **'Peveril'** Larger-flowered, dwarf and especially prolific. ‡36 in (90 cm). **'Purpurea'** Deep purple young shoots and foliage turning bronzed green. **'Velvet Night'** Purple-bronze foliage retaining its color especially well.

C. **'Rooguchi'** A very pretty form. The nodding, shiny, purple or sometimes bluish, bell-shaped flowers, 2 in (5 cm) long, have blue insides, prominent ridges and daintily flared tips; the four petals are edged in silvery cream. Flowering prolifically from early summer to mid-fall, it is not self-clinging but can be guided into a sturdy shrub or small tree, supported discreetly or allowed to sprawl as ground cover. It is unusual in being content in part-shade and also being a good cut flower. A hybrid of *C. integrifolia* and *C. reticulata* raised in Japan, the name is sometimes seen spelled, incorrectly, as 'Rouguchi' or 'Roguchi'. ‡6½ ft (2 m). Z4–9 H7–1

C. songarica Ridged and grooved stems die back to a woody base and carry slightly grayish, lance-shaped 4 in (10 cm) leaves, sometimes smooth-edged, sometimes toothed, and with three noticeable veins. Sprays of about 30 white, star-shaped, hawthorn-scented flowers with four reflexed petals appear from midsummer to early fall; they are followed by silky seed heads. The central stamens are green and maroon, adding to the display. Introduced in 1880 but still undeservedly neglected. Rocky banks in northwestern China, Mongolia, and in and around Afghanistan. ‡5–6½ ft (1.5–2 m). Z4–9 H7–1

ABOVE 1 *Clematis tubulosa* 'Wyevale'
2 *Clinopodium vulgare*

C. stans Ribbed stems die back to a woody base and carry bold leaves divided into three lobes, the central lobe itself with three to five lobes and the outer ones also sometimes lobed. Clusters of ¾-in (2-cm) fragrant, pale blue tubular flowers with very reflexed petals are carried toward the ends of the branches from midsummer to early fall. Similar to *C. heracleifolia*, but stems are more lax and the flowers are paler and mostly on the ends of the branches, rather than in sprays from the leaf bases. Japan. ‡ 5–6½ ft (1.5–2 m). Z3–7 H7–1

C. 'Tapestry' see *C. integrifolia*

C. tubulosa Dies back completely in winter, or to a short woody base. The leaves are divided into three lobes, the largest in the center, with oval or elliptical toothed leaflets up to 8 in (20 cm) long. The four-petaled, highly fragrant, upright blue flowers, 1 in (2.5 cm) across, tubular at the base then dramatically flared, are carried in compact clusters in the upper leaf joints. Male and female flowers on separate plants. You will probably smell it before you see it. It differs from *C. heracleifolia* in a number of ways, the most obvious in the male and female flowers being on separate plants and being tightly bunched. The plant often listed as *C. heracleifolia* var. *davidiana* is now included here. From forest margins and scrub in northwestern China. ‡ 4 ft (1.2 m). Z4–9 H7–1. **Alan Bloom** ('**Albo**') Dark blue flowers that turn mauve with age. '**Wyevale**' Large, dark blue flowers with wavy petal edges.

C. viorna (Leather flower) A delightful, somewhat shrubby climbing species with ribbed stems, sometimes dying back almost to the ground. The leaves have two to four pairs of leaflets that may themselves be further divided and whose tips act as tendrils to aid climbing. Very pretty four-petaled, 1-in (2.5-cm), nodding, urn-shaped, flowers, flaring at the tips, appear in mid- and late summer. These are usually maroon, though they can vary from pale lavender to reddish purple, and are edged in pale yellow. Surprisingly large fluffy seed heads follow to extend the season. Best seen when allowed to grow through tall shrubs, or even through a large-flowered clematis. Native to moist woods in the eastern US. ‡ 10 ft (3 m). Z4–9 H7–1

CLINOPODIUM
LAMIACEAE

Resilient plants that are useful for dry, alkaline soil, producing a reliable display of summer flowers.

The ten species of herbaceous perennials and annuals, sometimes woody at the base, have smooth-edged or slightly toothed oval leaves and clusters of two-lipped flowers in the upper leaf joints; the lower lip of each flower is split into three lobes, with the largest in the center. It is usually known in gardens from one species with hairy, mildly aromatic foliage and dense clusters of pinkish purple flowers carried on upright stems. Closely related to *Calamintha*, and sometimes included with it in the genus *Satureja*. Mainly found growing in temperate areas of Europe, North Africa, the Azores, Madeira, and North America.

CULTIVATION Grow in full sun or part-shade; it performs best in dry, alkaline soil.

PROPAGATION From seed or by division in spring.

PROBLEMS Usually trouble-free.

C. vulgare (Wild basil) A spreading plant with a tolerant nature suitable for use as ground cover. The 1–2-in (2.5–5-cm) leaves are egg-shaped, usually toothed and covered with soft white hairs; despite its common name, it is only faintly, although pleasantly, aromatic. The bright flowers, pollinated by bees and butterflies, are produced from midsummer to early fall in tiers of clusters of up to 20; each above a pair of leaves and composed of two-lipped, pink-purple flowers up to ¾ in (2 cm) long; white forms sometimes occur. Easy to grow, but avoid waterlogged soil and deep shade. Found throughout much of the Northern Hemisphere. ‡ 24–32 in (60–80 cm). Z4–9 H7–1

CLINTONIA
Bluebead
CONVALLARIACEAE

Quietly appealing summer-flowering shade-lovers for acidic or neutral soil.

The four or five species of deciduous plants grow in woodlands in North America, the Himalaya, and northeastern Asia; one of them is sometimes grown in gardens. Loose rosettes of strap-shaped or oval leaves arise from slowly spreading underground stems. Separate flowering stems bear small bell- or star-shaped, white, greenish, or purple flowers in late spring or early summer, sometimes followed by black or blue berries. Named for a former governor of New York, the naturalist De Witt Clinton.

CULTIVATION Grow in moisture-retentive, acidic soil in part- or full shade.

PROPAGATION By division or from seed.

PROBLEMS Susceptible to damage by slugs and snails.

C. andrewsiana Slowly spreading plant forming a clump of glossy, oval, dark green leaves to 10 in (25 cm) long. In early summer and midsummer, clusters of bell-shaped, deep purple flowers ¾ in (2 cm) long appear on separate leafless stems, sometimes followed by steel-blue berries that give the plant its common name. Unusual plant for a shaded position, where it should be mulched with leaf mold each spring. From woodlands in California. ‡ 12–20 in (30–50 cm). Z8–9 H9–1

CODONOPSIS
CAMPANULACEAE

Intriguing and often delicately patterned, recent clarification of their names will help increase their popularity.

There are about 35 species of tuberous-rooted herbaceous perennials from central and eastern Asia. Rather variable in habit of growth, the majority are twining, while some are upright and erect and others are rather floppy. Their leaves may be either opposite or alternately arranged and are often hairy. There are two main groups, divided according to the shape of their flowers. One group has bell-shaped or tubular flowers, generally musty smelling and often in shades of green or brown with markings in various colors. The second group is smaller with unscented saucer-shaped flowers in shades of blue or purple, sometimes with white variants; these fascinating flowers repay close inspection and so are best planted by paths or in containers.

In the past there has been much confusion over their names but this has recently been clarified and should help bring them much-deserved attention.

CULTIVATION The non-climbing species such as *C. clematidea* and *C. ovata* will thrive in the majority of ordinary well-drained garden soils in a sunny or part-shaded position in the garden, while most of the climbing species prefer damper, more humus-rich soil in part-shade, thriving especially in places where at least the roots are shaded—for example, among shrubs. They also make unusual and fascinating subjects for containers. The slender, often threadlike young shoots can be easily overlooked and damaged; they require fine twigs for support.

PROPAGATION Readily grown from seed, which is often set by the plant in abundance. The tubers of some species can be divided, while those of others simply get larger gradually without dividing.

PROBLEMS Slugs and snails, aphids and, in containers, swift moth larvae.

C. cardiophylla More-or-less erect leafy stems carry heart-shaped, untoothed, leaves with a slightly thickened whitish margin and, at their tips, in early summer and midsummer, one or several, nodding, ¾–¾-in- (1.5–2-cm-) long bells in pale lavender-blue with purple markings near the base. Native to Hubei province, China. ‡ 20–32 in (50–80 cm). Z5–7 H7–5

C. clematidea Robust, with erect, somewhat downy stems that are branched near the base; these leafy lateral shoots rarely carry flowers. The bluish green or grayish, oval to lance-shaped, untoothed leaves are opposite or alternately arranged and generally ½–1 in (1–2.5 cm) long, with a short stalk. The upper half of the main shoots is well-branched to form a pyramid shape; in early and mid- summer, each branch terminates in a solitary, bell-shaped, pendent ⅝–1¼-in (1.5–3-cm) flower, milky or pale blue and marked with orange and purple at the base inside. A good and reliable border plant best raised from seed. From southern Central Asia and Afghanistan eastward into the western Himalaya. ‡24–32 in (60–80 cm). Z7–9 H9–7

C. convolvulacea see *C. forrestii*; 'Alba' see *C. grey-wilsonii* 'Himal Snow'

C. forrestii syn. *C. convolvulacea* var. *forrestii* Vigorous twining climber with bright green stems bearing firm, oval, 1¼–4-in (3–10-cm) deep green leaves with a grayish bloom beneath and with a coarsely toothed margin. The ¼–½-in (0.5–1-cm) flowers, which appear from late summer to mid-fall on the main shoots and some of the side branches, are saucer-shaped, with mid- to lavender-blue narrowly elliptical petals, often with slightly darker veins. Best trained up pea sticks or allowed to clamber into suitable shrubs such as species roses or rhododendrons. Often mistakenly sold as *C. convolvulacea*, a distinct but rarely seen species. Native to southeast Tibet, Xizang, and northwestern Yunnan province, China. ‡6½–11 ft (2–3.5 m). Z7–9 H9–7

C. grey-wilsonii A relatively robust twining perennial with filamentous stems bearing thin, pale green, oval to lance-shaped, ⅝–2¼ in (1.5–5.5 cm) leaves with a rounded to heart-shaped base and occasional teeth. The 2–2¾ in (5–7 cm) long, saucer-shaped flowers, carried singly on both main and side shoots, in mid- to deep blue with a prominent crimson or purple basal ring inside, open from midsummer to early fall. Individual petals are broadly oval and hairy inside in the lower third. Good among ericaceous shrubs, it also makes an excellent container plant. Often sold as *C. convolvulacea*. Native to western and central Nepal. ‡3–6½ ft (1–2 m). Z7–9 H9–7 **'Himal Snow'** syn. *C. convolulacea* 'Alba' Pure white flowers; come true from seed.

C. ovata Delicate, erect plant with lance-shaped to oval foliage and very attractive flared bell-shaped flowers in rich blue with darker veining, the lobes flaring out like a skirt. A relatively short-lived plant, easily raised from seed but much confused with *C. clematidea*, which is larger and less striking. Native to the western Himalaya, 9,800–13,800 ft (3,000–4,200 m). ‡2–14 in (5–35 cm). Z7–9 H9–7

C. rotundifolia A vigorous twiner with alternate, oval to lance-shaped, weakly toothed ¾–2¾-in (2–7-cm) leaves

RIGHT 1 *Codonopsis grey-wilsonii* **2** *C. grey-wilsonii* 'Himal Snow' **3** *C. ovata* **4** *Colocasia esculenta* 'Black Magic'

bearing scattered blackish hairs. The ⅝–¾-in (1.5–2-cm) bell-shaped flowers, from early summer to early fall, are carried singly on both main shoots and side branches and are yellowish green or whitish green, veined with dark purple. They have a strong fetid smell. Best when allowed to clamber up large shrubs. Native to the Himalaya from Pakistan to central Nepal. ‡6½–10 ft (2–3 m). Z7–9 H9–7

C. tangshen Vigorous, twining climber with slender, smooth stems, fleshy, oval to lance-shaped, finely toothed, leaves up to 2½ in (6 cm) long. From early summer to early fall, bell-shaped, 1¼–1½ in (3–3.5 cm) long flowers, held singly at the main shoot tips and on lateral shoots, are greenish with purple spots and stripes, often checkered inside, and have spreading, triangular lobes and a green calyx that sits like a cap on the nodding flower. Native to Hubei and Sichuan provinces, China. ‡10 ft (3 m). Z7–9 H9–7

C. vinciflora A delicate twining plant. Extremely slender stems bear alternate, occasionally opposite, oval to lance-shaped, thin, ½–1½ in (1–3.5 cm) leaves. The 1¼–1½ in (3–4 cm) wide, saucer-shaped flowers, carried singly on the main shoots from early summer to early fall, are mid- to deep blue or bluish violet. Good among low ericaceous shrubs or in containers. Native to central and eastern Tibet, Xizang province, and western China. ‡20–60 ft (50–150 cm). Z7–9 H9–7

COLOCASIA
Elephant ears, Taro
ARACEAE

Tropical evergreen perennials that are generally grown for their exotic foliage.

There are six species from swampy and moist areas of tropical Asia. The tuberous rootstocks produce bold, arrow-shaped, dark green leaves, some with prominent veins. Flowers are rarely produced in gardens and tend to be small, white, and insignificant, developing into single-seeded, glossy green berries. Widely grown as a staple food in some countries.

CULTIVATION Usually grown in greenhouses or planted outside for summer as tender perennials, though interest in trying colocasias outside as hardy perennials is growing following some success in southern zones. In mild areas, take a gamble and leave colocasias in the ground. Protect the tubers with a deep mulch and cover the mulch with polyethylene as protection against excessive moisture. Colocasias can overwinter outside in some areas where they have been rated as Z8—

they are even quoted as surviving 2°F (–18°C). However, experience of growing these as hardy perennials is still being accumulated.

In the greenhouse, they should be grown in light loamless potting mix at a minimum of 64°F (18°C), in light shade and high humidity. Water and fertilize heavily. As summer seasonal plants, start them in the greenhouse and plant out after all danger of frost is past in a warm, sheltered area with moist soil and a little shade. Tubers can be lifted and kept dry and frost-free over winter.

PROPAGATION By division of the tubers in spring.

PROBLEMS Red spider mite, aphids, thrips, and whitefly may be troublesome under glass.

C. antiquorum see *C. esculenta*

C. esculenta syn. *C. antiquorum* (Coco yam) Robust, fast-growing, and dramatic moisture-loving plant with large upright tubers from which spring bold, dark green, heart-shaped leaves 24 in (60 cm) long, borne on stalks up to 3¼ ft (1 m) long. Plants grown outdoors may be smaller. This is the main edible species, sometimes known as the "potato of the tropics." However, they are poisonous if eaten raw, and the sap can also be an irritant. Tropical East Asia. ‡ 5 ft (1.5 m). Z11–11 H12–10. ⚠ **'Black Magic'** Stupendous, very choice form with huge, inky black leaves that look stunning against a carpet of yellow-leaved *Lysimachia nummularia* 'Aurea'. Grows well in boggy areas and waterside locations but can be difficult to overwinter. ‡ 4–6 ft (1.2–1.8 m). **'Black Ruffles'** A spontaneous mutation of 'Black Magic' with large, inky black leaves. ‡ 4–6 ft (1.2–1.8 m). Z8–10 H10–8. (**'Burgundy Stem'** Dark green velvety leaves with crinkled edges on tall red-purple stems. **'Fontanesii'** Dark red to purple stems; probably the toughest form. ‡ 3–6½ ft (1–2 m). **'Illustris'** A 19th-century cultivar that is still very popular in the US. Excellent selection with bright green and purple leaves. ‡ 4–5 ft (1.2–1.5 cm). Z8–10 H 10–8

COMMELINA
Day flower
COMMELINACEAE

Uncommon plants that are best used for the front of a sheltered bed or border, both in formal and informal situations.

Most of the 100 or more species are from tropical to warm temperate areas, but a few are hardier and valued for their intense pure blue flowers. Most are perennial, some with dahlia-like tubers, and have narrow to grassy foliage and semierect to rather floppy stems. Three-petaled flowers emerge one at a time each day from modified boat- or purselike leaves and are usually, but not invariably, blue.

CULTIVATION Moderately fertile, well-drained soil in sun or shade. In cold areas, lift plants in late fall and keep them frost-free until spring.

PROPAGATION From seed, careful division in spring, or cuttings in early summer.

PROBLEMS Slugs.

C. coelestis see *C. tuberosa* Coelestis Group

C. dianthifolia A tuberous rootstock supports erect or semierect stems carrying narrow, 3½–5 in (9–13 cm) long tapered leaves that arch outward and often have inrolled margins. Bright blue, or rarely white, ¾–1¼ in (2–3 cm) wide flowers emerge throughout the summer and early fall. Related to better-known *C. tuberosa* but more upright in growth. Native to northern Mexico and southwestern US. ‡ 16–24 in (40–60 cm). Z7–10 H10–7.

C. **'Illustris'** Excellent selection with bright green and purple leaves. ‡ 4–5 ft (1.2–1.5 m). Z8–10 H 10–8

C. tuberosa This tufted to clump-forming, tuberous perennial has more-or-less prostrate, branching stems and narrowly lance-shaped, slightly fleshy 2½–3½ in (6–9 cm) long leaves. Flowering stems terminate in ¾–1¼ in (2–3 cm) long boat-shaped bracts, usually suffused or lined deep purple, which provide a succession of 1¼ in- (3 cm) wide rich blue flowers throughout summer and fall. Grows wild in Central and South America. ‡ 4–6 in (10–15 cm). Z9–10

BELOW 1 *Commelina tuberosa* Coelestis Group **2** *Convallaria majalis* 'Albostriata' **3** *C. majalis* var. *rosea*

H12–9. **'Alba'** White flowers. **Coelestis Group** syn. *C. coelestis* Erect stems. ‡ 24 in (60 cm).

CONOCLINIUM *see* EUPATORIUM

CONVALLARIA
Lily-of-the-valley
CONVALLARIACEAE

Much loved for its fragrant spring flowers, this tough shade-lover is ideal for seasonal ground cover in a woodland garden or under deciduous shrubs.

Around four species of deciduous plants grow in open woodlands or alpine meadows in north temperate regions; only one species is widely grown in gardens. Creeping steadily, the broad, lance-shaped foliage makes a good background for the exquisitely scented, little bell-shaped flowers that are superb for cutting.

CULTIVATION Thrives in part-shade; almost full shade is tolerated, with steadily moist, preferably slightly alkaline, humus-rich soil. Work abundant leaf mold into the soil before planting; mulch with leaf mold in fall, 1 in (2.5 cm) deep.

PROPAGATION By division in spring after flowering, or in fall. Seed (species only) is possible, but is not recommended as it is so slow.

PROBLEMS Gray mold.

C. majalis Makes good ground cover in early summer with its mid-green, elliptical basal leaves, 1½–8 in (4–20 cm) long, although it is sometimes uncomfortably vigorous. Pendulous, waxy, mainly white, highly scented flowers, ¼–½ in (5–10 mm) across, appear in late spring. They are carried

on elegant, arching stems and open just above the foliage, or are sometimes partially hidden by it; they are followed by scarlet berries. All parts, especially the berries and seeds, are toxic if eaten. Tolerates full sun if the summers are cool and the soil is steadily moist. Northern Europe but widely naturalized elsewhere. ‡ 9 in (23 cm). Z2–7 H7–1. ⚠ **'Albostriata'** Leaves striped lengthwise in cream-white; flowering shoots less dramatically striped. ‡ 6 in (15 cm). **'Dorien'** Large flowers on long stems and broad foliage. ‡ 12 in (30 cm). **'Flore Pleno'** Double flowers. ‡ 6 in (15 cm). **'Fortin's Giant'** Large leaves and flowers. ‡ 12 in (30 cm). **'Hardwick Hall'** Wide leaves with narrow, light green edges, large flowers. ‡ 10 in (25 cm). **'Prolificans'** Branching flowerheads; blooms, occasionally slightly misshapen, in tight clusters.

QUIRKS OF CULTIVATION

A familiar sight in old cottage gardens, often found in vigorous, deliciously fragrant clumps that may even invade paths, lily-of-the-valley seems easy to grow. But plant it in a part-shaded, fertile, slightly alkaline border—where you would expect it to thrive—and it may inexplicably languish. Indeed, it has been known to move, struggling weakly, along a border from where it was first planted and, in a few years, establish a thriving group some yards away from its planting site—or it may spring up, from a bird-dropped seed, in a parched place where it seems unlikely to thrive. Some recommend that rather than planting individual roots 1 in (2.5 cm) deep, it is best simply to cut out a square block of an old mass of roots with a spade and move it to a new site.

LEFT 1 *Convolvulus sabatius*
2 *Coreopsis* 'Schnittgold'

effect. Semidouble and double cultivars look especially ragged as they fade and benefit particularly from deadheading. Plants can be sheared over, just above the basal foliage, as the first flush draws to a close in midsummer to encourage reblooming into early fall. Cutting back hard in mid-fall helps to produce new basal shoots, encouraging successful overwintering. Do not allow *Coreopsis* with low basal foliage to be overshadowed by their neighbors.

PROPAGATION Divide clumps or take basal cuttings in spring. Species and some cultivars can be raised from seed, some blooming in their first season from an early sowing.

PROBLEMS Some are affected by mildew.

⬍ 7 in (18 cm). **var.** *rosea* Light mauve-pink flowers. ⬍ 8 in (20 cm). **'Variegata'** Leaves striped lengthwise with gold. **'Vic Pawlowski's Gold'** Dark green leaves closely striped lengthwise with gold on short plants. ⬍ 6 in (15 cm).

CONVOLVULUS
CONVOLVULACEAE

Prolific trumpet-shaped flowers and handsome foliage on attractive, durable, and sun-loving ground covers.

Around 250 species of mostly low scrambling perennials and annuals, plus a few shrubs, are primarily native to the Mediterranean. They are often confused with bindweed (*Calystegia*), from which they are distinguished by details of the pollen and flower structure, and with the morning glories (*Ipomoea*), whose blossoms close for part of the day. Only a few are grown in gardens. Their sometimes twining stems support leaves that may be divided or undivided, dark green or sometimes attractively silvered. The trumpet-shaped late spring and summer flowers, in blues, pinks, or white, are carried at the tips of the shoots or in the leaf joints. They are followed by round, dry seedpods. A few are disconcertingly vigorous, especially in warmer gardens, but make good container plants.

CULTIVATION Sun lovers; most tolerate hot or scorching conditions. Bloom nonstop throughout the summer with little or no grooming. Tolerant of drought and of poor soil, they prefer reasonably fertile, moist, but well-drained soil.

PROPAGATION By cuttings or seed.

PROBLEMS Occasionally invasive.

C. althaeoides (Mallow bindweed) A strong-growing, slim-stemmed tangle, featuring silvery gray leaves 1¼ in

(3 cm) long in a confusing diversity of shapes—from heart-shaped to arrow-shaped to deeply lobed—on 36 in (90 cm) twining stems. Up to five 1½ in (4 cm) long, trumpet-shaped flowers are gathered in the upper leaf joints and are always some shade of pink, dark or light. Less tidy than some other species and best interwoven with other trailers or denser, low-growing perennials; also good sprawling on a sunny bank. Cutting back encourages a denser presentation but also a greater spread; it has been accused of being invasive, especially in mild areas. Best in moist, well-drained soil. ⬍ 18–24 in (45–60 cm). Z6–8 H8–1 **subsp.** *tenuissimus* Brighter pink; more silvery and uniformly dissected foliage. Z6–8 H8–1

C. lineatus Trailing plant with long, rather variably shaped but often slender, grayish silver leaves on loose, whiplike growth of slender stems. The flowers, which appear in small clusters of three to four together or sometimes singly, are pink, trumpetlike, and with five creases from base to rim, similar to those of morning glories. Prefers sun and well-drained soil. From rocky shores in Russia and Greece. ⬍ 1¼–10 in (3–25 cm). Z6–8 H8–1

C. mauritanicus see *C. sabatius*

C. sabatius syn. *C. mauritanicus* Woody-based trailing plant with 1¼ in (3 cm), deep forest green, oval leaves on 12–24 in (30–60 cm) stems. Its primary claim to fame is the purple-blue, ⅝–1 in (1.5–2.5 cm) wide blossoms, like miniature morning glories, that line the trailing stems in clusters of up to three in summer and fall. Pink-flowered forms are said to exist but are not grown. Use cascading over walls or in containers; prune back to encourage more shoots from the base. Good in dry conditions. From North Africa and Italy. ⬍ 4–20 in (10–50 cm). Z7–9 H9–7 **'Blue Moon'** Darker blue flowers. **'Full Moon'** Light lilac-blue blossoms with a white eye. **'Moroccan Beauty'** Larger blue flowers. **'White Gladys'** White.

COREOPSIS
Tickseed
ASTERACEAE

Prolific and long-flowering daisies for use at the front of sunny beds and borders.

About 114 annuals and often short-lived perennials come from North and South America, most of the cultivated species coming from the US. The genus is closely related to *Bidens*, best known as a summer annual, and current research is likely to conclude that *Coreopsis* is so closely related to *Bidens* that it should be included in that genus.

Most species have flowerheads borne singly or on branched stems with a small central disk surrounded by usually eight ray florets that are often yellow but more rarely mahogany, red, pink, or white. The leaves are opposite, often narrow, and may be unlobed or divided into three or more lobes, sometimes giving a feathery effect. The roots are usually fibrous and a few species spread by rhizomes.

There are many garden cultivars, and more are being introduced. Many can be seed-raised but some must be vegetatively propagated because seed-raised plants are likely to be quite variable. Most are often treated as forms of *C. grandiflora* or *C. lanceolata*, but some may be hybrids, perhaps also involving annual *C. tinctoria*, which may contribute the red or mahogany blotch at the base of the petals of some cultivars. These species and hybrids tend to be short-lived but benefit from division every few years to maintain vigor.

CULTIVATION Most prefer sun and good drainage but perform best given consistent moisture. Deadheading helps promote longevity as well as longer flowering; cut the flower stems back to within the basal foliage to avoid an untidy

C. **'Astolat'** syn. *C. grandiflora* 'Astolat' Golden yellow single flowers with a mahogany blotch at the base of each petal. Vegetatively propagated by the Astolat Company, Guildford, Surrey, England, in 1946; Astolat, or Shalott, is the name of Guildford in Arthurian legend. Early summer to early fall. ⬍ 30 in (75 cm). Z5–9 H9–1

C. **'Autumn Blush'** Prolific, peachy yellow flowers with red eyes. Introduced by Terra Nova Nursery, OR. ⬍ 24 in (60 cm). Z6–9 H9–6

C. **'Baby Gold'** see *C.* 'Sonnenkind'

C. auriculata **'Schnittgold'** see *C.* 'Schnittgold'

FIRST-YEAR FLOWERS FROM SEED

As gardeners have become less patient while waiting for their plants to bloom, the plant breeders have worked hard to create perennials that can be raised from seed and will flower during their first year. Some of the very best of all perennials feature this valuable quality, including the superb Kompliment and Fan Series of *Lobelia*, and the 2005 All-America Selection winner *Gaillardia* 'Arizona Sun'. This approach has also produced some excellent *Coreopsis*.

The double flowered *C. grandiflora* 'Sunray' was the first of these to appear, followed by the earlier flowering 'Early Sunrise'. Both plants are neat and prolific in their first year, but taller, more open and straggly, and smaller-flowered in succeeding years. They are excellent plants for new gardens, often available from garden centers in late spring or early summer, and will flower for many months in their first season and bulk up to fill more space the following year. New introductions of this type continue; look for the Fleuroselect Gold Medal winner 'Heliot' (deep gold with bold red blotches), and the rather similar 'Unwins Gold'.

C. **'Calypso'** syn. *C. grandiflora* 'Calypso' Golden-yellow, single flowers, with a mahogany blotch at the base of each petal, are borne on stems bare of leaves in their upper half and bloom in early summer and midsummer, with some reblooming if deadheaded. The narrow, unlobed leaves are variegated creamy yellow. Vegetatively propagated and introduced by Bernwode Plants, Buckinghamshire, England. ↕14 in (35 cm). Z5–8 H8–1

C. **'Crème Brûlée'** A striking plant; forms a spreading, neat clump that is reliably persistent. Leaves, with three fingerlike lobes about ¼–⅜ in (5–8 mm) wide, are arranged in opposite pairs resembling a cluster of six leaves at each leaf joint, and are dark green, although they may turn a chlorotic yellow-green. From early to late summer, plants are covered with sulfur yellow daisies with gold disks. Each bloom has about eight overlapping petals, pleated twice lengthwise and with slightly notched ends. For well-drained soil in sun. Will rebloom into mid-fall if sheared over after the first flush. A hybrid of *C. verticillata* 'Moonbeam' from the Plantage nursery, Mattituck, NY, introduced by June Croon. ↕40cm. Z5–9 H9–1

C. **grandiflora** (Large-flowered tickseed) An upright, short-lived plant, the lowest leaves are undivided, becoming split into narrow or lancelike lobes farther up the stem, the upper half of the flower stalk lacking leaves. The yellow flowers, 1½–2½ in (4–6 cm) across, have about eight petals, each with three to five lobes at the tip, and appear from early summer to early fall. From damp soil in the eastern US. ↕12–40 in (30–100 cm). Z4–9 H12–1. **'Astolat'** see *C*. 'Astolat'. **'Calypso'** see *C*. 'Calypso'. **'Double Sunburst'** see 'Sunburst'. **'Early Sunrise'** Double or semidouble blooms with jagged-tipped gold petals, giving a ruffled effect. Flowers from late spring to early summer, with some later bloom if deadheaded or from early summer onward from a winter sowing. The flower stems are inclined to flop and plants are prone to mildew. Seed-raised, developed by renowned British plant breeder Ralph Gould and an All-America Selections Gold Medal Winner in 1989. ↕18 in (45 cm). **Flying Saucers ('Walcoreop')** Vigorous, compact, vegetatively propagated plant with plentiful, slightly cupped, golden-yellow, 3 in (7.5 cm) wide flowers on unbranched stems from early summer to mid-fall. The leaves can have up to five leaflets and are about ¾ in (2 cm) wide by 8 in (20 cm) long. Male-sterile—that is, only sets seed when pollinated by a different form—and therefore all offspring will be hybrids and highly variable, so propagate only by division or cuttings. Raised by David Tristram of Walberton Nursery,

RIGHT 1 *Coreopsis grandiflora* 'Sunray'
2 *C. g.* 'Sonnenkind' **3** *C. g.* 'Sterntaller'
4 *C*. 'Limerock Ruby' **5** *C. rosea*
6 *C. tripteris*

West Sussex, England. ‡18 in (45 cm).
'Golden Gain' see *C.* 'Schnittgold'.
'Mayfield Giant' A tall, single, gold-flowered, vegetatively propagated cultivar flowering into mid-fall with an unusually long length of leafless flower stem, making it especially useful for cutting. ‡36 in (90 cm). **'Schnittgold'** see *C.* 'Schnittgold' **'Sterntaler'** see *C.* 'Sterntaler'. **'Sunburst'** syn. *C. grandiflora* 'Double Sunburst', *C. lanceolata* 'Sunburst'. Seed-raised, with double or semidouble golden yellow flowers. ‡75cm. **'Sonnenkind'** see *C.* 'Sonnenkind'. **'Sunray'** (**Sonnenstrahl**). Short-lived, seed-raised cultivar with double golden yellow flowers from early summer to early fall, or from midsummer from a winter sowing. Fleuroselect Bronze Medal winner, 1980. ‡20 in (50 cm).

C. lanceolata (Lance-leaved tickseed) Short-lived plant with spoon- or lance-shaped leaves, usually undivided or occasionally with one or two pairs of side lobes; the flower stem is bare of leaves for more than half its upper length. The 1½–2¾-in (4–7-cm) yellow flowers, from early summer to early fall, have petals with about five lobes at the tip. Cutting back after the first flushand regular division are advisable. Best in full sun with some moisture. From both dry and moist soil in the central and eastern US and California. ‡8–30 in (20–70 cm). Z4–9 H9–1.
'Goldfink' (**Goldfinch**) Compact, vegetatively propagated cultivar with deep yellow single flowers from early summer to early fall. ‡10 in (25 cm)
'Schnittgold' see *C.* 'Schnittgold'.
'Sterntaler' see *C.* 'Sterntaler'.
'Sunburst' see *C. grandiflora* 'Sunburst'.

C. **'Limerock Ruby'** Perhaps the first *Coreopsis* with rich ruby red flowers. Masses of 1¼-in (3-cm) blooms from midsummer to early fall on compact, freely branching plants above dark green leaves, each with three radiating, threadlike lobes. Prefers consistent moisture and can be short-lived, but benefits from being trimmed back after the first flush of flowers. A vegetatively propagated hybrid of *C. rosea* and *C. verticillata* from Mary Ann Faria of Limerock Plant Farm, RI. ‡16 in (40 cm). Z7–9 H9–7

C. rosea (Pink tickseed) Spreads by rhizomes. The 1-in (2.5-cm) pink (rarely white) daisies with yellow disks are borne from early to late summer above dark green, threadlike leaves with up to three lobes. Enjoys sun but is intolerant of drought. Benefits from being clipped over after the first flush of flowers. From the eastern US. ‡12–24 in (30–60 cm). Z4–8 H8–1.
'American Dream' Popular cultivar with branched stems bearing, from mid- to late summer, 1½-in (4-cm) flowers with rose pink petals, jagged at the end, around a small golden yellow disk. Unusually drought-tolerant. Introduced by California horticulturist Roger Raiche in 1984. ‡14 in (35 cm).
'Sweet Dreams' From midsummer to early fall the 1½-in (4-cm) flowers have petals emerging whitish, with a

raspberry red base, around a mahogany disk. The ray florets expand and age through mauve-pink to magenta. A vegetatively propagated spontaneous mutation of 'American Dream' selected by Mark Leonard, CA. ‡14 in (35 cm).

C. **'Schnittgold'** (**Cutting Gold, Gold Cut**) syn. *C. auriculata* 'Schnittgold', *C. grandiflora* 'Schnittgold', *C. lanceolata* 'Schnittgold', *C. grandiflora* 'Golden Gain' Bright, prolific but short-lived seed-raised cultivar, developed as a cut flower. The 2-in (5-cm), single, golden yellow flowers, produced from early summer to early fall, have usually eight jagged-tipped petals. The simple, unlobed basal leaves are about half as wide as they are long, becoming narrower progressively up into the top half of the flower stem, unlike typical *C. lanceolata* or *C. grandiflora*. Less likely to die during winter if cut back in early fall. ‡36 in (90 cm). Z4–9 H9–1

C. **'Sonnenkind'** (**Baby Sun**) syn. *C. grandiflora* 'Sonnenkind', *C.* 'Baby Gold'. Seed-raised cultivar with single, gold flowers; reddish brown blotch at the base of each petal, flowering from early summer to early fall in its first year if sown early. Not to be confused with the rarely listed, unblotched *C. lanceolata* cultivar of the same name. ‡16 in (40 cm). Z4–9 H9–1

C. **'Sterntaler'** syns *C. grandiflora* 'Sterntaler', *C. lanceolata* 'Sterntaler' Seed-raised. Ribbed, golden-yellow petals, indented at the ends, each with a small mahogany blotch at the base, from late spring to early summer. Some later bloom if deadheaded. ‡16 in (40 cm). Z3–8 H8–1

C. **'Tequila Sunrise'** Broadly lance-shaped leaves edged creamy yellow. Flowers, from early summer to mid-fall, have about eight golden-yellow ray petals with lobed tips and a small red mark at the base. Reliably perennial, found in the garden of Kenneth and Linda Smith of Columbus, OH. ‡14 in (35 cm). Z5–9 H8–1

C. tripteris (Tall tickseed) Tall, upright and graceful, the flowers have lemon yellow petals around a chocolate disk, and are borne from midsummer to early fall on stems branched in their upper part. The foliage consists of opposite pairs of leaves, each leaf split into three to create the appearance of a cluster of six narrow leaves at each leaf joint and giving a repeated rhythm. Each lobe is 2–4 in (5–10 cm) long and up to 1 in (2.5 cm) wide. Prefers part-shade and woodland edge conditions and can make a handsome specimen plant. From eastern US. ‡6½ ft (2 m). Z4–9 H9–1. **'Pierre Bennerup'** Broader, slightly overlapping petals create more substantial flowers from midsummer to early fall. The leaf lobes are unusually broad. Named for the owner of Sunny Border Nurseries, CT. ‡6 ft (1.8 m).

C. verticillata (Whorled tickseed) Long-lived plant with opposite, dark green leaves each divided into three

radiating, threadlike parts, the 1–2-in (2.5–5-cm-) wide rich yellow flowers with a small yellow disk are borne on branched stems from midsummer to early fall. Likes full sun but tolerates some shade. From the eastern US. ‡12–36 in (30–90 cm). Z4–9 H9–1.
'Golden Gain' Prolific and compact; broad, slightly overlapping gold yellow petals, from Blooms of Bressingham Confusingly, this name had previously been used for other *Coreopsis* cultivars, including 'Schnittgold', so according to the international rules governing plant names, it should not be used for this plant. ‡18 in (45 cm) **'Grandiflora'** syn. *C. verticillata* 'Golden Shower' Golden yellow 2½-in (6–cm) flowers with overlapping petals are borne in great profusion on an upright plant. ‡36 in (90 cm). **'Moonbeam'** Exceptionally showy and prolific, the sulfur yellow flowers about 1½ in (4 cm) across, almost hiding the foliage. Selected by British horticulturist Bill Archer and chosen as Perennial Plant Association Perennial of the Year, 1992. Seed-raised plants under this name show some variability, often being less floriferous and tending to die over winter, so vegetative propagation is essential; plants should not be bought from batches that show signs of variability. ‡20 in (50 cm). **'Old Timer'** Tall and upright, benefiting from staking, with 1¾-in (4.5-cm) golden yellow flowers. ‡32 in (80 cm).
'Zagreb' Compact cultivar with plentiful 1½-in (4-cm) golden yellow flowers. ‡16 in (40 cm).

CORONILLA
Crown vetch
PAPILIONACEAE

Useful and attractive ground cover that will withstand poor conditions and is good for erosion control.

Of the 20 species of annuals, perennials and low shrubs native to woods, meadows, and dry cliff faces in Europe and North Africa, only one is grown in the perennial garden—a vigorous, spreading, ground cover with cloverlike flowers.

CULTIVATION Grow in any reasonably fertile soil in full sun to light shade. Overly rich soil will result in rampant growth.

PROPAGATION From seed or by softwood cuttings in spring, by division in fall.

PROBLEMS Anthracnose.

C. varia syn. *Securigera varia* A spreading plant with long narrow leaves composed of up to 25 individual oval leaflets on a central stalk. The pretty pink (occasionally white, purple, or bicolored) pealike flowers open from late spring to late summer in round heads of up to 20 individual flowers. They are followed by long seedpods that open explosively, throwing seed a considerable distance. The resulting seedlings can become invasive if allowed to mature. Best used as ground cover in poor soil or for stabilizing slopes and banks. Also attractive billowing from a large container. Widely naturalized in the US, even in areas much colder than its native range, where it has become notoriously invasive in many states and cited as a noxious weed that should no longer be planted. Native to Europe. ‡12–24 in (30–60 cm). Z7–9 H9–7. **'Penngift'** Less sprawling cultivar widely used for erosion control on sloping highway shoulders and banks but also good in the garden. Developed at the University of Pennsylvania.

BELOW *Coronilla varia*

CORTADERIA
POACEAE

Large, tussock-forming grasses with tall and spectacular plumes of late-season flowers.

Of the 24 fibrous-rooted species, most are from South America, with four (called toetoe, pronounced toy-toy) from New Zealand and one from New Guinea. A tough, woody crown supports evergreen or semievergreen, narrow foliage, often tinted in blue-gray; the edges of the leaves are minutely saw-toothed and can cut flesh, making the plants unsuitable for siting near paths. The plumelike flowers, which may be white, pink, or parchment-colored, are borne on stout stems; young plants produce upright flower stems, while older, larger clumps usually have stems more or less radiating for a fountainlike effect. Some cortaderia plants are female, the flower heads having sterile white pollen and spikelets with long, silky hairs toward the base, while others are bisexual and produce fertile yellow pollen; this differentiates them from *Chionochloa*, in which all plants are bisexual.

Cortaderias make striking specimen plants, effective against a background of dark foliage or lit from behind by the sun; in borders, they should be used toward the front to display their graceful habit. They are well suited for use in extended groups and large drifts in a naturalistic manner, and are especially effective with other large grasses such as *Miscanthus* and with late flowers such as many of the various *Aster* and *Eupatorium* species. Some species are pernicious weeds in hotter climates such as those found in California.

CULTIVATION The commonly cultivated species enjoy a waterside position, and reflections double their impact, and will tolerate winter rain; summer drought causes some species, especially the New Zealanders, to die off in patches, although *C. selloana* is more tolerant.

PROPAGATION Divide in mid-spring, after cutting back the clumps: forks are often not strong enough to deal with established clumps and a mattock may be required. The species can also be raised from seed sown in spring but cultivars rarely breed true.

PROBLEMS Usually trouble-free.

C. argentea see *C. selloana*

C. fulvida (Kakaho) Arching, one-sided slightly shaggy plumes emerge golden and age to pink or creamy white; 12–24 in (30-60 cm) long and borne above the 5 ft (1.5 m) high tussock of foliage from midsummer onward. Plumes retained until late winter. Mid-green, ¾ in (2 cm) wide leaves are ridged and have a white underside. Prone to dying out in patches when too dry. From moist areas, often seasonally partly submerged, in New Zealand. ↕8 ft (2.4 m). Z7–11 H10–7

RIGHT 1 *Cortaderia richardii*
2 *Cortaderia selloana* 'Renatleri'

CORTADERIA CONFUSIONS

Pampas grass (*Cortaderia selloana*) is one of the most distinctive of perennials, and although some gardeners find its crudely emphatic effect in Victorian gardening and its wide use in new housing projects in the 1950s and 1960s hard to forgive, it is enjoying something of a revival in naturalistic plantings, although its lateness of flowering limits its use.

Cortaderia is unusual in that individual species can produce plants that are either female or bisexual and look quite different from each other. Female plants tend to be more upright in habit, less arching, with an elliptic, rather solid-shaped plume, emerging white and aging to fawn, and shaped like a football on a stem rising up to 40 in (1 m) above the basal foliage; the upright habit tends to crowd the plumes. Bisexual plants have a rather shaggy, one-sided plume, emerging white to reddish, aging to white, fawn or pink, on a stem rising up to 6½ ft (2 m) above the foliage; the plumes are sometimes pendulous and generally more graceful, often with a silky sheen. Bisexual plants are sometimes thought to be male plants because the female parts of the plume are so small and hard to distinguish. Some plants seem to have neither male nor female parts but still feature fluffy plumes! Plumes of the females generally last until spring but lose much of their bulk; plumes of bisexual plants may be lost by late fall, or in some plants may persist until spring.

The result of this is that plants of the same species can look quite different from one another and, if grown from seed, they may also look different from their parents. What's more, seed that has been collected from female plants will have been created with pollen from a different individual, so, by definition, all plants raised from seed collected from female plants will be hybrids and likely to be variable. Sowing the seed inevitably gives both female and bisexual plants, with their differing forms, which itself creates confusion, as well as the usual seedling variation. Reluctant to propagate cultivars by division, because that method is relatively slow, nurseries have raised so many cultivars from seed that impenetrable tangles of identity have now been created, and it can be difficult to depend on plants being correctly labeled. The plants can also be invasive, particularly along the California coast, in New Zealand, and in South Africa, spreading by seed once both forms are established, as a consequence of nurseries having raised plants from seed.

C. richardii Graceful, arching, cream to fawn-colored plumes, without the substance and solidity of *C. selloana* but more elegant, and valuable for early blooming and lively movement in the slightest breeze. Flowers from early summer to mid-fall, bisexual plants flowering earlier than females. The narrow dark green leaves make an arching mound about 4 ft (1.2 m) high. From moist habitats in New Zealand. ‡ 10 ft (3 m). Z7–10 H10–7

C. selloana syn. *C. argentea, Gynerium argenteum* (Pampas grass) Very variable but always imposing plant with substantial fluffy plumes from early to late fall, sometimes earlier or later, which can vary in length, and thus showiness, from 12 in (30 cm) to 3¼ ft (1 m). Some plants carry only whitish female flowers, and these tend to be more upright and may have their plumes opening low down among the foliage. Other plants are bisexual, with both male and female fawn or pink-tinted flowers in each plume, and these are held more elegantly. In some plants the plumes last well, persisting into spring; in others they break during fall. Some so-called pink forms may actually be the closely related *C. jubata*. (see Cortaderia Confusions, p.136) Enjoying moisture but tolerant of drought, not all cultivars flower well in colder areas, where gardeners need to source good, reliable forms locally. Dead leaves can mar the effect if left: either cut back the plants or burn them off each year in mid-spring; a two-year or longer accumulation of dead matter will kill the plants when burned. From Argentina, Brazil, and Chile ‡ 4–12 ft (1.2–3.6 m). Z7–11 H12–7.
'Albolineata' syn. 'Silver Stripe' Foliage edged white, mounding to 3¼ ft (1 m), topped by showy white, upright plumes. A number of similar but distinct plants are grown under this name. ‡ 5 ft (1.5 m). Z7–11 H12–7

'Aureolineata' (syn. 'Gold Band') Leaves edged yellow, mounding to 4 ft (1.2 m), with graceful silvery plumes borne well above the foliage. A number of similar but distinct plants are grown under this name. ‡ 6½ ft (2 m). Z7–11 H12–7. **'Pink Feather'** (**Rosa Feder**). Tall, vigorous cultivar; plumes emerge rich pink. 11¾ ft (3.6 m). Z7–11 H12–7. **'Pumila'** Compact, upright, reliably floriferous female cultivar with creamy plumes borne just clear of the foliage from late summer to mid-fall. Introduced in 1875. Plants under this name but 6 ft (1.8 m) or taller are misnamed. ‡ 4 ft (1.2 m). Z7–11 H12–7. **'Rendatleri'** syn. 'Carminea Rendatleri', *Gynerium rendatleri* Tall, pink-flowered cultivar, imposing though weak-stemmed, flowering in early and mid-fall ‡ 10 ft (3 m). Z7–11 H12–7. **'Rosea'** Used for variable, often seed-raised, pink-flushed plants. 8–10 ft (2.4–3 m). Z7–11 H12–7. **'Silver Fountain'** Brightly white variegated leaves mound to 5 ft (1.5 m), topped by white plumes on green stems. ‡ 8 ft (2.4 m). Z7–11 H12–7. **'Sunningdale Silver'** Dramatically handsome, tall cultivar; large silvery plumes on sturdy stems and borne clear of the 5½-ft (1.7-m) mound of foliage from mid-fall to early winter. Shy-flowering near the northernmost limit of its hardiness. ‡ 10 ft (3 m). Z7–11 H12–7. **'White Feather'** A dubious name for a range of seed-raised, female or bisexual, white-flowered plants. ‡ 6–12 ft (2–3.6 m). Z7–11 H12–7

CORTUSA
PRIMULACEAE

Hardy woodland plants closely related to *Primula*, producing delicate flowers as spring merges into summer.

Eight species of deciduous clump-forming plants for the cool shade of a woodland garden or shrub border, they grow naturally in woodlands in mountainous areas, from western and central Europe to northern Asia. The long-stalked, lobed basal leaves are rounded, heart-shaped, or kidney-shaped. In late spring and early summer bell- or funnel-shaped flowers, dangling on thin stalks, are carried well above the leaves on one side of a slender stem. *Cortusa* differs from *Primula* in the details of the flower structure.

CULTIVATION For slightly acidic or alkaline, humus-rich, moist yet well-drained soil. Likes a cool position in part-shade; it is not suitable for hot, dry climates. Mulch with leaf mold or well-rotted garden compost in fall.

PROPAGATION By division in early spring. Sow ripe seed in an open cold frame, or take cuttings of thick, mature roots in late summer and place them in a cold frame.

PROBLEMS Slugs and snails.

C. matthioli Easily grown and the best-known species. The 4¾-in- (12-cm-)

ABOVE *Cortusa matthioli*

wide rich green leaves are kidney-shaped or rounded, covered in fine rust-colored hairs; edges jaggedly toothed. Nodding ½-in (1-cm) long, bell-shaped flowers in magenta, purple-violet or, more rarely, white, on rust-colored, hairy stems in late spring and early summer. From western Europe. ‡ 8–12 in (20–30 cm). Z5–8 H8–5. **'Alba'** White flowers. **subsp. pekinensis** Deeply cut, very hairy leaves, flowers sometimes darker in color. From China.

CORYDALIS
PAPAVERACEAE

Showy spring-flowering plants, many with pretty fernlike foliage, suitable for either woodland garden or borders.

About 300 deciduous and evergreen plants from Europe, Asia, and tropical Africa, mostly growing in scrub and woodlands. Several are commonly cultivated in gardens. From the usually tuberous or rhizomatous rootstocks arise slightly fleshy stems bearing finely dissected leaves; these are repeatedly split to give up to 27 leaflets that are often tinted or even brightly colored. The stems are topped with very dainty sprays of flowers that are quaintly shaped—two-lipped and usually with conspicuous spurs. They occur in a wide range of colors. In recent years, several excellent new introductions have been made, mostly from China and from central Asia (see New from China, p.139). Many are woodland plants well suited to planting beneath shrubs or

among ferns, but a few require more specialized conditions and are not covered here.

CULTIVATION Most are best grown in well-drained, humus-rich soil in part-shade. Some self-sow.

PROPAGATION From seed or by division.

PROBLEMS Slugs and snails may cause severe damage to young growth.

C. **'Blackberry Wine'** Vigorous; forms a clump of much-divided, blue-green leaves. From late spring or early to late summer, fragrant, straight-spurred, purplish pink flowers open in a dense spike. If sheared when flowering ceases in late summer, it may give a second flush of flowers in early and mid-fall. Origin uncertain, probably a hybrid

or selection of the variable *C. flexuosa*. ‡12 in (30 cm). Z5–8 H8–5

C. bulbosa see *C. cava*

C. buschii Rhizomatous plant with tubers. From each tuber grows a stem with long-stalked, blue-green leaves, much divided into narrow segments. In late spring and early summer, clusters of up to 25 dusky deep pink flowers, each 1–1½ in (2.5–3.5 cm) long with a long, straight spur. A recent introduction, easy to grow; forms a spreading clump with showy flowers. From damp woodlands in Korea, northeastern China, and far eastern Russian. ‡4–10 in (10–25 cm). Z5–8 H8–5

C. cashmeriana Deciduous perennial with fleshy roots, forming a tuft of upright stems with finely divided, pale bluish green leaves to 3 in (8 cm) long.

PATHSIDE PLEASURES

IN THIS PRETTY GROUPING the arrestingly pale ‘China Blue’ form of *Corydalis flexuosa* interknits delightfully with the bright-white variegated oat grass, *Arrhenatherum elatius* subsp. *bulbosum* ‘Variegatum’, in woodland soil and dappled shade. There seems to be only one problem with this late-spring and early-summer combination: both of these plants tend to die away in the summer, after the corydalis has flowered, and such a superb combination is bound to be in a prominent pathside place where an empty space in summer is very undesirable. The solution is to place a clump of an arching woodland perennial—*Gentiana asclepiadea* seems ideal—in the background. Erect in its early growth, and so not covering the low early display, it will later lean across the empty space, where its flowers will be easily visible.

Vivid blue flowers ⅝ in (1.5 cm) long, with down-curved spurs, open in small clusters in early summer and midsummer. Grow in part-shade, in well-drained soil that is rich in humus. At its best, this plant is one of the finest blue-flowered species, but it is not always easy to keep it going in warmer areas. From open scrub in the mountains of the Himalaya, from Kashmir to Tibet. ‡4–6 in (10–15 cm). Z6–8 H8–6. **‘Kailash’** Compact form; ‡2–4 in (5–10 cm).

C. cava syn. *C. bulbosa* Deciduous perennial with a rather large, hollow tuber; the upright stems feature two pale green leaves up to 4 in (10 cm) long, divided into many narrowly wedge-shaped leaflets. From early to late spring, each stem carries up to 20 purple or creamy white flowers 1 in (2.5 cm) long, with curved spurs. Beneath each flower is a simple, oval bract. Easy to grow; widespread in woodlands in central Europe. ‡8 in (20 cm). Z5–7 H7–5. **‘Albiflora’** White flowers.

C. cheilanthifolia Evergreen plant with fibrous roots supporting several fernlike, bronze-tinted oval leaves growing to 12 in (30 cm) or longer. From early spring or mid-spring to late summer or later, straight-spurred, bright yellow flowers up to ¾ in (2 cm) long open on erect stems, in dense clusters that are held well above the leaves. Grown as much for its beautiful foliage as for its flowers. It will often self-sow freely. From shaded, rocky places in central and western China. ‡8–12 in (20–30 cm). Z5–7 H7–3

C. elata Vigorous, partly evergreen plant forming a spreading clump of divided, fresh green leaves, growing from a fibrous root system. Intense deep blue, fragrant flowers are carried in dense clusters on upright stems in late spring or early summer and midsummer. Each flower is about 1 in (2.5 cm) long, with a straight spur that may be flushed with purple. Vivid lime-green young leaves appear in early spring, but are seldom affected by either frost or slugs, and the foliage remains delightful through hot weather and well into winter. Effective when planted so the flowering stems grow up through small shrubs. From forests in western China. ‡24 in (60 cm). Z5–7 H7–5. **‘Blue Summit’** Clear, deep blue flowers; may not be distinct from the species.

C. flexuosa Deciduous plant forming a spreading clump or mat from which arise dissected, usually bronze- or purple-tinged leaves up to 4 in (10 cm) long. In late spring and early summer, clusters of slender blue flowers 1 in (2.5 cm) long open on short leafy stems. Grows best in humus-rich soil in a fairly open situation, but the leaves tend to die down in summer, especially in dry weather, which can leave a gap in the border; new leaves then appear in fall. Variable in the wild, some plants being mat-forming, others making a compact clump. Easy to propagate from small pieces. Due to the

propensity of the various cultivars to self-sow and to hybridize, incorrect plants are sometimes sold under the following names, as well as others. From damp deciduous woodlands in western China. ‡8–12 in (20–30 cm). Z6–8 H8–6. **‘Balang Mist’** Clump-forming, with gray-green leaves; the downward-pointing flowers, which are whitish in bud, become palest blue with white tips to the petals. **‘Blue Panda’** Clump-forming, flowering from mid-spring into early fall. **‘China Blue’** Mat-forming, clear sky blue flowers, becoming purplish in cool weather. Tall, but less vigorous. ‡12 in (30 cm). **‘Golden Panda’** Like ‘Blue Panda’ but with yellow leaves, which are brightest during spring. **‘Nightshade’** Leaves are splashed with red along the midrib, flowers light blue. **‘Père David’** Mat-forming, with blue-green leaves that are splashed with red by the midrib; flowers are light greenish blue. ‡6 in (15 cm). **‘Purple Leaf’** Makes a compact mat of reddish purple leaves and purplish blue flowers; ‡6 in (15 cm).

C. linstowiana Fibrous-rooted, usually deciduous plant with blue-green leaves, divided into narrowly oval segments. In early summer and midsummer, light blue or mauve flowers 1 in (2.5 cm) long open in dense spikes at the tips of erect stems. A recent introduction to gardens, but appears reliable and may seed freely. From damp deciduous woods in western China. ‡12 in (30 cm). Z5–7 H7–5

C. lutea syn. *Pseudofumaria lutea* Vigorous and easy-going evergreen plant forming a spreading clump of prettily divided, light green 4–6-in (10–15-cm) leaves. Clusters of short-spurred, bright yellow flowers ⅝ in (1.5 cm) long open from mid-spring to early fall. Seeds freely and can be slightly invasive, but easily controlled. Few plants are better for brightening up a damp, shady corner, and it looks superb in shady stone walls. From shady rocky places in the foothills of the European Alps, and naturalized elsewhere in Europe. ‡12–16 in (30–40 cm). Z5–8 H8–4

C. malkensis Strong-growing tuberous plant with pale green leaves to 3 in (8 cm) long, divided into narrow leaflets. In late spring and early summer, broad-lipped, white flowers 1 in (2.5 cm) across open in loose clusters in the leaf joints. Vigorous enough to naturalize in grass, and often self-seeding. A recent introduction from damp, open woodlands in the Caucasus. ‡4–6 in (10–15 cm). Z5–8 H8–5

C. ochroleuca Strong-growing evergreen plant making a compact clump of leaves up to 4¾ in (12 cm) long, divided into oval light green leaflets, paler in color beneath. White ⅝-in (1.5-cm) flowers, tipped with bright yellow, open in dense clusters from late spring to midsummer or late summer. Tolerates full sun or part-shade, and often self-sowing freely. From limestone rocks in the mountains of

NEW FROM CHINA

Blue corydalis were once difficult to grow and short-lived, honored more in their remains than in their display. With the introduction of *C. flexuosa* from China, gardeners at last had a blue corydalis that anyone could grow.

First found by Père David of *Davidia involucrata* fame in Moupine (now Baoxing) in western China in 1865, it was over a century before this plant was introduced to western gardens. In 1985, American horticulturist Reuben Hatch collected a plant in the Wenhuan Wolong Nature Reserve, often known as the panda reserve, and called it 'Blue Panda'. Although a delightful plant, its tightly clump-forming habit did not lend itself to rapid propagation, so it did not become widely available.

Then, in 1989, James Compton, John d'Arcy, and Martyn Rix collected three more forms in the area of David's original discovery. Their Chinese hosts drove them through woods carpeted with blue but were reluctant to stop so that the visitors could examine the plants. Eventually, however, they were persuaded, and small pieces of three plants were packed in a moss-lined film canister. On their return, the three pieces were passed to three different nurseries which, between them, produced nearly 2,000 plants in two years. The success of this rapid propagation was largely due to the naturally creeping habit of these three forms.

At first grown under the reference numbers originally given to them by the collectors, they were then named 'Purple Leaf' (CD&R528a), 'Père David', (CD&R528b), and 'China Blue' (CD&R528c). Now widely grown in suitable climates all around the world, they have been followed by a further number of new forms collected from the wild, as well as by others that have arisen in gardens.

southern Europe, from Italy to the Balkans. ↕ 12 in (30 cm). Z6–8 H8–6

C. ophiocarpa Large, fibrous-rooted plant making a loose mass of much-divided large, 18 in (45 cm) leaves with gray-green leaflets. Greenish white to pale greenish yellow flowers ½–⅝ in (1–1.5 cm) long are borne in dense clusters at the tips of the stems from late spring to midsummer. From deciduous woodlands in low mountains in Japan, China, Taiwan, and northern India. ↕ 30 in (75 cm). Z5–8 H8–5

C. solida Tuberous-rooted plant forming a clump of erect stems bearing gray-green divided leaves to 3 in (8 cm) long. In mid- and late spring, spikes of pink, mauve, white, or reddish purple flowers ⅜–1 in (1.5–2.5 cm) long, with curved spurs, open in dense spikes. The leafy bract beneath each of the lower flowers is more or less divided. Very variable in flower color, leaf shape, and other characteristics, but most variants are easily grown and make good garden plants for part-shaded areas. Self-seeds, often producing seedlings in a variety of colors. From scrub and open woodlands in northern and central Europe and parts of the Middle East. ↕ 4–10 in (10–25 cm). Z5–7 H7–3. **subsp. incisa** Flowers usually white or pale purple, with more deeply cut, leaflike bracts; from the Balkans. **subsp. solida** Upper bracts are not divided; flowers dull purple. **subsp. solida 'Beth Evans'** Flowers pale pink with almost white spurs. **subsp. solida 'Dieter Schacht'** Compact, with light pink flowers that are flushed deeper pink on the lips. More robust than 'Beth Evans'. **subsp. solida 'George Baker'** Flowers are an unusual brick red color.

C. 'Tory MP' Vigorous plant forming a substantial clump with divided leaves. Reddish stems bear bright blue flowers 1 in (2.5 cm) long from late spring to mid- or late summer and occasionally again in mid-fall. A hybrid between *C. elata* and *C. flexuosa*, combining the best features of each; often proves more reliably perennial than *C. flexuosa*. ↕ 18–24 in (45–60 cm). Z5–7 H7–5

CORYNEPHORUS
Hair grass
POACEAE

Small, tufted, rather pretty grasses, which are good for edging, found in sandy places.

Five perennial and annual species grow on sand dunes and sea coasts from northern Europe to the Mediterranean and to Iran. They are clump-forming, often with inrolled, narrow bluish leaves and either loose or more compact feathery flowerheads.

CULTIVATION Very well-drained, sandy, acidic to neutral soil in a hot, sunny position.

PROPAGATION By division in spring or from seed.

PROBLEMS Usually trouble-free.

C. canescens (Gray or silver hair grass) Forms dense cushions of rough, quill-like gray leaves tinged purple-pink at the base and tightly inrolled, up to 2½ in (6 cm) long. In early summer and midsummer threadlike stems end in soft gray, narrow feathery flowers with purple stamens, 1½–3 in (1.5–8 cm) long. It is best grown in sandy, slightly acidic soil in full sun as an edging to a rock garden, on a dry path, or in a trough with other alpines. A rare grass of coastal sand dunes in Britain to Scandinavia and Russia. Naturalized in northwestern and northeastern US. ↕ 4–14 in (10–35 cm). Z7–10 H10–7

LEFT 1 *Corydalis cava* **2** *C. lutea* **3** *C. malkensis* **4** *C. solida* subsp. *solida* 'Beth Evans' **5** *C. solida* subsp. *solida* 'George Baker'

LEFT *Cosmos atrosanguineus*

almost dry sand, in cool, frost-free conditions.

PROPAGATION By basal cuttings in early spring.

PROBLEMS Slugs and snails, or aphids. Gray mold may be a problem.

C. atrosanguineus syn. *Bidens atrosanguinea* (Chocolate cosmos) Tuberous plant forming a mound of glossy, dark green leaves divided into toothed, angular leaflets and borne on sprawling, branched, deep red stems. The richly chocolate-scented, deep maroon flowerheads, 1¾ in (4.5 cm) across, open from midsummer to mid-fall, each consisting of about eight broad, petal-like ray florets of velvety texture. Originally from open scrub in Mexico, but now extinct in the wild (*see* Extinction and back). ‡16–24 in (40–60 cm). Z7–11 H12–1

COSMOS
ASTERACEAE

Tender summer-flowering plant that bring a unique color and a delightful scent to the garden.

About 26 species of perennial and annual plants grow in dry scrubland in the southern US and Central America, of which only one perennial species is cultivated in gardens. These plants have tuberous roots similar to those of *Dahlia*, supporting branching stems with paired, divided leaves. Solitary, long-stalked flowers with broad, petal-like ray florets open over a long period from summer through fall.

CULTIVATION Grow in full sun and well-drained, fertile soil. In cooler areas, it is safest to lift the tubers for winter and store them in in

EXTINCTION AND BACK

Cosmos atrosanguineus, widely grown in gardens around the world, is now thought to be extinct in its native Mexican pine and oak woods. To compound the problem, all plants in cultivation are derived from a single specimen that produces no seed when fertilized with its own pollen. None of the huge number of plants grown in gardens over the years had ever produced a single seed, so there was little point in considering reintroducing it to its natural habitat—it would be unable to develop a self-sustaining population.

However, in 1996 a fully fertile form was discovered in New Zealand by geneticist Dr. Russell Poulter of the University of Otago, thus creating the prospect of this extinct species being reintroduced into the wild. It also, of course, opens up the possibility of this appealing species being listed in seed catalogs and of new forms being introduced in the future.

CRAMBE
BRASSICACEAE

Large-scale plants easily grown in a sunny spot, with handsome, textured foliage and an abundance of small white flowers in summer.

Twenty species of sizable annuals and perennials related to the common cabbage are found in a range of habitats in Europe, Asia, Macaronesia, and tropical Africa. Two of the fully hardy European species are well established as garden plants of special merit. From deep, fleshy roots beneath a central crown, they typically form a mound of large, rounded or lobed, deciduous leaves. Above the foliage rise sturdy, branching flowerheads bearing masses of small, scented, white flowers with four petals, followed by green, beadlike fruits.

CULTIVATION For an open, sunny position in well-drained soil.

PROPAGATION By division or root cuttings, or from seed.

PROBLEMS Generally trouble-free but leaves may be damaged by cabbage white caterpillars.

C. cordifolia Resembling a vast gypsophila, this magnificent crambe needs plenty of space for its robust clumps of foliage, 5 ft (1.5 m) or more across, and its galaxy of flowers. The large, dark green basal leaves are heart-shaped, up to 24 in (60 cm) wide, with a wrinkled and bristly surface. In midsummer, a delicate, veil-like profusion of widely spaced, tiny white flowers floats above the foliage, suspended on huge, branching sprays. Each flower in the immense cluster is just ½ in (1 cm) across and sweetly

RIGHT **1** *Crambe cordifolia* **2** *C. maritima* **3** *Crepis incana*

scented. Performs best in well-drained, deep, fertile soil and a sunny position, but tolerates light shade. Strong wind may spoil the flowerheads. Spent flowering stems can be left on the plant, providing winter interest with their green pods. Native to the Caucasus, from steppes and open, rocky landscapes. ↕ 6½ ft (2 m). Z6–9 H9–6

C. maritima (Sea kale) Rich purple shoots unfurl in spring and develop into a striking mound of undulating, blue-gray foliage with a distinct look of the sea. Roundish in outline, the wavy-edged leaves are about 12 in (30 cm) long; they are hairless, slightly succulent, and covered with a silvery bloom. Thick, upright, flowering stems emerge from the clump, and by early summer the leaves are almost hidden beneath an impressive froth of fragrant white flowers. The small, ¼–⅜-in (1–1.5-cm) flowers are packed densely onto large, rounded heads. A coastal plant found mainly near the high tide line on sand or gravel beaches, it is adapted to survive salt spray and some degree of burial. Drought-resistant; suitable for seaside gardens. From western Europe, including the British Isles, as well as the Baltic region and the Black Sea. ↕ 16–24 in (40–60 cm). Z6–9 H9–6

CREPIS

Hawk's beard

ASTERACEAE

Orange and pink dandelion lookalikes for open, sunny situations.

There are around 200 species of predominantly yellow-flowered perennials and annuals native to the Northern Hemisphere, the majority being weeds or of a weedlike appearance; they contain milky sap. The leaves may be smooth-edged or deeply lobed and are either basal or borne on the stems—species vary greatly. The solitary flowerheads are borne on branched stems and consist only of ray florets.

CULTIVATION The two species below need an open, sunny, well-drained position and may be short-lived.

PROPAGATION From seed sown in spring at 59°F (15°C).

PROBLEMS Usually trouble-free.

C. aurea (Golden hawk's beard) Rosette-forming perennial with toothed, almost hairless, dandelion-like leaves to 4 in (10 cm). The flowerheads, to 1¼ in (3 cm) across, are orange with a paler eye and are normally borne singly on unbranched leafless stems from early summer to early fall. From the Alps and mountains of central southern Europe. ↕ 4–12 in (10–30 cm). Z5–7 H7–4

C. incana (Pink dandelion) The deeply toothed, dandelion-like leaves of this rosette-forming perennial are gray-hairy and grow to 5 in (13 cm). Pink flowerheads, to 1¼ in (3 cm) across, on branched leafy stems from early summer to early fall. From Greece. ↕ 4–6 in (10–15 cm). Z5–7 H7–4

CROCOSMIA

IRIDACEAE

Reliable, bold plants that bring fiery color to the border in mid- to late summer.

Eight species, all but one from South Africa, usually grow in moist soil in grassland or light forest shade. Forming a string of crocuslike corms with papery covering, each year's new corm being produced on top of the last, slender, shoelacelike growths may also extend from the corm for some distance and produce new plants at their tips. Round stems arise from the corm and carry deciduous, narrow, more or less sword-shaped foliage that may be smooth, with a central midrib, or distinctly pleated. The bases of the leaves clasp the stem, which is often branched above the foliage, so that the stem is visible only as it emerges from the topmost leaf to carry the flowers.

From midsummer the stems carry flowers that have three outer and three inner petals and may be starry or funnel-shaped, on upright or arching stems. The flower color is usually orange or red, though yellow is common, and many hybrids have purple or maroon spots and blotches. They are useful in the garden because of their attractive, upright foliage, producing sheaves of green, as well as their vibrant flowers, which bring vivid color in late summer.

There is an unusual degree of confusion among the cultivars of *Crocosmia*, with a number grown under incorrect names (*see* Hybrids and Confusions).

CULTIVATION Best in sunny places but most dislike soil that is dry in summer; in dry soil they often flower poorly and are susceptible to red spider mite. Most can be left undisturbed for several years but if flowering diminishes, they should be divided in early spring. They rarely need staking. Dry corms often fail to establish well, so buy growing plants, preferably in bloom so you can be sure they are correctly named. If you are starting with dry corms, plant early so they rehydrate well before warm temperatures encourage them to grow. In the past, many cultivars were considered to be frost-tender but have since proved hardier than previously believed. *Crocosmia paniculata*, *C. pottsii*, and *C. masoniorum* are the most cold-tolerant species, and *C. aurea* is the most tender, a trait that may be passed to its *C.* x *crocosmiiflora* hybrids, which may grow in mild falls only to be cut back by frost. In cold areas the hybrids of *C. paniculata* and *C. masoniorum* such as 'Severn Sunrise' should be planted first and then, if successful, the *C.* x *crocosmiiflora* hybrids can be tried. Deep planting will help plants overwinter in cold areas.

PROPAGATION Divide in early spring. Do not raise from seed—they are unlikely to come true.

PROBLEMS Red spider mite, especially in hot dry summers. *C. pottsii* in particular can sometimes prove invasive (*see* Naturalizing and Invasiveness, *p. 144*).

HYBRIDS AND CONFUSIONS

Crocosmias have had a confusing nomenclatural history. Now included in *Crocosmia* are plants that have previously been known as *Antholyza, Curtonus, Montbretia,* and *Tritonia*. To make matters worse, two of the hybrids have unusually confusing names, *C.* x *crocosmiiflora* and *C.* x *crocosmoides*, and there is also confusion among various groups of cultivars. Many similar, and not-so-similar, cultivars have been, and still are, sold under incorrect names.

This confusion has led to uncertainty over the parentage of some hybrids. 'Emberglow' and 'Vulcan', for example, are both said by raiser Alan Bloom to be hybrids between *C.* x *crocosmiiflora* and *C. masoniorum*, but more recent study has shown 'Emberglow' to be a cross between *C. pottsii* and *C. paniculata* and 'Vulcan' to be *C. aurea* x *C. paniculata*.

There is a long history of *Crocosmia* introductions. Victor Lemoine, the French horticulturist, was the first to introduce a range of hybrids, in the later years of the 19th century. The Earlham Hybrids from George Davison, George Henley, and Jack Fitt in Norfolk dominated the early decades of the 20th century. Alan Bloom rekindled interest with 'Lucifer' and other introductions from the 1960s, and more recently, Phillipa Browne, formerly of Treasures of Tenbury nursery, Worcestershire, raised a number, mostly with smoky foliage. In Holland, at various times over the years, breeders have been at work, and enthusiasts in Britain are also now making introductions.

***C.* 'Amberglow'** Bronze foliage sets off the 1½-in (4-cm) soft orange flowers, which are spotted with purple around the cream-colored center. A recent hybrid between 'Jackanapes' and 'Solfatare' raised by Phillipa Browne, in England. ↕ 28 in (70 cm). Z6–9 H9–6

***C.* Bressingham Beacon ('Blos')** Upward-facing red flowers, gold in the throat, are carried on horizontal branchlets. Rather slow to increase. Hybrid between *C. masoniorum* and *C. paniculata* raised by Alan Bloom in England. ↕ 36 in (90 cm). Z6–9 H9–6

***C.* 'Bressingham Blaze'** Rather narrow orange-red flowers with yellow throats are carried on unbranched spikes. Hybrid between *C. masoniorum* and *C. paniculata* raised by Alan Bloom in England. ↕ 24 in (60 cm). Z6–9 H9–6

C.* x *crocosmiiflora The familiar montbretia, with large bright orange flowers, paler in the throat, freely produced on branched stems above pale foliage only ⅜–⅝ in (8–15 mm) wide. Adaptable to both sun and light shade, and vigorous in growth, this hybrid between *C. aurea* and *C. pottsii* was first created at the French nursery of Victor Lemoine in 1879. It inherits its vigor from *C. pottsii* and is widely naturalized (*see* Naturalizing and Invasiveness, *p. 144*) and too vigorous for many gardens. Many of Lemoine's hybrids are still popular today and they formed the basis for the work of later hybridizers. ↕ 14–36 in (35–90 cm). Z6–9 H9–3. **'Babylon'** Bold, red flowers, 2¾ in (7 cm) across, with a dark, maroon ring round a yellow center. Can be uncomfortably vigorous. ↕ 32 in (80 cm). **'Bicolore'** *see* 'Jackanapes'.

BELOW *Crocosmia* x *crocosmiiflora* 'Emily McKenzie'

ECHOING ORANGES

BRIGHT AND BRILLIANT plant associations are now becoming fashionable as an alternative to the cool pastels that have always found favor with gardeners. Here, the deep purple foliage belongs to *Canna indica* 'Purpurea'—not so dark as to be deadening, while not so bright as to be distracting. It is topped by small orange flowers, but these are produced rather sparsely.

In front, *Crocosmia x crocosmioides* 'Castle Ward Late' repeats the color of the canna flowers but in spectacular profusion. The crocosmia flower stems arch across the vertical of the cannas and the slim fresh green foliage stands out against the purple paddles. This combination will work on a much smaller scale than illustrated here, with just one canna and a few crocosmia plants.

'Canary Bird' Light yellow 1-in (2.5-cm) flowers over narrow, green leaves on vigorous plants. Similar to 'Norwich Canary' but with narrower foliage. Introduced by Broadleigh Gardens in England. ↕24 in (60 cm). 'Carmin Brillant' Carmine red flowers, probably originating in Germany. Has been sold as 'James Coey'. ↕28 in (70 cm). 'Citronella' Pretty pale yellow with two maroon marks near the center. Plants bought under this name are rarely correct and may be 'Golden Fleece', 'Golden Sheaf' or 'Honey Angels', among others. Tall and vigorous. An Earlham Hybrid. ↕36–48 in (90–120 cm). 'Columbus' Fine and distinctive with 1½-in- (4-cm-) wide, gold flowers with small, dark blotches near the center, opening from violet bracts. ↕32 in (80 cm). 'Constance' Impressive Dutch bicolor. The outer petals are orange on the outside and red on the inside, the inner petals are orange with a yellow center. ↕28 in (70 cm). 'Custard Cream' Pale yellow flowers and green foliage, but requires good growing conditions or plants and flowers will be small and fade away. The similar 'Morning Light' is easier to grow well. Raised by

Phillipa Browne in England. ↕36 in (90 cm). 'Debutante' Small blooms face upward and are orange when first open but fade to pink with a yellow eye; the outsides are deep orange. Raised by Phillipa Browne. ↕32 in (80 cm). 'Dusky Maiden' Brownish rusty orange flowers above bronze foliage on dwarf plants. Raised by Phillipa Browne. ↕24 in (60 cm). 'Emily McKenzie' Large 2¾-in (7-cm) flowers in rich orange with crimson-purple blotches at the base of the petals, especially the inner three. The large flowers usually face horizontally or downward. One of the most popular and increasingly seen as a commercial cut flower. ↕30 in (75 cm). 'George Davison' Well-branched stems carry large 2¾-in (7-cm) pale yellow flowers touched with orange on tall and vigorous plants. One of the earliest to bloom. This name is often used for plants of 'Golden Sheaf' from which it was bred, 'Citronella', 'Golden Fleece', and 'Norwich Canary'. The first introduction from the eponymous Norfolk breeder whose triumph was 'Star of the East'. ↕36–48 in (90–120 cm). 'Gerbe d'Or' Tubular flowers of rich golden yellow on stocky plants,

vigorous and floriferous. One of the earliest hybrids, introduced by Lemoine in 1885. ↕24 in (60 cm). 'Golden Glory' Lovely apricot-yellow flowers with a dark red ring around the throat. ↕28 in (70 cm). 'His Majesty' Flowers up to 3 in (8 cm) across that are yellow in the center, shading through orange to scarlet at the tips with dark marks around the eye. Bred by George Henley and one of the best of the Earlham Hybrids (*see* Hybrids and Confusions, *p.141*) ↕28 in (70 cm). 'Jackanapes' Short, with masses of small, rather tubular flowers with dark orange outer petals and yellow inner petals. The leaves are often pale green. Introduced under this name by Alan Bloom, although almost certainly the true 'Bicolore' dating from 1895. ↕24 in (60 cm). 'James Coey' Strong-growing plant with deep orange-red 4 in (10 cm) flowers, blotched with crimson around the pale orange eye. Named for the owner of Slieve Donard Nursery in Northern Ireland. 'Carmin Brillant' has been sold under this name and these two, plus 'Mrs. Geoffrey Howard', are much confused in gardens and nurseries. The true plant may no longer be in cultivation. Z6–9 H9–6 'Jessie'

Prolific orange flowers, tinted with pink, with a pale yellow eye and purple spots. ↕28 in (70 cm). 'Lady Hamilton' Tall, with masses of yellow flowers with curved tubes, slightly orange in the throat at first and becoming peachier with age. An Earlham Hybrid raised by George Davison. ↕40 in (100 cm). 'Météore' Large, rounded 3-in (8-cm) flowers, opening dark yellow from dark red buds. An old Lemoine cultivar, from 1887. ↕32 in (80 cm). 'Mrs. Geoffrey Howard' Large, deep orange flowers with a yellow-flushed throat. Similar to 'James Coey', and may be the true plant. ↕24 in (60 cm). 'Norwich Canary' Small yellow flowers just 1 in (2.5 cm) across, often supplied as 'George Davison'. ↕24 in (60 cm). 'Queen Alexandra' Large, yellow-centered golden-orange flowers with reflexed petals on tall upright plants. An Earlham Hybrid. ↕36–48 in (90–120 cm). 'Queen of Spain' Flowers earlier than most with large 3½ in (9 cm) blooms of deep orange-red on red stems. Similar to, but deeper in color than, 'Star of the East'. One of the finest and most popular. ↕28 in (70 cm). 'Saracen' Bright red 1½-in (4-cm) flowers with neat yellow centers above bronze foliage. Raised by Phillipa Browne. ↕28 in (70 cm). 'Solfatare' Pale yellow flowers are freely produced above bronze foliage. Named, on account of the color combination, for the volcanic area south of Naples. Often misspelled, most often as 'Solfaterre'. Attractive and very useful in borders, a parent of the hybrids raised by Phillipa Browne. ↕24 in (60 cm). 'Star of the East' One of the most spectacular, with golden-orange 4 in (10 cm) flowers with a yellow eye opening from orange-red buds. An Earlham hybrid raised by George Davison, who turned to apple breeding after raising this, thinking it could never be surpassed. ↕28 in (70 cm). 'Sulphurea' Deep yellow, otherwise unusually similar to one parent, *C. pottsii*, and as vigorous but with larger flowers and more prolific. From Victor Lemoine. ↕28–40 in (70–100 cm). 'Sultan' Deep red, 1½-in (4-cm) flowers with purple-spotted, yellow centers, bronze foliage. A hybrid between 'Jackanapes' and 'Solfatare' raised by Phillipa Browne. ↕28 in (70 cm). 'Venus' Flowers with reddish outer petals and deep yellow inner petals, tipped with red. ↕28 in (70 cm).

C. x crocosmoides syn. *C. latifolia* Faintly pleated leaves, about two-thirds the height of the stems, with a sheath of openly branched arching stems carrying generous quantities of trumpet shaped, slightly curved orange-red flowers. These are relatively small, at ¼ in (5 mm) across, slightly flared, and with the upper petal longer than the others. Increasing more slowly than *C. x crocosmiiflora*, this hybrid between *C. aurea* and *C. paniculata* was created by Max Leichtlin and was distributed in 1890. ↕20–40 in (50–100 cm). Z6–9 H9–6 'Castle Ward Late' Vigorous with pleated leaves and flowers late in the season. 40 in (100 cm). 'Vulcan'

Deep orange-red flowers with a yellow
eye. ↕ 48 in (120 cm).

C. 'Emberglow' Very dark, dusky red,
tubular flowers above pleated foliage.
Unusually for a hybrid, it sets seeds
readily and is sold in fruit as a cut
"flower." Introduced by Blooms
Nursery in England, a hybrid of
C. pottsii and *C. paniculata*. ↕ 36 in
(90 cm). Z6–9 H9–6

C. 'Firebird' Upward-facing deep
red flowers on arching stems. A
hybrid between *C. masoniorum* and
C. x *crocosmiiflora* and generally similar
to *C. masoniorum* but with larger
flowers. Raised in England by Alan
Bloom. ↕ 30 in (75 cm). Z6–9 H9–6

C. 'Honey Angels' Small, trumpet-
shaped yellow flowers on vigorous
plants. Sometimes confused with
'Golden Fleece', 'Citronella', and the
other small, yellow-flowered cultivars, it
is basically a yellow-flowered *C. pottsii*.
↕ 28 in (70 cm). Z6–9 H9–6

C. Jenny Bloom (**'Blacro'**) Upright,
eventually arching, very elegant and
floriferous plant with branched stems
of upward-facing yellow flowers. A
hybrid of *C. pottsii* from Alan Bloom
selected by, and named for, his daughter.
↕ 30 in (90 cm). Z6–9 H9–6

C. 'John Boots' Yellow flowers that
open to flat, slightly paler-centered
stars 1½ in (4 cm) across. Increasingly
popular Dutch hybrid. ↕ 28 in (70 cm).
Z6–9 H9–6

C. 'Jupiter' Pale orange flowers
streaked with deep orange. A hybrid
of *C. masoniorum* and *C. crocosmiiflora*.
↕ 28 in (70 cm). Z6–9 H9–6

C. latifolia see *C.* x *crocosmoides*

C. 'Lucifer' The best-known of all
crocosmia cultivars, with masses of
brilliant, deep red flowers along the
top of the branching stems. This plant
is vigorous and it is said to breed
true from seed—which seems highly
unlikely. Hybrid of *C. masoniorum* and
C. paniculata. Introduced in England
by Alan Bloom in 1969. ↕ 4 in
(120 cm). Z6–9 H9–6

C. 'Marcotijn' Vigorous, sometimes
overly so, with orange-red flowers
featuring a dark ring around the eye.
Sometimes sold as 'Sonate'. Hybrid of
C. masoniorum and *C. pottsii*. ↕ 40 in
(100 cm). Z6–9 H9–6

C. 'Mars' Deep red flowers borne in
compact spikes. A Dutch hybrid of
C. masoniorum and *C. paniculata*. ↕ 24 in
(60 cm). Z6–9 H9–6

C. masoniorum Chains of corms
produce pleated, bright green leaves

RIGHT 1 *Crocosmia* x *crocosmiiflora*
'George Davison' **2** *C.* x *crocosmiiflora*
'Star of the East' **3** *C.* 'Lucifer'
4 *C. masionorum* **5** *C. masionorum*
'Rowallane Yellow' **6** *C.* 'Spitfire'

NATURALIZING AND INVASIVENESS

Some crocosmias are extremely vigorous, especially the original hybrid, *C. x crocosmiiflora*, usually known as montbretia. Raised in France in 1879, it was first found in the wild in 1911 and in recent years it has spread to areas with warm, moist climates, favorable for aggressive growth. Other especially vigorous forms include *C. pottsii* and its cultivars 'Red King' and 'Red Star', *C. x crocosmiiflora* 'Meteore' and 'Marcotijn', and *C. paniculata*, first recorded in the wild in 1961 and now spreading in many areas.

Montbretia is a familiar sight, especially where there is moisture, and is often seen along riverbanks and moist to wet roadside areas. Although some seed is produced, spread is usually from corms moved by soil disruption. The corms easily break apart when dug and some corms usually remain creating more plants the next year. However, its lack of hardiness prevents it from being a problem in zones below about 6.

This plant is invasive to the warm and moist areas of North America such as parts of California. Gardeners in these areas will find that they need to thin and divid *Crocosmia* every couple of years, and should watch it carefully.

and slightly taller arching stems, usually with a few branches, crowded with upward-facing orange flowers all pointed toward the tip of the stem. Vigorous and forming dense clumps, it extends by underground shoots and flowers freely. Tolerates drier conditions than most crocosmias. Found in only a few places in the Transkei, South Africa. ‡ 32 in (80 cm). Z6–9 H9–2. **'Dixter Flame'** Red flowers. **'Rowallane Yellow'** Bright yellow flowers.

C. **'Mistral'** Stems crowded with red flowers, similar to *C. masoniorum* 'Dixter Flame' but this plant is a Dutch hybrid between *C. masoniorum* and *C. paniculata*. ‡ 40 in (100 cm). Z6–9 H9–6

C. paniculata syn. *Antholyza paniculata* Bold plant with short chains of corms carrying distinctly pleated foliage. The branched, erect or sometimes slightly arching stems are topped with two rows of orange-red flowers with curved tubes lining the horizontal tips of the stems. Although the flowers are small, the plant makes quite a feature. Easy to grow and tolerates some dryness in summer. A parent of 'Lucifer' and other fine hybrids. From eastern South Africa. ‡ 48 in (120 cm). Z6–9 H9–2

C. pottsii Corms, in short chains, carry flat sword-shaped foliage with a noticeable central midrib. This is topped by rather lax, arching, branching flowering stems that carry up to 30 nodding, orange-red flowers in two rows. Not commonly grown but is easy and vigorous and can spread

too widely when happy. It prefers moist soil and may be suitable for wet soil and as a marginal pond plant. Hybrids with the larger flowered *C. aurea* have led to the many cultivars of *C. x crocosmiiflora*. Grows near shady streams in eastern South Africa. ‡ 40 in (100 cm). Z6–9 H9–6 **'Culzean Peach'** syn. 'Culzean Pink' Vigorous, with masses of small, rather tubular flowers of soft orange, tinged with pink. Perhaps a self-sown seedling of *C. pottsi*. Pronounced "kill-ain." ‡ 42 in (110 cm).

C. **'Severn Sunrise'** Vigorous but neat, upright plant with upward-facing orange flowers with yellow eyes. The flowers fade after opening and take on a pink tinge. A hybrid of *C. masoniorum* and *C. paniculata*. ‡ 40 in (100 cm). Z6–9 H9–6

C. **'Sonate'** see *C.* 'Marcotijn'

C. **'Spitfire'** Neat and prolific plant with flaring, fiery orange flowers. An Alan Bloom hybrid of *C. masoniorum* and *C. x crocosmiiflora* from 1966. ‡ 28 in (70 cm). Z6–9 H9–6

C. **'Tangerine Queen'** Vigorous with rich orange flowers on upright stems among compact pleated leaves. A Dutch hybrid of *C. masoniorum* and *C. pottsii*, introduced by Gary Dunlop. ‡ 40 in (100 cm). Z6–9 H9–6

C. **'Voyager'** Neat, floriferous plant forming tight clumps with relatively large 2½-in (6-cm) rich yellow flowers. Robust but slow to increase. ‡ 30 in (75 cm). Z6–9 H9–6

C. **Walberton Yellow** (**'Walcroy'**) Small bright yellow flowers on slow-growing plants. Probably a hybrid of *C. masoniorum*, which it resembles. Raised by David Tristram of Walberton Nursery in England; two other cultivars with the Walberton prefix were withdrawn and stock destroyed by the breeder because he considered them inferior. ‡ 28 in (70 cm). Z6–9 H9–2

'Zeal Tan' Prolific, bearing orange-red flowers with a yellow eye. ‡ 24 in (60 cm). Z6–9 H9–6

CRUCIANELLA *see* PHUOPSIS

CRYPTOTAENIA
Hornwort, Mitsuba
APIACEAE

Creeping ground-cover plant for moist places with clusters of tiny white flowers in summer.

There are four species with a wide distribution across the north temperate zone to the African mountains. The stout, creeping roots carry leaf stalks that clasp the base of the hollow stems and bold leaflets divided into three broad lobes. Higher up the stem, the leaves are less divided or may be toothed or smooth-edged. The stems are topped with clusters of tiny white

flowerheads in summer. These plants usually grow wild in moist places such as rich woodlands or streamsides; often cultivated in Japan as a salad crop or herbal seasoning and for the edible roots. It is rather surprising, then, that the leaves may irritate the skin. ⚠

CULTIVATION Best in moisture-retentive soil in sun or part-shade; hates drought.

PROPAGATION From sowing fresh seed in fall, by dividing the roots in spring, or lifting and transplanting young, self-sown seedlings.

PROBLEMS Usually trouble-free.

C. japonica Upright, rather succulent, but often short-lived plants with stout, branching, hollow stems; the leaves are divided into three broad, more or less equal-sized, oval, slightly lobed, 2–4-in (5–10-cm) segments. The flowerheads are unusual in the family in being asymmetrical—the tiny individual flowers are held on stalks of differing lengths. Needs moisture-retentive soil, where it will self-seed freely. Not often grown except in the vegetable or herb garden. From Japan. ‡ 28–36 in (70–90 cm). Z6–9 H9–4. **f. *atropurpurea*** The whole plant is dramatically flushed with deep purple, almost black; seedlings may vary in color.

CYNARA
ASTERACEAE

Spectacular foliage and handsome flowers are provided by this statuesque sun-lover.

About ten species of robust, thistlelike, deciduous plants grow in dry grassland and waste places in the Mediterranean region and the Canary Islands; only one is commonly grown in gardens. Huge, white-hairy, spiny-margined leaves grow in a bold, arching mass, from which a sturdy, branched, leafy flowering stem arises. The large, thistlelike, violet-blue flowerheads open in summer and early fall.

CULTIVATION Thrives in any well-drained soil in full sun. A thick winter mulch of dry pine bark or needles will help survival of *Cynara* in cold areas.

PROPAGATION By basal cuttings in spring, by root cuttings, or from seed.

PROBLEMS Slugs and snails may damage the young growth in early spring; aphids may infest plants.

C. cardunculus (Cardoon) (Artichoke) Vigorous plant forming a striking clump of arching, deeply cut, spiny leaves to 20 in (50 cm) long, covered

RIGHT 1 *Cynara cardunculus*
2 *C. cardunculus* 'Florist Cardy'
3 *C. cardunculus* Scolymus Group

with woolly gray or white hairs. From early summer to early fall, glowing violet-blue flowerheads 2½–3 in (6–8 cm) across, with spiny bracts, open on the branched, woolly stems. A very handsome plant, sometimes grown for the foliage alone, the flowering stems being cut off at the base. Also makes a good cut flower, fresh or dried. The leaf stalks and midribs may be eaten if blanched. From rocky places and dry grasslands in southwestern Europe and North Africa. ↕5–6½ ft (1.5–2 m). Z7–10 H9–1. **'Cardy'** Although used as a cultivar name, it appears to be an alternative common name for the species in Europe. **'Florist Cardy'** Extra-large flowerheads, grown for cutting. **Scolymus Group** syn. *C. scolymus* (Globe artichoke) Developed as a vegetable; both the rounded fleshy bracts under the flowerheads and the flowerhead base are cooked. ↕3¼–6½ ft (1–2 m).

C. scolymus see *C. cardunculus* Scolymus Group

CYNOGLOSSUM
Hound's tongue
BORAGINACEAE

A pleasing and popular border perennial among mostly short-lived annuals and biennials.

Cynoglossum has some 50–60 species of hardy to half-hardy deciduous perennials, biennials, and annuals. They are found in a wide range of habitats, from woodlands and grasslands to waste ground and seaside, throughout the temperate regions and mountains in the tropics. Usually upright in habit, they have hairy, long-stalked basal leaves and alternate stem leaves, usually lance-shaped to oblong or oval. The flowers are either funnel-shaped or cylindrical, with a short tube and five spreading, overlapping lobes, carried in one-sided terminal clusters; they are usually blue or purple. The seeds are covered with hooked spines; in the wild they are dispersed by attaching to animal fur or human clothing. This is a good plant for a herbaceous or mixed border. Some species attract bees.

CULTIVATION Will grow on any well-drained soil, but prefers deep, fertile soil. Most require full sun.

PROPAGATION Mainly from seed in fall or spring, although some species can be propagated by division or root cuttings.

PROBLEMS Can be short-lived.

C. nervosum White-hairy plant with basal rosettes of narrow, oval or oblong leaves to 1½ in (4 cm) long, and upright stems clothed in lance-shaped leaves, the lower ones to 4¾ in (12 cm) in length, all bright green. Branching sprays of many small deep blue flowers, each to ⅜ in (8 mm) across, similar to those of forget-me-nots, with scales in the throat, in early summer. Needs a

sunny position in any well-drained soil that is not too fertile; in rich soil, plants tend to flop. From the Himalaya. ↕24–32 in (60–80 cm). Z5–8 H8–5

CYPERUS
Umbrella sedge
CYPERACEAE

U mbrella-like rosettes of leaves and flowers top the stems of these sedges, hailing mainly from the warmer parts of the world.

About 500 species of perennials, and some annuals, are native to wet areas in mainly warm and tropical regions. There is some confusion in the naming of the different species. They are clump-forming or slowly creeping, sometimes with nut-shaped tubers; flat grasslike leaves, often with rough edges, sometimes form a basal tuft. The flower stems are solid and triangular and are topped with a rosette of flat, pointed leaves, with the flowers rising out of the joint of each leaf like the spokes of an upturned umbrella. Gardeners are beginning to appreciate that many are hardier than was thought.

CULTIVATION Best in moist soil in a warm, sheltered situation. In colder areas, grow in rich, moist soil or heavy clay loam in a pot standing in shallow water in a sunny situation, or place as an exotic addition to the water garden.

PROPAGATION By division in spring or by upper stem cuttings; alternatively, remove the seed heads and turn them upside down in water until new plantlets emerge.

PROBLEMS Usually trouble-free.

C. eragrostis (American galingale) Broad, pale, evergreen rushlike leaves up to 24 in (60 cm) long form a basal tuft, from which grow the flower stems. These are topped in mid- and late summer by an upturned umbrella of long, pointed leaves and short-stemmed spiky bunches of yellowish to pale green flowers. Prefers moist conditions but is a prolific self-seeder even in drier areas. Needs protection in cold areas over winter. Native to tropical America. ↕24 in (60 cm). Z9–10 H10–9

C. esculentus (Tiger nut) Bright green evergreen leaves ½ in (1 cm) wide and up to 36 in (90 cm) long are matched in height by the flower stems; these are topped by clusters of many lightweight yellowish brown to green flowerheads, ripening to reddish gray seed heads. An invasive root system has made this sedge a pernicious weed in some temperate regions. These plant needs damp, sandy soil; grow in a large pot to prevent spreading. Found in southern Europe to eastern Asia and North America; cultivated in some areas for the edible tuberous roots. ↕36 in (90 cm). Z4–9 H9–4

C. glaber A short-lived perennial with a basal clump of 18-in (45-cm) leaves ⅛–¼ in (3–6 mm) wide. The flower stem is topped from late spring to early winter with an umbrella of long, pointed leaves and short spokes ending in up to eight dense flower clusters. Good for cutting. Hardier than many, it does best in moist soil or pond margins in sun or part-shade. From central and southeast Europe and western Asia. ↕10–20 in (25–50 cm). Z7–10 H10–7

C. longus (Sweet galingale) Sweet-smelling, creeping, often invasive roots ⅛–½ in (3–10 mm) thick carry clumps of shiny, bright green evergreen leaves that are rough-edged, elegantly arching, and ½ in (1 cm) wide. In late summer and early fall the stems bear gracefully bending umbrellas of long, thin leaves

ABOVE 1 *Cynoglossum nervosum*
2 *Cyperus eragrostis*

and delicate sprays of spiky, olive green to brown flowers, ripening to black-brown seed heads. A graceful plant for the margins of lakes and large ponds, or grow in a large pot to prevent problems from the invasive roots. Native to northern temperate regions. ↕5 ft (1.5 m). Z3–11 H12–1

C. rotundus Edible tubers and thin roots form clumps with narrow, ¼ in (6 mm) wide leaves. From early summer to early fall, spiky flowers in reddish brown, edged with green, form umbrella-like heads with pointed green leaves on a slightly arching flower stem. Similar to *C. longus* but with edible tubers and fatter roots. Grows best in moist sandy soil. From southern and western central Europe. ↕4–24 in (10–60 cm). Z9–11 H11–9

CYPRIPEDIUM
Lady's-slipper
ORCHIDACEAE

S howy spring orchids with balloonlike pouches guaranteed to make visitors think you are a horticultural magician.

The most beautiful of garden orchids, the temperate lady's-slippers have a reputation for being difficult to grow, although in fact many are relatively easy. Some 45–50 species are found worldwide, the majority in China, also through Europe and the Americas to the Arctic Circle. They need climates with distinct seasons and a two-to-three-month dormancy at near or below freezing. Deciduous, with a shallow underground rhizome forming a chain of yearly growths, most have two or more broadly elliptical, soft, ribbed, strongly veined leaves that are sometimes hairy, twisted up along an erect stem. Up to 12 (but usually one to three) exotic-looking spring flowers last one or two weeks. The broad topmost petal is flanked by long, narrower, sometimes twisted or Mandarin-mustached, side petals with a bold pouch beneath. Petal colors are often dramatically different from that of the prominent shoelike lip pouch.

The lip pouches are what truly distinguish *Cypripedium*. They range from deep plum to red, yellow, pink, green, and white, with veining and mottling, and appear to be inflated with air. The pouch is often scented. It entices pollinators, usually bees, to fall into the circular and slippery mouth opening, forcing them to crawl out by the easiest escape route past the pollen, which latches on for a ride to the next flower. Related to the tropical slipper orchids, *Paphiopedilum* and *Phragmipedium*, all three are sufficiently different from other orchids for some taxonomists to wish to place them in an entirely new family. Many of the available cypripediums are hybrids (*see* Choosing Cypripedium).

Certain species, such as *C. acaule*, are a huge challenge to grow, but others are much less demanding and

CHOOSING CYPRIPEDIUM

Sometimes even the supposedly easy lady's-slipper species can be difficult; adaptability is the issue. Many species have an extensive natural distribution and may grow in dry woodlands in one area, while the same species chooses much wetter, colder sites in another. The trick to finding tolerant garden plants may lie in buying offspring from crosses of the same species, but from different climate zones.

For beginners, and even the avid gardener, the real key to success is to grow hybrids rather than species. Growing hybrids not only helps to protect species plants in the wild, but hybrids are far more tolerant, with the added attraction of larger flowers in more colors; choices are increasing rapidly. But, as with most orchids, *Cypripedium* hybrids are often very variable, and will only become more variable as further crosses are made; therefore, do not expect your flowers to look exactly like those of the picture in the catalog.

The danger of new garden successes with *Cypripedium* is the greatly increased chance of wild species bring ripped from their native habitats. Beware of inexpensive mature plants, undoubtedly taken from wild populations rather than nursery-propagated; besides the environmental issues, they are a waste of money, since vigor is often poor and infections abound. Beware also the words "nursery-grown" versus "nursery-" or "laboratory-propagated"; "nursery-grown" is highly suspect.

surprisingly rewarding. Nurseries are now successful not only in raising them from seed in laboratories, but also in growing them to large sizes for sale. As new hybrids become more robust and more affordable, cypripediums will be found in far more perennial gardens. In the meantime, given that large plants are expensive, cultural advice is given in some detail below.

Nearly all lady's-slippers are threatened or endangered in at least part of their ranges, but few are endangered everywhere. ⚠

CULTIVATION Humid woodlands that never completely dry out, protected from midday sun, suit most, with loose crumbly soil with a pH between 6.5 and 7.5. If ferns like the conditions, so, probably, will cypripediums. If the soil is heavy clay, add sharp sand and organic matter; add loam and organic matter to sandy soil. Avoid peat. It may be best to replace all of the soil in a large hole with a better mix.

Plant preferably in fall, or early spring, being careful not to break the root tips or expose them to sun or drying winds. Spread the roots out in the top 4 in (10 cm) of soil, with the rhizome just below the surface when mulch is used, ¾ in (2 cm) if not. Roots usually grow horizontally and only go deeper if they are dry. Summer temperatures should not regularly exceed 86°F (30°C) but should fall below 40°F (5°C) for two to three months in winter. Mulch with pine needles in areas where winter conditions mean the soil is subject to several cycles of freezing and thawing.

Cypripediums usually need to be five or six years old to bloom, so buy the largest plants you can afford. Even then, plants can be slow to establish, seeming near death for the first year or so, then finally perking up. Most are hardy to Z3–7 H7–1.

PROPAGATION Most resent division, but divide in fall if you must. Make large divisions—the more growths the better—so that each piece has three years' growth behind it. Never dig them up from the wild. Growing from seed is usually possible only in laboratories.

PROBLEMS Prone to many problems, but most are cultural—frosted growth, waterlogged winter and spring soil, damage to root tips, nutrient deficiencies, and the use of pesticides (which they hate). However, nematodes, whitefly, and squirrels can also be damaging.

C. calceolus (Lady's-slipper orchid, Yellow lady's-slipper orchid) A most widespread species, now distinguished from similar American species; the short, fat rhizome bears three to five

RIGHT 1 *Cypripedium calceolus*
2 *C. kentuckiense* **3** *C. macranthos*
4 *C. reginae*

hairy lily-of-the-valley-like leaves, 2½–7 in (6–18 cm) long, and one to three large flowers, intensely scented of overripe peaches, from late spring to midsummer. The bright yellow pouch, 1½–2½ in (3–6 cm) long, juts forward, often with a green cast, and the slender greenish, usually spirally twisted, petals are overlaid with russet brown to near black. A well-drained site in light shade and a pH of 6.9 are best. From dryish, alkaline slopes or light open woods through Europe to Siberia and Japan. ‡6–28 in (15–70 cm). Z3–7 H7–1

C. formosanum Glorious, and very easy, with an unusual and highly ornamental pair of 8-in (20-cm) fan-shaped, pleated leaves near the top of the stem. Extremely beautiful, single soft pink or white flower with pink or red mottling or spotting; the 2¼–2½ in (5.5–6.5 cm) long pouch looks poked in with a finger, like a balloon the day after the party. Blooming very early, between late winter and late spring, it tolerates higher summer temperatures in warmer climates. In cold areas it is crucial to protect the exceptionally early spring growth from frost damage if it tries to emerge during midwinter thaws. Requires abundant fertilizer, preferring, open, sandy, humus-rich loam in light shade. Spreads widely, often with 6 in (15 cm) between growths. Found in open damp forests of Taiwan. ‡4–12 in (10–30 cm). Z3–7 H7–1

C. Gisela Superb, robust, variable 1991 hybrid. One of the easiest cypripediums to grow, rapidly forming clumps. Large, fairly early (late spring) blooms often variously striped white and cherry with green or red accents, sometimes flushed creamy yellow, with twisted cherry-burgundy petals. Likes regular fertilizer and cool, moist, rich, well-drained soil. A hybrid between *C. macranthos* and *C. parviflorum*. Yellow-flowered forms are sometimes listed as Gisela Yellow ‡14–24 in (35–60 cm). Z3–6 H7–1

C. kentuckiense (Kentucky lady's-slipper) Tall, stately clump-former and the largest-flowered of all—the flower span is up to 8 in (20 cm) with a wide-mouthed pouch the look and size of a chicken egg. One of the latest to open, from late spring to midsummer, its usually solitary flower (there may be up to three), lasts up to three weeks. Raspberry-scented on opening, the pouch is creamy white to butter yellow with contrasting russet petals dangling like twisted shoestrings; topmost petal held over the pouch like an awning. Easy in light to full shade, sandy soil with pH of 6, and moderate moisture; tolerant of higher summer temperatures. From deciduous woods and periodically inundated streamlands from Virginia to Ohio and south to Texas. ‡16–36 in (40–90 cm). Z3–8 H7–1

C. macranthos Flowers usually deep red, purple, sometimes vivid to pale pink or white, on a tall stem, for an exceptional show. The single flower (rarely two) has flat, striped, mustache petals that curve forward; the top petal often falls over the 1¼–2½-in- (3–7-cm-) long,

THE LADY'S-SLIPPER ORCHID

Cypripedium calceolus (lady's-slipper orchid) was reduced to a single wild-growing specimen largely as a result of people picking the flowers for home decoration and for the market, and especially by collecting for gardens. Later, overenthusiastic inspection by those wishing simply to look at what became a celebrated rarity led to compacted soil and damage. The lady's-slipper orchid was declared extinct in 1915—then a single remaining plant was discovered 15 years later.

The road to recovery began with regular protection of that last site, including the presence of wardens during flowering time from the 1970s onward. More recently, this has been augmented by a thoughtfully planned and carefully executed plan of propagation, based on British native stock, and a reintroduction to habitats where the plant is known to have once grown.

Over 1,500 plants have now been reintroduced, and although many fall prey to slugs and the natural perils of the wild, many still survive, and there is now an increasing number of flowering-size plants in various, mostly secret, locations. In addition, there is good news for gardeners, who can now buy plants that have been produced in the laboratory. Although these plants can be expensive, we may now grow these exquisite plants in our gardens without plundering wild populations. A disaster followed by success—but how much simpler it would have been not to have destroyed all but a single plant in the first place.

somewhat checkered pouch. It can be recalcitrant, preferring a pH of 6.5 and a very open mix of coarse particles, low in organic matter, but can take more cold than most. A parent of many spectacular hybrids, it occasionally self-sows at the base of the mother plant. From sloping woods and damp meadows in Asia, China, and Russia. ‡6–18 in (15–45 cm). Z3–8 H7–1. **f. albiflorum** White. **f. rebunense** Pale yellow or cream. **f. speciosum** Pink.

C. parviflorum (Yellow lady slipper) Bright yellow and small-mouthed, the lip pouches vary in size but often exhibit a reddish cast and interior red spotting, and twisted petals of a slightly different color. Used medicinally by Native Americans but can be toxic. var. *parviflorum* (syn. *C. parviflorum*, *C. calceolus* var. *parviflorum*) (Small yellow lady's slipper) Rare and dainty, the one or two flowers have a lip ¾–1¼ in (1.5–3.4 cm) long and purple to maroon petals. Flowers, in late spring and early summer, may be rose-scented or intensely sweet. From neutral to acidic drier woodlands or cold bogs. Especially resents warm winters. From North Carolina to Maine and Wisconsin. ‡4–14 in (10–35 cm). Z3–7 H7–1. var. *pubescens* (syn. *C. pubescens*, *C. calceolus* var. *pubescens*) (Large yellow lady's slipper) Widespread and variable, this easy clumpformer has a large solitary flower with a ½–2½ in (2–6 cm) lip, smelling distinctly musty, for two to three weeks from mid-spring to late summer. Petals yellow or greenish, usually overlaid with rusty-red or dull brown streaks. Prefers neutral pH, up to three hours of direct sun, and can take less moisture than most. From open woods from Minnesota north to the Canadian coast and south to Georgia. ‡4–32 in (10–80 cm). Z3–7 H7–1

C. pubescens see *C. parviflorum* var. *pubescens*

C. reginae (Showy lady's-slipper) An easy-to-grow bicolored beauty. The three to seven hairy, strongly ribbed, lime green leaves, 4–9½ in (10–24 cm) long and 2½–6 in (6–15 cm) wide, cause an allergic reaction in some people. One of the finest American lady's-slippers, the large plants carry a single yellow-centered bloom per stem, from late spring to late summer, depending on the climate, although well-established plants can produce colonies with two flowers per stem and sometimes even multiple stems. The 3 in (7.5 cm) wide flowers have a 1–2 in (2.5–5 cm) long, sprightly held, cherry pink inflated pouch and broad, white, blunt-tipped petals 1–2 in (2.5–5 cm) long and ½–¾ in (1–2 cm) wide. Lip color is more intense in colder seasons. Prefers more moisture than most—keep damp but well-drained in neutral to slightly alkaline, nutrient-rich soil. Avoid midday heat, mulch in order to keep the roots cool, and avoid fertilizer; resents being disturbed. From the margins of swampy woods, cedar bogs, wet open ditches, and meadows from Newfoundland to New England south to North Carolina, west to North Dakota and Saskatchewan. ‡12–36 in (30–100 cm). Z2–7 H7–1. **f. albolabium** White or creamy.

C. Ulla Silkens Variable, cherry pink and white early summer and midsummer-bloomer considered the best of the new garden hybrids. Very like the *C. reginae* parent but the flowers are far more colorful and often spotted; they are held more elegantly and are easier to grow. Lip color is often richer in cool springs. Likes

fertilizer, damp feet in a potting mix, and more direct sun than most (three to six hours a day). A hybrid between *C. flavum* and *C. reginae*. ‡18–26 in (45–65 cm). Z3–6 H7–1

CYRTOMIUM
Holly fern
DRYOPTERIDACEAE

Striking, boldly divided fronds contrast well with the many more lacy ferns.

Most of the 20 similar evergreen ferns are from deep shade in damp forests in eastern Asia. A short, erect rhizome bears several large fronds with several large, leathery, sickle-shaped, lance-shaped, or triangular leaflets, usually toothed, on either side of the midrib. Spore-heaps are scattered over the underside of the leaflets. Closely related to *Polystichum* and sometimes included in that genus.

CULTIVATION Grow in moist but well-drained soil, in dappled shade.

PROPAGATION By spores.

PROBLEMS Usually trouble-free.

C. falcatum (Japanese holly fern) Almost erect fronds of up to 20 pairs of glossy, dark green, oblong, finely pointed leaflets, usually not lobed. The most handsome of the generally available species, often offered cheaply as a house plant and thus not believed to be hardy, but it has thrived in many gardens over many years. From open, rocky places at low altitudes from India to China and Japan. ‡16–28 in (40–70 cm). Z6–15 H12–10

C. fortunei Evergreen plant forming an upright tuft of dull mid-green fronds, divided into up to 20 pairs of narrowly lance-shaped leaflets. A robust grower and the best choice for gardens; the dull green color can contrast well with more glossy-fronded ferns. From mountain forests in Japan, South Korea, and China. ‡24 in (60 cm). Z7–10 H10–7. **var. clivicola.** Fewer, broader leaflets, with a lobe at the base, on more spreading fronds. ‡16 in (40 cm).

BELOW *Cyrtomium falcatum*

D

DACTYLIS
Cocksfoot
POACEAE

Distinctive and familiar evergreen grass of fields and hedgerows with a charmingly variegated form.

One species is found from Europe to Asia, and has been introduced as a pasture grass to many other parts of the world. It forms clumps of dark, smooth, bluish leaves, 4–18 in (10–45 cm) long and ⅟₁₆–⅝ in (2–14 mm) wide, and flattened at the bases. From late spring to early fall, tall, robust stems bear slender branches opening to a loose spikelet of purplish green, tufted, one-sided flowerheads. These are ¼–⅜ in (5–9 mm) long and become shaggy with yellow or purple stamens.

CULTIVATION Any fertile, well-drained soil in sun or part-shade. Cut back untidy growth in spring.

PROPAGATION From seed, or by division in spring.

PROBLEMS Usually trouble-free.

***D. glomerata* 'Variegata'** Leaves with white vertical stripes. A cool-season grass that looks best in fall and early summer. Cut back foliage and flowers in summer to encourage fresh leaves in fall. Effective ground cover in open woodlands and moist areas, especially with spring bulbs. Pull up any green seedlings—they will soon take over. ↕24 in (60 cm). Z5–9 H9–5

DACTYLORHIZA
Marsh orchids
ORCHIDACEAE

Stunning candles of small pink to purple blooms top the grassy green stems in these climatically adaptable, temperate, deciduous terrestrial orchids.

Named for underground tubers that resemble hands, with two to five carrot-thick fingers (*dactylos* is Greek for "finger"), this is a baffling blend of 35 to as many as 75 species, found from Europe and the Middle East through Siberia and Asia, and North America. Different species interbreed eagerly with each other in the wild, making them more like actively evolving "species groups" rather than truly distinct species in the usual sense. Plants also hybridize in gardens, and many commercially available species and hybrids are mislabeled—although hybrid vigor is usually outstanding.

These are unexpectedly unfussy and graceful plants, with succulent, slender to broad swordlike leaves,

ABOVE 1 *Dactylorhiza elata*
2 *D. foliosa* **3** *D. fuchsii*

sometimes purplish-spotted, often in a rosette at the base then arranged in decreasing size up a thick central stem topped by a dense head of many small to medium-sized hooded flowers that range in color from deep purple through pink to cream and white. Each flower is marked in patterns or lines, and has a broad, spurred, three-lobed lip and downward-pointing spur. Hybrid cultivars, often particularly vigorous and colorful, are sometimes listed but not consistently available.

These are among the easiest and often the least expensive of orchids and, in gardens with damp areas, are ideal first orchids for gardeners.

CULTIVATION Easy in open spots in well-drained but damp soil of pH 6–7, in sun or very light shade; do not allow the roots to dry out or continually stand in stagnant water. Good next to ponds, but add grit to open the soil mix, and in poor soil, feed in spring and summer. Leaf spotting patterns vary, with more in shade than in full sun.

PROPAGATION Divide or pull off new tubers from old plants in summer; often self-sows when happy. Tubers should double in number annually.

PROBLEMS Slugs and snails; treat with parasitic nematodes. Digging and grazing by small mammals and deer, especially when first planted, can be frustrating—enclose with cages to allow unhindered establishment.

D. elata syn. *Orchis elata* (Robust marsh orchid) One of the best garden species, slender and tall with five to fourteen generally unspotted, erect leaves to 10 in (25 cm) long at the bottom half of the hollow stem. Often making large clumps from which, from mid-spring to early summer, dense spikes of flowers appear, each like a neon purple flying seagull with a bulky pelican bill

strongly marked with dark slashes. The flower lip can have three tentative lobes or be undivided. Very attractive to bees and birds. Often confused with *D. foliosa*. Must be kept damp; best in moist soil in light shade. From wet meadows and bogs in Spain, France, Corsica, Sicily, and North Africa. ↕12–42 in (30–110 cm). Z6–8 H8–6

D. foliosa syn. *Orchis maderensis* (Madeiran marsh orchid) A superb garden species, with four to ten glossy, unspotted leaves and soaring, dark purple to pink, 1-in (2.5-cm) blooms, generally in midsummer, although it can flower at any time between mid-spring and late summer. Commonly misidentified; *D. elata* is often sold under this name, but everything about *D. foliosa* seems stouter than its confusing relative: the broader leaves, slightly shorter growth, and more hooded flower with wider though less strongly marked lip, which is more distinctly three-lobed. Can triple in size annually if growing well. Prefers full sun. Only from Madeira. ↕16–28 in (40–70 cm). Z7–8 H8–7

D. fuchsii syn. *D. maculata* subsp. *fuchsii* (Common spotted orchid) Very easy to grow, and lovely naturalized in a meadow, this is the plant for newcomers. Between seven and twelve spotted leaves are on each flowering stem, which from late spring to midsummer is topped by a dense pyramid of many flowers. These come in many shades of usually pale pink, sometimes white, with three strong lobes to the lip, the mid-lobe being distinctly the longest. The whole flower is covered in purple-red spots and lines, and the spike resembles an ascendancy of glistening flying angels. Generally best in alkaline soil and tolerates less dampness and less sun than other species. From Europe and Scandinavia. ↕8–24 in (20–60 cm). Z5–8 H8–5. **'Bressingham Bonus'** Slender-leaved, with variable spots, deep pink flowers more dense than the species, and beautifully held. Multiplies rapidly. Possibly a form of *D.* x *grandis*. ↕16 in (40 cm).

D.* x *grandis This beautiful natural hybrid between *D. fuchsii* and *D. praetermissa*, occuring in the wild and in gardens, usually sports purple-spotted, 8 in- (20 cm-) long leaves and long-stemmed, dense lavender plumes of artistically splashed flowers often so markedly and widely three-lobed that the parts seem to be trying to escape the bloom. Resents full sun. ↕12–28 in (30–70 cm). Z5–8 H8–5

D. maculata (Heath spotted orchid) Five to twelve good-looking, slender, usually purple-spotted leaves can reach 8 in (20 cm) long by 1¼ in (3 cm) wide. From mid-spring to late summer, the ¾-in (2-cm) flowers could pass for a horde of Little Red Riding Hoods, but in mauvey pink with candy spots. Often confused with *D. fuchsii*, and often hybridizing in the wild, it is distinguished by its middle lobe being the shortest of the three lip lobes. Though nectarless and thus fooling insects, this is the flower Charles Darwin dissected to prove that bee pollinators, more intelligent than credited, were indeed finding hidden sap behind an inner membrane, forcing them to spend a great deal of time at the flower and so allowing the pollen to harden slightly on their bodies to make it more viable: "…it appears to me one of the most wonderful cases of adaptation which has ever been recorded," he wrote. Can grow into magnificent clumps, splendid even out of bloom. Prefers acidic soil of pH 6.5 or less. From northern and central Europe and western North Africa. ↕8–28 in (20–70 cm). Z5–8 H8–5. **'Madam Butterfly'** Deep pink with broad lobes and lovely form. **subsp. *fuchsii*** see *D. fuchsii*.

D. majalis subsp. praetermissa subsp. purpurella see *D. praetermissa*, *D. purpurella*

D. praetermissa syn. *D. majalis* subsp. *praetermissa* (Southern marsh orchid) Exceptionally showy and large, forming large colonies. Fabulous in the garden, especially at pond margins, the southern marsh orchid stands supreme, with a dense shock of pale garnet blooms that individually look like little flying hooded seagulls dotted with purple. With five to seven unspotted leaves, the plants range from small to giant-sized, blooming in summer. The flower lip can be unlobed or with a midlobe marginally the more prominent of the three. Prefers damp acidic soil. From southern Europe, the British Isles, and coastal Norway. ‡ 12–32 in (30–80 cm). Z5–7 H7–5

D. purpurella syn. *D. majalis* subsp. *purpurella* (Northern marsh orchid) Deep rich violet blooms highlight the broad, bluish, unspotted leaves of this somewhat smaller, stocky, fleshy marsh orchid, one of the hardiest species. Blooming from late spring to late summer in colors ranging from pale red to deep violet-red, the flower lip is more like a pointed diamond than lobed. The top of the short flower stem is often stained purple, and the top of the flower head can appear flattened, as if it refused to keep growing. It does not like to be hot or dry and grows taller in richer soil. From northern Britain and Scandinavia. ‡ 8–16 in (20–40 cm). Z4–8 H8–4

DAHLIA
ASTERACEAE

Wild dahlias have a unique simplicity and a charm missing from so many of the highly bred hybrids.

There are 28 species of deciduous, tuberous perennials from dry habitats in Mexico and Central America, four of which are occasionally seen in gardens. These species include the ancestors of the many garden dahlias, most of

BELOW 1 *Dahlia sherffii*
2 *D.* 'Forncett Furnace'

HYBRID DAHLIAS

The worldwide tally of dahlia cultivars runs well into five figures. Some of these—particularly the cultivars with small flowers and dark leaves—are commonly integrated into herbaceous and mixed plantings. However, the vast majority of those available from garden centers and from mail order specialists, while theoretically good hardy perennials, are not. In some areas, usually zone 8 and below, few of these hybrid dahlias are reliably hardy. Consequently, the tubers must be dug up in fall, washed off, and stored dry in a frost-free place over winter; although even here, they sometimes succumb to rots. In more favored areas, even a deep mulch of bark chips may not always provide a sufficient amount of insulation.

All of this would not necessarily dictate the exclusion of dahlias from this book. However, many exhibition dahlias are viewed by perennials enthusiasts as gaudy, brash, inelegant, and singularly unsuited to being grown with "normal" perennials, so these have been excluded. Only the few really tough species, therefore, are covered here. I leave the remainder to the admirable dedication of the dahlia specialist.

which have showy, often double flowerheads in a wide range of colors. The deeply cut or divided leaves grow in pairs on stiffly erect stems. The flowers appear in late summer and fall and, in these species, consist of an aggregate of small, tubular, disk florets surrounded by a ring of broad outer ray florets. All species are almost tender, so the flowers and the foliage are destroyed by the first frosts, but they can often be overwintered in the ground in many areas, especially if given a thick, dry

RIGHT *Dahlia coccinea*

mulch in winter. Alternatively, the tubers can be lifted and stored in dry sand in a frost-free place. The colorful, usually less hardy hybrid dahlias, of which tens of thousands have been introduced (*see* Hybrid Dahlias), are not covered here.

CULTIVATION A sheltered, sunny position in well-drained, fertile soil. Stake taller species.

PROPAGATION By basal cuttings taken in early spring, by dividing the clusters of tubers, or from seed.

PROBLEMS Slugs and aphids.

D. coccinea Upright, bushy plant with dark, branched stems and undivided, or variably divided, rich green leaves up to 16 in (40 cm) long. From late summer to mid-fall or later, yellow-centered flowerheads, to 3½ in (9 cm) across, are borne in small clusters. The broad ray florets are usually scarlet or, occasionally, yellow or orange. Large-flowered dahlia cultivars are derived almost entirely from this species and the rarely grown *D. pinnata*. From dry places in low mountains from Mexico to Guatemala. ‡ 3¼–5 ft (1–1.5 m). Z7–8 H8–1. **'Forncett Furnace'** Orange-red flowers with yellow highlights and golden eyes. Introduced by John Metcalf of Four Seasons Nursery in Norfolk, England.

D. imperialis Very large plant with stout, bamboolike stems and much-divided, purple-tinged leaves to 24 in (60 cm) across. Flowerheads are 6 in (15 cm) across with light pink ray florets surrounding yellow or reddish central disk florets. Very late-flowering, from mid-fall to early spring in frost-free localities, but also makes a handsome foliage plant in cooler areas.

‡ to 10 ft (3 m) or more in ideal conditions, and to an amazing 28 ft (9 m) in its wild habitats, from Mexico to Colombia. Z7–8 H8–1

D. merckii Much-branched, slightly sprawling plant with reddish stems, bearing 8–16 in (20–40 cm) long leaves that are divided into pairs of toothed, oblong leaflets. From late summer to mid-fall, broad-rayed, lilac-pink flowerheads, 2½–2¾ in (6–7 cm) across, open in loose clusters above the foliage. Delightful, but difficult to support effectively. The hardiest, most popular species, from which a number of named selections have been fleetingly noted. From Mexico. ‡ 6½ ft (2 m). Z7–9 H8–1. *alba* White flowers.

D. sherffii Loosely branched; typical divided leaves and from late summer to mid-fall, yellow-centered, purplish pink flowerheads with broad, wavy ray florets. Similar in garden value and hardiness to *D. merckii*, but the flowers are slightly more dramatic. From rocky oak scrub in northern Mexico. ‡ 28–60 in (70–150 cm). Z7–8 H8–1

1

2

DARMERA
Umbrella plant
SAXIFRAGACEAE

Sparkling pink flower clusters in spring, followed by spectacularly large leaves, characterize this handsome and hardy, waterside perennial.

The one species is from woodlands and stream banks in western US. It is related to *Tolmiea,* but differs from it in having five petals, rather than four, and ten stamens rather than three—not to mention its strikingly large, round, leaves. A robust plant that slowly spreads by rhizomes to form a substantial clump.

CULTIVATION Thrives in moist to wet soil, in sun or light shade; will tolerate normal, fertile soil.

PROPAGATION By division in early spring, or from seed.

PROBLEMS Flowers may suffer from late frosts.

D. peltata syn. *Peltiphyllum peltatum* Large, clump-forming plant, slowly spreading by means of stout rhizomes, thus ideal for binding soil of a pond or stream margin. Round, lobed, and coarsely toothed leaves with long central stalks unfurl in early summer. In good conditions, they may reach 24 in (60 cm) across, coloring in fall to glowing, deep red shades. In late spring, before the leaves unfold, rounded heads of small, dark-centered, pale pink flowers, ⅝ in (1.5 cm) across, are borne on erect, hairy, reddish stalks. It is a striking foliage plant for the margin of a large pool, streamside, or bog garden, it also thrives in wet areas of woodland gardens. From California, Oregon, and Utah. ↕ 36–60 in (90–150 cm). Z5–9 H9–5. **'Nana'** Dwarf, with leaves to 10 in (25 cm) across. ↕ 12 in (30 cm). Z7–8 H8–7

DATISCA
DATISCACEAE

Marijuana lookalike with which to amuse friends and visitors.

There are two species of these leafy perennials from Asia and America, of which just one is usually grown. They make interesting summer foliage plants, useful as a green background to more colorful subjects. The alternately arranged leaves are divided into three, or opposite pairs, of lance-shaped leaflets. Male and female flowers, without petals, are carried on separate plants, though neither are especially dramatic.

CULTIVATION Moisture-retentive soil and a sunny, sheltered site.

PROPAGATION From seed in warmth or by division in spring.

PROBLEMS Usually trouble-free.

ABOVE *Darmera peltata*

D. cannabina Wandlike stems bear dissected leaves composed of lance-shaped, deeply toothed and taper-pointed leaflets, 2½–5½ in (6–14 cm) long. The stem tips produce many short, slender spikes of tiny, greenish flowers in late summer. As its species name suggests, this plant resembles a perennial version of *Cannabis.* It is found wild from the eastern Mediterranean to the Himalaya. ↕ 6½ ft (2 m) or more. Z6–10 H10–5

DEINANTHE
HYDRANGEACEAE

Choice relatives of the hydrangea, easily grown in cool borders, with appealing flowers held above bold foliage.

There are only two species, both clump-forming perennials from moist, shaded woodlands in Japan and China. Short rhizomes produce upright shoots in mid- to late spring. The paired, soft green, lush leaves are large and slightly hairy, with a slightly puckered texture and toothed edges. Flowers in sprays are carried at the tips of the shoots. As in hydrangeas, two types of blooms are produced: the larger, fertile flowers are fleshy, cup-shaped, and rather nodding, with five petals, while the smaller, outer sterile blooms have no petals and are insignificant. The most popular species is *Deinanthe caerulea,* but other species and hybrids are slowly becoming available and are well worth a place in woodland gardens.

CULTIVATION Hardy and easily grown in woodlands, in cool, moist but well-drained, humus-rich, and ideally acidic soil in light shade. Best

with shelter from winds that might bruise the soft foliage. Mulch annually in spring with very well rotted manure or leaf mold.

PROPAGATION By division in early spring as shoots begin to emerge; replant in improved soil. Plants will take a year to establish. Alternatively, from seed sown when ripe. Germination is erratic and the seedlings will take several years to reach flowering size.

PROBLEMS Slugs and snails can destroy emerging shoots in spring.

D. caerulea A slow clump-former. Purplish stems bear bristly, 6 in (15 cm) oval leaves and clusters of rounded, rather somber, downward-facing but charming, slate-blue or rarely white flowers, up to 1½ in (4 cm) across. From China. ↕ 16 in (40 cm). Z5–9 H9–5

DELPHINIUM
RANUNCULACEAE

Traditional favorites for herbaceous borders and cottage gardens, especially loved for their majestic spires of beautiful flowers, mostly in hues of blue.

From the Northern Hemisphere, with a few species found below the equator along the mountain ranges of East Africa. There is a particularly rich diversity of wild delphiniums in California and in western China. Most are perennials; a few are annuals or biennials. Many species are attractive, yet few are regularly grown in gardens, although interest is increasing. After many generations of hybridizing and selection in cultivation, garden delphiniums have diverged dramatically from their wild ancestors.

The stems grow from buds on a woody crown, formed from the bases of old stems, below which is an extensive, semipermanent system

of fibrous roots. Spring-flowering species, especially those from North America, often have tuberous roots with buds from which stems develop; these produce new fibrous roots each year.

Leaves are normally divided into three to five lobes with toothed margins, and are arranged spirally on stalks around the lower stem. In some species, they are repeatedly divided into many narrow segments. On the upper part of the stem, leaves become very small; flowers on stalks of decreasing length develop at each leaf joint to form a spike of spirally arranged florets. Subsidiary flower spikes may develop below the main one; in some species, this branching occurs at the base of the stem. The whole spike is sometimes described as a "bloom."

Flower colors cover the whole spectrum including shades of blue, lavender, violet, and purple, as well as white, yellow, pink, and red. As in many members of the Ranunculaceae (the buttercup family), the flower parts have become modified so that it is not the petals that are the most colorful parts (*see* The Delphinium Flower). Although garden delphiniums are usually considered to be flowers of early summer, many species flower as soon as snow melts in spring, while others bloom from midsummer onward.

Many wild delphiniums produce a large amount of nectar, but flowers are rarely scented. After pollination, three or more seedpods develop from each flower. This feature distinguishes delphiniums from the closely related, annual larkspurs, *Consolida,* which have only one seedpod per flower.

All delphiniums should be considered toxic, although extracts from the plants have been widely used in folk medicine. Wild species growing in western US have been associated with acute poisoning of grazing cattle in spring. ⚠

THE DELPHINIUM FLOWER

The appearance of a delphinium flower is dominated by the shape and color of the five large sepals. The uppermost sepal has a spur that extends behind the flower. To confuse matters, these large, colored sepals are commonly called petals. The two pairs of much smaller true petals are modified into an "eye" at the center of the flower, sometimes called a "bee"; this is often white or brown. The upper pair of petals in the eye both extend backward into spurs that lie closely together to form nectaries that fit inside the sepal spur.

Spur   *Sepal*   *Petal*

Delphinium (Belladonna Group) **'Volkerfrieden'**

CULTIVATION Best in a sunny site with good, free-draining soil. Many species especially require sun and good drainage, while relatively poor soil helps stop them from growing too lush, which can inhibit survival over winter. Needs of individual species vary greatly. Always support delphiniums to prevent the stem from breaking, especially where it joins the roots, which can be fatal. Place a cage of canes inserted in the soil and interlaced with twine around tall plants. A few twiggy branches suffice for dwarf types.

PROPAGATION Propagation of species from seed is often difficult because seeds may need long periods of chilling or germinate only at very low temperatures. The best of the tall border delphiniums are increased from cuttings (*see* Cuttings and Division, *p. 153*), but plants produce few cuttings so high-quality, named forms are relatively scarce and stocked mainly by specialist suppliers. Seed-raised forms are far more widely available, but much more variable in quality.

Entries for individual delphinium cultivars indicate those that are best propagated vegetatively, from cuttings or by division, and those that should be raised from seed. Seed-raised plants from a spring sowing will often be shorter, and flower later, in their first season.

PROBLEMS Slugs, snails, leaf miner, spider mite, black leaf spot in spring, caterpillars eating foliage, developing flowers or seed, powdery mildew (especially on cultivars with purple or violet flowers and wild species), viruses, and root and crown rots. An alarming list—but most gardeners only have to deal with slugs and powdery mildew.

***D.* 'Alice Artindale'** (Elatum Group) Slender spikes of pink-flushed, blue, double flowers of rosebud form, sometimes with a hint of green, in early summer to midsummer. Introduced in 1936, and still a favorite of flower arrangers. Division or cuttings. ↕ 5 ft (1.5 m). Z3–8 H7–1

***D.* 'Astolat'** (Pacific Hybrids Series) From late spring to early summer, flowers arrive in pink shades from pale blush to deep raspberry-rose with fawn or black eyes. Seed. ↕ 4–6½ ft (1.2–2 m). Z3–8 H7–1

***D.* Belladonna Group** Excellent compact garden delphiniums, with leaves usually extensively divided into narrow lobes. Their much-branched stems and delicate flowers make them ideal for informal borders, where their massed, small flowers flutter like clouds of butterflies. The many short spikes of loosely spaced, single flowers in blue,

RIGHT **1** *Delphinium* 'Blue Nile'
2 *D.* 'Can-can' **3** *D.* 'Galileo'
4 *D.* 'Gillian Dallas' **5** *D.* 'Lord Butler'
6 *D.* 'Loch Leven'

BORDER DELPHINIUMS FROM SEED

Delphinium seeds deteriorate unless kept dry and cool. Sow seeds soon after harvest or store it in sealed containers in a refrigerator at approximately 39°F (4°C). It is wise to store the seeds that are obtained from commercial suppliers in this way because the packaging does not always prevent seed deterioration. Sow the seeds in trays of moist seed mix, covering them only lightly with the mix or with vermiculite. Keep the trays at 62–68°F (17–20°C) and cover them to

keep the medium moist throughout the germination period, which can range from seven days up to four weeks or so. Prick out the seedlings when they produce their first true leaves. Seedlings from sowings in late winter or early spring should provide good-quality blooms in late summer to mid-fall, provided they are grown in fertile soil. In the eastern US, seeds that are sown in early fall will produce plants that flower in the spring.

white, and violet have five petals and small eyes, often with showy white or yellow hairs. When established, most bloom in late spring and early summer, with flowers on sideshoots prolonging the display; they flower again in fall.

These cultivars are excellent for cutting. In overly rich soil, they tend to lose their bushy habit. Space them 28 in (70 cm) apart and support with twiggy sticks. Cut down to ground level after flowering for a second flush of fall blooms. Raised from seed or cuttings. From spring sowings, plants flower between midsummer and early fall when 24–36 in (60–90 cm) tall in their first year, and in late spring and early summer at 54 in (1.3 m) in subsequent years. Their origin is uncertain; some are thought to be hybrids between tall border types and *D. grandiflorum,* but some may have a quite different hybrid origin. All have the look of a distinct group. ‡ Very variable. Z3–8 H7–1. **'Atlantis'** Deep blue flowers with a purple flush. Vigorous; quickly develops a large crown and many stems with dark green leaves. Division or cuttings. ‡ 4½ ft (1.4 m). **'Bellamosum'** Large, dark blue flowers with yellow hairs on eyes. Seed. ‡ 4½ ft (1.4 m). **'Blue Shadow'** Gentian blue flowers with yellow hairs on the eye petals. Seed. ‡ 54 in (1.3 m). **'Casa Blanca'** Pure white flowers, a favorite for cutting. Seed. ‡ 54 in (1.3 m). **'Cliveden Beauty'** Large, pastel blue flowers with a white eye. One of the first fertile Belladonna cultivars, introduced in 1931. Seed. ‡ 54 in (1.3 m). **'Connecticut Yankee'** syn. 'Steichen Strain' Flowers in a range of blues, mauve, and white; dwarf plants with tough stems. All American Selection 1963. Seed. ‡ 54 in (1.3 m). **'Delft Blue'** Pretty flowers with blue stripes over a white background. A spontaneous mutation of 'Volkerfrieden'. Division or cuttings. ‡ 5 ft (1.5 m). **'Moerheimii'** Pure white flowers. Arose as a spontaneous mutation of a pale blue variety; introduced in 1906. By division or from cuttings. ‡ 4 ft (1.2 m). **'Oriental Blue'** Gentian blue flowers, sometimes with a rosy purple flush in some seasons. Seed. ‡ 54 in (1.3 m). **'Oriental Sky'** Pale blue flowers. Seed. ‡ 4 ft (1.2 m). **'Piccolo'** Bright blue, short-growing. Division or cuttings. ‡ (1 m). **'Steichen Strain'** see 'Connecticut

Yankees'. **'Volkerfrieden'** Brilliant gentian blue flowers that make a fine spectacle in a border. The plant is widely grown for cutting. Division or cuttings. ‡ 5½ ft (1.7 m). **'West End Blue'** Deep sky blue with pink flush, from late spring to midsummer. Division or cuttings. ‡ 54 in (1.3 m).

D. **'Black Knight'** (Pacific Hybrids Series) Round, dark violet florets with a velvety texture; flower in late spring to early summer. Seed. ‡ 4–6 ft (1.2–2 m). Z3–8 H7–1

D. **'Blue Bird'** (Pacific Hybrids Series) Mid-blue with white eyes and small, 2½-in (6-cm) florets; flower in late spring to early summer. Seed. ‡ 4–6 ft (1.2–2 m). Z3–8 H7–1

D. **'Blue Dawn'** (Elatum Group) Long, tapering spikes of pink-flushed, pale blue flowers with brown eyes, in early summer to midsummer. Division or cuttings. ‡ 7¾ ft (2.4 m). Z3–8 H7–1

D. **Blue Fountains Group** One of the first seed strains yielding compact plants that are less than 3¼ ft (1 m) tall, with short spikes of semidouble flowers in blue shades, in early summer. Seed. ‡ 32–40 in (80–100 cm). Z3–8 H7–1

D. **'Blue Jay'** (Pacific Hybrids Series) Dark blue florets with dark brown eyes, in late spring to early summer. Seed. ‡ 4–6½ ft (1.2–2 m). Z3–8 H7–1

D. **'Blue Nile'** (Elatum Group) Mid-blue flowers with white eyes, early summer to midsummer. Division or cuttings. ‡ 5½ ft (1.7 m). Z3–8 H7–1

D. **'Blushing Brides'** see *D.* New Zealand hybrids

D. **'Bruce'** (Elatum Group) Large, violet-purple florets, 3¼ in (8.5 cm) across with brown eyes, carried in long, broad-based spikes in early summer to midsummer; exhibition quality. Division or cuttings. ‡ 6 ft (1.8 m). Z3–8 H7–1

D. **'Cameliard'** (Pacific Hybrids Series) Lavender bicolor with white eye. Late spring to early summer. Seed. ‡ 4–6½ ft (1.2–2 m). Z3–8 H7–1

D. **'Can-can'** (Elatum Group) Purple and blue, eyeless, double flowers, early summer to midsummer. Division or cuttings. ‡ 6 ft (1.9 m). Z3–8 H7–1

D. **cardinale** (Scarlet larkspur) A spectacular but short-lived delphinium with flowers, widely spaced on slender spikes, in late spring and early summer. Small, red, 1-in (2.5-cm) flowers have long spurs and the upper part of each eye is yellow with red lips. Forms in yellow and peachy shades are available and there is a rare double form. These have been a starting point for many attempts to breed red-flowered delphiniums (*see* Red Delphiniums, *p. 155*). Plants need dry conditions during dormancy after flowering. Sow

USING DELPHINIUMS IN THE GARDEN

Delphiniums' distinctive feature is the way in which they spiral dramatically skyward. Disadvantages include the rather short flowering season and the need for careful staking. For best results, choose an open site away from shrubs, trees, and walls, which encourages the plants to grow taller, and interplant small groups of two or three delphiniums with later-flowering phlox and dahlias. To complement delphinium colors, plant with herbaceous perennials such as yellow thalictrums or purple salvias, orange alstroemerias, or, for a structural contrast too, drifts of flat-topped achilleas—for example, these butter yellow *Achillea millefolium* 'Taygetea'. Site the smaller delphiniums among low-growing perennials such as dwarf campanulas. These can also make good plants for containers, red-flowered *D. nudicaule* and dainty *D. grandiflorum* 'Blue Butterfly' being among the best for this purpose.

CUTTINGS AND DIVISION

To divide a selected delphinium, dig up a mature plant and split the crown into several pieces with both roots and shoots. Trim off diseased root or crown material before replanting.

Taking cuttings is preferable to division and easiest from plants lifted when growth starts in spring. Cut 1½–4-in (4–10-cm) shoots from the base where they join the old, woody crown. Rooting in moist sand or a jar of water takes four to five weeks. Pinch out the shoot tip to encourage basal buds, either when

potting up a rooted cutting, or a few days later. Cuttings should be ready to plant about four weeks after rooting. If planted in late spring or early summer, cuttings, or young plants of named cultivars from a nursery, should soon send out strong stems. Allow these shoots to grow for good blooms in late summer to mid-fall, or pinch them out in order to develop the crown. Support stems of young plants carefully to avoid damage to the crown from stems breaking off.

seed in early spring for flowers in late summer and early fall. Support slender stems discreetly. From southern California and Baja California, Mexico. ↕ 36 in (90 cm) in first year, then 5–6½ ft (1.5–2 m) subsequently; can be taller in the wild. Z3–7 H7–1

D. 'Cassius' (Elatum Group) Flowers are dark blue with a seasonally variable purple flush and brown eyes, carried in broad tapering spikes on a short stem. Durable; starts into growth and flowers late—in midsummer. Division or cuttings. ↕ 5½ ft (1.7 m). Z3–7 H7–1

D. 'Celebration' (Elatum Group) Large, parchmentlike, cream flowers with dark brown eyes, in early summer and midsummer. Division or cuttings. ↕ 5 ft (1.5 m). Z3–7 H7–1

D. Centurion Series In early summer and midsummer, large, well-formed, semidouble, 2½–3 in (6–8 cm) flowers, which have the quality of good vegetatively propagated cultivars. 'Centurion White', 'Centurian Gentian Blue', and 'Centurion Sky Blue' offer specific colors, while 'Centurion Formula Mixture' includes these and other colors not available separately. Raised by Sahin Zaden of Holland. Seed. ↕ 6 ft (1.8 m). Z3–7 H7–1

D. 'Cherub' (Elatum Group) Pale pinkish mauve florets with white eyes, early summer to midsummer. Division or cuttings. ↕ 5 ft (1.5 m). Z3–7 H7–1

D. Clear Springs Series Commercial cut-flower series, also good in the garden. Flowers with white eyes, well-spaced around the spikes. Borne late spring to early summer. Colors available are 'Clear Springs Lavender', 'Clear Springs Light Blue Shades', 'Clear Springs Mid-Blue Shades', 'Clear Springs Rose Pink Shades', and 'Clear Springs White', plus a mixture. Essentially, a more compact, higher-quality version of the Pacific Hybrids Series; raised by Ball Seed in Illinois. ↕ 30–42 in (75–110 cm). Z3–7 H7–1

D. 'Conspicuous' (Elatum Group) Pale mauve and blue flowers with prominent, dark brown eyes, in early summer and midsummer. Division or cuttings. ↕ 5 ft (1.5 m). Z3–7 H7–1

D. 'Constance Rivett' (Elatum Group) Lovely, large white florets with white eyes, in tapering spikes sit on compact plants, early summer to midsummer. Division or cuttings. ↕ 54 in (1.3 m). Z3–7 H7–1

D. 'Coral Sunset' (University hybrid) Ruffled flowers in pale orange-red color, redish tips to older flowers. Division or cuttings. ↕ 40–48 in (100–120 cm). Z3–7 H7–1

D. 'Cupid' (Elatum Group) Pale sky blue with a white eye; early summer to midsummer. Division or cuttings. ↕ 3¼ ft (1 m). Z3–7 H7–1

D. 'Darwin's Blue Indulgence' (Elatum Group) Mid-blue, eyeless, double flowers in early summer and midsummer. Intended for cutting. Division or cuttings. ↕ 54 in (130 cm). Z3–7 H7–1

D. 'Darwin's Pink Indulgence' (Elatum Group) Eyeless, pink double flowers, early summer to midsummer. Good for cutting. Division or cuttings. ↕ 54 in (1.3 m). Z3–7 H7–1

D. 'Dreaming Spires' see New Century hybrids

D. 'Dusky Maidens' see New Zealand hybrids

D. elatum Quite small, violet-blue or blue flowers, variable in color, with dark brown eyes; closely spaced in long spikes. Hollow stems, hairy toward base, smooth or almost smooth above, rise from a woody, fibrous-rooted crown. Leaf size decreases from base to flower spike and partially divided into five lobes with toothed margins. A native of forest margins and clearings, ravines, and meadows with tall vegetation. Deemed predominant in the development of today's tall stately, perennial garden delphiniums, but the true species is rarely seen in cultivation. After a few generations, self-sown seedlings from unselected garden delphiniums can resemble *D. elatum*. From seed or cuttings. From the mountains of central and eastern Europe and Central Asia. ↕ 5–10 ft (1.5–3 m). Z2–7 H7–1

D. Elatum Group Umbrella name for all border delphiniums in the traditional style *(see panel, p.154)*.

D. Elatum hybrids Alternative collective name for all border delphiniums in the traditional style *(see Elatum Group, p.154)*.

D. 'Elizabeth Cook' (Elatum Group) White flowers with white eyes; elegant, tapering blooms of exhibition quality; early summer to midsummer. Division or cuttings. ↕ 5½ ft (1.7 m). Z3–7 H7–1

D. 'Emily Hawkins' (Elatum Group) Flat, pale mauve florets with fawn eyes, on tapering spikes in early summer. Perhaps the best of the excellent introductions from British breeder David Bassett, which also include 'Gillian Dallas' and the Summerfield cultivars. Division or cuttings. ↕ 6½ ft (2 m). Z3–7 H7–1

D. 'Faust' (Elatum Group) Dramatic, long, tapering spikes of intense ultramarine blue flowers with black eyes, from early summer to midsummer. Ideal for the back of a border. Division or cuttings. ↕ to 7¾ ft (2.4 m). Z3–7 H7–1

D. 'Fenella' (Elatum Group) Small, brilliant gentian blue florets with black eyes, from early summer to midsummer. Unusually long-lived. Division or cuttings. ↕ 5½ ft (1.7 m). Z3–7 H7–1

D. 'Finsteraarhorn' (Elatum Group) Single-flowered, violet-blue with brown eyes, from early summer to midsummer. Introduced in 1936 by German breeder Karl Foerster. Division or cuttings. ↕ 5½ ft (1.6 m). Z3–7 H7–1

D. 'Galahad' (Pacific Hybrids Series) Glistening white flowers of heavy texture with white eyes, from late spring to early summer. Seed. ↕ 4–6½ ft (1.2–2 m). Z3–7 H7–1

D. 'Galileo' (Elatum Group) Long, tapering spikes of large, frilled florets in mid-blue, sometimes heavily flushed mauve, and brown eyes; early summer to midsummer. Division or cuttings. ↕ 6 ft (1.8 m). Z3–7 H7–1

D. 'Gillian Dallas' (Elatum Group) From early summer to midsummer, large florets, 3½ in (9 cm) across, ruffled edges in pale violet and white eyes—an especially excellent spike. Division or cuttings. ↕ 6 ft (1.8 m). Z3–7 H7–1

D. 'Giotto' (Elatum Group) Purple and blue florets with light brown eyes; compact growth. Early summer to midsummer. Division or cuttings. ↕ 5½ ft (1.7 m). Z3–7 H7–1

D. 'Gordon Forsyth' (Elatum Group) Long, slender spikes in pure amethyst-blue with dark gray eyes. Late-flowering (early summer to midsummer) and fairly susceptible to mildew. Division or cuttings. ↕ 6 ft (1.8 m). Z3–7 H7–1

D. grandiflorum Branched stems end in short spikes of pretty, disklike, blue flowers with straight, slender spurs. Leaves are dissected to bases into many narrow segments. Known in cultivation for several hundred years, this species has given rise to plants that range from dwarf, rounded mounds to tall, elegant

sprays with blue, violet, or white flowers. Many delightful seed strains have been developed. Support stems with twiggy sticks. Plants in well-drained soil survive winter well, but crowns must be protected from slugs. Best raised from seed in early spring for flowers in late summer. Native to rocky slopes and dry meadows across Asia, from Siberia to China. ↕ 8–32 in (20–80 cm). Z3–8 H8–1. **'Amour'** Dwarf mixture in range of blues, as well as white and a pretty, pale pink shade with violet-tinged spurs. **'Blue Butterfly'** Elegant, upright stems with feathery foliage and blue flowers. **'Blue Mirror'** Dwarf plants with unusual, upward-facing, brilliant gentian blue flowers that have no spurs or eyes. ↕ 10 in (25 cm). **'Tom Pouce'** Exceptionally dwarf plants with large flowers in three colors, 'Tom Pouce Gentian Blue', 'Tom Pouce Sky Blue' and 'Tom Pouce Snow White', as well as a mixture. ↕ 4 in (10 cm). **'White Butterfly'** Elegant, upright stems with feathery foliage and white flowers.

D. Green Expectations Group (Elatum Group) Semidouble, or eyeless, white flowers, tinged with green, from early summer to midsummer. Some seedlings have blue or white flowers. Seed. ↕ 4 ft (1.2 m). Z3–8 H8–1

D. Guardian Series Developed as a cut flower, but also suitable for garden use. Unusually uniform, with thin, strong stems; flowering early, 20 weeks from sowing. Colors are 'Guardian Blue', 'Guardian Early Blue' (earlier and shorter than 'Guardian Blue'), 'Guardian Lavender', and 'Guardian White'. Raised by Ball Seed in Illinois. Seed. ↕ 30–40 in (75–100 cm). Z3–8 H8–1

RIGHT *Delphinium* 'Lucia Sahin'

ELATUM GROUP

Most perennial garden delphiniums come under this umbrella name, including the Pacific Hybrid Series (see Pacific Hybrids Series, p.159), and are derived from *Delphinium elatum*, perhaps with *D. exaltatum* and *D. formosum*. Upright, hollow stems with many large leaves grow from a woody crown with fibrous roots. The long-stalked leaves are divided into three or more broad lobes with toothed margins; each cultivar has slightly different foliage. The 8–51-in (20–130-cm) flower spike consists of 20–100 or more florets on individual, 2–8-in (5–20-cm) stalks arranged spirally, with a small leaflet at the base of each stalk. Up to five smaller spikes develop from leaf joints just below the main one. Mature plants normally flower between late spring and midsummer, with significant variations between cultivars and local climates. One flower spike gives color for 10 to 14 days, but flowers on sideshoots extend flowering by about two weeks.

Delphinium blooms can be slender, parallel-sided columns or be broad-based and taper to a point. The best cultivars have been selected for long-lasting florets of good form with clear colors and compact eyes, as well as regular placement of florets in the spike. The florets at the base of the spike should still be attractive when buds at the top open. Colors include blues of many hues, brilliant purple, violet, dusky pink, creamy yellow, or white; they can be uniform or patterned, in tones of one color or in a mixture of colors. The eyes may be black, shades of brown, white, or striped with the petal color.

Elatum Group plants are tetraploids so they have twice as many chromosomes as most delphinium species, creating larger flowers with more petals. Most high-quality delphiniums have "semidouble" flowers with 13 petals and extra petals in the eye, or "double" ones with no distinction between the eye and petals.

Grow these plants in well-drained, fertile, near-neutral or slightly acidic soil, incorporating compost or fertilizer dug in well before planting. Space them at least 30 in (75 cm) apart and at a similar distance from neighboring plants. In following years, apply a complete fertilizer in spring to maintain fertility and mulch with leaf mold or mushroom compost to retain soil moisture for sturdy growth. The plants also grow well in containers, if the soil has adequate nutrients (try the slow-release fertilizers for this purpose) and is watered regularly.

Selected delphiniums of this group, such as a named cultivar, can be replicated only by division or cuttings. Seed-raised strains are designed to yield plants of a specific size and flower color and are easily raised from seed strain (*see* Border delphiniums from Seed, *p.152*), but seedlings may not be identical to the parent, even if it is from a true-breeding seed strain.

D. 'Guinevere' (Pacific Hybrids Series) Pinkish lavender florets with white eyes, in late spring and early summer. Seed. ‡4–6½ ft (1.2–2 m). Z3–8 H8–1

D. 'Innocence' see New Zealand hybrids

D. 'King Arthur' (Pacific Hybrids Series) Royal purple, velvety texture, and large, white eyes; the long flower spikes are carried on thin, woody stems in late spring and early summer. Seed. ‡4–6½ ft (1.2–2 m). Z3–8 H8–1

D. 'Langdon's Royal Flush' (Elatum Group) Broad spikes of magenta pink with white eyes, early summer to midsummer. Division or cuttings. ‡5 ft (1.5 m). Z3–8 H8–1

D. 'Loch Leven' (Elatum Group) Pale blue with white eyes; late spring to early summer. Division or cuttings. ‡5 ft (1.5 m). Z3–8 H8–1

D. 'Lord Butler' (Elatum Group) Bears slightly cupped, mid-blue flowers with white eyes on neat, packed spikes; early summer and midsummer. Division or cuttings. ‡5 ft (1.5 m). Z3–8 H8–1

D. 'Lucia Sahin' (Elatum Group) Deep dusky-pink florets with dark brown eyes, on long, tapering spikes of exhibition quality. Early summer to midsummer. Division or cuttings. ‡6½–7 ft (2–2.2 m). Z3–8 H8–1

D. Magic Fountains Series Seed-raised series offers a full range of hues; in effect, a dwarf version of the Pacific Hybrid Series; 2-in (5-cm) flowers on spikes 12–20 in (30–50 cm) long, from early summer. Available as a color mixture and in specific colors with bulky names: 'Magic Fountains Cherry Blossom with White Bee', 'Magic Fountains Dark Blue with Dark Bee', 'Magic Fountains Dark Blue with White Bee', 'Magic Fountains Lavender with White Bee', 'Magic Fountains Lilac Pink with White Bee', 'Magic Fountains Sky Blue with White Bee', 'Magic Fountains White with Dark Bee', and 'Magic Fountains Pure White'. Pinch out first stem of young plant to encourage root development and stronger flower stem. Readily repeat-flowers by forming new stems from the base; support these stems with twiggy sticks. Also good in patio pots. Seed. ‡36–40 in (90 –100 cm). Z3–8 H8–1

D. 'Michael Ayres' (Elatum Group) Purple. Blue-tipped outer petals, brown eyes; broad, tapering flower spikes in late spring and early summer. Division or cuttings. ‡6 ft (1.8 m). Z3–8 H8–1

D. 'Mighty Atom' (Elatum Group) Deep lavender with dark gray and lavender eyes, in slender spikes in mid-summer. Late, compact growth. Division or cuttings. ‡4½ ft (1.4 m). Z3–8 H8–1

D. 'Min' (Elatum Group) Florets in shades of lavender-blue, darkest at the

RIGHT *Delphinium nudicaule*

edge; brown eyes; spikes up to 40 in (100 cm) long; early summer to midsummer. Division or cuttings. ‡5½ ft (1.6 m). Z3–8 H8–1

D. New Century hybrids (Elatum Group) Tall, seed-raised delphiniums in a wide range of hues, developed from named British cultivars. Mainly available as 'Dreaming Spires' mixture, although separate colors are occasionally seen. Flowers in early summer and midsummer. Raised by Sahin Zaden in Holland. Seed. ‡6 ft (1.8 m). Z3–8 H8–1

D. New Millennium (Elatum Group) This name covers all plants bred by Terry Dowdeswell of Dowdeswell's Delphiniums in New Zealand, including plants intended to be grown from seed and from cuttings. The name "New Millennium hybrids" is also sometimes used for the mixture of seed-raised plants from this source.

D. New Zealand hybrids (Elatum Group) Vigorous plants with strong stems that carry long, elegant spikes of large good quality flowers in a full range of delphinium shades. These hand-pollinated seed strains from Dowdeswell's Delphiniums in New Zealand are similar in style to the best vegetatively propagated cultivars; they are selected to tolerate humid summers and flower in early summer and mid-summer. Many colors are available by reference number; some are also named, although supplies are usually limited. This name is also sometimes used for seed in a mixture of colors. Seed. ‡4–6 ft (1.2–1.8 m). Z3–8 H8–1. **'Blushing Brides'** Shades of pink with white and brown eyes. **'Dusky Maidens'** Dusky pink with brown eyes. **'Innocence'** White with white or black eyes. **'Pagan Purples'** Eyeless, double flowers in dark blue, purple, and mauve.

'Royal Aspirations' Shades of dark blue, flashes of purple, and mainly white eyes.

D. nudicaule (Red larkspur) Dwarf, variable plant with mainly basal leaves with broad, rounded lobes. Branched stems carry short spikes of small, almost tubular, red flowers on long stalks—unusually early in the wild, late winter and early spring; later in gardens. Sow in early spring and plant in well-drained soil, or grow in pots, for flowers in late summer and early fall. Use twiggy sticks to support the stems. Keep pot-grown plants dry after flowering; poor winter survival in wet ground. Grows on cliff faces and moist scree slopes in northwest California and southwest Oregon. ‡12 in (30 cm). Z5–7 H7–5. **'Laurin'** Uniform and compact plants with better branching.

D. 'Olive Poppleton' (Elatum Group) Creamy-white florets, honey eyes; in broad spikes in early summer. Division or cuttings. ‡6 ft (1.8 m). Z3–8 H8–1

D. 'Oliver' (Elatum Group) Translucent, rounded, light blue florets, with mauve stripes and black eyes, loosely packed in broad spikes from late spring to early summer. Division or cuttings. ‡5 ft (1.5 m). Z3–8 H8–1

D. 'Our Deb' (Elatum Group) Pale lilac-pink with pink-striped brown eyes, in loose, broad spikes from early summer to midsummer. Division or cuttings. ‡6 ft (1.8 m). Z3–8 H8–1

D. Pacific Hybrids Series (Elatum Group) There is now little justification for the use of the original names for individual color strains (*see* Pacific Hybrid Series, *p.155*). Plants sold under these labels continue to be widely available, but flowers are often single or of incorrect color, so any link to

original strains may be tenuous. Descriptions here refer to cultivars as they were when first introduced see *D.* 'Black Knight', *D.* 'Blue Bird', *D.* 'Blue Jay', *D.* 'Cameliard', *D.* 'Galahad', *D.* 'Guinevere', *D.* 'King Arthur', *D.* 'Percival', *D.* 'Summer Skies'. ‡4–6½ ft (1.2–2 m). Z3–8 H8–1

D. 'Pagan Purples' see New Zealand hybrids

D. 'Percival' (Pacific Hybrids Series) Glistening white flowers with black eyes, from late spring to early summer. Seed. ‡4–6½ ft (1.2–2 m). Z3–8 H8–1

D. 'Princess Caroline' (University hybrid) Deep salmon-pink with hints of red. First of the University hybrids to be widely available; first revealed at the 1994 Chelsea Flower Show in London, England. Division or cuttings. ‡3¼–4 ft (1–1.2 m). Z3–8 H8–1

D. 'Red Caroline' (University hybrid) Rose red flowers, the closest to scarlet yet available. Introduced in 2002. Good for cutting. Division or cuttings. ‡3¼–4 ft (1–1.2 m). Z3–8 H8–1

D. 'Rosemary Brock' florets with brown eyes, in tapered spikes from early summer. Division or cuttings. ‡5½ ft (1.7 m). Z3–8 H8–1

D. 'Royal Aspirations' see New Zealand hybrids

D. x ruysii 'Pink Sensation' In early summer, rose pink, violet-tinged, sterile flowers appear, widely spaced on branched stems. Similar in habit and look to the Belladonna Group, but the single flowers remain cupped and growth is less vigorous. Introduced in 1936; the first commercially successful

PACIFIC HYBRIDS SERIES

The Pacific Hybrids Series was developed by Vetterle and Reinelt of Capitola, California, between 1935 and 1970, to tolerate the high summer temperatures and humidity of many areas where delphiniums had failed to thrive. Rigorous selection and careful hand pollination resulted in vigorous, uniform plants with a wide color range that came true from seed and produced high-quality, large blooms in their first season. They had large, semidouble flowers, typically 3 in (7.5 cm) across and regularly spaced in long spikes, with sturdy stems up to 5 ft (1.5 m) tall. Mature plants tend to come into growth and flower two or three weeks earlier than other-named cultivars. Since their introduction, Pacific Hybrids has revolutionized the supply of garden delphiniums, and directly or indirectly influenced breeding of them, all over the world. However, longevity has never been a priority in the breeding of these and most other seed strains and they have deteriorated dramatically in recent years.

ABOVE *Delphinium* 'Sunkissed'

pink delphinium, raised in a breeding program from Elatum Group border delphiniums and red-flowered *D. nudicaule*. Division or cuttings. ‡24–36 in (60–90 cm). Z3–8 H8–1

D. 'Sandpiper' (Elatum Group) White, with dark brown eyes, fading in sunlight; late spring to early summer. Division or cuttings. ‡5 ft (1.5 m). Z3–8 H8–1

D. 'Sarita' (Elatum Group) Lavender-blue, double flowers tinged with pink, from early summer to midsummer. Raised by Terry Dowdeswell in New Zealand. Division or cuttings. ‡4¼ ft (1.3 m). Z3–8 H8–1

D. semibarbatum syn. *D. zalil* Spikes of pale primrose, or deeper yellow, flowers on slender, branching stems rise from a tuberous root. Extensively divided leaves with long, narrow lobes wither when flowering. Seedlings from early sowings may flower in late summer or early fall; mature plants flower earlier in cooler climates. Needs moisture when growing, but dry conditions after flowering; very susceptible to mildew. From semi-desert slopes in northern Iran, Afghanistan, and adjacent regions of Central Asia. ‡30–40 in (75–100 cm). Z8–9 H9–8

D. 'Skyline' (Elatum Group) Tall, and late-flowering in midsummer, with double, sky blue florets. Division or cuttings. ‡7 ft (2.2 m). Z3–8 H8–1

D. 'Spindrift' (Elatum Group) Fascinating mauve-flushed blue flowers, with greenish tinges and white eyes, in long spikes, from late spring to early summer. Division or cuttings. ‡5 ft (1.5 m). Z3–8 H8–1

D. 'Strawberry Fair' (Elatum Group) Mulberry pink with white eyes, in early summer and midsummer. Division or cuttings. ‡5 ft (1.5 m). Z3–8 H8–1

D. 'Summerfield Miranda' (Elatum Group) Flat, rounded, pale lilac-pink florets with brown eyes, in long blooms of exhibition quality, from early summer to midsummer. Division or cuttings. ‡6 ft (1.8 m). Z3–8 H8–1

RED DELPHINIUMS

Many breeders have attempted to create a red delphinium. The lovely pink *D. x ruysii* 'Pink Sensation' is the only survivor from the first attempt in the 1930s; recently, red-flowered plants have been bred in the style of traditional border delphiniums. Known collectively as University hybrids, these complex hybrids result from work begun in 1953 by Professor R.A. Legro at Wageningen in Holland, and continued at the Royal Horticultural Society's Garden at Wisley, England. Hybrids between red-flowered Californian species, *D. cardinale* and *D. nudicaule*, were crossed with selected garden delphiniums. Many more generations of crosses resulted in plants similar to conventional garden delphiniums in habit and foliage, but with flowers in pink, brilliant red, and orange-red shades. They are less vigorous than those in more traditional colors and highly susceptible to mildew. Only a few selected cultivars, including 'Coral Sunset', 'Princess Caroline', and 'Red Caroline', are now seen, primarily as commercial cut flowers propagated by tissue culture. In the garden, treat them as other delphiniums but fertilize well, ensure that they are not waterlogged, and take steps to prevent mildew.

D. 'Summerfield Oberon' (Elatum Group) Brilliant deep purple with contrasting white eyes, in tapering spikes, from late spring to early summer. Division or cuttings. ‡to 7 ft (2.2 m). Z3–8 H8–1

D. 'Summer Skies' (Pacific Hybrids Series) Pale sky blue with white eyes, from late spring to early summer. Seed. ‡4–6½ ft (1.2–2 m). Z3–8 H8–1

D. 'Sungleam' (Elatum Group) Cream florets with yellow eyes, in rather short spikes, in early summer and midsummer. Division or cuttings. ‡5½ ft (1.7 m). Z3–8 H8–1

D. 'Sunkissed' (Elatum Group) Well-formed, pale yellow florets with yellow eyes, in neat tapering spikes, in early summer and midsummer. Division or cuttings. ‡5½ ft (1.7 m). Z3–8 H8–1

D. 'Susan Edmunds' (Elatum Group) Large, fully double florets feature pale lavender outer petals shading to cream inner petals, in tapered spikes. early summer to midsummer. Division or cuttings. ‡5½ ft (1.7 m). Z3–8 H8–1

D. tatsienense Elegant sprays of purple-blue flowers with long spurs; slender stems, of variable height, with highly dissected leaves, arise from thickened roots. Seed sown in early spring yields flowering plants in late summer. To ensure good survival over the winter, grow in free-draining soil and protect crowns against slug attack. From high, grassy mountain slopes and alpine meadows in China. ‡12–32 in (30–80 cm). Z3–7 H7–1.

'Mediterranean Seas' Mixture in a

range of shades, including pale and dark blues, violets, and white.

D. University hybrids see Red Delphiniums.

D. 'Walton Gemstone' (Elatum Group) Very pale lavender with white eyes and dark violet veins on the back of flowers; early summer to midsummer. Division or cuttings. ‡6 ft (1.9 m). Z4–8 H8–1

D. 'White Swan' (Elatum Group) Dwarf plants with spikes of close-packed, pure white flowers in early summer, on 12 in (30 cm) spikes. Seed. ‡30 in (75 cm). Z4–8 H8–1

D. zalil see *D. semibarbatum*

DENNSTAEDTIA
DENNSTAEDTIACEAE

Attractive ground-covering ferns, thriving well in full sun as well as shadier situations.

About 50 mainly tropical species include just one deciduous species from cooler regions. Most develop into colonies of creeping rhizomes, which can sometimes spread too invasively, carrying fronds that are finely divided two, three, or four times into opposite pairs of leaflets. Typically the spore-bearing structures consist of two cups at the edges of the frond segments.

CULTIVATION Grow in an open situation in well-drained, humus-rich, preferably acidic soil. Tolerates full sun when established.

PROPAGATION By division or from spores.

PROBLEMS Usually trouble-free.

D. punctilobula (Hay-scented fern) Deciduous fern with long-stalked, erect fronds borne singly along far-creeping rhizome. Fronds are lance-shaped, pale green, and divided two or three times into pairs of small oblong segments. Gland-tipped whitish hairs cover fronds and give off scent of hay when touched. This fern is not always easy to establish, but should grow rapidly in well-drained soil and may become invasive. Attractive in late spring and early summer, but becomes untidy in late summer. The specific name is sometimes spelled *punctiloba*. One of few plants deer never eat. Native to open habitats. ‡12–24 in (30–60 cm). Z3–8 H8–1

DESCHAMPSIA
Hair grass
POACEAE

Early-flowering, shade-loving grasses that bear masses of delightful, airy flowerheads.

There are about 40 mainly perennial species, with some native annuals, growing in a range of temperate and cool regions

A GRASSY GROVE

GROWING A RANGE of different grasses together can be delightful if the plants are chosen carefully—but it can be a disaster if sufficient forethought has not been given to the selection. In particular, avoid grouping a vigorous grass with more retiring ones. Here, three clump-forming grasses in three different foliage shades make an attractive grove, the clumps separated sufficiently to show off their habit, but not so far apart as to be isolated from each other. In the back are the russet tones of *Deschampsia cespitosa*, in the front the yellow-edged *Alopecurus pratensis* 'Aureomarginata' and in between the two is the sharp blue foliage of *Helictotrichon sempervirens*.

throughout the world in meadows, woodlands, and moorlands. Only two species are generally grown in gardens, often forming dense tussocks of narrow leaves attractively arranged in a bold inverse cone, with slender flower stems hanging above them in airy profusion.

CULTIVATION Tolerant of damp to dry shade but in most soils grows equally well in full sun; they perform less well in hot, dry climates. Trim back untidy growth in spring.

PROPAGATION By division in spring, though they resent being split into small pieces, or from seed.

PROBLEMS Usually trouble-free

D. cespitosa (Tufted hair grass) Densely tufted, often forming hummocks up to 5 ft (1.5 m) tall. Evergreen leaves are dark, blue-green, 4–24 in (10–60 cm) long and up to ¼ in (5 mm) wide, with rough, sharp edges. From late spring to late summer, flower stems bear shimmering plumes, 4–20 in (10–50 cm) long, which open into a greenish purple haze, turning bronze to give a lovely fall display. It prefers a damp spot in semishade and looks lovely either planted in drifts or with ferns and hostas, especially with the sun filtering through the airy flowerheads. Good for drying. Found throughout temperate to arctic regions in marshy fields, rough pasture, and moors. Sometimes incorrectly spelled *D. caespitosa*.
↕ 8–78 in (20–200 cm). Z5–9 H9–1
'**Bronzeschleier**' (**Bronze Veil**) Silver-green flowers turning bronze; good for warmer climates, but needs moisture.
'**Fairy's Joke**' see var. *vivipara*.
'**Goldgehänge**' (**Gold Shower, Gold Pendant**) Flowers becoming golden-yellow on arching stems. '**Goldschleier**' (**Gold Veil**) Golden yellow flowers with a silver sheen. '**Goldtau**' (**Gold Dew**) Leaves and flowers warm gold in late summer, best in neutral to acidic soil.
↕ 30 in (75 cm). '**Northern Lights**' Leaves with vertical cream stripes sometimes tinged with pink or red in cooler climates; only flowers occasionally. Effective in containers.
↕ 10 in (25 cm) (leaves only). **var. *vivipara*** syn. '**Fairy's Joke**' Stems end in tiny plantlets, not flowers, weighing stems to the ground and rooting.

D. flexuosa (Wavy hair grass) Forms slowly spreading, loose to dense tufts of threadlike, tightly inrolled evergreen leaves, ⅛–⅜ in (3–8 mm) wide and up to 8 in (20 cm) long. In early summer and midsummer, thin flower stems bear wavy hairlike branches of shimmering plumes, 1½–6 in (4–15 cm) long, which open into billowing purple-pink clouds, turning bronze toward fall.

Lovely if grown in drifts in open, dry woodlands. Found in sandy or peaty acidic soil, usually in dry situations, on moors, heathlands, and open woodlands throughout Europe, northern Asia, and the northwest US ↕ 8–40 in (20–100 cm). Z4–9 H9–1. '**Tatra Gold**' Bright yellow-green arching leaves with pale reddish bronze flowers. Best in acid, well-drained but moist soil.
↕ 30 in (75 cm). Z4–9 H9–1

DIANELLA
Flax lilies
PHORMIACEAE

These exotic looking evergreens, with grasslike foliage, are mainly grown for their brilliant blue or purple fruits. Around 30 perennial species occur naturally in tropical Asia, East Africa, Madagascar, Polynesia, and Australasia, in habitats including rain forest, temperate woodlands, heathlands, and coastal sand dunes. Exotic-looking dianellas grow from branched rhizomes, though upright stems topped with tufts of foliage may be produced. The tough, straplike leaves fan out from the soil surface and were used by Australian aborigines for basket-making. Small, starlike, usually blue flowers are produced in open branching clusters in early summer, followed by succulent, glossy, blue or purple berries that make a surprising feature. Flax lilies can be difficult to tell apart and vary greatly within species; plants are often offered under the wrong names.

CULTIVATION Best in a warm, sheltered position; unsuitable for cultivation outdoors in areas experiencing hard frosts. They enjoy chalk-free, humus-rich, well-drained soil; damage from hard frosts is worsened by water-logging. Most species prefer good light, but *D. tasmanica* grows well in semishade and makes unusual ground cover for warm gardens.

PROPAGATION Clumps can be divided in spring. Sometimes small plantlets can be found on the flower stems, and these can be removed and rooted in a gritty potting mix. Sow seed under glass in spring, though berries are often seedless.

PROBLEMS Usually trouble-free.

D. caerulea A spreading species with a thick rootstock that forms colonies of upright, lance-shaped foliage, rough at edges; 4–24 in (10–60 cm) long. The ⅝-in (1.5-cm) blue or white flowers are carried in loose clusters in late spring and early summer, followed by striking ½–¾-in (1–2-cm) berries that are often stated to be light blue but may be deep blue or purple. Requires well-drained soil and good light to thrive. Propagate from seed, by division, or by rooting plantlets that are frequently produced among flowers. Native to mainly coastal areas in Australia from Tasmania, Queensland, New South Wales, and the Northern Territory. ↕ 20–24 in

RIGHT *Deschampsia flexuosa* 'Tatra Gold'

(50–60 cm). Z9–10 H10–9

D. nigra Upright lance-shaped foliage and blue or white flowers as seen in *D. intermedia,* from which it differs only by being a little smaller, having narrower flowering stems, and smaller petals. It also tolerates more shade and moisture than some of its relatives, and is a little hardier, though it prefers drier conditions in humid areas. From New Zealand. ↕ 12–28 in (30–70 cm). Z9–10 H10–9. **'Margaret Pringle'** syn. 'Variegata' Foliage variously marked with creamy-white stripes, the margins often pinkish. ↕ 16 in (40 cm).

D. tasmanica Bold, spreading or clump-forming species with a thick rootstock from which emerge lance-shaped leaves, 12–48 in (30–120 cm) long, with sharp teeth along margins. Many branching stems carry pale blue, ⅝-in (1.5-cm) flowers, opening in late spring and early summer in lax clusters. In good forms, the ¾-in (2-cm) berries are a stunning deep blue, though pale forms are also seen. Probably the hardiest species, enjoying a position in filtered light in humus-rich, slightly acidic soil. From cool, moist woodlands in southeast Australia and Tasmania. ↕ to 5 ft (1.5 m). Z12–13 H12–10. **'Variegata'** Originally a plant with pale yellow stripes on leaves, this name is now usually applied to a plant with variable white markings prone to reversion. **'Yellow Stripe'** Excellent 2004 introduction; the leaves striped in bright yellow; dark blue-black fruits.

DIANTHUS
Carnation, Pink
CARYOPHYLLACEAE

Indispensable, often long-flowering, fragrant, and silver-leaved evergreens for borders, containers, and path edging.

There are around 300 evergreen perennial species, with a few annuals and shrubs, almost all from the drier areas and mountains of Europe and Asia with a small number from Africa and one species from North America. Although a number of species are grown, it is mainly the several thousand cultivars that are known. Dianthus fall into convenient categories (*see* Defining Dianthus) although the boundaries have now become blurred.

From fibrous roots, fat, often woody-based stems with swollen, fragile leaf joints carry oppositely arranged, long and slender, pointed leaves that often have a bluish or silvery bloom; in some species, and a few cultivars, foliage is green and may be dark and shiny. Stems, very short and tight in clump- or mat-forming species, taller and ususallly floppy in many grown as border perennials, carry flowers singly or in small clusters; each flower has a tubular base sheathing the lower part of the petals (the calyx), above which, at their simplest, five petals extend at right angles, although in fully double forms there may be

RIGHT *Dianthus* 'Becky Robinson'

50–60 crowded petals. The petals are usually pink or white, often fringed at their tips, and frequently scented, usually of cloves. They are followed by capsules containing many seeds.

Most cultivars either from an open rounded plant or a spreading mat, or, in carnations, are taller with double flowers weighing down stems, which need support. Silver foliage makes many valuable foliage plants in addition to their delightful flowers.

In the species, the majority of flowers are simple singles with a natural charm; cultivars feature many doubles and semidoubles; some are flat, with overlapping petals forming a disk. Others are more fluffy, making them into a rounded, frilly pompon. In cultivars, the color range is based on pink and white with a few creams and even yellows. The pink varies in intensity from the palest, faintly blushed white through to dark purple-pinks and reds of various shades. Some are all one color, others have varying patterns and markings in other colors (*see* Color Forms and Patterning, *p.159*). Colors often fade and patterns change as flowers age.

Dianthus cultivars have long been grown in gardens. In the distant past in the herb garden, when pinks were important for their clove scent and taste, used to flavor food and drinks—often to disguise a bad or bland taste. These old-fashioned pinks tend to have a short flowering season around midsummer, with a few producing the odd later flower. Many of the modern cultivars derive from pinks grown in the 19th or earlier centuries and have come to us through cottage gardens. The naming of many of these is confused and a number of different forms may be found under the same name. Recently, there has been a constant supply of valuable new cultivars that continue to appear. Modern pinks have been bred to have a longer season, and many flower throughout the summer and often into the fall. They fall into a number of fairly distinct categories (*see* Defining Dianthus).

CULTIVATION *Dianthus* do best in alkaline soil, but can be grown successfully in other soils if they have good drainage. Wet soil, in winter or summer, is their downfall. They appreciate plenty of sun, with well-circulating air and without overhang from other plants. Remove flower stems when flowers have faded and lightly prune straggly plants. A general fertilizer can be added to poor soil in spring, but be cautious—they do not respond well to overfeeding. Pinks can be short-lived, so take cuttings regularly to ensure their continuance.

Pinks thrive in a variety of garden situations—at the front of mixed and perennial borders, as path edging, and in containers—and

many of them make excellent cut flowers. Smaller cultivars make good rock garden plants; some of the taller ones can be naturalized if the surrounding grass is not too vigorous.

PROPAGATION Can be grown from seed sown in early spring, but for the majority of species and cultivars the normal method of increase is to take cuttings. These are usually taken from nonflowering shoots in summer, but many can be rooted at almost any time of year. Cuttings can be prepared in the usual way, or as "pipings," where the top section of a stem is gently pulled so that it parts at a swollen leaf joint like a plug coming out of an outlet.

PROBLEMS Usually trouble-free; in bad seasons, aphids and slugs may need controlling. Problems are usually due to wet soil or old age.

D. **'Allspice'** An old-fashioned pink introduced during 17th century. The flowers, 1½-in (3.5-cm), which appear in early summer: single, have overlapping petals and a slightly ruffled appearance. Mottled purple petals pale with age, with two almost white spots and a thin white margin. ↕ 12 in (30 cm). Z3–8 H9–1

D. amurensis A variable plant, spreading, sometimes lax, with 1-in (2.5-cm) deeply fringed flowers in summer; single, pink or mauvish pink, with narrow, deep purple markings around the center. Short-lived but easily grown from seed. From eastern Asia. ↕ 14 in (35 cm). Z3–9 H9–1

D. **'Arctic Star'** (Star Series) Beautiful, glistening white double flowers, 2 in (5 cm), fringed and slightly fragrant, are set against good foliage through the summer. ↕ 10 in (25 cm). Z5–8 H9–1

DEFINING DIANTHUS

Border carnation Fully frost-hardy carnations, not treated here, since they are mostly grown by enthusiasts and very rarely in perennial borders. Perhaps they should be considered for the garden. Above, 'Forest Treasure'.

Modern or border pink First raised by Montagu Allwood by crossing the white 'Old Fringed' with a perpetual flowering carnation. Noted for vigor, extended flowering season, and fully double flowers. 'Joy' (above).

Mule pink Sterile hybrids (above, *D.* 'Emile Pare') between a sweet William (*D. barbatus*) and the garden pink (*D. plumarius*), raised in the 19th century. Highly scented, impressively prolific, they sometimes deploy so much energy to flower that they die. Few available.

Old-fashioned pink This term is usually reserved for cultivars that were introduced before the arrival of the modern or border pink in about 1910, for example, *D.* 'Mrs. Sinkins', above, and mainly derived from *D. plumarius*.

D. arenarius A delightful tufted species with small ½ in (1 cm) or slightly more, flowers with narrow, gapped, deeply fringed petals. White, highly perfumed flowers, with a green mark at the petal's base, are carried, usually singly, in early summer over green foliage. Surprisingly tolerant of shade. From eastern Europe. ‡12 in (30 cm). Z3–9 H9–1

D. barbatus (Sweet William) Upright, short-lived plant, often grown as an annual or biennial. Stout stems branch from the base and carry relatively broad green, often purple-tinted foliage with a noticeable midrib and two parallel veins. Topped, in early summer, by dense, flat or slightly domed heads up to 3 in (7.5 cm) across with prominent leafy bracts. Small flowers are highly scented and either red, pink, or white, usually with a pale eye, but often in attractive bicolors. Often treated as a biennial, when seed is sown in early summer and later young plants are transplanted in fall to their flowering positions. Many annual cultivars have recently appeared. From southern Europe; naturalized in the US. ‡24 in (60 cm) (often shorter). Z3–9 H9–1.
'Heart Attack' One of the most

reliably perennial, the flowers red tinged with black above green foliage.
Nigrescens Group Very dark red, almost black, flowers that contrast well with the purple foliage and stems.
'Sooty' Very dark red, almost black, flowers that take on a sooty metallic sheen as they age. Green foliage.

D. 'Bath's Pink' Single-flowered, with a mass of 1-in (2.5-cm), fragrant, fringed flowers that are pink with a ring of red dots toward the center; they appear in early summer in great profusion over a neat mat of slightly bluish foliage. Good in hot, humid summers. A cultivar of D. gratianopolitanus and similar to 'Bewitched' and 'Icomb'. Selected by Jane Bath of Georgia. ‡10 in (25 cm). Z4–8 H8–1

D. 'Becky Robinson' A strongly clove-scented modern pink with an old-fashioned appearance. The 1½-in (3.5-cm) double flowers are rose pink with crimson zones and lacings. ‡16 in (40 cm). Z5–9 H9–5

D. 'Betty Morton' From the 1920s, from early to late summer bearing single, 1¼-in (3-cm), fragrant flowers, deep pink with a maroon eye, the edges fading to white as the flowers age. Sometimes listed as 'Betty Norton'. ‡12 in (30 cm). Z3–8 H9–1

D. 'Bewitched' A typical seedling pink (in this case of D. 'Feuerhexe') in which the single flower has fringed pink petals and a magenta central ring. Lightly-scented flowers appear in early summer. Similar to 'Bath's Pink', 'Icomb', and other hybrids of D. gratianopolitanus. ‡10 in (25 cm). Z4–7 H8–1

D. 'Bovey Belle' Fragrant, modern double pink. Flowers in summer, up to 2 in (5 cm) across. Toothed petals, vibrant purple, slightly paler toward middle. ‡18 in (45 cm). Z4–7 H8–1

D. 'Bridal Veil' Reputed 17th-century pink, still very popular. Highly fragrant, double, 2-in (5-cm) flowers of white, deeply fringed petals with mauvish red eye. They have a short, early summer flowering season. ‡12 in (30 cm). Z4–7 H8–1

D. 'Brilliant Star' (Star Series) Summer-flowering, flowers 1½ in (3.5 cm) wide, fragrant, semidouble to double, with fringed petals that glisten white and a rich, velvety maroon center. Summer-flowering. ‡6–10 in (15–25 cm). Z4–8 H8–1

D. 'Brympton Red' A superb fragrant single pink with overlapping petals which are a rich pinkish purple with chestnut brown markings and lacing. The flowers are 1¾ in (4.5 cm) across and appear in early summer. Z5–9 H8–1

D. 'Calypso Star' (Star Series) Single, slightly fragrant, fringed, with deep

---

RIGHT **1** *Dianthus* 'Bovey Belle'
2 *D. deltoides* 'Leuchtfunk' **3** *D.* 'Doris'
4 *D.* 'Fettes Mount'

pink 1½ in (3.5 cm) flowers with paler pink blotches and lacing, borne in early summer. ‡ 12 in (30 cm). Z4–8 H8–1

D. 'Carmine Letitia Wyatt' Large, fringed double flowers in a rich salmon pink with a pleasant but not powerful fragrance. ‡ 11 in (28 cm). Z4–8 H8–1

D. carthusianorum Long, wiry, usually unbranched, four-angled stems with short, slender pale green leaves carry flat clusters of small, deep pink to red (occasionally white) single fringed flowers, in summer. Rather variable. Good for naturalizing in poor soil. From southern and central Europe. ‡ 16 in (40 cm). Z5–9 H9–5

D. 'Chastity' Old semidouble with well-scented, flat, 1¼-in (3-cm) white flowers, creamier toward center, in early summer. Plants with double flowers, or with red spots around the center of the flower, are sometimes offered under this name. ‡ 4 in (10 cm). Z4–8 H8–1

D. 'Chetwyn Doris' Slightly fringed double 1¾-in (4.5-cm) flowers, pink with a red eye and flecked and striped with mauvey purple. Only slightly fragrant Flowers throughout the summer. A spontaneous mutation of 'Doris' with similar habit, vigor, and perfume. ‡ 16 in (40 cm). Z4–8 H8–1

D. 'Claret Joy' Large fragrant flowers up to 2 in (5 cm) across, all through summer: double, bright scarlet, perhaps crimson (but not claret), paling toward the center. A spontaneous mutation of 'Joy'. ‡ 12 in (30 cm). Z4–8 H8–1

D. 'Cranmere Pool' Pure white—or at least described as such by its raiser, Cecil Wyatt of England, in about 1971. The plants now grown under this name are pale pink, almost white, with the occasional red spot on the petals.

Slightly fragrant; flowers are large, up to 2 in (5 cm), making it a floppy plant. ‡ 10 in (25 cm). Z4–8 H8–1

D. 'Dad's Favorite' An old, much-loved semidouble or flat double with a white background and velvety maroon central zone and lacing, usually fading to purple. The flowers, from midsummer, can be up to 2 in (5 cm) across. 'Hope' and 'Paisley Gem' are sometimes grown under this name. Also sometimes known as 'A. J. Macself', after the former editor of *Amateur Gardening* magazine who found the plant in a Northumberland, England garden. ‡ 12 in (30 cm). Z4–8 H8–1

D. 'Dawlish Joy' Double modern cultivar, the prolific fragrant pink flowers are striped in carmine pink and appear over a long season. Good for cutting. A spontaneous mutation from 'Joy'. ‡ 10 in (25 cm). Z4–8 H8–1

D. deltoides (Maiden pink) Forms tight, flat mats of dark green, sometimes bluish, foliage, with small red, white, or pink flowers, sometimes with a darker or different colored eye. Petals toothed at the tips are carried singly on short leafy stems in summer. Good for the front of a border. Cultivars are intended to be raised from seed and may be variable. Found in Europe and Asia. ‡ 8 in (20 cm). Z3–10 H10–1. **'Albus'** White. **'Brilliant'** Cerise red with a darker eye. **'Leuchtfunk'** (**Flashing Light**) Red with a darker central ring. **'Vampir'** Scarlet.

D. Devon Series A series of modern pinks with large double flowers in a range of colors. Bred by John Whetman of H. R. Whetman of Houndspool in Devon, England, mainly with long stems for cut flower growers. They flower all summer, with a varying fragrance. Some have been judged a

RHS Award of Garden Merit standard but may still be rarely available. ‡ 12 in (30 cm). Z5–9 H9–5. **'Devon Cream'** Soft creamy yellow with slight magenta tints and streaks, vigorous but coarse; less prolific than many—but a unique color. Unscented. **'Devon Dove'** Glistening pure white scented flowers with noticeably lacy petal tips. **'Devon General'** A brilliant crimson red, and well scented, with flowers over a long season on a vigorous yet not straggly plant. **'Devon Glow'** Well-scented, semidouble or flat double in lavender purple, fading at slightly fringed petal tips, flowering prolifically all summer on bushy, compact plants. **'Devon Pearl'** Large-flowered, highly fragrant, well-shaped, double, palest pink flowers, with a slight touch of magenta in the center, over a long season. **'Devon Wizard'** Well-scented purple flowers with a ruby-red center on a vigorous strong-stemmed plant. See also 'Pink Devon Pearl'.

D. 'Dewdrop' Very well-scented, single flowers with a pale yellowish green eye over many weeks from early summer. ‡ 6 in (15 cm). Z4–8 H8–1

D. 'Diane' Deep salmon-pink double; pale toward the center. Large flowers, up to 2½ in (6 cm) wide, appear over a long period. A spontaneous mutation of 'Doris' introduced by Montagu Allwood, creator of the modern pink, in 1964. Six other *Dianthus* have, at one time, been given the same name! ‡ 12 in (30 cm). Z4–8 H8–1

D. 'Doris' A classic and favorite, the fragrant flowers fully double, pink with a salmon-pink band, up to 2 in (5 cm) wide. 'Doris' has a very long flowering season, from early summer into fall. It has produced many spontaneous mutations including 'Chetwyn Doris', 'Diane', 'Houndspool Ruby', and 'Old Mother Hubbard'. One of the most popular and best of the modern pinks, raised by Montagu Allwood of England in 1945. ‡ 12 in (30 cm). Z4–8 H8–1

D. 'Emile Paré' Clusters of beautifully scented, slightly double, pale pink flowers with darker salmon are set off by bright green foliage. Highly prolific,

ABOVE 1 *Dianthus* 'Gran's Favourite'
2 *D.* 'Haytor White'

with an unusually long flowering season, the result of being a sterile hybrid, or "mule" (see Defining Dianthus, p.157). ‡ 10 in (25 cm). Z5–9 H8–1

D. 'Evening Star' (Star Series) Very short, deep pink, noticeably jagged semidouble flowers with a burgundy red eye. ‡ 4 in (10 cm). Z5–9 H9–5

D. 'Fenbow Nutmeg Clove' Semidouble flowers in midsummer of a deep rich crimson red with a superb nutmeg fragrance and set against blue-green foliage. A very old pink, going back to at least 1652. Although generally similar, it is not clear if the plants currently offered under this name match the original exactly—especially since seed is now offered. ‡ 10 in (25 cm). Z5–9 H9–5

D. 'Fettes Mount' Prolific double pink from the early 20th century with, in early to midsummer, very fragrant flowers that darken with age. ‡ 12 in (30 cm). Z5–9 H9–5

D. 'Feuerhexe' syn. '*Firewitch*' Single-flowered, with a prolific show of 1-in (2.5-cm), intensely fragrant, fringed magenta flowers all summer and into fall, especially if deadheaded, over a broad tight mat of lovely silvery-blue foliage. Best in hot, humid summers. A German hybrid of *D. gratianopolitanus* and the 2006 Perennial Plant of the Year. ‡ 8 in (20 cm). Z3–8 H9–1

D. 'Fusilier' Neat, bushy, dwarf plant with 1¼-in (3-cm), fragrant, rosy-red single flowers with a deep crimson eye in early summer. Plants of similar habit but with bright red semidouble flowers have recently been sold under this name. Often grown in rock gardens, but good in sunny, well-drained borders. ‡ 6 in (15 cm). Z4–8 H8–1

D. 'Gran's Favorite' Large, fragrant, 2-in (5-cm), double white fringed flowers with a bright pinkish purple center and narrow paler lacing. Very pretty set against its grayish foliage, but

COLOR FORMS AND PATTERNING

Both old-fashioned and modern pinks come in colors ranging from pure white through every shade of pink, to deep red or purple and even yellow. The flowers themselves have also been developed into a wide range of flower forms from single-flowered to a variety of different doubles.

Self (self-colored) The flower is entirely one color, as in the old fashioned, double fringed 'White Ladies', above.

Bicolor Each flower features an eye in a color contrasting with the remainder of the flower (above, 'Old Square Eyes').

Fancy A variable pattern of streaks, stripes, or flecks contrasts with the background color and often makes a zone of solid color at the edge.

Laced The eye color is extended around its rim, usually with a slender zone of the main color at the very edge (above, 'Dad's Favourite').

Picotee Each flower features a narrow rim in a color contrasting with the remainder of the flower (above, the border carnation 'Pierrot').

weak-stemmed and may need support. Introduced by Mrs. Desmond Underwood of Ramparts Nursery, Essex, in England who specialized in pinks and gray foliage plants. ‡14 in (35 cm). Z5–9 H8–1

D. gratianopolitanus (Cheddar pink) Neat mats of slim, gray-green leaves support short stems carrying solitary, ¾-in (2-cm), single, very fragrant light pink to light purple flowers in early to midsummer. Parent of many unusually heat- and humidity-resistant cultivars including 'Bath's Pink', 'Bewitched', 'Feuerhexe', 'Greystone', and 'Mountain Mist', though since often raised from seed, it is not always possible to distinguish between them or to know you have the right plant. From western and central Europe. ‡8 in (20 cm). Z4–8 H8–1. **'Flore Pleno'** Double flowers.

D. 'Greystone' A white single pink with deeply fringed petals, sometimes tinged pink in cool conditions. The early summer flowers are just over ½ in

(1 cm), fragrant, held above steel-gray foliage. Good in hot, humid summers. A hybrid of *D. gratianopolitanus.* ‡8 in (20 cm). Z3–9 H9–1

D. 'Gypsy Star' (Star Series) Single, fragrant, deep cerise-pink flowers with a dark maroon ring around a pale center. In summer. ‡6 in (15 cm). Z4–8 H8–1

D. 'Haytor Rock' Long-flowering modern pink with rather large, 2½-in (6-cm), very pale pink, fringed double flowers streaked with scarlet. ‡15 in (38 cm). Z4–8 H8–1

D. 'Haytor White' A classic, modern, large-flowered and long-flowering pink with 2½-in (6-cm), double, almost carnation-like flowers of glistening pure white. The petals of the flower are noticeably toothed. Raised by Cecil Wyatt of Bovey Tracey in Devon, England. ‡15 in (38 cm). Z4–8 H8–1

D. 'Hot Spice' Modern, double-

flowered, deepish pink; deepens further toward red in the center. Large, 2½-in (6-cm), fragrant flowers appear over a long season. ‡12 in (30 cm). Z4–8 H8–1

D. 'Houndspool Cheryl' Fringed, double flowers, 1¾ in (4.5 cm) wide, velvety red with a slight clove fragrance are produced over a long flowering season. A spontaneous mutation of 'Houndspool Ruby', and so a descendant of the much-loved 'Doris', raised by John Whetman of Houndspool in Devon, England. ‡15 in (38 cm). Z5–9 H8–1

D. 'Houndspool Ruby' Excellent modern double pink with a long season of lightly scented fringed, bright pink 1¾-in (4.5-cm) flowers with a ruby center. Spontaneous mutation of 'Doris' introduced by John Whetman. ‡13 in (33 cm). Z5–9 H8–1

D. 'Inchmery' Superb old-fashioned pink from the 18th century, with highly scented, clear pale pink, flat

double flowers, 1½ in (4 cm) across, in early summer over blue-green foliage. Does better than most on clay. ‡8 in (20 cm). Z4–9 H9–1

D. 'India Star' (Star Series) Dwarf, single pink with scented, dark pink 1¼-in (3-cm) flowers, each with a ruby red center, throughout summer. ‡4 in (10 cm). Z3–8 H9–1

D. 'James Portman' Modern full double with large, highly scented, crushed raspberry flowers with maroon lacing. ‡12 in (30 cm). Z4–8 H8–1

D. 'Joy' Dark pink double, slightly paler toward the center and occasionally with orange flecks or streaks. The coarsely fringed flowers are about 2 in (5 cm) across and come throughout the summer. One of Montagu Allwood's modern pinks. ‡10 in (25 cm). Z4–8 H8–1

D. 'Kesteven Kirkstead' A beautiful, clove-scented pink with single flowers that have a pure white ground and a wide crimson central zone that fades to purple as the flower ages. The flowers are unusually wide, up to 2 in (5 cm) across, and set against good blue-green foliage. ‡10 in (25 cm). Z4–8 H8–1

D. knappii Short-lived, summer-flowering, with slender, rather straggly stems bearing slim leaves, each of which has a prominent midrib, and topped with a cluster of small pale yellow flowers, each petal with a purple spot at the base. Unique in its flower coloring, but hardly dramatic, although it has been used by hybridizers. From Bosnia and Herzegovina. ‡18 in (45 cm). Z3–7 H7–1

D. 'Laced Joy' Semidouble or double, rose pink, clove-scented, 1½-in (4-cm) flowers with lacing and a central zone of maroon, reminiscent of blackberries in raspberry ice cream. The best known of Montagu Allwood's laced pinks. ‡12 in (30 cm). Z3–9 H9–1

D. 'Laced Monarch' Dark pink, slightly fringed, 1½-in (4-cm) double flowers with brownish maroon lacing that becomes less pronounced and redder as the flowers age. Vigorous and well-branched, but only lightly scented. From Montagu Allwood. ‡12 in (30 cm). Z5–9 H8–1

D. 'Letitia Wyatt' Large, strongly scented, double flowers, up to 2½ in (6 cm) wide, with fringed, blush-pink petals, deepening toward the center. Introduced by Cecil Wyatt of England. ‡11 in (28 cm). Z4–8 H8–1

D. Mendlesham Series Neat, fragrant, single or semidouble pinks for the front of border or for containers, raised by Mill Farm Plants of Mendlesham in Suffolk. Colors vary from white to maroon; all are easy to grow and trouble-free. ‡8 in (20 cm). Z4–8 H8–1. **'Mendlesham Belle'** Very pale pink single flowers with red center. **'Mendlesham Maid'** Pure white, semidouble, exceptionally fragrant

A NEW WAY WITH AN OLD FAVORITE

TWO OLD FAVORITES make a really delightful combination in a sunny, well-drained site. *Dianthus* 'Doris' is the best known and one of the most reliable of garden pinks; it is grown around the world, often simply as a path edging. Here, self-sown wild love-in-a-mist, *Nigella papillosa*, with its rounded blue petals, is peeping through and opening among the fragrant pink dianthus flowers. As it first grows in spring, the

feathery, dark green leaves of love-in-a-mist are pretty with the slender, bluish foliage of the dianthus, and later its inflated seed pods capture the interest. Self-sown seedlings spring up unpredictably and may need to be moved to more advantageous places where pretty combinations like this can be created. Try to move them while they are still small and will settle quickly.

RIGHT 1 *Dianthus* 'Houndspool
Ruby' **2** *D. knappii* **3** *D.* 'Mrs. Sinkins'
4 *D. superbus* **5** *D.* 'Unique'

flowers over a long season from spring
to fall. **Mendlesham Minx** (**'Russmin'**)
Dwarf, neat semidouble, rich ruby with
white lacing and markings, flowering
over a very long season. ↕6 in (15 cm).

D. **'Miss Sinkins'** Smaller version of
the famous 'Mrs. Sinkins', a scented,
frilly white double flowering in early
summer. ↕5 in (12 cm). Z5–9 H8–1

D. **'Monica Wyatt'** A modern frilly
double cultivar with deep pink flowers,
with a central red zone that bleeds into
the pink. Fragrant 2-in (5-cm) summer
flowers; raised by Cecil Wyatt of
England. ↕11 in (28 cm). Z5–9 H8–1

D. **'Moulin Rouge'** Pretty and
strongly clove-scented, modern laced
double in pale pink-purple with deep
burgundy red center and lacing. Raised
by John Whetman of England. ↕12 in
(30 cm). Z5–9 H8–1

D. **'Mountain Mist'** Deeply fringed,
semidouble, slightly misty sugary-pink
flowers in early summer over silvery
foliage. A hybrid of *D. gratianopolitanus*;
tolerant of high summer temperatures.
↕10 in (25 cm). Z4–8 H8–1

D. **'Mrs. Sinkins'** One of the best, and
best known, old-fashioned pinks. Frilly
double, pure white flowers have a
superb scent, but can often burst their
calyx, giving a lopsided appearance and
showing the pale green center. Short
flowering season in early summer.
↕10 in (25 cm). Z5–9 H8–1

D. **'Musgrave's Pink'** A superb old-
fashioned pink with single, 1½-in
(4-cm), fragrant flowers in early
summer, creamy white with a pale
green eye. ↕10 in (25 cm). Z5–9 H8–1

D. **'Night Star'** (Star Series) Very
dwarf plant with single flowers of
overlapping cherry-red toothed petals
with pale silvery-pink lacing and
markings. Summer-flowering. ↕5 in
(13 cm). Z4–8 H8–1

D. **'Oakington'** Prolific semidouble or
flat-double purple-pink flowers in early
summer over low carpeting foliage.
Introduced by Alan Bloom of England
in 1928 and still popular. Sometimes
known as 'Oakington Hybrid'. ↕6 in
(15 cm). Z3–8 H8–1

D. **Oakwood Series** An extensive
series of large-flowered, mostly fragrant
doubles with flowers up to 2 in (5 cm)
across raised by Seed Hall of New
Ollerton, Nottinghamshire, England.
'Oakwood Gillian Garforth' (crimson),
'Oakwood Romance' (purple cerise),
and **'Oakwood Splendour'** (purplish
pink with a crimson center) have
received the Royal Horticultural
Society Award of Garden Merit but
are often difficult to track down and
so are not listed individually.

D. 'Old Square Eyes' Single pink with white petals, each has a triangular pink patch at the base; when seen at a quick glance, gives the impression of a square central eye (in fact, it is a five-sided "square"!) The fragrant, 1¾-in (4.5-cm) flowers appear in midsummer. ↕16 in (40 cm). Z4–8 H8–1

D. 'Pink Devon Pearl' (Devon Series) Large-flowered, highly fragrant, well shaped double in soft rose-pink, darkest in the center, flowering over a long season. ↕12 in (30 cm). Z4–8 H8–1

D. 'Pink Mrs. Sinkins' A lilac-pink form of 'Mrs. Sinkins' with a touch of rose pink in a central band and a pale green eye. Flowers up to 2 in (5 cm) across in early summer to midsummer. Fragrant. There are several variants around. ↕12 in (30 cm). Z4–8 H8–1

D. plumarius Loose, slightly bluish plant with slender wiry stems and slim, grasslike leaves. A solitary, 1¼-in (3-cm), highly fragrant, pink flower is held on each stem in summer, though garden plants may have two or three; each petal is deeply fringed. A distant parent of the many hybrid pinks grown today. From eastern Europe. ↕16 in (40 cm). Z3–8 H9–1. **'Albiflorus'** White.

D. 'Queen of Henri' Single, fragrant, 1¼-in (3-cm), reddish purple flowers with two pink eyes on each petal and delicate pink lacing. Very similar, if not identical, to 'Waithman's Beauty' and has also been known as 'Queen of Hearts'. ↕8 in (20 cm). Z4–8 H8–1

D. 'Red Dwarf' Single, rich red flowers with a maroon eye over neat gray foliage. Raised by John Whetman of England. ↕4 in (10 cm). Z4–8 H8–1

D. 'Rose de Mai' An excellent mauvey pink French double from

about 1900 with, from early to midsummer, 1¾-in (4.5-cm) flowers that may be darker in the center and show spotting in wet weather. Often sold, mistakenly, as 'Lilian'. ↕12 in (30 cm). Z4–9 H9–1

D. 'Rose Joy' Large-flowered double with purple-pink flowers, 2 in (5 cm) across, that pale toward the center with age. Fragrant, with a long flowering season. A spontaneous mutation of 'Joy'. ↕10 in (25 cm). Z4–8 H8–1

D. 'Rose Monica Wyatt' A frilly double in rose pink with a darker center. The fragrant, 2-in (5-cm) flowers appear in summer. A spontaneous mutation of 'Monica Wyatt'. ↕11 in (28 cm). Z4–8 H8–1

D. 'Sam Barlow' A much-loved old-fashioned pink with large, 2-in (5-cm), strongly clove-scented, double white flowers. Each flower has a dark maroon central blotch, in early to midsummer. Won its first award in 1933. ↕8 in (20 cm). Z4–8 H8–1

D. 'Siskin Clock' Spectacular, single laced flowers that open light pink, with a deep maroon-laced edge and eye, then fade to white with the lacing becoming magenta—all set off by a loose mound of gray-green foliage. Raised by John Whetman. ↕12 in (30 cm). Z4–8 H8–1

D. 'Sops in Wine' Very old, strongly clove-scented, double pink with frilly white petals that have a deep maroon center. The 2-in (5-cm) flowers open in midsummer. Originally 'Sops in Wine' was a general name used for a variety of pinks; several different plants have been sold under this name, including 'Queen of Henri' and 'Waithman's Beauty'. ↕10 in (25 cm). Z4–8 H8–1

D. Star Series Neat, dwarf, very hardy, usually single-flowered plants derived from rock garden types but good in sunny borders and in containers. The plentiful flowers, carried over slender gray foliage, are small compared to the blowzier doubles but produced in generous quantities, often over a long period. Raised by John Whetman, of H.R. Whetman & Sons in England, the series includes a number of award-winners and is still expanding see 'Arctic Star', 'Brilliant Star', 'Calypso Star', 'Evening Star', 'Gypsy Star', 'India Star', and 'Night Star'.

D. 'Strawberries and Cream' Large, pale pink double with salmon-colored flecks and a center that is slightly tinged with yellowy buff. The fragrant flowers are up to 2 in (5 cm) across. ↕12 in (30 cm). Z4–8 H8–1

D. superbus One of the tallest species, with floppy stems growing out of slender basal foliage, then turning up to carry one or two fragrant, pink or purple, 2–3-in (5–7.5-cm) flowers, with each petal dramatically dissected to give a delightful ragged appearance. A good intermingler. Found in Europe and Asia. ↕36 in (90 cm). Z3–8 H8–1. **'Crimsonia'** syn. 'Red Feather' Scarlet flowers. **'Snowdonia'** syn. 'White Feather' Pure white.

D. 'Sweetheart Abbey' An old, fragrant, flat, deeply fringed double in crushed raspberry with a silvery sheen, fading away to white around the margins. The flowers, up to 1¾ in (4 cm) wide, come from early summer to midsummer. Similar to the less often seen 'Hope', but more deeply fringed. ↕10 in (25 cm). Z4–8 H8–1

D. 'Unique' An old, coarsely fringed single from the 17th century with raspberry red flowers and a dark

crimson central zone and lacing. Eyes form in each petal as it ages. The 1¾-in (4-cm) flowers open in early summer to midsummer. Not easy to propagate. Four other pinks, none now grown, and 17 carnations have also been given this name! ↕12 in (30 cm). Z5–8 H8–1

D. 'Ursula Le Grove' Single white flowers up to 1¾ in (4 cm) wide have a narrow crushed raspberry central zone and lacing for a short early-summer-to-midsummer season. It was introduced by the Rev. C. Oscar Moreton, author of the classic *Old Carnations and Pinks*, and named for his daughter. ↕10 in (25 cm). Z4–9 H9–1

D. 'Valda Wyatt' (**Miss Pinky**) Well known modern double, fragrant, 2-in (5-cm), purple-pink, darkening toward the center, with a redder central zone. Raised by Cecil Wyatt and named for his wife. ↕12 in (30 cm). Z5–9 H8–1

D. 'Waithman Beauty' Deep raspberry-red fragrant single with two irregular pinkish white "eyes" on each petal and a thin lacing of the same color. Flowers are about 1¼ in (3 cm) wide and appear in summer. Similar, or identical, to 'Queen of Henri'. Introduced by Reginald Kaye of Waithman Nurseries in England around 1951. ↕8 in (20 cm). Z4–9 H9–1

D. Whatfield Series A large series of dwarf rock garden pinks raised by Mrs. Joan Schofield of Whatfield in Suffolk, England, including some superb plants. There are both single and double flowers up to 1¼ in (3 cm) across in a wide range of colors. However, they are mostly for the rock garden, so are not treated individually here. ↕4–6 in (10–15 cm) Z3–8 H9–1

D. 'White Joy' Prolific double in the palest of pink shades, especially when in bud, that fades to creamy white. The fragrant flowers are up to 2 in (5 cm) across and good for cutting. ↕12 in (30 cm). Z4–8 H8–1

D. 'White Ladies' An old, fragrant white double, slightly creamier toward the center, very similar to 'Mrs. Sinkins' but with the petals less finely cut. Often raised from seed, so variable. ↕10 in (25 cm). Z4–8 H8–1

D. 'Widecombe Fair' Fringed pale pink double with a touch of cream and occasional darker flushes and streaks; fragrant flowers are up to 2½ in (6 cm) across. ↕15 in (38 cm). Z4–8 H8–1

DIASCIA
Twinspur
SCROPHULARIACEAE

Small, prolific, long-flowering plants in an increasing range of growth habits and flower colors. There are 50 species of these southern African annuals and

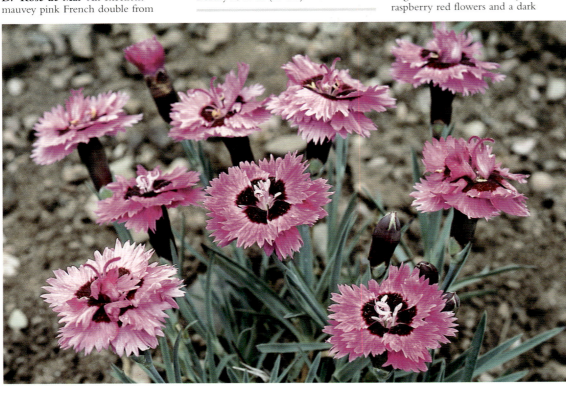

LEFT *Dianthus* (Whatfield Series) 'Whatfield Gem'

perennials, which have increased rapidly in popularity in recent years. Plants often have a spreading, suckering habit, their upright, or more frequently rather sprawling, stems lined with pairs of small, toothed leaves, varying in shape from heart-shaped to almost threadlike. These slender stems are topped with clusters of ⅝–¾ in (1.5–2 cm), open-mouthed, five-lobed flowers with two backward-pointing spurs, giving the plants their common and botanical names. At the base of the upper two lobes are two yellow windows, often almost merging into one; *Diascia* is often confused with *Nemesia,* which can be distinguished by having just one spur. The flowers of most species come in various shades of rose pink, but the many cultivars now available encompass lilac-pinks, deep red, salmon, and white.

Diascias' long flowering season is one of their main attractions. Away from their natural habitat, and the long-legged bees that are their natural pollinators, plants rarely set seed; this helps prolong flowering. New cultivars are introduced every year, and these increasingly tend to have flowers close to the mat of foliage rather than held on upright stems high above the leaves. Many of the most familiar cultivars were bred in England, on Humberside, by amateur enthusiast Hector Harrison. It is to him that we owe the current range of colors. Penhow Nurseries in Wales and Graham Brown in New South Wales, Australia, are continuing development.

CULTIVATION Rather short-lived, and often grown as annual container plants, as perennials they prefer sun and rich, well-drained soil. They will grow well in part-shade but flowering is best in full sun. In well-drained soil, diascias will survive several degrees of frost, although plants often look miserable in cold weather. Young, vigorous plants produce the best displays. If flowering ceases, most can be encouraged to flower again if trimmed back and given extra fertilizer and water. They vary in their hardiness (*see* Diascias in Borders and Baskets).

PROPAGATION Species can be grown from seed, if available. For cultivars, take short cuttings of new growth in spring or summer.

PROBLEMS Slugs and snails; aphids may infest young shoots.

D. barberae Low, dense green mats often comprise slim wiry stems laying flat and turning up at the tips to carry the flowers; plants may be more erect in poor, dry conditions. The overall effect is often rather ragged. Pairs of

LEFT 1 *Diascia barberae* 'Blackthorn Apricot' **2** *D.* Coral Belle **3** *D.* Ice Cracker **4** *D. rigescens*

DIASCIAS IN BORDERS AND BASKETS

When diascias first became popular, beginning with the appearance of 'Ruby Field' in the 1970s, they were viewed just as perennials on the borderline of hardiness. Even when given an RHS trial at Wisley, England in 1995, it was as perennials for the border.

Now, it is as plants for containers that their popularity has soared, with, for example, series like Sun Chimes which was introduced specifically for hanging baskets. But astute gardeners will also use diascias bred for containers in the garden. The neater forms are ideal at the front of borders, spilling onto a stone edging. Trailing types are quite delightful

billowing over a low retaining wall.

In colder areas, however, such cultivars may prove relatively fleeting. *D. barberae, D. fetcaniensis* and *D. integerrima* seem to be the hardiest of the species, with 'Appleby Apricot', 'Ice Cracker', and 'Ruby Field' considered the hardiest cultivars. Cold, wet winter conditions are detrimental, as is disturbance or dividing late in the season, and the microclimate of the garden can have a significant influence. Try them all, but be prepared to take late-season cuttings of favorites as a precaution and to keep them warm over the winter.

oval leaves line the stems, which are topped in summer by prolific dark, salmon pink flowers with two dark glands and short spurs, often with a second, later flush. Seed-raised cultivars are usually intended as half-hardy annuals. From South Africa. ↕8 in (20 cm). Z8–9 H9–8. **'Belmore Beauty'** Leaves broadly edged with yellow. A spontaneous mutation of 'Ruby Field'. ↕10 in (25 cm). **'Blackthorn Apricot'** Delicate flowers of light orange; hardier than the similar 'Hopley's Apricot' (below). A spontaneous mutation of 'Ruby Field'. ↕10 in (25 cm). **'Fisher's Flora'** Deep pink, darker than 'Ruby Field'. ↕12 in (30 cm). **'Hopley's Apricot'** Pale apricot flowers. Raised in New Zealand by Hokonui Alpines and originally introduced in the UK simply as 'Apricot' by Hopleys Plants of Hertfordshire, England, it has been used to breed better plants, such as 'Joyce's Choice'. ↕30cm (12cm). **'Katherine Sharman'** Coral-red flowers, with grayish leaves with a white edge. Not vigorous. Tends to revert. A spontaneous mutation of 'Ruby Field'. **'Ruby Field'** Deep coral red flowers held above flat mats of foliage on wiry stems. Raised by John Kelly in 1971; introduced by his Stanton Alpine Nursery of England. He reported it as a hybrid between *D. barberae* and *D. cordata* but there is doubt about the true identity of the plants involved; it seems to fit here best.

D. **Blue Bonnet** ('Hecbon') The first diascia to have a hint of blue coloration: there is a grayish lilac tinge to the pink flowers, which is most pronounced in cool weather. Raised by Hector Harrison. ↕10 in (25 cm). Z8–9 H9–8

D. **Coral Belle** ('Hecbel') Bright, coral-orange flowers are held over apple-green foliage on a spreading plant. Raised by Hector Harrison in England. ↕10 in (25 cm). Z8–9 H9–8

D. **'Dark Eyes'** Short spikes of deep pink flowers, named for the shadows produced inside the spurs. ↕8 in (20 cm). Z7–9 H9–7

D. **'Elizabeth'** Deep pink flowers with a purplish flush in 6 in (15 cm) long clusters above mounds of green foliage. ↕12 in (30 cm). Z8–9 H9–8

D. fetcaniensis A suckering plant with hairy, oval leaves, which tend to be heart-shaped at the base, on slim, rather wiry stems. These are topped by loose spikes of rose pink flowers in summer, each flower with broad flat lips and a downward-pointing spur. A determined plant that will creep along cracks in paving to make billowing lines across a patio. From South Africa and Lesotho. ↕10 in (25 cm). Z8–9 H9–8

D. **'Frilly'** Strong, purplish pink flowers on 3 in (8 cm) spikes; named for the frilly edge to its narrow petals. ↕14 in (35 cm). Z8–9 H9–8

D. **'Hector's Hardy'** Deep pink flowers appear above bushy plants with a moundlike habit. This is one of Hector Harrison's first hybrids. ↕10 in (25 cm). Z8–9 H9–8

D. **Ice Cracker** ('Hecrack') Pure white flowers showing a faint hint of pink on the lower petal. ↕10 in (25 cm). Z8–9 H9–8

D. **Ice Cream** ('Icepol') Palest pink flowers that are often pure white, are freely produced on wiry stems above mounds of vigorous foliage. ↕12 in (30 cm). Z8–9 H9–8

D. **Iceberg** ('Hecice') Pure white flowers on long stems over an upright plant. Bred from *D. integerrima* 'Blush'. ↕12 in (30 cm). Z8–9 H9–8

D. integerrima Taller than most diascias, with narrow, sparsely toothed and crowded leaves. Wiry stems are topped with tapering spires of deep pink flowers. Often among the last to start flowering in summer, but one of the hardiest. Spreads by underground stems, often forming perennial patches. From South Africa. ↕18 in (45 cm). Z8–9 H9–8. **'Blush'** Palest pink flowers.

D. **'Jacqueline's Joy'** Mauve-pink flowers on long stems over bushy plants all summer. ↕10 in (25 cm). Z7–9 H9–7

D. **'Joyce's Choice'** Pale apricot flowers held on wiry stems above a mat of foliage. Late spring throughout summer. A hybrid between 'Salmon Supreme' and *D. barberae* 'Hopley's Apricot'. ↕12 in (30 cm). Z7–9 H9–7

D. 'Lady Valerie' Large soft apricot flowers with long, darker spurs on wiry stems top mats of pale green leaves. It begins to flower in midsummer, over a month later than 'Joyce's Choice', but is a better color. A cross between 'Salmon Supreme' and *D. barbarae* 'Hopley's Apricot'. ↕10 in (25 cm). Z7–9 H9–7

D. 'Lilac Belle' The first purple-pink cultivar. Flowers are distinctive for their large lower petal, tiny upper petals, and winglike side petals. Bred from the small-flowered, rarely seen, and straggly *D. stachyoides*, with its unique mauve-tinted flowers, and *D. barbarae* 'Ruby Field'. ↕9 in (22 cm). Z7–9 H9–7

D. 'Lilac Mist' Their dense spires of small, purplish pink flowers are at their best in late summer. They combine the color of 'Lilac Belle' and the height of *D rigescens*. ↕16 in (40 cm). Z7–9 H9–7

D. Little Dancer ('Pendan') Masses of bright pink flowers with darker eyes and paler lips smother the deep green leaves. ↕10 in (25 cm). Z7–9 H9–7

D. Pink Panther ('Penther') Profuse, pale, clean pink flowers with dark "eyes" appear above deep green leaves. ↕10 in (25 cm). Z7–9 H9–7

D. Red Ace ('Hecrace') Freely produced deep, bright red flowers cover the deep green leaves. It is unusually vigorous and makes good ground cover. One of Hector Harrison's finest cultivars. ↕10 in (25 cm). Z7–9 H9–7

D. Redstart ('Hecstart') Large, orange-red flowers with prominent golden anthers top the apple-green foliage and have a long season from late spring to fall. ↕10 in (25 cm). Z7–9 H9–7

D. rigescens Creeping roots support branching, sometimes rather floppy stems, which carry close-set toothed, heart-shaped, stalkless leaves. These are tipped with tall upturned flower stems carrying ¾-in (2-cm) pink flowers below crowded buds. Can be short-lived. One of the most dramatic, and at its best in late summer. From South Africa. ↕18 in (45 cm). Z7–9 H9–7

D. 'Ruby Field' see *D. barbarae* 'Ruby Field'

D. 'Rupert Lambert' Deep pink flowers on 6 in (15 cm) spikes start to bloom in early summer. A hybrid of *D. integerrima* found as a seedling at the Royal Botanic Gardens, Kew, England. ↕16 in (40 cm). Z8–9 H9–8

D. 'Salmon Supreme' Very short with apricot flowers featuring a few dark freckles at the top of the lip. This was the first of Hector Harrison's apricot cultivars and although popular for many years, is no longer supreme and has been superseded by 'Joyce's Choice'. A hybrid of *D. barbarae* 'Ruby Field' and *D. stachyoides*. ↕6 in (15 cm). Z8–9 H9–8

D. Sun Chimes Series Vigorous, spreading, free-flowering plants in an increasing range of colors from reds and pinks through lavender and apricot to white. Bred by Graham Brown in New South Wales, Australia. ↕18 in (45 cm). Z7–9 H9–7

D. 'Twinkle' Tight spikes of purple-pink flowers and flushed with violet, open from late spring throughout summer. Bred from 'Lilac Belle'. ↕12 in (30 cm). Z7–9 H9–7

D. vigilis Large mats of fleshy, oval, deeply toothed leaves support loose clusters of large flowers, up to 1 in (2.5 cm) across, that are pink with purple stippling at the top of the lower petal, with pale spurs and white windows. One of the hardiest species in this genus, it flowers throughout the summer and into fall. From South Africa and Lesotho. ↕12 in (30 cm). Z7–9 H9–7. **'Jack Elliott'** Larger flowers. Collected in the Drakensburg Mountains, South Africa.

D. Wink Series A compact habit with upright flowers over dense mounds of deep green foliage. The colors include coral, salmon, and strawberry-red. ↕10 in (25 cm). Z7–9 H9–7

D. Whisper Series Free-flowering, vigorous and complementary to the Wink Series but with laxer growth. The colors include cranberry-red, lavender-pink, and pure white. Intended for baskets, but also good tumbling over low walls. ↕10 in (25 cm). Z7–9 H9–7

DICENTRA
Bleeding heart
PAPAVERACEAE

Shade- and moisture-lovers whose elegant foliage and arching stems of heart-shaped flowers grace the spring garden.

The 20 or so species of hardy annual and deciduous perennial dicentras grow mainly in moist places, including forests and mountains, in North America and Asia. Many are essential plants for borders and woodland gardens, and the more vigorous cultivars make fine ground cover among shrubs in a border. Perennials may have rhizomes or tubers, or even a thick, fleshy root. The foliage is often prettily divided, making a pleasing background for the dangling flowers, which range in hue from pink, red, and purple, to yellow and white. All parts are mildly toxic; some people may have an allergic reaction to the foliage. ⚠

CULTIVATION Thrives in rich, moist, neutral to slightly alkaline soil with abundant humus. Part-shade is best for most. Early spring growth is prone to frost damage, so grow in a sheltered site. Many self-seed freely, giving highly variable seedlings: rogue them out, or deadhead promptly, to keep plants true to type.

PROPAGATION By division in early spring or early fall, or after leaves die down in summer. Take root cuttings of *D. spectabilis* in winter; place in a cold frame. From seed for species, sown as soon as ripe or in spring, at 50°F (10°C).

PROBLEMS Slugs and snails attack spring foliage.

D. 'Adrian Bloom' Spreading rhizomes form clumps with gray-green leaves up to 20 in (50 cm) long. These

WOODLAND TREASURES

THE ELEGANT ARCHING SHOOTS of the pure white *Dicentra spectabilis* 'Alba', held on fresh green stems, are unusually lovely, lighting up dappled spring shade, and nearby trees and shrubs provide protection from late frosts and spring breezes, which can damage the relatively fragile growth. What a treat, stretching into the striking upright shoots of *Disporum uniflorum* with its yellow, tubular bells clustered at the top of the stems and steadily spreading right into, and under, the dicentra. In the background, a few blue sparks from *Brunnera macrophylla* are visible; later, its broad and rough-textured foliage will contrast nicely with that of the divided dicentra and glossy disporum. An annual mulch of weed-free organic matter will keep them all content.

set off 1¼-in- (3-cm-) long, glowing crimson flowers that appear in late spring and often again in early fall. Originated as a seedling from 'Bountiful' at Alan Bloom's Bressingham Gardens in Norfolk, England, and was named for his son, Adrian. Ideal choice for a border or woodland garden. ↕15 in (38 cm). Z4–8 H8–1

D. 'Bacchanal' Rhizomatous plant with ¾-in- (2-cm-) long, gray-green lobed leaves. Crimson flowers, to 1 in (2.5 cm) long, appear in mid- and late spring. Perhaps the darkest-flowered of all. ↕18 in (45 cm). Z3–9 H9–1

D. 'Boothman's Variety' see *D.* 'Stuart Boothman'

D. 'Bountiful' Forms clumps of fleshy, spreading rhizomes. The finely divided, gray-green leaves are up to 20 in (50 cm) long. Deep rose red flowers, about 1 in (2.5 cm) long, open in late spring and early summer and again in early fall. Needs good soil for best growth. ↕12 in (30 cm). Z4–8 H8–1

D. canadensis (Squirrel corn) Thread-like rhizomes produce many small, yellow tubers, giving rise to finely cut, somewhat triangular, green leaves with a hint of gray that grow to 12 in (30 cm). Fragrant, white, 1-in (2.5-cm) long flowers, tinged with mauve, appear in mid- and late spring. Thrives in a neutral to slightly acidic soil. From damp woods in North America. ↕12 in (30 cm). Z4–8 H8–4

D. cucullaria Compact, clump-forming, tuberous plant. Deeply lobed or cut, blue-green leaves, up to 10 in (25 cm) long. These are overtopped in early or mid-spring by stems of white, yellow-tipped flowers, up to ¾ in (2 cm) long. Needs gritty, well-drained, yet humus-rich soil in part-shade. Soon dies down after flowering. Best kept virtually dry during summer dormancy. Can be unexpectedly robust in the wild. From eastern areas of North America (Nova Scotia to North Carolina and Kansas). ↕8 in (20 cm). Z4–8 H8–1

D. eximia This excellent plant has fleshy rhizomes that form a matted clump of gray-green, parsleylike leaves up to 20 in (50 cm) long. Magenta-rose, 1¼-in- (3-cm-) long flowers are carried in stumpy sprays in late spring, and sparingly to early fall. Performs best in cool summers; in hot, dry summers, it tends to look bedraggled and die back, but revives when the weather cools. Much confused with *D. formosa* (*see* Which is Which?). From the mountains of the eastern US. ↕24 in (60 cm). Z7–3 H10–1. **'Snowdrift'** Pure white flowers, pale gray-green foliage. ↕12 in (30 cm).

D. formosa Very similar to *D. eximia* (*see* Which is Which?) 1 in (2.5 cm) long, in late spring and early summer. Often self-seeds prolifically. From western areas of North America. ↕18 in (45 cm). Z4–8 H10–1. ***alba*** White flowers. **'Aurora'** Large, white flowers. **subsp. *formosa*** Leaves gray below, but rarely above, and flowers rosy purple to pink, rarely white. From Washington, Oregon, and California. **subsp. *oregana*** Leaves gray above and below; flowers cream, occasionally pale yellow, with pink tips. Restricted to two small areas in Oregon and California.

D. 'King of Hearts' Exceptionally blue leaves, up to 12 in (30 cm) long, make a superb background for the dark pink-red flowers. These are about 1 in (2.5 cm) long and are borne from mid- or late spring to mid-fall. A robust, yet compact hybrid and a much-sought-after plant—beware paler-flowered impostors. Hybrid between the rather fussy *D. peregrina* from Japan and a hybrid of two North American species, *D. formosa* subsp. *oregana* and *D. eximia*. ↕10 in (25 cm). Z5–9 H8–1

D. 'Langtrees' Vigorous, spreading plant with rhizomes that give rise to silver-gray, lobed leaves up to 12 in (30 cm) long. Pink-tinted white flowers, ¾ in (2 cm) long, appear from mid-spring to early summer, or into midsummer. Said to be a later renaming of 'Pearl Drops'—certainly very similar. ↕12 in (30 cm). Z4–8 H8–1

D. 'Luxuriant' Spreading plant with fresh green, ferny leaves up to 12 in (30 cm) long, and 1-in (2.5-cm) red flowers from mid-spring to early summer or midsummer. ↕12 in (30 cm). Z4–8 H8–1

D. macrantha Spreading plant with ferny, light green to pale yellow-green leaves. Slim, 3 in (8 cm) long, creamy yellow flowers hang from stems in late spring. Especially prone to frost and wind damage in spring. From eastern China. ↕24 in (60 cm). Z4–8 H8–1

D. macrocapnos Unusual climber for walls and fences, or for growing through a large shrub, with delicate, ferny foliage. Clusters of 1-in (2.5-cm), bright yellow flowers are borne prolifically from early summer to early fall, and brown as they fade. Fairly recent introduction from Nepal. Needs shelter. ↕10 ft (3 m) or more. Z6–8 H8–1

D. 'Pearl Drops' Spreading fairly freely by rhizomes, with handsome, lobed, blue-gray leaves up to 12 in (30 cm) long. White, pink-tinted flowers, ½ in (1 cm) long, from mid-spring to early summer or midsummer. A seedling raised by Japanese nurseryman Dr. Tsushenige Rokujo and introduced by Alan Bloom of England. ↕12 in (30 cm). Z3–9 H8–1

D. scandens syn. *D. thalictrifolia* Climber for sheltered walls and fences. Deeply lobed leaves up to 14 in (35 cm) long, some with tendrils. Yellow, or sometimes white, 1-in- (2.5-cm-) long flowers, occasionally tipped with pink or purple-pink, emerge from mid-spring to mid-fall. From the Himalaya. ↕10–12 ft (3–4 m). Z6–8 H10–1. **'Athens Yellow'** Brighter yellow flowers, very floriferous, and more vigorous.

D. Snowflakes ('Fusd') Fresh green, very finely cut leaves make a superb foil for the pure white flowers, about 1 in (2.5 cm) long, that appear in late spring and early summer. A beautiful, cool-hued plant, but can be uncomfortably vigorous. Found in a garden in Yorkshire, England. ↕10 in (25 cm). Z3–8 H10–1

D. spectabilis (Bleeding heart) Extremely elegant, tight clumps of light green leaves, with cut or lobed leaflets, that grow up to 16 in (40 cm) long. Early in the season, tall, rather succulent shoots emerge; in late spring and early summer, rose-pink to purple-pink and white lockets, about 1¼ in (3 cm) long, are carried in long, arching sprays. Very susceptible to spring frosts, but tolerates sun if the soil stays moist; best in fertile soil with good drainage. Fleshy, fanglike roots resent division. From northern

WHICH IS WHICH?

Two North American species, *Dicentra eximia* and *D. formosa*, are very similar and often confused.

Dicentra eximia is confined to eastern areas of the US, mainly in the Appalachian Mountains from North Carolina and Tennessee to Maryland and a few sites in Pennsylvania and New Jersey. It is threatened or endangered in northern parts of its range. Plants in other areas are likely to be misidentified, or be garden escapes.

D. formosa is confined to western regions of North America, with two subspecies. *D. formosa* subsp. *formosa* occurs from Vancouver Island and British Columbia in the north through the Cascades and Coast Ranges, and along the Sierra Nevada into California. There is also a race with twice as many chromosomes, which grows from Oregon's Cascade Mountains south through the Coast Ranges into central California. Flowers of both races vary in size, shape, and color. *D. formosa* subsp. *oregana* has a highly restricted distribution, found in just four counties straddling the California–Oregon state line.

The two species also differ in their flowers, particularly in the size of reflexed portions of the outer petals: in *D. eximia,* they are ⅙–⅓ in (4–8 mm) long, while in *D. formosa,* they are only 1⁄12–⅕ in (2–5 mm).

This is all very arcane, but the similarity of the two species has led to much misidentification and also to confusion. This would not matter, however, if there were not also major differences that gardeners would appreciate. For example, *D. formosa* is less tolerant of hot, humid summers, and more tolerant of drought; it is also more aggressive, spreading by rhizomes and self-seeding profusely.

1

2

3

RIGHT 1 *Dicentra* 'Bacchanal' **2** *D. cucullaria* **3** *D. scandens*

China, Korea, and Siberia. ↕4 ft (1.2 m). Z3–9 H9–1. **'Alba'** Pure white flowers until midsummer. **'Gold Heart'** Yellow leaves and pale pink flowers.

D. 'Spring Morning' Clumps of spreading rhizomes produce ferny medium- or deep green leaves, to 20 in (50 cm) long. Pale pink flowers, 1¼-in- (3-cm-) long, in late summer and early fall. ↕12 in (30 cm). Z3–9 H9–1

D. 'Stuart Boothman' syn. *D. 'Boothman's Variety'* Spreading vigorously by rhizomes, this first-class plant has ferny, blue-gray leaves up to 8 in (20 cm) long. Leaves contrast beautifully with deep pink flowers, about 1 in (2.5 cm) long, from mid-spring to early summer or midsummer. Plants with deeper colored flowers are listed under the probably invalid name of 'Dark Stuart Boothman'. 'Boothman's Variety' is said to be paler, but this is an indication of only how freely the plants self-seed and how the seedlings vary. ↕12 in (30 cm). Z3–9 H9–1

D. thalictrifolia see *D. scandens*

DICLIPTERA
ACANTHACEAE

Uncommon foliage and flowering plants that add a touch of distinction to a sheltered border.

About 150 species of climbers, shrubs, perennials, and annuals are found in tropical and warm temperate regions. Most of those cultivated are grown as potted plants in the greenhouse and home. All are typified by usually six-sided stems, terminal clusters of long, slender two-lipped flowers, and opposite pairs of untoothed, velvety leaves.

CULTIVATION Fertile, well-drained but not dry soil and a sunny or part-shaded position. In cold areas, these plants are best overwintered in a frost-free place.

PROPAGATION From cuttings, any time from spring to late summer.

PROBLEMS Usually trouble-free.

D. suberecta Semierect, woody-based perennial with slender, velvety gray stems set with pairs of equally downy oval green leaves, to 2¾ in (7 cm) long. In summer and fall, each stem terminates in elongated clusters of 1¼ – 1½ in (3–3.5 cm) long brick-red flowers which also spring from the upper leaf joints. From Uruguay. ↕12–20 in (30–50 cm). Z8–11 H11–8

DICTAMNUS
Burning bush, Dittany, Gas plant
RUTACEAE

Showy and imposing plants for any sunny border, with an intriguing reputation.

The species most commonly grown, which is found naturally across a wide range from southern Europe to China and Korea, makes a large, long-lived clump. Stems, woody at the base arising from tough roots, carry aromatic foliage topped with dramatic spikes of flowers in early summer. These plants get their common names from a volatile oil, given off by the flowers and seed pods, that, in theory, can be ignited on a calm evening and will burn off without harming the plant. Although it rarely works as expected, the oil causes a reaction in some people that may lead to photodermatitis. All parts of the plant are slightly toxic if swallowed. ⚠

CULTIVATION Grow in well-drained, rich soil in sun. Plants take a couple of years to become established.

PROPAGATION From seed, sown outside in fall promptly when ripe. Germination is sporadic and it may be 18 months before all the viable seeds germinate. Division of plants can be attempted, but new plants are very slow to establish. Root cuttings can be used but the parent plant seldom recovers. If propagation were easier, it would be more widely grown.

PROBLEMS Usually trouble-free.

D. albus A stiff, upright plant, with glossy green leaves composed of up to 11 leaflets in pairs along a slightly flattened main rib. They have a distinctive citrus smell if rubbed. In early summer, white flowers open in terminal spikes, the lower of their five petals bent down to reveal upward-curved stamens. These are followed by star-shaped seed pods that persist until fall and can be cut for winter decoration. Seldom requires staking. ↕4 ft (1.2 m). Z3–8 H8–3. **var. purpureus** syn. *D. fraxinella* Pinkish mauve flowers with darker veins.

D. fraxinella see *D. albus* var. *purpureus*

DIERAMA
Angel's fishing rod, Wandflower
IRIDACEAE

Beautiful and increasingly popular sun-lovers with spectacular dancing flowering sprays.

About 44 species, all evergreen, grow in moist grasslands from sea level to around 9,800 ft (3,000 m) in South Africa's Kwazulu-Natal and Cape regions, and the northeastern area surrounding Pretoria, but also in Zaire, Uganda, Kenya, and Malawi. Growing from corms that build up year by year into chains, rather like those of *Crocosmia,* plants produce grassy tufts of long, often arching, narrow, tough, greeny gray 3–6-ft (1–2-m) leaves. In summer, graceful sprays of dainty bell-shaped flowers, usually protected by papery bracts, dangle loosely from slender stems—which accounts for the common names. Although the pendulous flowers are, individually, quite short-lived, they appear in considerable numbers, and in succession, during mid- and late summer. They usually come in shades of purple, pink, or mauve, but species and selections with dark red, white, and even yellow flowers have been recorded. Once the flowers fade, dangling, rounded seed capsules appear, which are themselves attractive until the seeds are shed.

The naming of garden dieramas is rather confused, with plants often incorrectly named in nurseries and garden centers; many are seedlings of mixed parentage. Naming of wild species, too, is less than straightforward, since all are very similar and occasional confusing variants occur—plants with upward-facing flowers, for example, may occasionally appear in a species with otherwise pendulous flowers.

CULTIVATION Dieramas are easy to grow, but fussy. That sounds contradictory, but what it means is that if their basic requirements are fulfilled, they will do well without

LEFT 1 *Dicliptera suberecta*
2 *Dictamnus albus*

LEFT 1 *Dierama dracomontanum*
2 *D. pulcherrimum*
3 *D. pulcherrimum* 'Blackbird'

much attention. Most are reasonably frost-hardy when established, but none survive frozen, waterlogged soil. Make sure they receive plenty of water during summer, but are kept drier in winter—fertile, free-draining soil is ideal. Planting in spring, adding gravel and compost before planting and working it in deeply, is a big help. They come from open, sunny sites in the wild, and enjoy similar conditions in gardens. Cut off, rather than pull off, old foliage in spring.

Grow dieramas at the front of borders, or in gravel gardens, where they associate particularly well with grasses. They have more impact if planted in drifts of several plants. Dieramas are attractive by water, provided plants are not allowed to get too wet in winter, and emerging from cracks in paving they look especially elegant and appreciate both the summer moisture and winter protection. Being deeply rooted, they do not, unfortunately, succeed in containers.

PROPAGATION From seed or by division. Dry corms are sometimes sold, but avoid them—they rarely grow. Seedlings do not come true, and will take about three years to establish before they start to flower freely. Cultivars, or good seedlings, are best propagated by division in spring, but this can be tricky, since clumps are deep-rooted and resent disturbance.

PROBLEMS Usually trouble-free.

D. 'Candy Stripe' Flowers distinctively striped in sugar pink and deep rose. A hybrid of *D. pulcherrimum*. ‡5 ft (1.5 m) Z7–10 H10–7

D. cooperi From small clumps of leaves, about 28 in (70 cm) tall, emerge much taller, usually solitary flowering stems, toward the tips of which dangle downward-facing, dainty flowers in bright pink, occasionally white. From Free State and Kwazulu-Natal

provinces, South Africa. ‡5–6½ ft (1.5–2 m). Z7–10 H10–7

D. dracomontanum The most familiar garden species, easily grown and increasing freely. Making quite large, dense clumps, this is one of the shorter dieramas, with grassy foliage 12–24 in (30–60 cm) high. Established plants produce many, often fairly upright, much taller flowering stems. Nodding, open flowers are quite variable in color varying from mauve, rose pink, or coral pink to almost red. From altitudes to 9,200 ft (2,800 m) in South Africa's Drakensberg Mountains. ‡3¼ ft (1 m). Z8–9 H9–8. **Wisley Princess Group** Compact plants with flowers in shades of dusky pink. One of the 2004 Royal Horticultural Society Bicentenary Plant Collection. ‡24 in (60 cm).

D. galpinii Through clumps of leaves, to 3¼ ft (1 m) high, taller erect flowering stems emerge carrying unexpectedly upward-facing, bright magenta-pink flowers clustered tightly on short branchlets. From the eastern Pretoria area and Kwazulu-Natal, South Africa. ‡5 ft (1.5 m). Z7–10 H10–7

D. 'Guinevere' Pure white-flowered hybrid of great beauty. The large dangling blooms are carried elegantly above the foliage between early and late summer. Unusual, some find it enjoys a moist site. Raised by Jim Cave of England. ‡3¼ ft (1 m). Z7–10 H10–7

D. igneum Forms small clumps with leaves 12–32 in (30–80 cm) tall, with arching flower stems reaching much higher. Flowers are open, rather flared bells in rich to pale lilac or even white (never at all fiery as the misleading name suggests). Similar to the more commonly cultivated *D. pendulum* but has more flowers, more densely clustered. From up to 5,000 ft (1,500 m) along the coast of Kwazulu-Natal to the eastern Cape, South Africa. ‡4¼ ft (1.3 m). Z7–10 H10–7

D. 'Knee-High Lavender' Delightful lavender, bell-shaped flowers. This

cultivar was raised by South African plant breeder Jim Holmes. ‡20 in (50 cm). Z7–10 H10–7

D. 'Lancelot' Large, dangling, bell-shaped shell-pink flowers are borne on arching stems in great profusion. Raised by Jim Cave of England. ‡4 ft (1.2 m). Z7–10 H10–7

D. latifolium Rather broad foliage reaches 5 ft (1.5 m) in height, with much taller, gently arching flowering stems. The rather open flowers are crowded toward the ends of the flowering branchlets and are quite variable in color. Most common are shades of pink, but deep wine-red-flowered individuals are also found. In the wild, forms spectacular clumps to 10 ft (3 m) in diameter, but plants in cultivation are generally smaller. Found to around 6,600 ft (2,000 m) in central Kwazulu-Natal, South Africa. ‡8 ft (2.5 m). Z7–10 H10–7

D. medium A dainty species forming little more than a grassy tuft of leaves. Clusters of mauve flowers dangle from delicate, arching flowering stems. From moist, almost marshy areas in northeastern South Africa and Swaziland. ‡24 in (60 cm). Z7–10 H10–7

D. 'Merlin' Impressively sultry hybrid producing wonderful, dark blackberry purple, bell-shaped flowers that are almost black, from the plant's arching stems. From Jim Cave, probably derived from *D. pulcherrimum*. ‡3¼ ft (1 m). Z7–10 H10–7

D. pauciflorum Forms dense clumps of short leaves about 12–16 in (30–40 cm) high. The slightly taller, arching flowering stems are branched, with each branchlet bearing one to three dangling flowers, which are open, rather starry, and reddish pink in color. One of the smaller species, seen increasingly in gardens, widely distributed in eastern Zimbabwe and the Pretoria area and Free State province, South Africa. ‡24 in (60 cm). Z7–10 H10–7

D. pendulum Forms small clumps of foliage to around 32 in (80 cm). The much taller elegant flower stems carry purplish pink, bell-shaped blooms, the petals flaring at the base. A number of other species are thoughtlessly sold under this appealing name. ‡6½ ft (2 m). Z8–10 H10–8

D. 'Puck' Rose-colored flowers on compact yet graceful plants. They are similar to *D. dracomontanum* but a little taller and more vigorous. Named for one of the Shakespearean fairies (*see* Dierama Development). ‡28 in (70 cm) Z7–10 H10–7

D. pulcherrimum Eventually forms dramatic clumps of narrow leaves to almost 3¼ ft (1 m) high, topped by tall flower stems carrying large, distinctively tubular, pendulous flowers, the petals flaring at the tips. Flower color is variable and ranges from pale pink and magenta to rich purple. The most widely cultivated of *Dierama* species: large, mature plants make spectacular garden features and bloom for several weeks in summer. ‡6 ft (1.8 m). Z8–10 H10–8. **var. album** Pure white. **'Blackbird'** Darkest purple flowers,

DIERAMA DEVELOPMENT

Discovered in 1772, and first grown in Europe in 1825, it was not until William Slinger at the Slieve Donard Nursery, Newcastle, County Down, Northern Ireland, began to introduce named cultivars that interest and enthusiasm for *Dierama* grew. At first, he used existing forms of *D. pendulum* and *D. pulcherrimum* to create a series named after birds. Introduced in the 1920s and 30s, most of these are now lost (even the three that received Royal Horticultural Society awards—'Falcon', 'Kingfisher', and 'Windhover'), but 'Blackbird' may still be with us.

In the 1960s, Slinger then acquired the much shorter *D. dracomontanum*, and crossed this with *D. pulcherrimum* to create a series of graceful plants of intermediate height that he called the Slieve Donard Hybrids. Named for Shakespearean fairies, 'Puck' is still widely grown; 'Oberon' and 'Titania' are occasionally seen.

More recently, Jim Cave of Fir Tree Farm Nursery in Cornwall, England, has introduced a number of impressive selections named for figures in the legends of King Arthur: 'Guinevere', 'Lancelot', and 'Merlin' were the first.

Dieramas do not multiply rapidly, so the propagation of these named forms by division of the corms is very slow. For this reason, both gardeners and nurseries collect their seed and pass on the resulting plants under the parents' names. However, these seedlings are by no means guaranteed to resemble their parents.

most desirable. Seedlings in various darkish (and not so dark) shades have been sold under this name, and it is possible that the original plant may no longer be in cultivation (*see* Dierama Development, *p.167*). **Slieve Donard Hybrids** A name misused. Correctly, refers only to the series of named cultivars raised at Slieve Donard Nursery during the 1920s and 30s but now incorrectly given to almost any mixed colored seedlings.

D. reynoldsii A tall, fairly slender, beautiful species. Flowering stems reach above foliage, almost 3¼ ft (1 m) high. Dangling, bell-shaped flowers, a deep, sultry wine red, contrast with silvery, papery bracts. From Kwazulu-Natal and the eastern Cape, South Africa. ↕6½ ft (2 m). Z7–10 H10–7

D. robustum A tall, slender species with tufts of foliage up to 3¼ ft (1 m) high and taller upright flower stems. The dangling flowers are large and bell-shaped, flared at the opening, and usually pale in color, ranging from near white to pale mauve pink. From high ground in Free State province, Lesotho. ↕6½ ft (2 m). Z7–10 H10–7.

D. trichorhizum Small tufts of leaves no more than 12 in (30 cm) high, with erect flowering stems usually branching in two, each with up to three nodding flowers of pale mauve, pink, or light purple. From the mountains of notheastern South Africa. ↕20 in (50 cm). Z7–10 H10–7

DIGITALIS

Foxglove

SCROPHULARIACEAE

Statuesque plants for both formal borders and light woodlands, the taller species making impressive specimen groups.

About 20 species, including evergreen perennials, a few biennials, and one shrubbier species, are native to woodlands or meadows in Central Asia, northwest Africa, and Europe. All form a rosette of leaves in their first year and flower the next. Perennials form clumps of oval, oblong, or lance-shaped leaves, sometimes toothed, with smaller versions arranged alternately up the stems. The elegant one-sided spikes have nodding, two-lipped tubular flowers, often spotted or patterned within, in a variety of colors. They are generally rather short-lived. ⚠

CULTIVATION All do well in ordinary garden soil; they tolerate part-shade but do better in sunnier situations.

PROPAGATION From seed and, for the more persistent perennials, by basal cuttings or careful division.

PROBLEMS Usually trouble-free.

D. ambigua see *D. grandiflora*

D. ciliata A neat species, distinct in forming relatively long-lived, slow-spreading clumps and having small, lance-shaped, hairy leaves up to 4 in (10 cm) long. The stems may be green or purple-tinted and, in summer, carry ¾-in- (2-cm-) long, usually pale yellow or off-white flowers—which are more attractive than they sound. They are held more horizontally than in most species. Restricted to the Caucasus. ↕16–24 in (40–60 cm). Z5–8 H8–5

THE BIENNIAL FOXGLOVE

The most familiar foxglove, *Digitalis purpurea,* is not included here because it is generally recognized as, and grown as, a biennial rather than a perennial. It is, of course, a fine garden plant and has been used as a parent of some good garden hybrids like, *D.* x *mertonensis* and 'John Innes Tetra'.

D. purpurea can be encouraged not to die after flowering, as it is naturally inclined to do, by very prompt deadheading. However, this will probably only give an extra year's flowers, since the crown tends to rot in the winter after flowering, infection beginning at the base of the old flower stems. It is better, frankly, either to allow plants to self-seed (in which case the offspring may be unpredictable in color) or to buy fresh seed each year.

D. davisiana Narrow, finely toothed leaves, 3–4¾ in (8–12 cm) long, support the wandlike stems in early summer and carry numerous pale yellow flowers, about 1½ in (4 cm) long, with orange veining and a pronounced tonguelike lower lip. From coniferous forests of southern Turkey. ↕20–28 in (50–70 cm). Z8–10 H10–8

D. dubia Short-lived, and resembling a miniature version of the familiar biennial foxglove, *D. purpurea,* the 2–4¾-in- (5–12-cm-) long leaves are somewhat wrinkled above and hairy beneath. Rose pink or rarely white, 1½-in- (4-cm-) long flowers appear in short loose spikes from early to midsummer. From rocky hillsides in the Balearic Islands. ↕12–16 in (30–40 cm). Z8–10 H10–8

D. ferruginea (Rusty foxglove) An elegant and distinctive but short-lived, occasionally biennial, species. Basal leaves, 4–8-in- (10–20-cm-) long, are narrowly oblong; stem leaves are smaller. In summer, 1–1½-in- (2.5–3.5-cm-) long flowers, appear in dense spikes; they vary from yellowish to reddish brown with darker veining within, and a tonguelike lower lip covered with long white hairs. From southeastern Europe, Turkey, and the Caucasus. ↕3–4 ft (1–1.2 m). Z4–9 H9–1. **'Gelber Herold'** Flowers the color of Dijon mustard. **'Gigantea'** Larger, 1½-in (4-cm) flowers. **subsp. *schischkinii*** Smaller, ⅝-in (1.8-cm) flowers.

***D.* 'Glory of Roundway'** Instantly appealing, the attractive, slightly grayish foliage supports a long season of well-branched spikes of generally slightly pendulous tubular flowers, rich apricot-pink on the outside and paler inside, with a scattering of rusty speckles. Sterile, but long-lived and easily divided, though slow to propagate on a commercial scale, and so less commonly grown than it deserves. A hybrid between *D.* x *mertonensis* and *D. lutea* from The Botanic Nursery, Wiltshire, England. ↕4 ft (1.2 m). Z3–8 H8–1

D. grandiflora syn. *D. ambigua* (Yellow foxglove) Somewhat glossy green, narrowly oval to lance-shaped basal leaves to 8 in (20 cm) long, those on the stems smaller. The 1½–2-in- (4–5-cm-) long yellow flowers have a pretty network of brown veins within and appear in loose spikes in summer. The most widely grown and best of all the truly yellow-flowered foxgloves, despite being relatively short-lived. From eastern Europe to southwest Asia. ↕24–32 in (60–80 cm). Z3–8 H8–1. **'Carillon'** Very compact. ↕6 in (15 cm). **'Temple Bells'** Larger flowers.

***D.* 'John Innes Tetra'** An unusual hybrid between the pale, white-lipped *D. lanata* and the yellow-flowered *D. grandiflora,* it blends the characters of the two, giving attractive gray-green foliage below striking spikes of yellow, white-lipped flowers veined in honey brown. Raised at Britain's John Innes Institute in 1926; due to spontaneous chromosome doubling, breeds true. ↕24–36 in (60–90 cm). Z6–8 H9–3

D. laevigata Dark basal foliage, broadest toward the tip, supports rather lax stems that are occasionally branched, carrying a scattering of yellow flowers veined in reddish brown with just a few hairs on the contrasting white lip. Similar to *D. ferruginea* but with fewer flowers and far fewer hairs on the lips. Usually short-lived. Native to the Balkan peninsula. ↕36 in (90 cm). Z7–9 H9–3

D. lamarckii A very pretty foxglove with strap-shaped leaves, to 5 in (13 cm) long, often curved like a sickle. In summer, the sticky, downy stems bear loose spikes of rather fat, 1–1¼-in- (2.5–3-cm-) long bells, fawn with purplish veins inside. From Turkey. ↕20–32 in (50–80 cm). Z6–8 H9–3

D. lanata Unbranched stems, often reddish purple, carry dense spikes of white or pale yellow flowers, about 1 in (2.5 cm) long, with a longer, arching white lip, above a rosette of oblong or lance-shaped foliage. Closely related to both *D. laevigata* and *D. ferruginea,* but with much paler flowers. From Eastern Europe and Turkey. ↕36–40 in (90–100 cm). Z3–9 H9–1

D. lutea Forms clumps of oblong- to lance-shaped, somewhat glossy deep green basal leaves. Tough stems bear dense spikes of 1-in- (2.5-cm-) long, pale yellow, sometimes almost white, flowers from early to midsummer. One of the longer-lived perennial species,

RIGHT **1** *Digitalis ferruginea* **2** *D. grandiflora* **3** *D. mertonensis*

from western and central Europe and northwest Africa. ↕24–36 in (60–90 cm). Z3–8 H8–1. **'Flashing Spire'** Cream-variegated leaves.

D. × mertonensis An unusual hybrid between the pink-flowered, usually biennial *D. purpurea* and the yellow-flowered, short-lived, perennial *D. grandiflora*. The result is like a shorter version of *D. purpurea* with bold crowded spikes of 2–2½-in- (5–6-cm-) long flowers of a shade described as crushed strawberry pink. Raised at Britain's John Innes Institute and introduced in 1926; due to spontaneous chromosome doubling, this hybrid is fertile. (*See* also 'John Innes Tetra'.) ↕28–36 in (70–90 cm). Z3–8 H8–1

D. parviflora Slender perennial. Lance-shaped to oblong, deep green leaves. White downy stems are closely packed in summer. Narrow flowers, about ½–¾ in (1–2 cm) long, are an unusual brownish red with purple veining and white hair; an attractive slender spike. Restricted to the mountains of Spain. ↕16–24 in (40–60 cm). Z4–9 H9–1

D. stewartii Something of a mystery: this is not a plant that has ever been formally named by botanists and may well be a selection or hybrid that has somehow acquired this name. It resembles a fine form of *D. ferruginea*, and could be a variant of that species or a hybrid with the closely related *D. laevigatus.* Narrow, dark green

RIGHT **1** *Diphylleia cymosa* **2** *Disporopsis pernyi*

basal foliage supports the handsome spikes of orange flowers that set it apart from both its relatives. ↕36–48 in (90–120 cm). Z4–10 H9–1

D. viridiflora The least showy, but still charming, species, with slightly downy parts. Rosettes of oblong to lance-shaped leaves, 3–6½ in (8–17 cm) long, support tough, slender stems. Long greenish yellow flowers, ½–¾-in- (1.2–1.8-cm-), are darker-veined and carried in long, dense spikes from early summer to midsummer. A fairly persistent perennial. From the Balkan peninsula. ↕24–32 in (60–80 cm). Z6–8 H9–3

DIPHYLLEIA
BERBERIDACEAE

Seldom-grown shade-lovers with distinctive leaves, charmingly simple flowers, and unusual fruits.

Three species of these deciduous plants grow in deciduous woodlands in the mountains of eastern North America and northeast Asia; one is occasionally grown in gardens. Slowly spreading branching rhizomes support the large, elegant, rounded leaves. In late spring, clusters of pure white flowers appear on unbranched stems just above a pair of smaller leaves. The short-lived flowers are followed by bloomy dark blue berries. Bold but refined, these attractive shade-lovers deserve to be planted more widely.

CULTIVATION Best in a sheltered situation in full or part-shade, with moist, humus-rich soil.

PROPAGATION By division or from seed.

PROBLEMS Young growth may be badly damaged by slugs and snails.

D. cymosa (Umbrella leaf) Slowly spreads to form a large clump. Long-stalked, rounded leaves, to 24 in (60 cm) across, are divided almost to the stalk into two coarsely toothed lobes. Simple stems carry two smaller leaves above which, in late spring and early summer, six-petaled white flowers ¾ in (2 cm) across open in rounded clusters. The petals soon fall, but flowers are followed by bloomy deep blue berries ½ in (1 cm) across. From mountain woods in the eastern United States from Virginia to Georgia and Tennessee. ↕12–24 in (30–60 cm). Z7–10 H10–7

DISPOROPSIS
CONVALLARIACEAE

Shade-tolerant plants resembling a small, evergreen Solomon's seal (*Polygonatum*), and forming compact colonies.

About five species, all evergreen and spread by rhizomes, are found in woodland habitats in tropical and

subtropical parts of East Asia, from the Philippines to southeastern China. Just one, *D. pernyi*, is widely grown, but more are becoming available. Stout, branching rhizomes give rise to arching stems bearing oval or lance-shaped, evergreen leaves. Nodding, bell-shaped, white or greenish flowers arise singly or in pairs at the base of each upper leaf. Each petal has a characteristic scale on the inside below the tip, on which the stamen sits. Each flower is followed by a dark purplish berry. Attractive in a shade garden, it tolerates dry conditions once established; especially valued as an evergreen, although old stems can be removed in late winter if untidy.

CULTIVATION Thrives in fairly moist, humus-rich soil in part-shade.

PROPAGATION By division, or from seed.

PROBLEMS Usually trouble-free.

D. fuscopicta A characteristic knobby rhizome, contracted between the nodes, carries tall, arching stems lined with oval or elliptic 4-in (10-cm) leaves and solitary or paired flowers in the upper leaf joints. Flowers are followed by purple berries. The ⅝–¾-in (1.5–2-cm), creamy white flowers are tinged with

---

SYMPHONY IN YELLOWS

AFTER THE SPRING sunburst of yellow, when daffodils are so dominant, it is always interesting to try yellows again later in the season. Here, at Hadspen Garden in Somerset, England, the rambling rose 'Wickwar' up on the wall falls into the brilliant *Spartium junceum* in buttercup yellow, best pruned regularly to prevent it from becoming large, floppy, and overdominant, while thrusting toward it is another rose, 'Graham Thomas'. This is all viewed through an open curtain of the dependable perennial foxglove, *D. lutea*, with its small creamy bells lining long lengths of vertical stems, while in front creamy-centered leucanthemums lean in toward the path.

purple on the upper side. From hillside forests in southern China. ↕16–32 in (40–80 cm). Z7–9 H9–7

D. pernyi Makes a loose clump. Stiff but arching stems are clad in shiny dark green, lance-shaped or elliptic leaves to 4¾ in (12 cm) long. Slightly fragrant, bell-shaped flowers, ⅝ in (1.5 cm) long, appear singly or in pairs in leaf joints. Opens in early summer and midsummer. Creamy-white flowers are tipped with green on each petal, and may be followed by dark brownish purple berries. Sometimes misidentified as *Polygonatum cyrtonema*. From rocky places in forests and along shaded streambanks in southern China. ↕16 in (40 cm). Z6–9 H9–6

DISPORUM
Fairy bells
CONVALLARIACEAE

Elegant shade-lovers with attractive foliage and dainty flowers which usually followed by showy berries.

About 20, perhaps as many as 30, species of these mostly deciduous plants grow in forests and thickets in Asia, from the Himalaya through China to Japan, and also in North America. About eight are fairly commonly cultivated. Spreading by rhizomes and forming a clump of arching, usually branched stems, they carry lance-shaped to oval leaves and small clusters of tubular bell-shaped to bowl-shaped flowers. Spring or summer flowers may be white, greenish, yellow, pink, or dull purple, and are followed by black, orange, or red berries. They are generally easily grown, and ideal for planting in light shade beneath shrubs or small trees, or among other perennials such as hardy ferns. American species are sometimes separated into their own genus, *Prosartes*, mainly on details of genetic makeup and molecular structure.

LEFT Disporum uniflorum

RIGHT 1 *Dodecatheon meadia* f. *album*
2 *D. pulchellum* subsp. *pulchellum* 'Red Wings'

CULTIVATION Grows well in woodland conditions of part-shade, in well-drained, humus-rich soil.

PROPAGATION By division or from seed.

PROBLEMS Young growth may be damaged by slugs and snails; vine weevils may damage roots.

D. cantoniense syn. *D. pullum* Forms a compact clump of sparingly branched, arching stems with lance-shaped leaves to 4¾ in (12 cm) long. In late spring and early summer, tubular ⅝–1-in (1.5–2.5-cm) flowers open in a cluster of up to 10 at the tips of the stems. Flowers are usually purplish, sometimes creamy white or brownish red, and are followed by dark red berries. Rather a variable species, growing in forests in much of southern Asia from the Himalaya to southeast China. 20–48 in (50–120 cm). Z4–9 H9–1. "**Aureovariegata**" Leaves with a pale yellowish green center. Creamy flowers, tinged purple. This name is invalid. ↕14 in (35 cm).

D. flavens see *D. uniflorum*

D. hookeri syn. *Prosartes hookeri* (Small-flowered fairy bell) Variable clump-former, the tall, arching stems bearing slender-pointed, broadly lance-shaped 5½-in (14-cm) leaves, heart-shaped at the base. Pendulous, tubular, greenish white ½–¾-in (1–2-cm) flowers with slightly flared petals open in clusters of up to three at the tips of the stems, in late spring or early summer, followed in fall by orange-red berries. From forest clearings in northwestern North America. ↕12–32 in (30–80 cm). Z4–9 H9–1. **var. oreganum** Leaves hairy beneath, stamens protruding from flowers. Possibly not genuinely distinct.

D. maculatum syn. *Prosartes maculata* Low, clump-forming plant with arching stems bearing oval leaves to 4 in (10 cm) long. In late spring and early summer, narrowly bell-shaped ¾-in (2-cm) white flowers open, the petals spotted with purple. Each flower is followed by a hairy, yellow to orange berry, ripening in early fall. From woodlands in eastern North America. ↕12–20 in (30–50 cm). Z4–9 H9–1

D. pullum see *D. cantoniense*

D. sessile Vigorously spreading plant with narrowly oval, slender-pointed 2–6-in- (5–15-cm-) leaves borne on arching, branched stems. In late spring and early summer, small clusters of up to three tubular creamy-white 1–1¼-in (2.5–3-cm) flowers open at the tips of branches, each tinged green toward the tip; fall berries are blue-black. A lovely and useful colonizer, the green-leaved wild species is not often grown. From

woods in hills throughout Japan and Sakhalin. ↕12–24 in (30–60 cm). Z4–9 H9–1. '**Aureovariegatum**' Leaves striped with creamy yellow. This cultivar name is invalid. '**Variegatum**' Leaves neatly striped with white toward the apex. Other similar variegated forms exist, more than one of which may be sold under this name. ↕12–18 in (30–45 cm). '**White Lightning**' Leaves streaked with pale yellow in the center, becoming almost white with a narrow green margin. Weak. Sometimes, incorrectly, listed under *D. smithii*. ↕12 in (30 cm).

D. smithii syn. *Prosartes smithii* Clump-forming plant with arching, reddish branched stems bearing wavy-edged, oval 2–4¾-in (5–12-cm) leaves. Small clusters of up to six narrowly bell-shaped, greenish white flowers to 1¼ in (3 cm) long open in late spring and early summer, followed by striking orange berries. From moist woods in northwest North America. ↕12 in (30 cm). Z4–9 H9–1

D. uniflorum syn. *D. flavens* A slender, creeping rhizome sends up arching, simple or branched stems with short-stalked, elliptic leaves. One to three nodding, narrowly bell-shaped, pale yellow, ¾–1¼-in (2–3-cm) flowers open at the tips of the branches in mid- and late spring, followed in fall by oblong, blue-black berries. A very elegant plant in flower and in fruit. From forests in northeast China and Korea. ↕12–24 in (30–60 cm). Z5–9 H9–1

DODECATHEON
American cowslip, Shooting star
PRIMULACEAE

Hardy and very elegant spring- or early summer-flowering moisture-lovers.

There are 14 species of these deciduous plants, all of which are native in North America, where they grow in moist meadows (including high alpine meadows) or woodlands, making them ideal

for woodland gardens, shrub borders, or pool surrounds and streamsides. Closely related to *Primula,* they have either basal rosettes or tufts of oval, spoon-shaped or lance-shaped leaves, and round-topped heads of long-stalked nodding flowers. The flowers always attract attention because they look remarkably like those of cyclamen, with their swept-back petals and similar colors. The long, cone-shaped reproductive organs are another distinctive feature of the flowers.

CULTIVATION They thrive in damp yet well-drained soil, with plenty of moisture during the growing period. Dry soil when growing is the most common cause of disappointment. Make sure that the soil contains abundant humus, preferably leafmold. Thrives in sun or part-shade; plants become dormant in summer; some prefer to be kept dry during this period.

PROPAGATION By division in early spring. From seed for species only, sown as soon as ripe in an open cold frame.

PROBLEMS Slugs and snails.

D. amethystinum see *D. pulchellum*

D. 'Aphrodite' A large robust hybrid, ideal for woodland gardens and shrub borders, with light green leaves up to 12 in (30 cm) long and larger-than-average flowers on thick, sturdy stems. Clusters of several nodding mauve-pink flowers are carried on each stem during late spring and early summer. A hybrid or selection of *D. meadia*. ↕20 in (50 cm). Z4–8 H8–2

D. dentatum A small, very hardy species. Light to mid-green, lance-shaped leaves with jagged edges to 3 in (8 cm) long are carried on long stalks. The white flowers ½–¾ in (1–2 cm) long, have conspicuous dark anthers and are borne on slim stems in late spring. Best in moist shady conditions. From the Pacific Northwest south to Arizona, often growing near water. ‡ 8 in (20 cm). Z4–8 H8–2

D. hendersonii syn. *D. integrifolium* Relatively vigorous, fleshy deep green longish oval leaves grow up to 2½ in (6 cm) long, and in early summer, stout stems carry purple-pink, dark-centered 1-in (2.5-cm) flowers with a white basal ring. Can be propagated by detaching the tiny bulblets at the base of the roots. From western North America, from Vancouver Island, Canada, to California. ‡ 16 in (40 cm). Z5–7 H7–5

D. integrifolium see *D. hendersonii*

D. jeffreyi syn. *D. tetrandrum* Robust plant with light or mid-green, longish (to 12 in/30 cm) oval leaves, slightly fleshy and sticky. Red or magenta to deep purple flowers, 1 in (2.5 cm) long, with maroon and yellow stamens, appear in late spring and early summer. From western North America, from Alaska to California. ‡ 20 in (50 cm). Z4–8 H8–1. **'Rotlicht'** Bright red.

D. meadia syn. *D. pauciflorum* A very tough clump-former, and by far the most widely grown species, with oval, light to mid-green leaves, to 10 in (25 cm) long, with toothed edges. In mid- and late spring, heads of magenta-pink flowers to ¾ in (2 cm) long are borne on sturdy stems. Over 100 flowers have been counted in one head of a well-grown plant. *D. pulchellum* is sometimes sold under this name. From the eastern US, from Pennsylvania to Alabama. ‡ 16 in (40 cm). Z4–8 H8–1. **f. album** Creamy-white, dark-centered flowers with yellow anthers. **'Goliath'** Very large, lilac-rose flowers on stout stems; good for cutting. ‡ 28 in (70 cm). **'Queen Victoria'** Lilac-pink, unusually dwarf. ‡ 12 in (30 cm).

D. pauciflorum Name used for plants correctly found under *D. meadia* or sometimes *D. pulchellum*.

D. pulchellum syn. *D. amethystinum, D. radicatum* Very variable, hardy clump-former with oval to spoon-shaped mid-green leaves to 8 in (20 cm) long. Heads of deep cerise pink, or sometimes magenta, lavender, or white, dark-centered flowers, to ¾ in (2 cm) long, appear in mid- and late spring. Found at high altitudes in western North America and Mexico, and has become naturalized in the eastern US. Best in moist, shady conditions. ‡ 14 in (35 cm). Z4–7 H8–2. **subsp. pulchellum 'Red Wings'** Dark magenta-pink flowers in late spring and early summer, and light green leaves. ‡ 8 in (20 cm).

D. radicatum see *D. pulchellum*

D. tetrandrum see *D. jeffreyi*

DORONICUM
Leopard's bane
ASTERACEAE

A profusion of cheerful yellow daisies is the key attraction of these easy-going spring and early summer-flowering plants.

About 35 species, all deciduous and growing from rhizomes or tubers, grow in glades in mountain woodlands, in Europe and Asia as far east as Tibet. Five species are commonly grown in gardens, forming compact or spreading clumps of soft, oval or heart-shaped leaves that give rise to erect stems bearing smaller leaves and solitary or loosely clustered, daisylike flowerheads with yellow centers and many narrow, spreading ray florets. Plants grow best in part-shade, and work well interplanted among deciduous shrubs and small trees. Traditional cottage garden favorites for early in the season, the cultivars are seen listed under a variety of species in catalogs, but their origins are uncertain, so most are treated alphabetically here.

CULTIVATION Grow in any reasonably fertile, free-draining soil in dappled shade, preferably sheltered from the strongest summer sunshine.

PROPAGATION By division or, in some cases, from seed.

PROBLEMS Susceptible to root rots and powdery mildew; may be damaged by slugs and snails.

D. columnae 'Miss Mason' see *D. 'Miss Mason'*

D. x excelsum 'Harpur Crewe' syn. *D. plantagineum* 'Excelsum' Spreads by rhizomes to make a good-sized, rather open clump of softly hairy, strongly toothed, oval leaves. Erect, branched stems each bear up to four golden yellow flowers 4 in (10 cm) across in

mid- and late spring. Tolerates full sun in many areas but generally best in part-shade. *D. x excelsum* is thought to be a complex hybrid of *D. x willldenowii* (*D. pardalianches* x *D. plantagineum*) and *D. columnae*, but doubts linger. ‡ 24–32 in (60–80 cm). Z4–8 H8–1

D. 'Finesse' Compact clump of heart-shaped leaves, the bright yellow flowers with elegant, narrow ray florets. The long flower stalks make it good for cutting. Sometimes listed under *D. orientale*. ‡ 20 in (50 cm). Z4–8 H8–1

D. 'Little Leo' Very short, compact, bushy plant with typical heart-shaped mid-green leaves. In mid- and late spring, yellow flowers with a double layer of ray florets open above foliage. Sometimes listed under *D. orientale*. ‡ 10 in (25 cm). Z4–8 H8–1

D. 'Miss Mason' Spreads by rhizomes to make a neat clump a little broader than tall. The heart-shaped dark green leaves are 3 in (8 cm) long, the margins with rounded teeth. From mid- to late spring, bright yellow daisies 3 in (8 cm) across open on the leafy stems well above the main leaves. Sometimes listed under *D. columnae*. ‡ 16–24 in (40–60 cm). Z4–8 H8–1

D. orientale Compact plant, spreading by rhizomes, with rather pale green, heart-shaped leaves to 4 in (10 cm) long. In mid- and late spring, solitary, narrow-rayed bright yellow flowers, 1¼–2 in (3–5 cm) wide, open on sparsely leafy, upright stems. More tolerant of dry summer conditions than other species. Grows in rocky woods in southeast Europe and Central Asia. ‡ 12–24 in (30–60 cm). Z4–8 H8–1. **'Frühlingspracht'** (**'Spring Beauty'**) Compact plant with fully double flowers, longer-lasting but less elegant than single-flowered forms. ‡ 16 in (40 cm). **'Goldcrest'** Tall plant with golden-yellow flowerheads, each with two or three layers of comparatively broad, flat petals. Comes true from seed. ‡ 24 in (60 cm). **'Magnificum'** Flowers

1½–2 in (4–5 cm) across on multi-branched stems. Comes true from seed. ‡ 20 in (50 cm). **'Spring Beauty'** see 'Frühlingspracht'.

D. pardalianches (Great leopard's bane) Tuberous plant spreading by underground runners. The softly hairy mid-green basal leaves are 4¾ in (12 cm) long; among them rise erect stems with smaller leaves and loosely branched clusters of light yellow flowers, 2 in (5 cm) across, opening from mid- or late spring to early summer. Although tending to be invasive, it is a handsome and elegant plant and ideal for naturalizing in open woodlands. From woods in western and central Europe, frequently naturalized elsewhere. ‡ 36 in (90 cm). Z4–8 H8–1

D. plantagineum 'Excelsum' see *D. x excelsum* 'Harpur Crewe'

DRACOCEPHALUM
Dragon's-head
LAMIACEAE

Clump-forming plants with aromatic foliage topped by attractive blue to violet summer flowers, superficially resembling a large-flowered, slightly coarser *Nepeta* (catmint).

About 45 species of annuals, herbs, and dwarf shrubs from Europe, Asia, North Africa, and North America, only a few of which are commonly grown in gardens. Their natural habitats are rocky slopes, sunny dry meadows, and dry woodlands. The generally lance-shaped leaves are in opposite pairs with toothed or lobed edges; the flowers are in terminal spikes up to 12 in (30 cm) long, or in short sprays from the leaf bases.

CULTIVATION Thrives in dry locations with morning sun and shade during the heat of the day. Additional moisture is required in sunnier sites.

PROPAGATION From seed sown in fall or spring, or cuttings of new growth in spring.

PROBLEMS Occasionally, downy mildew and mites.

D. argunense syn. *D. ruyschianum* var. *speciosum, D. speciosum* A tough, bushy plant with more or less linear leaves to 2 in (5 cm) long, stalked at the base, but smaller and almost stalkless in the leafy spikes. The soft blue flowers are carried toward the tips in midsummer. Neglected, yet probably the showiest of all the dragon's-heads, worth a place at the front of any border. Best in slightly acidic soil. Native to northeast Asia. ‡ 30 in (75 cm). Z4–8 H8–1. **'Fuji Blue'** Bright blue flowers with a paler tip toward the lower petal. ‡ 12 in (30 cm). **'Fuji White'** Snow white, but with a pale blue flush on the lower petals. ‡ 12 in (30 cm).

D. grandiflorum A bushy plant, as wide as it is tall; the oblong basal leaves have

RIGHT **1** *Doronicum pardalianches*
2 *Dracocephalum argunense*

long stalks, the oval stem leaves have none. Intensely dark blue flowers appear on short, 3-in (8-cm) spikes in mid- and late summer with upper petals forming a pronounced hood over lower ones. From Siberia, but many of the plants sold under this name prove to be the Chinese *D. rupestre,* with wider, more heart-shaped basal foliage and violet-blue flowers. ‡ 12 in (30 cm). Z4–8 H8–4

D. ruyschianum (Siberian dragon's-head) The tallest species, and also the latest to flower. Slightly downy stems carry long and narrow leaves with their edges rolled under, and are tipped by short, 1-in (2.5-cm) spikes of flowers in the blue-purple to purple range, although white forms exist. Often grown from seed, so flower color can be unpredictable. Found from central Europe to Siberia. ‡ 24 in (60 cm). Z3–7 H7–1. **var. *speciosum*** see *D. argunense*

D. speciosum see *D. argunense*

DRACUNCULUS
Dragon arum
ARACEAE

Large, tuberous plant grown for its distinctly patterned foliage and its enormous and smelly flower; its botanical name means "little dragon."

Two species of *Dracunculus* are found in open sun to dryish part-shade in the eastern Mediterranean, but only one is widely cultivated. Its stout, distinctive shoots emerge from the tuberous roots in early spring, opening to rich green foliage, much divided and often highlighted by silver-white streaks. The single flower, with its typically aroid look (*see The Arum Family p.74*), is intensely colored and may have a strong and

BELOW 1 *Dracunculus vulgaris*

offensive smell that can be detected over a large area. After flowering, the plants go dormant by midsummer. A fine plant for a Mediterranean or gravel garden, but its strong smell at peak bloom would suggest that the best planting site be away from the house (or neighbors). ⚠

CULTIVATION Requires ample spring moisture and good drainage in dry, warm summers. Hardier in climates with hot summers than those with cool summers.

PROPAGATION By division of tubers.

PROBLEMS Usually trouble free.

D. vulgaris syn. *Arum dracunculus* Large, dramatic, tuberous perennial. Leaves, up to 30 x 10 in (75 x 25 cm) with many long narrow leaflets, are silver-white marked, and emerge early on stems. One flower, produced by each shoot, is rich blood red with a velvet surface and up to 24 in (60 cm) long. It stays open for four to five days, on one or more of which it has an intense, unpleasant fragrance that attracts flies for pollination. It then usually goes fully dormant in the heat of summer. In good growing conditions, it spreads to form a clump with multiple stems and flowers. A distinctive, colorful, and attractive plant, but not one for the faint-hearted. There are no cultivars, although pale, cream, white, or marbled flower forms occur in the wild. From the Mediterranean. ‡ 4–6 ft (1.2–1.8 m). Z8–10 H10–8

DRYOPTERIS
Male fern
DRYOPTERIDACEAE

Mostly robust, easily grown ferns that can form the backbone of any fern collection and mingle with shrubs.

Between 250 and 350 species of these tufted ferns grow mostly in woodlands or swampy places throughout the northern temperate regions of the world. Short rhizomes bear shuttlecock-like tufts of erect or arching, oval or lance-shaped fronds, divided once or more into segments that are usually toothed. Kidney-shaped spore-bearing structures are found on the undersides of the fronds. Most species are deciduous, some evergreen. Along with *Polystichum,* the male ferns comprise the largest number of species suitable for temperate gardens. Many are valuable garden plants: bold, often impressive, and generally tough ferns, many are unexpectedly drought-tolerant, especially when well established.

CULTIVATION Grow in moist woodlands or in dappled shade in a border with humus-rich soil. Many species withstand dry periods well.

PROPAGATION By division of crowns,

or from spores.

PROBLEMS Usually trouble-free, but may be damaged by thrips in dry weather.

D. affinis (Golden male fern) Robust, tufted evergreen fern with upright rhizomes, which in damp conditions may form a short trunk, carrying almost erect, oblong to lance-shaped, dark green fronds, twice divided into alternately arranged oblong segments that are somewhat squared at their tip. The frond midrib is covered with golden brown scales. Where the side stems join the midrib, there is a dark spot, easily seen on the underside: a characteristic distinguishing *D. affinis* and its allies from the somewhat similar *D. filix-mas.* A complex species with several subspecies and, to complicate matters further, *D. affinis* commonly hybridizes with *D. filix-mas* to produce *D. x complexa.* These plants are currently under investigation. Easy in most garden soil, it grows better in acidic soil but will tolerate alkalinity if given plenty of organic matter. Once established, will tolerate fairly dry conditions. Good where a large fern is required as background in dry shade. Native to woodlands and grassy banks in most of Europe. ‡ 28–48 in (70–120 cm). Z6–8 H8–6. **'Congesta Cristata'** Dwarf form; the fronds are crispy with the main leaflets partially overlapping and the tips of the fronds and leaflets neatly crested. ‡ 8 in (20 cm). **Crispa Group** Selected crispy forms with pale fronds, the segments are turned up at the edges. 28 in (70 cm). **'Crispa Gracilis'** Dark green crispy fronds, broadest at the midpoint. ‡ 8 in (20 cm). **'Cristata'** Dark green fronds that are neatly crested at the tips of the leaflets. A very handsome plant, known as "the king of the male ferns." ‡ 3¼–4 ft (1–1.2 m). **'Cristata Angusta'** Fronds are narrow, crested. ‡ 36 in (90 cm). **'Pinderi'** Erect, dark green, narrowly lance-shaped fronds. ‡ 20 in (50 cm). **'Polydactyla Dadds'** Fronds lance-shaped with fingered crests on all main frond segments (pinnae) and a heavy crest on the frond tip. The fingered crests of this cultivar are both larger and less uniform than the neat crests of 'Cristata'. ‡ 28 in (70 cm). **'Polydactyla Mapplebeck'** Fronds lance-shaped, heavily crested on all main frond segments and the frond tip. Like 'Polydactyla Dadds' but with heavier crests. ‡ 4 ft (1.2 m).

D. carthusiana (Narrow buckler fern) Deciduous with a short horizontal rhizome, so the fronds arise slightly separated rather than in a shuttlecock. The fronds are narrowly lance-shaped, pale grayish green, three times divided into opposite pairs of divisions, the main ones triangular. Distinguished from *D. dilatata* by its neater, narrower fronds and by the uniformly pale straw-colored scales near the base of the stalk. Needs a moist position. Native to marshes and bogs in much of Europe. ‡ 20 in (50 cm). Z6–8 H8–6

D. clintoniana (Clinton's wood fern)

Deciduous fern that has a short horizontal rhizome that bears tall, long-stemmed, erect, twice-divided, narrowly lance-shaped fronds with triangular main divisions. This plant needs a sheltered, moist, shady position. Grows in marshes and wet woodlands in eastern North America. ‡ 32 in (80 cm). Z3–8 H8–1

D. x complexa **'Stablerae'** Evergreen, nearly erect, narrow, lance-shaped, twice-divided fronds forming a shuttlecock with the leafy parts of the fronds wavy or crisped. There is more than one form, some being more compact. A British selection from the hybrid between *D. affinis* and *D. filix-mas* that is common through most of Europe. ‡ 36–48 in (90 cm–120 cm). Z6–8 H8–6

D. cristata (Crested buckler fern) A shortly creeping rhizome bearing slightly spreading sterile fronds and more erect fertile deciduous fronds that are narrowly lance-shaped and twice-divided. Triangular main segments are arranged up the main midrib in pairs that resemble a series of butterflies. Will grow in normal, reasonably dry borders, but for best results, the plant needs wet conditions and plenty of light, including some sun. Native to raised mossy hummocks in reed swamps and fens in Europe and eastern North America. ‡ 16–24 in (40–60 cm). Z6–8 H8–6

D. cycadina Distinctive semievergreen fern forming a tuft of erect to arching, lance-shaped fronds, with copious dark brown or black scales on the stalk and midrib. The narrow main divisions of the frond are undivided, but regularly toothed. Sometimes considered a form

CULTIVAR NAMES IN LATIN

Since 1959, international regulations governing the style of cultivar names have prevented plants from being given cultivar names in Latin; they must be in everyday language. Names coined in Latin before that date are, however, allowed to stand. In the 19th century, newly discovered forms of ferns in particular were routinely given names, in Latin, that are difficult to reconcile in these days of 'Amber Queen' and 'Razzmatazz' being applied to perennials: *Dryopteris filix-mas lux-lunae polydactyla* may be descriptive, if the Latin is familiar, but hardly rolls off the tongue. These Latinate names have been retained, albeit sometimes a little modified in their presentation, to make them easier to understand (and to say). Many of the cultivars of *Dryopteris,* and other ferns, that we grow today are tough and persistent plants and have been in gardens for well over a hundred years; so, more so than most perennials, these Latinate names are still in use. They serve as a reminder of the great days of fern hunting and of how fortunate we now are to have a more regulated system of naming.

of the more tender *D. atrata*. Grows in deep woodlands in Asia from the Himalaya to China and Japan. ‡ 24 in (60 cm). Z6–9 H9–6

D. dilatata (Broad buckler fern) Robust semievergreen fern with an erect rhizome bearing a tuft of arching, dark green fronds that are broadly lance-shaped to triangular, and divided three times into opposite pairs of strongly toothed segments. Distinctive scales on the base of the leaf stalk are dark in the center and paler brown at the edges, unlike the similar *D. carthusiana*. Luxuriates in moist shady conditions, and is probably the easiest fern to grow. Very common in Europe. ‡ 20–40 in (50–100 cm). Z6–8 H8–5. **'Crispa Whiteside'** Frond segments are attractively crisped. ‡ 16 in (40 cm). **'Grandiceps'** Rather upright fronds with a broad crest at the tip and on the ends of main segments. ‡ 20 in (50 cm). **'Lepidota Cristata'** Elegant, with all the frond segments narrowed and neat crests at the tips of main segments and frond. ‡ 16 in (40 cm).

D. erythrosora (Fall fern) Splendid evergreen fern with slightly glossy, long-stalked, triangular fronds that are divided two or three times into opposite pairs of leaflets. The young fronds are a bright red, gradually turning pink before becoming pale green. Justifiably one of the most popular garden ferns. Grows in woodlands in northeast Asia. ‡ 24 in (60 cm). Z2–6 H9–5. **var. prolifica** All frond segments narrower and more leathery. Occasionally produces bulbils on the frond, from which new plants can be raised.

D. filix-mas (Male fern) Robust, upright deciduous fern, with erect rhizomes forming clumps of mid-green, lance-shaped or oblong fronds twice divided into opposite pairs of leaflets. Frequently arrives uninvited in gardens; when established, it tolerates dry conditions better than most ferns,

and is a useful "filler" under trees. The common name refers to the robustness of this species compared to the similarly common, but more delicate-looking lady fern *(Athyrium filix-femina)*. Grows in woodlands and more open habitats in Europe, west Asia and North America, and is a very common native fern. ‡ 36–48 in (90 cm–120 cm). Z4–8 H8–1. **'Barnesii'** Tall, with narrower fronds and well-spaced main divisions. ‡ 4 ft (1.2 m). **'Crispa Cristata'** Fronds slightly crisped and crested at the tips and ends of the main segments. ‡ 24 in (60 cm). **'Cristata'** Fronds crested at tips and ends of divisions. ‡ 28 in (70 cm). **'Cristata Martindale'** Small twisted crests at frond tips and at ends of segments. The upper frond divisions curve gracefully toward the tip of the frond. ‡ 32 in (80 cm). **'Grandiceps Wills'** Fronds with a broad, often branched, terminal crest and small crests on the frond segments. ‡ 28 in (70 cm). **'Linearis'** Fronds dark green and more leathery with narrow ultimate segments. ‡ 24 in (60 cm). **'Linearis Polydactyla'** Long, fingered crests at tips of fronds and segments. ‡ 12 in (30 cm).

D. goldieana (Goldie's wood fern) A large, deciduous fern with long-stalked and broadly triangular-oblong, pale green fronds, twice divided, the main divisions being quite broad and oblong. This is a beautiful fern, but the plant requires a sheltered position in the garden in order to avoid wind damage. Grows in damp woodlands in northeastern North America. ‡ 3–4 ft (1–1.2 m). Z6–8 H8–5

D. marginalis Tufted semievergreen or deciduous fern with a short, upright rhizome bearing lance-shaped, dark bluish green fronds, which are twice divided, with the spore-heaps close to the edges of the finely scalloped frond segments. Will tolerate drier conditions when it is well established. Found in rocky woodlands in northeastern

ABOVE 1 *Dryopteris affinis*
2 *D.* 'Cristata Angustata'

North America. ‡ 20 in (50 cm). Z3–8 H8–1

D. sieboldii Very distinctive evergreen fern with pale green fronds composed of up to four pairs of very leathery, narrowly lance-shaped leaflets with a similar terminal leaflet—quite unlike most other *Dryopteris* species. A spectacularly different fern that deserves to be more widely grown, unexpectedly preferring moist shade in gardens; it comes from dry mountain forests in Japan and China. ‡ 16 in (40 cm). Z7–10 H10–7

D. tokyoensis Tall, deciduous fern with a short rhizome, forming a narrowly vase-shaped rosette of pale green, upright fronds that are divided into many narrow, well-spaced, tapering leaflets, each deeply scalloped on the margin. Makes a striking accent plant, but the tall fronds require shelter from the wind. Native to moist woods and clearings throughout Japan; also found in Korea and China. ‡ 3¼ ft (1 m). Z6–8 H8–6

D. wallichiana Large, handsome evergreen fern forming an erect crown of fronds, the stout rhizome sometimes forming a short trunk. The fronds are oblong to lance-shaped and twice-divided into oblong, slightly glossy green segments. The plant resembles *D. affinis*, but the copious scales on the stalk and midrib of this fern are dark brown to black—golden brown in *D. affinis*—and very conspicuous on the crozierlike unfurling fronds. This is rightly one of the most popular garden ferns, a group of well-grown plants creating an eye-catching effect. It grows best in moist shade, or in dappled shade in soil with added organic matter. Native to forests in Asia from the Himalaya to China and Japan (where

it may be extinct); also Jamaica, Mexico, and Hawaii. ‡ 4¼–5½ ft (1.3–1.6 m). Z5–7 H11–10

DUCHESNEA
ROSACEAE

Modest, summer-flowering ground cover with a long season of foliage interest.

Two species of sprawling, strawberry-like perennials native to India and southeast Asia are found in meadows, on mountain slopes and river banks. Lax stems root as they run along the ground, supporting plantlets with short-stemmed leaves composed of three wedge-shaped leaflets. From base of leaves, separate shoots each bear a single, bowl-shaped flower with five rounded petals, from which develops a spongy, rounded fruit. A durable ground cover under trees and shrubs, or over banks; also used to trail from hanging baskets. Tolerant of summer drought, but spreads most rapidly in moderately fertile soil that is moist yet well-drained. May become a nuisance where planted in unsuitable places, yet is easily curbed by pulling out the surface-rooting runners. Named in honor of the 18th-century French botanist Antoine Nicolas Duchesne, author of a natural history of strawberries; some botanists now suggest that *Duchesnea* may be better placed within *Potentilla* (along with *Fragaria*, *see* Hybrids and a Name Change, *p.201*) where its nearest relatives lie.

CULTIVATION Adapts to most soils, in full sun or light shade.

PROPAGATION By division, rooting plantlets at the tips of runners, or seed.

PROBLEMS Usually trouble-free.

D. indica syn. *Fragaria indica* (Indian strawberry, Mock strawberry) Semievergreen rosettes of leaves throw out long runners that root at intervals along their length, enabling the plant to spread widely. The three leaflets forming the leaves are dark green, serrated along the edge, and up to 1½ in (3.5 cm) long. For weeks in summer, the foliage is dotted with golden flowers, about 1 in (2.5 cm) across, sitting within green, leafy ruffs. Attractive fruits, brilliant red and shiny, follow in early fall. The plant is very similar to the strawberry (*Fragaria*), except for its yellow flowers and tasteless fruit. Variegated cultivars tend to be less rampant. Naturalized in Africa, North America, and southern Europe; native to India and Afghanistan east through China to Japan, and south to Indonesia. ‡ 2–4 in (5–10 cm). Z6–8 H8–6. **'Harlequin'** Leaves mottled creamy white, with slight pink tints most pronounced in full sun. Surprisingly, comes true from seed. **'Snowflake'** White-edged leaves. Propagate by either rooted plantlets or division.

E

ECHINACEA
Coneflower
ASTERACEAE

Striking summer daisies beloved by butterflies, with their prominent central cones held on sturdy stems.

Nine species of these deciduous perennials are found in a variety of dry habitats, including prairies, rocky hillsides, gravelly areas, and open woodlands in central and eastern North America. The thick, black rootstocks carry basal clumps of dark green, rough-textured leaves and stiff, erect, bristly, generally unbranched stems bearing alternate leaves and large, solitary flowerheads. These consist of a prominent, hemispherical to broadly cone-shaped disk of green, brown, or purple florets interspersed with stiff, yellow to brown spinelike scales. These emerge above the disk florets, giving the cone a prickly and often orange-brown appearance.

The angle at which the ray florets are held gives the plants real character: some are stiffly horizontal on emergence while others will droop languidly with the upstanding cone held proudly above. The ray florets are usually in shades of purplish pink to reddish purple, but they can be white or yellow. Many species have a honey scent and attract bees and especially butterflies. The name *Echinacea* derives from *echinos*, from the Greek for "hedgehog," for the resemblance of the plant's cone to the spines of a hedgehog.

All species are reputed to hybridize with each other; breeders are starting to exploit the yellow of *E. paradoxa* to create orange shades.

Echinacea is an important source of a herbal medicine used to stimulate the immune system. This is mainly extracted from the roots of *E. angustifolia*, but *E. purpurea* and *E. pallida* are also used.

CULTIVATION Thrive in deep, humus-rich, well-drained soil in full sun; poor drainage in winter will lead to losses, and a dry mulch is advisable in extremely cold areas. Echinaceas are unusually tolerant of hot summers. Cut back flowered stems to encourage a longer display, but leave the plants to develop into substantial clumps, since the plants resent disturbance.

PROPAGATION Sow seed of *E. purpurea* at 68°F (20°C) in spring. The seed of other species may need a cold spell before it will germinate. Root cuttings can be taken in late fall or in early winter. Division can be attempted in spring but it can be unreliable.

PROBLEMS Usually trouble-free.

E. angustifolia (Narrow-leaved coneflower) Deciduous perennial with a less compact rootstock than some species and hairy, untoothed, narrowly lance-shaped leaves to 6 in (15 cm). The flowerheads, produced from early to late summer, have an orange-brown cone and pale purple to pink, drooping, narrow ray florets to 1 in (2.5 cm). Native to plains, prairies, and open woodlands of central North America. ‡12–32 in (30–80 cm). Z4–9 H9–1

E. 'Art's Pride' see *E.* Orange Meadowbrite

***E.* Mango Meadowbrite** (‘CBG Clone 3’) Horizontal mango-yellow rays surround an unusually well-scented orange cone. It is a spontaneous mutation of Orange Meadowbrite from the Chicago Botanic Garden, IL. ‡24–36 in (60–90 cm). Z4–9 H9–1

***E.* Orange Meadowbrite** (‘Art's Pride’) A breeding breakthrough: the horizontal rays are deep orange, the cone is brown. A hybrid of *E. paradoxa* and *E. purpurea* bred by Dr. Jim Ault of the Chicago Botanic Garden, IL. ‡24–32 in (60–90 cm). Z4–9 H9–1

E. pallida (Pale coneflower) Taprooted deciduous perennial with hairy, untoothed linear to elliptical leaves to 8 in (20 cm). Flowerheads, produced from midsummer to early fall, consist of an orange-brown cone and slender, drooping ray florets, 1½–3½ in (4–9 cm) long, like the trails of a jellyfish. Pink but quickly fading to pale pink, or near-white at the tip. Native to prairies and hillsides of eastern US. ‡3¼–4¼ ft (1–1.25 m). Z4–8 H8–1

E. paradoxa (Bush's coneflower) A tightly spreading, deciduous, virtually hairless perennial with linear or lance-shaped leaves to 8 in (20 cm). The flowerheads, produced from midsummer to early fall, have a dark brown cone and drooping, narrow, yellow ray florets to 2¾ in (7 cm) long. Native to the prairies of south-central US; protected in Arkansas. ‡3¼ ft (1 m). Z4–8 H8–1

E. purpurea syn. *Rudbeckia purpurea* (Purple coneflower) The most widely grown species. Slowly expanding crowns carry roughly hairy, toothed leaves to 6 in (15 cm); basal leaves are egg-shaped, those on the stem narrower. Rigid stems carry flowerheads to 4¾ in (12 cm) across from midsummer to mid-fall, with an orange-brown cone and ray florets ¼–3 in (3–8 cm) long. Ray florets are

BOLD AND BEAUTIFUL

THE PURPLE CONEFLOWER, *Echinacea purpurea*, is a dependably dramatic plant: determinedly upright, endearingly robust, and with unmistakable broad-centered flowers. The dark stems also add appeal, but the plant cries out for something frothy and mounding to disguise what is often deteriorating basal foliage and provide a colorful launch pad for those skyward stems. Hardy geraniums fit the bill well, especially as the long season of so many cultivars matches that of the echinacea. Geraniums in a wide variety of pink shades will compliment this pink echinacea, and white echinaceas, too, will take many companions. With the more recent orange shades, a vivid blue geranium like G. ‘Anne Thomson’ would provide contrasting flower color with more harmonious yellow foliage.

ECHINACEA FLOWER STRUCTURE

Echinaceas are recognizably members of the daisy family, Asteraceae. The central part of the flower, known as the cone or more correctly the disk, is made up of tightly packed florets without petals, known as the disk florets, interspersed with stiff pointed scales. The shape and anatomical character of these pointed scales distinguishes *Echinacea* from *Rudbeckia*. The scales stand proud of the florets and they give the disk its color. Surrounding the disk are the rays or ray florets, which give the flower its attractive coloring.

Echinacea purpurea ‘White Swan’

Spiky scales give disk its color

Disk floret

Ray floret

typically reddish purple (or white) but many shades have been developed and cultivars also vary in the width, length, and poise of the rays. White cultivars may have a yellowish green cone; stems of deeper-colored flowers are often deep maroon. Cultivars are often very variable, even if not intended, through having been grown from seed and not selected for purity (*see* Fashion and Variability, *p. 168*). The species is native to prairies and open woods of eastern US. ‡20–60 in (50–150 cm). Z3–9 H9–1. **'Alba'** Ray florets white. ‡32 in (80 cm). **'Augustkönigin'** Ray florets horizontal, narrow, numerous, rose-pink with gray overlay. ‡3¼ ft (1 m). **Bressingham hybrids** Seedlings of 'Robert Bloom' ranging from pale pink to carmine red, though should be the same shade as 'Robert Bloom'. ‡36 in (90 cm). **'Doubledecker'** syn. 'Indiaca' Deep rose pink with an extra tuft of florets emerging from the top of the cone. Startling. ‡3¼ ft (1 m). **'Fragrant Angel'** Strongly branched flower stems carry white flowers with many overlapping, horizontal white ray florets. Well scented. ‡3¼ ft (1 m). **'Indiaca'** *see* 'Doubledecker'. **'Kim's Knee High'** Small flowerheads, ray florets reflexed, and a clear, bright pink. Selected by North Carolina horticulturist Kim Hawkes. ‡24 in (60 cm). **'Kim's Mop Head'** Ray florets white, disk yellowish green. A spontaneous mutation of 'Kim's Knee High'. ‡24 in (60 cm). **'Leuchtstern'** Ray florets horizontal, dark purple-red. ‡30 in (75 cm). **'Little Giant'** Flowerheads 3–4¾ in (8–12 cm) across, ray florets horizontal, pink. ‡16 in (40 cm). **'Magnus'** Numerous broad, overlapping, horizontal ray florets in deep reddish pink. ‡3¼ ft (1 m). **'Prairie Frost'** Leaves variegated with a narrow, white margin. Flowerheads 2¾ in (7 cm) across, ray florets horizontal, broad, purplish pink. ‡3¼ ft (1 m). **'Razzmatazz'** Ray florets purplish pink, disk transformed into a large pompon of short, slightly darker florets. Distinctive, the first of its kind. ‡36 in (90 cm). **'Robert Bloom'** Ray florets reddish purple. Selected by Alan Bloom. ‡36 in (90 cm). **'Rubinglow'** Ray florets numerous, overlapping, horizontal, carmine-red. ‡28 in (70 cm). **'Rubinstern'** Flowerheads 4¾ in (12 cm) across, ray florets horizontal, ruby-red. ‡34 in (85 cm). **'Ruby Giant'** Branched flower stems, flowerheads 4¾ in (12 cm) across, ray florets in two rows, reddish pink fading to grayish pink. ‡34 in (85 cm). **'Sparkler'** Rose pink flowers; foliage speckled and splashed in cream. ‡24 in (60 cm). **'Vintage Wine'** Short, very deep pink ray florets held slightly above the horizontal, around a relatively flat cone. Raised by Piet Oudolf in Holland. ‡36 in (90 cm). **'White Lustre'** Ray florets creamy

RIGHT 1 *Echinacea* Orange Meadowbrite
2 *E. purpurea* 'Pallida'
3 *E. purpurea* 'Augustkönigin'
4 *E. purpurea* 'Kim's Knee High'
5 *E. purpurea* 'Kim's Mop Head'
6 *E. purpurea* 'Robert Bloom'

white, cone yellowish green. ‡ 24 in (60 cm). **'White Swan'** Ray florets reflexed and white, cone orange-brown. ‡ 28 in (70 cm).

E. 'Sunrise' Pale, vivid yellow rays surround a golden cone. A hybrid of *E. paradoxa* and *E. purpurea* bred by Itsaul Nurseries in Atlanta, GA. ‡ 3¼ ft (1 m). Z4–9 H9–1

E. 'Sunset' Bright orange rays, broader than those of Orange Meadowbrite. A hybrid of *E. paradoxa* and *E. purpurea* bred by Itsaul Nurseries in Atlanta, GA. ‡ 3¼ ft (1 m). Z4–9 H9–1

E. tennesseensis (Tennessee coneflower) Shortly rhizomatous, deciduous, hairy perennial; linear leaves to 7 in (18 cm). Flowerheads with narrow, horizontal, purplish pink ray florets to 1 in (2.5 cm) long are produced from midsummer to early fall. Endangered species found in open clearings in limestone soil in conifer woodlands. Restricted to five protected populations in Tennessee. ‡ 12 in (30 cm). Z3–9 H9–1. **'Rocky Top'** Petals curve upward around the coppery cone.

FASHION AND VARIABILITY

Echinaceas are fashionable. As wilder styles of gardening caught on, they were seen as ideal members of naturalistic plantings. And when a plant becomes more popular, plant breeders produce new variants and the new introductions themselves fuel the fire. So dwarf forms, the pompon *E. purpurea* 'Razzmatazz', and hybrids between *E. purpurea* and *E. paradoxa* that have produced new colors, have brought echinaceas to a broader range of gardeners.

But while breeding continues in a number of countries, propagation by division is slow. Some cultivars are propagated by tissue culture, but many small nurseries, eager to have plants for sale, choose to raise plants from seed. The problem is that echinaceas are self-incompatible; that is, an individual plant cannot produce seed when pollinated with its own pollen. So all *Echinacea* seed is the result of hybridization. This is not necessarily a bad thing, but good-quality seedlings depend on careful selection of the plants that provide the seed and on removing all seedlings that are not true to type.

Unfortunately, as was demonstrated at the trial of *Echinacea* held at the RHS Garden at Wisley in 2002/2003, some nurseries are selling seed-raised plants without checking that their features match those that go with their cultivar name. The result is that plants can be variable in color, height, flower form, and vigor. For the gardener, the answer is not to eschew echinaceas but to check plants in flower before buying and to be prepared for variation when raising echinaceas from seed— and to enjoy the fruits of the plant breeders' art.

ECHINOPS
Globe thistle
ASTERACEAE

Architectural, undemanding, ornamental thistles are useful as a feature plant and attractive to wildlife.

There are some 120 species of perennials, biennials, and, rarely, annuals, found from the Mediterranean to Central Asia and the mountains of Africa, where they grow in grasslands or on rocky sun-baked hillsides. Stems are tall, erect, grooved, usually hairy, and carry leaves at the base and alternately up the stem. They are divided into up to three pairs of opposite lobes and are attractively, but sharply, spiny, often white with hairs beneath. The terminal flower buds are attractive, as perfect spheres that, in summer, open from the base upward and around, revealing the blue or white flowers to create a globe of color. When mature, each tubular floret has a stigma and blue-gray anthers protruding from it. The flowers are attractive to bees, last well in a vase, and are also suitable for drying (when cut before the flowers open). *Echinops giganteus*, from northeast Africa, is the tallest species, growing to a huge 9 ft (2.8 m), but is very rarely seen.

CULTIVATION A hot position in well-drained soil in full sun is preferred but will grow well in almost any soil or situation, except heavy shade. Tall forms may require support when grown in moist, fertile soil.

PROPAGATION By division in spring or by root cuttings in the dormant season. Species can also be raised from seed.

PROBLEMS Aphids.

E. bannaticus (Blue globe thistle) Branched or unbranched stems carry egg-shaped or elliptical leaves; their upper surfaces are hairy, the undersides white, and the margins have short rough hairs. Grayish blue flowerheads are 1–2 in (2.5–5 cm) across. Sometimes confused with *E. ritro*, but taller and broader in habit, and a much less spiny plant with broader, flatter leaf segments. Native to southeast to eastern Europe. ‡ 32–60 in (80–150 cm). Z5–9 H9–5. **'Albus'** White flowers. **'Blue Globe'** syn 'Blue Ball' Large, dark blue flowerheads, reliably repeat-flowering. ‡ 5 ft (1.5 m). **'Taplow Blue'** Intense flowers that are steel blue flowers. ‡ 5–6 ft (1.5–1.8 m). Z5–9 H9–5

'Nivalis' syn. 'Niveus' Slender habit, with white flowers and deeply cut silvery foliage. May be a hybrid of the rarely seen *E. tournefortii*. ‡ 5–6½ ft

RIGHT 1 *Echinops bannaticus*
2 *E. bannaticus* 'Taplow Blue'
3 *E. ritro* **4** *E. ritro* 'Veitch's Blue'
5 *E. sphaerocephalus*

(1.5–2 m). Z5–9 H9–5

E. ritro (Small globe thistle) Branched stems carry metallic blue flowerheads up to 1¾ in (4.5 cm) across from midsummer. The elliptical leaves are white and woolly beneath and feature sharp spines to ⅝ in (1.5 cm) long. It is native to central and eastern Europe through to central Asia. ↕36–40 in (90–100 cm). Z3–9 H12–1.
subsp. ruthenicus syn. *E. ruthenicus* Taller, with unbranched or few-branched stems and the leaves are more deeply divided. The flowers are bright blue. From northern Europe and northern Asia. Z6. **subsp. ruthenicus 'Platinum Blue'** Bright blue flowers on a smaller plant. Comes true from seed. ↕32–36 in (80–90 cm). **'Veitch's Blue'** Reliably repeat-flowering. ↕32–36 in (80–90 cm).

E. ruthenicus see *E. ritro* subsp. *ruthenicus*

E. sphaerocephalus (Great globe thistle) Sturdy gray, hairy stems with leaves which are hairy above, white-woolly beneath, and with short, narrow marginal spines. Grayish white flowerheads, up to 2½ in (6 cm) across. Native to south and central Europe through to Russia and naturalized in western Europe. ↕6½ ft (2 m). Z3–9 H9–1. **'Arctic Glow'** Dwarf, with dark red-brown stems. Comes true from seed. ↕3¼ ft (1 m).

ELYMUS
Wheat-grass, Wild rye
POACEAE

Attractive grasses for hot, dry areas with eye-catching blue foliage and tall, ryelike flowerheads.

About 50 species are found in meadows, woods, prairies, and sand dunes throughout temperate regions but mainly in Asia. Only a few are cultivated. Either clump-forming or with a vigorous, creeping root system, most have large, straplike blue-gray leaves. The flowerheads are similar to those of cultivated rye, with spikes comprising a single row of flowers (sometimes two to four rows). The leaves, with their sometimes intense steely blue coloring, make an arresting addition to dry areas, gravel gardens, and hard landscaping. There is some confusion with *Leymus*, which differs only in small botanical details and is not always considered distinct; cultivated species of *Agropyron* are now considered to belong here.

CULTIVATION Grow in sunny, exposed areas in well-drained, moderately fertile soil. Some of the more vigorous species need a large area to run or to be contained with barriers, or their roots will have to be hacked back in spring.

PROPAGATION By division in spring, or from seed.

PROBLEMS Relatively trouble-free,

though will be prone to fungal diseases in moist, shady conditions.

E. canadensis (Nodding or Wild Canadian rye) Forms evergreen clumps of dark green to gray-green flat leaves, up to 18 in (45 cm) long and ¾ in (2 cm) wide, through which grow tall, nodding stems carrying, in late summer and early fall, heads of brown-gray flowers up to 10 in (25 cm) long. The flowerheads are similar to those of rye flowerheads but with many outward-curving bristles. A good candidate for prairie plantings or informal gardens where it can seed itself freely. Found along river banks and on the prairies on dry, open ground throughout North America. ↕30–72 in (75–180 cm). Z3–8 H8–1. **'Glaucifolius'** syn. var. *glaucus* Leaves more intense blue-gray. Plants sold under this name are often the highly invasive *Leymus racemosus* or *L. arenarius*.

E. glaucus see *E. hispidus*

E. hispidus syn. *E. glaucus* (Wild blue rye) Forms dense, erect, evergreen clumps of intense silvery blue-green 10 in (25 cm) leaves with inrolled edges, through which straight, velvety green flower stems bear ryelike flowers with soft bristles around ½ in (1 cm) long. Good in gravel gardens or other dry areas. Found in dry, sandy, and rocky soil in sun or semishade across northern temperate regions. ↕12–48 in (30–120 cm). Z7–9 H9–7

E. hystrix see *Hystrix patula*

E. magellanicus syn. *Agropyron magellanicus, A. pubiflorum* (Magellan wheat-grass, Blue wheat-grass) Forms slowly spreading lax clumps of semi-evergreen or deciduous intense silver to sky blue leaves, ¼ in (7 mm) wide. Stiff erect stems topped with dense purple-blue flowerheads up to 8 in (20 cm) long, turning straw-colored as seeds ripen. Grows in well-drained soil. Looks stunning in gravel gardens and is useful for coastal and other exposed areas in summer. Dislikes excessive summer humidity, winter moisture, and heavy clay. From coastal sands and gravels and lowland saline grassland in Chile, Argentina, and the Falklands. ↕12–24 in (30–60 cm). Z7–8 H8–7

ENSETE
False banana
MUSACEAE

Six species of giant evergreen plants from Africa, Madagascar, and southern Asia. The species are closely related to bananas and have large paddlelike leaves that grow from a trunklike false stem.

The stem is actually composed of the bases of leaf stalks with the growing point, surprisingly, down at ground level. Very quick-growing when happy, foliage brings a drama

seen in few perennials. Cup-shaped flowers may be produced on mature plants followed by banana-like fruits that are dry and unpalatable; dies after flowering. Frequently used outdoors in subtropical bedding displays and increasingly being tried as a hardy perennial. Species previously untried as perennials are becoming available. Distinct from the closely related *Musa* in dying after flowering (*Musa* is a true perennial), and in the size of seeds.

CULTIVATION It is only fair to say that this is not the ideal plant for many North American gardens. It can be possible to overwinter plants outdoors in zones 8 and 9. Plant in rich, well-drained soil in a sunny, sheltered position in early summer. Keep the plants well-watered and fertilize until late summer. In fall, when the leaves begin to look ragged or are touched with frost, the plant needs protection. The aim should be to protect both the ground-level growing point and the "stem." Cut off the foliage and wrap the stem with bubble wrap, or with straw held in place by netting, as insulation against the cold. Try to seal the insulation to keep rain out, and finish with a deep mulch. In spring, unwrap the plant and allow new foliage to develop. The more risk-averse gardener can dig up the whole plant and overwinter it in a frost-free place.

PROPAGATION Sow seed at 64–70°F (18–21°C). First, soak seed in warm water for 24 hours. Germination is erratic.

PROBLEMS Usually completely trouble-free outside.

E. glaucum (Snow banana) Introduced from high altitudes in Yunnan Province, China, in 1999. Potentially one of the hardiest species. There is not enough experience to be precise as to its frost tolerance, but as it becomes more widely available, its degree of hardiness will become clear. A very large, impressive plant with a blue-green stem growing to around 15 ft (5 m); the blue-green leaves may reach 6½ ft (2 m) long and 20 in (50 cm) wide, making a dramatic and impressive plant, although height and leaf size will be less in temperate gardens. From China, India, and Vietnam; also known as "elephant hip" in China from the swollen base of the stem. ↕15 ft (5 m). Z8–10 H10–8

E. ventricosum syn. *Musa ensete* (Abyssinian banana, Ethiopian banana) A magnificent foliage plant; the "stem" can reach 15 ft (5 m) or more and leaves may be 6½ ft (2 m) long and 3½ ft (1 m) wide—although rarely achieves quite such glory in gardens. The leaves are red-tinted as they emerge, then become dark green, with the undersides of the midribs deep red. This coloring extends in varying degrees to the rest of the leaf. White flowers, enclosed in bronzy cups, are carried on 3¼ ft (1 m) spikes in summer but will not be seen on plants growing outside in temperate areas. Valued since Victorian times, this is a fast-growing and very rewarding, if somewhat variable, plant, best in full sun or dappled shade in rich, moisture-retentive soil. From eastern Africa, from Ethiopia to Zimbabwe; in some countries it is grown to produce a starch that is a human staple food. ↕6–12 ft (2–4 m). Z10–11 H12–1. **'Maurelii'** The most spectacular of all the ornamental bananas, with huge leaves richly colored in shades of red, ruby, and chocolate through to almost black. Bring inside in northern areas.

EOMECON
Snow poppy
PAPAVERACEAE

A vigorous woodlander with fleeting flowers and handsome bold foliage. There is just one,

RIGHT **1** *Elymus magellanicus*
2 *Ensete ventricosum*

RIGHT *Epilobium glabellum*

distinctive Chinese species, related to *Sanguinaria* and *Chelidonium*, and more surprisingly to *Bocconia*; although the flowers are rather small and ephemeral, the handsome leaves make interesting and effective ground cover among mature shrubs in conjunction with other woodlanders. With its determinedly spreading habit, the snow poppy colonizes briskly in shady situations.

CULTIVATION Enjoys leafy, humus-rich, moist soil and is especially good in woodlands among shrubs and other vigorous perennials.

PROPAGATION By division of the rhizomes in early spring or summer.

PROBLEMS Usually trouble-free.

E. chionantha A handsome, vigorous perennial, spreading rapidly and oozing red sap when cut. All the leaves arise from the base on long stalks, the blades heart-shaped to kidney-shaped with a scalloped margin, gray-green and rather fleshy, often with a lilac flush. The small, lax, branched clusters of flowers arise on stems just clear of the foliage; each flower is small, white, poppylike, 1¼–1½ in (3–4 cm) across, with four oval petals and a central boss of yellow stamens. Flowers appear, fleetingly, in late spring or early summer. Best in moist soil in dappled shade; in sunny or exposed positions the foliage may scorch. Too invasive for smaller gardens. Restricted to woodlands in eastern China.
↕16–20 in (40–50 cm). Z7–9 H9–7

EPILOBIUM
Willowherb
ONAGRACEAE

Modestly attractive plants for borders and informal areas, some of which can become invasive.

About 200 annuals and perennials, some woody at the base, grow in temperate zones of both hemispheres; some are prostrate and mat-forming, some are erect. All have opposite pairs or clusters of simple leaves and four-petaled flowers borne singly or in terminal spikes. Each flower arises from the tip of a long slender ovary that later becomes the seedpod, bearing many minute soon-to-be-airborne seeds.

CULTIVATION Almost any garden soil that does not get too dry, ideally in sun.

PROPAGATION By division, cuttings, or from seed.

PROBLEMS Usually trouble-free.

E. angustifolium see *Chamerion angustifolium*

E. californicum see *Zauschneria californica*

E. canum see *Zauschneria californica*

E. dodonaei see *Chamerion dodonaei*

E. glabellum Forms patches of slender, reddish stems with ½–¾ in (1–2 cm) long, glossy, toothed, elliptic to oval, sometimes bronze-tinted leaves. In summer, outward-facing, cup-shaped, ⅝–¾ in (1.5–2 cm) wide flowers appear in short, branched spikes. In the wild, the flowers are usually white, but in gardens, pink, rose-purple, and pale yellow forms are known. Best in a raised bed or at the front of a border. From the mountains of New Zealand.
↕8–12 in (20–30 cm). Z5–8 H8–5

EPIMEDIUM
Barrenwort
BERBERIDACEAE

Captivating, low-growing, spring-flowering woodlanders become more popular as the range increases.

Fifty-four evergreen or deciduous species are found mainly in woodlands and scrub in northeast Asia, with a few in western Asia and Europe. Most are shade-lovers, but a few are adaptable and tolerate more open positions. Clump- or mat-forming plants, they grow from a tough, much-branched rhizome, which may be short and stout or thin and fairly long. From this arise wiry stems carrying elegant leaves divided, in most species, into three, nine, or sometimes more oval, lance-shaped, or arrow-shaped leaflets with finely spine-toothed margins. The leaves are often shaded or mottled with attractive coppery tints, most conspicuously in spring.

The characteristic spidery flowers, usually carried in open sprays from mid- or late spring to early summer, are held above or just below the foliage. Although relatively small, they have an alluring delicacy and poise, their color ranging through white, yellow, shades of pink and purple; some strikingly bicolored.

There is nothing quite like them. Flowers consist of several colorful petals (see Epimedium Flower Structure), sometimes with nectar-secreting spurs. In Japan, they are called *ikari-so*, which translate as "anchor plant": the flowers of some look like the four-clawed anchor of traditional fishing boats. Small black seeds are carried in slender pods.

Plants are self-sterile—flowers require pollen from a different plant to set seed. The species are largely interfertile and easily hybridize with each other when grown in proximity; it pays to buy from a specialist who will propagate plants in the most appropriate way and should be able to ensure that your plant is correctly named.

Epimediums also have the advantage of giving more than one season of interest—the foliage, both young and old, is often attractive

and dense enough in the evergreen sorts to make effective and beautiful ground cover. This is an exciting time to grow epimediums. Recently, we have seen a superb monograph on them (see Professor William T. Stearn, p. 179). Fresh discoveries include plants with undivided foliage, and new and rediscovered species, mainly from China, continue to be introduced along with new hybrids and cultivars.

CULTIVATION Epimediums prefer humus-rich, moist but well-drained soil; most are tolerant of all but the extremes of acidity or alkalinity. Some, such as *E. alpinum*, *E. pinnatum* subsp. *colchicum*, and *E. pubigerum*, and particularly those from the Mediterranean region and the Caucasus, are drought-resistant when established, and will tolerate sunny conditions, although they may flower less freely. Those from the East Asia, however, grow well in shade or semishade, with humus-rich soil. All repay care through their first year, especially with watering. Waterlogged soil may result in the rhizomes rotting in winter. A spring mulch of leaf mold or composted bark will help maintain vigor and protect the rhizomes in cold climates.

Some gardeners prefer to shear evergreen types of epimediums in early spring in order to remove old foliage before the new leaves and flowers appear. However, this leaves a bare patch, and exposes the new growth to frost and cold winds. The leaves of truly evergreen types, such as *E. x perralchicum* and *E. pinnatum* subsp. *colchicum*, remain in good condition well into the new year. These should be left alone. Many of the Chinese species flower above the old leaves, which can be left on to protect the young growth. Deciduous types tend to produce

EPIMEDIUM FLOWER STRUCTURE

The flowers of epimediums show little sign of their relationship to *Berberis*, although they are in the same family. In the center of the flower is the ovary in which seeds will form, surrounded by four pollen-producing stamens. Next come four petals, with a tubular spur which secretes nectar. Then there are four inner sepals. Because both these groups of organs are colored, rather than green, we have referred to them in this book as "inner petals" and "outer petals" respectively. Finally, the outermost layer of the flower has four much smaller outer sepals. Pollination is by bees, especially bumble bees, which are attracted by the nectar. Although each flower contains male and female parts, they will not fertilize themselves or others on the same plant (or a division of it).

Inner petal with brown spur

Outer petal

Stamens surrounding the ovary

Epimedium perralderianum

PROFESSOR WILLIAM T. STEARN

For Professor William T. Stearn, a unique and mostly self-taught botanist, the study of epimediums was a life's work. His first monograph on the group, published in 1938, included a total of 21 species. Such was the influx of introductions that his second book, completed shortly before his death in 2001, covered 54 species.

At the age of just 22, Stearn became Librarian at the RHS and then Professor of Botany at the Natural History Museum, London. His first magazine

article on epimediums came in 1932, his first paper, on the then little-known Chinese species, in 1933, and he continued to study them over the years. Toward the end of his life, he published details of a number of new species, often based on wild collections by the Japanese botanist and collector Mikinori Ogisu. Finally, his invaluable final monograph has proved indispensable in helping the many enthusiasts around the world to understand these sometimes confusing plants.

flowers and new leaves slightly later.

PROPAGATION Increase named cultivars only by division, preferably in early fall, as species and cultivars hybridize easily. Those forming a tight clump eventually lose vigor and should be divided every four years or when flowering less freely. Those with a more creeping habit grow well for years. Wash off soil, expose the rhizomes, and cut into pieces with small pruners. Remove some leaves to reduce water loss. Replant, and keep moist and shaded until established. Division in early spring is possible, but young growth is brittle; early fall is safer.

Seed should be sown as soon as it is shed, still green, in pots or trays, but division is preferable because of the likelihood of hybridizing.

PROBLEMS Prone to damage by vine weevil, slugs, snails, aphids, rabbits, leaf-cutter bees, and deer. Mottled leaves may indicate a virus disease.

E. acuminatum Evergreen, with leaves composed of three finely pointed, lance-shaped leaflets up to 7 in (18 cm) long, heart-shaped at the base and spiny-margined. The young leaves are a soft, pale green marked conspicuously with reddish brown, becoming dark green and leathery. Each flowering stem carries two leaves and many large flowers, opening in late spring or early summer and, in good conditions, spasmodically later, on spreading branches. Flowers, to 2 in (5 cm) across, have pale purple, pinkish, or white outer petals, and deeper dusky purple inner petals with long down-curved spurs. Yellow-flowered forms are occasionally seen. From mountain woods in western China. ↕ 20 in (50 cm). Z5–9 H9–4

E. 'Akebono' A small deciduous plant with coppery red young leaves, turning mid-green with red edges, then mid-green. The three or nine leaflets, 3½ in (9 cm) long, have spiny edges and red stems. Sprays of up to 12 white flowers appear in late spring or early summer and often again in fall, the inner petals tinted pale rose. It is thought to be one of the best of many Japanese hybrids. The plant may be a selection of *E. grandiflorum*, or of *E. x youngianum*. ↕ 14 in (35 cm). Z5–9 H9–4

E. alpinum (Barrenwort) A deciduous plant spreading by slender rhizomes to form a loose clump. The leaves, usually with nine oval leaflets, to 4¾ in (12 cm) long, are thin, with spiny edges. Bright green in spring, often with red margins, they become mid-green in summer and usually color crimson in fall. The flowers first appear above the leaves but are soon overtopped by them. Although flowers are numerous, they are only about ½ in (1 cm) wide and not very showy, with dull red outer petals and yellow, small-spurred inner petals.

Tough and tolerant of some sun. From open woodlands in southern Europe, from the Balkans to northern Italy. ↕ 16 in (40 cm). Z4–9 H9–4

E. 'Beni-kujaku' Deciduous, with small, rounded, pale green leaflets in threes and up to 2 in (5 cm) long. The flowers, which open widely giving a starlike appearance, are pale pink shading to a darker purple-pink edge, the cupped inner petals with short white spurs. A recent Japanese hybrid, probably a selection of *E. x youngianum*. Weak, needing good conditions. ↕ 12 in (30 cm). Z5–9 H9–4

E. brevicornu Deciduous, and forming a compact clump; leaves usually of nine oval leaflets to 3 in (8 cm) long, thin-textured and sometimes blotched with copper when young and later mid-green and firmer. Many small, starry white flowers, ½ in (1.5 cm) wide, form a loosely branched spray above leaves. Inner yellow petals with short white spurs. Very hardy. From woodlands and scrub in central and western China. ↕ 24 in (60 cm). Z5–9 H9–4

E. x cantabrigiense An evergreen that slowly makes a spreading leafy clump. The leaves have nine or more oval leaflets to 4 in (10 cm) long, at first pale green, then darkening slightly in summer. Numerous, dull pinkish red flowers with yellow inner petals, about ½ in (1 cm) across, are held above the foliage. It is strong-growing, and makes useful ground cover in part-shade, but it is unexciting in flower. Plants with yellow-mottled leaves are infected with a virus and should be destroyed. A hybrid of *E. alpinum* and *E. pubigerum* that arose by chance in the garden of St. John's College, Cambridge, England. ↕ 24 in (60 cm). Z5–8 H8–5

E. davidii A clump-forming evergreen with leaves of three (sometimes five) blunt, oval leaflets to 2½ in (6 cm) long, coppery when young, later mid-green and slightly leathery. The flowering stem carries up to 24 bright yellow flowers, to 1¼ in (3 cm) wide, held above the foliage. The outer petals are small and dull red, the inner petals yellow, forming a cup, with slender, curved spurs. In good conditions, it may flower on and off through to early fall. Dwarf forms have now been discovered. From mountain woods

MINGLING IN THE SHADE

THE WOODLAND TAPESTRY that works so well as we allow shade-loving plants to intermingle, here has the bright emerging foliage of that dependable old favorite *Hosta* 'Albomarginata' providing a good anchor. Intermingling in front are *Epimedium* x *youngianum*, in a form with the pink buds opening to white flowers and with

delicate emerging foliage fluttering in the breeze—a nice contrast to the robust hosta clumps. The blue and white forms of *Viola sororia* self-seed contentedly, and their flowers stretch toward the light. The pattern could also be augmented by wood anemones, choice primroses, and trilliums.

in western Sichuan, China. ↕ 18 in (45 cm). Z5–9 H9–4

E. diphyllum A neat and rather delicate, usually evergreen plant, making a tidy clump of leaves, each composed of two pointed, oval leaflets to 2 in (5 cm) long. Coppery olive-green when young, then mid-green in summer, and often color well in fall. The flowering stem bears a single leaf and up to nine white flowers in mid- and late spring, held just above the foliage. Nodding, cup-shaped, and ½ in (1 cm) across, with spreading outer, and spurless inner petals. Dainty but not vigorous; best in a sheltered position in light shade in acidic or neutral soil. The first Japanese species to reach Europe, in about 1829, from woodlands in southern Japan. ↕ 10 in (25 cm). Z5–9 H9–4

E. 'Enchantress' An evergreen plant, its leaves usually have three leaflets which are variable in size but up to 4 in (10 cm) long, and arrow-shaped with pointed tips. They have a somewhat crinkly surface with distinct veins, an undulating edge, and few spines, and are mottled reddish copper when young, later mid-green, glossy, and rather leathery. Up to 10 flowers, about ¾ in (2 cm) across, are carried on a stem above a single stem-leaf. The outer petals are lilac-pink, with purple-lipped, pale pink inner petals beneath, the spurs shading to white at the tips. A hybrid between *E. dolichostemon* and *E. leptorrhizum* raised by Elizabeth Strangman at Washfield Nursery, England. ↕ 16 in (40 cm). Z5–10 H9–4

E. epsteinii Evergreen; makes a clump of leaves with three leaflets to 2 in (5 cm) long, pale green when young, glossy mid-green in summer. Leaflets are narrowly oval with pointed tips and finely spiny margins. Up to 15 flowers borne on a stem carrying one or two leaves. The flowers, about 1¼ in (3 cm) across, have unusually broad white outer petals and dark reddish purple inner petals; the spur protrudes beyond the outer petals and curves downward. One of the finest flowered epimediums and named for Harold Epstein, an epimedium enthusiast from New York State. From Hunan province, central China. ↕ 10 in (25 cm). Z5–10 H9–4

E. fargesii Evergreen and forming a compact clump, with leaves composed of three narrow, lance-shaped leaflets to 4 in (10 cm) long, the outer pair very asymmetrical. Pale green with coppery tinges when young, they become dark green and leathery with age. The flowers, about ½ in (1.5 cm) across, have narrow, strongly reflexed, white outer petals and smaller, dark purple inner petals. Their distinctive shuttlecock shape reveals the long stamens. From Sichuan province in western China.

LEFT 1 *Epimedium grandiflorum* 'Lilafee'
2 *E. grandiflorum* 'White Queen'
3 *E. x perralchicum* 'Frohnleiten'
4 *E. pinnatum* subsp. *colchicum*
5 *E. pubigerum* **6** *E. x setosum*

FASHIONS CHANGE

Once, only the brightest, most flamboyant and colorful perennials filled the catalogs. Around 100 years ago, one listed over 200 *Phlox paniculata* cultivars, and no epimediums. Things have changed.

While phlox listings have declined significantly, almost 150 epimediums are now offered by nurseries, about a third of them species. This is five times as many as in 1990 and reflects the increased accessibility of China in recent years and the work of various collectors, most notably Mikinori Ogisu from Japan and Darrell Probst from the US. Indeed, new species are still being found in China, along with new forms of already familiar species. Many were first described and named by Professor

William Stearn (*see panel, p.179*); no fewer than 43 of the 54 species he lists come from China.

This influx of species has greatly increased the diversity of form and habit available to gardeners. A bonus has been the increasing flow of new hybrids, some chance seedlings, others the result of deliberate hybridization. Elizabeth Strangman, when at Washfield Nursery, Kent, England, was an early enthusiast for the genus, as was Harold Epstein in New York State, and David Barker in Essex, who did much to foster early interest in the UK. Long-time enthusiasts Robin White at Blackthorn Nursery, Hampshire, Darrell Probst in Massachusetts, and others continue to grow and introduce new forms.

‡ 20 in (50 cm). Z4–8 H9–4. **‘Pink Constellation’** Longer leaflets, blotched with brownish red when young; flowers larger, with lilac-pink outer petals and purple inner petals. ‡ 18 in (45 cm).

E. franchetii A large evergreen plant with lance-shaped leaflets to 5½ in (14 cm) long, three to a leaf, which are pale green with coppery shadings, becoming darker and leathery by midsummer. They have a pointed tip, spiny margins, and very unequal basal lobes on the outer pair. Unbranched flowering stems bear up to 25 flowers to 1¾ in (4.5 cm) across, held above the leaves. The pale yellow outer petals are small, the inner petals much longer, slightly deeper yellow with long, sharply down-curved spurs. Variable in hardiness, from central China. ‡ 24 in (60 cm). Z4–8 H9–4. **‘Brimstone Butterfly’** Large spiny-edged leaves, with coppery markings when young; flowers with reddish brown outer petals above yellow inner petals. Later flowering. ‡ 26 in (65 cm).

E. grandiflorum syn. *E. macranthum* A very variable deciduous plant forming a compact clump of leaves each with nine oval leaflets to 4¾ in (12 cm) long, with finely spiny edges and pointed tips. Young leaflets are light green, often with reddish coppery tints, becoming mid-green. A second, taller flush of leaves often develops after flowering. Up to 16 flowers are produced on a leafy stem, each flower ¾–1¾ in (2–4.5 cm) wide, in shades of rose-lilac, white, or pale yellow. The paler inner petals have long, slightly curved spurs. Much used in hybridization, in both Europe and Japan, and a parent of *E.* x *youngianum*, *E.* x *rubrum*, and *E.* x *versicolor*. From deciduous woodlands in Japan, northern Korea, and Manchuria. ‡ to 14 in (35 cm). Z5–8 H8–5. **‘Crimson Beauty’** Probably identical to ‘Rose Queen’. **‘Crimson Queen’** Probably identical to ‘Rose Queen’. **subsp. koreanum** A variable plant with green or dark coppery young leaves of nine leaflets, and light yellow flowers rather hidden by the foliage. Much confused in gardens with a distinct, pale yellow variant of *E. grandiflorum*. Sometimes

listed as *E. koreanum*. ‡ 12 in (30 cm). Z5–8 H8–5. **‘Lilacinum’** Purple-flushed young foliage, and large flowers with pale purplish pink outer petals and long-spurred, white inner petals. ‡ 16 in (40 cm). **‘Lilafee’** Purple-tinted young foliage; flowers deep violet-purple with paler inner petals and white-tipped spurs. Later into growth than most. ‡ 12 in (30 cm). **‘Mount Kitadake’** Young leaves pinkish purple, becoming light green with a rosy edge; flowers deep rose-violet, the inner petals edged and tipped with white. ‡ to 10 in (25 cm). **‘Nanum’** Dwarf, with rounded, coppery-edged leaflets and small white flowers. ‡ 10 in (25 cm), often shorter. **‘Rose Queen’** Young foliage purple-bronze; flowers large, rose-purple with white spur tips. ‘Crimson Beauty’ and ‘Crimson Queen’ are probably the same. ‡ 18 in (45 cm). **‘Roseum’** Young foliage coppery, becoming pale green with faint coppery edges; flowers rose and white. ‡ 18 in (45 cm). **‘Rubinkrone’** Flowers deep rose, the large spurs tipped with white. ‡ 12 in (30 cm). **‘Sirius’** Small arrow-shaped light green leaflets; flowers pale pink with long, narrow, whitish spurs. ‡ 6 in (15 cm) when in flower, later 18 in (45 cm). **f. violaceum** Large lilac-purple flowers held above the foliage. ‡ 14 in (35 cm). **‘White Queen’** Later-flowering, with large white flowers and mid-green leaves. ‡ 14 in (35 cm). **‘Yellow Princess’** Young leaves mottled with copper; flowers pale yellow with cream outer petals. Late flowering. Introduced by renowned Massachusetts *Epimedium* collector and breeder Darrell Probst. ‡ 12 in (30 cm).

E. **‘Kaguyahime’** Evergreen: the leaves, with their three arrow-shaped leaflets, to 4 in (10 cm) long, are pale green when young, later mottled with dull red, becoming bronzed in winter. Up to 40 flowers, about ¾ in (2 cm) wide, are borne in branched sprays well above the foliage, the outer petals broad and pale lavender, and the inner petals dark purple with paler, strongly curved spurs. A chance hybrid of *E. acuminatum* and *E. dolichostemon* from a Japanese nursery. ‡ 20 in (50 cm). Z5–8 H9–4

E. latisepalum An evergreen plant making a low mound of leaves composed of three leathery, dark green, narrowly oval leaflets to 3½ in (9 cm) long, with coppery blotches when young. The flowering stems bear two leaves and up to eight well-spaced, nodding white flowers 1½–2 in (4–5 cm) across. Outer petals are broad, and inner ones tinged yellow or purple at the base with long, straight spurs. From western China. ‡ 12 in (30 cm). Z5–8 H9–4

E. leptorrhizum An evergreen with a long slender rhizome forming a spreading clump. Leaves are leathery, each with three conspicuously veined, narrowly oval leaflets up to 4½ in (11 cm) long, tinged bronze when young. Drooping flowers, 1½ in (4 cm) across, have light pink outer petals and pale pink or almost white inner petals, with long curved spurs. Needs a position where the rhizome will not dry out. From woodlands in western China. ‡ 12 in (30 cm). Z5–9 H9–4

E. **‘Little Shrimp’** Deciduous; making a dense clump of foliage. Pale green young leaves, each usually with nine oval leaflets to 2¾ in (7 cm) long, have unequal, rounded lobes at the base. The ½ in (1 cm) wide flowers, with coral pink outer petals and yellow inner petals, appear mid- and late spring, and often appear again in late summer. Possibly a compact form of *E.* x *cantabrigiense*. ‡ 10 in (25 cm). Z5–8 H9–4

E. macranthum see *E. grandiflorum*

E. membranaceum An unusually long-flowering evergreen with leathery leaves composed of six or nine oval leaflets to 4 in (10 cm) long. Sprays of up to 35 pale yellow, rarely pink, flowers, 1¼–2 in (3–5 cm) across, open from mid-spring until mid- or late summer and are held well above the leaves. Their small, narrow outer petals are faintly shaded red, the inner petals are larger, with long spurs curving sharply downward. From deciduous woodlands in western China. ‡ 26 in (65 cm). Z4–9 H9–4

E. ogisui An evergreen with leaves of three oval leaflets to 2½ in (6 cm) long, splashed with coppery red when young, then turns mid-green. Flowering stems bear two leaves and up to 12 white flowers, 1 in (2.5 cm) across, with spreading outer petals and inner petals with slightly curved spurs, their bases forming a cup. Named for Mikinori Ogisu (*see* Fashions Change). From the moist, shady limestone cliffs in Sichuan province, western China. ‡ 14 in (35 cm). Z5–8 H8–5

E. x *omeiense* Evergreen, with large, leathery leaves composed of three finely spiny, oval leaflets to 3½ in (9 cm) long, with rounded tips. The flowering stems bear a pair of leaves and up to 25 flowers, 2 in (5 cm) across. The narrow outer petals are dull rose pink and the inner petals are pale yellow and shaded red near the base, with long, sharply curved, whitish spurs tipped with yellow. It is a natural hybrid of *E. acuminatum* and *E. fangii* from Emei Shan (Mount Omei) in Sichuan province, western China. ‡ 20 in (50 cm). Z5–9 H9–4. **‘Akame’** syn. ‘Emei Shan’ Taller, with coppery mottled young foliage; up to 70 flowers. ‡ 24 in (60 cm). **‘Stormcloud’** Dull brownish purple flowers.

E. x *perralchicum* A vigorous evergreen that makes a dense, spreading clump of leathery leaves, each with three or five broadly oval or rounded leaflets to 4 in (10 cm) long, their wavy margins having few spines. The leafless flowering stems bear their bright yellow flowers, about ¾ in (2 cm) wide, above the foliage. The outer petals are rounded, with the much smaller, brown inner petals, with tiny curved spurs, hidden beneath. Very drought-tolerant once well established, making excellent ground cover. Often supplied as *E. perralderianum*, especially in the US. A chance hybrid of *E. perralderianum* and *E. pinnatum* subsp. *colchicum* originating in the UK at RHS Garden, Wisley. ‡ 16 in (40 cm). Z5–8 H8–5

BELOW *Epimedium versicolor*

ABOVE 1 *E. x youngianum* 'Merlin'
2 *E. x youngianum* 'Niveum'

'Frohnleiten' Young foliage has coppery red shading between striking green veins; flowers are slightly deeper yellow. **'Wisley'** The name given to the original form described above.

E. perralderianum An evergreen plant that slowly spreads to make good ground cover. Each leaf has three rather glossy, oval 2½ in (6 cm) leaflets with spiny margins, often copper-shaded between green veins when young, becoming darker green and leathery. The flowers are bright yellow, ½–¾ in (1.5–2 cm) across, with up to 25 per stem carried above the leaves. The outer petals are oval, with the tiny inner petals beneath having a yellow, cup-shaped base and very short, curved brown spurs. Tolerates dry and open situations well once it has become well established. *E. x perralchicum* is often supplied under this name, especially in the US. From mixed forests in the mountains of Algeria. ‡ 12 in (30 cm). Z5–8 H8–5

E. pinnatum A vigorous, usually evergreen plant with leaves composed of nine (or five or eleven) oval leaflets, to 3 in (8 cm) long, setting off up to 30 small but long-lasting, outward-facing flowers, ½ in (1.5 cm) across, borne on a simple, leafless stem well above the leaves. Bright yellow, broadly oval outer petals cover very small yellow inner petals with tiny brown spurs. A tough plant, happy in dry conditions when established. From mountain woods in northern Iran and Azerbaijan. ‡ 16 in (40 cm). Z5–9 H9–4. **subsp.** *colchicum* Leaves composed of three or five broadly oval leaflets, to 6 in (15 cm) long. Up to 20, sometimes more, bright yellow flowers, ¾ in (1.8 cm) across, borne well above the leaves, have tiny, curved brown spurs on the inner petals. A tough plant, thrives in some sun and a parent of the well known hybrids *E. x perralchicum*, *E. x versicolor*, and *E. x warleyense*. From woods in western Georgia and northeast Turkey. ‡ 14 in (35 cm). **subsp.** *colchicum* **'Black Sea'**

Leaves dark, becoming almost purple-black in winter; flowers paler, creamy yellow. Perhaps a hybrid.

E. pubigerum An unusually drought-tolerant evergreen making a compact clump; leaves of mostly nine oval or rounded leaflets, sparsely spiny on the margins. The 2–3½ in (5–9 cm) leaflets are pale green, but turn darker, glossier, and more leathery, while remaining softly hairy beneath. Flowering stems bear a single leaf and up to 30 flowers, about ½ in (1 cm) across, held well above the foliage. The boat-shaped, pale pink outer petals almost hide smaller, pale yellow, short-spurred inner petals. Tolerates some sun when established. Found in damp beech woodlands in southeast Bulgaria, Turkey, and along the Black Sea coast to western Georgia. ‡ 26 in (65 cm). Z4–8 H8–1

E. rhizomatosum An evergreen forming a spreading clump of leaves each with three spiny-edged leaflets, 1½–2½ in (4–6 cm) long. Oval leaves with tapering tips, sometimes lightly mottled with copper when young. Up to 30 pale yellow flowers, 1½–2 in (4–5 cm) across, are borne on stems with one pair of leaves. The tiny outer petals are white or tinted red; long spurs on the pale yellow inner petals curve abruptly downward giving flowers a spiderlike appearance. Similar to *E. membranaceum*, but with a more running habit. From mountain woodlands in Sichuan province, western China. ‡ 16 in (40 cm). Z5–9 H9–5

E. x rubrum Evergreen, with leaves composed of nine or more oval leaflets to 5½ in (14 cm) long when mature; flushed bright red when young, they often turning reddish brown in fall. Flowering stems bear a single leaf and up to 25 flowers, ½–1 in (1.5–2.5 cm) across, in a loose spray. Bright crimson outer petals partially hide short-spurred, pale yellow inner petals. An easy plant with striking young foliage; a hybrid of *E. alpinum* and *E. grandiflorum* made in Belgium around 1850. ‡ 16 in (40 cm). Z4–8 H8–1

E. x setosum Evergreen plant with pale,

oval leaflets to 3½ in (9 cm) long, varying in number from two to six per leaf, sometimes with dark bronze tints. The leafy flowering stem bears up to 20 small, pendulous, bell-shaped white flowers about ½ in (1 cm) wide, the outer petals spreading, the inner petals spurless, similar to those of *E. diphyllum*. A natural hybrid of *E. diphyllum* and *E. sempervirens* from southern Japan. ‡ 12 in (30 cm). Z5–9 H9–5

E. stellulatum An evergreen forming a compact clump, with leaves composed of three oval leaflets about 3½ in (9 cm) long. These have coppery markings when young, later becoming mid-green and leathery, and have well-marked veins and spiny margins. The flowering stem, with two leaves, carries a spray of up to 40 (and sometimes considerably more) beautifully poised, star-shaped flowers. The outer petals are white and almost hide the tiny, yellow, short-spurred inner petals; the protruding stamens are yellow. From central China. ‡ 18 in (45 cm). Z5–9 H9–5. **'Wudang Star'** The name given to the original introduction, by Roy Lancaster, from crevices in shady old walls and rocky places in Hubei province, China.

E. x versicolor A variable hybrid, which may be evergreen or deciduous, with leaves with three, five, nine, or more oval leaflets, often coppery red when young. The flowering stems carry a single leaf and up to 20 usually sterile flowers, ¾ in (2 cm) across, which vary in color from pale yellow to coppery pink, the inner petals having medium-sized spurs. Easy-going plant, thrives in dry conditions when established. A hybrid of *E. grandiflorum* and *E. pinnatum* subsp. *colchicum* first raised in Belgium in around 1850. ‡ 16 in (40 cm). Z5–9 H9–4. **'Cupreum'** Deciduous, usually with nine leaflets, often a deep copper when young; the outer flower petals are coppery red. ‡ 10 in (25 cm). **'Neosulphureum'** Evergreen, usually with three leaflets, coppery when young; the outer petals of the pale yellow flowers are longer than the spurs. ‡ 14 in (35 cm). **'Sulphureum'** Evergreen, usually with nine leaflets, coppery when young; pale yellow flowers have outer petals and spurs of similar length. Tough and popular; makes good ground cover. ‡ 14 in (35 cm). **'Versicolor'** Deciduous, with nine leaflets, which are usually red-shaded when young, later light green with reddish edges. Flowers have rose-colored outer petals and shorter yellow inner petals. ‡ 14 in (35 cm).

E. x warleyense Evergreen plant, making a loose clump of leaves, usually with five or nine oval leaflets to 5 in (13 cm) long. The flowering stem is leafless or with one leaf and carries up to 30 outward-facing flowers, ½ in (1.5 cm) across, well above the leaves. Unique in coloring, they have vivid coppery orange outer petals, with small, short-spurred, yellow inner petals, and greenish stamens. Quite drought-tolerant once established. A chance garden hybrid of *E. alpinum* and

E. pinnatum subsp. *colchicum* introduced from Miss Ellen Willmott's famous garden at Warley Place, Essex, England, in the 1930s. ‡ 20 in (50 cm). Z5–9 H9–5 **'Orangekönigen'** More compact, with leaves often with three leaflets and paler orange flowers. ‡ 18 in (45 cm).

E. wushanense An evergreen that makes a clump of leaves with three narrowly lance-shaped leaflets up to 5 in (13 cm) long, with tapering tips and conspicuous spines along the wavy edges. The leaflets are olive green when they are young, becoming darker and leathery. Dark stems bear up to 100 flowers, to 1½ in (4 cm) wide, in a loose spray held well above the foliage. Their outer petals are white to pale yellow, the inner petals sulfur yellow, with long, straight or curved spurs. A very striking plant from Sichuan province, western China. ‡ 36 in (90 cm). Z6–9 H9–6. **'Caramel'** The leaves are mottled with purple; the flowers have green outer petals shaded with red, and light orange-yellow inner petals, edged purple by the spur opening.

E. x youngianum A compact, deciduous plant with leaves composed of up to nine thin, oval leaflets often tinged purple when young. The flower stems bear a single leaf and from three to 12 nodding, bell-shaped, white or pink flowers to ¾ in (2 cm) across, their outer petals lance-shaped and spreading and inner petals slightly longer, with no spur or a short one. A hybrid between *E. diphyllum* and *E. grandiflorum*; more cultivars are being introduced. ‡ 12 in (30 cm). Z5–9 H9–5. **'Lilacinum'** *see* 'Roseum'. **'Merlin'** Coppery young leaves and deep rosy mauve flowers, paler in the center. **'Niveum'** Coppery purple leaves when young, turning green; white flowers. **'Pink Ruffles'** *see* 'Tamabotan'. **'Roseum'** syn. 'Lilacinum'. Leaves with two to nine leaflets; flowers light rosy mauve. **'Tamabotan'** syn. 'Pink Ruffles' Dark coppery purple young leaves with nine leaflets; flowers pale rose, the inner petals similar to the outer ones, so appearing double.

EPIPACTIS

Helleborine
ORCHIDACEAE

The easiest garden orchids, with tall slender spikes of summer blooms: a rather primitive flower in an ancient genus. About 25 species are found from Europe to Ethiopia and east to Japan, with one North American species and another a widespread American invader. Just a few are generally grown. The common name of helleborine covers both *Epipactis* and the similar *Cephalanthera*, with which it can cross. It refers to a similarity to *Helleborus*, since all had the same ancient medicinal uses.

The underground rhizomes and fleshy roots can creep unexpected distances and throw up leafy stems bearing spirally arranged, veined

leaves, and long spikes of flowers, held on one side of the stem. The flowers have a two-part lip with a cup at the bottom and a heart-shape or triangle at the top, and bloom in late spring through summer into fall, attracting wasps and bees.

The European *E. helleborine* has become widely established in North America.

CULTIVATION Extremely adaptable, but insist on constant moisture and good garden soil. They prefer sun with damp soil, or cooler woodland conditions with dappled shade. Plant just below the soil surface.

PROPAGATION Divide in spring.

PROBLEMS None unless too dry.

E. gigantea syn. *E. americana* (Giant helleborine, Chatterbox orchid) Possibly the easiest garden orchid to grow, and wonderfully adaptable. Although not at all gigantic, it is quick to clump into colonies of slender, 10 in (25 cm) long, glossy, pleated green leaves, 4–12 per stem, enduring for many years. Free-flowering from mid-spring to mid-fall, depending on climate, the 5–20 successive, fly-pollinated, 1½-in (4-cm) blooms, flushed and veined rosy brown and greenish yellowish, resemble a swan diving off the tall stem. The three-lobed, hinged red lip oscillates in the breeze like a talkative mouth, inspiring the "chatterbox" nickname. Best in organic amended soil and most vigorous in part-shaded damp conditions; tolerates drier conditions and full sun but becomes dormant in drought. Can take a year or two to establish before blooming. From wet spots, some at high altitudes, in northeast Asia and western North America to Texas. 8–40 in (20–100 cm). Z4–8 H8–1. **'Serpentine Night'** Desirable dark-leaved form with a rich

red cast to the foliage, discovered in California. ↕8–32 in (20–80 cm).

E. palustris (Marsh helleborine) The 4–8 narrow, stiff, upright, sharp-edged leaves, 1–1½ in (2.5–4 cm) wide, are arranged spirally on the stem. The flirty, white, ruffled-apron lips are eye-catching from a distance from early summer to early fall, since each plant is capable of bearing 100 loose flower spikes boasting 5–20 very pretty rose pink ¾-in (2-cm) nodding flowers; the lip is also strikingly marked with a yellow half circle or V, and the inner cup is striped red. Usually light pink, the flower color can range from green to dark red. Adaptable, preferring open sunny marshes in loamy alkaline soil; add limestone and leaf mold and keep moist. From Europe to North Africa and the Middle East, also Japan. ↕4–28 in (10–70 cm). Z4–8 H8–1

E. 'Sabine' Large, full, richly colored pink-red, burgundy-brown, and green flowers with yellow and white lips. The first, very showy hybrid between the two most garden-worthy species, *E. gigantea* and *E. palustris,* from Werner Frosch of Germany in 1984, and even more vigorous than either parent. ↕20–36 in (50–90 cm). Z4–8 H8–1

EQUISETUM
Horsetail
EQUISETACEAE

Discreetly attractive but mostly rampant foliage plants for a wild, moist site.

About 30 species of deciduous and evergreen plants, growing in a range of habitats from meadows and woodlands to marshes and shallow water, are found worldwide, except Australasia. Deep-running rhizomes support erect, jointed, hollow stems, often with whorls of slender branches at each of the upper joints. Leaves are reduced to tiny scales at joints. Spore-bearing, conelike fruiting bodies appear at the tips of

the stems. The curiously primitive appearance is attractive but, once established, horsetails are ineradicable, so site with great care, or grow in a container.

CULTIVATION Any moist soil in sun or light shade; best in a pot.

PROPAGATION By careful division.

PROBLEMS Usually trouble-free.

E. camtschatcense see *E. hyemale*

E. hyemale (Scouring rush, Dutch rush) Unbranched, rough-surfaced green stems, banded with black at each joint, end in a black cone. Less relentlessly spreading than some horsetails, but still safest grown in a container. From moist, part-shaded places in Europe, Asia, and North America. ↕24–54 in (60–130 cm). Z3–11 H12–1. **var. *affine*** Stems pink-flushed when young. ↕3¼–4 ft (1–1.2 m). *E. camtschatcense* is a name used for a plant of uncertain origin, resembling a neater form of *E. hyemale*, forming a more compact clump of erect, hollow, cylindrical, black-ringed stems. ↕3¼ ft (1 m).

E. scirpoides Dwarf plant making a spreading tangle of fine, wiry green sinuous shoots, occasionally tipped with tiny black cones. Safer than most to grow in the garden, but also good in a damp trough or container. From wet woodland banks in northern Europe, North America, and eastern Asia. ↕4–6 in (10–15 cm). Z3–11 H12–4

ERAGROSTIS
Love grass
POACEAE

Airy and delicate grasses from open dry grasslands.

About 350 annual and deciduous perennial species are found in dry, weedy places in tropical and subtropical areas throughout the world. These clump-forming,

drought-tolerant grasses have loose and often graceful flowerheads, varying from dense to more sparse sprays of flowers. Many species of the plant have blue-green foliage, making lovely airy additions to gravel gardens, either in drifts or as specimen plants. Use them also to soften hard landscapes or plant in a tall container.

CULTIVATION Prefer a dry, open, sunny spot in well-drained, moderately fertile soil.

PROPAGATION From seed, or by divisions, not too small, in late spring.

PROBLEMS Usually trouble-free if given plenty of open space.

E. airoides (Fly grass, Darnel fly grass) Forms dense, soft mounds of bright green leaves, from which grow fine wiry stems. From late summer to mid-fall, many branches bear, gossamer clouds of tiny pink-purple flowers. This plant grows in drifts in a sunny well-drained position where sun can filter through the smoky flowers. From Argentina. ↕18 in (45 cm). Z7–10 H10–7

E. chloromelas (Boer love grass) A densely tufted plant, the graceful arching mounds of very fine blue-gray leaves, which turn buff in winter, make a lovely foundation for the slightly arching, branched, gray flower stems bearing tiny, delicate, purple to olive-green flowers that float in airy sprays above the foliage in late summer. Drought-tolerant; grow in a sunny position in fertile soil. A good weed suppressor in gravel gardens if grown in drifts, and lovely as a specimen plant or grown in a container. Seeds freely. Used as a pasture grass on dry plains in South Africa. ↕3¼ ft (1 m). Z7–10 H10–7

E. curvula (Weeping love grass, African love grass) Dense, arching clumps of fine, dark green in-rolled leaves, turning buff in winter, underpin green, arching branched flower stems that in late summer bear one-sided airy plumes of tiny, dark gray to purple flowers, hanging above the foliage. Drought-tolerant; a beautiful addition to wild prairie gardens or where the foliage can flow over stones. Can be short-lived, but self-seeds freely. Grows in south and tropical Africa, and naturalized over all but the coldest parts of North America, where it was introduced as a stabilizer for sandy soil. ↕4 ft (1.2 m) Z9–12 H12–10. **'Totnes Burgundy'** Leaves turn a deep burgundy red; sprays of green-beige flowers. Deciduous. ↕36 in (90 cm).

E. trichodes syn. *Poa trichodes* (Sand love grass) Slowly creeping clumps of shiny, flat green leaves, ¼ in (5 mm) wide. In midsummer to early fall, flower stems grow up from the foliage bearing airy, arching heads of shiny bright green, red-tinted flowers, which float among the leaves. Attractive in

drifts in well-drained areas of the garden, and in open dry woodlands where sun can filter through the delicate flowers. A native from Illinois to Texas, growing on dry sand, prairies, and woodlands. ↕4 ft (1.2 m). Z5–9 H9–5

EREMURUS

Desert candle, Foxtail lily

ASPHODELACEAE

In early summer, magnificent upright flower spikes in pastel shades tower above the low rosettes of leaves.

These clump-forming plants hail mainly from the dry, rocky steppes of mountainous central and western Asia. Only three of the 45 or so species are widely grown, but these are among the most imposing, making impressive garden plants.

All have thick, fleshy roots radiating out horizontally like the arms of a starfish from a central bud that produces a loose tuft of long, strappy leaves, which are smooth, pointed, and usually ridged underneath. Stiff, leafless, unbranched stems emerge from the clump, soaring to 10 ft (3 m) or more in some species. In late spring to early summer they are topped with spectacular tapering plumes composed of hundreds of densely packed buds which open gradually, the lowest first, revealing starry short-stalked flowers in white, pink, or yellow, with showy stamens (*see* The Eremurus Flower). After flowering, the plant dies down—to survive searing summer heat in its native habitat—and lies dormant until the following year. The cultivated species and garden hybrids differ mainly in flower color and height; many last well as cut flowers. Improvements in *Eremurus* are largely the work of Dutch hybridizer N.C. Ruiter. Unfortunately, many of his named cultivars have been raised from seed and now vary in color and quality.

CULTIVATION Need rich, well-drained soil in a sunny, preferably sheltered, position. Plant in a broad, shallow hole and sit the rootstock on a 2-in (5-cm) mound of coarse sand so the crown is at soil level. Place toward the back of borders or among deciduous shrubs where clumps can die down without being seen, or grow with plants from similar habitats in widely spaced, prairie-style plantings. Young growth is vulnerable to damage from late spring frosts, so protect on cold nights. Tolerates very alkaline soil.

PROPAGATION By division in summer or early fall, when the leaves have died down. Established clumps with many stems have extra rooted crowns that can be divided or cut apart, taking care not to damage the fragile roots. Species can also be raised from seed, which germinates best when fresh. Seedlings reach flowering size in 3–5 years.

PROBLEMS Usually trouble-free.

E. bungei see *E. stenophyllus* subsp. *stenophyllus*

***E.* 'Emmy Ro'** Flowers lemon-yellow inside, tinged with apricot orange from the reverse of the petals, with a rusty brown central vein. Long stamens with orange anthers. Raised by N.C. Ruiter of Holland. ↕6 ft (1.8 m). Z5–8 H8–5

E. himalaicus From a basal clump of smooth-edged, bright green leaves, up to 1½ in (4 cm) wide and 20 in (50 cm) long, tall flower stems bear 36 in (90 cm) spikes of many white florets, each about 1½ in (3.5 cm) across. May need staking. From Afghanistan and northwest of the Himalaya. ↕6½–8 ft (2–2.5 m). Z5–8 H8–5

E.* x *isabellinus A wide range of relatively tough hybrids with slightly dull green, lance-shaped, 6–12 in (15–30 cm) leaves and elegant spikes of flowers in white, yellow, orange, bronze, or pink on relatively short stems. Created by crossing *E. stenophyllus* with the rarely grown pale pink *E. olgae*. ↕5–6 ft (1.5–1.8 m). Z5–8 H8–5. **'Cleopatra'** Burnt orange buds open into glowing, peachy orange flowers, with a dark red midrib on the backs of the petals and orange anthers. A selection by N.C. Ruiter, from his hybrids. **'Obelisk'** White flowers with pale green centers and green midribs. Also raised by Ruiter. **'Pinokkio'** Deep daffodil-yellow with orange anthers. Darker than 'Emmy Ro'. **Ruiter hybrids** A mixture of striking pastel spikes in pinks, yellows, and golds, raised by N.C. Ruiter. **Shelford hybrids** Shorter plants bearing long spires in soft tones of off-white, pink, yellow, and orange. From one of the first *Eremurus* hybridizers, Sir Michael Foster of Great Shelford, Cambridge, England. ↕3¼–5 ft (1–1.5 m).

***E.* 'Oase'** Light pink flowers with dark brown midribs. Originally a selection by Ruiter, though dark pink-flowered plants also seem to be circulating under this name. ↕6 ft (1.8 m). Z5–8 H8–5

E. robustus A giant, the blue-green leaves slightly rough-edged, up to 1½ in (4 cm) wide and 3¼ ft (1 m) long, and the flowers in dramatic columns up to 3¼ ft (1 m), atop tall stems. Blooms for several weeks; each spike is studded with around 800 flowers, light pink with a brown blotch at the base and about 1½ in (4 cm) wide. May need staking. From Afghanistan and Central Asia. ↕8–10 ft (2.5–3 m). Z5–8 H8–5

***E.* 'Romance'** Long, dense spikes of flowers are in a salmony orange-pink color. Raised by N.C. Ruiter. ↕5 ft (1.5 m). Z5–8 H8–5

E. stenophyllus Smaller in scale than some. Linear leaves, up to ⅝ in (1.5 cm) wide and 12 in (30 cm) long, rough-edged, and may be covered in fine hairs. Slender, 12-in (30-cm) foxtails of brilliant yellow flowers, each ¾ in (2 cm) across, bristle with protruding, orange-tipped stamens. As upper buds open, the lower flowers age to rusty brown, giving a two-toned effect. The species most used for hybridizing. From central Asia, Afghanistan, Iran, and western Pakistan. ↕3¼–5 ft (1–1.5 m). Z5–8 H8–5. **subsp. *stenophyllus*** syn. *E. bungei* Leaves are hairless.

ERIGERON

Fleabane

ASTERACEAE

Reliable, underrated, long-flowering daisies that are unfortunately rather out of favor.

Approximately 200 species, most of which are herbaceous perennials

LEFT **1** *Eremurus himalaicus* **2** *E.* x *isabellinus* 'Cleopatra' **3** *E.* 'Oase'

THE EREMURUS FLOWER

An upright, unbranched, leafless flowering stem rises from ground level, studded at the top with many densely or loosely held flowers, each borne on individual ½–1½-in (1–4-cm) stalks with a narrow, papery bract at the base, the lower buds opening first. The six-pointed flowers are composed of three outer sepals and three inner petals, together known as tepals; each is marked with one, three, or five dark central veins. In the center of the flower, around a single-styled ovary, project six stamens which in some species are much longer than the tepals. Seeds are wind-dispersed and usually winged.

Eremurus robustus

ABOVE 1 *Erigeron karvinskianus*
2 *E.* 'White Quakeress'

with a few annuals and biennials, are widely distributed, with the majority native to North America, where they grow in meadows, open prairies, woods, and rocky places. The leaves are produced in a basal rosette, or are confined to the stems, where they are arranged alternately, and are either entire or slightly toothed, usually lacking a noticeable stalk.

The daisylike flowers feature brightly colored ray florets in a range of colors include violet, pink, orange, white, and mauve-blue around a yellow eye; single flowers have one row of rays, semidoubles have two. These are followed by seeds tipped with a parachute of bristles. Some species, including *E. karvinskianus*, are considered invasive weeds in certain parts of the world. The larger types are suitable for the herbaceous border and flower for most of the summer; they look superficially like asters, but bloom several months earlier. The smaller ones are better suited to raised beds or for use on walls.

The name *Erigeron* is pronounced with a soft "g," as in "Germany," and means "old man." This may refer either to the hairy leaves of some species or, perhaps more likely, to the whiskered seeds.

CULTIVATION Prefer a sunny position and moderately fertile, free-draining soil that remains moist through the summer. They grow well near the sea. Many grow best in a raised bed, and some cultivars, such as *E.* 'Dimity', can be killed by excessive winter rain. Some need support with twigs; all benefit from deadheading, and should be cut back in fall. They are inclined to become rather woody as they age and are best dug up, propagated, and replanted every 2–3 years. Avoid excessive feeding because this will reduce the number of flowers.

PROPAGATION Cultivars are generally propagated by division or from basal softwood cuttings in the spring. Species can be grown from seed, sown at 59–68°F (15–20°C).

PROBLEMS Powdery mildew.

E. **'Adria'** Semidouble, pale violet flowers; golden-orange eye in early summer and midsummer. Good ground cover. ↕ 30 in (75 cm). Z5–8 H8–5

E. aurantiacus (Orange daisy) A mat- or clump-forming perennial with untoothed, velvety, spoon-shaped basal leaves and lance-shaped stem leaves. The basal leaves have a short stalk, which is missing from the stem leaves. Flowers, each with a bright orange center and darker orange rays, are borne singly on erect stems from late spring to midsummer. Often short-lived. A parent, with *E. glaucus*, of hybrid cultivars such as *E.* 'Dimity'. From the mountains of Turkestan. ↕ 12 in (30 cm). Z5–8 H8–5.
'Bressingham' Golden yellow flowers; longer-lived.

E. **'Azurfee'** syn. *E.* 'Azure Fairy' Pale mauve flowers with narrow rays and yellow eyes on strong stems from early to late summer. Good for cutting, but varies as grown from seed. ↕ 18 in (45 cm). Z5–8 H8–5.

E. **'Black Sea'** see *E.* 'Schwarzes Meer'

E. **'Dignity'** Single, slightly orangey-yellow-centered, mauve flowers from late spring to midsummer. Earlier than most hybrids. Raised by Alan Bloom of England. ↕ 20 in (50 cm). Z2–7 H7–1

E. **'Dimity'** Semidouble, bright pink flowers that develop from orange-tinted buds in early summer and midsummer. Easily damaged by winter rain and usually short-lived. From Alan Bloom. ↕ 10 in (25 cm). Z5–8 H8–5

E. **'Dunkelste Aller'** syn. 'Darkest of All' Semidouble, deep violet-blue flowers with a yellow center above grayish green leaves from early to late summer. The name is no longer accurate—'Schwarzes Meer' has a deeper violet-colored flower. ↕ 24 in (60 cm). Z5–8 H8–5

E. **'Foerster's Liebling'** syn. 'Föerster's Darling' Very deep rose pink, semi-double flowers in early summer and midsummer, carried on erect stems above grayish green leaves. Noticeably short and clump-forming. Raised by Karl Foerster of Germany. ↕ 24 in (60 cm). Z5–8 H8–5

E. **'Four Winds'** Yellow-centered, lilac-pink flowers on compact plants with short stems in early summer and mid-summer. ↕ 10 in (25 cm). Z5–8 H8–5

E. glaucus (Beach aster) Rather succulent, with fat, often sprawling stems emerging from a dense basal mound of reverse egg-shaped, gray-green, 6 in (15 cm) leaves and carrying similar but smaller stem leaves. The flowers, carried singly or in small clusters, are lilac or violet with yellow centers and produced from late spring to midsummer. Very salt-tolerant. From seasides along the western coast of the US. ↕ 12 in (30 cm). Z5–8 H8–5.
'Arthur Menzies' Bright bluish green leaves are covered with pink daisies with large greenish yellow eyes from late spring to early fall. Selected by Wayne Roderick. ↕ 8 in (20 cm).
'Elstead Pink' Pink, fine-rayed daisies. Raised at Ernest Ladham's nursery at Elstead in Surrey, England, origin of many fine plants. **'Sea Breeze'** Rich red-purple flowers on compact plants from late spring to early fall. **'Wayne Roderick'** Branched stems carry large lavender flowerheads with yellow centers. Found by Mr. Wayne Roderick

ORIGINS

There are two main groups of hybrid erigerons. The first group consists of hybrids with *E. speciosus* subsp. *macranthus*; these are relatively tall-growing with brightly colored flowers and include the thirteen hybrids, including 'Dignity' and 'Prosperity', raised by Alan Bloom at Bressingham Gardens in England from crosses with *E. aurantiacus*. Other species involved include *E. glaucus*, which brings a dwarf habit and thicker, often blue-tinted leaves and also *E. aurantiacus*, which is also short and brings, among other things, orange coloring, including in the buds, but is short-lived.

Alan Bloom was one of the most prominent breeders and, with Percy Piper, introduced 13 cultivars, all ending in the suffix "-ity," although some of the less resilient cultivars have been lost. Most are extremely robust and flower from early summer or midsummer, sometimes to late fall. All should be deadheaded regularly and will often produce a second flush of flowers if they are cut back immediately after flowering. However, the plants may fail to produce any flowers in the first year after planting, and this can also happen if the soil is impoverished.

of England. Sometimes known as 'W.R.'. Perhaps a hybrid.

E. karvinskianus syn. *E. mucronatus* Forms a vigorous mound of wiry, somewhat woody, rather floppy stems. The bright green leaves, slightly downy toward their tips, are untoothed or slightly toothed, narrowly elliptical, lance-shaped or reverse-egg-shaped. The flowers are similar to those of the common lawn daisy and carried singly or in clusters of up to five. Each has a bright yellow center and pink-flushed, white ray petals that gradually turn reddish purple as they age. Much daintier than the hybrids. Readily self-seeds and is excellent for softening stone edges and naturalizing in walls. Cut back in the fall to keep it neat and tidy. Often flowers 2–3 months after a spring sowing. Considered a serious weed in New Zealand where its sale is prohibited. Found in rocky places from Mexico to Panama. ↕ 32 in (80 cm). Z5–7 H7–5. **'Profusion'** Free-flowering seed strain. May not be distinct from the species.

E. mucronatus see *E. karviskianus*

E. **'Nachthimmel'** Deep violet semi-double flowers with a hint of blue and a yellow eye from June to August. ↕ 24 in (60 cm).

E. **'Pink Jewel'** see *E.* 'Rosa Juwel'

E. **'Prosperity'** Semidouble, almost fully double, mauve flowers with yellow centers are carried on erect and compact plants in early summer and midsummer. From Alan Bloom. ↕ 24 in (60 cm). Z5–8 H8–4

E. **'Quakeress'** Masses of single, pale pink, daisylike flowers with slender rays and small yellow centers are carried over grayish green foliage in early summer and midsummer. An old and vigorous cultivar, still worth growing but needs supporting with twigs or sticks. ↕ 24 in (60 cm). Z5–8 H8–5

E. **'Rosa Juwel'** syn. *E.* 'Pink Jewel' Large, pale pink semidouble flowers with a bright yellow center. Raised from seed and variable—even listed as pale blue. ↕ 24 in (60 cm). Z2–7 H7–1

E. **'Schneewittchen'** syn. *E.* 'Snow White' Pure white, threadlike petals: raised, bright yellow center. Very pretty. A cleaner white than 'White Quakeress'. ↕ 24 in (60 cm). Z5–8 H8–5

E. **'Schwarzes Meer'** syn. *E.* 'Black Sea' Semidouble, deep violet flowers with a yellow center in early summer and midsummer. The darkest of all. ↕ 24 in (60 cm). Z2–7 H7–1

E. **'Shimmering Sea'** see *E.* 'Strahlenmeer'

E. **'Snow White'** see *E.* 'Schneewittchen'

E. **'Strahlenmeer'** syn. *E.* 'Shimmering Sea' Masses of pale violet, threadlike petals with small yellow centers.

Attractive, strong-growing; an upright
habit. ↕ 28 in (70 cm). Z2–7 H7–1

E. 'White Quakeress' White flowers
with bright yellow centers, above
grayish green foliage. Not always pure
white, perhaps because it is often raised
from seed. Needs support. ↕ 24 in
(60 cm). Z5–7 H7–5

E. 'Wuppertal' Large, semidouble, deep
mauve flowers above tight clumps.
↕ 24 in (60 cm). Z5–7 H7–5

ERIOPHYLLUM
Woolly sunflower
ASTERACEAE

Vibrant, brilliant yellow-flowered
daisies that make a stunning
summer display in a sunny border.

Of twelve species of annuals and
perennials, some woody-based, from
open, generally sandy, scrubland in
the western US, northwest Mexico,
and southwest Canada, only one is
widely grown. Branching from the
base, a dense, rounded clump is
formed of usually alternate leaves
covered to varying degrees in white
wool. Golden yellow starlike flowers
are held on long stalks above the
foliage; each flowerhead consists of
six to eight outer female ray florets,
broad and overlapping at the base,
narrowing rapidly toward the tip,
surrounding a central cone of dark
golden yellow, bisexual disk florets.
They can be short-lived in gardens,
in warm, wet summers. Birds may
line nests with the woolly foliage.

CULTIVATION Best in full sun in dry,
light, infertile to moderately fertile
soil; tolerates most soils except those
that are wet or cold for long periods
in winter. Cut back after flowering
to help maintain a compact habit.

PROPAGATION From seed, by division,
or cuttings.

PROBLEMS Slugs and snails.

E. lanatum (Oregon sunshine) Clump-
forming, woolly perennial, usually as
wide as tall, with many-branched,
numerous stocky, lightly woolly stems
arising from a woody base. Spoon-
shaped basal leaves can be undivided,
lobed, or dissected; stem leaves decrease
in size up the stem, but are as variable,
and are white-woolly on their lower
surface. The flowerheads, up to 1½ in
(4 cm) across, are brilliant yellow and
produced in succession from late spring
through the summer. Drought-tolerant,
favoring sandy or gravelly, well-drained
soil. From western North America.
↕ 16–24 in (40–60 cm). Z5–8 H8–5.
'Pointe' Dwarf. 12–16 in (30–40 cm).

ERODIUM
Heron's bill
GERANIACEAE

Hardy sun-lovers valued for their
attractive foliage and long
flowering period in summer.

ABOVE 1 *Erodium chrysanthum*
2 *E. manescauii*

About 60 species, including annuals,
alpines, and evergreen or semievergreen perennials, some with a
noticeably woody base, are found in
limestone mountains in Europe and
Central Asia and also in North
Africa, North and South America,
and cooler parts of Australia. The
greatest concentration is around
the Mediterranean. Some are best
in rock or scree gardens or troughs;
larger types are well suited to mixed
or herbaceous borders.

Generally similar in appearance
to hardy geraniums, erodiums have
rounded, five-petaled, pink, purple,
red, white, or yellow flowers in
summer. They are distinct: their
leaves are divided into opposite
pairs of leaflets, or gently and
irregularly lobed, while geraniums'
leaves are more sharply divided
from a central point. Also, geraniums
have 10 fertile stamens; erodiums
have only five.

CULTIVATION Best in full sun, in
neutral to alkaline soil with good
drainage and rich in humus; plants
may suffer in winter if the soil is
poorly drained.

PROPAGATION Divide mat- or
clump-forming kinds in spring;
also take basal stem cuttings in
spring. For species only, sow seed
as soon as it is ripe.

PROBLEMS Vine weevils.

E. carvifolium An excellent front-of-
border plant. Green basal leaves, 2–6 in
(5–16 cm) long, that consist of
numerous leaflets in opposite pairs.
Red saucer-shaped flowers, about ¾ in
(2 cm) wide, in clusters on upright
stems in mid- and late spring, or later.
From central Spain. ↕ 14 in (35 cm).
Z6–8 H8–6

E. chrysanthum Tufted, forming a
dense mound, often seen in rock
gardens but suitable for well-drained
raised borders. Silver-green oval
leaves, 1⅜ in (3.5 cm) long consisting
of many leaflets in opposite pairs; a
superb background for the ¾ in
(2 cm) wide, saucer-shaped, pale
yellow, rarely pink flowers; from
early summer onward. From Greece.
↕ 6 in (15 cm). Z7–8 H8–7

E. hymenodes see *E. trifolium*

E. manescauii A tallish, clump-forming
plant, ideal for the front of a border.
Somewhat lance-shaped, or more oval,
mid-green hairy leaves, to 12 in
(30 cm) long, consist of many leaflets
with toothed edges in opposite pairs.
Clusters of 1¼ in (3 cm) wide, saucer-
shaped flowers in magenta-purple, with
dark spots on upper petals, are freely
produced on long stems, early summer
to early fall. Self-seeds, especially if
mulched with gravel. From the
Pyrenees. ↕ 18 in (45 cm). Z6–8 H8–6

E. pelargoniiflorum Useful for the front
of a border, its woody base carrying
long-stalked, 1½-in (4-cm), lobed,
apple-green, heart-shaped leaves whose
edges have rounded teeth. As the name
indicates, the flowers resemble those of
a *Pelargonium*. Carried in clusters and
about ¾ in (2 cm) in diameter, the
blooms are white, the upper two petals
spotted with purple, and appear from
early summer onward. From Turkey.
↕ 12 in (30 cm). Z6–8 H8–6

E. trifolium syn. *E. hymenodes* A short-
lived evergreen perennial, or sometimes
biennial, of slightly shrubby habit
suitable for the front of a border. Gray-
green, three-lobed leaves, about 2 in
(5 cm) long, have deeply toothed edges.
Flowers, carried in clusters, are about
1 in (2.5 cm) across; pink, with spotted
brown upper petals at the base. They
appear in late spring or early summer.
Often self-seeds freely. From Morocco.
↕ 14 in (35 cm). Z7–10 H10–7

ERYNGIUM
Eryngo
APIACEAE

Striking and distinctive flowers,
their impact often increased by
metallic blue coloring, and popular
for cutting and for borders.

About 240 species of perennials,
biennials, or annuals are found
worldwide, except in tropical and
southern Africa. The leaves are
mostly basal and can be undivided,
deeply lobed, or divided into
leaflets. The flower stems are
ascending and branched, carrying
flowerheads with individual florets
gathered together in a round, egg-
shaped, or cylindrical structure,
usually with a ring of bracts below
that are generally tipped, and
sometimes edged, with spines. Most
have a few thick, fleshy, rather brittle
roots and resent disturbance. The
South American species are very
different from the more commonly
cultivated Old World species, having
parallel-veined, strap-shaped leaves
like those of a bromeliad. The roots
of some species, including the two
native to the British Isles, were
traditionally candied and are
referred to as "eringoes" by
Falstaff in Shakespeare's *The Merry
Wives of Windsor*.

Many cultivars of species such as
E. alpinum, E. bourgatii, and *E. planum*
have been re-raised from seed so
many inferior seedlings masquerade
under the original name: the true
cultivars are often rare, in some cases
extinct. The hybrids, however, are
generally sterile, and are therefore
propagated vegetatively. They should
be true to type.

CULTIVATION Most need good
drainage, dislike nutrient-rich soil,
tolerate alkalinity, and thrive in sun,
although the South American
species are less tolerant of drought.
Some species benefit from staking.

Short twigs worked through the base of the plant work well for shorter species; taller species or cultivars can be supported by larger twigs if they make fairly dense clumps. For those that only produce a few stems, bamboo canes can be used, one per stem; the stems need anchoring only a short way up, perhaps a quarter to a third of their height, to prevent them from toppling at the base.

PROPAGATION Propagation is by division in spring, by root cuttings or, in the case of the species, from seed sown as soon as it is ripe.

PROBLEMS Blackfly, powdery mildew, and leaf miner.

E. agavifolium Evergreen, with strap-shaped leaves to 20 in (50 cm) long, the edges coarsely toothed and spined. The stout, branched flower stems are clasped and almost sheathed by the stem leaves. From midsummer to early fall, each stem has as many as 20 thumb-sized, greenish flowerheads, up to 2 in (5 cm) high, with grayish blue anthers above a ruff of narrow, rather short bracts. Often known, incorrectly, as *E. bromeliifolium*. From Argentina. ‡5 ft (1.5 m). Z6–9 H9–6

E. alpinum Deciduous, with irregularly-toothed, egg- or heart-shaped basal leaves, and stem leaves with radiating lobes. In mid- to late summer, several blue, egg-shaped to cylindrical flowerheads, up to 1½ in (4 cm) tall, are borne on stout stems that are blue-flushed above and often carry strikingly blue-white veined stem leaves. Each head has an extravagant ruff up to 5 in (13 cm) wide of more than 25 bracts, with spiky lobes often divided again to give a lacy effect; they are soft to the touch and not prickly. From the Jura, the Alps, and the mountains of west and central former Yugoslavia. ‡20–32 in (50–80 cm). Z6–9 H9–6. **'Amethyst'** Small, dark violet flowerheads and more divided foliage. Raised by Georg Arends of Germany. ‡24 in (60 cm). **'Blue Star'** Rich blue

flowerheads, the color extending well down the stems. ‡28 in (70 cm). 'Slieve Donard' see *E. × Zabelii* 'Donard Variety'. **'Superbum'** Large, dark blue flowerheads. ‡30 in (75 cm).

E. amethystinum (Italian eryngo) Usually evergreen, with leathery, thistlelike basal leaves, divided into lobes along the midrib; the upper stem leaves are cut into radiating lobes. In mid- and late summer, branched stems bear many egg-shaped to roundish flowerheads, about ¾ in (2 cm) tall, each with five to nine spreading bracts up to 4 in (10 cm) across and usually blue, more rarely amethyst. The best selections have richly colored upper stems as well as flowers. From Italy, Sicily, and the Balkans. ‡20–32 in (50–80 cm). Z3–8 H8–1

E. **'Blue Jackpot'** In mid- and late summer, sturdy stems carry flowerheads consisting of a blue cone surrounded by large and showy metallic-blue bracts, each with a number of unbranched spines down the sides. A hybrid derived principally from *E. alpinum*. ‡24 in (60 cm). Z4–8 H8–1

E. bourgatii Much-divided dark green basal leaves surround stems bearing divided stem leaves, often more pale-veined up the stem. From early to late summer, the stems bear up to seven flowerheads, each with an egg- or flattened globe-shaped cone of florets surrounded by seven to fifteen spine-tipped bracts, often with further spines along their edges, giving an overall diameter of about 4 in (10 cm). The flowerheads can be whitish green, dull grayish green (not effective and best avoided), or, in the most desirable selections, rich blue or violet, with the coloration extending down the flower stem, sometimes into the veins of the upper leaves. Some selections benefit from staking. Sun-loving, native to Spain, the Pyrenees, and northwest Africa. ‡12–22 in (30–55 cm). Z5–9 H9–5. **Graham Stuart Thomas's selection** Exceptionally divided, narrow-lobed leaves with pronounced white veins, a neat habit, and, in mid-

and late summer, good blue coloration of flower heads and upper stems. Selected from plants raised from seed collected by Jim Archibald in about 1980. ‡20 in (50 cm). **'Oxford Blue'** Richly colored, rather dwarf selection with much divided, pale-veined foliage, flowering in mid- and late summer. Demands sun and good drainage. Selected and named by Primrose Warburg in 1980. ‡16 in (40 cm). **'Picos Amethyst'** Prolific deep amethyst-blue flowers on sturdy stems in early summer and midsummer, darkening as the flower ages. Introduced from the Picos de Europa in Spain's Cantabrian Mountains by Dr. Ronald Mackenzie. **'Picos Blue'** Sturdy, floriferous, and relatively easy to grow, with rich lavender-blue flowers on sturdy stems in early summer and midsummer. Introduced by Dr. Ronald Mackenzie. ‡20 in (50 cm).

E. bromeliifolium see *E. agavifolium* and *E. eburneum*

E. campestre (Field eryngo) Leathery, rather blue-gray, sometimes evergreen basal leaves are egg-shaped in outline and divided into three lobes, each of these further cut into spiny, saw-toothed lobes. The stem leaves become more divided and the blade more reduced up the plant toward the flowers, so that the uppermost may consist of little more than white veins with green flanges. In mid- and late summer, the upper-most, branching, whitish stems bear many pale greenish, egg-shaped flowerheads on branching, winged stems. Each is ½–¾ in (1–2 cm) across, with five to nine lance-shaped, spine-tipped bracts ¼–2 in (2–5 cm) long, each with up to two pairs of lateral spines. From central and southern Europe extending to southern England. ‡8–28 in (20–70 cm). Z5–8 H8–5

DRAMA AND FLAIR

ERYNGIUM ALPINUM IS A DRAMATIC and distinctive plant. The silver foliage of artemisias is often used as a partner—*A*. 'Powis Castle' with its finely cut leaves, perhaps—and this works well creating a billowing contrast. Here, there is a different approach associating flowers rather than flowers and foliage. The spiky-looking, but soft-to-the-touch, ruffs around the flower cones are contrasted with the rounded double flowers of *Geranium pratense* 'Plenum Violaceum'. Slender geranium stems lean into the more vertical eryngium, each geranium flower like a dancer throwing up her skirts, and the fresh green upper stem leaves, divided jaggedly, picking up a similar shape in the ruff of the eryngium.

ERYNGIUM FLOWER STRUCTURE

Eryngium flowers have florets gathered closely together in a cone- or egglike structure, usually surrounded by a ruff of spiny bracts that discourage grazing animals. In this they differ from typical umbellifers (in the family Apiaceae), which usually have flowers like Queen Anne's lace with a plate or dome of florets, usually white, above a branched structure of floret stalks. Individual *Eryngium* florets have a calyx of five spiny teeth alternating with five shorter tiny petals in blue, mauve, white, or green.

Florets

Eryngium X oliverianum   Spiny bracts

***E.* 'Delaroux'** see *E. proteiflorum*

E. decaisneanum see *E. pandanifolium*

E. ebracteatum Strap-shaped leaves 8–40 in (20–100 cm) long and ¼–½ in (0.5–1.5 cm) wide, are edged with a few spines. In mid- and late summer, the widely branching stems bear many columnar, wine-colored flowerheads, measuring ¼–1¼ x 1/16–¼ in (5–30 × 2–5 mm). The bracts at the base of each flower are tiny or absent. Dramatic and distinctive, from South America. ↕ 6½ ft (2 m). Z7–10 H10–7

E. eburneum Sword-shaped basal leaves 3¼ ft (1 m) long by 1¼–2 in (2–5 cm) wide, are edged with stout spines in their upper half. The stems have leaves slightly clasping at the base and, in mid- and late summer, carry a branched spray of many small, round, greenish white flowerheads, ½–¾ in (1–2 cm) long. Sometimes known, incorrectly, as *E. bromeliifolium*. From South America. ↕ 6½ ft (2 m). Z9–11 H12–10

E. horridum At least three different species are grown under this name, but it seems likely that none is the extremely spiny South American agricultural weed to which this name correctly applies.

E. maritimum (Sea holly) A striking blue-gray-green, rather short-lived perennial. Its leathery, silvery blue-green leaves, about 4 in (10 cm) across and roughly round in outline, have up to five sharply pointed, triangular lobes, usually twisted to one side or the other, giving a lively play of light and shade. The branching flower stems tend to be woody at the base and carry, in mid- and late summer, numerous almost round, pale blue flowerheads, each with 4–7 bracts resembling the leaves beneath. Demands full sun, sharp drainage, and nutrient-poor soil; site at the front of the border or in the gravel garden. Like another blue-gray seasider, *Crambe maritima*, it has potential for superlative beauty that it rarely achieves, often developing a loose, open habit. From sand dunes on the coasts of western Europe (including the British Isles), the Mediterranean, and the Black Sea. ↕ 12 in (30 cm). Z5–10 H10–5

E.* × *oliverianum Vigorous and easy deciduous perennial with heart- to egg-shaped, slightly three-lobed, long-stemmed, dark green basal leaves with forward-pointing spines. The stem leaves have three to five radiating lobes, each of which is again lobed. In mid- and late summer, the branched stems bear 1½ in (4 cm-) tall, vivid blue, egg-shaped to cylindrical heads, each with 10–15 violet-blue spiny bracts beneath. Perhaps the most remarkable feature is the intense steel blue of the upper flower stems, more than compensating for the rather coarse foliage. Generally needs staking. Tolerates heavy clay. A seedling of *E. alpinum* reputedly pollinated by *E. planum* or the biennial *E. giganteum*, though *E. amethystinum* seems more likely. ↕ 3¼ ft (1 m). Z5–8 H8–5

E. pandanifolium syn. *E. decaisneanum* Clump-forming, evergreen perenneial with linear, parallel-veined leaves, ⅝–1 in (1.5–2.5 cm) long by ¾–1½ in (2–4 cm) wide, are edged with weak spines. The much-branched flower stem bears similar but smaller leaves; from late summer to mid-fall, many small, purple-red, egg-shaped heads, about ¼–½ in (7–10 mm) wide and ⅛–⅜ in (4–8 mm) across with 1/16-in (2-mm) bracts beneath, just showing beneath the heads. From South America. ↕ 5–12 ft (1.5–4 m). Z9–10 H12–10

E. planum (Blue eryngo) Variable deciduous plant; the rather leathery, dark green, oblong to egg-shaped basal leaves are 2–4 in (5–10 cm) long and have forward-pointing teeth. The stem leaves have radiating lobes and become smaller, more spiny, and blue-tinged toward the top of the stem. From midsummer to early fall, the branching stems bear many round, usually bluish heads about ½–⅝ in (1.5–2.5 cm) across, each with six to eight bracts, each ⅝–2 in (15–25 mm) long and edged with one to four pairs of spinelike teeth. Coming from dry, nutrient-poor soil in wild, pampered garden plants may need support. From Germany and Austria eastward to Russia, the Caucasus, and Central Asia. ↕ 10–40 in (25–100 cm). Z5–9 H9–5. **'Bethlehem'** A floriferous selection with a profusion of relatively small, slate-blue flowerheads. ↕ 3¼ ft (1 m). **'Blauer Zwerg'** (**Blue Dwarf**) Intensely blue flowerheads on a compact plant. The true plant is now rare, having been

CUTTING AND DRYING

Eryngiums are increasingly popular as cut and dried flowers. *Eryngium planum* and its cultivars are the most widely grown; some recent introductions have been raised with cut-flower growers in mind, but even tall species like *E. yuccifolium* are sometimes cut for the house.

All should be cut when they have reached their maximum coloring; placing the cut flowers in cool temperatures, around 39°F (4°C), will improve the color. Flowers should last about ten days, or slightly more; the foliage of some is less resilient and may need to be removed while the flowers are still in good condition. Eryngiums can also be dried: simply hanging them upside-down in a warm, dry and airy place works well, though small sprigs dry very well in silica gel and this approach retains the best color. The only drawbacks are that some people find they have an unpleasant smell when dried, and, being spiny, they can also be uncomfortable to handle.

RIGHT 1 *Eryngium agavifolium*
2 *E. alpinum* **3** *E. bourgatii*
4 *E. bourgatii* 'Oxford Blue'
5 *E.* x *oliverianum*

superseded by inferior seedlings. ‡20 in (50 cm). **'Blaukappe'** syn. 'Tetra Blue' Rich blue flowerheads on a compact plant. ‡24 in (60 cm). **'Blue Ribbon'** Violet-blue, prolific "hen-and-chickens" flowerheads, an amusing effect that obscures the shape of the individual heads but makes the display last longer. A spontaneous mutation of 'Flüela'. ‡3¼ ft (1 m). **'Flüela'** Tall, with rich violet-blue flowerheads. ‡4 ft (1.2 m). **'Seven Seas'** Narrow upright habit. Flowers intensely blue but fade with age. ‡38 in (95 cm). **'Silver Stone'** Grayish green flower-heads on stout stems. ‡38 in (95 cm).

E. proteiflorum syn. *E.* 'Delaroux' Rosette-forming evergreen, with lancelike, parallel-veined, mid- to dark green basal leaves, 4–12 in (10–30 cm) long by ½–1 in (1–2.5 cm) wide, edged with spiny lobes. The flower stems bear similar but shorter alternate leaves, their bases clasping the stem. Bluish, egg-shaped to cylindrical flowerheads ½–1¼ in (1–3 cm) tall, usually borne one to a stem, are surrounded by 15–30 spiny bracts up to 5 in (12 cm) long, usually silvery, occasionally near white or tinted sea-green or greyish-blue. With the showiest bracts of the South American species, this is a plant of supreme floral beauty with the main flush in mid- and late summer and sporadic later flowering into mid-fall. Unfortunately, it rarely has enough blooms to make a large-scale impact. The synonym is often styled as a cultivar name but this is a double error; François Delaroche (not Delaroux) was the botanist who first gave this plant its species name. Its lushness in gardens belies its origin in poor, dry, gravelly volcanic soil, and it is tolerant of summer drought. Its unexpected frost tolerance derives from its high altitude native habitat on the slopes of volcanoes in Mexico. ‡20–40 in (50–100 cm).

E. serra Hairless perennial with lancelike, parallel-veined basal leaves, 12–24 in (30–60 cm) long by ¾–2 in (2–5 cm) wide, edged with spine-tipped teeth separated by rather spiny marginal hairs. The numerous ½-in (1-cm), round white flowerheads are borne in late summer and early fall on a branched stem, each of these with six to nine, lance-shaped ¼-in (5-mm) bracts beneath. A number of different species seem to be grown under this name. From Brazil to Argentina. ‡6½ ft (2 m). Z6–9 H9–6

E. × tripartitum The basal leaves are three-lobed, dark green and spiny-edged, while the stem leaves lack stalks and are more deeply divided into lobes and tipped with spines. The much-branched, slender, wiry stems bear, in mid- and late summer, roundish heads, ½–¾ in (1–2 cm) across, above six to nine narrow, radiating bracts about 1¼ in (3 cm) long. The upper stems and heads are silvery gray-green before assuming a rich violet-blue tint when in full bloom, coloring best when grown in well-drained soil in full sun. May need staking. An outstandingly

elegant, sterile hybrid perhaps derived from *E. amethystinum* and *E. planum*. ‡24–36 in (60–90 cm). Z5–8 H8–5

E. variifolium Evergreen, with oblong to circular mid- to dark green, toothed basal leaves, about 2 in (5 cm) long and marbled with pale veins. The stem leaves, with spiny lobes at intervals along the midrib, become progressively narrower, whiter, and more spiky up the plant. Many blue-gray, round to egg-shaped flowerheads, up to ¾ in (2 cm) across, with five to seven spiny whitish bracts ¾–2½ in (2–6 cm) long beneath, are borne on stiffly erect, branched stems in mid- and late summer—though its early season foliage is, perhaps, its chief attraction. From North Africa. ‡12–18 in (30–45 cm). Z5–9 H9–5

E. yuccifolium (Rattlesnake master) Variable evergreen with parallel-veined, straplike, bluish green basal leaves, 8–40 in (20–100 cm) long, toothed with ¼-in (5-mm) spines. The stem leaves are similar, clasping the stem at their base and becoming progressively smaller up the plant. From midsummer to early fall, the branched stems bear from a few to many round to egg-shaped heads, ½–1 in (1–2.5 cm) across, opening blue-gray, whitish, or green, above five to ten short bracts, scarcely showing beneath the heads and toothed all along their margins. From the eastern United States. ‡4–6 ft (1.2–1.8 m). Z4–9 H12–1

E. × zabelii Clump-forming with semievergreen basal leaves divided into three deep lobes, each of them further lobed and lobed again, and toothed with spines. The stem leaves become more narrowly lobed, spiny, pale-veined, and blue-tinted up the stem. Egg-shaped to cylindrical heads in blue or violet, usually several to a branched stem, flower in mid- and late summer, each with a ruff of long, rigid bracts with forward-pointing spines. A hybrid of *E. alpinum* and *E. bourgatii*. ‡24–40 in (60–100 cm). Z5–8 H8–5. **'Donard Variety'** syn. *E. alpinum* 'Slieve Donard' Large, gray-blue flowers with extra-large cones and long, recurved bracts with few subsidiary lobes. The whole plant appears silvery gray when mature. Introduced by the Slieve Donard Nursery, Northern Ireland, in about 1945. ‡3¼ ft (1 m). **'Jos Eijking'** Vigorous and easy, with richly blue-tinted flowerheads and upper stems. The usually 12–15 bracts are straight and rather broad, giving a starry appearance. ‡28 in (70 cm). **'Violetta'** Upright plant with rich violet blue flowers and silvery blue bracts. ‡24 in (60 cm).

EUPATORIUM
Hemp agrimony, Joe Pye weed
ASTERACEAE

Underrated sun-loving plants that have a long, late flowering season.

Forty species of annuals, evergreen and deciduous perennials, subshrubs

BIG, BOLD, AND BODACIOUS

Eupatoriums are big plants. Although *E. coelestinum*, *E. purpureum* subsp. *maculatum*, 'Gateway', and 'Purple Bush' allow their butterfly-friendly fall flowers to be brought into small spaces, at well over 6½ ft (2 m), *E. fistulosum* 'Atropurpureum' and the taller forms of *E. purpureum* rule themselves out for planting in small gardens. Yet, in a more expansive situation, they are spectacular. They support themselves unexpectedly well, although the stems can arch alarmingly when their flowerheads become saturated with rain.

However, their height can be reduced by cutting back in early summer. Cut the whole plant back to 12–18 in (30–45 cm) and it will flower at about the usual time, or a little later, on much shorter stems. The resulting flowerheads are usually smaller and more manageable for flower arranging. This approach also works well with 'Chocolate', whose flowers are a less pure white than we would like; cutting back as the buds appear creates a flush of dark foliage, so maintaining the foliage effect for longer.

Cutting back also helps in another respect. It is far easier to deadhead an aggressive self-seeder when it is a short plant in the middle or front of the border than if it is a tall plant at the back.

and shrubs, native to Europe, Africa, Asia, and North and South America, are found in a range of habitats including woodlands, sunny places, and swamps. They are deciduous and form compact clumps. Their foliage shows great diversity, but most have paired or clustered leaves with toothed margins. Flowers are tiny and grouped in flat or domed heads like those of closely related *Ageratum*; they are followed by fluffy seed heads.

Botanists have recently been re-examining eupatoriums and have split them into a number of new genera, including *Ageratina* and *Conoclinium*, on the basis of small but important botanical features. They may be found listed under these names in some catalogs.

Eupatoriums are much beloved of butterflies—peacocks, small tortoiseshells, and painted ladies in particular—although double-

flowered cultivars produce less nectar and so are less attractive. *E. purpureum* is one of the relatively few shade-loving perennials the butterflies appreciate.

The height of most eupatoriums dictates their place at the back of the border, but once planted, removal can prove difficult. They are useful for their long flowering season, which often continues into late summer and fall, although by then the foliage may look tired; fortunately, it will be hidden by more forward plants. Coarser types are well suited to a wildlife or seminatural garden (they attract butterflies, beetles, and other insects) but may self-seed irritatingly, so deadheading is advisable.

CULTIVATION Most thrive in

BELOW *Eupatorium cannabinum*

LEFT 1 *Eupatorium purpureum* subsp. *maculatum* 'Atropurpureum'
2 *E. rugosum*

moderately moist soil in full sun or part-shade. In hot summers, may need watering to prevent wilting.

PROPAGATION By division.

PROBLEMS Usually trouble-free, but can prove invasive.

E. album Compact with rough, hairy stems bearing paired, coarsely toothed, oval leaves to 2 in (5 cm) long. From midsummer to mid-fall, fluffy white flowerheads are produced in flat or domed clusters. A shorter eupatorium, it also thrives in dry conditions. From open or part-shaded places in sandy soil in the eastern US, listed as endangered in some areas. ‡ 3¼ ft (1 m). Z4–8 H8–1. **'Braunlaub'** Dark stems and brown-flushed young leaves with ivory white flowers. Shade-tolerant. Sometimes listed under *E. rugosum*.

E. cannabinum (Hemp agrimony) An upright plant forming a large, dense clump of reddish stems. Paired leaves are divided into narrow, fingerlike segments to 4¾ in (12 cm) long, and resemble the foliage of marijuana. From mid- to late summer or early fall, it bears flat sprays of light purple, pink, or white flowerheads, to 4 in (10 cm) across, that attract butterflies and other insects, making it a fine plant for a wildlife garden, though it can prove invasive. Grows in sunny, wet places in most of Europe. ‡ 5 ft (1.5 m). Z3–9 H9–1. **'Flore Pleno'** Long-lasting, double pink blossoms above red-tinted leaves. Does not set seed.

E. capillifolium (Dog fennel) Tall with feathery leaves divided into very narrow segments, like fennel. Greenish white flowers are borne in loose, waving plumes in early fall. Weedy in appearance, but quietly elegant and suitable for a wild corner where its late flowering would be an asset. From pastures and fields in the southeastern US, where it is an agricultural weed. ‡ 8 ft (2.5 m). Z3–10 H8–2. **'Elegant Feather'** More compact, with handsome, plumelike, white flowers, tinged pink at maturity. ‡ 6 ft (1.8 m).

E. coelestinum syn. *Conoclinium coelestinum* (Hardy ageratum, Mist flower) A vigorously spreading plant. Upright, brownish stems bear paired, broadly oval, light green leaves to 4 in (10 cm) long, the margins bluntly toothed. From late summer to mid-fall, flat sprays of fluffy blue, purple, or white flowers open at the tips of the branching stems. Although compact, stems tend to flop and it benefits from a position where nearby plants give some support. Good for a herbaceous border or wild garden; unexpectedly drought-tolerant; good for cutting. From moist places in the central and southeastern US and the West Indies. ‡ 36 in (90 cm). Z5–11 H9–1

RICH COLORINGS IN FALL SUNSHINE

FALL PERENNIAL PLANT ASSOCIATIONS have a great deal of competition—from fiery fall foliage in particular—so bold, dramatic, and intriguing combinations like this are especially valuable because they catch the rich, low light. *Eupatorium purpureum* subsp. *maculatum* makes an imposing clump with its dark, mottled stems and prolific, slightly rounded heads of purplish pink flowers. But alongside, making a contrast in both color and form, is the underrated

Sanguisorba tenuifolia 'Alba', its pendulous tails on slender stems weaving into the eupatorium to bring added distinction. In spring, bulbs can be scattered through the clumps; then, after flowering, their fading foliage will be masked by the developing leaves of both perennials.

E. fistulosum 'Atropurpureum' (Hollow-stemmed Joe Pye weed) Tall, erect, red-brown stems bear clusters of lance-shaped, light green, vanilla-scented leaves to 25 cm (10 cm) long. From midsummer to early fall, stems are crowned by large, domed sprays of dusky deep pink or wine red flowers. Too tall for most borders, but a striking plant for a wild garden and much loved by butterflies. The species itself is rarely grown. Grows in sunny, damp places in the eastern US, south to Texas. ‡ 10 ft (3 m). Z3–8 H8–2

E. perfoliatum Upright with hairy stems bearing paired, lance-shaped, prominently veined leaves to 8 in (20 cm) long, joined by their bases across the stem. Flat, branched sprays of white or purple-tinted flowers appear at the tips of stems from mid- or late summer to early fall. A good plant for the back of a damp border, or a wild area. From wet places in eastern North America. ‡ 5 ft (1.5 m). Z3–9 H8–1

E. purpureum (Joe Pye weed) A tall plant with stems bearing clusters of long-stalked, oval or lance-shaped, finely toothed leaves to 10 in (25 cm) long, often tinged purple when grown in full sun. In late summer and early fall, rounded sprays of small pale or purplish pink (occasionally white) flowers open at the tips of stems. The foliage tends to be past its best by flowering time, but is useful for the back of a border. It prefers alkaline soil and tolerates more shade than other species. The curious common name is said to be a corrupted form of the name of a native American who reputedly used this plant for medicinal purposes. From damp meadows in eastern North America. ‡ 10 ft (3 m). Z3–9 H9–1. **'Album'** Flowers white. **subsp. maculatum** Stems spotted purple with more flowers in flatter clusters. **subsp. maculatum 'Album'** Flowers white; may be the same as 'Album', above. **subsp. maculatum 'Atropurpureum'** Stems deep reddish purple, flowers purple. **subsp. maculatum 'Gateway'** Shorter form, with purple stems and light purple flowers. Selected by Maryland horticulturist Kurt Bluemel. ‡ 6½ ft (2 m) **subsp. maculatum 'Glutball'** Stems tinged pink; flowers mauve-pink, in rounded clusters. **'Purple Bush'** Compact form with smaller, light purple flower clusters. Raised by Piet Oudolf in Holland. ‡ 5 ft (1.5 m).

E. rugosum syn. *Ageratina altissima* (White snakeroot) A clump-forming plant with brown stems bearing paired, oval leaves to 4 in (10 cm) long, which are nettlelike, deeply veined, and coarsely toothed. From midsummer to early fall, rounded sprays of pure white flowers open at the tips of stems. Needs moist soil or part-shade to prevent wilting but survives in dry shade. From damp, open places in eastern North America. ‡ 6½ ft (2 m). Z4–8 H8–2. **'Braunlaub'** see *E. album*. **'Braunlaub' 'Chocolate'** Leaves and stems deep purple; a superb foliage plant, but the flowers are off-white. ‡ 3¼ ft (1 m).

EUPHORBIA
Spurges
EUPHORBIACEAE

Striking flowering and foliage plants for borders, ground cover, and dry gardens.

Nearly 2,000 species show a wider variety of growth forms than any other plant and grow on every continent, with the exception of Antarctica. The majority are spiny, leafless, succulent plants that are easily mistaken for cacti. The leafy perennials that bring a unique range of colors to our gardens have two important characters in common with these succulent tropical and subtropical plants.

First, they have a distinct and very unusual flower structure, without the showy petals of many other plants in this book, but, unfortunately, with its very own terminology (*see* Unique Flower Structure). The second common feature of euphorbias is that they all exude white sap when damaged. In some people this sap can provoke a very unpleasant rash when it comes into contact with the skin, so care should be taken when handling the plants. Keep the sap off your skin and wash it off immediately. Never rub the sap into your eyes, and never let it drop into water containing fish.

Plants covered here fall into two main groups: hardy perennials in the traditional style, such as *E. polychroma*, and evergreen perennials that produce biennial shoots, such as *E. characias*. Woody species like *E. acanthothamnos* are more correctly shrubs and have been excluded; *E. mellifera*, technically a shrub but generally included as a perennial by gardeners, is included.

In general, the euphorbias treated here either have fat roots, which also contain the milky sap, with a few fibrous roots, or tap roots, supporting a tight, often woody crown or sometimes a network of running roots, which, in a few cases, can be invasive.

The stems, which vary from stiffly upright to laying flat on the ground, are lined with leaves that vary relatively little in shape between species: they tend to be linear or lance-shaped, usually alternately or spirally arranged, without stalks, and gather into a cluster just below the flowers. They may be various shades of green, sometimes with a central white or pink stripe, or blue-gray.

The flowers are gathered into a branched flowering head. Usually, there are five initial branches, which are then themselves branched into three, then again into two, and sometimes into three again. The flowers are very distinctive (*see* Unique Flower Structure) and the predominant color is usually chartreuse, with many species exhibiting yellower, red or orange, or rusty tones.

Different species have different roles in garden: some make good ground cover in shade, some are ideal for dry, sunny Mediterranean-style gardens, and some are excellent in mixed or perennial borders. It is important to choose the right species for the right place.

Euphorbias are sometimes dramatic, often intriguing, and always valuable, and while they are rarely the stars of the show, they are vital members of the garden chorus, providing a range of colors that act as a perfect foil and contrast to other flowers. ⚠

CULTIVATION Species vary in the soil they require and the light levels they appreciate. There is no evidence that the acidity or alkalinity of the soil is important, and any reasonable fertile soil will do. Most of the deciduous perennials require staking, but the evergreens should be allowed to sprawl or stand up for themselves. Deadheading is only necessary either if the plant looks untidy or if you want to prevent too many self-sown seedlings.

PROPAGATION Many are very easily grown from seed, best sown in its first winter. The seedlings often resent disturbance, so sow two seeds to each 3-in (7-cm) pot, then thin to one. Division can be tricky due to the woody nature of the roots, but is best carried out at the end of the winter. Cultivars must be propagated by spring cuttings, since seedlings will not come true.

PROBLEMS Powdery mildew, rust, aphids, and thrips. Slugs can also be a problem to seedlings—a remarkable fact given the toxicity of the sap.

E. amygdaloides (Wood spurge) Evergreen, self-supporting ground-cover plant with stout shoots producing their flowers in their second year and then dying to the base. In their first year, the 4-in (10-cm) green leaves are softly hairy; in their second year they are less hairy and sometimes hairless. The chartreuse-colored flowerheads grow up to 12 in (30 cm) in diameter in mid-spring, on the

RIGHT *Euphorbia amygdaloides* var. *robbiae*

UNIQUE FLOWER STRUCTURE

The flowers of all euphorbias follow the same, unique design. Superficially, they look like many other flowers, with an ovary in the center, for seed production, surrounded by a ring of pollen-bearing stamens. Around the stamens is a ring of glistening glands that produce nectar. There are neither sepals nor petals, but there are normally small leaves around the flowers that attract pollinators, performing the same function. The nectaries are attached to the rim of a cup known as a cyathium. A capsule grows from inside this, containing three ovaries. When the flowers first appear, stamens can also be seen growing inside these cups, but once they have released their pollen, they wither and fall away. The botanical reality of this arrangement is that each capsule is one female flower and each stamen is one male flower. At the base of each cup there are a number of leaves. Shoots grow from the base of these leaves, and these shoots will end in another cup and leaves. The result is a complex flowerhead or inflorescence, and it is this, complete with leaves, that provides the color in our gardens, rather than the flowers themselves.

Male flower
Female flower
Nectaries on rim of cup
Cyathium
Cyathium leaf

Euphorbia palustris

shoots from the previous year. The pair of leaves at the base of the cyathium is often fused; the glands are crescent-shaped. Thrives in semishade in fertile soil rich in organic matter. Remove spent flowering shoots at the base when they become unsightly. May seed around and often forms large drifts. From woodland edges and glades in western Europe, including Britain, to Central Asia and the Mediterranean. ↕ 40 in (100 cm). Z6–9 H9–2.
'**Cragieburn**' Purple leaves with yellow flower heads contrasting strongly with the leaves. '**Golden Glory**' Acid yellow flowers, exceptionally dark green leaves; more resistant to mildew than most.
'**Purpureum**' A range of seed-raised plants are grown under this name; they are variable in size and very prone to mildew. **var. robbiae** Very dark green, hairless leaves form tight spirals on the top half of the stems. Roots run boldly, making it a fine, though sometimes aggressive, ground cover; good in dry shade. A parent of *E. x martinii*. ↕ 28 in (70 cm). '**Variegata**' Leaves edged cream; a weak plant of no garden merit but valued by collectors. ↕ 16 in (40 cm).

E. barrelieri see *E. beselicus*

E. beselicus syn. *E. barrelieri*, *E. flavicoma* Sprawling, evergreen with silver-gray leaves up to 2 in (5 cm) long, often sparsely arranged, along 24 in (60 cm)

shoots. The very open, 4 in (10 cm) heads of dull yellow flowers are produced in late spring on one-year-old shoots. The cyathium leaves may turn a bright pink in late summer, especially when grown in a pot. Best in full sun but will tolerate semishade. It requires well-drained soil and is ideal for a gravel garden. The shoots should be removed when they become tattered. From France to northwest Turkey. ↕ 6 in (15 cm). Z6–9 H9–2

E. characias (Frog-spawn bush) Very variable, evergreen, shrubby perennial that flowers on shoots produced the previous year. At its best a mature plant can develop into a huge hemispherical dome, 12 ft (4 m) in diameter, but the stems may fall over, especially when in full flower. Leaves, up to 8 in (20 cm) long, vary from dark green to densely hairy and appear silvery blue-gray. The flowerheads also vary enormously in size and shape, but most have shoots that branch twice into two. The nectaries vary from yellow to black; the two extremes have been described as different species, but even in the wild, populations are so variable that the names are now irrelevant—although still widely used. The glands may or may not have slender horns. The leaves at the base of the cyathium are normally fused. Grows best in full sun to semishade, in fertile, well drained

soil. Remove flowering shoots as low as possible after seeds have been shed, or the crown may become very congested. Propagate by cuttings (essential for cultivars) or seed. Most cultivars of *Euphorbia characias* are clones that have subsequently been propagated by seed, so may not be true to type. Some nurseries indicate whether seeds or cuttings have been used. From dry rocky places in the Mediterranean region, but naturalized elsewhere in Europe, including Britain, where it was first recorded in 1797. ↕ 6½ ft (2 m). Z7–10 H10–7. '**Black Pearl**' Compact form with black nectaries. ↕ 30 in (75 cm). **subsp. characias** Name originally used to describe the plants from the western end of the Mediterranean region, with black nectaries. **subsp. characias 'Blue Hills'** Compact plant with blue-gray foliage. Introduced by Jim Archibald and Eric Smith of England. ↕ 4 ft (1.2 m). **subsp. characias 'Burrow Silver'** Compact, with a clean cream edge to the leaves right into the flowerhead. In open ground it is a weak plant, but it does well in a container when it can be brought in for the winter. ↕ 4 ft (1.2 m). **subsp. characias 'Humpty Dumpty'** Very compact plant with green-gray foliage. ↕ 3¼ ft (1 m). **subsp. characias 'Portuguese Velvet'** Very compact, with gray velvety foliage and tight flowerheads, 5 in (12 cm) in diameter, with black glands. Best in full sunshine and well-drained soil; superb in a gravel garden. Introduced from Portugal by the photographer John Fielding. ↕ 24 in (60 cm). '**Goldbrook**' Longer than normal leaves and a chartreuse-yellow flowerhead, up to 12 in (30 cm) in diameter. Short. ↕ 3¼ ft (1 m). **Silver Swan** ('**Wilcott**') Good variegated plant with a clean cream edge to its leaves. '**Tasmanian Tiger**' Dramatic white variegation extending into the flower heads. Found in a garden near Hobart, Tasmania. ↕ 36 in (90 cm). **subsp. wulfenii** Originally used to describe the plants from the eastern end of the Mediterranean region, with yellow nectaries. Forms of this subspecies tend to be taller that those of subsp. *characias*. **subsp. wulfenii 'Emmer Green'** Cream-edged leaves. In well-drained soil this is the hardiest variegated form of *E. characias* and a good plant for a gravel garden. ↕ 36 in (90 cm). **subsp. wulfenii 'Jimmy Platt'** The cyathium leaves are yellow and the glands red, in compact 8-in (20-cm) heads. **subsp. wulfenii 'John Tomlinson'** Large, bright yellow inflorescences up to 14 in (35 cm) in diameter. Often propagated from seed, so plants under this name vary but are usually good. **subsp. wulfenii 'Lambrook Gold'** Tall, with dark yellow flowerheads up to 12 in (30 cm) in diameter. Selected by Margery Fish of England. ↕ 6½ ft (2 m). **subsp. wulfenii 'Lambrook Yellow'** Tall, with yellow flowerheads up to 12 in (30 cm) in diameter. Paler than 'Lambrook Gold'. Selected by Margery Fish. ↕ 6½ ft (2 m). **subsp. wulfenii Margery Fish Group** Seedlings from the two Lambrook cultivars. Can be good garden plants but, of course, variable.

subsp. wulfenii 'Purple and Gold' syn. 'Purpurea' Purple winter foliage fading through the spring to dull green in the summer, then returning in fall. Flowerheads bright yellow, contrasting well with the foliage in mid-spring.

E. cognata Delicate, under used herbaceous plant with 2-in (5-cm) dark green leaves, each with a cream central vein. The cyathium leaves are bright yellow from late spring to early fall, and their color persists even if grown in part-shade. Prefers good fertile soil and the shelter of other plants in a mixed or herbaceous border, otherwise it will need staking. Propagate by spring cuttings or careful division. From Afghanistan to the western Himalaya. ↕ 5 ft (1.5 m). Z6–9 H9–2

E. coralloides (Coral spurge) Sparse, rather loose, short-lived, sometimes biennial plant. The leaves on the young shoots are flushed with pink, hence the name, but the majority of the stem leaves fall off as the plant starts to flower. Most of the plant is hairy when young, including the young seed capsules, and the plants have a very loose, much-branched flowerhead, up to 24 in (60 cm) across, accounting for half of the height of the plant. The cyathium leaves share the coral tones of the stem leaves. Plants can flower from spring to fall. Best in well-drained soil in full sunshine. Will seed around if happy, otherwise may fade away. From central and southern Italy (including Sicily). ↕ 5 ft (1.5 m). Z10–11 H11–10

E. cornigera A robust herbaceous perennial: the dark green, 3 in (7.5 cm) leaves have a pale central vein and the clear yellow flowerhead, attractive from late spring to late summer, is up to 5 in (12 cm) in diameter. Prefers full sunshine but will tolerate semishade. It may grow taller, and need supporting, in rich conditions. Especially useful as a background for other, more brightly colored plants. Propagate from seed, cuttings, or careful division. Very similar to *E. wallichii* and confused with it in gardens. From northern Pakistan and Kashmir. ↕ 24 in (60 cm). Z6–9 H9–2

E. cyparissias (Cypress spurge) An aggressive plant, pretty in flower and foliage, with narrow, pale green, 1½-in (4-cm) leaves that rarely reach ¼ in (0.5 cm) wide and turn bright yellow in the fall. It produces loose, bright yellow 8-in (20-cm) flowerheads in spring, and in summer the cyathium leaves turn red. Unfortunately, it produces runners below the soil, often secretly during the winter; shoots can appear in the spring in the middle of its neighbors as much as 3 ft (1 m) from the original plant. Also irritatingly floppy but too short to stake, it prefers full sunshine and fertile soil but should never be planted near delicate plants. Cultivars are no less dangerous; attractive with significant drawbacks. Naturalized in most of North America; cited as noxious in Colorado. Beware. From Europe to northwestern Turkey. ↕ 16 in (40 cm). Z4–9 H9–1. '**Fens Ruby**' syn. 'Purpurea' Purple foliage, coloring best

EUPHORBIA CHARACIAS FORMS

Even within just this one species, there is a great deal of variation. In foliage, it is shown here at its most blue, its most noticeably hairy, in a short length in 'Portuguese Velvet', and in a strikingly variegated form in 'Emmer Green'. The broad, clear heads of 'Jimmy Platt' contrast with the dark-eyed flowers of 'Blue Hills'.

E. characias subsp. *wulfenii* 'Portuguese Velvet'

E. characias subsp. *wulfenii* 'Emmer Green'

E. characias subsp. *wulfenii* 'Jimmy Platt'

E. characias subsp. *wulfenii* 'Lambrook Gold'

in full sun, with contrasting yellow flowers. **'Orange Man'** The cyathium leaves turn red in summer; stem leaves turn clear yellow with red tips in fall. Taller. ‡18 in (45 cm). **'Purpurea'** *see* 'Fens Ruby'.

E. donii syn. *E. longifolia* Tall herbaceous perennial with leaves up to 8 in (20 cm) long, their length further emphasized by being relatively narrow at just ¾–1¼ in (2–3 cm) wide. The stem leaves are a dark green, while the cyathium leaves are a bright chartreuse color. Flowering in early summer and midsummer, it will normally require staking, especially when in full flower. Requires moisture-retentive soil in full sunshine; will suffer in winter if the soil is too dry. Propagate from seed, cuttings, or by careful division. From Nepal, Bhutan, and Tibet. ‡6 ft (1.8 m). Z6–7 H7–6. **'Amjilassa'** Larger, more robust. Named for the Pakistani village near where it was found. ‡6½ ft (2 m).

E. dulcis Neat, clump-forming herbaceous perennial, the stem leaves up to 2 in (5 cm) long and half as wide; both stem and cyathium leaves are the same matte green. The flowerheads are much branched but compact, and completely obscure the stem leaves when fully open. Takes full sun to semi-shade. From Europe. ‡28 in (70 cm). Z4–9 H9–1. **'Chameleon'** Purple leaves, and a looser habit. Self-seeds freely. Cut down in midsummer, after flowering, to produce a second flush of foliage. Found in a roadside ditch in France and immediately popular, but now very prone to rust.

E. epithymoides see *E. polychroma*

E. **Excalibur** (**'Froeup'**) Herbaceous perennial forming open clumps that need staking. The 3-in (8-cm) leaves have purple edges, while the flower-heads have yellow cyathium leaves and are produced from late spring to midsummer. Best in fertile soil and full sun. Propagate by division or cuttings. A hybrid of *E. cornigera* and *E. schillingii*. ‡4¼ ft (1.3 m). Z6–8 H8–6

E. flavicoma see *E. beselicus*

E. griffithii One of the finest euphorbias. Distinctive dusky gray-

green stem leaves, to 5 in (13 cm), have a noticeable pink midrib. Orange to red cyathium leaves are produced in early summer and midsummer, the glands on the rim of the cyathium are yellow and rounded. In dry soil, it runs extensively but thinly; an untidy plant with less impact. In moist soil, it stays more tightly clumped and is far more impressive; it also appreciates rich conditions and full sun or part-shade. May need staking. Propagate by division or from cuttings. From the eastern Himalaya and northern Burma, Tibet, and south-central China. ‡3¼–5 ft (1–1.5 m). Z4–9 H9–2. **'Dixter'** Bright red cyathium leaves and smoky gray-green leaves. ‡3¼ ft (1 m). **'Dixter Flame'** Bright red cyathium leaves and smoky gray-green leaves. ‡36 in (90 cm). **'Fern Cottage'** Orange cyathium leaves; produces good fall color after a warm summer. **'Fireglow'** Clear orange cyathium leaves and dull green stem leaves. Often raised from seed, sometimes results in inferior color.

E. hyberna (Irish spurge) Congested, generally self-supporting stems carry dark green stem leaves, almost all on upper stem, up to 2 in (5 cm) long and ¾ in (2 cm) wide. Cyathium leaves are also dark green. Flowers from spring to late summer and, if cut back in mid-summer, plants may produce a second flush. Best in semishade and moist, fertile soil. Propagate from seed, from cuttings in the spring or by careful division in the fall. Native to western and southwestern Europe, including Ireland. 36 in (90 cm). Z6–9 H9–6

E. longifolia Plants under this name may be *E. cornigera, E. donii,* or *E. mellifera*.

E. x *martinii* Variable evergreen hybrid, flowering on shoots produced in the previous year. The leaves are up to 4 in (10 cm) long and normally hairy, giving the foliage a silver sheen. The cyathium leaves are normally fused into a cup and the glands are often red, with two pointed horns. A hybrid between the sun-loving *E. characias* and the shade-loving *E. amygdaloides*; very variable and adaptable. It is smaller than the former with a habit that is intermediate between the two parents. A very tolerant plant, enjoying full sun or shade but preferring well-drained soil. Flowering shoots should be removed when the flowerheads begin to look untidy. Propagate from cuttings. ‡36 in

LEFT 1 *Euphorbia griffithii* 'Dixter'
2 *E. mellifera* **3** *E. palustris*

HANDLE EUPHORBIA WITH CAUTION

Hundreds of species of *Euphorbia* can be found around the world. Members of this genus comprise a fascinating collection of succulent as well as non-succulent plants. They range from annual weeds, to ornamental perennials, to Mediterranean shrubs and small trees. A significant number of euphorbias are used in North American landscapes, although most originate from either Africa or Madagascar. All euphorbias produce a sap that is similar to white latex. In fact, the genus is named after a

Greek surgeon called Euphorbus. As a physician he was supposed to have used the milky latex as an ingredient of his potions. However, this milky latex can cause skin burns and should always be treated with respect. Euphorbia latex should never be allowed to come into contact with eyes and any latex should be washed immediately from the skin. For this reason, it is an excellent idea to make a habit of washing one's hands immediately after handling or planting any species of *Euphorbia*.

(90 cm). Z7–10 H12–7. **'Blue Lagoon'** Bright yellow flowerheads fade to burnt orange; blue foliage with red-tinted new growth. From Oregon's Dan Heims. **'Orange Grove'** Chartreuse flowers fade to citrus orange; red-tinted foliage. From Dan Heims. **'Red Dwarf'** Cyathium leaves retain red color throughout the summer. ↕ 24 in (60 cm). **Redwing** (**'Charm'**) Very compact form, with flowerheads completely obscuring the foliage. Requires full sunshine. ↕ 16 in (40 cm).

E. mellifera (Honey-scented spurge) Correctly an evergreen shrub, but usually considered with perennials by gardeners. Branching from the base and sending up new shoots from the base very freely if happy, the soft, pale green leaves can be 8 in (20 cm) or more long but fall from lower parts of the stems. The flowers, in early and mid-spring, have a powerful honey scent but the cyathium leaves are insignificant, and often fall before flowering. The seedpods are often flushed red on one side and are covered in "warts"; the seeds germinate easily. Best in full sunshine if the scent is to be fully appreciated, and needs a sheltered site to help it through hard winters. Older stems should be cut to ground level in the spring, leaving strong young shoots. From Madeira and the Canary Islands. ↕ 6½ ft (2 m). Z9–10 H10–9

E. myrsinites A dwarf, sprawling, silver-leaved evergreen; stems radiate out in a circle from the crown; lasting only two growing seasons. Leaves are up to 1½ in (4 cm) long and ¾ in (2 cm) wide; on young shoots they are arranged in compact spirals, but tend to drop as the flowers develop. The shoots overwinter, then flower in the spring, as with the rather different-looking E. characias. Flowerheads are up to 5 in (12 cm) across, with bright chartreuse cyathium leaves. Best in full sun in well-drained soil; it can be grown in containers. Cut out spent flowered shoots to allow new shoots to develop. Propagate by cuttings in late spring, or from seed. Naturalized in North America; a noxious weed in some states. From southern Europe to northern Iran. ↕ 4 in (10 cm). Z5–8 H8–5

E. nicaeensis Evergreen that is not quite a shrub. The silver-gray, 3-in- (8-cm-) long, sometimes pink-tinged leaves are carried on upright, red-tinged stems that can become very congested and intertwined. The yellow-green flowerhead is produced in early summer, and some feel that it contrasts unpleasantly with the stem leaves. Best in full sunshine and fertile, well-drained soil. The flowering shoots should be removed when untidy. Propagate from seed or take cuttings in spring. Native to the Mediterranean region and Turkey. ↕ 24 in (60 cm). Z5–8 H8–5

E. oblongata Neat, clump-forming herbaceous perennial, the dark green stem leaves are relatively small, rarely

ABOVE *Euphorbia sikkimensis*

more than 2 in (5 cm) long and ¾ in (2 cm) wide. Yellow-chartreuse cyathium leaves are produced on flat heads, 6 in (15 cm) wide at almost any time of the year. Grows in almost any situation, but is particularly effective on the edge of woodlands or under large, leggy shrubs. Can be cut down at any time except winter and will regrow. Used by flower arrangers to hide stem supports. Self-sows. From Balkans to northwestern Turkey. ↕ 24 in (60 cm). Z6–9 H9–6

E. palustris Robust but rather variable, clump-forming herbaceous perennial. Matte green stem leaves are relatively long, up to 8 in (20 cm); when grown in full sun may produce very bright fall color. The bright yellow flowerhead, up to 12 in (30 cm) in diameter, can account for half the height on short specimens. In late summer, there may be a second flush of flowers. Prefers moist soil in full sunshine but will also grow well in dry semishade. Propagate from seed, cuttings, or by careful division in the winter. Similar to E. villosa, but bushier and with leaves that are not downy. From Europe to northwestern China ↕ 6½ ft (2 m). Z7–9 H7–6. **'Walenburg's Glorie'** Smaller and more compact, with larger brighter flowerheads. ↕ 36 in (90 cm).

E. polychroma syn. E. epithymoides Very reliable, clump-forming herbaceous perennial, at its best forming hemispherical domes. The 2-in (5-cm)

LEFT 1 *Euphorbia polychroma*
2 *E. rigida* **3** *E. schillingii*

stem leaves are hairy when young and pale green. Flat-topped flowerheads feature very bright yellow cyathium leaves in mid- and late spring, then fade to a range of shades through the summer (hence *polychroma*) and are followed by seed capsules with red, sausagelike protuberances in late summer. Often needs careful staking, otherwise it falls apart, leaving a bare open center. At its best grown in full sunshine in fertile soil, but will tolerate some shade—though the fall color will be less bright. Propagate from seed, cuttings, or by careful division in spring. From central and southeastern Europe, northwestern Turkey, and Libya. ‡24 in (60 cm). Z5–9 H9–5. **'Candy'** syn. 'Purpurea' Young leaves prettily flushed purple but fading in the summer. **'First Blush'** Spring foliage green, pink, and white. **'Lacy'** syn. 'Variegata' Cream-edged variegation requiring full sunshine. **'Major'** Paler yellow flowers, later-flowering. **'Midas'** Very bright yellow. **'Sonnengold'** The brightest yellow of all. **'Purpurea'** *see* 'Candy'. **'Variegata'** *see* 'Lacy'.

E. rigida Sprawling evergreen forming plants up to 4 ft (1.2 m) across when in flower. The silver-gray leaves are up to 3 in (8 cm) long with sharp points, and are arranged in perfect neat spirals all along the stems in the first year. Bright yellow flowerheads are produced in late winter and early spring on the previous year's shoots. These are best removed once the seed has been ejected from the seedpods (or sooner if you wish to avoid seedlings). Needs a sunny situation and fertile soil; it also thrives in containers if fertilized through the summer as it grows its new shoots. Propagate from seeds and cuttings. Similar to, but generally larger than, *E. myrsinites*. Native to the Mediterranean region and into Turkey and Iran. ‡12 in (30 cm). Z7–11 H12–7

E. schillingii Tidy, clump-forming herbaceous perennial; stem leaves are pale green with a paler central vein and grow up to 4 in (10 cm) long. The flowerheads are 8 in (20 cm) in diameter and are produced in late summer, their bright yellow cyathium leaves forming an almost perfect circle. Thrives in full sunshine in fertile, water-retentive soil. Propagate from seed, cuttings, or by careful division in spring. Discovered and introduced by Tony Schilling, formerly in charge of Kew's satellite garden at Wakehurst Place in England. From central Nepal. ‡32 in (80 cm). Z7–9 H9–7

E. sequieriana Delicate, clump-forming herbaceous perennial, the narrow blue-green leaves, to 2½ in (6 cm) long, are packed densely along the stems. Flowers are borne in mid- and late summer on the previous year's shoots; the cyathium leaves are pale yellow and can clash with the grayish leaves. Tolerant of drought, so can be grown in full sunshine on poor soil, but is happier in more fertile conditions. Propagate from seed or cuttings in late spring. Europe to Northwestern China. 4 ft (1.2 m) wide. ‡24 in (60 cm). Z8–11 H12–8. **subsp. *niciciana*** Greener leaves, and

slightly tougher. Z8–11 H12–8

E. sikkimensis Spreading herbaceous species, distinguished by the bright pink young shoots that emerge in early spring and which are sometimes caught by late frosts. The shoots form an untidy sprawling plant that is best grown through more robust neighbors. The pink coloring fades and is restricted to the leaf stalks by the time the plant starts producing its 8-in (20-cm) diameter, bright yellow inflorescences in early summer. Prefers full sunshine and moisture-retentive, fertile soil. Grow from cuttings, in spring. Found in Nepal, Sikkim, Bhutan, Tibet, China, and North Vietnam. ‡6 ft (1.8 m). Z6–9 H9–6

E. villosa Variable, robust, clumping, herbaceous perennial; can be from 4 ft (1.2 m) to 6½ ft (2 m) tall, with the flowerhead accounting for one-third of its height. The stem leaves are dull

matte green and relatively long, up to 8 in (20 cm), and when grown in full sun can produce very bright orange fall color. The bright yellow flowerhead can be up to 12 in (30 cm) in diameter. The young seed capsule is very hairy— hence *villosa*. Similar to *E. palustris* but more erect, with slightly downy leaves. In late summer there may be a second flush of flowers, produced on branches from the tops of the stems. Best in full sun or semishade in fertile soil. Propagate from seed, cuttings, or by careful division in winter. A European native. ‡6½ ft (2 m). Z4–8 H8–1

E. virgata Herbaceous perennial with running roots and flimsy stems carrying narrow, pale green leaves ¼ in (7 mm) wide and up to 2¾ in (7 cm) long. In early summer, 4 in (10 cm) flowerheads feature cyathium leaves in pale yellow. Staking is essential. Best grown in a container; in an open border it will

quickly spread. Propagate by separating the runners. Confused with *E. esula*, *E. x waldsteinii* and *E. x pseudovirgata*. From Europe and temperate Asia. ‡24 in (60 cm). Z6–9 H9–6

E. wallichii Confusingly variable, robust, often self-supporting herbaceous perennial with dark green leaves up to 3 in (7.5 cm) long, each with a pale central vein. Flowerheads 5 in (12 cm) across are produced from late spring to late summer. The clear yellow cyathium leaves are in threes, making a triangular shape. Prefers fertile soil in full sunshine but will tolerate semishade. Propagate from seed, cuttings, or by careful division in the spring. *E. donii* and *E. cornigera* have been distributed under this name. From Afghanistan to China. ‡24 in (60 cm). Z6–9 H9–6

EURYBIA see ASTER

STALWART FAVORITES MAKE GOOD COMPANY

TWO DEPENDABLE, SHADE-LOVING ground covers, both thriving in less-than-ideal conditions, mingle together in spring. In the back, the dusky, dark flowers of *Geranium phaeum* turn to face the light and are just taller than the evergreen *Euphorbia amygdaloides* var. *robbiae,* with its similarly rounded flowers but in cool chartreuse. Earlier in the season, the low domes of

sharply cut geranium foliage make an attractive contrast with the heavy, slightly leathery leaves of the euphorbia. The geranium makes slowly expanding clumps that die down in winter, while the euphorbia is a well-clothed evergreen that steadily spreads at the root. Both plants grow well in shade, but the euphorbia will withstand more drought than the geranium.

F

FALLOPIA
Knotweed
POLYGONACEAE

Although bold and statuesque, *Fallopia* is best admired *from* your garden, rather than in it—or not admired at all.

The nine species of erect and climbing perennials and woody climbers are native to the northern temperate zone and are typified by alternate, simple, often large, triangular or oval leaves and a spectacularly invasive habit. The tiny, creamy white, angular, apparently petalless flowers are carried in terminal, often conspicuous clusters, and in the upper leaf joints.

Some botanists and many gardeners still consider these to be included in other genera. For example, over the years Japanese knotweed, *F. japonica*, has been

THE CLASSIC INVASIVE PLANT

Japanese knotweed, *Fallopia japonica*, is the most invasive plant of the temperate world. Introduced into North America in the late 1800s as a landscape ornamental, for screening, and to control erosion, it was also known as Japanese Fleeceflower and, rather mysteriously, Mexican Bamboo. It has proved to be an aggressive colonizer in a wide variety of habitats but is at its most destructive, in terms of disrupting native ecology, along watercourses. It hybridizes with the much larger, but less widespread, *F. sachalinensis* to produce *F. x bohemica*.

Variegated forms of *F. japonica* and *F. x bohemica* are available from nurseries but should not be planted; some nurseries even sell the plain green form and this too should, of course, be avoided. The variegated forms may be less aggressive than the plain green leaved forms—although they will still creep into the lawn and persist in spite of weekly mowing—they can also revert back to plain green forms.

It is found along roadsides and also in riparian areas, where it thrives in the moist soil and forms new populations when the flow of water breaks off portions of rhizomes or stem growth and takes them downstream. Land managers have difficulty removing it once it is established due to rhizomes continually producing more stems.

These are attractive plants, but not so irresistible that we can not forgo them for the sake of helping protect our native species—and of avoiding our concrete paths being fractured from below.

shifted from one genus to another by taxonomists, and this can obscure the huge amount of information available on this plant. It has been known widely as *Polygonum cuspidatum* but has also appeared as *Persicaria japonica, Pleuropterus cuspidatus, Pleuropterus zuccarinii, Polygonum reynoutria, Polygonum zuccarinii,* and *Reynoutria japonica*.

CULTIVATION Any reasonably moist garden soil in sun or shade.

PROPAGATION By division when dormant.

PROBLEMS Very invasive.

F. x bohemica This natural hybrid between *F. japonica* and *F. sachalinensis* is intermediate in overall size and in leaf and flower characteristics but often more rampageous than either parent. **'Spectabilis'** Foliage prettily marbled with white and pink. Can revert to plain green, especially in poor soil.

F. japonica (Japanese knotweed) Densely and vigorously colony-forming, annually producing thickets of erect, often reddish stems which become woody with age. Bright green oval leaves with an abrupt base and slender pointed tip can reach 6 in (15 cm) in length. In late summer and early fall, white to cream flowers, often aging pinkish, arise in 2½–6 in (6–15 cm) long frothy clusters from all the upper leafy joints. Undoubtedly attractive and conspicuous but very invasive with an extensive, woody root system almost impossible to control. Extensively naturalized in many areas of the US. The best advice is not to plant this species or its cultivars (*see* The Classic Invasive Plant). From Japan. ‡6–10 ft (2–3 m). Z4–10 H10–4. **var.**

BELOW 1 *Fallopia japonica* var. *compacta* **2** *Farfugium japonica* 'Argenteum'

compacta Darker green, more rounded leaves and reddish flowers. ‡32 in (80 cm). **var. *compacta* 'Milkboy'** syn. 'Fuji Snow', 'Variegata' Conspicuously white-variegated foliage. May revert. **var. *compacta* f. *rosea*** Pink flowers.

F. sachalinensis Red-brown stems form loose clumps developing from an open root system that spreads extensively. Oval or oblong leaves are up to 12 in (30 cm) long with a pointed tip; the compact, 2½–6-in (6–10-cm) clusters of flowers are white with a greenish tinge. The giant of its race, resembling an expanded version of *F. japonica*. It grows largest in wetter soil. The best advice is not to plant it. The larger size makes it a greater problem than *F. japonica*. From the Sakhalin islands off the coast of eastern Siberia. ‡8–12 ft (2.5–4 m). Z3–10 H10–3

FARFUGIUM
ASTERACEAE

Striking architectural plants for a lightly shaded situation or as interesting container specimens.

The two species of herbaceous perennials grow in woodlands and grasslands, in damp meadows, and by streams in northeastern Asia. They spread slowly by rhizomes. The evergreen basal leaves, on long stalks rising from a short, erect stock, are rounded to heart-shaped, with short hairs when young. The daisylike flowers, above the foliage, have bright yellow female ray florets around a darker yellow center consisting of bisexual disk florets. Only one species is widely grown.

CULTIVATION Prefers fertile, moist, humus-rich, but well-drained soil in part-shade and dislikes cold, drying winds. The leaves can become slightly scorched if grown in full sun, especially if allowed to dry out. Resistant to salt spray. Protect from

severe frost during winter with a heavy mulch. In marginal areas, grow as a specimen container plant and move under shelter in winter.

PROPAGATION Divide variegated cultivars, and species, in spring, or raise species from seed.

PROBLEMS Slugs.

F. japonicum syn. *F. tussilagineum, Ligularia tussilaginea* Clump-forming perennial with thick rhizomes and long-stalked, shiny, leathery leaves up to 6 in (15 cm) long by 12 in (30 cm) wide, the margins either untoothed or with shallow teeth. Flower stems carry yellow, 1½–2½-in (4–6-cm) flowerheads in late summer through fall, even into early winter. Sometimes known collectively by the Japanese common name, tsuwabuki. The variegated cultivars are particularly popular in Japan, where more are being developed but, sadly, they are less hardy. Many duplicate names have been coined for the cultivars. Native to Japan. ‡30 in (75 cm). Z7–8 H8–6. **'Argenteum'** syn. 'Albovariegatum', 'Variegatum' Leaves irregularly mottled with gray-green and cream, particularly around the margins. At times, half a leaf or more may appear cream. **'Aureomaculatum'** syn. 'Leopard', 'Spotted Leopard' Dark green leaves randomly spotted with yellow. **'Crispatum'** syn. 'Crested Leopard', 'Cristatum' Dark green leaves crumpled, ruffled, and crisped at the margins. **var. *giganteum*** Larger, thicker, glossier, and more rounded leaves. ‡3¼ ft (1 m). **'Kagami-jishi'** Dark green leaves randomly spotted with yellow but with fewer spots than 'Aureomaculatum' and with a ruffled leaf margin. **'Leopard'** *see* 'Aureomaculatum'. **'Spotted Leopard'** *see* 'Aureomaculatum'. **'Variegatum'** *see* 'Argenteum'.

F. tussilagineum see *F. japonicum*

FERNS

Ferns are relatively primitive plants that are quite unlike the other species in this book. In evolutionary terms, they predate the arrival of flowering plants on the planet and, lacking flowers, they have an entirely different method of reproduction. There is also a unique terminology to describe it.

Ferns have two specific stages in their life cycle. In the stage with which we are all familiar, during which they make attractive foliage plants, fine dustlike spores are released from special organs that are usually found on the undersides of the leaves—which in ferns are usually referred to as fronds—or sometimes on different modified fronds.

The spores are released in huge quantities and are carried on the wind. When they come to rest in a moist place, the spores germinate. Each develops into a tiny, flat, green, usually heart-shaped organ, called a prothallus, that lies flat on the soil. This tiny structure is hardly noticeable in itself, but when many spores germinate together, as often happens, the effect can be like a film of green over the soil.

On different parts of each tiny prothallus, the sexual organs develop: male parts in one area, and female parts in another. In damp conditions, the male sperm swims in the moisture film to the female eggs and fertilizes one. From this fertilization the green plant develops, first as a single small rudimentary frond, then developing into a familiar fern plant.

Fern hybrids are created when spores from two different species germinate alongside each other, and the sperm from one prothallus swims to a different prothallus and fertilizes its egg. As in flowering plants, hybrids are relatively uncommon but they do sometimes occur, as in the recent hybrids between *Athyrium* species (*see p.83*).

Moisture is a crucial element in the process, for not only do the sperm require moisture to swim to the egg, but the prothallus itself has only a few tiny hairlike roots and may shrivel and die in prolonged dry conditions. Consequently, in nature many ferns inhabit shady sites, where the soil dries out less quickly, or waterside habitats where there is a constant supply of soil moisture. Alternatively, they are found in climates where there is consistent seasonal moisture. Some ferns are aquatic. However, while ferns require moisture for sexual reproduction, some can be remarkably tolerant of dry conditions once they are established, so you will not necessarily have to provide any of these habitats in order to succeed in growing ferns in your garden.

Sixteen ferns are covered in this book: *Adiantum, Asplenium, Athyrium, Blechnum, Cyrtomium, Dennstaedtia, Dryopteris, Gymnocarpium, Matteuccia, Onoclea, Osmunda, Phegopteris, Polypodium, Polystichum, Thelypteris,* and *Woodwardia.*

FERN STRUCTURE

Ferns reproduce from spores, not seeds, hence they do not have flowers. The fronds of most ferns are regularly divided into several main leaflets or pinnae, often comprising many smaller divisions—pinnules—that may be further divided into segments. In most ferns, the spores are produced on the undersides of the fertile fronds. Spores develop in capsules known as sporangia, often clustered under a protective indusium. Each cluster of sporangia, called a sorus, has a distinctive shape, circular in some ferns, linear, dash- or comma-shaped in others. When ripe, the sporangia burst open to release the spores (*see* Ferns).

Frond (whole leaf)

Rolled immature frond (crozier)

Leaflet (pinna)

Polystichum setiferum

FERULA
Giant Fennel
APIACEAE

Huge, bold, remarkable plants that make a dramatic impression even in dry gardens.

Over 170 varied species are extensively distributed in the summer-dry regions of the Mediterranean across to Central Asia, but only very few are grown in gardens. Many are stout, though sometimes short-lived, perennials, with a thick, deep rootstock. The majority form strong clumps of finely dissected leaves made up of threadlike segments, though a few feature broad-bladed, deeply divided leaves, resulting in a quite different appearance. The basal foliage persists in winter in mild areas. The base of the leaf broadly sheaths the stem, with upper leaves progressively reduced to little more than the sheathing base. In early summer, mature plants produce a dramatic flowering spike reaching up to 12 ft (4 m) or more. The flowers are bright to deep yellow and carried in large hemispherical to spherical heads, often grouped together in an upright, multibranched structure. Many fennels are used medicinally in eastern countries, most particularly in Iran, Afghanistan, Pakistan, and Turkestan.

CULTIVATION Grow in deep, fertile soil in full sun; fennels are best established as young plants to allow the deep taproot to develop naturally. Such specimens are more likely to flower year after year rather than die after their first flowering, as sometimes happens. A long life can also be fostered by removing the flower spike before it sets seed. The evergreen winter foliage may be vulnerable in colder climates.

PROPAGATION Sow fresh seed in late summer and fall. Germination usually occurs in early winter, but plants take several years to reach flowering size.

PROBLEMS Usually trouble-free.

F. chiliantha see *F. communis* subsp. *glauca*

F. communis (Giant fennel) A remarkable but variable plant. The leaves are repeatedly divided into opposite pairs of narrow, bright green, flat, threadlike lobes up to 2 in (5 cm) long. The umbels are made up of 20–40 rays and are up to 8 in (20 cm) across, the terminal umbel of each branch being stalkless and surrounded by smaller stalked umbels. After flowering, the foliage rapidly dies down, leaving the developing seeds to ripen by early fall. Plants make a striking feature in late winter and spring as the foliage develops prior to throwing up the dramatic flower spike. Found in open sunny scrub, rocky ground, grassy places, roadsides, and ditches around the Mediterranean. ↕6–10 ft (2–3 m). Z6–9 H9–6. **subsp. *glauca*** syn. *F. chiliantha* Blue-green foliage is pale silvery green below; the developing flower spike is notably tall and amethyst-red, with the flowers a deeper orange-yellow. Sometimes dies after flowering and setting seed. Very distinct from the typical species. ↕10–12 ft (3–4 m). Z9–10 H10–9.

F. tingitana A bold plant with bright distinctive green leaves repeatedly divided into short opposite lobes ¼–½ in (6–10 mm) long with their edges turned under. The stout flower spikes carry rounded heads of umbels of yellow flowers gathered in branched heads. Similar to *F. communis* but less robust, with the edges of its shorter leaves rolled over, and less often encountered in gardens. Best in a warm and sheltered spot. Native to Portugal, southern Spain, and northwest Africa. ↕6½ ft (2 m). **'Cedric Morris'** Leaves with a shiny varnished upper surface, noticeably distinct. Grown by the artist Sir Cedric Morris and distributed by Beth Chatto of England.

RIGHT *Ferula communis*

FESTUCA
Fescue
POACEAE

Colorful grasses for exposed dry positions, forming delicate clumps and carpets.

Some 450 perennial species are found throughout temperate regions of the world, on tropical mountains, hills, plains, and meadows, usually in exposed places. Relatively few are grown. Clumps or slowly creeping carpets of thin, inrolled leaves have either loose or more compact plumes, usually held above the foliage on slender stems. Some species have long been used to make lawns, but in the modern garden are increasingly grown as delicate and colorful foliage plants for dry areas as edging or, with taller species, as architectural additions. These are cool-season plants looking best in spring and fall, dying back in hotter, more humid conditions. There is some confusion over the naming of the smaller blue-leaved forms.

CULTIVATION Grow in exposed dry locations in well-drained, light soil. For best color, trim back in the spring and summer. Clumps tend to die out in the middle, so divide every three years.

PROPAGATION From seed or by division.

PROBLEMS Ants often take over older clumps, so divide regularly.

F. amethystina (Tufted fescue, Hair fescue, Large blue fescue) Dense evergreen tufts of thin, blue-green, in-rolled leaves to 6 in (15 cm) long; in exposed areas the color may tend to gray-blue. The flower stems grow above foliage, in late spring to mid-summer, ending in small, green flower spikes tinged pink-purple, then buff as seeds ripen. Good in open areas such as gravel gardens, or as edging. From dry places in central Europe, the Alps, and the Balkans. ‡24 in (60 cm). Z4–8 H8–1

F. caesia see *F. glauca*

F. crinumursi see *F. gautieri*

F. eskia (Bear-skin grass) Dark green, slowly spreading carpets of stiff needle-like leaves up to 6 in (15 cm) long keep their green color through the winter. Short, slender flower stems in early summer and midsummer support small, nodding, reddish brown flower spikes. Perfect ground cover for sunny, well-drained beds. Grows on screes and rocky pastures in acidic soil in the Pyrenees. ‡6 in (15 cm). Z5–7 H7–5

F. gautieri syn. *F. crinumursi* (Spiky fescue) Dense, undulating cushions of bright green, sharply pointed, ⅟₁₆ in

LEFT 1 *Festuca eskia* **2** *F. glauca*
3 *F. glauca* 'Elijah Blue'

(1 mm) wide needles, which are often curved and sometimes covered with a white bloom, turn yellow in winter. Silver flower stems in midsummer carry compact, yellow-green flower spikes 2–3½ in (5–9 cm) long. Good covering for path edges. From rocks and scrub in southwest France and northeast Spain. ‡14 in (35 cm). Z4–8 H8–1

F. glauca syn. *F. caesia, F. ovina* 'Glauca' (Blue fescue, Gray fescue) Small cushions of fine, inrolled, ice-blue leaves become greener in the winter. Upright stems grow in late spring and early summer, bearing narrow, bristly, blue-green flower plumes up to 2 in (5 cm) long, turning golden brown. A cool-season plant dying back in hot, humid conditions, the blue coloring protects it from weather extremes and intensifies if its natural growing conditions are mimicked by planting in not-too-fertile, well-drained soil in sun. Comb out dead leaves in early spring or midsummer for a flush of new color. Short-lived: divide every three to four years. Grow in drifts with contrasting red- or yellow-colored grasses. There are many forms, in varying degrees of blue to silver-blue, many incorrectly named in gardens and nurseries. From exposed, rocky soil in southern France. ‡16 in (40 cm). Z4–8 H8–1. **'Azurit'** Very tight clumps of steely-blue foliage. ‡12 in (30 cm) **'Blaufuchs'** (**Blue Fox**) Silvery-blue leaves. ‡10 in (25 cm). **'Blauglut'** (**Blue Glow**) Intense but pale blue. ‡14 in (35 cm). **Blue Fox** *see* 'Blaufuchs'. **Blue Glow** *see* 'Blauglut'. **'Elijah Blue'** Best, most intense icy-blue of all. Tends to live longer than many. ‡12 in (30 cm) **'Golden Toupee'** Soft gold leaves, semievergreen. ‡6 in (15 cm) **'Harz'** Blue-green leaves with purple tips; purple flowerheads. ‡12 in (30 cm). **'Seeigel'** (**Sea Urchin**) Very fine blue-green leaves. ‡6–12 in (15–30 cm). **'Silbersee'** *see F. valesiaca* 'Silbersee'.

F. idahoensis (Blue bunch grass, Idaho grass) Dense tufts of inrolled, thread-thin, blue-green leaves; upright flower stems appear above the foliage in early summer and midsummer; pale green plumes of zigzag, nodding flowers. Easier to grow than *F. glauca,* less liable to die out in the middle, and more tolerant of wet conditions. Should be more widely grown. Found in grasslands, sage desert, rocky mountain slopes and meadows in the eastern US. ‡14 in (35 cm). Z3–8 H8–1

F. mairei (Atlas festuca) Handsome, tall mounds of silvery gray-green, needle-thin leaves. Very fine flower stems spray out over the foliage, bearing slender green flowers in early summer. More tolerant of hot weather than many species, equally good as an accent plant or in drifts in gravel gardens. Comb out the dead leaves regularly. From the Atlas Mountains in Morocco. ‡40 in (100 cm). Z4–8 H8–1

F. ovina (Sheep fescue) Very dense, evergreen tufts of green to gray-green, thread-thin leaves 1¼–5 in (3–13 cm) long. Erect flower stems grow above

the foliage from late spring to mid-summer, carrying narrow, loose spikes of blue-green flowers sometimes tinged purple. Drought-tolerant and with-standing heavy cutting, it is a familiar lawn grass; also a valuable ingredient of wildflower lawns and meadows. Common in poor soil in exposed areas in northern temperate regions. ‡2–24 in (5–60 cm). Z2–8 H8–1. **'Glauca'** see *F. glauca.* **var** *vivipara* see *F. vivipara.*

F. valesiaca Dense clumps of very fine, gray-blue leaves often with a silver bloom. In late spring and early summer stiff flower stems end in narrow plumes of silvery blue-green flower spikes tinged with mauve, turning brown as they mature. Plant with spring bulbs or along path edges. Found on dry, grassy slopes from central Europe to central Asia. ‡10–16 in (25–40 cm). Z5–9 H9–5. **var.** *glaucantha* (Wallis fescue) Blue-green leaves. ‡6–10 in (15–25 cm) **'Silbersee'** (**Silver Sea**) Pale silver-blue leaves. ‡15–8 in (3–20 cm).

F. violacea Thick tufts of metallic, bright blue-green, very fine leaves are topped with narrow plumes carrying purple-green flowers, turning golden as the seeds ripen. Lovely planted as edging, or underplanted with spring bedding and bulbs, or in tubs in a sunny spot. From the mountains of Europe. ‡12 in (30 cm). Z4–8 H8–1

F. vivipara syn *F. ovina* var. *vivipara* Dense tufts of green, or slightly bluish, threadlike leaves usually 4–12 in (10–30 cm) long, lead to flower stems that, instead of flowers, carry mainly tiny green plantlets which gradually arch

BELOW *Festuca glauca* 'Golden Toupee'

toward the ground, where they fall off and root. A few fertile flowers may appear at the base of the spike. The little plantlets give a fluffy appearance that some think attractive and delicate, others rather strange. Very similar to *F. ovina* but with plantlets instead of flowers. Grow in a container for closer inspection or in drifts as an unusual edger. From fertile soil on cliffs and moors in Wales and northern Scotland to the Arctic, Asia, and North America. ‡2–24 in (5–60 cm). Z4–8 H8–1

FILIPENDULA
ROSACEAE

Easy-going plants for damp soil; frothy sprays of summer flowers above attractively lobed leaves.

About 16 deciduous species grow in moist habitats in North America, northern Europe, and Asia east to China and Japan, about seven of which are commonly grown. Most form a compact clump of erect stems bearing leaves with a large maplelike, lobed leaflet at the tip and much smaller side leaflets in opposite pairs down the stalk. Tiny, five-petaled flowers in loose or compact clusters in early summer create a fluffy or foamy effect. The naming of some species and cultivars has fallen into confusion.

CULTIVATION Best in full sun in permanently moist to wet soil; tolerates border conditions in part-shade if not too dry.

PROPAGATION By division. Most will seed quite freely but may not come true to type.

PROBLEMS Sometimes disfigured by a fungal leaf spot and may suffer from mildew in dry soil.

F. camtschatica Robust plant forming a large clump of bold, lobed leaves to 10 in (25 cm) across. White flowers in frothy sprays to 12 in (30 cm) wide open in early summer and midsummer. Best in really moist soil in sun or part-shade. It tolerates border conditions in light shade; foliage may scorch in hot weather. The name is often missspelled, with a K. From Japan, Korea, and Kamtchatka. ‡6–8 ft (2–2.5 m). Z3–7 H8–1

F. hexapetala see *F. vulgaris*

F. 'Kahome' Fairly compact plant with typical, maplelike, lobed leaves and loose clusters of tiny vivid pink flowers in sprays 6 in (15 cm) across in early summer and midsummer. A hybrid derived from *F. multijuga,* perhaps crossed with *F. purpurea.* ‡24 in (60 cm). Z4–9 H9–1

F. multijuga syn. *F. palmata* 'Digitata Nana' Compact plant with hairless basal foliage, divided into opposite pairs of neatly toothed leaflets and pale or mid-pink flowers in sprays 6 in (15 cm) across in early summer and midsummer. From Japan. ‡12–24 in (30–60 cm). Z6–8 H8–6

F. palmata Clump-forming plant with lobed leaves densely covered with fine white hairs on the underside. Small white flowers are borne in irregular loose sprays in early summer. The name is more common than the true plant as this is much confused with *F. rubra, F. purpurea,* and *F. multijuga.* From eastern Russia, China, and North Korea. ‡4 ft (1.2 m). Z3–9 H9–1. **'Digitata Nana'** see *F. multijuga.* **'Rosea'** Forms of *F. purpurea, F. multijuga, F. rubra,* and, probably most often, hybrids are grown under this name. **'Rubra'** see *F. rubra* 'Venusta'.

F. purpurea Smooth, often purple-tinted stems rise through compact clumps of neatly lobed leaves, usually without side leaflets. Small, deep pink flowers in dense clusters open in mid- and late summer. From Japan. ‡3–4 ft (1–1.2 m). Z4–9 H9–1. **f. albiflora** Flowers white and leaves paler green. ‡24 in (60 cm). **'Elegans'** More compact, with deep rose pink flowers. ‡24 in (60 cm).

F. rubra (Queen of the prairie) Tall, dramatic, very vigorous plant, spreading quickly to form an extensive colony. Deeply lobed leaves, to 8 in (20 cm) across, form a striking feature throughout summer, and typical foamy clusters of small light pink flowers open in early summer and midsummer. It is best suited to a large, semi-wild area or lakeside. From the eastern US. ‡6–8 ft (2–2.5 m). Z3–9 H9–1. **'Venusta'** syn. *F. palmata* 'Rubra' Deep, bright, rose pink flowers fading slightly with age.

F. ulmaria (Meadowsweet) Vigorous plant forming a clump of erect stems with leaflets in opposite pairs and usually white beneath. Branched sprays of creamy white flowers open in early summer and midsummer. The plant is likely to seed freely in boggy conditions. From a variety of wet places in Europe and western Asia. ‡36 in (90 cm). Z5–9 H9–1. **'Aurea'** The leaves are bright yellow in spring then become paler and eventually become light green by summer. It is often scorched in dry, hot spells, especially in spring. **'Flore Pleno'** Flowers double, longer-lasting. **'Variegata'** Leaves margined and splashed with yellow.

F. vulgaris syn. *F. hexapetala* (Dropwort) Distinct in its leaves tapering to the tip, each one of the of the many oppositely paired leaflets are boldly toothed. Foamy sprays of attractive, creamy white flowers, to ⅝ in (1.5 cm) across, are very often tinged pink in bud. It grows better in less moist positions than the larger species and is excellent for the front of a border in fertile soil. From alkaline meadows in Europe and Central Asia. ‡24 in (60 cm). Z4–7 H8–1. **'Multiplex'** Flowers fully double and longer-lasting.

RIGHT 1 *Filipendula purpurea*
2 *F. rubra* 'Venusta' **3** *F. ulmaria* 'Aurea'
4 *F. ulmaria* 'Variegata'

FOENICULUM
Fennel
APIACEAE

An attractive, adaptable, aromatic long-season foliage plant with the bonus of yellow flowers.

Just one species, found growing in much of Europe, is the wild progenitor of the culinary herb, the vegetable, and the perennial. The whole plant is famously aromatic—the smell of aniseed can sometimes be detected from quite some distance on hot days—and the flavorful leaves often accompany fish dishes. It is also used to flavor drinks, including ouzo and Pernod. The strong aniseed flavor of both the leaves and seeds has given fennel a long history of herbal and medicinal use, making it essential in the herb garden.

CULTIVATION Grow in well-drained soil in a sunny position.

PROPAGATION From seed, or by digging up seedlings from the garden while still small.

PROBLEMS Prolific self-seeding.

F. vulgare A tall, erect, grayish green perennial with deeply questing tap roots. The leaves repeatedly divide into oppositely arranged fine feathery lobes, the base of each leaf sheathing the stem. At first the crowded leaves make a mass of delicate green laciness through which the stems surge, carrying more leaves to create a tall foliage fountain. By the time the flat-topped umbels of yellowish green flowers appear, the stems have become hollow; they stiffen as the seeds form. It is wise to remove the developing seedheads—plants can produce forests of self-sown seedlings. Native to waste ground, roadsides, and rocky places, often close to the sea, in much of Europe, especially the Mediterranean, and widely naturalized eastward into India and in eastern North America. ↕5–6½ ft (1.5–2 m). Z4–9 H9–6. **'Giant Bronze'** Robust form with bronze-purple foliage. **'Purpureum'** Stems and leaves flushed dark maroon-purple, later becoming bronze-green. **'Smokey'** Probably not distinct from 'Purpureum'.

FRAGARIA
Strawberry
ROSEACEAE

Attractive relations of the garden strawberry, particularly useful as ground cover in informal situations.

There are twelve semievergreen species with a wide distribution in European woodlands and hedgerows and also in Asia, China, and Chile, usually in alkaline soil. The leaves of of all are divided into three leaflets and have toothed edges. White or sometimes pink flowers, usually with five rounded petals, are produced over a long period in the summer and are carried in short, open heads, usually at the same level as the foliage. They are followed by fleshy, usually red, fruits.

Plants can quickly colonize large, even inhospitable, areas, spreading over the ground by rooting from the leaf joints of the stems and then producing plantlets that become established, resulting in an excellent, though combative, ground cover. In small gardens, flowers or fruits are managed more easily in containers.

CULTIVATION Plants like a fertile, moist but well-drained, alkaline soil to thrive, although they will grow in acidic soil and even in dry conditions. They generally do best in light, dappled shade and are ideal under established shrubs, in woodland gardens, or even in cracks between paving slabs. They are also useful for the front of borders, in pots or herb gardens. When happy, plants can become invasive and may need to be kept in check, but they form interesting plant combinations, especially with more traditional ground-cover plants. In rich soil, variegated selections may revert.

PROPAGATION Simply lift and replant rooted plantlets, detaching them from the runner.

PROBLEMS Vine weevil, powdery mildew.

F. x ananassa The cultivated strawberry, a hybrid between *F. chiloensis* and *F. virginiana*. The original hybrid is not grown but is represented in gardens by

ABOVE *Foeniculum vulgare* 'Purpureum'

the many cultivars grown for their fruit and this ornamental form. **'Variegata'** Leaflets are up to 3 in (8 cm) long and strongly splashed with cream. They are usually retained, at least partially, over the winter, especially in mild seasons. White flowers are up to 1¼ in (3 cm) across. ↕6 in (15 cm). Z4–8 H8–1

F. chiloensis Wrinkled evergreen leaflets, shiny above and quite soft beneath, are about 2 in (5 cm) long, held on long stalks. White flowers, male and female on separate plants, are produced on erect stems and followed by pinkish fruits if plants of both sexes are grown. Tends to spread, but is generally less invasive than *F. vesca*. From the US and South America. ↕12 in (30 cm). Z5–9 H9–5. **'Chaval'** Fine female selection with pink leafstalks and particularly glossy foliage. The flowers are slightly larger and growth is lower than usual, forming excellent ground cover. ↕8 in (20 cm).

F. indica see *Duchesnea indica*

F. **'Lipstick'** A fast-growing plant that produces rich cherry pink flowers with golden stamens during summer and fall. It thrives in part-shade and is excellent as ground cover or in containers, where it can better be restrained. Developed in Holland, this cultivar is the result of a cross between an unnamed strawberry, *F. x ananassa,* and *Potentilla palustris* (*see* Hybrids and a Name Change). ↕6 in (15 cm). Z4–9 H8–1.

F. **Pink Panda ('Frel')** Extremely vigorous ground-cover plant producing

BRINGING TEXTURES TOGETHER

THIS IS A CLASSIC COMBINATION of shapes and textures. Two bold and broad-leaved hostas—one bluish, one edged in cream—are separated by a fountain of self-sown seedlings of fine and feathery green fennel, probably self-sown from the larger plant behind. The contrast in shape and texture is delightful. The determinedly upright spikes of white foxgloves also provide contrast to both the broad hostas and the finely filigreed fennel, while their white flowers meld into the soft colorings of the nearby foliage. If any foxglove seedlings should come purple, they would best be removed to avoid disrupting the harmony.

HYBRIDS AND A NAME CHANGE

In 1962, British strawberry breeder Dr. Jack Ellis described a cross he had made between an unnamed white-flowered cultivated strawberry, *Fragaria x ananassa,* and the purple-flowered *Potentilla palustris.* The resultant plants had flowers of intermediate color. He then crossed his hybrids with the original strawberry and produced the plants now known as *Fragaria* Pink Panda ('Frel'), widely grown as a ground-cover plant. At Blooms of Bressingham, they repeated the original cross and named the result *F.* 'Franor' ('Red Ruby'). For convenience, these plants have all been grown under the name *Fragaria.*

However, as early as 1760 some botanists saw *Fragaria* as so similar to *Potentilla* that they could not justify their separation and treated them both as *Potentilla.* In spite of this, on the whole they continued to be treated separately, the edible fleshy fruits of the strawberry seen as too different from the dry pods of the potentilla to unite them.

Now, nearly 250 years after it was first suggested, it seems that the two may finally be united. Not only do these hybrids indicate a close relationship, there are many important features, some at the molecular level, common to both, and even a species with fruits that are between the two types in structure. Consequently, it may not be long before all these plants are transferred to *Potentilla.*

bright pink flowers 1¼ in (3 cm) across, with up to seven petals. They appear over a long period from spring until mid-fall, but rarely produce fruit. Can be invasive, moving into and flowering in lawns, but can be impressive in a tall container. A hybrid between *F.* x *ananassa* and *Potentilla palustris* (*see* Hybrids and a Name Change) introduced by England's Blooms of Bressingham in 1989. ↕6 in (15 cm). Z5–9 H9–5

Red Ruby (**'Samba'**) Mounds of glossy leaves bear deep rose, almost red flowers, with golden anthers from early summer until fall, and may be followed by red berries. A selection developed by Blooms of Bressingham. ↕6 in (15 cm). Z4–8 H8–1

F. vesca Vigorous, sometimes invasive perennial forming dense ground cover composed of rosettes of neat, attractive, more or less evergreen, bright green leaves divided into three leaflets. The small white flowers sprays appear amid foliage in spring and are followed by attractive, red, sweet ½-in (1-cm) fruits. From Europe. ↕10 in (25 cm). Z5–9 H9–5 **'Golden Alexandria'** Yellow foliage and a long season of fruits. **'Monophylla'** A strange form; one, simple undivided leaf, and a range of other leaves with up to three leaflets. **'Multiplex'** Small but attractive double white flowers resembling pompons. **'Muricata'** (Plymouth strawberry) Flowers are composed of green bracts followed by bizarre spiky red fruits. Recorded by plant collector Tradescant in Plymouth, England in 1620. **'Variegata'** Gray-green leaves with broad creamy yellow edges. Less invasive.

FRANCOA
Bridal wreath
SAXIFRAGACEAE

These frost-hardy cliff-dwellers are valued for their evergreen foliage and for their bold spikes of summer flowers.

Five clump- or mat-forming species inhabit partially shady cliffside crevices in Chile. They are valuable in open spots in a woodland garden, for planting around shrubs in a border, or in containers. Egg-shaped or broadly lance-shaped lobed leaves, up to 5 in (13 cm) long, are covered with soft hairs and form rosettes, above which rise dense spikes of small, cross-shaped, white or pink flowers. An attractive plant; good for cutting.

CULTIVATION Best in mild climates and moist yet well-drained, humus-rich soil in part-shade or full sun. Protect from cold, drying winds and excessive winter moisture. Containers need to be large, with free-draining potting mix.

PROPAGATION By division or, for species, from seed sown in spring.

PROBLEMS Usually trouble-free.

F. appendiculata Curving, wandlike spikes of palest pink flowers, ¾ in (2 cm) wide, often marked inside with deeper pink, wave in the breeze from midsummer onward above rosettes of wide, lance-shaped leaves. ↕36 in (90 cm). Z7–9 H9–7

***F.* 'Confetti'** Long, lance-shaped, apple green leaves form rosettes from which arise pink-stemmed wands of densely packed white flowers, ¾ in (2 cm) wide, from midsummer to early fall. Does well in dry shade and in tubs. ↕30 in (75 cm). Z7–9 H9–7

F. glabrata see *F. ramosa*

***F.* 'Purple Spike'** see *F. sonchifolia* Rogerson's form

F. ramosa syn. *F. glabrata* Candelabras of white ¾ in (2 cm) wide flowers, marked with deep pink, are held well above the rosettes of wide, lance-shaped leaves from midsummer onward. ↕36 in (90 cm). Z7–9 H9–7

F. sonchifolia Rosettes are formed from wide, lance-shaped leaves that are

ABOVE *Francoa sonchifolia*

lobed. The leaves support the spikes of ¾ in (2 cm) wide pink flowers. The flowers have somewhat deeper pink spots or blotches from midsummer onward. ↕36 in (90 cm). Z7–9 H9–7. **'Alba'** White flowers. **Rogerson's form** syn. *F.* 'Purple Spike' Purple flowers.

BELOW 1 *Fragaria* Pink Panda **2** *F. vesca* 'Multiplex' **3** *F. vesca* 'Variegata'

G

GAILLARDIA
Blanket flower
ASTERACEAE

Brilliantly colorful, though often short-lived, sparklers for summer sun.

Thirty species of these annual, biennial, and perennial plants are all natives of the prairies and other open grasslands of the Americas. Their common name is derived from the plants' ability to cover the ground with a mass of colorful flowers. Each plant has a basal rosette of hairy leaves that may be entire, lobed, or toothed, and erect stems with alternate leaves. The daisylike flowers have brown, red, yellow, or purple centers and brightly colored petals. They produce their sometimes dazzling flowers throughout the summer and make good cut flowers. Best planted in groups of four to five in the middle or front of the herbaceous border.

CULTIVATION Grow in full sun, in any moderately fertile but well-drained soil. Deadhead regularly.

PROPAGATION By division or root cuttings, or from seed (which will produce variable offspring).

PROBLEMS Downy mildew, slugs. Roots may rot in wet soil.

G. x *grandiflora* An attractive but short-lived, hairy plant with a basal rosette of entire, toothed, or lobed, lance-shaped leaves. The flowers, from midsummer to late fall, are borne on erect stems and can measure up to 4 in (10 cm) across. Usually needs staking; cut back in fall to improve winter survival. A hybrid between the perennial species *G. aristata* and the annual *G. pulchella*, which rarely lives beyond its fourth

year. The cultivars are very vigorous, usually with bright yellow, orange, or red flowers. Deadhead them regularly and cut down to a height of 6-in (15-cm) at the end of the summer to stimulate the development of new buds at the base and increase longevity. Often raised from seed, so some cultivars may prove variable. ‡ 14–30 in (35–75 cm). Z3–8 H8–1. **'Bijou'** Dwarf, with yellow tipped, orange-red petals. ‡ 18 in (45 cm). **'Bremen'** Bright scarlet petals with yellow tips. ‡ 30 in (75 cm). **'Burgunder'** Deep wine-red petals with yellow tips. ‡ 14 in (35 cm). **'Dazzler'** Deep mahogany-red flowers with yellow-tipped ray florets. ‡ 30 in (75 cm). **'Fanfare'** Deep reddish brown center and bright red, tube-shaped petals, with bright yellow tips. ‡ 24 in (60 cm). **'Goldkobold'** (**Golden Goblin**, **Yellow Goblin**) Free-flowering with relatively large golden yellow flowers with a slightly darker center. ‡ 14 in (35 cm). **'Kobold'** (**Goblin**) Red disk florets, red ray florets and yellow tips. ‡ 15 in (38 cm). **'St. Clements'** An important color break: the flowers have a peach and orange center with yellow petals tips, in late spring and early summer. Raised by Hardy's Cottage Garden Plants in Hampshire, England. ‡ 24 in (60 cm). **'Tokajer'** Rusty-orange flowers, flushed with purple toward base of the petals. ‡ 24 in (60 cm). **Yellow Goblin** see 'Goldkobold'.

GALAX
Beetleweed, Galaxy
DIAPENSIACEAE

Shade-loving plant with slender spires of small white flowers held just above a mat of tough, glossy evergreen foliage.

The single species grows in rich, moist forests in the eastern US, spreading by short runners to form

a creeping mat of abundant dark green leaves; pretty, tiny white flowers appear in late spring and early summer.

CULTIVATION Very useful in moist, humus-rich, acid soil under trees or among shrubs. Will not tolerate prolonged drought.

PROPAGATION By dividing rooted pieces in early spring, or from seed.

PROBLEMS Usually trouble-free.

G. aphylla see *G. urceolata*

G. urceolata syn. *G. aphylla* Good ground cover is provided by the slowly spreading, dense mat of leathery foliage, comprising rounded, glossy, dark green, toothed leaves, to 3 in (8 cm) across, carried on wiry stalks, and becoming tinted with red in fall. Erect, leafless spikes hold the small, 5-petaled, white flowers above the foliage in spring and early summer. Leaves were once collected from the wild for flower arranging. From the southeastern US. ‡ 12 in (30 cm). Z5–8 H8–5

GALEGA
Goat's rue
PAPILIONACEAE

Robust and reliable cottage garden favorites with bold foliage and a mist of pastel pea-flowers over a long summer season.

Six deciduous species come either from the mountains of East Africa

or from meadows, scrub, and open forest in Europe and southwest Asia. Two fairly similar species and their hybrids are grown in gardens. These include some survivors from the Edwardian era, when *Galega* was held in high regard. Bushy in habit and deep-rooting, plants produce abundant, lush, bright green foliage on upright stems, the leaves composed of slender, oval to oblong leaflets arranged in opposite pairs. Long flower spikes rise from stem tips and the base of leaf stalks from early to late summer, bearing many small, sweet-pea-type flowers in blues and whites, often with a coconut scent. These are much underrated border perennials, although sometimes invasive, and are also ideal in wild gardens and fall-cut meadows.

CULTIVATION Easy to grow in almost any garden soil. Prefer an open, sunny position but will also tolerate light shade. Need staking in flower borders and may self-sow.

PROPAGATION By division in spring or late fall, or from seed soaked in warm water before sowing.

PROBLEMS Pea and bean weevil, powdery mildew, and aphids.

G. bicolor see *G. officinalis*

G. x *hartlandii* Similar to *G. officinalis*, under which it is often classified. The foliage is irregularly edged with silver in spring but gradually fades to plain

ABOVE 1 *Galega officinalis* 'Alba'
2 *G. orientalis*

green by the time the flowers appear in summer. Abundant flower spikes, up to 7 in (18 cm) long, are like miniature wisterias in color, producing their bicolored white-and-mauve blooms well into fall without setting seed. In its vigorous growth, upright form, and bold mounds of oval leaflets, it differs little from *G. officinalis* (except in its sterility). Introduced in around 1901 by Hartland's nursery of Cork, Ireland, it attracted attention for its seasonally variegated leaves. It arose as a chance seedling, so parentage is unrecorded. It may be a cross between *G. officinalis* and *G. orientalis*, although earlier accounts give it as a hybrid of *G. officinalis* and *G. bicolor*. However, since *G. officinalis* and *G. bicolor* are now judged identical; in effect, a form of *G. officinalis*. Final pronouncement is awaited. Can be cut to the ground after flowering to produce a fresh flush of leaves. Propagate by division. ‡5 ft (1.5 m). Z5–10 H10–1. **'Alba'** Striking white flowers. **'Candida'** White. Probably now the same as 'Alba' but originally an 18th-century name for a white form of *G. officinalis*. **'Lady Wilson'** Two-toned flowers in periwinkle-blue and cream. **'Spring Light'** White flowers, but with springtime variegation of its leaves, fading to green. A recent spontaneous mutation of 'Alba'.

G. 'His Majesty' Well-loved old cultivar White buds open to bicolored flowers in pinkish lilac and white. Coconut-scented and non-seeding. Variously attributed to *G. officinalis* or *G. x hartlandii*. ‡5 ft (1.5 m). Z5–11 H12–5

G. officinalis syn. *G. bicolor* (French lilac) A vigorous, clump-forming perennial with more or less erect, hairless or slightly downy stems. The soft-textured leaves are divided into 9–17 oblong or elliptical leaflets, slightly downy underneath, their tips abruptly ending in a fine, short point. The flower spikes, up to 7 in (18 cm) long, are crowded with some 50 flowers, varying in color from white to pale lavender-blue or purple, from midsummer to early fall. Deadhead

promptly to avoid self-seeding; cut to the ground after flowering to produce a fresh flush of attractive leaves. Fast growth, deep roots, and its capacity to fix atmospheric nitrogen make this plant a good green manure. Classified as a noxious weed. Native to central and southern Europe, eastward to Iran and western Pakistan. ‡5 ft (1.5 m). Z5–10 H10–5. **'Alba'** Scented, white flowers. Usually comes true from seed. **'Bicolor'** Bicolored white-and-blue flowers. **Coconut Ice ('Kelgal')** White-edged leaves and pale pink, scented flowers. Raised by Kelway's Nursery in Somerset, England. Slow to propagate.

G. orientalis A more or less erect plant, spreading by rhizomes, with branching stems and divided leaves, each leaf with 13–25 egg- or lance-shaped leaflets. In late spring and early summer it produces fragrant blue-violet flower spikes to 6 in (15 cm) long. Similar to *G. officinalis* but its flowers are a more intense shade of blue-violet, and the slightly larger leaflets have a tapering rather than abrupt point. Best in full sun, but can be invasive. New agricultural cultivars are being developed as this species is under evaluation as a fodder crop in northern Europe. From the Caucasus. ‡4 ft (1.2 m). Z5–8 H8–5

GALEOBDOLON *see* LAMIUM

GENTIANA
Gentian
GENTIANACEAE

Elegant summer- or fall-flowering shade- or sun-lovers. They are highly valued for their often vivid blue flowers.

About 400 species, widely spread throughout temperate parts of the world, include annuals, biennials, and deciduous, partially evergreen, or evergreen perennials. Many are from mountain habitats; others, especially North American and Japanese species, are woodlanders. The simple leaves are unremarkable,

RIGHT 1 *Gentiana asclepiadea*
2 *G. lutea*

forming basal rosettes or arising from the stems in pairs or tiered clusters (whorls). Fall-flowering gentians usually have overwintering rosettes; flower stems dye back when seeds have formed. The flowers are relatively large and showy, generally trumpet-shaped, but sometimes bell- or urn-shaped. Blue is the usual color, often intense, but other colors include white, pink, purple, red, and yellow. The woodlanders, in particular, are appreciated as they are at their best when most woodland flowers are past their peak.

Tall species are ideal for a woodland garden or among shrubs in a border; small species are effective planted in bold drifts in similar settings.

CULTIVATION Most are best shaded from the strongest sun, unless summers are cool and moist, although we prefer full sun. Provide humus-rich, steadily moist, acidic or neutral soil, ensuring good drainage for the small fall-flowering mountain gentians.

PROPAGATION For species, sow seed in summer or early fall, as soon as ripe, in a cold frame. All types can be divided in early spring. To increase mat-formers, detach rooted offsets.

PROBLEMS Slugs and snails, aphids, stem rots, gentian rust.

G. asclepiadea (Willow gentian) Easily grown. One of the best for woodland gardens or for naturalizing in long grass. A deciduous clump-former, its willowlike leaves, to 3 in (8 cm) long, are arranged in pairs or whorls up the stems. Trumpet-shaped flowers, 2 in (5 cm) long, in deep or pale blue, open from midsummer to early fall. Suitable for dappled shade but thrives in sun. Expect some variability—all cultivars have, at times, been raised from seed. From central and southern Europe and Turkey. ‡24–36 in (60–90 cm). Z6–9 H9–6. **var. alba** White flowers; green throat, pale foliage. **'Knightshayes'** Deep blue, white-throated flowers.

Named for the Devon garden of the same name. ‡24 in (60 cm). **'Phyllis'** Pale blue flowers. **'Pink Swallow'** White-tipped pink flowers, but variable. **'Rosea'** Pink flowers.

G. lagodechiana see *G. septemfida* var. *lagodechiana*

G. lutea (Great yellow gentian) Robust, clump-forming, fleshy-rooted, deciduous border perennial, enhancing pond- or streamsides and quite unlike the familiar blue species. The 12 in (30 cm) long elliptical or oval basal leaves are blue-green and distinctively ribbed and pleated, the stem leaves being carried in pairs. Clusters of star-shaped yellow flowers, 1 in (2.5 cm) across, open in midsummer. The root is used in herbal medicine and is also an ingredient of liqueurs and aperitifs. Best in an open sunny spot. Dislikes disturbance, so propagate from seed. From alpine meadows in the Pyrenees, Alps, Apennines, and Carpathians. ‡5 ft (1.5 m). Z7–8 H8–7

G. septemfida "Everybody's gentian," for planting in bold drifts among shrubs. Spreading modestly, the prostrate or upward-growing deciduous stems carry pairs of 1½ in (3.5 cm) long oval leaves. Clusters of 1½ in (3.5 cm) long narrowly bell-shaped flowers, vivid blue or purple-blue with dark stripes and white throats, open in late summer. Best in sun, but grows equally well in part-shade, and in any moist soil. From the Caucasus, Turkey, Iran, and Central Asia. ‡6–8 in (15–20 cm). Z6–8 H8–6. **'Alba'** White flowers. **var. lagodechiana** syn. *G. lagodechiana* Ground-hugging stems, each bearing one to three flowers.

G. tibetica Rosette-forming plant for an open border or wild garden, with broad, shiny foliage. The lance-shaped basal leaves reach 12 in (30 cm) in length, the stem leaves 6 in (15 cm). Tiered clusters of 1¼ in (3 cm) long, narrow, funnel-shaped, greenish white flowers open from mid- to late summer. Best grown in a sunny spot. From the Himalaya. ‡24–36 in (60–90 cm). Z5–9 H9–5

GERANIUM
Cranesbill
GERANIACEAE

The most popular of all hardy perennials—invaluable components of bed, border, and ground-cover plantings, in sun or shade.

About 300 mostly annual, biennial, or perennial species, a few of them perennials with woody stems, are found mostly in the temperate Northern Hemisphere, with a few Australasian and South African species, and some from tropical mountains.

The rootstock consists of a much-shortened stem, often woody, from which both the flower stem and the roots themselves develop. The roots are usually thick and penetrate deep into the soil, with finer roots near the surface. Some species produce stout, slow-spreading rhizomes on the surface; some make far-creeping rhizomes above ground; some have slender underground rhizomes. A few species have tubers that help them survive dry summers.

The above-ground habit is usually one of two types: either they produce many basal leaves in spring followed by erect flowering stems, or they have few or no basal leaves and their stems trail across the ground.

Basal leaves usually form a rosette and have about five or seven radiating divisions, often cut almost to the base of the leaf, each division often being lobed and each lobe often further toothed or sometimes deeply cut. The result is often that the foliage looks lacy or feathery. A few species take on attractive fall tints before the leaves die. The smaller leaves on the stems may be opposite or alternately arranged and are also usually divided and lobed. The form of the leaf is often related to habitat: species growing naturally in shade tend to have shallow divisions and lobes and many small teeth, a rather hairy, wrinkled surface, and yellowish green coloring; those from dry, sunny habitats tend to have dark green leaves with narrow segments. A few species have very silvery or very hairy foliage as an adaptation to a hot, dry climate.

The flowering spray can be very spreading and diffuse, in which case flowering may continue for some time, as is usual for trailing species. In more upright species, the flowers may be carried more densely, in which case the plant is likely to flower for a shorter season. In many cases, the flowers seem to be adapted to particular pollinators, often bees and hoverflies, more rarely wasps, beetles, or butterflies.

The flowers themselves (*see* Geranium Flower Structure) range from ⅜ to 1½ in (1.5 to 4 cm) in diameter, and are generally borne in pairs, each usually having five identical petals alternating with five sepals beneath, giving them a fivefold symmetry as opposed to closely related *Pelargonium,* which is symmetrical in only a single plane with two petals at the top of the floret and three beneath.

The petals vary in color from blue through purplish red to white, and most shades in between. They are often notched at the tip, and frequently have a network of deeper or paler veins, or a series of guidelines radiating from the petal base to lead pollinating insects to the pollen and nectar. There may also be similar markings that are only visible in ultraviolet light, seen by insects but invisible to humans.

At the center of the flower, ten stamens in two rings of five surround the style, at the base of which are the five seed-bearing organs (carpels), in each of which usually a single seed forms. After pollination, the style elongates to produce the "crane's bill" that gives the genus its common name. When ripe, the strips running from the carpel to the top of the style split away explosively from the bottom of the beak and upward, dispersing the seeds.

Species and cultivars of *Geranium* do not vary dramatically and gardeners often find it difficult to distinguish one from another. So the descriptions in this entry include more detail than is the case with

BELOW **1** *Geranium albanum* **2** *G. asphodeloides*

GERANIUM FLOWER STRUCTURE

Geranium sylvaticum is typical of the more upright cranesbill, with flowers clustered together, which makes them more visible to pollinating insects over the relatively short season. Each flower has five outer sepals enclosing the flower in bud, five petals, five stamens, in this case with a dark anther held on a slender filament and with a nectary at the base, and five carpels in the center of the flower. The carpels, fused together and topped by a five-part style, develop into the fruit.

Sepal
Five-part style
Developing fruit
Petals
Anther

Geranium sylvaticum

most plants in this book, in the hope that readers will find this helps them appreciate the distinctions.

CULTIVATION Geraniums grow naturally in a wide range of habitats. There are low-growing alpines, requiring sun and excellent drainage under cultivation—although most of these are not discussed here. A few grow naturally in deciduous woodland, where summer drought and dense shade favor species that grow and flower mainly in spring; some of these die back in summer to withstand seasonal drought. Species from woodland edges in dappled shade are often adapted to scramble toward the light, a characteristic that suits them to ground cover. Species whose natural habitat is meadowland will grow in full sun, shoulder to shoulder with other plants, and so are able to compete in a border. Most will grow in any good soil, including quite alkaline ones, but adequate moisture throughout the growing season is preferable for all but the most drought-tolerant.

Plant between early fall and early spring. In heavy soil, early spring is best since plants can rot over winter after fall planting; silvery-leaved kinds are also generally better planted in early spring. Early-leafing types need to be well established by the time they come into leaf and generally prefer fall planting.

Many species flop if not supported (*see* Staking Geraniums, *p.215*) and benefit from deadheading after flowering: to keep them neat and well furnished with fresh foliage; to discourage a plethora of seedlings; and in some cases to encourage reblooming.

The best way to remove faded flowers varies. For most, all the leaves look decidedly tired once the first flush has finished and the easiest treatment is to shear off all the top-growth. New foliage will generally grow within a couple of weeks. In a few cases, all the top-growth can be pulled off, removing the flowering stems and basal foliage entirely without breaking the basal stems. This works for 'Johnson's Blue' and a few others but backfires if the basal stems come away with the tops. Geraniums whose basal foliage lasts throughout the summer without becoming untidy can be deadheaded by snapping off each flowering stem at a low node beneath the dome of basal leaves, a technique that works, for example, with *G. psilostemon*. At the end of the season, cut plants to the ground.

PROPAGATION Division is perhaps the easiest and most generally satisfactory method of propagation, between early fall and early spring. An alternative is to cut back plants after flowering in summer, then divide, replant, and water well.

For tuberous species, the tubers can be separated, in fall for those that remain in leaf through summer

or, for those that die back in summer and become dormant, shortly after the foliage is lost but before fall.

Geraniums are promiscuous and generally do not come true from seed; even species often show variation when seedlings are raised, especially when grown, as they usually are, in gardens with other species or cultivars nearby. In general, division is recommended for wild species and all their cultivars and for all hybrids. Some can be raised from cuttings but, unless specifically mentioned, only species should be raised from seed, preferably when grown in isolation, and even then some variation should be expected. Only a few, mentioned where relevant, come reliably true from seed.

Basal cuttings are recommended for those that are relatively slow to increase, such as 'Mavis Simpson', and root best if taken about 2–2½ in (5–6 cm) long with a woody base from late winter to mid-spring. Most geraniums can be rooted from flowering stems, but the resulting plants are not always able to form the usual perennial rosette and tend to continue flowering until they die in their first winter. However, a few species and their hybrids have the potential to make normal plants from cuttings of the flowering stems, including *G. procurrens* and its hybrids 'Anne Folkard' and 'Ann Thompson' (though these two are rather slow to root); also, *G. wallichianum*. Root cuttings may be used for some, including more choice double selections of *G. pratense*.

PROBLEMS Rust, powdery mildew, slugs, snails, aphids, and vine weevil can all be troublesome, along with virus diseases, but in general cranesbills are robust and reliable plants that tolerate any problems with which they may be afflicted. Cultural methods such as regular dividing and replanting, avoiding overcrowding, and maintaining adequate moisture levels help plants avoid and tolerate problems.

G. albanum Scrambling, wide-spreading, slender-stemmed semievergreen. The mid-green leaves glisten through a light covering of fine hairs and are cut beyond halfway into nine divisions, each of them lobed. Small flowers in vibrant mauve-pink, slightly paler at the center, with three to five slightly branched magenta veins, the petals notched at the tip, open in early summer and midsummer. For sun or part-shade. Can be used to cover a bank or scramble into shrubs; best cut back after flowering to produce fresh foliage. From the southeast Caucasus and neighboring parts of Iran. ↕ 18 in (45 cm). Z5–8 H8–5

G. anemonifolium see *G. palmatum*

G. angulatum see
G. sylvaticum 'Angulatum'

VIVID INTERMINGLING

GERANIUM 'ANN FOLKARD' is undoubtedly a very vivid color, and while some gardeners may be tempted to choose companions to try to tone it down, others work to capitalize on its vibrancy. Here, a middle course has been steered with the flat heads of the soft yellow *Achillea* 'Taygetea', and the more upright spikes of the buttery *Lysimachia punctata*, picking up the tones in the geranium foliage as it greens from its spring gold. Their flowers are bright, but less dramatic than the orange or scarlet tones that are sometimes used with 'Ann Folkard' to startle visitors.

G. 'Ann Folkard' Vigorous hybrid with leaves emerging golden green, darkening a little to green as they age, and cut almost to the base into five divisions, each of them lobed and further toothed. The rather large flowers, appearing in early summer and midsummer though with some bloom into fall, open magenta with a black center and veins, aging toward deeper purple. Allowed to sprawl, it covers a large area without rooting where it touches the ground, making it more manageable than its parent *G. procurrens*. Tolerates shade, though the foliage color is best in full sun. Propagate by division, though it is slow to produce new crowns, or cuttings which are slow to root and develop. A chance hybrid of *G. procurrens* and *G. psilostemon*

selected by the Reverend Oliver Folkard in Lincolnshire, England. ↕ 20 in (50 cm). Z5–9 H9–5

G. 'Anne Thomson' Vigorous, sprawling hybrid with young leaves flushed golden yellow, this coloring mostly lost as they age to mid-green. The leaves are cut almost to the base into five divisions, each of them lobed and further toothed. The flowers open in early summer and midsummer, in magenta with a black center and black veins, aging to purple; the petals do not quite overlap. A less bright, less spreading and more solid plant than 'Ann Folkard', its flowers a little smaller but attractive, and useful for ground cover on a smaller scale. Divide, or take cuttings from the flowering stems.

A hybrid of *G. procurrens* and *G. psilostemon* raised by Alan Bremner of England. ↕20 in (50 cm). Z4–9 H8–1

G. x *antipodeum* Tufted plant with numerous basal leaves and many stems with tiny stem leaves. The basal leaves are 1 in (2.5 cm) across, or a little less, cut two-thirds or a little more toward the base into about seven crowded divisions, not lying flat, and further lobed; they are minutely downy with the upper surface bright green or, if derived from *G. sessiliflorum* subsp. *novae-zelandiae* 'Nigricans', flushed with bronze or black. The stem leaves are less than ¾ in (2 cm) across, carried in much-branched, trailing sprays. The ⅛– ¾ in (1.5–2 cm) flowers, from early summer to mid-fall, are white or flushed with rose pink. Prefers full sun with good drainage; dark-leaved selections are less hardy than green-leaved forms. Propagate by basal cuttings or division. Plants may be sterile, or may produce viable seed that produces variable seedlings. A hybrid of *G. traversii* and *G. sessiliflorum*, so named because two Southern Hemisphere species crossed in the Northern Hemisphere (see also 'Stanhoe'). ↕8 in (20 cm). Z4–7 H7–1.
'Chocolate Candy' Mounds of rich, deep brown foliage are topped with pale pink flowers. A seedling of 'Stanhoe' selected by Coen Jansen. **Crûg strain** Dark-leaved seed strain with rather small pink to white flowers, continually being selected at Crûg Farm Plants for rich foliage color.
'Pink Spice' syn. *G.* 'Pink Spice' Spreading plant with bronzed foliage, very dark in full sun, appearing lustrous and satiny. The petals are rose pink, deeper at the center, near-white toward the base, and with about five unfeathered purple veins. Good in containers. ↕6 in (15 cm). **'Sea Spray'** Blackish green leaves and pale pink flowers. From Alan Bremner. ↕6 in (15 cm). **'Stanhoe'** Blackish green leaves and very pale pink flowers. The first form, named for the Norfolk,

England garden of Ken and Gillian Beckett where it was found.

G. *aristatum* A grayish, hairy plant. The leaves are large, cut about three-quarters of the way into seven or nine divisions, and further coarsely lobed and toothed. The flowers, usually borne in threes in early summer and midsummer, are nodding, with backswept petals in the manner of a cyclamen, and are white or pale lilac at the tips, merging to deep lilac or reddish purple at the base and with parallel lilac or red-purple veins. For sun or part-shade. From the mountains of Albania, the former Yugoslavia, and northern Greece. ↕20 in (50 cm). Z5–8 H8–5

G. *asphodeloides* Very spreading, leafy perennial, sometimes a biennial, with a stout rootstock and many thick roots. The basal leaves are cut to two-thirds or more into five to seven divisions and further lobed and toothed. The stem leaves are borne in opposite pairs. In late spring and early summer, rather small, narrow-petaled, mauve to white flowers with about three magenta veins are borne in profusion. For sun or part-shade, and will tolerate drought. Best cut back after the first flush of flowers, reblooming from late summer. Self-sows, but not prone to hybridizing with other species. From southern Europe from Sicily eastward to the Caucasus, Iran, and Turkey. ↕16 in (40 cm). Z6–9 H9–6. **subsp.** *asphodeloides* **'Prince Regent'** Hairy stems and leaf stalks, and pale mauve-pink flowers with darker veins. Less spreading and slightly earlier in flower. ↕12 in (30 cm).

G. **'Bertie Crûg'** Low-growing, creeping plant with tiny, glistening leaves flushed blackish brown and cut into five divisions, each with roundish lobes. Vibrant mauve-pink flowers are produced over a long period from late spring to late fall. Best in sun with good drainage. Roots readily at the leaf joints and so is easily propagated

by cuttings or layering as well as by division. A chance seedling at Crûg Farm Plants believed to be a hybrid of *G.* x *antipodeum* Crûg strain and *G. papuanum*, and named for a terrier belonging to the nursery owners. ↕4 in (10 cm). Z5–8 H8–5

G. **'Blue Cloud'** Very spreading plant, the 4 in (10 cm) basal leaves cut almost to the base into about seven overlapping rhomboid divisions, each is again deeply cut and cut again; they emerge flushed gold but wither early. Stem leaves, also very dissected, become smaller and bractlike up the plant, and are missing from the uppermost joints. Abundant, dished, pale lavender-blue flowers with purple veins, quite large in diameter but with rather narrow petals that do not overlap, are borne in a diffuse spray from late spring to midsummer. Plants tend to open up in the center unless staked. A chance seedling introduced by David Hibberd. ↕32 in (80 cm). Z5–8 H8–5

ABOVE *Geranium* 'Blue Cloud'

G. **'Blue Pearl'** Upright, with leaves cut almost to the base into about seven divisions, then cut and cut again to give a deeply dissected appearance. Plentiful large, dished, soft lavender-blue flowers with radiating violet veins are borne in early summer and midsummer. Seems to dislike full sun and to prefer shade. Named by David Hibberd; probably a chance seedling of *G.* 'Brookside'. ↕24 in (60 cm). Z5–8 H8–5

G. Blue Sunrise (**'Blogold'**) Sprawling with young foliage emerging yellow-green flushed with orange-red, mostly at edges, maturing to a bright yellow-green if grown in sun. Basal leaves are deeply cut into five to seven divisions, each further cut about halfway in into pointed lobes. Stem leaves are similar but smaller, borne in opposite pairs. Flowers, from early summer to mid-fall, are quite large, cupped, lavender-blue shading to purple toward the center with a white eye and purple veins. Foliage color best in sun, though it will tolerate shade. Outstanding flowering and foliage plant for the front of beds or borders, and good in tall containers. A chance seedling from Holland believed to be a hybrid of *G.* 'Ann Folkard' and *G. wallichianum* 'Buxton's Variety'. ↕16 in (40 cm). Z5–8 H8–5

G. **'Bob's Blunder'** Rather spreading with black-flushed leaves cut into three or five lobed divisions and from late spring to late fall, broadly trumpet-shaped flowers with notched petals emerging bright mauve-pink and aging to near-white. Tolerant of a wide range of conditions but flowers most prolifically and has best foliage color in sun. Supplied by Bob Brown as 'Rosie Crûg' to Crûg Farm Plants where it was recognized as different and named. ↕12 in (30 cm). Z5–8 H8–5

LEFT 1 *Geranium* Blue Sunrise
2 *G.* 'Brookside'

G. 'Brookside' Vigorous, floriferous plant with basal leaves cut almost to the base into seven, scarcely overlapping divisions and again deeply lobed to about halfway, appearing very dissected. Lower stem leaves are in opposite pairs and similar but smaller, decreasing in size and becoming very small toward the top of the stems. The rather downy leaves and buds have an attractive silvery cast when young. Large, dished, lavender-blue flowers appear from early to late summer and have a small white center, reddish purple veins, and overlapping, almost round, smooth-edged petals. A very spreading plant suitable for ground cover in sun or part-shade. A hybrid of *G. clarkei* and *G. pratense* found as a seedling in the University of Cambridge Botanic Garden at Cambridge, England. Named for the street on which the garden is situated. ‡ 24 in (60 cm). Z5–8 H8–5

G. caffrum Bushy, leafy evergreen becoming woody at the base with a long, thick taproot. Lower leaves are without hairs and divided to the base, or nearly so, into five or seven narrow divisions, each of which has a few lobes on either side, some of the lower ones with one or two teeth. Upper leaves are smaller and sometimes divided into three. It forms a sprawling plant with diffuse sprays of plentiful white or pale pink blooms on slender stems held well above the foliage. However, the plant usually grown has rich pink flowers shading to a white center with faint darker veins. For well-drained soil in full sun. Stems root where they touch the ground and thus are easily layered, or plants can be raised from seed. From Natal and Cape Provinces, South Africa. ‡ 24 in (60 cm). Z5–8 H8–5

G. x cantabrigiense An aromatic carpeter. Trailing stems retain their foliage into winter. Light green leaves are almost invisibly hairy, the largest of them cut three-quarters or more toward the base into seven divisions, each of which has three lobes with up to two teeth each. The flowering stems have leaves at the first and sometimes the second leaf joint, and bear, from late spring to midsummer, clusters of five to ten flowers, usually held above the foliage, with roundish petals varying in color from magenta-pink to white, paler selections showing faint veins. Sepals are usually flushed red or brown. Suitable for the front of beds and borders and for ground cover or underplanting. Useful for small gardens, where its parent, *G. macrorrhizum*, would be too spreading. For sun or shade, and tolerant of most soils. Divide, or layer the stems. A hybrid of *G. dalmaticum* and *G. macrorrhizum* first made at the University of Cambridge Botanic Garden, then subsequently found wild in Croatia, where both parents are native. ‡ 10 in (25 cm). Z5–8 H8–5. **'Biokovo'** Blush pink with contrasting deep pink stamens. Found by Dr. Hans Simon in the Biokova Mountains, Croatia. **'Cambridge'** Very deep pink, near magenta, flowers. Original plant raised at Cambridge, England. **'Karmina'**

Dark pink, almost magenta flowers; like 'Cambridge', but a little larger in all its parts and a little less floriferous. Introduced by German horticulturist Ernst Pagels. **'St. Ola'** The flowers, among the largest of the species, are almost pure white, aging to light rose pink, with overlap-ping petals. Remains in flower later than other cultivars. A hybrid of *G. macrorrhizum* 'Album' and *G. dalmaticum* 'Album' raised by Alan Bremner. **'Westray'** Floriferous, with small leaves and flowers, each deep pink bloom opens from a brown calyx. From Alan Bremner.

G. 'Chantilly' Upright, with sage-textured, light green leaves, cut a little more than halfway into about five divisions, each of them with shallow lobes bearing a few teeth. The flowers are borne well above the leaves in late spring and early summer; their heart-shaped petals have a deep notch at the tip and are vibrant mauve with a white base and about five radiating purple veins. Flowers best in full sun but will tolerate a little shade. A hybrid of *G. gracile* and *G. renardii* raised by Alan Bremner. ‡ 18 in (45 cm). Z5–8 H8–5

G. clarkei Spreading by rhizomes; long-stalked basal leaves are cut almost to the base into seven divisions, each of them with numerous deep lobes, which may in turn have a few pointed teeth, giving a heavily dissected effect. The stem leaves are similar and smaller, borne in opposite pairs. In early summer and midsummer the stems branch to form a many-flowered but not dense display, each flower usually dished, upward-facing, and purplish-violet, less commonly white or pink, borne above the foliage on slender stalks. Similar to *G. pratense* but distinct in its lower growth, producing a carpet of basal leaves, and in its more diffuse display. Good in sun or part-shade. From Kashmir. ‡ 20 in (50 cm). Z5–7 H7–5. **'Kashmir Blue'** see *G.* 'Kashmir Blue'. **'Kashmir Green'** see *G.* 'Kashmir Green'. **'Kashmir Pink'** Cupped, mauve-pink flowers have about five radiating purple veins on each petal. A seedling of *G. clarkei* 'Kashmir Purple' raised at Blackthorn Nursery, Hampshire, England. ‡ 16 in (40 cm). **'Kashmir Purple'** *see* Purple-flowered Group. **'Kashmir White'** syn. *G. rectum* 'Album' Less vigorous, with bowl-shaped flowers with lightly feathered radiating purple veins, giving the flower a muted grayish cast. Growing from seed produces a proportion of purple-flowered plants. ‡ 16 in (40 cm). **Purple-flowered Group** Rather variable, generally with lavender flowers becoming more purple toward center and with a white eye and about seven radiating purple veins on each petal. Both sides of outer margins of each petal are often slightly turned upward and inward. Result of many generations of raising the now rare 'Kashmir Purple' from seed. Rather invasive.

RIGHT **1** *Geranium* x *cantabrigiense*
2 *G.* x *cantabrigiense* 'Cambridge'
3 *G.* 'Chantilly'

G. collinum A variable, bushy but diffuse plant growing from a compact rootstock with very thick roots. Basal leaves sometimes emerge tinged pale yellow and pink before becoming grayish green, and are cut nearly to the center into seven divisions, each of them with a few pointed lobes spaced out along either side; these in turn have a few to several pointed teeth. The stem leaves are paired and become smaller up the plant, the uppermost ones greatly reduced and nearly stalkless. The flowers, from early to late summer, are of medium size, pale to deep mauve-pink, with or without undivided or feathered red veins. Not the showiest species, but tough and long-flowering; suited to the wild garden. Prefers sun and is tolerant of drought. Similar to *G. pratense* but the leaves have fewer, coarser teeth and lobes. Widespread from southeastern Europe eastward to Siberia and the northwest Himalaya. ‡ 24 in (60 cm). Z5–8 H8–5

G. 'Coombland White' Mound-forming plant with attractively marbled, finely downy foliage, the leaves cut to about halfway into five divisions, each with three pointed-tipped lobes. From early to late summer, upward-facing flowers appear with violet-veined, palest mauve-pink petals, cerise at the base, overlapping only at their broadest point. The flowers are of exceptional beauty when seen at close range and are produced over a long period. Prefers good drainage and sun. Propagate by division or basal cuttings. A hybrid of *G. lambertii* 'Swansdown' and *G. traversii* var. *elegans* raised at Coombland Nursery, West Sussex, England. ‡ 16 in (40 cm). Z5–8 H8–5

G. 'Dilys' Very spreading, sprawling ground-cover plant remarkable for its late and long flowering. The stems are strongly flushed red and do not root where they touch the ground. Mid-green, rather shiny, clean and healthy-looking leaves are relatively small, oppositely arranged, and cut three-quarters or more of the way to the base into five divisions, each has three lobes

which may have one or two teeth. The broadly funnel-shaped, magenta-pink flowers with narrow purple veins are borne a little sparsely but continuously from late summer until frost, continuing into early winter in mild climates. Best in part-shade with adequate moisture, but will tolerate wet or poorly drained soils. A hybrid of *G. procurrens* and *G. sanguineum* raised by Alan Bremner and named for Hardy Plant Society stalwart Dr. Dilys Davies. ‡ 16 in (40 cm). Z4–8 H8–1

G. 'Diva' Spreading ground-cover plant for the front of the border or underplanting. The opposite leaves, borne on reddish stems, emerge yellow-green before becoming mid-green and are cut three-quarters of the way or more toward the base into five divisions, each with three lobes. The rather small, light purple flowers with violet veins are borne from early summer to early fall. The scattering of flowers is enough to maintain interest if not to dazzle; the fresh, clean appearance of the foliage adds to its appeal. For sun or part-shade and tolerant of most soils that are not waterlogged. A hybrid of *G. sanguineum* and *G. swatense*, raised by Alan Bremner. ‡ 20 in (50 cm). Z5–8 H8–5

G. 'Elizabeth Ross' Low-growing, semievergreen sprawler; mid-green leaves with a yellowish cast, cut three-quarters of the way or more toward the base into five divisions, each of which usually has three lobes with about three teeth each. Vibrant magenta flowers, with a little white at the base of each petal, are borne on short flower stems from early summer to early fall. Prefers well-drained soil in sun or part-shade. Propagate by division or basal cuttings. A hybrid of *G. x antipodeum* and *G. x oxonianum* raised by Alan Bremner. ‡ 8 in (20 cm). Z5–8 H8–5

G. endressii Rather small, hairy perennial with elongated rhizomes at, or just below, the surface. The partially evergreen basal leaves are cut almost to the base into five divisions, each of

which is lobed about halfway to the midrib, the lobes having two or three teeth which, like the tips of the lobes, have pointed ends. The notch between the divisions is not brown or red as it is in the related *G. versicolor*. Stem leaves, solitary at the base of the stem but paired above, are similar but become smaller up the plant. The rather large trumpet-shaped flowers are rose pink or salmon (rarely magenta) with a silvery sheen; the color usually deepens with age. They open from early summer to early fall. Petal veins are colorless in the lower part of the petal and slightly darker and netted above. Vigorously colonizing, and good as ground cover, it may fill too much space in a small garden. Many plants seen under this name prove to be its hybrid with *G. versicolor*, *G. x oxonianum*. Except in its choicest selections, this can be rather a dull species. For sun or part-shade in any good garden soil, but best if not too dry. From the western half of the Pyrenees, mainly in France. ‡ 10–20 in (25–50 cm). Z5–8 H8–5. **'Beholder's Eye'** see *G. x oxonianum* 'Beholder's Eye'. **'Betty Catchpole'** syn. *G. x oxonianum* 'Betty Catchpole' Spreading, with dark green foliage and plentiful mauve-pink flowers with faint veining from late spring to mid-fall. The almond-shaped petals have gaps between and blooms tend to bleach in full sun. Plants tend to open up in the center unless provided with short stakes. Long grown at Tatton Park in Cheshire and introduced by Judith Bradshaw. ‡ 16 in (40 cm). **'Castle Drogo'** Salmon pink flowers from late spring to mid-fall, silvering with age to reveal darker veins. Very similar to *G. x oxonianum* 'Wageningen', but considerably more spreading. The plants tend to open up in the center unless staked. Commemorates the Devon, England garden of this name. ‡ 18 in (45 cm). **'Rosenlicht'** see *G. x oxonianum* 'Rosenlicht'. **var. thurstonianum** see *G. x oxonianum* f. *thurstonianum*. **'Wageningen'** see *G. x oxonianum* 'Wageningen'. **'Wargrave Variety'** see *G. x oxonianum* 'Wargrave Pink'.

HYBRIDIZATION

Geraniums are unusual in that even quite different species will often hybridize with each other. This has given rise to hundreds of new cultivars in recent decades, sometimes merely chance seedlings that gardeners have recognized as different and left in place to see whether they had potential. The hybrids often have a much longer flowering season than the species, aided sometimes, if they prove sterile, by their not wasting their resources on seed production.

There have also been some ambitious hybridization projects, working through as many species as possible, preferably in their most desirable forms, and crossing them with other species. A notable success for this approach has been the work of Alan Bremner, who, from his garden in Scotland's Orkney Isles, has produced a steady stream of new cultivars, several of which have already become classics.

The hundreds of cultivars now existing are only a beginning: much natural variation—in, for instance, species from China—has yet to be exploited. Most of the existing crosses are primary hybrids between two species: making hybrids between hybrids and capitalizing on natural variation will offer even wider possibilities in the future.

G. erianthum Variable plant with leaves cut as far as about three-quarters into seven to nine overlapping divisions, each with several pointed-tipped lobes, each lobe having several pointed teeth. The stem leaves are similar, opposite, with five to nine divisions, forming ruffs beneath the flowers and each stem branch. The rather large flowers face outward, with white to light to deep lavender petals and deeper veins that are sometimes feathered; they often have a white center. The display is congested, usually from late spring to early summer but sometimes as early as mid-spring; some later reblooming. The foliage can color attractively in fall. For part-shade and well-drained soil, although it will tolerate full sun. From eastern Siberia, Japan, Alaska, northern British Columbia, and islands in between. ‡ 18–24 in (45–60 cm). Z4–8 H8–1. **'Calm Sea'** Attractive light lavender flowers with striking, slightly feathered, darker veins and dark green, firm-textured leaves. ‡ 24 in (60 cm).

G. eriostemon see *G. platyanthum*

G. 'Espression' see *G. 'Tanya Rendall'*

G. 'Frances Grate' A hybrid between *G. incanum* and *G. robustum*; named for Frances Grate of Monterey, CA. Woody, semi-upright stems with narrowly lobed leaves that are gray-green above and silvery beneath; pale mauve flowers open from spring to early summer. ‡ 15 in (38 cm). Z8–11 H11–8

LEFT 1 *Geranium clarkei* 'Kashmir White' **2** *G. himalayense* 'Plenum'

G. gracile Rather hairy plant with a tangle of rhizomes. The leaves are light green with a wrinkled, slightly glossy surface, the basal ones cut by about two-thirds into five, scarcely lobed, more or less evenly toothed divisions. The paired stem leaves are smaller, and may have only three divisions. Above the basal foliage, the flower stems branch repeatedly, the upper part of the stem lacking leaves so that the display seems airy and diffuse. The individual flowers, opening from early summer to early fall, are upward-facing with wedge-shaped, notched petals, vertical at the base, then bend sharply outward to form a very flared trumpet. Petals are pale pink at the tip, shaded to white below, or a bright deep pink shading to white, the zone of the petal that bends outward being marked with about five short parallel purplish-red veins. An attractive species for the woodland garden or for ground cover in shade, looking superficially like a bigger, stouter cousin of *G. nodosum*. From northeastern Turkey and the Caucasus. ‡16–28 in (40–70 cm). Z5–8 H8–5

G. grandiflorum var. *alpinum* see *G. himalayense* 'Gravetye'

G. grevilleanum see *G. lambertii*

G. himalayense Rather variable carpeting plant spreading by underground rhizomes. Basal leaves, up to 8 in (20 cm) wide, are cut three-quarters of the way in or more into seven divisions, each usually with three rather spreading lobes cut up to halfway to the midrib of the division, usually with a few rather blunt lobes. Stem leaves are paired, becoming smaller and more cut in appearance up the plant. The outward-facing, 1½–2½-in (4–6-cm), saucer-shaped flowers vary from deep blue to white, though are typically a deep campanula blue, purplish at the center; they open from late spring to midsummer. For any soil with adequate moisture in sun or part-shade. With the largest flowers of all cranesbills, this is useful for the front of beds and borders and for ground cover. Similar to *G. pratense,* which is distinct in its more compact rootstock, more deeply divided leaves and less diffuse display of flowers. From the Himalaya, from northeastern Afghanistan to central Nepal, and the Pamir region of Tajikistan. ‡10–18 in (25–45 cm). Z4–7 H7–1. **'Baby Blue'** Exceptionally large, 2½-in (6-cm), lavender-blue flowers shading to purple toward the center, with a small whitish green eye and purple veins. Found at Ingwersen's Birch Farm Nursery. in England ‡12 in (30 cm). **'Birch Double'** see 'Plenum'. **'Derrick Cook'** Large, handsome, palest lilac-gray flowers with purple-gray veins in late spring and early summer. The stems are reddish, and it makes a very spreading plant that is inclined to flop unless staked. Collected by Derrick Cook and his sister Rowlatt in Nepal. ‡12 in (30 cm). **'Gravetye'** syn. *G. grandiflorum* var. *alpinum* A name now being applied to several spreading plants with 2½-in (6-cm), lavender-blue flowers with a

FIRE AT SEA

IN SOME SITUATIONS there is simply a need for plants that will cover the ground well, look attractive for a long season, not require too much care and attention, and mingle well together informally. Here, in a wilder border where strict formality is not required, the upright stems and fiery orange flowers of *Euphorbia griffithii* 'Fireglow' are surrounded, and at times almost swamped, by a blue sea of *Geranium* 'Johnson's Blue'. The euphorbia, however, is a robust plant, spreading determinedly, and while the geranium is cut back every spring to allow space for bulbs to flower, it soon sparkles again in its wave of blue.

pronounced reddish purple center and reddish purple veins, flowering in late spring and early summer and again in early fall. Leaves are smaller than in the species, with sharper and narrower lobes and teeth. Thought to originate before 1903; only the plant from Ingwersen's Birch Farm Nursery at Gravetye, England is considered to be the true cultivar. ‡12 in (30 cm). **'Irish Blue'** Vigorous, with 1½-in (4-cm) flowers in late spring and early summer that are closer to primary blue than lavender and rather paler than usual for the species; they shade to violet toward the center and have faint purple veins. Introduced by English horticulturist/writer Graham Stuart Thomas. ‡16 in (40 cm). **'Plenum'** syn. 'Birch Double' Informal and slightly muddled 1½-in (3.5-cm) double flowers, unfurling lavender purplish, suffused lilac and with reddish veins when fully open. It flowers in late spring and early summer, with some later flowers. Rather invasive. Named by English nurseryman Walter Ingwersen. ‡12 in (30 cm).

G. ibericum Hairy plant with leaves cut from two-thirds to seven eighths toward the base into nine to eleven overlapping divisions. Each split has about three toothed lobes on either side of the midrib, the main lobes being further lobed and toothed, the

tips of the lobes and teeth being pointed. The stem leaves are similar but decrease in size up the plant, the upper ones being stalkless. The hairs are not tipped with pinhead glands (*see* subsp. *jubatum, below*). The upward-facing flowers, in late spring and early summer, are usually lavender with purple veins, shading to a purple center, and may be rather open. For any soil in sun, tolerating dry conditions. Plants under this name often prove to be *G. x magnificum,* the hybrid with *G. platypetalum.* From northeastern Turkey and the Caucasus. ‡16–24 in (40–60 cm). Z5–8 H8–5. **subsp.** *jubatum* Distinct only in that some hairs on the flower stalks are tipped with pinhead glands, some not. From northern Turkey.

G. incanum Showy, relatively tender, aromatic bushy perennial showing no distinction between flowering and non-flowering shoots and becoming woody below. The leaves are cut to the base into five divisions that are lobed and lobed again into very narrow segments no more than $\frac{1}{16}$ in (1 mm) wide, giving a lacy effect; they are green above and silvery-hairy below. From early summer to mid-fall, bears deep magenta-pink or white, ¾–1½ in (2–3.5 cm) flowers with notched petals. For well-drained soil in full sun;

suitable for gravel gardens, raised beds, and containers. Propagate from seed, or stem cuttings taken in midsummer. From Cape Province, South Africa. ‡9 in (23 cm). Z5–8 H8–5. **var.** *incanum* Generally smaller white flowers. **var.** *multifidum* Deep magenta-pink flowers with darker veins and a white V-shaped mark at the base of the petals. The variety usually grown. **'Sugar Plum'** Green, very dissected leaves and rub-colored flowers. This selection named by Monique Simone of Weidner's Nursery, Encinitas, CA. ‡8 in (20 cm). Z8–11 H11–8

G. 'Ivan' Showy, with mid-green basal leaves, about 7 in (18 cm) across, divided beyond three-quarters into five divisions that are further lobed and toothed; stem leaves are paired, becoming smaller up the plant. Large, 1¾-in (4.5-cm), magenta flowers with black veins are borne in profusion on much-branched stems from early to late summer. Grows in any soil that is not dry in sun or part-shade. A hybrid of *G. endressii* and *G. psilostemon,* like a shorter, slower-growing version of *G. psilostemon.* ‡36 in (90 cm). Z5–8 H8–5

G. 'Jean Armour' syn. *G. x riversleaianum* 'Jean Armour' Very vigorous, semievergreen ground cover; leaves are slightly downy and cut two-thirds of the way or more toward the base into five to seven divisions, usually with a lobe to either side, all with a few blunt teeth. Stem leaves are borne in pairs. Flowers, from late spring to mid-fall, have rose pink petals, paler toward the center, and about five faint magenta veins on each petal. Like G. 'Mavis Simpson', with which it is much confused. Now believed to be a hybrid of G. x oxonianum and G. traversii; it differs in its greater vigor and less pronounced silvery sheen to the petals. It is also prone to die in mild, wet winters, probably as a result of fungal disease. Prefers sun and well-drained soil. Propagate by division or basal cuttings. ‡ 12 in (30 cm). Z5–8 H8–5

G. 'Johnson's Blue' Sprawling ground-cover plant with underground rhizomes. Leaves are deeply cut almost to the base into seven divisions, usually with a lobe to either side, and all with a few rather pointed teeth. The cupped, lavender-blue flowers, shading to lilac and becoming paler toward the center, have near-white veins; they appear from late spring to midsummer, with some later blooming. Several similar plants are grown under this name. Once among the most esteemed of cranesbills, it is now challenged by newer cultivars producing even more bloom over a yet longer season, though these tend to be rather larger plants. For any good soil in sun or part-shade, and easily deadheaded by pulling off the spent stems. Raised by Bonne Ruys of Holland from seed of G. pratense from A.T. Johnson and perhaps a hybrid with G. himalayense. ‡ 18 in (45 cm). Z4–8 H8–1

G. 'Jolly Bee' Exceptionally vigorous sprawler suitable for large-scale ground cover. The paired mid-green leaves are about 4 in (10 cm) across, less toward the extremities of the plant, cut three-quarters of the way into five divisions, each with a lobe to either side, all with a few rather blunt teeth. The foliage is marbled with pale flecks below each notch around the margin and also at the junction of the larger veins. The

saucer-shaped, 2-in (5-cm) flowers open from early summer to mid-fall, in rich campanula blue with a white center, each petal having about five radiating purple veins. Suited to any soil in sun or part-shade; its size and tendency to swamp neighbors can be a limitation. Much confused with the very similar G. Rozanne. A hybrid of G. wallichianum 'Buxton's Variety' and G. shikokianum var. yoshiianum raised by Dutch horticulturist Marco van Noort. ‡ 24 in (60 cm). Z4–8 H8–1

G. 'Joy' Evergreen, sprawling, mound-forming plant; marbled leaves cut about three-quarters of the way into five divisions, usually with one lobe to each side, all edged with a few blunt teeth. Cupped, pale mauve-pink flowers, beautiful at close range, with about seven, radiating purplish red veins on each petal; from early to late summer but seldom in great profusion. For well-drained soil in sun; propagate by division or basal cuttings. A hybrid of G. lambertii and G. traversii var. elegans raised by Englishman Alan Bremner. Named for Geranium specialist and author Joy Jones. ‡ 18 in (45 cm). Z5–8 H8–5

G. 'Kashmir Blue' syn. G. clarkei 'Kashmir Blue' Dissected leaves are cut almost to the base into seven divisions, each rather deeply lobed and sharply toothed. The dished, outward-facing, soft campanula-blue flowers open from late spring to midsummer and have a white center and colorless, slightly feathered veins that appear grayish against a dark background. For any good garden soil in sun or part-shade; adequate moisture and frequent replanting help prevent mildew. A hybrid between two white-flowered plants, G. pratense subsp. pratense f. albiflorum and G. clarkei 'Kashmir White', it generally resembles G. pratense. ‡ 24 in (60 cm). Z5–8 H8–5

G. 'Kashmir Green' syn. G. clarkei 'Kashmir Green', G. 'Piet's White' Rather sprawling plant with pale stems and feathery dark green leaves cut almost to the base into seven narrow

divisions, each further cut into narrow lobes with a few pointed teeth. In sun, the margins of the leaves sometimes roll inward, contrasting the apple green undersides with the darker upper surface. The flowers, in late spring and early summer, shade from pure white to a green-tinted center, each almond-shaped petal having about seven lightly feathered translucent veins that appear grayish against a dark background. The flowers have a slightly untidy outline but the contrast of the cool white blooms with the holly-green leaves is effective. For sun or part-shade, with adequate soil moisture. Staking prevents flower stems from collapsing outward. A hybrid of G. clarkei and G. pratense introduced by Coen Jansen of Holland. ‡ 22 in (55 cm). Z5–8 H8–5

G. 'Khan' syn. G. 'Wisley Hybrid' Very spreading; the vibrant green leaves age darker and are divided three-quarters or more of the way into five divisions, each with two lobes that may be untoothed or have one or two teeth. The magenta-purple, 1¾ in (4.5 cm) flowers have petals with a shallow notch at the tip and about five deep red-purple veins; they open from early to late summer. For any reasonable soil in sun. Propagate by division or basal cuttings. Resembling a large G. sanguineum, from the garden of Allan Robinson, formerly of the RHS Garden at Wisley, England. ‡ 18 in (45 cm). Z5–8 H8–5

G. kishtvariense Bushy, with slowly creeping rhizomes; the bright green, wrinkled basal leaves are cut about two-thirds or more of the way into three to five rhomboid, toothed divisions. The stems have swollen nodes and smaller leaves, becoming paired up the plant and three-lobed, with the central lobe dominating. The flowers, from early summer to early fall, vary in color from shocking pink to rich mauve or lilac, and the petals, their surface with the finish of glossy lipstick, have five or seven narrow, slightly feathered, red-purple veins and a white V-shaped mark at the base. Not easy to grow, and not sufficiently floriferous to be showy, though the flowers are beautiful at close range. Prefers a well-drained but moisture-retentive soil in

part-shade. Introduced by English horticulturist Roy Lancaster. From Kashmir. ‡ 12 in (30 cm). Z6–9 H9–6

G. lambertii syn. G. grevilleanum Moderately hairy sprawler with rather sparingly borne, nodding flowers whose beauty is best appreciated at close range. The few, rather wrinkled basal leaves are cut just beyond halfway into five divisions, each lobed and further toothed, the tips of the lobes and teeth being sharply pointed. The stem leaves are paired and similar but rather smaller. The nodding, saucer-shaped flowers open from midsummer to early fall and may be pink or white, sometimes with a deep rose or crimson stain at the center; the anthers are black. For moist soil in part-shade; it seems to flourish and flower more freely when allowed to scramble over shrubs. From the Himalaya, from central Nepal to Bhutan and adjacent Tibet. ‡ 12–18 in (30–45 cm). Z5–8 H8–5. **'Swansdown'** White, more strongly inverted flowers with a deep rose or crimson stain at the base. Less prolific, but even more beautiful. Comes true from seed.

G. libani syn. G. peloponnesiacum var. libanoticum Summer-dormant, spreading by rhizomes, flowering with the later spring bulbs in mid- and late spring, then dying back until its foliage reappears in fall. The leaves are glossy mid-green above, differentiating it from its close relative G. peloponnesiacum, which has hairy foliage, and cut three-quarters or more into five or seven rather open divisions and further lobed and toothed to give a broken outline. The lavender flowers have about five indistinct veins on each heart-shaped petal and are sometimes paler at the center. For sun or part-shade and happy under deciduous trees. The plant leaves a gap after flowering that can be filled by sprawling neighbors or annuals. From Lebanon, western Syria and south-central Turkey. ‡ 16 in (40 cm). Z6–9 H9–5

G. 'Little Gem' A compact plant, the leaves are bluish-green, slightly downy and cut two-thirds of the way or more toward the base into five to seven divisions, usually three-lobed, all with a few blunt teeth. The stem leaves are borne in pairs. Bright magenta-pink flowers are borne in profusion from late spring to midsummer with some later blooms. Best in well-drained

LEFT 1 *Geranium* 'Johnson's Blue'
2 *G.* 'Kashmir Blue'

though not very dry soil, in sun; prone to die during winter. Propagate by division or basal cuttings. A hybrid of *G. x oxonianum* and *G. traversii* raised by Alan Bremner of England and much smaller than others of this parentage. ↕6 in (15 cm). Z5–8 H8–5

G. macrorrhizum Spreading, sticky, semievergreen, famously aromatic perennial, with thick underground rhizomes and, above ground, stout, persistent, sprawling stems. The whole plant is covered with minute sticky hairs, plus longer hairs both with and without pinhead glands at their tips. The mid-green leaves are divided two-thirds or more of the way to the base into seven divisions, each has spreading lobes on its outer half, each with a few usually blunt teeth. The foliage can take on attractive fall tints. In late spring and early summer, more or less upright stems hold densely arranged, usually magenta-pink, ¾–1¼-in (18–30-mm) flowers, each emerging from a red-tinged, inflated calyx, well above the foliage. From the center of the more or less vertical petals, the long filaments swoop downward, sometimes extending beyond the bottom of the flower and often turning up at the tips. Suitable for large-scale ground cover or underplanting, and tolerant of wide range of conditions, including drought, in sun or shade. Forms a dense mat and tends to spread inexorably outward, so needs occasional reduction. From the southern Alps, Apennines, Balkan Peninsula, and Carpathians. ↕12–18 in (30–45 cm). Z4–8 H8–1. **'Album'** Plentiful white flowers with the faintest blush of pink, with a pink eye and pink filaments, emerging from a strongly red-brown calyx. Rather less spreading than usual. Collected by Englishman Walter Ingwersen in Bulgaria. ↕16 in (40 cm). **'Bevan's Variety'** Rather large, vibrant, magenta-pink flowers with veined petals, clashing slightly with the red-brown calyx. Floriferous, though tends to flower most freely on the outside of the clump. Collected by Dr. Roger Bevan and introduced by Elizabeth Strangman of England. ↕16 in (40 cm). **'Czakor'** Vibrant magenta-pink flowers from red-brown calyces on reddish flower stems, like 'Bevan's Variety' but with fewer, larger, flatter flowers. Introduced by Dr. Hans Simon from the Czakor Gorge, Montenegro. ↕16 in (40 cm). **'Ingwersen's Variety'** Light pink flowers with contrasting rich pink filaments accompany lighter green, slightly glossy leaves. Collected by Walter Ingwersen in Montenegro. ↕16 in (40 cm). **'Lohfelden'** Compact, with small, blush pink flowers with darker veins and filaments, resembling *G. x cantabrigiense*. ↕14 in (35 cm). **'Pindus'** Low-growing, small, hairless plant; its magenta-pink flowers with scarlet filaments emerge from a large, glossy sealing-wax-red calyx. Collected by Bill Baker in the Pindus Mountains, Greece. ↕12 in (30 cm). **'Ridsko'** Magenta-pink flowers and rather glossy, rounder, deciduous leaves. ↕14 in (35 cm). **'Snow Sprite'** Pure white flowers, each with a green calyx and petals a little larger and more

overlapping than in 'White-Ness' (*below*). ↕12 in (30 cm). **'Spessart'** White flowers with a brownish calyx, similar to 'Album' but with larger, more overlapping petals. A pink-flowered plant is sometimes wrongly grown under this name. Introduced by Dr. Hans Simon and named for the Spessart Mountains, Germany. ↕16 in (40 cm). **'Variegatum'** Less vigorous, with mauve-pink flowers and leaves edged cream and overlaid with gray-green. Foliage can look distorted if grown in poor, dry soil in sun, but can be quite handsome in moist, dappled shade. ↕14 in (35 cm). **'White-Ness'** Floriferous, with rather small, pure white flowers emerging from pale green calyces. Named for the University of Liverpool Botanic Gardens, Ness, England. ↕12 in (30 cm).

G. macrostylum **'Leonidas'** syn. *G. tuberosum* 'Leonidas' This cultivar is a tuberous plant, the basal leaves cut almost to the base into five or seven divisions that have numerous narrow, toothed or entire lobes almost throughout their length, giving a feathery effect. Stem leaves are similar and paired. It differs from *G. tuberosum* in having red-tipped pinhead hairs, in being in leaf from fall through to spring, and in having tiny, elongated tubers. In 'Leonidas', the large, saucer-shaped flowers, appearing on upright stems in mid- and late spring, have bright mauve-pink, notched and ruffled petals, with darker veins slightly feathered at the tips. Prefers well-drained soil in sun. Can be weedy, since its tiny tubers are so easily scattered. Propagate by separating and replanting the tubers. Collected by Antoine Hoog in Greece. ↕16 in (40 cm). Z5–8 H8–5

G. maculatum (Spotted cranesbill) Sparsely leafy and upright, growing from a compact rootstock. Basal leaves are cut almost to the base into five or sometimes seven widely separate divisions, with spreading, toothed lobes. Tips of the lobes and the teeth are sharply pointed. The few stem leaves are paired and widely spaced, decreasing in size up the stem. The common name refers to the faint pale spots sometimes seen on the mid-green leaves. Flowering in late spring and early summer, sometimes reblooming in fall, the upward-facing, saucer-shaped flowers are usually pale mauve-pink, rarely deeper pink, lilac, or lavender, with a white eye and faint veins. For sun or part-shade, in any good soil that is not dry. Dark-leaved kinds color best in sun. From most of eastern North America, from Quebec south to Alabama. ↕20–28 in (50–70 cm). Z4–8 H8–1. **f. *albiflorum*** syn. var. *album* Rather paler leaves and pure white flowers with transparent veins that appear grayish. Comes true from seed if grown in isolation. ↕24 in (60 cm). **'Beth Chatto'** Large, pale lilac flowers with a central white zone and a green

RIGHT **1** *Geranium macrorrhizum* 'Ingwersen's Variety' **2** *G. macrorrhizum* 'Variegatum' **3** *G. maculatum*

LEFT 1 *Geranium maderense*
2 *G.* x *magnificum*
3 *G.* 'Mavis Simpson'

veins. The flowers of *G. palmatum*, with which it is sometimes confused, lack these veins and are closer to a primary pink. Enjoys full sun with frost protection and can be grown in a large container, but needs frequent transplanting to prevent a check to growth. Raise from seed. From Madeira. ‡3¼ ft (1 m). Z8–9 H9–8

G. x **magnificum** Vigorous and very hairy; the leaves are cut to about two-thirds into about seven overlapping divisions, each lobed and the lobes toothed. Flowers, produced in great profusion for a short time in early summer, are dished, lavender-blue shading to lilac in the center, and with purple veins, often with a notch at the end of the petal. There are many types, some named, though the individual cultivars are hard to identify. For any reasonable soil in sun or part-shade. Some plants flop and are best staked. New foliage quickly appears if plants are sheared after flowering. A sterile hybrid between *G. ibericum* subsp. *ibericum* and *G. platypetalum*, sometimes mistakenly sold as *G. platypetalum*. Grown at the Botanic Garden of Geneva, Switzerland as early as 1871. ‡20–30 in (50–75 cm). Z4–8 H8–1. **'Peter Yeo'** Leaf divisions are not, or only slightly, overlapping, are more abruptly tapered beyond the middle of the division, and only shallowly lobed. Flowers are not obviously clustered and are outward-facing with overlapping petals, rather bluer than lavender. Close to *G. platypetalum*. Once informally referred to as "Wisley Variety" and occasionally seen under this name. ‡30 in (75 cm). **'Rosemoor'** Relatively compact with deeply notched, heart-shaped, lavender-blue petals just touching, scarcely overlapping. The best cultivar, less inclined to flop and with some later bloom. ‡24 in (60 cm).

G. malviflorum A tuberous species, the foliage usually emerges in fall and dies away in summer, each leaf having seven overlapping divisions, these deeply lobed along both sides of the midrib. Lower lobes have teeth, the upper ones sometimes lack them. Flowers are lilac to violet (a glowing violet is often seen), paler toward the center, with about five lightly feathered, deep purple veins on each petal. Similar to *G. tuberosum* but with larger leaves; sometimes sold as *G. atlanticum*. Best in full sun with good drainage; tolerates nutrient-poor soils. Can be used much like spring bulbs, using annuals or neighboring plants to occupy the space in summer. From southern Spain, Morocco, and Algeria. ‡12 in (30 cm). Z7–9 H9–7

G. 'Mary Mottram' Compact, neat and free-flowering. Pure white flowers, with a pale green eye, age to pale blush pink at the tips of the narrow petals and are held well above the mid-green leaves from late spring to midsummer, with some later bloom if clipped back

after the first flush. For sun or part-shade in any reasonable soil. A hybrid between *G. endressii* and *G. sylvaticum* 'Album'. ‡16 in (40 cm). Z5–8 H8–5

G. 'Mavis Simpson' syn. *G.* x *riversleaianum* 'Mavis Simpson' Exceptionally long-flowering, semievergreen, sprawling ground cover. The flowers, from early summer to mid-fall, have rose pink petals with a silvery sheen, slightly paler toward the center, and faint magenta veins. Leaves are slightly grayish and rather downy, cut into five to seven divisions with reddish brown marks at the base of the notches between. The stem leaves are borne in pairs on a very spreading plant. Prefers sun and good drainage. Propagate by division or basal cuttings. Prone to winter losses, as much in a mild winter as a harsh one, probably caused by fungal disease. A hybrid of *G.* x *oxonianum* and *G. traversii* var. *elegans*, found as a chance seedling on the Rock Garden at Kew, England and named for one of Kew's gardeners. ‡8 in (20 cm). Z6–8 H8–6

G. x **monacense** A variable, upright plant, its basal leaves, with or without brown blotches, are cut about two-thirds into seven divisions that are shallowly lobed and toothed. The rather small, downward-tilted flowers open in late spring and early summer and with their backswept petals resemble a *Dodecatheon*. They are a dark, dull purplish red or dusky mauve with a white basal zone, above which is a dull bluish violet zone crossed by darker veins. Some selections have very attractively zoned and marked flowers and are worth growing where they can be seen at close quarters. Seems to set fertile seed. For sun or shade in any reasonable soil. A hybrid of *G. phaeum* and *G. reflexum* grown by E. A. Bowles of England and sometimes sold as *G. punctatum*. ‡24–48 in (60–120 cm). Z4–8 H8–1. **var. anglicum** Mauve flowers have a narrow whitish petal base and a broad, slaty, violet-blue zone above, crossed with conspicuous veins. The leaves are usually unblotched, with long, narrow divisions. It is a hybrid of *G. phaeum* var. *lividum* and *G. reflexum*. **'Muldoon'** Leaves have strongly blotched leaf notches and usually dusky purple flowers. It was once circulated as '*G. punctatum* hort,' the name has also been misapplied to *G. phaeum* 'Variegatum'. It refers to the character Spotty Muldoon, invented by comedians Peter Cook and Dudley Moore and immortalized in a gloriously inane eponymous ballad. ‡32 in (80 cm).

G. nepalense var. **thunbergii** see *G. thunbergii*

G. 'Nicola' Vigorous, long-flowering plant; basal leaves cut three-quarters to the base into five to seven divisions. The rich magenta-pink flowers, from late spring to late summer, have petals shallowly notched at the tip, a paler zone toward the base, and a deep red-purple, near-black V at the bottom, with about five feathered veins in the

eye borne on red flower stalks. the leaves are vibrant mid-green with five to seven straplike divisions. Named by Coen Jansen for the Essex, England author and gardener. ‡24 in (60 cm). **'Elizabeth Ann'** Lilac, outward-facing, flat, rather large flowers with a greenish white center above chocolate-flushed leaves with five straplike divisions. A handsome plant developed by Maryland's Carol Tyssowski. ‡24 in (60 cm). **'Espresso'** Dark leaves with five narrowly rhombus-shaped divisions and rather small, mauve flowers with a whitish green center. Found by Dale Hendricks of North Creek Nurseries, PA, in his local woods. ‡24 in (60 cm). **'Heronswood Gold'** Gold leaves hold their color well through the season. A selection from Dan Hinkley, Heronswood Nursery, WA. ‡12 in (30 cm). Z5–8 H8–5

'Vickie Lynn' Cupped, soft lilac flowers with a white center are borne above glossy leaves with seven broad divisions, making the leaf appear more

solid in outline. Foliage turns brilliant orange in fall. ‡20 in (50 cm).

G. maderense A gigantic, aromatic rosette that tends to die after flowering, this is one of the few cranesbills that is dramatically architectural. The single stout stalk is succulent when young, becoming woody by flowering time, and about 24 in (60 cm) high. The leaves, borne on long, thick, succulent stalks, are the largest of any species, up to 24 in (60 cm) wide, and cut into five divisions, the central one stalked. Lobes are cut to the midrib of the divisions and are themselves lobed and toothed. As flowering approaches, the older leaves wither but their stalks remain, angled downward and propping up the plant in a very distinctive manner. The flowers are produced on a short central stalk from the center of the rosette, bearing one or two clusters of branches that fork repeatedly to produce a dome of color. The individual flowers are mauve with a darker reddish purple center and pronounced reddish-purple

LEFT **1** *Geranium* 'Nimbus'
2 *G. nodosum*

same color radiating toward the tip. The petals do not touch, giving the flower a starry appearance. Prefers sun and adequate moisture; benefits from staking. A hybrid of *G. psilostemon* and *G. x oxonianum* raised by Englishman Alan Bremner. ↕ 24 in (60 cm). Z5–8 H8–5

G. 'Nimbus' Extremely vigorous and floriferous ground cover. The basal leaves, emerging yellow-flushed before becoming mid-green, are cut into about seven divisions and deeply lobed, giving a heavily dissected effect. The rather large, lavender-blue flowers with a white center and purple veins have petals not overlapping, touching only at the base, and open from early to late summer. A hybrid of *G. clarkei* and *G. collinum* found at the University of Cambridge Botanic Garden in England. ↕ 3¼ ft (1 m). Z5–8 H8–5

G. nodosum Upright, with elongated rhizomes at or just below the soil surface. Bright green, rather glossy basal leaves are cut by about two-thirds into three or five divisions that are scarcely lobed but evenly toothed, except at the base. The stem leaves are paired, mostly with three divisions, decreasing in size up the stem. Flowers, from early to late summer, are of average size, sparsely produced, and mauve-pink to magenta, usually with a paler zone at the center and three radiating dark reddish-purple, scarcely feathered veins. The petals are deeply notched or, more rarely, irregularly lobed. Good ground cover without being unduly invasive, and valuable for woodland or the wild garden. For sun or shade, and moist or dry soil—an adaptable plant. Divide or raise from seed; the cultivars breed more or less true if grown in isolation. From mountain woodlands from central France to the Pyrenees, to central Italy and central former Yugoslavia. ↕ 8–20 in (20–50 cm). Z4–8 H8–1. **'Svelte Lilac'** Mauve flowers with a satin sheen, paler at the center, with petals touching or overlapping slightly with three dark reddish purple slightly feathered veins. A fairly common variant recognized and named by Monksilver Nursery of Cambridgeshire, England, but becoming rather variable.

↕ 18 in (45 cm). **'Swish Purple'** Starry flowers have elongated heart-shaped petals, rich magenta-pink at the tip shading to pale lilac at the base, with three to five slightly feathered, red-purple veins. Another frequently grown variant recognized and named by Monksilver Nursery of Cambridgeshire, England. ↕ 18 in (45 cm). **'Whiteleaf'** Dark-leaved; the marbled magenta and magenta-pink petals are traversed by three smudgy deep magenta veins on each petal. The petals are edged palest mauve, with irregular lobing around the tips. ↕ 14 in (35 cm).

G. 'Nunwood Purple' syn. *G. pratense* 'Nunwood Purple' Spreading with large flowers. Mid-green basal leaves are cut almost to the base into seven divisions and further lobed and toothed. Large, dished flowers in lavender, shading to lilac toward the center and with a whitish eye, appear in late spring and early summer. Each petal has about seven lightly feathered deep purple veins. The flowers become more purple before the petals are shed. A hybrid of *G. pratense* subsp. *pratense* f. *albiflorum* and *G. himalayense* 'Gravetye' raised by John Ross of Scotland's Charter House Nursery. ↕ 18 in (45 cm). Z5–7 H7–5

G. oreganum Upright plant growing from a compact rootstock. Basal leaves are cut nearly to the base into seven divisions with several deep-cut lobes on either side, each with few or several teeth. Stem leaves are paired, decreasing rapidly in size after the first few pairs. Flowers are up to 2 in (5 cm) across, upward-facing and saucer-shaped, borne in a diffuse display in early summer and midsummer, vary in color from pale mauve pink to almost magenta with a paler center, or to lavender-blue. Most garden forms have deep magenta-pink flowers. Similar to *G. pratense* but the leaves look more coarsely cut. Good in borders or wildflower meadows, in sun or part-shade. From the western US. ↕ 24 in (60 cm). Z5–7 H7–5

G. 'Orion' A superlative, very spreading plant suitable for ground cover with plentiful bloom over a long

period. Basal leaves are cut almost to the base into seven divisions and again deeply lobed, giving a very dissected appearance. The stem leaves are very divided, becoming smaller up the plant. The plentiful, very large, lavender-blue flowers have purple veins, a white center, and almost round, overlapping petals, and are borne from early to late summer. A seedling of *G.* 'Brookside'. ↕ 32 in (80 cm). Z5–8 H8–5

G. 'Orkney Pink' Compact, cushion-forming plant for the front of the border. The few semievergreen basal leaves are similar to the paired stem leaves: minutely downy, bluish-green slightly flushed bronze, cut halfway or a little more into seven divisions and scarcely lobed but evenly toothed. The bright magenta-pink flowers with a white eye are borne profusely in late spring and continue less prolifically until first frosts. For well-drained soil in sun, but dislikes drought. Propagate by division or basal cuttings. A hybrid of *G. x antipodeum* and *G. x oxonianum* raised by Englishman Alan Bremner. ↕ 6 in (15 cm). Z5–8 H8–5

G. x oxonianum (Druce's cranesbill) Leafy, sometimes downy or hairy plant best used as ground cover and in the wild garden. The basal leaves are more or less wrinkled and cut almost to the base into about five divisions and further lobed. The notches between the divisions are sometimes stained reddish-brown. The ⅜–1½ in (1.5–4 cm), usually funnel-shaped flowers may be white to rich magenta-pink, often with a network of deeper veins. The best garden selections, made for extra flower size, long season, attractive petal markings, good foliage, or neat habit, usually far exceed the typical species in appeal. The spread varies from about 18 in (45 cm) to almost 6½ ft (2 m): the broadest are clearly too big for small gardens but many make good ground cover. Most flower from early summer to midsummer; some start in late spring, others continue until mid-fall. Best in dappled shade with adequate moisture; some will tolerate full sun, others have petals that bleach unattractively. A tricky group: some cultivars are so similar that they are difficult to distinguish, and some are represented in gardens and nurseries by incorrect plants, probably seedlings. A fertile hybrid of *G. endressii* and *G. versicolor*, occurring in the wild

A CHOICE OF G. x OXONIANUM

Geranium x oxonianum 'Lace Time'

Geranium x oxonianum 'Rebecca Moss'

Geranium x oxonianum 'Rose Clair'

Geranium x oxonianum 'Rosenlicht'

Geranium x oxonianum f. thurstonianum

Geranium x oxonianum 'Walter's Gift'

wherever the parents are native but also becoming naturalized in France and the British Isles. ‡ 12–32 in (30–80 cm). Z4–8 H8–1. **'A. T. Johnson'** Compact and long-flowering; the flowers open silvery pink with faint darker veins, deepening a little with age, and appear over a shorter season. Plants with salmon pink flowers are sometimes incorrectly grown under the name. Selected by A. T. Johnson and introduced by Walter Ingwersen of England. ‡ 12 in (30 cm). **'Ankum's White'** Spreading plant with the leaves darkly notched between the divisions, and plentiful, almost pure white flowers with faint gray veins. Petals roll back at the tips, giving an irregular outline. The most prolific white-flowered form. Introduced by Coen Jansen, the name commemorates his home village in Holland. ‡ 18 in (45 cm). **'Anmore'** Light, olive-green foliage; very light pink flowers. A beautiful and vigorous selection from the garden of Phoebe Noble, distributed by The Perennial Gardens, Maple Ridge, British Columbia. ‡ 15 in (38 cm). Z4–8 H8–1. **'Beholder's Eye'** syn. *G. endressii* 'Beholder's Eye' Plentiful, small, vibrant deep pink flowers approaching magenta on a neatly domed, small-leaved, spreading plant. Exceptionally neat and attractive. ‡ 18 in (45 cm). **'Betty Catchpole'** see *G. endressii* 'Betty Catchpole'. **'Breckland Sunset'** Vigorous, spreading, useful for ground cover, with pale stems and small-veined flowers in mauve-pink, deepening with age. Flowers bleach in full sun. ‡ 16 in (40 cm). **'Bregover Pearl'** Spreading and long-flowering; rather small, silvery mauve-pink, faintly veined flowers deepen with age, the petals turning back at the tip. ‡ 16 in (40 cm). **'Bressingham's Delight'** Floriferous, with rather small, salmon-pink flowers, the tips of the petals tending to roll back. Retention of the dead petals slightly mars the effect. Introduced by Blooms of Bressingham. ‡ 16 in (40 cm). **'Claridge Druce'** Common,

vigorous, and represented by many similar but not identical clones, this downy plant has slightly blue-green leaves and large mauve-pink flowers with a pronounced network of purple veins. Effective ground cover, but not the showiest or most refined. Commemorates Oxford, England botanist George Claridge Druce, who first noticed this hybrid. ‡ 12–32 in (30–80 cm). **'Cream Chocolate'** Spreading plant with pale rose pink flowers and green leaves heavily overlaid with chocolate brown. ‡ 18 in (45 cm). **'Frank Lawley'** Large, pale mauve-pink flowers with faint darker veins and a satin sheen; petals are narrow, giving a open effect. Found by Robin Moss and introduced by Axletree Nursery in England. ‡ 18 in (45 cm). **'Hexham White'** Spreading; foliage darkly notched between divisions; white flowers of average size, with only the faintest hint of blush at the tip of the petals, open on slender stems well above foliage. Clean and elegant; from Robin Moss. ‡ 18 in (45 cm). **'Hollywood'** Robust, downy plant with bright green foliage and large, plentiful, pale pink flowers with a network of purple veins, borne over a long period. A back-cross to *G. versicolor* introduced by the Essex, England nursery Langthorns Plantery. ‡ 24 in (60 cm). **'Julie Brennan'** Downy plant with deep green leaves and large, mauve, rather narrow-petaled flowers with a pronounced network of purple veins. Probably a seedling of 'Claridge Druce', from Judith Bradshaw. ‡ 28 in (70 cm). **'Katherine Adele'** Leaves cut into five more or less rhomboid divisions, heavily flushed chocolate except at the edges. Flowers rather small, pale mauve-pink with magenta veins and with a white center veined gray. A seedling of 'Walter's Gift'. ‡ 16 in (40 cm). **'Kurt's Variegated'** see 'Spring Fling'. **'Lace Time'** Spreading plant with foliage shaded yellow when young. Near-white, rather small flowers aging to pink are overlaid with network of dark

veins. Introduced by Croftway Nursery in Sussex, England. ‡ 16 in (40 cm). **'Lady Moore'** A vigorous, spreading plant with rather small mauve flowers with a network of purple veins. Given by Lady Moore to Margery Fish but not named until after Mrs. Fish's death. ‡ 24 in (60 cm). **'Lambrook Gillian'** Rather small, pale mauve-pink, faintly veined flowers on a spreading plant. From the garden at East Lambrook Manor, Dorset. ‡ 20 in (50 cm). **'Laura Skelton'** Extravagantly marked, with elongated white petals in a trumpet shape and overlaid with a very bold network of mauve-purple veins leaving an unmarked white edge. Very striking. ‡ 18 in (45 cm). **'Lutzie'** Large, deep pink flower, a white throat, and deep red-rose veins. A seedling 'Claridge Druce' raised by The Perennial Gardens, Maple Ridge, British Columbia. ‡ 24 in (60 cm). Z4–8 H8–1 **'Meryl Anne'** Spreading, long-flowering plant with rather glossy, light green foliage and large, rose pink, satin-sheened flowers aging to deeper pink, the petals curled back at the edges. ‡ 20 in (50 cm). **'Miriam Rundle'** Compact, with almost evergreen foliage emerging yellowish green, aging darker, and producing vibrant magenta-pink flowers, paler at the center and base of heart-shaped petals and with deeper veins. Introduced by David Hibberd of England. ‡ 12 in (30 cm). **'Old Rose'** Medium-sized, pale mauve-pink, magenta-veined flowers from late spring to late summer deepen with age to near-magenta. A hybrid of 'A. T. Johnson' and *G. versicolor* introduced by David Hibberd. ‡ 16 in (40 cm). **'Pearl Boland'** Pale mauve pink flowers with magenta veins, a silvery sheen, and a paler eye, deepening with age. Remains neat and attractive over a long period. ‡ 16 in (40 cm). **'Phoebe Noble'** Small but intensely colored flowers in magenta-pink with deeper veins, borne on a sprawling plant for a long season. ‡ 20 in (50 cm). **'Prestbury Blush'** A dense-growing, long-flowering cultivar with small, pale blush flowers. ‡ 16 in

ABOVE *Geranium* 'Patricia'

(40 cm). **'Rebecca Moss'** Spreading plant with very pale pink, glistening flowers of average size, faintly veined greenish gray, aging to rose pink, the petals slightly deeper pink at the margins. Selected by Robin Moss of England. ‡ 18 in (45 cm). **'Rose Clair'** A compact form selected by A. T. Johnson and introduced by Englishman Walter Ingwersen, who described the flowers as "a clear rose-salmon with just a trace of veining." Several plants with flowers not matching that description have been distributed under the name, including cyclamen red *G.* x *oxonianum* 'Rødbylund'. The true plant may be lost. ‡ 18 in (45 cm). **'Rosenlicht'** syn. *G. endressii* 'Rosenlicht' Spreading but fairly neat, producing deep magenta-pink flowers of average size from early to late summer. ‡ 18 in (45 cm). **'Spring Fling'** syn. 'Kurt's Variegated' Compact, with leaves emerging broadly edged cream and flushed pink, becoming yellowish green, with dark reddish marks at the base of the notches between the leaf divisions. Produces rather sparse, small pink flowers. Introduced by Bob Brown, Cotswold Garden Flowers, England. ‡ 14 in (35 cm). **'Summer Surprise'** Floriferous, spreading, downy plant with very large, vibrant mauve-pink flowers with faint veins. Plants tend to open out unless staked. Raised by Piet Oudolf. ‡ 20 in (50 cm) in Holland. **f.** *thurstonianum* syn. *G. endressii* var. *thurstonianum* Petals narrowed to just ⅛–¼ in (3–6 mm), sometimes quilled or fluted, pink to magenta-purple, usually with a network of darker veins. the stamens may become like petals, producing double flowers. Apart from the flower shape, this form embraces the full range of variation of the species. A variable plant, more interesting than beautiful, that occurs sporadically where both parent species are found or as a seedling of *G.* x *oxonianum*. ‡ 12–32 in (30–80 cm). **f.** *thurstonianum* **'Sherwood'** Strap-shaped, ½–¼ in (12 x 5 mm) petals, scrolled back at the edges, are mauve-pink at the tip with deeper veins, and white at the base.

LEFT *Geranium palmatum*

Raised by Alan Bremner. ‡28 in (70 cm) in England. **f. _thurstonianum_ 'Southcombe Double'** Slow-growing, with small, starry, carmine-pink flowers veined darker; usually double, though single flowers are sometimes produced for part of the season. ‡18 in (45 cm). **f. _thurstonianum_ 'Southcombe Star'** Vigorous, with small, carmine-pink, narrow-petaled flowers veined purple, double early in the season. Introduced by Trevor Wood of Southcombe Garden Plants, England. ‡22 in (55 cm). **'Trevor's White'** Spreading plant with light green leaves and white flowers of average size, the petals tipped pale blush-pink, borne over a long period. From Englishman Trevor Bath. ‡18 in (45 cm). **'Walter's Gift'** Small, pale pink, near-white flowers are veined magenta, aging to rose pink; leaves have a large central blotch of chocolate-brown. Seed-raised plants may have the blotch much reduced or missing. Commemorates horticulturist Mary Ramsdale's former home in Essex, England. ‡16 in (40 cm). **'Wageningen'** syn. _G. endressii_ 'Wageningen' Superlative, rather downy, upright plant close to _G. endressii_ with glistening rich salmon flowers over a long period from early summer to mid-fall; unfortunately, they bleach in strong sun. Found by Dr. Hans Simon of Germany. 18 in (40 cm). **'Wargrave Pink'** syn. _G. endressii_ 'Wargrave Variety' Vigorous, with glistening salmon pink flowers of average size, bleaching with age. ‡20 in (50 cm). **'Winscombe'** Compact, the average-sized flowers open silvery rose pink aging to deep rose, giving a two-toned effect; they also become more noticeably veined with age. Good for small-scale planting. Discovered by Margery Fish in the Somerset garden, England of this name. Introduced by Elizabeth Strangman. ‡12 in (30 cm).

G. palmatum syn. _G. anemonifolium_ A succulent species in its first year when it is prone to dying out in winter; the rootstock becomes woody and very perennial if it survives. Leaves are up to 10 in (25 cm) across, divided into five, the central division stalked, the others with short or no stalks, each division lobed almost to the base and again lobed and toothed. The leaves are borne on long, stout stalks, radiating to form a gigantic rosette, and these are retained after the leaf blade withers, propping up the plant. The much-branched flowering display forms an imposing dome above the foliage from early to late summer, each flower having rich pink (tending to mauve), almond-shaped petals shaded magenta at the base, not overlapping. Its first flowering is spectacular; in successive seasons, the woody rootstock gives rise to a number of smaller rosettes. For sun or part-shade. Old plants that have become comparatively shy-flowering are best replaced with seedlings. From Madeira. ‡5 ft (1.5 m). Z7–9 H9–7

G. palustre An adaptable, sprawling perennial with a compact rootstock, its bright green leaves are cut by about three-quarters into seven divisions that are rather deeply lobed, the lobes furnished with a few or no teeth. The stem leaves are paired and similar, decreasing in size toward the apex of the plant, with three or five divisions. The upward-facing, rather large flowers can be dished or widely trumpet-shaped, with petals either open or slightly overlapping, in vibrant mauve to magenta or lilac, with a small white eye and dark red-purple, slightly feathered veins. They appear over a long season from early summer to early fall. For sun or part-shade; will cope with wet soil but tolerates relatively dry conditions. From eastern and central Europe. ‡16 in (40 cm). Z5–8 H8–5

G. 'Patricia' Slightly sprawling, vigorous plant with large, rather rough-textured basal leaves cut by about two-thirds into five or seven divisions that are shallowly lobed, the lobes having a few or no teeth. The stem leaves are similar, paired and becoming smaller up the plant, the uppermost with three or five divisions. The broadly trumpet-shaped, shining magenta-pink flowers have petals barely touching or slightly overlapping, each with a glistening purple-red V at the base from which five lightly feathered veins of the same color run about three-quarters of the way toward the apex. They open in early summer and midsummer with some later bloom, especially if deadheaded. Benefits from staking. A hybrid of _G. endressii_ and _G. psilostemon_ raised by Englishman Alan Bremner; in effect, a shorter, less fiercely-colored alternative to _G. psilostemon_. ‡30 in (75 cm). Z4–8 H8–1

G. peloponnesiacum var. _libanoticum_ see _G. libani_

G. phaeum (Dusky cranesbill) Medium-sized and upright, with a stout rootstock on the soil surface; the stems are often dotted purple, sometimes even entirely blackish violet. The large basal leaves may be blotched or unblotched, cut by about two-thirds into seven or nine divisions that are rather shallowly lobed, the lobes each with two to five teeth. The flowers, appearing in late spring and early summer, are ¾–1¼ in (2–3 cm) across, nodding or horizontally held. The petals sometimes have a pointed tip and may be slightly reflexed; all with a whitish base, they may be lilac, pinkish, violet, maroon, or nearly black, the paler colors usually impure, grayish, or slaty. Dark-flowered variants are known by the common name "mourning widow," which may be invalidly styled as a cultivar name. A useful species for deep shade, but also happy in sun; those with variegated or yellow-green leaves thrive best in part-shade, and all prefer adequate moisture. From the mountains of southern and central Europe, and naturalized in many areas. ‡12–42 in (30–110 cm). Z4–8 H8–1. **'Album'** Large, outward-facing, flat, pure white flowers, with petal edges usually slightly crimped and ruffled. The petals overlap, giving a round outline. The bright green leaves are without dark blotches. ‡30 in (75 cm). **'Aureum'** _see_ 'Golden Spring'. **'Blauwvoet'** Pale green leaves and clean, pale lilac, rather large flowers, the petals slightly reflexed, smooth-edged and lightly ruffled, white toward

BELOW 1 _Geranium phaeum_
2 _G. phaeum_ 'Album'

STAKING GERANIUMS

Many geraniums flop if not supported. They fall outward, exposing a bare crown, or they lean sideways and fall into their neighbors. The most effective, and least obtrusive, support is by pea-staking. This staking method uses stout and twiggy tree branches worked through the clump before the basal foliage has reached its full height. It can be put in place early, and the leaves then hide the stakes as they develop. In time, a dome of flowers overtops the foliage and supports.

Taller species such as _G. pratense_ and its cultivars can be supported with branches of, for instance, filbert or birch. Large clumps of tall plants such as these can sometimes benefit from twine looped between the branches to create a matrix of support.

For species such as _G._ × _magnificum_, larger twigs work well and will especially be needed on fertile soil. Some, like the inherently sprawling 'Anne Thomson', can be supported on groups of tall branches. Various steel and plastic horizontal mesh supports are also effective, though some can be obtrusive.

One approach to avoid is the series of bamboo canes set in a ring around the clump with two tiers of twine making a constrictive enclosure. Not only is this obtrusive, but plants have a habit of leaning over one side.

the center with a ring of slaty veins. A sport of *G. phaeum* 'Album' named for the blue petrel, a bird symbolic of the Flemish people's struggle for cultural independence. ↕ 28 in (70 cm). **'Calligrapher'** Rather small, dusky pink petals, edged and shaded purple, with a ring of slaty purple veins around a white eye. The leaves have a chocolate blotch at the center of each division. Introduced by David Hibberd of England. ↕ 28 in (70 cm). **'Chocolate Chip'** Exceptionally dark satiny maroon, near-black, slightly nodding flowers with a small whitish eye open from mid-spring to early summer. Overlapping petals have a few irregular notches around the margin. Named by Robin Parer, Geraniaceae Nursery, CA. ↕ 3¼ ft (1 m). **'Golden Spring'** syn. 'Aureum' Rather shiny leaves with dark notches emerge yellow-green before becoming mid-green. Reflexed, nodding flowers, in mid- and late spring, are dusky deep mauve-pink with a slaty lavender zone and a starry white center traversed by gray veins. Raised by Robin Moss, and introduced by Judith Bradshaw. ↕ 18 in (45 cm). **'Lily Lovell'** Unblotched leaves emerge yellowish but become bright green, then, from late spring to midsummer, large, violet flowers nod only a little and have a white eye surrounded by a deep purple zigzagged line. The slightly reflexed petals touch or overlap only a little and have a slightly wavy margin. Introduced by Trevor Bath and named for his mother. ↕ 36 in (90 cm). **var. lividum** Usually with unblotched leaves; the flowers are often slightly reflexed, rather pale lavender, lilac, or pink, with a small white base. The lowest part of the colored zone is crossed by slaty-violet or lavender veins, smudged at their upper end and forming a bluish halo around the white eye. From Croatia westward along the south side of the Alps into France. ↕ 24–36 in (60–90 cm). **var. lividum 'Joan Baker'** Vigorous, with large, nodding, soft mauve-pink flowers, paler around the

DARK-LEAVED VARIANTS OF GERANIUM PRATENSE

All today's dark-leaved *G. pratense* variants are probably derived from a seed strain originally developed by San Francisco horticulturist Victor Reiter Jr. (1903–86). He gave it to Robin Parer of Geraniaceae Nursery, CA, who called it 'Victor Reiter'. As it embraces some variation it is not a distinct and uniform cultivar.

The dark-leaved types have reduced vigor, perhaps due to long-time inbreeding, and are mildew-prone. They need sun for best foliage color. The 16 in (40 cm) 'Victor Reiter' is seed-raised, but can produce green-leaved and dwarf plants that should not carry the name; the same may be true of 'Purple-haze'. Dwarf, 8 in (20 cm) dark-leaved plants are known as Midnight Reiter strain (the very dark-leaved 'Purple Heron' is a selection) and propagated by division. The taller Black Beauty ('Nodbeauty'), at 16 in (40 cm) is easier to grow than most, and less prone to mildew. 'New Dimension', 12 in (30 cm), and 'Hocus Pocus', 16 in (40 cm), should be divided. Choose good individual plants and propagate by division.

Geranium pratense 'Black Beauty'

Geranium pratense 'Midnight Reiter'

Geranium pratense 'Purple-haze'

Geranium pratense 'Victor Reiter'

edge of the lightly frilled, slightly reflexed petals and with a crown of slaty lilac veins around the eye. Collected by Bill Baker and named for his wife. ↕ 30 in (75 cm). **var. lividum 'Majus'** Vigorous, with unblotched leaves and slightly nodding and reflexed large, deep mauve flowers, becoming near white above the crown of slaty lavender veins that surrounds the eye. ↕ 32 in (80 cm). **'Margaret Wilson'** Compact, with pale stems and leaves netted with creamy yellow veins and edged creamy green. The flattish violet flowers have a white eye. Reputed to breed true from seed if grown in isolation. Introduced by David Hibberd.

↕ 16 in (40 cm). **'Mrs. Withey Price'** Foliage emerges bright yellow-green in spring, deepening to green, with small dark red blotches between the divisions. The light purple, flattish, slightly nodding flowers have a white center. A seedling from the Seattle garden of horticulturist Jerry Flintoff. ↕ 20 in (50 cm). **'Raven'** From Rainforest Gardens, Maple Ridge, British Colombia. A seedling selection of *G. phaeum* 'Lily Lovell'. Leaves mid-green and unblotched; flowers are purple-brown. Raised by The Perennial Gardens, Maple Ridge, British Columbia. ↕ 18 in (45 cm). Z4–8 H8–1. **'Rose Air'** Compact with, from late spring to

midsummer, slightly nodding and reflexed flowers in pale, dusky mauve-pink with a ring of slaty lavender veins around a white eye. Introduced by John Sirkett of Mallorn Gardens, Cornwall, England. ↕ 18 in (45 cm). **'Rose Madder'** Bold, light green leaves are darkly blotched between the divisions and have reddish brown spots scattered around the edge of the leaf. Nodding flowers are a curious dusky pinkish red (similar to raw meat that is just on the turn) with a slaty violet zone around a white eye, red-purple feathered veins running from this to the edge of the petals. Raised by Englishman Trevor Bath. ↕ 20 in (50 cm). **'Samobor'** Somberly handsome, upright selection with leaves with a broad chocolate zone. Nodding maroon flowers with obtusely pointed petals are borne on slender flower stalks from early summer to midsummer. Introduced by Elizabeth Strangman of England from Samobor, Croatia. ↕ 36 in (90 cm). **'Séricourt'** Very compact, with, from late spring to midsummer, bright yellow-green, almost pure yellow foliage and small, outward-facing maroon flowers with a white eye. Scorches in full sun but very showy in a shady spot. Said to come true from seed if grown in isolation. Found in the French village of Séricourt. Introduced by Bob Brown, Cotswold Garden Flowers, England. ↕ 12 in (30 cm). **'Springtime'** Leaves emerge heavily marbled with cream, less so at the leaf edges, and overlaid with a bold red zone. The nodding, slightly reflexed deep maroon flowers have a white eye. A chance seedling

LEFT 1 *Geranium phaeum* var. *lividum* 'Joan Baker' **2** *G. phaeum* 'Samobor' **3** *G.* 'Philippe Vapelle'

discovered by Dutch nurseryman Piet Oudolf. ‡24 in (60 cm). **'Stillingfleet Ghost'** Pale green, unblotched foliage and, from mid-spring to early summer, pale grayish mauve flowers with a central white eye and translucent veins appearing grayish. Unusual in lacking a darker zone around the eye. The gently reflexed petals are slightly frilled at their edges. Raised by Vanessa Cook of Yorkshire's Stillingfleet Lodge Nurseries, England. ‡24 in (60 cm). **'Taff's Jester'** Brown-blotched leaves are irregularly splashed with cream: sometimes half or whole leaf is without chlorophyll and often no variegation. Nodding, deep maroon-purple flowers with slightly reflexed petals open from late spring to midsummer. Found by variegated plant enthusiast Stephen Taffler of England. ‡28 in (70 cm). **'Variegatum'** Leaves unevenly edged cream and overlaid with gray green; dark red blotches between the divisions. Variegated areas may curl in dry conditions or in sun. Nodding flowers are deep maroon. ‡24 in (60 cm).

G. 'Philippe Vapelle' Hairy, spreading plant. Mid-green basal leaves, their hairs giving a blue-gray cast, are cut to about halfway into seven divisions, shallowly lobed and regularly toothed, giving a solid outline. Their surface is covered with a pronounced, even network of veins. Sparse flowers, in late spring and early summer, have pale lavender, heart-shaped petals with five prominent, feathered, deep lavender veins. Prefers sun; will tolerate drought. A hybrid of G. renardii and G. platypetalum. ‡16 in (40 cm). Z5–8 H8–5

G. 'Piet's White' see G. 'Kashmir Green'

G. 'Pink Delight' Cushion-forming, compact with minutely downy, blue-gray-green leaves that are cut about halfway toward the base into five divisions, only sparsely and shallowly further lobed or toothed. Flowers, from late spring to mid-fall, open pale pink, almost white around the edges of the petals, and age to mauve-pink. Red sepals remain after the petals are shed, adding to the display. Believed to be a hybrid of G. x antipodeum and G. x oxonianum and introduced by Jenny Spiller of Elworthy Cottage Plants, Somerset, England. ‡8 in (20 cm). Z5–8 H8–5

G. 'Pink Spice' see G. x antipodeum 'Pink Spice'

G. platyanthum syn. G. eriostemon Upright, hairy plant growing from a thick rootstock. The light green leaves, sometimes edged red, are cut to halfway or more into five to seven divisions with shallow, toothed lobes or merely unevenly toothed. The few stem leaves are similar with three or five divisions, solitary below but paired farther up the plant. Light violet-blue flowers, borne in dense clusters, are nodding or held horizontally, with petals spreading or sometimes slightly reflexed, with a white base. They appear for only a month between mid-spring

and early summer with some later bloom. Not the showiest species but with extremely handsome foliage that often colors well in fall. For sun or part-shade. From eastern Siberia to Tibet, China, Korea, and Japan. ‡24 in (60 cm). Z5–8 H8–5

G. platypetalum Hairy, with a thick, compact rootstock; the wrinkled basal leaves are rounded in outline and divided about halfway into seven or nine divisions, broadest near the apex, with lobes that are broader than they are long, usually with a tooth on either side. The stem leaves are usually paired, the upper ones with three or five divisions. Large flowers, in early summer, are flat or saucer-shaped and outward-facing, the petals lavender-blue, sometimes paler and tending to purple at the base, with about five feathered deep violet veins; they are notched or weakly three-lobed at the apex. Similar to G. ibericum, with which it has produced the hybrid G. x magnificum, but differing in its less deeply cut leaves. Will rebloom if deadheaded. For reasonably well-drained soil in sun or part-shade. From Turkey and the Caucasus. ‡12–20 in (30–50 cm). Z3–8 H8–1

G. pratense (Meadow cranesbill) Tall, upright, and growing from a compact rootstock; leaves are cut almost to the base into seven or nine divisions and further deeply lobed, the lobes sometimes having several teeth. The medium-sized to large outward-facing flowers make a compact display from late spring to midsummer, with some later bloom if deadheaded, and are usually violet-blue, campanula-blue, or white, usually with a white eye; the unnotched petals have translucent or pinkish veins. A showy and useful species, suited to close planting with other plants in borders or flowery meadows. Plants with especially attractive foliage may be seen listed as G. transbaicalicum. For sun or light shade, and tolerant of chalky soils. Adequate moisture and regular replanting help prevent mildew. Best

LEFT *Geranium pratense*
'Mrs. Kendall Clark'

divided, though some variants come true from seed. From Europe (including the British Isles), the Altai mountains of central Asia, western China and possibly western and eastern Siberia. ‡8–66 in (20–160 cm). Z4–8 H8–1. **'Bicolor'** see 'Striatum'. **'Bittersweet'** Pale, dusky mauve-pink flowers with even paler veins, in early summer and midsummer. Selected by former Royal Horticultural Society botanist Alan Leslie. ‡3¼ ft (1 m). **Black Beauty** ('Nodbeauty') Strongly purple-flushed leaves and cupped lavender-blue flowers, with petals scarcely touching or slightly open and with faint paler veins, are borne from early to late summer on reddish flower stalks with scarlet bracts beneath each flower. Easier to grow and less prone to mildew than other dark-leaved types. Raised by Nori Pope, Hadspen Garden, Dorset, England. ‡16 in (40 cm). **'Cluden Sapphire'** Neat, with almost primary blue flowers shading to lilac at the center with white veins in early summer and midsummer. Raised by Englishman John Ross. ‡30 in (75 cm). var. *flore-pleno* see 'Plenum Violaceum'. var. *flore-variegato* see 'Striatum'. **'Hocus Pocus'** Purple leaves and, from early summer to late summer, lavender flowers with slightly overlapping petals, a white eye and pale veins. Selected from 'Purple-haze' by Dutch horticulturist Marco van Noort. ‡16 in (40 cm). **Midnight Reiter strain** Dwarf plant with very dark purple leaves and lavender flowers from early to late summer. Occurs as a proportion of seedlings in the Victor

Reiter strain and can also be increased by division. Not easy to grow well. ‡8 in (20 cm). **'Mrs. Kendall Clark'** Confusing, seed-raised plant with pale lavender flowers networked with white veins, flowering in early summer and midsummer, and again in fall if deadheaded. Not now the original plant of this name, introduced by Walter Ingwersen and described in 1946 as having pearl gray flowers flushed rose, with no mention of veining. Also, in some areas, plants under this name have the color scheme reversed, with whitish petals and pale lavender veins. ‡3¼ ft (1 m). **'New Dimension'** Bronze leaves the shallowly cupped, lavender flowers from early to late summer have a paler center and translucent veins that appear grayish. ‡12 in (30 cm). **'Nunwood Purple'** see G. 'Nunwood Purple.' **'Plenum Caeruleum'** Small, soft violet-blue, double flowers, usually with about 15 petals pinkish at the base. The flowers are retained as they die, marring the effect. ‡3¼ ft (1 m). **'Plenum Violaceum'** syn. 'Purpureum Plenum', var. *flore-pleno* Attractive small, pompon flowers in rich lavender shading to reddish purple at the bases of the petals and at the center of the flower. Flowers in early summer and midsummer, with good reblooming if deadheaded. Some flowers are retained as they die, marring the effect. Found by Lady Charlotte Murray (1754–1808) near Athol House, Scotland. ‡36 in (90 cm). **subsp. pratense f. albiflorum** syn. G. pratense var. album The name for all variants of the species that are predominantly white-flowered. **subsp. pratense f. albiflorum 'Laura'** Vigorous, with double flowers, in pure white but for a green eye, in early summer and

ABOVE 1 *Geranium psilostemon*
2 *G. pyrenaicum* 'Bill Wallis'

midsummer. A great improvement on 'Plenum Album' but does not shed all the spent flowers cleanly. ‡ 3¼ ft (1 m).
subsp. *pratense* f. *albiflorum* 'Galactic' Pure white flowers in early summer and midsummer, the translucent veins scarcely feathered and seeming grayish; the plant is completely without dark pigment. Does not come entirely true from seed. ‡ 3¼ ft (1 m). **subsp. *pratense* f. *albiflorum* 'Silver Queen'** Very pale, grayish-lavender flowers with translucent veins that appear grayish and with black anthers. The name was originally used for a possibly different plant with large silver-blue flowers. ‡ 36 in (90 cm). **'Purple-haze'** Leaves emerge purple, aging to green, and are flushed and edged bronze or purple while from early to late summer the flowers open in shades of lavender. Very variable and doubtfully distinct from Victor Reiter strain. ‡ 16 in (40 cm).
'Purple Heron' Very dark-leaved clone with dark purple foliage and lavender flowers, with pale veins and slightly sparse petals, from early to late summer. Selected from Midnight Reiter strain. ‡ 8 in (20 cm).
'Purpureum Plenum' *see* 'Plenum Violaceum'. **'Rose Queen'** Near-white flowers with pronounced carmine-pink veins and coral pink anthers on a plant of relatively neat habit in early summer and midsummer. Introduced by David Hibberd of England. ‡ 36 in (90 cm).
'Splish-splash' *see* 'Striatum'.
subsp. *stewartianum* 'Elizabeth Yeo' A selection of a Himalayan subspecies that differs in its earlier flowering and its wider leaf divisions, lobes, and teeth. Handsome, glossy, mid-green foliage and large, glistening, vibrant pink flowers with faint translucent veins in late spring and early summer. Named

by Peter Yeo after his wife. ‡ 32 in (80 cm). **'Striatum'** syn. 'Bicolor', 'Splish-splash', var. *flore-variegato* Flowers open in early summer and midsummer, the white petals irregularly spotted and streaked with lavender-blue; grayish, translucent veins. Named by Daisy Hill Nursery, Newry, County Down, England in 1897, though a much older plant. ‡ 3¼ ft (1 m)
Victor Reiter strain Seed-raised variant. Leaves emerge purple and age to green, flushed and edged bronze or purple. Flowers lavender, sometimes with a paler eye, from early to late summer. Seedlings will include a few plain green-leaved plants that should be rejected and a similar proportion of very dwarf, very dark-leaved plants, the Midnight Reiter strain. ‡ 16 in (40 cm).
'Wisley Blue' Pale lavender flowers, greenish white at the center, with faint purple veins. Among the tallest of hardy cranesbills but may suffer from mildew. ‡ 5½ ft (1.6 m).

G. 'Prelude' Upright clump-former with basal leaves cut by about four-fifths into five or seven divisions, the outer part of the divisions further lobed, the lobes usually have a few teeth. Stem leaves are paired; divisions reduce to three at the top of plant. The much-branched flower stems produce a cloud of rather small, sparse, lilac flowers, quite deep as they open, becoming pale, with about three purple veins on each petal. Strongly red-flushed flower stalks and calyces add to the effect, though this coloring is less pronounced in full shade. A very pretty plant, fleeting in its late-spring flowering though it will rebloom if deadheaded. Best grown in part-shade with adequate moisture. A hybrid of *G. albiflorum* and *G. sylvaticum* that was raised by Alan Bremner of England. ‡ 24 in (60 cm). Z7–9 H9–7

G. procurrens Exceptionally vigorous scrambler with red stems rooting at leaf joints, thus aggressively invasive. There are few basal leaves but stem leaves are paired; lower ones cut by about two-thirds into five (rarely seven) divisions, each with three apical lobes with or without one or two teeth. Flowers, borne in pairs from midsummer to mid-fall, open dull magenta, each petal having a black V at its base and about seven near-black veins. Flowers expand as they age, becoming more purple. The scarcity of flowers is too thin to be showy but its late season is useful, though its invasiveness suits only the largest-scale sites. For sun or shade in any reasonable soil. Propagate by detaching rooted stems. From eastern Nepal, Bhutan, and Sikkim. ‡ 12 in (30 cm). Z7–9 H9–1

G. psilostemon Handsome plant; shoots emerge in spring encased in bright, primary red stipules, from which unfurl very large basal leaves, cut by about four-fifths into seven divisions, further divided into lobes with several often deep teeth. The stem leaves are similar, paired, with five divisions, becoming smaller up the plant. The upright, diffuse flowering display, in early summer and midsummer, comprises large, magenta, saucer-shaped flowers with a deep red, near-black eye from which radiate about eleven slender veins per petal. Pink and white selections from Turkey are as yet unnamed. Upright enough for close-planted borders and enough punch for the most sumptuous color schemes. For sun or dappled shade with adequate moisture. Staking is usually necessary and deadheading encourages later blooms. From northeastern Turkey and southwestern Caucasus. ‡ 32–48 in (80–120 cm). Z5–8 H8–5.
'Bressingham Flair' Magenta-pink flowers with rather crumpled petals are in a slightly softer shade than the species and are useful in cooler color combinations. Introduced by Alan Bloom of England.

G. pylzowianum Dwarf, and spreading by underground rhizomes bearing tiny tubers. Basal leaves are cut almost to the base into five or seven wedge-shaped divisions and further deeply lobed; lobes usually have a few teeth. The broadly funnel-shaped mauve-pink flowers are borne a few to a stem in early summer with a green eye and purple veins. Dies back after flowering, to appear again the following spring. Good at the front of beds and borders. May intertwine with neighbors, though its absence for most of the year makes this less of a problem. Well-drained, nutrient-poor soil in sun encourages more flowering and less invasiveness,

BELOW 1 *Geranium renardii*
2 *G.* x *riversleaianum* 'Russell Prichard'

"WHEN IN DOUBT, PLANT A GERANIUM"

So said Margery Fish of East Lambrook Manor in Somerset, England one of the leading enthusiasts for hardy geraniums in the 1950s and 60s. Their unobtrusive form, with many small flowers, a roundish and rarely spiky outline, and usually quiet foliage, suits them to combinations with almost any other sort of plant. And although this unassuming charm means that most are "always the supporting actor, never the star," they look quite good in many situations.

Nor are they suitable solely as companions to plants with deficits of form, such as roses, where an extra element with bold foliage needs to be added: as irises, hostas, or daylilies, could oblige. Most cranesbills cannot really dazzle, only a few having the dramatic architecture of *G. maderense* or the fierce color of magenta *G. psilostemon*. Even so, they are invaluable in plant combinations, separating bolder companions so that these have room to express themselves, and harmonizing with most other plants (though there are few that could contribute to a hot-colored scheme).

Geraniums are justly valued as ground cover, many kinds providing dense cover that is hard for weeds to penetrate. However, there are some common pitfalls. Very dry situations, perhaps under trees or in the rain shadow of a wall or building, suit only a few. If they are invasive types, they may destroy the balance with other plant groups. While ground cover should be attractive for as much of the year as possible, few cranesbills can fulfill this criterion, though good foliage alone and a long flowering season is usually desirable. Most cranesbills are late enough into growth to permit an underplanting of snowdrops or wood anemones. Though some geraniums can be used to underplant shrubs or bush roses, vigorous ones can pull themselves up into their hosts by several times their normal height; this may smother frailer shrubs, but if the host is robust enough, it will provide a startling high-level show.

So although cranesbills rarely have the pizzazz or the boldness of habit to stand alone as specimens, they are invaluable as ground cover and as weavers with other plants so that, especially now that so many more good plants have been developed, Margery Fish's enthusiasm remains justified.

though this may cause it to die back sooner. Raise from seed, or remove and replant the tubers. From western China. ‡8 in (20 cm). Z5–8 H8–5

G. pyrenaicum (Pyrenean cranesbill) Sprawling, slender, and densely hairy; basal leaves are roundish in outline, cut by half or more into seven or nine divisions that are three-lobed at the apex. Lobes usually have a pair of teeth. From the compact rootstock are borne stems up to 28 in (70 cm) long, forming a diffuse display from late spring to mid-fall. Stem leaves pair like the basal leaves but become smaller up the plant. Flowers are variable in size, up to ¾ in (2 cm) across but usually less, deep mauve-pink with a white base and purple veins. Petals have a notch at the apex. Can be pretty in the wild garden, though the flowers of some plants may be too small to make an impact. Best avoided where self-sowing would be a nuisance. For sun or part-shade; raise from seed. Originally from southwestern and western Europe eastward to the Caucasus. ‡12 in (30 cm). Z5–9 H9–5. **f. albiflorum** White flowers, faintly tinged pink in cool weather. **'Bill Wallis'** Exceptionally richly colored, glowing purple flowers, with purple-flushed stems and leaf-stalks and darker foliage. Named for the Cambridgeshire, England, horticulturist who introduced it. **'Isparta'** Larger selection with paler leaves and larger, lighter, and bluer flowers with a large white eye. Introduced by Peter Yeo of England from the Turkish province of this name. ‡24 in (60 cm).

G. Rambling Robin Group syn. *G.* 'Silver Cloak' Bushy perennials with a woody base, not forming a basal rosette and with no distinction between flowering and nonflowering stems. This Group covers the slightly variable offspring combining the silvery filigree foliage of *G. incanum* with the greater vigor of *G. robustum*. The silvery-hairy leaves are cut to the base into about five divisions that are lobed and toothed again, divisions, lobes, and teeth all in the form of narrow, straplike filaments, giving the filigree effect. Nodding buds open into upward-facing flowers, in vibrant mauve or light magenta-purple with a white eye, for a long season from late spring to late fall. For sun and well-drained soil; useful in very hot climates and in hanging baskets. Propagate by cuttings; seed is sometimes sold as 'Silver Cloak'. A hybrid first raised by Englishman Robin Moss. Plants sold as 'Silver Shadow' probably belong here too. ‡18 in (45 cm). Z5–8 H8–5

G. rectum 'Album' see *G. clarkei* 'Kashmir White'

G. reflexum Adaptable, clump-forming, medium-sized, upright, leafy plant growing from a stout rootstock. Basal leaves are cut to two-thirds or a little more into seven divisions and shallowly lobed; lobes have a few teeth, and are usually strongly blotched brown where the divisions, and sometimes the lobes, meet. Stem leaves are solitary and similar, becoming smaller up the plant. The flowers are inverted, with narrow, reflexed petals in rose pink to dark violet, separated from a white base by a slaty blue band. Similar to *G. phaeum* but with smaller flowers and suited to the woodland garden. They thrive in sun to deep shade with adequate moisture. From Italy, via Montenegro, Kosovo, and north Greece to Bulgaria. ‡24–36 in (60–90 cm). Z5–8 H8–5

G. regelii Slightly creeping, tufted plant with crowded shoots and distinct offsets. Basal leaves are cut by about four-fifths into five or seven divisions that are three-lobed at the apex, the lobes often turned outward with one or two teeth. Paired stem leaves are cut a little more deeply into five divisions. Medium-sized to large outward-facing flowers are borne in a very loose display in early summer and midsummer, and are usually campanula-blue with a paler eye and radiating, slightly feathered violet veins, the petals unnotched. An attractive species, like a smaller, more slender *G. pratense*. For sun or light shade. From the mountains of Tien Shan and Pamir Alai, northeast to Afghanistan, and the western Himalaya. ‡12 in (30 cm). Z5–8 H8–5

G. renardii Low-growing perennial with a thick, woody rootstock trailing above ground. Basal leaves are gray-green, sage-textured, downy and with a network of fine wrinkles, cut about halfway into five or seven divisions that are shallowly three- or five-lobed. Lobes furnished with blunt teeth. Stem leaves are similar, diminishing rapidly in size up the plant. In late spring and early summer, the once- or twice-forked stems bear dense clusters of more or less flat, outward- or slightly upward-facing flowers with wedge-shaped, notched, open petals usually in white (sometimes tinted gray or blue) or in lavender with about seven bold, feathered violet veins on each petal. Pleasing foliage for the front of the border; flowers are especially attractive when examined closely. Best in a sunny spot; poor, rather dry soils aid flowering and produce grayer foliage. From the Caucasus. ‡14 in (35 cm). Z6–8 H8–6. **'Tcschelda'** Large lavender-lilac flowers with ruffled petals and violet veins. Collected in the Caucasus.

'Whiteknights' Lavender flowers with violet veins, and a rather looser habit of growth. Named after England's University of Reading's campus. ‡16 in (40 cm). **'Zetterlund'** Large, pale lilac flowers heavily veined in violet on a compact plant. ‡12 in (30 cm).

G. x riversleaianum A short, stout rootstock carries leaves divided as far in as three-quarters into about seven divisions, each of them tapered and lobed up to about a third of their length. The whole plant is covered in short hairs, giving it a grayish appearance, and produces trailing or scrambling flowering stems with paired leaves and usually pink flowers. For well-drained soil in sun. The hybrid of *G. endressii* and *G. traversii*, first raised at Russell Prichard's Riverslea Nursery, Hampshire, England. ‡6–16 in (15–40 cm). Z6–8 H8–6. **'Jean Armour'** see *G.* 'Jean Armour'. **'Mavis Simpson'** see *G.* 'Mavis Simpson.' **'Russell Prichard'** Unusual in its magenta flowers, which are much more strongly colored than either parents; the flowers, in early summer and midsummer with some reblooming in mid-fall, are set against grayish foliage on a widely spreading plant. ‡12 in (30 cm).

G. rivulare syn. *G. sylvaticum* subsp. *rivulare* Erect clump-former with basal leaves cut almost to the base into seven or nine divisions. The dense display is composed of numerous erect, funnel-shaped flowers, their white petals lined with fine violet veins reaching nearly to the tip. Differs greatly from the closely related *G. sylvaticum* in its leaves having long, narrow, almost toothless lobes. For sun or part-shade, preferably in moist soil. From the western and

BELOW *Geranium* 'Salome'

central European Alps. ↕8–18 in (20–45 cm). Z5–8 H8–5

G. robustum Large, bushy, leafy evergreen, growing from a woody base rather than a rosette; stems up to 5¾ ft (1.75 m) long but lax and sprawling. Leaves are solitary below, paired above, cut almost to the base into five divisions and deeply lobed, with several teeth to each lobe, giving a filigree effect; they are green on the upper surface and white-felted beneath. Large mauve to lavender flowers with a white eye open erect from nodding buds over a long season from late spring to late fall. For well-drained soil in sun. From South Africa. ↕24 in (60 cm). Z5–8 H8–5

G. Rozanne ('Gerwat') Very vigorous sprawler suitable for large-scale ground cover. Paired mid-green leaves are about 4 in (10 cm) across, less toward the tips of stems, cut three-quarters of the way into five divisions, each with a lobe to either side, all with a few blunt teeth and marbled with pale flecks below each notch around the margin and at the junction of the larger veins. Saucer-shaped flowers, from early summer to mid-fall, are about 2 in (5 cm) across, rich campanula-blue with a white center, each petal having about five radiating purple veins. Good in any soil in sun or part-shade, though vigorous enough to smother neighbors. Much confused with the very similar G. 'Jolly Bee'. Can be propagated by division but is slow to make a productive crown; cuttings might be successful. A hybrid of G. wallichianum 'Buxton's Variety' and G. himalayense from Gomer and Rozanne Waterer of Somerset, England, introduced by Blooms of Bressingham. ↕24 in (60 cm). Z5–8 H12–2

G. Sabani Blue ('Bremigo') Hairy clump-former with basal leaves cut about three-quarters toward the base into about seven divisions and further lobed and toothed. Similar stem leaves decrease in size up the plant, the upper ones being stalkless. Upward-facing flowers, in mid- and late spring, are lavender with violet veins and a whitish eye; some later bloom if dead-headed. For sun or part-shade. A very early-flowering hybrid of G. ibericum and G. libani raised by Alan Bremner of England. ↕16 in (40 cm). Z5–8 H8–5

G. 'Salome' Sprawling with gold-flushed foliage, especially when young, that is slightly marbled and rough-surfaced. Few basal leaves. Paired lower stem leaves are cut by about three-quarters into five, sometimes seven, divisions, each shallowly cut into three divisions that have a few teeth. Cupped, rather sparsely produced mauve flowers are borne in pairs from midsummer to mid-fall; their petals are open at the base, and heavily marked with deep red-purple veins, coalescing at the base to make a bold, dark V. Best in shade in

good soil, though will tolerate sun given adequate moisture. The stems do not root where they touch the ground, but can be used as cuttings. A seedling of G. lambertii and G. procurrens found by Elizabeth Strangman of England. ↕12 in (30 cm). Z4–8 H8–1

G. sanguineum (Bloody cranesbill) Variable, low, bushy perennial with shortly spreading underground rhizomes. There are few basal leaves, these differing from the stem leaves in that they are less deeply divided and havw blunt-tipped lobes. The stem leaves are paired, cut almost to the base into seven divisions that are mostly deeply three-lobed; lobes have up to two teeth. Some cultivars show good fall leaf color. In early summer and midsummer, the saucer-shaped flowers, up to about 1½ in (4 cm) across, are borne singly rather than in pairs, an unusual feature for this genus that is usually passed on to its hybrids. The color varies between carmine red, magenta-purple, and white, usually deepening with age, and the veins may be conspicuously reddish purple or faint and translucent. The flowering stems continue to grow even after flowering has stopped. An attractive plant for the front of the border, in well-drained soil in sun, and often also grown in walls and gaps in paths. From most of Europe (including the British Isles), the Caucasus and northern Turkey. ↕6–20 in (15–50 cm). Z3–8 H8–1. **Alan Bloom** ('Bloger') Large, rich mauve-pink flowers with broad-lobed, deep green leaves. Raised by Blooms of Bressingham, England. ↕8 in (20 cm). **'Album'** syn. var. album Large, pure white flowers with no red pigment and with translucent veins appearing grayish, borne above the dark foliage on pale green flower stalks in late spring and early summer. ↕10 in (25 cm). **'Ankum's Pride'** Outstanding, compact, spreading plant with large, vibrant, deep rose pink flowers with faint darker veins, held over pale foliage

from late spring to midsummer. Raised by Coen Jansen of Holland and named for his home village. ↕6 in (15 cm). **'Aviemore'** Spreading plant with large, rich mauve-pink flowers over mid-green, narrow-lobed foliage in early summer and midsummer. Raised by Englishman Jack Drake. ↕6 in (15 cm). **'Belle of Herterton'** Large flowers opening a deep, vibrant mauve, unusual in aging paler, on a neat, compact plant from late spring to midsummer. Discovered by Robin Moss. ↕6 in (15 cm). **'Cedric Morris'** Spreading plant with large, light magenta-purple flowers over light green leaves. Collected by the artist gardener Sir Cedric Morris on the Gower Peninsula, South Wales. ↕6 in (15 cm). **'Connie Hansen'** Large, light pink flowers with a pale center. From the garden of Connie Hansen, Lincoln City, OR. Flowers with a pale center. ↕15 in (38 cm). Z4–8 H8–1 **'Cricklewood'** Light magenta flowers, resembles G. sanguineum although it is sterile and more vigorous. Selection made by Dennis Thompson of Cricklewood Nursery, Seattle, WA. ↕18 in (45 cm) Z4–8 H8–1. **'Elsbeth'** Large, light magenta-purple flowers in late spring and early summer on a very spreading plant. ↕10 in (25 cm). **'Feu d'Automne'** Magenta-purple flowers of good size, with a little later flower until mid-fall, above foliage that colors well in fall. ↕12 in (30 cm). **'Glenluce'** Mound-forming, with mauve flowers from late spring to midsummer; the petals have a shallow indentation at the apex. Found by A.T. Johnson near Glenluce, Stranraer, Scotland. ↕12 in (30 cm). **'John Elsley'** Rich mauve-pink flowers from late spring to midsummer, of average size with pronounced red-purple veins, on a compact plant. Introduced by Blooms of Bressingham and named for the South Carolina horticulturist. ↕6 in

BELOW *Geranium sanguineum* var. *striatum*

GERANIUM PEOPLE

Many enthusiasts for hardy geraniums—gardeners, nurserypeople, and plant breeders—are mentioned here.

Bill Baker collected plants in many countries and grew them in his crowded horticulturist's garden in Berkshire, England; a number carry his name.

Trevor Bath is a specialist in cottage garden plants who gardens in Surrey, England and is the joint author of *The Gardener's Guide to Growing Geraniums.*

Judith Bradshaw is holder of an NCCPG National Geranium Collection at her garden near Preston, Lancashire, England.

Alan Bremner, the leading raiser of new cranesbills, has developed a wide range of exceptional hybrid cultivars at his garden in the Orkney Isles.

Bob Brown, Worcestershire, England horticulturist with a sharp eye for a good plant, popularized many fine cranesbills.

Jack Drake was the founder of the Inshriach Alpine Plant Nursery at Aviemore, Scotland and introduced a number of smaller cranesbills.

David Hibberd ran Axletree Nursery in Sussex, England (now closed), and selected, named, and introduced many fine new cranesbills.

The Ingwersens Walter Ingwersen founded the Sussex, England firm known as W. E. Th. Ingwersen Ltd. at Birch Farm Nursery, which has introduced a number of good cranesbills. He was succeeded by Will Ingwersen, then Paul Ingwersen.

Coen Jansen is a horticulturist and plant breeder from northern Holland who has introduced many good new plants.

A.T. (Arthur Tysilio) Johnson was a horticulturist and writer who gardened in North Wales and is the author of *A Woodland Garden.*

Robin Moss has introduced a number of good cranesbills, often named for members of his family, from his garden in Hexham, Northumberland, England.

Piet Oudolf is a renowned garden designer, plant breeder, and writer based in eastern Holland with a wide range of plant introductions to his name.

Robin Parer has long been a champion of cranesbills from her Geraniaceae Nursery near San Francisco.

Dr. Hans Simon is a plant-hunter and grower with a nursery in Germany.

Elizabeth Strangman, a pioneer breeder of hellebores, introduced hardy geraniums and many other plants at Washfield Nursery in Kent, England (now closed).

Bleddyn and Sue Wynn-Jones have collected plants in many far-flung places and introduced them at their nursery, Crûg Farm Plants, in Wales

Peter Yeo is a pioneering botanist who established the modern classification of Geranium in his book, *Hardy Geraniums.*

(15 cm). **'Jubilee Pink'** Large, glowing fuchsia pink flowers. Raised by Jack Drake and named for the Silver Jubilee of Queen Elizabeth II. ‡8 in (20 cm). **var. *lancastrense*** see var. *striatum.* **'Max Frei'** Small, light magenta-purple flowers on a compact plant in late spring and early summer. Good fall color. ‡6 in (15 cm). **'New Hampshire Purple'** Light magenta-purple flowers of average size on a spreading plant from late spring to midsummer. Raised by Joe Eck of North Hill Garden Design, VT. ‡8 in (20 cm). **'Nyewood'** Small, light purple flowers on a neat, mounded plant, from late spring to midsummer. Introduced by Monksilver Nursery, Cambridgeshire, England. ‡6 in (15 cm). **'Rod Leeds'** Very large magenta flowers with dark veins over deep green foliage, with some later bloom. ‡12 in (30 cm). **'Shepherd's Warning'** Very low-growing, spreading plant with large flowers of glowing fuchsia pink; similar in hue to 'Jubilee Pink', but a touch deeper and redder. Raised by Jack Drake of England. ‡8 in (20 cm). **var. *striatum*** syn. var. *lancastrense* Small, pale rose pink flowers, lightly veined crimson, from late spring to early summer. Native to Walney Island and other sites along England's Cumbrian coast. ‡8–10 in (20–25 cm). **var. *striatum* 'Splendens'** Very spreading form with large flowers and long season from late spring to midsummer. ‡8 in (20 cm). **'Vision Light Pink'** syn. 'Vision Pink' (Visions Series) Small but plentiful pale pink flowers with red veins. **Visions Series** Vigorous and spreading but smaller, seed-raised plants with tiny, lacy-looking leaves and flowering from late spring to midsummer. Very distinctive.

Raised and introduced by Ernst Benary Samenzucht GmbH, Germany. ‡12 in (30 cm). **'Vision Violet'** syn. 'Vision' (Visions Series) Small but plentiful magenta flowers with deep red-purple veins. ‡12 in (30 cm).

G. sessilifolium* subsp. *novae-zelandiae Dwarf, semievergreen, with a stout, compact rootstock and flowering stems either very short or absent. The ½–¾ in (1–2 cm) wide leaves are cut halfway or a little more into five or seven divisions, each usually with three blunt lobes and no teeth, and are minutely hairy but not sufficiently to appear downy or velvety. Flowers, from late spring to early fall, are about ½ in (1 cm) across, in pink or white. A tiny species, not showy, for the front of gravel gardens or troughs, or other well-drained places in sun. Raise from seed or take basal cuttings. From grassland and coastal dunes in New Zealand. ‡1¼ in (3 cm). Z8–9 H9–8. **'Nigricans'** Naturally occurring variant with brownish leaves, the hairs imparting a slight satin sheen, and white flowers. A technically incorrect but well-established name used for a plant from New Zealand, introduced by The Plantsmen Nursery in Dorset, England in 1967; applied to subsequent introductions with brownish leaves. An important parent of much darker-leaved variants of G. x *antipodeum.* **'Porter's Pass'** The name encompasses all plants from Porter's Pass in New Zealand, with reddish leaves, but excludes brownish or green-leaved plants from the same locality.

G. 'Silver Cloak', 'Silver Shadow' see G. Rambling Robin Group

G. sinense A thick, compact rootstock supports wide-spreading branches; the slightly glossy, faintly marbled basal leaves are cut by three-quarters or more into seven (sometimes five), more or less rhomboid divisions that are further lobed or just unequally toothed. Stem leaves are similar but smaller and solitary or paired. Nodding flowers, in mid- and late summer, are small, with a prominent "bill," around the base of which is a circular nectary, attracting wasps and hoverflies. Backswept petals are velvety maroon-black with a narrow fuchsia pink zone at the base resembling those of the unrelated G. *phaeum.* Sometimes distributed as G. *delavayi.* A fascinating flower, though not showy. Barely visible from a distance. For part-shade, or sun if adequately moist. From Yunnan and Sichuan provinces, southwestern China. ‡24 in (60 cm). Z5–8 H8–5

G. 'Sirak' Spreading plant growing from a compact rootstock. Basal leaves are cut by about two-thirds into seven (sometimes nine) roughly rhomboid divisions that are shallowly lobed and further irregularly toothed. Stem leaves are similar, becoming smaller up the plant, the uppermost with only three divisions. Flowers open from hairy buds in late spring and early summer in vibrant mauve-pink with a white eye, the petals usually notched and with radiating red-purple, unfeathered veins. For sun or part-shade. Stems tend to sprawl, so that flowers end up around the perimeter; staking helps. A hybrid of G. *gracile* and G. *ibericum* collected by Hans Simon. The same cross raised by Alan Bremner produced an almost identical clone that was circulated under the same name; this might prove to be distinct and need a separate name. ‡24 in (60 cm). Z5–8 H8–5

G. soboliferum Deeply dissected leaves grow from a thick, compact rootstock. Basal leaves are cut almost to the base into seven divisions that are further dissected into narrow lobes, each with a few long, pointed teeth. Paired stem leaves are similar, decreasing in size up the plant. The medium-sized, saucer-shaped flowers, densely borne in midsummer to early fall, have light magenta-purple petals, heavily veined red-purple to either side so the center of the petal appears paler. For moist soil in sun or part-shade; intolerant of drought; perhaps best in a waterside planting. From the Pacific coast of Russia, Manchuria, and mountains of central and southern Japan. ‡12–16 in (30–40 cm). Z4–8 H8–1

G. 'Spinners' Clump-forming plant with basal leaves that emerge gold-flushed in spring, cut almost to the base into seven divisions, with numerous deep lobes which may in turn have a few pointed teeth, giving a very dissected effect. Paired stem leaves are similar, becoming smaller up the plant. Richly-colored, cupped flowers, opening in late spring and early summer, are among the closest of all to a true blue, shading through lilac to a near-white eye, the petals, lightly veined purplish-red almost to their tips. For sun or part-shade; regular division and adequate moisture help prevent mildew. Raised by Peter Chappell. Named for his Hampshire, England garden. Originally distributed as both G. *bergianum* and G. 'Kashmir Purple'; perhaps a hybrid of G. *pratense* and G. *clarkei* 'Kashmir Purple'. ‡36 in (90 cm). Z5–8 H8–5

G. 'Stephanie' Hairy, spreading plant, its mid-green, hairy basal leaves cut to about halfway into five or seven divisions, shallowly lobed and regularly toothed, their surface covered with a pronounced and even network of veins reminiscent of sage, or G. *renardii.* The open flowers, flowering in late spring and early summer, have pale lavender, heart-shaped petals with five prominent, feathered, deep violet veins. Prefers sun; will tolerate drought. A chance seedling grown at the Royal Botanic Garden, Edinburgh, Scotland; probably a hybrid between G. *peloponnesiacum* and G. *renardii.* ‡20 in (50 cm). Z5–8 H8–5

BELOW 1 *G. sessilifolium* 'Nigricans'
2 *G.* 'Spinners'

G. striatum see *G. versicolor*

G. 'Sue Crûg' Sprawling plant with exceptionally beautifully marked flowers. Few basal leaves, but the lower stem leaves are cut by two-thirds of the way or a little more into five rhomboid divisions that are further lobed and toothed. These leaves become smaller up the plant. The flowers, opening from early summer to mid-fall, are mauve-pink, paler to near-white at the center of the petals, deeper and quite rich at the outer edges. Petals are notched and heavily veined in deep purple-red, the veins coalescing to either side of the base of the petal. For part-shade, or sun if given adequate moisture. Can be allowed to scramble into shrubs or weave among other plants, though it can smother hosts if left unchecked. Perhaps the most beautifully marked blooms, produced sparingly over a long time. A hybrid of *G. x oxonianum* and *G. 'Salome'* raised by Englishman Bleddyn Wynn-Jones and named for his wife. ‡16 in (40 cm). Z4–9 H8–1

G. Summer Skies ('Gernic') Clump-former resembling *G. pratense*, with basal leaves cut almost to the base into seven divisions and further deeply lobed and toothed. Florets, densely borne in early summer and mid-summer, vary in color between lilac and lavender and resemble pompons, with 20–30 narrowly reddish purple veined petals, shading to white at the center with a green eye. Truly beautiful as they open, their display can be marred by rain, causing flowers to develop botrytis, or by drought, causing mildew. Some of the flowers are retained as they die, spoiling the later part of the flowering season. A flawed beauty. Best in sun but appreciates moisture. A hybrid of *G.* 'Spinners' and, probably, *G. himalayense* 'Plenum'. ‡24 in (60 cm). Z5–8 H8–5

G. sylvaticum (Wood cranesbill) Medium-sized, upright plant with a compact rootstock, the leaves are cut almost to the base into seven or nine divisions that are lobed and toothed almost to the base. The stem leaves are similar, the lower ones solitary, paired above, diminishing in size up the plant. The numerous, saucer-shaped 1–1½-in (2.5–4-cm) flowers are densely borne in late spring and early summer and are usually lavender blue with a white center. Its erect habit suits borders, though it flowers before most other border plants but after the spring bulbs; can also be grown in light shade in the woodland garden. From Europe. ‡16–54 in (40–130 cm). Z8–8 H9–8 **f. albiflorum** White flowers but retaining some dark pigments in sepals, stamens, and stigmas. **'Album'** Pale-leaved variant with white flowers but lacking dark pigment. Breeds true from seed if grown in isolation. Collected by Englishman Walter Ingwersen in northern Sweden. ‡28 in (70 cm). **'Amy Doncaster'** Bold leaves and

AN UNLIKELY INFLUENCE

From the coastal cliffs of the Chatham Islands, located almost 400 miles (650 km) east of New Zealand, where it grows with the Chatham Island forget-me-not (*Myosotidium hortensia*) and, more surprisingly, the Scotch thistle (*Cirsium vulgare*), *Geranium traversii* var. *elegans*, an unassuming, low-growing, gray-leaved variety with pink or white flowers, has had an unexpected influence on garden geraniums.

A pretty, spreading plant that grows best in sunny, well-drained conditions, it also has a crucial role as parent of a number of fine garden-worthy hybrids. Crossing *G. traversi* with its close relative *G. sessiliflorum* and, in particular, its brown, bronze, and coppery-leaved forms, results in *G. x antipodeum*. It is in this group that all of the dark-leaved, pink-flowered forms like 'Stanhoe', 'Sea Spray', 'Chocolate Candy', and more, fall.

A hybridization of *G. traversi* with *G. lambertii* has produced the unusually long-flowering 'Joy' and a hybridization with *G. argenteum* has produced the rare 'Silver Pink'.

With an even more distantly related parent, *G. endressii*, this plant has made one of the finest of all hardy geraniums, the exceptionally long flowering magenta-flowered *G. x riversleaianum* 'Russell Prichard' and, with *G. x oxonianum* as the other parent the similar pink flowered 'Mavis Simpson'; both are superb.

The indefatigable Geranium hybridizer Alan Bremner has successfully crossed *G. traversii* with a number of other species, including *G. versicolor*, *G. cinereum*, and *G. x lindavicum*, so we can surely look forward to more good plants derived from this attractive species from its lonely outpost in the southwest Pacific.

exceptionally beautiful, richly colored flowers approaching true blue, with slightly overlapping petals and a large white center. Named for the Hampshire, England gardener who raised it; introduced by Elizabeth Strangman. ‡28 in (70 cm). **'Angulatum'** syn. *G. angulatum* Large, palest blush pink, outward-facing flowers with a network of deep pink veins. Elegant and lovely. Named for its angled stems, in 1792. ‡28 in (70 cm). **'Birch Lilac'** Medium-sized flowers in lavender (not lilac), with a small white eye. Introduced by Rainforest Gardens (now The Perennial Gardens), British Columbia, Canada. ‡28 in (70 cm). **'Mayflower'** Larger lavender-blue flowers with a white eye, scarcely distinguishable from 'Birch Lilac' but a touch purer blue. ‡28 in (70 cm). **subsp. rivulare** see *G. rivulare*. f. *roseum* **'Baker's Pink'** syn. 'Wengen' Medium-sized flowers with overlapping, faintly veined, rose pink petals, in early summer and midsummer. Collected by

Englishman Bill Baker near Wengen in Switzerland. ‡54 in (130 cm). **subsp. sylvaticum var. wanneri** Pale rose pink petals with bright rose veins that are feathered and looped. Similar to 'Angulatum', but shorter. From the Alps around Geneva. ‡16 in (40 cm). **'Wengen'** see f. *roseum* 'Baker's Pink'.

G. 'Tanya Rendall' syn. *G.* 'Expression', *G.* 'Obsession' Sprawling. Suitable for ground cover, growing from a compact rootstock. The basal leaves are small, cut about halfway into five or seven divisions that have three blunt lobes, each with one or two blunt teeth. The leaf surface is minutely hairy, giving a lustrous satin appearance, flushed with brown unless grown in shade, and with a network of recessed veins. Stem leaves are similar, smaller, and usually paired. Magenta flowers, over a long season from late spring to late fall, have a white eye and prominent radiating white veins. For well-drained soil in sun. Propagate by division or basal cuttings. A hybrid of *G. x antipodeum*. 6 in (15 cm). Z5–8 H8–5

G. 'Terre Franche' Hairy, clump-forming plant, the mid-green basal leaves cut a little beyond halfway into five or seven divisions, shallowly lobed and regularly toothed, their surface is covered with a pronounced and even network of veins, as in *G. renardii*. The stem leaves are similar and paired, becoming smaller further up the plant. The flat, lavender-blue flowers, in late spring and early summer, are shaded to lilac in the center, the heart-shaped petals having about five slightly feathered violet veins. For sun or light shade. A hybrid of *G. platypetalum* and *G.* 'Philippe Vapelle', from which it differs in its less open, deeper colored flowers. Raised in Belgium. ‡16 in (40 cm). Z5–8 H8–5

BELOW 1 *Geranium sylvaticum*
2 *G. traversii* var. *elegans* **3** *G. tuberosum*

G. thunbergii syn. *G. nepalense* var. *thunbergii* Sprawling, hairy semi-evergreen, growing from a small rootstock. Basal leaves are cut by two-thirds or a little more into five divisions that are shallowly lobed toward the apex; the lobes have a few shallow teeth. Stem leaves are similar and paired. The small, funnel-shaped, white to deep mauve-pink flowers are borne in diffuse sprays from midsummer to mid-fall, their petals having a few radiating darker red-purple veins. Stems root where they touch the ground. A tolerant species, useful for difficult positions in the wild garden and for ground cover, though not showy. Easily propagated by detaching rooted pieces. Sometimes sold as *G. yoshinoi*. From northern China, Taiwan, and Japan. ‡ 16 in (40 cm). Z5–8 H8–5. **'Jester's Jacket'** The leaves unfurl irregularly splashed and mottled with cream and pink, the pink fading to cream, with mauve-pink flowers. A seed-raised cultivar introduced from Japan by Sue and Bleddyn Wynn-Jones, probably the same as *G. yoshinoi* 'Confetti'.

G. traversii var. **elegans** Minutely hairy, semievergreen plant growing from a compact rootstock, the hairs giving a silky, grayish cast to dark green foliage. Basal leaves are cut by about three-fifths into seven divisions that are three-lobed; lobes have one or two small teeth. Stem leaves are similar, paired, and become smaller up the plant. From late spring to mid-fall, the diffuse flower sprays are held above the basal leaves before sprawling outward. Flowers are pink, in varying shades in the wild, but usually pale mauve-pink in cultivation, paler still at the slightly curled-back edges of the petals, which have a few dark veins toward the base. Quietly pleasing species for troughs or well-drained soil in sun; an important parent of some showy, long-flowering

hybrids (*see* An Unlikely Influence). Propagate from seed, division, or basal cuttings. From the Chatham Islands. ‡ 10 in (25 cm). Z8–9 H9–8

G. tuberosum Tuberous plant coming into leaf in spring, becoming dormant after flowering; the roundish tubers are ¼–⅜ in (7–15 mm) thick. Basal leaves are cut almost to the base into five or seven divisions that have numerous narrow, toothed or entire lobes almost throughout their length, giving a feathery effect. Stem leaves are similar and paired. Saucer-shaped flowers are borne on upright stems in mid- and late spring, and have light magenta-purple, notched petals with darker veins, slightly feathered at the tips. Its growth habit and flowering season parallel that of spring bulbs; it can be used in the same way, though inclined to become weedy because the tubers are easily scattered. Best in well-drained soil, in sun when it is in leaf. Propagate by separating and replanting tubers. Similar to *G. macrostylum*, but without its red-tipped pinhead hairs. From the Mediterranean region eastward to Iran. ‡ 10 in (25 cm). Z8–9 H9–8. **'Leonidas'** *see G. macrostylum* 'Leonidas'

G. versicolor syn. *G. striatum* Semievergreen with compact rootstock. Fresh green basal leaves are cut by two-thirds or more into five broad divisions that are cut into lobes about a third of the way to the midrib and further toothed. There are usually reddish-brown blotches between divisions. Stem leaves are paired and similar, decreasing in size up the plant. Erect, trumpet-shaped white flowers with a network of purple veins dot the plant from late spring to late summer; they are beautiful at close range, but rarely make a striking display. From central and southern Italy, Sicily, and the southern part of Balkan Peninsula. ‡ 18 in (45 cm). Z5–8 H8–6.

ABOVE 1 *Geranium versicolor*
2 *G. walllichianum* 'Buxtons Variety'

'Snow White' syn. 'White Lady' Satin-sheened white flowers and colorless veins appearing grayish, giving a delicate silvery effect. Introduced by David Hibberd of England.

G. viscosissimum (Sticky cranesbill) Upright perennial from a deep and woody rootstock and with pinhead hairs. Basal leaves are cut by four-fifths or more into five to seven broadly wedge-shaped divisions that are three-lobed in their upper half; lobes have up to two teeth. Stem leaves are paired, becoming smaller up the plant. Flowers, in early summer and midsummer, are flat, mauve-pink to magenta-purple (rarely white), sometimes paler at the center, and with red-purple, slightly feathered veins. An attractive plant, suited to sunny borders; fairly tolerant of drought but thrives in sun or part-shade. Difficult to divide, so propagate from seed. Often reblooms if dead-headed. From western North America. ‡ 12–24 in (30–60 cm). Z5–8 H8–5

G. wallichianum Very variable scrambler growing from a stout rootstock, lacking a rosette of basal leaves. Lower stem leaves are divided by two-thirds or more into five (sometimes three) more or less rhombic divisions that are shallowly lobed, the lobes sharply toothed. Stem leaves are paired and more or less wrinkled and marbled. At each leaf joint, the two pairs of large stipules fuse to make, in effect, two stipules. Large, saucer-shaped, upward-facing flowers, appear from late summer to late fall, and may be mauve-pink, magenta, blue, white, or any color between; marked with dark veins, they have blackish stamens and stigmas, and often a white eye. Petals are sometimes notched.

Best in light shade with adequate moisture. Some forms are relatively low-growing, others more vigorous and mounding. Propagate from seed or stem cuttings. From the Himalaya, from northeast Afghanistan to Kashmir. ‡ 8–16 in (20–40 cm). Z4–8 H8–1. **'Buxton's Variety'** syn. 'Buxton's Blue' Seed-raised, low-growing form with long, running stems and blue flowers with violet veins and a white center. The color can tend to purple in hot, dry weather but approaches primary blue as the weather cools in fall. Arose in Wales in the Betws-y-Coed garden of E. Charles Buxton. ‡ 8 in (20 cm). **'Syabru'** Vigorous, slightly downy, with leaves lightly mottled lime green; flowers are rich magenta-pink with deep red veins and no central white zone, the petals having a slight notch. Seedlings show some variation. Collected in Nepal, named for the village (pronounced "shoe brew") near where it was found. Introduced by Elizabeth Strangman of England. ‡ 16 in (40 cm).

G. 'Wisley Hybrid' *see G.* 'Khan'

G. wlassovianum Bushy, with hairy leaves, and growing from a compact rootstock. Basal leaves are cut by about two-thirds into seven divisions that have lobes usually with one or two teeth, the lobes and teeth pointed at the tip. Paired stem leaves have five divisions and become smaller up the plant. Foliage emerges copper-tinted in spring and flushes reddish brown in fall before coloring fiery red. The magenta-purple flowers are diffusely borne from early to late summer and have violet veins and a white eye. Thrives in damp ground in sun or part-shade, but tolerates dry conditions in sun. From far eastern Russia, Mongolia, and northern China. ‡ 12–18 in (30–45 cm). Z4–8 H8–1. **'Blue Star'** Vigorous, coloring well into fall, with rich lavender-blue flowers from midsummer to early fall. ‡ 18 in (45 cm).

G. yesoense Bushy, growing from a compact rootstock. basal leaves are cut almost to the base into seven divisions that are deeply lobed; the lobes may be narrow or wide and overlapping, further furnished with pointed teeth. Though the dissected leaves resemble those of *G. sanguineum*, the flowers, opening from early to late summer, differ in being borne in pairs and are saucer-shaped or slightly funnel-shaped, pink with fine darker veins or white. Not showy but suited to the woodland garden or water garden, in moist soil in sun or shade. From central and northern Japan, Kuril Islands. ‡ 12–18 in (30–45 cm). Z5–9 H9–5

G. yoshinoi Sprawling, slender plant with spreading upper branches, the basal leaves cut by about four-fifths into five or seven roughly rhomboid divisions that are shallowly lobed; lobes have one or two shallow teeth. Lower stem leaves are solitary, the upper ones paired, similar but smaller and with five or three divisions. Flower stems are very branched and bear small, upward-

facing, flat, sometimes sparse, mauve-pink flowers with a network of darker veins. Sometimes confused with *G. yoshinoi*, a stouter plant with funnel-shaped flowers and a few radiating veins on each petal. From Honshu, Japan. ↕ 16–28 in (40–70 cm). Z6–9 H9–6. **'Confetti'** see *G. thunbergii* 'Jester's Jacket'.

GEUM
Avens
ROSACEAE

Familiar favorites with a range of uses, producing hot-colored flowers from early in the season.

About 50 species of fiery-flowered perennials are native to cool parts of Europe, Asia, North and South America, New Zealand, and Africa. In the wild, most species are found on moist, rich soils in meadows or around woods, although others occur in more open, rocky habitats. Geums are generally hardy and adaptable plants, producing clumps of leaves divided into opposite pairs of leaflets that are toothed and scalloped, and leafy, branched or unbranched flower stems carrying five–petaled flowers that are doubled in many of the cultivars. Left uncut, the flowers are followed by small, dry fruits with hooklike appendages that readily catch on clothes.

Hybrids between species arise freely in gardens and most available cultivars are of hybrid origin—though it is not always possible to determine the identity of both parents. Plants derived from the scarlet-flowered *G. chiloense* are often hairy, with the leaflet at the end of the leaf only slightly larger than the other leaflets. Plants derived from *G. coccineum*, with its brick red flowers, may inherit its large, kidney-shaped leaflet at the end of the leaf and conspicuous yellow stamens. Hybrids of *G. rivale* frequently have three large leaflets at the end of the leaf, and drooping, bell-shaped, orange-pink flowers.

Though sometimes short-lived, geums are of great worth, reliably producing bright flowers over a long period and with representatives to suit a number of different situations. The showy *G. coccineum* and *G. chiloense* hybrids are eye-catching at the front of borders and in island beds or containers, while *G. urbanum* and *G. rivale* cultivars are useful for more naturalistic plantings combining well with the linear foliage of grasses.

Most cultivars are habitually, or have occasionally been, raised from seed. It is important to be aware that the inherent tendency of geums to hybridize can result in some unexpected variation in plants grown from home-saved seed, or

LEFT 1 *Geum* 'Dolly North'
2 *G.* 'Fire Opal' **3** *G.* 'Flames of Passion' **4** *G.* 'Lady Stratheden'
5 *G.* 'Lemon Drops' **6** *G.* 'Marmalade'

GROWING GEUMS FROM SEED

Geums are easily raised from seed and grow quickly to flowering size, so this is a means of propagation often used by both nurseries and home gardeners. Several of our favorite cultivars, such as 'Lady Stratheden' and 'Mrs. J. Bradshaw', will come reliably true from seed; many others usually vary little, if they have not been allowed to hybridize. However, to avoid the retail and cultivation of misnamed plants, it is important that plants that are not true to type are discarded, or at least not grown under the same cultivar names as their parents.

If space is available, geums can be raised like summer bedding plants from an early spring sowing at about 70°F (21°C), in which case they will flower in their first summer. However, with space at a premium in spring, a later sowing in early summer is often more practical, and this will still allow plants to become established before winter and flower prolifically the following year. Germination can be slow, perhaps taking four weeks, so you need to be patient.

even some surprisingly different plants appearing.

CULTIVATION Most species and cultivars enjoy a moist but well-drained soil rich in organic matter. Most tolerate some shade, but flower best in good light, when staking should not be required; *G. montanum* must have well-drained soil and an open site. Divide every few years to avoid congestion and reinvigorate aging plants. Plants can be encouraged to continue flowering into fall by frequent deadheading.

PROPAGATION Divide in fall or spring. Some cultivars will come true from seed but their promiscuity means variation is frequently encountered in other seed-raised cultivars.

PROBLEMS Sawfly larvae, leaf miner and mildew.

G. 'Beech House Apricot' Forms low clumps of foliage and bears ruffled, upward-facing, soft yellow flowers edged in apricot from mid-spring to midsummer. Possibly a *G. x intermedium* seedling. ‡ 10 in (25 cm). Z5–8 H8–5

G. 'Bell Bank' Lovely, nodding, double pink flowers, make good ground cover but require a cool spot. This cultivar, a *G. rivale* hybrid, was lost to cultivation but recently reintroduced by Dove Cottage Nursery in West Yorkshire, England. ‡ 12 in (30 cm). Z5–8 H8–5

G. 'Blazing Sunset' Very large, fluffy, double scarlet flowers borne from late spring, and often repeat-blooming until fall. Similar to 'Mrs. Bradshaw' but usually with larger, more double flowers. A hybrid of *G. chiloense* introduced by Thompson & Morgan

Seed Company and often offered as seed. ‡ 24 in (60 cm). Z5–8 H8–5

G. 'Borisii' A widely used name applied to a range of plants, including the entirely unrelated, and rarely seen, *G. x borisii* and variants of *G. coccineum*. It is unclear to which plant this name should be correctly applied. It would be helpful if nurseries and gardeners could eschew this name and try to identify their plants more correctly.

G. bulgaricum Spreading on thick rhizomes, and producing large, softly hairy, grayish green leaves, each with one large, toothed, kidney-shaped leaflet at the end and five to seven pairs of much smaller lateral leaflets. The flowering stems are upright, bear small leaves, and carry three to seven, nodding, 1 in (2.5 cm) flowers in shades from white to orange. Rare in gardens: the yellow-flowered plant sold under this name is probably *G. x heldreichii*, a hybrid between *G. coccineum* and *G. montanum*. From mountains in the Balkans ‡ 20 in (50 cm). Z5–8 H8–5

G. coccineum Clump-forming, softly hairy perennial producing leaves to 8 in (20 cm) long divided into five to seven leaflets, the leaflet at the end being kidney-shaped, sharply toothed or lobed, and much larger than the other, oppositely paired leaflets. Distinctively brick-red, spreading flowers, to 1½ in (4 cm) across, are borne late spring to midsummer, or later, on erect two- to four-flowered stems. Best in damp soils, but tolerates drier conditions, where it may be short-lived. From almost boggy habitats in southern Europe. ‡ 18 in (45 cm). Z5 **'Cooky'** Flowers bright orange. **'Werner Arends'** Compact growth habit and profusely borne, semidouble orange flowers, tinted red. ‡ 10 in (25 cm). Z5–8 H8–5

G. 'Coppertone' Nodding, double flowers, 2 in (5 cm) across, in an unusual copper-apricot color are produced from late spring to midsummer. A hybrid of *G. rivale*. ‡ 12 in (30 cm). Z5–8 H8–5

G. 'Dingle Apricot' Low-growing and producing an abundance of pale apricot flowers with darker markings from late spring to midsummer. ‡ 8 in (20 cm). Z5–8 H8–5

G. 'Dolly North' Large peachy orange flowers from late spring to late summer. A hybrid of *G. chiloense*. ‡ 20 in (50 cm). Z5–8 H8–5

G. 'Farmer John Cross' Low-growing, with nodding golden yellow flowers from dark buds carried on red stems, late spring to late summer. A hybrid of *G. rivale*. ‡ 12 in (30 cm). Z5–8 H8–5

G. 'Feuerball' see 'Mrs. Bradshaw'

G. 'Fire Opal' Dark stems bear semi-double, orange-red flowers to 1½ in

RIGHT *Geum rivale* 'Leonard's Variety'

(3.5 cm) wide. Petals are paler on the reverse; not found in similar cultivars. Good for front of border where can be appreciated. A hybrid of *G. chiloense*. ‡ 30 in (75 cm). Z5–8 H8–5

G. 'Flames of Passion' Attractive recent introduction forming mounds of foliage. Dark stems carry semidouble, rich red flowers from mid-spring to midsummer. Bred by Dutch breeder Piet Oudolf; likely a hybrid between *G. chiloense* and *G. rivale*. ‡ 20 in (50 cm). Z5–8 H8–5

G. 'Georgenburg' Large, single, orange-washed yellow flowers. Hybrid of *G. chiloense*. ‡ 12 in (30 cm). Z5–9 H9–3

G. 'Gold Ball' see 'Lady Stratheden'

G. x intermedium Variable, sometimes hairy plants. Short, thick rhizomes, carry leaves about 10 in (25 cm) long with a roundish terminal leaflet 2–3 in (5–8 cm) across and two to five pairs of lateral leaflets. Slightly hairy stems carry two to four, yellow, amber, or orange, usually nodding flowers, perhaps with pink overtones, in summer. A variable hybrid between *G. rivale* and *G. urbanum* with features intermediate between the two. ‡ 24 in (60 cm). Z5–8 H8–5

G. 'Karlskaer' Compact, neat mounds of foliage above which are carried single, upright apricot-orange flowers on dark stems, from late spring to late summer. ‡ 12 in (30 cm). Z5–8 H8–5

G. 'Lady Stratheden' syn. 'Gold Ball' Semidouble, rich yellow flowers throughout summer. Excellent hybrid of *G. chiloense* coming reliably true from seed. ‡ 20 in (50 cm). Z5–9 9–5

G. 'Lemon Drops' Low-growing with nodding, pale yellow flowers and prominent orange stamens. A hybrid of *G. rivale*. ‡ 10 in (25 cm). Z5–8 H8–5

G. 'Lionel Cox' Nodding, primrose-

colored, wavy-edged flowers emerge from dark buds over a long period in the summer. Forms attractive, compact mounds of soft green leaves but is sometimes weak in growth. A hybrid of *G. rivale*. ‡ 12 in (30 cm). Z3–8 H8–1

G. 'Marmalade' A neat plant producing single flowers with orange- and yellow-washed petals from dark buds from late spring to late summer. ‡ 16 in (40 cm). Z5–8 H8–5

G. 'Mrs. Bradshaw' A famous and favorite hybrid of *G. chiloense*, producing clusters of bright scarlet, semidouble flowers with ruffled petals, each up to 1¾ in (4.5 cm) across, from late spring into late summer. Raised from seed for many years, but usually grows fairly true. ‡ 20–28 in (50–70 cm). Z5–9 H9–5

G. 'Mrs. W. Moore' Pretty, nodding, semidouble, pink-flushed flowers, from late spring to midsummer. A hybrid of *G. rivale*. ‡ 12 in (30 cm). Z5–8 H8–5

G. 'Paso Doble' Large, frilly, very double blood red flowers are carried from late spring to midsummer on nodding stems. A hybrid of *G. chiloense*. ‡ 28 in (70 cm). Z5–8 H8–5

G. 'Prinses Juliana' Semidouble bright orange flowers, to 1¾ in (4.5 cm) across, flushed red on the margins, and produced from early to midsummer. A hybrid of *G. chiloense* dating back to 1923. ‡ 24 in (60 cm). Z5–8 H8–5

G. 'Red Wings' Bright scarlet, semi-double flowers up to 1¾ in (4.5 cm) across, produced freely from late spring to midsummer. Larger-flowered than 'Mrs. Bradshaw', but not with as many petals; more upright habit. A *G. coccineum* hybrid. ‡ 28 in (70 cm). Z5–9 H9–5

G. 'Rijnstroom' An attractive cultivar that produces brassy orange, semidouble

flowers over fresh green foliage during early and midsummer. ‡24 in (60 cm). Z5–8 H8–5

G. rivale (Water avens) Moisture-loving, rather variable, hairy perennial spreading on short, thick rhizomes from which emerge leaves that may be up to 14 in (35 cm) long but are usually smaller. The leaflets are toothed and in 3–6 unequal pairs, the top pair often considerably larger than the others, with a large, almost circular leaflet at the end of the leaf. Opening from dark buds, the attractive, nodding, bell-shaped, orange-pink, ¾ in (2 cm) flowers are carried in groups of 2–5 throughout the summer. Adaptable, enjoying moist conditions and tolerating a fair degree of shade, this is an excellent wild garden plant. From Iceland, North America, Europe, including Britain, and parts of Asia Minor. ‡8–32 in (20–80 cm). Z3–8 H8–1. **'Album'** White flowers. **'Leonard's Variety'** Orange-pink, brown-tinted flowers on dark stems. Perhaps a hybrid. ‡18 in (45 cm). **'Marika'** Very tall, graceful, pale-flowered variant found growing in Devon. ‡32 in (80 cm).

G. 'Rubin' Tall-growing. Large, double red flowers of a deeper, richer, more glowing color than similar cultivars; from late spring to late summer. Probably a hybrid of *G. chiloense*. ‡36 in (90 cm). Z5–8 H8–5

G. 'Sigiswang' Modestly sized but profusely borne orange flowers from late spring to late summer on a compact plant. Probably a hybrid of *G. coccineum*. ‡12 in (30 cm). Z5–8 H8–5

G. triflorum (Purple avens) An exceptionally hardy, silky-haired perennial with 6 in (15 cm) leaves; the unequal leaflets, in up to 15 pairs, are narrowly wedge-shaped and can be very hairy and gray, the leaflet at the end of the leaf being about the same size as the others. From early summer onward, the wiry flower stems carry up to three cream to purple, 1 in (2.5 cm) wide flowers that may have red margins and emerge from buds that are often attractively flushed with either red or purple. From cool, damp places or mountainous screes in North America. ‡18 in (45 cm). Z4–7 H7–1. **var. campanulatum** Smaller and less hardy, the petals tinged and veined crimson. ‡10 in (25 cm). Z4–7 H7–4

G. urbanum (Herb bennet, Wood avens) A hairy, spreading perennial on short rhizomes and producing leaves with only two or three pairs of oppositely arranged, unequal leaflets and a large leaflet at the end, to 3 in (8 cm) across. The flower stems are upright and carry up to three yellow-petaled flowers, to ⅝ in (1.5 cm) across, from late spring to late summer. Best in naturalistic settings, it may spread unwelcomingly. Found in scrub, woods, and other shady places in damp, usually fertile soils throughout most of Europe, including the British Isles, and also in western Asia and North Africa. ‡8–24 in (20–60 cm). Z5–8 H8–5. **'Checkmate'** Variegated with irregular white markings.

GILLENIA
Indian physic
ROSACEAE

A galaxy of delicate, shimmering stars decorates plants that are as tough as nails.

Both species are valued for their ornamental appeal as well as their medicinal prowess: Indian physic has a long history of use for both internal and external ailments, but is poisonous, so beware. Native to shady situations in the eastern and southeastern US, their compact crowns produce thick and spreading roots that carry wiry stems, sparsely clothed in toothed leaves with three leaflets. Delicate flowers with four slender, twisted petals are enchanting massed in their broad, airy clusters, reminiscent of *Gypsophila*, and complement coarse-textured flowers and foliage in beds and borders as well as looking good in informal cottage and meadow gardens. Rich yellow fall foliage adds to the plants' appeal. ⚠

CULTIVATION Best in moist, fertile soil in sun or part-shade, but, once established, plants are quite drought-tolerant and will tolerate full sun in all but the hottest areas. They spread slowly to form tight clumps that seldom need dividing.

PROPAGATION Take stem cuttings in spring or sow seed outdoors; germination occurs the next spring. Plants take three to four years to reach their best.

PROBLEMS Spider mites can occasionally be debilitating.

G. stipulata (American ipecac, Indian physic) Like *G. trifoliata* (below) but more delicate and noticeably more

open in form. As well as the three-lobed leaflets, the wiry stems carry persistent leaflike structures, called stipules, at each leaf joint, giving them a distinctive winged appearance. The flowers are carried in more open clusters and make less of a show than their more floriferous relation. Found in open woods and clearings and on roadsides from New York to Illinois, south to Georgia and Texas. ‡12–36 in (30–90 cm). Z5–9 H9–5

G. trifoliata (Bowman's root, Indian physic) An erect, shrublike perennial with thick, deep roots from which grow slim but strong stems. Broad terminal clusters of starry, white or pinkish, fragrant flowers smother the plant in late spring or early summer. Grows most densely in full sun to light shade; plants tend to lean toward the light in shaded situations, but bloom well. From open woods, clearings, rocky slopes, and roadsides from southern Ontario and New England, south to Georgia, Kentucky, and Alabama. ‡4 ft (1.2 m). Z5–9 H9–5. **'Pixie'** Dwarf form with full-sized flowers. ‡6 in (15 cm).

GLAUCIDIUM
GLAUCIDIACEAE

Large, poppylike, mauve or occasionally white flowers held above attractive foliage distinguish this enticing shade-lover.

The only species is a deciduous perennial from Japan that has distinctive jaggedly-lobed leaves and late spring flowers, followed by paired green seedpods. Especially valuable for its bold presence, it is good for use as a specimen plant among smaller species.

LEFT *Gillenia trifoliata*

ABOVE *Glaucidium palmatum*

CULTIVATION Best in moist, acid soil in light shade.

PROPAGATION Either from seed or by careful division in early spring.

PROBLEMS Slugs and snails.

G. palmatum From a short, stout rhizome grow two or three long-stalked, maplelike, lobed leaves up to 8 in (20 cm) wide. Solitary light purple or lilac flowers, 2½–3 in (6–8 cm) across and enhanced by a boss of deep yellow stamens, open just above the leaves in late spring and early summer. The plant needs cool, sheltered, woodland conditions, with a soil rich in humus. The seed offered may sometimes be a mix of the lilac and white forms. From mountain woodlands of central and northern Japan. ‡18–24 in (45–60 cm). Z6–9 H9–6. **var. leucanthum** Large, pure white flowers.

GLECHOMA
LAMIACEAE

Hardwearing ground cover or hanging basket plants best known in gardens for their pretty variegated forms.

Approximately 12 species are widespread in Europe and have extended into parts of temperate Asia. They have also escaped from cultivation in North America. *Glechoma* are plants of woodlands and hedgerows, that spread vigorously on long, slender stems that root readily wherever they touch the soil. The roughly toothed leaves may be either hairy or hairless. Tubular, usually blue or purple flowers are carried on short upright stems in spring or summer. Only one species is widely grown.

CULTIVATION Grows well in sun or shade, preferably in moist but well-drained soil.

PROPAGATION By division in spring or fall, by taking soft cuttings in spring, or by detaching rooted shoots.

PROBLEMS Slugs and snails.

G. hederacea Spreads vigorously on straggling, mat-forming stems up to 3¼ ft (1 m) or more in length, with small, toothed, kidney-shaped to almost round leaves. The two–lipped deadnettle-like flowers are usually violet or mauve, sometimes white or pink, and carried in clusters on upright stems from early to late summer. Reverted shoots of variegated cultivars should be removed. Found on heavy soils in woodlands and rough ground in Europe, including Britain. ↕12–20 in (30–50 cm). Z5–9 H9–5. **'Barry Yinger Variegated'** Leaves broadly margined and blotched with cream. **'Variegata'** Leaves irregularly edged and marbled with pure white. Reluctant to flower.

GLYCERIA
Sweet grass
POACEAE

A succulent, graceful, and resilient, if vigorous grass for wet places. Some 40 perennial species are found in temperate regions throughout the world in wet places and shallow water, but only one—is grown in gardens. Most spread by strong-growing creeping rhizomes. The flowerheads vary from loose, graceful plumes to more compact spikes with small nodding flowers.

CULTIVATION Grow in moisture-retentive soil or shallow water in full sun to part-shade. The trick is to achieve a balance between

RIGHT *Glycyrrhiza glabra*

providing sufficient moisture to prevent plants from losing lower leaves, but not so much that it spreads everywhere.

PROPAGATION From seed sown in spring; by division for var. *variegata*.

PROBLEMS Usually trouble-free

G. maxima (Hay grass) A tall, creeping bog grass. Thick vigorous rhizomes, form large stands of bright green, sharp-edged leaves, ¾ in (2 cm) wide. From early to late summer, stout stems carry many-branched feathery flowerheads hung with green, purple-tinged flowers. It prefers slightly alkaline condition; can be grown in any moisture-retentive soil in sun and slow-running water, large ponds, and marshes in water up to 18 in (45 cm) deep. Can be invasive, but is useful for preventing soil erosion on river and pond banks. Common in most of Europe and Asia; introduced elsewhere. ↕4 ft (1.2 m). Z4–9 H10–3. **var. *variegata*** Leaves with white or creamy yellow vertical stripes, paler in drier conditions; new leaves are pale pink in spring. ↕30 in (75 cm).

GLYCYRRHIZA
PAPILIONACEAE

P ale, late-summer blooms contrast well with more strident colors in large borders or wild gardens.

About 20 species of these rather coarse perennials are found in the Mediterranean region, North Africa, and North and South America, in habitats as varied as dry scrub and swamp. Their sticky foliage is either three-lobed or has small leaflets on either side of a central rib, in the same way as in Solomon's seal (*Polygonatum*). The flowers are pealike and in short, upright spikes arising from the leaf joints. Suitable for a wild garden or informal border.

CULTIVATION Best in deep, fertile soils and full sun.

PROPAGATION From seed sown in spring or fall, or by division in spring.

PROBLEMS Powdery mildew and rust are sometimes troublesome.

G. glabra syn. *G. glandulifera* (Licorice) A deep-rooting, steadily spreading

perennial, with leaves with up to 17 oblong to oval leaflets arranged alternately along the central stalk. The pale blue to lilac flowers bloom on short stems that are up to 3 in (8 cm) long in late summer and are followed by small brown seedpods. The plant's woody roots are the source of licorice, used in the manufacture of candy and medicines. From the Mediterranean region and south-western Asia. ↕4 ft (1.2 m). Z9–11 H12–10

G. glandulifera see *G. glabra*

GUNNERA
GUNNERACEAE

P lants of two foliage extremes: massive-leaved moisture-lovers for a dramatic waterside statement, or demure, creeping mat-formers.

About 40 species of deciduous and evergreen perennials (and even one annual) are native to moist areas of South America, southern Africa, Malaysia, Australia, New Zealand, Hawaii, and some southern hemisphere islands. The giant species are deciduous and clump-forming, eventually forming substantial colonies of massive, rounded,

LEFT 1 *Glechoma hederacea* 'Variegata'
2 *Glyceria maxima* var. *variegata*

jaggedly lobed leaves on tall stalks. The low-growing species form dense mats of small leaves and often have attractive fruits. In both types, tiny individual flowers are borne on spikes proportionate to the size of the plant. Some of the smaller species have male and female flowers on different plants, so both sexes are required in order to appreciate the fleshy, colored fruits.

CULTIVATION All require damp soil, the larger species preferring waterside or boggy areas and the smaller ones needing humus-rich soil in an open area. Protect the crown of larger species over winter in frost-prone areas; this is best done with layers of their own leaves secured with twine or straw held down with netting. A sheltered site and fertile soil with regular feeding encourages huge growth in the large species.

PROPAGATION Divide in spring. In the larger species, take cuttings of basal leaf buds—though these are difficult to manage. Sow fresh seed when ripe in cool, frost-free conditions. Dried seed may take a year to germinate but is often not viable.

PROBLEMS Usually trouble-free.

G. flavida Evergreen and mat-forming, its spreading stems root as they go and carry broadly elliptical, brownish green, long-stalked 1-in (2.5-cm) leaves with scalloped margins. Short spikes of greenish flowers in early summer and midsummer are followed in late summer by yellow fruits that persist into winter. Needs a moist site free from competition. From New Zealand. ‡6 in (15 cm). Z8–10 H10–8

G. hamiltonii Evergreen, forming patches of overlapping rosettes of brownish-green, triangular, raggedly toothed, 2-in (5-cm) leaves with distinctive winged leaf stalks. Spikes of greenish flowers are produced in early summer and midsummer; female plants bear small orange-red fruits if male plants are present. Needs moist conditions. Extremely rare in the wild; restricted to small populations in damp, sandy hollows on South Island and Stewart Island, New Zealand. ‡4 in (10 cm). Z8–10 H10–8

G. magellanica Deciduous and mat-forming, its stems spread widely across the soil to form extensive colonies. Emerald green, kidney-shaped 3½-in (9-cm) leaves, cup-shaped when young, with scalloped, wavy margins, are borne on erect stalks. The red-flushed flowers are produced in conical clusters just above the leaves in mid- and late spring. Male plants are more common in gardens, but flowers of females, if successfully pollinated, produce small, spherical, fleshy, orange-red fruits. Prefers a moist, open site, but is tolerant

of drier conditions, where it tends to form clumps. From southern South America and the Falkland Islands. ‡6 in (15 cm). Z8–9 H9–8

G. manicata (Brazilian giant rhubarb) The largest of the hardy species, and one of the largest herbaceous perennials cultivated in temperate gardens. Thick, compact rhizomes form large clumps with large, rounded to kidney-shaped, jagged-toothed, sharply lobed leaves, 5–6½ ft (1.5–2 m) or more across, and are carried on substantial leaf stalks, 5–8 ft (1.5–2.5 m) tall, with reddish prickles. Large, usually erect, conical to narrowly egg-shaped flowerheads, to 4 ft (1.2 m) in length, are more than three times as long as they are wide. Slender branches, the longest about 4 in (10 cm), bear small greenish flowers in late spring. Requires fertile, permanently moist soil in sun or part-shade. From colder parts of southern Brazil. ‡5–8 ft (1.5–2.5 m). Z7–10 H12–7

G. prorepens (Creeping gunnera) Deciduous and mat-forming, its stems spread widely to form a slowly expanding colony. The brownish green, egg-shaped, 1¼-in (3-cm) leaves with scalloped margins have stout leaf stalks. Dense spikes of flowers, in early summer and midsummer, are followed by reddish purple, raspberry-like fruits, often lasting until early winter. Best in sun or part-shade and moist soil, preferably slightly drier in winter. From New Zealand. ‡4 in (10 cm). Z8–10 H10–8

G. tinctoria (Chilean giant rhubarb) The slightly less giant of the "giant rhubarbs," similar to *G. manicata* but smaller in all its parts. The jagged-lobed leaves are typically no more than 5 ft (1.5 m) across and the 5-ft (1.5-m) leaf stalks have green prickles. The cylindrical, 3¼-ft (1-m) flowerheads are more than four times as long as they are wide, with stout branches, the

SURPRISES WITH GIANT RHUBARB

Some *Gunnera* species are widely referred to as "giant rhubarbs"—in particular, *G. manicata* and *G. tinctoria*. They are, of course, not real rhubarbs at all. Rhubarbs, both ornamental and culinary, belong to the genus *Rheum*, to which *Gunnera* is not even distantly related—a reminder that a superficial resemblance of foliage is no guide to true botanical relationships. In fact *Gunnera* is, rather surprisingly, more closely related to *Buxus*.

Even more surprisingly to many, some *Gunnera* species are exactly the opposite of "giant"; *G. hamiltonii* and many others are low, creeping plants.

Gunneras are sometimes grown in surprising ways, too. The huge *G. tinctoria* is, albeit only occasionally, seen grown in a patio container placed in a constantly refilled saucer of water; the astonishment of visitors is worth the at times daily attention. And some of the small creeping species are even grown in pans in the alpine greenhouse.

LEFT 1 *Gunnera magellanica*
2 *G. manicata* **3** *G. tinctoria*

ABOVE *Gymnocarpium dryopteris*

About 100 annual and perennial species, ranging from upright border plants to low, trailing ones suitable for the rock garden, occur in the wild mostly on rocky or sandy alkaline soils in the eastern Mediterranean, Central Asia, and northwestern China. Slender wiry stems, with a slight bluish sheen, spring from unusually tight crowns supported by deep fleshy roots, and carry generally lance-shaped leaves, held in opposite pairs, also with a gray-blue sheen. The tiny, five-petaled flowers in pink or white are carried singly or in many-flowered sprays, at their best creating billowing clouds with many hundreds of blooms on each stem. Ideal for expanding into border spaces left empty by earlier-flowering perennials, such as Oriental poppies. Gypsophilas also make superb cut flowers and can be dried for winter decoration (*see* Growing for Cutting). Many cultivars, developed as commercial cut flowers, are becoming available to gardeners.

CULTIVATION Best in a deep, well-drained, preferably alkaline soil in full sun, *Gypsophila* does unusually well in clay loam soil; in heavy ground, plants tend to be short-lived. Cut back after flowering to promote a second flush. Do not bother trying to move a mature plant; it will probably die.

PROPAGATION Difficult. Seed of species should be sown in warmth in winter, or outside in spring. Due to the very compact woody crown and deep roots, cultivars were traditionally grafted onto seedlings. Now they are raised commercially by tissue culture. In the garden, cuttings of young sideshoots taken with a small heel should root in sandy soil and some success can be had with root cuttings. But either

longest no more than 3 in (8 cm), and bear small reddish green flowers aging to reddish brown, in late spring. The green prickles are usually enough to distinguish it from the red-prickled *G. manicata*. Needs fertile, permanently moist soil in sun or part-shade. Starting to show invasive tendencies in California, especially along Tomales Bay in the Point Reyes National Seashore. From southern Chile and Argentina. ‡5 ft (1.5 m). Z8–10 H10–8

GYMNOCARPIUM
Oak Fern
WOODSIACEAE

Delicate, carpet-forming ferns; a delightful ground cover in cool, shady woodlands or among shrubs.

About 10 species of these small deciduous ferns occur throughout northern temperate regions. Well-separated, thin-textured, triangular fronds arise from slender creeping rhizomes. Naked spore clusters are scattered on the frond's underside.

CULTIVATION Grow in well-drained, humus-rich acidic to neutral soil in moist shade.

PROPAGATION By division or from spores.

PROBLEMS Usually trouble-free.

G. dryopteris (Oak fern) Creeping deciduous fern with a wide-spreading rhizome. Broadly triangular fronds, to 8 in (20 cm) long and two to three times divided, with blunt lobes, are a beautiful fresh green and are carried on a leaf stalk that is at least as long as the frond again, and almost without scales. Will spread through a border if

RIGHT *Gypsophila paniculata* 'Happy Festival'

conditions are suitable, but unwanted patches are fairly easily removed. Once established, can stand dry conditions, although fronds will be shorter. Grows wild in cool deciduous, coniferous, or mixed woodland in Europe, North America, and Asia east to China and Japan. ‡4–12 in (10–30 cm). Z4–8 H8–1. **'Plumosum'** Fronds more leafy with broader segments.

GYNERIUM *see* CORTADERIA

GYPSOPHILA
Baby's breath
CARYOPHYLLACEAE

Masses of tiny flowers on thin, airy stems make these popular plants much appreciated both in borders and in vases.

GROWING FOR CUTTING

Gypsophila is one of the most important commercial cut-flower crops, and is just as valuable for the home grower. Double-flowered perennials last particularly well—annual forms (of *G. elegans*), though, are decidedly inferior. However, the stems are intertwined and removing individual sprays without damage is difficult. Serious flower-arrangers shoiuld set aside a row of plants and cut from just one of them each time stems are needed. This will usually also promote another flush of flowers.

For immediate use, stems can be cut when 80 percent of their flowers are open. They are unusually sensitive to the growth of bacteria in the water; flower preservative will help preserve them. For drying, cut at about the same stage or a little later. The simplest method of drying *Gypsophila* is to stand the stems in a container in a lighted area with their bases just covered with water. A temperature of about 50°F (10°C) is ideal.

way, the success rate is low and buying commercially propagated plants is simpler.

PROBLEMS Crown gall may develop on grafted plants. Leafhoppers may spread virus as well as themselves debilitating the plants.

G. Festival Series Double or semidouble flowers appear in early summer and midsummer on plants that are more productive and more compact than many older cultivars. Cutting back the stems may well produce repeat flowers. Good for the border, for cutting, for containers, or even for large hanging baskets. ‡30 in (75 cm). Z5–9 H9–1. **'Festival'** Rich pink. **'Festival Pink'** Pale pink. **'Festival Star'** White and more compact. ‡14 in (35 cm). **'Happy Festival'** White with a faint pink blush. **'White Festival'** Pure white.

G. paniculata A deep-rooted perennial that resents disturbance once established, forming a rounded mound with thin stems covered with small single flowers in midsummer. The species is rarely grown, since the blooms of the double-flowered cultivars last longer and have more impact. From central and eastern Europe. ‡4 ft (1.2 m). Z5–9 H9–1. **'Bristol Fairy'** Large, white flowers like tiny powder-puffs. Introduced in 1928, for many years this was the first choice of flower arrangers. ‡36 in (90 cm). **'Compacta Plena'** Shorter, double soft pink to white flowers, less prolific than 'Bristol Fairy'. ‡18 in (45 cm). **'Flamingo'** Prolific double pale pink. **'Pink Fairy'** Shorter, long-flowering pale pink double, blooming into fall. ‡18 in (45 cm). **'Schneeflocke'** (Snowflake) Early-flowering white double, unusually heat-tolerant. Raised from seed. **'Viette's Dwarf'** Compact, long-flowering, light pink flowers. ‡16 in (40 cm).

H

HACQUETIA
APIACEAE

Intriguing early woodlander for shady situations, where it will seed around, forming small colonies.

The single, very dwarf species is related to but quite unlike *Astrantia* in appearance. This unique and distinctive perennial, native to the eastern Dolomites from eastern to northern Italy into Croatia and Slovenia and the Carpathians, grows naturally in damp, open deciduous woodlands and on moist, grassy slopes. Its bright yellow flowers are attractively set off by fresh green foliage. Delightful in association with other woodland perennials, such as anemones, hellebores, epimediums, erythroniums, pulmonarias, and snowdrops.

CULTIVATION Prefers shady, moist but well-drained conditions, although it tolerates summer drought well due to its strong and substantial root system. Best near a path where close inspection is possible. Do not allow it to be overwhelmed by more vigorous neighbors.

PROPAGATION From seed sown fresh in early summer; germination occurs early the following spring. Seedlings should be pricked out while still small as they quickly produce an extremely long root. Established plants can also be divided in early spring or after flowering, although the resultant divisions are slow to grow away.

PROBLEMS Usually trouble free.

H. epipactis A small clump-forming perennial, flowering for many weeks from late winter to early spring. The delightful heads of tiny yellow flowers are surrounded by five to seven fresh green, petal-like leaves (bracts), 1½ in (4 cm) across, held on short stems up to 4 in (10 cm) high. The three to five broad, lobed leaves develop after the flowers blossom and form a weed-smothering carpet until they begin to die away in fall. ↕4–10 in (10–25 cm). Z5–7 H7–5. **'Thor'** syn. 'Variegata' Leaves and floral bracts are pale gray-green and strongly margined and streaked with creamy white. Propagate carefully, by division only.

RIGHT **1** *Hacquetia epipactis*
2 *Hakonechloa macra* 'Aureola'

HAKONECHLOA
POACEAE

A clump-forming, smooth-leaved grass somewhat resembling a rather floppy miniature bamboo.

The one species is from a very specific habitat and area in Japan, but adapts well to gardens. A number of slightly confusing variegated forms are most widely grown.

CULTIVATION Grows best in well-drained, moisture-retentive, fertile soil, in sun to semishade. Allow space for its slow spread.

PROPAGATION Divide in spring as the new growth begins to appear.

PROBLEMS Usually trouble-free.

H. macra Forming low, deciduous mounds, the long-stemmed, bright green leaves, up to ¼ in (8 mm) wide, become red-tinged in fall. In late summer and early fall, wiry arching stems bear small loose flowerheads that flutter among the foliage. Best in a cool, damp spot and, in hotter climates, in shade. Variegated forms also look superb as specimen plants in large, low containers, and with blue and red foliage plants. Their names are confused both in gardens and nurseries and most have been sold under each other's names. From damp clefts on wet cliffs on Honshu Island, Japan. ↕14 in (35 cm). Z5–9 H9–5. **'Alboaurea'** syn. 'Aurea', 'Variegata' Long white and deep yellow stripes with thinner green stripes. Less vigorous than the species. Often confused with 'Aureola'. **'Albolineata'** syn. 'Albovariegata', 'Variegata' Green foliage, white edges and midrib. **'Aurea'** *see* 'Alboaurea'. **'Aureola'** Bright yellow leaves with very thin green stripes and pink tint in fall. In cooler climates, leaves may turn creamier. The most widely grown form. **'Mediovariegata'** Green, with a broad central cream stripe. **'Variegata'** *see* 'Alboaurea', 'Albolineata'.

HEDYCHIUM
Butterfly flower
ZINGIBERACEAE

Increasingly popular subtropicals grown for their exotic foliage and bold, colorful flowers.

About 50 species of these steadily spreading perennials are native to largely subtropical regions of Asia, the Himalaya, and Madagascar. Found in forests and forest margins in light shade or some sun, they

THE SIMPLER, THE BETTER

TWO WELL-KNOWN, RELIABLE, and attractive plants are here simply set side by side to create a very attractive picture. Both are tightly clump-forming and create weed-smothering mounds. The elegant, yellow waterfall of variegated *Hakonechloa macra* 'Aureola' complements the broad, deep green leaves of *Hosta* 'Francee' with its neat white edging. The hosta leaves overlap like fish scales, or strike out sideways, allowing the grass blades to slip between and arch down in slender ribbons. Fertile soil and a little shade will help this combination look its best all summer.

often grow alongside streams and in other wet places. The fat rhizomes grow on or just below the soil surface and send up fleshy, erect, reedlike stems. The shoots and, especially, the roots give off a gingery smell. Stout stems, up to 10 ft (3 m) high, carry luxuriant, usually lance-shaped foliage that may be topped, in late summer, by spectacular spikes of usually fragrant flowers held in green leaflike bracts; in some species, several flowers open at the same time, in others only one or two. Each bloom is slender and usually orange, yellow, white, or near-red, and may be followed by rounded fruit capsules.

Hedychiums are of particular use in creating a subtropical effect, and those that are not fully hardy may be planted outdoors for the summer, then lifted in the fall, the rhizomes stored in frost-free conditions over winter. Many species, however, may survive outdoors in southern zones, especially if some form of winter protection is provided. Stems will be blackened by the first frost, but shoots should appear from the roots the following spring.

Plants are sometimes confused in cultivation and are hard to identify; this is exacerbated by the fact that the species can be variable and plants hybridize readily.

They associate well in borders not only with other subtropical plants such as cannas, dahlias, and bananas, but also with *Crocosmia*, bold grasses such as *Miscanthus*, and even asters, which flower at a similar time.

CULTIVATION Plant in hot, sunny, sheltered borders, especially against a wall or fence, to help promote flower production. Many will also succeed in light shade around trees. They need rich, well-drained soil and plenty of moisture in summer, but are best kept rather dry in winter to prevent the fleshy roots from rotting. Cut back in fall and protect the roots with a deep mulch (*see* Tropicals in Temperate Gardens).

PROPAGATION. Divide in spring or, for the species, sow ripe seed at 70°F (21°C).

PROBLEMS Slugs and snails.

H. coccineum A variable but noticeably vigorous species, its stout stems carrying sharply pointed, lance-shaped foliage 1½ x 18 in (3.5 x 45 cm) with a distinctive gray bloom. The flowers range from yellowish orange to rich red. One of the hardier species, it tolerates some light frost, especially if given winter protection. Worth growing in sheltered gardens. From the Himalaya, extending into India and Bangladesh. ‡6½ ft (2 m). Z8–10 H10–8. **'Tara'** Magnificent, with large heads of reddish orange flowers and hardier than most. Sometimes listed as a form of *H. gardnerianum*. Most desirable; introduced from Nepal by horticulturist Tony Schilling and named for his daughter. Z4–10 H10–9

H. coronarium Superb, if rather tender species. The distinctive lance-shaped leaves, up to 24 in (60 cm) long, have downy undersides. The deliciously fragrant flowers are white and yellow, held in elliptical flowerheads up to 8 in (20 cm) long, but may only be freely produced in hot summers. From mostly tropical regions at altitudes to 6,200 ft (1,900 m). ‡6½ ft (2 m). Z9–11 H11–7

H. densiflorum One of the hardiest but shortest species. Fat clumps carry smooth, oblong or lance-shaped leaves up to 12 in (30 cm) long. It flowers early—in late summer—when short spikes of small, scented flowers appear at the end of each stem, usually pale orange-red, although in some plants flowers can be yellowish or even pinkish. The flowers usually open in one brilliant flush. From Nepal and the eastern Himalaya. ‡3¼ ft (1 m). Z8–11 H11–7. **'Assam Orange'** Large flower spikes of rich orange blooms, and rather narrower leaves than the species. Collected by Frank Kingdon-Ward in 1938. Z9–11 H11–9. **'Stephen'** Flowers about twice as large, in 8-in (20-cm) spikes, are primrose yellow with orange centers and have a delicious nocturnal perfume. Collected in Nepal by Tony Schilling and named for his son. Exceptional and highly distinctive. Z9–10 H10–9

H. 'Dr. Moy' (syn. 'Robustum') A show-stopper for variegation lovers with white streaks and speckles on deep green leaves. Butterfly-shaped flowers, pale peachy-orange with a

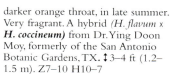

ABOVE 1 *Hedychium densiflorum*
2 *H. gardnerianum*

darker orange throat, in late summer. Very fragrant. A hybrid (*H. flavum* x *H. coccineum*) from Dr. Ying Doon Moy, formerly of the San Antonio Botanic Gardens, TX. ‡3–4 ft (1.2–1.5 m). Z7–10 H10–7

H. 'Elizabeth' Stunning ginger lily, huge raspberry pink flowers with delightful honeysuckle fragrance. Hybrid developed by Tom Wood, FL. ‡7–9 ft (2.1–2.7 m). Z7–10 H10–7

H. flavescens The lance-shaped leaves, about 24 in (60 cm) long, have long slender points and are downy underneath. Spicy-smelling, 8-in (20-cm) spikes of creamy yellow flowers, usually in early fall. Suitable for outdoor cultivation in sheltered locations with protection where, as long as the frost holds off for long enough, the exotically scented blooms will be produced. From the eastern Himalaya. ‡6½ ft (2 m). Z9–11 H11–8

H. gardnerianum Probably the finest species, it is certainly one of the largest and most vigorous, and in many warmer countries has become an invasive weed. A rather variable plant; the bold, oval, 16-in (40-cm) leaves have a faint blue tint, and the huge flowerheads, through summer and fall, are sweetly scented and may be bright yellow or orange with red stamens. In frost-prone regions. it is less invasive and makes a fine garden plant. It is also often seen in conservatories and greenhouses. From Nepal and Assam. ‡5 ft (1.5 m). Z9–10 H11–8

H. greenii More often seen than most species, the dramatic maroon-red, slender-pointed oblong leaves, carried on maroon stems, are its main feature. Bulbils are often produced along the stems and simplify propagation. The attractive orange-red flowers have no perfume and appear very late, well into mid-fall, when they can be damaged by frost (or it may be too cool for flowers to form at all); but the foliage is value enough. Given a thick mulch and a

warm corner, plants should survive outside over winter in mild areas. From Bhutan and northern India. ‡6½ ft (2 m). Z9–11 H11–9

H. 'Peach Delight' Peach-colored flowers with darker orange throats. Fabulously fragrant. Introduced by Tony Avent, Plant Delights Nursery, NC. ‡6–7 ft (1.8–2.1 m). Z7–10 H10–7.

H. 'Pradhanii' One of the oldest ginger lily cultivars that remain in cultivation. Large spikes of creamy peach-colored flowers bloom from late summer to frost. Light fragrance. ‡6–7 ft (1.8–2.1 m). Z7–10 H10–7

H. spicatum The hardiest species and short in stature, so it is one of the most useful in the garden. The slender-pointed, 16-in- (40-cm-) long, oblong or lance-shaped leaves have a scattering of hairs on their undersides and are 1¼–4 in (3–10 cm) across. Small, lightly scented, orange and white flowers appear in early fall, followed by seed capsules that are orange inside and split open to reveal red seeds. Widespread in China, Nepal, and much of the Himalaya. ‡3¼ ft (1 m). Z7–11 H11–9

HEDYSARUM
PAPILIONACEAE

Sweetly scented plants for the back of a border, attracting butterflies and making unexpectedly good cut flowers.

More than 100 small deciduous shrubs and perennials are native to meadows and the edges of woodlands in Europe and Asia. Many are suitable for the rock garden (but may be invasive), and just one perennial is usually grown. From its deep roots rise erect, generally self-supporting stems carrying more or less elliptical leaves

TROPICALS IN TEMPERATE GARDENS

Hedychiums come from areas that experience monsoons in summer and much drier, cooler winters—difficult conditions to emulate in many temperate gardens. However, in climate zones 8 and 9 they can be treated as hardy perennials and will bring impressive tropical style if given the hottest corners. To flower freely outside before frosts, plants need to receive as much sun as possible, so limit competition from neighboring plants. Plant in late spring or early summer when any danger of frost has passed and the plants are growing well. In cool areas it is wise to plant rather deeply, at about 4 in (10 cm)

for added protection. Soak bare tubers in water for several hours, then start them off in pots of well-drained potting mix in a conservatory or greenhouse to encourage growth.

Before planting, improve the soil by adding plenty of well-rotted manure, and if it is not well drained, some sand or gravel. In late fall, after the flowers have faded and the shoots are frosted, cut them to the ground and apply a thick mulch of straw, fallen leaves, or bracken. New shoots often appear rather late in spring, so remember where plants are positioned to avoid damaging them when cultivating the soil.

ABOVE *Hedysarum coronarium*

with several oval to lance-shaped leaflets arranged in opposite pairs along a central rib. The pealike flowers appear in the leaf joints and at the ends of the shoots. A showy plant, it is especially valuable for dry, high-limestone soil situations.

CULTIVATION Grow in light to sandy, well-drained soil. Avoid disturbing the plant once established.

PROPAGATION From seed, sown as soon as ripe or in spring. Division is generally impractical owing to the tight, deep root system.

PROBLEMS Slugs.

H. coronarium (French honeysuckle) Upright, bushy perennial with slightly bluish green leaves divided into three to seven pairs of leaflets with one at the tip. In summer, dense, fragrant spikes of 10–40 bright red, rarely white, pea flowers open among the leaves. May be grown as a biennial. From the western Mediterranean and Italy; French honeysuckle is an important food for honey bees in southern Europe. ↕ 4 ft (1.2 m). Z4–9 H9–4

HELENIUM
Sneezeweed
ASTERACEAE

Tough daisies that provide long-lasting color and are particularly valued for their bronze-orange and copper-red tones.

Forty species, including some annuals and biennials, grow on damp grassland, streamsides, and woodland edges in North and Central America. Typically clump-forming, they produce erect, leafy, branching stems bearing alternate, lance-shaped to egg-shaped leaves. The flowerheads, on wiry stems just above the foliage, have a prominent, central sphere of brown or yellow

disk florets surrounded by a collar of broad-tipped ray florets in yellow, orange, or red. As the flowers age, the rays gradually turn back (reflex), emphasizing the spherical center. The color of the disk florets and the degree of overlapping, width, and number and color of the ray florets help distinguish the cultivars, as does the degree of toothing in the leaves. In some, the rays are dramatically bicolored with the second color forming longitudinal streaks or contrasting marks at the base and tip. The mostly hidden undersides of the rays may be a different color.

Some begin flowering in midsummer; others, particularly the taller ones, start in early fall and many continue into mid-fall. They make good cut flowers and are favored by bees. The most widely grown cultivars are mainly derived from *H. autumnale*, itself popular in wild gardens and prairie borders, and the rarely encountered *H. bigelovii* and *H. flexuosum*. Many were raised in Holland and Germany and do not have English names; the translations sometimes used are confusing. The American common name, sneezeweed, is derived from the false belief that the flowers cause hay fever. All parts are toxic if eaten, and contact with foliage or sap may irritate skin. ⚠

CULTIVATION Ideal for herbaceous or mixed borders or more informal schemes, heleniums are extremely tough but need full sun and fertile, moisture-retentive soil. Leggy or bare stems and mildew at flowering time may need screening with other plants, but such problems can be minimized by digging in plenty of organic matter when planting to aid

PINCHING

Pinching improves the appearance of the plants. By flowering time, some heleniums lose their lower leaves, or are infected by mildew; in addition, some plants have grown too tall for smaller gardens. All of these difficulties can be dealt with by pinching the plants toward the end of May in order to reduce height and delay flowering. By pinching only the stems toward the front of the clump, the resulting short, bushy growth will hide any bare and mildewy stems on the rest of the plant. The flowering time is not usually delayed by the pinching. The plants can also be cut back later, in midsummer, to approximately 12 in (30 cm). This scheduling delays flowering by a few weeks, which is actually an asset in some situations, on much shorter plants. Alternatively, 4–6 in (10–15 cm) can be cut from the stems at the time that the flower buds first appear, putting back flowering by just a couple of weeks. Similar techniques can be applied to some other tall summer- and fall-flowering perennials, including cultivars of *Aster novae-angliae* and *A. novi-belgii*, *Phlox paniculata*, and *Solidago*.

water retention, and by fertilizing in early spring. Divide clumps in spring every two to three years to maintain vigor. Taller types usually need staking, and even the shorter ones benefit from discreet support. Prolong flowering by deadheading; snip back to the next bud.

PROPAGATION Sow seed of species in spring at 59°F (15°C). Divide cultivars in spring or take basal cuttings of young growth.

PROBLEMS Slugs and snails may attack emerging shoots. Occasionally afflicted by powdery mildew, leaf spot, and virus.

H. autumnale (Common sneezeweed) Erect, branched, winged stems bearing lance-shaped to elliptic, toothed leaves, to 6 in (15 cm) long, carry flat-topped clusters of flowers from late summer to mid-fall. The individual flowerheads, to 2 in (5 cm) across, have yellow centers and yellow rays. This species is tall and late-flowering, but all its features can be found among the wide choice of hybrid cultivars. Some *H. autumnale* cultivars may be hybrids. Native to most of North America. ↕ 5 ft (1.5 m). Z3–8 H8–1. **'Helena Gold'** Shades of pale gold with a yellow center. Seed-raised. ↕ 38–49 in (95–125 cm). **'Helena Rote Tone'** Shades of reddish brown. Seed variety. ↕ 38–48 in (95–125 cm) Z4–8 H8–1 **'Rotgold'** ('Helena Mix', 'Red and Gold', 'Sunshine Hybrid'). Seed-raised mixture in a full range of colors and color combinations. Seed-raised. ↕ 38–48 in (95–125 cm).

H. **'Baudirektor Linne'** Rich orange-red rays, copper-red on the undersides and aging a darker copper, surround a brown center. Flowers from late summer; foliage is very slightly toothed. ↕ 30–36 in (75–90 cm). Z4–8 H8–1

H. **'Biedermeier'** Red ray florets with long yellow tips and a narrow yellow zone surround the brown center. They open slightly reflexed, becoming more so with age. Flowers from late summer; the leaves are noticeably toothed. ↕ 3¼–4 ft (1–1.25 m). Z4–8 H8–1

H. **'Blütentisch'** Deep yellow rays with reddish brown streaks, especially on opening, and a reddish brown reverse, surround a brown center. The taller 'Gartensomme' is sometimes sold under this name. ↕ 3¼–4 ft (1–1.25 m). Z4–8 H8–1

H. **'Bruno'** Slightly messy-looking, brown-red ray florets that surround a honey brown center. Raised by English nurseryman Alan Bloom and introduced in 1960. ↕ 3¼–4 ft (1–1.25 m). Z4–8 H8–1

H. **'Butterpat'** Deep yellow ray florets, similar on the undersides, eventually reflexing, surround a green center

RIGHT **1** *Helenium* 'Butterpat'
2 *H.* 'Moerheim Beauty'
3 *H.* 'Wyndley'

opening to yellow, from midsummer. Raised by Alan Bloom and introduced in 1960. A number of taller, coarser plants are circulating under this name. ↕30–40 in (75–100 cm). Z4–8 H8–1

H. 'Chipperfield Orange' Orange-red ray florets, with darker undersides, have a narrow yellow ring around the dark center; they open from late summer and reflex strongly with age. The leaves have a few small teeth. Definitely needs support. ↕5 ft (1.5 m). Z4–8 H8–1

H. 'Coppelia' Deep orange rays with a few yellow flecks at the tips and brown undersides surround a brown center. Flowers from midsummer; the leaves have a few small, scattered teeth. Raised by Alan Bloom and introduced in 1965. ↕30–40 in (75–100 cm). Z4–8 H8–1

H. 'Dunkelpracht' (**Dark Beauty**) Dark, brown-tinted, orange-red rays with yellow tips surround a brown center. Flowers from late summer; the petals are not reflexed. Leaves neatly toothed. ↕30–48 in (75–125 cm). Z4–8 H8–1

H. 'Feuersiegel' Deep yellow rays; an orange-red band of variable width around pale brown center; undersides are more strongly marked. Flowers from mid- or late summer; the slightly rolled edges of the petals curl upward. ↕30–48 in (75–125 cm). Z4–8 H8–1

H. 'Flammendes Käthchen' The rays show a variable combination of deep yellow and orange-red, with the reverse more orange, around a brown center. Flowers from late summer. ↕3¼–4 ft (1–1.25 m). Z4–8 H8–1

H. 'Goldene Jugend' (**Golden Youth**) Pale yellow ray florets around a yellow center from mid- or late summer. ↕28–36 in (70–90 cm). Z4–8 H8–1

H. hoopesii syn. *Hymenoxys hoopesii*, *Dugaldia hoopesii*. (Owl's claws) Forms tight clumps; deciduous. Grayish leaves mostly basal, lance-shaped, untoothed, to 12 in (30 cm). Flowering stems with similar, clasping leaves; 3–10 flowerheads up to 3 in (8 cm) in width. Flowers in mid- and late summer. Disk florets yellowish brown; narrow ray florets yellow to orange, become reflexed and papery as flowers set seed. Unlike other species, forms attractive foliage clumps and is best in an open site. Often treated as a separate genus, *Hymenoxys*, or *Dugaldia*. From western North America. ↕3¼ ft (1 m). Z3–7 H7–1

H. 'Indianersommer' Brown-red rays above and below fade to yellow and orange, the edges of the petals rolled at first; the green center darkens to brown. The leaves are very slightly toothed. Flowers from late summer. ↕34–42 in (85–115 cm). Z4–8 H8–1

H. 'Kanaria' Bright, clean yellow ray florets, the undersides similar, with notched ends and the occasional gap between them; only slightly reflexed. The leaves are unusually large. Flowers from mid- or late summer. ↕38–48 in (95–125 cm). Z4–8 H8–1

H. 'Karneol' Flat heads of deep red rays fade to orange-red, the reverse darker, with a green center aging to brown. Large, toothed leaves. ↕38–48 in (95–125 cm). Z4–8 H8–1

H. 'Königstiger' Rich but bright orange-red rays with a yellow inner ring and tiny yellow points, the undersides similar, around a brown center. Boldly toothed foliage. ↕3¼–5 ft (1–1.5 m). Z4–8 H8–1

H. 'Kupferzwerg' Wide ray florets around a brown center are reddish brown front and back and open strongly reflexed. The leaves are untoothed. Flowers from late summer. ↕28–36 in (70–90 cm). Z4–8 H8–1

H. 'Moerheim Beauty' Strongly reflexed, rich orange-red rays fade to dark ocher; the reverse is dark red. The center is brown; the leaves are a little toothed. Flowers from late summer. ↕38–48 in (95–125 cm). Z4–8 H8–1

H. Pipsqueak (**'Blopip'**) Distinctive large yellow-brown cone dominates short, reflexed yellow petals. Flowers, held in a flat plane, open in midsummer.

↕16–24 in (40–60 cm). Z4–8 H8–1

H. puberulum (Rosilla) Short-lived; clumps of loose, erect, branched stems, narrow, untoothed, stalkless leaves to 6 in (15 cm) long. Unusual spherical flowerheads, with yellow to brown disk florets above a short skirt of yellow to brown rays, held horizontally or pointing down, to ¾ in (2 cm) across; produced singly or in few-flowered clusters from midsummer to early fall. Native to southwest North America. ↕20–60 in (50–150 cm). Z4–8 H8–1. **'Autumn Lollipop'** Yellow ray florets point down. Seed-raised. ↕3¼ ft (1 m).

H. 'Pumilum Magnificum' Rays reflexed, pale yellow, red ring around the brown eye; yellow on the reverse with a red tip. Plants without the red base to the petals are often sold under this name. Flowers from late summer. ↕30–40 in (75–100 cm). Z4–8 H8–1

H. Red Dwarf *see H.* 'Rubinzwerg'

H. 'Rubinzwerg' (**Red Dwarf**) Reflexed, dark red ray florets around a brown center, tips slightly lobed or

split, may show a light pinkish tinge. Neat growth; flowers from midsummer. ↕30–40 in (75–100 cm). Z4–8 H8–1

H. 'Sahin's Early Flowerer' Long ray florets yellow and brownish red in irregular streaks, around a brown center. Flowers from midsummer to mid-fall, *H.* 'Wyndley' often flowers earlier. ↕30–40 in (75–100 cm). Z4–8 H8–1

H. 'The Bishop' Ray florets are a bright golden yellow, on both sides, around a brown center. Flowers from midsummer; leaves are unusually broad. ↕30–40 in (75–100 cm). Z4–8 H8–1

H. 'Waltraut' Copper-orange rays have a deep yellow outer ring, the color becoming richer with age; the reverse is more evenly orange-brown. The brown-centered flowers open from midsummer, on plants with short leaves. ↕30–40 in (75–100 cm). Z4–8 H8–1

H. 'Wyndley' Deep yellow rays with brown-red streaks, more so on the reverse, are held more horizontally than most around a brown center. The leaves are untoothed. Very early, sometimes flowering from early summer. ↕20–

THOUGHTFUL STAKING DISGUISES THE GAP

GARDENERS HAVE BECOME much less cautious about bright and fiery combinations in recent years, and our gardens are much more exciting as a result. Here, in front, *Crocosmia* 'Carmin Brilliant' is strikingly upright, its carmine red flowers flaring from dark buds on dark stems among narrow leaves. Leaning in from behind,

Helenium 'Moerheim Beauty', with its orange-red flowers, is discreetly supported by small branches set at an angle to hold the helenium so that it sways toward the crocosmia without falling into it. This simple technique also disguises the space between the two plants in spring, before the flowers open.

30 in (50–75 cm). Z4–8 H8–1

H. 'Zimbelstern' Ray florets, held horizontally, yellow with brown-red marks, browner on the reverse, around a brown center. The leaves are slightly toothed. Flowers from late summer. ↕4–5 ft (1.2–1.5 m). Z4–8 H8–1

HELIANTHELLA
ASTERACEAE

Bright, drought-tolerant plants with more refinement than many tall yellow daisies.

Eight clump-forming species are native to meadows and forest clearings in western North America. Leafy stems, usually unbranched, carry narrow, unstalked, untoothed leaves and, at the top, flowerheads with yellow disk and ray florets. The flowers are held individually or in few-flowered, flat-topped heads. Similar to the coarser *Helianthus*, but the fruits are flattened.

CULTIVATION Needs full sun and fertile, well-drained soil, preferring neutral to alkaline conditions. Drought-tolerant, it suits herbaceous or mixed borders or can be naturalized in wilder areas. Divide clumps every three to four years in spring to maintain vigor.

PROPAGATION In spring, from seed sown at 59°F (15°C) or by basal stem cuttings.

PROBLEMS Slugs and snails may attack emerging shoots.

H. quinquenervis (Fivenerve helianthella) A deciduous, clump-forming perennial with mostly opposite leaves, to 20 in (50 cm) long, with two prominent pairs of lateral veins. Pale yellow, nodding flowerheads to 4 in (10 cm) across borne from mid- to late summer. *Helianthus* 'Lemon Queen' is sometimes sold under this name. Native to the central US and Mexico, especially along streams. ↕5 ft (1.5 m); up to 15 ft (5 m) in the wild. Z3–9 H8–1

HELIANTHUS
Sunflower
ASTERACEAE

Tough, reliable plants, all with cheery yellow daisy flowerheads; some are coarse, some invasive, but many are well behaved and some are even spectacular.

Approximately 70 species, including annuals, are native to a wide variety of habitats in North and South America. Growing from either tubers or rhizomes, and either clump-forming or running (especially some of the hybrids), some spread vigorously, while others grow much more tightly. All produce erect, sparsely branched stems, normally with large, alternate, egg-shaped leaves, topped by yellow daisy flowers held singly or in loose clusters above foliage. Flowerheads

RIGHT 1 *Helianthus* 'Lemon Queen'
2 *H.* 'Loddon Gold' **3** *H.* 'Morgensonne'

consist of a yellow or brown central disk and prominent yellow ray florets; the disk florets are enlarged, for an anemone-like center, or replaced by ray florets, creating a double flower. Most start to flower in late summer, but some are very late and flower only in hot falls.

The cultivars are sometimes variously assigned to *H. atrorubens*, *H. decapetalus*, *H. x laetiflorus*, or *H. x multiflorus* but most do not fit comfortably into these classifications, which are of little help to gardeners, so they are listed alphabetically. Contact with foliage or sap may irritate skin. ⚠

CULTIVATION Although tough, perennial sunflowers need full sun and fertile, well-drained soil, preferring neutral to alkaline conditions. Relatively drought-tolerant, they suit herbaceous or mixed borders or can be naturalized in wilder areas. Clumps should be top-dressed annually with garden compost, and divided every three to four years in spring to maintain vigor or to control spread. Deadhead to prevent self-seeding, which results in different seedlings. The taller types need staking.

PROPAGATION In spring, sow seed of the species at 59°F (15°C) or divide cultivars or take basal stem cuttings.

PROBLEMS Slugs and snails may attack emerging shoots. Sometimes afflicted by powdery mildew.

H. angustifolius (Swamp sunflower) Clump-forming, often short-lived plant with hairy stems, branched toward the top, carrying 6-in (15-cm), mostly alternate, rough, slender leaves. The 2-in (5-cm) flowerheads have yellow ray florets surrounding a purple-red, occasionally yellow, disk. Native to damp habitats in eastern US and more tolerant of wet soil than other species. ↕6½ ft (2 m). Z6–9 H9–4

H. atrorubens (Purpledisk sunflower) Spreads vigorously; its rough stems becoming smoother higher up the plant. The large, oval, generally opposite, usually hairy, 12-in (30-cm) toothed leaves are mostly gathered toward the base. The 2-in (5-cm) flowerheads have yellow or orange-yellow ray florets surrounding a purple-red eye. May be worth trying in wild woodland: its preference for dry woodland habitats in southeastern US indicates shade-tolerance. ↕5 ft (1.5 m). Z7–9 H9–5

H. 'Capenoch Star' A slow-spreading but not invasive plant with single flowerheads, 6–8 in (15–20 cm) across, from late summer to mid-fall. The ray florets are light yellow and notched at the tip, and the disk florets dark yellow. It occasionally mutates to produce an anemone-centered flower, and this

spontaneous mutation is sometimes sold under this name, as are a number of other plants; look for the notched petal tip. ↕5 ft (1.5 m). Z4–9 H9–1

H. 'Gullick's Variety' A relatively compact, slowly spreading plant, with upward-facing, semidouble flowerheads to 4 in (10 cm) across. Dark red disk florets; numerous yellow ray florets. Plants sold under this name with ray florets that are narrow and inrolled as they open are often *H.* 'Miss Mellish'. ↕5–6½ ft (1.5–2 m). Z4–9 H9–1

H. x kellermanii (Kellerman's sunflower) Spreads steadily but not aggressively. The tall, gray-green stems bear many narrow, lance-shaped, 8-in (20-cm) leaves that show the influence of *H. salicifolius*. Mainly grown for its foliage: the yellow flowerheads, 4 in (6 cm) across, are rarely produced. A hybrid between *H. grosseserratus* and *H. salicifolius*, native to central and eastern US. ↕10 ft (3 m). Z4–9 H9–1

H. 'Lemon Queen' A vigorous but rarely aggressive, bushy, clump-forming plant with hairy, dark green leaves. The prolific pale yellow flowers are long-

lasting and 2 in (5 cm) across. Rarely needs support; said to be a natural hybrid between two native species, *H. pauciflorus* and *H. tuberosus*. ↕5¾–6½ ft (1.75–2 m). Z4–9 H9–1

H. 'Loddon Gold' Clump-forming or steadily spreading; deep yellow, fully double, 3-in (8-cm) flowerheads are sterile, with no disk, and reminiscent of double chrysanthemums. Introduced by Thomas Carlile's Loddon Nurseries of England in about 1920. Not usually invasive. *H.* 'Triomphe de Gand' is sometimes sold under this name. ↕5¾ ft (1.75 m). Z4–9 H9–1

H. maximiliani (Maximilian sunflower) A variable, clump-forming perennial with tuberous roots and hairy stems carrying lance-shaped leaves, sometimes as much as 18 in (45 cm) long. Both disk and ray florets in the 3-in (8-cm) flowerheads are yellow. Native to prairies and waste ground, usually in dry soil, in central US and southern Canada. ↕10 ft (3 m). Z4–9 H9–1

H. 'Miss Mellish' Compact but slowly spreading, with semidouble flowerheads up to 4½ in (11 cm) across; the disk florets are deep yellow; the many ray florets are mid-yellow, distinctively inrolled as they emerge, flattening later. ↕6 ft (1.8 m). Z5–9 H9–5

***H.* 'Monarch'** Dramatic, but can be invasive in good soil. The semidouble flowerheads, the largest among perennial sunflowers, can be more than 6 in (15 cm) across, and even up to 12 in (30 cm) if side buds are removed. The disk florets are dark red and the ray florets golden yellow. Sometimes listed as 'The Monarch'. ↕8–10 ft (2.5–3 m). Z4–9 H9–1

***H.* 'Morgensonne'** A neat, slowly spreading clump-former; the yellow flowerheads have enlarged disk florets, giving it an anemone-flowered look. ↕3¼ ft (1 m). Z4–9 H9–1

H. salicifolius (Willowleaf sunflower) Clump-forming perennial with a mass of distinctive linear to lance-shaped, willowy leaves, to 8 in (20 cm) long. Large clusters of small yellow flowers are produced at the tops of stems late in the season, but it is primarily grown for the attractive "waterfall" effect of its foliage. All three cultivars were raised by New Zealand plant breeder Dr. Keith Hammett by crossing the species with the little-known *H.* 'Golden Pyramid'. They are not, as is sometimes stated, forms of *H. angustifolius*. Native to the central and eastern US. ↕8–10 ft (2.5–3 m). Z6–9 H9–6. **'First Light'** Prolific, compact form with 2-in (5-cm) brown-centered flowers, the rays the palest yellow of the three cultivars but still very bright, from early through mid-fall. ↕3¼–4 ft (1–1.2 m). **'Low Down'** Dwarf form with a dome-shaped habit. Shorter foliage and 2-in (5-cm), bright yellow flowers with brown disk florets, flowering in mid-fall. ↕12–20 in (30–50 cm). **'Table Mountain'** Compact form with 2-in (5-cm) bright yellow flowers with brown disk florets held on flat-topped plants from early through mid-fall. ↕3¼–4 ft (1–1.2 m).

***H.* 'Triomphe de Gand'** Slowly spreading; the 6-in (15-cm) flowerheads are semidouble with dark yellow disk florets and paler yellow ray florets. ↕5 ft (1.5 m). Z5–9 H9–5

HELICHRYSUM
Everlasting flower
ASTERACEAE

About 500 species, including annuals, biennials, perennials, shrubs, and small trees, are found in Europe, Africa, West Asia, South Africa, and Australia, usually growing in dry, open situations, such as grasslands, sand dunes, and poor fertility soils.

The stems are woolly or hairy, with alternate or occasionally opposite leaves, which sometimes form a basal rosette and occasionally have a rolled-back margin. The foliage is often densely woolly beneath and sometimes also above, and in some species has a powerful aroma. The flowers are solitary or in clusters, daisylike or a little like tiny shaving brushes. There are no "petals" (ray florets), but leafy bracts around the flowers may provide color. Very few of the species are grown.

CULTIVATION Best in a sunny position and well-drained soil toward the front of the border. They will suffer in waterlogged conditions and lose their character in fertile soil.

PROPAGATION Divide in spring or take cuttings in late summer.

PROBLEMS Powdery mildew.

***H.* 'Schwefellicht'** (**Sulphur Light**) Erect or slightly spreading stems covered with white woolly hairs carry narrowly lance-shaped, silvery green leaves with a strong aroma of curry, and compact clusters of ⅜–¾-in (8–15-mm) hemispherical flowers, which appear in late summer. The flowers are bright sulfur yellow when they open, turning orange-yellow with age. ↕16 in (40 cm). Z10–11 H11–10

H. thianschanicum Attractive mound-forming plant with erect, branched, woolly stems and silver-gray, alternate leaves, lance-shaped at the base of the plant, becoming linear and very narrow farther up the stems. Clusters of papery, yellow, egg-shaped or hemispherical flowers, about ½ in (1 cm) across, are borne in dense clusters on the tips of the shoots and on sideshoots from early to midsummer. Although it prefers a sunny position, will take a little shade. From Turkestan. ↕16 in (40 cm). Z10–11 H11–10. **'Goldkind'** (**Golden Baby**) Shorter, with golden yellow flowers. ↕12 in (30 cm). **'Icicles'** Short, with silvery gray foliage—like a miniature silver pine. ↕12 in (30 cm).

RIGHT *Helichrysum* 'Schwefellicht'

HELICTOTRICHON
Oat grass
POACEAE

Impressive and elegant blue-leaved grasses for dry areas.

There are about 100 perennial species, mainly from Europe and Asia but found throughout temperate regions of the world, growing on dry hillsides, in meadows, and at woodland margins. Mainly tightly clump-forming, the dense mounds are made up of leaves that are often blue on top and deep green on the underside. Tall, graceful flower stems carry fluttering oatlike flowers with short, twisted, bristly hairs.

CULTIVATION Grow in fertile, well-drained soil in a dry open position, although plants will take some shade. They dislike hot, humid conditions and wet winters, and may rot at the base if drainage is inadequate. Rake out dead foliage in spring to ensure good air circulation around the new leaves.

PROPAGATION From seed or by division in spring; cultivars by division only.

PROBLEMS Rust. Ants sometimes nest in plants that are starting to die out in the middle.

H. sempervirens (Blue oat grass) Forms shapely evergreen clumps of stiff, upright, pointed, steely blue leaves, ¾ in (2 cm) wide and up to 12 in (30 cm) long. Slightly arching flower stems grow high above the foliage, ending in delicate, one-sided, blue-gray flowers, becoming yellowish brown as the seeds ripen. Grow in drifts in dry gardens or as specimen plants with other colored grasses or smaller blue flowers. Often self-sows, and may be semievergreen in cool areas. From alkaline soil on rocks and rocky pastures in the southwest Alps. ↕3¼ ft (1 m). Z4–9 H9–1. **var. *pendulum*** Pendulous flower stems with more flowers. **'Saphirsprudel'** (**Sapphire Fountain**) Intensely bright blue foliage, with some rust resistance.

HELIOPSIS
Oxeye
ASTERACEAE

Reliable, robust, long-lived, and prolific yellow daisies related to perennial sunflowers (*Helianthus*).

Thirteen perennial species are native to open woodlands, dry meadows, and prairies in the US and Mexico. Erect, clump-forming plants, their three-veined leaves are held oppositely on the stems, and the yellow flowerheads of disk and ray florets are borne on loosely branched stems from midsummer to fall. They differ from *Helianthus* in the blunt-tipped bracts (like tiny leaves) around the flowerhead, and their fertile ray florets, which wither but persist after the seeds form.

ABOVE *Helictotrichon sempervirens*

CULTIVATION The only cultivated species, it prefers full sun and fertile, well-drained soil; once established, plants are drought-tolerant. Ideal for herbaceous borders: most do not require staking, but clumps should be divided every three years, in spring, to maintain vigor. They respond well to being cut back in early summer to reduce height at flowering time. If they look ragged after flowering, cut them back hard.

PROPAGATION In spring, sow seed of species at 59°F (15°C); divide or take basal stem cuttings of cultivars.

PROBLEMS Slugs and snails may attack emerging shoots. Shoots emerging white are thought to indicate a latent virus infection.

H. helianthoides Deciduous and clump-forming, with egg- to lance-shaped leaves to 6 in (15 cm) long. Flowerheads to 3 in (8 cm) across, with disk and ray florets in shades of yellow, semi- or fully double in some cultivars, are held solitarily on branched stems. Flowers early summer to early fall. Native to Canada, central and eastern US, and Mexico. ↕3¼–5 ft (1–1.5 m). Z4–9 H9–1. **var. *helianthoides*** Distinguished by its smooth stems and leaves. **Loraine Sunshine** (**'Helhan'**) Single and yellow, the strangely variegated leaves are silvery white with contrasting green veins. Weaker-growing and less tolerant of winter rain than other cultivars. Coloring is less pronounced in shade. ↕3¼ ft (1 m). **'Prairie Sunset'** Impressive, well-behaved plant: the 2-in- (5-cm-) wide flowers have golden-orange ray florets, the edges whitening with age, and brown disk florets, held on contrasting black-purple stems. Introduced by Prairie Nursery, WI. Flowers from early summer to early fall. ↕5¾ ft (1.75 m). Z4–8 H8–4. **var. *scabra*** Distinguished

ABOVE *Heliopsis helianthoides* var. *scabra* 'Light of Lodden'

from the less frequently grown var. *helianthoides* by its roughly hairy stems and leaves. **var. *scabra* Ballerina** *see* var. *scabra* 'Spitzentänzerin'. **var. *scabra* 'Goldgefieder'** (**Golden Plume**) Fully double, dark yellow. ‡ 4¼ ft (1.3 m). **var. *scabra* 'Light of Loddon'** Single, neat, well-shaped yellow flowers. ‡ 4¼ ft (1.3 m). **var. *scabra* 'Sommersonne'** (**Summer Sun**) Single, orange-yellow; both single and double-flowered forms are grown under this name. Thrives in hot climates. ‡ 4 ft (1.2 m). **var. *scabra* 'Sonnenglut'** Semidouble, golden yellow. ‡ 4½ ft (1.4 m). **var. *scabra* 'Spitzentänzerin'** (**Ballerina**) Semidouble, dark yellow ray florets with recurved margins and slightly divided, twisted tips. ‡ 4½ ft (1.4 m). **var. *scabra* 'Summer Nights'** Deep yellow, sometimes with an orange ring around the flower's eye, and a deep mahogany disk. Stems purple-red, foliage tinted red. **var. *scabra* Summer Sun** *see* var. *scabra* 'Sommersonne'. **var. *scabra* 'Venus'** Single, orange-yellow. ‡ 5 ft (1.5 m). **var. *scabra* 'Waterperry Gold'** Semidouble, deep yellow fading to pale yellow. ‡ 4 ft (1.2 m).

HELLEBORUS
Hellebore
RANUNCULACEAE

Essential and fashionable winter and spring plants available in an increasing range of colors, patterns, and forms.

Sixteen species of tightly clump-forming evergreen or deciduous plants are distributed across Europe, with outposts in China and Syria. Some are shade-lovers, others enjoy sunny situations, and some are more adaptable. There are two groups: Most species are long-lived, stemless with leaves and flowerheads arising separately from the woody crown, and rarely more than 18 in (45 cm) high. The others (*H. argutifolius*,

H. lividus, H. x sternii, and *H. foetidus*) are relatively short-lived plants (four to five years), with upright, semiwoody stems up to 4 ft (1.2 m) with both the foliage and, at the top, clusters of flowers; these stems die away after seeding and are replaced by new shoots from the base.

Hellebore leaves are important in distinguishing the species. Held on a distinct stem, each is divided into leaflets and these lobes are often again divided, giving anything from three leaflets to over 100. The leaves may be 3–20 in (7.5–50 cm) across, thick and rather leathery when mature, although often soft when young, most often a rich green, and usually toothed or notched.

The flowers are displayed in clusters that may be open and airy or tightly grouped; they may be carried on individual stems growing from the crown or, in the stemmed species, at the top of semiwoody stems that also carry the leaves. The individual flowers are superficially similar to those of a buttercup (*see* Hellebore Flower Forms).

Flowering is in late winter and spring. In most species, the flowers are green or brownish, less often white, pink, or purple, but in garden forms they can be white, cream, yellow, green, pink, red, purple, slatey blue, or almost black; many paler and a few darker forms are spotted in red or purple. In double forms, the nectaries revert to the size and color of petals, while in anemone-centered forms the nectaries have become partially enlarged and colored and make a ruff around the center of the flower.

A few hybrids have been available for some years, but recently a number of unexpected hybrids have been developed, especially by Kevin Belcher at Ashwood Nurseries, Warwickshire, England. These include 'Pink Ice' (*H. niger* x *H. thibetanus*), 'Briar Rose' (*H. niger* x *H. vesicarius*), *H. niger* x *H. viridis*, and *H. niger* x *H. foetidus* 'Wester Flisk'. These are proving slow to propagate, but experimentation in developing seed strains and production by tissue culture should see these plants eventually become available.

Hellebores are poisonous if eaten; foliage contact may irritate skin. They are resistant to deer browsing. ⚠

CULTIVATION Most hellebores grow well in any reasonably fertile soil that is not dry or waterlogged, but in general, the more open and sunny their situation, the more moisture they require. Many grow best in shade and alkaline or neutral soil. All appreciate thorough and deep soil preparation, although the stemmed, semiwoody species are generally less particular.

Remove the foliage of all stemless kinds in late fall to improve their look and as a precaution against leaf spot disease. Cut off the leaves of the semiwoody kinds as they deteriorate and remove the whole stem at ground level after flowering or seeding. Mulch with well-rotted organic matter in the fall.

PROPAGATION Stemless hellebores can be propagated from seed and, in early fall, by division. Semiwoody kinds are increased from seed. The recommended methods for cultivars and various groups are given in the following entries.

Seed of all species is best sown in pots while fresh, in summer, and placed outdoors in a cold frame or sheltered corner and kept moist. Germination usually takes place during the following winter, often with a high success rate. Hellebores are highly promiscuous, so plants grown from seed collected from garden plants are unlikely to resemble the parent.

PROBLEMS Aphids, viral diseases including "black death" (*Helleborus net necrosis* virus), slugs and snails, and vine weevil.

HELLEBORE FLOWER FORMS

In hellebore flowers, the true petals are modified into a ring of nectaries at the center of the flower to attract pollinating insects, while the sepals, which normally enclose the flower in bud, have become enlarged and petal-like and are usually referred to as petals.

Nectary (modified petal)

Petal (enlarged, colored sepal)

Helleborus hybridus cream

Anemone-centered Flowers with nectaries that have become slightly enlarged and colored to form a noticeable ruff around the center of the flower. In various colors and color combinations. Above: *H. hybridus* anemone-centered.

Double Flowers with nectaries that have reverted to their origins as petals; flowers have up to thirty "petals" and usually no nectaries at all. Increasingly available in a range of colors. Above: *H. hybridus* Party Dress Group.

Picotee Pale flowers with a red or purple edging on the petals and sometimes purple veins and purple nectaries. Above: *H. hybridus* Party Dress Group.

Spotted Single or double flowers with spotting on the inside; flower color and degree of spotting vary. Above: *H. hybridus* spotted, yellow.

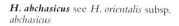

H. abchasicus see *H. orientalis* subsp. *abchasicus*

H. argutifolius syn. *H. corsicus* (Corsican hellebore) The tallest of the semiwoody group: its upright stems spring from a tight, slowly spreading rootstock and carry bold, leathery, evergreen leaves, 3–9 in (8–23 cm) across, each split into three spiny leaflets. From midwinter to mid-spring the stems are topped with crowded clusters of up to 30 green, bowl-shaped flowers, each 1–2 in (2.5–5 cm) across, which vary from fully rounded to open. Distinguished from *H. lividus* by being taller, and without pink tints. Plant in sunny situations in good, preferably well-drained soil. Relatively short-lived and best replaced by seedlings after four or five years. May need discreet staking with canes and string. From Corsica. ↕4 ft (1.2 m). Z6–9 H9–6. **'Janet Starnes'** Foliage speckled with gold, yellow, or cream and shoot tips tinted pink; rather variable. Remove plain green-leaved plants. May not be genuinely distinct from 'Pacific Frost'. Seed. ↕24 in (60 cm). **'Pacific Frost'** Foliage speckled with cream and white and shoot tips tinted in pink; rather variable. Reject plain green-leaved plants. From Pam Frost in Vancouver, British Columbia. Seed. ↕24 in (60 cm). **'Silver Lace'** Foliage bluish green but with rather open flowers. Introduced by Lynda Windsor of R&D Plants, Devon, England. Seed. ↕24 in (60 cm).

H. atrorubens One of the less showy of the stemless species, and variable in leaf shape and in flower color and pattern. The deciduous foliage is divided into seven to nine leaflets, the outer again subdivided into ten to fifteen elliptical divisions; the emerging leaves may be purple-tinted. Outward-facing flowers, not more than 2 in (5 cm) across, are carried on open, branched heads in late winter and early spring; usually green with purple backs, they can also be all-green or all purple. Sometimes confused with *H. orientalis* subsp. *abchasicus* 'Early Purple', once widely known, although incorrectly, as

H. atrorubens. Prefers a well-drained, humus soil in dappled or part-shade. Slow-growing and prone to slug damage. From southeast Slovenia and Croatia. ↕14 in (35 cm). Z6–9 H9–6.

H. x *ballardiae* syn. *H.* x *nigriliv* Hybrid combining the foliage shape of *H. niger*, with up to eight divisions, and the silvery leaf sheen and pale veins of *H. lividus*. From early winter to mid-spring, short stems carry three or four, 2½–3½-in (6–9-cm) sterile flowers, usually creamy green with pink tints inside and pinkish green outside— although these three shades may all be present in varying degrees. Shorter than the similar *H.* x *nigercors*, and with pink tints in the flowers. Good outside in well-drained, sunny, sheltered borders in warmer areas, also in containers. Prone to blackspot. Cultivars are very occasionally available. Can only be propagated by division. Named for the pioneer British hellebore breeder Helen Ballard, who first created this hybrid. ↕14 in (35 cm). Z5–9 H9–5.

H. cyclophyllus Bold deciduous species; the emerging foliage is covered in silver hairs, then matures to a striking leaf about 12 in (30 cm) across with seven segments, the outer ones repeatedly split to give about 25 divisions in all. Up to seven bright green, occasionally yellowish or creamy flowers, about 2 in (5 cm) across, appear from midwinter to early spring, sometimes with a flowering-currant scent. Enjoys more sun than many, but likes fertile, moisture-retentive soil. Susceptible to blackspot and to sudden spring frosts. Similar to *H. odorus*, which is usually evergreen. From Greece, Macedonia and Serbia, Albania, and southern Bulgaria. ↕22 in (55 cm). Z6–9 H9–6.

H. corsicus see *H. argutifolius*

H. x *ericsmithii* syn. *H.* x *nigristern* Variable, evergreen and often short-lived, the leaves split into three to five broad, dark green divisions with spiny edges and silvery veins; there may be pink tints in some plants. The long-

lasting flowers, from midwinter to mid-spring, appear singly or in twos on short stems, but also in taller, branched clusters of up to 20. Up to 4 in (10 cm) across, they are usually white or pale pink inside, sometimes striped green, and darker and tinted green or pink on the back. Pinker in flower, with silver leaf veins and less hardy compared with *H.* x *nigercors*. Good in fertile, well-drained soil, preferably with at least half the day's sunshine; also good in a low raised bed and as a container plant. Cut off older foliage in fall as a precaution against blackspot. Can be propagated only by division. A hybrid of *H. niger* and *H.* x *sternii* first made by Eric Smith. ↕15 in (38 cm). Z6–9 H9–6. **'Ivory Prince'** Pink-tinted creamy flowers over bluish green leaves. Raised by British plant breeder David Tristram.

H. foetidus (Stinking hellebore) Striking, rather short-lived, semiwoody species with an increasing number of stems developing from a slowly spreading rootstock. The evergreen, narrowly divided, slightly toothed 9–12-in (23–30-cm) leaves are divided into about 12 slender, slightly toothed leaflets. They are often rather leaden in color, smelling unpleasant when bruised. From midwinter to late spring, up to about 40 green, ¾-in (2-cm) tubular flowers top the stems, usually rimmed in reddish purple and flaring as they age. The leafy bracts in the flowerhead can be a striking feature. Best in good soil in part-shade, but can develop well in dry shade. Can only be raised from seed. From Britain east to Switzerland and south to Spain, Portugal, and the Balearics. ↕24–36 in (60–90 cm). Z6–9 H9–6. **'Gold Bullion'** syn. 'Chedglow' Dramatic, slow-growing form with golden-yellow foliage. Susceptible to blackspot. Probably identical to 'Chedglow', although perhaps more robust. Seed. **'Green Giant'** Tall, with finely divided foliage and pale bracts. Seed. ↕5 ft (1.3 m). **'Miss Jekyll's Scented'** Leaflets are noticeably narrow and the flowers sweetly scented, although not all the time. Sometimes listed simply as

ABOVE 1 *Helleborus argutifolius*
2 *H.* x *ericsmithii*
3 *H. foetidus* Wester Flisk Group

"Scented Form." Introduced by Gertrude Jekyll. Seed. **'Piccadilly'** Glossy, blackish green foliage, with reddish markings on the flower stem and leaf joints, and pale, whitish green flowers. From Piccadilly Farm, in Georgia. Seed. **'Red Silver'** Finely silvery gray dissected leaves with red stems. From Ernie and Marietta O'Byrne at Northwest Garden Nursery, Eugene, OR. Seed. ↕36 in (90 cm). **'Sopron'** Large, pale, unmarked flowers and dark metallic green foliage. Seed. **Wester Flisk Group** Striking, red-tinted main stems and leaf stems, with the staining continuing up into the flowerheads. Beware of impostors without red coloring. Seed.

H. x *hybridus* (Lenten rose, Orientalis Hybrids) Plants in this extensive and florally diverse group make dense, slowly expanding, rather woody clumps with bold, dark, leathery, evergreen, 16–20-in (40–50-cm) foliage, the central leaflet remaining undivided and the outer leaflets variously split, giving a total of up to 11 coarsely toothed segments. The upright flower stems usually carry four or five flowers, 2–4 in (5–10 cm) across, in late winter and spring. Flower colors range from white and cream to bright yellow; from blushed white through a full range of pinks and peachy shades to reds; silvery mauve shades, plum purples, slate blues, and even almost black. Double-flowered and anemone-centered forms in all these shades are becoming widely available. All colors are also seen with spotting on the inside of the flowers. Variegated forms are sometimes seen, but are usually infected with a virus. Divide in late summer or early fall. Growing from seed is not difficult; self-sown seedlings often appear around plants, but the results are unpredictable in both color and form. *H.* x *hybridus* is the name now agreed for all the hybrids involving *H. orientalis* and,

principally, *H. torquatus* and *H. odorus*. Many plants are sold under simple descriptive names like "anemone-centered" or "spotted." ‡18 in (45 cm). Z6–9 H9–6. **'Amber Queen'** *see* Queen Series. **'Apple Blossom'** A name used by many growers to describe a range of forms: blush pink flowers prettily dusted darker; blush pink with red edges to the petals; various blush pink seed strains, sometimes with spots. Division, seed. **Ashwood Garden Hybrids** High-quality plants in separate colors with single, anemone-centered, or double flowers in a wide range of shades, clear and spotted. Seed. **Ballard's Group** A name covering plants of any color derived from cultivars or unnamed seedlings raised by Helen Ballard. Variable and unpredictable. Division, seed. **'Blue Lady'** *see* Lady Series. **'Blue Metallic Lady'** *see* Lady Series. **H. Brandywine Hybrids** Blend containing singles, doubles, and semi-doubles. Bred by David Culp, PA. **'Emerald Queen'** *see* Queen Series. **'Gala Queen'** *see* Queen Series. **'Ice Queen'** *see* Queen Series. **Kochii Group** Small-flowered, early-flowering, white or cream forms, often with long flower stems. Division, seed. **Lady Series** Singles in seven separate colors: 'Blue Lady' (purple with a hint of blue), 'Blue Metallic Lady' (metallic blue–purple shades), 'Pink Lady' (shades of pink), 'Red Lady' (shades of red), 'White Lady' (white), 'White Lady Spotted' (white with bold red spots), 'Yellow Lady' (creams and yellows, some spotted). Developed in Germany by Gisela Schmiemann from original stock from Helen Ballard. Seed. **'Mrs. Betty Ranicar'** Double, pure white with a little green tinting at the base. Division, although seed is widely sold and produces variable results. **Party Dress Group** Small, neat, slow-growing plants derived from double-flowered forms of *H. torquatus* and well-colored forms of *H. x hybridus*. Colors include white, pink, yellow, red, purple, and blue-black, many with spots. Developed

by Robin White at Blackthorn Nursery, Hampshire, England. Seed. **'Picotee'** A name used for various forms with pale flowers with purple or dark pink edging to the petals and, sometimes, purple veins and purple nectaries. Division, seed. **H. Pine Knot Strain** Hand-pollinated strain with a wide array of rich colors and flower forms. Bred by Dick and Judith Tyler, VA. **'Pink Lady'** *see* Lady Series. **'Queen of Hearts'** *see* Queen Series. **'Queen of Spades'** *see* Queen Series. **'Queen of Night'** *see* Queen Series. **'Queen of the Night'** Deep purple, purple-tipped nectaries. Raised by Elizabeth Strangman (*see panel*). Division; similar seed-raised plants are sometimes sold as 'Queen of Night'. **Queen Series** Series of singles in nine colors: 'Amber Queen' (apricot-amber), 'Emerald Queen' (green, spotted purple), 'Gala Queen' (blush, spotted purple), 'Ice Queen' (white), 'Queen of Hearts' (rich rose), 'Queen of Spades' (dusky mauve), 'Queen of Night' (slatey purple), 'Washfield Queen' (pink, heavily veined). All developed by hellebore breeder Elizabeth Strangman (*see panel*). **'Red Lady'** *see* Lady Series. **'Royal Heritage'** A range of colors from white to maroon, strong on reddish shades. Developed by John Elsley of South Carolina. Seed. **'Snow Queen'** Large, vigorous double-flowered white with a few tiny red spots. Parent of many doubles. Division. **H. Sunshine Selections** Series of hand-pollinated F1 hybrids by Barry Glick, W.V. Singles of various colors. **'Ushba'** Pure white, rounded flowers with a very few small red spots. Raised and introduced by Helen Ballard. Division. **Washfield Doubles** Blend of fully double forms in reds, pinks, peachy shades, purples, blacks, greens, yellows, and white; some are spotted. Developed by Elizabeth Strangman (*see panel*). Seed. **'Washfield Queen'** *see* Queen Series. **'White Lady'** *see* Lady Series. **'White Lady Spotted'** *see* Lady Series. **'Yellow Lady'** *see* Lady Series. **Zodiac Group** Pink with a white edge and an inner zone of bold reddish purple spots. Raised by Eric Smith of England. Seed.

LEFT 1 *Helleborus* x *sternii* Ashwood Strain **2** *H.* x *hybridus* Party Dress Group **3** *H.* x *hybridus* 'Snow Queen' **4** *H.* x *hybridus* 'Ushba'

H. 'Ivory Prince' see *H.* x *ericsmithii* 'Ivory Prince'

ELIZABETH STRANGMAN

Elizabeth Strangman was the first breeder to create high-quality forms of *Helleborus* x *hybridus* that could be produced by nurseries in large quantities. Previously, named forms had been propagated by division, a very slow process, and were expensive and rarely available. Elizabeth realized that by using carefully controlled hand-pollination techniques of well-chosen parents, uniformly high-quality plants could be raised from seed and made available to far more gardeners.

At Washfield Nursery in Kent, England, she created "seed strains" in white, pink, yellow, slate, purple, peach, and many other shades, followed by veined and picotee types and then

doubles. The plants she created were not only uniform in color but also featured superior flower shape, evenness of markings, and vigor in the garden.

Elizabeth was also the first breeder to create double-flowered cultivars, by crossing greenish double forms of *H. torquatus,* which she collected in Montenegro, with *H.* x *hybridus* to create 'Belinda', the first double with pink flowers. She was unusually generous in explaining her techniques to other growers, and so influenced hellebore development all over the world. In 2003 she was awarded the Reginald Cory Memorial Cup by the Royal Horticultural Society in recognition of her pioneering work with hellebores.

CHOOSING AND RAISING HELLEBORES

Cultivars of *H. x hybridus* fall into two groups: clones propagated by division, and what are usually referred to as "seed strains," forms intended to be raised from seed. Most nurseries now grow plants for sale from seed, rather than propagating named cultivars by division, and this allows far greater numbers of high-quality plants to be offered.

Many specialists have developed their own strains and series, and chosen names for them—for example, Ashwood, Ballard, Blackthorn, Brandywine, Crûg, Farmyard, Hadspen, Harvington, Heronswood, Homelea, Kaye, Lady, Pine Knot, Mardi Gras Parade, Royal Heritage, Queen, Southern Belles, Sunshine, Winter Joy, Winter Queen, and more. The series name is usually coupled with another indicating the color—for example, 'Red Lady'. When these cultivars are bought from the original source, they can be the finest of all hellebores, although they may become unavailable if the nursery ceases production in the future.

Unless definite information is available from the supplier on the precise color of plants bought by mail order (increasingly, photographs on websites are proving

valuable), it pays to visit the nursery and select plants in flower. Look for balanced flowers with equal-sized petals and, if marked, matching patterns on those petals. Uneven, unbalanced flowers are the least effective. Look, too, for clear colors: green tints can ruin otherwise good, pure whites and clean pinks.

Plants raised from seed not created by hand-pollination may be somewhat different. Most hellebores hybridize readily, both between species and between forms of an individual species. The result is that plants raised from seed collected in the garden, and seedlings that self-sow in the garden, are highly unlikely to be identical to their parent.

Seed listed in the seed lists of specialist societies and some nurseries may also be suspect, being listed under a species or cultivar name when no care has been taken to prevent cross-pollination with other plants. Only hand-pollination can guarantee a true species plant, and some suppliers will make a point of stating that they do this. It is important to emphasize, however, that most hellebores now available are good plants—whether true to name or not.

H. lividus A beautiful, neat but short-lived and slow-growing species in the semiwoody group, the pink-tinted stems carrying neat, smooth-edged, 8–10-in- (20–25-cm) long foliage, divided into three leaflets. Each leaf is pewter green with silver veins, and dark pink on the back. The apple green flowers, sometimes pink on the inside and pink or purplish pink on the reverse, appear from early winter to early spring, and are up to 1½ in (4 cm) across. Much shorter than *H. argutifolius* and with striking pink tints. Grow outside in a sheltered, sunny, well-drained raised bed or a terra-cotta pot of sandy potting mix. Susceptible to blackspot. Can only be raised from seed, and in gardens it hybridizes readily with *H. argutifolius* to create the variable *H. x sternii*. From Majorca; very rare. ‡ 15 in (38 cm). Z6–9 H9–6

H. multifidus Plants of this confusing species make dense, slowly expanding clumps with woody rootstocks and deciduous foliage, about 8–12 in (20–30 cm) across, repeatedly divided to give 30 to 40 toothed leaflets. The branched flower stems usually carry three to eight green flowers, 1½ in (4 cm) across, in late winter and spring. Best in light shade in a rich but fertile soil, with shelter from icy winds. From Slovenia and Croatia. ‡ 10–12 in (25–30 cm). Z8–9 H9–8. **subsp. bocconei** Green or greenish white, elderflower-scented flowers up to 2½ in (7 cm) across. The leaves are split into about 20 slender, coarsely toothed divisions. From Italy. **subsp. hercegovinus** Valuable for its striking, repeatedly dissected foliage, often over 100 divisions in a single leaf on mature specimens. Flowers usually less than 2 in (5 cm) across, pale or slightly yellowish green. From Bosnia and Herzegovina.

H. niger (Christmas rose) Short, evergreen species with dark, leathery leaves, 10–12 in (25–30 cm) across, split into seven to nine leaflets, often toothed toward the tips. The flat, pure white flowers, occasionally with pinkish tones, are 1½–3 in (4.5–8 cm) across, more in some cultivars, and held on stout stems between midwinter and early spring—very occasionally at Christmas time. The leaves often overtop the flowers. Difficult to grow well, and often short-lived, preferring a part-shaded site on deep, humus-rich, well-drained but not dry or alkaline soil. Prone to blackspot. Mulch well in fall. From Switzerland, Austria, and Germany, Slovenia, Croatia, and northern Italy. ‡ 12 in (30 cm). Z4–8 H9–1 **Blackthorn Group** Tall, vigorous plants with reddish black stems and pink buds opening to white flowers that blush as they age. From Robin White of Blackthorn Nursery, Hampshire, England. Seed. **Harvington Hybrids** Large, white, sometimes pink-edged flowers standing above the foliage. From Liz and Hugh Nunn of Harvington Gardens, Worcestershire, England. Seed. **subsp. macranthus** Large flowers, 3–4 in (7.5–10 cm) across, slightly blue-tinted foliage, and stems up to 18 in (45 cm) tall. **'Potters Wheel'** Flowers pure white, 4–5 in (10–12.5 cm) across, with overlapping petals. Beware of less impressive impostors. Seed. **'Praecox'** Supposedly flowering more dependably at Christmas, but still variable. Division. **Sunrise Group** White or tinged pink, sometimes slightly creamy flowers, occasionally faintly striped. Seed. **Sunset Group** White flowers fade to deep pink as they age. Seed. **'White Magic'** White flowers about 3 in (7.5 cm) across, developing pink tints as they age. Small foliage and very prolific. Seed.

H. x nigercors Quickly making an impressive clump, the 10–14-in (25–35-cm) foliage splits into three to five bold, broad, matte green, evenly toothed segments. The flowers, from midwinter to mid-spring, appear singly or in twos on short stems and also in taller, branched clusters of up to 30 but more usually 10–20. Flowers are usually flat, 3–4 in (7.5–10 cm) across, and may be white or white tinted with green or cream, often striped in green along the center of each petal. The flowers fade to green and often develop peachy tints as they age, and maintain their color for many weeks. Thrives in most conditions from full sun to light shade, but in dry or poor soil, plants may be short-lived. Remove leaves in late fall to deter blackspot and to prevent the flowers from being hidden. Cultivars come and go, many hardly distinguishable from each other; few are poor. Names occasionally listed include 'Alabaster', 'Ashwood Strain', 'Blackthorn Strain', 'Honeyhill Joy', 'Le Maxx Crème', 'Moonshine', 'Valentine Green', 'White Beauty'. Tissue culture is now making them more widely available. A sterile hybrid between *H. niger* and *H. argutifolius*; propagate by division. ‡ 15 in (38 cm). Z4–9 H9–1. **double-flowered** With an extra inner row of short petals.

H. x nigriliv see *H. x ballardiae*

H. x nigristern see *H. x ericsmithii*

H. odorus Tall, often impressive, usually evergreen species, the young foliage silvered in fine hairs and sometimes slightly coppery; it expands into leaves 14–18 in (35–45 cm) across with five main divisions, the outer ones again divided to give about ten leaflets. The flowers may be either bright green or slightly yellowish, up to 2½ in (6.5 cm) across, and open from early winter to early spring. The scent varies; it may be sweet or a little acrid. Best in moisture-retentive soil in full sun, and also good in part-shade. Soon makes a substantial clump. From Bulgaria, Romania, and Slovenia. ‡ 18 in (45 cm). Z4–8 H8–1

H. orientalis Densely clumped with large, dark, evergreen, 12–18-in (30–45-cm) leaves that are split into seven to eleven roughly toothed divisions, the central leaflet remaining undivided. Flowers, from midwinter to early spring, are 2–3 in (5–7.5 cm) across and greenish white. Good in the shade, but thrives in full sun with sufficient moisture. The leaves should be cut off in fall in order to help prevent blackspot. Forms of *H. x hybridus* are often sold under this name. From Turkey. ‡ 18 in (45 cm). Z4–8 H8–3. **subsp. abchasicus** Flowers a blend of green and red. From the mountains of the Caucasus. **subsp. abchasicus Early Purple Group** Purple-flowered forms of subsp. *abchasicus*, known for many

RIGHT **1** *Helleborus niger* **2** *H. orientalis* subsp. *abchasicus* Early Purple Group **3** *H. purpurascens* **4** *H. torquatus* 'Dido'

years as 'Atrorubens', which flower dependably from early winter. Division. **subsp.** *guttatus* Flowers greenish white variably spotted in red or purple. From the mountains of the Caucasus.

H. purpurascens A short but undeservedly neglected, deciduous species. The 10–12-in (25–30-cm) foliage is hairy when young, then becomes rounded and, uniquely among the hellebores, all of the five main leaflets are joined at the tip of the leaf stalk, and are then split into about 15 elliptical toothed segments. The flowers, from early winter to early spring, are 2–3 in (5–7.5 cm) across, the first opening at soil level, then rising as the stem stretches. They may be soft or rich purple, grayish blue, pinkish purple, or brown on the back and a paler shade, or green, within. Best in full sun in good soil, or in dappled shade. Plant this species at the front of a sheltered

border where the early flowers can best be seen. Spray against blackspot as soon as the buds start to emerge. From eastern Europe. ↕ 12 in (30 cm). Z4–8 H8–3

H. x sternii This variable hybrid in the semiwoody group has a tight, slowly spreading rootstock, upright, green, pink, or pink-tinted stems, and bold, evergreen leaves, 3–9 in (8–23 cm) long, divided into three spiny leaflets. Leaves may be green, with faint silver veins, to almost entirely silver, some with pink tints. From midwinter to mid-spring, stems are topped with crowded clusters of up to 30 bowl-shaped flowers, each 1–2 in (2.5–5 cm) across, in green with a hint of pink to deep pink, sometimes dusky. Taller, robust types thrive in full sun in any reasonable soil but may need staking; smaller, more silvered forms do better in fertile but well-drained soil in full sun,

or in pots. Raise from seed; forms readily hybridize with each other and with parents, *H. argutifolius* and *H. lividus*. ↕ 12–48 in (30–120 cm). Z5–8 H8–5. **Ashwood strain** Green flowers flushed pink with grayish green, marbled leaves. Ashwood Nurseries, Warwickshire, England. ↕ 12–15 in (30–40 cm). **Blackthorn Group** Pink-tinged, pale green flowers; marbled leaves on purple stems. Blackthorn Nursery, Hampshire, England. ↕ 18 in (45 cm). **'Boughton Beauty'** Robust plant, gray-green, pink-backed foliage, pink stems, pink-tinted green flowers. From legendary British horticulturist Valerie Finnis. ↕ 36 in (90 cm).

H. thibetanus Slowly increasing; 8–12-in (20–30-cm) leaves, each with seven to nine saw-toothed divisions, die down in late summer, earlier than other species. Flowers are bell-shaped, then flatten out, 1½–2½ in (4–6.5 cm) across, in late winter and early spring, in white, white with pink veins fading to pink, or pink darkening with age. Seed ripens earlier than in other species. Best in carefully cultivated woodland gardens, in dappled shade and leafy soil. Early development of seedlings is slow. Newly introduced from China. ↕ 15 in (38 cm). Z5–8 H8–5

H. torquatus Slow-growing and quietly attractive; deciduous foliage, hairy and sometimes purple-tinted at first, matures to a generally rounded shape, 12–18 in (30–45 cm) across and split into as many as 80 leaflets. Flowers are 1½ in (4 cm) across in a range of colors and combinations: purple, brown, slaty blue, or green outside, with paler shades, or purple, or green, sometimes darkly veined, within. Best in a raised bed in part-shade, but will take more sun in moisture-retentive soil. Division, seed. From Bosnia, Herzegovina, Croatia, and Serbia and Montenegro. ↕ 15 in (38 cm). Z6–9 H9–6. **'Dido'** Double flowers, brown on the back and green within. Introduced from Serbia and Montenegro by Elizabeth Strangman (*see panel*, p.239). Division. **Party Dress Group** see *H. x hybridus* Party Dress Group.

WINTER INTO SPRING

SNOWDROPS AND HELLEBORES ARE natural companions, and both open in any winter weather. In wilder gardens—as here at Margery Fish's garden at East Lambrook in Somerset, England—hellebores and snowdrops self-sow freely and spring up in intimate combinations that will last from winter into spring. The hellebores, *H. x hybridus*, will vary in their shape and coloring—poor forms can simply be removed; the snowdrops, in this case *Galanthus nivalis*, will vary much less. They flower together before the smothering hellebore foliage has unrolled and, once the leaves spread, the snowdrops will have secured their strength from the early sun.

HELONIOPSIS
MELANTHIACEAE

Quietly attractive woodland plants with spikes of pink or white flowers in spring.

Four species of evergreens come from woodlands and meadows in mountains of Japan, Korea, and Taiwan. Short rhizomes give rise to rosettes of leathery, lance-shaped leaves, which sometimes bear small plantlets at the tips. Nodding star-shaped flowers are carried in one-sided clusters on erect purplish stems that are leafy toward the base. The petals persist, changing color as the fruit develops.

CULTIVATION Grow in moist soil in light shade.

PROPAGATION By removing leaf-tip plantlets, by division, or from seed.

PROBLEMS Slugs and snails.

H. orientalis In May and early summer, from a rosette of strap- or lance-shaped pale green leaves, to 6 in (15 cm) long, rise erect dull red stems, leafy at the base, each bearing a one-sided cluster of nodding, rose pink flowers, ¾ in (1.5 cm) across, with prominent stamens. As fruits develop, flower stalks straighten and petals fade to buff or pale green. From Japan and Korea. ↕ 6–8 in (15–20 cm). Z7–9 H9–7

HEMEROCALLIS
Daylily
HEMEROCALLIDACEAE

Amazingly diverse, tough, low-maintenance plants with summer flowers in a vast variety of shapes, colors, and patterns.

About 20 species grow in meadows, forest margins, and watersides in China, Japan, and Korea. Written records of the daylily

BELOW *Heloniopsis orientalis*

go back as far as Confucius, who died in 479 BCE, and today, daylilies are grown around the world. A vast profusion of highly bred cultivars has now been developed and the species are rarely grown.

Either evergreen or deciduous, sun-loving but shade-tolerant, plants vary from short and compact to very tall with lanky flower stems. Dense, long, and narrow, arching, dark green leaves, which can be from 9 in (22 cm) to 48 in (120 cm) in length, form an attractive fan and are supported by fibrous to tuberous roots, slowly increasing in compact clumps or with rhizomes that spread more expansively.

Cultivars described as evergreen retain their foliage during the winter, although in cold areas it may collapse and rot after severe frosts. The foliage of deciduous daylilies dies away at the onset of winter and reappears in spring. Those described as semievergreen respond to local conditions, dying down fully in cold areas but remaining evergreen in milder regions.

Flowers resemble true lilies, with three outer and three inner petals. In the wild species, most flowers are yellow, orange, or rusty red shades, but modern hybrids show almost every color, including slate blue, near-black, and near-white. Flowers vary in size from under 1 in (2.5 cm) to over 12 in (30 cm) and are classified in various forms, including single, double, polytepal, and spider (*see* Flower Forms in Daylilies). Singles are by far the most common, followed by doubles; the others are seen much less often. They are carried on erect or arching, usually branched stems and may come in a flush lasting two or three weeks, or rebloom to provide a summer-long succession.

Each flower lasts only one day, although in nocturnal types (*see* Nocturnal and Fragrant Daylilies) the flowers open in the afternoon and remain open until the following morning. Some cultivars produce just one flowering stem from each fan of foliage, others produce more. In some cultivars the flowers are "self-cleaning"—they drop off naturally—while in others the dead flowers are best removed to ensure a clean display.

Daylilies are tolerant of salt spray, so they are invaluable in seaside gardens. Unlike many perennials, they will grow near walnut trees. Nontoxic plants, daylilies have been used in medicine and foods. The flowers are sometimes eaten: paler colors are said to be sweet, the darker colors more peppery.

The creation of new cultivars has become a substantial industry—over 1,500 new ones are registered with the American Hemerocallis Society every year. With over 50,000 cultivars registered and some widely grown cultivars, particularly some popular in Europe, not having been registered, and therefore lying outside the mainstream, choosing

FLOWER FORMS IN DAYLILIES

Many specific terms are used by specialists to describe daylily plants and the way they grow, their foliage, and their flowers.

Double daylilies have additional inner petals. In some, the stamens remain intact and fertile, while in others they are converted to petals as in H. 'Double River Wye', above.

Polytepal daylilies have four (or more) outer and inner petals instead of the typical three, as demonstrated in H. 'Hypnotized', above.

Petal

Sepal

Eye or eyezone

Throat

Single daylilies have three outer colored sepals and three alternating inner petals (collectively sometimes known as tepals, but often all simply referred to as petals), forming triangular to round flowers, as in H. 'Paper Butterfly', above.

Spider daylilies resemble single daylilies, but with long, narrow petals, like those of H. 'Pink Charm', above.

Unusual-form daylilies have narrow petals that show pleating or twisting, as in H. 'Spoons for Escargots', above.

cultivars can be difficult. Those described here can, of course, be depended upon, but a number of lists, including records of award-winning cultivars, have been added to further inform choice.

CULTIVATION Daylilies are not picky about soil conditions, although they perform best in moist but well-drained soil. Although tolerant of a wide soil pH range, they do best in a neutral to slightly acidic soil, but it is rare for daylilies not to flourish in the average garden because of an unfavorable pH. They also thrive in loose soil, with lots of aeration, rather than densely packed soil, so the soil should be loosened prior to planting, by adding organic matter. Daylilies should be planted 18–36 in (45–90 cm) apart and the leaves trimmed to about half their original height when transplanted.

Daylilies prefer full sun, although they will grow well in part-shade. A minimum of four to six hours of direct sunlight, preferably in the morning, is generally recommended. If grown in full shade, they will usually survive, but will produce fewer or no flowers. Daylilies do not require staking or wind protection, and deadheading of spent flowers is only done for cosmetic purposes.

Species and cultivars vary greatly in their hardiness. While most do well across a wide climatic range, some perform better in extreme climates. In very cold climates, deciduous daylilies thrive; although some pure evergreens may not survive in these conditions, many modern evergreens are quite cold-hardy. Mulch plants following the first hard frost, particularly those

newly moved. In very hot climates, evergreens tend to perform better; however, many deciduous daylilies also perform very well in areas that receive only mild frosts.

PROPAGATION Divide plants in late summer or early fall, about six weeks before hard frost is likely. Dig up the clump, remove as much soil as possible from the root mass, then often they can just be pulled apart; if the plants do not separate by hand, you can divide them with a knife. Many older and tougher cultivars and species can be split and replanted while in growth, especially if watered well, although favorites should be treated with more care.

PROBLEMS Aphids, spider mites, leaf streak, thrips, tarnished plant bugs, earwigs, snails, slugs, rust (*see* Daylily Rust, *p.248*), and gall midge. Where winters are marked by alternating frost and thaw, bacterial leaf and stem rot (spring sickness) may be

troublesome; in areas with high humidity and high temperatures, crown rot may cause damage. In spite of these problems, daylilies are actually among the toughest and most reliable perennials.

H. altissima (Diploid) Bright, buttery yellow, trumpet-shaped, 3 in (8 cm) flowers, fading to apricot in the throat, are nocturnal and fragrant; the long flowering season begins in midsummer. The arching, erect foliage is deciduous, with individual leaves ranging from 24 to 48 in (60–120 cm) in length. A day-blooming plant with a distinct band in the flower is sometimes sold under this name. From Kaing-shu Province, China. ↕5 ft (1.5 m). Z3–9 H8–1

H. 'Always Afternoon' (Tetraploid) Medium-mauve, 5½-in (14-cm) flowers, edged in buff with a purple eye zone above a honey-edged green throat, from early summer onward. Well branched, often producing more than one flower stem above its semievergreen

NOCTURNAL AND FRAGRANT DAYLILIES

The flowers of daylilies open for just a single day—hence the name. Most cultivars, sometimes called diurnal, open during the morning and close in the early evening. Nocturnal cultivars, however, have a different cycle, usually opening late in the afternoon, remaining open during the night, and closing the following day. Breeders are working on extending the time the flowers remain open in both groups so that more flowers are open at a time. Cultivars whose flowers remain open for more than 16 hours are sometimes termed extended bloomers.

Scent is often strong in nocturnal cultivars, being obvious as soon as the flowers open; in diurnal cultivars it becomes stronger as temperatures rise during the day. The fragrance is similar to that of honeysuckle and on warm nights can be very heavy. On cool days and in cool climates, cultivars capable of producing a good scent may not develop their full fragrance. Nocturnal cultivars are very useful in mixed garden plantings, especially if fragrant. Those of us who work during the day welcome the opportunity to enjoy daylilies and their fragrance in the evening.

foliage; one of the most prolific of all daylilies. ‡22 in (55 cm). Z4–10 H9–1

H. 'American Revolution' (Diploid) Prolific, velvety black-red, 5½-in (14-cm) blooms with brighter red streaks and a deep green throat open from blackish red buds in midsummer, making a relatively narrow-petaled, six-pointed star. Flowers over a long season above its deciduous foliage. ‡28 in (70 cm). Z3–9 H8–1

H. 'Arctic Snow' (Tetraploid) Ivory to off-white, sometimes slightly blushed, 5½-in (14-cm) flowers with a green throat and black anthers open from midsummer above deciduous foliage. Raised by daylily breeder Pat Stamile, FL. One of the largest-flowered white daylilies. ‡23 in (58 cm). Z3–9 H8–1

H. 'Barbara Dittmer' (Tetraploid) Nocturnal, coral-orchid-rose pink, 4-in (10-cm), flowers with a gold edge and a slim magenta-rose eye zone above a yellow to bright green throat open from early summer. Flowers for a long season above semievergreen foliage. ‡24 in (60 cm) Z4–9 H9–1

H. 'Barbara Mitchell' (Diploid) Pink, 6-in (15-cm) flowers with a green throat open from midsummer over a long season. Petals recurve strongly; foliage semievergreen. Winner of the Stout Silver Medal *(see panel, p.246)* in 1992. ‡20 in (50 cm). Z4–10 H8–1

H. 'Beautiful Edgings' (Diploid) Nocturnal, fragrant, 7-in (18-cm) rose-edged cream blooms and a green throat open from midsummer for a long season from among semievergreen foliage. The flowers open unusually early in the day for a nocturnal. ‡30 in (75 cm). Z4–10 H9–1

H. 'Bela Lugosi' (Tetraploid) Deep purple, 6-in (15-cm), thick-petaled flowers with a vivid green throat and slightly ruffled edges open above semievergreen foliage from midsummer and retain their color well. Named for the star of the 1931 movie version of *Dracula.* ‡33 in (85 cm). Z4–10 H9–1

H. 'Betty Woods' (Diploid) Double, fragrant, Chinese yellow, 5½-in (14-cm) flowers with green hearts open over a long season from early summer above semievergreen foliage. Given the Stout Silver Medal, the highest award of the American Hemerocallis Society, in 1991. ‡26 in (66 cm). Z5–10 H10–5

H. 'Bill Munson' (Tetraploid) Fragrant 5-in (13-cm) pink flowers with green throats open from midsummer above semievergreen foliage. Raised by Toronto and Florida breeder Ted Petit and named for one of the pioneers of tetraploid daylily breeding. ‡27 in (68 cm) Z4–9 H9–1

H. 'Black Eyed Stella' (Diploid) Small,

nocturnal, gold to yellow, 3-in (8-cm) flowers, with a dark red (far from black, but still attractive) eye zone above a yellow to gold throat, are carried on endearingly dwarf plants. They flower prolifically for a long season, beginning in early summer, above deciduous foliage. A hybrid of *H.* 'Stella d'Oro'. ‡13 in (33 cm). Z4–9 H8–1

H. 'Black Magic' (Diploid) Dark blackish red, sometimes disconcertingly pale, starry flowers with pale-edged petals and a green throat begin to open in midsummer above deciduous foliage. ‡38 in (95 cm). Z4–9 H8–1

H. 'Blue Sheen' (Diploid) Lavender-blue with an almost white central streak in each front petal; rear petals equally pale. Large green to yellow throat. The 4-in (10-cm) flowers begin to open in midsummer; foliage deciduous. ‡20 in (50 cm). Z3–9 H8–1

H. 'Bonanza' (Diploid) Fragrant, orange-yellow, 5-in (12-cm) blooms; dark purple triangular eye zone split by a central yellow streak and green throat. Opens from midsummer above deciduous foliage. Still popular after 50 years. ‡34 in (85 cm). Z4–9 H8–1

H. 'Bumble Bee' (Diploid) Neat-growing. Small, light yellow, 2-in (5-cm) flowers with a rose eye zone begin to open early, in early summer,

FATHER OF THE MODERN DAYLILY

Dr. Arlow Burdette Stout is the Father of the Modern Daylily. Employed at the New York Botanical Garden as Director of Laboratories from 1911 to 1948, Dr. Stout worked creatively and diligently on the hybridization of daylilies and, in the process, also introduced several species to the gardening world, including *Hemerocallis fulva* var. *rosea*, *H. multiflora*, and *H. altissima*.

His breeding program produced nearly one hundred new daylily hybrids, many introduced through the Bertrand Farr Nursery Company of Pennsylvania. It is fair to say that through Dr. Stout's efforts the daylily has become a favorite plant for flower gardens across the United States.

Dr. Stout worked on attributes of color, long bloom time, hardiness, and double flowers, among other characteristics. His first cultivar was 'Mikado', a rich orange-colored daylily with mahogany blotches in the center of each petal, introduced in 1929. The first red daylily, 'Theron' (1934), was one of his selections. He was so successful in his efforts that today's daylily breeders rely upon the genetic material that he made available through his program.

The Stout Silver Medal is the highest award that a daylily can receive from the American Hemerocallis Society. First awarded in 1950 to 'Hesperus', this medal was named to honor the accomplishments of daylily breeding pioneer Dr. Arlow B. Stout.

LEFT **1** *Hemerocallis* 'Always Afternoon' **2** *H.* 'American Revolution' **3** *H.* 'Buzz Bomb' **4** *H.* 'Cartwheels'

and last for a long season Evergreen foliage. ‡ 12 in (30 cm). Z5–10 H10–5

H. 'Burning Daylight' (Diploid) Fragrant, glowing orange, 6-in (15-cm) flowers, with broader, wavier inner petals, are carried relatively low among deciduous foliage from midsummer. ‡ 28 in (70 cm). Z4–9 H8–1

H. 'Buzz Bomb' (Diploid) Slightly orangey red, 5-in (13-cm) flowers with yellow throats begin opening in midsummer and usually have a long season. Deciduous foliage. ‡ 24 in (60 cm). Z4–9 H8–1

H. 'Calling All Angels' (Tetraploid) A huge cranberry red eye and edge leave little space for creamy white zone between; 4-in (10-cm) bloom often shows tiny gold teeth and a wire gold edge. Long flowering season begins in midsummer; above evergreen foliage. ‡ 21 in (53 cm). Z4–9 H9–1.

H. 'Canadian Border Patrol' (Tetraploid) Cream, 6-in (15-cm) flowers with strongly contrasting purple edge and purple eye zone above a green throat. Begins to open in midsummer; flowers for a long season. Semievergreen foliage. Prolific and increases well. ‡ 28 in (70 cm). Z5–10 H10–5

H. 'Cartwheels' (Diploid) Deep yellow to orange, 6-in (15-cm) flowers with widely spreading petals and a small green throat, from midsummer over narrow, erect deciduous foliage. A popular classic from Orville Fay, IL. ‡ 30 in (75 cm). Z4–9 H8–1

H. 'Catherine Woodbery' (Diploid) Fragrant, 6-in (15-cm), orchid-pink flowers with a green throat begin to open in midsummer above deciduous foliage. Once much used as a breeding parent. ‡ 30 in (75 cm). Z3–9 H8–1

H. 'Champagne and Caviar' (Tetraploid) Creamy peach, 6-in (15-cm) flowers with contrasting grape-purple eye zone, green throat, and thick, rubbery purple picotee edged in gold. Opens from midsummer and blooms for a long season. Deciduous foliage. ‡ 24 in (60 cm). Z4–9 H9–1

H. 'Cherry Cheeks' (Tetraploid) In shades of rose pink, above a green to yellow throat, these 6-in (15-cm) flowers, with almost black anthers, begin flowering in midsummer. Deciduous foliage. Raised by noted tetraploid breeder Virginia Peck, TN. ‡ 28 in (70 cm). Z3–9 H8–1

H. 'Chicago Apache' (Tetraploid) Rounded and ruffled, scarlet, 5-in (12-cm) flowers with a green throat and black anthers begin to open in midsummer above lush deciduous foliage. Popular for 25 years, vigorous, thrives in all climates, and rarely fades in the sun. ‡ 27 in (70 cm). Z3–9 H8–1

H. 'Chicago Blackout' (Tetraploid) Green-throated, blackish red, 6-in (15-cm) flowers with narrow petals, each with a pale midrib, begin opening

TAPESTRY IN MAGENTA AND GOLD

THIS IS A THOUGHTFUL TAPESTRY of color in a wild but disciplined border. At its center is an ever-expanding clump of *Hemerocallis* 'Cherry Cheeks', the slightly magenta-tinted, rosy pink flowers featuring a golden yellow throat. Scrambling through the hemerocallis, from a tight crown, are the tangling trails of *Geranium* 'Ann Folkard', whose bright flowers echo the color of the daylily, and whose young yellow foliage reflects the color in their throats. The black anthers in the daylily even match the black eyes in the geranium. Peeping through the group are the dainty pink fireworks of *Allium carinatum* subsp. *pulchellum*.

in midsummer over semievergreen foliage. ‡ 30 in (75 cm). Z4–10 H9–1

H. 'Chicago Knockout' (Tetraploid) Velvety purple, 6-in (15-cm) flowers begin to open in midsummer; deciduous foliage. ‡ 25 in (65 cm). Z4–10 H9–1

H. 'Chicago Royal Robe' (Tetraploid) Slightly scented, plum-purple, 5½-in (14-cm) flowers with a green throat begin to open in early summer over semievergreen foliage. Reliable and prolific. ‡ 25 in (65 cm). Z4–10 H9–1

H. Chicago Series (Tetraploid) A large series of tetraploids developed by James Marsh of Chicago, who worked from the mid-1950s to 1978 and was especially noted for his lavender and purple introductions. He also raised diploids that carry the "Prairie" prefix.

H. 'Chicago Sunrise' (Tetraploid) Orange, 6-in (15-cm) flowers with a red haze around the green throat begin a long season of bloom in midsummer

above semievergreen foliage. ‡ 28 in (70 cm). Z3–9 H8–1

H. 'Chief Sarcoxie' (Diploid) Bright red, sometimes slightly brownish, 5½-in (14-cm) flowers with reflexed petals and a green throat start their season in midsummer above slender deciduous leaves. ‡ 32 in (80 cm). Z3–9 H8–1

H. 'Christmas Is' (Diploid) Vigorous, but sometimes shy-blooming, deep Christmas red, 4½-in (11-cm) flowers have a very large, dramatic green throat and begin to open in midsummer for a long season over deciduous foliage. ‡ 26 in (66 cm). Z3–9 H8–1

H. citrina Blue-green, semi-erect, deciduous foliage, with leaves 30–43 in (75–110 cm) long, shows off nocturnal-blooming, fragrant, 5½-in (14-cm) flowers, slender, trumpet-shaped and

RIGHT *Hemerocallis* 'Catherine Woodbery'

pale lemon yellow with a green throat; outer petals green on the outside with purple tips. From 30 to 50 flowers are carried on each stem. Open from midsummer. From Shen-si province, China. ‡ 45 in (114 cm). Z4–9 H8–1

H. **'Colorado Zs'** (Tetraploid) Fragrant, magenta lavender rose, 5-in (13-cm) blooms with wine magenta rose band and cream white edge above a greenish yellow throat; the long season starts in midsummer. Deciduous foliage. ‡ 26 in (66 cm). Z4–9 H9–1

H. **'Condilla'** (Diploid) Classic double with 4½-in (11-cm), deep gold flowers with black anthers from midsummer over deciduous foliage. Well-branched; prolific. ‡ 20 in (50 cm). Z3–9 H8–1

H. **'Cool It'** Large, fragrant, soft white, lily-shaped, 6-in (15-cm) flowers have broad and ruffled edges above a green throat. The foliage is deciduous, and blooming begins in midsummer, with a second flush in late summer, over deciduous foliage. Not registered with the American Hemerocallis Society. ‡ 20 in (50 cm). Z3–9 H8–1

H. **'Corky'** (Diploid) Small, 3-in (8-cm), bright lemon to yellow flowers with brown backs carried on brown stems that branch repeatedly toward their tips; open from midsummer over deciduous foliage. A European favorite raised by Herbert Fischer, who also raised the similar, but darker, 'Golden Chimes'. ‡ 34 in (85 cm). Z3–9 H8–1

H. **'Cream Drop'** (Diploid) Small, fragrant, slightly ruffled, 3-in (8-cm) cream flowers with a green throat open from midsummer over deciduous foliage. ‡ 17 in (43 cm). Z3–9 H8–1

H. **'Crimson Pirate'** (Diploid) Long season of scarlet, 5-in (12-cm) flowers with long, slender petals (spider-form), each with a narrow, orange central stripe. The flowers are held high over the deciduous foliage from midsummer. ‡ 30 in (75 cm). Z3–9 H8–1

H. **'Crystal Blue Persuasion'** (Diploid) Pale lavender, 3-in (7-cm) blooms with slate blue eye and pencil edge, green throat. Flowering for a long season from midsummer over evergreen foliage. ‡ 18 in (45 cm). Z4–9 H9–1

H. **'Custard Candy'** (Tetraploid) Small, nocturnal, creamy yellow, wide-petaled, 4½-in (11-cm) flowers; maroon eye zone, green throat. Blooms for a long season from midsummer. Deciduous foliage. ‡ 24 in (60 cm). Z3–9 H8–1

H. **'Divine Comedy'** (Tetraploid) Large, fragrant, rose-purple 6-in (15-cm) blooms; yellow watermark above a lemon yellow to green throat. Often produces more than one flower stem in a season over semievergreen

LEFT 1 *Hemerocallis* 'Cherry Cheeks' **2** *H.* 'Chicago Apache' **3** *H.* 'Chicago Royal Robe' **4** *H. citrina* **5** *H.* 'Condilla' **6** *H.* 'Cream Drop'

foliage. ↕30 in (78 cm). Z4–9 H9–1

H. 'Double River Wye' (Diploid) Pale yellow, double, 4½-in (11-cm) flowers; green throat. Blooms from midsummer for many weeks. Deciduous foliage. Easy and dependable. ↕30 in (75 cm). Z3–9 H8–1

H. 'Dragons Eye' (Diploid) Small, pastel pink, nocturnal, 4-in (10-cm) flowers; red eye zone and green throat. Open from midsummer; often produces more than one flush of flower stems over a long season. Semievergreen foliage. Prolific and bulks up well. From small-flowered daylily specialist Elizabeth Salter, FL. ↕24 in (60 cm). Z4–10 H9–1

H. dumortierii (Diploid) Low-growing, compact, deciduous foliage grows stiffly erect, 6–24 in (15–60 cm) in length, with two to four deep orange, trumpet-shaped flowers, 4 in (10 cm) across, on each stem from early summer. From Japan, Korea, Manchuria, and eastern Siberia. ↕24 in (60 cm). Z4–9 H9–1

H. 'Edge of Darkness' (Tetraploid) Dramatic lavender blooms; purple eye zone and picotee edge, above a yellow throat. The 5-in (13-cm) flowers begin to open in midsummer. Evergreen foliage. ↕25 in (65 cm). Z5–10 H10–5

H. 'Eenie Allegro' (Diploid) Apricot-edged, rose pink, 2½-in (6-cm) flowers have a chartreuse throat and open from midsummer over deciduous foliage. ↕13 in (33 cm). Z3–9 H8–1

H. 'Eenie Fanfare' (Diploid) Lightly scented, rich plum-red, 2¾-in (7-cm). White-edged above a green throat open from midsummer. Deciduous foliage. ↕12 in (30 cm). Z3–9 H8–1

H. Eenie Series A small series of dwarf daylilies raised in the 1970s by Paul Aden, NY, much better known for his many *Hosta* introductions.

H. 'Eenie Weenie' (Diploid) Tiny, 1¾-in (4.5-cm) yellow flowers with a green throat open in crowded heads from midsummer, often for a long season, above deciduous foliage. The most popular of the Eenie cultivars. ↕10 in (25 cm). Z3–9 H8–1

H. 'El Desperado' (Tetraploid) Dramatic, nocturnal, mustard yellow, 4½-in (11-cm) flowers with a wine-purple eye zone above a green throat open usefully late, from late summer, for a long season above deciduous foliage. ↕28 in (70 cm). Z3–9 H8–1

H. 'Elegant Candy' (Tetraploid) Small, fragrant, sugar-pink 4½-in (11-cm) flowers with a red eye zone above a green throat begin to open from midsummer, often for a long season, above deciduous foliage. ↕25 in (65 cm). Z3–9 H8–1

H. 'Elizabeth Salter' (Tetraploid) Very popular, nocturnal, highly ruffled, pink, 5½-in (14-cm) flower with a green throat. Flowering from midsummer, often for a long season. Semievergreen foliage. Raised by Jeff Salter, FL, and named for his wife (also a noted daylily breeder). ↕22 in (55 cm). Z4–10 H9–1

H. 'Eyes Wide Shut' (Tetraploid) Dramatic, cream to near white, 5-in (13-cm) flowers with a wine purple eye zone filling most of the flower and knobbly wine-purple picotee edge. Flowers from midsummer for a long season, semievergreen foliage. ↕26 in (66 cm). Z4–9 H9–1

H. 'Ferengi Gold' (Tetraploid) Popular, nocturnal, extravagantly ruffled, yellow, 5½-in (14-cm) flowers,

with flesh-pink overtones and a yellow eye zone above a green throat, open very early in the day. Flowers for a long period from midsummer. Deciduous foliage. The exact coloring may vary with the local climate. ↕19 in (48 cm). Z3–9 H8–1

H. 'Fire And Brimstone' (Tetraploid) Rich crimson red, 5-in (12-cm) flowers from midsummer feature a yellow gold border above a large, bright green throat and are produced over a long season above evergreen foliage. ↕26 in (66 cm). Z4–9 H9–1

H. 'First Degree' (Tetraploid) Sultry, clear crimson red, 15.2 cm (6 in) flowers with a brilliant green throat open from midsummer for a long season above evergreen foliage. ↕28 in (70 cm). Z4–9 H9–1

H. 'Forsyth Aristocrat' (Tetraploid) Fragrant, prolific, purple, 7-in (15-cm) bloom; white watermark above green throat; slim white edge on all petals. Opens from midsummer. Deciduous foliage. ↕34 in (86 cm). Z4–9 H9–1

H. 'Frans Hals' (Diploid) A bright rust and orange bicolor with bold creamy orange midribs, the rear petals in the same creamy orange shade completing a very striking, 4½-in (11-cm) flower that opens from midsummer over deciduous foliage. Popular for 50 years. ↕24 in (60 cm). Z3–9 H8–1

H. fulva (Diploid) Deciduous leaves with a noticeable "V" profile are up to 36 in (90 cm) long. Outer leaves arch outward, inner ones are held erect. Large numbers of rusty orange to red and rose pink, 5-in (13-cm) flowers are carried on each stem from midsummer. From China. ↕40 in (100 cm). Z3–10 H8–1. **'Flore Pleno'** (Triploid) Double, burnt orange, 6-in (15-cm) blooms with a red eye zone from midsummer. Often found naturalized in the US. The best for eating, deep-fried. ↕30 in (75 cm). **'Green Kwanso'** (Triploid) Orange reddish brown flowers with a darker eye zone from midsummer. ↕36 in (90 cm). **'Variegated Kwanso'** (Diploid) Deciduous, erect, green and white striped foliage up to 36 in (90 cm). Rusty orange, double flowers with a darker eye and light veining open from midsummer. Originally found in Japan. ↕36 in (90 cm).

LEFT *Hemerocallis fulva* 'Flore Pleno'

H. 'Gentle Shepherd' (Diploid) A classic near-white, and one of the whitest of all daylilies, with a yellow to green throat. These popular, 5-in (13-cm) flowers begin to open in midsummer above semievergreen foliage. Not vigorous. ↕30 in (75 cm). Z3–10 H8–1

H. 'Golden Prize' (Tetraploid) Golden yellow, 7-in (18-cm) flowers begin to open in late summer above deciduous foliage. An old favorite, the flowers more starry than those of many more modern cultivars. ↕26 in (66 cm). Z3–10 H8–1

H. Golden Zebra (**'Malja'**) Small, golden yellow, 3-in (7.5-cm) flowers above striking, stable, variegated, 30 in (75 cm) long, deciduous foliage that is green and white in shady conditions, but green and yellow in full sun. Not registered with the American Hemerocallis Society. ↕18 in (45 cm). Z5–9 H9–5

H. 'Green Flutter' (Diploid) Canary yellow, 3-in (7.5-cm) flowers with a green throat open for a long season in late summer above semievergreen foliage. One of the greenest, unusually prolific, and increases well. ↕20 in (50 cm). Z3–9 H8–1

H. 'Happy Returns' (Diploid) Early, small, light yellow, fragrant 3-in (8-cm) flowers open from early summer. Deciduous foliage. Popular. Long season if kept growing well. Descendant of the even more popular 'Stella d'Oro'. Introduced by Darrel Apps, NJ. ↕18 in (45 cm). Z3–9 H8–1

H. 'How Beautiful Heaven Must Be' (Tetraploid) Very wide petals, peach pink with ornate heavy gold ruffling extending deep into the throat. Fragrant 6 in (15 cm) flowers open for a long season from midsummer. Evergreen foliage. 26 in (66 cm). Z4–9 H9–1

H. 'Hyperion' (Diploid) Extremely popular daylily; supremely fragrant, light canary yellow blooms are produced in abundance above deciduous foliage for a short season starting in midsummer. Still going strong after more than 80 years. ↕40 in (100 cm). Z3–9 H8–1

H. 'Ice Carnival' (Diploid) Fragrant, white, green-throated, 6-in (15-cm), noticeably triangular flowers open from midsummer, often producing more

than one flush of flower stems in a season. Deciduous foliage. ↕ 28 in (70 cm). Z3–9 H8–1

H. 'Ida's Legacy' (Tetraploid) Clear lavender, 6 in (15 cm) flowers with a ruffled gold edge, lighter watermark and a green throat open from midsummer over semievergreen leaves. ↕ 24 in (60 cm). Z4–9 H9–1

H. 'In the Navy' (Diploid) Nocturnal, lavender 3-in (7.5-cm) flowers with a complex slate navy blue eye—one of the bluest in daylilies—above a green

throat. Opens from midsummer; long season. Semievergreen foliage. Invaluable breeder. ↕ 18 in (45 cm). Z4–9 H9–1

H. 'Invitation to Immortality' (Tetraploid) Burgundy flowers; lighter watermark above bright green throat, 6 in (15 cm) across. Opens from early summer for a long season. Evergreen foliage. ↕ 30 in (75 cm). Z3–9 H8–1

H. 'Jamaican Music' (Tetraploid) Fragrant, cream pink, 5 in (12.5 cm) blooms have a huge red eye and thick red ruffled picotee edge above a green throat. Opens for a long season from midsummer. Evergreen foliage. ↕ 36 in (90 cm). Z4–9 H9–1

H. 'Janice Brown' (Diploid) Very popular, bright pink, 4½-in (11-cm) flowers have a rose pink eye zone and a green throat. Flowering begins in midsummer. Semievergreen foliage. Prolific but sometimes slow to establish. ↕ 21 in (53 cm). Z3–9 H8–1

H. 'Jason Salter' (Diploid) Yellow blooms 2¾ in (7 cm) across, washed lavender purple eye zone, less distinct in cool climates, above a green throat. Open from midsummer. Evergreen foliage. ↕ 18 in (45 cm). Z5–10 H10–5

H. 'Jedi Dot Pierce' (Diploid) Fragrant, rose pink, lightly ruffled flowers, 6-in (15-cm), with a darker rose eye zone and a green throat, open from midsummer for a long season just above semievergreen foliage. Increases well. ↕ 20 in (50 cm). Z4–10 H9–1

H. 'Jenny Wren' (Diploid) Small brown flowers with an oxblood halo and an orange throat open from midsummer on well-branched stems over deciduous foliage. Distinctive and prolific. ↕ 36 in (90 cm). Z3–9 H8–1

H. 'Jerry Nettles' (Tetraploid) Extravagant, full, flat, lavender-purple, 6-in (15-cm) flowers with heavily ruffled gold edges, which glow across the garden, open from midsummer for a long season. Evergreen foliage. ↕ 28 in (70 cm). Z5–10 H10–5

H. 'Joan Senior' (Diploid) A classic: almost white, with a lime green throat, 6 in (15 cm) across. Opens from midsummer and often produce more than one flush in a season. Evergreen foliage. A good all-rounder. ↕ 26 in (65 cm). Z5–10 H10–5

H. 'John Peat' (Tetraploid) Prolific, dramatic, burgundy-purple flowers, 6 in (15 cm) across, with heavy gold edge and lighter watermark above the green throat. Open from midsummer and rebloom heavily. Evergreen foliage. ↕ 22 in (55 cm). Z4–10 H9–1

H. 'Jolyene Nichole' (Diploid) Rosy, green-throated, 6-in (15-cm) flowers with darker veins open in midsummer, just above evergreen foliage. Bleaches

in fierce heat and grows taller in cool climates. ↕ 14 in (36 cm). Z5–10 H10–5

H. 'Kate Carpenter' (Tetraploid) Pale pink, cream throat; fragrant 6-in (15-cm) blooms open from midsummer for a long season. Evergreen foliage. Slow to increase. ↕ 28 in (70 cm). Z3–9 H8–1

H. 'Kindly Light' (Diploid) Very narrow, clear yellow petals above a lime green throat make a 7½-in (19-cm) spider-form flower opening from midsummer on slender, rather weak stems over deciduous foliage. ↕ 28 in (70 cm). Z3–9 H8–1

H. 'Lady Betty Fretz' (Tetraploid) Striking, ivory cream, 6 in (15 cm) flowers, with a large red eye zone and picotee with a heavy gold edge, open in midsummer. Semievergreen foliage. ↕ 26 in (66 cm). Z4–9 H9–1

H. lilioasphodelus (Diploid) Large, widely spreading plants comprise strong tufts of deciduous foliage with leaves 30 in (75 cm) long. Very fragrant, lemon yellow, 4-in (10-cm) flowers open early summer, for a long season. From China. ↕ 30 in (75 cm). Z4–9 H9–1

H. 'Little Grapette' (Diploid) Tiny, 2-in (5-cm), grape-colored flowers open from early summer. Semievergreen foliage. Neat, prolific, and vigorous. ↕ 12 in (30 cm). Z4–10 H9–1

H. 'Little Maggie' (Diploid) Rose pink flowers with a burgundy eye zone above a green throat are 3 in (7.5 cm) across and open from early summer for a long season among evergreen foliage. ↕ 12 in (30 cm). Z4–10 H9–1

H. 'Little Red Hen' (Diploid) Red, yellow-throated, 3½-in (9-cm) flowers open from midsummer on relatively tall stems. Deciduous foliage. ↕ 30 in (75 cm). Z4–10 H9–1

H. 'Little Wine Cup' (Diploid) Tiny 2-in (5-cm) wine red flowers, with pale midribs and a green throat, open from early summer above deciduous foliage. ↕ 20 in (50 cm). Z3–9 H8–1

H. 'Lullaby Baby' (Diploid) Fragrant, 3½-in (9-cm), ruffled, pale pink, with green throat. Open from midsummer for a long season. Semievergreen

STOUT SILVER MEDAL

The highest award given in the US for a *Hemerocallis* cultivar, it is named for Dr. Arlow Burdette Stout, the father of modern daylily breeding in North America. The Stout Silver Medal has been annually awarded since 1960 by the American Hemerocallis Society to plants growing in gardens, not cut material. A few may be difficult to find in nurseries. Cultivars that have been received this award include: ,'Betty Woods', 'Custard Candy', 'Janice Brown', 'Siloam Doble Classic', 'Stella d'Oro', and 'Strawberry Candy'.

foliage. ↕ 19 in (48 cm). Z4–10 H9–1

H. 'Lusty Lealand' (Tetraploid) Red, 6-in (15-cm) blooms, yellow to green throat and orange backs to the petals, open from midsummer. Evergreen foliage. ↕ 28 in (70 cm). Z5–10 H10–5

H. 'Luxury Lace' (Diploid) Mars-orange with a deep green throat, the 3½-in (9-cm) flowers open from midsummer; often more than one flush of fragrant flowers per season. Deciduous foliage. A vigorous classic from pioneer Louisiana breeder Edna Spalding. ↕ 32 in (80 cm). Z3–9 H8–1

H. 'Malachite Prism' (Diploid) Relatively small, 4 in (10 cm) flowers in lavender and green; purple chevron eye zone above a large dramatic green throat; open from midsummer for a long season among semievergreen foliage. ↕ 36 in (90 cm). Z4–9 H9–1

H. 'Mallard' (Tetraploid) Classic, 6-in (15-cm) red flowers on strong stems open from midsummer over deciduous foliage. ↕ 26 in (66 cm). Z3–9 H8–1

H. 'Mary Todd' (Tetraploid) An old but popular buff-orange, with 6-in (15-cm) flowers opening from early summer. Semievergreen foliage. ↕ 26 in (66 cm). Z4–10 H9–1

H. 'Mauna Loa' (Tetraploid) In shades of amber-gold with a fine edge of deep red above a light green throat, the 5-in (13-cm) flowers open for a short season in midsummer over deciduous foliage. ↕ 22 in (55 cm). Z3–9 H8–1

H. 'Merry Moppet' (Tetraploid) Golden yellow, 3½-in (9-cm) flowers with a blood red eye zone and picotee edge open from midsummer and often for a long season over semievergreen foliage. ↕ 27 in (86 cm). Z4–9 H9–1

H. 'Michael Miller' (Tetraploid) Opulent, white, wide-petaled flowers, 6 in (15 cm) across, with ruffled and looped gold edges above a contrasting green throat. Open for a long season from midsummer. Evergreen foliage. ↕ 30 in (76 cm). Z4–9 H9–1

H. middendorffii (Diploid) The smooth, flat, deciduous foliage is erect, bent at the tops, and significantly overtops the intense, clear, glowing, light orange 3-in (7.5-cm) flowers, which open from early summer on 14-in (36-cm) stems. From Siberia, Japan, and Sakhalin Island. ↕ 36 in (90 cm). Z4–9 H9–1

H. 'Midnight Magic' (Tetraploid) A classic; dark black-red, 5½-in (14 cm) with striking green throat,. Opens early in the day from midsummer. Evergreen foliage. Prolific, well-branched, increases well, but may bleach in very hot conditions. ↕ 28 in (70 cm). Z4–9 H9–1

H. 'Mildred Mitchell' (Tetraploid) Fragrant, 6-in (15-cm) lavender blooms, known for their bluish eye zone and matching edge above a green throat, open from midsummer, often for a long season, over evergreen foliage. Not

vigorous. ‡26 in (66 cm). Z5–10 H10–5

H. 'Ming Porcelain' (Tetraploid) A classic pastel ivory-pink with a peach blush, fine gold edge, and wide yellow halo above a lime-green throat. The 5-in (13-cm) flowers open in early summer, often for a long season. Broad, lush evergreen foliage. ‡28 in (70 cm). Z5–10 H10–5

H. 'Mini Pearl' (Diploid) Blush pink, with a lemon yellow to green throat, the 3-in (7.5-cm) flowers open early in the day from midsummer, often for a long season, over the deciduous foliage. Prolific. ‡16 in (40 cm). Z4–10 H9–2

H. 'Mini Stella' (Diploid) Tiny, yellow, nocturnal, 1¼-in (3-cm) flowers with a burnt orange eye zone above a green throat begin to open in early summer, often for a long season, among deciduous foliage. A shorter, paler version of H. 'Stella d'Oro'. ‡10 in (25 cm). Z3–9 H8–1

H. minor (Diploid) Low, compact, deciduous 22-in (55 cm) foliage. Bell-shaped 3½-in (9-cm), bright cadmium yellow flowers, brownish red on the back of outer petal, open from midsummer. From eastern Siberia, northern China, Mongolia, and Korea. ‡24 in (60 cm). Z4–9 H9–1

H. 'Moonlit Masquerade' (Tetraploid) Dramatic, 5½-in (14-cm) flowers, cream with contrasting dark purple eye zone above a green throat, open at night from midsummer and are often produced for a long season. Semievergreen foliage. Vigorous. ‡26 in (66 cm). Z4–9 H9–1

H. 'Mort Morss' (Tetraploid) A dramatic dark purple with a striking, contrasting white toothy edge and a green throat, the 15.2 cm (6 in) flowers open from midsummer for a long season over semievergreen foliage. ‡68.6 cm (27 in). Z4–9 H9–1

H. multiflora (Diploid) The widely spreading, drooping, deciduous leaves are 30 in (75 cm) long, but their height is only about 18 in (45 cm), and through them, from late summer and for a long season, emerge medium orange to cadmium yellow, 3-in (7.5-cm) flowers. From Hunan, China. ‡40 in (100 cm). Z5–9 H9–5

H. 'My Darling Clementine' (Tetraploid) Popular, heavily ruffled, 4½-in (11-cm) yellow flowers with a green throat are held on well-branched stems well above the evergreen foliage from early summer over a long period. ‡21 in (53 cm). Z5–10 H10–5

H. 'Myla My Love' (Tetraploid) Fragrant, deep lavender grape, 6 in (15 cm) flowers with a lightly ruffled edge above a darker eye zone open from midsummer over deciduous

LEFT 1 *Hemerocallis* 'Joan Senior'
2 *H.* 'Little Grapette' **3** *H.* 'Moonlit Masquerade'

foliage. ‡34 in (86 cm). Z4–9 H9–1

H. 'Neyron Rose' (Diploid) Rich raspberry red, 4½-in (11-cm) blooms with striking white midribs above a tangerine throat open from midsummer. Semievergreen foliage. ‡30 in (75 cm). Z4–9 H9–1

H. 'Night Beacon' (Diploid) Dark, blackish purple flowers with white midribs, a large chartreuse center, and a green throat. The 4-in (10-cm) blooms open from midsummer, and often for a long season. Evergreen foliage. Vigorous. ‡28 in (70 cm). Z5–10 H10–5

H. 'Olive Bailey Langdon' (Tetraploid) The 5-in (13-cm), purple flowers with a yellow to green throat begin to open in midsummer, often for a long season, above semievergreen foliage. ‡28 in (70 cm). Z3–9 H8–1

H. 'Pandora's Box' (Diploid) Fragrant, cream, 4-in (10-cm) flowers with a purple eye zone above a green throat, often carried for a long season, open above evergreen foliage from midsummer. Adaptable and reliable. ‡19 in (48 cm). Z5–10 H10–5

H. 'Paper Butterfly' (Tetraploid) Creamy peach, starry blooms, 6 in (15 cm) across, with a patterned blue-violet eye zone above a green throat Open, often for a long season, in early summer above semievergreen foliage. Elegant, but not always dependable. ‡24 in (60 cm). Z4–10 H9–1

H. 'Pardon Me' (Diploid) Small but fragrant, nocturnal, bright red 2¾-in (7-cm) flowers with a yellow to green throat open from midsummer, often for a long season, over deciduous foliage. Bred by Darrel Apps, NJ. Prolific. ‡18 in (45 cm). Z3–9 H8–1

H. 'Pink Charm' (Diploid) A large pink with nice ruffling above a green throat; the 6-in (15-cm) spider-form flowers open in midsummer, often for a long season, over semievergreen foliage. ‡40 in (100 cm). Z4–10 H9–1

H. 'Pink Dream' (Diploid) Light red

to dark pink flowers, often carried on more than one flush flower stems in a season well above deciduous foliage, and opening from midsummer. ↕ 40 in (100 cm). Z3–9 H8–1

H. 'Prairie Blue Eyes' (Diploid) An older-style, triangular-shaped lavender flower with a bluish lavender eye zone above a green throat. The 5-in (13-cm) flowers open in midsummer above semievergreen foliage. Vigorous and prolific. ↕ 28 in (70 cm). Z4–10 H9–1

H. 'Promised Day' (Tetraploid) Deep purple flowers, 7 in (18 cm), have a large orange watermark and a rubbery tangerine edge above a small green throat. Open from midsummer, often for a long season. Semievergreen foliage. ↕ 21 in (53 cm). Z4–10 H9–1

H. 'Purple Waters' (Diploid) Lightly ruffled, plum-purple flowers, darker purple eye zone above yellow to green throat. Open in midsummer, often with a second flush later in the season. Semievergreen foliage. ↕ 36 in (90 cm). Z4–10 H9–1

H. 'Raspberry Candy' (Tetraploid) Nocturnal, fragrant, cream, 4¾-in (12-cm) flowers; raspberry red eye zone, green throat. Open in early summer, often for a long season. Deciduous

DAYLILY RUST

Discovered in the southeast in 2000, daylily rust (*Puccinia hemerocallidis*) is a new pathogen in the US, although it has been known in Asia since 1880. By the fall of 2001, this disease had been identified in over 30 states. The popularity and widespread distribution of daylilies are factors in the rapid spread of this disease.

The most recognizable symptom of the rust infection is the presence of yellow to brown streaks on the plant leaves. When the plant is infected, the undersides of the leaves will have many small bright yellow spots, or pustules. These pustules will mature and release many dusty, orange spores. Eventually the leaves turn yellow before drying up.

Rust diseases often have two separate hosts for different stages of their life cycles. The alternate host for daylily rust is *Patrinia*, an herbaceous perennial. Some speculation exists that *Hosta* species also might be alternate hosts for this rust and research continues to attempt to confirm this.

Management strategies for daylily rust include sanitation, both contact and systemic fungicides, and resistant varieties of *Hemerocallis*. Only a small number of cultivars have been tested, but the following are known to be resistant to daylily rust:
'Barbara Mitchell'
'Happy Returns'
'Joleyne Nichole'
'Prairie Blue Eyes'
'Siloam Double Classic'
'Siloam Ury Winniford'

foliage. ↕ 26 in (66 cm). Z3–9 H8–1

H. 'Reyna' (Tetraploid) Very large, extravagantly ruffled, cream flowers, 7½ in (19 cm), with faint violet cast and a darker violet eye zone and matching picotee. Open from midsummer, often for a long season. Semievergreen foliage. ↕ 25 in (64 cm). Z4–10 H9–1

H. 'Rose Dazzler' (Tetraploid) A blend of lavender and rose pink, the 6 in (15 cm) flowers open in early summer, often carried on more than one flower stem in a season, above semievergreen foliage. ↕ 20 in (60 cm). Z4–10 H9–1

H. 'Royal Renaissance' (Tetraploid) Rose red, 14 cm (5.5 in) flowers with a lighter watermark and a heavy white gold edge open from midsummer, often producing more than one flower stem in a season above semievergreen foliage. ↕ 71 cm (28 in). Z4–10 H9–1

H. 'Royal Braid' (Tetraploid) Lavender blooms with silver edging and royal purple braid and eye zone above a green throat. Nocturnal, fragrant, 5-in (13-cm) flowers open from midsummer, often for a long season. Semievergreen foliage, Best in hot conditions. ↕ 26 in (65 cm). Z4–10 H9–1

H. 'Russian Rhapsody' (Tetraploid) Violet purple with a yellow throat, the 6-in (15-cm) flowers open from midsummer over semievergreen foliage. ↕ 30 in (75 cm). Z4–10 H9–1

H. 'Sammy Russell' (Diploid) Brick red with lighter midribs above an orange to yellow throat, and old-fashioned looking with narrow petals, the 4-in (10-cm) flowers start to open relatively late, in late summer, Deciduous foliage. 30 in (75 cm). Z3–9 H8–1

H. 'Seminole Wind' (Tetraploid) Large, wide-petaled, fragrant, nocturnal, ruffled pink 6-in (15-cm) flowers, green throat; opens for a long season from midsummer over semievergreen foliage. Used by breeders as a parent plant. ↕ 23 in (58 cm). Z4–10 H9–1

H. 'Siloam Baby Talk' (Diploid) Tiny, pale pink blooms, 2 in (5 cm) across, with a deep rose halo above a green throat, open from midsummer just above deciduous foliage. Vigorous and prolific. ↕ 15 in (38 cm). Z3–9 H8–1

H. 'Siloam Bo Peep' (Diploid) Fragrant, relatively small, 4½-in (11-cm) flowers in shades of orchid pink, with deep purple eye zone and green throat, open from midsummer. Deciduous foliage. ↕ 18 in (45 cm). Z3–9 H8–1

H. 'Siloam David Kirchhoff' (Diploid) Small, 3½-in (9-cm), orchid pink flowers with a cerise pencil eye zone and a green throat open from midsummer over deciduous foliage. Lovely coloring, but can flower thinly.

RIGHT **1** *Hemerocallis* 'Stoke Poges'
2 *H.* 'Tetrina's Daughter'
3 *H.* 'Whichford'

‡16 in (40 cm). Z3–9 H8–1

H. 'Siloam Double Classic' (Diploid)
Fragrant, bright pink, double, 5-in
(13-cm) blooms; green throat. Opens
from midsummer. Deciduous foliage.
One of the most popular doubles,
although the first few flowers may be
single. ‡16 in (40 cm). Z3–9 H8–1

H. 'Siloam Royal Prince' (Diploid)
Reddish purple, 4-in (10-cm) flowers
with a green throat and white midribs
open in midsummer. Deciduous foliage.
Vigorous. ‡19 in (48 cm). Z3–9 H8–1

H. Siloam Series A large series of
mainly (not exclusively) miniature and
small-flowered daylilies developed by
Pauline Henry of Siloam Springs, AK.

H. 'Siloam Show Girl' (Diploid) Red
blooms with a deep red eye zone above
a green throat. The 4½-in (11-cm)
flowers begin to open in midsummer
over arching deciduous foliage. ‡18 in
(45 cm). Z3–9 H8–1

H. 'Siloam Ury Winniford' (Diploid)
Deep cream, 3-in (8-cm) flowers with
large purple eye zone and green throat
open from midsummer. Deciduous
foliage. Bold, attractive, dependable
plant. ‡23 in (58 cm). Z3–9 H8–1

H. 'Siloam Virginia Henson'
(Diploid) Pink blooms feature a ruby
red eye zone above a green throat, the
4-in (10-cm) flowers opening from
midsummer over deciduous foliage.
Bright, clean, and a popular breeding
parent but rather slow to increase, and
flowers may not always open properly.
‡18 in (45 cm). Z3–9 H8–1

H. 'Smoky Mountain Autumn'
(Diploid) Fragrant, 6-in (15-cm)
flowers, in mingled rosy oranges with a
rose-lavender halo and an olive green
throat open from early summer over
deciduous foliage. A good, popular
daylily, often flowering for a long
season. ‡18 in (45 cm). Z3–9 H8–1

H. 'Smugglers Temptation'
(Tetraploid) Nicely ruffled, greenish to
yellow, 5 in (13 cm) flowers, with a
lavender rose blush and often pale
toothed edges to the petals open from
midsummer over deciduous foliage.
‡24 in (60 cm). Z4–10 H9–1

H. 'Stella d'Oro' (Diploid) Extremely
long-blooming, small, fragrant, gold,
2¾-in (7-cm) flowers; very small green
throat open in midsummer over
deciduous foliage. The best known of
all daylilies and excellent in containers.
Introduced by Walter Jablonski. ‡11 in
(28 cm). Z3–9 H8–1

H. 'Stoke Poges' Fragrant, funnel-
shaped, salmon pink, 5-in (13-cm)
flowers with recurved petals have a
deeper pink eye zone and are carried
on slender stems over narrow foliage
from midsummer. Not registered with
the American Hemerocallis Society.
‡28 in (70 cm). Z3–9 H8–1

H. 'Strawberry Candy' (Tetraploid)

Very popular, with strawberry pink
flowers featuring a rose red eye zone
above a gold to green throat. The
nocturnal, 4½-in (11-cm) flowers open
from midsummer, often for a long
season, above semievergreen foliage.
‡26 in (66 cm). Z4–10 H9–1

H. 'String Bikini' (Tetraploid) Large,
7 in (18 cm) spider flowers have such a
huge green throat that the very slender
petals appear dark green tipped in
orchid lavender. Open, often for a long
season, from early summer. Evergreen
foliage. ‡30 in (76 cm). Z5–10 H10–5

H. 'Strutter's Ball' (Tetraploid) A
classic blackish purple with a very
small, silvery white watermark and a
silky halo above a small lemon-green
throat; the 6-in (15-cm) flowers open
from midsummer. Deciduous foliage.
‡28 in (70 cm). Z3–9 H8–1

H. 'Summer Wine' (Diploid) Pale
wine red, 5½-in (14-cm) flowers; with
a greenish yellow throat open in
midsummer over deciduous foliage.
‡24 in (60 cm). Z3–9 H8–1

H. 'Susan Pritchard Petit' (Tetraploid)
Rich burgundy-purple, double flowers
have a pronounced bubbly gold edge.
Each large, 6-in (15-cm) bloom opens
from midsummer, often for a long
season, above semievergreen foliage.
‡20 in (50 cm). Z3–9 H8–1

H. 'Tetrina's Daughter' (Tetraploid)
Nocturnal, fragrant, yellow, 5-in
(13-cm) flowers open from midsummer.
Semievergreen foliage. Unusually well-
branched and very prolific. ‡36 in
(90 cm). Z4–9 H9–1

H. 'Thin Man' (Tetraploid) A huge,
narrow petaled, bright red flower, 12 in
(30 cm); bold yellow midribs and edges,
green throat. Open from midsummer,
often for a long season. Evergreen
foliage. Classified as an Unusual Form
daylily. ‡42 in (107 cm). Z5–10 H10–5

H. 'Thumbelina's Carriage'
(Tetraploid) Pink, 5 in (13 cm) blooms,
rose eye zone above a green throat.
Open from midsummer. Semievergreen
foliage. ‡18 in (46 cm). Z4–10 H9–1

H. thunbergii Compact, dark green,
graceful, deciduous foliage forms a
mound 34 in (85 cm) high, the leaves
bending at the tip. Nocturnal, fragrant,
bright lemon yellow, 4-in (10-cm)
flowers have a green throat and open
from midsummer. From China and
Japan. ‡45 in (110 cm). Z4–9 H9–1

H. 'Unending Melody' (Tetraploid)
Fragrant, creamy peach, 6 in (15 cm)
flowers with a wine red eye zone and
picotee edge open from midsummer,
often for a long season. Evergreen
foliage. ‡30 in (75 cm). Z4–10 H9–1

H. 'Whichford' Fragrant, clear lemon
yellow, trumpet-shaped, 4-in (10-cm)
flowers, greenish throat. Not registered
with the American Hemerocallis
Society. ‡28 in (70 cm). Z3–9 H8–1

H. 'Wineberry Candy' (Tetraploid)
Fragrant, nocturnal, orchid-pink, 4¾-in
(12-cm) flowers; purple eye zone above
a green throat. Open from midsummer,
often for a long season. Deciduous
foliage. ‡22 in (55 cm). Z3–9 H8–1

HEPATICA
RANUNCULACEAE

An ever-expanding range of
captivating shade-lovers,
harbingers of spring.

Ten pretty species, all dwarf and
clump-forming, grow naturally on
woodland slopes in temperate parts
of the Northern Hemisphere
including North America, Europe,
and Asia. The deep green, three- to
five-lobed, leathery, hairy leaves,
often purple below and sometimes
with white or silvery marbling
above, are usually kidney-shaped.
They persist throughout winter,
replaced by a crop of new leaves in
spring immediately after flowering.
The bowl- or star-shaped blue,
purple, pink, or white flowers open
above the old foliage early in spring.

For best effect, plant them in
large groups, or as neat specimens
where they can be viewed close-up.
Allow the plants to mature into
clumps that will sparkle with a
galaxy of dainty spring stars. Often
grown in a shady spot in a rock
garden, but even more suitable for a
woodland garden in combination
with other small woodlanders.

CULTIVATION Best in part-shade but
will grow in slightly acidic, neutral,
or slightly alkaline, moist yet well-
drained soil with abundant humus.
May be found in clay soils in the
wild and tolerates heavy soil in
gardens. Mulch annually in fall with
fine leafmold or composted bark, or
well-rotted garden compost. Remove
old leaves just before flowering, so
that the blooms show up well. Once
planted, do not disturb.

PROPAGATION Divide mature plants
in spring after flowering; divisions
are slow to settle down and must
have ample roots. Sow seed of
species as soon as ripe in an open
cold frame.

PROBLEMS Slugs and snails, aphids.

H. acutiloba Slowly spreading; the
rounded or kidney-shaped, mid-green
leaves, 3 in (8 cm) long, have deeply
cut, sharply pointed lobes. Bowl-
shaped, blue, lavender, pink, purple, or
white flowers, to 1 in (2.5 cm) across,
are held on very erect hairy stems in
Early and mid-spring. From alkaline
soils in woods of eastern North
America. ‡6 in (15 cm). Z4–9 H9–3

H. americana Rounded, 1½–2½-in (4–
6-cm), three-lobed leaves, tinged purple
below, are sometimes marbled above.
Flowers, ¾ in (2 cm) across and pale
blue-purple, pale pink, or white, in
early and mid-spring. Found in acid
soil woodlands, eastern North America,

ABOVE **1** *Hepatica nobilis*
2 *H. nobilis* var. *japonica*

from southeast Canada to Florida.
‡4–6 in (10–15 cm). Z3–8 H8–1

H. angulosa see *H. transsilvanica*

H. x media A variable natural hybrid
between *H. transsilvanica* and *H. nobilis*
and intermediate between them,
flowering in early and mid-spring. It
occurs in the wild in central Romania
and is also made in gardens. ‡6 in
(15 cm). Z5–8 H8–5. **'Ballardii'** Slow
grower of dome-shaped habit, with
rounded, three-lobed, mid-green 4-in
(10-cm) leaves and 1¼-in- (3-cm-)
wide, semidouble, bowl-shaped, sky
blue flowers. **'Harvington Beauty'**
Dense, deep green, kidney-shaped
leaves, 1¼–2½ in (3–6 cm) long, make
good ground cover. The light to mid-
blue flowers, 1¼ in (3 cm) across and
reminiscent of *Anemone blanda*, are
very freely produced.

H. nobilis syn. *H. triloba* Slow growing
with a dome-shaped habit, the 1¼–
2½ in (3–6 cm) long, rounded or
kidney-shaped, lobed leaves are mid-
green, glossy, purple below and covered

with silky hairs. They may also be attractively marbled. The bowl-shaped flowers, 1 in (2.5 cm) across, may be blue, blue-purple, pink, or white, and open in early spring. Found in most of Europe. ‡4 in (10 cm). Z5–8 H8–4. **'Cobalt'** Deep blue flowers. **double pink** see 'Rubra Plena'. **var. *japonica*** Smaller plant with deep green leaves with pointed lobes and star-shaped blue, pink, or white flowers. From Japan. ‡3 in (8 cm). **var. *pyrenaica*** Compact habit, silver-marbled leaves, and pink, pale blue, or white flowers. From the Pyrenees. ‡3–4 in (8–10 cm). **'Rubra Plena'** syn. double pink Double, deep purple-red flowers.

H. transsilvanica syn. *H. angulosa* Slowly spreading. Hairy, light green, 2½–4 in (6–10 cm) long, oval leaves lobed with scalloped edges. Bowl-shaped, 1½ in (4 cm) wide flowers in pale blue, pale pink, or white in early spring; usually up to 12 petals, more than other species, although all vary. From Romania. ‡6 in (15 cm). Z5–8 H8–5. **'Blue Jewel'** Deep blue flowers. **'De Buis'** Mid-blue flowers. **'Eisvogel'** White flowers; a light blue flash on the petal undersides. **'Elison Spence'** Semidouble, anemone-centered, rich blue flowers fade to pale blue.

H. triloba see *H. nobilis*

HESPERIS
BRASSICACEAE

An attractive and fragrant favorite with great romantic appeal for cottage gardens.

Of the 14 species of biennials and perennials growing in Europe and Asia, only one has gained a permanent place in gardens.

Reminiscent of both stocks (*Matthiola*) and honesty (*Lunaria*), the smooth or slightly hairy stems carry toothed leaves or leaves partially split into opposite pairs of leaflets. Cross-shaped, four-petaled flowers may be reddish violet, lilac, white, or pale yellow. Single-flowered forms are very pretty, self-sowing in cottage-style borders and in part-shade; the doubles have more impact, last longer, and have been grown for 500 years. Their fragrance is captivating.

CULTIVATION Thrives in sun or shade in most soils, especially if slightly alkaline.

PROPAGATION From seed—singles often self-sow if not deadheaded— or by cuttings for the doubles (*see* Rediscovering the Doubles).

PROBLEMS Sometimes attacked by caterpillars of white butterflies.

H. matronalis (Dame's rocket, Sweet rocket) Short-lived perennial producing clusters of erect, more or less branched stems bearing stalked, oval to oblong, toothed, pointed leaves, to 10 in (25 cm) long. Carried in terminal spikes, the ¾-in- (2-cm-) wide flowers are lilac to purple or white and appear in late spring and early summer. Often grown as a biennial, but double-flowered cultivars produce no seed. Has naturalized across the US and is listed as a noxious weed in Colorado and Connecticut. From open woodlands and other partially shaded sites in Europe to Central Asia. ‡20–36 in (50–90 cm). Z4–9 H9–1. **var. *albiflora*** White flowers. **'Alba Plena'** Double white flowers. **'Lilacina Flore Pleno'** Double lilac flowers.

HEUCHERA
Coralbells, Alum root
SAXIFRAGACEAE

Neat evergreens for all-season interest in both flowers and increasingly varied foliage color.

About 50 North American species are native to slopes and rocky ledges from New England to western Canada and Mexico, with most in the Appalachians and the mountains of the West. Only a few species are grown in gardens; hybrids predominate. Varying in height from tiny alpines only 2–4 in (5–10 cm) tall in bloom to sizable plants 16 in (40 cm) across and 16–32 in (60–80 cm) tall, woody, branching and steadily expanding rootstocks support mounds of rounded, heart-shaped or lobed evergreen foliage

held on long wiry stalks and often toothed and noticeably veined. Tiny, tubular, ⅟₁₆–½-in (2–10-mm) flowers, some with five petals, others with none, may have a colorful calyx and are held in upright feathery sprays in spring and summer on self-supporting stems that may have a few small leaves.

Individual plants are usually self-sterile—that is, they will only produce seed when pollinated by a different individual. The result has been that both in the wild and in gardens, the delineation between species has become blurred by hybridization. Also—important for the gardener—if a number of different heucheras are grown in the same garden, they are likely to cross with each other, not come true from seed. The development of hybrid cultivars has been so rapid in recent years that the species themselves are rarely grown. (*see* Recent Breeding in Heuchera, *p.252*).

The flowers are attractive to bees, butterflies, and, in their natural habitat, hummingbirds, and last for up to two weeks in water. The leaves are excellent in arrangements and last for up to six weeks.

All mound sizes are given width first, height second. Maximum heights include flower stems.

CULTIVATION Best in well-drained, fertile, neutral to slightly alkaline soil; intolerant of waterlogged conditions. They grow well in full sun to light shade, but in hot climates some protection from hot sun is desirable to prevent leaf scorching in midsummer. Many of the bronze-leaved cultivars have insignificant flowers on long stems; these can be trimmed off for a neater look. Removal of spent flower stems may prolong blooming. High humidity, wet soil, and heavy shade may lead to rotting.

PROPAGATION From seed, or by division or cuttings, although seedlings rarely come true (*see* Recent Breeding in Heucheras, *p.252*), and commercially by tissue culture. For gardeners, the best method of propagation of cultivars is to remove side crowns in the late summer from established clumps.

PROBLEMS Mealy bug and vine weevil (*see* Daylily Rust, *p.255*).

H. 'Amber Waves' Ruffled, sharply lobed leaves, 3 in (8 cm) across, yellow on the upper surface, bronze on reverse, make an 8-x-12-in (20-x-30-cm) mound. Tiny pinkish flowers. Slow-growing and weak. Terra Nova Nursery, OR. ‡12 in (30 cm). Z4–8 H8–1.

H. americana (Alumroot) Rounded, slightly hairy leaves 3 in (8 cm) wide are plain green, or with silvery patches and, sometimes, maroon veining; they

LEFT 1 *Hesperis matronalis*
2 *H. matronalis* var. *albiflora*

make a 10-x-12-in (25-x-30-cm) mound. The coloration is brightest in the cooler months, and the best leaf color forms are attractive foliage plants. Tiny green flowers carried on leafless stems in late spring. Excellent for the woodland garden. Naturalizes by self-sowing in humus-rich soil in light shade. Native to shaded cliffs and ledges and wooded slopes in eastern North America, from Ontario to Georgia. ‡ 32–36 in (80–90 cm). Z4–8 H8–1. **'Beauty Color'** Silvered green foliage with contrasting maroon markings along the veins. A Dutch selection from Dale's strain. **Dale's strain** Variable seed strain; foliage well-silvered. Selected from wild plants of the southern Appalachians by Dale Hendricks of North Creek Nurseries, PA.

H. **'Amethyst Myst'** Sharply lobed, burgundy leaves, 3 in (8 cm) wide, are often suffused with beet shades and silvered between the veins and form a 16-x-10-in (40-x-25-cm) clump. Small whitish flowers. Terra Nova Nursery, OR. ‡ 24 in (60 cm). Z4–9 H8–2

H. **'Autumn Haze'** Sharply lobed leaves about 2 in (5 cm) across, soft pink, bronze, and silver on the upper side, reddish purple on the reverse, form a 12-x-8-in (30-x-20-cm) mound with small light pink flowers carried loosely above. Terra Nova Nursery, OR. ‡ 24 in (60 cm). Z4–9 H8–2

H. **'Blackbird'** Sharply lobed, purple-bronze leaves 3 in (8 cm) across; mound 16 x 8 in (40-x-20-cm). Small pale pink flowers. ‡ 20 in (50 cm). Z4–9 H8–2

H. **Bressingham hybrids** Rounded green leaves 3 in (8 cm) across make a 14-x-8-in (35-x-20-cm) mound with pink, red, and white flowers. Seed strain from Blooms of Bressingham, England, derived mostly from *H. sanguinea.*

‡ 24 in (60 cm). Z4–9 H8–2

H. **'Burgundy Frost'** One of the first recent introductions; leaves 3 in (8 cm) across, purple-bronze, silver mottling between the veins and reddish purple underneath, make a 16-x-8-in (40-x-20-cm) clump. Like 'Pewter Veil' but with smaller leaves. Insignificant flowers. Terra Nova Nursery, OR. ‡ 28 in (70 cm). Z4–9 H8–2

H. **'Can Can'** Ruffled leaves about 3 in (8 cm) across are silver with dark bronze veins on the upper surface, bronze turning green in summer, and reddish purple below. Forms a tight 12-x-8-in (30-x-20-cm) clump. Tiny greenish flowers. Terra Nova Nursery, OR. ‡ 24 in (60 cm). Z4–9 H8–2

H. **'Cappuccino'** Rounded, slightly ruffled leaves about 3 in (8 cm) across, evenly light bronze on the upper

surface and red-purple below, form a 12-x-8-in (30-x-20-cm) clump. Tiny white flowers. Terra Nova Nursery, OR. ‡ 20 in (50 cm). Z4–9 H8–2

H. **'Cascade Dawn'** Angular leaves 3 in (8 cm) across, almost totally silvered, dark purple veins and lavender shading above, reddish purple below, make a 14-x-10-in (35-x-25-cm) mound. Tiny, greenish flowers. Terra Nova Nursery, OR. ‡ 26 in (65 cm). Z4–9 H8–2

H. **'Cathedral Windows'** A 14-x-10-in (35-x-25-cm) mound is made up of angular leaves 3 in (8 cm) across with silvered patches between dark purple veins and reddish purple below. Like 'Cascade Dawn,' but the leaves appear more checkered and less silvered. Tiny greenish flowers. Terra Nova Nursery, OR. ‡ 26 in (65 cm). Z4–9 H8–2

H. **'Champagne Bubbles'** Green

leaves about 3 in (8 cm) across make a 16-x-10-in (40-x-25-cm) mound of foliage, which underpins exceptionally prolific and showy, small, light pink flowers. Terra Nova Nursery, OR. ‡ 32 in (80 cm). Z4–9 H8–2

H. **'Checkers'** see *H.* 'Quilters' Joy'

H. **'Cherries Jubilee'** Sharply lobed, bronze-green leaves 2½ in (6 cm) across make a 14-x-6-in (35-x-15-cm) mound and set off the loose spikes of small, cherry-red flowers. Terra Nova Nursery, OR. ‡ 16 in (40 cm). Z4–9 H8–2

H. **'Chocolate Ruffles'** Angular, ruffled leaves about 4¾ in (12 cm) across, evenly red-chocolate above and reddish purple below, form a 16-x-10-in (40-x-25-cm) mound. Tiny greenish flowers. Terra Nova Nursery, OR. ‡ 32 in (80 cm). Z4–9 H8–2

H. **'Chocolate Veil'** Rounded, lobed, leaves 6 in (15 cm) across, a smooth chocolate-bronze, make a 16-x-8-in (40-x-20-cm) mound. Tiny green-white flowers. Terra Nova Nursery, OR. ‡ 32 in (80 cm). Z4–9 H8–2

H. **'Coral Bouquet'** Loose, 12-x-6-in (30-x-15-cm) mound. Rounded, light green, 2-in- (5-cm-) wide leaves with silver markings; large pink flowers in cattail-shaped wands. The Primrose Path, PA. ‡ 16 in (40 cm). Z4–9 H8–2

H. **'Crimson Curls'** Highly ruffled, crisp bronze leaves about 2½ in (6 cm) across make a compact 12-x-6-in (30-x-15-cm) tuft. Small cream flowers. Ray Brown of Plant World in Devon, England. ‡ 16 in (40 cm). Z4–9 H8–2

H. cylindrica Oval, slightly fuzzy, evenly green leaves 1½–2½ in (4–6 cm) across form a dense, 10-x-6-in (25-x-15-cm) mound. Flowers greenish to creamy white, in substantial tight clusters on stiffly erect stalks. Plants in the wild are variable in size and coloration; those

LEAF COLORS

The silver patterns seen in the foliage of so many attractive *Heuchera* cultivars are caused by bubbles of air trapped under the surface of the leaf. These bubbles are neatly contained by the regular pattern of veins, which are sometimes tinted red, to create a very distinctive look. This feature is found occasionally in wild forms of *H. americana*, and plant breeders have used them to add this characteristic to modern cultivars.

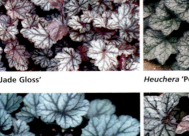

Heuchera 'Jade Gloss'

Heuchera 'Pewter Moon'

Heuchera 'Quilters' Joy'

Heuchera 'Silver Light'

Heuchera 'Silver Scrolls'

of good habit and clear flower color are well worth growing. Needs especially good drainage. From rocks and cliffs in western North America. ↕32 in (80 cm). Z4–8 H8–1. **'Greenfinch'** Large green flowers, popular for cutting. Blooms of Bressingham, England.

***H.* 'Ebony and Ivory'** Distinctive leaves, 2½ in (6 cm) across, are ruffled, jaggedly toothed, and long relative to their width. Dark green-bronze with a large central silvered area and dark veins above, red-purple below. Forms a low, loose 12-x-6-in (30-x-15-cm) mound. Small white flowers. Coloration especially striking in cool summer climates. Terra Nova Nursery, OR. ↕20 in (50 cm). Z4–9 H8–2

***H.* Firefly** see *H.* 'Leuchtkäfer'

***H.* 'Fireworks'** Sharply lobed, slightly ruffled leaves 2½ in (6 cm) across in a 14-x-8-in (35-x-20-cm) tuft. Small pink flowers. Terra Nova Nursery, OR. ↕16 in (40 cm). Z4–9 H8–2

***H.* 'Florist's Choice'** Green leaves about 3 in (8 cm) across in a 24-x-16-in (60-x-40-cm) mound, with showy pink flowers in loose spikes. Good cut flower. Terra Nova Nursery, OR. ↕36 in (90 cm). Z4–9 H8–2

***H.* 'Frosted Violet'** Sharply lobed leaves about 2¾ in (7 cm) across are pinkish violet mottled with silver in the spring, becoming bronze-purple in the summer, and form a 16-x-10-in (40-x-25-cm) mound. Small pink flowers from late spring into summer on open, arching stems that are clothed in dense purple hairs. Clearly derived

from *H. villosa.* The Primrose Path, PA. ↕20 in (50 cm). Z4–9 H8–2

***H.* 'Harmonic Convergence'** Round-lobed leaves 3 in (8 cm) across, with a central area of silver and bronze veining above and reddish purple below, form a 16-x-6-in (40-x-15-cm) clump. Large, frilly, light pink flowers. The Primrose Path, PA. ↕18 in (45 cm). Z4–9 H8–2

***H.* 'Helen Dillon'** Foliage 3 in (8 cm) across with rounded lobes; almost totally silver, green veining above, green below, in a 12-x-8-in (30-x-20-cm) mound. Small red flowers. Found in Vancouver, British Columbia; named for the Dublin, Ireland horticulturist. ↕20 in (50 cm). Z4–9 H8–2

***H.* 'Huntsman'** Green leaves 3 in (8 cm) across, marbled with gray and with dark gray-brown veining make a 12-x-6-in (30-x-15-cm) tuft of foliage. Salmon pink flowers. Bred by Dennis Davidson. ↕16 in (40 cm). Z4–9 H8–2

***H.* 'Jade Gloss'** Silvery, round-lobed leaves about 2¾ in (7 cm) across with heavy bronze veining make a 12-x-6-in (30-x-15-cm) mound, the leaves often curling to show red-purple undersides. Small white flowers from pink buds in dense sprays. The Primrose Path, PA. ↕18 in (45 cm). Z4–9 H8–2

***H.* 'Leuchtkäfer'** (**Firefly**) Medium-sized red flowers over light green leaves 3 in (8 cm) across. A seed strain derived mostly from *H. sanguinea* and similar to red-flowered forms of the Bressingham hybrids. 24 in (60 cm). Z4–9 H8–2

***H.* 'Lime Rickey'** Deeply lobed, yellow-green, ruffled leaves 2¾ in (7 cm) across. Forms 16-x-8-in (40-x-20-cm) clump. Very small white flowers. Terra Nova Nursery, OR. ↕18 in (45 cm). Z4–9 H8–2

LEFT 1 *Heuchera* 'Coral Bouquet'
2 *H. cylindrica* 'Greenfinch'
3 *H.* 'Frosted Violet'
4 *H. micrantha* 'Palace Purple'

RECENT BREEDING IN HEUCHERA

Very few wild *Heuchera* species are considered garden-worthy, since most have plain green foliage and diminutive greenish flowers. However, decorative foliage is found in a few, especially *H. americana,* from the southern Appalachians. Silvery mottling, due to an air space below the upper leaf surface, may be combined with reddish coloration, the background varying from blue-green to yellow-green to create very attractive foliage plants. Wild individuals have been found in *H. villosa* and *H. micrantha* in which the bronze to reddish purple coloration of new spring foliage is retained into the growing season. In addition, there are forms in which the leaf margin is ruffled or cut.

Some named selections have been made of wild plants with especially decorative foliage or showy flowers, but the great majority of garden forms are complex hybrids that emphasize the best traits of the wild plants. In the 1930s and 1950s, Alan Bloom, founder of Blooms of Bressingham in Norfolk, England, raised a number of hybrids

selected mainly for their flowers, partly with the cut-flower market in mind. Some of these are still among the best that are available.

Combination of the various leaf forms began in the late 1980s, and in the 1990s an explosion of cultivars with decorative foliage came onto the market. Two American sources in particular—Dan Heims at Terra Nova Nurseries of OR and Charles Oliver at The Primrose Path Nursery in PA—have, with their carefully planned breeding programs, between them developed most of the heucheras grown today.

The parent species used in hybridization for selection toward decorative foliage have some of the smallest and least conspicuous flowers in the genus, whereas those used for breeding toward showy flowers have undistinguished foliage. As a result, *Heuchera* cultivars have usually been grown either for flowers or for foliage. Only recently have cultivars appeared that combine good flowers with good foliage.

H. **'Magic Wand'** Green leaves about 3 in (8 cm) wide in a 16-x-18-in (40-x-20-cm) mound with large, dark pink flowers in tight, poker-shaped spikes. An improved version of 'Raspberry Regal'. Terra Nova Nursery, OR. ↕30 in (75 cm). Z4–9 H8–2

H. **'Marmalade'** Ruffled leaves 3 in (8 cm) across are reddish purple when young, becoming yellowish bronze with purple undersides, and make a 16-x-8-in (40-x-20-cm) foliage clump. Small red-brown flowers. Larger than 'Amber Waves' and considered more vigorous. Terra Nova Nursery, OR. ↕16 in (40 cm). Z4–9 H8–2

H. micrantha Sharply lobed, angled, often ruffled, usually hairy leaves about 2¾ in (7 cm) across make a 10-x-8-in (25-x-20-cm) mound of foliage. Tiny, greenish, or pinkish flowers carried in open sprays. Thrives among rocks with a northern exposure; the cultivars are easier to grow. From moist shaded cliffs and rock crevices in western North America. ↕16 in (40 cm). Z3–8 H8–1. **Bressingham Bronze** (**'Absi'**) Bronze, color-retentive foliage in a 12-x-8-in (30-x-20-cm) clump. Selected from 'Palace Purple' by Blooms of Bressingham. Less vigorous, but a better color. ↕12 in (30 cm). **'Emperor's Cloak'** Bronzed and ruffled foliage. **'Molly Bush'** Dark bronze foliage, the color retained all season. Selected from 'Palace Purple' by horticulturist Allen Bush at Holbrook Nursery, NC. **'Palace Purple'** Hairy bronze leaves, 4¾ in (12 cm) wide, form a 16-x-14-in (40-x-35-cm) mound. The first bronze-leaved selection, found at the Royal Botanic Gardens, Kew. Now widely raised from seed and variable in the intensity of leaf coloration, usually becoming an unattractive murky green by summer. This may be derived from *H. villosa* f. *purpurea*. ↕20 in (50 cm).

H. **'Midnight Burgundy'** Round-lobed leaves 2¾ in (7 cm) across, in dark slate-violet with light gray markings between the veins above and dark reddish purple below, make a 12-x-6-in (30-x-15-cm) tuft of foliage. Tiny pinkish cream flowers. The Primrose Path, PA. ↕16 in (40 cm). Z4–9 H8–2

H. **'Mint Frost'** Highly silvered green leaves 3 in (8 cm) across on red stems in a 14-x-6-in (35-x-15-cm) mound. Foliage develops pink tones in fall. Tiny white flowers. Terra Nova Nursery, OR. ↕28 in (70 cm). Z4–9 H8–2

H. **'Montrose Ruby'** Sharply lobed, 4¾-in- (12-cm-) wide leaves in dark reddish purple, silver-gray markings above and reddish purple undersides, make an open 16-x-10-in (40-x-25-cm) clump. Open sprays of tiny white flowers. Very vigorous and enduring. Raised at Nancy Goodwin's Montrose Nursery, NC, in the late 1980s, and an important breeding plant. ↕30 in (75 cm). Z4–9 H8–2

H. **'Neptune'** Slightly ruffled, angular leaves about 4 in (10 cm) across, pewter with dark veining above, red-purple

RIGHT *Heuchera* 'Midnight Burgundy'

below; make a 16-x-8-in (40-x-20-cm) mound. Small white flowers. From Holland. ↕16 in (40 cm). Z4–9 H8–2

H. **'Oakington Jewel'** Green leaves 3 in (8 cm) across with silver and bluish markings in a 12-x-8-in (30-x-20-cm) mound. Small pink flowers. Probably the most attractive foliage of the green-leaved cultivars. Introduced by Blooms of Bressingham, Diss, England, in 1932. ↕24 in (60 cm). Z4–9 H8–2

H. **'Obsidian'** Round-lobed, uniformly very dark green—nearly black—leaves 4 in (10 cm) across in a 16-x-10-in (40-x-25-cm) mound. Sprays of tiny cream flowers. Terra Nova Nursery, OR. ↕24 in (60 cm). Z4–9 H8–2

H. **'Persian Carpet'** Red-purple leaves mottled with gray above and evenly colored below are about 3 in (8 cm) across and form a 16-x-10-in (40-x-25-cm) clump overtopped with tiny cream-green flowers. Similar to 'Pewter Veil' but with more contrasting coloration. Terra Nova Nursery, OR. ↕32 in (80 cm). Z4–9 H8–2

H. **'Petite Lime Sherbet'** (Petite Series) Green leaves boldly veined in silver, plus bright pink flowers. ↕12 in (30 cm). Z4–9 H8–2

H. **'Petite Marbled Burgundy'** (Petite Series) Purple-bronze foliage with silver markings and large, pale pink flowers. ↕16 in (40 cm). Z4–9 H8–2

H. **'Petite Pearl Fairy'** (Petite Series) Dense bronze foliage with silver marbling and medium-sized light pink flowers. ↕12 in (30 cm). Z4–9 H8–2

H. **'Petite Pink Bouquet'** (Petite Series) Green foliage misted in silver, pink flowers. ↕12 in (30 cm). Z4–9 H8–2

H. **'Petite Ruby Frills'** (Petite Series) Bronze leaves patterned in silver; pink flowers. ↕12 in (30 cm). Z4–9 H8–2

H. **Petite Series** Dwarf, compact cultivars bred at The Primrose Path

SPRING FLOWERS AND A FOLIAGE TAPESTRY

IN A SMALL, DAPPLED, and moist corner overhung by tiers of white viburnum, the contrasting lustrous leaves of *Heuchera* 'Palace Purple' merge into the more rounded foliage of its elegant, creamy-spired relation, *Tellima grandiflora*. As the flowers of these and the pink geum alongside pass their prime, they can be cut out low to leave a tapestry of intermingling foliage for the rest of the season. In fact, the disappointing flowers of 'Palace Purple' are often best removed before they even open, to show off the leaves better and avoid inferior self-sown seedlings.

Nursery, PA, from dwarf alpine species and bronze-leaved types. All have small, ½–1¼-in- (1–3-cm-) wide leaves, marked with silver above, in 8-x-4¾-in (20-x-12-cm) mounds. Z4–9 H8–2

H. 'Pewter Moon' Rounded leaves 3 in (8 cm) across are silvery with dark bronze veining above, reddish purple below; form a 12-x-6-in (30-x-15-cm) mound. Open sprays of small white flowers. Like 'Silver Scrolls' but leaf markings less crisp and flowers smaller and in more open sprays. Not vigorous. Selected in the Netherlands by Piet Oudolf. ↕20 in (50 cm). Z4–9 H8–2

H. 'Pewter Veil' Pinkish bronze 4-in- (10-cm-) wide leaves, mottled light gray with a dull metallic sheen, form a 16-x-8-in (40-x-20-cm) mound. Tiny greenish flowers. The first bronze introduction from Terra Nova Nursery, OR, largely superseded by more colorful cultivars but still popular. ↕32 in (80 cm). Z4–9 H8–2

H. 'Pluie de Feu' (**Rain of Fire**) Rounded green leaves marked with silver are about 2½ in (6 cm) across and make a compact, 12-x-6-in (30-x-15-cm) foliage tuft. Medium-sized, bright red flowers. A classic derived from *H. sanguinea* in the 1930s by the Lemoine nursery in France. ↕24 in (60 cm). Z4–9 H8–2

H. 'Plum Pudding' Deeply lobed, 3-in- (8-cm-) wide leaves, glossy beet-purple with indistinct silvery mottling, relatively long stems; open 14-x-10-in (35-x-25-cm) mound. Insignificant flowers. Regarded as one of their best introductions by Terra Nova Nursery, OR. ↕26 in (65 cm). Z4–9 H8–2

H. 'Purple Petticoats' Very ruffled, evenly bronze-purple leaves, 3 in (8 cm) across, retain good leaf color throughout summer. Forms dense 16-x-10-in (40-x-25-cm) mound, Tiny cream flowers. Terra Nova Nursery, OR. ↕24 in (60 cm). Z4–9 H8–2

H. 'Quilters' Joy' Deeply lobed leaves, 3 in (8 cm) across, with crisp, dark bronze-green veining and light gray mottling above, dark red-purple below; make 14-x-8-in (35-x-20-cm) mound. Small white flowers. An early Primrose Path hybrid widely distributed under the incorrect name 'Checkers.' ↕24 in (60 cm). Z4–9 H8–2

H. 'Rachel' Bronze leaves about 3 in (8 cm) across in a 16-x-8-in (40-x-20-cm) clump with small pink flowers in open sprays. Bred by British enthusiast Mary Ramsdale, a hybrid of 'Palace Purple' with an *H. sanguinea* form. ↕20 in (50 cm). Z4–9 H8–2

H. Rain of Fire see *H.* 'Pluie de Feu'

H. 'Raspberry Ice' Rounded, sharply toothed leaves, 3 in (8 cm) across, with

LEFT **1** *Heuchera* 'Petite Lime Sherbet'
2 *H.* 'Petite Marbled Burgundy'
3 *H.* 'Petite Pearl Fairy'

ALUM ROOT

The roots of heucheras, most usually *H. americana*, were used by native Americans as a treatment for chronic diarrhea, dysentery, and other digestive and bowel complaints, as well as for diabetes and hemorrhoids. A tea made from this powerful astringent, sometimes sweetened with honey to mask the taste, was widely used by hunting parties of both native people and settlers. This plant, or its relatives *H. cylindrica*, *H. hispida*, and the related *Mitella caulescens*, are common and widely distributed, and digestive troubles regularly arose from drinking unusually alkaline or impure water while away hunting. It was sometimes mixed with *Geranium maculatum*, which often grows in similar situations. The powdered root was made into a gargle used to treat sore throats and mouth ulcers. External wounds and ulcers were treated with powdered root.

The roots of heuchera are a powerful astringent and should not be taken without advice from a qualified medical or herbal practitioner.

crisp, metallic silver markings on a purple-bronze; red-purple beneath. Makes a 20-x-10-in (50-x-25-cm) mound. Medium-sized pink flowers in open sprays. The Primrose Path, PA. ↕16 in (40 cm). Z4–9 H8–2

H. 'Raspberry Regal' Hairy green leaves, 3 in (8 cm) across, in a 16-x-8-in (40-x-20-cm) mound; greenish red flowers in poker-shaped spikes. Like the newer 'Magic Wand' but flower color less clear. ↕32 in (80 cm). Z4–9 H8–2

H. 'Red Spangles' Medium-sized intensely blood red flowers, green leaves 2½ in (6 cm) across in a 12-x-6-in (30-x-15-cm) tuft. An *H. sanguinea* hybrid from Blooms of Bressingham in 1950. ↕20 in (50 cm). Z4–9 H8–2

H. 'Regina' Round-lobed, angular leaves to 4 in (10 cm) across are reddish purple with silvery mottling and an

overall metallic sheen, and reddish purple below. They make dense, 16-x-10-in (40-x-25-cm) mounds. Small pink flowers. The Primrose Path, PA. ↕32 in (80 cm). Z4–9 H8–2

H. 'Ruby Veil' Large, sharply lobed leaves 4¾ in (12 cm) across, red above, reddish purple below, slate-gray veining and light gray mottling, in 14-x-8-in (35-x-20-cm) mounds. Insignificant flowers. Like 'Cascade Dawn' and 'Cathedral Windows'; not readily distinguished. Terra Nova Nursery, OR. ↕26 in (65 cm). Z4–9 H8–2

H. sanguinea (Coralbells) Rounded, shallowly lobed, dark green, hairy leaves to 2¾ in (7 cm) across make 12-x-10-in (30-x-25-cm) mound. Showy pink to red flowers in diffuse sprays; two or three small stem leaves. Best in well-drained neutral soil. Some grow elongated trunklike crowns that need to be replanted every couple of years. Selections and hybrids usually grown instead of the true wild species. Found on cliffs and ledges in the mountains of Arizona and northern Mexico. ↕16 in (40 cm). Z3–8 H8–2. **'Alba'** White flowers. **'Geisha's Fan'** Silver leaves, dark veins rolled over at the edges. Pink flowers. Possibly a hybrid. **'Monet'** Dark green leaves heavily splashed in white; red flowers on pink stems. **Ruby Bells** Dense spikes of dark red flowers. Seed strain. ↕16 in (40 cm). **Sioux Falls** Medium-sized, pink flowers above a tuft of green foliage. Seed strain. ↕24 in (60 cm). **'Snow Storm'** Green leaves mottled in white; cerise flowers. Weak, best in sun and well-drained soil. ↕12 in (30 cm). **'Taff's Joy'** Green, pink, and cream foliage all year; pink flowers. Best in well-drained soil and part-shade. Found by Stephen Taffler of England. ↕10 in (25 cm). **White Cloud** White flowers. Seed strain. ↕24 in (60 cm).

H. 'Sashay' Ruffled, 3-in- (8-cm-) wide, leaves, green on top and bronze below, in a 16-x-10-in (40-x-25-cm)

BELOW *Heuchera* 'Regina'

THE PROBLEM WITH VINE WEEVILS

Heucheras are naturally long-lived plants, and although they may look less attractive as the years go by, their woody roots have the capacity to keep extending over many, many years—or they did, until vine weevil became a common garden pest.

The black vine weevil, *Otiorhynchus sulcatus*, became widespread as powerful insecticides used by nurseries to control it were withdrawn for safety reasons. Having been kept under control for decades, it soon spread widely and established itself in nursery hedges from which it is difficult to eradicate.

Heucheras are among its favorite foods. It burrows into the woody crown so that a plant that looks perfectly

healthy one day, may the next day be decapitated by a gust of wind, its foliage blowing off the root. Foliage may wilt before this dramatic separation as its connection with the roots becomes increasingly tenuous. Notches in the foliage are also a giveaway; primroses, bergenias, sedums, and some evergreen shrubs like rhododendrons are also commonly attacked.

Vine weevil is less of a problem in cold areas (Zone 6 and below), where only a single generation may hatch in a year, and overwintering grubs are often killed by prolonged frost. Now that biological controls and safer chemicals are available to both nurseries and gardeners, the problem is decreasing.

mound. Tiny cream flowers. Except for the upper surface leaf color, like 'Purple Petticoats', of which it is a spontaneous mutation. Terra Nova Nursery, OR. ↕24 in (60 cm). Z4–9 H8–2

H. 'Scintillation' Forms a 12-x-6-in (30-x-15-cm) clump of 2½-in- (6-cm-) wide green leaves; the medium-sized flowers are deep pink with a coral rim and borne in attractive sprays. An *H. sanguinea* hybrid from Blooms of Bressingham, England, introduced in 1950. ↕16 in (40 cm). Z4–9 H8–2

H. 'Silver Light' A 10-x-6-in (25-x-15-cm) mound of angular, deeply lobed, very silvery leaves 3 in (6 cm) across, with a tracing of dark bronze veins above, reddish purple below, supports medium-sized, frilly, light pink flowers. The Primrose Path, PA. ↕18 in (45 cm). Z4–9 H8–2

H. 'Silver Lode' Rounded, matte silver leaves, 3 in (8 cm) across, have bronze veining above and are red-purple below. The 14-x-6-in (35-x-15-cm) mound is topped with small white flowers in narrow spikes. The Primrose Path, PA. ↕32 in (80 cm). Z4–9 H8–2

H. 'Silver Scrolls' Rounded leaves 3 in (8 cm) across, metallic silver with contrasting bronze veining on the upper surface, reddish purple below, make a 14-x-6-in (35-x-15-cm) clump. The new foliage has a pink-purple glow in spring. Medium-sized white flowers in narrow spikes. The Primrose Path, PA. ↕26 in (65 cm). Z4–9 H8–2

H. 'Stormy Seas' Angular, ruffled leaves, 4 in (10 cm) across, greenish bronze with some lighter mottling, turn green in summer, in a 16-x-10-in (40-x-25-cm (40-x-25-cm) clump. Tiny greenish flowers. Terra Nova Nursery, OR. ↕32 in (80 cm). Z4–9 H8–2

H. 'Strawberry Candy' Rounded green leaves 1½ in (4 cm) across marked with silver and form a 12-x-6-in (30-x-15-cm) tuft. Large, pink flowers. Terra Nova Nursery, OR. ↕14 in (35 cm). Z4–9 H8–2

H. 'Strawberry Swirl' Very ruffled and sharply lobed, 4-in- (10-cm-) wide

green leaves form a low 20-x-8-in (50-x-20-cm) mound, with abundant small pink flowers. An early Terra Nova Nursery, OR, hybrid between *H. micrantha* and an *H. sanguinea* form. ↕16 in (40 cm). Z4–9 H8–2

H. 'Velvet Night' Angular, round-lobed leaves, 3 in (8 cm) across; slate-purple, areas of light gray above, reddish purple below. Makes an open 16-x-8-in (40-x-20-cm) mound topped with insignificant flowers. Similar to 'Cascade Dawn', 'Cathedral Windows', and 'Ruby Veil', but with darker leaf markings. Terra Nova Nursery, OR. ↕26 in (65 cm). Z4–9 H8–2

X HEUCHERELLA
Foamybells
SAXIFRAGACEAE

Superb, ground-covering hybrids with attractive foliage and flowers, combining the features of two much-loved woodlanders.

These hybrids between *Heuchera* and *Tiarella* are all sterile, and none occur in the wild. The cultivars combine the traits of *Heuchera* and *Tiarella* in various ways, although most are intermediate in general appearance. The leaves, 2½–4 in (6–10 cm) across, usually have rounded lobes, but some have deeply cut leaves like those of some *Tiarella*. Foliage may be green or the purple-bronze of some *Heuchera*. The silvery gray mottling of *Heuchera* and the maroon mottling of *Tiarella* may be combined to make new leaf patterns. The flowers are borne in foamy sprays about 16–20 in (40–50 cm) tall; the individual ¼–½-in (5–12-mm) pink, white, or greenish cream flowers resemble star-shaped TV satellite dishes. Since no seed is set, the bloom period may be long. Some cultivars are much more vigorous and enduring than others.

CULTIVATION Best in moist, light shade in well-drained, neutral soil, but nearly full sun is tolerated in cooler areas. Will grow better and longer with high soil fertility.

PROPAGATION By cuttings or division.

PROBLEMS Vine weevil.

x **H. alba** Compact; rounded, gently lobed, 2¾-in (7-cm) leaves make a clump about 12-x-6 in (30-x-15 cm) and sprays of pink or white flowers. A hybrid between *Heuchera* x *brizoides* and *Tiarella wherryi*. ↕12–16 in (30–40 cm). Z4–9 H9–3. **'Bridget Bloom'** Slightly lobed leaves lightly marked with maroon. Sprays of small, pink flowers. Alan Bloom, UK, in 1953. ↕16 in (40 cm). **'Rosalie'** Rounded leaves marked with maroon and pink flowers in narrow spikes. ↕12 in (30 cm).

x **H. 'Burnished Bronze'** Glossy, bronze, deeply lobed 4-in (10-cm) leaves form a mound 14 in (35 cm) across by 8 in (20 cm) high; small, light pink flowers. Especially vigorous and enduring cultivar from Dan Heims, Terra Nova Nursery, OR. ↕18 in (45 cm). Z4–9 H9–3

x **H. 'Dayglow Pink'** Lobed, green, 2¾-in (7-cm) leaves with central maroon blotch make a 12-in- (30-cm-) wide by 8-in- (20-cm-) high mound; medium-sized, light pink flowers open from dark pink buds in dense spikes resembling those of *Tiarella*. Dan Heims, Terra Nova Nursery, OR. ↕16 in (40 cm). Z4–9 H9–3

x **H. 'Heart of Darkness'** Rounded, heart-shaped, 3-in (8-cm) leaves, maroon in the center surrounded by silver and green. Form a 14-in- (35-cm-) wide by 8-in- (20-cm-) high mound. White *Tiarella*-like flowers in airy sprays. Needs to be well fertilized to maintain size and vigor. Charles Olive, The Primrose Path, PA. ↕20 in (50 cm). Z4–9 H9–3

x **H. 'Kimono'** Very deeply lobed, green, silver, and maroon, 4–4¾-in (10–12-cm) leaves make a clump 12 in (30 cm) wide and 8 in (20 cm) high. Small, greenish cream flowers in long, lax sprays. The flower stems detract from the appearance of this spectacular foliage plant and are best removed. A vigorous and enduring cultivar from Dan Heims of Terra Nova Nursery, OR. ↕16 in (40 cm). Z4–8 H9–3

x **H. 'Party Time'** Deeply lobed, green, 2¾-in (7-cm) leaves marked with maroon and with a silver overlay, make a mound 10 in (25 cm) wide by 6 in (15 cm) high. Abundant light pink flowers open from dark pink buds in loose sprays. Dan Heims, Terra Nova. ↕12 in (30 cm). Z4–9 H9–3

x **H. 'Quicksilver'** Rounded, 2¾-in (7-cm) bronze leaves, mottled silver and with metallic overlay. Clumps 12 in (30 cm) across and 6 in (15 cm) high. Medium-sized white flowers open from pink buds in *Tiarella*-like spikes. Charles Oliver of The Princess Path, PA. ↕16 in (40 cm). Z4–9 H9–3

RIGHT 1 x *Heucherella* 'Heart of Darkness' **2** x *H.* 'Quicksilver' **3** x *H. tiarelloides*

x *H*. **'Silver Streak'** Deeply lobed, bronze and silver, 2¾-in (7-cm) leaves form a clump 12 in (30 cm) wide by 6 in (15 cm) high. Small, white flowers in irregular sprays. Not very vigorous and largely replaced by later cultivars. An early Dan Heims introduction. ‡12 in (30 cm). Z4–9 H9–3

x *H*. **'Sunspot'** Lobed, yellow-green, sometimes bright yellow, 2¾-in (7-cm) leaves, with a central maroon blotch, make a 12-x-8-in- (30-x-20-cm-) wide mound; medium-sized light pink flowers open from dark pink buds in dense spikes like those of *Tiarella*. A sport of 'Dayglow Pink' differing only in its foliage color. Dan Heims of Terra Nova, OR. ‡16 in (40 cm). Z4–9 H9–3

x *H*. *tiarelloides* Creeping; rounded, gently lobed and toothed, green, 2¾-in (7-cm) leaves, may be brownish at first. Mound is 12 in (30 cm) across by 6 in (15 cm) high. Brownish stems carry pink flowers in *Tiarella*-like spikes. A hybrid of *Heuchera* x *brizoides* and *Tiarella cordifolia* raised by Lemoine in 1912, but now superseded. ‡16 in (40 cm). Z5–8 H8–5

x *H*. **'Viking Ship'** Deeply lobed, 2¾-in (7-cm) green leaves, mottled with silver, form a clump 12 in (30 cm) across and 6 in (15 cm) high. Small pink flowers in tight spikes. Lobes of the leaves sometimes form detached leaflets. Dan Heims of Terra Nova, OR. ‡16 in (40 cm). Z4–8 H9–3

HEXASTYLIS *see* ASARUM

THE BEST OF BOTH WORLDS

Although a hybrid between *Heuchera* and *Tiarella* was first made in 1912, it is only in recent years that such hybrids have come into their own. The two oldest cultivars, from the Lemoine nursery and from Alan Bloom, predate the many recent introductions by many decades, but once significant improvements were made in the two parent genera in the 1980s and 1990s, it was natural to look at crossing the two again.

As with *Heuchera* and *Tiarella*, most recent heucherellas have been introduced by two American breeders, Dan Heims of Terra Nova Nurseries in OR or Charles Oliver at The Primrose Path in PA. The makeup of the new heucherellas involves many species and cultivars, the best combining the most desirable traits of *Heuchera* and *Tiarella*, themselves including material from a number of species. It is therefore impractical to give each hybrid a botanical name, as was done with the two original pairings. The result of bringing these two genera together again has been spectacular. There is now a large and varied assemblage to choose from, many impressive in both foliage and flowers, and many inheriting a tendency to spread a little more widely than some wild *Tiarella* variants.

HIERACIUM
Hawkweed
ASTERACEAE

Yellow daisies, with just a select few grown for their rosettes of attractive foliage.

This large genus is native to grassy or rocky habitats, particularly in mountainous zones, throughout the Northern Hemisphere. It is notorious for the 10,000 microspecies that reproduce asexually—seeds ripening without fertilization—grouped into 500 aggregate species. Hawkweeds form rosettes, sometimes in clumps from a branched rootstock but without creeping stems or roots, and contain milky sap. Stalked basal leaves range from linear to broadly egg-shaped in outline and from being untoothed to deeply lobed. Erect stems, leafy or without leaves, bear clusters of yellow, dandelion-like flowerheads.

CULTIVATION Requirements are as varied as the plants' original habitats. Those covered here perform best in full sun in poor, well-drained soil. Remove flower stems so as not to detract from the foliage.

PROPAGATION From seed sown in fall or spring, or by division in spring.

PROBLEMS Usually trouble-free.

H. aurantiacum see *Pilosella aurantiacum*

H. lanatum Clump-forming, mostly evergreen; lance-shaped to egg-shaped, white-felted leaves, usually untoothed, 4 in (10 cm) long. Leafy, wiry, branched stems carry up to twelve 1-in (2.5-cm) flowerheads, late spring to midsummer. Tolerant of most dry soils and even some shade. Native to limestone cliffs and rocks in southeast France, western Switzerland, and northwest Italy. ‡20 in (50 cm). Z5–8 H8–5

H. maculatum see *H. spilophaeum*

H. spilophaeum syn. *H. maculatum* (Spotted hawkweed) Clump-forming, deciduous; leaves lance- to egg-shaped, untoothed or shallowly toothed, 3½-in (9-cm) green or grayish green, spotted or blotched with purple. Leafy, branched stems bear 20 ¾-in (2-cm) flowerheads from early to late summer. Tolerant of most dry soils and best in full sun. May self-seed but rarely a nuisance. From open, alkaline grassland in central and western Europe. ‡32 in (80 cm). Z5–8 H8–5. **'Blue Leaf'** Leaves notably bluish green with dark brown spots fading to maroon as they age. Variable. ‡10 in (25 cm). **'Leopard'** Leaves gray-green with red-brown blotches. Variable. ‡10 in (25 cm).

HIEROCHLOE
POACEAE

Forms sweet-smelling carpets of creeping grass that grow well in woodland areas.

ABOVE *Hieracium lanatum*

Some 30 perennial species are found through much of the world in temperate and Arctic areas, from woodland to marshes, grassland to tundra. From spreading mats of leaves with an invasive root system grow sparse, insignificant flowers. All species contain coumarin, released as a sweet vanilla-like scent when the leaves are crushed or dried.

CULTIVATION Grow in moisture-retentive, humus-rich soil in shade.

PROPAGATION From seed or by division.

PROBLEMS Usually trouble-free.

H. odorata (Holy grass) Slender, white rhizomes produce carpets of loose evergreen tufts of flat, dark green leaves, ½ in (1 cm) wide and 12 in (30 cm) long. From early spring to early summer, slender stems carry sparse purple-green flowerheads above the foliage. Can be invasive. Use as ground cover with spring bulbs in woodland areas or at the edges of paths where the leaves will be crushed. Strewn on church floors; used to flavor Polish vodka. Found in some New England states. ‡24 in (60 cm). Z3–9 H9–3

HOLCUS
POACEAE

Soft-textured grasses, common in meadows and fencerows and best known for their variegated forms.

Six annual and perennial species are found in open woodland and wasteland in Europe, North Africa, and the Middle East, and have been introduced into North America. Plants form clumps or mats of soft, hairy leaves, with upright stems carrying dense, soft, feathery flower plumes. Some species are invasive weeds, but the variegated forms make highly desirable ground cover.

CULTIVATION Any soil in sun or part-shade. Cool-season species die back in summer, so trim the foliage in early spring and in midsummer.

PROPAGATION From seed or by division in spring (division only for variegated forms).

PROBLEMS Usually trouble-free, although fungal diseases can occur in hot and humid weather.

H. mollis **'Albovariegatus'** (Variegated soft grass) The species is an invasive weed with long, creeping rhizomes, common in grasslands and open woodlands in Europe. Only the much less intrusive variegated forms are treated here. 'Albovariegatus' forms low-growing carpets of soft green, ½-in- (12-mm-) wide leaves, heavily striped with white and with a broader central green stripe. In midsummer, the flower stems carry fluffy, gray-green plumes. A cool-season grass, its blazing white variegation is most attractive from late winter to early summer; cut back flowers and foliage in summer. For the best coloration, remove any that is dying back in the center of carpets every three years and replant the outer growth. Use as edging, as ground cover on rock gardens, as underplanting for spring bulbs, or in a multicolored lawn. ‡14 in (35 cm). Z5–9 H9–5. **'White Fog'** is another garden-worthy cultivar of similar hardiness with brilliant white variegation, flushed purple from early to late summer, and pink-tinged flowers. ‡12 in (30 cm).

HOSTA
Plantain lily
HOSTACEAE

Preeminent shade-lovers grown as specimens and ground cover for their variety of foliage color and form, habit, and flowers.

About 40 species are native to Japan, Korea, and China. Over 6,000 cultivars can be grown in most temperate areas of the world, and are popular in the US, Canada, Europe, East Asia, and New Zealand.

They are grown almost exclusively for their mounds of foliage, held on distinct stems and emanating from a woody crown supported by a coarse

BELOW *Holcus mollis* 'Albovariegatus'

but well-branched root system. The height of the mound of foliage ranges from 3 in to 40 in (8–100 cm) and is given for each of the entries. The width tends to be about twice the height, although a few hostas spread by rhizomes to cover large areas. The leaf size ranges from 2 in to 21 in (5–53 cm) long by 1 in to 16 in (2.5–40 cm) wide.

Foliage colors fall into two categories: solid and variegated. Solid leaves can be green, blue-green, or gold, with many different shades, while patterns of variegation vary widely. Margined forms combine a white, yellow, or gold margin with a green, gold, or blue-green center. Center-variegated cultivars have a white, yellow, or gold center with a chartreuse, green, or blue-green margin. Variations include streaking, misting, and mottling. The color of some hostas changes from spring to summer, either lightening or darkening, and can also vary with the amount of light the plants receive. A few recently introduced cultivars have variegation patterns that completely reverse during the growing season—for example, emerging gold-edged with a green center in spring, then becoming green-margined with a gold center by midsummer.

The lilylike flowers, each with six petals, last only one day, on stems from 12 in (30 cm) to 6½ ft (2 m) tall. Most are funnel-shaped, but some are trumpet- or bell-shaped or even spidery. Some are fragrant.

Flowering starts in early summer for *H. sieboldiana, H. tokudama* and related cultivars. The majority flower in mid- and late summer, while in early and mid-fall, those related to *H. longipes* and *H. longissima* bloom. Some hostas develop many seed pods; others are completely sterile. Seed propagation has been heavily used by breeders in developing new cultivars but is not recommended for home gardeners.

Hostas are indispensable for the shade garden, valuable as ground cover, excellent as border specimens, and superb in containers. The foliage is used in flower arrangements.

Some hostas are complex hybrids; others are more closely related to individual species. These affiliations are shown in parentheses after each hosta's name in the entries. Some are thought to be pure species, or forms of them. The naming of some hostas incurs much controversy and strong feeling. This especially applies to those, such as *H. fortunei* and *H. undulata,* that have been grown for many years and considered to be true species but many people now classify them as cultivars.

CULTIVATION Hostas are especially suited to part-shade or dappled shade situations, benefiting from one or two hours of direct sunlight in cool climates. Although they will survive, they will not thrive in deep shade. Hostas usually prefer cool, moist soil that is heavily

supplemented with organic matter, such as leaf mold, garden compost, or well-rotted manure. Dried or slow-release fertilizers improve growth, especially in new plantings. The soil moisture should be kept at a high level, but avoid standing water. Permanent mulches are not recommended because they harbor many pests and diseases that afflict hostas.

PROPAGATION Hostas are widely propagated by division, which can be done at any time during the growing season, but early spring is best, just as the plants are starting to grow. The traditional method—using two garden forks, inserted back-to-back then forced apart—may work, but the crowns can be so woody that slicing through with a spade is often necessary. A large knife can also be effective. Split the plant so you have individual shoots with roots attached for replanting. Cultivars vary enormously in how many divisions they will produce.

Tissue culture, employed by some nurseries to mass-propagate newer cultivars, is partly responsible for the rapid increase in the popularity of hostas. Cultivars do not come true from seed, and most species will also yield variable offspring.

PROBLEMS The main pests are slugs and snails (*see* Slug-resistant Cultivars, p.264), which eat small holes in the foliage as the buds emerge and also during the summer months. Leaf and root knot eelworms, vine weevils, cutworms, and a variety of other leaf- and root-eating pests can also cause damage. In some areas, they are eaten by voles, mice, rabbits, and deer, the latter favoring fragrant forms. Virus diseases are becoming increasingly common.

H. **'Abba Dabba Do'** Makes a huge 48-in (120-cm) mound of green-centered, gold-margined, slightly waved

and corrugated, oval, 12-x-8½-in (30-x-20-cm) foliage with curved tips, and bears pale lavender flowers in midsummer. A spontaneous mutation of 'Sun Power' introduced by Tony Avent of Plant Delights, NC. ‡ 28 in (70 cm). Z3–8 H8–1

H. **'Abiqua Drinking Gourd'** Heavily corrugated, deeply cupped, oval to rounded, blue-green foliage to 11 x 11 in (28 x 28 cm) makes large 24-in-(60-cm-) mound. Tightly clustered, near-white flowers in early summer among, or just above, leaves. A hybrid of *H. tokudama* and *H. sieboldiana.* ‡ 30 in (75 cm). Z3–8 H8–1

H. **'Abiqua Moonbeam'** Slightly corrugated, 9-x-8-in (22-x-20-cm), oval foliage of good substance, green center with 1–2-in (2.5–5-cm) gold margin, in 20 in (50 cm) mounds. Pale lavender flowers in mid- and late summer. A spontaneous mutation of 'August Moon'. ‡ 30 in (75 cm). Z3–8 H8–1

H. **Abiqua Series** A diverse collection of plants originating as seedlings or spontaneous mutations from a wide range of species and cultivars. The Abiqua prefix indicates plants developed by hosta breeders Charles Purtyman and Jay Hyslop, OR. The first Abiquas were registered in 1987.

H. **'Albomarginata'** (*fortunei*) Large, 23-in (57-cm) mound of oval, green, 10-x-6-in (24-x-15-cm) leaves with a ¾-in (2-cm) white margin and a long curved tip and without a wavy edge. Pale lavender flowers appear in midsummer. Formerly known as *H. fortunei* 'Albomarginata' and also often sold as 'Silver Crown'. ‡ 40 in (100 cm). Z3–8 H8–1

H. **'Allan P. McConnell'** Distinctive, dense, rounded, 13-in (33-cm) mound of leaves that are green with a very slender white margin. Produces lavender flowers from mid- to late summer. Sometimes misspelled Alan or Allen. ‡ 19 in (48 cm). Z3–8 H8–1

ABOVE **1** *Hosta* 'Allan P. McConnell' **2** *H.* 'Antioch'

H. **'American Dream'** Slightly corrugated, oval, 9-x-6-in (23-x-15-cm) white-margined, gold-centered leaves make a 24-in (60-cm) mound. Lavender flowers in late summer. From Van Wade, OH. ‡ 30 in (75 cm). Z3–8 H8–1

H. **'Antioch'** syn. *H.* 'Moerheim', 'Spinners' (*fortunei*) Green, oval, 11-x-7-in (27-x-18-cm) foliage; chartreuse margins, no more than 1¼ in (3 cm) wide, turn yellow, then white, Makes a 24-in (60-cm) mound. Lavender flowers in midsummer. Originated in 1920s; sold under various names. Often confused with *H.* 'Albomarginata', which has a narrower white leaf margin. ‡ 30 in (75 cm). Z3–8 H8–1

H. **'Aphrodite'** (*plantaginea*) Light green, broadly oval, 11-x-7½-in (28-x-19-cm) foliage; mound 24 in (60 cm) high. Fragrant, double white flowers in late summer. Keep well watered as the stems develop. A double-flowered version of *H. plantaginea,* which originated in China before 1940. ‡ 34 in (85 cm). Z3–8 H8–1

H. **'August Moon'** Classic hosta with broadly oval, 9-x-8-in (23-x-20-cm), slightly corrugated, gold leaves in a 20-in (50-cm) mound; pale lavender flowers in midsummer. The first significant gold-leaved hosta; a source of many seedlings and spontaneous mutations. ‡ 28 in (70 cm). Z3–8 H8–1

H. **'Aureomarginata'** (*montana*) Large, vase-shaped, 27-in (68-cm) mound of green-centered, 15-x-8-in (38-x-3-cm), oval foliage with 1–2-in (2.5–5-cm) gold margins. Pale lavender flowers in midsummer. Emerges very early in spring. ‡ 45 in (110 cm). Z3–8 H8–1

H. **'Aureomarginata'** (*ventricosa*) Bold, shiny, dark green, broadly oval, 9-x-8-in (22-x-20-cm) foliage, with a lightly rippled, heart-shaped base, and 1–1½-in

(2.5–4-cm) white margins, yellow at first. Makes a spectacular 22-in (56-cm) mound. Purple flowers in midsummer. ‡45 in (110 cm). Z3–8 H8–1

H. 'Baby Bunting' Unusually dense and wide, 11-in (28-cm) mound of round, 3-in (7.5-cm), green leaves. Bright purple flowers in midsummer. Size varies noticeably according to soil conditions. Robert P. Savory, Edina, MN. ‡19 in (48 cm). Z3–8 H8–1

H. 'Beauty Substance' Green-centered, gold-edged, broadly oval, 16-x-14-in (40-x-35-cm) foliage is slightly cupped and corrugated and makes a massive mound 30 in (75 cm) high and twice as wide. A spontaneous mutation of H. 'Sum and Substance'. ‡54 in (130 cm). Z3–8 H8–1

H. 'Big Daddy' Large mound 25 in (64 cm) high and over twice as wide, of slug-resistant, heavily corrugated, blue-green, broadly oval, 15-x-10½-in (38-x-25-cm) foliage, deeply lobed at the base, with dense heads of almost white flowers in early summer. A hybrid of H. sieboldiana introduced by Paul Aden, NY. ‡30 in (75 cm). Z3–8 H8–1

H. 'Big Mama' Thick, heavily corrugated, blue-green, 13-x-10-in (33-x-25-cm) foliage; 28-in (70-cm) high mound; near-white flowers in early summer. A hybrid of H. sieboldiana. ‡30 in (75 cm). Z3–8 H8–1

H. 'Birchwood Parky's Gold' Dense, symmetrical, 17-in (43-cm) mound of medium-gold, noticeably heart-shaped, 6-x-5-in (15-x-13-cm) foliage, which turns bright yellow in fall. Lavender flowers in midsummer. Probably a hybrid of H. nakaiana. Florence Shaw. ‡30 in (75 cm). Z3–8 H8–1

H. 'Black Hills' Deep green, rounded, 8-x-7-in (20-x-18-cm) foliage, heavily corrugated silver below, makes a 22-in (56-cm) mound. Pale lavender flowers, darker at the tips, in midsummer. From Robert P. Savory, Edina, MN. ‡30 in (75 cm). Z3–8 H8–1

H. 'Blonde Elf' Low, very dense, 20-in (50-cm) mound of wavy, lance-shaped, gold foliage and pale purple flowers in midsummer. Outstanding low ground cover. ‡20 in (50 cm). Z3–8 H8–1

H. 'Blue Angel' Large, 16-x-12-in (40-x-30-cm), broadly oval, blue-green leaves, thick-substanced and deeply lobed at the base, make a 32-in- (80-cm-) high mound. Prolific near-white flowers, each petal with a lavender midrib, in midsummer. Shows traits of both H. sieboldiana and H. montana. From Paul Aden, NY. ‡40 in (100 cm). Z3–8 H8–1

H. 'Blue Belle' (Tardiana Group)

Thick, wavy-edged, corrugated, deep blue-green oval foliage, 7 x 5½ in (18 x 14 cm), makes mounds 19 in (48 cm) high. Purple flowers in midsummer. Raised by Eric Smith, England. ‡20 in (50 cm). Z3–8 H8–1

H. 'Blue Boy' Dense, round, 18-in-(45-cm-) high mound of bluish green, 8-x-5-in (20-x-12.5-cm) foliage. Pale lavender flowers in midsummer. A hybrid of H. nakaiana and H. sieboldiana, that has features of both parents. from David Stone. ‡30 in (75 cm). Z3–8 H8–1

H. 'Blue Cadet' Fast-growing, dense mound, 15 in (38 cm) high, of slightly corrugated, heart-shaped, 5-x-4-in (13-x-10-cm), blue-green foliage coloring gold in fall. Lavender flowers in midsummer. A very popular hybrid of H. nakaiana from Paul Aden, NY. ‡24 in (60 cm). Z3–8 H8–1

H. 'Blue Diamond' (Tardiana Group) Excellent, thick, bright blue, slightly corrugated and wavy-edged, oval, 7-x-4-in (18-x-10-cm) foliage makes a 22-in- (56-cm-) high mound. Pale lavender flowers in midsummer. The largest of Eric Smith's Tardianas from England. ‡30 in (75 cm). Z3–8 H8–1

H. 'Blue Dimples' (Tardiana Group) Slug-resistant, deep blue, slightly wavy, oval, 9-x-5½ in (23-x-14 cm) foliage makes a mound 18 in (45 cm) high. Very pale lavender flowers in late summer. One of the bluest; similar to 'Blue Wedgwood' but with longer leaves. From British plant breeder Eric Smith. ‡20 in (50 cm). Z3–8 H8–1

H. 'Blue Mammoth' (sieboldiana) Massive, 34-in (85-cm) mound of slug-resistant, broadly oval, 16-x-12-in (40-x-30-cm) blue-green foliage; deeply lobed base, heavy corrugation, strong white bloom. Whitish flowers in early summer. Raised by Paul Aden, NY. ‡36 in (90 cm). Z3–8 H8–1

H. 'Blue Moon' (Tardiana Group) Small, dense, 10-in- (25-cm-) high mound of very thick, deeply cupped and corrugated, heart-shaped, deep blue-green, 5-x-4-in (13-x-10-cm) foliage. Off-white flowers in late summer. The much larger H. 'Blue Splendor' is also sold under this name. Raised by British plant breeder Eric Smith. ‡12 in (30 cm). Z3–8 H8–1

H. 'Blue Shadows' Thick, heavily corrugated, chartreuse-centered, blue-margined, almost round, 8-x-7-in (21-x-18-cm) leaves, 16-in- (40-cm-) high mound. Near-white flowers in early summer. A spontaneous mutation of H. tokudama f. aureonebulosa. ‡28 in (70 cm). Z3–8 H8–1

H. 'Blue Umbrellas' (sieboldiana) Huge, slightly confused mound, 33 in (84 cm) high and more than twice as wide, with bluish green, broadly oval, 15-x-12-in (38-x-30-cm), foliage with a heart-shaped base. Pale lavender flowers in midsummer. Raised by Paul Aden, NY. ‡36 in (90 cm). Z3–8 H8–1

LEFT 1 *Hosta* 'Birchwood Parky's Gold'
2 *H.* 'Blue Cadet'
3 *H.* 'Buckshaw Blue'
4 *H.* 'Carnival' **5** *H.* 'Cherry Berry'

HOSTAS FROM TISSUE CULTURE

The revolution that made a wide range of hostas available at reasonable prices, and allowed stocks of new introductions to be built up and distributed quickly, was the advent of tissue culture. Previously, hostas were propagated by division, which, while reliable, is slow and does not allow new introductions to be bulked up quickly.

Propagation in the laboratory by tissue culture allows a large number of plants to be created relatively quickly from a single original. They must still be grown to a good size for sale, but without this technique, both availability and affordability would be greatly restricted.

When hostas are propagated in the lab, two additional things happen. First, until they become established in the garden, the young plants may look less typical of the mature cultivar than young plants propagated by division—so think twice before returning a plant because it looks wrong. Second, occasional plants may appear that are slightly different from the parent.

These spontaneous mutations, or sports, may be reversions back to the cultivar from which a variegated or golden-leaved form was originally developed, or they may show new features; for example, H. 'Golden Sunburst' is a gold-leaved tissue-culture sport of H. 'Frances Williams'; 'Mountain Snow' is a white-edged tissue-culture sport of H. montana; and H. 'Golden Scepter' is a gold tissue-culture sport of H. 'Golden Tiara'.

H. 'Blue Wedgwood' (Tardiana Group) Vigorous, deep blue, thick, slug-resistant, gently waved, oval, 8-x-7-in (20-x-18-cm) foliage; heavy bloom on the upper surface. Makes an 18-in- (45-cm-) high mound. Bluish lavender flowers in late summer. Like H. 'Blue Dimples', but leaves shorter, more triangular. Raised in England by Eric Smith. ↕ 26 in (66 cm). Z3–8 H8–1

H. 'Borwick Beauty' (sieboldiana) Gold-centered, 14-x-9-in (35-x-23-cm), oval foliage, moderately corrugated, chartreuse early in the season with a 1–1½-in (2.5–4-cm), bluish green margin; makes a 24-in (60-cm) mound. Near-white flowers in early summer. Golden markings may burn; 'Great Expectations' burns less, but is less gold. The first gold-centered spontaneous mutation of H. sieboldiana 'Elegans'; often listed under H. sieboldiana. ↕ 30 in (75 cm). Z3–8 H8–1

H. 'Bressingham Blue' Large mound, 28 in (70 cm) high; heavily corrugated, blue-green, 6-x-4-in (15-x-10-cm), heart-shaped foliage; near-white flowers in early summer. Its introducer, Alan Bloom, said it was the bluest-leaved hosta but his enthusiasm later waned. Similar to H. sieboldiana 'Elegans' and its many seedlings; probably a hybrid of H. sieboldiana and H. tokudama. ↕ 28 in (70 cm). Z3–8 H8–1

H. 'Bright Lights' Of good substance. Gold-centered, 9-x-7-in (22-x-18-cm), oval foliage, with ¾–1½-in (3–3.5-cm) blue-green edges. Makes mounds 18 in (45 cm) high. Off-white flowers in midsummer. Similar to H. tokudama f. aureonebulosa but more vigorous and foliage less rounded. Raised by Paul Aden, NY. ↕ 20 in (50 cm). Z3–8 H8–1

H. 'Brim Cup' Dramatic mound, 14 in (35 cm) high, of broadly oval, 7-x-6-in (18-x-15-cm) dark green-centered, leaves with a ½-in (1-cm) white margin. Pale lavender flowers in midsummer. Leaves are cupped, but the margins tear and turn brown when they are mature (although this is less common on container-grown specimens). The rarely seen H. 'Cherub' is similar, but without this flaw. ↕ 24 in (60 cm). Z3–8 H8–1

H. 'Buckshaw Blue' Very corrugated, oval leaves, 8-x-7-in (20-x-18-cm); thick, deep blue bloom turns dark green as summer progresses. Makes a 19-in- (48-cm-) high mound, with near-white flowers in early summer. Slow; more vigorous in hotter climates. A hybrid of H. tokudama from Eric Smith of England. ↕ 18 in (45 cm). Z3–8 H8–1

H. 'Candy Hearts' Slightly corrugated, heart-shaped, 6-x-5-in (15-x-13-cm) green leaves. Dense, symmetrical, 17-in- (43-cm-) high mound. Pale lavender flowers in midsummer. A seedling of H. nakaiana. Eunice Fisher, WI. ↕ 20 in (50 cm). Z3–8 H8–1

H. 'Carnival' Slightly wavy, deep green-centered leaves, broadly oval, 9-x-7-in (22-x-18-cm) with creamy yellow margins that are paler in bright light. Dramatic but sparse, 18-in- (45-cm-) high mound Lavender flowers in midsummer. Bill and Eleanor Lachman, MA. ↕ 30 in (75 cm). Z3–8 H8–1

H. 'Carol' (fortunei) Medium-large mound, 21 in (53 cm) high, of green-centered, 8-x-6-in (20-x-15-cm) oval foliage narrowly but inconsistently margined in white. Pale lavender flowers in midsummer. Best in rich conditions. Similar to 'Francee' but with a less even margin. Frances R. Williams. ↕ 36 in (90 cm). Z3–8 H8–1

H. 'Chartreuse Wiggles' Low, dense, wide, 10-in- (25-cm-) high mound of very slender, 5-x-1-in (13-x-2.5-cm), elliptical gold leaves with a curved tip and a rippled edge. Pale purple flowers in late summer. Good for edging. A seedling of H. 'Wogon' from Paul Aden, NY. ↕ 20 in (50 cm). Z3–8 H8–1

H. 'Cherry Berry' Green-edged, elliptical, 6-x-3-in (15-x-8-cm) foliage is boldly splashed with white, creamier in spring, leaving a slender, ½-in (1-cm) green margin, and makes a 12-in- (30-cm-) high mound. Brilliant red stems carry purple flowers in late summer, followed by red pods. Best in a little sun. Bill and Eleanor Lachman, MA. ↕ 24 in (60 cm). Z3–8 H8–1

H. 'Chinese Sunrise' (lancifolia) Vigorously spreading; dense, medium-sized, 18-in- (45-cm-) high mound. Elliptical, 6-x-3-in (15-x-8-cm) leaf gold-centered in spring, completely green by early summer. Lavender flowers in late summer. A spontaneous mutation of H. lancifolia. ↕ 24 in (60 cm). Z3–8 H8–1

H. 'Choko Nishiki' (montana) Only slightly corrugated. Late-emerging, gold-centered, 13-x-8-in (33-x-20-cm), slightly wavy leaves have a ¼–⅜-in (6–9-mm) green edge. Makes a 22-in- (56-cm-) high mound. Without some light, the leaves turn green by midsummer. Very pale lavender flowers in midsummer. A seedling of H. montana found wild in Japan. Almost identical to H. 'On Stage'. ↕ 40 in (100 cm). Z3–8 H8–1

H. 'Christmas Tree' Round, 10-x-9-in (25-x-22-cm), dark green foliage, its ¼–⅜-in (6–9-mm) yellow edge becoming

ELEGANCE IN PERMANENCE

ONCE PLANTED, SOME PERENNIALS can simply be left alone to increase slowly and provide months of color. Here, in dappled shade with damp soil, established groups of just two plants make an impressive impact. In front, one of the best of the blue hostas, 'Big Daddy', makes dramatic clumps of puckered foliage and is best left undisturbed to develop real presence. Behind, with contrastingly golden green, lacily divided, much more upright foliage, is the shuttlecock fern, *Matteuccia struthiopteris*, which spreads to develop a network of roots, throwing up elegant ostrich fern fronds. Occasionally, fronds will emerge through the hosta as the roots spread farther afield.

creamy white later. Makes dense 22-in-
(56-cm-) high mound. Lavender
flowers in midsummer are followed by
purplish red seed pods. A hybrid of
H. 'Frances Williams'. Kevin Vaughn,
OH. ‡ 30 in (75 cm). Z3–8 H8–1

H. 'Color Glory' Heavily streaked
foliage of average substance; lavender
flowers in midsummer. Medium-large,
26-in- (65-cm-) high mound. The
plant usually sold as H. 'Color Glory is
a spontaneous mutation of *H. sieboldiana*
'Elegans' with thick-substanced, gold-
centered leaves, near-white flowers in
early summer; very similar to 'Borwick
Beauty'. ‡ 30 in (75 cm). Z3–8 H8–1

H. crispula Strongly waved, narrowly
oval, 11-x-6-in (28-x-15-cm) green
foliage; a slender, ½-in (10-mm) white
edge occasionally streaks into the
center. The tip of each leaf curls at
right angles to the blade. Large, 25-in
(65-cm) mound. Pale lavender, 2½-in-
(6-cm-) long flowers in midsummer.
Sometimes sold as 'Fortunei Marginata'.
‡ 45 in (115 cm). Z3–8 H8–1

H. 'Crusader' Vigorous, roundish,
6-x-5-in (15-x-13-cm) foliage with
narrow white margin. Dense, 18-in-

(45-cm-) high mound. Abundant
lavender flowers in late summer. Similar
to 'Tambourine' but leaf margin
narrower. A hybrid of *H.* 'Halcyon'
raised by Bill and Eleanor Lachman,
MA. ‡ 30 in (75 cm). Z3–8 H8–1

H. 'Daybreak' Large, spreading,
24-x-60-in (60-x-150-cm) mound of
bright gold, slightly waved, oval,
14-x-10-in (35-x-25-cm) foliage,
retaining its color late into the season
and rarely burning. Lavender flowers in
late summer; the stems tend to fall into
the foliage. One of the finest yellow-
leaved hostas. From Paul Aden, NY.
‡ 36 in (90 cm). Z3–8 H8–1

H. 'Decorata' Strongly spreading,
15-in- (38-cm-) high mound of blunt-
tipped, 6-x-4 in (15-x-10 cm), broadly
elliptical foliage with a neat, distinct,
¼-in (6-mm) white margin. Bell-
shaped, bright purple flowers in late
summer. Known in US as *H.* 'Thomas
Hogg'. ‡ 30 in (75 cm). Z3–8 H8–1

H. 'Devon Green' Dense 20-in
(50-cm) mound of shiny, dark green,
oval, 8-x-5-in (21-x-13-cm) foliage
with a slightly lobed base. Pale lavender
flowers in late summer. A spontaneous

mutation of *H.* 'Halcyon' from Ann and
Roger Bowden in Devon, England.
‡ 20 in (50 cm). Z3–8 H8–1

H. 'Diamond Tiara' Oval, slightly
corrugated, 5-x-4-in (13-x-10-cm),
green-centered foliage, with 1⁄16–½-in
(2–10-mm) white margins and slightly
wavy edges, makes a dense 18-in-
(45-cm-) high mound. Purple flowers
in midsummer, and later if promptly
deadheaded. A spontaneous mutation of
H. 'Golden Tiara' from Mark Zilis, IL.
‡ 28 in (70 cm). Z3–8 H8–1

H. 'Dorset Blue' (Tardiana Group)
Small, dense, very slow-growing, 10-in
(25-cm) mound of very thick, slug-
resistant, heavily corrugated, deep blue,
5-x-4-in (13-x-10-cm) foliage. Very pale
lavender flowers in late summer. The
smallest of Eric Smith's Tardianas.
‡ 16 in (40 cm). Z3–8 H8–1

H. 'Elvis Lives' Vase-shaped, semi-
upright, 20-in (50-cm) mound of wavy,
blue-green, 9-x-4-in (22-x-10-cm)
foliage with pale purple flowers from
midsummer into late summer. May
make a large, broad clump up as much
as 72 in (180 cm) across. Raised by
Tony Avent, Plant Delights, NC. ‡ 30 in
(75 cm). Z3–8 H8–1

H. 'Emerald Tiara' Very dense,
medium-sized, 17-in- (43-cm-) high
mound of gold-centered, 4½-x-3½-in
(11-x-9-cm), gently waved, oval leaves
with a ¾-in (2-cm) gold margin. Purple
flowers in midsummer. A spontaneous
mutation of *H.* 'Golden Scepter', itself
a spontaneous mutation of 'Golden
Tiara'. Walters Gardens, Zeeland, MI.
‡ 24 in (60 cm). Z3–8 H8–1

H. 'Eric Smith' (Tardiana Group)
Small, dense, 16-in (40-cm) mound of
blue-tinted, heart-shaped, slightly
waved foliage, a little bluer in spring.
Dark lavender flowers in midsummer.
The least blue of the Tardiana Group,
but considered by its raiser, Englishman
Eric Smith, to be the best. ‡ 30 in
(75 cm). Z3–8 H8–1

H. 'Fire and Ice' White-centered,
green-margined, 8-x-6-in (20-x-15-cm)
oval foliage with slightly wavy margins

ABOVE 1 *H.* 'Christmas Tree'
2 *H.* 'Devon Green' **3** *H.* 'Fire and Ice'
4 *H. fortunei* var. *albopicta*

makes a small- to medium-sized 23-in
(57-cm) mound. Lavender flowers in
midsummer. Can be slow-growing and
difficult. A spontaneous mutation of
H. 'Patriot' with the coloring reversed.
From Hans Hansen, MN. ‡ 24 in
(60 cm). Z3–8 H8–1

H. fluctuans 'Variegated' see
H. 'Sagae'

H. fortunei Controversial; sometimes
treated as a species, sometimes as a
cultivar. Green, oval leaves, 9 x 6 in
(23 x 15 cm), each with nine to eleven
pairs of veins. Pale lavender, narrowly
funnel-shaped, 2-in (5-cm) flowers are
held high above foliage in midsummer.
Makes medium to large, 20-x-48-in
(50-x-120-cm) mounds. Plants are
tough, vigorous, and will take more sun
than most. Variable, often producing
spontaneous mutations but little seed.
‡ 24–36 in (60–90 cm). Z3–8 H8–1.
var. albopicta syn. *H.* 'Fortunei
Albopicta' Slightly larger plant; heart-
shaped leaves change from gold-
centered and green-edged in spring
to all-green by early summer. **var.
albopicta f. aurea** syn. 'Fortunei Aurea'
Smaller plant; foliage gold in spring,
turning green by early summer. **var.
aureomarginata** syn. *H.* 'Fortunei
Aureomarginata', *H.* 'Gold Crown'
Smaller; green leaves have 1⁄8–½-in (3–
10-mm) gold edge. An old variety
still good by modern standards.
var. gigantea see *H. montana*. **var.
hyacinthina** syn. 'Fortunei Hyacinthina'
Slightly larger mound; bluish green
foliage. Often sold as *H.* 'Fortunei'.
Parent of spontaneous mutations
including *H.* 'Gold Standard'.

H. 'Fortunei Albopicta' see *H. fortunei*
var. *albopicta*

H. 'Fortunei Aurea' see *H. fortunei* var.
albopicta f. *aurea*

H. 'Fortunei Aureomarginata' see
H. fortunei var. *aureomarginata*

GROWING HOSTAS IN CONTAINERS

Although most often considered as
plants for ground cover, edging, or as
specimens in borders, hostas also make
superb plants for containers; a well
grown container specimen can make an
tremendous impact.

However, there is one important
factor of which the gardener should
be aware. A mature hosta carries an
enormous amount of foliage. This foliage
loses a great deal of moisture, and in a
container, with its limited root space, the
roots can very quickly suck out all the
moisture from the soil to supply the
foliage, from which moisture is constantly
being lost. When the soil dries out, the
plant wilts, and even when the moisture
is replenished the quality of the foliage
will be sadly diminished.

So regular watering is essential,
especially as the dense foliage often
throws rainwater off the plant and onto

the ground around the container. A
trickle or drip system, which can be
operated with one turn of the faucet, is
ideal. Using a potting mix based on loam
rather than peat or coconut fiber is also
advisable. Not only will it be heavier,
which improves stability in windy
situations, but it will be more easily
rewetted should you allow it to dry out.

Another advantage of growing hostas
in containers—apart from the spectacle
they create— is the ease with which they
can be pampered. The soil can be kept
consistently moist; feeding is likely to be
more regular; and slug and weevil
damage can be prevented.

Finally, do not be restricted to big or
bold hostas in containers. Many of the
smallest cultivars are best appreciated in
pots sited by doorways or on shady
patios where they can be appreciated at
close quarters.

H. 'Fortunei Hyacinthina' see
H. fortunei var. *hyacinthina*

H. 'Fortunei Marginata' see
H. crispula

H. 'Fragrant Blue' Blue-green, oval or heart-shaped, 8-x-6-in (20-x-15-cm) leaves slowly turn green. Makes 20-in- (50-cm-) high mound Fragrant, pale lavender flowers in late summer. Paul Aden, NY. ‡ 30 in (75 cm). Z3–8 H8–1

H. 'Fragrant Bouquet' Striking, 22-in- (55-cm-) high mound of chartreuse-centered, slightly wavy, 10-x-8-in (25-x-20-cm) leaves with ½–¾-in (1–2-cm) creamy white margins. Large, fragrant, pale lavender flowers produced in late summer in dense clusters. Source of several significant spontaneous mutations including 'Fragrant Dream' and 'Guacamole'. Paul Aden. ‡ 40 in (100 cm). Z3–8 H8–1

H. 'Francee' (*fortunei*) Impressive, popular and reliable, making a 20-in- (50-cm-) high mound of green-centered, 8-x-6-in (20-x-15-cm), oval foliage with a ⅛-⅜-in (3–15-mm) white margin. Lavender flowers in midsummer. Widely grown for its good color and durability. Parent of the excellent 'Minuteman' and 'Patriot'. Minnie Kopping, Nebraska. ‡ 28 in (70 cm). Z3–8 H8–1

H. 'Frances Williams' (*sieboldiana*) Blue-green-centered, corrugated, 13-x-10-in (33-x-25-cm), slug-resistant, oval foliage with a heart-shaped base; the pale green 1½–2-in (4–5-cm) margins change to gold by midsummer; may burn in spring. Makes large, open, 28-in (70-cm) mound. Dense clusters of near-white flowers in early summer. Spontaneous mutation of *H. sieboldiana* 'Elegans' found in CT by Frances R. Williams, in 1936. ‡ 30 in (75 cm). Z3–8 H8–1

H. 'Fried Green Tomatoes' Vigorous. Medium-green, slightly wavy, 11-x-8-in (28-x-20-cm), broadly oval foliage. Makes 24-in (60-cm) mound Fragrant, pale lavender flowers in dense clusters. Spontaneous mutation of 'Guacamole'. Robert M. Solberg, Chapel Hill, NC. ‡ 48 in (120 cm). Z3–8 H8–1

BELOW *H.* 'Fragrant Blue'

H. 'Frosted Jade' (*montana*) Green-centered, oval, 14-x-10-in (35-x-25-cm), rippled leaves with a heart-shaped base and ¼–½-in (6–10 mm) white margins. Makes 32-in- (80-cm-) high mound. Pale lavender flowers in midsummer. ‡ 40 in (100 cm). Z3–8 H8–1

H. 'Geisha' Dense, 18-in- (45-cm-) high mound of wavy, 7-x-4-in (18-x-10-cm), elliptical to narrowly oval foliage with a 1½-in (4-cm) green margin and a center that changes from gold in spring to pale green by late summer. Bright purple flowers in late summer. Originated in Japan, where it is known as "Ani Machi Giboshi." ‡ 28 in (70 cm). Z3–8 H8–1

H. 'Ginko Craig' syn. *H. helonioides* 'Albopicta' Deservedly popular and vigorous plant making a low, wide, 14-x-44-in (35-x-114-cm) mound of narrow, 6-x-2-in (15-x-5-cm), elliptical, wavy, white-margined foliage, becoming broader with age and with wider margins and corrugations to the leaves. Purple flowers in late summer. Sometimes mistakenly sold as 'Ginkgo Craig'. ‡ 28 in (70 cm). Z3–8 H8–1

H. 'Gold Crown' see *H. fortunei* var. *aureomarginata*

H. 'Gold Drop' (*venusta* hybrid) Small, dense, 12-in (30-cm) mound of oval, chartreuse to medium gold, 5-x-4-in (13-x-10-cm) foliage with a heart-shaped base. Lavender flowers are carried in dense clusters in midsummer. An outstanding garden plant and source of many spontaneous mutations and seedlings. Ken Anderson, MN. ‡ 20 in (50 cm). Z3–8 H8–1

H. 'Gold Edger' Heart-shaped foliage changing from pale green to chartreuse or gold and with yellow fall color. Makes small, dense, 13-in (33-cm) mound of 5-x-4-in (13-x-10-cm). Lavender flowers in midsummer. A source of many spontaneous mutations and seedlings; fine garden plant. Paul Aden, NY. ‡ 22 in (55 cm). Z3–8 H8–1

H. 'Gold Regal' Erect oval, 11-x-8-in (27-x-20-cm), leaves with squared base change from pale green to chartreuse or gold over the season; gold fall color. Makes large, almost statuesque, 32-in- (80-cm-) high mound. Lavender flowers in midsummer. Best in bright light to bring out the foliage color. One of Paul Aden's best introductions. ‡ 40 in (100 cm). Z3–8 H8–1

H. 'Gold Standard' (*fortunei*) Vigorous, dense, 22-in (56-cm) mound of gold-centered, slightly corrugated, 9-x-6-in (22-x-15-cm) oval leaves with rounded base, contrasting, ¼–½-in (6–10-mm), dark green margin. Pale lavender flowers in midsummer. Perhaps the most significant cultivar of the last 100 years. From Pauline Banyai. Parent of many spontaneous mutations including 'Moonlight' and 'Striptease' and itself a spontaneous mutation of *H. fortunei* var. *hyacinthina,* from 1976. ‡ 30 in (75 cm). Z3–8 H8–1

H. Goldbrook Series A group of a dozen or so cultivars originating with Sandra Bond of Goldbrook Plants, Suffolk, England. Most significant in the series are 'Goldbrook Glimmer', a spontaneous mutation of 'Halcyon' with narrow, pale green-centered leaves, and 'Goldbrook Glamour', with creamy margined foliage.

H. 'Golden Medallion' (*tokudama*) Medium-sized, 16-in (40-cm) mound of thick, 8-x-7-in (20-x-18-cm), broadly oval, slightly wavy foliage, chartreuse at first, becoming gold. Near-white flowers in early summer. A relatively slug-resistant spontaneous mutation of *H. tokudama* f. *aureonebulosa*. ‡ 28 in (70 cm). Z3–8 H8–1

H. 'Golden Prayers' (*tokudama*) Boldly corrugated, thick, bright gold, 8-x-8-in (20-x-20-cm), broadly oval, rather wavy leaves make a 20-in- (50-cm-) high mound. Near-white flowers in early summer. The much smaller 'Little Aurora' has been sold under this name. ‡ 24 in (60 cm). Z3–8 H8–1

H. 'Golden Scepter' (*nakaiana*) Golden, oval, 5-x-3¾-in (13-x-9.5-cm) foliage makes a 14-in- (36-cm-) high mound, chartreuse at first, becoming more golden. Pale purple flowers in midsummer. A gold-leaved spontaneous mutation of 'Golden Tiara', but less vigorous. Robert P. Savory, MN ‡ 26 in (65 cm). Z3–8 H8–1

H. 'Golden Sunburst' (*sieboldiana*) Forms a 20-in- (50-cm-) high mound of thick, heavily corrugated, 11-x-10-in (28-x-25-cm), broadly oval foliage, strongly lobed at the base; leaves open chartreuse in spring and turn gold by summer. Near-white flowers in early summer. Foliage tends to burn in spring and often becomes unsightly and brown-spotted. 'Piedmont Gold' and 'Zounds' are good alternatives. A spontaneous mutation of 'Frances Williams'. ‡ 29 in (74 cm). Z3–8 H8–1

H. 'Golden Tiara' (*nakaiana*) A classic, fast-growing, 16-in- (40-cm-) high mound of green-centered, 4-x-3-in (10-x-8-cm), oval foliage with a ⅛-¾-in (3–20-mm) gold margin. Purple flowers in midsummer. Popular ground cover and edging. Robert P. Savory, MN. ‡ 30 in (75 cm). Z3–8 H8–1

H. gracillima 'Variegated' see *H.* 'Vera Verde'

H. 'Great Expectations' (*sieboldiana*) Blue-green, slightly wavy and cupped, 12-x-10-in (30-x-25-cm) foliage boldly splashed in yellow or cream. Large, dramatic, 29-x-58-in (73-x-148-cm) mound. Dense clusters of near-white flowers in early summer. Slow-growing, thrives on rich soil and high moisture levels when young. A spontaneous mutation of *H. sieboldiana* 'Elegans'

RIGHT 1 *Hosta* 'Fragrant Bouquet'
2 *H.* 'Frances Williams'
3 *H.* 'Frosted Jade'
4 *H.* 'Golden Tiara'

A SHRUB, A PERENNIAL, AND A HARDY ANNUAL

HOSTA 'GOLD STANDARD' IS ONE of the most popular of all hostas, and here its fat clump of puckered, boldly golden-centered, blue-green foliage shows why hostas are best left undisturbed. Alongside, in a complete contrast of form, the twiggy stems of *Lonicera nitida* 'Baggeson's Gold' are lined with pairs of tiny, rounded golden leaves that pick up the color of the hosta leaf. Peeping out all through this pairing are the white-edged yellow flowers of a self-sown hardy annual, the poached-egg plant, *Limnanthes douglasii*, whose seed germinates both in spring and in fall.

developed by John Bond, Savill Gardens, England. ↕ 30 in (75 cm). Z3–8 H8–1

H. 'Green Fountain' (*kikutii*) Distinctive, fountainlike mound, 22 in (56 cm) high, with long, 11-x-4-in (28-x-10-cm), broadly elliptical, bright green leaves with long slender tips. Lavender flowers in late summer on arching stems. Paul Aden, NY. ↕ 36 in (90 cm). Z3–8 H8–1

H. 'Ground Master' Green-centered, wavy, elliptical, 6-x-3-in (15-x-8-cm) foliage with ½–¾-in (1–2-cm) creamy white margin. Fast-growing, medium-sized, 16-x-40-in (40-x-105-cm) mound. Bears bright purple flowers on straight leafy stalks in midsummer. Excellent for ground cover or edging, although susceptible to slug damage. ↕ 24 in (60 cm). Z3–8 H8–1

H. 'Guacamole' Broadly oval, slightly wavy leaves, 11-x-9-in (27-x-22-cm), chartreuse center and ⅝-in (1.5-cm) green margin; foliage most intense in bright light. Fast growing, 24-in- (60-cm-) high mound. Large, fragrant, pale lavender flowers in late summer. Spontaneous mutation of 'Fragrant Bouquet'. Robert M. Solberg, Chapel Hill, NC. ↕ 40 in (100 cm). Z3–9 H9–1

RIGHT 1 *Hosta* 'Green Fountain'
2 *H.* 'Ground Master'
3 *H.* 'Hadspen Blue'

H. 'Guardian Angel' Bold, 23-in- (58-cm-) high mound; the 16-x-12-in (40-x-30-cm), broadly oval foliage, deeply lobed at the base, misted green and white in the center with a blue-green margin in spring, then turns dark green by midsummer. Dense clusters of near-white flowers in midsummer. A spontaneous mutation of 'Blue Angel'. Rick and Criss Thompson, VA. ↕ 36 in (90 cm). Z3–8 H8–1

H. 'Hadspen Blue' (Tardiana Group) Thick, cupped, broadly oval, 7-x-6-in 18-x-15-cm), deep blue leaves; heart-shaped base. Makes 18-in- (45-cm-) high mound. Pale lavender flowers in late summer. Fairly slow growing. One of the most popular Tardianas, relatively slug-resistant, and one of the bluest hosta. ↕ 24 in (60 cm). Z3–8 H8–1

H. 'Hadspen Heron' (Tardiana Group) Thick, deep blue, 5-x-2-in (13-x-5-cm) leaves, narrowly elliptical when young then considerably wider with age. A modest 14-in- (36-cm-) high mound. Pale lavender flowers in late summer. ↕ 14 in (35 cm). Z3–8 H8–1

H. Hadspen Series Ten cultivars with the Hadspen prefix developed by Eric Smith, gardener at Hadspen House, Somerset, England and later a partner with Jim Archibald in The Plantsmen nursery. Some are derived from a cross between *H. tardiflora* and *H. sieboldiana* 'Elegans', other plants derived from the same cross have names without the Hadspen prefix; some with the Hadspen prefix are other crosses.

H. 'Halcyon' (Tardiana Group) A dense blue mound, 18 in (45 cm) high, with deep blue-green, 8-x-5-in (20-x-13-cm), oval leaves, gently lobed at the base. Pale lavender flowers in late summer. The most popular of Eric Smith's Tardianas and origin of many seedlings and spontaneous mutations. ↕ 28 in (70 cm). Z3–8 H8–1

H. 'Happiness' (Tardiana Group) Makes an 18-in- (45-cm-) high mound of thick, rich blue, 8-x-6-in (20-x-15-cm), slightly corrugated, oval leaves with pale lavender flowers in late summer. One of Eric Smith's lesser known Tardianas from England. ↕ 30 in (75 cm). Z3–8 H8–1

H. helonioides 'Albopicta' The plant originally grown under this name was misidentified and is *H. rohdeifolia*. More recently this plant was named and widely distributed as 'Ginko Craig' but the cultivar name has been retained.

H. 'Honeybells' A large, fast-growing, 24-in (60-cm) mound of wavy, light green, 10-x-6-in (25-x-15-cm), elliptical foliage, slightly puckered at the margins and broadening with age, sets off fragrant, pale lavender flowers in late summer. A superb *H. plantaginea* hybrid introduced in 1952. ↕ 40 in (100 cm). Z3–8 H8–1

H. 'Hydon Sunset' (*nakaiana*) A low, dense, 8-x-22-in (20-x-55-cm) mound of heart-shaped foliage that is bright gold in spring, becoming green by midsummer, when the purple flowers are borne. Confusingly, at least three different plants have been grown under this name, most often 'Dawn', which stays gold all season. ↕ 24 in (60 cm). Z3–8 H8–1

H. hypoleuca Shiny, rippled, oval, green foliage, deeply lobed at the base and intensely white on the underside. An unusual species in that it forms a very open, 20-in- (50-cm-) mound. Lavender flowers in late summer weigh down 30-in (75-cm) stems almost to ground level. Native to cliffs in central

Japan. ↕20 in (50 cm). Z3–8 H8–1

H. 'Inniswood' Broadly oval, slightly wavy, 11-x-7-in (28-x-18-cm), gold-centered foliage with a neat, ½–1½-in (1–4-cm), dark green margin makes a striking, relatively slug-resistant, 22-in- (56-cm-) high mound. Pale lavender flowers in midsummer. A fine specimen plant. ↕30 in (75 cm). Z3–8 H8–1

H. 'Invincible' A 20-in- (50-cm-) high mound of shiny, dark green, 8-x-6-in (20-x-15-cm), slightly rippled, oval foliage with a deeply lobed base. Fragrant, pale lavender flowers in late summer. An *H. plantaginea* hybrid, but less invincible than its name suggests. ↕30 in (75 cm). Z3–8 H8–1

H. 'Jade Cascade' Large, impressive, 30-in- (75-cm-) high, upright, arching mound of unusually large, up to 19-in (48-cm), bright green, lance-shaped, foliage. Pale purple flowers in midsummer. Dan Heims, OR. ↕54 in (130 cm). Z3–8 H8–1

H. 'Janet' (*fortunei*) Medium-sized, 17-in (43-cm) mound of oval foliage that broadens with age. Chartreuse leaves in spring, deepens to light gold; a ⅛-in (3-mm) green margin. Lavender flowers in midsummer. Similar to *H.* 'Gold Standard' but slightly smaller and a paler gold. ↕30 in (75 cm). Z3–8 H8–1

H. 'Julie Morss' (*fortunei*) Oval, 10-x-7-in (25-x-18-cm) foliage, with a rounded base; chartreuse-centered and green-edged in spring but all-green by midsummer. Pale lavender flowers in midsummer. Makes a 21-in (53-cm) mound. ↕30 in (75 cm). Z3–8 H8–1

H. 'June' (Tardiana Group) Medium-sized mound of gold-centered, 6-x-4-in (15-x-10-cm) foliage with a ⅛–¾-in (3–20-mm), blue-green margin. Leaf center is pale green with a bluish haze in spring but becomes more golden. Pale lavender flowers in late summer. A popular spontaneous mutation of 'Halcyon'; 'Goldbrook Glimmer' is similar, but leaf center slightly greener. ↕24 in (60 cm). Z3–8 H8–1

H. 'Just So' Corrugated, oval, 4-x-3-in (10-x-8-cm), gold-centered foliage; ¼-in (5-mm) green margin. Very small, neat, but vigorous, 10-in (25-cm) mound Pale lavender flowers in midsummer. ↕18 in (45 cm). Z3–8 H8–1

H. 'Knockout' Bold, but flawed, plant making an 18-in (45-cm) mound of blue-centered, creamy white-margined 7-x-7-in (18-x-18-cm) foliage. Near-white flowers in early summer. Striking as a juvenile plant, but at maturity the white margins fall away, leaving an unattractive, sawtooth leaf edge. The less often seen 'Heart's Content' is similar but without this flaw. ↕30 in (75 cm). Z3–8 H8–1

H. 'Krossa Regal' Dramatic plant making 30-in (75-cm), vase-shaped mounds, which may reach 70 in (175 cm) across, of slug-resistant,

powdery blue, 11-x-7-in (28-x-18-cm), oval, wavy-edged foliage with a slightly lobed base. Lavender flowers open on tall stems in late summer. Tremendous for its foliage color, habit, and tall stems. A seedling of *H. nigrescens*. Gus Krossa. ↕60 in (150 cm). Z3–8 H8–1

H. 'Lacy Belle' Medium-sized, 16-in (40-cm) mound of wavy, 7-x-4-in (18-x-10-cm), elliptical foliage; ¼-in (6-mm) creamy white margin. Pale purple flowers in late summer. A hybrid of *H.* 'Halcyon'. Bill and Eleanor Lachman, MA. ↕28 in (70 cm). Z3–8 H8–1

H. Lakeside Series The "Lakesides" are a broad group of over 100 cultivars from Mary Chastain of Ooltewah, TN. They cover a wide range of forms, originating from such species as *Hosta ventricosa*, *H. hypoleuca* and *H. yingeri*. Most prominent are 'Lakeside Symphony', a light gold-centered spontaneous mutation of 'Piedmont Gold'; 'Lakeside Black Satin', a dark-leaved descendant of *H. ventricosa*; 'Lakeside Accolade', a large mound of shiny, dark green foliage; and 'Lakeside Blue Jeans', a large, upright mound of blue foliage.

H. lancifolia Narrow, shiny, elliptical or oval, 7-x-3-in (18-x-8-cm), medium green leaves overlap like fish scales. Neat, vigorous, dependable, and attractive, making a 16-in (40-cm) mound. Lavender flowers on tall stems in late summer. The most widely grown hosta of all time, and one of the first to be grown outside East Asia. From China. ↕24 in (60 cm). Z3–8 H8–1

H. 'Lemon Lime' Slightly wavy, narrowly oval, 4-x-2-in (10-x-5-cm), greenish gold foliage, rounded at the base. Fast-growing, small, dense, 12-in- (30-cm-) high mound. Bright purple flowers in profusion in midsummer. Cut off stems after flowering for reblooming in early fall. From Robert P. Savory, MN. ↕24 in (60 cm). Z3–8 H8–1

H. 'Leola Fraim' A bold, adaptable, underrated plant making a 22-in- (56-cm-) high mound of 10-x-7-in (25-x-18-cm), dark green, oval leaves gently lobed at the base, each with a ¾–1½-in (2–4-cm) white margin. Lavender flowers in midsummer. Good both as a specimen plant and as ground cover. Bill and Eleanor Lachman, MA. ↕36 in (90 cm). Z3–8 H8–1

H. 'Little Black Scape' Striking 10-in- (25-cm-) high mound of heart-shaped, 6-x-4-in (15-x-10-cm) chartreuse foliage changes to medium gold during the growing season. Lavender flowers on blackish purple stems in midsummer. A seedling of 'Sum and Substance', best in sun. Tony Avent, NC. ↕18 in (45 cm). Z3–8 H8–1

RIGHT 1 *Hosta* 'Halcyon'
2 *H.* 'Inniswood'
3 *H.* 'Jade Cascade'

H. 'Little Wonder' Very dense, round, 9-in- (23-cm-) high mound of green, waved, narrowly oval, 4½-x-2-in (11-x-5-cm) foliage with a ⅛–¼-in (3–6-mm) white margin. Purple flowers held neatly in midsummer. Vigorous, and the ideal edging plant. Bill and Eleanor Lachman, MA. ↕ 24 in (60 cm). Z3–8 H8–1

H. 'Love Pat' An impressive, relatively slug-resistant, medium-large, 20-in (50-cm) mound of thick, heavily corrugated, 9-x-9-in (22-x-22-cm), blue-green, rounded foliage, which eventually becomes dark green. Dense clusters of near-white flowers in midsummer. Paul Aden, NY. ↕ 26 in (65 cm). Z3–8 H8–1

H. 'Midas Touch' (*sieboldiana*) Intensely corrugated, deeply cupped, broadly oval, 8-x-7-in (20-x-18-cm) foliage is bright gold throughout the season. Makes 20-in- (50-cm) high mound. Near-white flowers in early summer. Paul Aden, NY. ↕ 24 in (60 cm). Z3–8 H8–1

H. 'Midwest Magic' Fast-growing and making a 20-in- (50-cm) high mound of gold-centered, slightly waved and corrugated, 8-x-6-in (20-x-15-cm), oval leaves with a ½–¾-in (1–2-cm) green margin; the center greener in summer. Lavender flowers in midsummer. ↕ 26 in (65 cm). Z3–8 H8–1

H. 'Mildred Seaver' Large, 27-in- (68-cm-) high mound of green, 10-x-7-in (25-x-18-cm), very slightly

LEFT 1 *Hosta* 'June' **2** *H. lancifolia* **3** *H.* 'Mildred Seaver' **4** *H.* 'Morning Light'

wavy, broadly oval foliage, with a ½–¾-in (1–2-cm) rim that changes from yellow to white during the season. Pale lavender flowers in midsummer. The name honors the Massachusetts hosta breeder who created so many good plants. ↕ 30 in (75 cm). Z3–8 H8–1

H. minor Tiny creeping plant making a 6-in- (15-cm-) high mound of 3-x-2-in (8-x-5-cm), medium green, oval leaves with red dots on their ridged stalks. Purple flowers in midsummer. Native to Korea, but naturalized in Japan where it is known as "Keirin Giboshi." ↕ 22 in (55 cm). Z3–8 H8–1

H. 'Minuteman' (*fortunei*) Dark green, 8-x-6-in (20-x-15-cm), thick, oval, slightly wavy foliage, deeply lobed at the base, with a ½–1-in (1–2.5-cm) white margin, makes a 23-in- (58-cm-) high mound. Lavender flowers in midsummer. John Machen, VA; similar to 'Patriot' but a darker green and a purer white and, like 'Patriot', a spontaneous mutation of 'Francee'. ↕ 30 in (75 cm). Z3–8 H8–1

H. 'Moerheim' see *H.* 'Antioch'

H. montana Large, vase-shaped, 28-x-78-in (70-x-200-cm) mound of deeply veined, medium-green, oval, 12-x-9-in (30-x-22-cm) foliage with very slender tips. Very pale lavender, 2¾-in- (7-cm-) long, openly funnel-shaped flowers in midsummer with a white leafy bract beneath each one. Origin of many spontaneous mutations from the wild and gardens. From woodlands and mountainous areas in Japan. ↕ 50 in (125 cm). Z3–8 H8–1

H. 'Moon River' Dense, 11-in- (28-cm-) high mound; round, 4-x-4-in

(10-x-10-cm), blue-green foliage that puckers slightly as it matures with a ⅛–½-in (3–10-mm) edge that changes from yellow to almost pure white. Pale lavender flowers in midsummer. From Bill and Eleanor Lachman, MA. ↕ 24 in (60 cm). Z3–8 H8–1

H. 'Moonlight' (*fortunei*) Dense, 20-in- (50-cm) high mound of oval, 9-x-5-in (22-x-13-cm) foliage with a rounded base, opening chartreuse and becoming gold with a ⅛-in (4-mm) white edge. Lavender flowers in late summer. A spontaneous mutation of 'Gold Standard' from the late Pauline Banyai, MI. ↕ 30 in (75 cm). Z3–8 H8–1

H. 'Morning Light' Small, 14-in- (36-cm-) high mound of thick, gold-centered, 6-x-4-in (15-x-10-cm), oval foliage; 1-in (2.5-cm) green margin. Lavender flowers in midsummer. A spontaneous mutation of 'Twilight'. ↕ 17 in (43 cm). Z3–8 H8–1

H. 'Mountain Snow' (*montana*) Large, vase-shaped, 24-in (60-cm) mound of 12-x-8-in (30-x-20-cm), medium-green, oval, slightly wavy leaves; slender, ¹⁄₁₆-in (1-mm) pure white margin. Very pale lavender flowers in midsummer. One of the latest hostas to emerge in spring. A spontaneous mutation of *H. montana*. Mark Zilis, Q&Z Nursery, IL. ↕ 40 in (100 cm). Z3–8 H8–1

H. 'Nancy Lindsay' (*fortunei*) Medium-sized, 19-in- (48-cm-) high mound of 8-x-6-in (20-x-15-cm), oval foliage, gold with green splotches in spring, medium-green by late summer. Lavender flowers in midsummer. ↕ 33 in (84 cm). Z3–8 H8–1

H. 'Niagara Falls' Large, semi-upright

SLUG-RESISTANT CULTIVARS

Slugs (and snails) are the number one pests of hostas and can reduce a clump to shreds overnight. Especially insidious is when they eat the emerging shoots in spring and ever-enlarging holes are revealed as the shoots unfurl. Slugs and snails tend to avoid those hostas with thick foliage, usually preferring plants with thinner, more tender leaves. These hostas, although not immune to slug damage, are relatively resistant.

'Abiqua Drinking Gourd'	'Invincible'
'Big Daddy'	'June'
'Blue Angel'	'Krossa Regal'
'Blue Dimples'	'Love Pat'
'Blue Mammoth'	'Northern Exposure'
'Blue Moon'	'Sagae'
'Blue Umbrellas',	'Sea Lotus Leaf'
'Blue Wedgwood'	*H. sieboldiana* and its forms
'Dorset Blue'	'Spilt Milk'
'Fragrant Bouquet'	'Sum and Substance'
'Gold Edger'	*H. tokudama* and its forms
'Gold Regal'	'Zounds'
'Great Expectations'	
'Hadspen Blue'	
'Halcyon'	

Hosta 'Blue Wedgwood'

Hosta 'Great Expectations'

Hosta 'Krossa Regal'

Hosta 'Love Pat'

mound 26 in (66 cm) high with rippled, dark green, 14-x-10-in (35-x-25-cm), broadly oval leaves with a deeply lobed base and a pretty "piecrust" finish along the edge. Pale lavender flowers in midsummer. Olga Petrysyzen and Bill Brincka, IN. ↕45 in (110 cm) Z3–8 H8–1

H. 'Night Before Christmas' Large, vigorous, and impressive 25-in (65-cm) mound of 12-x-7-in (30-x-18-cm), oval, slightly wavy, dark green leaves with a 2-in- (5-cm-) wide white splash in the center. Lavender flowers in midsummer. A tetraploid spontaneous mutation of 'White Christmas'. John Machen, VA. ↕36 in (90 cm). Z3–8 H8–1

H. nigrescens Large, vase-shaped, 30-x-66-in (75-x-160-cm) mound of thick, corrugated, cupped, oval, blue-green, 12-x-9½-in (30-x-23-cm) foliage with a heart-shaped base and noticeable pointed tip. The leaves become dark green by midsummer. Funnel-shaped, 2½-in (6-cm) lavender flowers in late summer. From northern Japan (Kuro Giboshi) ↕5 ft (1.5 m). Z3–8 H8–1

H. 'Northern Exposure' (*sieboldiana*) Blue-green, 14-x-10-in (35-x-25-cm), broadly oval foliage with a heart-shaped base, heavy corrugations, and slightly wavy edges, features a wide, 1–1½-in (2.5–4-cm) creamy margin and makes a 28-in- (70-cm-) high mound. Dense clusters of near-white flowers in midsummer. Like 'Northern Halo', but with much wider margins. Spontaneous mutation of *H. sieboldiana* 'Elegans'. ↕30 in (75 cm). Z3–8 H8–1

H. 'Olive Bailey Langdon' Large, open, 30-in (78-cm) mound of blue-green-centered, corrugated, 13-x-10-in (33-x-25-cm), slug-resistant, oval foliage with a heart-shaped base; the 1½–2-in (4–5-cm) margin starts pale green then changes to gold by midsummer. Clusters of near-white flowers in early summer. In effect, identical to 'Frances Williams' but with gold margins that do not burn in spring. Russ O'Harra, IA. ↕30 in (75 cm). Z3–8 H8–1

H. 'On Stage' see *H.* 'Choko-Nishiki'

H. 'Opipara' Impressive, 24-in- (60-cm-) high mound, spreading by rhizomes to make a plant 64 in (160 cm) wide with green, 12-x-8-in (30-x-20-cm), oval foliage with a rounded base and ¾–1½-in (2–4-cm) yellow margins. Purple flowers in late summer. Makes a vigorous and spectacular specimen. From Japan. ↕40 in (100 cm). Z3–8 H8–1

H. 'Pacific Blue Edger' Dense, medium-sized, 15-x-38-in (38-x-95-cm) mound of bluish green, heart-shaped, 5-x-4-in (13-x-10-cm) foliage. Lavender flowers in midsummer. A spontaneous mutation of 'Gold Edger'; very similar to 'Blue Cadet'. Dan Heims, OR. ↕24 in (60 cm). Z3–8 H8–1

H. 'Pandora's Box' Small, very dense, 4-in (10-cm) mound of 2¼-x-2-in (5.5-x-5-cm), almost round, white-centered foliage; ½-in (1-cm) green margin. Purple flowers in midsummer. More vigorous than many white-centered hostas and good in troughs and the garden. Spontaneous mutation of 'Baby Bunting'. Hans Hansen, MN. ↕12 in (30 cm). Z3–8 H8–1

H. 'Paradigm' Gold-centered, green-edged, 11-x-9-in (28-x-22-cm), oval, corrugated, sometimes cupped foliage of thick substance makes a 22-in- (56-cm-) high mound. Near-white flowers in midsummer. A descendant of 'Sum and Substance'. Walden West, OR. ↕34 in (85 cm). Z3–8 H8–1

H. 'Paradise Joyce' Gold-centered spontaneous mutation of 'Halcyon' with a ¾-in (2-cm), blue-green edge to the 8-x-5½-in (20-x-14-cm), oval leaves, which are slightly lobed at the base, and a pale gold center, making a 14-in- (36-cm-) high mound. Lavender flowers in late summer. Dutch hosta breeder Marco Fransen; similar to 'June' but with a brighter gold center. ↕20 in (50 cm). Z3–8 H8–1

H. 'Patriot' Green, oval, 8-x-6-in (20-x-15-cm) leaves; ½–1-in (1–2.5-cm) margins are creamy yellow at first, then become white. Mound is 23 in (58 cm) high. Lavender flowers in midsummer. A tetraploid sport of 'Francee' differing in its thicker leaves with wider, white margins. ↕28 in (70 cm). Z3–8 H8–1

H. 'Paul's Glory' A large, 25-in- (65-cm-) high mound of gold-centered, 9-x-7-in (22-x-18-cm) oval foliage, deeply lobed at the base, with a ⅜–¾-in (0.8–2-cm), blue-green edge that is greener by midsummer. Pale lavender flowers in midsummer. More dramatic version of 'Gold Standard'. Paul Hofer and Peter Ruh, OH. ↕36 in (90 cm). Z3–8 H8–1

H. 'Pearl Lake' Dense, vigorous, 16-in- (40-cm-) high mound of 6-x-5-in (15-x-13-cm), heart-shaped, slightly wavy, green foliage; slightly grayish at first and becoming slightly corrugated. Lavender flowers in midsummer. David Stone. ↕24 in (60 cm). Z3–8 H8–1

H. 'Piedmont Gold' (*sieboldiana*) Outstanding, slug-resistant plant making a 25-in- (65-cm-) high mound of heavily corrugated, bright gold, 11-x-9-in (28-x-22-cm), broadly oval foliage with a deeply lobed base and slightly rippled edges. Off-white flowers in early summer. Colors best in light shade, and does not burn. ↕36 in (90 cm). Z3–8 H8–1

H. 'Pilgrim' Dense, 12-in- (30-cm-) high mound of green-centered, oval, 4-x-3½-in (10-x-9-cm) leaves with ¼-in (6-mm) margins that fade from yellow to creamy white. Attractive show

RIGHT **1** *H.* 'Night Before Christmas'
2 *H. nigrescens* **3** *H.* 'Paradigm'
4 *H.* 'Paradise Joyce' **5** *H.* 'Patriot'
6 *H.* 'Piedmont Gold' **7** *H.* 'Pilgrim'
8 *H. plantaginea* var. *grandiflora*

of pale purple flowers in midsummer. George Rasmussen, NY. ‡18 in (45 cm). Z3–8 H8–1

H. 'Pizzazz' Distinctive 20-in- (50-cm-) high mound of broad, 10-x-8-in (25-x-20-cm), dark green, oval leaves with a neat, pointed tip and a ¾–1¼-in (2–3-cm) yellow edge, becoming creamier and sometimes with a few streaks in the center. Off-white flowers in midsummer. Paul Aden, NY. ‡24 in (60 cm). Z3–8 H8–1

H. plantaginea A large, 22-in (56-cm) mound of shiny, light green, 11-x-7-in (28-x-18-cm) oval foliage with deeply lobed base and with a neat tip. Nocturnal, fragrant, pure white, 5-in (13-cm), trumpet-shaped flowers in dense clusters in late summer. Has the largest flowers of any hosta, and is the only fragrant species, flowering best with a few hours of sunlight per day. China. ‡30 in (75 cm). Z3–8 H8–1. **var. japonica** syn. var. *grandiflora* Narrower, wavier foliage and narrower petals. From Japan.

H. 'Purple Dwarf' Small, 12-in (30-cm) mound of 2½-x-2-in (6-x-5-cm), medium green, flat, heart-shaped foliage. Purple flowers in late summer. A seedling of *H. minor*, but making a larger mound and with taller stems. ‡40 in (100 cm). Z3–8 H8–1

H. 'Queen Josephine' Thick, dark-green-centered, 7-x-5-in (18-x-13-cm), oval leaves, slightly lobed at the base, feature slightly wavy, 1-in (2.5-cm) white margins to make an 18-in- (45-cm-) high mound. Pale purple flowers in midsummer. Bob Kuk, OH. ‡30 in (75 cm). Z3–8 H8–1

H. 'Radiant Edger' Green-centered,

ABOVE **1** *Hosta* 'Regal Splendor'
2 *H.* 'Remember Me'
3 *H.* 'Revolution'

4-x-4-in (10-x-10-cm), rounded leaves with a ½-in (1-cm) gold margin make 14-in- (35-cm-) high mound. Lavender flowers in midsummer. A slower-growing, green-centered spontaneous mutation of 'Gold Edger'. Mark Zilis, IL. ‡24 in (60 cm). Z3–8 H8–1

H. 'Red October' (*kikuti*) Medium-sized, 16-in (40-cm) mound. Lance-shaped, 8-x-4-in (20-x-10-cm) medium-green leaves, intensely purple-red stems in early fall. Roy Herold, MA. ‡24 in (60 cm). Z3–8 H8–1

H. 'Regal Splendor' Large, vase-shaped, 30-in (75-cm) mound of 11-x-7-in (28-x-18-cm), blue-green, oval, wavy-edged leaves with ¼–¾-in

(0.5–2-cm), yellow margins that turn creamy white and are narrow toward the tips of the leaves. Lavender flowers on tall stems in late summer. A white-edged spontaneous mutation of 'Krossa Regal'. Walters Gardens, MI. ‡60 in (150 cm). Z3–8 H8–1

H. 'Remember Me' Low, wide, 10-in- (25-cm-) high mound of oval, 5-x-3½-in (13-x-9-cm) leaves, each with a ¼-in (6-mm) blue-green margin and a creamy yellow to white center. Lavender flowers in midsummer. A seedling of 'June'. ‡20 in (50 cm). Z3–8 H8–1

H. 'Reversed' Slow-growing, 16-in (40-cm) mound of puckered, creamy yellow- to white-centered, heart-shaped, 8-x-6-in (20-x-15-cm) leaves with a ½-in (1-cm) dark green margin, the center gold but becomes creamier. Lavender flowers in midsummer. ‡24 in

(60 cm). Z3–8 H8–1

H. 'Revolution' Wavy-edged, oval, 7-x-5-in (18-x-13-cm) leaves; ½-in (1-cm) green margin has a white center with many green speckles, all making a 15-in- (38-cm-) high mound. Lavender flowers in midsummer. Better grower than most white-centered forms. A spontaneous mutation of 'Loyalist'. Van Wade, OH. ‡23 in (56 cm). Z3–8 H8–1

H. 'Richland Gold' (*fortunei*) Green at first, the 8-x-6-in (20-x-15-cm) foliage, oval with a rounded base, becomes a 20-in- (50-cm-) high mound of bright gold by midsummer. Lavender flowers in midsummer. A gold-leaved form of 'Gold Standard' and slower-growing. ‡30 in (75 cm). Z3–8 H8–1

H. 'Robert Frost' Large, 24-in (60-cm) mound of thick, slug resistant, broadly oval, 11-x-8½-in (28-x-21-cm) foliage with blue-green centers and ½–1-in (1–2.5-cm) creamy white margin. Near-white flowers in midsummer. Hybrid of 'Frances Williams'. ‡30 in (75 cm). Z3–8 H8–1

H. rohdeifolia Medium-sized, 14-in- (35-cm) high mound of 7-x-3-in (18-x-8-cm), elliptical green leaves with a slim ⅛–¼-in (3–6-mm) yellow margin that changes to creamy white. Light purple, 2-in (5-cm), slightly bell-shaped flowers in late summer. Species name comes from the resemblance of the foliage to that of *Rohdea japonica*, but is sometimes spelled *H. rhodeifolia*. From Japan. ‡30 in (75 cm). Z3–8 H8–1. **f. albopicta** see *H. helonioides* 'Albopicta'

H. 'Royal Standard' Fast-growing, 24-in- (60-cm-) high mound of bright green, 10-x-6-in (24-x-15-cm), oval foliage with a lobed base and a slightly wavy margin sets off a prolific show of fragrant, 3 in (7.5 cm) long flowers in late summer. An *H. plantaginea* seedling that is both outstanding in foliage and magnificent in flower. ‡36 in (90 cm). Z3–8 H8–1

H. 'Sagae' syn. *H. fluctuans* 'Variegated' Dramatic and increasingly popular. Vase-shaped 30 in (75 cm) high

SUN-PROOF HOSTAS

Hostas are naturally shade-loving plants. To some extent, they will take more sun in soil that is consistently moist than in soil that quickly dries out, but the foliage can still be damaged. In general, hostas with thin leaves, especially if they have white margins, are the most likely to be damaged, and those with thick foliage tend to be more resistant. This is selection of relatively sun-proof hostas.

'Abba Dabba Do'
'August Moon'
'Birchwood Parky's Gold'
'Blue Umbrellas'
H. fortunei var. *aureomarginata*
'Fragrant Bouquet'
'Francee'
'Fried Green Tomatoes'
'Ginko Craig'
'Gold Drop'
'Gold Edger'
'Green Fountain'
'Guacamole'

'Honeybells'
'Invincible'
H. lancifolia
'Lemon Lime'
'Midas Touch'
H. plantaginea and its forms
'Royal Standard'
'September Sun'
'So Sweet'
'Sugar and Cream'
'Sum and Substance'
'Sun Power'
'Zounds'

Hosta 'Fragrant Bouquet'

Hosta 'Francee'

Hosta 'Invincible'

Hosta 'Royal Standard'

mound. Green-centered, gold-margined, 13-x-10-in (33-x-24-cm), oval, almost triangular foliage, with a deeply lobed base. Lavender flowers in midsummer, stems later drooping under the weight of seed pods. Known for many years as *H. fluctuans* 'Variegated'. ↕50 in (125 cm). Z3–8 H8–1

***H.* 'Saint Elmo's Fire'** Strong-growing, 18 in (45 cm) high mound. Oval 9-x-6-in (22-x-15-cm), foliage has wavy, ½-in (1-cm), gold margin that turns green by early summer. Lavender flowers in late summer. Sometimes listed, incorrectly, as 'St. Elmo's Fire'. ↕28 in (70 cm). Z3–8 H8–1

***H.* 'Samurai'** (*sieboldiana*) Puckered, relatively slug-resistant, oval, 13-x-10-in (33-x-25-cm) leaves. Blue-green centers and heart-shaped base; 1½–2-in (3.5–5-cm), pale green margins change to gold by midsummer. Makes bold, 26-in- (65-cm-) high mound. Dense clusters of near-white flowers in early summer. Identical to 'Frances Williams' but has less tendency to burn along leaf margin. ↕30 in (75 cm). Z3–8 H8–1

***H.* 'Sea Dream'** Fast-growing, makes a 20-in- (50-cm-) high mound of wavy, gold-centered, 9-x-6-in (22-x-15-cm), oval leaves, rounded base; ⅛-in (4-mm) white margin. Lavender flowers held high above the leaves in midsummer. ↕40 in (100 cm). Z3–8 H8–1

***H.* 'Sea Lotus Leaf'** Blue-green, 10-x-9-in (25-x-22-cm), almost round foliage that is also heavily corrugated, thick-substanced, and attractively cupped, making a 24-in- (60-cm-) high mound. Near-white flowers in early summer. ↕28 in (70 cm). Z3–8 H8–1

***H.* Sea Series** Mildred Seaver of Needham Heights, MA, developed this impressive group of over 50 cultivars. Though most are open-pollinated seedlings descended from 'Neat Splash', *H. sieboldiana*, or *H. tokudama*, their value lies in Mildred's careful selection process. This resulted in the introduction of colorful, attractive hostas that perform well in the garden. Notable in the series are 'Sea Dream', 'Sea Drift', 'Sea Fire', 'Sea Lotus Leaf', 'Sea Monster', 'Sea Sapphire', 'Sea Sunrise', and 'Sea Thunder'.

***H.* 'September Sun'** Makes a 22-in- (55-cm-) high mound of gold-centered, 9-x-7-in (22-x-18-cm), slightly wavy and slightly corrugated, broadly oval or oblong foliage with a ½–1-in (1–2.5-cm) green edge. Pale lavender flowers in midsummer. A spontaneous mutation of 'August Moon'. ↕30 in (75 cm). Z3–8 H8–1

***H.* 'Serendipity'** Heart-shaped, 5½-x-4-in (14-x-10-cm), bluish green foliage; slightly wavy edges. Makes a dense, 16-in- (40-cm-) high, rounded mound. Lavender flowers in midsummer. Excellent ground cover. ↕30 in (75 cm). Z3–8 H8–1

***H.* 'Shade Fanfare'** Vigorous and deservedly popular, the light green, 9-x-6½-in (22-x-17-cm), oval foliage with its slightly lobed base is edged with a ¾–1-in (2–2.5-cm) creamy white margin and makes a bold, 20-in- (50-cm-) high mound. Excellent as a specimen or in a container. Pale lavender flowers in midsummer. Paul Aden, NY. ↕30 in (75 cm). Z3–8 H8–3

***H.* 'Sharmon'** (*fortunei*) Oval, gold leaves, with a slight blue bloom, are 8 x 6 in (20 x 15 cm) with a rounded base and make a 20 in (50 cm) high mound. The margin is green in spring, then the whole plant turns green. Lavender flowers in midsummer. Similar to *H. fortunei* f. *albopicta* and equally outdated. ↕30 in (75 cm). Z3–8 H8–1

H. sieboldiana Variable plant making a large, 24–66-in (60–160-cm) mound of very large, 17-x-10-in (43-x-25-cm), broadly oval foliage, with slightly rippled edges, that ranges from medium-green to deep blue-green in color. Near-white, 2½-in (6-cm), funnel-shaped flowers are carried just above the foliage in early summer, followed by many seed pods. From northern Japan. ↕22–35 in (55–85 cm). Z3–8 H8–1. **'Elegans'** Thick, heavily corrugated, blue-green foliage makes a larger, 28-in (70-cm) mound with densely clustered flowers. Introduced by Georg Arends, Germany *(see panel, p.87)* in 1905, but still the standard for large, blue-green hostas. ↕30 in (75 cm).

H. sieboldii Green, elliptical or narrowly oval, 6-x-3-in (15-x-7.5-cm), slightly wavy foliage making a mound about 13 in (33 cm) high. Purple, 2-in- (5-cm-) long, openly funnel-shaped flowers in late summer. Sometimes the variegated form, 'Paxton's Original', is known as *H. sieboldii,* with the green-leaved form known as *H. sieboldii* f. *spathulata*. This confusion arose because the variegated form was the first to be introduced from the wild, although most wild plants are green. From Japan. ↕22–30 in (55–75 cm). **'Paxton's Original'** Leaves with a 1/32–⅛-in- (0.5–4-mm-) white margin. **var. *sieboldii* f. *kabitan*** Narrow, gold-centered, green-edged, rather thin foliage. Lavender flowers in late summer. ↕18 in (45 cm). Z3–8 H8–1

***H.* 'Silver Crown'** see *H.* 'Albomarginata'

***H.* 'Snow Cap'** Bluish green, 7-x-6-in (18-x-15-cm), heart-shaped leaves have wide, white ½-in (1-cm) margin and make a 19-in- (48-cm-) high mound. Near-white flowers in midsummer. Leaf margins often tear in mature specimens, leaving a jagged brown edge. ↕25 in (65 cm). Z3–8 H8–1

***H.* 'Snow Flakes'** (*sieboldii*) Small, 14-in- (35-cm-) high mound of narrow, rather thin, green, 5-x-2-in (13-x-5-cm) foliage with pretty, pure white flowers in late summer. A hybrid of *H. sieboldii* and *H. plantaginea*. ↕18 in (45 cm). Z3–8 H8–1

***H.* 'Snowden'** Large mound, 27 in (68 cm) high, of wavy, blue-green, 14-x-10-in (35-x-25-cm), narrowly heart-shaped foliage with near-white flowers in early summer. An imposing hybrid of *H. fortunei* var. *albopicta* f. *aurea* and *H. sieboldiana*. Eric Smith, England. ↕40 in (105 cm). Z3–8 H8–3

***H.* 'So Sweet'** Vigorous, 20-in (50-cm) mound of green, elliptical 7-x-5-in (18-x-13-cm), foliage, broadening with age and edged with a ¼–½-in (0.6–1-cm) white margin. Fragrant, pale lavender flowers in late summer. Excellent for mass plantings. A seedling of 'Fragrant Bouquet'. ↕28 in (70 cm). Z3–8 H8–1

***H.* 'Spilt Milk'** Broadly oval, 10-x-8-in (25-x-20-cm) leaves with a deeply lobed base are edged with a 1–2-in (2.5–5-cm) blue-green margin; the center is misted in green and white. Makes an unmistakable 24-in- (60-cm-) high mound. Near-white flowers in midsummer. Best as a specimen. Mildred Seaver, MA. ↕30 in (75 cm). Z3–8 H8–1

***H.* 'Spinners'** see *H.* 'Antioch'. Sometimes, wrongly, said to differ from 'Antioch' in its slightly narrower leaves.

***H.* 'Spritzer'** Cascading, 22-in (55-cm) mound of gold, narrowly oval, 9-x-5 in (23-x-13 cm) foliage with a rounded base and with a 1-in (2.5-cm) green margin that may streak into the center. Lavender flowers in midsummer. A seedling of 'Green Fountain'. Paul Aden, NY. ↕30 in (75 cm). Z3–8 H8–1

***H.* 'Stiletto'** Heavily rippled, narrow, elliptical 5-x-1½-in (13-x-4-cm), green leaves that have a ⅛-in (3-mm) white margin. The rapidly growing, dense,

RIGHT 1 *Hosta sieboldii* 'Paxton's Original' **2** *H.* 'Snowden' **3** *H.* 'Snow Flakes' **4** *H.* 'Stiletto'

12 in (30 cm) high mound. Purple flowers open in midsummer. An excellent edging plant. ↕ 24 in (60 cm). Z3–8 H8–1

H. 'Striptease' (*fortunei*) Makes a 20 in (50 cm) high mound of slightly wavy, oval, 8 x 6 (20 x 15 cm) foliage; narrow gold center and 2 in (5 cm) green margin. Lavender flowers in midsummer. A tetraploid spontaneous mutation of 'Gold Standard' with wider margins. Rick and Criss Thompson, VA. ↕ 30 in (75 cm). Z3–8 H8–1

H. 'Sugar and Cream' Large, vigorous mound 24 in (60 cm) high of slightly wavy, 12-x-5 (30-x-13 cm), elliptical foliage widening with age and with a ¼–½-in (0.5–1-cm) white margin. Fragrant, pale lavender flowers in late summer. A spontaneous mutation of 'Honeybells' from Mark Zilis, IL. ↕ 45 in (110 cm). Z3–8 H8–1

H. 'Sum and Substance' Deeply lobed, slightly cupped, broadly oval, 16-x-14-in (40-x-35-cm), chartreuse to medium gold foliage. Massive, mound up to 40 x 110 in (105 x 280 cm). Lavender flowers in midsummer on drooping stems. Paul Aden, NY. ↕ 50 in (125 cm). Z3–8 H8–1

H. 'Summer Fragrance' Large, 26-in- (65-cm-) high mound of green, 12-x-9-in (30-x-22-cm) leaves with a ¼-in (0.5-cm) white margin. Fragrant, pale lavender flowers in late summer. A hybrid of *H. plantaginea* from Kevin Vaughn, OH; the first hosta with both variegated foliage and fragrant flowers. ↕ 40 in (100 cm). Z3–8 H8–1

H. 'Summer Music' Strong-growing, and making a 16-in- (40-cm-) high mound of 8-x-1½-in (20-x-4-cm), broadly oval, slightly wavy foliage with a ½-in (1-cm) green edge and the center splashed in creamy white. Lavender flowers in midsummer. Roy Klehm, IL. ↕ 24 in (60 cm). Z3–8 H8–1

H. 'Sun Power' Dramatic plant, making a 28-in- (70-cm-) high, vase-shaped mound of wavy, bright gold, 12-x-7-in (30-x-18-cm), broadly oval foliage with a cupped base. Lavender flowers in midsummer. Makes a very bright and striking specimen plant. Paul Aden, NY. ↕ 36 in (90 cm). Z3–8 H8–1

H. 'Super Nova' Large, 24-in- (60-cm-) high mound of thick, gold-centered, 13-x-9-in (33 -x-23-cm), very broadly oval foliage with a 2-in (5-cm) green edge. Near-white flowers in early summer. A spontaneous mutation of the rarely seen 'Aurora Borealis' but does not burn as easily as many of this type. ↕ 30 in (75 cm). Z3–8 H8–1

H. 'Tall Boy' Unusually dramatic in flower, the 28-in- (70-cm-) high, vase-shaped mound comprises green,

13-x-8-in (33-x-20-cm), oval, slightly wavy foliage. Lavender flowers open in late summer on very tall stems, especially when well watered. ↕ 6 ft (1.8 m). Z3–8 H8–1

H. Tardiana Group The Tardianas are the most significant group of hosta cultivars ever developed. They started with a cross between *H. tardiflora* and *H. sieboldiana* 'Elegans' made by Eric Smith of Hadspen House, Somerset, England in 1961. Thirty-two cultivars resulted from three generations of seedlings, most notably **'Halcyon'**, **'Hadspen Blue'**, **'Blue Wedgwood'**, **'Dorset Blue'**, and **'Blue Moon'**. In general, the Tardianas are medium-sized, fast-growing plants with thick-substanced, blue-green foliage. The flower color is typically a pale bluish lavender, but a few are white, near-white, or purple. Flowering times range from early summer to early fall.

H. tardiflora Thick, very shiny, dark green, 7-x-3-in (18-x-8-cm), slightly wavy, elliptical foliage. Mound 12 in (30 cm) high. Lavender, 2-in (5-cm), narrowly funnel-shaped flowers with turned-back tips open in early fall and later. Sometimes classified as a cultivar. A parent of the Tardiana Group, from Japan. ↕ 20 in (50 cm). Z3–8 H8–1

H. 'Tattoo' Quietly distinctive plants making a 12-in- (30-cm-) high mound of gold-centered, green-margined foliage with a noticeable darker watermark between the margin and the leaf center, seeming to create the outline of an inner, maplelike leaf. Lavender flowers in midsummer. Needs good drainage to prevent rotting. ↕ 18 in (45 cm). Z3–8 H8–1

H. 'Thomas Hogg' see *H.* 'Decorata'

H. tokudama Heavily corrugated, thick, blue-green, slug-resistant, 9-x-7-in (22-x-18-cm), slightly cupped, broadly oval foliage makes a slow-growing 16-in (40-cm) mound. Near-white, 2¼-in- (5.5-cm-) long, narrowly funneled flowers in early summer. Sometimes treated as a cultivar. From Japan. ↕ 24 in (60 cm). Z3–8 H8–1. **f. aureonebulosa** syn. 'Tokudama Aureonebulosa' Gold-centered foliage makes a 14-in- (36-cm-) high mound. Very slow-growing, often taking ten years to reach maturity. **f. flavocircinalis** syn. 'Tokudama Flavocircinalis' Foliage with a 1–1¾-in (2.5–4.5-cm) gold margin in a 17-in- (43-cm-) high mound. Moderate growth rate.

H. 'Torchlight' Semi-upright, 20-in- (50-cm-) high mound of dark green, 6-x-4 in (15-x-10 cm), oval foliage with ½-in (1-cm) white margin and red dots on leaf stem. Lavender flowers in late summer. Bill and Eleanor Lachman, MA. ↕ 36 in (90 cm). Z3–8 H8–1

H. 'True Blue' Medium-large, 20-in- (50-cm-) high mound of heavily corrugated, deep blue-green, broadly oval, 11-x-8 in (27-x-20 cm) foliage. Produces very pale lavender flowers in dense clusters in midsummer. Paul

LEFT 1 *Hosta* 'Striptease'
2 *H.* 'Sum and Substance'
3 *H. tokudama* f. *aureonebulosa*
4 *H.* 'Torchlight' **5** *H. ventricosa*

ABOVE 1 *Hosta venusta*
2 *H.* 'Whirlwind' **3** *H.* 'Wide Brim'

Aden, NY. ↕ 30 in (75 cm). Z3–8 H8–1

H. 'Twilight' (*fortunei*) Medium-sized, 18-in- (45-cm-) high mound of green, 9-x-6-in (22-x-15-cm), oval leaves with a distinct tip and a ½–1-in (1–2.5-cm) gold edge. A spontaneous mutation of *H. fortunei* var. *aureomarginata*, with more intense foliage colors and thicker substance. ↕ 24 in (60 cm). Z3–8 H8–1

H. undulata Small, 12 in (30 cm) high mound of twisted and curled, white-centered, narrowly elliptical foliage, with a ⅛–½-in (4–10-mm) wide green margin. The leaves often turn green in midsummer. Lavender, 2.5 in (6 cm) long, narrowly funnel-shaped flowers in midsummer, but rarely forms seedpods. Sometimes listed as a cultivar. From Japan. ↕ 30 in (75 cm). Z3–8 H8–1. **var. albomarginata** syn. *H.* 'Undulata Albomarginata', *H.* 'Thomas Hogg' Fast-growing, making 18 in (45 cm) high mound of foliage, green-centered with a ¼–½-in (5–10-mm) white margin. ↕ 40 in (100 cm). **var. erromena** syn. *H.* 'Undulata Erromena' Fast growing, 20-in- (50-cm-) high mound of medium-green foliage. ↕ 45 in (110 cm). **var. undulata** see *H. undulata.* **var. univittata** syn. *H.* 'Undulata Univittata' Vigorous 16-in- (40-cm-) high mound with 1½-in (3.5-cm) green margins. With its broader green margins, this grows more strongly than *H. undulata.* ↕ 36 in (90 cm).

H. 'Valentine Lace' Bluish green, heart-shaped, 8-x-6½-in (20-x-15-cm) leaves. Mound eventually 20-in- (50-cm-) high. Lavender flowers in midsummer. Maxine Armstrong, NE. ↕ 30 in (75 cm). Z3–8 H8–1

H. ventricosa Bold, shiny, dark green, 9-x-8-in (22-x-20-cm), broadly oval foliage, with a heart-shaped base and lightly rippled, makes a mound 22 in (55 cm) high. Bell-shaped, 2½-in (6-cm)

purple flowers in midsummer. Seedlings identical to the parent. One of the first hostas to reach Western gardens from China. ↕ 45 in (110 cm). Z3–8 H8–1. **var. aureomaculata** Leaves gold-centered in spring, all green by early summer.

H. venusta Dwarf, making a neat, dense, 6-in- (15-cm-) high mound of green, 2½-x-1¾-in (6-x-4.5-cm), oval foliage with a rounded base. Purple, 1¾-in- (4.5-cm-) long, funnel-shaped flowers in midsummer. The smallest *Hosta* species, it is an superb breeding plant. From Korea. ↕ 18 in (45 cm). Z3–8 H8–1. **'Variegated'** syn. 'Masquerade'. Slightly longer, wavy, white-centered leaves. From Japan. ↕ 20 in (50 cm).

H. 'Vera Verde' syn. *H. gracillima* 'Variegated') Low, dense, 13-in- (33-cm-) high mound of narrow, rippled, 4-x-1½-in (10-x-4-cm), wavy green foliage with very slender, 1⁄₁₆-in (1-mm) white margins. Purple flowers in late summer. From Japan. ↕ 20 in (50 cm). Z3–8 H8–1

H. 'Whirlwind' (*fortunei*) Distinctive 16-in- (40-cm-) high mound of 8-x-6-in (20-x-15-cm), broadly oval, strikingly wavy foliage, gold-centered with green veins and with 2-in (5-cm) green margins in spring, becoming completely green by midsummer. Lavender flowers in midsummer. John Kulpa, MI. ↕ 30 in (75 cm). Z3–8 H8–1

H. 'Wide Brim' Bold and vigorous, making an 18-in- (45-cm-) high mound of green, broadly oval, slightly wavy, 8-x-6-in (20-x-15-cm) foliage with a 1–2-in (2.5–5-cm) creamy yellow margin. Lavender flowers in late summer. Paul Aden, NY. ↕ 30 in (75 cm). Z3–8 H8–1

H. 'Wogon' (*sieboldii*) Small, 14 in (35 cm) high mound of narrow, thin, gold, 6-x-2-in (15-x-5-cm), lance-shaped foliage less bright in summer.

RIGHT *Houttuynia cordata* 'Chameleon'

Lavender flowers in midsummer. Formerly known as 'Wogon Gold'. ↕ 20 in (50 cm). Z3–8 H8–1

H. 'Wolverine' Vigorous, making a 16 in (40 cm) high mound of 7-x-3-in (18-x-8-cm) leaves that are blue-green in the center with a boldly contrasting ¼-in (5-mm) wide gold margin. Lavender flowers in late summer. A hybrid of 'Dorset Blue'. Jim Wilkins, MI. ↕ 24 in (60 cm). Z3–8 H8–1

H. 'Yellow River' Large, 30 in (75 cm) high, vase-shaped mound of dark green, 12-x-8-in (30-x-20-cm), broadly oval, slightly wavy foliage, with a ⅜–1⅛-in (8–14-mm) yellow margin. Near-white flowers in midsummer. An Eric Smith hosta that has only recently become popular. ↕ 40 in (100 cm). Z3–8 H8–1

H. 'Yellow Splash' Medium-sized, 18-in- (45-cm-) high mound of 7-x-3-in (18-x-8-cm), broadly elliptical foliage heavily streaked in yellow,

cream, and green. Purple flowers in late summer. Widely used as a breeding plant. Like 'Neat Splash', but slightly larger. ↕ 30 in (75 cm). Z3–8 H8–1

H. yingeri Smooth, very shiny, dark green elliptical foliage from 6 x 4 in (15 x 10 cm) to 11 x 6 in (28 x 15 cm); slightly wavy, sometimes corrugated, it makes a 12-in- (30-cm-) high mound. Purple, 1½-in- (4-cm-) long, spiderlike, narrow-petaled flowers in early fall. An unusual species discovered by Asian plant specialist Barry Yinger in 1989. From among shaded rocks on a few Korean islands. ↕ 20–30 in (50–90 cm). Z3–8 H8–1

H. 'Zounds' Dense, bold mound, 22 in (55 cm) high; heavily corrugated, bright gold, 10-x-9-in (25-x-22-cm), broadly oval leaves, deeply lobed at the base, that do not burn in spring. Very pale lavender flowers in midsummer. Paul Aden, NY. ↕ 30 in (75 cm). Z3–8 H8–1

HOUTTUYNIA
SAURURACEAE

An unusual deciduous perennial for the wild garden or pondside, or for ground cover.

A single species from Asia, it forms wide colonies, spreading by branching underground stems, and can be very invasive. The smooth, heart-shaped leaves have a sharp orange scent when bruised and are edible, either raw or cooked. Tiny white flowers without petals are held in dense, cylindrical spikes backed by petal-like bracts, creating the appearance of a single bloom rather like that of an anemone.

CULTIVATION Tolerant of a wide variety of soils from the driest to the wettest, in sun or shade. Also good in containers, where its spread can be restricted.

PROPAGATION By division when dormant, or by cuttings of young basal shoots.

PROBLEMS Trouble-free, except for its invasiveness.

H. cordata Unbranched or sparingly branched stems bear rich green, heart-shaped leaves, to 3½ in (9 cm) long, with slender, pointed tips. The flower spikes, carried at the tips of the shoots in summer, up to 1¼ in (3 cm) long, each with three to five white petal-like bracts about ¾ in (2 cm) long. From the Himalaya to Japan, Taiwan, and Java. ‡24 in (60 cm). Z5–11 H11–1. **‘Boo-Boo’** Leaves marbled gray-green and red. **‘Chameleon’** syn. ‘Tricolor’ Less vigorous; the leaves splashed and margined cream, often heavily red-flushed. **‘Flore Pleno’** syn. ‘Plena’ Pagoda-shaped flower spikes formed of many petal-like bracts. **‘Joker’s Gold’** Leaves patterned orange, gold, and green. **‘Pied Piper’** Variegated foliage in contrasting shades of red, orange, and yellow against a green background. **‘Plena’** *see* ‘Flore Pleno’. **‘Tricolor’** *see* ‘Chameleon’. **Variegata Group** Leaves variegated white, cream, or red.

HUMULUS
Hop
CANNABACEAE

Valuable foliage climbers with the bonus of hops for brewing or indoor decoration.

Two or three tough and vigorous deciduous species from woodlands, hedgerows, and scrub in Europe and Asia; *H. lupulus* has been long cultivated for brewing. A tough, fleshy, strongly spreading rootstock supports twining stems, which have a bristly surface, assisting the plant when climbing through shrubs and trees; they may reach 20 ft (6 m) or more in length. The rough, rounded, lobed leaves are a fresh green, especially when young. Male and female flowers on separate plants in mid- to late summer and are wind-pollinated; males bear insignificant clusters at the ends of shoots, while female plants bear the dense, attractive conelike heads of flowers that are of commercial value. The dried female stems are often used to make attractive garlands, and the soft young shoots are edible.

CULTIVATION Thrives in almost any fertile soil as long as it is not waterlogged, growing in sun and semishade, although golden-leaved selections are most vivid in full sun. Train stems up screens or trellises or along wires. Beware: these plants are very vigorous once established and may easily swamp smaller, slower, more delicate plants. In late fall, cut down old stems to the ground. Easy and very hardy.

PROPAGATION Divide the fleshy rootstock of mature plants in spring. Species can be grown from seed.

PROBLEMS Verticillium wilt.

H. lupulus Rampant climber with oppositely held, green, lobed leaves on bristly stems. Rather coarse for the garden, but it may be of use in wilder areas for covering unattractive structures, for brewing or culinary purposes, or for cutting, drying, and bringing indoors as decoration. The forms with colored foliage are those most often seen. Native or naturalized in much of the US. ‡20 ft (6 m). Z4–8

H8–1. **‘Aureus’** Fine, golden foliage is especially eye-catching in spring. Both male and female plants in cultivation; the male is the most widely grown, having been in cultivation for longer, but the female is more desirable, with attractive flowerheads in late summer. **‘Diva’** Shorter, female cultivar with attractive golden foliage; more easily managed than most other forms. ‡10 ft (3 m). **‘Prima Donna’** Compact, female form has smaller green leaves; excellent for garlands and brewing. ‡12 ft (4 m). **‘Taff’s Variegated’** Leaves splashed with gold: some leaves are almost entirely yellow, others mostly green with a few yellow streaks. Found by the English plant breeder Stephen Taffler, who has introduced many fine variegated plants. ‡12 ft (4 m).

HYDRASTIS
Golden seal
RANUNCULACEAE

Hardy shade-lovers whose bold, hand-shaped leaves combine well with the flowers and foliage of many other woodlanders.

Two species of deciduous plants spreading by thick rhizomes grow naturally in shady places such as mountain valleys in eastern North America and Japan. The lobed leaves far more distinctive than the small, solitary petal-less flowers appearing in spring and summer. A valuable mingler in woodland gardens.

CULTIVATION Best in rich, moisture-retentive yet well-drained, slightly acidic to neutral soil containing plenty of leafmold, and partial or dappled shade.

PROPAGATION By division in very early spring, or from seed sown as soon as ripe in an open cold frame (germination is slow and erratic). Pieces of rhizome can also be removed and grown on in a cold frame before planting out.

PROBLEMS Usually trouble-free.

H. canadensis (Golden seal, Yellow root, Turmeric root) A vigorous plant spreading by thick, yellow rhizomes, which have antibiotic properties and have long been used in herbal medicine. They support deep green basal leaves growing up to 8 in (20 cm) across, each with five to nine deeply toothed lobes. Green-white flowers, ⅝ in (1.5 cm) long, may be tinged with pink and backed by bold leaves, on stiff stems from April or May onward, followed by red berries. From eastern North America, where it is endangered over much of its range, having been overcollected for medicinal use. ‡15 in (38 cm). Z4–9 H8–4

HYLOMECON
PAPAVERACEAE

A delightful quiet woodlander, sometimes called the forest poppy, and the first poppy to flower.

GOLDEN CLIMBER COMES DOWN TO EARTH

ONE OF THE ATTRACTIVE features of the golden hop, *Humulus lupulus* ‘Aureus’, is its tendency to stray from its supports and to send yellow trails down into nearby plantings. Sometimes this can overwhelm its neighbors, but here it forms a perfect partnership with a drift of blue love-in-a-mist, *Nigella* ‘Miss Jekyll’. The intricately divided nigella foliage makes a nice contrast with the bolder hop leaves, and there are glimpses of blue-leaved dicentra, grasses, and variegated euonymus.

The one spring-flowering, patch-forming, herbaceous species, related to *Chelidonium* and *Stylophorum*, comes from shaded moist woodlands of China, Japan, and Korea. Introduced into cultivation in 1870, it has long been a popular woodland plant although it has a very short flowering season. Its green mat of foliage carpets the ground between shrubs during the summer months.

CULTIVATION Requires moist, yet well drained leafy soil in dappled shade; ideal in shaded parts of the garden or beneath trees and shrubs.

PROPAGATION From seed or by division, after flowering or in fall.

PROBLEMS Usually trouble-free.

H. japonicum syn. *Chelidonium japonicum* Slow-spreading; forms carpets of lush, deep green foliage in spring and summer. Leaves have five elliptical to lance-shaped, sharply toothed leaflets like a rose leaf. Four-petaled, saucer-shaped, 1½–2 in (3.5–5 cm) across, bright yellow poppy flowers open from erect, pear-shaped buds. They are borne singly on slender stalks just above the mat of foliage in mid- and late spring. Needs moisture-retentive soil in dappled shade and adequate moisture is summer. Dislikes exposed, dry positions. From eastern China (including Manchuria), Japan, and Korea. ‡8–12 in (20–30 cm). Z5–8 H8–5

HYLOTELEPHIUM *see* SEDUM

HYPERICUM
St. John's wort
CLUSIACEAE

Sparkling yellow stars on plants that have been used for their medicinal properties.

A varied group of over 400 annuals, perennials, shrubs, and small trees of cosmopolitan distribution; the perennials described here add a range of yellow shades to the garden. All have simple leaves in opposite pairs and terminal four- to five-petaled flowers, each with a central boss of many threadlike stamens. Many species have black or sometimes red glands on the leaves.

St. John's wort is increasingly used as a herbal treatment for depression (*see panel*) but is not universally recommended.

CULTIVATION Grow in ordinary garden soil; many thrive in alkaline conditions. A sunny position is best, although some shade is tolerated.

PROPAGATION From seed in spring under glass, or by basal cuttings.

ST. JOHN'S WORT

In recent years St. John's wort has been increasingly recognized as an alternative treatment for depression. It is approved, and widely used, in Germany and Britain and has attracted a growing following in many other countries. However, not all physicians are so enthusiastic, some having doubts about the result of combining it with other medications.

One species in particular, *Hypericum perforatum*, is used to produce the remedy. This is not one of the most colorful species, though it is a familiar European wild flower that is also naturalized in North America. In fact, in British Columbia, *H. perforatum* is listed as a pest plant: it contains a toxin that can cause cattle and sheep to become unusually sensitive to sunlight, resulting in intense skin irritation. To a limited extent, the same effect has been observed in people taking this plant as an herbal cure, so it is important that it should not be taken without prior consultation with a qualified practitioner.

Long ago, St. John's wort was also used to ward off evil spirits and, when they wore the herb in a pouch around their neck, to give warriors in battle heightened resolve.

PROBLEMS Usually trouble-free.

H. perforatum (Common St. John's wort) Clumps of erect, two-ridged stems bear opposite, narrowly oval to oblong, ½–1¼-in (1–3-cm), mid-green leaves that, when held up to the light, display many translucent, dotlike glands that give the appearance of perforations, hence the botanical name "perforatum". Broadly pyramidal clusters of bright yellow, ¾–1¼-in- (2–3-cm-) wide, star-shaped flowers appear in summer. This familiar wayside plant makes a colorful addition to the informal or wild garden. Widespread in Europe and western Asia, and naturalized in North America. ‡ 40 in (100 cm). Z7–9 H9–7 ⚠

H. tetrapterum (Square-stemmed St. John's wort) Erect four-winged stems that look square in cross-section carry ½–1¼ in (1–3 cm) long, oval to oblong leaves, which are similar to those of *H. perforatum* but even more thickly dotted with glands. Open pyramidal heads of pale yellow flowers in summer. Native to damp areas in Europe and North Africa. ‡ 32 in (80 cm). Z4–8 H8–1

HYSTRIX
Bottle brush grass
POACEAE

Attractive bristly woodland grasses, especially decorative when dried.

Nine perennial species of bottle brush grass are found in North America, temperate Asia, and New Zealand, growing in woodland and meadows. From deciduous clumps of flat and very wide leaves rise slender flower stems that support cylindrical flowerheads, which bristle like a porcupine with rigid hairs. Although the plant can look somewhat untidy, it is attractive in naturalistic plantings.

RIGHT *Hystrix patula*

ABOVE 1 *Hylomecon japonicum*
2 *Hypericum perforatum*

CULTIVATION Needs moderately fertile, damp soil in some shade.

PROPAGATION In spring, either from seed or by division.

PROBLEMS Usually trouble-free.

H. patula syn. *Elymus hystrix* (Bottle brush grass) Loose tufts of green, pointed leaves up to ½ in (1 cm) wide are tinted red in spring. In late summer to mid-fall, blue-gray flower stems carry the unusual baby-bottle-brush-shaped flowers, up to 6 in (15 cm), with stiff pink-green hairs, aging to brown. Best in an open woodland setting in drifts where the sun can filter through the spiky flowers. Needs a cool position; hot weather can make flowers turn brown and messy. Good for drying if picked while the flowers are green. Collect seeds before fully ripe, since they shatter quickly. From moist rocky woodlands in North America. ‡ 4 ft (1.2 m). Z3–9 H9–3

I

IMPATIENS
Balsam
BALSAMINACEAE

Valuable relatives of the summer seasonal bedding favorites, bringing bright colors to the border.

About 1,200 annual and perennial species are scattered throughout temperate and tropical zones (with the exception of Australasia and South America), mostly in shady or part-shaded places. The perennial species are tufted or spreading, sometimes rooting at leaf joints, with a fibrous or tuberous rootstock. Stems can be simple or variously branched; stems and leaves are generally succulent and readily wilt in dry conditions.

Leaves may be spirally arranged or borne in distinctive clusters (whorls), often lance-shaped or elliptical in outline, with a toothed margin. Each generally has one or more pairs of sticky glands at the base, which can be attractive to ants.

The flowers can be flat, cupped, or variously pouched, and are borne singly or clustered among the upper leaves, or in distinctive sprays, sometimes well above the foliage. With glistening, fleshy petals, the flowers come in a wide range of colors, although yellow, pink, purple, and red tend to dominate. They open from midsummer well into fall, often until the first frost.

The shapes of the flower parts vary enormously, but the flowers have two particular features. They are nearly always spurred behind, the spur varying from long and slender, either straight or curved, to short, incurved, and two-pronged. The succulent, club- or spindle-shaped fruits explode when ripe, expelling the seeds far away from the plant. This makes them a source of great delight to children, and indeed, some to adults, too.

CULTIVATION Best in deep, moist, humus-rich soil and dappled shade, in a woodland garden or shady border. Taller species such as *I. tinctoria* require shelter from buffeting winds. All need ample water during the growing season. The addition of a good layer of mulch (of leaf mold or sifted garden compost) is a great help in conserving moisture around the plants and helps protect them during the winter months.

PROPAGATION Take cuttings of vigorous, green, nonflowering shoots at any time from late spring to the end of summer. Strong, young basal shoots can be removed from tuberous species in spring to root as cuttings.

PROBLEMS Slugs and snails, aphids, and vine weevil.

I. arguta Sparingly branched herbaceous perennial, with erect to spreading, deep green or purple-flushed stems. The leaves are deep green, oval to lance-shaped, with a serrated margin, up to 6 in (15 cm) long and 2 in (5 cm) wide. The 1–1½ in (2.5–3.5 cm) flowers may be solitary, or paired at the base of the upper leaves and partly concealed by them; they are pink to purplish red with a whitish pouch that terminates in a short incurved spur. The upper petal has a hornlike crest. For woodland gardens, in dappled shade. Take cuttings or sow seed; it does occasionally self-sow. From the central Himalaya eastward to southwestern China. ‡ 20–28 in (50–70 cm). Z7–11 H11–7

I. omeiana A patch-forming evergreen perennial with rather thick, fleshy stems. The oval to lance-shaped, deep green leaves with their coarsely toothed margins are up to 6 in (16 cm) long and 2 in (5 cm) wide and tend to be crowded toward the shoot tips; in cultivated forms they are variegated with white along the midrib and veins. Clusters of up to eight creamy yellow, 1–1½ in (2.5–4 cm) flowers are held just clear of the foliage, each with an abruptly incurved spur. Excellent in moist, leafy soil beneath low shrubs, or makes an attractive container plant. Divide or take cuttings in early summer. From western China. ‡ 20 in (50 cm). Z6–9 H9–6

I. tinctoria A bold and impressive tuberous-rooted herbaceous plant with stout, very thick, erect, generally purplish or reddish stems, often with a few short branches above. The large, spirally arranged leaves are oblong to lance-shaped or elliptical, up to 10 in (25 cm) long and 4 in (10 cm) wide, with a serrated margin. The white flowers, with some purple markings in the center, are held clear of the foliage in clusters of up to nine, and have a large flattish lip up to 3 in (7.5 cm) across and a long, slender and incurved spur 3–5 in (7.5–12.5 cm) long. For a sheltered position in dappled shade. Divide tubers in spring or take cuttings in late spring or early summer. Tubers can be lifted and overwintered in sand in a dry frost-free place. From eastern and northeastern Africa. ‡ 6½ ft (2 m). Z10–11 H11–10

IMPERATA
POACEAE

Tropical yet fairly hardy grasses grown for their vibrant red-purple foliage.

Of the eight perennial species found growing in open cultivated and disturbed areas from the tropics to warm temperate regions, only one is generally grown in gardens. The loose, creeping clumps have strong underground roots and die back over winter. Many-branched flower stems carry spikes of tiny

ABOVE *Imperata cylindrica* 'Rubra'

flowers enveloped in long white hairs, although in cooler climates it is rarely warm enough for them to develop. Some species, mainly in tropical climates, are invasive and considered noxious weeds.

CULTIVATION Grow in a sunny position in well-drained fertile soil with plenty of moisture available. Protect in the winter with a mulch.

PROPAGATION By division in late spring.

PROBLEMS Usually trouble-free.

I. cylindrica (Halfa grass) A slowly creeping grass that forms loose clumps on short, stout roots with upright, usually in-rolled leaves, ⅝ in (1.5 cm) wide and up to 24 in (60 cm) long. These turn salmon pink to bright purple in fall before dying back over winter. Occasionally flowers in late summer to early fall in hot summers; the dense white plumes, 8 in (20 cm) long with silky white hairs, are hung with purple stamens. Plant in drifts to appreciate the fall color, or in containers, as they do in Japan. There are sometimes said to be two forms of this species, one invasive and one better-behaved, but these differences may simply be related to climate. Found in open sandy ground near rivers and the sea in hot tropical and warm temperate regions from southern Europe to Japan and Australasia. ‡ 20 in (50 cm). Z5–9 H9–3. **'Rubra'** syn. 'Red Baron' (Japanese blood grass) Foliage green at the base, striping up to deep red at the tips, and increasing in intensity through the fall. Stunning when backlit by sun or in drifts with foliage of contrasting color. This cultivar is not invasive.

INCARVILLEA
BIGNONIACEAE

Bold, trumpet-shaped flowers on neat plants that, despite their slightly exotic appearance, are easy to grow.

There are about 17 species, originating mainly from the Hindu Kush, the Himalaya, and western and northern China, but with one found in Kazakhstan. Evergreen or herbaceous, often tuberous perennials, they sometimes have an intricately branched, rather woody base (subshrubs); the leaves are undivided or divided into opposite lobes. The flowers are borne in clusters, occasionally branched, or are solitary, on strong, leafy or leafless stems. The showy funnel- or trumpet-shaped flowers are two-lipped, with the upper lip split into two lobes, and the lower into three. The fruit capsule is papery, leathery, or woody, and splits in two lengthwise to expel numerous winged or hairily tufted seeds.

BELOW *Incarvillea delavayi*

CULTIVATION The hardy species are tuberous-rooted and showy; the larger ones for herbaceous borders, the smaller for raised beds. They thrive in well-drained, loamy soil in an open, sunny, sheltered position.

The tuberous-rooted species, particularly *I. delavayi* and *I. mairei*, are often sold dried as a "bulb" and are readily grown on in the open garden or in containers. The tubers, which are carrot-shaped, should be placed thick end upward, with the top just below soil level.

PROPAGATION Sow seed in late winter or early spring, or take the summer cuttings of nonflowering shoots.

PROBLEMS Slugs and snails.

I. delavayi Herbaceous with a large basal tuft of deep green leaves, each split into 6–11 pairs of lateral leaflets with a small end leaflet. Up to ten pinkish purple to deep purple flowers, 1½–2¼ in (3.5–5.5 cm) across, with a yellowish throat and purple lines, in erect clusters from late spring to early summer, occasionally later. From southwestern China. ‡ 20–28 in (50–70 cm). Z6–10 H9–3. **'Alba'** *see* 'Snowtop'. **'Bee's Pink'** Clear pink flowers; comes true from seed. **'Snowtop'** syn. 'Alba' Pure white flowers; comes true from seed.

I. mairei Herbaceous perennial with large basal leaves divided into up to five pairs of small lateral leaflets, with one very large end leaflet. Each stem carries up to six deep pink or rose-purple flowers, 1¾–2½ in (4.5–6.5 cm) across. Plant in any reasonable, well-drained garden soil. Distinguished from *I. delavayi* mainly by its foliage. From western and southwestern China. ‡ 12–20 in (30–50 cm). Z4–8 H8–1

I. olgae An erect, herbaceous perennial with leaves split into three to four opposite pairs of narrowly elliptical lobes. From early to late summer, branched stems are topped by clusters of up to ten rose pink, rarely white, narrow funnel-shaped flowers, 1¼–1¾ in (3–4.5 cm) long overall. Can only be raised from seed. Hardy in mild areas, or grow in a cool greenhouse in gritty loam. From Turkmenistan to Tajikistan and northeastern Afghanistan. ‡ 28–39 in (70–100 cm). Z6–9 H9–6

I. zhongdianensis Tufted herbaceous perennial with shiny to matte green leaves in a large basal tuft. Each leaf is split into five to nine pairs of lance-shaped to elliptical, faintly toothed leaflets, with an end leaflet that is marginally larger than the others. In early summer and midsummer, one or several erect stems each carry up to three deep magenta or crimson-magenta flowers, 2½–3¼ in (6.5–8.5 cm) across, with a yellowish throat and white flares at the base of each lobe. Plant in well-drained soil in full sun, preferably in a sheltered position. From southwestern China (northwestern Yunnan province). ‡ 16–24 in (40–60 cm). Z6–9 H9–6

INULA
Elecampane, Fleabane
ASTERACEAE

Robust yellow daisies, the taller species useful as a strong structural element in the garden.

About 100 species, mostly perennial, are native to habitats from dry mountain slopes to moist lowlands in Europe, Africa, and Asia. They are clump-forming or spread by means of rhizomes. Taller species have bold, broad, alternate, unlobed leaves and stout, erect stems with large yellow daisies held solitarily up the stem or spaced out in clusters. The flowerheads have slightly darker yellow centers, while the ray florets are numerous and characteristically narrow, giving a spidery appearance. The shorter species tend to have narrower leaves and solitary flowerheads at the apex of each stem; others are stemless. The three giants are *I. helenium*, *I. magnificum*, and *I. racemosa*. They are distinguished from the otherwise similar *Telekia* and *Buphthalmum* by the absence of scales between the disk florets.

CULTIVATION All prefer deep, fertile, moisture-retentive soil in full sun or part-shade. The taller species need plenty of space in a large border or informal area. The tallest of all may need support in windy situations.

PROPAGATION By division in early fall or spring.

PROBLEMS Usually trouble-free.

I. ensifolia Clump-forming, deciduous, virtually hairless; sometimes spreading slowly by rhizomes, with unbranched stems bearing linear to narrowly lance-shaped, parallel-veined, untoothed leaves to 3½ in (9 cm) long. A yellow flowerhead, up to 2 in (5 cm) across, is borne at the apex of each stem between early and late summer; the ray florets clearly spiraled in bud, unfurling prettily. Mature plants form a dense mound studded with flowers. Tolerant of dry soil. Native to dry slopes from southern and central Europe to the Caucasus. ‡ 10–15 in (20–35 cm). Z4–9 H9–1

I. helenium (Elecampane) Robust, deep-rooted, deciduous with short rhizomes and large, toothed, broadly elliptic leaves, hairless and wrinkled above, white-hairy beneath, up to 32 in (80 cm) long. Stout, angular, hairy, leafy stems branch at the apex, where they produce large yellow flowerheads up to 3½ in (9 cm) across from early to late summer. Differs from *I. magnifica* in its longer, broader leaves with their white-hairy undersides and its smaller flowerheads. Prefers moisture-retentive soil and tolerates part-shade. Colonies are renowned for being long-lived. The aromatic rhizomes have a long history of medicinal use. Native to western and central Asia, but widely naturalized in Europe and western and eastern North America. ‡ 3¼–6½ ft (1–2 m). Z5–8 H8–5

ABOVE *Inula helenium*

I. hookeri Clump-forming, deciduous, hairy perennial, sometimes spreading slowly by rhizomes. The leaves are lance-shaped to narrowly elliptical, up to 6 in (15 cm) long, and margined with small, glandular teeth. Normally unbranched stems bear solitary yellow flowerheads up to 2½ in (6 cm) across, from whiskery, hairy buds in mid- and late summer. The ray florets are a paler, more greenish yellow than those of other species, the disk florets orange-yellow. Prefers cool temperate climates and moisture-retentive soil. Native to open woodlands in the Himalaya. ‡ 30 in (75 cm). Z4–8 H8–1

I. magnifica Clump-forming, deciduous perennial with large, elliptical to egg-shaped, coarsely hairy, toothed leaves to 10 in (25 cm) long. Erect, hairy, purple-flushed leafy stems branch widely at the apex, where they bear large flowerheads, to 6 in (15 cm) across, from early summer to midsummer. Differs from *I. helenium* in the shorter, narrower leaves and larger flowerheads. Suitable for waterside or boggy conditions. Native to alpine meadows and woodland clearings in the eastern Caucasus. ‡ 6½ ft (2 m). Z5–8 H8–5. **'Sonnenstrahl'** More floriferous; raised by Ernst Pagels, Leer, Germany.

I. orientalis Deciduous perennial spreading by rhizomes with stalkless, elliptical to egg-shaped, toothed leaves to 5½ in (14 cm) long. Unbranched, erect, leafy stems bear solitary orange-yellow flowerheads, to 3½ in (9 cm) across, from densely hairy buds for a short period between early summer and midsummer. Best in rich, moisture-retentive soil. Native to damp places in the Caucasus and Turkey. ‡ 16–32 in (40–80 cm). Z4–8 H8–1

I. racemosa Clump-forming, deciduous perennial with large, elliptic to lance-shaped, toothed leaves to 12 in (30 cm)

long. The lower leaves have short stalks, while the upper are stalkless. Short-stalked or stalkless, yellow flowerheads, up to 2½ in (6 cm) across, are borne close to the main axis of the sturdy, erect, leafy, purple-flushed stem, forming an imposing spirelike head from mid- to late summer. Prefers deep, rich soil. From disturbed habitats in the western Himalaya. ‡ 6½–8 ft (2–2.5 m). Z6–9 H9–6. **'Sonnenspeer'** Taller: ‡ 10 ft (3 m).

I. rhizocephala Rosette-forming perennial with broadly lance-shaped, untoothed, blunt-tipped, ground-hugging leaves to 4¾ in (12 cm) long with wide yellowish-green midribs. The stalkless, yellow flowerheads, ranging from ¾–1½ in (2–4 cm) across, are borne in tight clusters at the center of the rosette in early summer. The central flowerhead is usually larger than its satellites. Grows best in a sunny, well-drained site but can be short-lived. Native to high-altitude rocky slopes in eastern Iran, Afghanistan, and Central Asia. ‡ 4 in (10 cm). Z4–8 H8–1

I. royleana (Himalayan elecampane) Clump-forming, deciduous perennial bearing egg-shaped leaves, up to 10 in (25 cm) long, with deeply impressed veins. The basal leaves have long, winged leaf stalks. Erect stems with smaller, stalkless leaves bear large, solitary, orange-yellow flowerheads to 4¾ in (12 cm) across with long, drooping ray florets, emerging from dark buds between early summer and early fall. A choice plant with oversize flowers, but slow-growing, needing a deep, rich, moist soil and preferring cool temperate climates. Native to forests and scrub in the western Himalaya. ‡ 24 in (60 cm). Z4–8 H8–1

IRIS
IRIDACEAE

Internationally popular and often flamboyant plants for a variety of garden situations.

About 300 species are found wild in a wide range of habitats throughout the Northern Hemisphere. All are perennials, with stolons (rhizomes that creep along or under the soil) and these may be fleshy and thick or wiry and woody; alternatively, they develop bulbs (not included here). A few are evergreen or partially so; most are deciduous, with slender, even grass-like to broadly sword-shaped foliage usually held upright and often making an attractive feature in its own right.

Iris flowers are unmistakable. Individually, they last only a few days, but most plants carry branched stems and most species flower for several weeks. The majority of herbaceous species and cultivars bloom from early to midsummer, but some remontant (reblooming) cultivars flower again later in the season (*see Remontant Irises, p.283*). Flowers often give way to fat seed-pods with three or six angles.

Irises are classified primarily according to whether they are rhizomatous or bulbous. Those with rhizomes (which form the majority) are then split into groups according to whether or not they have a beard (*see table, p.275*) and other characteristics. Bulbous irises are not covered here except for Juno irises, which, while sometimes described as bulbous, have fat fleshy roots as well as bulbs.

Usually represented in gardens by bearded irises that flower in early

BEARDED IRISES GROUPED BY SIZE

Bearded irises are classified according to their height and flower size (the abbreviations below appear in their entries). In order of flowering time, they are:

Miniature Dwarf Bearded (MDB)
Flowers up to 2¾ in (7 cm) across, with narrow falls, on stems up to 8 in (20 cm) tall. The first to bloom.

Standard Dwarf Bearded (SDB)
Flowers up to 3 in (8 cm) across on branched stems 8–16 in (20–40 cm) tall. They tolerate shade better than taller hybrids but flower best in full sun.

Intermediate Bearded (IB) Flowers up to 4¾ in (12 cm) across on stems 16–28 in (40–70 cm) tall.

Miniature Tall Bearded (MTB)
Flowers up to 3 in (8 cm) across on 16–26-in (40–65-cm) stems.

Border Bearded (BB) Flowers up to 5 in (13 cm) across on stems 16–28 in (40–70 cm) tall.

Tall Bearded (TB) Flowers up to 6 in (15 cm) across, sometimes as large as 9 in (22 cm), on 28–34-in (70–85-cm) stems though sometimes as tall as 39 in (100 cm). Later-flowering.

BEARDED AND BEARDLESS IRISES

Irises are divided into two distinct groups—bearded irises and beardless irises—although the flowers of both groups are still unmistakably irises and have their own unique terminology. Bearded irises are themselves classified by height and flower size (*see Bearded Irises Grouped by Size*) and also by flower pattern (*see Flower Patterns in Bearded Irises, p.276*); these patterns can be found across most of the groups. Beardless irises are divided into a number of botanical groups (*see p.275*).

Fall   Haft   Beard   Standard

Bearded iris (*I. 'Rajah'*)

Standard

Petal-like style ("stigma flap")

Signal

Fall

Beardless iris (*I. douglasiana*)

summer, the genus *Iris* includes plants for dry soil and wet. Some are easy to grow, others challenge even experienced enthusiasts. They show some resistance to deer and rabbits. ⚠

CULTIVATION Mainly sun-lovers, but different types are suited to different situations (*see table p.275*), from sunny, well-drained beds at one extreme to damp watersides at the other. It is important to choose the right type for the right situation.

PROPAGATION Species by division and from seed; cultivars by division only (*see table, p.275*).

PROBLEMS Bearded irises are affected by slugs and snails, and viruses as well as the major problems of iris borer and bacterial soft rot on some species (*see table, p.275*).

I. **'Acoma'** (TB, Plicata) Sky blue standards with ruffled white falls edged violet and a small yellow beard. Broad, elegant, scented, but not an especially prolific flowerer, with five or six buds per stem from late spring to early summer. ↕ 32 in (80 cm). Z3–9 H9–1

I. **'Action Front'** (TB, Bicolor) Copper-red standards, mahogany-maroon falls with creamy veins, and a bold, bright orange beard. Soft scent, with up to eight flowers per stem. Early summer. ↕ 32 in (80 cm). Z3–8 H9–1

I. **'Afternoon Delight'** (TB, Blend) Honey-tan standards flushed lavender, tan-edged lavender falls, and a yellow beard open from rusty brown buds in early summer. Vigorous and well-ruffled. ↕ 32 in (80 cm). Z3–8 H9–1

I. **'Alcazar'** (TB, Bitone) Pale purple standards, deep purple falls, and yellow beards, on strongly striped petal stalks. Narrow petals. Introduced by Vilmorin in 1910 and still popular. Early summer. ↕ 32 in (80 cm). Z3–8 H9–1

I. **'Alizes'** (TB, Amoena) Pure white, ruffled standards, faintly tinted blue in some situations, above white falls

broadly edged with sky blue and with a yellow beard. Early summer. ↕ 34 in (85 cm). Z3–8 H9–1

I. **'Amber Queen'** (MDB, Bitone) Pale primrose standards and narrow yellow-amber falls with an amber beard. Rather small flowers. Late spring. ↕ 8 in (20 cm). Z3–8 H9–1

I. **'Amethyst Flame'** (TB, Self) Ruffled lavender-blue, a lavender beard, and fiery orange-red flares at sides of petal stalks. An early award-winner. Early summer. ↕ 32 in (80 cm). Z3–9 H9–1

I. **'Apricot Drops'** (MTB, Self) The incurved wrinkled standards are pale apricot, tinted more yellow around the margin; the rather drooping falls are a grayed orange with a deep orange beard, tipped yellow. Vigorous, with bluish-green leaves. Late spring. ↕ 26 in (65 cm). Z3–8 H9–1

I. **'Arctic Fancy'** (IB, Plicata) White waved standards with broad violet margins, white falls with a narrower violet edge then dark veins fading into white; a white beard with a yellow tip. Superb. Late spring/early summer. ↕ 18 in (45 cm). Z4–9 H8–1

I. **'Ask Alma'** (IB, Self) Standards and falls pale coral orange, prettily veined then more richly colored at the base, with white and tangerine beards. Elegant and vigorous. Late spring/early summer. ↕ 24 in (60 cm). Z3–8 H9–1

I. **'Austrian Sky'** (SDB, Neglecta) The standards are pale blue with darker veins. The falls are darker blue with white in the throat. Floriferous and reliable. Mid-/late spring. ↕ 12 in (30 cm). Z3–8 H9–1

BELOW *Iris* 'Alcazar'

BEARDED IRISES

This is by far the most popular group around the world. Bearded irises have thick, woody, branching rhizomes carrying, at their tips, fans of upright, sword-shaped foliage. Their flowers, usually several to a stem, are distinguished by a furry "beard" on the falls, usually in a contrasting color. The standards may be upright or, more commonly, curve inward at the top. Traditionally, the falls hang down vertically, showing the most color on tall cultivars when viewed from the side. However, in modern cultivars they may "flare" and be presented almost horizontally—more effective when dwarf cultivars are viewed from above. The majority are fragrant, but some have a strong scent which, while welcome in the garden, may seem less pleasant when flowers are picked for the home.

The species are not commonly grown but there are thousands of hybrids, originally derived from *I. pallida* and other species. They flower for about two months from mid-spring to early summer, the smaller-growing cultivars blooming earlier. New patterns and shapes are constantly being bred. Both standards and falls may be ruffled; some are laced, frilled with small, needlelike growth; the upper part of the fall (haft) is usually striped but modern cultivars may have "clean" hafts. "Space-age" irises have extra petal tissue at the end of their beards, though its appearance is often erratic. Remontant (reblooming) irises (*see Remontant Irises, p.283*) do not follow a fixed pattern of growth and flowering and can, if conditions allow, flower later in summer; this feature can be unpredictable in cool climates.

Cultivation Bearded irises prefer well-drained ground in a sunny spot. Alkaline soil is best but not essential. They do not thrive in wet soil or when crowded; debris must be cleared from around the rhizomes in fall and winter.
Propagation Divide every 3–4 years, preferably about a month after flowering when root growth begins again. Plants can be divided in early spring but flowering will be affected that summer. When dividing, select strong fans, trim the rhizome to about 4 in (10 cm) (less for dwarf types) and trim back the foliage by at least half to prevent plant movement while the roots establish.
Problems Prone to slugs and snails. Susceptible to iris borer, which subjects the rhizome to bacterial soft rot. Plants degenerate when affected by virus. Rhizomes suffer from fungal and bacterial rots when grown in wet soils. Leaves can be harmed by leaf spot in wet seasons.

Aril irises An exotic-looking, demanding, rarely grown group, often known by their botanical classification of *Oncocyclus* and *Regelia*. They include *I. hoogiana*, *I. iberica*, and *I. paradoxa*. They come from areas with dry, cold winters, dry summers, and wet springs; plants are difficult to grow in most temperate areas because wet winters encourage

early leaf growth vulnerable to frost. Although these species have beards, in other ways they are very different from the more familiar bearded irises above. Some aril irises have been hybridized with bearded irises to produce **aril bred** irises. These combine some of the exotic appearance of the aril irises with the ease of cultivation of bearded irises.

Cultivation Because of the difficulty in cultivating them in the garden, aril irises are often grown in a bulb frame with demanding bulbs.
Propagation By division after flowering, or from seed.
Problems Flower stems may be subject to aphid attack. Most are vulnerable to virus diseases, so propagation from seed is advisable.

BEARDLESS IRISES

Large group of valuable, generally summer-flowering plants suitable for either moist or wet soils. Two

exceptions are *I. foetidissima*, which has colorful seedpods, and winter-blooming *I. unguicularis*.

Pacific Coast Irises (PCI) and California Hybrids (CH) About 15 species from the west coast of the US, mostly small, neat plants, ideal for edging and small borders, that flower in early summer. They have thin foliage and stems with two or three flowers in a wide range of colors. *I. douglasiana* is the most robust and easiest to grow. Some, from more southerly parts, are not reliably hardy in most temperate gardens.

Hybrids among the species, with bright flowers with flaring falls, usually delicately veined, are called California Hybrids (CH); their need for a neutral or acidic soil has restricted their popularity. Modern cultivars have larger flowers than the species with broad, often ruffled petals in bright, often contrasting colors. Newer hybrids between PCIs and Siberian irises (Calsibs) are not yet widely available.

Cultivation Generally easy, given well-drained, neutral or slightly acidic soil in full sun or part-shade.
Propagation Easy from seed (though the resulting plants may be variable) and easy to divide. In general, they dislike root disturbance and, once established, should be divided only when essential, preferably in spring or early fall.
Problems Usually trouble-free.

Siberian irises Eleven species of clump-forming plants with narrow leaves and tall stems of elegant flowers, usually blooming in midsummer. They are divided into two groups according to the number of chromosomes: those with 28 (noted as Siberian/28), are most familiar and include the western *I. sibirica* and *I. sanguinea*. Those with 40 chromosomes (Siberian/40), including

I. chrysographes from Asia, have smaller flowers and flower slightly later, but their drooping, rather than flaring, falls give an elegant appearance. The two groups have been hybridized to create the Sino-Sibs (usually listed under *I. sibirica* for convenience). Modern hybrids tend to have broad, horizontal falls. Some are remontant (repeat-flowering).

Cultivation Best in sun or part-shade in moist soil that does not dry out in summer.
Propagation Divide in fall or spring.
Problems Usually trouble-free.

Spuria irises These tall plants with bold, upright foliage form creeping, woody rhizomes. In the wild, most are found in damp places. They bloom with and after Siberian irises; their large flowers have

narrow falls and standards. The species are not grown as often as hybrids, except for two unusual plants, smaller than most: *I. graminea* and *I. kerneriana*. These stylish plants should be more widely grown.

Cultivation Growth best in full sun; thrive in any fertile garden soil, or clay enriched with organic matter.
Propagation Division in spring or late summer.
Problems Usually trouble-free.

Laevigata (Water irises) Range of species that prefer full sun and generally require soils that are moist in summer. Two are widely grown for their spectacular and beautiful flowers. *Iris ensata*, the Japanese water iris, has flowers to 10 in (25 cm) wide in midsummer.

It has been highly bred and double cultivars, with flowers resembling large clematis, are prized. *Iris laevigata* is similar but has smaller flowers. Others in this group include the European yellow flag, *I. pseudacorus*, and the North American *I. versicolor*.

Cultivation Will not thrive in cold winter areas or in dry soil.
Propagation By division in spring or late summer or from seed.
Problems Usually trouble-free.

Louisiana irises This small group of species from the southeastern US and their hybrids need moist soil, full sun, and warm summers. Their rather flat,

often large, flowers are produced on zigzagging stems. *Iris fulva* is the easiest to grow, but is not as spectacular as the hybrids.

Cultivation Not for cold-winter areas or dry soil.
Propagation Divide in spring or late summer; from seed.
Problems Usually trouble-free.

Crested irises This group produces branched stems of rather flat flowers with horizontal standards and, instead of a furry beard on the falls, a toothed crest or crests. The flowers are usually white or blue and

are produced in late spring or summer. Predominantly Asian, they vary from small, creeping plants to unusual perennials with fans of foliage on upright stems.

Cultivation Most prefer moist, humus-rich soil and sun or light shade.
Propagation By division in spring or after flowering.
Problems Usually trouble-free.

Juno irises About 50 spring-flowering species with bulbs with just a few scales, thick, fleshy roots, and fleshy leaves in two ranks, looking rather like leeks. The stems have several flowers, distinguished by small, drooping standards. Most are from areas with

cold, dry winters and hot summers, and, hating winter rain, are suitable only for bulb frames or alpine houses, but a few, notably *I. magnifica* and *I. bucharica*, can be grown outside, in a raised rock garden or sunny bed at the base of a wall.

Cultivation They demand a sunny spot and soil that is well drained, especially in winter.
Propagation From seed, or by division when dormant.
Problems Slugs and snails may eat new growth.

I. **'Autumn Circus'** (TB, Plicata) Intricately patterned, ruffled flowers with white standards, stippled in deep blue, coalescing into a solid edge. Falls white, densely colored at the edge, with strong deep blue veins and yellow-tipped beards. Late spring. Remontant. Gorgeous. ‡34 in (85 cm). Z3–9 H9–1

I. **'Baby Blessed'** (SDB, Self) Standards and falls pale yellow, the falls with a pale beard from which radiate white veins. Mid-spring. Vigorous and remontant. ‡10 in (25 cm). Z3–9 H9–1

I. **'Batik'** (BB, Broken Self) Eccentric, deep purple-blue flowers with erratic white stripes through the standards and falls with an orange beard. A striking, but a love-it-or-hate-it plant. Early summer. ‡28 in (70 cm). Z3–9 H9–1

I. **'Bedford Lilac'** (SDB, Self) Neat, pale blue, inward-curving standards and almost horizontal, slightly pointed, pale blue falls, prettily veined in darker blue with a slightly darker blue beard. Mid-spring. ‡12 in (30 cm). Z4–9 H8–1

I. **'Bee's Knees'** (SDB, Self) Slightly wrinkled flowers. The standards are pale peachy yellow, fading to cream at the center with purple veins; the horizontal falls are palest peach, deepening at the base and veined in maroon with a maroon beard. Late spring. ‡16 in (40 cm). Z3–8 H9–1

I. **'Before the Storm'** (TB, Self) Lavish, lightly fragrant, velvety blooms, lightly ruffled, in dark deep purple with raised falls and matching beard tipped in brown. Pictured as true black in some catalogs, but not quite. Early summer. ‡32 in (80 cm). Z3–8 H9–1

I. **'Berkeley Gold'** (TB, Self) Bright golden yellow, slightly ruffled standards with golden falls veined in deeper gold and a bright orange beard. The leaves are strongly purple-tinted at the base. Slightly scented. Late spring/early summer. ‡38 in (95 cm). Z3–8 H9–1

I. **'Berlin Tiger'** (Laevigata) Small, deep yellow flowers overlaid with dark, brownish purple veins borne on tall branched stems in summer. Better in rich moist soil than in water. A seedling from 'Holden Clough'. Midsummer. ‡4 ft (1.2 m). Z3–8 H9–1

I. **'Best Bet'** (TB, Bitone) Ruffled flowers, pale blue standards; deep purple-blue flaring falls tend toward horizontal. Prolific, scented seedling of 'Titan's Glory'. Sometimes remontant. Early summer. ‡34 in (85 cm). Z3–8 H9–1

I. **'Betty Simon'** (TB, Bicolor) Lightly ruffled flowers with lemon yellow standards and lilac falls, with bronze petal stalks. Yellow beards match standards. Well-branched stems. Late spring/early summer. ‡34 in (85 cm). Z3–9 H9–1

I. **'Beverly Sills'** (TB, Self) Large, ruffled and laced, bright coral pink standards and falls with a paler zone in the center of the falls and an orange beard. Vigorous and free-flowering with a sweet scent. Superb. Late spring/early summer. ‡34 in (85 cm). Z3–9 H9–1

I. **'Bibury'** (SDB, Self) Large, ruffled, creamy white standards and falls with a pale yellow petal stalk and a blue beard. Free-flowering and vigorous. Mid-/late spring. ‡12 in (30 cm). Z3–8 H9–1

I. **'Big Money'** (PCI/CH) Vigorous, clump-forming, evergreen iris with long, narrow, grassy leaves and yellow flowers. The standards are pale yellow with darker veins and the falls have a central, darker patch and delicate brown veins. Late spring. ‡18 in (45 cm). Z3–8 H9–1

I. **'Black Gamecock'** (Louisiana) Large, 4 in (10 cm) inky purple flowers with horizontal standards and falls sparked with a bright gold flash. Evergreen and extremely vigorous. Midsummer. ‡38 in (95 cm). Z5–10 H10–5

I. **'Black Swan'** (TB, Self) Medium-sized flowers with deepest purple standards and black, partially raised falls. Introduced in 1960. Still popular, although more recent introductions are darker. Early summer. ‡34 in (85 cm). Z3–8 H9–1

I. **'Blackbeard'** (BB, Self) Elegant, pale blue standards, partially raised falls and inky blue beards around a few dark lines. Vigorous and prolific. Late spring/early summer. ‡26 in (65 cm). Z3–8 H9–1

I. **'Blenheim Royal'** (TB, Self) Deep, rich blue, pretty waved, ruffled standards and falls, and six or seven buds per stem. Fragrant, and moodily stylish. Early summer. ‡3¼ ft (1 m). Z3–8 H9–1

I. **'Blue Ballerina'** (PCI/CH) Clump-forming evergreen with narrow foliage. White flowers with purple veins radiating from the small orange signal on the falls. Late spring. ‡16 in (40 cm). Z3–8 H9–1

I. **'Blue Denim'** (SDB, Self) Pretty, pale blue standards and falls; darker veins, especially at sides of falls, a white beard, and an orange throat. Mid-/late spring. ‡12 in (30 cm). Z3–8 H9–1

I. **'Blue Line'** (SDB, Self) White, slightly incurved standards and white falls, both slightly honeyed at the base; sometimes faintly tinted blue, with a bright blue beard. Sweetly scented. Late spring. ‡16 in (40 cm). Z3–8 H9–1

I. **'Blue Luster'** (TB, Self) Large, silky, lightly ruffled flowers, the standards violet-blue and falls deeper violet with darker veins and a blue beard. Early summer. ‡3¼ ft (1 m). Z3–8 H9–1

FLOWER PATTERNS IN BEARDED IRISES

Amoena ('Alizes') Colored falls; paler standards. Reverse Amoenas have the opposite coloration.

Bicolor ('Edith Wolford') Standards and falls of differing colors.

Bitone ('Party Dress') Standards the same color as the falls, but paler.

Blend ('Brown Lasso') Two or more colors are intermixed.

Luminata ('Fancy Woman') Wash of color in falls with paler white or yellow veining.

Plicata ('Stepping Out') Pale ground "stitched" with a contrasting dark color around the edge.

Self ('Amethyst Flame') Predominantly one color. A pattern of irregular stripes and lines of a (usually paler) color is called "broken self."

Variegata ('Bumblebee Delite') Yellow falls and maroon standards—the typical coloration of *I. variegata* (see p.289).

I. **'Blue Pools'** (SDB, Self) White with a dark purple-blue blotch on the falls around a pale yellow beard. Mid-/late spring. ‡12 in (30 cm). Z3–8 H9–1

I. **'Blue Rhythm'** (TB, Self) Mid-blue, narrow-petaled blooms, the standards slightly paler; falls with an orange beard. Despite an "old-fashioned" shape, popular because of its ease of growth, long season, and lemon scent. Early summer. ‡3¼ ft (1 m). Z3–9 H9–1

I. **'Blue Shimmer'** (TB, Plicata) Pale blue-purple standards, stippled over white toward the center. Narrow white falls broadly edged and in turn stippled with pale blue-purple, with yellow beards. Very fragrant and prolific. Early summer. ‡36 in (90 cm). Z3–8 H9–1

I. **'Blue Suede Shoes'** (TB, Self) Large, ruffled, navy blue flowers with yellow beards tipped in white. Bold, dramatic, scented, very vigorous, prolific, and remontant. Early summer. ‡3¼ ft (1 m). Z3–8 H9–1

I. **'Bold Print'** (IB, Plicata) Neat, dainty, gently waved white flowers, the standards with a bold purple edge, the falls with a prettily stitched slimmer margin and a white, blue-tipped beard. Neat and pretty. Late spring/early summer. ‡22 in (55 cm). Z3–8 H9–1

I. **'Boogie Woogie'** (TB, Amoena) Unusual, with ruffled white standards slightly purple-tinted at the base, and raised blue falls striped with purple, more densely toward the edge, and a yellow beard. Early summer. ‡3¼ ft (1 m). Z5–9 H9–5

I. **'Braithwaite'** (TB, Amoena) Pale blue standards, velvety, deep royal purple falls and yellow beards. Classic, unruffled, and traditional with a fruity scent. Early summer. ‡34 in (85 cm). Z3–8 H9–1

I. **'Brassie'** (SDB, Self) Slightly brassy yellow standards and slightly paler, green-tinted falls with a few dark mustard veins to the sides and a pale primrose beard. Mid-/late spring. ‡12 in (30 cm). Z3–8 H9–1

I. **'Brazilian Holiday'** (TB, Amoena) White, lavender-flushed standards and sumptuous rich plum falls with orange beards and mustard style arms. Vigorous, well-branched stems with large, ruffled flowers. Very vigorous, with branched stems and a mass of buds. Early summer. ‡3¼ ft (1 m). Z3–8 H9–1

I. **'Breakers'** (TB, Self) Large, heavily ruffled flowers of rich uniform blue with a white beard tipped in pale yellow, carried on well-branched stems. Early summer. May bloom again in the fall. ‡3¼ ft (1 m). Z3–9 H9–1

I. **'Bright White'** (MDB, Self) Pure white standards and falls, with a slightly creamy beard. Mid-/late spring. ‡8 in (20 cm). Z3–8 H9–1

I. **Broadleigh Series** (PCI/CH) A valuable range of Pacific Coast Irises

raised by Christine Skelmersdale at Broadleigh Gardens, Somerset, England. Always featured at the Chelsea Flower Show, a few are widely popular, some are rarely seen. **'Broadleigh Rose'** (CH) Clump-forming, with narrow foliage and rich, mulberry-pink blooms with paler standards. Falls have maroon-veined, bright yellow signals. Late spring. ‡16 in (40 cm). Z3–8 H9–1

I. **'Bromyard'** (SDB, Bicolor) Blue-gray standards; the falls also blue-gray with a large ocher-yellow patch and a yellow beard. Late spring. ‡12 in (30 cm). Z3–8 H9–1

I. **'Bronzaire'** (IB, Bitone) Ruffled, incurved, honey gold standards with lightly ruffled falls in golden bronze with a few purple flecks and a brown beard. Late spring/early summer. ‡28 in (70 cm). Z3–8 H9–1

I. **'Brown Lasso'** (BB, Blend) Striking and unusual. Lightly ruffled, perfectly formed flowers have butterscotch standards and horizontal lilac falls, edged brown, and a golden beard. Early summer. ‡24 in (60 cm). Z3–8 H9–1

I. *bucharica* (Juno) Glossy, bright green, leeklike, 8-x-1¼ in (20-x-3 cm) foliage in two ranks with branched spikes of up to six, 1½–2½ in (4–6 cm) flowers, opening downward from the top, in mid-spring. Each flower has upright, outward-reaching, white or yellow standards and yellow falls, the white petal stalk striking upward and the yellow blade curving downward. The all-yellow form is sometimes, incorrectly, grown as *I. orchioides*. The easiest Juno iris to grow outside, requiring well-drained soil and full sun. Ideal for raised beds, especially if protected from early winter rains. From rocky places in northeastern Afghanistan and Central Asia. ‡16 in (40 cm). Z5–9 H9–5

I. *bulleyana* (Siberian/40) Neat with very slender, 6–18 in (15–45 cm) leaves that remain over winter, turning reddish brown. One or two 2½–3 in (6.5–7.5 cm) flowers appear in early summer on unbranched stems when foliage has expanded. The erect, pale violet standards are slightly outward-facing and the blue-purple falls are marked with white and yellow. For moist soils in sun or part-shade. From China. ‡18 in (45 cm). Z5–9 H9–5

I. **'Bumblebee Deelite'** (MTB, Variegata) Startlingly patterned, petite flowers with yellow incurved standards and maroon falls, edged bright yellow with striped petal stalks and a yellow beard. Easy to grow. Late spring/early summer. ‡20 in (50 cm). Z3–8 H9–1

I. **'Butterscotch Kiss'** (TB, Self) Very large, ruffled flowers with pale honey-caramel standards, similar falls, but mauve-shaded with an orchid beard and spicy scent. Early summer. ‡3¼ ft (1 m). Z3–8 H9–1

RIGHT 1 *Iris* 'Before the Storm'
2 *I.* 'Blue Denim' **3** *I.* 'Braithwaite'

IRISES AND MIMULUS IN A DAMP BORDER

THE VARIEGATED FORM of the yellow flag iris, *I. pseudacorus* 'Variegata', can be a spectacular plant in moist conditions like these, especially when grown with a bushy neighbor in a complementary color, like this cheeky mimulus, around the base. But there are lessons here... On the right, the iris foliage has reverted to plain green, and this part of the plant is already growing vigorously; it may not take over from its more attractive variegated parent entirely, but it should have been removed when it first appeared. While the iris has been allowed to revert, the mimulus has clearly been dead-headed efficiently, for these hybrid mimulus tend to vary in the coloring of the self-sown seedlings, and this detracts from the display. Prompt dead-heading, as here, prevents the problem and also extends the flowering season of the parent.

I. **'Cannington Bluebird'** (TB, Plicata) Superb large flowers. White-centered blue standards, white-centered blue falls, and violet edges. Sadly, neglected. Early summer. ↕ 36 in (90 cm). Z3–8 H9–1

I. **'Carolyn Rose'** (MTB, Plicata) Lovely, old-fashioned-looking, with white incurved standards heavily veined in rosy purple, especially toward edges. Almost circular arching falls are less patterned with an orange beard. ↕ 24 in (60 cm). Early summer. Z3–8 H9–1

I. **'Cee Jay'** (IB, Plicata) Ruffled white standards broadly margined in deep violet-blue, ruffled white falls with a narrower violet-blue edge, and a violet beard. Good form. Late spring. ↕ 24 in (60 cm). Z3–8 H9–1

I. **'Celebration Song'** (TB, Bicolor) Large, ruffled flowers with apricot-pink standards and lilac falls, paler around the orange beard. Vigorous, well-branched, and long-flowering, with many buds per stem. Early summer. ↕ 38 in (95 cm). Z3–8 H9–1

I. chamaeiris see *I. lutescens*.

I. **'Champagne Elegance'** (TB, Amoena) Large, ruffled, fragrant flowers, white standards, and pale pink-buff falls with a yellow beard. Color varies with temperature: often tinged with lilac in cool weather. Remontant. Early summer. ↕ 38 in (95 cm). Z3–8 H9–1

I. **'Change of Pace'** (TB, Plicata) Broad, ruffled, fragrant, flaring flowers. Rose-pink standards and broad, almost rounded white falls, broadly edged with purple. Caramel style arms. Early summer. ↕ 41 in (105 cm). Z3–8 H9–1

I. **'Chanted'** (SDB, Self) Soft, muted pink standards; similar falls with striking, deep lavender-blue beards enhanced by a surrounding, paler area. Mid-/late spring. ↕ 12 in (30 cm). Z3–8 H9–1

I. **'Chantilly'** (TB, Blend) Frilly-edged, pinkish standards shading to golden-bronze at the base; white falls, yellow-striped petal stalk, shading to pinkish-bronze at the frilly edges and with an orange beard. Scented and beautifully shaped, but sparse. Early summer. ↕ 32 in (80 cm). Z3–8 H9–1

I. **'Cherry Garden'** (SDB, Bitone) Rare cherry-purple standards and purple falls with a bold, darkly veined, deep cherry zone around a purple beard. Mid-/late spring. ↕ 12 in (30 cm). Z3–8 H9–1

I. **'Chickee'** (MTB, Self) Small, neat flowers with golden yellow standards and similar falls with a paler center, all with darker veins. Grayish foliage. Early summer. ↕ 20 in (50 cm). Z3–8 H9–1

I. chrysographes (Siberian/40) Slowly spreading clumps support narrow, gray-green, 10–28 in (25–70 cm) foliage and unbranched stems, each carrying two fragrant, 2¾–4¾ in (7–12 cm) flowers, each 2¾ (7 cm) across. The color varies from rich wine-purple to almost black, typically with gold marks and veins on falls. Supposedly "black" seedlings may prove variable in color. Early summer/midsummer. From hillsides and forest edges in China. ↕ 20 in (50 cm). Z3–9 H9–1. **'Black Knight'** Dark violet flowers. **'Inshriach'** Darker than 'Black Knight'. **'Kew Black'** Free-flowering. **'Mandarin Purple'** Deep purple with gold markings. Sometimes classified as a Sino-Sib (*see table p.275*). ↕ 18 in (45 cm). **'Rubella'** Rich, deep plum-maroon with yellow streaks on the falls.

I. **'City Lights'** (TB, Self) Bright, large, ruffled flowers; white petals suffused with rich violet-blue at edges; falls with pale yellow beards. Early summer. Vigorous. ↕ 3¼ ft (1 m). Z3–8 H9–1

I. **'Clara Garland'** (IB, Self) Heavily ruffled, incurved, bright yellow standards are framed by slightly drooping, yellow falls, prettily veined in brown and with a creamy yellow beard. Raised by British breeder Cy Bartlett. Late spring/early summer. ↕ 20 in (50 cm). Z3–8 H9–1

I. **'Clarence'** (TB, Amoena) White standards edged pale blue, darker blue falls, and a white zone around the white beard. Large, flaring, vanilla-scented but slightly sparse flowers. Dependably remontant. Late spring/early summer. ↕ 3¼ ft (1 m). Z3–8 H9–1

I. **'Classic Look'** (TB, Plicata) Large, heavily ruffled, vanilla-scented flowers. The white standards and falls are boldly rimmed with deep blue stitching. Well-branched and vigorous. Early summer. ↕ 3¼ ft (1 m). Z3–8 H9–1

I. **'Clear Morning Sky'** (TB, Self) Very elegant, large, lightly ruffled flowers with palest blue falls, blue beards, and slightly darker standards. Early summer. ↕ 3½ ft (1.1 m). Z3–8 H9–1

I. **'Cliffs of Dover'** (TB, Self) Well-formed, pure white, ruffled flowers with a hint of yellow in the falls and a yellow beard. Early summer. ↕ 36 in (90 cm). Z3–8 H9–1

I. confusa (Crested) Unusual, bamboo-like evergreen, forming large clumps of upright stems and fans of about ten, shiny green, sword-shaped, 8–16 in (20–40 cm) long leaves. In spring and early summer, branched stems carry up to 30 flat, white, 2 in (5 cm) flowers, marked with yellow and blue spots, that open over many weeks. Early summer. After flowering the fans and stems die, but are constantly replaced. From China. ↕ 4 ft (1.2 m). Z9–11 H11–9. **'Martyn Rix'** Lilac flowers.

I. **'Conjuration'** (TB, Amoena) A dramatic, moderately-sized flower; white standards, flushed with lilac around the edge. Falls are white, edged with deep

ABOVE 1 *Iris chrysographes* **2** *I. confusa* **3** *I.* 'Dusky Challenger'

lilac, and tend to the horizontal. The orange beard has fuzzy white horns. Space-age iris with up to 12 scented flowers per stem. Early summer. Vigorous. ‡ 3½ ft (1.1 m). Z3–9 H9–1

I. **'Cranapple'** (BB, Self) Bright, rich, velvety flowers with cranberry red standards, slightly darker falls, and deep rusty beards. Early summer. ‡ 24 in (60 cm). Z3–8 H9–1

I. cristata (Crested) Small clumps will form broad patches of fans of bright green, 6 in (15 cm) long leaves. Small, 1½ in (4 cm), lilac-blue flowers in spring are marked with white and have a yellow or orange crest. Other color forms, including pink, may be seen. Ideal for shade in well-drained, acidic soil. Mid-spring. ‡ 6 in (15 cm). From the eastern US. Z3–8 H9–1. **'Alba'** White flowers, marked with gold.

ANGLES AND FALLS

In irises, one of the features that breeders have worked on is the angle at which the falls are held. Falls tend to hang down vertically, and this is especially advantageous in taller types such as Spurias and tall *I. sibirica* cultivars, since the flowers show up well when viewed from the side, as is most usually the case. Cultivars with broad falls are even more impressive when seen from a distance.

On the other hand, cultivars with falls that stand out horizontally are most attractive when viewed from above. Most Standard Dwarf Bearded types have been developed in this way, and they are very effective in the garden for this reason.

I. crocea (Spuria) Robust plant, forming spreading clumps of tough, upright, sword-shaped, 30 in (75 cm) foliage, with tall stems carrying clusters of up to 20 large, 6 in (15 cm), bright yellow flowers on up to three branches opening over several weeks in early summer. Easy in moist soil in sun. From Kashmir. ‡ 4 ft (1.2 m). Z3–8 H9–1

I. **'Crowned Heads'** (TB, Reverse Amoena) Unusual, large, heavily ruffled, fragrant flowers with deep purple-blue standards; pale blue falls with pale blue beards. Vigorous, strong stems. Early summer. ‡ 3¼ ft (1 m). Z3–8 H9–1

I. **'Cutie'** (IB, Blend) Pure white standards, with incurved white falls streaked in denim blue, sometimes a bit smudged toward the base. Yellow-tinted toward the sides. Late spring/early summer. ‡ 24 in (60 cm). Z3–8 H9–1

I. **'Dancer's Veil'** (TB, Plicata) Ruffled flowers, white standards, heavily flushed with violet, the falls white with much narrower violet edges; brownish stripes on petal stalks and a white beard. Early summer. ‡ 36 in (90 cm). Z3–8 H9–1

I. **'Dark Passion'** (TB, Self) Small ruffled, flared flowers. Standards and falls are deep, inky black, the falls with dark beards. Well-branched and vigorous with a sweet, grapey scent. Early summer. ‡ 3¼ ft (1 m). Z3–8 H9–1

I. **'Dazzling Gold'** (TB, Variegata) Compact with large, bright yet deep gold standards and yellow, ruffled falls, suffused and striped with red. Early summer. ‡ 28 in (70 cm). Z3–8 H9–1

I. **'Deep Black'** (TB, Self) Rather small flowers with narrow, reflexed falls—not as black as its name implies. Unruffled flowers with dark purple standards and

deep indigo purple falls, lighter around the orange-tipped beard. Early summer. ‡ 34 in (85 cm). Z3–8 H9–1

I. delavayi (Siberian/40) Steadily creeping clumps carry 20–40 in (50–100 cm), grayish-green, strap-shaped leaves and, in summer, stems with three branches each carrying two 3 in (8 cm), lightly fragrant flowers in purple-blue with yellow and striped petal stalks. Grow in moist, fertile soil in sun or part-shade. The tallest of the 40-chromosome Siberian irises. From ditches and meadows in China. ‡ 5 ft (1.5 m). Z4–8 H9–1

I. **'Demon'** (SDB, Self) Very dark maroon-purple standards and falls with contrasting blue beards. Mid-/late spring. Prolific and scented. ‡ 12 in (30 cm). Z3–8 H9–1

I. **'Diabolique'** (TB, Self) Beautifully and evenly ruffled, thick-textured, weather-resistant flowers with reddish purple standards and slightly darker falls with bluish purple beards. Vigorous and easy to grow, with strong stems. Early summer. ‡ 3¼ ft (1 m). Z3–8 H9–1

I. douglasiana (PCI) Variable, forming vigorously spreading clumps carrying glossy, evergreen foliage up to 24 in (60 cm) long, sometimes reddish at the base. Branching stems bear up to eight, 4 in (10 cm) wide flowers, usually in lavender or lilac. Tolerates drier and more alkaline soil than most of its type, but ideally, plant in moist soil, in sun or part-shade. Easiest, most robust, leafiest, and most coarse of the group, from the coasts of California and Oregon. Late spring. ‡ 24 in (60 cm). Z7–9 H9–7

I. **'Dusky Challenger'** (TB, Self) Huge, silky, elegantly ruffled flowers open from jet black buds on well-branched stems. The open standards, falls, and

beards are all darkest purple. Vigorous, prolific, and chocolate-scented. Early summer. ‡ 3½ ft (1.1 m). Z3–8 H9–1

I. **'Early Light'** (TB, Plicata) Large, ruffled white flowers; hazy white standards broadly edged in yellow, with a crisper, narrower edge and pale yellow beards. Slightly scented, carried on strong stems. Early summer. ‡ 3¼ ft (1 m). Z3–8 H9–1

I. **'Edith Wolford'** (TB, Bicolor) Superb, large, heavily ruffled flowers with pale yellow, slightly incurved standards, flushed lavender through the

BELOW *Iris* 'Early Light'

midrib; slightly raised lavender falls with yellow beards. Vigorous, prolific, and scented. Early summer. ↕3¼ ft (1 m). Z3–9 H9–1

I. 'Edward of Windsor' (TB, Self) Peach standards with a hint of beige and narrow reflexed falls in a similar shade with honeyed veins and orange beards. Old-fashioned in style, but with nine flowers per stem. Early summer. ↕32 in (80 cm). Z3–8 H9–1

I. 'Eileen Louise' (TB, Self) Soft pink standards, and soft pink falls that are slightly paler in the center and have an orange beard. Early summer. ↕36 in (90 cm). Z3–8 H9–1

I. 'Eleanor's Pride' (TB, Self) Elegant, slightly waved, soft blue flowers; very pale yellow beard. A hybrid of 'Jane Phillips' and 'Blue Rhythm'. An award-winner in England and the US. Early summer. ↕36 in (90 cm). Z3–8 H9–1

I. 'Elizabeth Poldark' (TB, Self) Ruffled white with yellow flushing in the heart of the bloom and with a yellow beard tipped in white. Early summer. ↕36 in (90 cm). Z3–8 H9–1

I. 'English Charm' (TB, Self) Cream standards are flushed coppery buff with paler edges; falls are apricot-copper with paler edges and dark veins around the orange beard—odd but attractive coloring on these moderately ruffled flowers. Sometimes remontant. Early summer. ↕34 in (85 cm). Z3–8 H9–1

I. 'English Cottage' (TB, Plicata) Almost white: the white standards are faintly tinted in pale lilac-blue at the edges, more noticeably veined in the falls with a yellow beard. One of the most reliable remontants. Early summer. ↕36 in (90 cm). Z3–8 H9–1

I. ensata syn. *I. kaempferi* (Laevigata) Clump-forming perennial with narrow, 8–24 in (20–60 cm) long foliage with a distinct midrib. Flower stems are unbranched, or may branch once, with three or four 4–6 in (10–15 cm) flowers, in midsummer. Typically purple with yellow marks on the falls and small, erect standards, this species has been developed for centuries in Japan, where different regions favored different flower shapes. Flowers of cultivars may be single or have no standards and six falls, often very broad and ruffled. There are also double, multipetaled cultivars with nine or more petals. They were classified into groups in Japan: **Edo** irises have moderately sized flowers with petals that do not overlap. They may be single or double with arching falls. Flowers are held above the foliage on branched stems and are the oldest form; **Higo** irises were developed in the 1860s from Edo irises and produce solitary flowers, often up to 12 in (30 cm) across. They may be single or double, with over-lapping petals and horizontal falls. Modern cultivars may have branched stems; **Ise** were developed from 1800 but formally classified in 1910. They may be single or double, have flowers

the same height as the foliage tips and the falls are pendant. Grow in moist soil in full sun. Not tolerant of their crowns being submerged by water in winter, though this will do no harm in summer. With cultivars being imported from Japan, there are uncertainties about the naming of some. Propagate the species from seed and the cultivars by division. From China, Japan, and eastern Russia. ↕36 in (90 cm). Z3–9 H9–1. **'Activity'** Large, single flowers in lilac with deep purple veins and yellow signal. **'Barr Purple East'** Vivid purple, 8-in (20-cm) single flowers with a bright gold signal. ↕4 ft (1.2 m). **'Caprician Butterfly'** Double, pale, almost white flowers with violet veins radiating from the yellow blotch. Purple style arms. **'Cry of Rejoice'** Large, single flowers in lilac with lavender coloration around the yellow signal. ↕24 in (60 cm). **'Darling'** Single, pale pink veined in darker pink; pale yellow signals. ↕32 in (80 cm). **'Eden's Blue Pearl'** Large, double purple flowers, streaked with white; bright yellow signals. ↕32 in (80 cm). **'Eden's Charm'** Large, double flowers in pure white; yellow signals. ↕32 in (80 cm). **'Eden's Harmony'** Large, double flowers in white with a flush of blue; yellow signals. ↕32 in (80 cm). **'Eden's Paintbrush'** Large, double flowers, speckled purple on white; yellow signals and pale style arms. ↕32 in (80 cm). **'Eden's Picasso'** Large, double, purple flowers with white veins and mottling; neat yellow signals. ↕32 in (80 cm). Z4. **'Eden's Purple Glory'** Large, double purple flowers; bright yellow signals. **'Emotion'** Large, double flowers in lilac-pink with white around the yellow signals. **'Gracieuse'** Large, single white flowers edged with lilac-blue; yellow signals. ↕32 in (80 cm). **'Hercule'** Large, double, pale blue flowers with purple veins and conspicuous yellow signals. **'Hue and Cry'** Large double, each reddish purple petal with white lines radiating from the yellow signal. **'Innocence'** Large, double white flowers; yellow signals. ↕32 in (80 cm). **'Iso-no-nami'** Large, single flowers with a white flare around the yellow signals. ↕32 in (80 cm). **'Laughing Lion'** Large, double, deep reddish purple flowers with contrasting bright yellow signals, with darker purple borders. ↕32 in (80 cm). **'Light at Dawn'** Large, double white flowers lightly speckled purple-rimmed; yellow signals. ↕32 in (80 cm). **'Moonlight Waves'** Large, double, pure white flowers with yellow signals. ↕32 in (80 cm). **'Pink Frost'** Large, double, pale pink-white flowers; yellow signals. ↕28 in (70 cm). **'Rose Queen'** Single, veined pink flowers, small standards; yellow signals. Primitive, but popular. **'Sensation'** Large, double, deep purple flowers with narrow yellow signals. ↕32 in (80 cm). **'Summer Storm'** Almost black buds open to velvety purple flowers with more rudimentary petals in the center and yellow signals.

RIGHT 1 *Iris ensata*
2 *I. ensata* 'Rose Queen'
3 *I.* 'Florentina'

Unusually late-flowering. ‡3¼ ft (1 m).
'The Great Mogul' Dark reddish
purple with a yellow signal. ‡32 in
(80 cm). **'Variegata'** Narrow foliage
striped with white, and purple flowers.
'Waka-murasaki' Large, double, violet-
blue flowers with a narrow white edge;
yellow signals. ‡32 in (80 cm).

I. **'Eyebright'** (SDB, Bicolor) Brightly
colored flowers, deep yellow standards,
similar falls, with bold maroon whiskers
sometimes merging into a patch. White-
flowered, with a blue thumbprint on
falls. May be seen under this name. Mid-
spring. ‡12 in (30 cm). Z3–8 H9–1

I. **'Fancy Woman'** (TB, Bicolor)
Almost black buds open to large,
ruffled flowers; plummy purple
standards with white streaks to the
edges and a white rim. Falls in a richer
shade with white rim and white splash
and lines around the orange beard.
Fragrant. ‡3¼ ft (1 m). Z3–8 H9–1

I. **'First Interstate'** (TB, Bicolor)
Dramatic, beautifully formed, ruffled,
fragrant flowers with golden-yellow
standards and white falls, edged
with the same yellow; yellow beards.
Vigorous. Early summer. ‡3¼ ft (1 m).
Z3–8 H9–1

I. **'Florentina'** syn. *I. florentina*,
I. germanica 'Florentina' (IB/TB, Self)
Palest blue standards and falls, fading
to white, with a pale yellow beard. An
ancient plant that may be a hybrid or a
species that has long been domesticated:
it is the source of orris root, providing
violet perfume from its dried rhizomes.
Long cultivated in northern Italy. Late
spring. ‡32 in (80 cm). Z3–8 H9–1

I. foetidissima (Beardless) Robust
evergreen, forming clumps of tough,
dark green foliage to 30 in (75 cm);
smells unpleasant only when crushed.
Flowers, up to five per stem, are small,
brown and purple, and not showy, but
are followed by large seedpods that
burst open in fall to reveal scarlet
(rarely orange, yellow, or white) seeds
that remain attractive for months. Easy
to grow and thrives in shade but may
harbor leaf spot fungus that can spread
to bearded irises. Divide in spring or
sow seeds. Native to the western
Mediterranean, and North Africa. Late
spring. ‡18 in (45 cm). Z4–9 H9–2. **var.
citrina** Pale yellow and brown flowers,
said to fruit more freely. **'Fructu Albo'**
White fruits. **var. lutescens** Buttercup
yellow flowers. **'Variegata'** White and
gray striped foliage, but rarely flowers
or sets seed: propagate by division.

I. forrestii (Siberian/40) Steadily
spreading clumps support linear,
yellowish green, 8–20 in (20–50 cm)
leaves to ¼ in (7 mm) wide. In summer,
slenderer, unbranched stems carry pairs
of brown-lined, yellow, 2–2½ in (5–
6 cm) blooms, with drooping falls atop
the foliage. Grow in sun or part-shade
in moist soil. Divide in spring or sow
seed. From ditches and stream-sides in
Tibet, Yunnan, and Sichuan provinces
in China, and in Burma. Early summer.
‡16 in (40 cm). Z6–9 H9–6

I. **'Frost and Flame'** (TB, Self) Large,
pristine white flowers, the falls
enhanced by a tangerine beard. An old
cultivar but vigorous, aging well. Fruity
scent. ‡36 in (90 cm). Z3–9 H9–1

I. fulva (Louisiana) Slender rhizomes
form a spreading clump of strap-
shaped, pale green, 12–28 in (30–
70 cm) leaves with drooping tips. The
slender, slightly zigzagged stems carry
up to seven rusty-orange, 2¾ in (7 cm)
wide flowers with drooping falls and
standards in summer. The easiest and
hardiest of the Louisiana irises, growing
in most moist soils. From streamsides in
Mississippi. ‡28 in (70 cm). Z4–9 H9–2

I. x *fulvala* (Louisiana) Robust with
2¾ in (7 cm) reddish purple summer
flowers, somewhere between the purple
of one parent, *I. brevicaulis,* and the
coppery shade of the other, *I. fulva*.
‡28 in (70 cm). Z6–9 H9–6

I. germanica (Bearded) Fat rhizomes
support evergreen, gray-green leaves,
12–16 in (30–40 cm) long and 1–1¾ in
(2.5–4.5 cm) wide. In late spring, once-
or twice-branched stems carry 4 in
(10 cm) flowers with bluish violet
standards and falls, the latter with striped
petal stalks and yellow beards. Robust
and persistent, thriving in sunny, dry
soils. Probably an ancient hybrid
cultivated around the Mediterranean
for centuries, with some variants found.
It is not a parent of modern bearded
iris cultivars. ‡36 in (90 cm). Z3–9
H9–1. **'Florentina'** see *I.* 'Florentina'.

I. **'Gingerbread Man'** (SDB, Self) Pale
brown, incurved standards with ginger-
brown falls and a contrasting bright
blue-purple beard. Late spring. ‡14 in
(35 cm). Z6–9 H9–6

I. **'Going My Way'** (TB, Plicata) Large,
dramatic, ruffled, scented flowers, the
standards suffused purple around white
and the broad white falls edged purple,
with purple beards shading to orange at
the center. ‡34 in (85 cm). Z4–9 H9–2

I. graminea (Spuria) (Plum tart iris)
Dense, leafy clumps of arching, narrow,
flat, bright green, 12 in (30 cm) foliage.
Flattened stems carry purple, 2¾ in
(7 cm) flowers with narrow standards
and falls. The scent is of stewed plums,
hence the common name. Best in moist
soil in sun or part-shade, but easy to
grow in most soils. Propagate by division
in spring or from seed. Late spring and
early summer. Native to southern
Europe. ‡16 in (40 cm). Z6–9 H9–5

I. **'Green Spot'** (SDB, Self) Ivory-white
standards, falls with an olive-green spot
below a white beard. Very striking. Late
spring. ‡12 in (30 cm). Z3–8 H9–1

I. **'Gypsy Romance'** (TB, Self) Large,
ruffled standards and falls in mulberry
purple suffused with violet. Falls have
red petal stalks and a violet beard. Early
summer. ‡3¼ ft (1 m). Z3–8 H9–1

RIGHT 1 *Iris foetidissima*
2 *I. foestii* **3** *I. graminea*

EARLY SUMMER IN A SUNNY BORDER

CAREFUL PLANNING AND sheer chance here create a bright summer border grouping of irises, allium, and red valerian. The rounded purple drumsticks of *Allium* 'Purple Sensation', slightly bluish in bud, have sprung from bulbs carefully planted among the fat rhizomes of *Iris* 'Jane Phillips'; this mingled planting is easier to achieve if the irises are planted in distinct clumps rather than in one broad drift. The red valerian, *Centranthus ruber* 'Atrococcineus', has arrived by chance in exactly the right place, but could easily have been removed by overenthusiastic weeding.

I. 'Happy Mood' (IB, Plicata) Lightly waved, pale lilac flowers, standards hazed with white; lilac-edged white falls, with a neat yellow beard. Late spring/early summer. ↕ 24 in (60 cm). Z3–8 H9–1

I. 'Harriette Halloway' (TB, Self) Very large, fragrant flowers with clear blue standards; broad, clear blue falls shade to white in the center, veined in buff. A larger-flowered alternative to the popular 'Jane Phillips'. Late spring/early summer. ↕ 41 in (105 cm). Z3–8 H9–1

I. 'Headcorn' (MTB, Bitone) Small but elegant flowers have incurved yellow standards faintly veined in maroon; the cream horizontal falls are edged yellow and veined in maroon, with a bold orange beard. Vigorous and striking. Late spring/early summer. ↕ 32 in (80 cm). Z3–8 H9–1

I. 'Hello Darkness' (TB, Self) Huge ruffled flowers of evenly inky black,

including the beards, with stiff substance and velvet texture. Among the best "blacks" for color, but only seven buds per stem. Early summer. ↕ 3¼ ft (1 m). Z3–8 H9–1

I. 'Holden Clough' (Laevigata) Large, with arching, sometimes evergreen, slightly grayish foliage, and small, yellow flowers heavily veined in purple to give a brown-netted effect. More intriguing than it is flamboyant. Grow in moist soil in full sun; propagate by division. An unexpected hybrid of *I. chrysographes* and *I. pseudacorus* at Holden Clough Nursery in Lancashire, England. ↕ 3¼ ft (1 m). Z5–8 H8–5

I. 'Honey Glazed' (IB, Amoena) Attractive flowers with cream standards shading to yellow at the base above rich amber falls, prettily veined toward the sides at the base, and with a golden beard. Remontant. Late spring/early summer. ↕ 28 in (70 cm). Z3–8 H9–1

I. 'Honeyplic' (IB, Plicata) Cream standards and falls edged in honey brown and with brown veins, the falls with a white beard tipped in brown. Late spring/early summer. ↕ 18 in (45 cm). Z3–8 H9–1

I. 'Honky Tonk Blues' (TB, Self) Large, ruffled blooms with deep blue standards. Slightly paler mottled falls are streaked with white with blue beards. Strong stems, each with ten buds. Early summer. ↕ 38 in (95 cm). Z3–8 H9–1

I. hoogiana (Aril/Regelia) Robust, with fat rhizomes and erect, mid-green foliage, 20 in (50 cm) long and ½–⅜ in (1–1.5 cm) wide, with purple bases and stems. Two or three beautiful, silky-textured, clear mid-blue, fragrant 4 in (10 cm) flowers with yellow beards are borne in late spring. Requires well-drained soil in full sun. Propagate by division or seed. From Tajikistan. Late spring. ↕ 24 in (60 cm). Z7–9 H9–7

I. 'Immortality' (TB, Self) Compact plant with lightly ruffled, fragrant white flowers with the faintest hint of blue that fades rapidly; lemon beards. Popular, vigorous, and reliably remontant. ↕ 32 in (80 cm). Z3–9 H9–1

I. 'Impetuous' (BB, Self) Pale violet-blue waved standards, and flared, pale violet-blue, slightly waved falls, these with some darker zones; a white petal stalk with a few purple veins and a yellow-tipped white beard. ↕ 28 in (75 cm). Z3–8 H9–1

I. 'Indian Chief' (TB, Amoena) Large blooms with very pale, soft red standards. Rich deep red falls with golden beards. Tough and reliable. Late spring/early summer. ↕ 3½ ft (1.1 m). Z3–8 H9–1

I. innominata (PCI) Evergreen clump-former with narrow, ¹⁄₁₆–⅛ in (2–4 mm) leaves, 12 in (30 cm) in height and purple at the base. Unbranched stems bear one or two 3 in (8 cm) wide flowers in early summer. These are typically pale yellow or cream, but may be golden or purple or lavender, with frilly falls. Thrives in moist, acidic or neutral soil, in sun or part-shade. Can be divided in late summer if necessary, but it dislikes disturbance; best propagated from seed. From southwestern Oregon and northwestern California. ↕ 10 in (25 cm). Z7–9 H9–7

I. 'Jane Phillips' (TB, Self) Elegant, lightly ruffled, fragrant flowers with clear sky blue standards and falls and a golden beard. Popular, old, strong, and vigorous cultivar. Early summer. ↕ 36 in (90 cm). Z3–8 H9–1

I. japonica (Crested) Spreads vigorously by thin rhizomes that run across the soil surface, sometimes forming broad clumps of its attractive evergreen fans of broad, glossy green, 18 in (45 cm) foliage, clustered at the tips. In late spring, branched stems carry small clusters of usually white or pale lavender, 2 in (5 cm) flowers marked with blue around the orange crest. Grow in sun or part-shade in a sheltered spot, in moist soil; once flowered, leaf fans die and should be removed to keep clumps neat. Propagate by division in spring. From Japan and China. ↕ 18 in (45 cm). Z7–9 H9–7. **'Aphrodite'** *see* 'Variegata'. **'Ledger'** syn. 'Ledger's Variety' Reputedly hardier than the species. The name has been applied to a number of forms. **'Variegata'** syn. 'Aphrodite' Foliage boldly striped with white, and flowering freely.

I. 'Jazz Festival' (TB, Bicolor) Very large, ruffled, fragrant flowers with creamy buff standards and large, rich crimson falls with yellow beards and faint petal stalks stripes hold on stout, well-branched stems. Late spring/early summer. ↕ 3¼ ft (1 m). Z3–8 H9–1

I. 'Jazzed Up' (TB, Amoena) Large, ruffled flowers with good substance have pure white standards and broad, rosy-purple falls with a white patch

under the white beard. Well branched, unusually tall stems with nine buds. Late spring/early summer. ‡ 4 ft (1.2 m). Z3–8 H9–1

I. **'Jean Guymer'** (TB, Self) Large, lightly ruffled and laced flowers in peach, honey-tinted at the base of both standards and falls and with orange beards. Pretty, if dated, with its narrow falls, but with excellent fragrance and remontant habit. Early summer. ‡ 3¼ ft (1 m). Z3–8 H9–1

REMONTANT IRISES

Irises showing a tendency to bloom again after the main spring/early summer flush of flowers are termed "remontant." This habit is thought to derive from a lack of the usual requirement of a cold spell to initiate flower buds. Cultivars not needing this cold treatment will therefore tend to bloom again later in the season.

Although the first such cultivars are thought to have been introduced in the late 19th century, it was with the arrival of 'Autumn Flame' and 'Gibson Girl' in the 1940s that they began to find popularity. At first, the old-fashioned flower form deterred many from trying them, but there is now a wide range of excellent cultivars available.

A long growing season, a mild climate, and good growing conditions are all helpful in fostering reblooming; plants that are stressed or starved are unlikely to build up the substantial reserves required for a long flowering season. Cultivars that have proved to rebloom include:

'Autumn Circus',   'Golden Encore'
'Beverly Sills',   'Immortality'
'Breakers'   'Perfume
'Champagne   Counter'
  Elegance'   'Royal Summer'
'Chaste White',   'Victoria Falls'
'Clarence'

I. **'Jesse's Song'** (TB, Plicata) Large flowers with broad, ruffled petals; almost solid deep violet standards. White falls with violet edging shading to peppering around the central white zone with its lemon beard. Grows and flowers well for a long period, on branched stems. Fragrant. ‡ 3¼ ft (1 m). Z3–8 H9–1

I. **'Jitterbug'** (TB, Variegata/Plicata) Large, gently ruffled flowers with yellow, incurved standards faintly veined in brown, and yellow falls heavily overlaid with dark russet-red stripes and edged in solid color. Compact and prolific, with good branching. Late spring/early summer. ‡ 34 in (85 cm). Z3–9 H9–1

I. **'Jurassic Park'** (TB, Bicolor) Large, broadly ruffled and laced, boldly colored flowers with mustard yellow domed standards and flared violet falls. A descendant of 'Edith Walford' and 'Best Bet'. Fragrant. Early summer. ‡ 3¼ ft (1 m). Z3–9 H9–1

I. **'kaempferi'** see *I. ensata*

I. **'Katie-Koo'** (IB, Self) Waved, tightly packed, violet-purple standards and lightly ruffled horizontal falls in an even deeper shade, with a bright gray-white beard. Sweetly scented. Raised by British breeder Cy Bartlett. Late spring/early summer. ‡ 28 in (70 cm). Z3–8 H9–1

I. **'Kent Pride'** (TB, Self) Sultry, richly colored, scented blooms with reddish brown standards and reddish brown falls with a dark-veined, yellow-edged white patch around the bright gold beard. The leaf bases are stained purple. ‡ 34 in (85 cm). Z3–8 H9–1

I. **'kerneriana'** (Spuria) Deciduous, clump-forming, spreading slowly by rhizomes, with foliage to 16 in (40 cm) tall and only ¼ in (5 mm) wide. Slender stems produce clusters of two to four, 2¾–4 in (7–10 cm) flowers in early

summer. Narrow standards and falls in yellow or cream, with a dark yellow blotch on the falls, arch back to almost touch the stem. Smaller than most Spuria irises. Grow in moist soil, in sun or part-shade. Propagate by division or from seed. From northern Turkey. Early summer. ‡ 18 in (45 cm). Z6–9 H9–6

I. **'Knick Knack'** (MDB, Plicata) Small, delicately colored flowers, the standards white with dark blue edging; falls also white are more faintly marked. Mid-/late spring. ‡ 6 in (15 cm). Z3–8 H9–1

I. **'Laced Cotton'** (TB, Self) Huge, gently ruffled and laced flowers in pure white, with the slightest lilac tint on first opening, and with white beards. Well-branched but with only six buds per stem. Early summer. ‡ 3¼ ft (1 m). Z3–8 H9–1

I. lacustris (Crested) Dwarf and creeping by rhizomes from which grow fans of bright green leaves, up to 4 in (10 cm) long and ½ in (1 cm) wide. The ¾ in (2 cm) flowers, in late spring, are blue, the falls with a darker zone around the white patch surrounding the yellow crest. Similar to *I. cristata* but shorter, with narrower leaves, and more tolerant of dry conditions and sun. Propagate by division or from seed. From moist gravels and sands in the Great Lakes region. ‡ 3 in (8 cm). Z4–8 H8–1

I. **'Lady Friend'** (TB, Self) Large, ruffled, rosy maroon standards, slightly honeyed at the base, and falls with rich red beards and striped petal stalks. Strong, multistemmed plants. Early summer. ‡ 36 in (90 cm). Z3–8 H9–1

I. **'Lady Mohr'** (AB) Elegantly inrolled pale blue standards, with palest blue falls delicately veined in chestnut with a honey haze, and a rich brown beard.

ABOVE 1 *Iris* 'Holden Clough'
2 *I.* 'Jane Phillips'

Exquisite but scarce. Early summer. ‡ 32 in (80 cm). Z3–8 H9–1

I. laevigata (Laevigata) Steadily spreading clumps of 16 in (40 cm), sword-shaped leaves ⅝–1½ in (1.5–4 cm) wide. In early summer and midsummer, unbranched stems bear two to four purple-blue flowers, to 4 in (10 cm) across. Standards are short and upright and the falls are large and drooping, typically with a white or yellow stripe down the center. Grow in moist soil or in ponds. Prefers acidic or neutral soil, but tolerates some alkalinity and being submerged.

RIGHT *Iris* 'Kent Pride'

Flowers earlier than *I. kaempferi*; can be distinguished by the lack of prominent leaf midrib found in that species. From China and Japan. ↕ 32 in (80 cm). Z4. **var. alba** White flowers. **'Albopurpurea'** White standards and white falls flecked with purple spots. **'Atropurpurea'** Rich purple flowers. **'Colchesterensis'** Unusual, double flowers splashed with inky blue on white. ↕ 28 in (70 cm). Z3–9 H9–1. **'Monstrosa'** Large, deep blue flowers with white stripes through the falls. **'Snowdrift'** White flowers. **'Variegata'** Leaves boldly striped with white, and blue flowers. **'Weymouth Midnight'** Dark purple flowers.

I. Langport Series (IB) Series of Intermediate Bearded cultivars bred by Kelways Nursery at Langport, Somerset, in England, and introduced prior to 1940. They are still grown because of their vigor, trouble-free growth, and their wide range of often unusual color combinations. All have smooth, narrow, unruffled blooms. ↕ 24 in (60 cm). Z3–8 H9–1. **'Langport Storm'** (IB, Self) An unusual combination of slightly frilled lilac standards and lilac falls with a brownish maroon patch and darkly veined petal stalks around the yellow beard. Prolific, scented, and unusually early-flowering. Late spring. **'Langport Wren'** (IB, Self) Rich purple-brown standards and similarly colored falls with darker veins, enhanced by a bright yellow beard. Prolific. One of the best. Late spring/early summer.

I. lazica (Beardless) Forms untidy clumps of green evergreen foliage, 12 in (30 cm) high and ⅝ in (1.5 cm) wide. The 3 in (8 cm), unscented, lavender-blue and white flowers, with darker spots on the falls, open in late winter; they have no stems but instead an enormously elongated perianth tube, up to 4 in (10 cm) in length. Differs from the usually taller, closely related *I. unguicularis* in tolerating moist soil and some shade. Propagate by division

or from seed. From scrub in northern Turkey and the Black Sea area. ↕ 10 in (25 cm). Z8–10 H10–8.

I. 'Lemon Brocade' (TB, Self) Elegant, ruffled flowers with lemon yellow falls and standards, the falls paler in the center below dark yellow beard. All open from caramel buds. Scented and prolific. ↕ 34 in (85 cm). Z3–8 H9–1.

I. 'Lilli-White' (SDB, Self) Pure white, ruffled standards and pure white falls with white beards. Late spring. ↕ 12 in (30 cm). Z3–8 H9–1.

I. 'Local Color' (TB, Bicolor) Large bicolored flowers with domed violet standards and almost black ruffled falls, paler at the edges and enhanced by bright orange beards. Early summer. ↕ 3¼ ft (1 m). Z3–8 H9–1

I. 'Loop the Loop' (TB, Plicata) Large, ruffled white falls and standards that are neatly edged with deep violet-blue. Dark style arms and yellow-tipped beards. Early summer. ↕ 41 in (105 cm). Z3–8 H9–1

I. 'Lucy's Gift' (MTB, Plicata) Gently waved flowers with slightly incurved white standards, strongly veined purple especially at the edges, and drooping falls similarly patterned and with a bold yellow beard. Prolific and well-branched. Late spring. ↕ 24 in (60 cm). Z3–8 H9–1

I. lutescens syn *I. chamaeiris* (Bearded iris) Variable, early-flowering plant with sword-shaped foliage 12 in (30 cm) high and ¼–1 in (0.5–2.5 cm) wide. Branched stems, sometimes as short as 2 in (5 cm), have, typically, soft yellow 2½–2¾ in (6–7 cm) flowers, though they may be white, violet, or blue. The falls curl inward and feature a yellow beard. Grow in well-drained soil in full sun. From grassy and rocky places in northern Spain, Italy and southern

France. ↕ 12 in (30 cm). Z7–9 H9–7

I. magnifica (Juno) Robust, with two rows of arching, glossy leaves, 12–24 in (30–60 cm) long and 1¼–2 in (3–5 cm) wide, resembling those of leeks in shape. In spring, branched stems bear up to seven pale lilac, 2¾ in (7 cm) flowers with a yellow zone surrounding the white crest. One of the easiest Juno irises for a sunny, well-drained spot. From rocky places in Central Asia. ↕ 18 in (45 cm). Z6–8 H8–6

I. 'Mary Constance' (IB, Self) Lightly ruffled flowers in pure mid-blue with pale beards. Vigorous and fragrant. ↕ 24 in (60 cm). Z3–8 H9–1

I. 'Mary Frances' (TB, Self) Large, beautiful, ruffled, lilac-blue flowers with a paler area in the center of the falls and a pale lilac, yellow-tipped beard. Well-branched, with a long season. American hybridizer Larry Gaulter considered this his finest introduction. ↕ 36 in (90 cm). Z3–8 H9–1

I. 'Mary McIlroy' (SDB, Self) Ruffled deep yellow standards and falls with paler beards. Bright and buttery. Late spring. ↕ 12 in (30 cm). Z3–8 H9–1

I. 'Maui Moonlight' (IB, Self) Bright lemon yellow standards with paler falls, deeper yellow around the beards. Scented and well-ruffled. ↕ 24 in (60 cm). Z3–8 H9–1

I. 'Maui Surf' (BB, Self) Ruffled flowers in lavender-blue with darker, violet-blue veins, cupped standards and drooping falls, with a creamy blue beard. Vigorous and prolific. Late spring/early summer. ↕ 36 in (90 cm). Z3–8 H9–1

I. 'Meadow Court' (SDB, Bicolor) Rich yellow standards and maroon falls, edged in yellow and with a yellow beard. Prolific and long-flowering. Late spring. ↕ 12 in (30 cm).

ABOVE 1 *Iris laevigata* 'Snowdrift'
2 *I. missouriensis* **3** *I. orientalis*

I. 'Medway Valley' (MTB, Bicolor) Very unusually colored flowers. Slightly incurved, wrinkled standards are pale coffee brown; white horizontal falls are boldly veined in purple–maroon, more densely at the edge, with a pale orange beard. Very prolific. ↕ 6 in (15 cm). Late spring/early summer. Z3–8 H9–1

I. mellita see *I. suaveolens*

I. 'Melon Honey' (SDB, Self) Extraordinary cantaloupe standards and falls with a slim gold rim to the standards, broader on the falls, and a white flash under the white-tipped, orange beard. Late spring. ↕ 12 in (30 cm). Z3–8 H9–1

I. 'Mer du Sud' (TB, Self) Cupped, deep navy blue standards and drooping navy blue falls, both ruffled and with just a hint of violet, the falls more so and shading to yellow at the base. Vigorous, with spreading foliage and slightly zigzag stems. A hybrid of 'Dusky Challenger'. Late spring/early summer. ↕ 36 in (90 cm). Z3–8 H9–1

I. 'Mesmerizer' (TB, Self) Large, ruffled, scented, pure white flowers with almost horizontal white falls and large spoons or flounces at the tips of the beards. Bred by Monty Byers of California, who specialized in space-age irises such as this. Early summer. ↕ 38 in (95 cm). Z3–8 H9–1

I. 'Midnight Oil' (TB, Self) Lightly ruffled, inky-black standards and falls with a matte finish and inconspicuous beards. Among the darkest available. Bred from 'Before the Storm'. Early summer. ↕ 36 in (90 cm). Z3–8 H9–1

I. milesii (Crested) Conspicuous,

creeping green rhizomes support fans of lush, pale green leaves, 12–24 in (30–60 cm) long and 1½–2¾ in (4–7 cm) wide. Well-branched flowering stems carry 2¾ in (7 cm), flat blooms, with mottled lavender petals and yellow crests on the falls over several weeks. Plant in moist, acidic or neutral soil in sun or part-shade. From the Himalaya. Early summer/midsummer. ↕32 in (80 cm). Z5–8 H8–5

I. missouriensis (Beardless) Deciduous, variable iris forming clumps of 8-in (20-cm) leaves only ⅛–¼ in (3–7 mm) wide and usually taller than the flower stems. Each stem carries up to four blue or lavender, 2¾-in (7-cm) flowers with boldly veined falls and a yellow signal. Plants need spring moisture but drier conditions in summer, and dislike root disturbance—propagate from seed. From western and central North America. ↕20 in (50 cm). Z3–9 H9–1

***I.* 'Monspur Cambridge Blue'** (Spuria) Vigorous and prolific with blue-green foliage to 4–4½ ft (1.2–1.4 m) long and 1 in (2.5 cm) wide. Erect stems carry six to seven flowers, the standards pale blue with a slim white edge, the circular falls blue, tinted violet, with a bright yellow signal and dark purple veins. Plant in sun or part-shade, in moist, well-drained soil. A hybrid of *I. monnieri* and *I. spuria* introduced by the historic British nursery of Barr and Sons. Early summer. ↕5 ft (1.5 m). Z3–8 H9–1

***I.* 'Morwenna'** (TB, Self) Elegant, broadly waved, sky blue standards, darker toward the middle; downcurved sky blue falls, with a white beard. Early summer. ↕36 in (90 cm). Z3–8 H9–1

***I.* 'Mrs. Nate Rudolph'** (SDB, Bicolor) Unusual grayish blooms, with ruffled standards pale gray-blue. The falls are grayish gold with a white beard. Late spring. ↕16 in (40 cm). Z3–8 H9–1

***I.* 'Ola Kalá'** (TB, Self) Moderately sized, lightly ruffled blooms with standards and falls of bright yellow on well-branched stems. Once considered the best yellow, still valued for its sturdy habit. Early summer. ↕3¼ ft (1 m). Z3–8 H9–1

***I.* 'Orange Caper'** (SDB, Self) Bright flowers in golden orange, the falls faintly dark-veined and with bright orange beards. Dark foliage. Late spring. ↕12 in (30 cm). Z3–8 H9–1

I. ochroleuca see *I. orientalis.*

I. orchioides (Juno) The true species is rarely grown; the name is usually given to all-yellow forms of *I. bucharica*.

I. orientalis (Spuria) syn *I. ochroleuca* A robust, sometimes evergreen, clump-former with 36 in (90 cm) upright, narrow leaves ½–¾ in (1–2 cm) wide. In summer, tall stems carry clusters of up to five 4 in (10 cm) wide white flowers with upright standards and a yellow blotch on the falls. Easy to grow in moist, well-drained soil in sun or part-shade. Propagate by division or from seed. From Turkey and Greece. ↕3¼ ft (1 m). Z6–9 H9–5

***I.* 'Orinoco Flow'** (BB, Plicata) Large, densely ruffled flowers. White standards heavily edged with violet, and white falls with a narrower edge of violet and blue lines around the blue beard. Fragrant. One of the best from British breeder Cy Bartlett. Late spring/early summer. ↕24 in (60 cm). Z3–8 H9–1

***I.* 'Owyhee Desert'** (TB, Plicata) Intriguing ruffled flowers with pure white standards and white flaring falls, heavily shaded and lined with caramel brown and with yellow beards. Uniquely colored and fragrant, though small-flowered. ↕36 in (90 cm). Z3–8 H9–1

***I.* 'Pale Shades'** (IB, Amoena) Slightly scented flowers with upright, incurving, blue-tinted white standards and horizontal, pale greeny yellow falls, rippled or waved at the edges; a pale blue beard. ↕12 in (30 cm). Z3–8 H9–1

I. pallida (Bearded iris) Semievergreen clump-former with green or gray-blue, sword-shaped, 8–24 in (20–60 cm) leaves, ½–1½ in (1–4 cm) wide. In early summer, branched stems carry up to six beautifully scented 4 in (10 cm) flowers, either pale blue and yellow-bearded or bluish purple with a white beard tipped in yellow, emerging from distinctively dry, silver bracts. Easy to grow in well-drained soil in full sun. Valuable for its showy flowers and often good foliage. Propagate by division or from seed. The variegated cultivars are often muddled. From southern Europe. ↕4 ft (1.2 m). Z6. **'Argentea Variegata'** Leaves broadly striped with white but flowers less freely and is less vigorous. **'Aurea'** *see* 'Variegata'. **'Aurea Variegata'** *see* 'Variegata'. **var. *dalmatica*** *see* subsp. *pallida*. **subsp. *pallida*** Gray-green leaves and pale blue flowers with yellow beards. **'Variegata'** syn. 'Aurea', 'Aurea Variegata' Leaves broadly striped with primrose yellow. More vigorous than 'Argentea Variegata'; flowers freely.

***I.* 'Party Dress'** (TB, Bitone) Large, ruffled, fragrant; pale peachy standards, deeper colored falls with tangerine beards. Prolific and vigorous. Early summer. ↕32 in (80 cm). Z3–8 H9–1

***I.* 'Pastel Charm'** (SDB, Bitone) Oddly named, since the dark flowers have rich purple standards while the falls are darker with a deeper tone around the blue-tinted, purple beard. Late spring. ↕12 in (30 cm). Z3–8 H9–1

***I.* 'Pearly Dawn'** (TB, Self) Pale pink standards and falls, deeper in the center of the blooms, with orange, white-tipped beards. Old-fashioned form but robust and prolific. Early summer. ↕32 in (80 cm). Z3–9 H9–1

***I.* 'Peggy Chambers'** (IB, Plicata) Striking flowers, the standards violet and the white falls edged with violet. Late spring/early summer. ↕18 in (45 cm). Z3–8 H9–1

***I.* 'Pele'** (SDB, Bicolor) Bright orange standards and orange falls with a bold dark purple blotch covering most of the petal below the orange beards. Individual in appearance. Mid-spring. ↕12 in (30 cm). Z3–8 H9–1

***I.* 'Phil Keen'** (TB, Self) Well-ruffled, slightly incurved standards and almost horizontal ruffled falls, all in deep purple with a purple beard. Heavy-textured petals are quite weather-resistant. Early summer. ↕38 in (95 cm). Z3–8 H9–1

***I.* 'Pledge Allegiance'** (TB, Self) Large, ruffled dark blue-violet flowers, with standards slightly paler than falls. Well-branched, prolific, and scented. Early summer. ↕3¼ ft (1 m). Z3–8 H9–1

***I.* 'Pogo'** (SDB, Bicolor) Pale yellow standards with yellow falls, each with a deep chestnut maroon-fringed blotch below the yellow beard. Dramatic. Late spring. ↕12 in (30 cm). Z3–8 H9–1

***I.* 'Pond Lily'** (TB, Bicolor) Large, ruffled flowers with lilac-pink standards and darker lilac falls with a pale area below the orange-tipped beard. Early summer. ↕36 in (90 cm). Z3–8 H9–1

***I.* 'Prince of Burgundy'** (IB, Plicata) Small, gently ruffled flowers, the standards burgundy with a small white center, the falls more narrowly edged, with a broad white zone surrounding a white-tipped orange beard, and with petal stalks stippled with brown. Late spring. ↕24 in (60 cm). Z3–8 H9–1

***I.* 'Provencal'** (TB, Plicata) Fragrant, richly colored flowers. The standards are heavily infused with copper brown around a yellow center, and the falls are buff yellow, broadly edged brown, with a fiery beard. Prolific. From Cayeux of France. Early summer. ↕36 in (90 cm). Z3–8 H9–1

I. pseudacorus (Laevigata) Vigorous, robust, creeping plant with strong rhizomes. The 36 in (90 cm) tall foliage is ½–1¼ in (1–3 cm) wide, ribbed and bright green. In early summer, the flowering stems produce up to a dozen bright yellow flowers carried below the tops of the foliage, 3 in (8 cm) across, with brown veins on the falls around a darker yellow zone. Plant in sun or part-shade; commonly planted in water as a marginal aquatic, but also thrives in moist soil. Propagate by division or from seed. Can become invasive and is classed as a noxious weed in some areas. From Europe, western Russia and North Africa. ↕4 ft (1.2 m). Z5–8 H8–3. **'Alba'** Translucent cream flowers with dark veins. **var. *bastardii*** Pale yellow flowers. **'Flore Pleno'** Double flowers with six falls. **'Roy Davidson'** Large yellow flowers with brown veins and a brown crescent below the beard. A seedling of 'Holden Clough', so technically a hybrid with

RIGHT 1 *Iris pallida* 'Argentea Variegata' **2** *I. pseudacorus*

ABOVE **1** *I. sanguinea* 'Snow Queen'
2 *I. setosa*

I. chrysographes. **'Variegata'** Foliage brightly striped with yellow in spring, gradually fading to green by the time flowers open. Yellow areas of foliage may scorch in dry soils in full sun.

I. **'Quechee'** (TB, Self) Large, smooth flowers in rich garnet red. Standards are slightly paler, the beards are yellow. Very fragrant and lovely, but old-fashioned in form and not prolific. Early summer. ‡36 in (90 cm). Z3–8 H9–1

I. **'Rain Dance'** (SDB, Self) Broad, bright blue standards and falls with a matching blue beard and delicately veined petal stalks. Late spring. ‡10 in (25 cm). Z3–8 H9–1

I. **'Rajah'** (TB, Variegata) Large yellow standards and small, incurved falls in maroon, heavily striped around the petal stalk and with a pale tangerine beard. Old-fashioned in form, but fruitily fragrant and prolific. Early summer. ‡36 in (90 cm). Z3–8 H9–1

I. **'Rare Edition'** (IB, Plicata) Superb, neat Plicata flowers with bold mulberry-purple markings around the white standards and more slenderly edged falls with pale lilac-blue beards. Scented. Late spring/early summer. ‡24 in (60 cm). Z3–8 H9–1

I. **'Rare Treat'** (TB, Plicata) Large, ruffled, wide, pure white standards broadly edged in deep indigo. The falls are crisply edged with deep indigo with a blue beard. Early summer. ‡36 in (90 cm). Z3–8 H9–1

I. **'Raspberry Blush'** (IB, Bitone) Rich, lilac-tinted pink blooms, the standards slightly paler than the almost horizontal falls, with a deeper-veined zone around the orange beard. Early summer. ‡20 in (50 cm). Z3–8 H9–1

I. **'Ringo'** (TB, Amoena) Large, lightly ruffled, bicolored flowers, the standards are pure white and the falls a purple,

rimmed with white. Vivid tangerine beards. Sometimes remontant. Early summer. ‡3¼ ft (1 m). Z3–8 H9–1

I. x *robusta* **'Gerald Darby'** (Laevigata) Robust moisture-lover, its lush foliage deeply stained purple at the base; unbranched flower stems carry up to four flowers, are also purple. Blooms are violet-blue with upright standards; falls have rich yellow signals lined with blue and white. Easy to grow in moist soil, in sun or part-shade. Ideal for bog gardens. Hybrid of *I. versicolor* and *I. virginica.* ‡32 in (80 cm). Z4–9 H9–2

I. **'Rocket'** (TB, Self) Large, smooth flowers with buff-orange standards, the falls in a similar shade with a yellow flare around the bright orange beard. Fragrant. ‡32 in (80 cm). Z3–8 H9–1

I. **'Romantic Evening'** (TB, Bitone) Large ruffled flowers with domed violet standards. The velvety falls are darker in color and enhanced by a deep red beard. ‡36 in (90 cm). Z3–8 H9–1

I. rubromarginata see *I. suaveolens* 'Rubromarginata'.

I. **'Rustler'** (TB, Blend) Large, heavily ruffled flowers; bright coppery-brown standards, flaring falls a darker chestnut brown with occasional purple highlights and a lighter rim. Gold beards are flanked by chestnut veins on white. Vigorous and well-branched. Early summer. ‡3¼ ft (1 m). Z3–8 H9–1

I. **'Sable'** (TB, Bitone) Smooth, deep purple blooms, standards paler than reflexed falls; striped petal stalks and a blue beard. Old, dependable, and scented. ‡36 in (90 cm). Z3–8 H9–1

I. **'Saint Crispin'** (TB. Plicata) Large, ruffled flowers; pale yellow standards with white central zone, while more narrowly edged falls have matching yellow-tipped white beards. Vigorous and prolific. Early summer. ‡36 in (90 cm). Z3–8 H9–1

I. sanguinea (Siberian/28) Clump-forming plant with thick, creeping

rhizomes carrying slightly bluish, ½ in (1 cm) wide, grassy foliage as tall as the flower stems. These are unbranched and carry two, typically reddish purple, 2–3 in (5–8 cm) flowers with small, erect standards and falls with orange petal stalks in early summer. Plant in moist soil in sun or part-shade. Long-lived without much care. Propagate from seed or by division. It can be distinguished from *I. sibirica,* with which it hybridizes, by its unbranched flower stems with just two flowers. From southeastern Russia, Japan, Korea, and China. ‡30 in (75 cm). Z4–9 H9–2.

I. **'Sapphire Gem'** (SDB, Self) Bright, clear blue standards and falls with a neat white stripe below the paler blue beards. Mid-/late spring. ‡12 in (30 cm). Z3–8 H9–1

I. **'Sarah Taylor'** (SDB, Self) Scented, soft yellow flowers with paler standards, and bright blue beards with a paler stripe below. Altogether excellent. Mid-spring. ‡12 in (30 cm). Z3–8 H9–1

I. **'Seakist'** (TB, Amoena) Large, ruffled flowers with ivory white standards and broad falls flushed with sky blue, with a white zone around a yellow beard. Free-flowering. ‡3¼ ft (1 m). Z3–8 H9–1

I. **'Sea Power'** (TB, Self) Sweetly scented, exaggeratedly ruffled flowers; falls and standards are deep cornflower blue, paler at the edges. Early summer. ‡39 in (100 cm). Z3–8 H9–1

I. setosa (Beardless iris) Variable species. The 8–20 in (20–50 cm) foliage is bright green, often purple-tinted, and ½–1 in (1–2.5 cm) wide. In early summer, branched stems carry up to 12 blue or purple, 2–3½ in (5–9 cm) flowers with tiny standards and arching falls with a white mark at the base. Grow in moist, acidic or neutral soil in sun or part-shade. Easy to grow and hardy. Propagate by division or from seed. From eastern Russia, Japan, Alaska, and northeast North America. ‡6–32 in (15–80 cm). Z3–8 H8–1. **'Alba'** White flowers. **var. arctica** Dwarf; unbranched stems. Alaska. ‡6 in (15 cm).

I. **'Shelford Giant'** (Spuria) Robust, beardless iris forming large clumps of creeping rhizomes carrying upright, narrow foliage and yellow and white flowers with a large yellow blotch on the falls in summer. Grow in moist, rich soil in sun or part-shade. ‡6½ ft (2 m). Z3–8 H9–1

I. **'Sherbet Lemon'** (IB, Self) Lightly ruffled, lemon yellow flowers with flaring falls and a strong fragrance. ‡24 in (60 cm). Z3–8 H9–1

I. sibirica (Siberian/28) Tightly clump-forming, the thick rhizomes carry 8–16 in (20–40 cm), gray-green, ¼–½ in (0.5–1 cm) wide grassy foliage that is usually shorter than the flower stems. Branched stems carry up to six 3 in (8 cm) flowers, usually in blue or violet, with white veins around the petal stalk of the falls. Standards are upright and the falls hang down

vertically. Many cultivars customarily listed here are hybrids; the early ones were between this species and *I. sanguinea,* but hybrids with the 40-chromosome species, known as Sino-Sibs, have brought new forms, often with larger flowers with broader, thicker petals and flaring rather than vertical falls. Modern hybrids also have a wider color range, many by the renowned American hybridizer Currier McEwen of Maine. Grow in moist soil in sun or part-shade. Plants develop open centers after several years and need dividing. Propagate from seed, cultivars by division. From Europe and western Asia. 24–40 in (60–100 cm). Z3–8 H9–1. **'Alba'** White, often with purple veins. **'Annemarie Troeger'** Bright blue flowers with rounded falls with a white, veined signal. ‡36 in (90 cm). **'Anniversary'** Slightly ruffled white blooms with flaring falls and yellow signals. ‡36 in (90 cm). **'Baby Sister'** Light blue flowers with darker veins and white signals. Raised by Currier McEwen. ‡16 in (40 cm). **'Berlin Ruffles'** (Siberian-tetraploid) Deep blue flowers with large, silver-edged, flaring falls and ruffled standards. ‡30 in (75 cm). **'Blue King'** Deep blue-purple, ruffled flowers, oblique standards, white, deep-veined signals. ‡28 in (70 cm). **'Butter and Sugar'** Flaring flowers, oblique, creamy white standards, cream style arms, rich yellow, rounded falls. Can be remontant. Raised by Currier McEwen. ‡28 in (70 cm). **'Caesar'** Deep blue-purple flowers with yellow signal. ‡36 in (90 cm). **'Caesar's Brother'** Mid-purple-blue flowers, erect standards. ‡3¼ ft (1 m). **'Cambridge'** Light blue flowers, paler standards, yellow, striped signal on the wavy falls. ‡36 in (90 cm). **'Chartreuse Bounty'** White, green-veined standards, chartreuse yellow, flaring falls. Remontant. Raised by Currier McEwen. ‡38 in (95 cm). **'Crème Chantilly'** Flaring white, ruffled flowers with oblique standards and a yellow signal. ‡3¼ ft (1 m). **'Dance Ballerina Dance'** Flaring, ruffled blooms, oblique, palest pink standards, rosy falls, edged white. Bright golden yellow, veined signals. ‡32 in (80 cm). **'Dreaming Spires'** Ruffled deep blue flowers, oblique, purplish standards. ‡32 in (80 cm). **'Dreaming Yellow'** White flowers, narrow yellow petal stalks, wavy white falls. Raised by Currier McEwen. ‡32 in (80 cm). **'Ego'** Broad, bright sky blue flowers, oblique standards, ruffled falls, veined around the yellow and white signals. ‡36 in (90 cm). **'Exuberant Encore'** Flared blue standards, recurved blue falls, boldly patterned pale toffee throat, then white, with purple veins. Remontant. ‡32 in (80 cm). **'Ewen'** Wine-red flowers, striped white and yellow signals. Raised by Currier McEwen. ‡32 in (80 cm). **'Flight of Butterflies'** Old-fashioned flowers, narrow, drooping falls, bright blue, heavily veined. Exquisite and free-flowering. ‡36 in (90 cm). **'Fourfold White'** Large flowers, broad, smooth falls, crisp yellow signals, no veins. Raised by Currier McEwen. ‡32 in (80 cm). **'Gatineau'** Old-fashioned flowers with

1

2

upright standards, spoon-shaped falls, brownish-striped petal stalks. Mid-blue. ↕36 in (90 cm). **'Gelber Mantel'** syn. 'Gerbel Mantel' (Sino-Sib) Narrow-leaved, pale yellow, brown-veined flowers. Sometimes spelled "Gelbe." ↕36 in (90 cm). Z5. **'Harpswell Happiness'** Broad, flaring flowers in pure white, yellow signals. Raised by Currier McEwen. ↕36 in (90 cm). **'Helen Astor'** Rose pink flowers, upright standards, veined falls, yellow, veined petal stalks. ↕32 in (80 cm). **'Helicopter'** Horizontal, deep blue flowers, six narrow falls, no standards. ↕36 in (90 cm). **'Illini Charm'** Large, lilac-pink flowers, oblique standards and arching falls with a large, veined, yellow and white signal. ↕28 in (70 cm). **'Jewelled Crown'** Dark wine red flowers, falls heavily white-lined. ↕32 in (80 cm). **'Lady Vanessa'** Rosy purple flowers, paler standards, broad falls; white, veined signals. ↕30 in (75 cm). **'Lavender Bounty'** Pale lilac-purple flowers, rounded falls, yellow, striped petal stalks, paler, oblique standards. Raised by Currier McEwen. ↕34 in (85 cm). **'Limeheart'** Broad flowers, oblique standards, flaring falls in greenish white, lime green center. ↕32 in (80 cm). **'Marilyn Holmes'** Dark blue, lightly ruffled falls, paler standards. Raised by Currier McEwen. ↕28 in (70 cm). **'Melton Red Flare'** Deep wine red flowers, yellow signals. ↕36 in (90 cm). **'Mrs. Rowe'** Small, narrow-petaled flowers in grayish-pink. Free-flowering. ↕36 in (90 cm). **'Oban'** Deep velvety blue standards and falls. ↕30 in (75 cm). **'Orville Fay'** Large, broad, sky blue flowers, oblique standards and white and yellow, lined signals. Raised by Currier McEwen. ↕4 ft (1.2 m). **'Ottawa'** Deep blue flowers, white striped on the falls, yellow signals. ↕32 in (80 cm). **'Papillon'** Free-flowering with small, soft blue flowers, white veins on the falls. ↕36 in (90 cm). **'Parasol'** Flat, pale, lilac-pink flowers, six falls, no standards. ↕3¼ ft (1 m). **'Perry's Blue'** Pale blue flowers of old-fashioned form; vertical, striped falls. ↕34 in (85 cm). **'Pink Haze'** Pale mauve flowers, paler standards, arching falls. ↕36 in (90 cm). **'Plissee'** Flared deep blue standards; ruffled, velvety, deep blue falls, a hairline white edge. ↕3¼ ft (1 m). **'Ruffled Velvet'** Large, broad, ruffled flowers in deep purple-blue, white and yellow striped signals. Raised by Currier McEwen. ↕24 in (60 cm). **'Shirley Pope'** Very dark, inky purple, velvety flowers, flaring falls. Yellow signal on falls surrounded by a white zone, lined with purple. Raised by Currier McEwen. ↕34 in (85 cm). **'Showdown'** Rich, velvety flowers in wine purple, oblique standard, falls small; white, veined signal. ↕34 in (85 cm). **'Silver Edge'** Large, broad flowers; blue standards, dark blue falls edged with white. Raised by Currier

3

4

5

6

McEwen. ↕ 34 in (85 cm). **'Snow Queen'** Ivory-white flowers. **'Soft Blue'** Pale, blue flowers, upright standards. Remontant. Raised by Currier McEwen. ↕ 32 in (80 cm). **'Sparkling Rosé'** Lilac-pink flowers; broad, oblique standards, rounded falls, white, veined signal. ↕ 28 in (70 cm). **'Steve'** Large, broad deep blue, ruffled flowers, round falls, floppy standards. ↕ 26 in (65 cm). **'Summer Sky'** Free-flowering, small, narrow-petaled pale blue flowers. Falls have long, yellowish petal stalks. ↕ 32 in (80 cm). **'Tropic Night'** Small flowers, narrow, upright, deep blue standards, narrow arching falls, a large, yellow, striped signal. ↕ 3¼ ft (1 m). **'Tycoon'** Large, rich blue flowers, upright standards, rounded falls; dark veins around yellow signal. ↕ 30 in (75 cm). **'Vi Luihn'** Deep violet-blue flowers, oblique standards, rounded falls with yellow, veined signals. ↕ 36 in (90 cm). **'White Swirl'** Flaring white flowers, a yellow center. ↕ 34 in (85 cm).

I. 'Silverado' (TB, Self) Large, broad, heavily ruffled, scented flowers. Palest blue standards and falls with yellow beards. A prolific multiple award-winner from Schreiners of Salem, Oregon. Early summer. ↕ 3¼ ft (1 m). Z3–8 H9–1

I. sintenisii (Spuria) Forms clumps of ¾–2 in (2–5 cm) wide, upright leaves 12–16 in (30–40 cm) long. In summer, the 12 in (30 cm) stems carry one or two 2½ in (6 cm) flowers with narrow falls and standards in violet blue with white falls very densely veined in violet. Grow in sun or part-shade, in moist, well-drained soil. From dry scrub and woodland clearings in southeastern Europe. ↕ 16 in (40 cm). Z6–8 H8–6

I. 'Skating Party' (TB, Self) Large, heavily ruffled, pure white fragrant flowers. Standards are especially well ruffled, with pale yellow beards on the falls. Vigorous and prolific. Early summer. ↕ 38 in (95 cm). Z3–8 H9–1

I. 'Sky Hooks' (TB, Bitone) A space-age iris; large, ruffled flowers in soft apricot, a paler area on the falls and pale lilac horns and spoons from the base of the yellow beard. The progenitor of many space-age irises. Early summer. ↕ 38 in (95 cm). Z3–8 H9–1

I. 'Snowy Owl' (TB, Self) Large, ruffled, pure white flowers with no other color except for the yellow beard, tipped in white. ↕ 38 in (95 cm). Z3–8 H9–1

I. 'Somerset Blue' (TB, Bicolor) Waved, arching, violet-blue standards with horizontal, wavy, grayish white falls veined in pale maroon with a yellow-tipped white beard. Prolific. Early summer. ↕ 30 in (75 cm). Z3–8 H9–1

I. 'Song of Norway' (TB, Self) Large, scented, ruffled flowers with large cool, icy blue standards; white-tipped beard. ↕ 3¼ ft (1 m). Z3–8 H9–1

I. 'Sonoran Señorita' (Spuria) Vigorous; 4 ft (1.2 m) long, 1 in (2.5 cm) wide grayish foliage, three to five large, lightly ruffled flowers in bright gold, held clear of the foliage. Early summer to midsummer. ↕ 4 ft (1.2 m). Z4–9 H9–2

I. 'Splashacata' (TB, Plicata) Large, slightly ruffled flowers with palest blue standards and pale blue falls, heavily overlaid with purple-blue spots, most strongly around the edge. Pale yellow beards. ↕ 34 in (85 cm). Z3–8 H9–1

I. spuria (Spuria) Robust, variable; narrow, stiffly upright, 12 in (30 cm) foliage. In summer, branched stems bear up to four 3 in (8 cm) wide, blue, lilac, purple, or yellow blooms. Needs moist, well-drained soil in sun or part-shade. Underused, perhaps due to tall growth. Propagate from seed or by division. From southern Europe to Central Asia. ↕ 36 in (90 cm). Z6–9 H9–6

I. 'Stairway to Heaven' (TB, Amoena) Large, ruffled flowers with arching, near-white standards and flaring, mid-blue falls with pale blue beards. A hybrid of the great 'Edith Wolford' and 'Breakers'. Vigorous and prolific. Early summer. ↕ 3¼ ft (1 m). Z3–8 H9–1

I. 'Staplehurst' (MTB, Bicolor) Upright, slightly incurved, pale brown standards with white horizontal falls delicately veined in purple toward the edges; a small orange beard. ↕ 24 in (60 cm). Late spring. Z3–8 H9–1

I. 'Starship Enterprise' (TB, Amoena) Unique flowers have upright waved white standards, gold at the base, pure white flared falls, edged in magenta, and a gold petal stalk and beard. Early summer. ↕ 36 in (90 cm). Z3–8 H9–1

I. 'Staten Island' (TB, Variegata) Bright yellow standards and droopy, yellow-edged, maroon falls with striped petal stalks and a golden beard. An old-fashioned look, but delightfully scented. Early summer. ↕ 38 in (95 cms). Z3–8 H9–1

I. 'Stepping Out' (TB, Plicata) Large, lightly ruffled flowers; both standards and falls pure white with a broad, violet-blue edge. Well-branched. Early summer. ↕ 3¼ ft (1 m). Z3–8 H9–1

I. stylosa see *I. unguicularis.*

I. suaveolens syn. *I. mellita* (Bearded iris) Dwarf; fans of curved leaves 9 in (22 cm) long, ½ in (1 cm) wide. Short stems bear one or two 2 in (5 cm) flowers in late spring. Blooms, 1¾– 2¼ in (4.5–5.5 cm) may be yellow or purple, often marked with brown; beards yellow or purple. Grow in well-drained soil in sun. Propagate either from seed or by division. From northwestern Turkey and Balkans. ↕ 6 in (15 cm). Z6–8 H8–6. **'Rubromarginata'** Leaves edged red. Sometimes, wrongly, elevated to a species as *I. rubromarginata.*

I. 'Sun Doll' (SDB, Self) Vivid, ruffled, uniformly rich yellow flowers like roses

in bud with a sweet fragrance. Mid-spring. ↕ 12 in (30 cm). Z3–8 H9–1

I. 'Sunny Dawn' (IB, Self) Ruffled yellow flowers, paler at the base of the standards, bronzing on the falls and brilliant bright tangerine beards. Late spring. ↕ 22 in (55 cm). Z3–8 H9–1

I. 'Sunrise in Sonora' (Spuria) Vigorous, with 4 ft (1.2 m) long, ¾ in (2 cm) wide, erect, slightly gray foliage and four large flowers per stem, with deep maroon, erect standards and rounded falls in deep maroon around a golden yellow center. Early summer/midsummer. ↕ 4 ft (1.2 m).

I. 'Superstition' (TB, Self) Large, gently ruffled, dark indigo blooms with maroon hints, especially toward the base of the standards and sides of the falls. One of the closest to black, with a blue-black beard. Very fragrant. Early summer. ↕ 38 in (95 cm). Z3–8 H9–1

I. 'Supreme Sultan' (TB, Variegata) Massive, 8 in (20 cm), ruffled, lily-blooms; arched standards deep gold and falls mahogany-red with golden beards. Probably the largest flowers of any iris, stout stems support them well. Early summer. ↕ 38 in (95 cm). Z3–8 H9–1

I. 'Susan Bliss' (TB, Self) Old-fashioned-looking, fragrant, with lilac-pink standards and similar, narrow falls with striped petal stalks and a yellow beard. Vigorous. Late spring/early summer. ↕ 34 in (85 cm). Z3–8 H9–1

I. 'Swingtown' (TB, Self) Large, ruffled, and sweetly fragrant. Arching standards are mulberry red; the falls are of similar color and have purple beards. Prolific and stiff-stemmed. Early summer. Prolific. ↕ 38 in (95 cm). Z3–8 H9–1

I. tectorum (Crested) Attractive, creeping iris with fans of broad, sword-shaped, light green, 4¼ ft (1.3 m) leaves. In early summer, the fans produce sparsely branched stems with several 4 in (10 cm), pale lavender, rather orchidlike flowers, with floppy standards and horizontal falls with a toothed crest and pale signals. Grow in full sun, in well-drained soil. Prefers a sheltered, warm spot. From China. ↕16 in (40 cm). Z5–9 H9–3. **'Alba'** Beautiful white flowers with yellow crests and petal stalks. **'Variegata'** White-striped foliage. Plants sold under this name are often *I. japonica* 'Variegata'.

I. **'Templecloud'** (IB, Bitone) Lightly ruffled flowers, pale blue standards, and deep violet falls with deep blue beard. Free-flowering over an very long season. Late spring. ↕22 in (55 cm). Z3–8 H9–1

I. tenax (PCI) Clump-forming, with narrow, deep green, 12 in (30 cm) foliage, tinted red at the base. In early summer, slender, unbranched stems carry one or two 3 in (8 cm) blue, lavender, yellow, cream, or white flowers with yellow signals on the falls. Grow in moist, well-drained, acidic or neutral soil in sun or part-shade. Propagate by seed. From Washington and Oregon. ↕10 in (25 cm). Z5–9 H9–5

I. **'Thornbird'** (TB, Blend) Unique flowers the color of unbleached linen with waved standards, narrow, flaring, slightly darker falls, and curved purple hooks at the base of orange beards. Very free-flowering. Space-age iris. Early summer. ↕38 in (95 cm). Z3–8 H9–1

I. **'Thriller'** (TB, Self) Large, scented, lightly ruffled flowers in rich purple-claret with darker purple beards. Prolific and with petals of great substance. ↕36 in (90 cm). Z3–8 H9–1

I. **'Tiger Honey'** (TB, Broken self) Large, gently ruffled flowers, the lightly laced standards amber-caramel streaked with gold and the falls mustard yellow, heavily streaked with white. Strong-growing. ↕36 in (90 cm). Z3–8 H9–1

I. **'Tinkerbell'** (SDB, Bitone) Very pretty, medium-blue standards and slightly darker falls with a deeper blue zone, whiskered white at the sides around the white beard. Late spring. ↕12 in (30 cm). Z3–8 H9–1

I. **'Titan's Glory'** (TB, Self) Very large, broad, ruffled, silky flowers in rich, dark violet with swirling standards and dark blue beards. Strong-stemmed and fragrant. ↕38 in (95 cm). Z3–8 H9–1

I. **'Top Flight'** (TB, Self) Large and impressive, ruffled apricot flowers with partially reflexed falls; a bright orange beard. ↕38 in (95 cm). Z3–8 H9–1

I. unguicularis syn. *I. stylosa* (Beardless) Clump-forming, with tight rhizomes; narrow, evergreen, often scruffy foliage may reach 28 in (70 cm). The almost stemless, sweetly fragrant, flowers are on long, 6 in (15 cm) perianth tubes from winter to spring, the 3 in (8 cm) pale lilac-blue blooms nestle in the foliage marked with white around the petal

stalks with a yellow signal. They may be damaged by frost, but are replaced by new buds over several months. Easy in full sun in dry soil; requires summer baking and likes alkalinity. Can be slow to establish after transplanting. Propagate from seed or by division. From Algeria, Tunisia, east of the Mediterranean, and western Syria. ↕16 in (40 cm). Z7–9 H9–7. **'Alba'** Delicate-textured, white flowers with a yellow signal. **subsp. cretensis** Richly colored flowers in violet-blue and a dwarf habit, with grassy foliage. ↕5 in (12 cm). From Crete. Z8. **'Mary Barnard'** Large, bright violet flowers with yellow signals. **'Walter Butt'** Large 4 in (10 cm) flowers in pale, silvery lilac with yellow signals. Flowers earlier than most, often starting in late fall.

I. **'Vanity'** (TB, Self) Large, pale pink flowers with a hint of blue, the falls paler in the center and with deep coral pink beards. Vigorous and prolific. ↕34 in (85 cm). Z3–8 H9–1

I. variegata (Bearded iris) Sword-shaped, gray-green leaves, 12 in (30 cm) long and ½–1¼ in (1–3 cm) wide, spring from a stout rhizome that carries branched stems with up to six 2¾ in (7 cm) flowers in early summer. Each bloom has pale yellow standards, and pale falls densely lined with maroon, especially around the tips, with yellow beards. The parent of larger, brighter hybrids with the Variegata flower pattern (*see* Flower Patterns in Bearded Iris, *p.276*). Grow in sun, in well-drained soil. From central and eastern Europe. ↕16 in (40 cm). Z5–9 H9–5

I. versicolor (Laevigata) Robust, making a clump of arching, deep green, 14–24 in (35–60 cm) leaves, tinted

purple at the base and ½–¾ in (1–2 cm) wide. In early summer, branched stems carry small clusters of 3 in (8 cm) wide violet, purple, or lavender flowers with short, upright standards, narrow falls, and white, striped petal stalks and signals. Grow in moist soil, in sun or part-shade. Propagate from seed or by division. From the northeastern US. ↕32 in (80 cm). Z3–9 H9–1. **'Kermesina'** Bright reddish purple flowers.

I. **'Victoria Falls'** (TB, Self) Large, fragrant, bright blue, ruffled flowers with a white flare on the falls below the white beard. Vigorous, well-branched and very prolific. Remontant. Early summer. ↕3¼ ft (1 m). Z3–8 H9–1

I. **'Wabash'** (TB, Amoena) Old, unruffled cultivar with narrow petals. Standards are pure white and falls, deep purple with white rim, clearly striped petal stalks and a gold beard. Early summer. ↕34 in (85 cm). Z3–8 H9–1

I. **'White City'** (TB, Self) Old, fragrant cultivar with slightly ruffled standards and unruffled narrow falls, all in white gently flushed with blue, with a golden beard. Early summer. ↕36 in (90 cm). Z3–8 H9–1

I. **'White Knight'** (TB, Self) Old-fashioned-looking flowers with large, white standards. Drooping, paddle-shaped white falls suffused with cream and green, with a yellow beard. Early summer. ↕32 in (80 cm). Z3–8 H9–1

I. wilsonii (Siberian) Clump-forming, with narrow, grayish foliage 10–22 in

BELOW *Iris variegata*

(25–55 cm) long and 2–3 in (5–8 cm) wide. Hollow, unbranched stems carry two 2¼–3 in (6–8 cm) flowers in early summer, pale yellow with brownish veins on the falls. Similar to *I. forrestii*, but has larger flowers and spreading standards; some botanists say it is too similar—not a genuinely distinct species. Grow in sun or part-shade, in moist, humus-rich soil. Propagate from seed or by division. From western China. ↕28 in (70 cm). Z4–8 H9–2

I. **'Wyoming Cowboys'** (Spuria) Vigorous, with slightly bluish foliage, 4¼ ft (1.3 m) long and 1 in (2.5 cm) wide. Just overtopped by large flowers with erect yellow standards boldly edged in gray-brown and gold falls with a thin brown edge. Late spring/ early summer. 4 ft (1.2 m). Z3–9 H9–1

I. **'Yaquina Blue'** (TB, Self) Large, broad, ruffled, mid-blue flowers; paler area on falls below pale yellow beard. Vigorous. ↕38 in (95 cm). Z3–9 H9–1

ISOPYRUM
RANUNCULACEAE

Graceful woodland plants with pretty divided foliage and anemone-like flowers.

Thirty deciduous species grow in damp mountain woods and along shaded stream banks in Europe, northern Asia, and North America; two are sometimes cultivated. From tuberous or rhizomatous rootstock rise slender stems bearing leaves divided into several lobed leaflets. Small, anemone-like, white or pink-tinged flowers with five or six petals open in spring at base of the upper leaves. Need shelter from dry winds.

CULTIVATION Grow in moist, humus-rich soil in part-shade.

PROPAGATION From seed or by division.

PROBLEMS Slugs and snails.

I. biternatum A clump-forming plant with fibrous roots and small tubers that support slender, branched, leafy stems. The lower leaves are like those of *Thalictrum* (meadow rue), long-stalked and divided several times into broad, lobed leaflets ½–1 in (1–2.5 cm) long; stem leaves are smaller and less divided. White, ¾ in (2 cm) flowers, usually with five oval petals, open in late spring. From damp woodlands in eastern North America, from Ontario to Texas. ↕12 in (30 cm). Z3–8 H9–1

I. thalictroides A mat-forming plant, spread by rhizomes, with slender, branched stems bearing much-divided, blue-green leaves composed of three-lobed leaflets. In late spring, nodding white flowers, to ¾ in (2 cm) wide, appear from upper leaf joints. Each flower is followed by two small seed pods. Can be invasive, but useful for planting under shade-loving shrubs. From moist woods in Europe to Siberia. ↕12 in (30 cm). Z5–8 H8–5

J

JABOROSA
SOLANACEAE

Intriguing yet underused fragrant ground-cover plants that relish sun and arid conditions but need plenty of space to spread.

Twenty deciduous species are found in arid parts of South America. Only one is commonly grown, usually in a warm, dry part of the garden, such as a mixed border. Generally spreads by rhizomes; the basal leaves, usually oval or elliptical, make a good background for the fragrant, bell-shaped or tubular, lobed summer flowers.

CULTIVATION Choose a sheltered spot with plenty of sun and light, sandy, well-drained soil. In cold areas, protect roots from frost with a dry winter mulch, such as straw or salt hay.

PROPAGATION In spring, by division or from seed germinated at 55–61°F (13–16°C).

PROBLEMS Slugs and snails. The plant itself can be invasive.

J. integrifolia A fragrant, stemless species. Its clusters of deep green, fleshy, oval or elliptical basal leaves grow at least 8 in (20 cm) long and hug the ground. Green-to-white tubular flowers, about 2½ in (6 cm) across with star-shaped lobes, appear from June onward, giving off their scent at night. Good for a warm, sunny border, at the foot of a wall, or in a gravel garden. Beware its colonizing habits. From Argentina, southern Brazil, and Uruguay. ‡6 in (15 cm). Z8–10 H11–1

JASIONE
CAMPANULACEAE

Long-flowering plants for the front of a border, with round flowerheads resembling scabious.

About ten species of annuals, biennials, and perennials are found in open grasslands in Europe and Asia; only one of which is usually grown in gardens. Simple, alternate, lance-shaped leaves, mostly making a tufted mass at the base of the plant, support wiry, seldom-branched stems that are topped with pincushion flowers over a long period. They are good for cutting and attractive to insects, especially butterflies.

CULTIVATION Grow in neutral or acid, sandy soil in full sun to part-shade.

PROPAGATION From seed sown as soon as ripe in fall, or by division in spring.

PROBLEMS Slugs and snails in spring.

J. laevis syn. *J. perennis* (Shepherd's scabious) In spring, the new growth makes a dense mound of foliage about 6 in (15 cm) high from which, in early to late summer, grow stems of rather variable height topped with 2-in (5-cm) globes of softly spiky, misty blue flowers. Each has a protruding stigma, giving a dainty pincushion effect. ‡16 in (40 cm). Z6–8 H8–6.
'Blaulicht' (**Blue Light**) Bright blue flowers; more regular in height.

J. perennis see *J. laevis*

JEFFERSONIA
BERBERIDACEAE

A short-lived show of flowers is followed by a long season of attractive foliage.

There are two species, one North American, the other Asian. Not the showiest of plants, *Jeffersonia* is loved for its brief display of pristine petals that epitomize the ephemeral nature of spring flowers. A tough crown supports the naked flower stalks, which bear single, white or lavender, eight-petaled, cup-shaped flowers in early spring, emerging just as the foliage is expanding. American botanist Benjamin Smith Barton named *Jeffersonia* for president Thomas Jefferson because this was his favorite flower.

CULTIVATION Plant in humus-rich, moist, alkaline to moderately acidic soil in part- to full shade. Plants grow slowly but in time form broad, striking clumps. They take a year or two to establish after transplanting.

PROPAGATION Divide in fall using a sharp knife to cut the tough crown, leaving two or three new buds per clump. Sow fresh seed outdoors. Plants bloom in two to three years.

PROBLEMS Usually trouble-free.

J. diphylla (Twin leaf) Tough fibrous-rooted crowns support paired, 6 in (15 cm) wide leaflets on slender stalks. Several single, 1-in (2.5-cm), pure white, eight-petaled flowers appear in early spring on thin stalks, followed by a pipelike seed capsule that blows its top and expels the seed away from the parent. It prefers alkaline soil. Mature clumps make a fine foliage display in the summer garden. From deciduous woods, sheltered cove forests, and streamsides on limestone-derived soils in North America (from ONT and MN, south to VA and AL). ‡18 in (45 cm). Z5–7 H7–5

J. dubia Purple-stained, 4 in (10 cm) wide, shield-shaped to weakly two-lobed leaves emerge after the copious 1-in (2.5-cm) lavender flowers. Plants bloom in early spring, yielding multiple

RIGHT 1 *Jasione laevis* 'Blaulicht'
2 *Jeffersonia diphylla* **3** *J. dubia*

stems from fibrous-rooted crowns far tougher than they appear. Prefers evenly moist, neutral to moderately acidic soil. Established plants tolerate drought. More delicate than *J. diphylla*. From woods and rocky slopes from northern China to Siberia. ‡8 in (20 cm). Z5–8 H8–5. **'Alba'** White flowers.

JUNCUS
Rush
JUNCACEAE

Architectural foliage plants for wet areas or containers, with strong stem structures and striking colors and textures.

Over 800 species grow in wet and moist places in temperate regions throughout the world, with a few tolerating drier conditions. These grasslike plants often feature creeping root systems that form large clumps of cylindrical or flat, hairless, stemlike foliage, smooth or ridged and, unlike grasses, with pithy solid centers. The flowers open in tight clusters at the ends of the stems or appear to burst from the sides, though actually backed by a stem-like leaf. They are generally green or brown and very simple, with male and female parts on the same tiny flower. The fruits are usually roundish nutlets and their shapes are a useful way to identify the different species. A number of species are almost exclusively grown in their curly-leaved forms. *Juncus* make beautiful background plants for smaller, more colorful bog plants, and can also be grown to great effect in moist wildflower meadows or open woodlands. Curly-leaved forms are attractive in containers.

CULTIVATION Grow in moist, infertile soil in sun. Plants can be invasive; some are prolific self-seeders. In smaller gardens, best grown in pots of heavy clay loam and divided every three years in spring. Cut back untidy and dead growth in spring.

PROPAGATION Divide variegated and curly forms in spring. Species can be grown from fresh seed kept moist once sown.

PROBLEMS Usually trouble-free.

J. decipiens **'Curly-wurly'** syn. 'Spiralis' Bright, light green, evergreen mounds of fine, tightly curled, slender leaves are like plastic-coated springs. Best grown in containers in moist, infertile soil, with water left standing in the saucer. It also looks good at the edge of small ponds in sheltered areas. The wild species grows in damp, acidic soil in Japan, China, Korea, and North America. ‡4 in (10 cm). Z6–9 H9–6

J. effusus (Soft rush) Slowly expanding evergreen clumps of bright, greenish yellow, rounded stems, up to 5 ft (1.5 m) high, arch out into a graceful fan of foliage. From late spring to late summer, small, loose, frothy round heads of green to brown flowers burst

from the sides of the stems. A handsome accent plant for ponds and bogs, it makes a good background in wilder areas; alternatively, grow in pots. Common in most temperate regions in damp woods and bogs, and in moist, overgrazed pasture. ‡5 ft (1.5 m). Z6–9 H9–6. **'Gold Strike'** With a single gold stripe on one side of its almost straight or slightly twisting stems. ‡12 in (30 cm). **f. *spiralis*** Dark green, corkscrewlike stems. ‡18 in (45 cm). **'Yellow Line'** Curling stems with a bold yellow stripe. ‡20 in (50 cm).

J. ensifolius Slowly creeping, bright green foliage with narrow, slightly flattened, two-winged stems. In late summer, glossy, brown to purple flowerheads make a dramatic contrast against the broad-bladed stems. Best grown as a marginal bog plant where it can be seen in flower. From damp moors in Japan and western North America. ‡20 in (50 cm). Z4–8 H8–4

J. filiformis **'Spiralis'** (Curling thread rush) Bright green, very fine, slightly ridged stems, spreading out in rows, carry small, tight heads of green-brown flowers, backed by a long stem leaf, from early summer to early fall. They are followed by round seedheads. A delicate marginal plant for small ponds; it is also attractive in containers of moist soil. The wild species is from wild wet places in northern temperate regions. ‡8 in (20 cm). Z6–9 H9–6

J. inflexus (Hard rush) Slowly expanding evergreen clumps are made up of gray-green, upright, ribbed stems, which carry flowers from May to July in loose, one-sided, brownish clusters backed by a longish stem leaf. Grow it as an impressive accent marginal bog plant, in moist wildflower meadows, or by path edges. Poisonous to livestock. Similar to *J. effusus* but with gray-green, rather than yellowish, stems. Grows in boggy land (though it will tolerate drier conditions), usually on heavy alkaline soil, throughout Europe to Iraq. ‡4 ft (1.2 m). Z4–10 H11–10. **'Afro'** Loose, coiling blue-gray stems. More vigorous than *J. effusus* f. *spiralis* and will tolerate drier conditions. ‡18 in (45 cm). Z6–9 H9–6

J. patens **'Carman's Gray'** Forms evergreen clumps of steely blue-gray sprays of cylindrical foliage, with profuse quantities of brown flowers bursting from the tops of the stems in summer. Looks best planted as an accent to contrast with gold and variegated bog plants. From marshy areas in CA and OR; however, the species will tolerate drier areas in full sun. ‡24 in (60 cm). Z7–10 H10–7. **'Silver Spears'** Silver-green, needlelike foliage. **'Unicorn'** Giant curly form with dark green stems; grows in drier conditions than *J. effusus* f. *spiralis*.

JUSTICIA *see* DICLIPTERA

RIGHT 1 *Juncus decipiens* 'Curly-wurly'
2 *J. effusus* **3** *J. effusus* f. *spiralis*
4 *J. patens* 'Carman's Gray'

K

KALIMERIS
ASTERACEAE

Elegant, billowy perennials for a sunny situation that reward with a long flowering period.

About ten adaptable but strangely unfashionable species come from open woodlands and grasslands in East Asia. *Kalimeris* has previously been included in *Aster, Asteromoea,* and *Boltonia,* and is clearly similar to the smaller-flowered asters. With creeping rhizomes, plants have an erect habit, usually only branching where there are flowers, giving a light and airy feel. Leaves are held alternately, but in other characteristics the foliage varies noticeably between species; narrow or rounded, toothed, lobed, or divided into pairs of leaflets, and with or without hairs. The leaves higher up the flowering stems are typically smaller and undivided. A rosette of the basal leaves often remains visible during the winter months. Loose masses of daisylike flowers are held on branched stems through summer into fall. The central disk florets are always in shades of yellow, but the outer ray florets vary from white through pinks and blues to purple.

CULTIVATION Easy: they grow best in full sun or part-shade in moderately fertile, well-drained soil and with shelter from wind, although moist soil is tolerated. Pinching out the tips encourages bushy, compact growth and increases the number of flowers; otherwise, plants may require staking in exposed situations. Prune lightly after flowering. Plants can age quickly, becoming woody after a few years, but they are easily propagated and can be replaced regularly.

PROPAGATION By division or removal of outer growth in spring; cuttings can also be taken in spring.

PROBLEMS Mildew.

K. incisa syn. *Aster incisus, Boltonia incisa* Clump-forming, slightly hairy perennial, with dark, erect stems and oblong leaves 1¼–3 in (3–8 cm) long, with finely toothed margins and with or without leaf stalks. Flowering from early summer and continuing into early fall, the ray florets of the 1¼–1½ in (3–4 cm) flowerheads are usually light purple or white. From East Asia. ‡ 24 in (60 cm). Z5–9 H9–1. **‘Alba’** White flowers. **‘Blue Star’** Pale blue flowers.

K. mongolica syn. *Aster mongolicus, Asteromoea mongolica* Erect, clump-forming perennial with oblong, deeply divided, stalked leaves, 4–6 in (10–15 cm) long with hairs on their

ABOVE *Kalimeris incisa*

margins. Flowerheads are ¾–1¼ in (2–3 cm) wide with pale ray florets tinged with purple. Flowers through the summer, but not for as long as *K. incisa.* From Mongolia and China. ‡ 36 in (90 cm). Z5–9 H9–1.

K. pinnatifida syn. *Asteromoea pinnatifida, Boltonia cantoniensis, B. indica* Tall, erect, clump-forming perennial with oblong to diamond-shaped, prominently divided, stalkless leaves to 3 in (8 cm) long. Flowerheads are 1¼ in (3 cm) wide, with pale pink to pale violet ray florets. Native to Honshu, Japan. ‡ 24–36 in (60–90 cm), occasionally to 5 ft (1.5 m). Z5–9 H9–1. **‘Hortensis’** Anemone-centered white flowers tinged with pale yellow in the center.

K. yomena **‘Shogun’** Two-tone green leaves are margined with creamy white and have a pink tinge in the spring.

During the summer, the yellow fades to cream before turning yellow again in the fall. Flowerheads 1¼–1½ in (3–4 cm) wide have light violet-blue ray florets. Originating in Japan, this cultivar is grown more often than the species itself. ‡ 18–28 in (45–70 cm). Z6–9 H9–6

KIRENGESHOMA
HYDRANGEACEAE

Unusual, attractive plant for the woodland garden, shady border, or as a specimen plant or group.

The single species of deciduous perennial is native to the mountain forests of Japan and Korea. Densely clump-forming, it has erect to somewhat spreading reddish purple stems that contrast well with the broad mid- to light green leaves. The somewhat lilylike yellow flowers make a welcome addition to an early fall display.

CULTIVATION Best in part-shade, needs moist, humus-rich soil to thrive.

PROPAGATION By division, or from seed sown as soon as ripe.

PROBLEMS Slugs are sometimes a nuisance.

K. palmata Densely clump-forming, the erect to somewhat spreading stems bearing pairs of rounded to oval leaves, 4–7 in (10–18 cm) long, with margins cut into pointed, triangular lobes. From late summer to fall, fleshy, five-petaled, 1½ in (3.5–4 cm) long, pale yellow to light apricot-yellow flowers open in loose terminal clusters. *K. koreana* was once considered a distinct species but is now treated as the Korean race of *K. palmata.* It tends to be a little taller and has flowers that open more widely. ‡ 36–48 in (90–120 cm). Z5–8 H9–5

KITAIBELA
MALVACEAE

Robust, leafy plant of bold and imposing stature, for large borders or for naturalizing in the wild garden.

Unmistakably a mallow, the one resilient and hardy species, from the Balkan region, has tough woody roots supporting tall stems; these carry large, attractive, vinelike leaves, which provide contrast to the white mallowlike flowers. This substantial, leafy plant is unsuited to small gardens, but is impressive in more expansive, informal settings.

CULTIVATION Easy to grow and thrives in most soils, in sun or part-shade. In fertile, moist soil, it is more prone to produce massive growth at the expense of flowers.

PROPAGATION From basal cuttings taken in spring or, more usually, from seed sown in spring or fall. The tough, tight woody rootstock makes division difficult, though not impossible.

PROBLEMS Usually trouble free.

K. vitifolia Forming a clump of strong, upright stems from a woody base, the 7 in (18 cm) long, five- or seven-lobed leaves are mid-green and softly hairy. The five-petaled, mallowlike flowers, 2 in (5 cm) across, are white, occasionally pink, with yellow stamens, and each petal is attractively separated from the next. They open in small clusters in the leaf joints, sometimes rather hidden by the foliage, over several months from midsummer and are surrounded by six to nine leafy bracts which enclose the seeds. Easily

BELOW 1 *Kirengeshoma palmata*
2 *Kitaibela vitifolia*

grown from seed and, though hardy, plants are often short-lived and should be regularly propagated. From scrub and grassland a from Slovenia to Macedonia. ‡6½ ft (2 m). Z6–8 H9–6

KNAUTIA
DIPSACACEAE

Long-flowering plants for the edge of a woodland, or on a sunny slope, and unusually attractive to butterflies.

Related to *Scabiosa*, the 60 or so annuals and perennials have similar heads of spiky flowers; the leaves are long and fairly narrow, and vary from simple to deeply dissected. They grow from a woody rootstock that spreads slowly to form a large clump. Foliage generally overwinters as a rosette, except in very cold climates, where it may die away completely. Good plants for a wild garden or wildflower meadow, but also suitable for a more formal border.

CULTIVATION Best in sandy, slightly alkaline soil and full sun.

PROPAGATION Sow seed in spring and give a cold period below 41°F (5°C); germination can be erratic and spread over a long period. Alternatively, take basal cuttings in spring.

PROBLEMS Rare, although aphids may sometimes occur.

K. arvensis syn. *Scabiosa arvensis* (Blue buttons) A deep-rooted perennial with soft stems that are bristly, especially toward the base, and hairy, dull green leaves that vary in shape from simple to deeply cut. Lilac flowers in small globe-shaped heads are carried on sparsely leaved stems from midsummer onward. Native to fields and waste ground in Europe, it has become established in North America from Newfoundland to Pennsylvania. ‡5 ft (1.5 m). Z5–9 H9–5

K. macedonica syn. *Scabiosa rumelica* (Macedonian scabious) Deep-rooted, with narrow, lance-shaped basal leaves, while those on the stems are divided into almost fernlike segments. Branching stems of crimson flowers appear in early summer and continue to be produced until fall. Seeds freely and can become somewhat invasive, but worth the effort of removing unwanted plants. Very drought-tolerant. Collections from the wild by Jim Archibald, of England, have added new shades to the long-familiar crimson. From the central Balkans and Romania. ‡32 in (80 cm). Z5–9 H9–5. **'Mars Midget'** Slightly paler flowers. ‡16 in (40 cm). **Melton pastels** Pink, red, rose, or salmon flowers. Cut back after the first flush of blooms to produce more flowers. ‡4 ft (1.2 m).

RIGHT 1 *Knautia arvensis*
2 *K. macedonica*
3 *K. macedonica* Melton pastels

KNIPHOFIA
Red-hot poker, Torch lily
ASPHODELACEAE

Familiar summer spikes of cool to hot colors that progressively change to lighter shades as the flowers open.

Around 70 species of evergreen or deciduous plants are found mainly in the mountains and upland grasslands of South Africa, but are also found as far away as Ethiopia, Arabia, and Madagascar. They are clump-forming plants with rosettes of long, thin, spiky foliage, above which the dense flower spikes are held clear on stout, erect stems. The foliage is generally untidy and the long, weak, strongly keeled leaves often bend irregularly at sharp angles; only in the two stemmed species, *K. caulescens* and *K. northiae*, can it be considered ornamental. Rather surprisingly, variegated cultivars are rarely grown.

The pendulous flowers, which open from the bottom of the spike upward, are long and tubular with the yellow stamens often slightly protruding. The color of the buds is usually in contrast to, and darker than, the fully open flower, but some cultivars have more or less uniformly colored spikes. The flowering period for many species and cultivars is confined to a short window, often less than a month. However, some have a propensity to produce another small flush of flowers earlier or later in the season.

The species themselves hybridize readily with each other, even in the wild, and seed from species grown in cultivation is very likely to be of hybrid origin; this means that very few true species are currently grown—whatever it may say on the label. Also, many spontaneous seedlings arise in gardens, further complicating the recognition of cultivars, and mixed seedlings of unknown origin are often sold by seed companies. Unless a plant is known to come from a reliable source, it probably is an unnamed cultivar masquerading under a familiar and reputable name.

There is no working classification for the numerous cultivars, but a distinction might be possible between the small semideciduous cultivars—probably of *K. triangularis* origin—and the taller cultivars, which are evergreen. This does, however, vary with the climate, and more study is needed.

Hardiness can seem unpredictable, but it is not simply a matter of winter temperature. Cool, wet winters, poor drainage, and alternate freezing and thawing are more damaging than a consistently dryer, colder period.

CULTIVATION Although most species grow in damp areas in the wild, they require very good drainage, especially over winter. Waterlogging can cause rotting during the cold dormant months, but plants can be watered plentifully during the summer. They require deep, fertile soil in full sun and benefit from good mulching to retain water during the summer and to protect the roots over the winter. Leaves can also be tied over the rosette during the winter to shield it from the rain, which is more likely to kill plants than cold.

PROPAGATION Divide in spring. Although propagation of species from seed is easy, it is best avoided since the probability of hybridization with other species and cultivars is very high if they are growing in the vicinity. Seed-raised cultivar strains are available, but are generally a melange of colors with little coherence apart from plant size.

PROBLEMS Usually trouble-free, if winter drainage is good. Mottled foliage can be caused by thrips. Violet root rot can be devastating.

K. **'Ada'** Rich golden orange flowers with darker stamens opening from orange buds and held on dark stems. Raised at Slieve Donard Nursery, Northern Ireland. Flowers in the late summer to early fall. ↕1m (3¼ ft). Z6–9 H9–6

K. **'Alcazar'** Dense spikes of orange-red buds with the tips of the open flowers turning yellow-orange and the stamens noticeably protruding. Flowers early summer to early fall. ↕24–48 in (60–120 cm). Z5–8 H9–4

K. **'Apricot Souffle'** Slim spikes of dark-tipped, peachy orange buds opening to off white. Blooms July to August. ↕36 in (90 cm). Z6–9 H9–6

K. **'Atlanta'** Dense, bicolored heads of red and yellow, set off by slightly bluish foliage. One of the best archetypal red-hot pokers. Found on the grounds of the Atlantic Hotel in Tintagel, Cornwall, England, in 1962. Flowers mid-spring to early summer. ↕4 ft (1.2 m). Z6–9 H9–4

K. **'Bees' Lemon'** Round heads of slightly misty lemon yellow flowers opening from greenish buds, and narrow foliage. Introduced by Bees of Chester, England, in the 1940s. Flowers midsummer to early fall. ↕34–36 in (85–90 cm). Z6–9 H9–6

K. **'Bees' Sunset'** Bronzed stems bearing spikes of orange buds opening to soft orange flowers, and narrow foliage. Introduced by Bees of Chester. Flowers early summer to early fall. ↕30–48 in (75–120 cm). Z6–9 H9–6

K. **'Border Ballet'** Unpredictable seed-raised mixture of assorted colors and sizes of variable quality. Consistently good when originally raised by Ralph Gould of the Hurst Seed Company, England; some plants are excellent and selections of particularly good forms have been made. One, a dusty coral, is, confusingly, seen under this name. ↕24–36 in (60–90 cm). Z6–9 H9–4

K. **'Bressingham Comet'** Red buds open to apricot-yellow flowers with red tips above grassy leaves. A hybrid of *K. triangularis,* it may also flower earlier in the year. Raised by Englishman Alan Bloom and introduced in 1963. Opens late summer to mid-fall. ↕18–30 in (45–75 cm). Z6–9 H9–4

K. **Bressingham Sunbeam ('Bresun')** Delicate spikes of white-tipped, pale apricot flowers on coppery stems open from slightly darker buds. Flowers midsummer to early fall. ↕24–30 in (60–75 cm). Z6–9 H9–4

K. **'Brimstone'** Slender yellow flowers opening from green buds and with narrow foliage. Flowers midsummer to late fall. ↕30–36 in (75–100 cm). Z6–9 H9–4

K. **'Buttercup'** Round heads of clear yellow flowers opening from slightly darker buds. Flowers from early

summer to midsummer. ↕30 in (75 cm). Z6–9 H9–4

K. **'Candlelight'** Yellow flowers opening from greenish yellow buds and and grassy foliage. Raised and introduced by Alan Bloom in 1975. Flowers early to late summer. ↕1½–3 ft (45–90 cm). Z6–9 H9–4

K. caulescens (Lesotho red-hot poker, Basuto torch lily) Short, thick, trailing, trunklike stems bear relatively stiff, keeled, blue-gray evergreen leaves, to 28 in (70 cm) long and 2 in (5 cm) wide. From early summer to mid-fall, coral red buds open to pale creamy yellow flowers with long protruding stamens; although in softer shades than typical red-hot pokers, the spikes complement the cooler-hued foliage. One of the few species that can be raised reliably from seed. From marshes and among rocks at high altitudes in the mountains of eastern South Africa

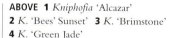

and Lesotho; the Basutos regard it as a charm against lightning and often plant it near their houses. ↕36–48 in (90–120 cm). Z6–9 H9–4

K. citrina (Yellow red-hot poker) Clumps of narrow, tapering leaves up to 28 in (70 cm) long and ½ in (1 cm) wide bear rounded heads of flowers, from July to August, that open a clear yellow from green buds. Vigorous. Related to *K. uvaria.* From coastal grasslands of the Eastern Cape province, South Africa. ↕20–24 in (50–60 cm). Z6–9 H9–4

K. **'Cobra'** Tall, bold, dense spikes of orange-brown buds fading to orange then opening to cream are noticeably broader at the top, hence the name. Good as a specimen. Raised by Alan

Bloom of Diss, England. Flowers July to September. ↕36–42in (90–105cm). Z6–9 H9–4

K. 'Dingaan' Tall, stout, bronze-tinged spikes carry green buds opening to yellow flowers. Flowers July to August. ↕5–6½ ft (1.5–2 m). Z6–9 H9–4

K. 'Dorset Sentry' Large, round heads of yellow flowers opening from greenish buds on bronzed stems over a long season. Flowers midsummer to mid-fall. ↕36–40 in (90–100 cm). Z6–9 H9–4

K. 'Drummore Apricot' Slender spikes of orange-yellow, tinged red in bud. Not "Drunmore," as sometimes seen. Flowers early to late summer. ↕30–36 in (75–90 cm). Z6–9 H9–4

K. 'Earliest of All' Slender, soft coral-red spikes that flower in early to late summer. Orange-flowered plants may be mistakenly sold under this name. ↕12–48 in (30–120 cm). Z6–9 H9–4

K. 'Early Buttercup' Dark yellow buds open to paler yellow flowers in rounded heads. Similar to 'Buttercup,' but flowers late spring to early summer. ↕30–40 in (75–100 cm). Z6–9 H9–4

K. ensifolia Clumps of erect, strongly keeled, bluish green leaves, up to 4 ft (1.2 m) long and 1½ in (3.5 cm) wide, send up tall, thin, cylindrical spikes of greenish white flowers from mid-spring to midsummer, tapering toward the green or reddish buds. From streambanks and marshy grasslands of northern South Africa. ↕to 6 ft (1.8 m). Z6–9 H9–4

K. 'Erecta' The most distinctive of cultivars, but rather a curiosity, with bright orange flowers that turn to point upward as they open. Flowers midsummer to early fall. ↕3¼–5 ft (1–1.5 m). Z6–9 H9–4

K. 'Fiery Fred' Slender, bright fiery red spikes from greenish buds over a long season. Named for English cricket player Fred Trueman. Flowers early summer to mid-fall. ↕26–48 in (65–120 cm). Z6–9 H9–4

K. 'Flamenco' Unpredictable seed-raised mixture of assorted colors and sizes of variable quality; plants may flower in their first year from seed. Theoretically taller than 'Border Ballet'. ↕30–40 in (75–100 cm). Z6–9 H9–4

K. galpinii Slender, grassy, fibrous leaves up to 24 in (60 cm) long, and bicolored flowerheads, from early summer to early fall. Red at the tip and orange-yellow lower down, the tips do not spread, unlike those in the orange heads of the similar *K. triangularis,* which is in fact the plant most often sold as *K. galpinii.* From grasslands and marshes of eastern South Africa and Swaziland. ↕20–24 in (50–60 cm). Z6–9 H9–1

K. 'Gladness' Uniform spikes of bright orange opening from burnt orange buds on slightly bronzed stems. Flowers early summer to midsummer. ↕3¼–5 ft (1–1.5 m). Z6–9 H9–1

K. 'Green Jade' Slender pale green spikes fading to greenish white. For lovers of the unusual, green flowers have never looked so elegant. Raised and introduced by Beth Chatto, England. Flowers midsummer to early fall. ↕4–5 ft (1.2–1.5 m). Z6–9 H9–4

K. hirsuta Rosettes of rather floppy, hairy leaves, up to 24 in (60 cm) long and 1 in (2.5 cm) wide, sit below dense spikes of orange to salmon pink buds opening to greenish yellow flowers in early summer and midsummer. Often grown from seed, when it can flower in its first year from an early sowing. From streambanks and grasslands in the mountains of Lesotho. ↕20–24 in (50–60 cm). Z6–9 H9–4. **'Traffic Lights'** Seed-raised selection that is little more than a marketing name for the species.

K. 'Ice Queen' Yellowish buds with a hint of green open to ivory white flowers. Raised and introduced by Alan Bloom. Flowers early summer to mid-fall. ↕3¼–5 ft (1–1.5 m). Z6–9 H9–6

K. 'Jenny Bloom' Salmon pink buds opening to peachy cream flowers tinged with salmon at the tips. Not strong. Raised by Englishman Alan

Bloom and named for his daughter. Flowers early summer to early fall. ↕24–36 in (60–90 cm). Z6–9 H9–4

K. 'John Benary' Tall spikes of an almost uniform coral red with a hint of yellow-orange on the tips of the open flowers. Blooms midsummer to early fall. ↕30–60 in (75–150 cm). Z6–9 H9–4

K. linearifolia (Common marsh poker) A typical red-hot poker with rather robust but untidy leaves up to 4½ ft (1.4 m) long and 1¼ in (3 cm) wide and, from midsummer to late fall, large, oblong, dense heads of scarlet red buds opening to bright yellow flowers. Widespread in southern Africa from the Eastern Cape to Malawi. ↕4–5 ft (1.2–1.5 m). Z6–9 H9–4

K. 'Little Maid' Dwarf, with prolific spikes of greenish yellow buds opening to creamy white above grassy foliage. A popular cultivar from Beth Chatto of England with flowers filling almost half the stem from early summer to early fall. ↕18–24 in (45–60 cm). Z6–9 H9–4

K. 'Lord Roberts' Uniformly colored, tall red spikes. Very similar to 'John Benary' and sometimes considered the

same. Flowers late summer to mid-fall. ↕4–6½ ft (1.2–2 m). Z6–9 H9–4

K. 'Mermaiden' Long, broad, and dense spikes of green buds opening to yellow flowers on stems that are sometimes branched. A hybrid of the majestic 'Prince Igor'. Flowers midsummer to early fall. ↕32–36 in (80–90 cm). Z6–9 H9–4

K. 'Minister Verschuur' Spikes of almost uniformly golden orange-yellow flowers only paling at the very base. Flowers early summer to midsummer. ↕24 in (60 cm). Z6–9 H9–4

K. 'Nancy's Red' Uniformly colored slender spikes of deep pinkish red with a hint of yellow on the open flowers. Flowers midsummer to mid-fall. ↕20–40 in (50–100 cm). Z6–9 H9–4

K. northiae (Broad-leaved poker, Marianne North's poker) A dramatic species for foliage, with very broad, blue-gray leaves up to 5 ft (1.5 m) long and 5 in (12 cm) wide, lacking the keels of *K. caulescens* and reminiscent of the leaves on an *Aloe.* The flower spikes, produced from late spring to late summer, are extremely dense but in

RICH FOLIAGE, BRILLIANT FALL COLORS

KNIPHOFIA ROOPERI is undoubtedly a dramatic plant, its tightly clustered vertical stems topped with unusually fat bicolored heads to create bold orange-yellow impact. Half-hardy summer plants gather around to create a fiery summer scene. The purple-leaved castor oil plant, *Ricinus communis,*

with its glossy foliage and spikes of spiny red seedpods, makes a revealing background, its leaf color picked up by the dark-leaved dahlias on either side; on one side their yellow flowers echo the yellow of the poker heads, on the other double reds match the *Ricinus* seedpods.

muted colors, with pale red buds opening to yellow-white flowers with long protruding stamens. From grasslands of eastern South Africa and Lesotho. ‡5–5½ ft (1.5–1.7 m). Z6–9 H9–6

K. 'Painted Lady' Long spikes with amber buds opening to golden yellow. Introduced by The Plantsman nursery (England). Flowers mid- to late summer. ‡4¼–5 ft (1.3–1.5 m). Z6–9 H9–4

K. 'Percy's Pride' Long dense spikes with green buds opening to greenish yellow flowers. Raised by Alan Bloom and named for his long-serving assistant, Percy Piper. Blooms early summer to mid-fall. ‡24–48 in (60–120 cm). Z6–9 H9–6

K. praecox see *K.uvaria*

K. 'Prince Igor' Spectacular, tall, robust, predominantly orange-red spikes opening to yellow at the tips. More than one plant may be grown under this name. Flowers midsummer to early fall. ‡1.3–3m (4¼–10ft). Z6–9 H9–4

K. rooperi (Winter poker) Large, almost spherical heads of bright red and yellow are held aloft on stout stems from early to late fall. The lax leaves, up to 3¼ ft (1.1 m) long and 1½ in (4 cm) wide, are an uninspiring green, filling the border without flowering for most of the summer. Often sold as 'C. M. Prichard'. From the marshy coast of eastern South Africa. ‡4–4½ ft (1.2–1.4 m). Z6–9 H9–9

K. 'Royal Castle' Orange-red buds opening to yellow flowers. Not 'Royal Caste' as sometimes seen. 'Royal Castle Hybrids', also known as 'Grandiflora Mixture', is a name sometimes incorrectly used for a mix of red, orange, and yellow shades. Flowers July to August. ‡24–40 in (60–100 cm). Z6–9 H9–4

K. 'Royal Standard' Tall red-hot poker with fat spikes of scarlet buds changing to lemon yellow flowers. One of the most strongly contrasting of bicolors. Raised by Prichard's Nursery of Christchurch, Hampshire, England in 1921. Flowers early summer to early fall. ‡34–48 in (85–120 cm). Z6–9 H9–6

K. 'Samuel's Sensation' Very long, soft coral-red spikes fading to yellow on opening. Raised by Watkin Samuel, also a noted English delphinium breeder, in the early 1950s. Flowers early summer to early fall. ‡30–60 in (75–150 cm). Z6–9 H9–6

K. sarmentosa Stiff, keeled, evergreen, grayish-green leaves, similar to those of *K. caulescens*, are up to 26 in (65 cm) long and 1¼ in (3 cm) wide. The flower spikes—appearing sporadically at any time of the year, especially in winter and sometimes year-round—form dense cones of green to reddish upward-facing buds opening to cream

LEFT 1 *Kniphofia northiae* **2** *K.* 'Percy's Pride' **3** *K.* 'Royal Standard' **4** *K.* 'Wrexham Buttercup'

HOT POKERS

Kniphofia selections are sometimes considered difficult to grow in cold climate areas of North America. Low winter temperatures and winter wet soils can contribute to plant decline. For success with this attractive species the following steps should be taken.

Select healthy-looking plants that show new growth in leaves and flower stems for spring planting. Fall planting does not allow for root establishment before the onset of winter conditions. Plant in well-drained soil in full sun. Remember that this species is native to South Africa, where the soils are rocky and well drained. Place the plants no deeper in the soil than they were growing in the containers. A light application of fertilizer should be applied at planting. An organic mulch should be placed around, but not on top of, the plant. Tie the foliage together in the fall to prevent water from entering the crown, which causes rot. Kniphofia rarely requires division and should not be disturbed unless necessary.

These red hot pokers are the more common and available hybrids for North American gardens:
'Bees' Sunset' (orange)
'Border Ballet' (coral)
'Bressingham Sunbeam' (yellow)
'Green Jade' (lime green)
'Ice Queen' (ivory white)
'Percy's Pride' (greenish yellow)
'Vanilla' (ivory white)
'Shining Sceptre' (clear yellow).

or buff. From streamsides and moist areas in the mountains of Western Cape province, South Africa. ‡ 20–24 in (50–60cm). Z7–9 H9–7

K. 'Shining Sceptre' Bluish green foliage with fat spikes of orange-yellow buds opening to a clear yellow. Vigorous. Raised by English nurseryman Alan Bloom and introduced in 1975. Flowers early summer to early fall. ‡ 36–48 in (90–120 cm). Z6–9 H9–4

K. 'Strawberries and Cream' Small, slender spikes of creamy flowers open from dusky pink buds. Selected and introduced by Beth Chatto. Flowers midsummer to early fall. ‡ 20–28 in (50–70 cm). Z6–9 H9–4

K. 'Sunningdale Yellow' Long-flowering yellow spikes with green buds held on slightly bluish stems and with broad bluish foliage. A hybrid of *K. triangularis.* Flowers early to late summer. ‡ 36–40 in (90–100 cm). Z6–9 H9–4

K. 'Tawny King' Buffish orange buds opening to creamy white flowers on bronzed stems. Prolific and long-flowering. Flowers midsummer to mid-fall. ‡ 4ft (1.2m). Z6–9 H9–4

K. thomsonii A tender species, spreading slowly by rhizomes. From rosettes of weak, long, thin leaves rise

tall spikes of loosely arranged but strongly curved orange flowers from early summer to late fall. Plants are often incorrectly sold as var. *snowdenii,* but the variety should have hairy flowers. From moist grasslands and marshes from the mountains of northern Tanzania to Ethiopia. ‡ 3¼–4ft (1-1.2m). Z7–9 H9–7

K. 'Timothy' Bronzed stems bearing uniform spikes of gorgeous pinkish orange flowers. From Carlile's Nursery of Twyford, Buckinghamshire, England. Flowers early summer to early fall. ‡ 28–40 in (70–100 cm). Z6–9 H9–4

K. 'Toffee Nosed' Brownish orange buds opening to cream flowers on dark stems. Raised and introduced by John Metcalf of Four Seasons Nursery, Norfolk, England. Flowers early summer to mid-fall. ‡ 3¼ ft (1 m). Z7–9 H9–7

K. triangularis (Mandarin poker) Fine grassy leaves up to 24 in (60 cm) long but less than ½ in (1 cm) wide stand below flowerheads with pendulous flowers in shades of orange to red from midsummer to mid-fall, with the buds usually in a similar color or redder. A very variable species that may have given rise to many of the dwarf cultivars found today. Widespread in moist and rocky areas in the uplands of eastern South Africa and Lesotho. ‡ 20–24 in (50–60 cm). Z6–9 H9–1. **'Light of the World'** Uniformly clear orange, narrow spikes from late summer to mid-fall. Perhaps a hybrid. ‡ 24 in (60 cm).

K. uvaria (Red-hot poker) Robust clump-former with lax, strap-shaped leaves, up to 32 in (80 cm) long and ¾ in (2 cm) wide. Egg-shaped heads of bright scarlet buds open to yellow flowers from midsummer to mid-fall. The original red-hot poker, its natural variability is compounded by the fact

that many plants sold under this name are of hybrid origin. From mountains of the Cape region of South Africa. ‡ 3¼–4 ft (1–1.2 m). Z5–9 H9–1. **'Nobilis'** Imposing, with tall, large red and yellow pokers from midsummer to mid-fall. Sometimes sold as *K. praecox.* ‡ 6–10 ft (2–3 m).

K. 'Vanilla' Slender elegant spikes of creamy yellow buds opening to ivory white over neat grassy leaves. Flowers early summer to early fall. ‡ 18–40 in (45–100 cm). Z6–9 H9–4

K. 'Wrexham Buttercup' Broad rounded spikes of yellow flowers open from greenish buds. Dramatic and impressive. From the raiser of 'Samuel's Sensation', Watkin Samuel. Flowers early summer to early fall. ‡ 3¼–4 ft (1–1.2 m). Z6–9 H9–6

K. 'Yellow Hammer' Bright yellow flowers opening from greenish buds. Flowers early summer to early fall. ‡ 30–54 in (75–130 cm). Z6–9 H9–6

KOELERIA
Hair grass
POACEAE

Invaluable spiky blue tufts for dry sites, topped with shimmering feathery flowers.

Some 35 perennial species, from temperate regions throughout the world, are found in dry grasslands and rocky places in limestone soil; only a few are generally grown. Their upright tufts of softly textured, very slender leaves are usually colored blue; the bases of some species are swollen into little bulbils. Erect stems bear early-blooming flowerheads with their soft silvery plumes of tiny shiny flowers carried high above the

foliage. This is a cool-season plant that dies back in hot, humid weather and looks best in gravel or at the edges of dry paths.

CULTIVATION Best in a dry, exposed position, in well-drained neutral to alkaline soil, otherwise they tend to rot at the base. Comb out untidy and dead leaves and trim back in late spring for good color.

PROPAGATION From seed or by division in spring.

PROBLEMS Sometimes affected by fungal disease in humid weather or rich soil, otherwise trouble-free.

K. glauca Low-growing, stiff, evergreen tufts of steely blue-gray, sometimes inrolled leaves are overtopped in midsummer with flower stems carrying dense, fluffy, silvery green plumes. Lovely in drifts where it can shimmer in the sun, by dry paths, and as edging for hot, dry borders. From sandy soil, especially sand dunes, throughout Europe to Siberia. ‡ 16 in (40 cm). Z6–9 H9–6

K. macrantha Green to blue-green, flat or inrolled leaves, ¹⁄₁₆–⅛ in (1–2.5 mm) wide, make loose, spiky evergreen tufts. The flower stems appear high above the foliage in early summer to midsummer, topped with dense, poker-shaped, shimmering plumes of purple-green, silver-edged flowers. Good in wildflower meadows and lawns where the wind and sun can run through the shimmering flowers. Common on dry and sandy grasslands in chalky soil in Britain, Europe, Asia, and North America. ‡ 4–20 in (10–50 cm). Z3–9 H8–1

BELOW 1 *Koeleria glauca*
2 *K. macrantha*

L

LAMIASTRUM *see* LAMIUM

LAMIUM
Dead nettle
LAMIACEAE

Rock-solid ground cover for shade or sun, with handsome leaves and noteworthy blossoms.

Fifty species of deciduous or evergreen ground-cover plants, both annuals and perennials, grow in damp woodlands or in drier, more open situations in Europe, Asia, and North Africa. Only a few are intentionally grown, and a number are considered to be weeds. Most grow from rhizomes, some are vigorous to the point of being invasive, with square stems bearing paired, oval, or triangular leaves, mottled with silver or gray in some taxa. The characteristic two-lipped, tubular flowers may be solitary or they may be carried in whorls among the upper leaves. Many make attractive ground cover in part-shade, and are grown primarily for their neat foliage, with the flowers a welcome bonus.

CULTIVATION Grow in moist soil in full or part-shade.

PROPAGATION By division, or detaching rooted stems.

PROBLEMS Usually trouble-free,

BELOW **1** *Lamium album* 'Friday'
2 *L. maculatum* 'Album'
3 *Lathyrus grandiflorus*

although the leaf-spot disease *Peronospora lamii* often disfigures cultivars of *L. maculatum*, especially those with almost entirely silvery foliage, by producing purple spots, usually on the lower leaves.

L. album (White dead nettle) Spreading by rhizomes, and often considered a weed, this species forms an evergreen clump with erect stems bearing strongly toothed, oval, light green leaves to 2½ in (6 cm) long, heart-shaped at the base. Creamy white flowers, ¾ in (2 cm) long, are borne in several whorls among the leaves toward the ends of the stems, opening intermittently over a long period from late spring to early winter. Easily grown, best suited to a semi-wild setting, planted in moist soil in full sun or dappled shade. Native to Europe and western Asia. ↕ 24 in (60 cm). Z4–8 H8–1. 'Friday' Leaves two-toned green with a central golden stripe. May revert to plain green.

L. galeobdolon syn. *Galeobdolon luteum*, *Lamiastrum galeobdolon* (Yellow archangel) Very vigorous evergreen, spreading rapidly by rooting stems and capable of colonizing a large area. Light green, bluntly toothed leaves to 2½ in (6 cm) long, sometimes with silvery blotches, are borne in pairs. Upright flowering stems are brightened by handsome light yellow flowers ¾ in (2 cm) long in late spring and early summer. Invasive in good conditions, but an excellent carpeting plant for damp, shady places. From damp woodlands, usually in heavy soils, in much of Europe, including the British Isles, and also western Asia. ↕ 20 in (50 cm). Z4–8 H8–1. 'Hermann's Pride' Leaves are narrow, silver between the veins, tending to hide the flowers. subsp. **montanum** 'Florentinum' Taller plant with large leaves heavily splashed with silver, tinged purple in winter. ↕ 24 in (60 cm). 'Silberteppich' (Silver Carpet)

Compact and clump-forming, leaves silver with green veins.

L. maculatum (Spotted dead nettle) Evergreen plant spreading both by rhizomes and by rooting stems, but not aggressively. Leaves paired, oval to triangular, dark green, usually with a central white or silvery stripe, and 1¼–3 in (3–8 cm) long with bluntly toothed margins. Deep purplish pink, two-lipped flowers form a tight spike at the tips of the upright stems from late spring to early or mid-fall. Good ground cover for part-shaded sites in moist soil, but also suitable for the front of a border if not too dry. From damp woodlands in Europe, North Africa, and western Asia. ↕ 10 in (25 cm). Z4–8 H8–1. 'Album' White flowers; leaves with a central whitish stripe. 'Anne Greenaway' Leaves irregularly yellow-variegated, with a central silver stripe. 'Aureum' syn. 'Golden Nuggets' Pale yellow leaves with a central silver stripe; flowers light pink. Best in light shade to prevent sun scorch. 'Beacon Silver' Silvery broad leaves with a fine dark green margin; flowers purple. 'Cannon's Gold' Compact, with yellow leaves and lilac-pink flowers. 'Chequers' Leaves broad, with a bold central silver stripe; flowers deep red-purple. Vigorous. A plant very similar to 'Beacon Silver' is also grown under this name. **Golden Anniversary** ('Dellam') Leaves smaller, with a central silver stripe and golden edge. Flowers purple. 'Golden Nuggets' see 'Aureum'. 'James Boyd Parselle' Compact, with leaves silver, narrowly edged dark green; flowers bright pink. 'Pink Nancy' Leaves silver with narrow green margin; flowers salmon pink. 'Pink Pearls' Leaves with narrow white stripe; flowers pink. 'Pink Pewter' Leaves silver, edged green; flowers salmon pink. Long flowering season,; tolerates sun better than many. 'Roseum' Leaves with central silver stripe; flowers pink. 'White Nancy'

Leaves broad, silver with narrow green margin; flowers white. 'Wootton Pink' Compact, with slightly larger, pale pink flowers; leaves silver with green margins.

L. orvala (Giant dead nettle) Clump-forming with broad, triangular leaves to 6 in (15 cm) long, prominently veined and toothed, and, like the stems, sometimes tinged with purple on the edges. Deep coppery pink flowers, 1¼–1½ in (3–4 cm) long, open in late spring and early summer in whorls in the upper leaf joints. Noninvasive and a very handsome plant. Native to central southern Europe. ↕ 24 in (60 cm). Z4–8 H8–1. 'Album' Flowers off-white. 'Silva' Dusky pink flowers; each leaf has a slender silver central stripe.

LASIAGROSTIS *see* STIPA

LATHYRUS
PAPILIONACEAE

Indispensable perennial relations of the familiar sweet pea, ranging from neat mounds to tall, vigorous climbers.

More than 100 annual and perennial species are native to grassy slopes and gravelly banks in Europe, North Africa, and temperate North and South America. They often have winged stems, and many climb by means of tendrils at the tips of the alternately arranged leaves. Each leaf is composed of one or more pairs of roughly oval leaflets and tipped by a tendril, which in some species is reduced to a point or bristle. The familiar flowers, which in a few species are scented, are carried singly or in small sprays on stems growing from the leaf joints. They are followed by flattish pods, which often snap open in dry weather and fling out the seeds. Some species have been included

UNFASHIONABLE COMPANIONS

LATHYRUS VERNUS IS A MUCH underrated spring perennial that comes in pretty shades of blue and pink, and in white. Here it is fronted by seed-raised bedding violas that can be planted either in the fall, in which case they will often flower during mild winter spells, or in spring. Enthusiasts for perennials are sometimes reluctant to use annuals or bedding plants from the garden center in plant associations, perhaps because they are less fashionable than they should be, but they can help create some delightful color harmonies. These charming violas are now available in an astonishing range of colors and color combinations, and precisely the right shade can be chosen to work best with the lathyrus you happen to be growing.

in a separate genus, *Orobus*, and some species are also difficult to separate from *Vicia*.

CULTIVATION Grow in fertile but well-drained soil in full sun to light dappled shade. Climbing species can scramble through a shrub or be supported by canes or twiggy branches. Deadhead frequently to promote further flowering.

PROPAGATION From seed in spring or by early spring division for non-climbing species.

PROBLEMS Thrips, aphids, midges, mildews, and a root rot may occasionally cause problems but are not common.

L. aureus syn. *L. gmelinii* 'Aureus', *L. luteus* 'Aureus', *L. vernus* 'Aurantiacus', *Orobus aureus* A bushy, robust, non-climbing species with an upright habit and flattened stems that are not winged. The leaves are composed of three to six, or more, pairs of oval leaflets up to 2 in (5 cm) wide that end in a point, not a tendril, and have brown glands on the underside. In late spring and early summer, sprays of up to 25 flowers ¾ in (2 cm) across open; they are usually yellow but may be tinted brown. Native to woodlands and areas of low trees and shrubs

growing in Greece and the surrounding area. ‡ 32 in (80 cm). Z5–9 H9–5

L. fremontii see *L. laxiflorus*

***L. gmelinii* 'Aureus'** see *L. aureus*

L. grandiflorus (Everlasting pea) A weak, slightly downy climber. Its stems, without wings but with prominent ridges, carry leaves with just one pair of oval leaflets up to ¾ in (2 cm) long, each leaf ending in a tendril. The cream buds open to give usually two, but sometimes up to four, 1¼ in (3 cm) flowers; each flower has a violet standard, purple wings and pink keel. Sometimes invasive, especially in light soil, but grows well in part-shade. Best allowed to sprawl through other robust plants. From shady places in the mountains of the Balkans and southern Italy. ‡ 5 ft (1.5 m). Z6–9 H9–5

L. latifolius (Perennial pea) A resilient, vigorous climber, the stems having wings that may be wider than the stems themselves. Each leaf is composed of a pair of linear to broadly oval leaflets, up to 6 in (15 cm) long and 2 in (5 cm) wide and with four to five prominent veins. There is a robust branched tendril at the tip. The 1¼ in (3 cm) purplish pink flowers, in sprays of 6–11 or sometimes even 15, are unfortunately not fragrant, but open in

a long season from early summer to early fall. Needs stout support, but if allowed to trail it makes good ground cover, especially on a bank. The cultivars are often mixed and usually raised from seed. Probably the most commonly grown of the perennial peas, this has become naturalized in many areas (*see* Naturalized Lathyrus) and is commonly seen on roadsides and waste areas in North America. Native to central and southern Europe and North Africa. ‡ 6½ ft (2 m). Z5–9 H9–5. **'Albus'** White flowers. **'Blushing Bride'** Pale pink and white. **'Red Pearl'** Magenta-red flowers. **'Rosa Perle'** Rose pink without a magenta cast. **'White Pearl'** White, with larger flowers than 'Albus'.

L. laxiflorus syn. *L. fremontii* A bushy, non-climbing species with an upright habit and unwinged stems. Each leaf has just one pair of lance-shaped leaflets up to 1½ in (4 cm) long. Two to six ¾ in (2 cm) bluish violet flowers are carried on short stems in the leaf joints. Grows well in sun and flowers for most of the summer if deadheaded, or can be cut back hard after the first flush of bloom to quickly reshoot and flower a second time. Native to woods and shady banks in southeastern Europe. ‡ 16 in (40 cm). Z5–9 H9–5

***L. luteus* 'Aureus'** see *L. aureus*

L. nervosus (Lord Anson's pea) Often sparse, short-lived, sometimes temperamental, but worth growing. Unwinged stems, almost stalkless leaves, each with one pair of 1½ in (4 cm) oval leaflets and a tendril branched into three. Three to seven flowers, in lovely shades of blue or bluish mauve, sometimes paler at the petal's base, are carried on relatively long stems in summer. Dislikes winter rain, but good in a raised bed or container where it can trail. From open fields and areas of low-growing trees and shrubs in South America. ‡ 4¼ ft (1.3 m). Z3–10 H10–1

L. niger (Black pea) Upright with wingless branched stems. Leaves have three to six pairs, or more, of elliptical leaflets to 1½ in (4 cm) long, without a tendril. The purplish, 1 in (2.5 cm) flowers are borne in sprays of four to ten in early summer and turn blue as they age. The name is from the foliage, which turns black as it dies. Native to most of Europe and into North Africa. ‡ 36 in (90 cm). Z5–9 H9–5

L. rotundifolius A climber with winged stems carrying leaves comprising a single pair of elliptical to almost round leaflets up to 2½ in (6 cm) long with parallel veins and a tendril at the tip branched into three. In summer, the dull red to purple-pink, ¾ in (2 cm) flowers are held in clusters of three to eight. Found in hedges and meadows, often on a north slope, in the Caucasus and Crimea. ‡ 5 ft (1.5 m). Z5–10 H10–1. **'Tillyperone'** Flowers of a rich pink, for a longer period. Also known by veined leaflets that join before reaching the leaf edge. Said to come from a garden of this name in Wales.

L. sylvestris A climber with winged stems and one pair of leaflets, about

NATURALIZED LATHYRUS

A familiar plant found scrambling on roadsides, railroad embankments, sea cliffs, and waste ground, *Lathyrus latifolius* is one of the most attractive and resilient garden escapes. It has become established in almost every state in the US and province in Canada. It was first discovered in Great Britain in 1670.

With lupines, this sweet pea is among the most attractive of naturalized perennials. Although it is usually seen in its natural pink form, some populations show the occasional white-flowered plants. It is a difficult plant to eradicate, due to its deep root system, that contains reserves allowing it to regrow after mowing. It spreads mainly by seed, which can be heard popping from the pods on hot summer days.

Other showy *Lathyrus* species that have also become naturalized, although much less widely, include *L. grandiflorus* and also *L. tuberosus*, which, in some climates, can be especially resilient.

four times as long as wide, and a branched tendril. The summer flowers, ¾ in (2 cm), have pink standards and keel with mauve wings and come in sprays of up to 15. Similar in growth and habit to *L. latifolius* but with narrower leaves. Native to woodlands and hedges in most of Europe, including Britain, and into Morocco. ‡ 6½ ft (2 m). Z6–9 H9–6

L. tuberosus (Fyfield pea, Earth-nut pea, Dutch mice) A scrambler, unusual in producing small, edible tubers that multiply rapidly and break off easily from the brittle roots. Slender unwinged stems trail along the ground or may climb into other plants. The leaves are composed of one pair of elliptical or oblong, 1¾ in (4.5 cm) leaflets with a three-branched tendril. Slightly fragrant, bright purple flowers are carried on long stems in clusters of two to seven in summer. Plant with great caution; it can be very invasive. First found naturalized in Britain in 1800 in Fyfield, Essex, hence one of its common names. Naturalized in the US. Found in much of Europe. ‡ 4 ft (1.2 m). Z5–9 H9–5

L. vernus syn. *Orobus vernus* (Spring pea, Spring vetchling) Upright, mound-shaped with slender but strong, erect, unwinged stems growing from a tight crown. The leaves are composed of 2–4 pairs of 2¾ in (7 cm) oval or lance-shaped leaflets, each ending in a point, and no tendril. In early spring, up to six or ten reddish purple ¾ in (2 cm) flowers, aging to a bluish tint, appear on one side of the flowering stem. An invaluable and easy woodlander. The flowers may open before the leaves appear, but this depends on the climate; where winters are harsh, flowers and leaves appear together. Flowering may also be curtailed by frost, but this seldom harms the plants. Found in woods, scrub, and on rocky ledges in most of Europe. ‡ 14 in (35 cm). Z5–7 H7–5. **'Alboroseus'** Two-toned flowers of blush pink and white. **'Aurantiacus'** see *L. aureus*. **'Caeruleus'** Blue flowers flushed with purple. **'Cyaneus'** Darker blue than 'Caeruleus'. **'Flaccidus'** Narrower leaflets and a drooping habit. **'Rosenelfe'** Pink and white flowers and red-tinged seedpods; shorter. ‡ 7 in (18 cm). **f. roseus** Mauve-pink. **'Spring Melody'** Candy pink and white flowers on a bushier plant.

LAVATERA
Mallow
MALVACEAE

Eager to please and prolific, quickly producing a mass of summer-long blooms and ideal for impatient gardeners.

The 25 species of annuals, biennials, and short-lived herbaceous perennials and shrubs have a wide-ranging distribution in both hemispheres, usually in coastal areas and in dry soil. The slightly downy, upright stems branch freely at the base and carry long-stalked, alternately arranged leaves that are

ABOVE 1 *Lavatera cachemiriana*
2 *Leonotis leonurus*

usually three- or five-lobed and softly hairy. They have the typical flowers of the mallow family, mainly in open clusters at the tops of the shoots, with five petals and a central cluster of stamens around the stigmas; flowers are typically pink or white. They are produced over a long period in summer and fall.

There has been some confusion in the nomenclature of *Lavatera*, although this has now been clarified (*see* Shrubs and Perennials). Those generally considered, and grown, as shrubs are not covered here.

CULTIVATION Easily grown in most well-drained soil in full sun, though plants often need staking, especially when grown in highly fertile soil.

Cut back by two-thirds in fall, then hard in early spring.

PROPAGATION By cutting of basal shoots in spring.

PROBLEMS Aphids, rust. Often short-lived.

L. cachemiriana Prolific but short-lived woody-based perennial. The vigorously upright stems carry downy, deeply veined leaves with three or five lobes. The flowers, produced for many months in mid- to late summer, are up to 3 in (8 cm) across with narrow, two-lobed, pale pink petals, white at the base, creating a flower with space betweeen the petals. From open, grassy places in the western Himalaya. ‡ 6½ ft (2 m). Z4–9 H9–1

L. thuringiaca A woody rootstock supports a bushy plant with a mass of

erect stems lined with 3½ in (9 cm) heart-shaped, lobed leaves, usually five-lobed at base and three-lobed on the flowering stems. Whole plant is covered in grayish hairs. The 2–3 in (5–8 cm) wide flowers are pale pink and open mid- to late summer. The shrubby cultivars once listed under this name are now more correctly considered under *L. x clementii*, of which *L. thuringiaca* is one parent (*see* Shrubs and Perennials). From eastern Europe and western Asia. ‡ 3¼–5 ft (1–1.5 m). Z7–9 H9–7. **'Ice Cool'** syn. 'Peppermint Ice' White flowers. ‡ 5 ft (1.5 m).

LEONOTIS
Lion's ear, Wild dagga
LAMIACEAE

These stately perennials with furry flowers provide unusual form for the back of a sheltered border.

Nine species of tall annuals or perennials, only three of which are usually grown, come mostly from Africa. Often woody at the base, the four-sided stems carry oppositely arranged, oval or lance-shaped, toothed leaves. Flowers are carried in whorls of up to 60 at regular intervals at the leaf joints in the upper reaches of the stem. In bloom for a long period from late summer to fall, the flowers are densely hairy and form a 1–2 in (2.5–5 cm) long arching tube with a very long protruding upper lip, perfectly adapted to pollination by sunbirds in its native habitat. Bright orange is the most common color, but some

SHRUBS AND PERENNIALS

The classification of *Lavatera* species has been the subject of much debate and is partly based on whether the plants are shrubby or die down in the winter. The shrubby types are now grouped under *L. olbia*, the herbaceous perennial types come under *L. thuringiaca*, and the hybrid between the two is *L. x clementii*. Following this classification, *L. olbia*, *L. x clementii*, and their cultivars are not covered here.

However, not only is the line between shrubby and herbaceous lavateras rather a blurred one, but some forms of *L. olbia* tend to die back for the winter while some forms of *L. thuringiaca* can be woody. The hybrid, as you might expect, can vary between the two extremes.

Also, climate plays a part. In colder climates, those that may otherwise tend to be shrubby can be cut back to the ground, while in warmer climates those tending to die back may remain partially woody. In areas colder than Zone 7, plants may simply be killed entirely. Consequently, there is scope for gardeners to treat shrubbier types as perennials in many areas, always keeping in mind that they tend to be extremely vigorous yet short-lived.

forms come in paler shades tending toward white or yellow.

While it is commonly known as wild dagga (marijuana) in South Africa, there is no evidence of any narcotic properties, though it is widely used there for a variety of medicinal reasons.

The botanical name of the most common species grown, *Leonotis leonurus,* has created confusion with the genus *Leonurus.* Although the flowers of both are in clusters, those of *Leonurus* are small and pinkish, in sharp contrast to the long, bright orange flowers of *Leonotis.*

CULTIVATION Needs full sun and well-drained soil in a sheltered position. Plants with a woody base should be pruned hard in early spring.

PROPAGATION From seed, or by cuttings in early summer for the woodier species.

PROBLEMS Usually trouble-free.

L. leonurus A tall, bushy plant, with a woody rootstock, its coarsely hairy leaves are long and narrow, up to 1 in (2.5 cm) wide, in contrast to the other two species, which have broadly diamond- to heart-shaped leaves. Dramatic, bright orange flowers make a bold impact in fall. Formerly grown mainly as a greenhouse plant, it is proving increasingly hardy in milder areas. From South Africa. ‡6½–10 ft (2–3 m) Z10–11 H11–6. **var.** *albiflora* Almost white flowers.

L. nepetifolia A very tall, short-lived perennial, grown as an annual in colder areas, that is naturally very variable in form and size depending on the source of the seed. One constant is that the coarse leaves are always noticeably broad, at 1½–6 in (4–15 cm). The flowers are usually orange, but may be yellow or cream. Found throughout the tropics. ‡10 ft (3 m). **'Staircase'** Robust selection with orange flowers. ‡24 in (60 cm).

L. ocymifolia Tall, sparsely branched but naturally very variable plant, woody at the base and with a large woody rootstock. The grooved, hairy stems carry velvety, more or less heart-shaped, toothed leaves, 3 in (8 cm) long, and orange flowers in up to five clusters. Similar to *L. leonurus* but with much broader foliage. Also differs, if you care to look, by having only a single ring of hairs at the base of the inside of its flower-tube—the other two species have three. From Africa. ‡6½–10 ft (2–3 m). Z10–11 H11–1

LEONTODON
Hawkbit
ASTERACEAE

Low-growing plants with broad leaf rosettes and clusters of small yellow daisies.

About 50 species of annuals and perennials come from a range of open or grassy habitats through Europe, North Africa, and south-western Asia to Iran; only one is generally grown. All have milky sap, are often coarsely hairy, and form basal rosettes of untoothed to deeply dissected leaves. Erect, almost leafless, stems bear solitary or, more commonly, clusters of, yellow flowerheads like dandelions. Most of species are weedy or have little ornamental potential, but are sometimes grown as wild flowers.

CULTIVATION Requirements vary with the species, but *L. rigens* prefers moisture-retentive soil in full sun and will survive only light frosts. It tends to be short-lived and is best propagated from seed regularly.

PROPAGATION Sow seed, at 59–68°F (15–20°C), or divide in spring.

PROBLEMS Usually trouble-free.

L. rigens syn. *Microderis rigens* (Bristle-leaved hawkbit) Striking, rosette-forming evergreen perennial with a stout rootstock. The rosette consists of crowded clusters of glossy, elliptic to egg-shaped leaves, each up to 12 in (30 cm) long, with sparse, bristly hairs on both surfaces and distinctive jagged, irregular teeth along the edge. In winter, it retreats to a rosette of smaller leaves. The yellow flowerheads, each 1–1¼ in (2.5–3 cm) across, are borne in a dense cluster of up to 120 on leafless stem from late summer to mid-fall. Each rosette will produce several flower stems. It is sometimes grown purely for its foliage, in which case the flower stems are best removed. Native to rocky or open habitats in the Azores. ‡16 in (40 cm). Z6–9 H9–6. **'Girandole'** Indistinguishable from the species.

LEONURUS
LAMIACEAE

An attractive plant for the herb garden or wildflower garden.

There are nine perennial and biennial species from Europe, Asia, and Central and South America, only one of which is generally grown. Erect stems carry opposite, deeply lobed or toothed leaves with the flowers grouped in distinctive, regularly spaced clusters (whorls) in the leaf joints. Each flower has a hooded upper lip and a lower lip split into three lobes. *Leonurus cardiaca* has been used in herbal medicine in Europe, while *L. sibiricus* is widely used in traditional Chinese medicine. Naturalized throughout the US.

CULTIVATION Easy to grow in any reasonable soil in either sun or part-shade.

PROPAGATION Sow seed in containers and keep seedlings in a cold frame until the summer, when the young plants can be planted outside. Alternatively, divide established plants in the spring.

PROBLEMS Usually trouble-free.

L. cardiaca (Motherwort) Erect, spread by wiry rhizomes, with hairless or more often slightly downy, branched stems. Leaves coarsely toothed; lower ones palm-shaped with five to seven lobes, higher ones with three lance-shaped lobes, the middle one longer than the outer two. From midsummer to early fall, pink, or occasionally white, ½ in (1 cm) flowers often speckled with purple spots and hairs on the upper surface of the top lip are clustered at leaf joints. Grown as a medicinal plant since the Middle Ages, is was used to reduce labor pain during childbirth and is also claimed to control stress-induced hypertension. Undemanding and only occasionally invasive. From fencerows, walls, and waste places in western Europe. ‡4 ft (1.2 m). Z4–8 H9–1

LEUCANTHEMELLA
ASTERACEAE

A statuesque and impressive late-flowering daisy for great fall color.

There are two species, increasing by rhizomes, from southeastern Europe to eastern Asia; one, *L. serotina,* is easily grown. Over the years, they have been classified in different genera but are now settled here. All leaves are undivided, alternate, stalkless and dotted with glands. The basal leaves are slightly lobed, while the stem leaves are oblong to lance-shaped with forward-pointing marginal teeth. The daisy flowerheads, which follow the sun, are made up of sterile outer ray florets around greenish yellow fertile disk florets, which bear stalkless glands. They benefit from a winter mulch of organic matter.

CULTIVATION Grows best in full sun and moist soils, but they will tolerate part-shade and most soils.

PROPAGATION From seed, or by division or basal cuttings taken in spring.

PROBLEMS Usually trouble-free.

L. serotina syn. *Chrysanthemum serotinum, C. uliginosum, Pyrethrum uliginosum, Tanacetum serotinum* A hairy-stemmed, clump-forming, bushy and erect plant, with leaves up to 4¾ in (12 cm) long. The 2¾ in (7 cm) wide flowerheads are produced in late summer or, more usually, in the fall, and make excellent cut flowers. The outer ray florets are usually white, tinged with red, and are ½–1 in (1–2.5 cm) in length, surrounding a greenish yellow central eye. Slowly spreading by its white rhizomes, it rarely requires division but often needs support, although its height and, therefore, its need for staking, can be reduced by pinching out earlier in the season. From beside ponds or streams and in other moist places from eastern Europe to China and Japan. ‡5–6½ ft (1.5–2 m). Z4–9 H9–1. **'Herbsterm'** (**Autumn Star**) White flowers, tinged with yellow in the center.

LEUCANTHEMOPSIS see RHODANTHEMUM

LEUCANTHEMUM
ASTERACEAE

An indispensable showy, usually white daisy that provides a profusion of blooms in the summer sunshine.

BELOW *Leucanthemella serotina*

ABOVE *Leucanthemum × superbum*
'Horace Read'

There are 25 species of summer-flowering annuals and sometimes short-lived perennials from Europe and northern Asia. The usually dark green leaves are held alternately on the stem but can be entire, lobed, or divided. Large, typical daisylike flowerheads are held singly, or more rarely in small groups, on long stalks and turn to follow the sun. Outer ray florets are female, fertile, and usually white; the inner disk florets that form the eye of the flowerhead are yellow and have a swollen, spongy base. Interestingly, plants are noted for having red tips to their roots. Most are good for cutting.

Originally, all cultivars were intended to be propagated vegetatively, by division or cuttings. However, in recent years, a number of dwarf cultivars of *L. × superbum* in particular have been introduced as plants to be raised from seed. When grown from the raiser's seed, these are often superb dwarf plants, flowering prolifically in their first summer but developing into large plants in succeeding years. Plants raised from home-collected seed are often more variable, as are those raised from seed from cultivars intended to be vegetatively propagated.

CULTIVATION Best in full sun, with a well-drained and rich fertile soil, although moderate fertility and light shade are tolerated. Single forms are good for naturalizing in long meadow grass; double-flowered cultivars are more suited to a sunny situation in any border. Many require hidden staking to prevent them from flopping over other plants.

PROPAGATION Species and some cultivars may be raised from seed, but division, in late summer or early spring, rather than in fall, is preferable.

PROBLEMS Aphids. In addition, young plants are susceptible to slugs, particularly in the spring, and leaves can suffer fungal infections in wet summers.

L. hosmariense see *Rhodanthemum hosmariense*

L. maximum syn. *Chrysanthemum maximum* Basal leaves can be untoothed or toothed; the stem leaves are often also toothed, and daisylike flowerheads, 3–3½ in (7–9 cm) in diameter, have white ray florets and yellow disk florets. Plants sold under this name are sometimes *L. × superbum* with its larger flowerheads. Well-suited to naturalizing in meadows. From the Pyrenees. ↕ 32–40 in (80–100 cm.). Z5–8 H9–1

L. nipponicum see *Nipponanthemum nipponicum*

L. × superbum syn. *Chrysanthemum superbum* (Shasta daisy) Dark green foliage sets off large, brilliant white daisies floating above on long stalks between early summer and early fall. The flowerheads, usually comprising white ray florets and yellow disk florets, can be 4 in (10 cm) or more in diameter and are larger than those of *L. maximum*. Easy to grow, but will become stressed by soils that are either too wet or too dry. Division of clumps every two to three years will help to retain flowering potential. Thought to be a hybrid between *L. lacustre* and *L. maximum* and similar to both. ↕ 10 in to 5½ ft (25 cm to 1.7 m), usually about 3 ft (1 m). Z5–8 H8–1. **'Aglaia'**

Shasta daisies were first introduced by the prolific American plant breeder Luther Burbank in 1901. He claimed to have first crossed the familiar ox-eye daisy (*Leucanthemum vulgare*) with a plant he knew as the English field daisy and which he referred to at the time as *Leucanthemum maximum*—an uncommon and relatively weak plant that actually grows wild in the Pyrenees Mountains and not in England. He is then said to have crossed the best of the resulting hybrids with *L. lacustre*, a relative from Portugal.

Dissatisfied with the lack of brilliance in the white coloring, he is then said to have crossed his best seedlings with a Japanese relative, *Nipponanthemum nipponicum*, the late-fall-flowering Montauk or Nippon daisy. Finally, after further selection, in 1901 he introduced his new plant, which he named for the snow-capped Mount Shasta in northern California.

The more recent view has been that only *L. maximum* and *L. lacustre* were involved in the hybrid, but now some botanists believe that all Shasta daisies may actually be selections from just one species, *L. lacustre*. It seems very probable that some of his original plants had been misidentified.

So, in spite of Burbank's account, it is perhaps more likely that whatever crosses Burbank actually made, and whatever the true identity of the plants he used, his years of rigorous selection and his eye for a good garden plant—he introduced about 800 different plants, ranging from plums and the first thornless blackberry to grains and forage plants as well as ornamentals—were the most crucial factors in his success.

In Britain, development of Shasta daisies continued after a lucky find by nurseryman Horace Read. Traveling on a train one day, he noticed a double-flowered plant of *L. vulgare* growing alongside the track. Having noted the spot, on his return journey he pulled the emergency cord, quickly left the train, dug up the plant and then returned to the train and continued his journey. This plant was used as a parent to produce 'Esther Read' and Horace Read also introduced 'Horace Read', 'Jennifer Read,' and 'Pauline Read' as well as 'Cobham Gold'.

Neat, frilly, nearly full double, white flowerhead though later flowerheads are often less fully double, with the yellow center becoming more prominent. Sometimes unexpectedly tender. ↕ 20 in (50 cm). **'Alaska'** Single flowerheads. From seed, but pleasingly uniform. ↕ 3¼ ft (1 m). **'Anita Allen'** Neat semidouble flowerheads with three rows of white ray florets. ↕ 22 in (55 cm). **'Barbara Bush'** Creamy yellow-margined dark green leaves, semidouble flowerheads. A less hardy spontaneous mutation of 'T. E. Killin'. ↕ 18 in (45 cm). Z6. **'Beauté Nivelloise'** syn. 'Old Court', 'Shaggy' Attractive, very narrow, white ray florets. ↕ 20 in (50 cm). **'Becky'** Single

LEUCANTHEMUM GALLERY

As in so many members the daisy family, the range of flower forms in shasta daisies, *Leucanthemum*, has been expanded from the basic familiar daisy shape to include a number of interesting variants seen here in a range of *L. × superbum* cultivars.

Single The basic daisy shape, (here in 'Snow Lady') consists of a ring of white ray florets around a bright yellow or orange eye packed with slender disk florets.

Double When the disk florets in the eye develop to resemble the white ray florets (here in 'Fiona Coghill') the result is an impressive fully double flower.

Double frilly A profusion of unusually narrow ray florets (here in 'Aglaia') creates an endearingly dissected look which may also affect the edge of the central disk.

Anemone-centred When the central disk, or edge of it, develops more like the white ray florets (here in 'Wirral Supreme') the result is an anemone-centered flower.

flowers, appearing in early summer or midsummer, rather than in late spring. Good in humid heat. Perennial Plant Association Perennial Plant of the Year, 2003. **'Christine Hagemann'** Large, anemone-centered, white flowerheads. ↕32–42 in (80–110 cm). **'Cobham Gold'** Creamy yellow double flowers. ↕18 in (45 cm). **'Crazy Daisy'** Variable, shaggy flowerheads. Perhaps the same as 'Snowdrift'. ↕24 in (60 cm). **'Droitwich Beauty'** Large double flowerheads; similar, and perhaps the same as, 'Aglaia'. ↕20 in (50 cm). **'Esther Read'** Short and less hardy; early-flowering, with fully double flowerheads. ↕16–24 in (40–60 cm). Z5–8 H8–1. **'Fiona Coghill'** Very large fully double creamy flowerheads. Requires shelter from wind to prevent the large flowers from being ruined. ↕24 in (60 cm). **'Horace Read'** Old-fashioned, fully double flowerheads; needs support. ↕32–42 in (80–110 cm). **'John Murray'** syn. 'Summer Snowball' Very even double, cream flowers. ↕34 in (85 cm). **Little Silver Princess** see 'Silberprinzesschen'. **'Manhattan'** Single, and very tall. ↕5½ ft (1.7 m). **'Old Court'** see 'Beauté Nivelloise'. **'Phyllis Smith'** Narrow ray florets, some curling inward toward the center. Similar to 'Beauté Nivelloise' but with slightly wider florets. ↕36 in (90 cm). **'Shaggy'** see 'Beauté Nivelloise'. **'Silberprinzesschen'** (**Silver Princess**) Small single flowerheads in proportion to the low stature. From seed, and variable. ↕12–18 in (30–45 cm). **'Silver Princess'** see 'Silberprinzesschen'. **'Snow Lady'** Dwarf, with single flowers and often short-lived. From seed, and variable. ↕10–24 in (25–60 cm). **'Snowcap'** Single flowers, prolific and dwarf. A self-sown seedling introduced by Alan Bloom of Bressingham, Norfolk, England, in 1978. Has been raised from seed, and so now variable. ↕16 in (40 cm). **'Snowdrift'** Shaggy, cream flowerheads. From seed, and variable. ↕36 in (90 cm). **'Sonnenschein'** (**Sunshine**) Primrose yellow single flowerheads; requires support. Reblooms late, if deadheaded. ↕3¼ ft (1 m). **'Summer Snowball'** see 'John Murray'. **Sunshine** see 'Sonnenschein'. **'Sunny Side Up'** Anemone-centered flowerheads. ↕15–20 in (38–50 cm). **'T. E. Killin'** Anemone-centered flowerheads with very broad ray florets. ↕3 ft (1 m). **'Thomas Killin'** see 'T. E. Killin'. **'Wirral Pride'** Tall, with anemone-centered flowerheads. ↕40–48 in (90–120 cm). **'Wirral Supreme'** Tall, with anemone-centered flowerheads featuring two outer rows of ray florets, the inner ring slightly shorter than the outer. ↕3¼–5 ft (1–1.5 m).

L. vulgare syn. *Chrysanthemum leucanthemum* (Ox-eye daisy, Moon daisy) Long-stalked, usually scalloped basal leaves and longer and narrower, stalkless stem leaves that can be entire or lobed and are usually green, though sometimes slightly bluish. The typical yellow and white daisylike flowerheads appear in summer and vary greatly in size, between 1 in (2.5 cm) and 3½ in (9 cm) in diameter. Lovely in a meadow, but easier to establish from young plants than from seed. Native to Europe and Asia but naturalized over much of North America. ↕24–40 in (60–100 cm). Z3–8 H8–1. **'Filigran'** Prolific, with very slender foliage. **'Maikönigin'** (**May Queen**) Very early. ↕28 in (70 cm).

LEYMUS
POACEAE

Invaluable intense ice-blue foliage on often invasive plants makes attractive ground cover.

Up to 40 perennial species are found mainly in northern temperate regions growing on rocky slopes and steppes and often adapted to saline, alkaline, and sandy habitats. Many species have very invasive root systems and, while useful in binding sand-dunes, may prove troublesome in gardens. Flat, pointed, wide leaves are often in eye-catching shades of icy blue; the tall, sturdy flower stems carry bristly ryelike flowers. The blue foliage is best grown in dramatic sweeps as ground cover or as background to darker-colored flowers in hot dry areas; plants are also useful as edging for salt treated drives and pathways.

CULTIVATION. Grow in light, well-drained soil in hot sunny positions or in part-shade.

PROPAGATION. From seed or by root division in spring.

BELOW **1** *Leymus arenarius*
2 *Liatris spicata* 'Kobold'

PROBLEMS Can suffer from fungal diseases in moist conditions.

L. arenarius (European dune grass, Lyme grass, Blue wild rye) A robust, invasive grass with long, stout rhizomes that spread over long distances. The rigid upright leaves, up to ¾ in (2 cm) wide and 24 in (60 cm) long, are an intense steely blue. In midsummer long, sturdy, blue-gray flower stems support the bristly ryelike blue flowers that soon turn pale yellow. One of Gertrude Jekyll's favorites, it needs a large area to run and produce its most stunning color effects, but can be grown in pots if repotted frequently. The flowerheads make good dried flowers if picked while still blue. Grows on most types of soil and is drought- and salt-tolerant; for the best color trim back the flowers and foliage in the summer. May suffer badly from stem smut, which covers the stems with black pustules in wet conditions. Introduced around the world to stabilize sand dunes but native to Europe. ↕5 ft (1.5 m). Z4–10 H10–1

LIATRIS
ASTERACEAE

Bold spikes of feathery blooms, unusual in opening from the top downward.

There are about 40 North American species, found mostly in dry prairies and open woods where the soil is poor and gravelly. Just a few are generally grown. They form a tuberous rootstock and are often sold packaged in spring as dormant plants alongside summer-flowering bulbs. The long, narrow, bright green leaves are gathered in a basal tuft and arranged alternately up the flower spike. Good border plants, they also do well in a wildflower meadow, where they attract bees and butterflies, and are also valued as cut flowers (*see* Cut Flowers, *p.304*).

CULTIVATION Plant in well-drained soil in full sun. Plants may rot over-winter if grown in heavy soil where winters are wet.

PROPAGATION From seed sown in fall or by division in early spring.

PROBLEMS Leaf spot and rust are occasionally troublesome.

L. aspera (Rough gayfeather) Drought-tolerant with upright, usually roughly textured stems emerging through the crown of unusually long, rough leaves that may reach 16 in (40 cm). Smaller, stalkless leaves carried on stems. The purple flowers are grouped in small clusters containing up to 40 individual blooms gathered in dense flower spikes up to 18 in (45 cm) long in late summer. Plants may need staking in exposed locations; they are particularly susceptible to winter wet. From Ontario to Florida and Texas, North America. ↕6½ ft (2 m). Z3–9 H9–1

L. callilepis see *L. spicata*

L. pycnostachya (Kansas gayfeather) Tall, floppy, hairy-stemmed. Lower leaves up to 14 in (35 cm) long but progressively smaller up the flowering stems. Bright reddish purple flower spikes up to 18 in (45 cm) long, are crowded with flowers opening from midsummer to fall. In hot climates, the plants may be short lived and are best treated as biennials. Less drought-tolerant than *L. aspera* but also suffers in wet, heavy soil in winter.

CUT FLOWERS

Liatris, especially forms of *L. spicata*, are becoming increasingly popular as cut flowers and are often raised from seed for this purpose. The Floristan Series from Germany was especially developed with this in mind, combining a shorter stature, so avoiding staking, with a long flower spike—in effect, the length of bare stem between the crown and the spike of flowers has been reduced. These are proving long-lasting and easy to grow, and their striking form is much appreciated, as is their relatively novel habit of the flowers opening from the top down.

For everyday use, stems are best cut when about half the flowers are open, but if they can be plunged in a solution of flower preservative immediately, they can be cut when just three or four have opened. Try to cut them as early in the day as possible. The use of preservative will ensure that the flowers last up to about 12 days. The leaves tend to deteriorate more quickly than the flowers, so it pays to strip the foliage before arranging.

Liatris also make very effective dried flowers. Wait until all the flowers on the spike are fully open before cutting, then dry them by simply hanging them upside down in small bunches in a dry, well-ventilated place.

Needs good support. From Wisconsin to Texas. ‡5 ft (1.5 m). Z3–9 H9–2. **'Alba'** White flowers.

L. spicata syn. *L. callilepis* (Blazing star) Erect, smooth or rarely slightly hairy stems emerge from a crown of slender 14 in (40 cm) foliage to carry smaller, narrower leaves. Spikes of pinkish purple flowers to 28 in (70 cm) long appear in late summer; excellent cut flowers. Better suited to moist soils but liable to rot in winter if too wet. Large clumps require staking. From New York to Florida. ‡5 ft (1.5 m). Z4–9 H9–1. **'Alba'** White flowers. **'Floristan Violett'** Violet. ‡36 in (90 cm). **'Floristan Weiss'** White. ‡36 in (90 cm). **'Kobold'** (**Goblin**) Rose pink. Flowers earlier; can rebloom if deadheaded promptly. ‡30 in (75 cm).

LIBERTIA
IRIDACEAE

Dense clumps of elegant, narrow leaves complement the attractive sprays of late-spring and summer flowers.

There are 20 species of evergreen plants from the southern hemisphere, mostly South America and New Zealand, several of which are frequently grown. The narrowly swordlike, upright leaves arranged in fans make a striking feature in themselves. In late spring and early summer, stiff stems appear, bearing one or more clusters of bowl-shaped flowers with three small outer petals and three showy inner ones. The small seed capsules, often orange or brown, are long-lasting and decorative.

CULTIVATION Grows well in full sun, and moist, fertile soil. Usually best when three or four years old, after which they often look ragged.

PROPAGATION From seed or by division in spring.

PROBLEMS Usually trouble-free.

L. **'Amazing Grace'** Slowly forms a substantial clump of narrowly sword-shaped, bronze-tinted leaves to 16 in (40 cm) long. In late spring and early summer, sprays of ¾ in (2 cm) white flowers on stems just longer than leaves. A hybrid of *L. chilensis* and *L. ixioides*. ‡24 in (60 cm). Z8–10 H10–8

L. caerulescens Forms a compact clump of tough, grasslike foliage, with dense clusters of ½ in (1 cm) flowers with three pale blue petals in late spring and early summer. Flower clusters are held along erect stems above the foliage. From open grassy places in Chile. ‡24 in (60 cm). Z9–10 H10–9

L. formosa Robust, tufted forming a fountainlike mass of narrow, dark green leaves. Erect stems carry several dense clusters of 1½ in (3.5 cm) bowl-shaped, white flowers over a long period from late spring to midsummer. Tolerates light shade; can be effective when mass-planted beneath mature deciduous trees. Dislikes hot, humid summers. From moist open places in Chile. ‡32–40 in (80–100 cm). Z7–9 H9–7

L. grandiflora Strong-growing. Narrow, leathery leaves, develop into a bold

clump. Erect leafy stems carry several open clusters of bowl-shaped ¾–1¼ in (2–3 cm) white flowers in late spring and early summer, followed by spherical seedpods that turn black when mature. Tolerates light shade. From stream banks and open woodlands in New Zealand. ‡40 in (90 cm). Z8–11 H12–8

L. ixioides Yellowish green, narrowly sword-shaped leaves form neat clumps to 20 in (50 cm) across, which are often attractively orange-tinged in winter. Pure white ½–¾ in (1–2 cm) flowers are borne in dense clusters on erect stems, followed by rounded yellow seed capsules. From stream banks in New Zealand. ‡18 in (45 cm). Z8–10 H10–8

L. peregrinans Striking clumps of narrow leaves, often become beautifully coppery orange when grown in full sun and look especially lovely with low light behind them. Bowl-shaped white flowers about ¾ in (2 cm) across are borne in late spring and early summer and slightly hidden among the leaves. Produces offsets some distance from the parent plant. From New Zealand,

growing in peaty or sandy soil. ‡24 in (60 cm). Z8–10 H10–8. **'Gold Leaf'** Leaves deep orange; grow in full sun for the best color.

L. sessiliflora Grasslike leathery leaves form compact clumps, with small, pale blue flowers borne in tight clusters on stems as tall as the leaves. Needs well-drained, fertile soil in full sun. From open grassy places in Chile. ‡24 in (60 cm). Z9–10 H10–9

LIGULARIA
ASTERACEAE

Statuesque foliage plants for a bog garden or moist border, with the bonus of striking summer flowers.

There are about 180 species of medium-sized and large, deciduous perennial plants, mostly with bold or attractively cut foliage, about ten of which are commonly cultivated. They grow wild from Europe to the Himalaya, China, and Japan, generally in wet places in the mountains. From a short rhizome arise numerous triangular, kidney-

WARM HUES FOR DAMP SOIL

THE BOLD, ROUNDED LEAVES and yellow flowers of these ligularias indicate daylilies as excellent partners, since the slender daylily foliage makes an attractive contrast and the flowers of their many cultivars in shades of yellow, orange, and red harmonize so well with the ligularias, as do the neighboring goldenrods. The dark-leaved cordyline and the plummy undersides of the ligularias add depth and solidity to the mix.

shaped or elliptical leaves, undivided or sometimes deeply divided, and with smooth or coarsely toothed margins. The leaves of several come in unusual and attractive shapes, and most are worth growing for the foliage alone. In mid- and late summer, showy yellow or orange, daisylike flowers are borne in sprays or spikes on unbranched, leafy stems. These handsome plants should be given plenty of space, and will repay good soil preparation. Along with rodgersias and astilbes, they are archetypal plants for a bog garden or pondside, but will grow well in any moist situation.

CULTIVATION Grow in a fertile, moist soil in part-shade; a more open position may be tolerated if the soil does not dry out. Most wilt in hot sun but revive in the evening.

PROPAGATION By division or from seed, although cultivars will not come true from seed.

PROBLEMS Slugs and snails.

L. dentata Robust plant with a short rhizome, from which arise several mid-green, coarsely toothed, kidney-shaped basal leaves to 16 in (40 cm) across, somewhat hairy beneath, and borne on stalks to 28 in (70 cm) long. From midsummer to early fall, bright deep yellow, daisylike flowers, 3–4 in (8–10 cm) across, open in flat-topped clusters on erect stems, each carrying two smaller leaves. Although the wild form is a striking plant, various cultivars with bronze-purple leaves are more popular in the garden. From wet mountain meadows in Burma, central and western China, and Japan. ‡5 ft (1.5 m). Z4–8 H8–1. **‘Britt-Marie Crawford’** Stems and leaves very dark blackish maroon, purple beneath; flowers deep orange-yellow. ‡3¼ ft (1 m). **‘Desdemona’** Leaves bronze-green above, deep purple beneath; flowers orange. ‡4 ft (1.2 m). **‘Othello’** Leaves deep purplish green above, reddish purple beneath, on rather long stems; flowers orange. ‡4 ft (1.2 m).

L. fischeri Large, rather variable plant forming a clump of long-stalked, kidney-shaped, mid-green leaves to 16 in (40 cm) wide, toothed on the margins. Rather starry, bright yellow, 2-in (5-cm) flowers are carried in narrowly conical sprays from midsummer to early or mid-fall, on erect stems with woolly hairs near the base. From wet mountain meadows in the Himalaya, Siberia, China, and Korea. ‡6½ ft (2 m). Z4–8 H8–1.

L. ‘Gregynog Gold’ Forming a clump of rounded, toothed leaves, heart-shaped at the base and up to 12 in (30 cm) across. The rich orange-yellow flowers, up to 4 in (10 cm) across, have brown centers and are carried in tall, conical sprays held well above the foliage, from midsummer to early fall or later. Its imposing demeanor and richly colored flowers make this one of the most striking plants for a moist

RIGHT 1 *Ligularia* ‘Gregynog Gold’
2 *L. przewalskii*
3 *L. dentata* ‘Desdemona’

border in late summer. A hybrid of *L. dentata* and *L. veitchiana,* originated at Gregynog, a country house in mid-Wales. ‡6½ ft (2 m). Z6–9 H9–6

L. × *hessei* Clump-forming, with rounded to kidney-shaped leaves up to about 12 in (30 cm) across, heart-shaped at the base. The 4-in (10-cm) orange flowers are held in impressively large conical sprays. Very similar to ‘Gregynog Gold’, but flowering slightly earlier and with paler orange flowers. A hybrid of *L. dentata* and *L. wilsoniana.* ‡6½ ft (2 m). Z4–8 H8–1

L. hodgsonii Compact clump-forming plant with long-stalked, kidney-shaped or rounded leaves up to 10 in (25 cm) wide in mid-green or tinged with purple beneath. From midsummer to early fall, 2-in (5-cm), yellow or orange-yellow flowers open in compact clusters. In effect, a miniature version of *L. dentata,* from which it differs also in that there are two small bractlike leaves beneath each flower. Its modest size makes it desirable for a smaller garden. From mountain meadows in northern Japan, the Kurile Islands, and Sakhalin. ‡36 in (90 cm). Z4–8 H8–1

L. japonica From a short rhizome arise several long-stalked leaves and erect, purple-spotted stems. Leaves grow to 16 in (40 cm) long, and are deeply divided into several pairs of coarsely toothed or lobed segments. Up to eight bright yellow flowers about 4 in (10 cm) across, each with several narrow ray florets and darker yellow centers, are carried in small clusters. Individual flowers are a good size, yet sparse and lack impact, but the deeply cut foliage is attractive and distinctive. From open, grassy places in the mountains of China, Korea, Taiwan, and southern Japan. ‡3¼ ft (1 m). Z6–8 H8–6

L. przewalskii Tall, clump-forming with almost black stems arising from a substantial clump of triangular leaves to 12 in (30 cm) across, each deeply divided into seven fingerlike, strongly toothed lobes. In mid- and late summer, erect, almost black stems carry slender wandlike spikes to 20 in (50 cm) long, composed of flowers, each ¾–1¼ in (2–3 cm) across, with just two or three clear yellow rays. Individual flowers are small, but are borne in long spires with contrasting dark stems, making a winning combination. From grassy hillsides in northwestern China. ‡6 ft (1.8 m). Z4–8 H8–1

L. sibirica Bold clumps of finely toothed, triangular or kidney-shaped leaves, up to 10 in (25 cm) wide, develop from a short, thick rhizome. Long, slender spires of dark-centered, starry yellow 1¼ in (3 cm) flowers open in mid- and late summer, and are held well above the foliage. A variable species, growing in damp meadows in low mountains over a wide area from

Europe to China and Japan. ‡4 ft (1.2 m). Z4–8 H8–1

L. stenocephala Clump-forming with a short rhizome and long-stalked triangular leaves up 8 in (20 cm) wide, the margins jaggedly toothed. Tall, upright stems, usually deep blackish purple, contrast beautifully with the long, narrow spires of small yellow flowers in mid- and late summer. Each flower has only one to three rays, but the dense spires give a fine effect, enhanced by the distinctively cut leaves. From wet meadows in the mountains of China, Taiwan, and Japan. ‡5 ft (1.5 m). Z4–8 H8–1

L. ‘The Rocket’ The long-stalked, triangular leaves, up to 10 in (25 cm) wide, are deeply and jaggedly toothed. From among them rise tall, blackish purple flower stems bearing long spires of many bright yellow flowers, ¾–1¼ in (2–3 cm) across, in mid- and late summer. A popular hybrid between *L. przewalskii* and *L. stenocephala,* and combining the best characteristics of each, with good foliage and imposing flower spikes. ‡6 ft (1.8 m). Z4–8 H8–1

L. tussilaginea see *Farfugium japonicum*

L. veitchiana A robust plant forming a clump of long-stalked, kidney-shaped leaves to 18 in (45 cm) wide, finely toothed on the margins, and with cobweblike hairs when young. The bright, deep yellow, 2 in (5 cm) flowers are carried in narrow spires up to 30 in (75 cm) long, in mid- and late summer, and are then followed by conspicuously fluffy seed heads. The bold, rounded leaves provide a fairly dramatic contrast to the rather slender flower spikes. From damp woods in western China. ‡ 6 ft (1.8 m). Z4–8 H8–1

L. wilsoniana Big, clump-forming, with spectacularly large, rounded leaves, to 20 in (50 cm) across, and sharply toothed on the margins. Bright yellow flowers are 1 in (2.5 cm) wide and are borne in profusion on long, branched spikes. From China; grows in moist woodlands, best given some shade in the garden. Height to ‡ 6½ ft (2 m). Z4–8 H8–1

L. x yoshizoeana 'Palmatiloba' Clump-forming plant with long-stalked, rounded leaves to 8 in (20 cm) wide, deeply divided into broad, coarsely toothed lobes. Bright, deep yellow, 4 in (10 cm) flowers are borne in flat-topped sprays from mid- to late summer or early fall. The handsome leaves are quite different in effect from other species. A hybrid of *L. dentata* and *L. japonica*, 'Palmatiloba' probably originated in western gardens, but the same hybrid occasionally occurs in the wild in Japan where parents grow together. ‡ 3¼ ft (1 m). Z5–9 H9–5

L. 'Zepter' Forming a large clump of long-stalked, rounded leaves to 12 in (30 cm) across, in mid- and late summer. Tall spires of deep orange-yellow flowers, ¾ in (2 cm) wide, rise on black stems, well above the foliage. A striking plant, raised in Germany, with the large leaves of *L. veitchiana* combined with the dark stems of *L. przewalskii* or, more probably, 'The Rocket'. ‡ 6 ft (1.8 m). Z5–9 H9–5

LIMONIUM

Sea lavender

PLUMBAGINACEAE

Drought-tolerant plants for sunny areas, with flowers keeping their color well after drying.

About 150 species of annuals, evergreen and deciduous perennials, and shrubs, mostly grow in dry plains and seaside locations throughout the temperate world. Several are commonly grown in gardens. Wiry stems bear simple or lobed, gray-green leaves, with branched sprays of flowers of papery, often showy tissue around the flower (calyx), the true flower being smaller and white, blue or yellow. Popular with flower arrangers: flowers retain their color well even when dried.

CULTIVATION Any free-draining soil in full sun.

PROPAGATION From seed or by root cuttings.

PROBLEMS Powdery mildew. Poor drainage may cause root rot.

L. bellidifolium Neat, dome-shaped, evergreen with rounded or spoon-shaped, dark green leaves to 2 in (5 cm) long. Blue-violet flowers, ¼ in (5 mm) across, are carried in many small clusters on branched, rough-surfaced stems in early summer and midsummer. Best grown at the front of a dry, sunny border or in a container. From salt-marshes in Europe, from England to Russia. ‡ 8 in (20 cm). Z7–9 H9–7

L. latifolium see *L. platyphyllum*

L. platyphyllum syn. *L. latifolium* An evergreen rosette of elliptic or broadly spoon-shaped, leathery, dark green leaves up to 18 in (45 cm) long supports large, branched, wiry stems bearing many ¼ in (6 mm) pale violet-blue flowers in open sprays in late summer and early fall. From steppes and dry grasslands in southeastern Europe. ‡ 3¼ ft (1 m). Z7–9 H9–7. **'Violetta'** Deep violet flowers.

LINARIA

Toadflax

SCROPHULARIACEAE

Brightly colored flowers on plants ranging from the small and prostrate to the tall and erect.

About 100 species of annuals, biennials, and herbaceous perennials are found in a range of open sunny situations, including sand dunes, grassland, waste ground, and rocky places in Europe, Japan, North Africa, and the Canary Islands. The basal leaves are produced in clusters or are oppositely arranged, while the stem leaves are alternate, entire, egg- or lance-shaped and without stalks. Brightly colored, long-spurred flowers, like those of antirrhinums,

MORE THAN ENOUGH

Linarias are undoubtedly valuable plants, but they can also be a nuisance. The purple and pink forms of *Linaria purpurea* in particular, but also *L. x dominii*, can cast their many seeds through borders, resulting in a forest of young plants. This can lead to some unexpectedly attractive associations with neighbors, but in general, they are not worth the trouble of having to remove them. It is better to deadhead regularly. This will also prevent the choice colors from throwing up purple seedlings that may tend to dominate.

Both *L. dalmatica* and *L. vulgaris* have been listed as a noxious weeds in many western states and are proving difficult to eradicate where they are troublesome. Both have the unexpected ability to withstand hotter summer temperatures than those found in their native European habitats, and their persistent creeping roots not only aid their spread but are difficult to remove or kill.

ABOVE **1** *Limonium platyphyllum* **2** *Linaria vulgaris*

are produced singly in the leaf joints or in long terminal spikes. The lower lip of each flower is divided into three lobes, often with a unique mark in a contrasting color toward the throat (known as the palate). The upper lip is divided into two lobes.

Some species can be a nuisance because of their aggressive spread or prolific self-seeding, but many are valuable border plants. Individuals are often short-lived but usually establish themselves by self-seeding, although hybrids and cultivars will often not come true.

CULTIVATION Generally fairly tolerant; all prefer a sunny position and good drainage and are useful for very poor soil that dries out in summer.

PROPAGATION Sow seed in early spring in an unheated greenhouse or cold frame; divide plants or take basal cuttings in spring.

PROBLEMS Aphids and downy and powdery mildew.

L. anticaria 'Antique Silver' Attractive. Covered with a waxy bloom and with branched, ascending, or floppy stems. Linear to narrowly lance-shaped silver-gray leaves. In spring it produces open spikes of grayish blue flowers. The wild species, with blue-striped white flowers each with a purplish palate, is rarely seen. For front of herbaceous border; it needs sun and well-drained soil. Protect in winter with a layer of conifer branches. Wild species is from southern Spain. ‡ 18 in (45 cm). Z5–8 H8–5

L. Blue Lace ('Yalin') A vigorous

trailing plant of uncertain origin with masses of small, fragrant blue and white flowers. Suitable for tumbling over low walls in a sunny well-drained site or for containers. ‡ 10 in (25 cm). Z5–8 H8–5

L. dalmatica (Dalmatian toadflax) A vigorous, short-lived plant with a long taproot supporting upright or rather floppy stems and rather erect, blue-gray, lance- or egg-shaped leaves, up to 1½ in (4 cm) across. In the summer it produces long, open spikes of widely spaced, long-spurred, bright yellow flowers followed by large quantities of seed. Best in dry, sandy soil; very drought-tolerant. Sometimes considered a subspecies of the less often seen *L. genistifolia*. Introduced into the US in the early 19th century and now a serious grassland weed, it is native to the Balkan peninsula, Italy, and Romania. ‡ 3¼ ft (1 m). Z5–8 H8–5

L. x dominii Erect or spreading stems carry slightly grayish green, opposite, linear or narrowly lance-shaped leaves to 2 in (5 cm) long. Branched spikes carry a long season of typically lilac or purplish violet, two-lipped, ⅝ in (1.5 cm) flowers. A naturally occurring hybrid of *L. purpurea* and *L. repens* and intermediate between the two. Only cultivars are usually grown. Propagate by division or by taking basal cuttings early in the year. From areas in Europe where both parents grow together. ‡ 3¼ ft (1 m). Z4–9 H9–1. **'Carnforth'** Pale lilac flowers; spreading habit. **'Yuppie Surprise'** Waxy blue foliage and slender spikes of lilac-pink flowers.

L. purpurea An easily grown, hairless, slightly grayish green herbaceous perennial with erect, branched stems. Lower leaves are in clusters, becoming alternate farther up the stem, and linear in shape. Small, ⅝ in (1.5 cm), purplish violet flowers are borne in long, slender, tapering spikes and have short curved spurs. It flowers from early summer to early fall and readily self-seeds, often arriving as an unexpected guest with other plants. From Italy. ‡ 36 in (90 cm). Z5–8 H8–5. **'Canon Went'** Silver-gray foliage and spikes of soft pink flowers from early summer to early fall. Self-seeds; difficult to keep true. **'Springside White'** Grayish green foliage and tall spikes of equally spaced white flowers on shorter plants. ‡ 20 in (50 cm).

L. repens (Pale toadflax) Vigorous, with creeping rhizomes and erect or floppy, hairless, branched stems. The leaves, arranged in clusters or more rarely alternately on the stems, are linear or slightly broader toward the tip, and have noticeable points. In summer, it produces long, tapering spikes of white to pale mauve flowers with violet veins and an orange mark in the mouth. An adaptable plant that can be grown in a herbaceous border or on walls. Found on walls and in rocky places and rough ground from northern Italy to northern Spain, Sweden, and British Isles. ‡ 32 in (80 cm). Z5–8 H8–5

L. triornithophora (Three birds flying) Erect in growth, with simple or branched stems that are stouter than those of most species, and carrying clusters of three or four gray-green, oval or lance-shaped leaves. The flowers are borne in groups of three in the leaf joints in distinctive isolated clusters. They vary from lavender-pink to pale purple, occasionally white, and have a very long, slightly curved brownish purple spur. There is a contrasting yellow palate. Less hardy than most, but more distinctive. Best raised regularly from seed. From Spain and Portugal. ‡ 36 in (90 cm). Z7–9 H9–7. **'Rosea'** Rose pink with cream spurs.

L. vulgaris (Common toadflax, Butter and eggs) Erect, spreading—sometimes vigorously—by runners, with stiff, simple or branched, upright stems and pale green, alternate, linear or narrowly elliptical leaves. Dense spikes of bright or pale yellow flowers, with an orange palate, have a long season from late spring to early fall or later. It readily self-seeds, and runs; unwanted plants should be removed before they become well established. Best in wild areas. Introduced to North America; now in all states except Hawaii, a noxious weed in some. Widespread throughout much of Europe. ‡ 36 in (90 cm). Z4–8 H8–1

LINDELOFIA
BORAGINACEAE

Unusual and attractive plants with nodding flowers held in elegant sprays.

About 12 deciduous, hairy plants come from mountainous habitats of Central Asia, the Himalaya, Pakistan, Afghanistan, and China; only one is commonly grown in gardens. They have rather stout rootstocks and more or less upright, usually softly hairy stems, with long-stalked basal leaves and alternate, oval to oblong,

lance-shaped, stalkless stem leaves. Flowers are bell-shaped, funnel-shaped, or cylindrical, with five lobes, often blue or purple, and carried on terminal shoots and sideshoots in smallish clusters that together can form a large head. The genus includes some lovely, though mainly uncommon, plants for a herbaceous or mixed border.

CULTIVATION Most require full sun in well-drained, ideally moisture-retentive soil, in a sheltered position with some protection from winds.

PROPAGATION From seed in spring or as soon as it is ripe; also by division in fall or spring, or root cuttings in winter.

PROBLEMS Powdery mildew.

L. longiflora A decorative plant with lance-shaped hairy leaves up to 12 in (30 cm) long at the base and shorter stem leaves to 3 in (8 cm), the upper ones clasping the bristly upright stem. The flowerhead is about 6 in (15 cm) long and comprises several clusters of vibrant gentian- or purple-blue flowers, each about ½ in (1.5 cm) across, in summer. An excellent perennial for a sunny border. From the western Himalaya (Pakistan, northwestern India, Kashmir, and western Nepal). ‡ 24 in (60 cm). Z4–8 H8–1

LINUM
Flax
LINACEAE

The prettiest blue flowers you could hope to see, produced over a long period.

About 200 species of annuals, biennials, and both evergreen and deciduous perennials are native to temperate areas of the Northern Hemisphere. *Linum* is unusual in having plants with bright yellow, blue, red, and white flowers among its species, a color range that few other genera can match. Their open, funnel or saucerlike, five-petaled flowers are produced in clusters at the shoot tips, or in the upper leaf joints, over a long period, although the individual flowers are generally short-lived, often opening for only one day. The plants are also short-lived, and seed freely without becoming invasive. The generally simple, narrow foliage is usually alternately arranged. In addition to their ornamental qualities, the annual *L. usitatissimum* is the source of flax used in linens, rope and cordage, and of linseed oil.

CULTIVATION Well-drained soil in full sun.

PROPAGATION From seed sown cool, or stem cuttings or by division in spring for the named varieties.

PROBLEMS Usually trouble-free.

L. flavum (Golden flax) A robust plant

with erect stems, slightly woody at the base, carrying ¾–1 in (2–2.5 cm) leaves, broadest at the tip, becoming more slender higher up. Open clusters of 25–40, bright yellow, 1 in (2.5 cm) flowers are borne in summer. It is sometimes confused with *L. capitatum*, which has a basal rosette of dark foliage. From central and southern Europe. ‡ 12 in (30 cm). Z5–7 H7–5. **'Compactum'** Much shorter. ‡ 6 in (15 cm).

L. narbonense (Narbonne flax) Prolific and unusually long-lived, the upright stems are lined with slender leaves, the whole plant having a slightly blue-gray tint. The funnel-shaped, 1¾ in (4.5 cm) azure-blue flowers have a white throat and come in sparse clusters. The best species for garden use because of its larger flowers, prolific blooming, and longer life. White-eyed, funnel-shaped flowers distinguish it from the similar *L. perenne*. Cutting the plants back to about 8 in (20 cm) after flowering will often promote rebloom. From the western and central Mediterranean. ‡ 24 in (60 cm). Z6–9 H9–5. **'Heavenly Blue'** Darker flowers on a slightly smaller plant. ‡ 20 in (50 cm).

L. perenne (Blue flax, Perennial flax) Usually erect, though sometimes rather floppy, plant with narrow blue-green leaves, up to 1 in (2.5 cm), that are shed as the plants grow, leaving the bases of the stems bare. The pale blue, saucer-shaped, 1 in (2.5 cm) flowers open for several weeks from early summer onward, opening in the morning and closing by mid-afternoon. Heat-tolerant, and good for hot, dry locations. A variable plant in the size of its leaves and flowers and in the number of flowers produced. From Europe and North America. ‡ 18 in (45 cm). Z7–9 H9–7. **'Album'** White with a slight blue tinge. **subsp.** *alpinum* **'Alice Blue'** Clear blue flowers; dwarf. ‡ 12 in (30 cm). **'Blau Saphir'** (**Blue Sapphire**) Sky blue; dwarf. ‡ 12 in (30 cm). **'Diamant'** White flowers with a small yellow center. **subsp.** *lewisii* Stouter, hardier, and with longer leaves. From western North America. **'White Diamond'** Pure white; dwarf. ‡ 12 in (30 cm).

LIRIOPE
Lily turf
CONVALLARIACEAE

Modest clump-formers or spreaders making excellent ground cover and adding a touch of color to the fall border.

About eight species of evergreen plants come from China, Japan, and Vietnam, where they inhabit woodland edges and scrub. Only three are commonly grown. All have fibrous roots with scattered tubers supporting narrow grassy-green foliage, but they vary in habit from tightly clumping to widely colony-

RIGHT 1 *Linum narbonense* **2** *L. perenne* **3** *Liriope muscari*

LEFT **1** *Liriope muscari* 'Okina'
2 *Lithophragma parviflorum*

forming. Small, bell-shaped flowers are held erect on upright spikes among or above the leaf tips and are followed by purple-black berries. They are appreciated as ground cover, for their fall flowers, and, increasingly, as foliage plants. Many are mistakenly listed in catalogs under the closely related *Ophiopogon*, which differs in its nodding flowers. The name 'Silvery Sunproof' has been used for a number of different variegated cultivars.

CULTIVATION Thrives in sun but best in part-shade; some sun required for fall-flowering species. Most soils are suitable if fertile and well-drained.

PROPAGATION Cultivars by division, species by division or from seed.

PROBLEMS Usually trouble-free.

L. exiliflora syn. *L. muscari* var. *exiliflora* Slowly forms dense, sodlike colonies that spread short underground stems; can be agressive. Leathery, deep green ⅜–½ in (9–12 mm) wide leaves arch, for a total height of 8 in (20 cm). Thin violet-brown stems bear loose spikes of ¼ in (5–7 mm) long mauve bells in fall. Different than *L. muscari*, which forms compact clumps and has dense flower spikes. From China and Japan. ↕12–16 in (34–40 cm). Z5–9 H9–1. **'Majestic'** see *L.* 'Majestic'.**'Silver Sunproof'** syn. 'Ariake Janshige' Leaves striped white to yellow.

L. graminifolia see *L. muscari*

***L.* 'Majestic'** syn. *L. exiliflora* 'Majestic' Flower spike has a thickened or crested tip. A popular cultivar.

L. muscari syn. *L. graminifolia* var. *densiflora, L. platyphylla, Ophiopogon muscari* Showy, and best-known forming dense clumps of deep green, leathery leaves 10–18 in (25–45 cm) long and ⅝–¾ in (1.5–2 cm) wide. Violet-flushed stems bear dense spikes of ¼–⅜ in (5–8 mm) wide violet-blue bells in fall, often into early winter. Sometimes listed, incorrectly, as *L. graminifolia.* Some cultivars here may mistakenly be sold under each other's names. Wild in China but long cultivated in Japan. ↕18–24 in (45–60 cm). Z6–10 H12–1. **'Big Blue'** A name often seen, but plants are no different from the typical wild species. **var. *exiliflora*** see *L. exiliflora.* **'Gold-banded'** Leaves with a greenish yellow central stripe; compact. ↕14 in (35 cm). **'Ingwersen'** Dense spikes of lilac-blue flowers. ↕12 in (30 cm). **'John Burch'** Leaves with a golden yellow central stripe. Wider leaves, and taller, than 'Gold-banded'. **'Monroe White'** Larger, pure white flowers. **'Okina'** Leaves 8–10 in (20–25 cm) long and white when young, aging frosty green with pure green tips. ↕14 in (35 cm). **'Royal Purple'** Dark purple flowers. **'Samantha'** Distinctive pink flowers in showy spikes. **'Silver Ribbon'** Intensely silvered foliage but rarely flowers. Compact. ↕10 in (25 cm). **'Variegata'** Leaves margined yellow. Often sold as 'Gold-banded' and 'Silvery Sunproof'.

L. platyphylla see *L. muscari*

L. spicata syn. *Ophiopogon spicatus* Best species for ground cover, spreads widely by slender, underground stems. Leaves are grasslike, 6–13 in (15–33 cm) long and only ⅙–¼ in (4–7 mm) wide, deep green and arching. Flowers, ⅙–¼ in (4–7 mm), vary from pale violet to almost white, in summer, in short spikes among the leaf tips. From China and Vietnam. ↕8–12 in (20–30 cm). Z6–10 H12–1. **'Alba'** White flowers. **'Silver Dragon'** syn. 'Gin-ryu' Compact, with silvery white striped foliage. ↕8 in (20 cm).

LITHOPHRAGMA

Woodland star

SAXIFRAGACEAE

Hardy, subtly elegant, shade-loving woodlanders enhancing the spring garden with charming campion-like flowers.

The nine species of deciduous plants are native to woodlands in western North America and suitable for a woodland garden, shrub border, or shady spot on a rock garden. Only one is commonly grown. They are rosette-forming plants, with long-stalked, lobed and toothed, rounded or kidney-shaped leaves, or with leaves consisting of three leaflets. Their growing season is short, and they disappear completely in summer. Small campion-like flowers with five petals open in the late spring. They often produce bulbils, on the stems after flowering, or below ground.

CULTIVATION Grows well in fertile very well-drained soil containing abundant humus, and in part- or complete shade.

PROPAGATION By division in spring or fall, bulbils separated and planted in spring or fall, or from seeds outdoors in fall.

PROBLEMS Slugs love the succulent new foliage in spring.

L. parviflorum Clump-forming. Dark green leaves rounded and three lobes or consisting of three leaflets, and ½–1¼ in (1–3 cm) long. They may be very hairy or hardly hairy at all. Heads of up to 14, white or light pink, sometimes scented flowers, 1¼ in (3 cm) wide with deeply cut petals, appear in late spring. Grows well with other woodlanders. From California. ↕20 in (50 cm). Z4–6 H6–1

LOBELIA

CAMPANULACEAE

Valued for their brightly colored flowers, lobelias vary enormously in their stature and habit of growth.

Lobelias are unusually diverse, with about 370 species of annuals, perennials (a few of which are aquatic), shrubs, and even trees from marshes and wet meadows to woodlands, hilly and mountainous slopes, and deserts throughout tropical and temperate areas worldwide, especially North, Central, and South America.

The perennials discussed here may have fleshy crowns or be woody at the base with upright, branched or unbranched stems, carrying simple, alternate, and often stalkless 4–6 in (10–15 cm) leaves that are often toothed. The flower is a tube flaring into five lobes, making a face 1–1½ in (2.5–3.5 cm) across, the three lower lobes large and fanlike, the upper two small and usually curved back. The flowers usually grow in unbranched spikes, dense and crowded in some species, longer and more sparsely arranged, though not necessarily less dramatic, in other species. The blooms open from the bottom up. The whole plant is generally poisonous and has a milky sap that may be an irritant.

There has been much uncertainty and confusion over the classification of species, cultivars, and hybrids of *Lobelia* that has now been clarified and is reflected here. In particular, the species formerly known as *L. fulgens* and *L. splendens* are no longer treated as distinct from *L. cardinalis.* Hybrids between *L. cardinalis* and *L. siphilitica* are confirmed as *L. x speciosa.*

With the exception of bedding lobelia, all species are poisonous and are an irritant to skin and eyes. ⚠

CULTIVATION The majority of the species and cultivars listed here require moist, well-cultivated, fertile soils and a situation in full sun or part-shade; all need adequate moisture in summer. If border types are allowed to wilt, their stems will recover but remain unattractively kinked. When grown on the borderline of hardiness, plants must either be well mulched before winter with a good open mulching

VIRUS AND VIGOR

Gardeners often find that some perennial lobelias thrive in the garden, but others do not; or they may thrive for a year or two and then decline. This reluctance to thrive may be caused by a virus infection.

It is not possible to cure virus diseases, but they can be prevented. In the case of lobelias, many of the latest introductions are propagated in the laboratory by tissue culture and removing the virus is a precursor to this process, so newly introduced cultivars are less likely to be infected.

The disease is transmitted by aphids, and can also be transmitted on pruning tools, so it is important to keep aphids under control and, when cutting back plants, clean your pruning tools

thoroughly before you start working on each new plant.

The other approach is to grow only seed-raised cultivars, which start off virus-free since viruses do not infect the seeds. These plants are astonishingly vigorous—one plant of 'Kompliment Scharlach' can produce four tall flower stems in its first summer from a spring sowing, and ten flower stems in its second summer. Plants in the Fan Series may produce even more. The range of colors of the seed-raised types, in both the flowers and the foliage, is, at the moment, less extensive than in the vegetatively propagated cultivars, but it is increasing, and they are certainly prolific.

---

material that will keep the roots warm, or lifted and overwintered in a frost-free greenhouse.

PROPAGATION Some species and cultivars can be grown from seed, which should be germinated at around 59–64°F (15–18°C). The seed is very fine and should be sown on the surface and not covered with soil. Some can be propagated by basal cuttings in spring or bud cuttings taken from the chopped-up stems later in the season. Virtually all types can be propagated by division of the crowns in the spring.

PROBLEMS Slugs, and crown rot in wet conditions, but virus diseases, spread by aphids and on tools, are the most destructive problem. Weak growth and leaf discoloration are the main symptoms. Infected plants should be promptly destroyed (*see* Virus and Vigor).

L. bridgesii syn. *L. excelsa* A robust perennial, with a stout, woody rootstock carrying tall stems with substantial, narrow mid-green leaves. These are topped by spikes of pinkish flowers with blue stamens, produced in summer. In appearance, rather like a pink version of *L. tupa*. Grows well in well-drained, slightly acidic soil in a sunny location. Needs a mulch for winter protection of its roots in many areas. Now quite rare in its native Chile. ‡5 ft (1.5 m). Z3–8 H8–1

L. cardinalis syn. *L. fulgens, L. splendens* (Cardinal flower) Short-lived clump-forming perennial growing from short rhizomes, that produce a basal rosette in spring, then reddish purple stems with long, narrow, sometimes bronze-tinted leaves up to 4 in (10 cm) long. From early summer to mid-fall, tall spires of bright scarlet to blood red flowers with reddish purple bracts are borne. It flowers freely on sideshoots after the main spike has finished flowering, especially if the dying spike is removed promptly. Suitable for a moist border or damp soil beside a pond. Hardiness varies according to the origin of the stock. Native to North America from Canada to Mexico.

‡36 in (90 cm). Z2–8 H8–1. **'Bees' Flame'** Narrow, slightly hairy leaves up to 6 in (15 cm) long. Both leaves and stems are beet red. Flowers from midsummer to early fall with spikes of bright crimson, two-lipped flowers. ‡30 in (75 cm). Z4–9 H9–1. **'Elmfeuer'** Dark leaves and brilliant red flowers. Claimed to be an improved and hardier version of 'Queen Victoria'. ‡18 in (45 cm). **'Eulalia Berridge'** An Irish selection with lovely, bright raspberry pink flowers. Described by California horticulturist M. Nevin Smith as "pink gone berserk." ‡36 in (90 cm). Z3–8 H8–1. **'Queen Victoria'** Deep purple stems, narrow beet red leaves, and vivid scarlet flowers throughout summer. Short-lived. Raised from seed, so variable. ‡36 in (90 cm). Z6–8 H8–6. **'Russian Princess'** The true cultivar has green leaves tinged red and flowers of a bright purple, but this may no longer be in existence. The plant now usually supplied under this name is a *L. x speciosa* cultivar with rich cerise pink flowers bordering on purple, and stems and leaves of rich burgundy. ‡30 in (75 cm). Z6–8 H8–6

L. Color Spires Cranberry Crush see *L. x speciosa* 'Cranberry Crush'

L. Color Spires Lilac see *L. siphilitica* 'Lilac Candles'

L. Color Spires White see *L. siphilitica* 'White Candles'

L. Compliment Series see *L. x speciosa* Kompliment Series

L. excelsa see *L. bridgesii*

L. fulgens see *L. cardinalis*

L. x gerardii see *L. x speciosa*

L. inflata (Indian tobacco) Short-lived plant with slender green stems carrying slightly hairy, relatively broad green leaves. The widely spaced, pale blue flowers appear from midsummer to mid-fall. As the seed pod develops, it swells into a ball, hence the species

RIGHT *Lobelia cardinalis* 'Bees' Flame'

name; these inflated seedpods are a clear distinguishing feature. It has long been used in a herbal medicine. Thrives in ordinary garden soil if given a cool, shady location; in hot areas, it may stop flowering in midsummer. Best propagated from seed sown in midwinter. From fields, roadsides, and open woods in the eastern US. ‡36 in (90 cm). Z4–8 H8–1

L. Kompliment Series see *L. x speciosa* Kompliment Series

L. laxiflora Rather variable perennial, often woody at the base, spreading by rhizomes to make extending clumps. Wiry, reddish, arching stems with very thin, finely toothed, light green leaves carry pendulous tubular flowers, each with a red tube and two yellow lips, from late spring to fall. Not a mass of color, but enough. From Central America and Mexico. ‡36 in (90 cm). Z9–10 H10–9. **var. angustifolia** A mass of slender stems bears very narrow leaves with fine points. Bright orange, tubular flowers, more delicate than the species, are freely produced throughout summer. Propagate from semiripe cuttings in fall. From Arizona. ‡24 in (60 cm).

L. polyphylla Woody-based, well-branched plant crowded with foliage that varies considerably from ⅛ in (4 mm) wide and linear in shape to 2 in (5 cm) wide and oval. Many of these forms, distinguished by their leaf shape, have been named, but variations show no correlation with distribution or habitat, and these names have now largely been abandoned. Terminal

INNOVATION

Three breeders have been crucial in the development of perennial lobelias. Wray Bowden of Ontario raised a number of hybrids between *Lobelia cardinalis* and *L. siphilitica* that are sometimes called the Canadian Tetraploid Group because they have double the number of chromosomes of previous lobelias. These are characterized by their hardiness, large flowers, luminous colors, and vigor. His introductions included 'Dark Crusader' and 'Will Scarlet'.

In more recent years, Thurman Maness from Pittsboro, North Carolina, introduced a number of very prolific, often dense and large-flowered cultivars including 'Monet Moment', 'Ruby Slippers', and 'Sparkle Divine'.

The German seed company Ernst Benary Samenzucht GmbH has created perennial lobelias that are raised from seed. Using the techniques more familiar in bedding plants like petunias and impatiens, two series of F1 hybrid lobelias have been created, the Fan Series and the Kompliment Series. While not featuring the range of flower and foliage colors of the Bowden and Maness introductions, these plants flower in their first summer from an early sowing. This allows them largely to avoid the problems of virus infection that have plagued so many cultivars, including those from Wray Bowden and Thurman Maness, which are propagated by cuttings or division.

clusters of attractive but curious curved wine-colored flowers appear in late spring and are much loved by bees. From dry regions of Chile. ‡ 24–36 in (60–90 cm). Z5–8 H8–5

L. sessilifolia Clump-forming, often without overwintering rosettes, with slender, erect, dark-colored stems and narrow, unstalked, lance-shaped green leaves, becoming smaller higher up the stem. Flowers in mid- and late summer with dense terminal spikes of mid-blue flowers without the two upper lobes on the flower seen in other species. Suitable for bog gardens and damp areas, but tolerates drier conditions than *L. cardinalis*. From wet areas of Japan, Taiwan, Korea, and Manchuria. ‡ 24 in (60 cm). Z5–8 H8–5

L. siphilitica (Great lobelia, Blue cardinal flower) Clump-forming, the erect stems are dense with slightly hairy, alternate, 4 in (10 cm), oval or lance-shaped green leaves. Mid-blue, two-lipped flowers, 1 in (2.5 cm) across with leafy green bracts, appear from midsummer to fall. Grow in moist situations such as the margins of a pond, in full sun or light shade. Native to eastern North America. ‡ 36 in (90 cm). Z4–8 H8–1. **'Alba'** Pure white. **'Lilac Candles'** (**Color Spires Lilac**) Sturdy stems with light green foliage, topped in midsummer with huge, chunky spikes of lilac flowers. ‡ 18 in (45 cm). Z3–9 H8–1. **'White Candles'** (**Color Spires White**) Sturdy, compact, with pale foliage and large crowded spikes in white with a hint of blue. ‡ 18 in (45 cm). Z3–9 H8–1

L. splendens see *L. cardinalis*

L. x *speciosa* syn. *L.* x *gerardii* Slightly hairy plant with a noticeable basal rosette and several erect stems with oblong or oval leaves. Flowering stems are crowded with 1¼ in (3 cm) violet flowers, tinged with pink to purple and with white marks on the lower lip, over a long period through summer. This is a robust wild hybrid between *L. cardinalis* and *L. siphilitica* that has also produced many excellent garden cultivars of variable hardiness. Many catalogs and books omit the specific name and just use the cultivar name. Easy to grow in both heavy and light soils. ‡ 5 ft (1.5 m). Z5–8 H8–5. **'Butterfly Blue'** Rich violet-blue flowers in late summer. One of the hardier hybrids. ‡ 36 in (90 cm). Z5–8 H8–5. **'Cherry Ripe'** Mid-green leaves often suffused with maroon and spires of tubular, cherry red flowers from mid- to late summer. Raised by Wray Bowden. ‡ 36 in (90 cm). Z5–8 H8–5. **'Cranberry Crush'** (**Color Spires Cranberry Crush**) Dense spikes on cranberry red flowers with green foliage. From Dan Heims, Terra Nova Nursery. ‡ 16 in (40 cm). Z5–8 H8–5. **'Dark Crusader'** Maroon stems and

LEFT 1 *Lobelia laxiflora* var. *angustifolia* **2** *L. siphilitica* **3** *L.* x *speciosa* 'Pink Flamingo'

SUMMER RICHNESS IN PURPLE

PURPLE AND BRONZE FOLIAGE with deep red flowers is always a dependable combination that adds richness and solidity to summer borders without being dark and somber. Here in the background, the purple hazel, *Corylus maxima* 'Purpurea', which keeps its color all season, sets off the upright spikes of scarlet *Lobelia* x *speciosa* 'Cherry Ripe' and the double red *Dahlia* 'Bloodstone'. It pays to renew the lobelia regularly, and, while some may be tempted to choose a dahlia with larger flowers, this small decorative type matches the scale of the other plants well.

leaves topped with velvety deep red flowers in mid- and late summer. From Wray Bowden, of Ontario, Canada. ‡ 28 in (70 cm). Z5–8 H8–5. **Fan Series** A series of F1 hybrid cultivars, intended to be raised from seed and flowering prolifically in their first summer. Compact, upright, noticeably well-branched plants produce green, sometimes red-tinted foliage and dense spires of flowers. Good in a sunny position and rich moist soil. Divide existing plants or grow from bought seed; home-saved seed will not come true. Raised by Ernst Benary in Germany. ‡ 24 in (60 cm). Z5–8 H8–5. **'Fan Blau'** (**Fan Blue**) Deep blue flowers and green leaves. ‡ 28 in (70 cm). **'Fan Burgundy'** Wine red flowers and green foliage. **'Fan Lachs'** (**Fan Salmon**) Pale salmon pink flowers and bronze leaves. **'Fan Orchidrosa'** (**Fan Orchid Rose**) Bright rose pink flowers and slightly bronzed leaves. **'Fan Scharlach'** (**Fan Scarlet**) Bright scarlet flowers, with coppery foliage. **'Fan Tiefrosa'** (**Fan Deep Rose**) Deep

rose pink flowers with green leaves. **'Fan Zinnoberrosa'** (**Fan Cinnabar Rose**) Deep rosy red flowers with deep green leaves. **'Grape Knee-Hi'** Deep purple flowers on a compact plant. Sterile flowers produce no seed so flowering is extended. From Dan Heims, Terra Nova Nursery. ‡ 16 in (40 cm). Z5–8 H8–5. **'Hadspen Purple'** Large, bright purple flowers all summer and fall. Light green, purple-flushed leaves. Raised by Nori Pope at Hadspen House, Somerset, England. ‡ 24 in (60 cm). Z5–8 H8–5. **Kompliment Series** (**Compliment Series**) A series of F1 hybrid cultivars, intended to be raised from seed and flowering prolifically in their first summer. From midsummer onward, upright, unbranched stems are clothed with green foliage and carry tall spikes of closely packed flowers in rich and pastel colors ranging from pale pink through rose, crimson, lilac, and purple. Spectacular in the border, they are also superb cut flowers. They are

best in a sunny position and in rich, moist soil. Divide existing plants or grow from bought seed; home-saved seed will not come true. Raised by Ernst Benary in Germany. ‡24–36 in (60–90 cm). Z6–9 H9–6. **'Kompliment Blau'** (Compliment Blue) Blue flowers. **'Kompliment Purpur'**® (**Compliment Purple**) Rich purple flowers. **'Kompliment Scharlach'**® (**Compliment Scarlet**) Large, very bright scarlet flowers on unbranched elegant spikes. Stunning. **'Kompliment Tiefrot'**® (**Compliment Deep Red**) Dark maroon red. **'Monet Moment'** Unusually massive heads of large, rich pink-violet flowers. Very vigorous. From Thurman Maness, NC. ‡36 in (90 cm). Z5–8 H8–5. **'Pink Elephant'** Deep, rich pink spikes with green foliage. Much more reliably perennial than many. ‡4 ft (1.2 m). Z5–8 H8–5. **'Pink Flamingo'** Spikes of attractive pink flowers in midsummer; pale green leaves. ‡4 ft (1.2 m). Z5–8 H8–5. **'Rosenkavalier'** Long spires of tubular, rose pink flowers, with a white eye. Leaves suffused red. ‡36 in (90 cm). Z5–8 H8–5. **'Ruby Slippers'** Compact, with upright stems topped with delicate ruby-garnet flowers from mid-spring through to midsummer. From Thurman Maness, NC. ‡18 in (45 cm). Z5–8 H8–5. **'Russian Princess'** see *L. cardinalis* 'Russian Princess'. **'Sparkle DeVine'** Vigorous, with green leaves and fuchsia-purple flowers in midsummer to late summer. From Thurman Maness, NC. ‡36 in (90 cm). Z5–8 H8–5. **'Tania'** Hot magenta flowers on burgundy stems; bronze-flushed green foliage. ‡36 in (90 cm). Z5–8 H8–5. **'Vedrariensis'** syn. *L* 'Vedrariensis' Long, tubular, violet-purple flowers in tall spires with dark green leaves suffused red. ‡36 in (90 cm). Z5–8 H8–5. **'Will Scarlet'** Mid-green leaves are suffused maroon with bright blood red flowers from midsummer to early fall. From Wray Bowden, Ontario. ‡36 in (90 cm). Z5–8 H8–5

L. splendens see *L. cardinalis*

L. tupa A robust, upright, clumping perennial with a woody rootstock carrying a few stiff, reddish purple stems with large, narrow, hairy, gray-green leaves that are up to 12 in (30 cm) long. From midsummer into early or mid-fall, there are narrow, tubular, curved and fleshy, brick red flowers that look like small parrot beaks. Needs a sunny position and grows best in well-drained but fertile soil with adequate moisture in summer. Mulch roots overwinter in borderline areas and protect from excess moisture. Easily raised from seed. Basal cuttings also possible but very few are produced. From sandy seaside hills in Chile. ‡6½ ft (2 m). Z8–10 H10–8

L. **'Vedrariensis'** see *L.* x *speciosa* 'Vedrariensis'

LOPHOSPERMUM
SCROPHULARIACEAE

Easily grown climbers with delicate trumpet flowers in pinks and reds.

There are eight species of evergreen perennial climbers and shrubs from South America with rounded to triangular leaves. The striking, solitary, usually pendulous, 2–3 in (5–8 cm) tubular flowers, in purple, pink, or white, resemble those of a foxglove and are borne in the upper leaf joints. They are attractive growing through twiggy shrubs but are for mild areas. The naming of plants in this genus has long been a subject for debate, and change, and some species have been moved between *Asarina, Maurandya*, and *Lophospermum* and back again.

CULTIVATION Thrives in sun and well-drained but fertile soil; keep dryish in winter. In cooler areas, grow in containers and move them to a protected area for the winter.

PROPAGATION From seed or semiripe cuttings.

PROBLEMS Usually trouble-free.

L. erubescens syn. *Asarina erubescens, Maurandya erubescens* Climbing. Clings by twining leaf-stalks that die to a tuberous root system in winter. Evergreen in mildest areas, otherwise deciduous. Triangular 2¾ in (7 cm) downy grayish green leaves. Rose pink, trumpet-shaped flowers, 2¾ in (7 cm) long, similar to foxgloves, throughout summer and fall. Fast-growing: may be grown from seed and treated as an annual; otherwise, over-winter frost-free under glass

in cooler and cold areas. Mexico. ‡10 ft (3 m). Z10–11 H11–10

L. **'Magic Dragon'** Pale green foliage and large red flared flowers. Sometimes raised from seed, which may yield pink-flowered forms. Hybrid of 'Red Dragon' and *L. erubescens* from Ray Brown of Torquay, England. ‡6½ ft (2 m). Z10–11 H11–10

L. **'Red Dragon'** Shining, carmine red, 2½ in (6 cm), trumpetlike flowers, smaller and less flared than 'Magic Dragon'. Soft, furry green leaves. ‡12 ft (4 m). Z10–11 H11–10

L. scandens syn. *Maurandya scandens* Vigorous climber, woody at the base, with smooth, or maybe slightly hairy, heart-shaped green leaves up to 4 in (10 cm) long, each with a long point. Purplish pink or lavender-blue trumpet-shaped flowers, 2¾ in (7 cm) long, with a white throat. From Mexico. ‡7½ ft (2.4 m). Z9–10 H10–9

LOTUS
PAPILIONACEAE

Low perennial plants that are suitable for both the front of a border, when used as a specimen in a gravel garden, or when used, very nicely, as ground cover.

There are about 150 species of annuals, perennials, and shrubs found in pastures and dry, rocky sites in Europe, Africa, and Australia. Only a few are grown as perennials, most of which are spreading in habit. The leaves may be simple or dissected into up to 15 opposite pairs of leaflets; the small pealike flowers, held singly or in clusters in the leaf joints, often only toward the tips of the shoots, come in a range

of colors. It is a diverse group, with some of the tropical species grown as house plants. Note that this is an entirely different genus from the aquatic sacred lotus, *Nelumbo*.

CULTIVATION Well-drained soil in full sun.

PROPAGATION From seed, sown in spring or fall, or by division.

PROBLEMS Usually trouble-free.

L. corniculatus (Bird's-foot trefoil) Bushy, or often widely spreading, rather variable plant, with a stout, usually compact rootstock. The leaves are split into three reverse egg-shaped leaflets ¼–⅝ in (5–15 mm) long and shaped like a bird's foot—hence the common name. In summer plants are covered in small heads of six to eight bright yellow flowers that darken to orange with age and are often streaked in red. This coloring is the source of its other common name—bacon and eggs. Excellent for the wild garden, being a good food source for butterflies and bees, but can become invasive. Native to Europe and Asia, it has become naturalized in the US. ‡8–12 in (20–30 cm). Z5–8 H8–5. **'Plenus'** Double flowers, but less vigorous and not invasive. Propagate by division in spring.

L. maritimus syn. *Tetragonolobus maritimus* A mat-forming plant for well-drained soil with upright flowering stems. The leaves are split into three 1¼ x-⅝ in (3 x 1.5 cm) leaflets each with one side larger than the other and may be shiny or slightly hairy. The 1¼ in (3 cm) pale yellow flowers are carried singly in summer. Native to Europe and Ukraine. ‡16 in (40 cm). Z5–8 H8–5

LUNARIA
Honesty
BRASSICACEAE

Perennial version of the well-known honesty that will enliven a natural gardens and informal settings.

There are three species of biennials and perennials native to rocky places in central and southern Europe, two are commonly grown. Erect stems bear large, toothed, heart-shaped to oval leaves, and four-petaled, white, lilac, or purple flowers in small terminal clusters. The flowers are followed by large, flat seedpods. The sides of these fall away to leave a silvery membrane—the seed heads of the biennial *L. annua*, especially, are useful for dried flower arrangements. Easily grown in a wide range of conditions and valuable in wildflower gardens and other informal spaces.

CULTIVATION Grow in any fertile, moist soil in sun or light shade.

PROPAGATION By division in spring, or from seeds.

PROBLEMS Clubroot and virus diseases.

L. rediviva (Perennial honesty) Forms a clump of upright stems bearing dark green, oval or triangular leaves to 8 in (20 cm) long, with finely toothed margins. The stems terminate in a loose cluster of sweet-scented, pale purplish white flowers 1 in (2.5 cm) across in late spring and early summer followed by elliptical seedpods 2½–3 in (6–8 cm) long, which become pale brown when ripe. As with the more familiar biennial honesty, seedpods from early flowers may coincide with blooming of later flowers, for a long season. From rocky places in much of continental Europe. ↕ 36 in (90 cm). Z6–9 H9–6

LUPINUS
Papilionaceae
LUPINE

Iconic cottage garden plants for well-drained sites, with flamboyant, vertical flower spikes in early summer.

Around 200 species of annuals, biennials, perennials, and shrubs have a wide natural distribution. Most, including many of the perennials, are concentrated in North, Central, and South America, while in the Old World, lupines are found mainly in the Mediterranean region and North Africa. Habitats are generally dry, rocky, and infertile, varying from grassland, to coastal sand and cliffs, or the banks of streams and rivers.

Lupines generally form upright clumps arising from taproots, with a basal mound of distinctive, fresh green leaves divided into fingerlike leaflets diverging from a single point, like spokes on a wheel. In late spring to early summer, showy spikes bearing short-stalked, bell-like flowers open from the bottom buds upward, held above the foliage on strong, hollow stems (*see* Lupine Flower Form). The flowers are either a single color or two-toned, usually in blues, purples, or white, and have a peppery fragrance. They are bee-pollinated.

The hybrid garden lupines, developed from the seed strain originally selected by George Russell (*see* The Origin of the Hybrid Lupine), are far more widely grown than species, either as clonal cultivars (raised from cuttings) or far more often as seed-raised plants in separate colors or mixtures (some of which are produced to a formula, for a balanced blend of colors). The generally dense flower spikes come in a spectacular range of shades, including varying tones of red, yellow, blue, white, pink, purple, and orange. Bicolors, where the standard and wings contrast, come in soft or vivid combinations. Breeders have also developed dwarf lupines, aimed at smaller gardens and exposed locations, which do not need staking in ordinary conditions. Garden hybrids tend to be short-lived, thriving for around five years before they need to be repropagated. They are sometimes seen in catalogs listed under *L.* x *regalis* or *L. polyphyllus*. Lupines give very good value as accent plants or in large drifts for exuberant color, and they also make good cut flowers. The species is also suitable for naturalizing in prairielike plantings.

Some species are used as green manure, since they are able to fix nitrogen by root nodules. They are also used for land reclamation, animal fodder, and, with increasing economic significance, as a source of protein for human consumption, particularly as flour produced from the seeds. Although it is wise to treat lupines as harmful if eaten, sweet lupines are strains of edible species with low levels of the bitter-tasting, toxic alkaloids, and their importance as a legume crop dates back to ancient times. Traditional uses of the Mediterranean annual *L. albus* include a snack made of its pickled seeds. ⚠

CULTIVATION Undemanding plants, preferring an open, sunny position in well-drained, neutral to slightly acidic soil, lupines will also tolerate part-shade, and are able to grow in relatively poor soil. They dislike drought while in growth, so ensure adequate water in spring, but they may rot in winter wet. Avoid covering the crown with mulch, and use bonemeal to fertilize rather than high-nitrogen type. Taller kinds may need staking. Remove faded flower spikes before the flat, hairy pods swell, to prevent self-seeding and encourage a second flush of (generally smaller) flowers later in the summer. Weed out self-sown seedlings: over several generations, seedlings tend to revert to plants with blue, open spikes. Plants often look tired after flowering, so screen with late-flowering perennials such as asters or Japanese anemones.

PROPAGATION Propagate selected forms by careful division of the crown in early spring, or by basal stem cuttings taken from new shoots in mid- to late spring, sliced off with a sliver of the tough yellow rootstock attached. Inserting the cuttings in pure perlite helps prevent rotting. Sow seed of species and purchased seed strains in modules in spring, summer, or fall, after soaking in cold water for 24 hours or nicking the hard seed coat to promote even germination. Seeds stay viable for a long time (excavated seeds of *L. arcticus* sprouted after 10,000 years) but germinate more quickly and uniformly when fresh. Some

THE GOOD AND THE BEST

The best lupines are spectacular. From the original cultivars raised by George Russell to the more recent introductions from Woodfield Brothers and Westcountry Nurseries, they are colorful, dramatic, and altogether astonishing. But finding these in nurseries can be difficult.

If you look at a lupine plant, you will see that the number of shoots arising from the crown is relatively small. These are the shoots that, in their young stage, make cuttings. However, taking the first cuttings does not promote a crop of even more cuttings a few weeks later, as happens with, say, penstemons. Consequently, the supply of the top-quality named cultivars is always going to be small.

This has severely limited the supply of the superb cultivars created by Morris Woodfield in Wolverhampton, England (*see* The Origin of the Hybrid Lupin, *p.313*) and more recently the excellent introductions of National Collection holder Sarah Conibear at Westcountry Nurseries, Devon, England. Propagation by tissue culture in the laboratory is being tested and may be the solution.

Raising lupines from seed is the alternative route, but quality can be variable. The dwarf Gallery Series is very dependable but is available in only a limited range of five separate colors and lacks the impact of taller kinds. The Band of Nobles series also comes in separate colors, but quality varies dramatically and is often poor. Some specialists supply mixed seed taken from their named cultivars and, although the quality is usually good, colors are left entirely to chance.

LEFT *Lunaria rediviva*

LUPINE FLOWER FORM

The stalked flowers arise from a single, upright stem, along which they may be spirally arranged or grouped into tiers of flowers (whorls) separated by a short space. The colorful parts of the flower are the broad upper petal known as a standard or flag, together with the inflated "bell" beneath it formed from two wings joined together over the inconspicuous, sickle-shaped keel that covers the reproductive structures. The fruit are flat hairy pods that shed their hard seeds as they dry and split.

Lupinus 'My Castle'

Buds

Standard

Main flower stem

Bell or wings

modern dwarf hybrids are bred to flower in their first year from an early sowing, although plants reach full quality from the second year onward.

PROBLEMS Lupine aphids and anthracnose (*see* Two Recent Lupine Probems, *p.314*) slugs and snails, powdery mildew, and virus diseases.

L. **Band of Nobles Series** Robust, dense flower spikes in a range of strong shades, including single colors and bicolors and also available in six popular, separate colors and a mixture. A well-established range of seed-raised tall, traditional Russell-type lupines, flowering in early summer and midsummer, which has been available for more than 30 years and, though originally selected in Holland, is now widely produced and consequently rather variable in height, and especially color. ‡ 36–48 in (90–120 cm). Z5–8 H8–5. **Band of Nobles Mixed** A blend of all the separate colors. **'Chandelier'** Yellow shades. **'My**

Castle' Brick red shades, usually with a darker standard. **'Noble Maiden'** Creamy white shades. **'The Chatelaine'** Pinks with white standards. **'The Governor'** Blues with white standards that may have purplish streaks. **'The Page'** Carmine red shades, often with paler standards. Often spelled as 'The Pages'.

L. **'Bishop's Tipple'** Dense spikes of mauve flowers with ivory-flecked standards mask the stem. A recent cultivar, to be propagated vegetatively; one of the first raised by Sarah Conibear. Introduced by Westcountry Nurseries, England. ‡ 36 in (90 cm). Z5–8 H8–5

L. **'Chandelier'** *see L* Band of Nobles Series

L. **Dwarf Gallery Series** see *L.* Gallery Series

RIGHT *Lupinus* Band of Nobles Series: **1** 'Chandelier' **2** 'Noble Maiden' **3** 'The Chatelaine'

THE ORIGIN OF THE HYBRID LUPINE

At the turn of the 20th century, the most ornamental lupine for gardens was blue *L. polyphyllus*, introduced in 1826, and its limited number of color variants, such as pink-and-white 'Moerheimii'. Some of the first hybrids were bred by horticulturist James Kelway, who was followed by G. R. Downer (whose red 'Downer's Delight' of about 1917 was much admired) and John Harkness.

The most lasting legacy, however, comes from the work of George Russell (1857–1951). A professional gardener with nursery experience, in 1911 Russell began to grow a mixture of *L. polyphyllus* with other lupines on his allotments near York, England, seeking to improve its open flower spikes and limited color range. He kept no record of what these other lupines were, but they probably included shrubby *L. arboreus* and annuals such as *L. hartwegii*, as well as existing hybrids and seed mixtures.

Russell left his thousands of plants open to pollination by bees, then collected seed of only the best plants, having disposed of the remainder before their pollen was released. In this way, he developed, over 25 years, a strain of lupines ever closer to his ideal: strong, weather-resistant perennials; mouth-watering new colors; long, tapering, solid-looking spikes densely packed with large flowers which, with their broad, upright standards and rounded "bells," hid the straight-backed stem beneath.

The Russell hybrid was launched commercially, to great excitement, in 1937 by Baker's Nursery, near Wolverhampton, England, and, in the years up to 1967, more than 150 cultivars selected from the Russell strain were also introduced and propagated vegetatively. Almost all of these have vanished, but the seed strain itself survived and forms the basis of the hybrid lupines in our gardens today.

TWO RECENT LUPINE PROBLEMS

In 1980, two problems of lupines appeared in England gardens. Lupine aphids (*Macrosiphum albifrons*), native to North America, arrived in the UK in 1981. These unusually large, gray-green aphids spend their whole lifecycle on lupines and can form dense colonies on flower spikes and the undersides of leaves in late spring to midsummer, causing the plant to collapse. Control by hand-picking or using insecticides or products containing fatty acids.

Anthracnose (*Colletotrichum acutatum*) was first seen in 1989. The distinctive symptoms include dieback of young shoots, dark brown dead patches toward the leaf edges, and brown scarring of stems and older foliage with rotting in the crown. It is troublesome in humid conditions. Severely infected plants usually die. There is no treatment for this disease. One main transmission route is by seed; some companies are now heat-treating seed to prevent infection, but it can be spread on home-saved seed. Fortunately, these diseases are not major problems in North America. Leaf spots may occur, but are not serious and infected leaves can be removed. Powdery mildew can be an occasional occurrence but is not serious.

L. Gallery Series syn. *L.* Dwarf Gallery Series Dwarf, seed-raised plants, with chunky, well-filled flower spikes in five vibrant colors, and a mix of them all, bred and introduced by French seed company Tézier in 1984 and still of dependably high quality. Sturdy and early-flowering, with a long bloom period; established plants can produce up to 12 spikes, around 10 in (25 cm) tall. Flowers in first year from an early sowing, before plants reach full size. Suitable for containers. ‡20 in (50 cm). Z4–8 H8–1. **'Gallery Blue'** Purple-blue shades, with some white bicolors. **'Gallery Mixed'** A blend of all five separate colors. **'Gallery Pink'** Rose shades, with some white bicolors. **'Gallery Red'** Bright red shades, with some white bicolors. **'Gallery Yellow'** Creamy to light golden shades. **'Gallery White'** White, opening from creamy buds.

L. 'Lulu' Dwarf Russell-style lupines with a long bloom period and well-filled spikes in a broad spectrum of solid and bicolors including warm orange tones, which distinguishes it from Minarette Group. Established plants produce 10–12 stems. Can flower in first year from a midwinter sowing. Well-known seed mixture bred by British horticulturist Ralph Gould at Hursts in the 1970s. ‡24 in (60 cm). Z4–8 H8–1.

L. Minarette Group Seed-raised, miniature lupines with plentiful, sturdy spikes in varying rainbow mixtures. Early flowering and suitable for containers. ‡20 in (50 cm). Z5–8 H8–5

L. 'Morello Cherry' Intense ruby red flowers, with standards a deeper shade than the wings, set in whorls around a dark stem to form slender spikes, around 16 in (40 cm) long. A tall, seed-raised cultivar introduced in 2001 by Thompson and Morgan. Flowers in its first year, from an early sowing. ‡36–48 in (90–120 cm) Z5–8 H8–5

L. 'My Castle' see *L.* Band of Nobles Series

L. 'New Millennium' syn. *L.* 'Sky Rocket' Impressive, shapely plumes up to 24 in (60 cm) long and 2¾–3 in (7–8 cm) across, produced in quantity on reliable, vigorous plants, and densely packed with flowers in a dazzling array of single and bicolor shades, including blue-black, old rose, brick red, and ivory. Will flower in first year from an early sowing, but reaches full quality from second year. Lasts well in water as a cut flower and also features improved weather tolerance. Seed-raised mixture from Dutch seed company Sahin. ‡4 ft (1.2 m). Z5–8 H8–5

L. 'Noble Maiden' see *L.* Band of Nobles Series

L. nootkatensis (Alaska lupine) A robust, upright perennial forming a low clump of velvety leaves divided into seven or eight slim leaflets, each up to 2½ in (6 cm) long and ⅝ in (1.5 cm) wide, tapering toward the base and with a short point at the rounded tips. In early summer and midsummer, 4 in (10 cm) spikes bear whorls of widely spaced flowers in single or mixed shades of purple-blue, white, and pink. Grizzly bears are known to dig up plants in order to feast on the roots. Needs sun and well-drained soil and dislikes hot, dry summers. Can self-seed to form colonies in ideal conditions. Closely related to *L. perennis* from eastern North America, which has smaller leaflets with smooth, hairless upper surfaces, and flower spikes up to 8 in (20 cm) long. Naturalized in Scotland, Ireland and Norway, and used to reclaim soils eroded by sheep grazing in Iceland, where it is also found to be invasive. Native to open slopes, meadows, tidal marshes, and gravel banks on the coast of Alaska and British Columbia, western North America, and also northeastern Asia. ‡20–28 in (50–70 cm). Z3–8 H8–1

L. 'Polar Princess' Plump spikes reaching about 20 in (50 cm) in length are tightly packed with snowy white flowers, giving a quilted effect. The spikes open fully before the lower flowers set seed. Compact, sturdy habit with good wind resistance. Selected for vegetative propagation from a seed-raised mixture by Arthur Hockin in his Devon garden in 1989, and introduced by Howard & Kooijs nursery, Norfolk, England. ‡30 in (75 cm) Z5–8 H8–5

L. polyphyllus (Blue-pod lupine, Marsh lupine) Stout, upright, producing a lush mound of large, long-stalked leaves divided into a fan of 9–17 slender leaflets, up to 4¾ in (12 cm) long and ¾ in (2 cm) wide. Stems, usually unbranching, are crowned in summer by imposing towers set with more or less loose whorls of blue, purple, or reddish flowers, the spikes reaching 7–16 in (18–40 cm). The stems may bend under the weight of the furry, violet seedpods. Various cultivars selected for flower color were grown around the turn of the 20th century, when this species was the main garden lupine. It was eclipsed in the 1930s by the multicolored, dense spikes of the hybrid Russell lupine (*see* The Origin of the Hybrid Lupine, *p.313*) and is now little grown. It is now under

GENTLE CONTRASTS IN PASTEL SHADES

LUPINES ARE NATURALLY dramatic plants, standing boldly upright in the border. While some have strong colors, even 'The Chatelaine', in these lovely soft pink and white tones, demands attention simply by the confident way it holds its flowers. Behind, clouds of soft blue hardy geraniums set them off nicely, while at the back the clustered yellow heads of *Phlomis russeliana* introduce another pastel shade. This is an example of how gentle distinctions, in both plant habit and flower color, can work together to create a harmonious whole.

LEFT *Lupinus* Gallery Series:
1 'Gallery Blue' **2** 'Gallery Red'

seed strain developed by George Russell, with tall spikes in a wide range of shades, as single colors and bicolors. Seed is produced by many companies and, since the strain is now maintained in different ways, the mixtures will vary in qualities such as fullness of spike and subtlety of color combinations. Since the 1950s, new, named strains have been developed from Russell hybrids, seeking, through reselection, to improve or change particular attributes such as height, weather resistance, or spike size. Plants available today are descended from the celebrated seed strain developed by George Russell, but rarely resemble his strain at the peak of its perfection. ‡36–48 in (90–120 cm). Z4–8 H8–1

L. 'Sky Rocket' see *L.* 'New Millennium'

L. 'The Chatelaine' see *L.* Band of Nobles Series

L. 'The Governor' see *L.* Band of Nobles Series

L. 'The Page' see *L.* Band of Nobles Series

L. 'Tutti Frutti' Seed mixture in a variety of colors, with an emphasis on attractive bicolor combinations, and selected for its many large flower spikes as well as improved spike form, a characteristic more difficult to obtain in seed-raised plants than in vegetatively propagated cultivars. First-year-flowering from an early sowing. From Thompson & Morgan Seeds. ‡3¼ ft (1 m). Z5–8 H8–5

L. variicolor syn. *L. versicolor* (Bluff lupine) Sprawling, herbaceous plant, sometimes woody at the base, forming a mat of delicate leaves with a silver sheen, composed of six to nine leaflets each ¾–1½ in (2–3.5 cm) long. Short 2½–6 in (6–15 cm) flower spikes rise above the foliage in summer, studded with small, typically blue-and-white bicolored flowers. The upper flowers are sometimes white, and combinations of purple, pink, and yellow are also found. Well-drained soil and sun are essential. One of the more widely available perennial lupine species. Native to fields and chaparral, slopes, strands, and sand dunes on the coast of California. One of three lupine species essential to the lifecycle of the endangered Mission blue butterfly. ‡8–20 in (20–50 cm). Z5–8 H8–5

L. versicolor see *L. variicolor*

LUZULA
Woodrush
JUNCACEAE

Fine white hairs on the leaves and delicate flowers mark out this useful rush for both wet and dry shade.

Some 80 species, mostly perennial, are found worldwide but mainly in Europe and Asia, growing in moist, rich woodlands and on wet river and stream banks. The foliage grows in tufts with flat evergreen leaves covered in white hairs. The flowers, generally similar to those of ordinary rushes (*Juncus*), come in loose, open-branched clusters and are usually green or brown, sometimes nearly white; they appear early in the year. These are generally slow-growing plants that prefer fertile soil, but they will survive in drought conditions. They make useful decorative ground cover for woodland and shady bog gardens, especially in spring, when their flowers and shimmering green leaves add delicacy to early spring bulbs; the colored-foliage forms look particularly effective.

CULTIVATION Fertile, moist soil enriched with leaf mold or other organic matter in part-shade to shade.

PROPAGATION From seed or by division in early spring; cultivars by division only.

PROBLEMS Usually trouble-free.

L. x borreri 'Botany Bay' Bright green clumps are densely packed with broad leaves that are vertically striped white, tinged pink when the new leaves emerge in spring, but fading to paler green. The flower stems carry loose clusters of dark brown flowers in early spring. A hybrid of *L. forsteri* and *L. pilosa* found growing in Botany Bay, Australia, in 1985, this tiny rush makes beautiful ground cover in dry shade with snowdrops and other early spring flowers. ‡8 in (20 cm). Z4–9 H8–1

review in New Zealand as a potential grazing crop for poor soils. In gardens, effective as seminatural colonies in grass and prefers sun to part-shade, in moist to average, well-drained soil. One of the 23 lupine species that was introduced from North America by plant-hunter David Douglas in the early 19th century and found in marshes or damp ground in meadows, forests, and stream banks in Canada and western US. ‡6–60 in (50–150 cm). Z5–8 H8–5

L. x regalis A name that is sometimes used for hybrid garden lupines, but should be restricted to hybrids between *L. polyphyllus* and *L. arboreus;* it is suspected that hybrid garden lupines also include other, perhaps annual, species in their background, so use of this name is perhaps best avoided except for known hybrids between these two species.

L. Russell hybrids Mixtures of tall lupines descended from the celebrated

AWARD OF GARDEN MERIT

When the Royal Horticultural Society held a trial of cuttings-raised lupines in 1991–93, eight out of ten Awards of Garden Merit went to cultivars bred by Woodfield Brothers, a specialist nursery near Stratford-on-Avon, Warwickshire, England. All the entries from the Woodfield Brothers nursery were impressive, and growing them together in the trial created an unforgettable spectacle. Their prize-winning lupines, from the trial, are listed below.

All their lupines, have become extremely scarce since the Warwickshire nursery closed. Hybrid lupine cultivars, with their short lifespan and the high chance of seedlings taking the place of mother plants, are prone to disappear without a nursery or another guardian to ensure their survival.

The other winners from the lupine trial were 'Royal Parade', a white and reddish purple bicolor, and 'Troop the Colour' in shades of brilliant orange and red.

'Anne Gregg'

'Esmerelder'

'Helen Sharman'

'Judy Harper'

'Kayleigh Ann Savage'

'Olive Tolley'

L. luzuloides Slowly creeping evergreen clumps grow from long thin roots, while the narrow, light green, ¼ in (6 mm) wide leaves feature long white hairs along the leaf edges. In early summer, tall flower stems are topped by airy clusters of off-white flowers tinged red or brown. Good as a decorative ground cover in woodlands and gardens where it will grow in moist and dry conditions. Found in woods, scrub, and grasslands throughout Europe. ↕ 32 in (80 cm). Z4–9 H8–1. **'Schneehäschen'** syn. *L. nivea* 'Schneehäschen' (meaning Little Snow Hare or Snow Leveret) Near-white flowers aging to pale brown. ↕ 18 in (45 cm).

L. nivea (Snowy woodrush) Loose, gently spreading, evergreen clumps are made up of narrow, hairy, dark green leaves just ⅛ in (4 mm) wide. In midsummer, tall flower stems appear bearing graceful arching clusters of pure white flowers that become reddish brown as the seeds ripen. A beautiful ground cover, or use as underplanting with shrubs in moist, rich soil; it is less tolerant of dry conditions than the similar *L. luzuloides*. Self-seeds very readily. From mountain woods and scrubland throughout central Europe. ↕ 12 in (60 cm). Z4–9 H8–1. **L. nivea 'Schneehäschen'** *see* *L. luzuloides* 'Schneehäschen'.

L. sylvatica (Great woodrush) Slowly spreading on strong rhizomes to eventually form thick tussocks of ¾ in (2 cm) wide, glossy, dark green leaves up to 24 in (60 cm) high, looking rather like the top of a pineapple. Tall flower stems in spring to early summer carry loose forked clusters of warm chestnut-brown flowers. Eventually makes a virtually weed-proof carpet in damp or dry shade and is a handsome ground cover with wild spring flowers. Common in damp woods and moorland among rocks, usually on acidic soil in Britain and Europe. ↕ 32 in (80 cm) Z4–9 H8–1. **'A. Rutherford'** *see* 'Taggart's Cream'. **'Aurea'** *see* 'Hohe Tatre'. **'Auslese'** syn. 'Select' Wide, light green leaves, twisted at the tips. **'Hohe Tatre'** syn. 'Aurea' Upright, acid-greenish yellow leaves in winter and spring, becoming greener in the summer. ↕ 18 in (45 cm). Z4–9 H8–1. **'Marginata'** syn. 'Variegata' Leaves narrowly edged in white. ↕ 20 in (50 cm). Z4–9 H8–1. **'Select'** *see* 'Auslese'. **'Taggart's Cream'** syn. 'A. Rutherford' New leaves emerge white with thin green edges, then become green in summer. ↕ 18 in (45 cm). Z4–9 H8–1. **'Tauernpass'** Broader, glossy green leaves, lower-growing and more compact. ↕ 12 in (30 cm). Z4–9 H8–1. **'Variegata'** *see* 'Marginata'.

L. ulophylla Tiny dense tufts form low mounds of long, thin, deep green leaves, with white hairs on the undersides and margins giving a silvery effect. In early summer, stiff flower stems carry loose clusters of dark

LEFT **1** *Luzula nivea* **2** *L. sylvatica* 'Hohe Tatre' **3** *L. sylvatica* 'Marginata'

RIGHT **1** *Lychnis* x *arkwrightii* 'Vesuvius' **2** *L. chalcedonica* **3** *L. coronaria* Oculata Group

brown flowers, also edged white. Plant at a shady path edge, or in a pot, where the shimmering leaves can be easily seen, especially when wet. Grows in moist woodlands in New Zealand. ↕ 16 in (40 cm). Z8–10 H10–8

LYCHNIS
Campion, Catchfly
CARYOPHYLLACEAE

Intensely colored, easy-to-grow, and sometimes dramatically colored plants for sunny sites.

There are about 20 species of biennial or perennial herbs closely related to *Silene* but differing in botanical details. They are found in a range of habitats in northern temperate and even arctic areas. Upright, branched stems carry simple leaves, which are often hairy, in opposite pairs; they are topped by five-petaled, flat-faced, sometimes star-shaped flowers carried singly, in flat heads or in open sprays. Deadheading prolongs flowering and helps control their spread by seed. The name *Lychnis* is from the Greek for "lamp," and refers to the fact that the feltlike leaves were formerly used for lamp wicks.

CULTIVATION Grow in full sun to part-shade in well-drained soil. Although some species thrive on the edge of a bog garden, most appreciate drier conditions.

PROPAGATION From seed sown as soon as ripe or in spring. Some cultivars can be grown from basal cuttings or by division in spring; others will come fairly true from seed if grown in isolation.

PROBLEMS Usually trouble-free.

L. x arkwrightii (Arkwright's catchfly) Short-lived and clump-forming, but blooming in its first year from seed, the stiff, upright stems carry hairy, oval or lance-shaped leaves, and both stems and foliage are noticeably brown-tinted. In early summer, the stems are topped by heads of three to ten 1½ in (4 cm) bright red flowers with a pronounced notch at the petal tip; these are followed by bronzed seedpods. Pinch out the growing tips early in the season to give a compact, bushy plant. Best in moist, fertile soil, with midday shade in hot areas. A hybrid between *L. chalcedonica* and *L.* x *haageana,* variable in its flower and foliage color and the degree of notching of its petals. ↕ 18 in (45 cm). Z5–8 H8–5. **'Orange Zwerg'** Dwarf form with orange-red flowers. ↕ 8 in (20 cm). **'Vesuvius'** Orange-scarlet flowers over very dark foliage. Best raised from cuttings, but often grown from seed then variable.

L. chalcedonica (Maltese cross, Jerusalem cross) Noticeably stiff,

upright-growing plant best in traditional herbaceous borders, the usually unbranched stems carry rough, oval, dark green, 3 in (8 cm) leaves, heart-shaped at the base and clasping the stem. Flattish, slightly domed heads of up to 50 scarlet flowers are carried at the top of the stems in early summer and midsummer, each ⅝ in (1.5 cm) flower with four petals arranged in the form of a cross. Best in moist soil. Easy to grow from seed, but cultivars are best raised from basal cuttings. From eastern Russia. ↕36 in (90 cm). Z3–8 H8–1. **var. albiflora** White flowers, but variable when grown from seed, and can be quite dingy. Seedlings will revert to scarlet if the seed parent is not grown in isolation. **'Carnea'** Pale flesh pink. **'Dusky Salmon'** Various salmon shades in the same head. Individual flowers open dark and fade to a lighter shade as they age. **'Flore Pleno'** Double flowers of a slightly duller red. Double white and double pink forms are also occasionally seen. **'Rosea'** Pale pink flowers with a darker eye. **'Salmonea'** Light salmon pink. **Summer Sparkle Series** Red, dusky pink, or white flowers. Intended to be grown from seed.

L. coronaria (Rose campion, Dusty miller) Short-lived perennial, sometimes a biennial, living longest where summers are cooler. A rather brittle crown supports 7-in (18-cm) basal oval or lance-shaped foliage, the stiff stems carrying similar leaves to just 4 in (10 cm). Both stems and leaves are covered with bright silvery wool. Through mid- and late summer, long-stemmed, 2-in (5-cm) flowers open continuously in much-branched heads and range in color from bright rose to red-purple. The effect can be intense and dramatic—place with care, since the color can clash with other flowers. Flowering is best in the second year, and plants then decline, especially where summers are hot, but there are usually plenty of self-sown seedlings. Easy to grow from seed. Best in well-drained soil in full sun; intolerant of winter rain. From southern Europe. ↕36 in (90 cm). Z3–8 H8–1. **'Abbotswood Rose'** see *L. x walkeri* 'Abbotswood Rose'. **'Alba'** White. **'Angel's Blush'** White with a pink eye. The size and intensity of the eye differs depending on summer temperatures and weather conditions. **Atrosanguinea Group** Carmine red or magenta flowers; the actual shade varies from plant to plant. **'Blushing Bride'** White with a pink eye. Similar to 'Angel's Blush' but with wider pink centers, covering most of the flower in some blooms. The petals tend to be reflexed, making the flower like an upside-down saucer. **'Dancing Ladies'** A mix of cherry, pink, white, rose, and two-toned blooms grown from seed and flowering the second year. **'Hutchinson's Cream'** White flowers; the foliage is splashed with cream. This will come true from seed, but not all seedlings will have good variegation. **Oculata Group**

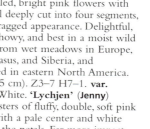

ROSE CAMPION

Rose campion, *Lychnis coronaria*, boasts some of the best gray foliage in the perennial border, and in sun, showing off its rose pink to magenta flowers, the whole plant makes quite an impact. It tolerates shade, too—indeed 'Alba', the white-flowered form, is quite a good brightener for dark places.

But like a number of popular perennials, this is a short-lived plant and difficult to propagate except by seed. The result is that although there are seven named forms, there are really just three main types—purple/magenta, white, and white with a pink eye. A mixture of colors is available, known by a variety of names, and the three colors harmonize quite well together; some people like the blend because its balance changes from year to year as self-sown seedlings spring up. Others prefer to concentrate on just one color. Plant appropriately colored neighboring perennials or annuals, and weed out any seedlings in different colors that appear and take over from their short-lived parents. Gardeners, who choose either white or eyed types, will find that both throw magenta-flowered plants.

White flowers with pink eyes, but the amount of pink varies. 'Angels Blush' and 'Blushing Bride' are selections from this group.

L. flos-cuculi (Ragged robin, Cuckoo flower) Slim-stemmed, moisture-loving. Slender, sometimes slightly bluish basal leaves, up to 5 in (13 cm) long, give way to shorter broader leaves on the stems, their bases wrapping around the stalk. In late spring and early summer, the open, sparse heads are made up of four-petaled, bright pink flowers with each petal deeply cut into four segments, giving a ragged appearance. Delightful, but not showy, and best in a moist wild garden. From wet meadows in Europe, the Caucasus, and Siberia, and naturalized in eastern North America. ↕30 in (75 cm). Z3–7 H7–1. **var. albiflora** White. **'Lychjen'** (**Jenny**) Large clusters of fluffy, double, soft pink flowers with a pale center and white streaks in the petals. Far more impact than the species, and only slightly less charming. Found wild in France. **'Nana'** Very dwarf form. ↕6 in (15 cm).

L. flos-jovis (Job's flower) Mat-forming with 4 in (10 cm) spoon-shaped leaves. Through summer upright, unbranched stems covered in white, woolly hairs carry small, loose, slightly domed heads of reddish pink flowers, each with four notched petals. Grows best in well-drained soil and full sun. Native to Alps, but widely naturalized. ↕24 in (60 cm). Z4–8 H8–1. **'Hort's Variety'** Clear pink flowers and free-flowering; dwarf. ↕12 in (30 cm). **'Peggy'** Rosy red flowers on short plant. ↕10 in (25 cm).

L. x haageana Neat, usually short-lived plant forming a clump of rather hairy, lance-shaped leaves up to 3 in (7.5 cm) in length through which emerge upright stems clothed in downward-pointing hairs. In summer, the flowerheads are made up of a few bright orange-scarlet blooms, each of the four petals with two lobes and with small teeth on their edges. Thrives in full sun with constant moisture, although some shade is desirable where summers are hot. A hybrid between the rarely seen *L. fulgens* and *L. sieboldii*. ↕12 in (30 cm). Z6–8 H8–6

L. **'Molten Lava'** Neat, clump-forming but short-lived plant with bright orange-red flowers almost hiding the bronzy foliage. Eye-catching at the front of a sunny border and good in well-drained containers. Often listed as a form of *L. x haageana*, which it may well be. ↕8 in (20 cm). Z5–8 H8–5

L. viscaria syn. *Viscaria vulgaris* (German catchfly) Slowly creeping clumps of narrowly lance-shaped dark green leaves up to 3 in (7.5 cm) long support thin, erect stems that are sticky where the leaves arise and also just below the flowerheads. In summer, these carry open heads of flowers with notched petals, colored a vivid magenta that is sometimes difficult to place in a border. Grow in a moist, slightly acidic soil in full sun or part-shade; it thrives with heaths and heathers. From Europe and western Asia. ↕18 in (45 cm). Z3–7 H7–1. **'Alba'** White. **subsp. atropurpurea** Deep purple blooms, a slightly less hard shade. **'Feur'** (Fire) Bright red flowers, some of which are double. **'Plena'** Fully double magenta flowers. **'Splendens Plena'** Double flowers with a pinkish tone and foliage tinged with bronze.

L. x walkeri **'Abbotswood Rose'** Silvery, neatly clump-forming, with 3 in (7.5 cm) oval basal leaves and smaller leaves of similar shape on the stems. In summer, rounded, rose pink flowers, slightly reflexed at the edges and shallowly notched, are carried generously on stiff stalks. Its overall appearance is of a dwarf form of *L. coronaria*, under which name it is often listed. A hybrid of *L. coronaria* and *L. flos-jovis*. ↕16 in (40 cm). Z5–8 H8–5

L. yunnanensis Short, clump-forming plant featuring slender green foliage and bright pink, often outward-facing flowers held either singly or in small heads on upright stems in early summer. It needs moist soil and full sun and is attractive to butterflies. This plant may be more correctly named as *Silene linnaena*. Native to southwestern China. ↕8 in (20 cm). Z6–8 H8–6

LYSICHITON
Skunk cabbage
ARACEAE

Bold foliage and classic white or yellow flowers for spring impact in wet places.

There are two species of deciduous perennials with spreading rhizomes from moist to wet environments, one from western North America, the other from eastern Asia. Their large oval foliage is thick and lustrous. The very early spring flowerhead features a boat-shaped spathe in bright yellow, cream, or clear white and a shorter greenish spadix. Both the flowers and crushed foliage have a musky odor, and a large colony should be planted for distant, rather than uncomfortably close, viewing. ⚠

CULTIVATION Best grown in slowly moving water, a pond, or a marsh in humus-rich soil in the sun or,

alternatively, in part-shade. They do not grow well in pots.

PROPAGATION By division of offsets in spring or summer. Seed is rarely available.

PROBLEMS Usually trouble-free, but odor is unpleasant or "skunky."

L. americanus (Western or Yellow skunk cabbage) Bold, glossy, noticeably veined, oval leaves up to 48 in (120 cm) long and 24 in (60 cm) wide arise in basal rosettes, in spring when flowers are open and developing quickly. They mature to a leathery finish. Spathes are clear, bright daffodil yellow and up to 16 in (40 cm) long, the broad blade backing a yellow spadix and narrowing to 8–10 in (20–25 cm) stems. The flowers are very cheery in ponds in the early spring. In rich soil with abundant moisture they can produce enormous leaves and look almost tropical and exotic. From soggy habitats including shallow standing water in coastal North America from Alaska south to northern California and inland to Idaho. ‡ 36 in (90 cm). Z5–7 H7–5

L. camtschatcensis (Eastern or White skunk cabbage) Big, bold, strongly veined, oval leaves, 18–36 in (45–90 cm), appear in basal rosettes, in spring as the flowers are at their peak. Funnel-shaped spathes are pure white, 16 in (40 cm) tall on 12 in (30 cm) stems, and roll around, partially enclosing the greenish spadix. A little smaller than *L. americanus,* with white rather than yellow flowers, and a little more tolerant of drier conditions.

BELOW *Lysichiton americanus*

NATURALIZED LYSICHITON

The sight of *Lysichiton americanus* growing in boggy woods in the western part of the United States is quite impressive; it can look very much like the yellow sails of a cheery flotilla bobbing across the water and may seem unexpectedly unusual and exotic in what can be a very cold climate.

In gardens, this is a superb early-season streamside plant and it is also a valuable plant for naturalizing in informal garden settings. Plant it on the margins of a pond and there, it will slowly expand along the banks as its fat seeds are moved around by ducks, other wildlife, or your own propagation efforts. Plant it on a streamside and it will slowly appear farther and farther downstream as its seeds are washed along the banks, find a hold, and germinate.

In Scotland its spread is now beginning to cause concern.

The dark foliage and bright white spathe has a very classic appearance. Fertile moist soil produces the most luxuriant plants. From Japan north through far eastern Russia including Sakhalin and Kamchatka. ‡ 30 in (75 cm). Z5–9 H9–1

L. **'Devonshire Cream'** Oval leaves emerge when the creamy spathes do, and expand impressively. A lovely, vigorous hybrid of *L. camtschatcensis* and *L. americanus* sometimes sold without a cultivar name. ‡ 30–36 in (75–90 cm). Z5–9 H9–1

LYSIMACHIA
Loosestrife
PRIMULACEAE

A varied and attractive group, including indispensable border perennials and attractive ground-cover plants.

About 180 species come from a wide variety of habitats, mostly in Asia, especially China, and North America. The perennial species are generally very attractive and easy to grow, but a few may be too vigorous and need watching. They vary from erect to prostrate in habit, with mainly narrow leaves in opposite pairs or in clusters; the five-petaled flowers, usually yellow but also white, purple, or pink, are carried in terminal spikes or clusters or, in some of the prostrate types, simply from the leaf joints. Not to be confused with *Lythrum,* also known as loosestrife.

CULTIVATION Moist soil is favored, but ordinary garden soil is suitable, too. Good growth in part-shade, but most do best in the sun if the soil is moist.

PROPAGATION By division or from seed.

PROBLEMS Usually trouble-free, apart from the invasiveness of some species.

L. atropurpurea Upright stems carry distinctive narrow, gray-green leaves, up to 4 in (10 cm) long, with strongly waved edges. In summer they are topped by slender, open spikes of deep purple flowers, each one formed of five tiny petals. These are followed by globular, spine-tipped seed pods. Native to damp, sandy places in the Balkans. ‡ 24 in (60 cm). Z3–8 H8–1. **'Beaujolais'** Burgundy-colored flowers and more silvery foliage, developing autumnal tints as it ages.

L. barystachys Spreads vigorously, the upright stems carrying blunt-tipped, usually alternately arranged, lance-shaped leaves edged with tiny hairs. Small white flowers are borne in a wavy spike. Similar to the better known *L. clethroides,* but distinguished by less elegant spikes and a desire to form wide colonies. Best in the wild garden. Native to northern China, Korea, and Japan. ‡ 26 in (65 cm). Z5–9 H9–1

L. ciliata Forming compact colonies, this elegant plant produces slender stems clad with lance-shaped to oval leaves, fringed with tiny hairs and arranged in pairs or fours. Five-petaled, bright yellow flowers, to ¾ in (2 cm) across, appear from the uppermost leaf joints, forming open clusters in late summer. Thrives in most soils, though native to damp woods and lake and river margins in North America. ‡ 4 ft (1.2 m). Z5–8 H9–3. **'Firecracker'** Spectacular, with leaves richly suffused deep purple.

L. clethroides One of the most elegant species, forming sizable but compact colonies of erect stems bearing slender, pointed, lance-shaped mid- to light green leaves. In summer, terminal tapered spikes of white buds appear and gracefully arch over. As the white, ½ in (1 cm) wide flowers expand, each spike straightens and elongates. Best performance is in open or part-shaded sites. Agressive grower in garden soils. From eastern Asia. ‡ 36 in (90 cm). Z4–9 H9–1. **'Geisha'** Leaves edged with cream.

L. ephemerum Statuesque clump-former with strong, erect stems furnished with pairs of gray-green, narrowly oblong to lance-shaped, stalkless leaves. In summer, long, airy, wandlike spikes of ½ in (1 cm) wide, starry white flowers, tinted palest purple, provide a distinctive display. Moist soil is essential. Useful in being a gray-leaved plant that will tolerate some shade. From grassy sites near springs and streams in western Europe. ‡ 4 ft (1.2 m). Z7–9 H9–7

L. lichiangensis Erect, well behaved. with lance-shaped, mainly alternate

RIGHT 1 *Lysimachia atropurpurea*
2 *L. clethroides*
3 *L. punctata* 'Alexander'

leaves, showing distinctive dots, held on narrowly winged stalks; they clothe the clumps of erect stems that may branch at the base. Spikes of ½ in (1 cm) wide pink, sometimes white, flowers with darker veining appear in summer. From grassy slopes, woodland margins, thickets, and river valleys in Sichuan and Yunnan Provinces, China. ‡20 in (50 cm). Z8–10 H10–8

L. minoricensis Erect stems form small colonies and carry alternate leaves varying from lance-shaped to oval. In summer, slightly bell-shaped flowers open singly from the upper leaf joints, each petal being light pink at the base and greenish yellow at the tips. Best in damp but well-drained soil in sun or part-shade. Now extinct in its native Minorca (*see* Extinction of *Lysimachia Minoricensis*). ‡24 in (60 cm). Z7–9 H9–7

L. nummularia (Creeping Jenny, Moneywort) Perhaps the best-known species of all. Mat-forming, creeping stems reach 16 in (40 cm) or more in length and are clad with pairs of small rounded leaves. During summer, cup-shaped, bright yellow flowers, up to 1 in (2.5 cm) wide, arise singly or more rarely in pairs from the leaf joints. Highly adaptable as ground cover, or in a container or hanging-basket inside or out, or even as a short-term aquarium plant. Usually found in wet grassland, ditches, and lake shores in the wilds of Europe, including Russia. ‡2 in (5 cm). Z4–8 H8–1. **'Aurea'** The form usually seen, with foliage flushed bright yellow.

L. punctata A determined spreader, with erect stems bearing lance-shaped to elliptical, finely hairy leaves in pairs or clusters of three or four. These nicely set off the terminal leafy spikes of bright yellow, 1 in (2.5 cm) wide, cup-shaped flowers, which appear in summer. Vigorous and soon forming sizable but compact colonies, this is one of the showiest species and is often seen in gardens. Tolerant of most soils. From moist places in eastern Europe. ‡36 in (90 cm). Z4–8 H8–1. **'Alexander'** Leaves variegated cream and flushed pink, especially early in the season. Occasionally reverts. **'Golden Alexander'** Leaves boldly edged bright yellow; less vigorous and shorter than

'Alexander'. Perhaps the same as the occasionally seen 'Golden Glory'. ‡24 in (60 cm). **'Ivy Maclean'** Deep green leaves with yellow-green edges, more pronounced coloring on young growth.

L. thyrsiflora (Tufted loosestrife) More or less colony-forming, depending upon moisture. Erect stems bear pairs of narrowly oblong to lance-shaped, stalkless leaves peppered with minute black glands. Tiny bell-shaped, yellow flowers in dense, long-stalked heads from the middle leaf joints in early summer. Best in permanently moist or wet soil or in shallow water. From bogs and marshes in the temperate Northern Hemisphere. ‡24 in (60 cm). Z3–7 H8–1

L. vulgaris (Yellow loosestrife) A rapid colonizer. Self-supporting, slender stems appear in tufts or small clumps and are clad with pairs or clusters of lance-shaped leaves. Yellow flowers, ½ in (1 cm) or more across, appear in terminal, loose, broadly conical heads in late summer. It spreads by producing stems that creep along the soil surface, or just under it, reaching 3¼ ft (1 m) or more in a season and rooting at the tips like blackberries. The next season one or more stems arise from these tips. Rarely grown intentionally, but may be sold as *L. punctata*. It is native to permanently wet ground (but can survive brief droughts) throughout most of Europe. ‡5½ ft (1.6 m). Z4–8 H8–1

L. yunnanensis Forms clumps of oval to lance-shaped, deep green leaves, sometimes with paler veins. Contrasting well with the foliage, open pyramidal spikes of large, cup-shaped, sometimes pink-tinged cream flowers appear in summer, and are followed by reddish seedpods. The plant is only recently appearing in gardens, and rapidly becoming popular, but often confused with *L. lichiangensis*. From the mountains of Yunnan province, China. ‡30 in (75 cm). Z4–8 H8–1

LYTHRUM
Lythraceae
LOOSESTRIFE

Colorful and easily grown, long-flowering moisture-lovers make a bold impact in late summer.

RIGHT *Lythrum salicaria* 'Feuerkerze'

There are 38 annuals, deciduous perennials, and small shrubs, growing in moist, open places almost throughout the temperate regions. Two perennial species are commonly grown in gardens. Tough rhizomatous rootstocks form large clumps of erect, branching, four-angled stems bearing narrow, willowlike leaves that may be paired or alternate. In late summer, small rosy purple, pink, or white flowers open, either singly in the leaf joints or clustered into a terminal spike. The starry flowers have four to eight oval petals.

These are very hardy plants with a long flowering season, for use in moist sunny border. Some of the cultivars may be listed under either species, or may be of hybrid origin. In North America, where it has become naturalized, purple loosestrife, *L. salicaria*, has become aggressively invasive (*see* A Highly Invasive Plant).

CULTIVATION Grow in full sun, in moist or even wet, humus-rich soil.

PROPAGATION By division or by cuttings. Although plants may seed freely, but seedlings from cultivars are unlikely to be true to type.

PROBLEMS Usually trouble-free.

L. salicaria (Purple loosestrife) Strongly upright plant making a large clump of usually hairy stems clad in narrowly lance-shaped, mid-green, hairy leaves up to 4 in (10 cm) long. From early summer to late summer or early fall, a profusion of starry, purplish pink, ½ in (2 cm) flowers open in dense spikes up to 18 in (45 cm) long. When grown in a border, it is best deadheaded soon after flowering to prevent excessive seeding. In a spacious bog garden or wild setting, however, this may be an advantage. From marshy soils on the margins of lakes and slow streams and canals in Europe (including the British Isles), northern Asia, and North Africa; naturalized in North America (*see* A Highly Invasive Plant). ‡4 ft (1.2 m). Z4–9 H9–1. **'Blush'** Flowers clear light pink; good fall foliage color. ‡32–40 in (80–100 cm). **'Feuerkerze'** (Firecandle) Flowers vivid rose red. ‡36 in (90 cm). **'Lady Sackville'** Flowers bright rose pink. ‡36 in (90 cm). **'Morden Pink'** Clear pink flowers in loose spikes. ‡32 in (80 cm). **'Robert'** Flowers bright rose pink; good fall color. ‡36 in (90 cm). **'The Beacon'** Flowers carmine red. ‡32 in (80 cm). **'Zigeunerblut'** Flowers deep carmine red. ‡4 ft (1.2 m).

L. virgatum Clump-forming plant with erect stems bearing very narrow leaves up to 4 in (10 cm) long; both stems and leaves are hairless. Purplish pink flowers 6 in (15 mm) wide open from midsummer to early fall in loose spires. Similar to *L. salicaria*, but more slender and refined, with narrower hairless

leaves and more open flower spikes. It is also less liable to self-seed, so is better suited to a more cultivated setting. From marshes and other wet places in Asia and southern and eastern Europe. ‡4 ft (1.2 m). Z3–9 H9–1. **'Dropmore Purple'** Flowers reddish purple, in leafy spikes. ‡40 in (90 cm). **'Rosy Gem'** Long spikes of deep rose pink flowers. ‡40 in (90 cm). **'The Rocket'** Flowers bright rose pink. ‡32 in (80 cm).

A HIGHLY INVASIVE PLANT

In North America, *Lythrum salicaria* (Purple loosestrife) is one of the most invasive alien plants to colonize the continent. Originally brought from Europe for honey production and as an ornamental, it aggressively invades wetlands of and is now classified as a noxious weed in many states and has invaded much of Canada.

Purple loosestrife spreads extensively both by seed and with its creeping roots; it should not be sold or planted. Vast sheets of color may look attractive in the summer, but purple loosestrife chokes out many native species and has a damaging effect on the wildlife that depends on them, reducing the supply of both food and nest sites for waterfowl, for example.

Purple loosestrife has a long flowering season, generally June to September, which allows for the production of vast amounts of seed. A mature plant may produce as many as thirty flowering stems capable of producing thousands of seeds per year.

Small areas of young purple loosestrife plants may be pulled by hand, before the seed sets. Herbicides may also be used to kill this aggressive perennial. Biological control may be the most effective long-term control and research continues in this area.

EXTINCTION OF LYSIMACHIA MINORICENSIS

This lovely plant is extinct in its native Minorca. Following overcollecting, in about 1916 it finally disappeared from its only known site in a valley close to a watermill near the southern coast when the mill fell into disuse and the area was invaded by brambles and scrub. However, not long after, a few seeds were recovered from a dried specimen in a herbarium and were successfully germinated. Slowly, plants were multiplied and seed was eventually distributed to botanic gardens around the world.

This is a species known to have become completely extinct on its native island, the whole of which is now classified by UNESCO as a Biosphere Reserve. Attempts to reintroduce the plant into the wild have, in the long term, proved unsuccessful, perhaps because of the limited gene pool of cultivated stock and the change in the habitat of the area. Seed of this plant is now widely available to gardeners, however, and as more plants are grown it is possible that future attempts at reintroduction may prove successful.

M

MACLEAYA
Plume poppy
PAPAVERACEAE

Majestic plants with handsome foliage and large feathery plumes, but not very poppylike.

Two bold species are restricted to China and Japan, with a hybrid between the two grown in gardens. Creeping by rhizomes, and sometimes invasive, plants have rigid upright stems that exude an orange juice when damaged that will stain the skin like iodine, and can ruin clothing. The stems carry handsome, alternate, toothed, often attractively flushed, lobed leaves, to 8 in (20 cm) across. Small flowers without petals are carried in branched plumes, up to 12 in (30 cm) long, at the stem tops. Grown as much for their handsome foliage as for their airy plumes of tiny flowers, these robust, though aggressive, clump-forming perennials are ideal for the back of the herbaceous or mixed border.

CULTIVATION Thrives in any good moist garden soil, but greatly dislikes wind and drought; also performs well in dappled shade in open woodland conditions. Applying yearly compost mulches will help maintain vigor.

PROPAGATION From seed or by division; suckers can be carefully removed without necessarily disturbing the parent plant. Cuttings of one-node pieces of stem (each with a single healthy leaf) can be rooted in early summer.

PROBLEMS Slugs, botrytis.

M. cordata syn. *Bocconia cordata* Stout and vigorous, dense, patch-forming

perennial, the attractive leaves are more or less heart-shaped but with rounded and toothed, shallow lobes, the upper gray-green surface contrasting with the pinkish gray one beneath. Large, narrow, plumes of tiny buff, or creamy white flowers, each with 25–30 stamens, in early summer and midsummer and are followed by small fruit capsules that contain four to six seeds. An excellent plant for a bold feature in an herbaceous border. But it can be aggressive. Fertile soil will promote spread in the garden. From mountain woodlands in eastern China and Japan. ‡5–8 ft (1.5–2.5 m). Z4–8 H8–1

M. x *kewensis* Stout, patch-forming, with elegant erect stems, the alternate leaves are borne horizontally and are round to heart-shaped in outline but with five to nine bluntly toothed lobes. Large, airy plumes of very small cream or buff flowers appear in early summer and midsummer, forming a foamy mass above the handsome foliage. A hybrid of *M. cordata* and *M. microcarpa*. ‡6½–8 ft (2–2.5 m). Z4–9 H9–1.

LEFT *Macleaya microcarpa* 'Kelway's Coral Plume'

SEEDLING IN THE RIGHT PLACE

TWO IMPOSING BUT relatively compact perennials are joined by a self-sown foxglove seedling. The bold, gray-green lobed leaves of *Macleaya microcarpa* are held against the white-variegated arching leaves of *Miscanthus sinensis* 'Variegatus' in a cool grouping of contrasting foliage forms, but in harmonizing tones. Alongside, the creamy buds of the foxglove open to flared white bells held on a single stem. These will self-sow but may produce purple-flowered seedlings that will disrupt the cool effect of this association. Revealed by the red pigment in their leaf stems, these seedlings can be moved to a more appropriate spot when still small.

'Flamingo' The gray stems and leaves that are often suffused with pink, with buff-pink flowers.

M. microcarpa syn. *Bocconia microcarpa* Robust, sometimes invasive, forming crowded patches. The roughly heart-shaped, rounded leaves are toothed and with shallow lobes—the upper surface grayish green, the lower whitish gray. Before flowering, it is difficult to distinguish from *M. cordata*. Small flowers, in summer and midsummer, contain eight to twelve stamens, usually flushed in bronze, followed by one-seeded fruit capsules. Native to western and central China. ‡5–8 ft (1.5–2 m). Z4–9 H9–1. **'Kelway's Coral Plume'** Pink-flushed foliage, deep pink plumes. **'Spetchley Ruby'** Dark red flowers followed by ruby seed heads.

MAIANTHEMUM
CONVALLARIACEAE

Hardy shade-lovers, varying from the bold to the demure, that create attractive ground cover in cool, moist conditions.

Twenty-eight species of deciduous plants, spreading by rhizomes, that grow in moist woodlands in temperate regions of the Northern Hemisphere, including Europe, Asia, and Central and North America. The alternate, heart-shaped, oval or lance-shaped fresh green foliage is carried on usually arching stems, from 4 in to 5 ft (10 cm to 1.5 m) high, tipped with crowded, often rather stubby, spikes of tiny, fluffy white, cream, pink, or dark purple flowers in spring or summer. These are often followed by yellow, red, or bright orange berries. Fruiting can be more dramatic than flowering and is enhanced by having plants of different origin together in the garden. Similar in overall appearance to *Polygonatum* but with its flowers crowded at the ends of the shoots rather than in the leaf joints. Bold, attractive but relatively unknown species from the mountains of Central America also look exciting. Providing effective ground cover, bold foliage displays, and attractive flowers and fruits; invaluable plants for the woodland garden, around shrubs in a border, or under trees.

It has recently been realized that the plants formerly classified under *Smilacina* are not sufficiently different to stay separated from *Maianthemum*; they are included here.

CULTIVATION Best in cool, humus-rich, acidic to neutral soil with even moisture and good drainage. Heat tolerance is limited and drought is a killer. Some species may prove overly vigorous and not suitable for the carefully maintained garden.

PROPAGATION Divide in early spring before growth emerges. Propagation from seed is also possible; remove the flesh and sow the fresh seed as soon as possible in late summer or fall. Germination will normally occur the following spring; first flowering from seed takes two to five years.

PROBLEMS Slugs and snails, rust and leaf spot; deer and rabbits will find the new growth delectable.

M. bifolium Spreading moderately, slender stems carry usually only two thin, shiny, deep green, narrowly heart-shaped leaves, up to 6 in (15 cm) long, which are tipped with white fragrant flowers that open in late spring or early summer. These are followed by translucent, deep red fruits. Also produces many shoots that do not carry flowers. Some forms, from the western US, have larger, slightly downy foliage. Makes effective low ground cover. From western Europe to Japan, and western North America. ‡6 in (15 cm). Z3–7 H8–1. **subsp. *kamtschaticum*** syn. *M. dilatatum* Altogether larger in all its parts. ‡12 in (30 cm).

M. dilatatum see *M. bifolium* subsp. *kamtschaticum*

M. oleraceum syn. *Smilacina oleracea* Robust species with unusually large oval leaves, 8 in (20 cm) long, on often slightly zigzagged stems. In late spring or early summer, the large nodding terminal clusters of small purplish, pink, or white flowers are produced, resulting in crops of translucent red fruit. Difficult to establish and particularly dependent on cool, moist conditions and humus-rich soil. Similar to *M. racemosum,* but the individual flowers are larger. From the Himalaya. ‡ 4 ft (1.2 m). Z3–7 H8–1

M. racemosum syn. *Smilacina racemosa* Bold, sometimes even dramatic plants, the stems are crowded with fine-tipped, narrowly oval, elliptical leaves, 3 in (7.5 cm) long, and carry large heads of small, creamy white flowers in late spring or early summer, followed by handsome crops of red, rarely yellow, fruit. Essential in any shaded border where there is space. From both coasts of North America; plants in the west are taller, more robust and with more upright growth than those in the east. ‡ 24–60 in (60–150 cm). Z3–7 H8–1

M. stellatum syn. *Smilacina stellata* Short, demure but widely creeping with erect stems carrying elliptical to lance-shaped 2½ in (6 cm) leaves. Stems are tipped with small heads of white flowers in late spring, followed by red or pink striped fruit. Can spread rapidly, causing problems in some gardens, but suitable for ground cover in wilder situations, where it will effectively knit with other perennials. Also tolerates poor gravelly soil if provided with even moisture. From North America. ‡ 12 in (30 cm). Z3–7 H8–1

Malva

Mallow
MALVACEAE

Large showy, plants with bright and bold summer blooms in shades of purple, pink, white, and lilac.

About 30 species of annuals and generally short-lived, woody-based perennials from dry soil and waste ground in North Africa, Europe, and Asia. Some are widely naturalized around the world. Stiff, upright or spreading stems are clothed with alternate, rounded to heart-shaped to boldly lobed or divided foliage. The flowers have five petals, usually with a notch at the tip, making them heart-shaped, and a central cluster of stamens around the stigmas. The petals are often enhanced by deeper veins radiating from the base. They are carried singly, or more often in clusters, at the tips of the shoots and in the upper leaf joints. Similar to *Lavatera* but distinguished by the one to three leafy bracts at the base of each flower, which are completely separate in *Malva* but joined at the base in *Lavatera.*

CULTIVATION Thrives in light, well-drained, fairly fertile soil that does not dry out; in moist, fertile soil, they may be excessively leafy and prone to wind damage because of their luxuriant growth.

PROPAGATION From seed, or from cuttings of sterile forms. Many will naturalize in wild gardens and in rough grass and will frequently self-seed in well-drained soil in a sunny spot.

PROBLEMS Aphids, rust (which also attacks *Alcea,* hollyhock).

M. alcea (Hollyhock mallow) Bushy in habit, the rounded, five-lobed leaves are larger at the base of the plant and only slightly lobed, but are smaller and finely divided on the flowering stems. The 2 in (5 cm) flowers have frilly-edged petals and are held above the foliage on short, leafy stems, creating a cloud of bright pink flowers for many months, from early to late summer. Easy and reliable, thriving in sun in well-drained soil, and may self-seed in suitable conditions. Native to southern Europe, but naturalized in other areas, including the northeastern US. ‡ 32 in (80 cm).

Z3–8 H8–1. **var. *fastigiata*** More upright habit, deeper pink flowers, and may flower into fall.

M. moschata (Musk mallow) Always neat and attractive, the lower leaves are heart-shaped but the foliage on the flowering stems is finely divided. The clean pink flowers, 2 in (5 cm) across with five petals, each with a flat edge, appear in a long succession from early summer until early fall. One of the prettiest of all mallows, the musk mallow gets its name from the faint, musky scent of its foliage, though this is not strong enough to be offensive. From Europe, and northwestern Africa. ‡ 36 in (90 cm). Z3–8 H8–1. **f. *alba*** Beautiful white flowers with a touch of pink. **rosea** Deeper pink flowers.

M. 'Parkallee' Large with a woody base and triangular, three-lobed leaves. Cream flowers, with a central cluster of petals around the purple anthers, create a rosette shape. Perhaps not a *Malva,* or a hybrid with *Althaea* or *Alcea,* or between the latter two. Research continues. ‡ 5 ft (1.5 m). Z3–8 H8–1

M. sylvestris Short-lived, woody at the base, but sometimes grown as an annual; the habit varies from low and spreading to tall and bushy. A robust stem carries foliage, up to 4 in (10 cm) across, which is rounded with five to seven lobes and with long leaf stalks. Clusters of two to five flowers, to 2 in (5 cm) across, are borne over a long season—from early summer until fall—in the upper leaf joints and are usually pink or lilac, paler at the base, with a notch at the tip. In general, young plants are the finest and flower most freely, so plants are best propagated every year. Those with bluish flowers are often sterile. May become too leafy in highly fertile soil. Very prone to hollyhock rust. From the Mediterranean, east to the Middle East and Russia. ‡ 1–6½ ft (30 cm–2 m). Z4–8 H8–1. **subsp. *mauritiana*** Tall, with large purple flowers with deeper veins and glossy green leaves. ‡ 5 ft (1.5 m). **subsp.**

mauritiana **'Bibor Fehlo'** Robust, with rich purple, dark-veined petals. ‡ 6½ ft (2 m). **'Mystic Merlin'** Mixture with a wide range of flower colors, including violet blues and purples. Tall and upright. ‡ 5 ft (1.5 m). **'Primley Blue'** Low-growing, widely spreading plant, with pale violet flowers with three darker veins radiating out from the center of each petal. ‡ 12 in (30 cm).

Malvastrum

MALVACEAE

Creeping relatives of the hollyhock, with a long season of sun-loving summer flowers.

About 30 species of usually creeping, rather woody, mostly evergreen perennials from the Americas; only one is commonly grown. The alternately arranged leaves, 1–4½ in (2.5–11 cm) long, may be unlobed, heart-shaped, or lobed and, toward the end of the shoots, short spikes of flowers are formed in the leaf joints or at the shoot tips. The five-petaled, typically mallowlike, cup-shaped flowers open throughout summer, and may be red or yellow with short stalks or no stalks at all. At times, most have been included in other general.

CULTIVATION Grow in any well-drained soil in full sun. In cold winter areas, the plants should be protected in winter or overwintered as young plants from cuttings.

PROPAGATION From seed or cuttings.

PROBLEMS Slugs and snails.

M. lateritium Hairy, creeping, with generally rounded, three- to five-lobed, deep green leaves; each lobe wedge-shaped or oblong, forming large mats

BELOW 1 *Maianthemum bifolium*
2 *M. stellatum* **3** *Malva moschata*
4 *M. 'Parkallee'*

of growth. Produces a long succession of bowl-shaped, 2 in (5 cm), flowers of pale apricot with a deep red, sometimes pinkish, ring around the center and straight or slightly rounded petal edges. Useful for banks and summer containers. From Argentina and Uruguay. ‡8 in (20 cm). Z7–9 H9–1

MARRUBIUM

Horehound
LAMIACEAE

Woolly-leaved sun-lovers with mintlike flowers, providing an attractive, useful option for poor soil.

Around 40 species of herbaceous perennials, sometimes woody at the base, are found in dry, usually rocky habitats centered around the Mediterranean but are also present in other parts of Europe and Asia. They are not considered flamboyant plants and few are grown in gardens. Square stems carry silky or woolly, mostly egg-shaped, leaves that may be toothed and wrinkled and are often aromatic. The flower spikes, to about 20 in (50 cm) long, carry spherical clusters of rather small two-lipped flowers in shades of white, yellow, or purple.

CULTIVATION Provide full sun and well-drained soil, low in nutrients. Offer protection from cold winds and winter rain—water around the roots will not be tolerated.

PROPAGATION Separate rooted layers from established plants or take softwood cuttings in spring or fall.

PROBLEMS Usually trouble-free.

M. vulgare (Common horehound) Slowly spreading on short, stout rhizomes and producing upright, white-woolly stems, usually with many short branches. The wrinkly leaves are egg-shaped to almost round with a scalloped margin and heart-shaped base, growing to 2 in (5 cm), usually with a covering of white hair. The dense whorls of two-lipped white flowers, ⁵⁄₈ in (1.5 cm) long, are borne throughout much of the summer. When crushed, the leaves smell pleasantly of thyme. The most adaptable and widespread species; found in the Canary Islands, North Africa, Europe (including Britain), and Asia, and naturalized in North America. Height ‡20 in (50 cm). Z4–9 H10–2. **'Green Pompon'** Large flowers.

MATTEUCCIA

WOODSIACEAE

Elegant, hardy, and vigorous ferns for moist or wet, shady places.

About three species of deciduous fern that grow in damp woods and streamsides throughout much of the northern temperate zone. Stout, erect stocks either make clumps or spread widely to form colonies. Once- or twice-divided sterile fronds, and shorter spore-bearing fronds, appear in summer on long stems, maturing in midwinter. The fertile fronds are very different from the sterile fronds—maturing to black and much contracted. These are fine garden ferns for damp situations, often forming impressive and distinctive colonies of bold green shuttlecocks.

CULTIVATION Moist or wet shade. If grown in sun, fronds tend to discolor by mid-season.

PROPAGATION By division, removing outlying plants from the colonizing species, or by spores.

PROBLEMS Usually trouble-free.

M. orientalis syn. *Onoclea orientalis* Large and imposing plant with a shortly creeping rhizome bearing several arching, broadly egg-shaped fronds whose main leaflets are deeply lobed and carried on long stems up to 4 ft (1.2 m) long. Much shorter, blackish fertile fronds arise from the center of the crown in summer. Very handsome in early summer, but the fronds become weather-damaged rather easily. Grow in moist shade with ample leaf mold and shelter from cold winds. Propagate from spores. Native to the Himalaya and eastern Asia. ‡32 in (80 cm). Z6–8 H8–6

M. pensylvanica Short rhizomes quickly form an extensive colony. The lance-shaped, once- or twice-divided fronds are borne in a rather spreading shuttlecock; the base of their stems is slightly bluish. Erect, black spore-bearing fronds arise in summer in the center of the crown and are nearly as long as vegetative fronds. Spreads underground to produce new crowns, not single fronds as in most other creeping ferns. Very similar to *M. struthiopteris* in appearance and cultural requirements, and often included in that species, but differing in botanical details. The unfurling fronds—the fiddleheads—are the state vegetable of Vermont. It grows in damp woods and streamsides in eastern North America. ‡3¼–4 ft (1–1.2 m). Z3–8 H8–1

M. struthiopteris (Shuttlecock fern, Ostrich fern) Quickly spreading to make impressive colonies, the lance-shaped, almost erect fronds form a familiar shuttlecock and are divided once or twice into opposite pairs of segments. Short, compact, black, spore-bearing fronds arise in summer in the center of the shuttlecock. The bright green shuttlecocks of new fronds in spring make it one of the star plants in the garden. Wonderful in a bog garden or by water, it can be invasive but unwanted plants are easily removed. Avoid full sun, which quickly disfigures the fronds. From damp woods and river bottoms in sections of Europe, eastern Asia, and North America. ‡3¼–5 ft (1–1.5 m). Z3–8 H8–1

MAURANDYA

SCROPHULARIACEAE

Slender twiners for cozy situations, and lovely peeping from shrubby supports in containers, or on walls.

Two species of twining herbaceous perennial climbers from rocks and woodlands in Mexico and the central US. The fresh green leaves are triangular, heart-shaped, or broadly oval and sometimes five-lobed. Solitary trumpet-shaped flowers are carried in the leaf joints toward the tips of the stems for a long season in summer. Confused with *Asarina* and *Lophospermum*, under which they may be listed in catalogs; further study is required to positively place the species in all three genera. Valuable for clothing trellises in warm areas.

CULTIVATION Thrives in any moderately fertile, sandy loam in warm, sunny locations. In cold areas, grow under glass as a conservatory climber, or as a summer annual.

PROPAGATION From seed or cuttings.

PROBLEMS Usually trouble-free.

M. barclayana syn. *Asarina barclayana* (Mexican viper) Slender, erect, free-flowering climber with a woody base and pointed, angular, light green leaves up to 1¼ in (4.5 cm) long. From midsummer onward, white, pink, or purple trumpet-shaped flowers, about 2¾ in (7 cm) long and with greenish

BELOW **1** *Malvastrum lateritium* **2** *Marrubium vulgare* **3** *Matteuccia struthiopteris* **4** *Meconopsis betonicifolia*

tints to the tube, are produced in continuous succession. From Mexico. ‡8 ft (2.4 m). Z9–10 H10–9. **alba** White flowers.

M. erubescens see *Lophospermum erubescens*

M. scandens see *Lophospermum scandens*

M. 'Victoria Falls' Very short, twining, tuberous climber with soft gray-green leaves, 1 in (2.5 cm) long, and large mauve-pink snapdragon-like blossoms all summer and fall. Often listed as *Asarina* or *Lophospermum,* under one of which names it may, in fact, belong. ‡3¼ ft (1 m). Z9–10 H10–9

MECONOPSIS
PAPAVERACEAE

The fabled Himalayan blue poppy is just one of some exquisite, yet challenging, species.

About 50 species almost exclusively from the Himalaya, western China, and Tibet (Xizang), where they are mainly plants of the monsoon region, growing in places with high rainfall in summer, when most flower. They vary from small, tufted, short-lived plants to large multiflowered plants and robust clump-forming perennials. Over half the species are monocarpic, taking two or more years to reach maturity, then flowering, fruiting, and dying.

The species vary a great deal in leaf characters: some have untoothed leaves, while others have leaves that are variously toothed and dissected. Most are adorned with various hairs or bristles, sometimes densely, covering all parts of the plant except the petals, and occasionally the fruits. The flowers are typical poppy flowers with buds made up of two sepals that fall away as the buds open, and four or more (up to ten) thin, brightly colored petals and numerous stamens. *Meconopsis* is very closely allied to *Papaver, Meconopsis* differing in its ecological preferences as well as a number of botanical details.

Meconopsis are grown primarily for their beautiful flowers—indeed, the famous blue poppies are among the most exquisite flowers grown in temperate gardens. In addition, several are grown for their handsome evergreen leaf-rosettes, which are especially attractive during the winter months.

Because they prefer cool, moist conditions during summer months, these plants grow best in areas where these conditions are the norm, including northern Britain, Ireland, Norway, the northwestern US, British Columbia, and northern Quebec.

The classification of the blue-flowered species and cultivars has long been a matter of (sometimes strong-minded) discussion. Here, the species and cultivars are organized in a logical way, presenting a solution to the problem while the study of these plants continues.

A CLASSIC WOODLAND GARDEN ASSOCIATION

IN THE DAPPLED or part-shade of a woodland garden, meconopsis, candelabra primulas, and ferns make a combination that has been grown since these plants were first introduced to western gardens from Asia. Here, a mix of primulas in a colorful range of shades are planted in front of a drift of plants in the *Meconopsis* Infertile Blue Group. In the foreground are the elegant arching fronds of the shuttlecock fern, *Matteuccia struthiopteris*. This sparkling rainbow of color—the meconopsis providing the main shade that the primulas lack—needs the frame of greenery to help show it off, and prevent color clashes with other perennials and bulbs planted nearby.

CULTIVATION The western European *M. cambrica* is easy to grow in most gardens, but the Asian species are more demanding in that they require summer moisture, good drainage, and cool summer temperatures. (*see* Growing Asian Meconopsis, p.325).

PROPAGATION The large blue perennial species and cultivars can be propagated by division of the parent clumps. This is best undertaken the moment flowering ceases, or as plants come into growth in the early spring. Divided pieces should be replanted as soon as possible to avoid possible desiccation. Seed of species and some hybrids is best sown fresh, the moment it is ripe. It will germinate in ten days or so and the seedlings can be pricked out when large enough to handle, and overwintered in an unheated greenhouse or cold frame for planting out the following spring. When it is not possible to get fresh seed, it is best to sow in the late winter for subsequent pricking out in the spring. However, always beware of the possibility of hybridization.

PROBLEMS Slugs, snails and aphids—plus hot, dry summers and poor winter drainage.

M. baileyi see *M. betonicifolia*

M. betonicifolia syn. *M. baileyi* (Himalayan blue poppy) A tuft-forming herbaceous perennial, often behaves as a biennial, the leafy stems die down to a resting crown in the winter. Basal and lower leaves are long-stalked, paddle-shaped with a rounded to heart-shaped base, and coarse with rusty hairs. Upper and middle stem leaves are unstalked, the uppermost three or four in a close cluster beneath the flowers. In early summer and midsummer, the stems are topped by up to ten, occasionally more, shallowly cupped, sky blue to rose-lavender, horizontal to half-nodding, 3–4 in (7.5–10 cm) flowers borne on long, erect, bristly stems. The fruit pods that follow are oblong and densely bristly. Best in a cool position in dappled shade in a free-drained, yet moisture-retentive, organic amended soil that is never allowed to dry out. Readily raised from seed. Removing the flowers produced in the second year the moment the stems arise may persuade plants into a more perennial habit, but not guaranteed. From northern Burma, southwestern China (Yunnan province), and southeastern Tibet (Xizang). ‡3¼–5½ ft (1–1.6 m). Z6–8 H8–6. **var. alba** Pure white flowers. **'Hensol Violet'** Flowers smaller than normal and deep lilac.

M. 'Blue Ice' see *M.* Fertile Blue Group 'Lingholm'

M. cambrica (Welsh poppy) A tufted, clump-forming perennial with yellow-green, long-stalked leaves split into pairs of toothed segments; the leaves on the erect wiry stems are unstalked or short-stalked. From late spring to early fall—sometimes later—a succession of yellow, deeply cupped, four-petaled flowers, 2–2⅜ in (5–6.5 cm) wide, arise on long slender stalks followed by smooth, club-shaped fruit pods. The easiest and most tolerant species, thriving in a variety of garden soils in sun or part-shade, provided plants are neither excessively dry nor waterlogged. Will self-sow in most gardens. From western Britain (southwestern England, Wales), western Ireland, western France and northwestern Spain. ‡12–20 in (30–50 cm). Z6–8 H8–6. **var. aurantiaca** Orange flowers. **'Flore Pleno'** A name loosely applied to yellow and orange, semidouble forms. **'Frances Perry'** syn. 'Rubra' Single deep orange-crimson flowers. **'Muriel Brown'** Semidouble red flowers; does not come 100 percent true from seed. **'Rubra'** see 'Frances Perry'.

M. chelidonifolia A modest, patch-forming perennial species, not unlike a large greater celandine (*Chelidonium* *majus*), with pale, bristly leaves, divided into opposite lobes, each segment broad and lobed; the upper leaves are smaller and mostly three-lobed. In early summer and midsummer, airy sprays of small, clear yellow, saucer-shaped, semi-nodding 1–1½ in (2.5–3.5 cm) flowers are produced, followed by small, smooth, or slightly bristly fruits that are elliptical in outline. Ideal for a woodland glade or shrubbery in dappled shade and in moist organic amended, well-drained soil. Best from seed, normally produced in quantity. Alternatively, remove rooted pieces from the edge rather than dig up the entire plant. From Sichuan province, China. ‡3 ft (1 m). Z6–8 H8–6

M. 'Corrennie' see *M.* Fertile Blue Group 'Lingholm'

M. Fertile Blue Group Plants in this group have narrow, spear-shaped to elliptical leaves that are not purple-flushed on emergence, and pure blue flowers. The fruit capsule is oblong in outline and sparsely to moderately bristly, containing many seeds. It is these plants that are normally offered by nonspecialist nurseries. All fertile plants of hybrid origin but of unknown parentage belong here. ‡3–4 ft (1–1.2 m). Z6–8 H8–6. **'Lingholm'** syn. *M.* 'Blue Ice', 'Corrennie' Clump-forming, soundly perennial plant with elliptical, mostly stalked lower leaves, the uppermost unstalked; leaves tend to lean to one side and are occasionally Y-shaped, apparently due to the fusion of two leaf blades. The 4–6-in (10–15-cm) flowers are deep, rich sky blue. The most widely available hybrid, but quite variable according to source.

M. George Sherriff Group A distinct group with broad, oval, perhaps tending to oblong, leaves that emerge in the spring with a marked purple flush. The flowers are blue, often also with a purple flush, and the egg-shaped fruit capsules have dense bristles. Propagate by division. ‡3–4 ft (1–1.2 m). Z6–8 H8–6. **'Ascreavie'** Jagged-margined

leaves and extra-large, blue, with a hint of lilac, flowers with markedly ruffled petals. Sometimes six-petaled. **'Branklyn'** The identity of this plant, which originates from the Branklyn Botanic Garden in Scotland, is unclear; plants sold under this name generally turn out to be 'Lingholm' or 'Slieve Donard'. The original cultivar is probably lost. **'Jimmy Bayne'** Bold, leafy clumps have broad, paddle-shaped leaves and large, nodding, bowl-shaped flowers with unruffled, rounded, translucent blue petals with a hint of purple. ‡4 ft (1.2 m).

M. grandis A stout clump-former, dying down to overwintering buds, with long-stalked, spear-shaped, basal leaves with rusty bristles; the unstalked stem leaves are few, mostly in clusters of three to five, and much smaller. From late spring to midsummer, several large, rich blue to purple or wine-purple, sometimes white, nodding to half-nodding, cupped flowers are produced, each on a slender, erect stalk that elongates as the flowers fade, followed by an erect, bristly or smooth fruit capsule, narrowly oblong. There are normally four petals, occasionally five or six. Grows well in moist, loamy, preferably humus-rich soil in sun or part-shade. Propagate from seed when available, or by division as the plants come into growth in the spring, taking great care to avoid damage to the brittle rootstock. Various forms are sold, including those from eastern Nepal, which tend to have wine-purple or pinkish purple flowers; the finest, which tend to come from Bhutan and Tibet, have rich blue flowers. Found in the Himalaya, from western Nepal eastward to Bhutan and southeastern Tibet (Xizang). ‡24–32 in (60–80 cm). Z5–8 H8–5. **GS600** see George Sherriff Group (see Perennial Blue Poppies).

M. horridula Plants grown under this name are invariably *M. prattii*. The true *M. horridula*, native to the high Himalaya, is difficult to grow and very rarely seen.

M. Infertile Blue Group Relatively narrow, more or less spear-shaped leaves and usually pure blue flowers. The fruit capsules are narrowly club-shaped to elliptical in outline, and covered with rather sparse bristles, or at least not as dense as those in the George Sherriff Group. Sterile, propagate by division. ‡3 ft (1 m). Z6–8 H8–6. **'Crewdson Hybrid'** Bushy, leafy plants with narrowly elliptical to oblong leaves and rich blue, deeply cupped flowers that are sideways-facing or slightly nodding. Very similar to the rarely seen 'Mrs. Jebb'. **'Slieve Donard'** A vigorous clump-forming plant that has narrow, spear-shaped, pointed leaves and open, shallow, bowl-shaped, rich clear blue flowers that are sideways-facing or half-nodding. Vigorous and reliable.

M. integrifolia (Lampshade poppy) A monocarpic species overwintering as a resting bud at ground level and maturing in three to four years from seed. The basal leaves, in a single rosette, are elliptical, three-veined, and covered, like most parts of the plant, in golden or orange hairs. The flowering stems are erect and sparsely leafy, with the uppermost three to five leaves in a cluster beneath the flowers. From late spring to midsummer, each plant produces several large, erect to horizontal, goblet- to bowl-shaped, 5–9 in (13–22 cm) flowers on long, hairy stalks that elongate as the flowers fade, followed by oval, densely hairy fruit capsules. Best in moist, leafy, well-drained soil in dappled shade, particularly among shrubs; plants benefit from shelter from excessive winter rain, but should not be allowed to dry out. Seed must be resown annually to ensure that plantings continue. From western China (Gansu, Qinghai, Sichuan, and Yunnan provinces), and western and northwestern Tibet (Xizang). ‡16–32 in (40–80 cm). Z7–8 H8–7. Many plants in circulation, from recent introductions from China, are **subsp. lijiangensis** with leafless stems apart from cluster beneath the flowers and more open, cup-shaped flowers.

M. napaulensis An impressive monocarpic species with a large evergreen rosette, up to 24 in (60 cm) across, sometimes larger, in the first two to four years before flowering; the rosette leaves are long-stalked, lobed into opposite pairs of sharply toothed segments and generously adorned with stiff golden or fawn hairs. From early to late summer, flowering plants produce stately, candelabra-like panicles carrying many cupped, horizontal to half-nodding, generally four-petaled, 2½–3¼ in (6–8 cm), pink or red flowers with orange or yellow anthers and a green stigma. Requires a sheltered position in fertile, deep humus-rich soil in dappled shade; in more exposed positions, the plants are likely to be blown over in bloom. Propagate only from seed, which is copiously produced, but if grown near

PERENNIAL BLUE POPPIES

Almost all the perennial blue poppies of hybrid origin have now been classified into three groups. Many of these are extremely fine, clump-forming, fully perennial plants. In recent years work has been undertaken to classify these poppies (which mostly have rather obscure garden origins) in a logical way and the best selections have been named, although others will undoubtedly follow. These hybrids can be divided broadly into three main groups:

Fertile Blue Group All fertile perennial plants of hybrid origin but of unknown parentage, as distinct from *M. x sheldonii* (see entry), which is a known cross between *M. betonicifolia* and *M. grandis*, belong here. These certainly involve *M. betonicifolia*, *M. grandis*, and possibly *M. simplicifolia* and other species. Many of these are unnamed seed-raised plants and have been grown as *M. x sheldonii* and

M. grandis. 'Lingholm' is so far the only cultivar in this group.
George Sherriff Group Sterile plants formerly, and incorrectly, collectively known as *M. grandis* GS600 (from the reference number given by George Sherriff to seed he collected in eastern Bhutan in 1934) now belong here. The forms that were grown under this collector's number have now been named. 'Ascreavie', 'Branklyn', and 'Jimmy Bayne' (see entry) are more generally available than 'Huntfield' and 'Spring Hill'.
Infertile Blue Group All infertile plants (with the exception of those that fit into the George Sherriff Group) belong here and are generally long-established and often previously classified as *M. x sheldonii*. 'Crewdson Hybrid' and 'Slieve Donard' (see Infertile Blue Group entry) are more generally available than 'Crarae', 'Cruikshank', 'Dawyck', and 'Mrs. Jebb'.

RIGHT 1 *Meconopsis cambrica*
2 *M. grandis* **3** *M. napaulensis*

M. paniculata and *M. wallichii*, hybrids are highly likely. From central Nepal. ↕4–8 ft (1.5–2.4 m). Z8–9 H9–8

M. paniculata A large, monocarpic, taprooted species that forms large gray-green, evergreen, rosettes of oblong, deeply lobed and toothed leaves. to 24 in (60 cm) long, which are densely covered with stiff hairs. From early to late summer, flowering-sized plants, generally in the second or third year from seed, produce candelabra-like panicles carrying many half-nodding, deeply cupped, canary yellow flowers that are normally four-petaled, 2–3 in (5–7.5 cm) across, with yellow anthers and a pale purple stigma. Best in a fertile, humus soil in a sheltered position, propagate only from seed, which is copiously produced, but keep isolated from *M. nepaulensis* and *M. wallichii* to prevent hybridization. Found in the Himalaya, from central Nepal eastward to Sikkim, Bhutan, northwestern India (Assam), and neighboring parts of Tibet (Xizang). ↕5–6½ ft (1.5–2 m). Z8–9 H9–8

M. prattii A monocarpic species; overwintering as a bud at ground level and taking two to four years to flower from seed. The rosette, to 10 in (25 cm) across, consists of bright green or gray-green elliptical, ascending, very sharply bristly leaves. From early summer to early fall, the solitary, erect, bristly and leafy flower stem carries a slender spike of up to 30 saucer-shaped, blue to violet-blue or purplish blue, 2–3 in (5–7.5 cm) flowers with numerous white or cream stamens. The narrow, pear-shaped fruit capsules are covered with stiff, sharp bristles. Enjoys moist, gritty, humus soil in sun or part-shade. An excellent and relatively easy species which will sometimes self-sow, or seed can be sown promptly when ripe. Often distributed as *M. horridula*. From southwestern China (Yunnan and Sichuan provinces), northern Burma, and southeastern Tibet (Xizang). ↕18–39 in (45–100 cm). Z7–8 H8–7

M. punicea (Red poppywort) A tufted perennial, often behaving as a biennial or monocarpic species, with a solitary taproot and a dense basal tuft of oval to elliptical, softly hairy, grayish or ginger leaves. From late spring until mid-summer, occasionally later, a succession of vivid crimson, pendulous flowers—each one shaped like a flared skirt—arise on slender erect stems well above foliage, each 2–4 in (5–10 cm) flower has four, sometimes five or six, petals. The erect fruits are oblong and bristly. Grow as a colony in an open position in moist, humus-enriched soil. Raise from seed sown in early spring. From western China (Gansu, Qinghai, and Sichuan provinces). ↕20–24 in (50–60 cm). Z7–8 H8–7

M. quintuplinervia (Harebell poppy) A patch-forming herbaceous perennial with branching underground stems, the slender-stalked leaves are all basal, oval to lance-shaped, with often five parallel veins and covered with straw- or rust-colored hairs. From late spring until

GROWING ASIAN MECONOPSIS

With the exception of the western European *M. cambrica* (which is easy in most gardens, often in quite dry situations), the Asian species require fairly exacting conditions if they are to thrive. Plenty of moisture in summer is essential, while hot conditions are not to their liking. They mostly require a deep, humus-rich soil in sun or dappled shade: the addition of well-rotted manure and friable leaf mold to the soil is highly beneficial, while summer mulches—bark chips, weed-free compost, or leaf mold—all help to keep conditions moist around the plants. Excessive winter moisture is also to be avoided; it can be a difficult balance to strike.

The monocarpic evergreen species can succumb if conditions are too wet during the cold months of the year, but this can be easily prevented by placing a sheet of glass or stiff, clear plastic overhead to keep the rain off. At the same time, plants should not be allowed to desiccate during the winter. During dry summers, the species may fail to set seed: some growers overcome this by setting up misters to keep the atmosphere around their plants moist during the summer months, thus mimicking conditions in the wild.

The large monocarpic species, which can reach 6 ft (2 m) or more in height, require a sheltered position, otherwise they are likely to be damaged by wind as they come into flower.

If *M. betonicifolia* and *M. grandis*, or *M. napaulensis* and *M. paniculata*, are grown in proximity, they are likely to hybridize, and the resultant seed will be varied: some may be extremely fine plants, some not, but the species' purity will be lost.

early fall, a series of pendulous, pale lavender to deep lavender-blue, four- to six-petaled flowers, 1¼–2 in (3–5 cm) long, rise on slender, upright stalks, followed by erect, bristly, elliptical fruit capsules. Grows best in moist, humus-enriched soil in sun or part-shade. Divide as plants come into growth in the spring, or right after flowering. From western China (Gansu, Qinghai, Sichuan, and Shaanxi provinces) and northeastern Tibet (Xizang). ↕12–20 in (30–50 cm). Z7–8 H8–7

M. regia Many plants circulate in the trade under this name. A distinct monocarpic Nepalese species with spear-shaped, unlobed leaves and yellow flowers, but they invariably prove to be of hybrid origin (involving *M. napaulensis*, *M. paniculata*, and *M. regia*). It is doubtful whether the true species is at present in cultivation.

M. x sheldonii Tufted, forming lax rosettes of dark green, spear-shaped, lightly toothed, bristly leaves. Stems are erect and leafy; the uppermost leaves, in a cluster beneath the flowers, are similar to the basal leaves, but without stalks. Half-nodding, shallowly cup-shaped,

MECONOPSIS FOLIAGE ROSETTES

Meconopsis have some of the most captivating flowers you will find in this book, but they also have another valuable feature: their rosettes of spring foliage.

The leaves vary from being long and slender or boldly lobed to impressively divided, and some also feature a colorful coating of honey or golden or even black hairs, especially as the leaves unfold. The result is a plant that repays a leisurely walk in the shade garden long before those famous flowers open.

Meconopsis nepaulensis

Meconopsis paniculata x M. regia

Meconopsis Infertile Blue Group

mid-azure-blue flowers with a hint of green, appear in late spring to mid-summer on long slender stalks. Narrow, spindle-shaped fruit capsules are often formed but contain no viable seeds. It is quite rare in cultivation, despite its name appearing frequently in literature and catalogs. Plants found under this name are usually best classified under Infertile Blue Group. Best in moist, loamy, preferably humus-enriched soil in sun or part-shade. Divide large multicrowned plants in early spring or immediately after flowering. A sterile garden hybrid of *M. betonicifolia* and *M. grandis*, and generally with intermediate characteristics. ↕28–36 in (70–90 cm). Z7–8 H8–1

M. villosa syn. *Cathcartia villosa* Tufted with long-stalked, rounded basal leaves, partly cut into three- or five-toothed lobes, and covered with soft bristles; stem leaves are similar but short-stalked and alternate. Early to late summer, half-nodding, four-petaled, soft yellow flowers in lax, few-branched clusters. Smooth, cylindrical fruit capsules split their entire length. For humus-enriched woodland soil in dappled shade—best grown as a colony drifted between trees or shrubs. Often placed in the genus *Cathcartia*. From the Himalaya, from eastern Nepal to Bhutan. ↕20–24 in (50–60 cm). Z7–8 H8–7

MEEHANIA
LAMIACEAE

Vigorous carpeting plant for a shady place, with quietly attractive flowers in late spring.

Six species of deciduous plants grow in woodlands in East Asia and North America but only one

is commonly grown. Widely spreading, with clumps of light green, heart-shaped leaves; long runners develop after flowering. Showy, deadnettle-like, tubular, violet-blue flowers are borne in the late spring or early summer.

CULTIVATION Grow in moist, humus-enriched soil in part-shade.

PROPAGATION By division, or easy from cuttings taken from spring to late summer.

PROBLEMS Liable to damage by slugs and snails.

M. urticifolia Spreading, forming a wide mat of long stems with paired, light green, heart-shaped leaves to 2 in (6 cm) across. Short, erect leafy stems bearing light mauve 2½ in (5 cm) flowers, spotted darker on the lower lip, appear in late spring and early summer. Pink forms are sometimes seen in the wild. Unexpectedly, the leafy scales around the flower, the calyx, are pleasantly aromatic. Long, running stems develop in summer. From woodlands in Japan and China. ↕12–16 in (30–40 cm). Z5–8 H8–5. **'Wandering Minstrel'** syn. 'Silver Sprinter' Leaves neatly margined with creamy-white. Good in containers.

MELIANDRIUM *see* SILENE

MELIANTHUS
MELIANTHACEAE

Handsome foliage plants with great architectural presence, sometimes with a bonus of profuse, richly colored flowers.

Six species of tender evergreen shrubs from grasslands of southern Africa, of which only three are usually grown, but treated as perennials in cooler climates as they are usually cut down to the ground by frost. Striking blue-green leaves, held on stout stems, are composed of several boldly toothed leaflets, and have a curious nutty smell. The spikes of small, nectar-rich flowers are less important to gardeners. They are carried on the previous year's stems, which are often killed to ground level in winter, so are more likely to be seen in warmer gardens. Most effective in coastal gardens, sheltered courtyards or similar protected locations, and containers.

CULTIVATION Best in well-drained soil in full sun and shelter, with a protective dry mulch in fall.

PROPAGATION By division in early spring, or from seed.

PROBLEMS Red spider mite.

M. comosus Bushy, with large attractive blue-green leaves that are divided into toothed, oblong segments and tend to be gathered toward the tips of the stems. In a sheltered site, the old stems may bear spikes of red-brown flowers in mid- or late summer, followed by large four-winged seed capsules. The whole plant has a particularly unpleasant smell. Invasive in parts of Australia. From Namibia, southern Africa. ↕6½ ft (2 m). Z8–11 H11–8

M. major (Honey bush) Arching, soft, gray- or blue-green leaves, to 20 in (50 cm) long, composed of several pairs of coarsely toothed, oblong leaflets, are the main feature of this first-rate plant. After a hot summer, deep red-brown flowers may appear in spikes, to 32 in (80 cm) long, in late summer and early

fall. Can also be employed to add an exotic foliage effect to summer bedding. From Cape province in South Africa. ↕8 ft (2.4 m). Z8–11 H11–8. **'Purple Haze'** Leaves tinged with purple, on dark purple stems.

M. minor Rather open, slightly straggly plant, with gray-green leaves, 6–10 in (15–25 cm) long, and orange-red flowers in 14 in (35 cm) spikes in late summer and early fall. Although it is a little smaller overall, the habit of the plant's growth is less compact than *M. major*. From South Africa. ↕3¼–6½ ft (1–2 m). Z8–11 H11–8

M. villosus Compact plant with divided, gray-green leaves of distinctive appearance and, in warmer gardens, spikes of deep maroon flowers in late summer, sometimes followed by bright green, inflated fruits. From mountainous areas in South Africa. ↕4 ft (1.2 m). Z8–11 H11–8

MELICA
Melick Grass
POACEAE

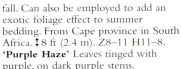

Delicate grasses for alkaline soil—some tiny, some making striking clumps, all with papery flowers good for drying.

At least 80 perennials growing throughout the world, except Australia, in dry woodlands and on rocky slopes. The leaves form clumps of rather coarse foliage, sometimes with very rough edges, and usually die back to some extent over the summer months. The flowerheads are often one-sided and are made up of papery little flowers that can be dried if picked soon after they open. A cool season plant that tends to flower early in the year. The foliage can become scruffy during the summer months, but this

can be hidden if the taller species are grown in a herbaceous border, where the flowers will still look impressive. Smaller species are good minglers for dry shady areas.

CULTIVATION Best in well-drained, fertile neutral to alkaline soil in open positions to light shade. Most species are drought-tolerant but prefer some moisture at the roots. Trim back untidy leaves in winter to early spring.

PROPAGATION From seed or by division; division only for cultivars and varieties.

PROBLEMS Usually trouble-free.

M. altissima **'Atropurpurea'** syn. 'Purpurea', 'Rubra' (Purple Siberian melick) Loose, slowly spreading clumps are made up of bright green leaves, hairy beneath, with rough edges. In early summer, stout, leafy flower spikes carry arching, one-sided flowerheads, up to 8 in (20 cm) long, hung with papery mauve-purple flowers like spiky tooth brushes that deepen in color before eventually turning buff as the seeds mature. Grown in gardens since at least 1888—as much for its value as a dried plant as for its decorative qualities in the flower border. ↕24 in–8 ft (60cm–2.4 m). Z5–8 H8–5

M. ciliata (Hairy or Silky melick) Makes clumps of thin, sometimes inrolled, rough ⅛-in (4-mm) leaves, which are green on top and blue-gray beneath. In late spring to early summer, the rather weak flower stems splay over the foliage and are topped with papery white to pale buff flowers shaped like chunky pipe cleaners. Mingle with other herbaceous plants so the flower-heads will have some support and the scruffy foliage will be hidden, or use to add interest to a wildflower

meadow. From open, dry, rocky places in the Middle East, eastern Europe, and Africa. ↕3¼ ft (1 m). Z5–8 H8–5

M. nutans (Mountain or Nodding melick) Slowly spreading evergreen clumps comprise branches carrying the bluntly pointed dark to bright green, flat, ¼-in (6-mm) leaves, tinted red and yellow in the fall. Slender, arching flower stems, in late spring and early summer, end in a one-sided row of shiny, papery purple-red beady flowers that nod above the foliage. A lovely delicate addition to woodland gardens. Found on limestone on shady banks and rocks in Europe, including Britain, and Asia. ↕24 in (60 cm) Z6–8 H9–6

M. transsilvanica Evergreen clumps of flat, green, ¹⁄₁₆–¼-in (2–6-mm) leaves with a prominent midrib. In late spring and early summer, stems carry woolly white bottle-brush shaped flowers, to ½ in (1 cm) long, which become more silvery and papery as the seeds mature. A lovely grass for dry, informal gardens either in shade or sun. Found on the edges of dry woodlands and steppes from central and eastern Europe to Central Asia. ↕1–3 ft (30–90 cm). Z5–8 H8–5. **'Atropurpurea'** Deep pink to purple flowers. **'Red Spire'** Deep red papery flowers, green leaves turning red-brown. ↕5½ ft (1.7 m).

M. uniflora (Wood melick) Slowly creeping deciduous patches of bright green pointed leaves, 8 in (20 cm) long by ¼ in (5 mm) wide; delicate, widely branched, purplish flower stems appear in late spring to midsummer, hung with little beady chocolate-brown flowers with yellow stamens that nod above the foliage. A graceful grass for dry shady paths and woodland margins. Found in dry alkaline woodlands throughout Europe to northern Iran. 8–24 in (20–60 cm). Z7–9 H9–7. **f. albida** White flowers. **'Variegata'** Foliage with fine white vertical stripes. Best grown in drifts in damp shade. Very slow. ↕6–12 in (15–30 cm).

MELISSA
Lemon balm
LAMIACEAE

Tough and leafy herbs, with a tangy, citrus scent, usually grown for their medicinal and culinary properties.

Three species of deciduous plants native to disturbed ground and roadsides in southern Europe, North Africa, and parts of Asia. The pleasantly aromatic, egg-shaped foliage is usually somewhat hairy and borne on upright, branching stems that form dense clumps. The unprepossessing two-lipped flowers are usually yellow or white, and are produced in the summer. Only one species is common in cultivation; its leaves are used in salads, sauces, and herbal teas, and to treat a range of maladies, including indigestion. Golden-leaved cultivars are much valued as ornamentals.

CULTIVATION Grow in an open, well-drained spot. Golden-leaved plants will color best in a little shade. Stems should be cut back after flowering to restrict the numbers of self-sown seedlings, and to promote new growth, which has better color and flavor.

PROPAGATION Divide clumps in spring or fall, or sow seed in spring. Self-sown seedlings are often produced and can be potted up.

PROBLEMS Usually trouble-free.

M. officinalis (Lemon balm) A bushy herb, dying back in the winter, with square, branching stems forming upright clumps. The leaves, up to 3¼ in (9 cm) long, are wrinkly, egg-shaped, hairy, toothed, and smell deliciously of lemon when bruised. Inconspicuous two-lipped flowers, produced intermittently throughout the summer, are about ⅗ in (1.5 cm) long and yellow fading to pink or white. Golden-leaved plants may burn or bleach in strong sun. Frequently naturalized in North America and northern Europe, including the British Isles, but native to the Mediterranean. ‡12–40 in (30–100 cm). Z4–9 H11–1. **'All Gold'** Leaves entirely golden and flowers pale lilac. Comes reliably true from seed. **'Aurea'** Leaves broadly and irregularly marked with gold on the margins. Seedlings seldom come true.

MELITTIS
Bastard balm
LAMIACEAE

Attractive, underrated woodlander whose name is derived from the Greek name for a bee.

One species of clump-forming deciduous perennial, which grows in European woods. Square stems carry opposite pairs of aromatic, nettlelike leaves, among which, toward the top of the plant, cluster very pretty two-lipped flowers; the individual flowers turning to face the light. This very pretty plant, a favorite with bees, deserves to be planted more widely in shady situations.

CULTIVATION Best in moderately fertile, moist, but well-drained soil and part-shade. Ideal in a woodland garden, or in herbaceous and mixed borders that do not dry out.

PROPAGATION Divide, or sow seed in containers and keep in a cold frame, during spring or fall.

PROBLEMS Usually trouble-free.

M. melissophyllum Upright, branched stems covered with long hairs carry opposite pairs of oval or egg-shaped leaves with deeply impressed veins and rounded scalloped teeth along the edge. Both stems and leaves are covered with

glandular hairs and have a strong honey scent that is retained for a long period when dry and used in potpourri. In late spring to early summer, the white, pink, purple, or bicolored 1½-in (4-cm) flowers are arranged in distinct clusters along the stem, each with a three-lobed lower lip and slight, hooded upper lip. The most widely grown form has white flowers with a large deep pink or purple blotch on the lower lip and originates from eastern Europe. Found in western, central, and southern Europe. ‡28 in (70 cm). Z6–9 H9–6.

MENTHA
Mint
LAMIACEAE

Strongly aromatic, most familiar in the kitchen garden, but including several ornamental species.

Twenty-five perennial and annual herbs, with strongly mint-scented foliage, are native to Eurasia and Africa and occur in various habitats, but most often in wet places. Paired leaves may be rounded, oval, or lance-shaped and hairy, or smooth. Tiny tubular flowers, mostly pale purple, gather into clusters, either at the leaf joints or forming a terminal spike. All are easy to grow, and favor damp soil, but care must be taken in siting them, since most can be very invasive. One option is to confine them to a large pot or another container, in which they will grow well given a good, fairly fertile potting mix. (*see* Invasive?, *p.328*).

CULTIVATION Grow in any moist, fertile soil in sun or part-shade.

PROPAGATION By division, or from cuttings, which root easily in water.

PROBLEMS Powdery mildew, and rust. Spraying is less of an issue when plants are grown only for ornamental purposes.

M. x *gentilis* 'Variegata' see *M.* x *gracilis* 'Variegata'

M. x *gracilis* **'Variegata'** syn. *M.* x *gentilis* 'Variegata' (Ginger mint) Vigorous plant forming a wide-spreading clump of upright reddish stems bearing dark green, oval leaves, to 2¾ in (7 cm) long, striped with deep yellow markings along the main veins, and with a strong gingery scent. Pale mauve flowers are borne in dense rounded clusters among the upper leaves in midsummer. Lovely leaves, but flowers are insignificant. Grows equally well, and retains its variegation, in sun or part-shade. A variegated hybrid of *M. gentilis* and *M. spicata.* ‡12 in (30 cm). Z6–9 H9–6

M. longifolia (Horsemint) Tall, wide-spreading plant with hairy upright stems bearing softly gray-woolly,

RIGHT 1 *Melissa officinalis* **2** *Melittis melissophyllum* **3** *Mentha longifolia* Buddleia Mint Group **4** *M.* x *piperata* f. *citrata*

LEFT 1 *Mentha spicata* var. *crispa* 'Moroccan' **2** *M. suaveolens* 'Variegata'

narrowly lance-shaped leaves to 3½ in (9 cm) long. Pale lilac flowers are borne in long, dense spikes at the ends of the stems in mid- and late summer. Grown for ornament only—the musty scent of the foliage is not pleasant—but the buddleia-like, grayish foliage complements the pale flowers well. Native to Europe, western Asia, East and South Africa, and naturalized throughout the US. ↕3¼ ft (1 m). Z6–9 H9–6. **Buddleia Mint Group** Leaves more silvery; flowers deeper mauve-pink. **'Variegata'** Leaves splashed with yellow. Slightly less vigorous.

M. x piperita (Peppermint) Strong-growing plant forming a spreading mat of usually hairless stems, sometimes flushed purple, with lance-shaped, dark green leaves to 3½ in (9 cm) long. Lilac-pink flowers form a dense terminal spike in mid- and late summer. As well as being ornamental, its true peppermint scent makes it a useful plant in the kitchen. A natural hybrid of *M. aquatica* and *M. spicata* from Europe. ↕12–24 in (30–60 cm). Z3–7 H7–1. **f. citrata** (Eau de Cologne mint, Orange mint) Leaves oval, flushed purple; eau de Cologne scent. **f. citrata 'Chocolate'** Leaves and stems deep reddish brown; scent has chocolate undertones. **'Logee's'** Leaves irregularly cream-variegated, sometimes flushed pink; peppermint-scented.

M. pulegium (Pennyroyal) Mat-forming plant with bright green, elliptical or rounded leaves, ½–1¼ in (1–3 cm) long, with a fresh, pungent mint scent. Lilac flowers open in late summer and early fall, in well-spaced clusters on erect stems. Best in full sun and quite distinct from other mints in its compact mat-forming style of growth. Native to wet places in sandy soil in western and central Europe, and western Asia. ↕4–16 in (10–40 cm). Z7–9 H11–2

M. spicata (Spearmint) Vigorous upright plant rapidly colonizing in almost any situation. The bright, deep green, lance-shaped leaves, to 3½ in (9 cm) long, have a fresh scent. In mid- and late summer, very pale lilac-pink flowers open in dense terminal spikes. Best grown in a container to curb its spread. From damp grassy places in central and southern Europe. ↕12–36 in (30–90 cm). Z5–9 H9–5. **var. *crispa*** Leaves broader, with crinkled edges. **var. *crispa* 'Moroccan'** Said to be more aromatic.

M. suaveolens (Apple mint) Tall, with softly hairy, rounded, light green leaves, to 1½ in (4 cm) long, with a distinct fresh apple scent. Pale lilac flowers open in dense spikes in late summer and early fall. Spreads freely, with shoots often arising some way from the original clump. Grows on wasteland in much of Europe. ↕36 in (90 cm). Z6–9 H9–5. **'Variegata'** (Pineapple mint) Leaves irregularly variegated with creamy-white. ↕8–14 in (20–35 cm).

INVASIVE?

We all know that mints can spread. Even growing them in buckets sunk into the ground often fails to contain them—their runners creep up and over the edge and set off vigorously across the garden.

However, one of the advantages of the variegated ornamental forms is that they grow less strongly. With the variegated part of each leaf lacking in chlorophyll, variegated mints, like other variegated plants, are inherently less vigorous. So *M. x gracilis* 'Variegata', *M. longifolia* 'Variegata', and *M. suaveolens* 'Variegata' can be planted with less fear that they will swamp their neighbors.

However, they can revert. *M. suaveolens* 'Variegata' regularly produces all-cream shoots (which if detached soon die), and these attractive forms may also produce plain green shoots. These are more vigorous and should be promptly removed, otherwise they will first take over the clump and then proceed to take over the garden.

M. x villosa var. *alopecuroides* (Bowles' mint, Woolly apple mint) Tall plant with soft, rounded, grayish green leaves up to 3½ in (8 cm) long, prominently toothed on the margins. Lilac-pink flowers open in leafy spikes during late summer and early fall. The leaves are strongly spearmint-scented. Spreads freely in moist conditions. A vigorous hybrid of *M. spicata* x *M. suaveolens*. ↕24–36 in (60–90 cm). Z5–8 H8–5

MERTENSIA
Bluebells
BORAGINACEAE

Charming blue-flowered plants of varied habits and habitats. From 40 to 50 species of deciduous perennials native to a wide variety of habitats, including mountains, streambanks, seashores, and woodlands in North America, Asia, and Europe. They are hairy or hairless plants, with one to many upright, arching, or sprawling stems arising from the rootstock. Leaves are untoothed, alternate, elliptical, oval, and heart- or lance-shaped, and range from light green to bluish and dark green. Flowers are funnel-shaped, tubular, or bell-shaped, with five lobes, are carried in loose or dense clusters; they are usually a shade of blue, often opening from pink buds, and are attractive to bees. Many are fine border and rock garden species, although only a few are commonly grown.

CULTIVATION Requirements differ widely between the species.

PROPAGATION From fresh seed, or by careful division in spring, and some from root cuttings in winter.

PROBLEMS Slugs.

M. ciliata An elegant deciduous plant, with numerous stems arising from a branched woody rootstock. Basal leaves, which may sometimes be absent, are long-stalked, oval to lance-shaped, bluish green, to 6 in (15 cm) long and 4 in (10 cm) wide; the stem leaves are somewhat narrow, the uppermost stalkless. Bears clusters of nodding tubular bell-shaped, sky-blue flowers ½–⅝ in (10–15 mm) long, opening from pink buds in late spring and early summer. Best in light shade but will tolerate full sun if the soil is continuously moist. Ideal by ponds. From the US and Mexico. ↕12–24 in (30–60 cm). Z3–8 H8–1

M. maritima (Oysterplant) A beautiful and unusual—though unpredictable—deciduous perennial, forming a mat of branched, trailing stems that spread to cover an area over 3¼ ft (1 m) across, and are clothed in bluish, oval, fleshy leaves ¾–4 in (2–10 cm) long. The terminal clusters of small, tubular funnel-shaped, turquoise-blue flowers,

about ⅜ in (8 mm) across, open from soft-pink buds. Requires gravelly or sandy soil in full sun; slugs love it. Raise from seed. From coasts of northern Europe, Greenland, and some northern parts of North America. ↕4 in (10 cm). Z3–7 H7–1

M. pterocarpa see *M. sibirica*

M. pulmonarioides see *M. virginica*

M. sibirica syn. *M. pterocarpa* Clump-forming, hairless, upright deciduous perennial with unbranched stems and rather fleshy, bluish green leaves. Lower leaves are oval with a heart-shaped base, up to 8 in (20 cm) long, and usually wither at flowering time. Stem leaves are oval, pointed, stalkless, and up to 2¾ in (7 cm) long. Paired, nodding clusters of more or less tubular, long-stalked, blue flowers, to ½ in (1 cm) long, are borne in spring and early summer. Needs a lightly shaded position on any well-drained but moist, humus-enriched soil. A very hardy and attractive plant. From Siberia and western Sichuan province in China. ↕12–18 in (30–45 cm). Z3–7 H7–1

M. simplicissima Beautiful blue-green deciduous perennial, with trailing stems growing up to 3¼ ft (1 m) long, clothed in elliptical, fleshy 3-in (8-cm) leaves. Bears small clusters of tubular, turquoise-blue flowers, to ½ in (1 cm) across, opening from pink buds in summer. Very similar to *M. maritima*, but much less hardy and easier to grow. From coasts of Japan, Korea, eastern Russia, and the Aleutian Islands. ↕4 in (10 cm). Z6–8 H8–6

M. virginica syn. *M. pulmonarioides* (Virginian bluebells, Virginia cowslip) Handsome deciduous plant, with upright stems arising from fleshy, thick rhizomes. The basal leaves are gray-green, long-stalked, lance-shaped to

RIGHT *Mertensia maritima*

THE BLUEBELL

This is the plant that makes the case for using botanical names. In the United States, the common name "bluebell" is regularly applied to *Mertensia virginica*, an attractive woodlander widely grown in other temperate climates.

Another woodland plant also known as the bluebell is a bulb, *Hyacinthoides non-scripta*. This relative of the familiar fragrant hyacinth is Britain's national flower and carpets deciduous woodlands in late spring. *Wahlenbergia* is also called bluebell—in particular, *Wahlenbergia gloriosa*, which is sometimes called the Royal Bluebell, and is the floral emblem of the Australian Capital Territory. In Scotland the bluebell is yet another plant, *Campanula rotundifolia*.

Wahlenbergia and *Campanula* are the most similar to look at and the closest botanically; *Mertensia* and *Hyacinthoides* are the closest in terms of habitat. And while when you see any two side by side, it is clear that they are different, casually referring to bluebells, or using the common name in a seed list or magazine article, is clearly likely to cause confusion.

oval, 1½–8 in (4–20 cm) long, and stem leaves are smaller, short-stalked, or clasping the stem. The nodding clusters of fairly large, purple-blue, funnel-shaped flowers, each ¾–1¼ in (2–3 cm) long, appear in spring. Pink, white, and misty lavender forms are very occasionally seen. Great for any lightly shaded spot on moist soil, but leaves gaps as it dies away completely in summer. This is an old garden favorite. From North America. ↕12–24 in (30–60 cm). Z3–7 H7–1

MILIUM
POACEAE

A graceful woodland grass with airy sprays of late spring flowers and some attractive foliage forms.

Some 45 annual and perennial species are native to moist woodlands in Europe, Asia, and North America. Sometimes slowly spreading clumps form a carpet of flat silky leaves—the flower stems carry branches with small, millet-like, airy flowers, usually early in the year. It is a lovely ground-cover plant for use in damp shady areas, especially if grown with early spring flowers. The colored forms make lovely eye-catching contrasts to blue-leaved hostas.

CULTIVATION Grow in dappled shade in moist, well-drained rich soil. Cut back untidy growth of cool season species in the summer.

PROPAGATION From seed or by division in early spring. Divide varieties and cultivars.

PROBLEMS Slugs and snails.

M. effusum (Wood millet) Loose tufts with flat somewhat pointed leaves, ⅝ in (1.5 cm) wide, spread slowly to form a soft carpet of pale green foliage. In late spring to midsummer, tall flower stems carry clusters of long wiry branches hung with nodding, pale green, milletlike flowers that flutter above the foliage. A cool-season grass dying back in summer, the foliage will last longer in damp part-shade and looks best where the sun can filter through the silky leaves and airy flowers. Found in damp oak and beech woods on heavy alkaline soil throughout northern temperate regions. ↕1½–3 ft (45cm–1.8 m) Z4–7 H7–1. **'Aureum'** (Bowles golden grass). Bright yellow leaves and flowers, opening in early spring to early summer, fading to pale yellow-green as the weather becomes hotter. Spectacular ground cover; comes true from seed. ↕20 in (50 cm) **'Yaffle'** Green leaves with narrow central yellow line. Named for the traditional name of the green woodpecker, with its yellow and green plumage. ↕18–30 in (45–75 cm).

MIMULUS
Monkey flower, Musk flower
SCROPHULARIACEAE

C heerful, often aromatic moisture-lovers in a wide range of colors, many with attractive speckling.

About 150 species of annuals, short-lived perennials, and some shrubs, from generally moist habitats in southern Africa, Asia, Australia, and North America, where they are established as aliens. A fibrous root system supports round or square erect stems carrying pairs of smooth-edged, toothed, or sometimes more deeply cut, leaves set at 90 degrees to each other. The open-throated flowers are tubular and divided into two lobes at the mouth, of which the lower is usually the largest and is split into three, the upper split into two; they are produced in the leaf joints in summer, or in small clusters at the top of the stems. Although yellow is the most familiar flower color, often spotted with red, the species also includes bright red, orange, pink, and lilac—as well as white—and the hybrids show a great diversity of colors and patterns. In moist soil they may spread to form large mats. The taller species often tolerate drier conditions and are more reliably perennial.

The low-growing, moisture-loving mimulus, which are popular as summer bedding plants, are not reliably hardy in areas with winter frost and, if grown in dry soil, may die after the effort of flowering and setting seed.

RIGHT **1** *Mimulus cardinalis*
2 *M. guttatus* **3** *M.* 'Highland Orange' (Highland Series) **4** *M. lewisii*
5 *M. ringens*

CULTIVATION Most require, fertile, moist soil, and some will tolerate being submerged in water when in growth. They will grow in light shade but flower best in full sun.

PROPAGATION From seed, basal cuttings, or by division. Most will bloom in their first year from seed.

PROBLEMS Slugs and snails. Mildew, especially on dry soil.

M. cardinalis A tall, erect, well-branched plant with bright green, softly hairy, oval to elliptical leaves, up to 4½ in (11 cm) long and with three to five veins. These complement the showy, 2-in (5-cm) scarlet flowers, tinged with yellow in the throat. Thrives in moist soil with its roots in water, but also grows well in a border if the soil is not too dry in summer. From Oregon south to Baja California, Mexico. ‡36 in (90 cm). Z6–9 H9–6

M. cupreus **'Whitecroft Scarlet'** Low, compact, well-branched little plant with small, green, coarsely toothed leaves, to 1¼ in (3 cm) long and ⅝ in (1.5cm) wide, and loose clusters of bright scarlet flowers, ¾ in (2 cm) wide, marked with yellow spots on the lower lip. It has a long flowering season in moist soil but is generally short-lived. ‡4 in (10 cm). Z8–9 H9–8

M. guttatus Vigorous, erect, or sometimes floppy, plant that may spread strongly in damp soil. Fleshy stems carry leaves to ⅝–6 in (1.5–15 cm) long and mostly reverse egg-shaped with small teeth. The 1¼–1¾-in (3–4.5-cm) bright yellow flowers are variously spotted with red, and with red ridges on the lower lobe that may almost close the throat. From the western, midwestern, and northeastern US. ‡12 in (30 cm). Z6–9 H9–6. **'Richard Bish'** Gray-green leaves with white edges, and yellow flowers with faint red spots.

M. x *harrisonii* An upright plant with

pale green foliage, sometimes partially clasping the stem, and glowing magenta-pink blooms—with a white throat speckled in pink and yellow ridges on the lip—produced throughout summer. A garden hybrid between *M. cardinalis* and *M. lewisii,* two species from western North America. ‡28 in (70 cm). Z6–9 H9–6

M. **Highland Series** Compact, free-flowering series, intended to be raised from seed; less fleeting than other modern hybrid series but still short-lived. Neat, tightly tufted plants carry small flowers in orange, deep pink, rose-pink, crimson, and yellow; a mixture is also available. ‡4 in (10 cm). Z6–9 H9–6

M. lewisii Upright with 1¼–2¾-in (3–7-cm) oblong or elliptical, slightly grayish leaves, sometimes partly clasping the stem. Bright magenta-pink flowers have maroon spots in the throat, two yellow stripes, and obvious hairs on the lower petal. It blooms throughout summer. From western North America. ‡24 in (60 cm). Z5–8 H8–5

M. luteus Spreading, fleshy plant with stout hollow stems that root at the base, and bright green, toothed, ¾–1¼-in (2–3-cm), oval or oblong leaves. The ¾–2-in (2–5-cm) yellow flowers, spotted with red or purple, are produced mainly in early summer. It thrives beside ponds and in shallow water, and self-seeds freely. From Chile, and naturalized elsewhere. ‡12 in (30 cm). Z10–11 H11–10

M. **'Orkney Gold'** Double-flowered, yellow form with one flower inside another. Derived from the Orkney garden of *Geranium* breeder Alan

Bremner, and sometimes listed as hose-in-hose. ‡12 in (30 cm). Z9–10 H10–9

M. ringens Smooth, square, sometimes slightly winged, stems create a distinctly upright, sparsely branched plant with 2–4-in (5–10-cm), roughly lance-shaped, sharply pointed leaves, becoming steadily smaller up the stem. Pale pink, white, or—more usually—violet, flowers, ¾ in (3 cm) wide, in summer. Best grown in moist soil or shallow water. From North America. ‡36 in (90 cm). Z4–9 H9–4

M. **'Threave Variegated'** Gray-green leaves with a cream edge and pale yellow flowers with faint red spotting. ‡12 in (30 cm). Z7–9 H9–7

MIRABILIS
Marvel of Peru, Umbrellawort
NYCTAGINACEAE

Deliciously scented afternoon and evening flowers, which are often curiously streaked.

A group of 50 species of annuals and tuberous perennials from dry, open places in the southwestern and central US, and South America. One species is generally grown. Tuberous roots, sometimes reaching a very large size, support branched, smooth, or sometimes sticky, stems clad with oval oppositely arranged leaves. Open heads of large, brightly colored, open trumpet-shaped flowers, often fragrant, appear throughout the summer. Often grown as annuals in cold areas. Handle with care; sap from damaged stems may cause minor skin irritation. ⚠

CULTIVATION Best in well-drained, fertile soil in sunny positions. Tubers can be overwintered frost-free, or grown afresh from seed each year.

ABOVE 1 *Miscanthus sinensis* var. *condensatus* 'Cosmopolitan' **2** *M. sinensis* 'Gracillimus'

PROPAGATION From seed or by division of tubers.

PROBLEMS Slugs, aphids.

M. jalapa (Four o'clock) Bushy perennial, sometimes grown as an annual, with green, oval, 2–4-in (5–10-cm) leaves that are heart-shaped at the base with a pointed tip. Fragrant circular flowers, up to 2 in (5 cm) across, open in late afternoon and fade by morning; they come in red, purple pink, yellow, or white, and are often streaked or speckled. From Peru, and tropical areas of North, Central, and South America. ‡24 in (60 cm). Z10–11 H11–1. **'Broken Colours'** Flowers in a range of colors splashed or marbled with cerise-red. ‡20 in (50 cm). **'Red Glow'** Bright red.

MISCANTHUS
Silver grass
POACEAE

Elegant and imposing large and small grasses for flower and foliage, border and container.

About 20 species of mostly deciduous grasses, clump-forming or spreading by rhizomes, usually from open hillsides and marshes in Southeast Asia but extending westward to Africa. Some are valuable garden plants, but a few are invasive.

Reaching up to 4-ft (1.2-m) in length, and varying from ¹⁄₁₂ to 1½ in (2–40 mm) across, the leaves of some species have tiny serrations along the margins sufficient to cut flesh, although not to the same extent as most cortaderias. The foliage often develops attractive fall tints of yellow, orange, or red. The leaf bases enclose the top of the developing flowerhead, which emerges from late summer to late fall and unfurls to a silky-looking plume, sometimes crimped, and usually beige, white, mahogany, or pink. It usually comprises from two to many fingers, and the plumes become fluffier, and often paler, with parchment or brownish tints later, often persisting well into the winter. Young plants tend to be more upright, becoming spreading and dome-shaped as the clumps mature.

Related to *Saccharum* (sugarcane), with which it hybridizes; both species and hybrids have become important for the production of biomass and fiberboard.

Often dramatic and imposing plants, much development has taken place in recent years, especially in Germany and the US (*see* Developments in Miscanthus, *p.334*).

Their usually graceful, fountain-like clumps are shown off best when given space to develop and, like other tall grasses, much of their appeal is due to their graceful movement in the breeze, giving life to any planting. Magical effects may be achieved by planting them where they can be seen backlit by the sun, either early in the morning or late in the day. Because single plants are so pleasing, there is a tendency not to use them to form drifts, ribbons or even screens, though they are equally suited to this approach

Their late flowering favors associations with Michaelmas daisies, crocosmias, Japanese anemones, sedums, tender perennials, and other grasses—such as cortaderias or molinias. A few cultivars and species have a habit that is narrow enough for them to be grown in densely planted borders graded by height. However, they are generally more attractive when planted in front of other plants of the same height and given space to develop their characteristic shape.

CULTIVATION Miscanthus are tolerant of most soils, often coping well with poor drainage or dry conditions, though drought will limit their growth. Most grow quite well in part-shade, but flowering tends to be reduced. The smaller species are suitable for pots and containers, though not all will stand being frozen at the root. They can be cut back once they become untidy, but it is advisable to leave the old growth on until mid-spring in areas where they are not as hardy. Staking is rarely necessary, though nitrogen-rich soil can lead to excessively lax growth and fewer flowers. Clumps generally benefit from dividing and replanting every three to five years, as growth starts in spring.

PROPAGATION By division in spring. Species can also be raised from seed.

PROBLEMS Some are rather prone to rust. Miscanthus mealybug is troublesome in North America. Some variegated cultivars, especially those with transverse bands, can scorch in sun.

M. x *giganteus* Upright in habit, without invasive rhizomes, its bold, strap-shaped leaves are about 1 in (2.5 cm) wide and arch over at their tips, giving the effect of a fountain. Its flowerheads appear from mid-fall (albeit shyly where summers are cool), opening pinkish and aging to silver. One of the most important species for biomass production, it is also useful for screens; it does not need clipping like a hedge, but is ineffective after cutting back in spring. When it is grown as a screen, horizontal wires held by stout posts can be used for support and to create a physical barrier. Useful for adding height to plantings, creating a dramatic, large-scale, almost tropical effect, and perhaps especially good near water, where its reflections can double the impact. Some have recently been bred for biomass production, but are not yet available to gardeners. This is a spontaneous natural hybrid occurring where both parents are native; also hybridized artificially. First seen in Denmark before 1930, most plants under this name are an enormous triploid, sometimes misidentified as *M. floridulus* or *M. sacchariflorus*, created by crossing tetraploid *M. sacchariflorus* with diploid *M. sinensis,* though the name also covers plants of more modest bearing. ↕ 11 ft (3.5 m). Z5–8 H8–5

M. nepalensis syn. *Diandranthus nepalensis* (Himalayan fairy grass) Variable plant grown not so much for its mid-green leaves as for its elegant tassels—their many silky fingers emerge light golden-brown in midsummer, each finger starting upward, then arching over to one side in unison. The seed-heads become fluffy and parchment-colored, remaining attractive for some months. This elegant species varies greatly in height and hardiness, the smaller types being suited to pot or container culture, although they are unlikely to survive being frozen at the roots. From northern India, Nepal, northern Burma, and western China. ↕ 2½–6 ft (75–180 cm). Z7–9 H9–7

M. oligostachyus Relatively short, thin-textured, mid-green leaves about ½ in (13 mm) wide, have a white midrib but this is less pronounced than in *M. sinensis*. Rich orange or red fall colors follow hot summers, and upright flowerheads with two to five fingers are produced in early fall. It dislikes drought but will tolerate shade. From the mountains of Honshu, Shikoku, and Kyushu, Japan. ↕ 3¼–4 ft (75–120 cm). Z5–8 H8–5. **'Nanus Variegatus'** Dwarf, with creamy-yellow variegation. This name may not be valid. ↕ 2½ ft (75 cm).

M. **'Purpurascens'** (Flame grass) An upright plant with grayish, slightly red-tinged summer leaves, about ½ in (13 mm) wide. Its chief glory is its fiery fall foliage, produced after fairly hot summers followed by cool fall temperatures. In mid- and late summer, upright, pink-flushed flowerheads with two to five fingers—like those of *M. oligostachyus*—appear, though they become broader and fluffier, aging to silver and then fawn as they mature. Full sun is needed for best fall color, but it is intolerant of drought and excessive heat. Much confused in cultivation with purple-tinged variants of *M. oligostachyus* and *M. sinensis*, and

MISTY FALL WITH MISCANTHUS AND ASTER

THIS MISTY FALL scene is made up of just two plants at the peak of their display. The foamy seed heads of *Miscanthus sinensis* 'Kleine Fontäne'— a relatively short cultivar that flowers and seeds reliably in cooler climates—here insinuates its arching, downy sprays among the almost black stems of a classic fall aster, 'Calliope', whose myriads of simple daisies last for many weeks. Both perform well in any good soil in a sunny place, and can be cut back in spring to reveal a carpet of spring crocuses that will provide a delightful early display.

sometimes incorrectly called *M. sinensis* var. *purpurascens*. A hybrid of *M. oligostachyus*, perhaps with *M. sinensis*, selected by Hans Simon (Germany). ‡5 ft (1.5 m). Z5–8 H8–5

M. sacchariflorus (Amur silver grass) Vigorous plant with invasive rhizomes and upright stems carrying arching, mid-green leaves, about 1¼ in (3 cm) wide, with a prominent white central vein and topped by flowerheads of numerous erect, silvery fingers borne well above the foliage in mid-fall. Shy-flowering where summers are cool. This text refers to tetraploid selections most often seen in gardens, but a range of other genetic variants is also grown. The invasive nature of these plants limits their use, though they can be planted in landscaping to colonize large sites quickly. From wetland areas of Japan and northeastern Asia. ‡10 ft (3 m). Z8–9 H9–8

M. sinensis syn. *Eulalia japonica* (Chinese silver grass) Clump-forming, without spreading rhizomes, varying considerably in size and hardiness, its leaves are typically mid-green, ½–¾ in (1–2 cm) wide, with a prominent white midrib, and turn yellow in fall. The flowerheads are silvery, or may start mahogany, aging through pale pink, eventually turning silver or parchment, and have many fingers making a showy display. In some, the plumes emerge crimped, more or less straightening themselves out as they age. Has been the subject of a number of breeding programs intended to produce floriferous cultivars for climates with cool summers. From slopes in the mountains and lowlands of East and Southeast Asia, including Japan. ‡12 in–10 ft (30 cm to 3 m). **'Adagio'** Relatively small and erect with narrow green leaves and rather slender, upright flowerheads in late summer and early

fall. Useful for the small garden, pots and containers. From Kurt Bluemel, MD. ‡4 ft (1.2 m). Z5–8 H8–5. **'Arabesque'** Compact, with slightly pink-flushed, upright flowerheads in early fall. From Kurt Bluemel, MD. ‡1.5 m (5 ft). Z5–8 H8–5. **'China'** Narrow, olive-green foliage with large plumes emerging mahogany-red in early fall and aging through pink to silver, borne in profusion well above the leaves. Considered by Ernst Pagels (Germany) to be one of his finest. ‡5 ft (1.5 m). Z5–8 H8–5. **var. *condensatus*** Taller and more robust with thicker stems that are bluish green at the base, broader, ⅝-x-1½-in (1.5-x-4-cm) leaves—bluish green underneath and denser flowerheads. Also less hardy, but its cultivars break to the very base of the plant so are valuable as specimens. From near seashores and sometimes in mountains of Hokkaido, Honshu, Shikoku, and Kyushu, Japan and perhaps more widely in Southeast Asia. ‡8–10 ft (2.4–3 m). Z5–8 H8–5. **var. *condensatus* 'Cabaret'** Dramatic leaves, to 1¼ in (3 cm) wide, have a broad central creamy white stripe, a third of the width of the deep green leaf or a little more. The variegation can scorch in full sun. Flowering, in mid- or late fall, tends to occur only after a hot summer. One of the least hardy variegated cultivars. An old Japanese cultivar, introduced to the west and named by Kurt Bluemel, MD. ‡8 ft (2.4 m). Z5–8 H8–5. **var. *condensatus* 'Cosmopolitan'** Leaves with creamy-white edges flanking a central deep green zone with a pale central vein—similar to 'Cabaret' but with the variegation reversed. Marginally less striking than 'Cabaret', but flowering more readily in mid- and late fall and scorching less, its leaves being constantly replaced by healthy new foliage. Altogether a more satisfactory garden plant—and one of

MISCANTHUS SINENSIS 'GRACILLIMUS'

First described in 1889—and said at the time, rather fancifully, to have been found in Tahiti—*Miscanthus sinensis* 'Gracillimus' was long grown in Japan before being introduced to the west. Having been raised from seed for more than 100 years, a number of different selections are now found under this name.

Although always narrow-leaved, with a central white vein, its habit may be narrowly upright, roughly three times as tall as it is wide, with foliage tending to arch outward elegantly toward the tips. Such plants are typical of some long-established American plantings, but plants can also be dome-shaped and

rather wider than they are tall, with copper-colored flowerheads in mid-fall where summers are hot. Some selections have a mixture of rather broader and narrower leaves, giving them a slightly untidy appearance, and some are inclined to flop, especially if grown in fertile soil or shade.

In utilitarian landscape situations, this variability may not be a problem. However, in gardens where dependability of form is more important, gardeners should perhaps look to *M. sinensis* 'Sarabande,' or variegated *M. sinensis* 'Morning Light' when a fine-leaved cultivar is required.

the best variegated cultivars—it retains its foliage late into fall. Found in the 1940s by Toyoichi Aoki of Tokyo and named by Kurt Bluemel, MD. ‡8 ft (2.4 m). Z5–8 H8–5. **var. *condensatus* 'Cosmo Revert'** syn. var. *condensatus* 'Central Park', var. *condensatus* 'Emerald Giant' Dramatic, with bold, vibrant green leaves down to ground level that retain their color well into fall, and large, dense plumes, although these are produced very rarely in areas with cool summers. A plain green reversion from 'Cosmopolitan' but propagated vegetatively so dependably uniform. ‡10 ft (3 m). Z5–8 H8–5. **'Dixieland'** Dramatically variegated with longitudinal creamy white stripes and reddish flowerheads in early fall. Similar to 'Variegatus' but freer-flowering, a little more compact, and with less arching leaves. From Kurt Bluemel, MD. ‡6 ft (1.8 m). Z5–8 H8–5. **'Ferner Osten'** Slim, olive-green foliage turning rich orange in fall, the plentiful large, arching flowerheads, borne in late summer well above the foliage, aging from mahogany through pink to silver. Very like 'China' but with wider leaves

and a white tip to each branch of the plume. From Ernst Pagels (Germany). ‡5½ ft (1.6 m). Z5–8 H8–5. **'Flamingo'** Foliage with a pronounced white midrib, turning golden-orange in fall, topped by large, loosely arching plumes emerging pink-flushed in late summer, later becoming fluffy and silver. From Ernst Pagels (Germany). ‡5½ ft (1.6 m). **'Gearmella'** Relatively short with arching plumes emerging pink-tinted in early fall, aging to silver and borne well above the foliage. From Ernst Pagels (Germany). ‡3½ ft (1.1 m). **'Gewitterwolke'** Big, beefy, narrowly upright plant with broad leaves, turning orange in fall, and dense flowerheads combining vinous purple and silver and appearing in late summer. Dramatic, but with a slightly "trussed up" look and rather congested plumes sometimes hidden in the foliage. From Ernst Pagels (Germany). ‡6 ft (1.8 m). **'Ghana'** An upright plant with

---

BELOW 1 *Miscanthus sinensis* 'Kaskade' **2** *M. sinensis* 'Rotsilber' **3** *M. sinensis* 'Silberfeder'

cascading leaves and feathery flowerheads emerging erect and tinged red in early fall. Its chief glory is its rich russet fall color. From Ernst Pagels (Germany). ↕6 ft (1.8 m). **'Giraffe'** Leaves with transverse bands of yellow variegation and silvery plumes emerging in early fall. Flowers are held well above the leaves. Foliage is less stiff than 'Strictus', but not as arching as 'Zebrinus', on a plant taller than either. From Ernst Pagels (Germany). ↕8 ft (2.4 m). **'Goldfeder'** Broad leaves with longitudinal gold variegation, rare in *Miscanthus*, and flowering freely in early fall, but inclined to be rather lax. A spontaneous mutation of 'Silberfeder' found in the 1950s by Hans Simon (Germany). ↕6 ft (1.8 m). **'Gold und Silber'** Compact, tidy plant—its foliage has faint transverse banding and blotching and turns golden-orange in fall. Brown-red plumes emerge in late summer, hung with myriad golden anthers like dewdrops. One of the best for small gardens. From Austria. ↕4½ ft (1.4 m). **'Goliath'** Handsome, its broad leaves have a prominent white central vein. Rich mahogany flowerheads are borne well above the leaves in early fall. From Ernst Pagels (Germany). ↕8 ft (2.4 m). **'Gracillimus'** syn. *M. sinensis* var. *gracillimus*, *Eulalia gracillima* (Maiden grass) Variable but always with relatively narrow leaves with a central white vein and brownish pink flowers in late fall (where summers are cool) scarcely overtopping the leaves—many of them buried in the foliage. Rarely flowers in climates with cool summers. Its habit may vary greatly (*see* Miscanthus Sinensis 'Gracillimus', *p.332*) but the narrow foliage gives all variants a subdued grace. ↕7 ft (2.2 m). **'Graziella'** Large, silvery flowerheads are borne well above the foliage in early fall, becoming shining white before aging to beige. The leaves turn orange in fall. From Ernst Pagels (Germany). ↕5 ft (1.5 m). **'Grosse Fontäne'** Very long, arching leaves that acquire richly varied fall colorings of reds, purples, oranges, and greens. The airy and elegant flowerheads, held well above the foliage, are rich pink at first, becoming silver. From Ernst Pagels (Germany). ↕8 ft (2.4 m). **'Kaskade'** Narrow foliage, with a pronounced central white vein, turns rich coppery-red in fall. Its cascading plumes, emerging silky and rich rose-pink in late summer, are borne well above the foliage, and age to silvery-beige. From Ernst Pagels (Germany). ↕6 ft (1.9 m). **'Kleine Fontäne'** Prolific and compact, the narrow leaves with white midribs turn golden-yellow in fall. A spectacular display of gracefully drooping red plumes in late summer quickly turns fluffy silver. From Ernst Pagels (Germany). ↕5½ ft (1.6 m). **'Kleine Silberspinne'** Neat and elegant, narrow dark green leaves with a white midrib turn to a blend of red, orange, and gold in fall. Upright flowerheads, borne on bright green stems, emerge dusky rose in late summer, turning fluffy and brown when mature. Good for the small garden, it remains attractive into winter. From Ernst Pagels (Germany). ↕4 ft (1.2 m). **'Little Kitten'** Very

narrow foliage and erect, light brown flowerheads in late summer. One of the smallest and neatest cultivars, similar in size to the later-flowering 'Yakushima Dwarf', though its blooms do not shine. Useful for pots and the small garden. From Greg Speichert, IN. ↕32 in (80 cm). Z5–8 H8–5. **Little Nicky** (**'Hinjo'**) Long, fairly broad, yellow-banded leaves curve down to touch the ground, making a mound about 3¼ ft (1 m) high; the creamy-yellow crossbands can scorch badly in sun, so grow in some shade. Upright stems carry flowerheads in early fall, though they are rarely produced where summers are cool. Suitable for containers and for small gardens. Like the other cross-banded cultivars—'Strictus' and 'Zebrinus'—but smaller. ↕6 ft (1.8 m). **'Malepartus'** The plumes, produced dependably in profusion in late summer even in cool summers, emerge reddish and mature to fluffy white above mid-green foliage that turns orange and gold in fall. Slightly untidy, and some stems may lean. This has long been regarded as a yardstick among modern hybrids, but has perhaps now been superseded. From Ernst Pagels (Germany). ↕6½ ft (2 m). **'Morning Light'** Outstandingly elegant and useful. The foliage, with its clean white margins, arches out at the top so that young plants in particular are broader above than below. Reddish flowerheads in mid-fall, although not where summers are cool. A century-old variegated sport of 'Gracillimus' from Japan, named by Kurt Bluemel, MD. ↕6 ft (1.8 m). **'Nippon'** Narrowly upright with erect flowerheads emerging pinkish in late summer before becoming silvery. The green leaves often take on attractive orange-red tints in fall. From Ernst Pagels (Germany). ↕5 ft (1.5 m). **'Pünktchen'** Cross-banded foliage produces its creamy-yellow markings rather late but compensates by its generous display of reddish plumes in mid-fall, even where summers are cool. Its foliage is intermediate in stiffness—between 'Strictus' and 'Zebrinus'—and its bands are spaced rather farther apart. From Ernst Pagels (Germany). ↕7 ft (2.2 m). **'Roland'** Big, broad leaves with a plentiful display of flowerheads emerging light pink and crimped in late summer, unfurling as they age to silver, giving a bold but tousled effect. From Ernst Pagels (Germany). 8¼ ft (2.6 m). **'Rotfuchs'** Narrow, dark green leaves tinged purple, followed by red fall color. Elegant, mahogany plumes emerge in late summer, becoming silvery with age. ↕6½ ft (2 m). **'Rotsilber'** Leaves with a pronounced white midrib, turn coppery-red in fall. Narrow, erect purple-pink plumes are produced in early fall, aging to grayish brown and held into winter. The stems have a slight tendency to flop. From Ernst Pagels (Germany). ↕6½ ft (2 m). **'Sarabande'** Upright plant, though tending to sprawl by late fall; the very narrow leaves have a marked white midrib. The erect, plentiful, coppery-brown flowerheads are produced in early fall. From Kurt Bluemel, MD. ↕6½ ft (2 m). **'Septemberrot'** Bold,

broad leaves, with a bright white midrib, turn orange and then copper in fall. Graceful, upright heads of mahogany-red flowers appear in early fall. One of the best cultivars for late-season color but can collapse before the display is over. ↕8 ft (2.4 m). **'Silberfeder'** Long popular for its absolutely regular and copious flowering even where summers are cool. Silver plumes emerge in late summer above broad green leaves and remain attractive for months, though they can be flattened by fall gales. Still a valuable cultivar; selected at the Munich Botanic Garden by Hans Simon in the early 1950s. ↕8 ft (2.4 m). **'Silberspinne'** Narrow, dark green leaves with a white midrib turn fiery shades in fall but, unlike the similar, slightly shorter 'Kleine Silberspinne' are held out at right angles to the stems. Erect plumes with reddish fingers emerge in early fall, becoming fluffy and silver as the blooms age. From Ernst Pagels (Germany). ↕4½ ft (1.4 m). **'Sioux'** Red-tinged foliage turns rich orange to red in fall, and narrow, nodding, reddish flowerheads are rather sparsely borne at varying heights in early fall. From Ernst Pagels (Germany). ↕3½ ft (1.1 m). **'Sirene'** Superlative early-flowering selection with proportionately very large flowerheads emerging mahogany in early fall, their spreading fingers drooping gracefully and becoming fluffy silver as they mature. Its movement in the slightest breeze gives it extra vitality. From Ernst Pagels (Germany). ↕4 ft (1.2 m). **'Strictus'** (Porcupine grass) Outstanding upright plant with yellow crossbands to the foliage but differing from 'Zebrinus' and other similar selections in having straight, upward-pointing leaves that do not generally arch or kink, giving a pronounced spiky effect. Crinkly plumes emerge in mid-fall. Its narrow habit allows it to be grown in closely planted borders. ↕6½ ft (2 m). **'Undine'** Tall and elegant with green leaves that arch gracefully toward the ground and turn to shades of orange and straw-yellow in fall, remaining attractive into the winter. The upright flowerheads emerge tinged red in late summer and age to rosy-beige. From Ernst Pagels (Germany). ↕6½ ft (2 m). Z5–8 H8–5. **'Variegatus'** syn. *Eulalia japonica* var. *variegata* Distinct in its bright white longitudinal stripes, which make this one of the showiest for foliage effect. Through the season, the clump builds up into an impressive fountain of foliage 5½ ft (1.6 m) high, though it may flop by fall. Crinkly reddish flowerheads emerge in early fall, but it is shy-flowering where summers are cool. Long cultivated in Japan and introduced to Europe in about 1873. Several similar selections are now grown under this name. ↕7 ft (2.1 m). Z5–8 H8–5. **'Vorläufer'** As its name, meaning "forerunner," suggests, this is one of the earliest to flower. Its bright green, downward-arching leaves

RIGHT **1** *Miscanthus sinensis* 'Variegatus'
2 *M. sinensis* 'Yakushima Dwarf'
3 *M. sinensis* 'Zebrinus'

DEVELOPMENTS IN MISCANTHUS

Until the 1960s, there were few *Miscanthus* cultivars, and only *M. sinensis* 'Silberfeder' could be relied upon to flower in areas with cool summers. By the late 1950s, Ernst Pagels in Germany had realized both the potential of the species and its shortcomings, and started to raise hybrids from the few cultivars that were available at the time, including the early-flowering 'Gracillimus', forced to produce its coppery blooms under glass, and 'Silberfeder'.

The impressive range of cultivars currently available includes dozens raised by Pagels, with some of his earlier hybrids already superseded by his more recent introductions. Paradoxically, the earlier, more prolific flowering of the new hybrids has meant that they are now considered a weed threat in certain areas of North America where the plain species would not be invasive. Kurt Bluemel, of Maryland, has also raised and introduced new cultivars, and named cultivars imported from Japan. Cultivars' country of origin is given where known.

turn yellow in fall, and red flowerheads emerge red in late summer, developing into silvery plumes. From Ernst Pagels (Germany). ‡4½ ft (1.4 m).

'Yakushima Dwarf' Very compact, the narrow foliage and upright, buff plumes emerging in mid-fall make it ideal for pots and containers. About the same height as 'Little Kitten' but showier. ‡32 in (80 cm). Z5–8 H8–5.

'Zebrinus' syn. *Miscanthus zebrinus, Eulalia japonica* var. *zebrina* (Zebra grass) Crossbanded selection; the bands across the leaves are pale creamy-yellow, and silvery-buff, upright flowerheads emerge in mid-fall. Much confused

with 'Strictus', but differs in having leaves that arch gently outward and are not stiff, making a wider, less erect clump. Long grown in Japan; introduced into Europe in 1877. ‡7 ft (2.2 m). Z6

M. transmorrisonensis (Taiwanese miscanthus, Evergreen miscanthus.) Broadly arching, dark evergreen leaves, and flowerheads, borne well above the foliage, that emerge over several months so they appear at different stages of development, the light brown, many-fingered, new blooms intermixing with the older, fluffy, buff plumes. Makes a wide clump and is a great boon for winter effect. The evergreen foliage can make plants look ragged if left—but if clumps are cut back in mid-spring, flowering will be delayed until late summer (though this is perhaps the best option). Introduced into cultivation in the west from Mount Daxue in Taiwan at an elevation of 9,425-ft (2,900-m), hence its relative hardiness. ‡7 ft (2.2 m). Z6–10 H10–6

M. zebrinus see *M. sinensis* 'Zebrinus'

MITELLA
Miterwort
SAXIFRAGACEAE

Quiet shade-lovers making intriguing ground cover that meanders among shrubs and chunkier perennials.

About 12 species of demure woodlanders from North America and East Asia, of which only a few are grown. Evergreen, long-stemmed, medium to dark green, heart-shaped, hairy leaves, 2–2½ in (5–6 cm) wide, make a basal clump from which, in summer, rise slim, often one-sided, spikes of very small flowers—the finely cut petals make each flower resemble a snowflake. Similar to *Tiarella*, but differing in the flower structure. They are

graceful plants but not very showy, best used in drifts along woodland paths or in shady rock gardens.

CULTIVATION Best in moist shade in a humus-rich soil.

PROPAGATION From seed or by division.

PROBLEMS Usually trouble-free.

M. breweri Rounded, 1¼-x-3-in (3-x-8-cm) leaves, with seven to eleven gentle lobes, make a loose clump about 8 in (20 cm) wide and 4 in (10 cm) high. In summer, small yellow-green flowers, that open from the bottom up, are carried in thin spikes on leafless stems. From the mountains of western North America. ‡10 in (25 cm). Z5–7 H7–5

M. caulescens Rounded, ¾-x-2¾-in (2-x-7-cm) leaves, with three to seven lobes, make a tuft, 8 in (20 cm) wide by 4 in (10 cm) high, through which emerge stems carrying two or three leaves and small yellow-green flowers opening from the top down. From the mountains of western North America. ‡10 in (25 cm) Z5–7 H7–5

MOLINIA
Moor grass
POACEAE

Elegant and valuable late-flowering grasses with tall, arching sprays of flowers, for damp acidic soil.

Two to four perennial species found on wet moorlands and heaths throughout Europe to western Russia, and east to Japan, only one of which is generally grown. A clump-forming grass with a dense root system and green, pointed deciduous leaves; the flower stems are swollen at the base and appear

late in the summer. They carry wiry branches of swaying airy cords of purple-green flowers hung with purple stamens. This handsome grass looks splendid moving in the wind, especially in a herbaceous border of late summer flowers, or in a wildflower or prairie-type garden. Later the foliage provides a short bonfirelike display of fall color.

Until recently, *M. caerulea* has been divided into two subspecies: subsp. *arundinacea* and subsp. *caerulea*. However, recent research at Kew has determined that these subspecies are not as distinct as previously thought. The two types grow together in the wild and the increased vigor of some plants, previously separated as subsp. *arundinacea*, is now seen to be the result of growing in unusually moist, fertile pockets of soil, while subsp. *caerulea* is found growing on the drier edges of the same boglands. The difference in appearance is now understood to be no more than the result of different growing conditions. This change is reflected here—all cultivars are grouped under *M. caerulea*.

CULTIVATION Plant in an open position in well-drained, fertile, neutral to acidic soil and provide plenty of water in hot, dry periods.

PROPAGATION From seed or by division. Divide cultivars and varieties. Difficult to divide because of the density of the root system, and slow to reestablish.

PROBLEMS Usually trouble-free.

M. caerulea (Purple moor grass, Purple melick) Compact tussocks, with dense, tough root systems, slowly build up in height. The leaves, which are completely deciduous, emerge from bright yellow shoots turning green. They are long, flat, and finely pointed, ⅛–½ in (3–10 mm) wide, and turn yellow to orange and red in fall. In late summer to early fall, tall, somewhat arching flower stems end in narrow, beady, purple-green flowerheads hung with purple stamens. Magnificent when grown in large groups or drifts, and taller cultivars look spectacular when backlit at night. Grows in acidic peat bogs, moorlands, and overgrazed pasture throughout Europe, through to Siberia, and introduced to the US where populations can be found in a few scattered states. ‡3¼ ft (1 m). Z5–9 H9–1. **'Bergfreund'** Leaves turning yellow in fall, shiny purple-green, airy flowerheads.‡5½ ft (1.7 m). **'Carmarthen'** Pale green leaves striped cream-yellow; gold-brown narrow flower spikes. **'Claerwen'** Yellow-cream striped leaves; dark green-purple narrow flower spikes. **'Edith Dudszus'** Green leaves, red-purple stems, and dark purple-brown flower spikes ‡24 in (60 cm). **'Fontäne'**

LEFT 1 *Mitella breweri* **2** *Molinia caerulea* 'Edith Dudszus' **3** *Molina caerulea* 'Moorhexe'

Arching purple flowerheads, yellow fall foliage. ↕6–6½ ft (1.8–2 m). **'Heidebraut'** Upright to arching flower stems with narrow pale purple flower spikes ↕4 ft (1.2 m). **'Karl Foerster'** Arching foliage; airy green to dark purple flowerheads on erect stems ↕7 ft (2.2 m). **'Moorhexe'** Erect foliage; dense narrow purple-green flowerheads ↕20 in (50 cm). **'Skyracer'** Broad leaves, gold in fall, and tall stiff flower stems with airy sparse flowerheads. ↕4–8 ft (1.2–2.4 m). **'Strahlenquelle'** Wide sprays of leaves and stems arching over with blue-green to purple flowers. ↕24–39 in (60 –100 cm). **'Transparent'** Yellow fall foliage; airy wide-spaced flowerheads. ↕6½ ft (2 m). **'Windspiel'** Yellow fall foliage; swaying golden-brown flowerheads ↕6½ ft (2 m). **'Variegata'** Erect yellow and cream striped leaves with yellow-green narrow flowerheads ↕18 in (45 cm).

MONARDA

Beebalm, Bergamot, Horsemint
LAMIACEAE

Bright, scented flowers and aromatic foliage for the summer garden, but beware of mildew.

About 15 species of annuals and perennials native to North America are found in scrub, prairie, and woodlands, mostly on the eastern side of the continent. The square stems carry opposite pairs of generally toothed, lance-shaped to oval leaves that may have a purplish tinge. Flowerheads, appearing from midsummer into fall, are in terminal clusters around a central disk, and the individual blooms are tubular with a hooded upper petal and a three-lobed lower one. The heads of flowers may be sitting on brightly colored bracts, which add to the display, are a good source of pollen and nectar, and are very attractive to bees, butterflies, and hummingbirds.

Plants increase by underground stems and can colonize a large area if not divided every two to three years. Keeping the clumps small also helps control mildew, by allowing more air movement through the plant. They are known as bergamots because their foliage, when crushed, smells like the bergamot orange (*Citrus bergamia*) which gives Earl Grey tea its distinctive flavor.

Many cultivars have been listed as forms of *M. didyma*. However, most are now considered hybrids and are listed individually. There has been some confusion over the cultivars from Dutch breeder Piet Oudolf, named for the signs of the zodiac—they are correct as given here, but some, for example 'Fishes', in translation of the more familiar Pisces and some, like 'Aquarius', given in their usual form.

CULTIVATION Grow in moderately moist soil in full sun where summers are cool, or in dappled shade where they are hot. Do not allow plants to dry out in summer but protect from excessive winter moisture.

TWO-TONE HARMONIES

OLD AND NEW come together in this interesting pairing, both perennials featuring pale and dark shades of the same color. *Monarda* 'Beauty of Cobham' is an old favorite, its broad purple bracts with pinkish highlights setting off heads of arching pale pink flowers. Behind is the first of the modern verbascums, 'Helen Johnson', with its almost brick-colored flowers, aging paler. Peeping through are a few pink flowers from a bedding nicotiana slipped between the two perennials in late spring to provide a consistency of bright, clear color all through the summer.

PROPAGATION Grow species from seed in spring, and species and cultivars by division or cuttings in early spring.

PROBLEMS Very prone to powdery mildew. Some wild individuals, and some cultivars, are at least partially resistant, although the resistance of the plant may breakdown as the mildew mutates. (*see* Powdery Mildew, *p. 336*) Occasionally rust may be a problem.

M. **'Adam'** A good cherry-red, the bracts have a purple tinge. It is less bright than 'Cambridge Scarlet' or 'Gardenview Scarlet'. The plant flowers from midsummer onward. ↕36 in (90 cm). Z4–9 H9–1

M. **'Aquarius'** Pale purple-pink flowers with green, purple-tinged bracts and bronzy foliage. Partially mildew-resistant. ↕4 ft (1.2 m). Z4–9 H9–1

M. **'Balance'** (**Libra**) Bright pink flowers over purplish bracts and it is slightly taller than many. ↕3½ ft (1.1 m). Z4–9 H9–1

M. **'Beauty of Cobham'** Pale pink with slightly purple bracts and the leaves often tinged with purple. ↕3½ ft (1.1 m). Z4–9 H9–1

M. **'Blaustrumpf'** (**Blue Stocking**) Deep violet flowers over purple bracts. Partially mildew-resistant. ↕36 in (90 cm). Z4–8 H8–1

M. **'Cambridge Scarlet'** Bright red. An old variety introduced early in the 1900s and for many years the brightest red. Now often raised from seed, so it is highly variable in color, and also prone to mildew. ↕32–36 in (80–90 cm). Z3–9 H9–1

M. **'Capricorn'** Clear pink flowers over dark bracts and purple-tinged leaves. At least partially mildew-resistant. ↕4 ft (1.2 m). Z4–9 H9–1

M. citriodora (Lemon bee balm) Short-lived perennial—or annual or biennial—with narrow, lance-shaped, slightly toothed leaves smelling of lemons when crushed, and carried in clusters around the stem; they were used by the indigenous peoples to flavor meats and also as a tea. White to pink flowers, ¾ in (2 cm) long and spotted with purple, are carried in two 1½-in (3.5-cm) clusters, one above the other. Native to the southern US, and northern Mexico. ↕24 in (60 cm). Z5–9 H9–2. **subsp.** *austromontana* Lilac with a slightly blue tinge. From New Mexico and Arizona.

M. **'Comanche'** Pale lilac-pink with rusty-brown bracts over slightly bronzed foliage. Taller than most pinks and partially resistant to mildew. One of a number of generally taller selections by Piet Oudolf in Holland; originally intended as cut flowers, they were given American Indian names. ↕4½ ft (1.3 m). Z4–9 H9–1

M. **'Croftway Pink'** Rose-pink flowers, slightly darker than 'Beauty of Cobham'. It is an older variety from 1932; prone to mildew. ↕3½–4 ft (1.1–1.2 m). Z4–9 H9–1

M. **'didyma'** (Bee balm, Bergamot, Oswego tea) Forms strongly spreading clumps; square, upright, branching stems carry sharply pointed, toothed, egg-shaped leaves, to 4 in (10 cm) long, on short stalks with soft hairs below. They have the characteristic bergamot flavor. From midsummer on, two flower clusters sit one above the other, each 1¼–1¾ in (3–4.5 cm), bright red flower opening over red-tinged bracts. Grows poorly in hot dry summers and

LEFT 1 *Monarda* 'Aquarius' **2** *M.* 'Beauty of Cobham' **3** *M.* 'Cambridge Scarlet' **4** *M.* 'Fishes' **5** *M. fistulosa*

susceptible to mildew when allowed to dry out. First collected by American botanist John Bartram, near Oswego, NY. Found on streambanks under branches from New England south to Georgia and Tennessee. ‡ 36 in (90 cm). Z4–10 H10–1

M. 'Elsie's Lavender' Soft-lavender-colored blooms that are slightly more blue in color than 'Aquarius'. ‡ 3¼ ft (1 m). Z4–9 H9–1

M. 'Fishes' (**Pisces**) Pale pink flowers, with green throats and pale green bracts make this a very distinctive variety. It is prone to mildew. ‡ 4 ft (1.2 m). Z4–9 H9–1

M. fistulosa (Wild bee balm, Wild bergamot) Vigorous, bushy clump-former; the slightly rounded stems carry more or less egg-shaped, slightly or un-toothed, softly hairy 1½–4-in (4–10-cm) leaves, and sometimes a single cluster of flowers—or sometimes two or three—one above the other. The flowers, 1¼ in (3 cm) long, range from lavender to white and emerge from a purple-tipped calyx. Tolerant of dryer conditions than *M. didyma*, less prone to mildew, and comes into bloom a little later. Native to North America from Quebec to Texas and Arizona. ‡ 4 ft (1.2 m). Z3–9 H9–1

'Gardenview Scarlet' Bright red, slightly brighter than 'Cambridge Scarlet', with pale green, pink-tipped bracts, which bronze after flowering, and distinct in its vigor and its better mildew resistance. A modern introduction from Henry Ross at Gardenview Park in Strongsville, OH. Rarely raised from seed, so dependably good. ‡ 36 in (90 cm). Z4–9 H9–1

M. Gemini see *M.* 'Twins'

M. 'Jacob Cline' The large heads of dark red flowers and bracts sit over dark green foliage. It is partially mildew-resistant and rust-resistant. ‡ 36 in (90 cm). Z4–9 H9–1

M. Libra see *M.* 'Balance'

M. 'Loddon Crown' Dark reddish purple flowers and purple bracts. ‡ 36 in (90 cm). Z4–8 H8–1

M. 'Mahogany' Very dark wine-red blooms above almost brown bracts. ‡ 36 in (90 cm). Z3–9 H9–1

M. 'Marshall's Delight' Bright pink flowers; shiny, light green foliage. A Canadian introduction quite resistant to mildew. 36 in (90 cm). Z4–9 H9–1

M. 'Mohawk' Light mauve with darker mauve bracts and bronzy foliage. ‡ 36 in (90 cm). Z4–9 H9–1

M. 'Ou Charm' Short plant with pink flowers over dark maroon bracts. Prone to mildew and rather fleeting. ‡ 16 in (40 cm). Z4–9 H9–1

M. Panorama Hybrids Unpredictable seed-raised mix in shades of red, pink, and salmon. ‡ 36 in (90 cm). Z4–9 H9–1

M. 'Petite Delight' Dwarf, with lavender-rose flowers and excellent mildew resistance. ‡ 24 in (60 cm). Z4–9 H9–1

M. 'Petite Wonder' Dwarf, with bright, clear pink flowers on rounded plants. Excellent mildew-resistance. ‡ 24 in (60 cm). Z4–9 H9–1

M. Pisces see *M.* 'Fishes'

M. 'Prärienacht' (**Prairie Night**) Dark lilac flowers and reddish bracts. The plant is partially mildew-resistant. Introduced in 1955 in Germany. ‡ 36 in (90 cm). Z4–9 H9–1

M. punctata (Dotted horsemint, Spotted

POWDERY MILDEW

The big issue with monardas is powdery mildew. This disfiguring disease is caused by *Erysiphe cichoracearum*—different strains of which attack brassicas as well as *Phlox paniculata* cultivars. Although the problem can to some extent be controlled by repeated spraying, this is hardly ideal; resistant cultivars would seem to provide a more acceptable route to combating the disease. Unfortunately, it is not quite that simple.

A number of cultivars have been introduced that are said to be resistant, and trials have taken place in various gardens in an attempt to establish which are the most reliable. But the severity of infection is influenced by a wide range of factors, so a cultivar that seems resistant in one location—and in one or two seasons—may be susceptible in other circumstances.

These factors include climate, weather, irrigation regimen, soil fertility, extent, density of planting, exposure, and the strain of mildew present. In particular, it is worth noting that mildew is an adaptable disease, and small mutations can overcome resistance in cultivars previously known to be mildew-free.

The result is that a particular cultivar may prove consistently resistant in one area for some time but not elsewhere—or in some seasons but not others—but that this resistance may break down. It is also worth noting that even the cultivars noted in one trial as "highly resistant" nevertheless experience 40–50 percent defoliation.

One approach that sometimes works well, but is not often tried, is to treat monardas as "annuals." Plants are raised from spring cuttings, are kept growing strongly, and are then planted out for a single season in an open situation and kept consistently moist. There is evidence that the vigor of such plants reduces the incidence of mildew—whatever the cultivar.

bee balm) Slightly downy, compact, with lance-shaped to oblong, slightly or untoothed leaves to 3½ in (9 cm) long. Pale pink flowers, ¾ in (2 cm) wide, liberally dotted with small, dark red spots, sit in two or more showy clusters of long pink bracts, and open from midsummer onward if deadheaded. Less invasive than most bergamots. Native in well-drained woods in sandy soil from Minnesota to Florida and New Mexico. ‡36 in (90 cm). Z4–9 H9–2

M. 'Raspberry Wine' Dull red flowers over a very long period and partially disease-resistant. Sent to White Flower Farm nursery in Connecticut by a customer. ‡32 in (80 cm). Z4–9 H9–1

M. 'Ruby Glow' Bright red flowers atop large red-tinged bracts. 36 in (90 cm). Z4–9 H9–1

M. 'Sagittarius' Very pale pink flowers that are darker at their base. Prone to mildew. ‡36 in (90 cm). Z4–9 H9–1

M. 'Schneewittchen' (**Snow White**) syn. 'Snow Maiden' White, and one of the best of that color, but often sold under several different translated names. An introduction by the great German horticulturist Karl Foerster. ‡36 in (90 cm). Z4–9 H9–1

M. 'Scorpion' Purple flowers with a tinge of red above very dark purple bracts. ‡4 ft (1.2 m). Z4–9 H9–1

M. 'Sioux' Very pale pink with leaves that have a slight purple tinge. Prone to mildew. ‡36 in (90 cm). Z4–9 H9–1

M. 'Snow Queen' White with a just a faint blush of pink. ‡36 in (90 cm). Z4–9 H9–1

M. 'Snow Maiden' see M. 'Schneewittchen'

M. Snow White see M. 'Schneewittchen'

M. 'Squaw' Scarlet flowers above dark bracts and yellow-green foliage on pale green stems. Good mildew resistance. ‡4 ft (1.2 m). Z4–9 H9–1

M. 'Twins' (**Gemini**) Pink flowers that have some mildew resistance. ‡36 in (90 cm). Z4–9 H9–1

M. 'Vintage Wine' Smaller plant. Maroon flowers over red bracts. Prone to mildew. ‡30 in (75 cm). Z4–9 H9–1

M. 'Violet Queen' Bright violet flowers over dull purple bracts; purple tinged foliage. ‡36 in (90 cm). Z4–9 H9–1

MONARDELLA
LAMIACEAE

Small, colorful, aromatic, very drought-resistant plants suitable for Mediterranean and dry gardens.

Nineteen species of annuals and perennials from mainly dry, open situations in western North America, only one is usually grown; many are very local in their distribution and particular in their soil requirements. Upright, usually square, stems carry small, oppositely arranged, lance- or diamond-shaped usually aromatic leaves. Spherical clusters of flowers, often surrounded by purplish, leaf-like bracts, are carried at the tips of the shoots; each flower is two-lipped, the lower lip split in three, the upper split into two. Very similar to Monarda, but generally smaller and more difficult to grow, and the upper lip of the flowers of Monarda are not split.

CULTIVATION Grow in poor, well-drained soil in full sun. Protect from winter rain.

PROPAGATION From seed, by division or basal cuttings.

PROBLEMS Rust, whitefly.

M. odoratissima (Western pennyroyal) Usually upright, the tall stems are gray and woolly, while the leaves are lance-shaped with very short stalks and have a minty fragrance. The 1¼-in (3-cm) heads of flowers appear in mid- to late summer and their color ranges from rose-pink to almost white. They were used for a tea and as a cold cure by the native peoples. Native to higher altitudes in the western US. ‡4–24 in (10–60 cm). Z5–10 H10–5

MONTBRETIA see CROCOSMIA

MORINA
MORINACEAE

Hardy, thistlelike plants making a dramatic statement in the border or gravel garden.

Seven or more evergreen species growing naturally in open situations, especially rocky areas and grassy slopes, in eastern Europe, Turkey to Central Asia, the Himalaya, and southwestern China. In summer, from evergreen rosettes of spiny, lance-shaped leaves, arise stems bearing pink, red, white, or yellow, tubular, five-lobed flowers arranged in whorled clusters around the stem and protected by spiny bracts (modified leaves). Their spiny texture contrasts well with smoother plants in mixed borders or gravel gardens.

CULTIVATION Best in very well-drained soil and full sun. Growth will be unduly lush in rich soil. Plants dislike disturbance.

PROPAGATION From seed, but avoid root disturbance later.

PROBLEMS Slugs and snails.

M. longifolia Rosette-forming plant with shiny, wavy-edged, or deeply cut dark green leaves to 12 in (30 cm). In midsummer, 1¼-in- (3-cm-) long white flowers appear, turning pale pink aging to bright crimson Suitable for moist soil, which must still be very well drained. From the Himalaya. ‡36 in

(90 cm). Z6–9 H9–6

M. persica Rosette-forming plant with dark green, toothed or deeply cut, very spiny 8-in (20-cm) leaves. Yellow-throated white, flowers, 1¼ in (3 cm) long, are freely produced during midsummer and late summer, and turn deep pink as they age. From the Balkan Peninsula. ‡12–36 in (30–90 cm). Z5–9 H9–5

MUHLENBERGIA
Muhly
POACEAE

Drought-tolerant grasses from the American prairies to the Mexican deserts.

Some 160 annual and perennial species found on dry, open grasslands and desert scrub, mainly in subtropical and warm temperate regions of the US and Mexico, with a few in South Asia. Foliage varies considerably in the different species, and the similarities can be seen in the flowers only when highly magnified—not much help to most gardeners. Leaves can be long and arching, or shrublike on branched stems; the flowers are either long, narrow spikes or smokelike clouds and are often shades of purple, or even pink, fading to buff or white. All are drought-tolerant and reasonably hardy despite coming from very warm regions. They make highly decorative plants for hot, dry areas, especially when grown in drifts.

CULTIVATION Plant in very well-drained, reasonably fertile soil improved with sand or grit if needed, in full sun in an open position.

PROPAGATION From seed or by division; by division only for cultivars. These are warm-season plants and should not be divided or

ABOVE **1** *Monardella odoratissima* **2** *Morina longifolia*

replanted until late spring.

PROBLEMS Usually trouble-free.

M. capillaris (Pink hair grass). Tufts of flat to inrolled, glossy dark green foliage; leaves, to 14 in (35 cm) long, taper to fine points. Flower stems are a bit taller, topped in fall by an ethereal pink-purple haze of open branches hung with tiny flowers with bristles, to ⅜ in (15 mm) long, fading to smoky-gray seed-heads. Spectacular in fall when grown in drifts, but in cold weather the flowers may not open fully. Grow in full sun; tolerates some shade. Native to open rocky woods, prairies, and pastures in the central and eastern US, and Mexico. ‡16–40 in (40–100 cm). Z7–10 H10–7

M. japonica 'Cream Delight' Loose mats of leaves dying back over winter, new leaf shoots grow to 12 in (20 cm) high before arching over to trail along the ground, sometimes rooting into the soil. Leaves are narrow and pointed, to ½ in (4 mm) wide with white margins and very thin, creamy-white to yellow vertical stripes. In late summer to mid-fall, flower stems grow high above the foliage with small, soft, dense, silvery-green plumes, 2¾–6 in (7–15 cm) long and tinged with purple. A beautiful ground cover for dry, open woodlands or as underplanting for shrubs in fertile soil. The original wild species grows in woods, fields, and roadsides. From Japan, China, and Korea. ‡6–20 in (15–50 cm) Z7–10 H10–7

M. mexicana Slowly spreading clumps of thin gray-green leaves, 6 in (15 cm) long and ¼ in (6 mm) wide, die back over winter. In midsummer to early fall, tall, branched, leafy flower stems carry shiny purple-green hairy plumes up to 6 in (15 cm) long. Grow in drifts

in a prairie-type garden, or near the edges of paths in moisture-retentive soil. Found in moist to wet soil by rivers and ponds, and in drier areas, from Canada to Mexico. ↕16–40 in (40–100 cm). Z4–7 H7–4

M. rigens (Deer grass) Arching, inrolled, dark gray-green leaves, ⅜ in (8 mm) wide, form evergreen clumps up to 14 in (35 cm) high, which turn buff-colored in the winter. In late summer, tall vertical stems end in whippy, narrow, silver-gray flowerheads, which mature to pale gold and hold upright over winter. Needs good drainage and humus-enriched soil, but is also drought-tolerant. Good as an accent plant in hard landscapes against walls and buildings where its gently arching stems will be emphasized. A native of dry open hillsides, moist gullies, and open woodlands in Arizona and Mexico. ↕28–72 in (70–180 cm). Z7–10 H10–7

MUKDENIA

SAXIFRAGACEAE

Quietly elegant woodlanders grown for their handsome leaves and small white flowers.

Two species of deciduous plants growing in mountain forests in northern China, Korea, and Manchuria. One of which is increasingly cultivated. Slowly spreading rhizomes form a clump of broad, nicely lobed leaves, providing a good backdrop for the compact sprays of tiny, white,

five-petaled flowers in spring. Well-suited to an informal planting in moist shade.

CULTIVATION Optimum growth occurs in full or part-shade, in well-drained but moist, humus-rich soil.

PROPAGATION By division in spring, or from seed.

PROBLEMS Slugs and snails.

M. rossii syn. *Aceriphyllum rossii* A short rhizome supports a clump of long-stalked, bronze-tinged leaves to 6 in (15 cm) across, divided maple-fashion into seven or nine lobes. In late spring, small, bell-shaped, white flowers, ¼ in (5 mm) across, open in dense clusters. A valuable woodland garden plant. From shaded cliffs and forests in mountain valleys in northern China and Korea. ↕16 in (40 cm). Z7–9 H9–7. **'Crimson Fans'** Leaves reddish bronze when young, becoming flushed with crimson in summer and fall.

MUSA

Banana
MUSACEAE

Spectacular foliage plants for milder climates or exotic summer containers.

About 55 species of large perennials, often spreading by rhizomes, that are found in light woodlands at forest margins in northeastern India and Bangladesh, and from Southeast Asia to Japan

and northern Australia. New species are still being identified. Grown for their gigantic leaf-blades, which are often paddle-shaped. The leaves are produced from a false stem that is made up of leaf-sheaths, giving a treelike effect. Small, tubular flowers with colored bracts are eventually formed. After flowering, the shoot will die, usually to be replaced by suckers from the base. Some species and cultivars are grown for the well-loved dessert banana fruit as well as for plantains and other cooking bananas. Commercially, bananas are grown over a huge area of the tropics, mainly by small-scale farmers, with an annual production of over 95 million tons. As interest in tropical-style gardening increases in less tropical areas, bananas have become more popular; an increasing range is being offered by nurseries and seed companies. Attempts to overwinter them outside in marginal areas are becoming more widespread—and more successful.

CULTIVATION Best in full sun or light shade and moist soil; a sheltered position is preferable, since strong winds will shred the leaves. Often lifted, potted, and overwintered in frost-free greenhouses; some species can be successfully grown outdoors in temperate climates with simple protection. Although the top growth is usually killed by frost, it is possible to retain the stature of the plant from year to year by protecting the false stem over the winter. In early fall, before the onset of frosts, all the

foliage should be removed from the top of the plant. The false stem is then enclosed in some form of insulation, such as a straw-filled tube of netting, with the top of this structure covered to keep the straw dry. The insulation is removed in late spring each year and the plant produces fresh leaves. In this way, large specimens have developed in many temperate gardens.

PROPAGATION Most species produce suckers that can be separated in the spring and grown on to form new plants. Plants can also be grown from seed, which should be soaked in warm water for 24 hours before being sown at 70–75°F (21–24°C).

PROBLEMS Red spider mite, mealy-bug and aphid, and strong winds.

M. basjoo Suckering, with slender false stems, which are green when young and eventually turn papery brown. The leaves are bright green and huge, growing to 6½–10 ft (2–3 m) long and about 12 in (30 cm) wide, eventually forming an impressive treelike plant. Pendulous cream flowers are followed by yellowish green, unpalatable fruits that are full of black seeds. This is one of the hardiest of all bananas and, although the top growth will be killed by frost, the rootstock will often survive even in areas down to Zone 7. With no additional protection, it will grow from ground level each year, producing a clump of shoots. Protecting the false stem allows substantial specimens to develop. Easily propagated from seed or suckers. From China. ↕15 ft (5 m). **'Sakhalin'** Particularly hardy, perhaps with slightly darker, thicker green leaves. Z8–11 H11–8

M. ensete see *Ensete ventrilosum*

M. itinerans A slender plant, spreading by rhizomes, the attractive, blue-green, leaves, 8–10 ft (2.5–3 m) long and 28–36 in (70–90 cm) wide, are carried on long stalks and create a somewhat waxy false stem that becomes purple with age; the undersides of the leaves may have a red flush when young. Plants may produce suckers six feet or more (two or more meters) from the parent plant, hence the name, so are difficult to grow in pots. Quite tough, but less hardy than *M. basjoo*; worth trying in sheltered gardens in mild areas, although the plant and its rootstock will need overwinter protection. This species grows better in the shade than other bananas. From China, particularly Yunnan province. ↕15–22 ft (5–7 m). Z8–11 H11–8

M. lasiocarpa (Chinese yellow banana) Stiff-looking with a chunky false stem and quite tough, rigid leaves, 20 in (50 cm) long, 8 in (20 cm) wide, held like a shuttlecock. Flowers when fairly young with a spectacular yellow flowerhead, like a giant waterlily, that can last over six months. Introduced relatively recently, its hardiness and heat tolerance have not yet been fully determined, but it is small enough to be grown in a pot and overwintered indoors. In sheltered areas, it may be worth leaving outside over winter with protection. Sometimes it is now placed in its own genus, *Musella*. From China, particularly Yunnan province. ‡6 ft (1.8 m). Z8–11 H11–8

M. sikkimensis A dramatic plant with glossy leaves, up to 6½ ft (2 m) long and 24 in (60 cm) wide, with a distinct purple flush on the underside. Rather variable, some seedlings may even have strong chocolate colored markings on the young leaves. Insignificant flowers are produced high on the plant and so are more or less irrelevant. Protect the stem over the winter. From Northeast India into northern Indo-China. ‡12 ft (4 m). Z8–11 H11–8

MYOSOTIDIUM
Chatham Islands forget-me-not
BORAGINACEAE

A striking and handsome evergreen that is grown for its glossy foliage and sparkling blue flowers.

Just one species of evergreen perennial endemic to the seashores of the Chatham Islands, New Zealand. It has a stout, cylindrical rootstock, and succulent, broadly oval leaves with a heart-shaped base; the stem leaves have stalks and alternate, the upper are stalkless. Blue flowers with a short tube and five rounded lobes resemble a giant forget-me-not. A demanding plant but well worth the effort.

CULTIVATION Grows best in lightly shaded, even woodland conditions with continuously moist but well-drained, humus-rich soil.

PROPAGATION From fresh seed. Very careful division in spring may be possible with large plants.

PROBLEMS Slugs and snails; cucumber mosaic virus.

M. hortensia syn. *M. nobile* (Chatham Islands forget-me-not, Giant forget-me-not). Magnificent evergreen plant that forms a mound of many large, fleshy leaves, 6–13 in (15–32 cm) long including the stout stalks. The upper surfaces of the leaves are shiny, hairless, and deep green, with prominent parallel veins. The forget-me-not-like flowers are dark to pale blue, or occasionally pure white, about ½–⅝ in (1.2–1.5 cm) across, carried in a dense terminal cluster 4–6 in (10–15 cm) across. Rare and endangered in its native habitat due to overgrazing by sheep and cattle. Endemic to the seashores of the Chatham Islands, New Zealand. ‡12–24 in (30–60 cm). Z10–11 H11–1

M. nobile see *M. hortensia*

MYOSOTIS
Forget-me-not
BORAGINACEAE

The familiar forget-me-not, but in a delightful perennial form that attracts bees and butterflies.

Between 50 and 100 hairy annuals, biennials, and perennials, native to a wide range of habitats— including woodlands, mountains, wetlands, seashores—and widely distributed in Europe, Asia, high altitudes in Africa and North America, and New Zealand. All have alternate, undivided, softly hairy leaves and wheel-shaped flowers with a short tube, five flat or slightly concave lobes, and five white or yellow scales at the throat. The flowers are typically in shades of blue or white, occasionally yellow or pink, and usually carried in paired, coiled clusters, which can sometimes be leafy, and they are attractive to many insects. A versatile group, with many short-lived forms, but some are reliable perennials.

CULTIVATION Best in a sunny or lightly shaded situation but requirements vary greatly.

PROPAGATION From seed, by division, or from cuttings.

PROBLEMS Powdery mildew.

M. alpestris **'Gold 'n' Sapphires'** Softly hairy, clump-forming; expands slowly by the spread of rhizomes. The striking, bright golden-yellow basal leaves are lance- to spoon-shaped, to 3 in (8 cm), and more or less pointed. The typical forget-me-not dark blue flowers are borne in compact clusters. This is a dramatic plant, sometimes incorrectly listed as a form of *M. sylvatica*. Thrives in a sunny or lightly shaded position, but the best foliage color is in full sun. Best in moist but well-drained, acidic to neutral soil. Propagate only from cuttings or by division. Introduced by Terra Nova Nurseries, OR. ‡8 in (20 cm). Z5–9 H9–5

M. scorpioides (Water forget-me-not) Semievergreen, marginal aquatic, or marsh plant, with shortly creeping rhizomes, ascending or upright stems, and oblong, hairy leaves to 2¾–4 in (7–10 cm) long. Clear sky-blue, yellow-centered forget-me-not flowers, to ½ in (10 mm) across, open from pink buds from spring into summer. For sun or light shade in moist soil or shallow water to 2 in (5 cm) deep. Will not tolerate drying out. From central and northern Europe, Asia, and North Africa. ‡6–20 in (15–50 cm). Z5–9 H9–5. **Maytime** ('**Blaqua**') Leaves have broad cream margins. ‡8 in (25 cm). '**Mermaid**' More compact, with sturdy stems. ‡6–9 in (15–23 cm). '**Pinkie**' Pink flowers. ‡12 in (30 cm). '**Snowflakes**' White flowers. ‡12 in (30 cm).

MYRRHIS
Sweet Cicely
APIACEAE

Elegant and aromatic plant bringing quiet confidence and subtlety to the summer border.

A single species that is native primarily to damp soil alongside streams and rivers, or on grassy roadsides and in woodlands, in the mountainous regions of Europe, and long naturalized in Britain and in other parts of northern Europe. Appealingly aromatic, the flat-topped umbels of the white flowers are bold, and are set against delicate fernlike foliage. Both the generic and the specific names of the only species derive from words for perfume and refer to the attractive aniseed-like scent of the leaves. An attractive plant to naturalize in woodlands as well as in moist, grassy places.

CULTIVATION Although this plant is native to habitats with fertile, damp soil, the deep roots of *Myrrhis* enable it to tolerate drier soil and protracted spells of drought, making it a versatile plant for a variety of garden situations.

PROPAGATION From seed.

PROBLEMS Usually trouble-free.

M. odorata A strong-growing aromatic perennial with fine, feathery fernlike leaves distinctly flecked with white— a good distinguishing feature. The leaves emerge in late winter and persist to the following early winter, giving an unusually long season of effective ground cover. Good heads of white flowers in small umbels, ⅝–1¼ in (1.5–3 cm) across, are borne in late spring and early summer and mature to distinctive, deep shiny brown ripe fruits, 1 in (2.5 cm) long, which have a wide variety of herbal uses. The plant self-seeds readily and should be deadheaded where this is likely to be a nuisance. ‡4 ft (1.2 m). Z3–7 H7–1

LEFT 1 *Myosotis scorpioides*
2 *Myrrhis odorata*

N

NASSELLA
POACEAE

A mountain grass with airy, decorative flowers that have long, wispy hairs.

The fifteen species are found from South America (mainly on Andean hillsides) to California, and naturalized in Australasia and parts of Africa, where some are considered noxious weeds. Dense, shallow-rooted, evergreen clumps are made up of very fine, sometimes in-rolled leaves arching into a mop-head of foliage. In late spring to early summer, thin flower stems carry loose, airy flowerheads with little pointed flowers, each with very long hairs that, in some species, make the grass appear misty and cloudlike. The seeds can be spread over large areas because of the hairs. Plant *Nassella* in drifts as an airy edging to paths and dry borders.

CULTIVATION Needs very well-drained, moisture-retentive, fertile soil mixed with sand or gravel, and an open, sunny position; if the base remains wet for too long, it will rot. Comb out dead foliage in the summer after flowering, taking care not to pull out the plant.

PROPAGATION From seed. Plants dislike being divided; if it has to be done, make large divisions and keep them well watered until established.

PROBLEMS Usually trouble-free, but excessive self-seeding can be a problem.

N. cernua (Nodding needle grass) Dense, gray-green clumps of very fine, inrolled leaves 1/16–1/8 in (1–4 mm) wide. In early spring, tall flower stems carry loose, nodding plumes of tiny flowers with purple hairs up to 4½ in (11 cm) long, turning silver, airy, and delicate before the seeds fall, when they are shuttled along the ground by the hairs. Effective in informal plantings with other prairie-type grasses and flowers. Found mainly in sandy, dry grasslands, chaparral, and juniper woodlands in California. ↕3¼ ft (1 m). Z8–10 H10–8

N. tenuissima see *Stipa tenuissima*

N. trichotoma Clumps of stiff, inrolled, thread-thin, ¼-in (5-mm) leaves arch over in a dense fountain of foliage. In late spring to early summer, numerous very thin, wiry flower stems are hung with shiny little purple flower-beads, each with a hair up to 1 in (2.5 cm) long. As the flower stems bend over the foliage, the whole plant seems covered with a luminous, smoky haze that trails down to sweep around the base of the grass. Blooms on and off through the summer, but never with the profusion of the first flowering. Looks spectacular in drifts softening hard landscapes. Introduced into New Zealand, where it is now considered a noxious weed. It is also a very aggressive grass in many areas of the US. Native to grasslands and scrub in Argentina and Uruguay. ↕8–20 in (20–50 cm). Z8–10 H10–8

LEFT *Nassella trichotoma*

NEPETA
Catmint
LAMIACEAE

Tough, easily grown plants, strong in character and neat in foliage, with a long flowering period.

Two hundred and fifty species of deciduous perennials are native to Europe, Asia, and North Africa; about 20 are frequently grown in gardens. Many come from dry, rocky places, others from woodlands or damp mountain slopes. Neat leaves arise in pairs on the stems; they may be toothed or entire, and are sometimes an attractive gray-green. Flowers are tubular, two-lipped, often borne in dense terminal clusters or spikes; they are usually purple or blue, occasionally light yellow, and attractive to bees. The calyces are sometimes colored, too, enhancing the overall effect. These tough plants blend readily into a perennial border, and are a useful alternative to lavenders. Most flower over a long period from early to late summer or into fall, and prefer sun and good drainage.

CULTIVATION Grow in well-drained soil in full sun unless stated otherwise.

PROPAGATION By division, or from soft cuttings in early summer.

PROBLEMS Powdery mildew. May be damaged by slugs or cats.

N. cataria (Catnip) Loose clump of branched gray stems, with toothed, long-stalked, oval gray-green leaves to 3 in (8 cm) long. From midsummer to early fall, white flowers spotted with violet, 7/16 in (1.2 cm) long, on dense spikes at the ends of the stems. Strongly aromatic leaves attractive to some cats, who may roll on, nibble, or even destroy the plant (*see* Catnip, *p.341*). From open places, usually in alkaline soil, in much of Europe and in western Asia. ↕36 in (90 cm). Z3–7 H7–1. **'Citriodora'** Leaves lemon-scented.

***N.* Cat Series** Derived from several species and not a true series, the various "Cat" nepetas, raised recently in the Netherlands, have little in common and are described here under their parent species. Examples include 'Candy Cat' and 'Cool Cat' (see *N. subsessilis*), 'Kit Cat' (see *N.* x *faassenii*), and 'Wild Cat' (see *N. grandiflora*).

N. clarkei (Himalayan catmint) Clump-forming, with toothed, oval leaves to 2½ in (6 cm) long; slender terminal spikes composed of clusters of flowers (whorls) open from midsummer to early fall. The flowers are ⅝ in (1.5 cm) long, violet-blue with a white lip, giving an attractive two-tone effect. Little known, but well worth a place in a sunny border. From open slopes in the Himalaya from Pakistan to Kashmir. ↕30 in (75 cm). Z5–9 H9–5

N.* x *faassenii Forms a clump of upright or spreading stems bearing gray-green leaves to 1¼ in (3 cm) long, with impressed veins. From early to late summer or early fall, long-lasting, pale violet-blue flowers, 7/16 in (1.2 cm) long, open in dense spikes. Grow in full sun. Benefits from a trim after the first flush of flowers; is sometimes damaged by cats. A hybrid between *N. nepetella* and *N. racemosa*. Most plants grown as *N. mussinii* belong here. ↕18–24 in (45–60 cm). Z4–8 H8–1. **'Alba'** Flowers white. **'Kit Cat'** Dwarf but spreading, with light violet-blue flowers and reddish calyces. ↕16 in (40 cm). **'Little Titch'**, **'Snowflake'**, and **'Walker's Low'** (all sometimes listed under *N.* x *faassenii*): see under *N. racemosa*.

N. govaniana Makes a loose clump of light green, oval leaves to 4 in (10 cm) long. Loose sprays of pale yellow flowers, to 2¼ in (3 cm) long, open from midsummer to early fall. Stands apart from other catmints in its graceful habit and unusual flower color. Best grown in part-shade, or in sun given a cool, moist root-run. From forests in the western Himalaya. ↕36 in (90 cm). Z5–9 H9–1

N. grandiflora (Giant catmint) A lax clump of sparsely branched, upright stems bear oval, green to gray-green leaves, heart-shaped at the base and up to 4 in (10 cm) long. They carry violet-blue, ⅝-in (1.7-cm) flowers in dense clusters, forming a long, interrupted spike, from early to late summer. From the Caucasus. ↕30 in (75 cm). Z3–8 H8–1. **'Bramdean'** Deep indigo-blue. **'Dawn to Dusk'** Flowers very pale mauve-pink, with dark reddish calyces. ↕26 in (65 cm). **'Pool Bank'** Flowers lavender-blue, with red-purple calyces. ↕32 in (80 cm). **'Wild Cat'** Taller, with lavender purple flowers and purple calyces. ↕3¼ ft (1 m).

N. longipes Slightly hairy, oval to oblong dark green leaves to 2¾ in (7 cm) long. Small, light blue-mauve flowers dark calyces, 7/16 in (1.2 cm) long, carried in dense spikes in mid- to late summer or early fall. Probably a hybrid. ↕3¼ ft (1 m). Z5–9 H9–5

N. mussinii see *N.* x *faassenii* and *N.racemosa*

N. nepetella Variable plant with green or gray-green, oval or lance-shaped leaves to 1½ in (4 cm) long, bluntly toothed on the margins. Flowers are curved, to 7/16 in (1.2 cm) long, pink or white, and borne in a long spike in mid- and late summer. Rather low in garden impact, but of interest as a parent of *N.* x *faassenii* and many fine hybrid cultivars. Native to southwestern Europe and southern Italy. ↕32 in (80 cm). Z5–9 H9–5

N. nervosa Dense clump of upright, unbranched stems bearing narrowly lance-shaped, dull green leaves to 4 in (10 cm) long. From midsummer to early fall, violet-blue (rarely yellow), ½-in (1-cm) flowers open in short, dense spikes to 6 in (15 cm) long. Trimming after flowering will help keep plants compact. Native to meadows and open slopes in the hills of Kashmir. ↕24 in (60 cm). Z5–7 H8–1. **'Forncett Select'** Compact; flowers deep sky-blue. ↕18 in (45 cm).

N. nuda Tall, clump-forming plant with purplish stems bearing hairless, oblong, mid-green leaves to 2¾ in (7 cm) long. White or pale violet, ⅜-in (8-mm) flowers are borne in well-separated whorls on the branching stems, forming long sprays, from early summer to mid-summer. Rather lax and rangy in habit, benefits from close planting with other perennials. Native to open,

grassy places in eastern Europe and western Asia. ‡36 in (90 cm). Z5–9 H9–5. **‘Snow Cat’** Flowers white, with green calyces.

N. parnassica Sticky stems bear scalloped, gray-green, triangular to oval leaves, to 1½ in (3.5 cm) long. White ⅝-in (1.3-cm) flowers, spotted with purple, open from midsummer to early fall. From sunny, grassy places in Greece and southern Albania. ‡4 ft (1.2 m). Z5–8 H8–5. **‘Porzellan’** Dwarf plant with narrow, grayish leaves to 1¼ in (3 cm) long, and spikes of light violet-blue flowers in mid- and late summer. Raised in the Netherlands; perhaps a form of *N. x faassenii*. ‡10 in (25 cm). Z5–9 H8–5

CATNIP

We are all familiar with the effect that catnip has on some cats. Less common in young kittens and in older cats, the catnip reaction is inherited, so not all animals are affected. The response is not limited to domestic cats; even tigers can show it.

The effect lasts about six minutes, with about three minutes of intense reaction followed by increasing lack of interest. It starts with investigation and sniffing, then physical contact and rolling, followed by a general loss of control! It may take a few hours for sensitivity to return, during which time the cat will show no reaction.

The response is caused by the chemical nepetalactone, found in the strongest concentrations in *Nepeta cataria* but also present in other species. Garden displays can be ruined and shoots broken. Some elements of the feline response are similar to predatory behavior, but the connection between this plant and hunting is not clear.

Catnip has been introduced into North America primarily for cat-lovers to plant in their gardens. In some areas it has escaped and become invasive.

N. prattii Tall plant with lance-shaped green leaves, scalloped on the margins. In mid- and late summer, blue or purple 1½-in (3.5-cm) flowers open in dense whorls at the tips of the stems. Seldom grown, and different in effect from most other catmint species and cultivars. From wet, grassy slopes at medium altitudes in western China. ‡36 in (90 cm). Z5–8 H8–5

N. racemosa syn. *N. mussinii* Variable plant with spreading or upright stems bearing oval, gray-green leaves, to 1½ in (4 cm) long, bluntly toothed on the margins. From early summer to early fall, ½–¾-in (1–1.8-cm) flowers, varying from pale to deep violet-blue, are carried in dense, well-separated tiers. Important as a parent of many cultivars. From open, rocky places in the Caucasus and Caspian regions. ‡12–20 in (30–50 cm). Z3–8 H8–1. **‘Little Titch’** Very dwarf, with pale lavender-blue flowers. ‡6 in (15 cm). **‘Snowflake’** Low and spreading, with gray leaves and white flowers. ‡12 in (30 cm). **‘Walker's Low’** Compact, bushy, non-flopping plant with violet-blue flowers from late spring or early summer to early fall. Good front-of-border plant. ‡24 in (60 cm).

N. sibirica Upright plant with running roots and aromatic, mid- to dark green leaves to 3½ in (9 cm) long, narrowly oblong or lance-shaped and bluntly toothed. Violet-blue, 1¾-in (4.5-cm) flowers are borne in loose spikes from midsummer to early fall. Very hardy, tolerating both sun and light shade, but can be invasive in good conditions. From sunny mountain slopes in Siberia and northern China. ‡36 in (90 cm). Z3–8 H8–1. **‘Souvenir d'André Chaudron’** syn. ‘Blue Beauty’ More compact, although also running underground, with light violet-blue flowers. ‡18 in (45 cm). **‘Six Hills Giant’** Tall, strong-growing plant. Leaves toothed, lance-shaped gray-green, to 1½ in (4 cm) long. Lavender-blue, ¾-in (2-cm) flowers in dense

tiered clusters, or whorls, forming long spikes. ‡36 in (90 cm). Z3–8 H8–1

N. stewartiana Upright plant with lance-shaped, dark green leaves to 4 in (10 cm) long, with finely scalloped margins. Curved, violet-blue 1-in (2.5-cm) flowers, white-spotted on the lower lip, are borne in loose whorls, forming a long spike at the end of each stem. From grassy mountain slopes in Yunnan province, western China. ‡36 in (90 cm). Z3–8 H8–1

N. subsessilis Tall plant; stiffly erect stems bear egg-shaped, pale green leaves to 4¾ in (12 cm) long, margins bluntly toothed. From mid- to late summer or early fall, pale mauve, or rarely white, ⅝–1 in (1.5–2.5 cm) wide flowers open in a long loose spike. Deadheading prolongs flowering. From wet, shady places on hills in southern Japan. 3¼ ft (1 m). Z4–8 H8–1. **‘Candy Cat’** Light rosy purple flowers in short spikes. ‡20 in (50 cm). **‘Cool Cat’** Pale lavender-blue flowers from early summer. ‡30 in (75 cm). **‘Sweet Dreams’** Flowers white with pink flush. ‡20 in (50 cm).

N. transcaucasica Bushy plant with gray-green, aromatic leaves, 1¼–1½ in (3–4 cm) long, the margins finely scalloped, and violet-blue flowers in dense spikes in mid- and late summer. From dry, rocky, open places and roadsides in the Caucasus. ‡8–16 in (20–40 cm). Z3–9 H8–1. **‘Blue Infinity’** Taller, with lavender-blue flowers, the lower lip white with purple spots, opening from early summer to early fall. ‡16–24 in (40–60 cm).

N. tuberosa Simple, gray-hairy stems arise from a tuberous rhizome and bear narrow, oval leaves to 3 in (8 cm) long, sometimes whitish with woolly hairs. Purple, ½-in (1-cm) flowers are carried in dense spikes from midsummer to early fall. Needs well-drained soil, disliking winter rain. From dry, sunny habitats in Spain, Portugal, and Sicily. ‡32 in (80 cm). Z7–10 H10–7

ABOVE 1 *Nepeta nervosa* **2** *N. racemosa* ‘Snowflake’ **3** *N. sibirica* ‘Six Hills Giant’ **4** *N. tuberosa*

NIPPONANTHEMUM
Nippon daisy
ASTERACEAE

Large, gleaming white daisies set against aromatic dark green foliage.

There is just one perennial species from coastal Japan, which often retains a woody basal structure. Thick, stalkless leaves are held alternately, mainly toward the tips of erect or spreading stems. In fall, daisylike flowerheads are held singly on long, leafless stalks. Tends to retain its woody framework in mild areas, but is cut down to the ground in colder areas and usually regrows from below ground.

CULTIVATION Grows best in full sun, in moderately fertile, very well-drained soil and a sheltered position, preferably against a wall, which will encourage earlier and more reliable flowers. In colder climates, flowers are sometimes lost in their prime to an early frost. Pinch out growing tips to encourage bushy growth.

PROPAGATION From seed or by division.

N. nipponicum syn. *Chrysanthemum nipponicum, Leucanthemum nipponicum* Clump-forming plant with thick, leathery, minutely hairy, aromatic, spoon-shaped leaves, sometimes with irregular marginal teeth near the broad apex. In late summer or fall, the elegant, 2½-in (6-cm), daisylike flowerheads are held singly on long, leafless stalks. The outer ray florets are white and the inner disk florets are yellow. Native to Japan. ‡20–40 in (50–100 cm). Z6–10 H10–6

O

OAKESIELLA *see* UVULARIA

OENANTHE
APIACEAE

Unremarkable plants redeemed by the inclusion of a single attractive variegated foliage form.

About 30 species of these moisture-loving plants are found across the Northern Hemisphere and in South Africa and Australia, growing mainly in marshlands, water meadows, and other damp habitats. They have alternately arranged leaves split into opposite pairs of leaflets, and small, star-shaped flowers, each with five petals notched at the apex, gathered into flat, rather open groups of umbels. Several wild species, such as *O. crocata*, are highly poisonous.

CULTIVATION Thrives in any reasonably fertile, moist soil in sun or part-shade.

PROPAGATION By division or spring cuttings.

PROBLEMS Slugs and snails; aphids.

O. javanica Spreads, sometimes vigorously, by rhizomes. The green, triangular, 2¾–6-in (7–15-cm) leaves are divided into pointed oval segments with irregularly toothed or sometimes lobed margins, rather like celery. The white umbels of star-shaped, ⅛-in (3-mm) flowers are produced in summer. Widely cultivated and collected from the wild as a vegetable

in its native regions, in pronounced contrast to its poisonous relations. From India and the Far East, including northern Australia. ‡12 in (30 cm). Z9–11 H11–1. **'Flamingo'** Leaves gaily colored with pink, cream, and white.

OENOTHERA
Evening primrose
ONAGRACEAE

A one-night stand of color and fragrance characterizes these fleeting, showy summer flowers.

There are about 80 species of annuals, biennials, and perennials, only a few of which have ornamental merit, from meadows, roadsides, and prairies in North America. The best have lovely saucer-shaped flowers with four wide, overlapping petals and a prominent stigma with diverging lobes. The upright or spreading, often succulent stems, growing from a thick taproot or fibrous, sometimes aggressive roots, are clothed in lance-shaped foliage and crowned with elongated terminal clusters of flowers. Individual flowers last just a day, often fading in early afternoon, but are often produced in good succession. Some are night-blooming and vanish with the dawn. Flowers of all species darken in color as they fade, creating an often showy contrast. Tall species are easily integrated into beds and borders, while shorter, bushier species are best toward the front.

This is a rather confusing group, with a number of hybrids becoming increasingly popular yet whose parentage is not always clear. As serious breeding work on oenotheras as an oil-yielding crop increases, understanding of their

LEFT *Oenanthe javanica* 'Flamingo'

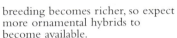

breeding becomes richer, so expect more ornamental hybrids to become available.

CULTIVATION Best in fertile, well-drained soil in full sun or light shade. Most spread by slow-creeping rootstocks to form dense clumps and are tough, drought-tolerant plants of easy culture. All self-sow freely.

PROPAGATION Divide the rosettes in early spring or after flowering in late summer.

PROBLEMS Usually trouble-free.

O. acaulis (Stemless evening primrose) Tufted biennial or perennial with 8-in (20-cm), lance-shaped, irregularly sized leaves in opposite pairs, the leaves, stems, and buds often tinged with red. Pointed buds open all summer to 3-in (8-cm) white flowers that fade to rose-pink. Attractive for raised beds or border edges. Plant in average to rich, well-drained soil in full sun. From rocky slopes and plains in Chile. ‡4–6 in (10–15 cm). Z5–9 H9–5. **'Aurea'** Yellow flowers.

O. **'Apricot Delight'** Upright plant with red stems carrying, from midsummer to early fall, a succession of 3-in (8-cm) wide, sweetly scented flowers that open pale yellow then gently mature through richer yellow to apricot and then pink. Probably a hybrid of *O. stricta*. ‡3½ ft (1.1 m). Z5–9 H9–5

O. berlandieri see *O. speciosa* 'Siskiyou'

O. **'Colin Porter'** Trailing stems carry red flowers narrowly edged in yellow and enlivened by a yellow eye. Best with good drainage in a hot and sunny site. ‡5 in (12.5 cm). Z5–9 H9–5

O. **'Crown Imperial'** Vigorous, with narrow upright stems clothed with rich

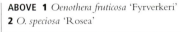

ABOVE 1 *Oenothera fruticosa* 'Fyrverkeri'
2 *O. speciosa* 'Rosea'

green, lance-shaped leaves. In late spring and summer, the stems are crowned with tight clusters of 1-in (2.5-cm) bright yellow flowers opening from rufous buds. Named for the resemblance of its habit to *Fritillaria imperialis*—the crown imperial—by Englishman Peter Moore, best known for his woody plant introductions. ‡24 in (60 cm). Z5–9 H9–5

O. fruticosa (Narrow-leaf evening primrose, Sundrops) Fibrous-rooted crowns creep to form dense clumps of evergreen winter rosettes, which slowly spread outward to form broad clumps with many leafy, upright, flowering stems carrying broadly lance-shaped, soft hairy leaves to 3 in (8 cm) long. Bright yellow, 1-in (2.5-cm), day-blooming flowers open from red-tinged buds. Can be uncomfortably vigorous and so needs restricting. Divide in early spring or after flowering in late summer. From meadows, clearings, roadsides, and disturbed fields from Nova Scotia and New York south to Florida and Alabama. ‡12–24 in (30-60 cm). Z4–8 H8–1. **'African Sun'** Prolific, summer-long yellow flowers above narrow foliage. ‡12 in (30 cm). **'Camel'** Foliage emerges almost orange, becoming green with yellowish blotches; yellow flowers open from red buds. ‡18 in (45 cm). **'Cold Crick'** Small but profuse, bright yellow, day-long flowers bloom all season above neat slender foliage on a tight clump. Unusually well behaved. Found on a Virginia farm; perhaps a hybrid. ‡10–12 in (25–30 cm). **'Fyrverkeri'** (**Fireworks**) Red buds open to 2-in (5-cm) yellow flowers on compact plants. ‡18 in (45 cm). **subsp.** *glauca* syn. *O. tetragona* Broader, smooth leaves that emerge red, and lemon-yellow flowers. **subsp.** *glauca* **'Erica Robin'**

Red shoot tips and reddish green young leaves become yellow and green, then fade to green. ‡ 12 in (30 cm). **subsp. *glauca* 'Longest Day'** Golden-yellow flowers in midsummer. ‡ 16 in (40 cm). **subsp. *glauca* 'Sonnenwende'** syn. 'Solstice' Clear yellow, compact, unusually restrained, with reddish fall foliage. ‡ 12 in (30 cm). **'Youngii'** Tall, upright, prolific. ‡ 24 in (60 cm).

O. kunthiana A rosette-forming short-lived perennial or annual, with 4-in (10-cm), lobed, linear basal leaves and smaller, less dissected stem leaves on lax stems. Clusters of ¾-in (2-cm) pink or white flowers open on summer evenings. Plant in average to fertile, well-drained soil in sun or light shade. From Texas and Arizona to Guatemala. ‡ 12–24 in (30–60 cm). Z6–10 H10–6

O. 'Lemon Sunset' In mid- to late summer, pink buds open to white, sometimes blushed flowers, stained yellow in the center, which darken to deep orange. Probably a wild species; further research is required. ‡ 36–40 in (90–100 cm). Z5–9 H8–1

O. macrocarpa syn. *O. missouriensis* (Ozark sundrops) A striking, sprawling to weakly upright plant forming broad clumps from a branched taproot with 2–4-in (5–10-cm) narrow, lance-shaped, light green leaves. Covered with glorious, large, rounded, 3–4-in (8–10-cm) lemon-yellow flowers that remain open until mid-afternoon and are lovely both in formal gardens and in wild settings, such as prairies, meadows, and rock gardens. These are tough, drought-tolerant plants of easy culture for average sandy or loamy, well-drained soil in full sun or light shade. Divide in early spring or after flowering. From open woods, cedar glades, savannas, and prairies in alkaline soil from Illinois and Colorado south to Missouri and Texas. ‡ 6–12 in (15–30 cm). Z5–8 H8–3. **subsp. *fremontii*** Gorgeous, lance-shaped, silvery-green leaves and paler yellow flowers on compact plants. **subsp. *fremontii* 'Lemon Silver'** Large flowers and silver leaves. ‡ 6–8 in (15–20 cm). **'Greencourt Lemon'** Soft-sulfur-yellow, 2–2½-in (5–6-cm) flowers. **subsp. *incana*** Broad, silver leaves and pale, lemon-yellow flowers. **'Silver Blade'** Silver-gray leaves and large, yellow, 3-in (8-cm) flowers. ‡ 4–6 in (10–15 cm).

O. missouriensis see *O. macrocarpa*

O. odorata see *O. stricta*

O. pallida (Pale evening primrose) Short-lived perennial or biennial, with sparsely toothed, lance-shaped leaves up to 2 in (5 cm) long lining stems that are crowned with fragrant, 2-in (5-cm) white flowers that age to pink. Flowers open in the evening and fade by mid-morning. Plant in average to fertile, well-drained soil in sun or light shade. Raise from seed. From open woods and on rocky slopes and roadsides from Manitoba and British Columbia south to Texas, Mexico, and Nevada. ‡ 12–18 in (30–45 cm). Z3–7 H7–1

'Innocence' Nearly flat, saucer-shaped flowers with pure white petals that fade to pink. ‡ 18–24 in (45–60 cm).

O. perennis (Little evening primrose) Thin stems are loosely clothed with 1–2-in (2.5–5-cm) linear leaves and topped with ¾-in (2-cm) yellow flowers held in open terminal clusters during the day. Of limited ornamental appeal compared to the showier species but surprisingly widely grown. The name tends to be applied by the unwary to many tall, upright, yellow-flowered plants. Plant in average to rich, well-drained soil in full sun or light shade. From open woods and on roadsides and waste places from Newfoundland and Ontario south to Georgia and Alabama. ‡ 12–24 in (30–60 cm). Z3–8 H8–1

O. speciosa (Showy evening primrose) A vigorously creeping perennial, quickly spreading outward by underground runners to form very wide, dense mats clothed with small, 1–3-in (2.5–7.5-cm) lance-shaped leaves with wavy or toothed margins. Large, 2-in (5-cm) pink flowers are borne during the day in late spring and early summer. Thrives in average to fertile, well-drained soil in sun or light shade. Shear plants in midsummer as

flowering wanes and new growth will rebloom. Once established, very difficult to eradicate, so plant only where it has room to spread, or where larger, even more pugnacious plants will keep it in check. Divide in spring. From open woods and on rocky slopes along streams from Missouri and Kansas south to Texas and Mexico. ‡ 12–24 in (30–60 cm). Z5–8 H8–1. **'Alba'** White flowers. **'Pink Petticoats'** Soft-rose with a white ring around a yellow eye. From seed, variable. **'Rosea'** White flowers, veined and edged pink. **'Siskiyou'** Rich-rose pink. Incorrectly listed under *O. berlandieri*, which is a rarely seen yellow-flowered species sometimes placed in a separate genus, *Calylophus*. **'Woodside White'** Opens white and fades to pink.

O. stricta syn. *O. odorata* (Chilean evening primrose, Fragrant evening primrose). Showy, short-lived perennial or annual with fibrous-rooted crowns supporting 6-in (15-cm), lance-shaped leaves, which are slightly bluish and form a basal rosette from which the flowering stems arise, with the leaves diminishing in size as they ascend. Large 1-in (2.5-cm) yellow flowers open in the evening and perfume the air as they fade to apricot. Plant in

fertile, well-drained soil in sun or light shade. Tolerant of very poor soils. Heavy clay soils may induce rot in winter. Widely naturalized, but wild in open situations and rocky slopes in Chile. ‡ 24–36 in (60–90 cm). Z5–9 H8–1. **'Sulphurea'** Cream, 2-in (5-cm) flowers.

O. 'Summer Sun' Extremely prolific with clusters of yellow flowers, from May to August, over red-flushed foliage—a very attractive combination. ‡ 18 in (45 cm). Z4–9 H8–1

O. tetragona see *O. fruticosa* subsp. *glauca*

O. versicolor A delicate short-lived perennial or annual, with linear, toothed leaves on stiffly upright, well-branched, wine-red stems. The summer flowers, borne in the first year from seed-grown plants, are carried in tight clusters at the top of the stems; they are 1 in (2.5 cm) across and vibrant yellow-orange, darkening with age. Plant in well-drained soil in full sun or light shade. Raise from seed. From South America. ‡ 24 in (60 cm). Z5–9 H8–1. **'Sunset Boulevard'** Tangerine flowers fading to red.

OMPHALODES
Navelwort
BORAGINACEAE

Pretty ground-covering woodlanders with flowers resembling forget-me-nots and attractive foliage.

There are up to 30 species of deciduous and evergreen annuals, biennials, or perennials, inhabiting mainly woodlands and mountains, and sometimes coastal habitats, of Europe, East Asia, North Africa, and Mexico. The plants are hairless or very finely hairy, usually clump- or tuft-forming or creeping, with simple, alternate, or lower opposite leaves that are often lance-shaped or oval, sometimes with prominent veins. Flowers are commonly blue or white, with a short tube, five rounded spreading lobes, and scales at the throat, and are usually carried in terminal clusters. The nutlets ("seeds") have a hollow on one side, somewhat resembling a human navel, which is reflected in the plant's common name.

CULTIVATION Best in wooded areas, in dappled shade on moist but well-drained, humus-rich soil.

PROPAGATION From seed or by division.

PROBLEMS Usually trouble-free.

O. cappadocica More or less evergreen, clump-forming plant spreading slowly by rhizomes, the hairy stems carrying long-stalked, oval, prominently veined, pointed leaves, 1¾–4 in (4.5–10 cm) long. Bright azure-blue, white-eyed, forget-me-not-like flowers, about ½ in (1 cm) across, are carried in sprays in spring. Good ground cover for cool, shady spots. Many plants sold under this

---

COLOR IN THE SUN

THRIVING IN PLENTY OF SUNSHINE and hot summers, the classic traditional lavender *Lavandula angustifolia* 'Hidcote', with its gray foliage topped by deep purple spikes, is becoming encircled by the contrasting bright lemony flowers of *Oenothera fruticosa* subsp. *glauca*. The oenothera will spread determinedly at the root and may smother the growth of the lavender at the base, causing the straggliness and bare lower stems that lavenders are prone to when they encounter competition. But, with a watchful eye, the oenothera can easily be restricted whenever it shows a tendency to become uncomfortably oppressive to its neighbor. If the lavender does become too leggy, it can be replaced with young plants rooted from cuttings.

name may belong to a different species, *O. lojkae*. Can be propagated from stem cuttings taken in mid- to late summer and rooted in a frame. From Turkey and the Caucasus. ↕4–6 in (10–15 cm). Z6–8 H8–6. **'Alba'** White flowers. ↕6 in (15 cm). **'Cherry Ingram'** Vigorous, with larger deep blue flowers and narrower dark green leaves. ↕10 in (25 cm). **'Lilac Mist'** Lilac-lavender flowers; a spontaneous mutation of 'Starry Eyes'. ↕6 in (15 cm). **'Starry Eyes'** White flowers, tinged very pale blue, with a deep-blue "star" in the middle of the flower. ↕6 in (15 cm).

O. nitida Upright, clump-forming plant, with dark green, lance-shaped, 2¾–8-in (7–20-cm) leaves on long brownish stalks. Bright blue flowers with yellowish centers, to ½ in (1 cm) across, are borne in late spring and early summer in loose clusters. From northern Portugal and northwestern Spain. ↕8–12 in (20–30 cm). Z6–9 H9–6

O. verna (Blue-eyed Mary) Fast-spreading, creeping plant, with oval, bright grass green, 1¾–4-in (4.5–10-cm) leaves. Abundant sprays of bright blue, white-centered flowers, about ½ in (1.2 cm) across, are carried in spring. Excellent ground cover for humus-rich soil in lightly shaded places. From Europe. ↕2–12 in (5–30 cm). Z6–9 H9–6. **'Alba'** Pure white flowers with yellowish centers. **'Elfenauge'** Pale blue flowers opening from pale pink buds.

ONOCLEA

WOODSIACEAE

Fronds of an unusual shape make this rapidly colonizing fern a must for a bog garden or any moist area in part-shade.

The single species, from Asia and North America, is closely related to *Matteuccia,* one species of which is sometimes included here. Some authorities consider Asian plants of *Onoclea* to differ enough from those from North America to be treated as a separate species. These colony-forming plants have deciduous vegetative fronds attached individually to the rhizomes and distinct fertile fronds that persist through the winter. They make valuable waterside plants.

CULTIVATION Grow in moist or very wet soil with plenty of humus, in part- or full shade.

PROPAGATION By division.

PROBLEMS Usually trouble-free.

O. orientalis see *Matteuccia orientalis*

O. sensibilis (Sensitive fern) Deciduous fern with a slender, branching rhizome quickly forming an extensive colony. The erect, broadly egg-shaped, vegetative fronds are borne singly along the rhizomes, and are divided into several pairs of lance-shaped, regularly lobed leaflets. They are a matte green in color, held on long coppery stalks, but are often pink-tinged in spring. Spore-bearing fronds are reduced to little more than a series of black "beads" along the leaflets. The vegetative fronds die down before the first frost, while the 12in(30cm) tall fertile fronds persist through most of the winter. Spreads rapidly and can be invasive. Native to wet habitats in eastern North America and Northeast Asia. ↕12–24 in (30–60 cm). Z3–8 H8–1. **Copper form** New fronds briefly red in spring.

OPHIOPOGON

Mondo grass

CONVALLARIACEAE

Dependable, low ground cover featuring dainty flowers and slender, prettily colored foliage.

About 65 evergreen, narrow-leaved perennials grow from China and Japan to Borneo and the Philippines, but of these only a few are hardy and generally available. They are clump-forming or determinedly spreading, with linear, grasslike foliage through which emerge upright spikes of white or lilac, six-petaled, conical flowers followed by blue berries. They were formerly included with *Liriope* but are now distinguished by their nodding flowers with spreading petals and blue to violet-blue fruits.

ABOVE 1 *Omphalodes cappadocica* 'Cherry Ingram' **2** *Onoclea sensibilis*

CULTIVATION Grows well in ordinary garden soil; best in part-shade, but also thrives in sun, in moist soil.

PROPAGATION By division or from seed. Variegated forms do not come true from seed.

PROBLEMS Usually trouble-free.

O. bodinieri syn. *O. formosanum* Tufted, colony-forming, and tuber-bearing, this is a plant with narrow leaves, 8–12 in (20–30 cm) or more long but rarely more than ⅙ in (4 mm) wide. About level with the leaf tips, or just below them, the spikes of ⅙–¼in- (4–6mm) long flowers appear in summer. They range from white to yellowish or purple-tinted, and may be followed by blue-purple berries. This plant thrives in shade and is native to forest scrub and ravines in much of China. ↕6–10 in (15–25 cm). Z7–10 H10–7

O. clarkei A good ground cover, spreading by stiff, horizontal stemlike runners, these bear fan-shaped tufts of rich green leaves, 8–12 in (20–30 cm) long by ¼ in (6 mm) wide. Appearing in summer, the ⅝in (1.5cm) wide white flowers are among the largest of all the mondo grasses. A distinctive species well worth looking for, from forest and scrub in Sikkim, India. ↕6–10 in (15–25 cm). Z7–10 H10–7

O. formosanum see *O. bodinieri*

O. intermedius Very variable, tufted to small clump-forming plant with very narrow, ⅛–⅜-in (3–5-mm) wide leaves, 18–24 in (45–60 cm) long. In summer, ½-in(1cm) wide lilac to white flowers appear in loose spikes among the leaves, followed by bluish fruits. From China, India, Sri Lanka, and the Himalaya. ↕16–24 in (40–60 cm). Z7–10 H10–7. **'Argenteomarginatus'** White-edged leaves. By far the most common form found.

O. jaburan Sizable clumps of arching, leathery leaves, 16–24 in (40–60 cm) long by ¼ in (5–6 mm) wide, set off the dense spikes of bell-shaped, white to palest purple, nodding, ⅜-in(8mm) wide flowers that appear among them in late summer. Broadly oblong, violet-blue fruits follow. Long known in cultivation, often as a durable potted plant. From woodlands in Japan. ↕16–24 in (40–60 cm). Z7–10 H10–7. **'Vittatus'** syn. 'Argenteovariegatus', 'Javanensis', 'Variegatus' Light green strap-shaped leaves striped and edged creamy-white.

O. japonicus Spreading steadily, with tuberous roots, the dark green, arching leaves, up to 16 in (40 cm) long and just ⅛ in (3 mm) wide, almost hide the white to lilac flowers on 2–4-in (5–10-cm) stems. These are followed by ¼-in (5-mm) small blue-black berries. Like a smaller version of *O. jaburan* with more arching leaves. Native to the shady forests and woodlands of Japan, China, and Korea. ↕8–12 in (20–30 cm). Z7–10 H11–1. **'Compactus'** Very dwarf form. ↕3–3½ in (8–9 cm). **'Gyoko-ryu'** Reputedly the smallest known cultivar, with very dark green foliage. ↕3 in (7.5 cm). **'Kigmafukiduma'** syn. 'Silver Mist' Narrower, more arching leaves with a central white stripe. **'Minor'** Very deep green leaves.

THOSE BLACK LEAVES

Unique in its almost black leaves (albeit usually slightly green at the base), *Ophiopogon planiscapus* 'Nigrescens' has been known as 'Arabicus', 'Black Dragon', 'Ebony Knight', and other appropriate names, though 'Nigrescens' is the correct one. It is also often called a grass, which it is not, in spite of its slender leaves. This is a determined plant, making good low ground cover and steadily making its way out of borders—even managing to emerge through nearby asphalt and other apparently impenetrable surfaces.

It needs careful placing, and not only because of its slow but relentless spread. The leaves do not show up well against soil, bark, or compost mulch, and black against black should be avoided. In fine or chunky gravel, however, it looks excellent. Better still, in a planting mulched with recycled glass chips in vivid blue or green, it really stands out. With a mulch of clear glass chips, the contrast is more stark, which is not to everyone's taste.

THE ORCHID FLOWER

An orchid flower has six petal-like parts: technically, two petals, three sepals (the topmost often called the dorsal), and a usually lower lip, containing a unique fused sexual organ—the column—that holds both the stamens (the male parts) and the female pistil. To ensure that the clumpy pollen is carried off by pollinators, orchids have evolved shapes, colors, and devices to seduce them. One of the most common adaptations is a flamboyant, attractive lip—for example, the large, colored pouch of the lady's-slipper orchids, *Cypripedium*, or the frilly landing platform of *Bletilla*. Some orchids fuse segments, making identification of parts confusing, such as the hood created by the dorsal sepal and petals in *Spiranthes*.

Bletilla striata

ORCHIDS

With more than 25,000 species, over 1,400 natural and man-made genera, and some 125,000 hybrids, orchids are the most diverse, and the most advanced, plants on Earth. Their diversity is enhanced by their ability to produce millions of wind-dispersible seeds in each seed capsule, the seeds containing a huge range of DNA. It is further compounded by the fact that, unlike most plant groups, orchids often interbreed between species and even between genera. Each plant from these crosses is different.

Most orchids are epiphytic—growing attached to trees or rocks for support—although all of those covered in this book grow in the soil. Epiphytic orchids usually possess thickened roots, which absorb rainwater and nutrients as they trickle by, and often have thickened stems (pseudobulbs) for storage. Even the gardenworthy types that grow in soil prefer loose, fast-draining soil and little fertilizer.

Orchid flowers are highly developed, and share a unique and recognizable structure, despite the fact that they have diversified into numerous shapes and spectacular color combinations (*see* The Orchid Flower).

Orchid seeds contain no nutrients, so they cannot grow without assistance; they need to be invaded by specific fungi (mycorrhizae) that convert starches into plant nutrients. Unless the fungus is present in the soil, seeds will not germinate, and only do so under laboratory conditions where nutrients are provided. Once seeds have germinated and are growing strongly, the relationship with the fungus is no longer necessary.

The naming of hybrid orchids is very different from the naming of other plants, and can confuse even veteran perennial growers. When two different orchid species or hybrids are crossed, the entire resulting group of hybrid plants is given a collective name, or grex name, which is always written in roman type, such as *Epipactis* Sabine. Yet the plants in that grex are not identical, so if you buy a plant based on a picture or description, it will probably be different from what was expected. The only way to be sure of receiving exactly what you see is to buy a division of that individual plant (or a clone of it made in a laboratory by tissue culture, although this is not yet possible for many types). These specific plants are given a cultivar name in the same way as other perennials, and the name is written, for example, as *Epipactis* Sabine 'Frankfurt', indicating a very specific plant in the Sabine grex. Orchid names are commonly misrepresented in perennial catalogs, even though they have been standardized since 1895, and the registration of orchid names is maintained by the Royal Horticultural Society.

The orchids covered in this book are *Bletilla, Calanthe, Cypripedium, Dactylorhiza, Epipactis,* and *Spiranthes.*

Dwarf. ↕ 4–4¾ in (10–12 cm). **'Nanus'** Dense, 4–6-in (10–15-cm), deep green leaves. Dwarf. ↕ 4–4¾ in (10–12 cm). **'Nippon'** Palest mauve flowers and blue fruit. Dwarf. ↕ 4 in (10 cm). **'Silver Mist'** *see* 'Kigmafukiduma'. **'Variegatus'** Clearly white-striped foliage and white flowers.

O. muscari see *Liriope muscari*

O. planiscapus Tufted, colony-forming, with dense, arching, 8–12in (20–30cm) long, dark green, grassy leaves. Among

or just above the leaf tips, short spikes of bell-shaped, ¼in (6mm) long, pale purple to white flowers appear in summer, followed by globular, dull blue fruits. From Japan. ↕ 6–8 in (15–20 cm). Z6–11 H11–1. **'Little Tabby'** Greenish cream leaves and small white flowers. ↕ 6 in (15 cm). **'Nigrescens'** Purple-black leaves and berries and purple flowers (*see* Those Black Leaves).

O. spicatus see *Liriope spicatus*

O. wallichianus Densely tufted, the narrow 18–24-in (45–60-cm) leaves almost hiding loose spikes of ⅜–¾-in (1.5–2-cm) white to lilac flared flowers (larger than *O. intermedius)* and followed by blue berries. From the Himalayas. ↕ 16–24 in (40–60 cm). Z7–10 H10–7

ORCHIS see DACTYLORHIZA

BELOW 1 *Ophiopogon jaburan* 'Vittatus' **2** *O. japonicus* **3** *O. planiscapus* 'Nigrescens'

ORIGANUM
Marjoram, Oregano
LAMIACEAE

Easily grown, oreganos perform many functions from purely ornamental ground-cover plants to hard-working culinary herbs.

About 20 deciduous perennials and deciduous or evergreen woody-based perennials are native to open habitats in the Mediterranean and southwestern Asia. Several are commonly grown, either for ornament or as kitchen herbs. Small, aromatic leaves are borne in pairs on the slender stems, which end in clusters of small tubular flowers, often with showy colored bracts. Recent years have seen an influx of garden hybrids, selected for habit, flower, and foliage effect. These range from low-growing plants suitable for ground cover and rock gardens to bushy upright plants for a sunny border. Most become woody at the base, and old flowered stems can be cut back in early spring to maintain a compact form.

The golden-leaved and variegated forms of *O. vulgare* are especially widely grown, being easy to propagate and having very effective colors. However, many of the yellow-leaved forms in particular are susceptible to disfiguring leaf scorch when grown in full sun. These are better in dappled or part-shade.

CULTIVATION Thrives in any well-drained soil in full sun.

PROPAGATION By division, or from cuttings.

PROBLEMS Usually trouble-free.

BELOW **1** *Origanum laevigatum* 'Herrenhausen' **2** *O. vulgare* 'Aureum' **3** *O. vulgare* 'Polyphant'

O. **'Gold Splash'** Low, spreading plant with green leaves splashed with gold; small heads of pink flowers are borne from midsummer to early fall. ‡ 12 in (30 cm). Z5–9 H9–5

O. laevigatum Slender, bushy plant with wiry purple stems bearing oval, gray-green, ½–¾-in (1–2-cm) leaves, often tinged with purple. Loose sprays of pink ⅜-in (1.5-cm) flowers open among small purple bracts at the stem tips from late spring or early summer to early fall. A drought-tolerant plant suitable for sunny raised beds or a well-drained border. From open, rocky places in southern Turkey, Cyprus, and Lebanon. ‡ 24 in (60 cm). Z5–9 H9–5. **'Herrenhausen'** Leaves purple-flushed in spring and winter, flowers mauve-pink in dense clusters. Z5. **'Hopleys'** Light green leaves; flowers ¾ in (2 cm) long, in showy hoplike clusters.

O. **'Norton Gold'** Low, mound-forming plant with strongly aromatic, bright golden-yellow leaves and mauve-pink flowers from midsummer to early fall. Elegant in containers. A hybrid of *O. laevigatum* and *O. vulgare* 'Aureum'. ‡ 16 in (40 cm). Z5–9 H9–5

O. **'Nymphenburg'** Gray-green leaves; cerise-pink flowers open from purple bracts, from late spring to late summer. ‡ 24 in (60 cm). Z5–9 H9–5

O. **'Rosenkuppel'** Compact, purple-flushed leaves. Purple flowers open among reddish purple bracts from June to August. A hybrid of *O. laevigatum*. ‡ 14 in (35 cm). Z5–9 H9–5

O. **'Rotkugel'** Compact hybrid with deep purple bracts bearing small, lilac-pink flowers from early summer to early fall. ‡ 16 in (40 cm). Z5–9 H9–5

O. vulgare (Wild marjoram, Pot marjoram) Spreads by rhizomes and forms a woody-based, bushy mound of slender stems bearing dark green, oval or rounded leaves up to 1½ in (4 cm) long. From midsummer to early fall, small pale or deep pink ⅜-in (4-mm) flowers open in loose sprays, among leaflike purple or green ½-in (1-cm) bracts. The strongly aromatic leaves are much used for flavoring and are easily grown in any sunny position. Native to dry grasslands and open scrub, usually on limestone or chalk soils, in most of Europe. ‡ 36 in (90 cm). Z4–9 H10–2. **'Acorn Bank'** Narrow, golden-yellow leaves and pink flowers from early to late summer. ‡ 12 in (30 cm). **var. *album*** Bushy, with pale green leaves and white flowers. ‡ 10 in (25 cm). **'Aureum'** Low, spreading plant with golden leaves and lilac-pink flowers. Needs shade from strong sun. ‡ 12 in (30 cm). **'Aureum Crispum'** Spreading, with curly, golden-yellow leaves. ‡ 18 in (45 cm). **'Country Cream'** Low-growing, with leaves edged with creamy-white. ‡ 14 in (35 cm). **'Gold Tip'** Leaves curled, green with a golden-yellow tip. ‡ 18 in (45 cm). **'Golden Shine'** Rounded, golden-yellow leaves and pink flowers. ‡ 12 in (30 cm). **'Polyphant'** Leaves gray-green, edged with creamy-white; flowers purplish pink. ‡ 18 in (45 cm). **'Thumble's Variety'** Larger pale yellow leaves becoming greenish yellow in summer and not scorching; flowers white. ‡ 14 in (35 cm)

OROBUS see LATHYRUS

OSMUNDA
Flowering fern
OSMUNDACEAE

Handsome and dependable clump-forming ferns, these rugged and adaptable plants are ideally suited to waterside planting.

About 15 species of these medium-sized to large deciduous ferns with large, erect rhizomes grow in wet habitats, especially in northern temperate regions. The fronds are once or twice divided, with spores borne on separate modified fronds or on parts of fronds lacking green leafy tissue. The spore-bearing structures, green when mature, turn orange-brown with age, hence the common name of flowering fern. In fall, the foliage briefly turns buttery-yellow before dying.

CULTIVATION Grow in wet or at least consistently moist sites, in humus-rich, preferably acidic or neutral soil in light dappled shade. Will tolerate sun if adequate moisture is available.

PROPAGATION From spores, which must be sown green very soon after collection, or kept cool in a refrigerator if immediate sowing is not possible.

PROBLEMS Usually trouble-free.

O. cinnamomea (Cinnamon fern) Compact, erect rhizomes bear a shuttlecock-like ring of slightly arching pale blue green fronds, narrowly lance-shaped and once to twice divided. The spore-bearing fronds are more erect with a cinnamon-colored plume of contracted segments. From moist habitats in North and Central America, the West Indies, and eastern Asia. ‡ 3¼ ft (1 m). Z4–8 H8–1

O. claytoniana (Interrupted fern) Stout, creeping rhizomes produce an erect rosette of lance-shaped, once-or twice-divided fronds similar to those of *O. cinnamomea*. However, the spore-bearing parts are confined to the central part of otherwise normal green fronds, giving it the name "interrupted fern." Unlike other osmundas, the spore cases are black when mature. The vegetative fronds make neat shuttlecocks encircling the more erect spore-bearing fronds. Perhaps less beautiful than *O. cinnamomea*, it is a

ABOVE **1** *Osmunda cinnamomea*
2 *O. regalis*

striking plant nevertheless and quite
a curiosity when producing spores.
Grows in damp woods in North
America and eastern Asia. ↕ 3¼ ft (1 m).
Z2–10 H8–1.

O. regalis (Royal fern, Flowering fern)
A magnificent deciduous fern with
an erect rhizome that frequently
branches, eventually forming a massive
rootstock, the fibers of which may
be found in potting mediums such as
orchid mix. The fronds are egg-shaped
to oblong, 3 ft (1 m) long, and twice
divided into narrow, well-spaced
segments that are rounded at the tips.
The spore-bearing fronds are modified
at the tips where the normal leafy
segments are replaced by much
reduced spore-bearing structures,
initially green, but soon turning
orange-brown. Best grown in a wet site,
and often develops good rusty-orange
fall color in an open situation—but
moisture is crucial. This is potentially
a very large fern, so give it plenty of
space, or place at the back of a border.
Equally at home in acidic or slightly
alkaline soils. Found in bogs and wet
woods virtually worldwide, but the
form most commonly grown is from
Europe and western Asia. ↕ 3¼–5 ft
(1–1.5 m). Z2–10 H9–1. **'Cristata'**
Tips of fronds and segments crested.
'Purpurascens' Fronds red purple in
spring. **var. *spectabilis*** The North
American form, with frond segments
spaced farther apart than in the
European plant, often red-tinted
when young. **'Undulata'** syn.
'Undulatifolia' Attractive cultivar
with wavy-edged frond segments.

RIGHT **1** *Ourisia* 'Loch Ewe'
2 *O. microphylla*

OURISIA
SCROPHULARIACEAE

Tufted or mat-forming plants for
cool, shady conditions, bearing
quietly attractive flowers in summer.
Twenty-five species of these grow
in scrub or open hill and mountain
habitats in New Zealand, Tasmania,
and the Andes of South America;
three species are frequently grown.
Slender rhizomes form a spreading
mat of dark, often prominently
veined green leaves. The slender-
tubed flowers with spreading lobes
may be solitary in the leaf joints, or
in clusters or elegant sprays. These
plants dislike dry heat, and benefit
from being divided and replanted
every few years.

CULTIVATION Grow in moist, humus–
rich soil in part-shade.

PROPAGATION By division, by
cuttings, or from seed.

PROBLEMS Slugs and snails.

O. caespitosa Prostrate plant with freely
branching, rooting stems bearing tiny,
crowded, dark green, leathery leaves less
than ½ cm (1 cm) long. In late spring
and early summer, erect stems carry
one or two pure white flowers, ⅝–¾ in
(1.5-2 cm) across. From damp rocks in
the mountains of New Zealand. ↕ 4 in
(10 cm). Z5–7 H7–5. **var. *gracilis*** Even
smaller, with thymelike foliage and
usually solitary flowers, ½ in (12 mm)
wide. From the South Island of New
Zealand. ↕ 2 in (5 cm).

O. coccinea Strongly veined, oval, light
green leaves, 1¼–2¼ in (4–6 cm) long,
are borne in rosettes, forming a loose
evergreen mat. Narrowly tubular, scarlet
1¼–1½-in (3–4-cm) flowers are carried
in loose clusters on slender stems from
early summer to late summer or early
fall. A showy plant that spreads well in
a cool, moist position. From damp peaty
places in low hills of southern Chile.
↕ 8–12 in (20–30 cm). Z7–9 H9–1

***O.* 'Loch Ewe'** Vigorous, making a mat
comprising several rosettes of broad,
bluntly toothed dark green leaves, to
2¼ in (6 cm) long. In late spring and
early summer, narrow-tubed, 1in
(2.5cm) wide, pale pink flowers are
borne in clusters on erect stems. A
hybrid of *O. coccinea* and *O. macrophylla*
from Inverewe Gardens, Scotland. ↕ 8 in
(20 cm). Z7–8 H8–7

O. macrophylla Robust plant forming
a clump of hairy, oval, dark green leaves
2–8 in (5–20 cm) long, the margins with
rounded teeth. White flowers, ¾ in
(2 cm) across and yellow in the throat,
are carried in several clusters on upright
stems in early- to mid-summer. From
damp streamsides in the mountains of
New Zealand's North Island. ↕ 12–24 in
(30–60 cm). Z7–9 H9–7

O. microphylla Heathlike plant, woody
at the base, with tiny leaves in four
rows, and solitary pale pink flowers,
½ in (1 cm) across, borne in early
summer and midsummer. From rocky,
open places in Chile and Argentina.
↕ 4 in (10 cm). Z7–9 H9–7

***O.* 'Snowflake'** Makes a low mat
of dark green, oval leaves ½ in (1 cm)
long, above which are carried clusters
of pure white flowers, ½–¾ in (1–
2 cm) wide, in late spring and early
summer. A hybrid of *O. caespitosa* var.
gracilis and *O. macrocarpa* from
Scotland's Inshriach Nursery; freer-
flowering than either of its parents.
↕ 4 in (10 cm). Z7–9 H9–7

P Q

PACHYPHRAGMA
BRASSICACEAE

Hardy shade-lover with good ground-smothering foliage, but the spring flowers are better seen than smelled.

One semievergreen species from moist beech forests in Turkey and the Caucasus makes pretty ground cover beneath shrubs and trees, either in a woodland garden or a more formal location, such as a border. Heart-shaped leaves cover the ground well and make a good background for the generous sprinkling of typical cabbagelike, white flowers that appear with the new foliage in early spring. A dependable spring sparkler.

CULTIVATION Best in reasonably fertile, moist yet well-drained soil with plenty of humus, in part-shade.

PROPAGATION By division in spring or basal stem cuttings in late spring, rooted with bottom heat, or from seed sown as soon as it is ripe in fall in a cold frame.

PROBLEMS Slugs and snails.

P. macrophyllum syn. *Thlaspi biebersteinii* Slowly spreading by rhizomes and

BELOW **1** *Pachyphragma macrophyllum*
2 *Pachysandra procumbens*

making effective ground cover, with 2–4 in (5–10 cm) long, shiny, dark green, heart-shaped basal leaves on long stalks that look best when young. Flat heads of four-petaled, ¾ in (2 cm) wide, bad-smelling white flowers with pale green veins appear in early or mid-spring, followed by flat seedpods. Often sold as *Cardamine asarifolia*, a different and uncommon plant. From northeastern Turkey and the Caucasus. ‡8–16 in (20–40 cm). Z5–9 H9–5

PACHYSANDRA
BUXACEAE

Pretty woodland perennial relation of the ubiquitous, if utilitarian, evergreen ground-covering shrub *P. procumbens*.

Four species of small evergreen shrubs and perennials are found in China, Japan, and the US. Just one of the perennials is grown, but is undeservedly neglected, perhaps suffering from disparagement of its shrubby relation. Its long, spreading rhizomes, forming large clumps, support foliage crowded toward the top of erect stems, from below which arise spikes of white flowers; each flower is either male or female but never both.

CULTIVATION Plant in moist, humus-rich, acidic soil in light to full shade. Plants spread slowly at first, but form broad clumps in a few years.

PROPAGATION By division.

PROBLEMS Usually trouble-free.

P. procumbens (Allegheny spurge) Clusters of satiny, broadly oval or rounded, 1¼–3 in (3–8 cm) leaves with

five to ten coarse teeth toward the tip. The new foliage is bright sea green mottled with pale blotches; in fall, frost induces a deep purple background with silvery mottling. The 3-in (8-cm) spikes of small, spidery, slightly blushed white flowers, the male flowers above the female ones, emerge among the leaves in spring. From rich deciduous or mixed coniferous woods in acidic soil, from North Carolina and Kentucky south to Florida and Louisiana. ‡6–12 in (15–30 cm). Z5–9 H9–3

PAEONIA
Peony
PAEONIACEAE

Extremely beautiful and elegant spring and summer perennials for borders and for cutting.

Between 25 and 45 herbaceous and shrubby plants grow mainly in scrub, meadows, steppe grasslands, and woodland clearings in Europe and Asia. Two very distinct species are found only in northwestern North America. Only herbaceous perennials are covered here. They can be very variable, and botanists are still debating their classification; research continues.

The roots are deep and tuberous and act as storage tissues, allowing established plants to tolerate drought. Plants are long-lived with a conspicuous crown and many erect stems, each bearing between five and ten large green leaves, larger at the base of the stem, smaller toward the top. Peony foliage is important in distinguishing species from each other. The leaves, which often emerge with rich reddish tones that then fade, are divided into nine or more leaflets, but in some species

each of these is divided again into three, and the resulting segments may be further divided into lobes. Flowers of wild species have eight to ten petals, 1¼–6 in (3–15 cm) across, while cultivated plants have flowers that range from single to fully double with more than a hundred petals. They close at night and in dull, overcast weather. Flowers of cultivars can be up to 6 in (15 cm) across, in red, pink, yellow, or white; among the several thousand cultivars, there are several distinct flower types (*see* Peony Flower Forms, *p.351*). The species tend to flower first, sometimes in mid-spring, and overlap with the first of the hybrid peonies, which flower from mid- to late spring. About a month later, the cultivars of *P. lactiflora* start to flower from early summer onward. The following entries include the flowering season. Most species have a single flower to a stem, but *P. lactiflora* has side buds that open later to extend the flowering period.

Mature fertile seed is usually dark bluish or brownish black, often mixed with red infertile seed in the same pod. As the pods split, these colors can increase the plants' appeal.

CULTIVATION Peonies grow best in well-drained soil and full sun, although a few tolerate some shade. Most prefer neutral or slightly alkaline conditions, but some thrive in slightly acidic soil.

Plant in fall, when plants become dormant; alternatively, if necessary, plant in early spring but be sure to water well in hot weather during their first summer. Cultivars of *P. lactiflora* and hybrid peonies are best bought as bare-root plants, with

ABOVE *Paeonia cambessedesii*

at least four or five buds on each. Plants with as few as two buds may take several years to establish.

Plant in a hole 12–24 in (30–60 cm) deep, mixing a handful of organic fertilizer with the soil at the bottom. Backfill carefully, leaving no air pockets among the roots, then water thoroughly to saturate the soil and fill any voids. Cultivars should be planted so that the top of the crown is about 2 in (5 cm) below the surface; young plants of species peonies are less vigorous, so plant at a depth of 1 in (2.5 cm). Mulch with composted bark to control weeds, but do not cover the crown.

Feed with a balanced fertilizer each fall. Growth is slow at first, hastens in the second year, and takes off in the third; plants reach maturity after four or five years. Contrary to popular belief, peonies can be moved successfully (*see* To Move or Not to Move?). However, they do not thrive in pots.

PROPAGATION Peonies are usually divided, but the species can also be grown from seed.

To divide, lift plants in the fall: after removing the dead foliage, remove all of the soil from the roots and leave the plant out of the ground for about two hours so that it becomes less rigid and easier to work with. Remove sections of the roots with at least four or five dormant buds from the crown attached to each. Cut through the roots with a clean, sharp knife, then dust the area with fungicide to prevent disease. Plant divisions with the buds approximately 2 in (5 cm) below the surface (1 in (2.5 cm) for species), and label carefully.

Peony seedlings usually take two years to emerge. Plant seeds in fall, 1 in (2.5 cm) deep in 5-in (13-cm) pots filled with loam-based seed mix. Cover with grit to prevent weed growth, label carefully, and leave outside. A root should develop during the following spring, but a shoot will not appear for another year. Growth is slow; seedlings may not flower for four or five years.

PROBLEMS Peony blight (*see panel*), verticillium wilt, leaf blotch, virus diseases, and swift moth larvae.

P. albiflora see *P. lactiflora*

P. **'America'** Slightly fragrant, vivid, single scarlet red flowers with a lovely sheen, held on strong stems. To many, the best single red peony. A seedling of 'Burma Ruby'. Early to mid-season. ↕36 in (90 cm). Z3–8 H8–1

P. **anomala** Deeply dissected, dark green leaves have fine hairs following the veins on the upper surface. A single red, or rarely pink, 2¾–3½-in (7–9-cm) flower with slightly waved petals is carried on each stem in late spring and early summer. In fall the foliage turns an attractive shade of orange-brown. The Chinese *P. veitchii* is very similar, but its flowers are pink or pale purple and there are usually two or more flowers to a stem. Prefers sandy, neutral

TO MOVE OR NOT TO MOVE?

It is often said that peonies should not be moved. This is not entirely true. If left to develop into substantial clumps, peonies certainly look very impressive and give a spectacular show, but they can be moved successfully if necessary. Two factors are important. First, they should be moved in fall, not spring. Peonies start into growth early in the season and may be set back severely if dug up at that time. Secondly, the less the roots are damaged, the better. They have a deep system of tuberous roots, so try to lift them with as much root system and as much soil as possible, although unfortunately the soil tends to fall off, since there are relatively few fibrous roots to hold it in place. Plants may flower less well, and grow less tall, in their first season after being moved, but will soon establish.

or acidic soil. One of the most widely distributed of all peony species, from Russia, Kazakhstan, and Mongolia. ↕20 in (50 cm). Z5–8 H8–5

P. **arietina** see *P. mascula* subsp. *arietina*

P. **'Belle Center'** *see P.* 'Buckeye Belle'

P. **'Buckeye Belle'** Semidouble with reddish brown, slightly crinkled flowers, that look fantastic when backlit by low sunshine. 'Belle Center' looks identical, but is a little shorter and flowers two weeks later. Early-flowering. ↕36 in (90 cm). Z3–8 H8–1

P. **'Burma Ruby'** Poppylike buds open to reveal fragrant single flowers, bright red with a faint purple tint. A parent of many good hybrids. Early flowering. ↕28 in (70 cm). Z3–8 H8–1

P. **cambessedesii** (Majorcan peony) Very distinctive grayish green leaves, up to 11 in (29 cm) long, reddish purple beneath and with wavy margin. Red-tinted stems, emerging very early in the year, carry 2½–4-in (6–10-cm) flowers, purplish pink with darker veins, in mid-spring. Many plants on sale are probably hybrids and less attractive than the true species. Needs extremely well-drained soil, and best planted at the foot of a sunny wall. From Majorca and Minorca; under threat in the wild due to coastal development of the Balearic Islands and depredations by feral goats, which are attracted to the seedpods. ↕24 in (60 cm). Z8–10 H10–8

P. **'Cherry Ruffles'** Strong stems carry pretty, very long-lasting, semidouble, crimson-scarlet flowers with a pale mark on the outside of the petals toward the base. Early to mid-season. ↕31 in (78 cm). Z3–8 H8–1

P. **corallina** see *P. mascula* subsp. *mascula*

P. **'Cora Louise'** (Itoh hybrid) Fragrant, semidouble white flowers held above the leave; dark lavender-colored blotches at the base of the petal. Mid-season. ↕24 in (60 cm). Z3–8 H8–1

P. **decora** see *P. peregrina*

P. **'Early Scout'** Deeply dissected, deep green foliage and single very deep red flowers. A hybrid of *P. tenuifolia*, from which it inherits the attractive foliage. Very early to flower. ↕21 in (53 cm). Z3–8 H8–1

P. **'Ellen Cowley'** Semidouble, bright pink flowers with a hint of orange above dissected foliage. Early-flowering. ↕28 in (70 cm). Z3–8 H8–1

P. **emodi** (Himalayan peony) Deeply divided leaves, bronzy green when they appear in the spring but turning mid-green by the summer. Leaves are 3–7 in (8–18 cm) long, the largest at the base divided into 20–30 segments, and the stems carry two to four, 2–4-in (5–10-cm), pure white flowers in mid-spring. The flowers are slightly cup-shaped and somewhat nodding, with a center of pretty yellow stamens. The

flowers have only one (occasionally two) seedpods. The hybrid peonies 'Early Windflower' and 'Late Windflower' are often sold as this plant, but *P. emodi* is more robust and has larger flowers. Will grow in dappled shade, although plants will be shorter and the foliage darker. It needs well-drained, fertile soil but is hardier than often thought. From northern India, northern Pakistan, and Afghanistan. ↕30 in (75 cm). Z6–8 H8–6

P. **'Flame'** Single, bright red flowers with a hint of orange and a white mark at the base on the outside of the petals. Good for cutting. Early-flowering. ↕32 in (80 cm). Z3–8 H8–1

P. **'Garden Treasure'** (Itoh hybrid) Vigorous, forming a low bush with mid-green foliage, and carrying double, golden yellow flowers with red blotches at the base of the petals. It blooms for up to a month, with up to three flowers per stem. A hybrid between the well-known 'Alice Harding' tree peony and a white form of *P. lactiflora*, and the only Itoh hybrid (*see* Itoh or Intersectional Hybrids, *p.351*) to have been awarded a Gold Medal by the American Peony Society. Mid-season. ↕30 in (75 cm). Z3–8 H8–1

P. **'Honor'** Pretty, single, bright pink, long-lasting flowers, which have a slightly spicy scent, over pale green leaves. Mid-season. ↕36 in (90 cm). Z3–8 H8–1

P. **'Illini Warrior'** Single or semidouble, glossy, slightly scented, red flowers with a pale streak through the center of each petal. Vigorous; early-flowering. ↕3¼ ft (1 m). Z3–8 H8–1

P. **lactiflora** syn *P. albiflora* Variable species from which over 5,000 cultivars are derived. Plants are generally hairless, with reddish brown stems carrying leaves that are usually split into three and then three again, giving nine or more elliptic or lance-shaped leaflets, dark green above and lighter beneath. The small bumps along the leaf edge that distinguish *P. lactiflora* from other species can be felt, but are invisible to the naked eye. The fragrant, 2¾–4-in (7–10-cm) white flowers are carried

PEONY BLIGHT

Peonies suffer from very few diseases, but are vulnerable to a fungus called peony blight (*Botrytis paeoniae*). This disease can affect any aerial part of the plant, which turns dark brown and wilts, and can be especially troublesome during wet weather. Infection can be greatly reduced by removing the foliage from all of your peonies in the fall and placing in the trash. This should reduce the number of spores in the soil and will reduce the risk of infection in the spring. It is also possible to achieve effective control by removing any infected material and destroying it when it first appears. The disease can also easily be controlled by spraying with an appropriate fungicide.

two or three to a stem in late spring or early summer. Wild plants of this species are rarely grown (the ones listed by nurseries are often impostors); most are hybrids between a few Chinese cultivars introduced in the early 19th century. Having been hybridized for many years, a huge number of cultivars have been introduced, although only a few hundred are available from nurseries. Many older cultivars have weaker stems, and need support, but they are still widely available and relatively inexpensive. The more recent cultivars are more robust, with stronger stems, and make superb cut flowers. The flowers range from white through various shades of pink, magenta, and magenta-red. They are often highly scented, and cultivars with semidouble or double flowers tend to have a stronger fragrance than singles. The flowers show a wide variety of forms (*see Peony Flower Forms, p.351*); the form for each cultivar is shown in parentheses. All peonies grow best in full sunshine; avoid waterlogged soil or areas prone to seasonal flooding. They require regular fertilizer applications and protection from peony blight (*see panel, p.349*). Propagate by division. From Siberia, Mongolia, China, and Tibet. ‡28–48 in (70–120 cm). Z3–8 H8–1. **'Albert Crousse'** (Double) Fragrant, free-flowering, and fully double, with globe-shaped, salmon pink flowers. Late-flowering. ‡38 in (95 cm). **'Barrington Belle'** (Anemone) Deep red guard petals (*see Peony Flower Forms, p.351*) encircle golden-edged, deep red staminodes. Mid-season. ‡34 in (85 cm). **'Bowl of Beauty'** (Japanese) Classically beautiful, with pink guard petals and masses of pale staminodes. Mid-season. ‡32 in (80 cm). **'Bunker Hill'** (Semidouble or double) Fragrant, with deep red petals. Vigorous. Mid-season. ‡36 in (90 cm). **'Charlie's White'** (Bomb) Large, slightly scented, pure white flowers. Vigorous; one of the best for use as a cut flower. Early-flowering. ‡4 ft (1.2 m). **'Cheddar Gold'** (Japanese) Strongly scented, with large, white guard petals around a large mound of yellow staminodes. Mid-season. ‡30 in (75 cm). **'Comanche'** (Japanese) Dark green leaves; flowers have bright magenta-pink guard petals and orange-yellow staminodes. Vigorous. Mid-season. ‡36 in (90 cm). **'Dinner Plate'** (Double) Very large, slightly scented, deep pink flowers on strong stems. Late-flowering. ‡36 in (90 cm). **'Doctor Alexander Fleming'** (Double) Sweetly scented full double with deep pink flowers, the central petals often curled into a tight ball. Some flowers may come semidouble. Mid-season. ‡3½ ft (1.1 m). **'Duchesse de Nemours'** (Double) Very fragrant; the white flowers have unusually large outer petals and a yellow heart. A good cut flower. Mid-season. ‡32 in (80 cm).

'Edulis Superba' (Crown) The sweetly scented flowers with magenta-pink petals, yellow at the base, make good cut flowers. One of the oldest *P. lactiflora* cultivars, introduced by Lemoine in 1824, and still widely grown. Early to mid-season. ‡38 in (95 cm). **'Felix Crousse'** (Double) Fragrant, with globe-shaped magenta-pink flowers in clusters. Mid- to late season. ‡30 in (75 cm). **'Festiva Maxima'** (Double) Pale pink, but quickly turning creamy white with splashes of carmine red on the central petals. Introduced in 1851 and still compares well. Mid-season. ‡3¼ ft (1 m). **'Gay Paree'** (Japanese) Striking flowers with vivid magenta-pink guard petals and pale pink, buff staminodes. Mid-season. ‡3½ ft (1.1 m). **'Honey Gold'** (Double) Fragrant, with large, white guard petals notched at the tip, and curly white inner petals emerging from the center of a large mound of narrow, yellow staminodes. Mid-season. ‡36 in (90 cm). **'Inspecteur Lavergne'** (Double) Fragrant, globe-shaped, crimson red flowers; large outer petals. Mid-season. ‡31 in (78 cm). **'Jan Van Leeuwen'** (Japanese) Small-flowered; pure white guard petals around golden yellow staminodes—all set off by dark green foliage. Mid-season. ‡36 in (90 cm). **'Kansas'** (Double) Fuchsia-purple petals, unusually strongly marbled on the backs. Vigorous, with strong stems. Mid-season. ‡36 in (90 cm). **'Karl Rosenfield'** (Double) Prolific, with bright crimson-red, globe-shaped flowers. Good for cutting. Mid- to late season. ‡31 in (78 cm). **'Kelway's Glorious'** (Double) Strongly rose-scented, the creamy white flowers have a yellow heart; some petals may be streaked with red. Widely grown for cutting. Mid- to late season. ‡3¼ ft (1 m). **'Krinkled White'** (Single) Elegant, with crinkled white petals and a center of golden yellow stamens. Early-flowering. ‡32 in (80 cm). **'Lady Alexandra Duff'** (Double) Highly fragrant double with lavender-pink outer petals and smaller, white inner petals that may have carmine markings. Several similar, but distinct, plants are sold under this name. Mid-season.

LEFT **1** *Paeonia lactiflora* 'Barrington Belle' **2** *P. lactiflora* 'Festiva Maxima' **3** *P. lactiflora* 'Karl Rosenfield' **4** *P. lactiflora* 'Sarah Bernhardt' **5** *P. lactiflora* 'Whitleyi Major'

HYBRID PEONIES

Breeders have attempted to cross all the peony species in order to bring together the best features of each. The first people to do this were Victor and Emile Lemoine. However, the majority of hybrid peonies are the result of crossing *Paeonia lactiflora*, *P. officinalis*, *P. peregrina*, and *P. wittmanniana*. There are a large number of hybrid peonies that have bright scarlet red flowers and several with unusual coral pink blooms, while others have pink, white, pale apricot, yellow, and even lavender-colored flowers.

Many plants that we now know to be hybrid peonies have in the past been listed for convenience as cultivars of *P. lactiflora*. All of these flower later than the fernleaf and tree peonies.

↕36 in (90 cm). **'Laura Dessert'** (Double) Strongly rose-scented, pale pink flowers, fading to white at the edges of the petals. Early to mid-season. ↕3¼ ft (1 m). **'Madame Calot'** (Double) Prolific, fragrant, and large-flowered, with pale pink inner petals surrounded by a ring of creamy white and flesh pink guard petals. Late-flowering. ↕30 in (75 cm). **'Miss America'** (Semidouble) Fragrant, pure white flowers become yellow toward the base of the petals; they open from blushed buds. Early-flowering. ↕36 in (90 cm). **'Monsieur Jules Elie'** (Crown) Reliable and fragrant with very large, rose pink flowers that retain their color in strong sun. Good for cutting, although the stems are little weak. Early to mid-season. ↕42 in (110 cm). **'Mr. G.F. Hemerik'** (Japanese) Magenta-pink guard petals surround crinkled, pale yellow staminodes. The leaves have distinctive crinkled edges. Slightly fragrant. Late-flowering. ↕34 in (85 cm). **'Mrs. Franklin D. Roosevelt'** (Double) Fragrant, with soft pink petals. The flowers appear semidouble at first, but more petals unfurl from the center to create a full double. Good for cutting. Mid-season. ↕33 in (83 cm). **'Nymphe'** (Single) The simple, fragrant, saucer-shaped flowers have large, flesh-pink petals. Late-flowering. ↕34 in (85 cm). **'Primevere'** (Anemone) Blush pink outer petals and a center of lemon yellow staminodes, becoming ivory with age. Prolific and fragrant. Mid-season. ↕36 in (90 cm). **'Raspberry Sundae'** (Bomb) Pale pink guard petals surround a collar of pale yellow staminodes with curly pink petals in the center. Very fragrant. Mid-season. ↕36 in (90 cm). **'Sarah Bernhardt'** (Double) Fragrant, apple-blossom pink flowers on stems not strong enough to

support the large, heavy flowers; plants ideally need ring supports that can be raised as they grow, yet will remain unobtrusive. Mid- to late season. ↕38 in (95 cm). **'Shirley Temple'** (Double) Pink buds open to reveal blush-white flowers, which fade to creamy white in strong sunshine. Fragrant with strong stem; very good for cutting. Mid- to late season. ↕33 in (83 cm). **'Solange'** (Double) Fragrant, globe-shaped, creamy white flowers held on strong stems. Very late-flowering. ↕34 in (85 cm). **'White Wings'** (Single) Slightly fragrant flowers with pure white petals on red stems. Late-flowering. ↕33 in (83 cm). **'Whitleyi Major'** (Single) Flesh pink buds open to reveal fragrant, pure white flowers carried in clusters. Good red fall foliage color. Early-flowering. ↕36 in (90 cm).

P. lobata see *P. peregrina*

P. **'Lovely Rose'** Strong, upright stems carry very large, deep pink, semidouble flowers, up to 8 in (20 cm) across, which lighten with age and develop distinctive marbling. One of the most striking hybrids. Early-flowering. ↕30 in (75 cm). Z3–8 H8–1

P. mascula (Male peony) A variable species in height; fat, tuberous roots support smooth stems carrying green or bluish green leaves with undivided leaflets. The 2½–4¾ in (7–12 cm) wide flowers, with five to nine petals, may be pink or white. The corresponding "female peony" is *P. officinalis*. From southern Europe. ↕10–24 in (25–60 cm). Z3–8 H8–1. **subsp.** *arietina* syn. *P. arietina* Hairy stems, the leaves elliptic or oblong in shape, light green and hairless above, slightly waxy and hairy beneath. The flowers are light magenta, but cultivars, most of which

are hard to find, may have white, pink, or even dark red petals. Research suggests that this plant is closer to *P. officinalis* than *P. mascula*. From Turkey. ↕28 in (70 cm). **subsp.** *arietina* **'Northern Glory'** Larger, more vigorous; single, magenta-carmine flowers and colorful fall leaves. **subsp.** *mascula* syn. *P. corallina* An adaptable plant, that will grow in most situations and even tolerate some shade. The upright stems have hairless, dark green, elliptical to egg-shaped leaflets and flowers that are usually dark magenta. Foliage turns apricot-brown in fall. From southern Europe plus Iran, Iraq, and Syria. ↕30 in (75 cm). Z5–8 H8–5

P. mlokosewitschii (Molly the Witch). Much sought-after for its single, 3–4¾-in (8–12-cm), primrose yellow flowers in mid- and late spring. It has hairless, reddish brown stems and leaves that are dark green or bluish green and hairless above, with a waxy finish and pale with a few hairs beneath; the leaflets are oval or egg-shaped. The fall foliage turns a wonderful shade of

orange-brown. Demand for this plant invariably exceeds supply—do not be tempted by cheap seedlings, which often have magenta-tinted flowers; choose divisions where possible. For full sunshine or part-shade, beneath deciduous trees or shrubs. From the Caucasus. ↕3¼ ft (1 m). Z5–8 H8–5

P. **'Moonrise'** Fragrant, single, creamy yellow flowers set against glossy light green foliage, which is relatively undivided with about a dozen leaflets. ↕28 in (70 cm). Z3–8 H8–1

P. obovata Pinkish brown, hairless stems carry leaves divided into seven to nine leaflets, dark green and hairless above, waxy beneath with a few scattered hairs. The leaflets are egg-shaped, with the broad end facing away from the stem (a shape known as obovate—hence *P. obovata*). Unusually, the foliage continues to grow and develop after the plant has finished flowering. Flowers from mid-spring to early summer; in the wild the 2¾-in (7-cm) flowers are purple or magenta, although the majority of garden plants have white flowers. For full sunshine or part-shade, under deciduous trees or shrubs. From China, Japan, Korea, and Siberia. ↕24 in (60 cm). Z3–8 H8–1. **var.** *alba* Pure white flowers. Most widely grown form comes true from seed.

P. officinalis (Female peony) Grown as an ornamental plant since the Middle Ages, the leaves are dark green and hairless above, paler and hairy beneath, with up to 35 narrow elliptic to oblong leaflets. Cultivars have completely hairless leaves. The wild plant has single, 3½–5-in (9–13-cm), bright magenta or reddish purple flowers with a sweet fragrance. The male peony is *P. mascula*. Easily grown from seed, or can be divided. From France, Italy, Switzerland, Hungary, Albania, and eastern Serbia. ↕24 in (60 cm). Z3–8 H8–1. **'Alba Plena'** Pure white double flowers that open with a blush tint. Slightly smaller than the better-known 'Rubra Plena'. **'Anemoniflora Rosea'** An anemone-form flower with bright purple guard petals and yellow-edged, purple staminodes. **subsp.** *humilis* Slightly smaller than the species, with hairy leaves and stems and magenta flowers. ↕16 in (40 cm). **'Rosea Plena'** Vivid pink flowers that gradually fade to almost white in bright sunshine.

ITOH OR INTERSECTIONAL HYBRIDS

Intersectional hybrids, often called Itoh hybrids in recognition of the Japanese breeder Toichi Itoh, the first person to make this cross successfully in 1948, are hybrids between hybrid tree peonies (*Paeonia x lemoinei*) and the herbaceous perennial Chinese peony (*P. lactiflora*). They have very short, woody stems, to which the plant dies back at the end of the season. The plants share the characteristics of their parents, with flowers in late spring and early summer, ranging in color from golden yellow to white, pink, bright red, and even copper. The flowers usually have distinctive

blotches at the bases of their petals called flares. They are produced over a longer period than most herbaceous perennial peonies, and have the potential to repeat-flower. Although vigorous, demand far exceeds supply, so they are currently very expensive. However, while for many years it was thought that peonies could not be propagated in the laboratory by tissue culture, recent advances should make Itoh hybrids more readily available. A number of breeders are continuing to develop new cultivars, and some spectacular plants have been produced.

PEONY FLOWER FORMS

Among the thousands of herbaceous peonies, there are several distinct flower forms. It is difficult to describe these without resorting to a technical term—the staminode. This is a stamen that has developed to look like a petal, although it may still be capable of producing pollen. The outer petals are also often referred to as "guard" petals.

staminode   guard petal

Paeonia lactiflora 'Cheddar Gold'

Single The flowers usually have two rings of petals, with between eight and ten petals in all. They are fully fertile. *P.* 'Peregrina' (above) is a single, as are all species peonies.

Japanese or Imperial Enlarged outer guard petals surround a mass of staminodes. This type of peony (here, 'Bowl of Beauty') may produce seed. Also incorporates the Anemone form.

Semidouble Flowers form by a multiplication of the floral structure, so that there are concentric circles of petals and stamens. Fully fertile. 'Miss America' (above) is typical.

Crown Flowers have a raised dome of petals in the center, which is surrounded by enlarged guard petals. Often infertile. 'Monsieur Jules Elie' (above) is a crown type.

Bomb Flowers resemble an ice cream bombe; a central raised mound of petals is often surrounded by a contrasting collar of staminodes. (Here, 'Raspberry Sundae'.)

Fully double All the flower parts within the ring of petals are converted into petal-like structures, as seen in the *P. lactiflora* cultivar 'Lady Alexandra Duff'. Usually infertile.

'Rubra Plena' Considerably larger than other forms with large, double, deep purplish red flowers that lack any stamens. Very tough, withstanding almost any abuse; however, the stems are too weak to carry the heavy flowers and need support from early spring. Perhaps a hybrid with *P. peregrina*.

P. **'Paula Fay'** Glossy foliage sets off vivid pink, semidouble flowers whose slightly crinkled petals have a white mark at the base. Vigorous. Early-flowering. ‡ 36 in (88 cm). Z3–8 H8–1

P. peregrina syn. *P. decora*, *P. lobata* (Byzantine peony, Red peony of Constantinople) An extremely important plant for breeding; its unusual combination of pigments is largely responsible for the development of coral-colored flowers in hybrid peonies. Spreading roots, developing into a diffuse clump, carry red-striped green stems with glossy dark green foliage that has distinctive notched leaflets. The uniquely bright scarlet red flowers open in late spring. Grows well either in full sunshine or in part-shade, under deciduous trees. From southern and eastern Europe. ‡ 24 in (60 cm). Z3–8 H8–1. **'Otto Froebel'** Bright coral red flowers. ‡ 32 in (80 cm).

P. **'Postilion'** Vigorous, with strongly scented, semidouble, bright scarlet red flowers and unusually large leaves on strong upright stems. A second flower may appear inside the first. Early-flowering. ‡ 36 in (90 cm). Z3–8 H8–1

P. **'Requiem'** Robust; large, scented, single, faintly blushed white flowers, against dark green foliage. Very early-flowering. ‡ 37 in (93 cm). Z3–8 H8–1

P. **'Scarlett O'Hara'** Dramatic, tough, vigorous single; long season of large, single, scarlet red flowers. Early to mid-season. ‡ 3½ ft (1.1 m). Z3–8 H8–1

P. tenuifolia (Fernleaf peony) Mass of deeply dissected, dark green foliage makes the plant valuable and easily recognizable, even when not in flower. The flowers are held just above the foliage, in late spring. Wild plants normally have single, 2½–3-in (6–8-cm) red flowers, but white and pink forms are available. Not as difficult to grow as is often rumored, although the buds can suffer from frost damage, and plants may take some years to reach their full height. Some botanists split *P. tenuifolia* into three species—*P. biebersteiniana*, *P. carthalinica*, and *P. tenuifolia*—but further research is needed to determine the validity of this approach. Prefers neutral to slightly acidic soil. From Romania, Ukraine, and Hungary. ‡ 24 in (60 cm). Z3–8 H8–1. **'Plena'** Double red flowers.

P. steveniana see *P. wittmanniana*

P. tomentosa see *P. wittmanniana*

P. veitchii One of the last peonies to appear in the spring. Deeply dissected foliage, bronzy green at first, turns dark green during the summer. The oblong or elliptic, narrow leaflets are hairless above and below, or have short hairs on the veins beneath. Two or more, slightly nodding, pink, magenta, or pale purple flowers, up to 2 in (5 cm) across, in late spring. Leaves turn orange-brown in fall. Ideal for the front of a herbaceous border; needs full sun to thrive. Very similar to *P. anomala*, but this species has more than one flower per stem. From China. ‡ 24 in (60 cm). Z3–8 H8–1. **var. *woodwardii*** Shorter, with magenta or pale purple flowers. ‡ 12 in (30 cm).

P. wittmanniana syn. *P. steveniana*, *P. tomentosa* A substantial plant needing plenty of space and often as wide as it is tall. The leaves are bronzy green, becoming dark green in the summer, with nine or more egg-shaped or broadly elliptic, hairy leaflets that can measure up to 6½ in (17 cm) long by 4½ in (11 cm) wide. The cream or pale yellow, 4–5-in (10–13-cm) flowers, which may be partly hidden by the leaves, come in mid- and late spring. Has been used to produce hybrids such as 'Requiem'. Forms with smooth foliage and flowers held well above the foliage are sometimes separated out as subsp. *nudicarpa* or *P. steveniana*. From Azerbaijan, Georgia, northern Iran, and Turkey. ‡ 39 in (100 cm). Z3–8 H8–1

RICH COLOR AS A SPECIMEN

PAEONIA LACTIFLORA 'KARL ROSENFIELD' is a tough, steadfast, and reliable old favorite and, when left undivided to develop into mature clumps, is very impressive in flower. When surrounded by other plants for which fine detail is the most consistent feature, as here with the developing green seed heads of *Veronica gentianoides*, held vertically on slender stems, the specimen quality of the peony is noticeably enhanced. The small flowers of the blue catmint behind and the neat habit of the pink dianthus in front both serve to emphasize the impressive stature of the peony.

LEFT 1 *Paeonia officinalis* 'Anemoniflora Rosea' **2** *P. officinalis* 'Rubra Plena' **3** *P. tenuifolia* **4** *P. veitchii*

PANICUM

POACEAE

Tall, delicate grasses with late summer flowers and colorful fall foliage.

Some 470 annual and perennial species are found in deserts, savannas, forests, and swamps throughout the tropics and temperate regions of North America. Foliage and growth habit varies considerably, though the flowers are much the same in all species. Some behave as woody shrubs, others are low cushions; most species suitable for gardens are clump-forming with glossy green to blue-pointed leaves. The flowers are usually shiny milletlike beads, nodding at the ends of wiry stems, either arching over in heavy swags or hanging in airy profusion. These warm-season grasses start into growth late in the spring and are best grown in groups or drifts in an open position with other late-flowering grasses and herbaceous flowers and seed heads. The taller species look particularly effective in prairie-style borders.

CULTIVATION Very well-drained, but moisture-retentive, fertile soil in an open position. Divide large clumps in late spring.

PROPAGATION From seed or by division. Cultivars by division only.

PROBLEMS In poor drainage, leaves can turn yellow at the tips in spring or summer and eventually blacken and die. Some blue-leaved cultivars prone to rust in very humid weather.

P. clandestinum (Deer-tongue grass) Evergreen clumps of bamboolike foliage with smooth, pointed, green to blue-gray leaves 3 in (8 cm) long and 1¼ in (3 cm) wide, turning purple in the fall. In mid- to late summer tall leafy flower-stems up to 60 in (1.5 m) high end in airy flowerheads hung with shiny brown, beady flowers, side branches carry somewhat more compact flowerheads. Looks best planted in drifts in open woods or informal gardens. Found in moist woods, thickets, and waste places in North America. ↕ 39–60 in (1–1.5 m). Z5–9 H9–1

P. virgatum (Switch grass, Panic grass) Slowly creeping clumps, sometimes spreading more rapidly in moist soil, with upright, purple-blue green to bright green, smooth, pointed leaves, 20 in (50 cm) long and ⅝ in (15 mm) wide. Tall, slender, bluish flower stems, sometimes lax and arching, or in cultivars usually more erect and sturdy, appear from late summer to early fall. The purple-brown flowers nod at the end of wiry branches in shimmering

clouds. Particularly associated with the American tallgrass prairies, and gave inspiration to the first German designers to create prairie-type gardens. Needs very good drainage and is reluctant to flower on heavy soil. Cut back dead foliage in spring. Found in open woods, prairies, and dunes from Canada to Mexico and the West Indies. ↕ 6–8 ft (1.8–2.4 m). Z5–9 H9–1.
'Cloud Nine' Rounded clumps of blue-gray leaves turning dark gold in fall. ↕ 5–8 ft (1.5–2.4 m). **'Dallas Blues'** Blue stems and leaves with pinkish flowers. ↕ 4–5 ft (1.2–1.5 m). **'Hänse Herms'** Green leaves turning deep burgundy, and airy, tiny, purple flowers. ↕ 3–4 ft (0.9–1.2 m). **'Heavy Metal'** Blue-gray to blue-purple leaves turning yellow in fall; stiff upright habit with pink flowers. Raised by Kurt Bluemel, MD. ↕ 4–5 ft (1.2–1.5 m). **'Northwind'** Upright, steel-blue foliage, drought-tolerant. From Northwind Perennial Farm, WI. ↕ to 6 ft 1.8 m). **'Prairie Sky'** Leaves more blue than 'Heavy Metal', more lax habit. ↕ 3–4 ft (0.9–1.2 m). **'Rehbraun'** Red-tipped green leaves becoming a mix of yellow and purple in fall. ↕ 3¼ ft (1 m). **'Rotstrahlbusch'** Leaves turning dark red in fall, light brown flowers ↕ 3¼–4 ft (1–1.2 m). **'Rubrum'** Red-tipped, green leaves turning bright red in fall, sparse but delicate pink to chestnut flowers. ↕ 3¼ ft (1 m). **'Shenandoah'** Leaves turn dark wine red in fall. ↕ 4 ft (1.2 m). **'Squaw'** Leaves green with red tints in fall, pink-purple flowers. Sterile. Raised by Kurt Bluemel, MD. ↕ 3¼–4 ft (1–1.2 m). **'Strictum'** Upright clumps, gray-green leaves turning yellow and red in fall, reddish flowers. ↕ 3–4 ft (0.9 –1.2 m). **'Warrior'** Leaves green developing dark red-brown tints in fall, large flowerheads with dark pink flowers. Sterile. Introduced by Kurt Bluemel, MD. ↕ 4 ft (1.2 m).

PAPAVER

Poppy

PAPAVERACEAE

Bold, decorative, and in a wide range of colors, poppies are easy in open, sunny places.

About 70 annual and perennial species distributed across the Northern Hemisphere, but especially in Europe and Asia, with one found south of the equator, in South Africa. The lowland species tend to be annuals, particularly associated with arable land or dry rocky places, whereas the perennial species are found in mountains, some reaching high alpine levels. The perennials are mostly clump-forming or tufted plants, although a few are monocarpic, forming handsome leaf-rosettes in the first two or three years before flowering—after which they die.

In general, the leaves come in basal tufts and, like the stems, are often rough and rather bristly. The flowers are borne singly, or in lax clusters, on leafless or leafy stems, and each is cupped or saucer-shaped with four petals, sometimes more

(especially in cultivated forms) surrounding a boss of many stamens. The petals are crumpled in the buds and expand like the wings of an emerging butterfly as the flowers open. The two or three, often bristly sepals, which completely enclose the flowers in bud, fall away when the flowers open. The poppy fruit varies greatly and is an important feature in accurate identification of the different species: the capsules are rather like pepper shakers, with a ring of pores at the top from which the numerous seeds are shaken by the wind.

CULTIVATION Perennial poppies thrive in a wide variety of garden soils, provided the soil is well-drained and not excessively acidic; a pH of 6–8 is ideal. Although a few species, for example, *P. rupifragum,* will grow well in dappled shade, most succeed best in full sun. All poppies thrive in a deeply dug soil with added humus as well as generous mulch of well-rotted organic matter in the late fall or early spring, depending on when growth starts. Too-fertile conditions will cause an abundance of foliage and lax, untidy growth. The larger types, especially the Oriental Poppy Group, mostly require some form of support, otherwise the clumps collapse outward as the stems flop apart, especially after heavy rain.

PROPAGATION Most species can be readily grown from seed, which is often produced in abundance, while division of some of the larger tufted species is also possible. The Oriental Poppy Group can be easily propagated from root cuttings. Seed of cultivars gives very mixed results; this is especially true of the Oriental Poppy Group, which are better propagated from root cuttings to ensure continuity of a particular cultivar. The multi-crowned perennial types can be divided in the late summer or early fall.

PROBLEMS Powdery mildew.

P. atlanticum (Moroccan poppy) A tufted evergreen forming a lax, spreading rosette of gray-green, rough-hairy, elliptical leaves that are somewhat lobed and coarsely toothed. The rather sparse flowers are borne on slender, upright, softly hairy, somewhat leafy stems; they are saucer-shaped or flattish, dull orange, 2–2¾ in (5–6.5 cm) across, and produced in succession from late spring until mid-fall. The fruit capsule is narrowly club-shaped and smooth. Often confused in gardens with the very closely related *P. rupifragum,* but *P. atlanticum* is far more often seen. For any good, moist, yet well-drained soil in full sun or part-shade, and excellent in gravel gardens, where it may prove invasive. Raise from seed. From the mountains of Morocco. ↕ 16–20 in (40–50 cm). Z5–7 H7–4.
'Flore Pleno' Dull orange, semidouble flowers; seedlings will produce both single and semidouble flowers and singles must be ruthlessly weeded out

CONTRAST AND HARMONY

THE LARGE FOUR-PETALED flowers of Oriental poppy 'Juliane'
create quite an impact in spite of their soft and delicate coloring.
However, being set against the prolific catmint *Nepeta* 'Six Hills
Giant', with its mass of tiny lavender blue flowers crowded on
to long stems that lean in among the stout stems of the poppy,
creates such a contrast in form that the poppy flowers stand out
in shape, yet blend well in color. Additional subtlety and intrigue
are provided by the unusual pale scarlet markings at the base of
the poppy petals.

if semidoubles are to be maintained
in the garden.

P. bracteatum syn. *P. orientale* var.
bracteatum A robust, leafy, deciduous
plant with a large basal tuft of bristly,
elliptical, lobed and sharply toothed
leaves to 14 in (35 cm) long. The erect
stems carry several similar, but smaller,
more or less unstalked leaves, the
uppermost three or four being bractlike
and held in a cluster immediately
beneath the flowers. The flowers,
appearing in late spring and early
summer, are large and deeply cupped,
5–7 in (12.5–17.5 cm) across, ranging
in color from blood red to purple-
crimson, the petals black-blotched at
the base. Distinct from *P. orientale* in the
ruff of two to four small, leaflike bracts
immediately beneath, and often closely
pressed to, the flowerbuds. Thrives in a
sunny position in well-drained soil.
Propagate either from seed or by root
cuttings. From eastern Turkey, northern

and northwestern Iran and the
Caucasus Mountains. ‡32–48 in (80–
120 cm). Z5–8 H8–5

P. heldreichii see *P. spicatum*

P. x hybridum 'Flore Pleno' see
P. lateritium 'Fireball'

P. lateritium (Armenian poppy) A
tufted deciduous plant, spreading by
stolons, with mostly roughly-hairy,
elliptical basal leaves, up to 8 in (20 cm)
long, which are divided into opposite
pairs of lobes, themselves coarsely
toothed. The cupped flowers, 1¾–2¾ in
(4–6 cm) across and borne singly on
slender wiry stems, are brick red or
occasionally apricot and open in late
spring and early summer, occasionally
later. The stamens are orange-yellow,
while the smooth fruit capsules are
more-or-less club-shaped. For a sunny
position in well-drained soil; plants
tend to spread from where they were

planted. Divide in late summer or
winter. From the mountains of Turkish
Armenia. ‡12–20 in (30–50 cm). Z4–9
H9–1. **'Fireball'** syn. *P. x hybridum*
'Flore Pleno', 'Nanum Flore Pleno',
'Nana Plena' Slender stems each carry
a solitary, fully double, pomponlike,
bright orange-scarlet, 1¼–1¾-in (3–
4-cm) flower. ‡8–12 in (20–30 cm).

P. miyabeanum (Japanese poppy)
A small tufted, short-lived, dainty
evergreen forming neat tufts of rough-
bristly, grayish, basal leaves split into
pairs of opposite lobes. The solitary,
pale yellow, deeply cupped, 1¼–1¾-in
(3–4-cm) flowers are borne on slender,
leafless, bristly stems and are followed
by small, rounded, bristly fruit capsules.
Thrives in a sunny position in well-
drained, gritty soil, though plants are
prone to rotting in excessive winter
rain, so a gravel garden is ideal, and
they will self-sow there. From the
Kurile Islands, northern Japan. ‡4–6 in
(10–15 cm). Z7–9 H9–5

P. orientale (Oriental poppy) A tufted,
multi-stemmed, bristly plant with basal
leaves, up to 12 in (30 cm) long, that
are lobed into opposite pairs of sharply
toothed segments and carried on long
stalks; the stem leaves are similar, but
often slightly smaller and unstalked.
In early summer and midsummer, the
leafy stems are topped with large,
individual cup- or bowl-shaped, 4–6-in
(10–15 cm)-flowers, each with four
overlapping, slightly frilled, orange-red
to blood red petals that sport a
handsome purplish black blotch at the
base. The boss of stamens is normally
violet-black. The smooth fruit capsule
is spinning-top-shaped with a row of
pores just below the rim. For a sunny
position in any good well-drained soil.
Ring with small branches to support
the stems as they elongate in early
summer, as the flowers can be heavy
when wet. Best propagated by root
cuttings. From eastern Turkey, northern
and northwestern Iran and the
Caucasus Mountains. ‡20–36 in (50–
90 cm). Z3–7 H9–1. **var. bracteatum**
see *P. bracteatum*

P. Oriental Poppy Group Bold, multi-
stemmed, rather bristly plants have a
cluster of leaves 12–14 in (30–38 cm)
long, variously lobed and toothed.
In late spring and early summer, and
sometimes later, the leafy stems are
topped with large, individual cup- or
bowl-shaped, single or semidouble,
sometimes frilly flowers in a range
of red, pink, purple and white shades
often with dark, boldly contrasting
blotches at the base of the petals. The
boss of dark stamens is often a feature
in itself and is followed by a large
capsule. For a sunny positions in any
good, well-drained soil. Best propagated
by root cuttings. These are hybrids
involving at least three western Asian
species, *P. bracteatum*, *P. orientale* and
the rarely seen *P. pseudo-orientale* (see
Oriental Poppies). ‡20–36 in (50–
90 cm). Z3–7 H9–1. **'Aglaja'** Bright
salmon pink, single flowers have
pleated, overlapping petals, each with
a small, dark basal blotch. Strong stems.

Sometimes misspelled 'Aglaya'. ‡28–
32 in (70–80 cm). **'Allegro'** Bright
orange-red, single flowers have papery
petals with a bold basal black blotch.
‡24–28 in (60–70 cm). **'Beauty of
Livermere'** Especially large, single
flowers of deep lustrous crimson-scarlet,
the markedly overlapping, thick-
textured petals have a large basal black
blotch. ‡36–44 in (90–110 cm).
'Beauty Queen' Rather delicate,
unblotched, single flowers are brownish
flushed with orange or apricot, the
petals thin and somewhat ruffled. ‡30–
40 in (75–100 cm). **'Black and White'**
Large, pure white, single flowers, with
overlapping, somewhat ruffled petals
with a prominent black blotch just
above the base. The whitest of all.
Sometimes mistaken for 'Perry's White',
which has pink-tinted petals. ‡28–32 in
(70–80 cm). **'Carneum'** Shallow bowl-
shaped, single flowers of bright salmon
pink; the petals are slightly pleated,
with a large basal black blotch. From
seed, and may be variable. ‡28–32 in
(70–80 cm). **'Cedar Hill'** A relatively
small plant with pink, unblotched
single flowers. ‡28–36 in (70–90 cm).
'Cedric Morris' syn. 'Cedric's Pink'
Large, deep bowl-shaped, single flowers;

the soft pink, gray-tinged, somewhat ruffled petals have a large basal black blotch. Introduced by the celebrated horticulturist-painter from Suffolk, England, Sir Cedric Morris. ‡28–36 in (70–90 cm). **'Charming'** Pale pink, medium-sized, single flowers have somewhat crumpled petals with an ill-defined, streaky basal blotch. ‡28–36 in (65–75 cm). **'Choir Boy'** Pure white, single flowers have ruffled petals with a bold, oblong, black basal blotch. Variable when sold as seed, as it often is. ‡32–36 in (80–90 cm). **'Coral Reef'** Vivid, coral pink, single flowers with overlapping, ruffled petals have a small purple-black basal blotch. Introduced by Thompson & Morgan Seeds and generally sold as seed, or seed-raised plants. ‡24–30 in (60–75 cm). **'Curlilocks'** Medium-sized, bright orange-red, single flowers, the petals have a deeply lacerated margin and a prominent, black basal blotch. ‡28–30 in (70–80 cm). **'Doubloon'** Medium-sized, bright orange-red, semidouble flowers. ‡30–36 in (75–90 cm). **'Effendi'** Large, bright salmon pink, single flowers; the petals are overlapping, somewhat frilled and pleated, reddish at the base but also with a uneven dark blotch above the base. ‡28–44 in (70–85 cm). **'Elam Pink'** Mid-blush pink, single flowers, the petals are somewhat ruffled and with a medium-sized, basal black blotch. ‡28–32 in (70–80 cm). **'Enchantress'** *see* 'Wunderkind'. **'Fatima'** White, single flowers margined with salmon pink; the petals are frilled and overlapping with a reddish purple basal blotch. Strong stems. ‡24–30 in (60–75 cm). **'Forncett Summer'** Single, bright salmon pink flowers, with overlapping, deeply lacerated petals, have a small, basal blotch. Introduced by John Metcalf of Four Seasons Nursery, Forncett St. Mary, Norfolk, England. ‡28–32 in (70–80 cm). **'Garden Glory'** Large, single, orange-pink flowers have a pale red flush, the petals markedly overlapping, frilled and fringed at the margin, unblotched but reddening toward the base. ‡30–36 in (75–90 cm). **Goliath Group** A group of similar, large, single flowered plants, with very large orange-scarlet flowers, the petals somewhat ruffled with a large, bold basal black blotch. Much confused with 'Beauty of Livermere', which is a stockier plant with crimson-scarlet flowers. ‡40–48 in (100–120 cm). **'Grauwe Witwe'** White single flowers are flushed with the palest gray-pink, eventually pure white, the petals somewhat ruffled with a distinct to indistinct purple or maroon blotch above the base. ‡28–34 in (70–85 cm). **'Harvest Moon'** Semidouble flowers are deep orange at first, but fade; petals strongly ruffled and overlapping, unblotched. ‡36–44 in (90–110 cm). **'Helen Ellis'** *see* 'Turkish Delight'. **'Helen Elizabeth'** *see* 'Turkish Delight'. **'Indian Chief'** Large, single, deep mahogany-red flowers have thick unblotched petals. ‡28–36 in (70–90 cm). **'John III'** Neat, shallow bowl-shaped, lustrous pinkish red, single flowers have an orange flush, the

unblotched petals pleated and overlapping. Raised and introduced by Countess von Stein-Zeppelin, Germany. ‡24–28 in (60–70 cm). **'John Metcalf'** Medium-sized, single, pale orange flowers have a whitish center, the unblotched petals somewhat pleated. Named for the owner of Four Seasons Nursery, Norfolk, England. ‡24–30 in (60–75 cm). **'Juliane'** Delicate, pale pink, single flowers have thick, overlapping, pleated petals, which are unblotched but flushed with red at the base. ‡28–34 in (70–85 cm). **'Karine'** Shallow, bowl-shaped, shell pink, single flowers, the petals slightly pleated, overlapping and unblotched but with a reddish purple basal zone. Raised and introduced Countess von Stein-Zeppelin, Germany. Strong stems. ‡24–28 in (60–70 cm). **'Khedive'** Large salmon pink, single flowers are flushed with orange and have a whitish center, the petals broad, overlapping, and very frilled, with a small purple blotch at the base. Another from Countess von Stein-Zeppelin. ‡24–30 in (60–75 cm). **'Kleine Tänzerin'** Single, relatively small, bowl-shaped, dark pink flowers with overlapping, frilled petals with a dark purple blotch toward the base. Like a small version of 'Mrs. Perry'. ‡24–30 in (60–75 cm). **'Ladybird'** Substantial vermilion-red, single flowers with a hint of orange, have ruffled, overlapping petals with a large bold, basal black blotch. Probably the cultivar with the largest flowers. ‡28–32 in (70–80 cm). **'Lady Moore'** syn. 'Lady Frederick Moore'. Wide, saucer-shaped, clear salmon pink, single flowers, the petals slightly ruffled and with a prominent basal black blotch. ‡28–34 in (70–85 cm). **'Lauren's Lilac'** Robust with large, single, mauve-purple flowers with a ruff of leaflike bracts; the petals are slightly ruffled and with a basal black blotch. Raised by NCCPG National Collection holder Sandy Worth, England. ‡35–40 in (87–100 cm). **'Lavender Girl'** *see* 'Lilac Girl'. **'Leuchtfeuer'** Lustrous reddish pink, single flowers with an orange flush; the petals are widely overlapping, slightly ruffled and with an oblong, purplish black basal blotch. ‡28–32 in (70–80 cm). **'Lighthouse'** Rather large, single floppy flowers are pale salmon pink, but fading with age, the petals slightly pleated and with a bold basal red blotch. ‡32–38 in (80–95 cm). **'Lilac Girl'** syn. 'Lavender Girl' Large, pale lilac purple, single flowers, fading in strong light, the unblotched petals pleated and overlapping. ‡32–40 in (80–100 cm). **'Manhattan'** Large, deeply cupped, rose pink, single flowers have somewhat ruffled petals with black basal markings. The most widely available of the New York Series, raised in Holland by Elinor de Konig. ‡28–34 in (70–85 cm). **'Marcus Perry'**

RIGHT 1 *Papaver lateritium* 'Fireball'
Papaver Oriental Poppy Group:
2 'Black and White' **3** 'Forncett Summer' **4** 'Karine' **5** 'Mrs Perry' **6** 'Patty's Plum' **7** 'Prinzessin Viktoria Luise' **8** 'Raspberry Queen'

Satiny, orange-scarlet, single flowers, the overlapping petals somewhat ruffled and with a dark basal blotch. ‡ 28–32 in (70–80 cm). **'May Queen'** Semidouble, saucer-shaped, unblotched, orange-red flowers have somewhat quilled petals. ‡ 26–30 in (65–75 cm). **'Mrs. Perry'** Large, rich salmon pink, single flowers have broad, overlapping, somewhat pleated petals with a prominent basal purple blotch that gradually fades. ‡ 32–40 in (80–100 cm). **'Orange Glow'** Single flowers in the brightest orange on a robust plant, the unblotched petals somewhat ruffled. ‡ 36–40 in (90–100 cm). **'Oriana'** Single, bowl-shaped, orange flowers; the somewhat overlapping and crumpled petals have a purple-mauve basal blotch. ‡ 30–34 in (75–85 cm). **'Patty's Plum'** syn. 'Mrs. Marrow's Plum' Deeply bowl-shaped, purple, single flowers but burnishing and fading with age, the petals overlapping, ruffled and slightly pleated, with a black basal blotch. Starts well but fades badly. ‡ 28–34 in (70–85 cm). **'Perry's White'** Large, white, single flowers with the faintest pink flush, the petals overlapping and somewhat ruffled, have a rather undistinguished purplish or reddish blotch or zone at the base. Perhaps not quite identical to the original plant found by a customer and introduced almost a hundred years ago by horticulturist Amos Perry of Enfield, Middlesex, England. ‡ 34–38 in (85–95 cm). **'Petticoat'** Single, saucer-shaped, salmon pink flowers have wide and overlapping, strongly frilled and pleated petals with a small, broken, purplish black basal blotch. ‡ 28–32 in (70–80 cm). **'Picotée'** Medium-sized, single, white flowers have an uneven salmon orange marginal zone, the unblotched petals frilled and pleated. The width of the marginal zone may vary with the weather. ‡ 26–32 in (65–80 cm). **'Pink Ruffles'** Compact, with medium-sized,

single, pink flowers with deeply fringed petals. ‡ 24 in (60 cm). **'Pinnacle'** Probably the same as 'Picotée'. **Pizzicato Group** syn. 'Pizzicato' A relatively dwarf selection of seed-raised plants with large, single flowers that range in color from red and scarlet to orange, salmon, mauve, pink and white, with petals that are usually dark-blotched at the base. ‡ 20–24 in (50–60 cm). **'Prinz Eugen'** Single, orange-pink flowers have overlapping frilled and fringed, unblotched petals, reddening toward the base. Very like 'Garden Glory' but a rather shorter. ‡ 28–32 in (70–80 cm). **'Prinzessin Viktoria Luise'** (**Princess Victoria Louise**) Very large, salmon pink, single flowers; the petals are thick and slightly pleated, with a purplish black basal blotch. ‡ 28–36 in (70–90 cm). **'Raspberry Queen'** Large, raspberry pink, unblotched, single flowers have darker streaks. ‡ 30–38 in (75–90 cm). **'Rembrandt'** Deep red, single flowers, the overlapping, slightly ruffled petals have an indistinct basal blotch. ‡ 30–34 in (75–85 cm). **'Rosenpokal'** Pink, single flowers, the petals are slightly ruffled, with a small, purplish black basal blotch. ‡ 30–36 in (75–90 cm). **'Royal Chocolate Distinction'** Large, deeply cupped, single flowers of deep chocolate-maroon with slightly ruffled petals. ‡ 28–34 in (70–85 cm). **'Royal Wedding'** Pure white, single flowers, the petals overlapping and somewhat ruffled with a prominent black basal blotch. ‡ 30–34 in (75–85 cm). **'Salmon Glow'** Large, semidouble, orange-salmon flowers have a silvery sheen; the petals are very frilled and with a small basal black blotch. ‡ 34–38 in (85–95 cm). **'Scarlet King'** Large, scarlet-red, single flowers; the unblotched petals are somewhat ruffled. ‡ 32–36 in (80–90 cm). **'Sindbad'** syn. 'Sinbad' Single, orange-red flowers; the unblotched petals are somewhat frilled, paler and almost whitish toward the red-flushed base. Strong stems. ‡ 34–42 in (85–105 cm). **'Snow Goose'** Pure white, semidouble flowers; the ruffled petals have a black basal blotch. Raised by NCCPG National Collection holder Sandy Worth, England. ‡ 32–36 in (80–90 cm). **'Springtime'** Pale salmon, single flowers merge to a white center, the unblotched petals somewhat ruffled. ‡ 28–32 in (70–80 cm). **'Sultana'** Large, single, cerise-rose flowers, redder on the exterior and toward the base, the petals frilled and somewhat crumpled, with an indistinct, blackish purple basal blotch. ‡ 26–30 in (65–75 cm). **Super Poppy Series** A series bred in California over thirty years by James DeWelt, with the aim of producing plants whose flowers lasted well in the hot, bright California sun. He is said to have used *P. atlanticum*, *P. bracteatum*, *P. californicum*, *P. orientale*, *P. rupifragum*, and *P. somniferum* in his breeding program, but it seems unlikely that the resulting introductions actually have blood from all these species. There are now well over a dozen cultivars starting

to become available. **'Türkenlouis'** Single, deep scarlet-orange flowers have deeply fringed, ruffled petals with a blackish red basal blotch. Very similar to 'Curlilocks' but without blotched petals. Strong stems. ‡ 28–32 in (70–80 cm). **'Turkish Delight'** ('Helen Ellis', 'Helen Elizabeth') Bowl-shaped, single, soft salmon pink flowers, the unblotched petals are somewhat ruffled. ‡ 24–30 in (60–75 cm). **'Watermelon'** Single, bowl-shaped, pale pinkish purple flowers, the petals are somewhat ruffled and have a large black basal blotch. ‡ 32–40 in (80–100 cm). **'Wunderkind'** ('Enchantress') Single, bright raspberry pink flowers. The petals are somewhat frilled with a prominent, black basal blotch. ‡ 26–32 in (65–80 cm).

P. pilosum A handsome, tufted plant with softly hairy, oblong to elliptical, coarsely toothed basal leaves up to 8 in (20 cm) long. In early summer and midsummer, stiff, erect, sparsely leafy stems arise, candelabra-like, from the basal tuft of leaves, and these carry clusters of orange-red to deep orange or lurid scarlet flowers, the petals often with a whitish basal blotch. Each flower is rather flat, 1¼–1¾ in (3–4.5 cm) across, with somewhat crumpled petals and orange-yellow anthers. The narrowly oblong fruit capsules are small, not more than ⅝ in (1.5 cm) long, smooth and with a distinctive flat top. For well-drained, light soil in full sun, but in a sheltered position. Plants resent disturbance once established, so raise from seed. From Bithynia and Galatia in Turkey. ‡ 20–24 in (50–60 cm). Z5–7 H7–5

P. rupifragum (Spanish poppy) A tufted, tap-rooted perennial forming a lax rosette of gray-green, elliptical, lobed and sharply toothed, rough, sparsely hairy leaves to about 6 in (15 cm) long. From late spring until early fall, a succession of slender, ascending, flowering stems arise, each bearing just a few leaves and up to five brick red, upright, saucer-shaped flowers, 1½–1¾ in (3.5–4.5 cm) across. The fruit capsules are narrowly oblong. Flourishes in any moist, yet well-drained, soil in sun or part-shade, it also thrives in gravel gardens, though it may prove invasive. Easily raised from seed. Very closely related to *P. atlanticum*, which is slightly hairier. From Andalucia (southern Spain). ‡ 20 in (50 cm). Z6–9 H9–6. **'Double Tangerine Gem'** Semidouble, tangerine-colored flowers. **'Flore Pleno'** Semidouble, brick red flowers. The form that is most common and most often seen in gardens.

P. spicatum syn. *P. heldreichii* A handsome plant with large tufts of softly hairy, oblong to elliptical, coarsely toothed basal leaves up to 8 in (20 cm) long. In early summer and midsummer, stiff, erect, sparsely leafy stems carry a slender spike of pale brick red flowers, each rather flat, 1¼–1¾ in (3–4.5 cm) across, and with somewhat crumpled petals. The anthers are orange-yellow. The narrowly oblong fruit capsules are

small, not more than ⅝ in (1.5 cm) long, and smooth. For well-drained, gritty soil in full sun and in a sheltered position. Dislikes excessive winter rain. Division is not possible—plants have a single, stout taproot—so they must be raised from seed. From the Taurus Mountains in southern Turkey. ‡ 20–28 in (50–70 cm). Z5–7 H7–5

PARADISEA
St. Bruno's lily
ASPHODELACEAE

Hardy and elegant plants that have grassy foliage and sprays of small lilylike flowers in the early summer.

Two species of these compact, deciduous plants are native to the damp meadows in the mountains of southern Europe, and both of them are frequently grown. Rather fleshy rhizomes produce clumps of narrow, gray-green, grasslike leaves. Separate stems bear graceful sprays of pure white, fragrant, trumpet-shaped flowers.

CULTIVATION Grows well in sun or part-shade in any fertile, well-drained soil rich in humus.

PROPAGATION By careful division or from seed.

PROBLEMS Slugs and snails.

P. liliastrum (St. Bruno's lily) Compact plant forming a clump of narrow, gray-green leaves to 10 in (25 cm) long. Up to ten, trumpet-shaped, white flowers, 1½–2 in (4–5 cm) long, each petal tipped with green, are borne in a one-sided spike in early summer and midsummer. From damp mountain meadows in Southern Europe. ‡ 12–24 in (30–60 cm). Z7–9 H9–7

P. lusitanica Robust plant with narrow leaves to 16 in (40 cm) long in a compact clump. During early summer and midsummer, tall stems bear up to 25 open funnel-shaped, white flowers ¾ in (2 cm) long in a loose spike. From damp, open woods and meadows in southwestern Europe. Easily grown in damp, fertile soil. ‡ 3¼–4 ft (1–1.2 m). Z7–9 H9–7

PARAHEBE
SCROPHULARIACEAE

Unusual, sprawling evergreen offering an exotic ground-cover alternative for the Mediterranean garden.

Around thirty species of shrubs and shrubby perennials, closely related to *Hebe*, growing in rocky soil from New Zealand, Australia, and Papua New Guinea. Often low-growing plants, they produce toothed leaves and pretty, saucer-shaped flowers in shades of pink, white, or blue, on sprawling stems that root readily where they touch the ground. *P. perfoliata* is strikingly different from other members of

LEFT *Papaver* Oriental Poppy Group 'Türkenlouis'

LEFT **1** *Parahebe perfoliata* **2** *Paris incompleta* **3** *Patrinia scabiosifolia*

PATRINIA
VALERIANACEAE

Easily grown shade-loving plants with sprays of small flowers above attractively divided leaves.

Fifteen deciduous species from open mountain woodlands and meadows from Europe to East Asia, three of which are increasingly being grown. Compact clumps of toothed or lobed leaves provide a good background to the large sprays of tiny, cup-shaped, bright yellow or white flowers in late summer. Most are plants for cool shade rather than a sunny border.

CULTIVATION Grow in humus-rich soil in part- or full shade.

PROPAGATION From seed or by division.

PROBLEMS Slugs and snails.

P. gibbosa Clump-forming. Erect stems bear attractive, jaggedly lobed, oval leaves. In late summer and early fall, small, curiously scented yellow flowers, each ¼ in (5 mm) across, open in branched sprays reminiscent of lady's mantle (*Alchemilla mollis*). From mountain woodlands in northern Japan. ‡ 18 in (45 cm). Z5–8 H8–5

P. scabiosifolia Stout rhizomes form a loose clump of ladderlike, divided, light green leaves. In late summer and early fall, slender, upright leafy stems bear branched clusters of small flowers ¼ in (5 mm) across, Grows in a more open situation than the other species, and can be used as a "see-through" plant in the same way as *Verbena bonariensis*. From sunny meadows in China, Japan, Korea, and Taiwan. ‡ 24–36 in (60–90 cm). Z5–8 H8–5

P. triloba Clump-forming plant with broad, deeply lobed, almost maplelike, light green leaves. In late summer and early fall, upright leafy stems carry large, branched clusters of fragrant, yellow flowers, ¼ in (5 mm) across. Good foliage and showy in flower. From rocky woods in the mountains of central and western Japan. ‡ 18–24 in (45–60 cm). Z5–8 H8–4

PELARGONIUM
GERANIACEAE

Hardy summer-flowering, more elegant perennial relations of the familiar pelargoniums of containers and bedding schemes.

Approximately 250 mainly frost-tender species of woody-based evergreen or herbaceous perennials, and annuals, growing in a variety of open, sunny places from mountains to deserts. Most are South African, although some hail from Australia and the Middle East. The few hardy

---

the group in having large, hairless, blue-green leaves.

CULTIVATION Grow in full sun or light shade in well-drained, acidic soil.

PROPAGATION From seed, by division or semiripe cuttings.

PROBLEMS Leaf spot; slugs may eat young growth.

P. perfoliata Evergreen perennial, becoming woody at the base in old plants, producing sprawling or arching stems. The leathery leaves are opposite, broadly egg-shaped, often toothed on the edge, and overlap with each other, becoming joined at the base, so that they completely encircle the stem. The bright blue-green color of the leaves complements beautifully the blue saucer-shaped flowers, to about ½ in (12 mm) across, which are carried in nodding sprays in late summer and early fall. Useful ground cover for well-drained, not-too-fertile soil. Rejuvenate old plants by cutting back to ground level in spring, or replace with new plants raised from cuttings taken in summer. From New South Wales and Victoria, Australia. ‡ 24–28 in (60–70 cm). Z9–11 H12–3. **'Pringle'** Flowers white with a purple ring.

PARIS
TRILLIACEAE

Uncommon yet elegant and charming woodlanders that are valued for foliage, fruit, and their intriguing flowers.

About 30 species of deciduous woodland plants from the Old World, primarily Asia and the Himalaya, are closely related to *Trillium*, but their classification is still confused. Creeping rhizomes carry upright stems with up to twelve

---

oval or lance-shaped leaves to 6 in (15 cm) long, clustered toward the top and just under the flower. Each understated but fascinating flower comprises a ring of broad, pointed, green segments below a second ring of narrow, threadlike segments. The fruits vary dramatically from a single fleshy berry to a many-seeded capsule, with some species having fruits intermediate in form. Many of the plants recently introduced from China are incorrectly named, and the naming in general is still very confused.

CULTIVATION Best in deep shade in cool, humus-rich soil. Some plants emerge very early in spring and must be protected from frost.

PROPAGATION Divide the widely creeping species in early spring before, or just as, growth resumes; tighter-growing species can be split with a knife in fall, although new shoots may not appear for one or two growing seasons. Propagation from seed is slow; germination may take as long as three years.

PROBLEMS Slugs.

P. incompleta Vigorously spreading; forms lush colonies of stems, each carrying an elegant whorl of four to six leaves and small but charming green flowers. As the botanical name implies, this species is incomplete: the flowers lack the tier (whorl) of narrow petals that is found in most other *Paris* species. The large, succulent, multiple-seeded, black-purple berries ripen in midsummer. From Turkey and the Caucasus. ‡ 12 in (30 cm). Z5–8 H8–5

P. polyphylla A widely distributed and remarkably diverse species, it is under this name that the majority of *Paris* are grown, sometimes erroneously. Shoots emerge in very early spring,

---

carrying five to nine oval leaves to 8 in (20 cm) long. Each flower comprises a ring of broad green segments below another ring of longer, wispy, golden segments. These are followed by clusters of red fruits. Some plants from the western Himalaya emerge later and are considerably taller. From the Himalaya. ‡ 15 in (38 cm). Z5–8 H8–5

P. quadrifolia (Herb Paris) Vigorously spreading at the root and forming substantial colonies in cool, moist, humus-rich soil. Cluster of four to five oval leaves to 6 in (15 cm) long topped by small, but charming flowers. These consist of a ring of green, lance-shaped segments to 1½ in (3.5 cm) under a ring of slender whitish or yellowish green segments. Flowers are followed by large, plump, blue-black berries that attract many birds. From woods in Europe. ‡ 12 in (30 cm). Z5–8 H8–5

P. thibetica Distinctive, very narrow lance-shaped leaves, up to 8 in (20 cm) in length, which are held in clusters of five to nine. The green flowers have a lower ring of four or five narrow 2 in (5 cm) segments but the usual second row of floral segments either may be missing, or it may be similar to the lower ones but longer and slimmer. The fruits of this species are green, splitting to expose bright orange-red flesh-covered seeds. From northwestern China. ‡ 24 in (60 cm). Z5–8 H8–5

P. verticillata A compact plant, often forming sizeable colonies, with clusters of five to nine, narrow, lance-shaped leaves to 6 in (15 cm) long. The much shorter, 2-in (5-cm), relatively broad, green flower segments reflex strongly downward soon after opening; the upper ring of more slender segments is yellowish green. Glossy black berries follow in midsummer. From Korea, northern Japan, and China. Z5–8 H8–5

perennials grow outdoors year-round in mild climates, in sheltered borders or containers. They have the typical five-petaled pelargonium flowers, the upper two petals usually larger than the lower three, and lobed, often aromatic leaves.

CULTIVATION Choose a sheltered position in full sun, with very well-drained and reasonably fertile soil. Plants will not tolerate wet soil during the winter, so protect them from excessive rain.

PROPAGATION From seed, in spring at 59°F (15°C), or by softwood cuttings in spring.

PROBLEMS Aphids, caterpillars and thrips.

P. endlicherianum Spreads by rhizomes. Rounded, shallowly lobed, gray-green, hairy basal leaves are about 2½ in (6 cm) across; heads of bright purple-pink, fragrant flowers produced from early to late summer. The two upper petals turn back and are about 1 in (2.5 cm) long, while the three lower petals are tiny or even absent. From Turkey. ↕18 in (45 cm). Z4–8 H8–4

P. sidoides A newly popular species with long-stalked, 2 in (5 cm) wide, heart-shaped, aromatic, velvety gray-green leaves with scalloped edges. Fairly large, deep red-purple flowers, ¾–1½ in (2–3.5 cm) across, are produced from early summer to mid-fall. From South Africa. ↕12–16 in (30–40 cm). Z8–9 H9–8

PELTIPHYLLUM *see* DARMERA

PELTOBOYKINIA
SAXIFRAGACEAE

Two species of charming, if not flamboyant, shade-lovers native to Japan.

Clump-forming woodlanders that are closely related to *Tellima*, and previously included in *Boykinia*, from which they are distinguished by their leaf stems that join the leaf toward the center of the blade rather than at the edge. Delightful in the woodland garden, both species in this genus are grown for their attractive leaves, enhanced by sprays of small, yellowish flowers in early summer.

CULTIVATION Optimum growth in moist, but not soggy, humus-rich soil in part-shade.

PROPAGATION By division in spring, or from seed sown in fall.

PROBLEMS Usually trouble-free.

P. tellimoides Compact; forms clump of olive-green leaves that expands after flowering to 12 in (30 cm) across. Leaves have up to thirteen broadly triangular lobes. In early summer, erect stems carry five-petaled creamy yellow flowers, ¼–⅜ in (6–8 mm) across. From mountain woodland in Honshu, Japan. ↕24–36 in (60–90 cm). Z6–9 H9–6

P. watanabei Clump-forming plant with glossy, rounded leaves, rich bronze in spring, and much more deeply divided into several coarsely-toothed lobes. Small, bell-shaped, creamy yellow flowers are carried on the leafy stems in early summer. From hilly woodlands in Kyushu and Shikoku, southern Japan. ↕24 in (60 cm). Z6–8 H8–6

PENNISETUM
Fountain grass
POACEAE

Fountains of feathery bristly flowers adding drama and color to the late summer garden.

About 80 annual and perennial species are found throughout the tropics and warm temperate regions of the world in woodlands, savannas, and weedy places; many species are drought-tolerant. Usually forming dense clumps and their tough root systems sometimes spreading; the smooth, flat, glossy leaves may be evergreen or deciduous. In late summer to fall, arching flower stems end in distinctive cylindrical, or somewhat rounded flowerheads, a little like bristly bottle brushes with sideways-pointing hairs and often prominent stamens. They look dramatic when grown in drifts in the herbaceous border or at the edges of dry and informal gardens, or can be used to soften hard landscapes and path edges. They

LEFT *Peltoboykinia watanabei*

SURPRISING SPIKES

BRINGING TOGETHER PLANTS that have superficially similar flowerheads, but differ in almost every other way, can create an intriguing, and rather surprising, grouping. Here, at the back, the slender purple spikes of *Salvia leucantha*, held on white stems above narrow, slightly grayish leaves, lean persuasively toward the light. In front, the broader, fluffy brown spikes of *Pennisetum alopeuroides* 'Moudry', like a battery of furry rockets streaking into the sky, are not only similar in shape but have enough purple tinting to connect them to the much brighter, more striking purple in the salvia spikes.

are equally beautiful as specimen plants in containers. Some species self-seed very freely and are best planted away from lawns or paths.

CULTIVATION Grow in well-drained but moisture-retentive fertile soil in full sun to part-shade.

PROPAGATION From seed or by division; cultivars by division only. These are warm-season grasses; if plants need dividing, leave until late spring.

PROBLEMS Usually trouble-free.

P. alopecuroides syn. *Pennisetum japonicum* (Fountain grass, Swamp foxtail grass) Large clumps of arching, dark green, rough-edged leaves, ½ in (12 mm) wide, taking on red and orange tints in the fall and fading to buff in the winter. In late summer to early fall, tall flower stems splay out from the base bearing fat, caterpillar-like flowers bristling with green to purple-brown 1¼-in (3-cm) hairs. Grow in drifts at path edges and in wildflower gardens in dry areas. The flowers make lovely dried bouquets if picked when they have just opened. A native of sunny, open lowlands and

ABOVE 1 *Pennisetum alopecuroides*
2 *P. setaceum* 'Rubrum'

wasteland in Japan, and other parts of eastern Asia from Korea to the Philippines. ↕3¼ ft (1 m). Z5–9 H9–5. **'Cassian'** syn. 'Cassian's Choice' Rich yellow-orange fall foliage; dusty, light brown flowers. Introduced by Kurt Bluemel, MD. **'Foxtrot'** Arching, rose-colored, 6–9 in (15–23 cm) flowers, gold fall color. Introduced by Kurt Bluemel, MD. ↕4–5 ft (1.2–1.5 m) **'Hameln'** syn. 'Hamelin'. Deep yellow fall foliage; creamy white flowers with prominent orange stamens. ↕24–36 in (60–90 cm). **'Herbstzauber'** Bronze poker-shaped flowers. ↕30 in (75 cm). **'Little Bunny'** Slender leaves; fluffy, green flower cylinders with whitish bristles. ↕18 in (45 cm). **'Little Honey'** Very slim, white edged leaves; flowers similar to 'Little Bunny'. ↕12 in (30 cm). **'Moudry'** (Black fountain grass) Compact clumps of glossy, dark green leaves turn yellow to red in fall, arching dark purple to almost black flowers. Self-seeds freely in warmer climates. Introduced by Kurt Bluemel, MD. ↕24 in (60 cm). **'National Arboretum'** Wide glossy leaves, very dark bristles make the flowers seem almost black; self-seeds very freely. Introduced by Kurt Bluemel, MD. ↕24 in (60 cm). **f. viridescens** Bright green leaves and flowerheads. ↕30 in (75 cm). **'Weserbergland'** Green flowers with white hairs. ↕3¼ ft (1 m) **'Woodside'** Early, light green flowers with dark purple hairs and orange stamens; looks pinkish from a distance. ↕24–36 in (60–90 cm).

P. flaccidum syn. *Pennisetum incomptum* Loose clumps, spreading with an invasive root system that can travel quite long distances, the pale green, 16-x-⅝-in (40-x-1.3-cm), arching leaves turn yellow in fall. In midsummer, erect, leafy flower stems carry soft pale pink to off-white, pencil-thin flowerheads like pokers above the foliage. Best grown where it has space to run in an informal setting, such as prairie-type gardens, or grow in a bed where it can be contained. From rocky slopes, screes, and among rocks on mountain sides in northeastern Iran to the Himalaya and China. ↕4 ft (1.2 m). Z5–9 H9–5

P. macrourum Loose clumps, slowly spreading from large runners, which can become very invasive, with pale green, 24-x-5-in (60-cm-x-13 mm) leaves turning yellow in the fall. In late summer to early fall, sturdy erect flower stems bear the bristly, greenish, pencil-shaped flowerheads that sway gracefully above the foliage. Best in well-drained but moist soil in full sun in drifts among other herbaceous plants as a soft contrast to spiky seed heads. Found in damp patches in mountainous regions of South Africa. ↕4–6 ft (1.2–1.8 m). Z5–9 H9–5

P. orientale (Oriental fountain grass) Dense, low growing clumps with stout roots and fine, arching, gray-green leaves, ⅛ in (4 mm) wide, that turn rich yellow to deep brown in fall. In midsummer to early fall, numerous slightly arching flower stems carry the long, white, pipe-cleaner flowers, fluffy with hairs tinged pink-purple. The flowers are good dried. Best in a sheltered but open location in well-drained soil; plant in drifts or large groups to soften paths or walls, or grow in a container as a specimen plant. Native to dry rocky slopes, screes, rocks, and scrub from lowland to mountains in central to northwestern Asia and North Africa to Iran and the Caucasus. ↕30–36 in (75–90 cm). Z6–10 H10–4. **'Karley Rose'** Taller, more erect, more hardy, and with darker foliage, the flowers last longer and are a deeper dusky pink than the species. ↕3¼–4¼ ft (1–1.3 m). **'Tall Tails'** Gray leaves and long fluffy pink-brown flowers aging to white. ↕4¼ ft (1.3 m).

P. setaceum syn. *Macrostachyum, P. ruppellianum, P. reppelii* Dense arching clumps, dying back in winter in colder climates, have stiff, rough, pale green leaves, ⅛ in (3 mm) wide. In early to mid-fall, tall arching stems carry the green, poker-shaped flowerheads with soft pink and purple bristles up to 1½ in (4 cm) long. In marginal areas, grow in very sheltered places such as walled gardens where plants are protected from winter cold and wet. In cold areas, grow as an annual. Native to dry slopes in tropical Africa and southwestern Asia. ↕4¼ ft (1.3 m). Z8–11 H12–8. **'Burgundy Blaze'** Dark red leaves, long soft burgundy-red poker flowers, very similar to 'Rubrum' but possibly more tender. ↕3¼ ft (1 m). **'Burgundy Giant'** Looks like a red-leaved corn plant. Flower head 12 in (30 cm). ↕4–5 ft (1.2–1.5 m). Z9–10 H11–1 **'Rubrum'** syn. 'Atropurpureum', 'Atrosanguineum', 'Cupreum' Deep red to burgundy foliage and stems, arching red-purple flowers. Seeds are not usually viable. ↕3¼–5 ft (1–1.5 m). Z8–11 H11–8

P. villosum (Feather top, Feather grass, Ethiopian grass) Loose clumps slowly spreading on a tough root system have gray-green leaves ¼ in (6 mm) wide dying back over winter. In late summer, the foliage is hidden by a mass of flower stems carrying the roundish, fluffy, white flowerheads, like rabbit tails, sprouting hairs up to 1 in (2.5 cm) long. May need protection from cold, wet winters; it looks spectacular grown in large groups at the edges of borders and paths. A native of North African mountains, also found in Italy and the Azores. ↕18 in (45 cm). Z9–11 H11–1

PENSTEMON

SCHROPHULARIACEAE

Colorful, prolific and increasingly popular summer stalwarts in a wide range of shades.

About 250 perennial species, some woody at the base, from a variety of habitats from open plains through to alpine areas, generally in North and Central America. Varying in height from 4 in to 10 ft (10 cm to 3 m), they are mainly evergreen and the leaves are generally narrow, lance-shaped and often borne without stalks in opposite pairs. Tubular or bell-shaped flowers with five lobes are borne on a vertical flower spike; each flower has five prominent stamens, which may have given penstemons their name, although some scholars question this simple explanation. The fifth stamen is infertile and so technically referred to as a staminode.

Popular as border and bedding plants since the 19th century, during the first half of the 20th century penstemons gained popularity slowly. As the needs for bedding plants waned, interest focused more on hybrids with a long flowering season and increasing hardiness. The names of many older introductions have become corrupted; and occasionally older plants have been raised from seed, leading to additional confusion. They are now widely hybridized both in Europe and the US, and a myriad of garden cultivars have been, and continue to be, produced. Dale Lindgren at the University of Nebraska West Central Research and Extension Center at North Platte has been active in the breeding and introduction of quality garden penstemons.

However, gardeners should be aware of the many hundreds of other penstemons that are available. In particular, many of the small, alpine types will succeed in any sunny well-drained situation and are worth trying. However, some species, like *P. glaber*, tend to be short-lived or behave more as biennials and do not form a basal crown of foliage.

CULTIVATION Most border types, particularly the hybrid cultivars, should be grown in well-drained, fairly fertile soil in an open sunny position. Soil should be well prepared, incorporating generous amounts of organic matter and a balanced preplanting fertilizer. They

will tolerate part-shade, especially in warmer climates. Deadheading significantly prolongs the flowering season, which may extend to late fall. Their hardiness varies (*see* Hardiness, *p.361*).

Some of the border species can also be pot-grown as summer patio plants using good sized containers; some species can also be used successfully with grasses and other perennials in prairie plantings.

PROPAGATION Penstemons can be propagated from seed or by cuttings or division. Cuttings can be taken at almost any time of year, but spring and fall are best. Prepare tip cuttings about 3–4 in (7.5–10 cm) long, removing the lower leaves and trimming just below a node. Those rooted in the spring will grow quickly and be ready for planting out by early summer; fall-rooted cuttings should be kept frost-free until spring. Seed is only suitable for species, when a cold period often hastens germination, and for commercially produced strains intended to be raised from seed. Cultivars will not come true. A few species can also be divided.

PROBLEMS Slugs, aphids, powdery mildew and eelworms (*see* panel, *p.362*).

P. **'Abbotsmerry'** (3B) Large, dark red flowers, paler inside the tube with fine penciled markings, have broad lobes with the upper lobes overlapping and a prominent white staminode. Discovered in a garden in Kent, England. ‡ 30 in (75 cm). Z7–9 H9–7

P. **'Agnes Laing'** (3B) Heavy heads of attractive carmine flowers with a silvery white throat are loosely held and tend to point downward. Raised in Scotland before 1870. ‡ 32 in (80 cm). Z7–9 H9–7

P. **'Alice Hindley'** (2B) syn. *P.* 'Lady Alice Hindley' Delicate mauve to violet flowers with white throats are held in strongly vertical spikes with loose tiers of flowers. Often makes a sparse clump, so plant closely and fertilize well. Well-known plant, introduced in 1931 by the Scottish horticulturist John Forbes. ‡ 4 ft (1.2 m). Z7–9 H9–7

P. **'Andenken an Friedrich Hahn'** (2A) syn. *P.* 'Garnet' Flowers are bright crimson with deep carmine penciling in the throat above masses of fine green leaves on a loosely mounded plant. Very hardy, dependable, and floriferous. Raised in Switzerland about 1918. ‡ 36 in (90 cm). Z7–10 H10–7

P. **'Apple Blossom'** (1) Pale flesh pink, darkening toward the tips of the lobes, with a creamy white throat lightly penciled with crimson. Forms a dense, upright, many-stemmed clump with

LEFT **1** *Penstemon* 'Alice Hindley'
2 *P.* 'Andenken an Friedrich Hahn'
3 *P. barbatus* subsp. *coccineus*

many dark green leaves, but inclined to be demanding. Like a paler form of 'Evelyn'. A shorter, large flowered plant (3B) similar to 'Thorn' is sometimes grown under this name. ‡ 30 in (75 cm). Z7–10 H10–7

P. **'Barbara Barker'** see *P.* 'Beech Park'

P. barbatus (Beardlip penstemon) Slender, erect, stems have semi-evergreen foliage at the base, each leaf being narrow, lance-shaped, and up to 3 in (8 cm) long. From early summer to mid-fall, small, bright red, 1¼–1½-in (3–4-cm) flowers, tinged pink with some yellow hairs on the lower lip; the lower lip of each flower is strongly reflexed, making the upper lip prominent. From low hills, dry canyons, and scrub forest from Colorado to Nevada, and south to Mexico. ‡ 36 in (90 cm). Z4–9 H9–2. **'Cambridge Mixed'** Seed-raised mix in shades of rose, pink, blue, and purple, all with gray-green foliage. Compact habit and flowers in 16–20 weeks from an early spring sowing. ‡ 12 in (30 cm). **subsp. coccineus** Bright scarlet flowers in mid- and late summer. ‡ 3–4 ft (90–120 cm). **'Elfin Pink'** Charming, rose pink, foxglovelike flowers in loose heads for much of the summer if deadheaded. ‡ 24 in (60 cm). **'Jingle Bells'** Bright scarlet; good cut flower. ‡ 4¼ ft (1.3 m). **'Navigator'** Very dwarf, compact, basal branching, seed-raised plants with many short spikes packed with flowers in wide range of clear colors. ‡ 10–12 in (25–30 cm). **var. praecox** An early-flowering seed-raised form. **var. praecox f. nanus** A compact early form, also seed-raised.

P. **'Beech Park'** (3C) Large flowered, the lobes are strong purplish red fading to cream, and the throat is white, which gives an overall pink and white effect. Originated at Beech Park, Dublin, Ireland. Very similar to the less often seen 'Barbara Barker' and stocks may be muddled. ‡ 24 in (60 cm). Z7–9 H9–7

PENSTEMON CLASSIFICATION

To simplify the descriptions of European-style *Penstemon* hybrids, and avoid undue repetition, the simple classification scheme devised during the last RHS trial—held between 1991 and 1993—has been used wherever possible. This divides cultivars into three main groups according to flower size, two of which are further split into secondary groups. The group to which each cultivar belongs is indicated alongside the name; a few cultivars show features from two groups. Precision is not always possible; some new introductions have not yet been classified.

GROUP 1: SMALL-FLOWERED
Flowers under 1¼ in (3 cm) in length, shape varying from narrow to bulbous. Compact flowerheads, leaves narrow and pointed. Pinks, mauves, and violets predominate. Usually under 24 in (60 cm).

GROUP 2: MEDIUM-FLOWERED
Flowers 1¼–1½ in (3–4 cm) in length, tubes expanding to wide mouths. May be subdivided by foliage type.

2A Narrow-leaved Leaves up to 3¼ x ¼ in (8.5 x 0.5 cm). Tall and spreading, up to 40 in (1 m) in height.
2B Broad-leaved Leaves up to 3 x ½ in (8 x 1.2 cm). Usually a spreading mound, up to 30 in (75 cm) in height.

GROUP 3: LARGE-FLOWERED
Flowers over 1½ in (4 cm) in length. May be subdivided according to flower shape.
3A Narrow trumpet Flowers long and narrow but less than ½ in (1.2 cm) wide at the mouth. Tall and erect, often noticeably shrubby if allowed to overwinter.
3B Wide trumpet Flower-tube expanding to greater than ½ in (1.2 cm). Bright purples and reds predominate, the throats often heavily marked. Reaching 36 in (90 cm).
3C Bell-flowered Flowers with a short tube expanding abruptly to a wide mouth with large, rounded lobes flared at right angles to the tube. Wide color range.

P. **'Bisham Seedling'** see *P.* 'White Bedder'

P. **'Blackbird'** (3A) Tall, with delicate stems hosting long flowerheads that move easily in the breeze, carrying flowers in deep reddish purple colorings. Very free-flowering. Raised by Ron Sidwell of Evesham, Worcestershire, England. ‡ 4 ft (1.2 m). Z7–9 H9–7

P. **'Burford Purple'**, *P.* **'Burford Seedling'** see *P.* 'Burgundy'

P. **'Burford White'** see *P.* 'White Bedder'

P. **'Burgundy'** (2B) syn. *P.* 'Burford Purple', *P.* 'Burford Seedling' Widely spaced flowers are deep magenta, the throat marked in brownish purple and featuring a vivid white staminode. Very reliable performer and persists well from year to year. Raised by Treasurer's of Tenbury, Worcestershire, England. ‡ 5 ft (1.5 m). Z7–11 H11–3

P. campanulatus Semievergreen species; upright, wiry stems with smooth, narrow green leaves up to 2¾ in (7 cm) long. This prolific plant carries long sprays of flared and slightly bulbous, tubular, lavender and white flowers, each one up to ½ in (1 cm) long, for a long season. A parent of many of the modern large-flowered hybrids. From Mexico and Guatemala. ‡ 24 in (60 cm). Z7–10 H11–3

P. **'Candy Pink'** see *P.* 'Old Candy Pink'.

P. **'Carolyn Orr'** Variegated foliage with a well-defined, broad cream margin. Large, pale-centered, lilac flowers. ‡ 24 in (60 cm). Z7–9 H9–7

P. **'Castle Forbes'** (3C) Rich scarlet flowers with a bluish tint and a white throat. An old cultivar, introduced by Scottish nurseryman John Forbes in 1925. ‡ 24 in (60 cm). Z7–9 H9–7

P. **'Charles Rudd'** (3C) Large flowers with a deep magenta tube, purple lobes, and a pure white throat. Often confused with 'Countess of Dalkeith', which has faint marks in the throat. ‡24 in (60 cm). Z7–9 H9–7

P. **'Cherry'** (3A) Clusters of narrow, tubular, rose red flowers have a white throat with well-defined magenta lines. Strong-growing and persists well over winter. Sometimes confused with 'Cherry Ripe', which is less vigorous. ‡30 in (75 cm). Z7–9 H9–7

P. **'Chester Scarlet'** (3B) syn. *P.* 'Mrs. Morse', *P.* 'Joy' Large, elegant red flowers with a narrowish tube; the white throat has deep carmine lines, which become smudges where the lobes meet. Quite distinct. Upright habit. ‡30 in (75 cm). Z7–10 H10–7

P. **cobaea** (Showy beardtongue, Purple beardtongue) Short-lived, the erect stems carry shiny, crisply toothed, green leaves up to 8 in (20 cm) long. Large, very showy 2-in (5-cm), pale to deep purple flowers with paler throat and rich maroon penciling appear in tight clusters through spring and early summer. A period of cold aids seed germination. From limestone glades and dry prairies in Texas, Oklahoma, Kansas, Nebraska, and Missouri. ‡12–24 in (30–60 cm). Z4–8 H8–1

P. **'Connie's Pink'** (3A) Bright rose pink, 1¼-in (3-cm) flowers are striped deep red in the white throats. Upright habit with light green foliage. A hybrid of *P. isophyllus* raised by Suffolk, England, horticulturist Ivor Dickings. ‡4 ft (1.2 m) Z7–9 H9–7

P. **'Cottage Garden Red'** *see P.* 'Windsor Red'

P. **'Countess of Dalkeith'** (3C) syn. *P.* 'Purple and White', *P.* 'Purpureus Albus' Large, bell-shaped, purple and white flowers over mid-green leaves.

Free-flowering and showy. Introduced by John Forbes in 1923. ‡24 in (60 cm). Z7–9 H9–7

P. **'Dazzler'** (3A/2B) Bright carmine flowers have a white throat irregularly penciled in crimson. Difficult to classify, with flowers as 3A but foliage as 2B. A vigorous old cultivar introduced by John Forbes in 1931. ‡3¼ ft (1 m). Z7–9 H9–7

P. **'Devonshire Cream'** (2B) Tall, with flowers in a delicate shade of rose pink with a paler underside; the white throat is lined with deep rose penciled markings. ‡4 ft (1.2 m) Z7–9 H9–7

P. **digitalis** (Foxglove beardtongue) Dense clumps with many stems, often flushed purple, carry mid-green lance-shaped, 4–6-in (10–15-cm) foliage that remains evergreen at the base. Delicate tiers of tubular, pale lavender or white flowers are freely produced in late spring and early summer, creating an overall misty appearance; each 1-in (2.5-cm) flower may be flushed in pale violet and marked with purple lines. Divide, or propagate from seed or cuttings. From Maine to South Dakota, south to Texas, Alabama, and Virginia. 30–36 in (75–90 cm). Z3–8 H8–1. **'Husker Red'** syn. *P.* 'Purpureus' Pure white flowers with deep wine red foliage and stems. Propagate by cuttings. Variable from seed; flowers are often a murky shade. Not 'Husker's Red'. ‡30 in (75 cm). **'Purpureus'** *see P.* 'Husker Red'. **'Ruby Tuesday'** Darker leaved and more free-flowering; white flowers have bluish blush. ‡18–24 in (45–60 cm).

P. **'Drinkstone'** syn. *P.* 'Drinkstone Red', *P.* 'Drinkwater Red' (2A) Free-flowering with a dense bushy habit; flowers are a deep scarlet-vermilion with the throat heavily penciled in magenta. A seedling of 'Andenken an Friedrich Hahn'. ‡32 in (80 cm). Z7–9 H9–7

P. **'Edithae'** Strong-growing and bushy with clear purple flowers. An early hybrid between *P. rupicola* and *P. barrettiae*. ‡12 in (30 cm). Z7–9 H9–7

P. **Etna** *see P.* Volcano Series.

P. **'Evelyn'** (1) syn *P.* 'Phyllis', *P.* 'Sissinghurst Pink' Sturdy, neat, bushy; small, mid-pink flowers penciled with deep magenta on tall wiry stems. Reliably overwinters and deservedly popular. ‡28 in (70 cm). Z7–9 H9–7

P. **'Firebird'** *see P.* 'Schoenholzeri'

P. **'Flame'** (3B) Nicely proportioned, bright crimson flowers rather like snapdragons have white throats. Persistent, prolific and vigorous. ‡36 in (90 cm). Z7–9 H9–7

P. **'Flamingo'** (3C) White flowers, suffused with bright rose, have a white throat penciled with deep carmine and are carried in elegant spires. One of the introductions named for birds by Ron Sidwell of Evesham, Worcestershire. ‡36 in (90 cm). Z7–9 H9–7

P. **Fujiyama** *see P.* Volcano Series.

P. **'Garden Red'** *see P.* 'Windsor Red'

P. **'Garnet'** *see P.* 'Andenken an Friedrich Hahn'

P. **'George Home'** (3B) Bright scarlet, its white throat is finely penciled in scarlet. An old cultivar making a vigorous but spreading plant. Not 'Lord Home' or 'George Holmes'. ‡36 in (90 cm). Z7–9 H9–7

P. **glaber** (Sawsepal penstemon) A small, woody-based clump carries several stems of narrow, glossy, dark green, leaves up to 4½ in (11 cm) long. Short, chunky spikes of deep blue to indigo, occasionally pink, 1½-in (3.5-cm) flowers with some maroon markings and sparse yellow hairs open in early

summer and midsummer. From dry, open grasslands and prairies from South Dakota to Nebraska and Wyoming. ‡12–24 in (30–60 cm). Z3–8 H8–1

P. **grandiflorus** (Large beardtongue) Pairs of large, smooth, waxy, blue-green leaves up to 3½ in (9 cm) long are topped with large, pink to lavender or pale blue flowers, up to 2 in (5 cm) long, with magenta markings, borne on nicely shaped open spikes in late spring and early summer. Best raised from seed. Thrives in dry conditions and ideal in prairie plantings. From North Dakota to Wyoming, Texas, and Illinois. ‡3¼ ft (1 m). Z3–9 H9–1

BELOW **1** *Penstemon* 'Chester Scarlet'
2 *P.* 'Connie's Pink' **3** *P.* 'Evelyn'
4 *P. glaber*

EELWORMS

An occasional pest of penstemons is a microscopic creature, the root knot nematode, *Meloidogyne* spp. or root knot eelworm. It can be recognized by the plants wilting and their foliage turning yellow and dying. Swellings (root knots), not unlike galls, will also be found on the roots. There is no treatment for this pest, so any infected plants are best pulled and destroyed.

Leaf and bud nematode (eelworm), which is the most common pest of penstemons in western Europe, is also sometimes a problem in the US. Starting at the base of the plant, the pest causes the foliage to develop yellowish blotches that lead to browning of the whole leaf, which then dries up and becomes distorted; brown leaves may drop off or they may remain attached to the plant. The damage progresses up the stem

and in severe cases can completely ruin the look of the plant, making plants look very sparse and leggy, although mature plants are rarely killed outright by leaf and bud nematodes. When young plants are attacked it can be fatal or, if not, it can prevent flowering.

The disease is exacerbated by overhead watering and is a familiar site on rooted cuttings and young plants in home gardeners' greenhouses. There is no cure, but it can be prevented by avoiding overhead watering in both greenhouse and garden and by choosing healthy stock from a retail nursery or garden center. Infected plants should be dug out and destroyed along with all plant debris. Since the eelworm also lives in the soil, penstemons should not be replanted in the same site for at least a year.

P. hartwegii (Hartweg's beardtongue) Bushy, with narrow, glossy green leaves to 4 in (10 cm) long and a succession of long, thin, brilliant scarlet flowers to 2 in (5 cm) long. Used as a parent for many seed strains and tends to be resistant to powdery mildew. From Mexico. ‡ 36 in (90 cm). Z9–11 H11–9. **'Albus'** White flowers open from creamy white buds. Reliable under most weather conditions. Probably the oldest surviving cultivar. ‡ 32 in (80 cm). **'Tubular Bells Rose'** Seed-raised, with very soft pale pink flowers, with deep rich maroon penciling broadening to large joined splashes on lower lips, over a long flower period. ‡ 24 in (60 cm).

P. heterophyllus (Foothill penstemon) Evergreen, strongly woody-based. Narrow, bluish green, glossy leaves, to 2 in (5 cm) long, and masses of rosy violet, funnel-shaped flowers, to 1½ in (3.5 cm) long, are produced in delicate spikes in midsummer. The stems are sometimes reddish, giving two-tone effect. Long-lived, and the parent of a number of good cultivars. From California. ‡ 16 in (40 cm). Z7–10 H10–7. **'Blue Gem'** Compact and bushy, producing sprays of blue, tubular flowers from early summer to early fall. Excellent. ‡ 18 in (45 cm). **'Blue Spring'** Glossy, bluish green evergreen foliage supports dense flower spikes of startling, sky blue flowers with a just touch of purple inside the bells. ‡ 18 in (45 cm). **'Catherine de la Mare'** Spreading semi-evergreen with dull, bluish green leaves and dense sprays of purplish blue flowers borne on reddish stems. ‡ 20 in (50 cm). **'Heavenly Blue'** Blue flowers tinged magenta from midsummer to October. ‡ 24 in (60 cm). **'Margery Fish'** *see* P. 'Margery Fish'. **'True Blue'** No different from the species; a redundant name. **'Züriblau'** Bushy, red-tinted stems carry a profusion of slim, bright blue, tubular flowers from early to late summer above narrow, bluish green foliage. ‡ 18 in (45 cm).

P. 'Hewell Pink Bedder' (2B) Upright habit with gray-green foliage, the reddish stems carry flowers with cerise

tubes and lobes and a white throat penciled in deep carmine. An old cultivar originally intended for bedding. Not 'Hewell's Pink Bedder'. ‡ 32 in (80 cm). Z7–9 H9–7

P. 'Hidcote Pink' (2B) Sturdy, upright with bright rose flowers, their creamy white throats penciled in cerise. Prolific and tough. Grown for many years at Hidcote Manor Garden, Gloucestershire, England. ‡ 3¼ ft (1 m). Z7–9 H9–7

P. 'Hidcote Purple' (2B) Prolific, multi-stemmed, carrying deep mauve flowers fading to bright mauve with bluish overtones. Persistent and reliable. Seems without connection to Hidcote Manor. ‡ 32 in (80 cm). Z7–9 H9–7

P. 'Hidcote White' (2B) Greenish buds open to pure or blushed white flowers. A feeble cultivar, like a poor version of 'White Bedder', with little persistence. Better known for the unprovable association indicated by its name than for any inherent quality. The superior 'White Bedder' may be supplied under this name. ‡ 24 in (60 cm). Z7–9 H9–7

P. hirsutus (Hairy beardtongue) A small spreading evergreen, woody at the base, the toothed, lance-shaped, dark green 4-in (10-cm) leaves are borne on slightly hairy, violet-tinged stems. Loose spires of delicate funnel-shaped, pale violet, occasionally white, 1-in (2.5 cm) flowers are carried on thin stems held well above the foliage in midsummer. Needs a well drained, sunny place. From northeastern North America. ‡ 18 in (45 cm). Z3–9 H9–1. **var. pygmaeus** Compact, with dense clusters of white tubular flowers, flushed outside with shades of lilac, mauve, and pale blue, set against purple-tinted leaves. ‡ 4¾ in (12 cm).

P. 'Hopleys Variegated' (2B) The large mid-green leaves are irregularly variegated with yellow; the deep mauve flowers fade to white, and the white throat is broadly streaked with mauve. Best in bright sun. A spontaneous mutation of 'Burgundy' introduced by Hopleys Plants, Hertfordshire, England.

‡ 36 in (90 cm). Z7–9 H9–7

P. isophyllus Tall, much-branched, woody-based evergreen, the reddish willowy stems carrying fleshy, glossy, mid-green, 1¼–2-in (3–5-cm), lance-shaped leaves, which are tinged purple. Widely spaced, slender, tubular, red flowers about 1½ in (4 cm) long have a cream throat streaked in red. Very free-flowering from early summer and unusually showy for a species. May be cut back to the ground in cold winters, but regrows well. From Mexico. ‡ 4 ft (1.2 m). Z8–11 H12–8

P. 'John Nash' (2B) Attractive white-throated, mauve to violet flowers in open vertical spikes. Almost identical to 'Alice Hindley' but bushier and shorter. ‡ 30 in (75 cm). Z7–9 H9–7

P. 'Joy' see P. 'Chester Scarlet'

P. 'June' see P. 'Pennington Gem'

P. 'King George V' (3C) syn. P. 'King George' Large, crimson flowers with white throats and reddish marks at the mouth. An old and popular cultivar introduced by John Forbes to mark the king's accession in 1910. ‡ 36 in (90 cm). Z7–9 H9–7

P. Kilimanjaro see P. Volcano Series.

P. kunthii Soft, velvety, dark fuchsia-pink flowers, about 1¼ in (3 cm) long with bright, white-striped throats, are held above long, slender, bright green leaves. Often confused with P. campanulatus, which has more bulbous, purplish flowers. Hybridizes freely with other species, so surprising plants may be found under this name. Only propagate from cuttings. ‡ 18–24 in (45–60 cm). Z7–9 H9–7

P. 'Lady Alice Hindley' see P. 'Alice Hindley'

P. 'Le Phare' (3A) syn. P. 'Phare' Compact, with a long flowering season and good persistence, the delicate flowers are rose red, shading to cerise at the lobes with a stark, silvery white throat marked with short streaks. ‡ 24 in (60 cm). Z7–9 H9–7

P. 'Lilac and Burgundy' (3B/3C) Strongly contrasted mauve tube with a white throat heavily marked in rich burgundy. Not easy to classify, with 3B habit and 3C flowers. Needs a sheltered position to overwinter well. ‡ 36 in (90 cm). Z7–9 H9–7

P. 'Lord Home' see P. 'George Home'

P. 'Lynette' (1) The small, deep magenta flowers, with white throats and deep magenta penciling, are carried in narrow, delicate spikes. Very persistent. Raised by *Aster* expert Paul Picton of Colwall, Worcestershire, England and a hybrid of 'Evelyn' and

RIGHT 1 *Penstemon kunthii*
2 P. 'Maurice Gibbs'
3 P. 'Mother of Pearl'

'Andenken an Friedrich Hahn'. ↕18 in (45 cm). Z7–9 H9–7

P. **'Madame Golding'** (2B) Rich rose red flowers with strongly marked throat. Perhaps the same as 'Old Candy Pink'. ↕24 in (60 cm). Z7–9 H9–7

P. **'Margery Fish'** Low-growing, almost spreading plant. Shiny green leaves and pale brown stems; pale blue to mauve flowers. A hybrid of *P. heterophyllus*. ↕20 in (50 cm). Z7–9 H9–7

P. **'Maurice Gibbs'** (3C) Short, chunky flower spikes filled with large, open-mouthed flowers in dark magenta with an unmarked white throat. Free-flowering older cultivar but with poor persistence. Raised by Vicary Gibbs of Elstree, Buckinghamshire, England before 1930—no connection with the Bee Gees. ↕3¼ ft (1 m). Z7–9 H9–7

P. **Mexicali hybrids** Unusual, seed-raised mixture comprising a full spectrum of penstemon colors with small and large flowers. Bred by Bruce Myers in Washington in the 1980's from his earlier 'Mexicana', itself a hybrid of *P. campanulatus*, and involving parentage of a number of diverse species. ↕18–48 in (45–120 cm). Z5–9 H9–5

P. **'Midnight'** (2B) A name widely used since the 1950s, but all current stocks are identical to 'Russian River'.

P. **'Modesty'** (2B) Shiny, olive green foliage on a loose clump shows off bright reddish pink flowers with a white throat heavily streaked in dark red. Not particularly persistent. From Scottish horticulturist John Forbes. ↕32 in (80 cm). Z7–9 H9–7

P. **'Mother of Pearl'** (2B) A strong, prolific clump, the many small, widely spaced, pale purple flowers have azure-blue tints at the base; the throat is paler and heavily striped in deep purple with a line running to the end of each lobe. Subtle, lovely. Raised and introduced in 1987 by Hopleys Plants, Hertfordshire, England. ↕3½ ft (1.1 m). Z7–9 H9–7

P. **'Mrs. Morse'** see P. 'Chester Scarlet'

P. **'Myddelton Gem'** (2B) syn. P. 'Myddelton Red' Neat bushy plants with gray-green foliage carry bright reddish pink flowers with a white throat, extending onto the lobes and with faint smudges of pink in the mouth. An old cultivar, raised very early in the 20th century and named for the garden in Enfield, Middlesex, England, of E. A. Bowles. Not Myddleton or Middleton. ↕30 in (75 cm). Z7–9 H9–7

P. **'Newbury Gem'** (2B) Slender stems carry carmine-scarlet flowers with a heavily lined throat on spreading plants. One of the old 19th century bedding types. ↕36 in (90 cm). Z7–9 H9–7

P. **'Old Candy Pink'** (2B) syn. P. 'Candy Pink' Medium to large flowers in bright crimson, shading paler on the underside of the tube, have a white throat with dark crimson

penciling merging into the color of the lobes. Free-flowering over a long season. ↕32 in (80 cm). Z7–9 H9–7

P. **'Osprey'** (3C) Substantial spikes are closely packed with creamy white flowers darkening to rose on the lobes. The throat is pure white and extends into the lobes as white lines across each of the three lower lobes. Makes a large, loose clump, best at the back of the border. From Ron Sidwell, of Evesham, Worcestershire, England. ↕3½ ft (1.1 m). Z7–9 H9–7

P. **ovatus** (Broad-leaved penstemon) Handsome rosettes are made up of large, almost oval, glossy, leathery green leaves, up to 6 x 1½ in (15 x 4 cm) wide, with toothed edges. In spring and early summer, tiers of bright, clear blue flowers that may appear purple in cloudy weather, the paler throat with distinct maroon markings. Needs very well-drained soil. From limestone rocks and woodlands from British Columbia to Oregon. ↕36 in (90 cm). Z4–8 H8–1

P. **'Papal Purple'** (1) Stiff stems carry small, evenly spaced, globular, bell-like flowers in a reddish violet with the throat penciled in deep magenta. A low-mounding cultivar very useful for the front of the border; persistent and maintains its winter foliage well. Found in the garden of Northamptonshire, England horticulturist Valerie Finnis. ↕18 in (45 cm). Z7–9 H9–7

P. **Patio Bells Series** Selected for their compact, upright growth and long display, from early summer to October. Intended for patio planters, also listed simply as Patio Series. ↕20–24 in (50–60 cm). Z7–9 H9–7. **'Patio Bells Coral'** Mid apricot-pink flowers. ↕18 in (45 cm). **'Patio Bells Pink'** Pink trumpets with white throats. The first in the series, a spontaneous mutation of 'Pink Endurance'. ↕20 in (50 cm). **'Patio Bells Red'** Almost pure red flowers with just a hint of white in the throat. ↕20 in (50 cm). **'Patio Bells Shell'** Pale pink flowers with magenta-veined throat. ↕20 in (50 cm). **'Patio Bells Wine'** Bright purple with pinkish white throat and dark markings. Strong. May be the best of the Patio Bells series but inclined to sprawl. ↕24 in (60 cm).

P. **'Peace'** (2B) Medium-sized, white flowers have lobes margined in cerise toning to paler pink, the throat is white and unmarked. Color is intense in the bud stage, appearing red on pale yellow. Forms a dense, spreading clump. ↕24 in (60 cm). Z7–9 H9–7

P. **'Pennington Gem'** (3B) A tall but very bushy, clump-forming plant with attractive grayish green foliage. The large, bright rose flowers, generally on one side of stem, and deepening toward the base of the tube, have faint bluish overtones. The throat is white with a few, faint magenta lines. Reliably persistent and very free-flowering. ↕3¼ ft (1 m). Z7–9 H9–7

P. **Pensham Series** An extensive, recently developed series of more than

30, mainly large-flowered hybrids developed by Edward Wilson, formerly a student at Pershore College, Worcestershire, England, and distributed by a number of nurseries in Worcestershire, England . Vigorous, and suitable for borders and large containers. ↕24–48 in (60–120 cm). Z7–9 H9–7. **'Pensham Blueberry Ice'** Vivid purple-pink (not blue) flowers with white-veined throats. ↕32 in (80 cm). **'Pensham Great Expectations'** Lilac flowers with a white throat. ↕24 in (60 cm). **'Pensham Just Jayne'** Vivid rose flowers with white-veined throat. Early flowering. ↕4 ft (1.2 m). **'Pensham Petticoat'** White flowers with rose edge. ↕24 in (60 cm). **'Pensham Plum Jerkum'** Purple flowers with a white throat. ↕32 in (80 cm).

P. **'Pershore Fanfare'** (2B) Vigorous, deep lilac flowers have a white throat,

flushed and penciled in lilac. Raised at Pershore College, Worcestershire, England and introduced in 1998. ↕36 in (90 cm). Z7–9 H9–7

P. **'Pershore Pink Necklace'** (3C) A tall, loose-growing clump carrying large, bright rose flowers with a white throat and rose lobes. There is an additional narrow band of white running through the rose coloring around the tube just behind the lobes, giving a distinctly jagged necklace effect. Raised at Pershore College, Worcestershire, England in 1995. ↕3¼ ft (1 m). Z7–9 H9–7

P. **'Phare'** see P. 'Le Phare'

P. **'Phyllis'** see P. 'Evelyn'

P. **'Pink Bedder'** Unfortunately, this name is used for both 'Hewell Pink Bedder' and 'Sutton's Pink Bedder'.

HARMONY IN PINK

PENSTEMONS VARY IN THEIR HARDINESS, and when you are creating plant pictures that are intended to repeat from year to year, it pays to choose the hardier types, such as this 'Pennington Gem' in a lovely rose-pink with a pale throat. *Achillea* 'Forncett Candy', in a slightly richer rose-pink but fading almost to white, is a lovely companion to create a harmonious group. Both benefit hugely from deadheading to ensure that the flowers keep coming and, in the case of the achilleas, this will also ensure that seedlings in less suitable colors do not disrupt the display. The addition of silver artemisias would expand this pastel partnership while retaining its quiet effectiveness.

P. 'Pink Endurance' (1) Low-growing, with fine, narrow foliage; the wiry stems carry small flowers in mid-purple with a penciled white throat. Very suitable for the front of the border, floriferous and reliably persistent. A seedling brought to Blooms of Bressingham, England by a customer and introduced by them. ↕ 20 in (50 cm). Z7–9 H9–7

P. 'Port Wine' (3B) Stiff and upright habit; the reddish flowering stems are topped with smallish heads of large flowers in a deep claret shading to a reddish purple on the lobes. The throat is white with fine parallel penciling in deep claret, the center line of which extends onto the lobes. Vigorous and persistent. ↕ 3¼ ft (1 m).

P. 'Prairie Fire' A low rosette throws up tall, strong-growing, and graceful heads of slightly pinkish red flowers with a white throat. An outstanding hardy hybrid of *P. barbatus*, and shows it. ↕ 3¼–5 ft (1–1.5 m). Z4–8 H8–1

P. 'Purple and White' see *P.* 'Countess of Dalkeith'

P. 'Purple Bedder' (2B) Unusually prostrate in habit, the stems turn to vertical and carry flowers whose tube and lobes are deep mauve, reddish toward the base, and whose throat is white with dark purple lines, the center of which extends into each lobe. ↕ 32 in (80 cm). Z7–9 H9–7

P. 'Purple Passion' (2B) Dense spikes of grape-purple flowers are arranged in noticeable tiers. Introduced by New Zealand's Bay Bloom Nurseries in 1989. ↕ 36 in (90 cm). Z7–9 H9–7

P. 'Purpureus Albus' see *P.* 'Countess of Dalkeith'

P. 'Raven' (3C) A very distinct and striking cultivar; erect stems carry small heads of large, blackish purple flowers with slightly lighter lobes, the white throats with smudgy penciling in red-purple. Of limited persistence. From Ron Sidwell of Evesham, Worcestershire, England. ↕ 3½ ft (1.1 m). Z7–9 H9–7

P. 'Razzle Dazzle' (2A) Bushy, with glowing, dark red flowers with indistinct penciling. See *P.* 'Schoenholzeri'. ↕ 36 in (90 cm). Z7–9 H9–7

P. 'Red Emperor' (3B) Robust grower with sparse foliage and bright scarlet flowers with white throats distinctly marked in carmine. Overwinters poorly. ↕ 36 in (90 cm). Z7–9 H9–7

P. 'Rich Ruby' (3B) Tall, with reddish purple stems thickly packed with flowers whose overall color is a rich crimson with bluish overtones and a heavily penciled, white throat. ↕ 3¼ ft (1 m). Z7–9 H9–7

P. 'Rosy Blush' (3C) Bright rose flowers and a creamy white throat on unusually dwarf plants. ↕ 18 in (45 cm). Z7–9 H9–7

P. 'Royal White' see *P.* 'White Bedder'

P. 'Rubicundus' (3C) A lovely, "big and brash" cultivar with huge, wide-mouthed, scarlet tubes with a silvery white throat irregularly marked with scarlet. Tall and vigorous but not reliably persistent. Said to have originated in 1908 at Lyme Park in Cheshire, England. Not to be confused with the species *P. rubicundus*. ↕ 4 ft (1.2 m). Z7–9 H9–7

P. 'Ruby Field' A confusing name that has been applied to a number of different forms. Sometimes incorrectly applied to 'Schoenholzeri' and also

used for a plant similar to 'Port Wine' and occasionally for other cultivars. The answer is to abandon this cultivar name altogether.

P. 'Russian River' (2B) An imposing plant, the dark purple stems carry deep green foliage and upward-pointing flowers in a deep reddish purple flushed with violet. The throat is white, heavily penciled in plum, merging into patches in the mouth. A strong grower with many stems producing an upright clump. Sometimes sold as 'Midnight'. ↕ 28 in (70 cm).

Scarlet Queen ('Scharlachkönigin') (3C) A fairly uniform seed strain in an intense scarlet with white throats and variable penciling type and color. The plant shows slight variation in earliness and throat marking. ↕ 32 in (80 cm). Z8–10 H10–8

P. 'Schoenholzeri' (2A) syn. *P.* 'Firebird' A bushy plant with lax, brownish stems bearing narrow green leaves, the flowers are a bright pinkish red with a throat heavily streaked in

ABOVE 1 *Penstemon* 'Rich Ruby'
2 *P.* 'Schoenholzeri'
3 *P.* 'Stapleford Gem'

deep magenta. A similar and possibly superior version of this, with very deep rose red coloring, is sometimes incorrectly offered under this name. It is suggested that the correct name for this should be 'Razzle Dazzle'. Raised and introduced in Switzerland in 1939. ↕ 36 in (90 cm). Z6–9 H9–6

P. Sea Series Large-flowered, white-throated cultivars in the traditional style but with a shorter, more compact habit, concentrating the flowering effect. Raised by horticulturist Fred Yates from Cheshire, England. ↕ 20 in (50 cm). Z6–9 H9–6. **'Sea Coral'** (3C) Coral pink. **'Sea Purple'** (2B/3C) Rich purple. **'Sea Red'** Magenta.

P. 'Sissinghurst Pink' see *P.* 'Evelyn'

P. smallii (Small's beardtongue) Broad, purple-veined green leaves up to 6 in (15 cm) long, on pinkish stems. Rich

ALTERNATIVE APPROACHES TO CUTTINGS

Tip cuttings with three or four pairs of leaves, and an active growing point, are the style of cuttings usually recommended for propagation. However, there are alternative ways in which to take cuttings.

Should you be fortunate enough to be given a flowering stem in a bouquet, cuttings can be taken from it. Simply cut pieces of stem, each with two pairs of leaves. Trim each cutting just above the top pair of leaves and just below the lower pair, nip off the lower pair of leaves, then treat the cutting in the normal way. This results in noticeably bushy plants, since not only do two

shoots grow from the upper leaf joints but shoots may also emerge from the lower leaf joint.

If material is very scarce, perhaps of a new cultivar, very small cuttings can be used. Cut a length of stem into pieces, each containing just one leaf joint; be sure to cut just above each pair of leaves—that is your cutting. It is even possible to cut such cuttings vertically down through the stem with a sharp blade, leaving a split stem with one leaf attached. While development can sometimes be slow using this method, it does allow large numbers of plants to be multiplied quickly.

'SOUR GRAPES'

There is a great deal of confusion relating to perhaps the best-known penstemon cultivar of all, 'Sour Grapes'. The origin and identity of the true plant has been unclear, and 'Stapleford Gem', or a plant very much like it, has often been sold under its name.

The plant that is generally becoming accepted as 'Sour Grapes' was given to Margery Fish of East Lambrook Manor, Somerset in the 1950s. It has a spreading habit, and the flower is a bright reddish violet toning to deep mauve with a white throat with clear maroon penciling. It was named because of its tendency to mass flowers at the top of the stem like a bunch of grapes. The green coloring of the buds enhances this effect.

Another form often sold as 'Sour Grapes' has a low-growing habit and dull violet-blue flowers with a white throat and clear maroon penciling. This was probably introduced by Washfield Nursery in Devon in the 1930s and is very similar to 'Stapleford Gem', suggesting that this 'Sour Grapes' was perhaps an improved shorter version.

One possible conclusion is that the same name was applied quite independently to different plants, but without clear documentary evidence it is not easy to prove the point. However, it is important to be aware that two distinct plants are circulating under this famous name. It has been suggested that the only really practical solution is to refer to the name with a descriptive suffix such as Lambrook form or Washfield form—cumbersome, but helpful.

purple buds with tinges of blue open to 1¼ in (3 cm) long, lavender to pink, tubular flowers, white throat striped with purple. Flowers in late spring and early summer in well-drained to dry soil in open or lightly shaded situation. From North Carolina and Tennessee. ‡ 30 in (75 cm). Z5–9 H9–1

P. **'Snow Storm'**, *P.* **'Snowflake'** see 'White Bedder'

P. **'Sour Grapes'** (2B) This name has long caused debate and there is still some doubt as to whether this is the correct cultivar. The flower is a bright reddish violet, toning to deep mauve with a white throat with clear maroon penciling. Given to Margery Fish of England in the 1950s, it was named for the bunching of its flowers at the top of the stems. ‡ 2 ft (60 cm). Z7–9 H9–7

P. **'Southgate Gem'** (2B) A graceful plant with a generous but open clump of delicate stems, carrying many widely spaced flowers with a slightly nodding habit. The color is bright rose red, with a white throat, lightly penciled in bright crimson, extending out onto the lower lobes. Originally raised before 1910. ‡ 30 in (75 cm). Z7–9 H9–7

P. **'Stapleford Gem'** (2B) A popular

bicolor cultivar with a bushy habit and sturdy, upright growth. The flowers are bright lilac suffused with blue and deeper reddish purple lobes, the white throat streaked in purplish red. Often masquerades as 'Sour Grapes' (*see panel*). ‡ 3¼ ft (1 m). Z7–9 H9–7

P. **Stromboli** see *P.* Volcano Series

P. **'Sutton's Pink Bedder'** (2B) Bushy and reasonably persistent, the well-shaped, open spikes of carmine-rose flowers have paler lobes and an unmarked white throat. Originally introduced as a seed strain by Suttons Seeds, of England in 1933, now only propagated by cuttings. ‡ 32 in (80 cm). Z7–9 H9–7

P. **'The Juggler'** (2B) Impressive display on strong, erect stems carrying light gray-green foliage and bright mauve flowers that fade to white on the underside of the tube. The white throat has magenta penciling. ‡ 3½ ft (1.1 m). Z7–9 H9–7

P. **'Thorn'** A pink and white cultivar reputed to retain a creamy or light yellow tint when the flowers are mature. Often confused with 'Appleblossom', 'Beech Park', and 'Peace' to the extent that it is difficult to authenticate the true plant. ‡ 32 in (80 cm). Z7–9 H9–7

P. **'Threave Pink'** (1) Slender stems carry small magenta flowers with a white throat clearly striped in dark magenta. Similar to 'Evelyn', but a darker color and less persistent. Named for the famous Scottish garden. ‡ 18 in (45 cm). Z7–9 H9–7

P. **'Torquay Gem'** (3A/2A) Loose spikes of deep rose red flowers have white throats marked with parallel carmine lines. Not vigorous but recovers slowly after hard winters. Difficult to classify, 3A flowers with 2A foliage. ‡ 24 in (60 cm). Z7–9 H9–7

P. **Vesuvius** see *P.* Volcano Series

P. **Volcano Series** Series of large-flowered cultivars developed horticulturist Fred Yates of Somerton, Cheshire, England and named for the mountains of the world. Their compact, upright habit makes them ideal for container display as well as border planting. They mix the qualities of the various classification groups. ‡ 24–30 in (60–75 cm). Z7–9 H9–7. **Etna** (**'Yatna'**) (3B) Fiery-red flowers, white inside the throat, and streaked with purple. ‡ 24 in (60 cm). **Fujiyama** (**'Yamaya'**) (2B/3C) Light cerise with a white throat, smudged with deep rose, opening from light yellow buds fading to creamy white on opening. 2B habit with 3C flowers. ‡ 24 in (60 cm). **Kilimanjaro** (**'Yajaro'**) Mid-red to bright pink with a white throat. ‡ 24 in (60 cm). **Stromboli** (**'Yaboli'**) Pearly white with mauve lips. Tall. ‡ 30 in (75 cm). **Vesuvius** (**'Yasius'**) Deep purple flowers with a white throat marked with purple penciling. ‡ 24 in (60 cm).

P. whippleanus (Whipple's penstemon) Slender stems bear shiny, soft green, lancelike leaves and striking, deep burgundy, almost purplish black flowers, to 1¼ in (3 cm) long, with pin-striped, cream-colored throats, in mid- to late summer. For a well-drained site and full sun, where it tends to be long-lived. From Montana, Wyoming, and eastern Idaho to Utah, New Mexico, and Arizona. ‡ 24 in (60 cm). Z3–8 H8–1. **'Chocolate Drop'** Marketing name for the species, not different.

P. **'White Bedder'** (2B) syn. *P.* 'Bisham Seedling', *P.* 'Burford White', *P.* 'Hidcote White', *P.* 'Royal White', *P.* 'Snowflake', *P.* 'Snowstorm' Bushy with greenish cream buds opening to pure white flowers with some pale pink suffusion, particularly as flowers age. Has been seed-raised, so color may vary with different sources. Probably the most widely available white cultivar, originally introduced by Scotland's John Forbes in 1912. ‡ 28 in (70 cm). Z7–10 H10–7

P. **'Whitethroat'** (2B) Dark pink flowers with a white throat and a strong upright growth. A purple-flowered form with a white throat is sometimes sold under this name. ‡ 36 in (90 cm). Z7–9 H9–7

P. **'Windsor Red'** (3A) syn. 'Cottage Garden Red', 'Garden Red' A vigorous, bushy, narrow-leaved cultivar, the delicate, upward-pointing flowers are deep rose-red, with white throats strongly penciled in magenta. Free-flowering over a long season. ‡ 28 in (70 cm). Z7–9 H9–7

PENTAGLOTTIS
Green alkanet
BORAGINACEAE

An attractive but aggressive ground cover plant, ideal for wilder parts of the garden.

BELOW *Pentaglottis sempervirens*

Only one species of evergreen, roughly hairy perennial, native to moist and shaded habitats of southwestern Europe. It has branched, upright or ascending stems, long-stalked basal leaves, and stalkless stem leaves. The bright blue flowers have a short tube and resemble forget-me-nots; they are attractive to bees. A fairly coarse plant, but good for wilder areas.

CULTIVATION Easy to grow in sun or shade in most soils.

PROPAGATION From seed, or by division or root cuttings.

PROBLEMS Can be very invasive, spreads by self-seeding and will re-sprout from any root fragments.

P. sempervirens syn. *Anchusa sempervirens* (Green alkanet) Stout, bristly, evergreen with deep green, oval leaves to 12 in (30 cm) long. Azure-blue, forget-me-not-like flowers, to ½ in (1 cm) across, are carried in paired clusters of five to fifteen, in late spring and summer. There is a rare pale blue form. Native to southwestern Europe. ‡ 12–40 in (30–100 cm). Z6–9 H9–6

PERSICARIA
Bistort, Knotweed
POLYGONACEAE

Sturdy, long-flowering moisture-lovers including some fine border perennials for carefree, late summer color.

Around 100 species of annuals and perennials are found in various habitats almost around the world and include agricultural weeds, and culinary and medicinal plants, as well as attractive ornamentals. Among the 17 or so species most widely cultivated as garden plants, many originate from the Himalaya and China, often growing in damp, grassy or wooded locations. This is a diverse group ranging from prostrate, miniature-leaved mats for the rock garden to burly giants up to 6½ ft (2 m) tall.

Many are medium-sized perennials, often spreading vigorously, those of the bistort-type forming bold clumps of deciduous, docklike, oval leaves. Separate, upright stems, sometimes also leafy, are tipped for many weeks from mid-summer into fall in spikes of clustered, red, pink or white, bell- to cup-shaped flowers only about ¼ in (5 mm) long. In other types, flowers are held in globes or branching sprays, turning rusty brown in fruit, and leaves also vary, some species displaying patterned foliage which changes color as the season progresses. The stems of most have swollen joints at the leaf bases, surrounded in an often papery sheath. Contact with all parts of the plant may irritate skin, and sap causes mild stomach upset if ingested. There has been uncertainty in recent years as botanists struggle to agree on exactly which plants belong under *Persicaria*. All persicarias were formerly included in *Polygonum* and may still be listed there by some; some *Persicaria* species have been known as *Aconogonon*, *Bistorta*, or *Tovara* and may still be listed there; some plants formerly included in *Persicaria* are now placed elsewhere—in *Fallopia*, for example. There are many synonyms, but the musical chairs now seems to be over. ⚠

CULTIVATION Prefers moist soil in either sun or part-shade. Many are spreading, some gradually so and easy to control, while a number are invasive and need careful siting. Their tendency to roam can be put to good use as ground cover or for naturalizing in woodland- or meadow-type plantings. *Persicaria*, however, also offers many hard-working border plants, including cultivars that are selected as being noninvasive.

PROPAGATION By division, from seed, or stem tip cuttings of non-flowering shoots.

PROBLEMS Usually trouble-free.

P. amplexicaulis syn. *Bistorta amplexicaulis*, *Polygonum amplexicaule* (Red bistort) Substantial mounds of foliage build from a woody rootstock producing long-stalked, mid-green, slightly wavy-edged, oval 10 x 4 in (25 x 10 cm) leaves, which are pointed at the tips and heart-shaped at the base. Above them rise a profusion of sturdy, branching stems well-dressed in smaller leaves and tipped in slim tapers, 1¼– 4 in (3–10 cm) long and often held in pairs, composed loosely of tiny, typically red flowers, but the color ranges from purple to white, from mid-summer to the first frosts. Adaptable and noninvasive but clumps steadily increase in size and needs plenty of room. May self-seed; be sure to propagate cultivars by division. From shady places among grass or in forests from the Himalaya to western China. ↕ 20–54 in (50–130 cm). Z3–8 H8–1. **'Alba'** Elegant white spires. ↕ 30–36 in (75–90 cm). **'Arun Gem'** *see* var. *pendula*. **'Atrosanguinea'** Deep purple-red flowers. Plants supplied

under this name may not differ from the species. ↕ 36–48 in (90–120 cm). **'Cottesbrooke Gold'** Yellow to lime foliage, coloring best in sun. Beware of propagating green shoots. Pinkish red flowers. ↕ 24–36 in (60–90 cm). **'Firedance'** Vivid salmon-red flowers, one of several selections by Dutch landscape designer Piet Oudolf. ↕ 24– 36 in (60–90 cm). **'Firetail'** Bright red, long-tapering spikes, but doubtfully distinct. Selected by Bressingham, England's Alan Bloom from seed of 'Atrosanguinea'. ↕ 36–48 in (90–120 cm). **'Inverleith'** Low-growing, with narrow leaves and blunt, purple-red heads. ↕ 12–24 in (30–60 cm). **var. *pendula*** syn. 'Arun Gem' Nodding spikes in magenta with bronze tips, on a shorter plant. Introduced by horticulturist Roy Lancaster from Nepal. ↕ 20–30 in (50–75 cm). **'Rosea'** Delicate, light pink flowers. ↕ 30–36 in (75–90 cm). **Taurus ('Blotau')** Fuller spikes of rich red with a neat habit and large leaves. Introduced by Bressingham's Alan Bloom. ↕ 30–36 in (75–90 cm).

P. bistorta syn. *Bistorta major*, *Polygonum bistorta* (Common bistort) A vigorous, variable and lush species. Thick, twisted rhizomes support mounds of wavy-edged, oval, 4–12-in (10–30-cm) leaves, with a white central vein and creased surface, and which are pale gray-green beneath, held on long, winged stalks. From late spring to early summer, slim, non-branching stems bear at their tips tiny, pale pink flowers clustered into dense, fluffy ¾–3-x-½-in (2–8-x-1-cm) bottlebrushes. May flower again in late summer. They may spread vigorously in moist soil, but are easy to control by digging up the rootstock. Propagate cultivars by division. Once grown as a medicinal plant and as a spring vegetable. Found through most of Eurasia. 12–40 in (30–100 cm). Z4–8 H8–1. **subsp. *carnea*** Smaller, with more rounded, ¾–1¼-in (2–3-cm) heads of deeper, salmon pink flowers. Spreads less and takes drier conditions. From the Caucasus and northern and eastern Turkey. ↕ 18–24 in (45–60 cm). **'Hohe Tatra'** Undeservedly ignored, noninvasive form with bright, reddish pink spikes. Named after the Tatra mountains between Poland and Slovakia. ↕ 14–20 in (35–50 cm). **'Superba'** Tall, with large, broad leaves

and pale pink, chenille-soft flowers in hefty 2–3-x-1-in (5–8-x-2.5-cm) spikes. May topple under the weight of the spikes. Needs ample moisture to thrive. ↕ 24–36 in (60–90 cm).

P. campanulata syn. *Aconogonon campanulatum*, *Polygonum campanulatum* (Lesser knotweed) Spreading determinedly and forming a thick mat of short-stalked basal leaves early in the season, the dark green, narrowly oval, 6-x-1½-in (15-x-4-cm) leaves are deeply veined on the upper surface, the undersides felted in buff or pinky brown. Attractive greenery also extends up the tall, branching flower stems as they develop during summer to culminate in loose clusters of tiny, pale pink, clearly bell-shaped flowers bursting from darker buds. Blooming extends into late fall. Shade-tolerant and suits woodland-type plantings, making attractive and effective ground cover, though easy to restrict. May also self-seed, propagate cultivars by division. Native to damp forests and valleys in the Himalaya and western China. ↕ 20–40 in (50–100 cm). Z5–8 H8–5. **Alba Group** White flowers. **'Rosenrot'** Deeper pink flowers. ↕ 32–48 in (80–120 cm).

P. japonica see *Fallopia japonica*

P. macrophylla syn. *Persicaria sphaerostachya*, *Bistorta macrophylla* The stout rhizomes support neat basal clumps of narrowly oval, 7-x-2½-in (18-x-6-cm), dark green, wavy-edged, and long-stalked leaves, which are paler beneath. In summer, almost leafless stems carry a single compact, rose pink, occasionally white, slightly shaggy, ¾– 2½-x-½-in (2–6-x-1-cm) spike, densely packed with tiny flowers. In bloom from early summer to the first frost. It is similar to the earlier-flowering *P. bistorta*, but lacking its winged leaf stalks, and the darker-flowered *P. milettii*, which does not have the stumpy leaf bases of *P. macrophylla*. It does not spread, and is good for sunny bog gardens. From alpine pastures in the Himalaya to western China. ↕ 8– 20 in (20–50 cm). Z5–9 H9–5.

P. microcephala Densely covering the ground in attractively patterned foliage, which spreads enthusiastically from stout rhizomes, the broadly oval, 4-x-1½-in (10-x-4-cm) leaves, held on short winged stalks, taper to a fine point. Red when young, they develop gray and brown zonal markings as they mature. From midsummer, the branching stems are topped with pairs of small, rounded, ¼-in (6-mm) heads of tiny white or pinkish flowers. Invasive, so best for wilder planting schemes. From forests and grassy places in China, Bhutan, India, Nepal, and Sikkim. ↕ 16–24 in (40–60 cm). Z5–8 H8–5. **'Red Dragon'** Spring foliage is deep burgundy with a silvery chevron, turning greener at the edges as the

---

RIGHT 1 *Persicaria amplexicaulis* 'Firetail' **2** *P. amplexicaulis* 'Rosea' **3** *P. bistorta* 'Superba'

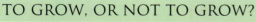

TO GROW, OR NOT TO GROW?

The fact that the infamous Japanese knotweed, *Fallopia japonica*, was once included here in *Persicaria* gives you a clue to the habits of this genus: some species can be a nuisance—and that, perhaps, is being generous.

Many are easy, well-behaved, and valuable perennials for soil that does not dry out, often smothering weeds both attractively and effectively. But a few, like *P. wallichii*, should be treated with more caution. Some say that because a plant is unusually vigorous and spreads thoughtlessly, then it should not be grown. But perhaps the answer, as is so often the case, is to plant it in the right place.

In the right situation, in wild areas bordered by mown grass, *P. wallichii* looks stunning. *P. campanulata* will smother woodland treasures in a horticulturist's shade garden, but as ground cover in sunless situations that are not intensively cultivated, it is attractive and valuable.

But news of the aggressive invasiveness of *P. wallichii* should alert us to the fact that as our climate changes and our landscape is degraded by our own activities, plants can escape from our gardens and impact our native flora. So we should be ever watchful once a plant hops over to the other side of our fence.

season progresses and held on red stems. The flowers are white. Propagate by stem tip cuttings or by division. A noninvasive cultivar introduced by Indiana horticulturist Greg Speichert. ‡24–30 in (60–75 cm).

P. milletii syn. *Bistorta milletii* Forming compact tufts, thick rhizomes support narrow, lance-shaped, 8-x-1¼-in (20-x-3-cm) leaves with wavy edges, which have a slightly leathery texture, and are held on long stalks. Above them, from summer into late fall on slender, almost leafless stems, sways a long succession of short, 1½-x-½-in (4-x-1-cm), rich crimson flower spikes, densely composed of tiny flowers with protruding stamens; the spikes have a slightly shaggy look. Could be confused with *P. macrophylla,* but in *P. milletii* the flowers are a deep red and the narrower leaves are wedge-shaped at the base, extending in narrow wings down the leaf stalk. Tough, noninvasive, and thrives on moisture but may self-seed. From scrub and alpine grass from the Himalaya to western China. ‡12–24 in (30–60 cm). Z5–8 H8–5

P. polymorpha A giant, forming a huge, bushy clump, as wide as it is high, of stout, branching stems bearing large, narrowly oval leaves that taper to a point, those near the ground reaching around 18 in (45 cm) in length. In summer, the stem tips are smothered in a fleecy mass of tiny cream flowers clustered together on large, branching heads about 6 in (15 cm) high. Continues to act as a feature plant into fall, when the flowers age to bronzy pink, then turn red-brown in fruit. Tough, self-supporting, and noninvasive, this is useful for mixed borders and naturalistic planting schemes, especially among grasses. Will tolerate some drought once established. From the Himalaya. ‡6½ ft (2 m). Z4–9 H8–1

P. polystachya see *P. wallichii*

P. runcinata Creeping vigorously from stout rhizomes, lowish mounds of upright stems are clothed in lobed, 3-x-1½-in (8-x-4-cm) leaves, held on short, winged stalks. The main leaf lobe is triangular, flanked by one to three pairs of much smaller lobes. Spring foliage emerges maroon, turning green, and the leaf undersides often have a pinkish tinge. From midsummer, tiny pink or sometimes white flowers, borne in ½-in (1-cm) pompons, bloom in abundance at the stem tips. Invasive, needing space to wander, or plunge plant in a pot to restrict its spread. Found on grassy mountain slopes and in woods from northern India and China, eastward to Indonesia. ‡12–24 in (30–60 cm). Z5–9 H9–5

P. sphaerostachya see *P. macrophylla*

P. virginiana syn. *Tovara virginiana* (Jumpseed) A variable plant forming bushy clumps of upright stems, clothed with leaves to the base. The short-stalked basal leaves are oval, up to 10 x 3½ in (25 x 9 cm), and marked in the center with dark brown patches,

particularly on spring foliage. Wispy flower spikes elongate above the foliage from late summer, with minute, beadlike, greenish to red flowers widely spaced along 4–12 in (10–30 cm) or more of the tall, wiry stems. Unobtrusive in itself, its more colorful cultivars are good for brightening shady, moist corners. Provide shelter from wind, which bruises the leaves. The leaves color best out of direct sun. May self-seed but is not spreading. Propagate cultivars by tip cuttings or division. Introduced from Virginia by plant collector John Tradescant the Younger in 1640. From eastern North America, the Himalaya, and Japan, in moist woods and thickets. ‡16–48 in (40–120 cm). Z5–9 H9–5. **Compton's form** Narrowly oval foliage emerges red in spring, with a deep red chevron, turning olive green with a broad brown chevron as the plant matures. Collected in Sichuan province by botanist James Compton ‡30–36 in (75–90 cm). Z4–9 H8–1. **'Lance Corporal'** Leaves have bold, dark chocolate chevrons. Discovered as a chance seedling at Rowden Gardens, Devon, England, home of the NCCPG National Collection of Persicaria. ‡36 in (90 cm). Z4–8 H8–1. **Variegata Group** Broad foliage irregularly blotched with creamy yellow. Several different plants are grouped under this name. Seedlings come variegated, but the quality varies. ‡18–24 in (45–60 cm). Z4–8 H8–1. **(Variegata Group) 'Painter's Palette'** Cream-and-green variegated leaves sport a central maroon chevron and pink tinges. Less striking plants raised from seed are sometimes offered for sale under this name. Has become one of the most popular persicarias, since its discovery in the 1970s by plant breeder and horticulturist Eric Smith. ‡18–24 in (45–60 cm).

P. wallichii syn. *Aconogonon polystachyum, Persicaria polystachya* (Himalayan knotweed) A spectacular but alarming plant spreading by a network of rhizomes, particularly in moist soil, to form a leafy thicket of sturdy, branching stems that may become woody at the base. They bear bold, conspicuously veined, lance-shaped 12-x-4-in (30-x-10-cm) leaves. Stems, leaf stalks, and leaf midribs are usually flushed red. In early fall the plant is covered in a sweetly scented froth of tiny, cream to pinkish flowers held in broad, branching sprays about 12 in (30 cm) high. Similar to the noninvasive *P. weyrichii* but in *P. wallichii* the flowerheads are loose and leafy. Wondrous at full height, but not widely grown because of its strongly invasive character and not advisable for borders. Best in large, wild spaces or planted in grass and controlled by mowing around it. Can regenerate from fragments of rhizome. Originally from mountain grasslands and forests from the Himalaya to western China ‡32 in to 7 ft (80 cm to 2.2 m). Z5–9 H9–5

P. weyrichii syn. *Aconogonon weyrichii* A tough, tall, compact species. Noninvasive rhizomes produce large basal, 12-x-8-in (30-x-20-cm), oval

leaves. The foliage extends up the robust stems, topped from late summer by huge, branching clusters dense with greenish white flowers. Impressive in late fall, as the flowers turn into papery, russet seed cases. Resembles *P. wallichii,* but *P. weyrichi* differs in being noninvasive and is also distinguished by its denser, unscented flowerheads. Another giant, and a pioneer species of volcanic deserts and from gravelly alpine slopes and coastal pebbles in Sakhalin and northern Japan. ‡3¼–6 ft (1–1.8 m). Z5–9 H9–5

ABOVE 1 *Petasites albus* **2** *P. fragrans*

PETASITES
Butterbur, Sweet coltsfoot
ASTERACEAE

Architectural, early flowering perennials with large leaves that make excellent ground cover.

About 15 species of winter- or early spring-flowering, usually vigorous, deciduous perennials, spreading by rhizomes, are found in all temperate areas of the Northern Hemisphere. Most flower before the large, long-stemmed, rounded to heart-shaped basal leaves appear, and it is these leaves for which many are valued. Stem leaves are present, but these are insignificant in comparison to the effect produced by the basal foliage. Flowers are usually white, or purple to pink, although yellow ones are also occasionally seen, and individual plants carry either male or female flowers (dioecious). These are held in fluffy spikes on long stems that elongate further when in fruit, and overall the flowers have a feathery appearance. Each spike is made up of many small flowerheads containing outer and inner florets. Male flowerheads have sterile outer florets and fertile inner florets; female flowerheads have many fertile outer florets surrounding a few sterile inner florets.

CULTIVATION Allow plenty of room, since many species have a tendency to be invasive. Best suited to wild gardens, for naturalizing, or for poor,

waste ground, even though they favor deep, fertile soil. Moist soil conditions in sun or part-shade are preferred.

PROPAGATION By division or from seed.

PROBLEMS Usually trouble-free.

P. albus (White butterbur) The 6–16-in (15–40-cm) leaves are orb to heart-shaped with angular marginal lobes and are densely woolly with hairs beneath. The immature leaves are sometimes hairy on both surfaces, but the hairs on the upper surface are quickly lost. Sweetly scented, creamy pale yellow to white flowers, about 12 in (30 cm) tall and later elongating, open in winter or early spring with the leaves appearing shortly afterward. Native to mountainous regions of Europe, North Africa, and southwestern Asia. ‡32 in (80 cm). Z6–9 H9–6

P. fragrans (Winter heliotrope) The leaves are a round heart-shape and softly hairy underneath. They start to appear between midwinter and early spring at the same time as the heads of pale pink, sweetly vanilla-scented flowers. Surprisingly, makes a good cut flower and is also more tolerant of drier soils than the other species, but can be uncomfortably vigorous. Best propagated by separation of the rhizomes. Native to the Mediterranean. ‡8–12 in (20–30 cm). Z7–9 H9–7

P. frigidus var. *palmatus* syn. *P. palmatus* Large, distinctive, rounded or kidney-shaped leaves, 12 in (30 cm) across, feature attractive, deep, coarsely toothed indentations and open after small, dense clusters of white, occasionally pink, flowers open in spring. From damp forests in northern US. ‡12–16 in (30–40 cm). Z6–9 H9–6. **'Golden Palms'** Yellow leaves and pink flowers.

P. giganteus see *P. japonicus* var. *giganteus*

P. hybridus (Butterbur) Large imposing, heart- or kidney-shaped, long-stalked foliage up to 24 in (60 cm) across opens in spring, before which the 4–16-in- (10–40-cm-) long flower spikes open, each carrying unscented, purple, male flowers and paler, mauve to brown female flowers. Vigorous and quickly spreading in its preferred moist conditions and is easily propagated by division. It is naturalized in northeastern and northwestern North America, where it is considered invasive, but native to Europe, northern Africa, and southwestern Asia. ↕ 32 in to 4 ft (80 cm to 1.2 m). Z5–9 H9–5

P. japonicus var. giganteus syn. *P. giganteus* Features the largest foliage of any *Petasites*—an individual near-round leaf can be 3¼–5 ft (1–1.5 m) in diameter, on stalks up to 6½ ft (2 m) tall. Flowers of very pale mauve to white fade into insignificance in comparison to the foliage. Requires moist conditions. From Japan. ↕ 6½ ft (2 m) Z5–9 H9–5. **'Nishiki-buki'** Variegated green leaves irregularly sectored and streaked with white to yellow. Less vigorous, with a tendency to revert to plain greens. **'Variegatus'** *see* 'Nishiki-buki'. **P. japonicus f. purpureus** Smaller, purple leaves.

P. niveus see *P. paradoxus*

P. palmatus see *P. frigidus var. palmatus*

P. paradoxus syn. *P. niveus* The dark green, heart-shaped leaves have prominent, spreading basal lobes and are noted for their undersides being densely covered in white hairs. Dense heads of bright pink to white flowers appear in spring. Native to wet places in the Alps and Pyrenees. ↕ 8–12 in (20–30 cm). Z6–9 H9–6

PETRORHAGIA
CARYOPHYLLACEAE

Small, neatly attractive plants that are ideal as edgings to sunny beds and borders.

About 25 species of annuals and perennials mainly native to rocky and sandy areas throughout Europe and Asia. They vary from erect and tufted to loosely mat-forming and have opposite pairs of simple, narrow leaves and tubular-based five-petaled flowers. The flowers seem to blend the characteristics of *Dianthus* and *Gypsophila*.

CULTIVATION Thrives in sun, in almost all soils if they are free-draining.

PROPAGATION From seed and cuttings.

PROBLEMS Usually trouble-free.

P. saxifraga syn. *Tunica saxifraga* Long cultivated for its mossy mats of needlelike leaves up to 12 in (30 cm) across, and frothy clusters of pink or white flowers in summer. Each flower is about ½ in (1 cm) across, formed of notched-tipped, darker veined petals. Native to southern and central Europe. ↕ 6–8 in (15–20 cm) Z5–9 H7–5 **'Alba Plena'** Rare, double white flower. From Switzerland. ↕ 8 in (20 cm).

PEUCEDANUM
APIACEAE

Bold, though rarely seen, moisture-lovers grown mainly for their foliage effect.

About 170 species widely distributed across usually moist habitats in Eurasia, and tropical and South Africa, only a few of which are grown in gardens, although others are also deserving. Strongly taprooted; the foliage is repeatedly split into pairs or trios of leaflets; the flowerhead is made up of a series of umbels, each comprising white, yellow or occasionally pink florets, the petals of which are long and turn down at the tip; the fruits are distinctly flattened. Most of these plants are more suitable for wild gardens and decidedly quiet or informal situations rather than formal borders.

CULTIVATION Moist soil in full sun or part-shade.

PROPAGATION From seed. Many are difficult to divide due to their parsniplike tap roots.

PROBLEMS Aphids, slugs, and snails.

P. ostruthium (Masterwort) Hollow stems marked with fine lines carry large fresh green leaves, which are triangular in outline and divided once or twice into groups of three leaflets, finely toothed at the margins. As in many members of the family, the bases of the stem leaves are strongly inflated, sheathing the stem at each leaf joint. The flowers may be white or pale pink and are held in large umbels with between 30 and 60 rays. Propagate by freshly sown seed. Native to damp meadows and streamsides in the mountains of central and southern Europe. ↕ 3¼ ft (1 m). Z4–7 H8–1. **var. angustifolium** Spreads widely by rhizomes, especially in moist soil. **'Daphnis'** Paler gray-green leaves variegated attractively around their edge with creamy white. Easily divided.

P. verticillare A tall and stately species, the young spring growth is flushed pink, maturing to a bluish shade as the shoots expand. The mature, waxy, twice-divided leaves, to 20 in (50 cm) long, are made up of oval to oblong, irregularly toothed leaflets. After several years, a stout flowering stem is produced topped by umbels of pale greenish yellow flowers. The maturing fruits are golden yellow with pronounced wings, very ornamental in their own right in the fall garden. After flowering, the plants die, maintaining themselves by self-seeding freely. A striking plant for wilder parts of the garden, especially in dry situations, and an alternative to the relatively coarse, and sometimes invasive, species of *Heracleum*. From the mountains of southeastern Europe and central Italy. ↕ 8 ft (2.5 m). Z6–9 H9–6

PHAENOSPERMA
POACEAE

Tall flower stems carry clusters of tiny, round seeds above handsome foliage.

Just one Asian species, closely related to bamboos from shady situations, this tall grass with steadily spreading rhizomes features erect stems clad with broad leaves that twist through 180 degrees at their base to present the lower side uppermost. The flowering stems seem disproportionately tall compared with the height of the foliage. The stems are topped with airy flowerheads and followed by noticeably shiny seeds from which the genus gets its name (*phaino*: to shine; *sperma*, a seed).

CULTIVATION Best in moisture-retentive, rich soil in full sun to part-shade.

PROPAGATION From seed, it self-seeds very readily. Dislikes division.

PROBLEMS Usually trouble-free.

P. globosa Slowly spreading evergreen clumps feature handsome foliage, the broad, pointed, rough and pleated 24-x-1¼-in (60-x-3-cm) leaves are dark green on the top surface and paler blue-green underneath. In late summer to mid-fall, tall flower stems grow high above the foliage and are hung with tiny flower spikes, maturing to shiny, round, ⅛-in (3-mm) seeds, clinging to wiry branches that whorl out from the main flower stems. Best grown in drifts in an open space, where the sun can catch the flowerheads and seed heads and the foliage can be seen. From woods of Japan, Korea, Taiwan, China, and Assam. ↕ 5 ft (1.5 m). Z5–9 H9–5

PHALARIS
POACEAE

Some highly decorative variegated forms of this adaptable grass make valuable ground cover.

Fifteen annuals and perennials are found in dry or damp soil in Mediterranean regions and north into Europe, also in California. Forming loose clumps or spreading on tough, vigorous root systems, the leaves are soft-textured and sometimes sweet enough to make it a useful pasture grass; some species were introduced into North America for this reason. The flower stems of some perennials are noticeably swollen at the base and carry compact flowerheads, sometimes in narrow cylindrical spikes and sometimes more rounded in shape.

CULTIVATION Best in moisture-retentive fertile soil, though also grows in drier ground in sun to part-shade. Cut back and divide in spring.

PROPAGATION From seed or by division. Divide cultivars and varieties.

PROBLEMS Usually trouble-free.

P. arundinacea (Reed canary grass) Loose evergreen tufts spread on an aggressive root system, with green, flat, bamboolike, pointed leaves ¼–¾ in (6–18 mm) wide feeling quite rough. In early to late summer, straight stems are topped with narrow, compact, lumpy spikes with pale greenish purple to whitish flowers, fading to buff in the fall. Reed canary grass has become a serious threat to native plant species in some regions. If grown in dry situations it is less difficult to control. Trim back variegated types in midsummer to promote a second flush of attractive pink-tinged young shoots. Found on the margins of rivers, streams, lakes, and marshes, where it can form impenetrable masses, throughout Europe, Asia, North America, and South Africa. ↕ 6½ ft (2 m) Z4–9 H9–3 **var. picta** (Gardener's garters, Ribbon grass) Dark

LEFT 1 *Petrorhagia saxifraga*
2 *Peucedanum ostruthium*

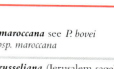

green leaves with pale green and white vertical stripes, tinged pink at the base in the spring. ‡ 24 in (60 cm). **var. *picta* 'Aureovariegata'** see 'Luteopicta'. **var. *picta* 'Feesey'** see 'Woodside'. **var. *picta* 'Luteopicta'** syn. 'Aureovariegata' 'Luteovariegata' Foliage has creamy yellow and green vertical stripes, becoming greener over summer. Low-growing and compact. ‡ 24 in (60 cm). **var. *picta* 'Streamline'** Green leaves edged white, especially in spring. **var. *picta* 'Tricolor'** Gray-green leaves edged white with white vertical white stripes, often with purple-pink tints in the spring and early summer. ‡ 24 in (60 cm) **var. *picta* 'Woodside'** syn. 'Feesey', 'Mervyn Feesey' 'Strawberries and Cream' Green-edged, nearly white leaves with thin green vertical stripes, sometimes with a pink flush on new leaves in the spring. ‡ 32 in (80 cm).

PHEGOPTERIS
THELYPTERIDACEAE

Delightful, rather lacy, small ferns that, despite their appearance, are surprisingly tough.

About three or four species of small, deciduous ferns from temperate regions of the Northern Hemisphere, formerly included in *Thelypteris*. Rhizomes are either erect or thin and creeping, and bear slightly hairy stalks and fronds. The fronds are oval or lance-shaped, divided into several pairs of leaflets that are themselves also lobed or divided. The naked spore-clusters on the underside of the frond are midway between the margin and the midrib. These are undeservedly neglected ferns, making attractive small-scale ground cover or more compact companions for other choice shade-lovers.

CULTIVATION Grow in moist shade, in neutral or acidic soil with plenty of humus.

PROPAGATION By division or from spores.

PROBLEMS Usually trouble-free.

P. connectilis syn. *Thelypteris phegopteris* (Beech fern) Slender, creeping rhizomes support long-stalked, oval, or almost arrow-shaped, pale green fronds. The lowest pair of leaflets points downward, away from the others. The main divisions are oblong and lobed. Good ground cover in light shade, making a very attractive feature with its densely packed fronds, and excellent on a shallow bank where the fronds can hang down in a pale green curtain. Native to damp woods and among shady rocks and on neutral soil in Europe, North America, and western Asia. ‡ 8–12 in (20–30 cm). Z4–6 H6–1

P. decursivepinnata syn. *Thelypteris decursive-pinnata* Clump-forming fern with short, upright, branching rhizomes bearing tufts of narrowly lance-shaped, pale green fronds, twice divided, with leaf tissue extending characteristically along the stems between the numerous main leaflets. Leaflets are further divided into many rounded lobes. A distinctive small fern forming tufts of pale green foliage. Usually propagated from spores, but offsets can be split from a mature clump. The same is sometimes written with a hyphen: *P. decursive-pinnata*. Grows among rocks and on walls in eastern Asia, from Kashmir to Thailand, and Japan. ‡ 16 in (40 cm). Z7–8 H8–5

PHLOMIS
LAMIACEAE

Regrettably underused but combining fine flowers with impressive foliage in bold clumps.

One hundred or more perennials, some woody based, and shrubs are native from the Mediterranean to central Asia and China. Extremely hardy plants with extensive root systems and some with large tubers form clumps, which expand slowly; their handsome leaves are often heart-shaped toward the base and long, slender, and more sparse as they go up the flower stalks. They are frequently felted or deeply textured; even without blossoms they look good. The pink, burgundy, or yellow flowers are grouped in clusters (whorls) encircling the flower spike and are accompanied by pairs of leaves. Jutting out from bracts that remain after the flowers have faded to look like the settings for jewels, the upper petal of each flower is hooded, the lower petal gaping open. Very attractive dried. Ideal where a plant with presence is required in the middle of the border.

CULTIVATION Easy to grow in full sun but tolerates part-shade. They require well-drained soil, wet conditions being fatal.

PROPAGATION Propagate by division, cuttings, or from seed.

PROBLEMS Usually trouble-free.

P. bovei subsp. *maroccana* syn. *P. maroccana* An erect plant, the attractive, slightly sticky, heart-shaped, 2½–3-in (6–8-cm) leaves have notched edges. A whorl of potbellied bracts backs handsome, pale lilac flowers, partly spotted with purple inside, the upper lip slightly longer than the lower. Worth growing for its foliage alone. Sometimes treated as a separate species. From the mountains of Morocco. ‡ 5 ft (1.5 m). Z9–10 H10–9

P. cashmeriana (Kashmir sage) Stunning, with erect, very woolly stems and long, slender, leaves that are forest green with a silver rim above, and silver below. The pale pink flowers, often with a darker lower lip, come in summer in densely packed whorls jutting from star-shaped bracts. Easy in sun in well-drained soil. Native to Kashmir and the western Himalaya. ‡ 36 in (90 cm). Z8–9 H9–8

P. maroccana see *P. bovei* subsp. *maroccana*

P. russeliana (Jerusalem sage) Handsome, forming large and impressive clumps even when immature; broad leaves, up to 10 in (25 cm) across, are thick, felted, and apple green, verging on silver at the base of the plant and becoming long and slender toward the top of the blooming spire. The plump, canary yellow summer flowers last for weeks and emerge from star-shaped bracts, that dry nicely for winter arrangements. Stubbornly hardy despite its warm native digs, but demands good drainage and is disconcertingly slow to emerge in spring. In fall, the foliage often remains intact long after most perennials are frosted. From western Syria. ‡ 36 in (90 cm). Z3–9 H9–1

P. samia (Greek Jerusalem sage) An upright, altogether sticky plant, the dark green, 4–8-in (10–20-cm) leaves are deeply textured and boldly heart-shaped at the base, losing the heart-motif and becoming wide and pointed on the upper flower spires. The blossoms, appearing in spring and summer, are burgundy on their lower lip and slightly pink on the upper hood. Resembles *P. bovei* subsp. *maroccana* but with a smaller lower lip to its blossoms. Native to North Africa, the Balkans, and Greece. ‡ 36 in (90 cm). Z4–9 H9–3. **var. *maroccana*** see *P. bovei* subsp. *maroccana*.

P. tuberosa Large, supposedly edible, tubers throw up tall stems, sometimes flushed with deep purple, carrying long, dark green, arrow-shaped leaves that are deeply veined and sharply serrated at the edges. Clusters of purple or pink flowers, with a straight upper

BELOW 1 *Phlomis russeliana*
2 *P. tuberosa* 'Amazone'

lip, appear in summer. From very well-drained slopes, fallow fields, and meadows in central and southeastern Europe and central Asia, $\updownarrow$4–5 ft (1–2–1.5 m). Z5–8 H8–5. **'Amazone'** Dependably tall. $\updownarrow$5 ft (1.5 m).

PHLOX
POLEMONIACEAE

Phlox fills the summer air with perfume and delights the eye with a rainbow of colors.

Over 60 annuals and evergreen and deciduous perennial species, with all but one native to North America, they were among the first plants sent to Europe from the New World. With dense, fibrous white roots, they may be tightly clump-forming, may spread by rhizomes, or prostrate stems may spread across the soil surface. Many species form basal carpets of opposite, short-stalked foliage with ephemeral flower stalks that wither away after seeds ripen. Others produce tall, persistent, rather woody, leafy stems with opposite foliage and crowned with dense, domed heads of flowers. The flowers are tubular at the base and flare at the end to form flat-faced, five-petaled flowers that open from gracefully twisted buds. Flowers may be white, pink, rose, red, violet, blue, or bicolored. They are as varied in form, flower color, and habitat as any group of garden plants. The perfume can be elusive; although many people find it strong, some can hardly detect it at all.

There are phlox suitable for a wide variety of garden situations. Woodland species, like *P. adsurgens* or *P. divaricata*, provide early color in the woodland or shady wildflower garden. Border phlox, like *P. maculata* and *P. paniculata*, are best placed in the middle or rear of herbaceous and mixed borders; give them ample room to spread and combine them with appropriate perennials, ornamental grasses, and shrubs. Not covered here are alpine species such as *P. douglasii* and *P. subulata* and the

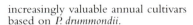

increasingly valuable annual cultivars based on *P. drummondii*.

CULTIVATION Cultivated phlox can be placed into three groups based on their requirements for growth. The woodland species, including *Phlox divaricata* and *P. stolonifera*, require evenly moist, humus-rich soil in light to full shade. They form evergreen ground covers that seldom need dividing unless they crowd other plants. Low, mounding species, like *P. adsurgens*, prefer average sandy or loamy, well-drained soil in full sun. Border phlox include *P. x arendsii, P. carolina, P. maculata,* and *P. paniculata*; plant in average to rich, evenly moist soil in full sun or light shade. Plants perform best where summer nights are cool, and they often bloom for weeks on end. With careful cultivar selection, garden phlox can be in flower from early summer through early fall.

PROPAGATION Propagate plants from stem cuttings in spring and early summer, though cultivars of *P. paniculata* are best propagated from root cuttings taken in fall and laid

horizontally in moist sand. Self-sown seedlings can be plentiful but will not come true, and cultivars must be propagated vegetatively.

PROBLEMS Powdery mildew, mites, occasionally leaf spot, botrytis, blight, and nematodes. All phlox are savored by rabbits and deer; use deterrent sprays or a fence.

P. adsurgens (Northern phlox) A mat-forming phlox developing from a taproot, ascending stems are clothed in 1¼-in (3-cm), hairless, oval leaves and, in late spring and throughout the summer, rather sparse, open clusters of 1-in (2.5-cm) bright pink to lilac flowers with rounded lobes. Plants form attractive clumps in and out of flower. Best in fertile, well-drained soil in sun to part-shade but intolerant of high night temperatures and excess humidity. From mountain meadows and clearings in Oregon and California. $\updownarrow$4–6 in (10–15 cm). Z4–8 H8–1. **'Wagon Wheel'** Narrow-lobed, pink flowers with pale eyes.

P. x arendsii An upright, mound-forming plant spreading from compact slow-creeping stems to form neat clumps of evergreen narrowly oval to lance-shaped foliage, 3–4 in (1¼–1½ cm) long. The ¾–1-in (2–2½-cm), fragrant, early summer flowers cover the stems and open for several weeks. Suitable for the front of the border or as an edging. An attractive hybrid combining the low stature of *P. divaricata* with the showy, brightly hued blooms of *P. paniculata*. Originally produced at Germany's famous Arends Nursery in the 1920s, most old selections have been superseded by new introductions that offer superior flower color, fragrance, and mildew resistance. Plant in rich, evenly moist soil in sun or light shade and cut the spent flower stems to the ground after flowering. Propagate by cuttings or division. Susceptible to powdery mildew, but modern selections are more resistant. $\updownarrow$12–24 in (30–60 cm). Z4–8 H8–1. **'Luc's Lilac'** Lavender-pink flowers. $\updownarrow$36 in (90 cm).

ABOVE 1 *Phlox maculata* 'Alpha'
2 *P. maculata* 'Natascha'
3 *P. maculata* 'Omega'

'Miss Jill' (Spring Pearl Series) White flowers with small, pink eyes. **'Miss Karen'** (Spring Pearl Series) Dark pink with a darker eye. **'Miss Margie'** (Spring Pearl Series) Lilac-blue flowers. **'Miss Mary'** (Spring Pearl Series) Rosy red flowers and dark foliage. **Spring Pearl Series** A range of named selections noted for mildew resistance in some areas, all prefixed Miss. **'Ping Pong'** Delicate pink with a darker rose eye. Mildew-resistant.

P. carolina (Carolina phlox) This stout, handsome phlox has glossy, broadly lance-shaped, 4–5 in (10–13 cm) long, deep green, pointed leaves on tall, straight stems topped with elongated flower clusters of ¾-in (2-cm) flowers; the flat faces are pink to purple, sometimes white. Plant in moist, rich soil in full sun or light shade; propagate from cuttings. From moist deciduous woods, clearings, and roadsides from North Carolina and Kentucky, south to Florida and Mississippi. $\updownarrow$36–48 in (90–120 cm). Z5–8 H8–5. **'Bill Baker'** White-eyed, medium-pink flowers. 20–24 in (50–60 cm). **'Magnificence'** Heat- and mildew-resistant with carmine-pink flowers. $\updownarrow$36 in (90 cm). **'Miss Lingard'** Fragrant, white flowers with pale yellow eyes; somewhat mildew resistant. **'Reine du Jour'** see *P. maculata* 'Reine du Jour'.

P. 'Charles Ricardo' Spreading by creeping rhizomes to form a good mat with deep lavender flowers. A hybrid of *P. divaricata* and *P. pilosa* and similar to 'Chattahoochee' but with a red eye, broader leaves, and longer-lived. For part-shade. $\updownarrow$15 in (38 cm). Z5–8 H8–5

P. decussata see *P. paniculata*

P. divaricata ♥ (Blue phlox) Slowly spreading clumps of 2-in (5-cm), glossy, evergreen, broadly lance-shaped leaves throw up erect, hairy flowering stems topped by open clusters of ¾-in (2-cm), fragrant, sky blue flowers with notched petals, each spaced from its neighbor. Stalks wither after flowering, leaving a tidy, glossy, evergreen ground cover. Good under flowering shrubs or with wildflowers, forming evergreen ground covers that seldom need dividing unless they crowd other plants. Self-sown seedlings vary widely in color, so propagate by cuttings or division if you want to perpetuate a specific color. From moist deciduous woods, clearings, floodplains, and roadsides from Quebec and Minnesota, south to Georgia and Texas. ‡ 10–15 in (25–38 cm). Z4–8 H8–1. **'Blue Dreams'** Lilac-blue flowers. **'Blue Moon'** Very full with overlapping petals of a deep violet blue. Introduced by the New England Wild Flower Society. **'Blue Perfume'** Sky blue, very fragrant flowers. **'Clouds of Perfume'** Intensely fragrant, ice blue flowers. **'Dirigo Ice'** Pale blue flowers. **'Eco Texas Purple'** Purple-blue flowers with a red eye. **subsp. *laphamii*** Periwinkle-blue flowers. From the eastern US. **subsp. *laphamii* 'Chattahoochee'** syn. 'Moody Blue' Lavender-blue flowers with cerise eyes that open in late spring as other selections are fading. Plants have stiff, narrow, hairy leaves and require full sun to light shade to flower well. Perhaps a hybrid with *P. pilosa*. **subsp. *laphamii* 'Chattahoochee Variegated'** Rare, rather weak, but dramatic white-edged form of 'Chattahoochee'. **'May Breeze'** Full-petaled, pure white flowers. **'Montrose Tricolor'** Powder blue flowers above white-edged leaves that emerge tinged with pink in spring. ‡ 4– 8 in (10–20 cm). **'Moody Blue'** *see* subsp. *laphamii* 'Chattahoochee'. **'Our Best Lavender'** Lavender flowers. Selected at the New England Wild Flower Society's Garden in the Woods. **'Purple Pinwheels'** Purple, with petals toothed along the margin and very full in shape. A seedling of 'Blue Moon' from the New England Wild Flower Society's Garden in the Woods. **'White Perfume'** Fragrant, white flowers with narrow petals.

P. maculata (Early phlox) Developing into broad clumps of open, tufted winter rosettes, the flowers open in early summer, filling the bloom gap between the spring species and the powerhouse bloom of *P. paniculata*. The fragrant, domed or cylindrical clusters boast tightly packed, 1-in (2.5-cm) flowers on often purple-spotted stems above glossy, broadly lance-shaped foliage to 5 in (13 cm) long. Generally mildew-resistant, but resistance can vary by region and season. Plant in evenly moist, humus-rich soil in full sun or light shade, deadhead to control unwanted seedlings, and propagate by cuttings or division. From low woods, moist meadows, and floodplains from Quebec to Minnesota, south to Georgia and Missouri. ‡ 24–36 in (60– 90 cm). Z5–8 H8–1. **'Alpha'** Rose pink flowers with slightly darker eyes. **'Delta'** Elongated, 12 in (30 cm) heads of white flowers with deep pink eyes. **'Natascha'** Dense clusters of small, though rather shocking flowers, each white petal with a central, pale magenta stripe. Not spelled 'Natasha'. **'Omega'** White flowers with lilac-pink eyes. Raised by Alan Bloom at Bressingham, Norfolk, England. **'Princess Sturdza'** Small, but abundant, deep mauve flowers. Vigorous and tall. ‡ 4½ ft (1.4 m). **'Reine du Jour'** Long season of pink-eyed white flowers. **'Rosalinde'** Vibrant, deep pink flowers.

P. paniculata syn. *P. decussata* (Border phlox) One of the most popular summer perennials. Slender, thongy roots form a tight crown supporting the rather woody stems, which carry oppositely arranged, 2–6-in (5–15-cm), broadly lance-shaped, slightly toothed, dull green leaves which are attractive all season. In mid- to late summer, huge domed clusters of fragrant, flat-faced, 1-in (2.5-cm), fragrant, magenta, pink or white flowers are held on erect, leafy stems. Hundreds of selections and hybrids have been made to increase the color range to violet, purple, rose, cerise, salmon, orange, and bicolors. Each plant flowers for as long as

5 weeks, with different cultivars blooming at different times. Plant in rich, evenly moist soil in sun to part-shade, they perform best where summer nights are cool. Plants bloom twice from each flower cluster; after the second flush of bloom, deadhead to control unwanted seedlings. Often susceptible to powdery mildew (*see* Powdery Mildew). Divide clumps every 3 to 4 years in spring or fall. Propagate all but variegated cultivars by root cuttings. From rich deciduous woods, clearings, floodplains, and roadsides from New York and Illinois, south to Georgia and Arkansas, and naturalized elsewhere. ‡ 36–48 in (90– 120 cm). Z4–8 H8–1. **var. *alba*** White flowers; white-flowered cultivars are generally superior to var. *alba*. **'Alba Grandiflora'** Long-established, large-flowered white. **'Amethyst'** Full heads of deep lilac flowers. **'Balmoral'** Large trusses of fragrant, pink flowers. **'Becky Towe'** Yellow-edged leaves and carmine flowers with dark eyes; a

spontaneous mutation of 'Windsor' found in Shropshire, England. **'Blue Boy'** The nearest to true blue. **'Blue Ice'** Dense trusses of white flowers with rosy blue eyes. **'Blue Paradise'** Medium blue flowers with a dark eye. **'Border Gem'** Dark violet flowers with a light eye. **'Brigadier'** Excellent salmon red flowers. **'Bright Eyes'** Red-tinged foliage and pink flowers with crimson eyes; mildew-resistant. **'Cotton Candy'** *see* 'Speed Limit 45'. **'Crème de Menthe'** Pink flowers and white-edged leaves. **'Darwin's Choice'** *see* 'Norah Leigh'. **'Darwin's Joyce'** *see* 'Norah Leigh'. **'David'** Huge heads of pure white flowers; excellent mildew resistance. Found in the garden at the Brandywine Museum, PA. Perennial Plant of the Year for 2002. **'Discovery'** Soft pink, highly scented flowers. ‡ 36 in (90 cm). **'Dodo Hanbury-Forbes'** Huge trusses open reddish purple and fade to lavender-pink. ‡ 36 in (90 cm). **'Duesterlohe'** syn. 'Nicky' Medium rose pink flowers.

NATIVE WOODLANDERS

Two quiet but captivating American woodland perennials, both tending to spread rather than stay in tight clumps, intermingle here into a delightful spring carpet around deciduous shrubs. The flowers of dainty *Phlox divaricata*, in a range of blue and purplish shades, look out in open clusters from the tops of their wiry stems, while the long, nodding bells of *Uvularia perfoliata*, spreading more widely at the root before sending up its flowering stems, add a contrasting flower shape in an equally pastel coloring. A mulch of leaf mold in early spring will help both of these plants to flower well.

VARIEGATED CULTIVARS

In recent years there has been a surge of introductions of variegated forms of *Phlox paniculata*. For many years there were only two, both raised by Alan Bloom at Bressingham, Norfolk. 'Nora Leigh' arose as a spontaneous mutation of the old favorite 'Border Gem', while 'Harlequin' was a seedling raised on the nursery.

Since then almost a dozen others have been introduced, although some quickly faded away. 'Becky Towe' is a mutation of 'Windsor'; 'Goldmine' is a mutation of 'Silvermine', which is itself a mutation of 'Popeye'. Others you may come across include 'Crème de Menthe', 'Darwin's Choice', and 'Darwin's Joyce' (which are both, in fact, 'Nora Leigh'), 'Frosted Elegance', 'Mary Christine', and 'Pink Posie'. Oddly enough, there are, as yet, no variegated forms of *P. maculata*. The latest are the three in the Mine Series, developed by Dutch horticulturist Rene van Gaalen. He first introduced

'Popeye', a mutation of 'Bright Eyes' with more contrasting coloring. This then mutated to the variegated 'Silvermine'; Goldmine is a mutation of 'Silvermine' and this has been joined by 'Rubymine'. One significant problem with variegated cultivars is that most forms of *P. paniculata*, especially in smaller nurseries, are propagated by root cuttings to avoid passing on phlox stem eelworm. But variegated cultivars cannot be propagated by this method as they usually revert to plain green leaves. Some nurseries use chemicals to control this pest, but for others propagation is difficult and this partly accounts for the relative scarcity of these cultivars in nurseries. The only other variegated cultivars are both forms of *P. divaricata* - 'Chattahoochee Variegated' and 'Montrose Tricolor'. Both are rather weak but are intriguing and colorful when well grown.

LEFT *Phlox paniculata*: **1** 'Brigadier'
2 'Bright Eyes' **3** 'Eva Cullum'
4 'Eventide' **5** 'Harlequin' **6** 'Mother
of Pearl' **7** 'Starfire' **8** 'Windsor'

PHLOX PANICULATA CULTIVARS

Many of the cultivars of *P. paniculata* grown today have been favorites in gardens for many years. In the 1940s and 1950s, Captain B.H.B. Symons-Jeune raised a large range, some still grown today, including 'Cecil Hanbury' (orange-salmon), 'Iceberg' (white), and 'Lilac Time' (lilac), but it is suspected that the success of his introductions owed more to good publicity than to their inherent quality. 'Lilac Time' is now the only one still widely grown. In the 1940s Fred Simpson of Otley in Yorkshire, England, who also raised Korean chrysanthemums, raised those named after the royal houses, including 'Balmoral', 'Barnwell', 'Sandringham', and 'Windsor', as well as 'Otley Choice' (all various shades of pink).

As Alan Bloom and his helper Percy Piper discovered, raising new forms of *P. paniculata* is not difficult; open pollinated seed from a collection of cultivars will inevitably turn up new forms. But they also discovered the other truth: finding ones which are better than those already being grown is more difficult. They raised a great many seedlings but selected and introduced only a few: 'Bill Green' (pink), 'Eva Cullum' (deep pink), 'Mary Fox' (salmon pink), and 'Franz Schubert' (violet) plus the variegated 'Harlequin'.

More recently the Dutch, in particular horticulturist Rene van Gaalen, have introduced the Mine Series of variegated forms and the Feelings Series, which are intended as cut flowers. New hybrids with *P. divaricata*, such as *P.* x *arendsii* Spring Pearls series are bringing new dwarfer forms to prominence.

'Eden's Crush' Bright pink with a dark eye; mildew-resistant. ↕ 24 in (60 cm). **'Eden's Smile'** Mauve with a dark eye; mildew-resistant. ↕ 24–30 in (60–75 cm). **'Empty Feelings'** (Feeling Series) Showy green bracts. **'Europa'** White flowers with a pink eye. **'Eva Cullum'** Stout, with rich pink, dark-eyed flowers. ↕ 36 in (90 cm). **'Eventide'** Lavender-blue flushed with lilac. ↕ 36 in (90 cm). **Feelings Series** Bred for flower arrangers and curious for its large sepals that make the tight flowerheads resembling goldenrods. In some, the tiny, sterile flowers never develop; others have small, narrow petals. Appears in need of deadheading rather than in need of adoring, but exceptionally long-lasting. From Holland's Rene van Gaalen who also introduced the Mine Series of variegated cultivars. **'Flamingo'** Bright pink flowers with a darker eye. **'Franz Schubert'** Lavender at the petal center, gradually fading to white at the edges. **'Frosted Elegance'** White-edged leaves and pale pink flowers with darker eyes. **'Goldmine'** (Mine Series) Gold-edged leaves and magenta flowers; a spontaneous mutation of 'Silvermine'. **'Graf Zeppelin'** Dark pink flowers with a lighter eye. **'Harlequin'** Creamy white leaf margins and hot pink flowers. A seedling raised by Alan Bloom at Bressingham, Norfolk, England. **'Hesperis'** Small but profuse, pale purple flowers with white eyes. ↕ 36 in (90 cm). **'Iris'** Flowers open magenta, aging to blue-violet. **'Jules Sandeau'** Deep rose flowers with a pale eye. **'Juliglut'** Dark carmine flowers and dark foliage. **'Katherine'** syn. 'Katarina' Compact lavender flowers with a white eye. ↕ 24–30 in (60–75 cm). **'Kirmesländler'** White flowers with red centers. ↕ 36 in (90 cm). **'Laura'** Deep rosy pink flowers with a starry white eye. **'Le Mahdi'** Violet-blue. Described by phlox breeder Capt. B. H. B. Symons-

Jeune as "Dull and miserly in the daytime, it goes a wonderful dark blue in the half lights." ↕ 24 in (60 cm). **'Lilac Time'** Good, lilac-blue flowers. ↕ 24 in (60 cm). **'Little Boy'** Compact, with violet-rose, white-eyed flowers; mildew-resistant. ↕ 30 in (75 cm). **'Little Princess'** Very short, with rosy pink, white-eyed flowers. ↕ 20 in (50 cm). **'Lizzy'** Very short, with bright pink flowers. ↕ 20 in (50 cm). **'Mia Ruys'** Compact, with large white flowers. ↕ 24 in (60 cm). **'Midnight Feelings'** (Feelings Series) Mahogany bracts and small, sterile flowers. **Mine Series** A series of three variegated cultivars with gold edges to the leaves, developed by Holland's Rene van Gaalen (*see* Phlox *paniculata* Cultivars). **'Miss Elie'** Impressive heads of rosy flowers. ↕ 36 in (90 cm). **'Miss Holland'** Late, with rose-eyed, white flowers. ↕ 36–48 in (90–120 cm). **'Miss Pepper'** Bright pink flowers with a red eye. **Miss Series** Most *Phlox* cultivars whose names begin Miss, other than those listed here, are cultivars of *P.* x *arendsii* in the Spring Pearls Series. **'Miss Universe'** Tall white. ↕ 36 in (90 cm). **'Monica Lynden-Bell'** Pale pink flowers, opening from dark buds. **'Mother of Pearl'** White suffused with pink. Raised by Alan Bloom at Bressingham, Norfolk, England. **'Mount Fuji'** Small, pure white flowers in narrow, upright clusters. ↕ 36 in (90 cm). **'Natural Feelings'** (Feelings Series) Small, rosy lavender flowers and exaggerated bracts. **'Nicky'** *see* 'Duesterlohe'. **'Norah Leigh'** syn. 'Darwin's Choice', 'Darwin's Joyce' Creamy yellow leaf margins and pale pink flowers with dark eyes. A spontaneous mutation of 'Border Gem' found at Broadwell, Gloucestershire, England and introduced by Alan Bloom. Z3–8 H8–1. **'Otley Choice'** Deep rose pink flowers. **'Prince of Orange'** Orange-red flowers. ↕ 24 in (60 cm). **'Prospero'** Medium lilac flowers with white-edged petals and a white eye. **'Red Feelings'** (Feelings Series) Small, narrow-petaled, red flowers with sepals making a dubious show. But good for cutting. **'Rijnstroom'** Salmon pink; an

excellent performer. ‡ 36 in (90 cm).
'**Robert Poore**' Giant flowerheads of
red-purple in midsummer. Mildew-
resistant, named for the Mississippi
landscape architect. ‡ 5–6 ft (1.5–1.8 m).
'**Rosa Pastell**' Large, soft pink flowers
with darker eyes. '**Rubymine**' (Mine
Series) White-edged leaves tinged red
when young and pink flowers with
rosy starburst centers; mildew-resistant.
'**Sandringham**' Medium pink flowers
with darker eyes. ‡ 36 in (90 cm).
'**Silvermine**' Gold-edged foliage and
white flowers with rosy reverse and
small red eyes; a spontaneous mutation
of '**Popeye**'. '**Speed Limit 45**' syn.
'Cotton Candy'. Hot pink. Found by a
road sign. '**Starfire**' Early, vibrant, deep
red with red-tinged foliage. '**Tenor**'
Early, with rosy scarlet flowers; a good
rebloomer. ‡ 24 in (60 cm). '**The King**'
Deep red-violet flowers. '**Tracy's
Treasure**' soft pink flowers on a
vigrous, disease-resistant plant. Selected
by Tracy DiSbato-Aust, OH. ‡ 4 ft
(1.2 m). '**White Admiral**' Late bloomer
with large, white flowers. '**Windsor**'
Carmine-rose flowers with a darker
eye. ‡ 24 in (60 cm).

P. stolonifera (Creeping phlox) Broad,
dense clumps of 3-in (8-cm), oval,
evergreen leaves line creeping stems
that root as they go to form attractive
mats. The ephemeral bloom stalks carry
open clusters of 1-in (2.5-cm) magenta
to pink flowers in early to mid-spring.
Plants look best when allowed to
develop without competition, but they
will weave gracefully among taller
clumping plants such as *Hosta* and
Polygonatum. Plant in moist, humus-
rich soil in light to full shade. After
seed set, trim any remaining bloom
stalks so the carpet of foliage can
ornament the garden through the
summer. Perennial Plant of the Year in
1990. From open woods and wooded,
rocky slopes from Pennsylvania and
Ohio, south to Georgia. ‡ 6–8 in (15–
20 cm). Z4–8 H8–1. '**Ariane**' White
flowers with a yellow eye. '**Blue Ridge**'
Full-petaled, lilac-blue flowers. '**Bruce's
White**' White, with yellow eyes. '**Fran's
Purple**' Royal purple with narrow
petals. '**Home Fires**' Iridescent pink
flowers. '**Mary Belle Frey**' Rose-pink
flowers with a dark eye. '**Pink Ridge**'
Mauve-pink flowers. '**Sherwood
Purple**' Purple-blue, fragrant flowers.
'**Violet Vere**' Pale violet flowers.

PHORMIUM
New Zealand flax
PHORMIACEAE

Statuesque specimen or accent
plants for foliage and structural
impact at the back of the large
border or in gravel.

Two species of evergreen plants
from New Zealand and Norfolk
Island, where they grow in a wide
range of habitats, from lowland
swamps to coastal cliffs and
mountain slopes. Clump-forming
with deep, fleshy roots, the long,
strap-shaped, strongly fibrous, very
leathery leaves, often with a keel
and drooping at the tips, are

arranged in elegant fans. Robust
stems, branching stiffly at right
angles well above the leaves, carry
numerous flowers, though it is the
foliage that is usually the main
attraction. Sometimes, mysteriously,
listed in catalogs under shrubs.

Many variegated and colored-
leaved forms have been introduced
and are now classified according to
their habit of growth (*see* Phormium
Shape Groups) The first arose as
spontaneous mutations on wild
plants and were cultivated by the
Maoris. Recently, breeding programs
have led to the introduction of
many plants in a wide range of
growth habits and foliage colors.

CULTIVATION Easily grown in
moisture-retentive soil, but surviving
periods of drought when established.
Often grown in areas on the
borderline of their hardiness and
may be damaged in hard winters.

PROPAGATION By division or from
seed (colored-leaves forms do not
come true to type).

PROBLEMS Usually trouble-free.

P. '**Alison Blackman**' (Spreading)
Olive green, gold-striped leaves with
narrow orange-red margins. ‡ 4 ft
(1.2 m). Z8–11 H11–1.

P. '**Apricot Queen**' (Spreading) The
young leaves shaded soft apricot,
maturing to shades of green and
yellowish orange with a brown edge.
‡ 28 in (70 cm). Z8–11 H11–1.

P. cookianum syn. *P. colensoi* Bold, erect
plant with arching leaves, usually pink
at the base, to less than 6½ ft (2 m)
long and up to 2½ in (6 cm) wide. In
summer, 1–1½-in (2.5–4-cm) long,
greenish blooms shaded yellow or
orange are borne more or less erect
on the flowering stem branches and
followed by slender, twisted, 4-in
(10-cm) or longer pods that hang
vertically. Clearly distinguished from
P. tenax by its arching, rather than erect,
leaves and its pendulous seedpods.
From New Zealand. ‡ 6½ ft (2 m).
Z8–11 H11–1. **subsp.** *hookeri* '**Cream
Delight**' (Arching) Leaves to 3¼ ft
(1 m) long and 2¾ in (7 cm) wide,
striped with cream, especially down
the middle. ‡ 36 in (90 cm). '**Tricolor**'
syn. *P. tenax* 'Tricolor' (Arching) The
leaves are strongly arched and
conspicuously striped with cream and
red margins. ‡ 4 ft (1.2 m).

P. '**Dazzler**' (Arching) Very dramatic
bronze leaves with conspicuous red
stripes. ‡ 36 in (90 cm). Z8–11 H11–1.

P. '**Duet**' (Spreading) The stiff leaves,
green in the center are creamy white
striped toward the margins. ‡ 3¼ ft
(1 m). Z8–11 H11–1.

P. '**Dusky Chief**' (Upright) Rich,
black-purple leaves with a paler
center and deep red edges. ‡ 36–48 in
(90–120 cm). Z8–11 H11–1.

P. '**Evening Glow**' (Arching) A
plant with a somewhat spreading
habit. The bright reddish pink-flushed
foliage is grayer at the edges. ‡ 36 in
(90 cm). Z8–11 H11–1.

P. '**Flamingo**' (Arching) Pale creamy
pink to dark pink with grayish green
stripes. May revert to brown. ‡ 36 in
(90 cm). Z8–11 H11–1.

P. '**Gold Sword**' (Spreading) Stiffly
erect leaves with a green margin and a
central yellow zone. It is similar to
'Apricot Queen' but paler. ‡ 3¼ ft
(1 m). Z8–11 H11–1.

P. '**Jack Spratt**' (Twisted) This plant
has somewhat arching leaves,
20–24 in (50–60 cm) long, with a
black midrib and purple-brown
margins. ‡ 18 in (45 cm). Z8–11 H11–1.

P. '**Jester**' (Arching) Bright pink and
green stripes, greener toward the edge,
with a pale midrib and orange margin.
‡ 4 ft (1.2 m). Z8–11 H11–1.

P. '**Maori Chief**' syn. *P.* 'Rainbow
Chief' (Spreading) Large, with bronze-
green, 4–5 ft (1.2–1.5 m) long leaves,
that are striped pink toward the sides
and with an orange margin. ‡ 6 ft
(1.8 m). Z8–11 H11–1.

P. '**Maori Maiden**' syn. *P.* 'Rainbow
Maiden', *P.* 'Rainbow Red' (Arching)
Low arching habit; the plant's long
leaves have a salmon pink central
zone that fades to yellow-pink later
in the season; the margins are greenish
bronze. ‡ 24–36 in (60–90 cm).
Z8–11 H11–1.

P. '**Maori Queen**' syn. *P.* 'Rainbow
Queen' (Spreading) A large plant with
erect, bronze-green leaves that are

pink-striped near the margins. ‡ 4–5 ft
(1.2–1.5 m). Z8–11 H11–1

P. **Maori Series** Selected in the 1980s
in New Zealand by Margaret Jones
from seedlings raised from the
Rainbow Hybrids.

P. '**Maori Sunrise**' syn. 'Rainbow
Sunrise' (Arching) Low, arching
mounds of 32-in (80-cm) leaves,
salmon pink in the center, fading to
yellow with greenish bronze margins.
‡ 36 in (90 cm). Z8–11 H11–1.

P. '**Merlot**' (Upright) Leaves dark wine
red above, silvery bronze beneath.
‡ 5–6 ft (1.5–1.8 m). Z8–11 H11–1

P. '**Pink Panther**' (Arching) Bright
pink leaves, striped in grayish brown
toward the edges with brown margins.
‡ 24–36 in (60–90 cm). Z8–11 H11–1

P. '**Pink Stripe**' (Spreading) Olive
green leaves strikingly margined in
vivid pink, especially low down. ‡ 4–6 ft
(1.2–1.8 m). Z8–11 H11–1

P. '**Platt's Black**' (Arching) Spreading
habit with leaves 3¼–4 ft (1–1.2 m)
long, rich brown, almost black above,
suffused white beneath. ‡ 3¼–4 ft (1–
1.2 m). Z8–11 H11–1

P. **Rainbow hybrids** *see*
P. 'Maori series'.

P. '**Sundowner**' (Upright) Popular
large cultivar with upright, 4–5 ft (1.2–
1.5-m), bronzy olive green leaves
variably striped red and pink but
mainly toward the edges. ‡ 7–9 ft (2.2–
2.8 m). Z8–11 H10–1

P. '**Surfer**' (Twisted) Erect, twisted, 24–
28 in (60–70 cm) long leaves suffused

PHORMIUM SHAPE GROUPS

To help gardeners choose
wisely from the increasingly
wide and varied range
of *Phormium* cultivars
available, and place them
thoughtfully in the garden,
the phormiums have been
divided into five groups
according to their growth
habit, and the way in which
they carry their dramatic,
leathery foliage.

Upright Foliage is rigid and upright,
as seen on 'Sundowner' (above); the
tips of the older leaves often arch
noticeably and may also split slightly.

Spreading Cultivars, such as 'Maori
Queen' (above), on which the foliage
is less rigid but stills grows upward,
although the tips may bend over.

Arching The foliage is softer and
less self-supporting, arching strongly
and with the tips often touching the
ground. (Here, *P. cookianum* 'Tricolor')

Twisted Leaves are relatively small
and rigid, often noticeably keeled,
wavy-edged, or twisted, as illustrated
here by 'Jack Spratt'.

Dwarf Plants, such as *P. tenax*
'Nanum Purpureum' (above) with
foliage in a tight cluster but sometimes
with an occasional larger leaf emerging.

LEFT 1 *Phormium tenax* Purpureum Group **2** *P.* 'Yellow Wave'

bronze-brown and with a central yellow-green zone. ‡ 18 in (45 cm). Z8–11 H11–1

P. **'Surfer Bronze'** (Twisted) Tall, wavy, bronze leaves with darker margins. ‡ 16–20 in (40–50 cm). Z8–11 H11–1

P. tenax Magnificent, usually pale at the base, with erect, gray-backed leaves, 6½–10 ft (2–3 m) long, often edged in red or orange; taller flowering stems with abundant dull red flowers, 1¼– 2 in (3–5 cm) long, decorating the horizontal branches in summer. The robust seedpods that follow are erect, 2½–4 in (6–10 cm) long, and roughly triangular in cross section. *P. cookianum* has arching leaves and erect seedpods. Thrives in most soils, though a wetland plant throughout its native New Zealand. ‡ 8–15 ft (2.5–5 m). Z8–11 H11–1. **'Alpinum Purpureum'** *see* 'Nanum Purpureum'. **'Atropurpureum'** *see* Purpureum Group. **'Co-ordination'** (Upright) Leaves to 5 ft (1.5 m) long with many fine, longitudinal lines of green and bronze plus a green margin. A spontaneous mutation of 'Purpureum'. ‡ 3¼ ft (1 m). **'Nanum Purpureum'** syn. 'Alpinum Purpureum' (Dwarf) The leaves are shaded purple-bronze. ‡ 18 in (45 cm). **Purpureum Group** syn 'Rubrum', 'Purpureum', and 'Atropurpureum' Maroon-purple foliage. ‡ 8–9 ft (2.5–2.8 m). **'Tricolor'** see *P. cookianum* 'Tricolor'. **'Variegatum'** (Upright) Leaves striped creamy yellow and white. Introduced in 1878. ‡ 8 ft (2.5 m).

P. **'Thumbelina'** (Twisted) Bronzy red with faint pale stripes and very dark edges. ‡ 12 in (30 cm). Z8–11 H11–1

P. **'Tom Thumb'** (Twisted) Spreading leaves up to 28 in (70 cm) long, are bronze-green with black margins. Despite its name, it is by no means the smallest cultivar. ‡ 24–36 in (60– 90 cm). Z8–11 H11–1

P. **'Yellow Wave'** (Arching) Broad, arching, 3¼ ft (1 m) long, yellow leaves, variegated green as they mature. ‡ 36 in (90 cm). Z9–10 H10–3

PHRAGMITES
POACEAE

Tall, waterside grasses with robust root systems and large, attractive, feathery flowers.

Three to four perennial species are found all over the world in temperate to subtropical climates, growing in marshes and on riversides. Stout stems grow on a vigorous, creeping root system with bamboolike, evergreen leaves, the bases of which wrap around the stems and unfurl into wide, pointed blades. In the late summer, the leafy stems carry large, pampas-grass–like flowers, but looser and fluffier with a mass of hairy flower spikes. *Phragmites* is a very tough, robust grass and the stems and leaves are still used for thatching and fencing in England. Caution should be exercised in using this species due to its strongly invasive tendency.

CULTIVATION Grow in moist, heavy soil and, if in containers, top with gravel. Will also survive in drier conditions producing a smaller, less robust plant.

PROPAGATION By division in spring.

PROBLEMS Usually trouble-free.

P. australis syn. *P. communis* (Common reed grass) Dense colonies are formed on a vigorous root system with tall, stout stems and bamboolike, gray-green, smooth leaves 8 in (20 cm) long

RIGHT 1 *Phragmites australis* **2** *Phuopsis stylosa*

and ½–1¼ in (1–3 cm) wide, unfurling from the stems at an almost horizontal angle. Late in the summer, the stems carry large, fluffy flowerheads with purple to dark brown flowers fringed with white hairs that give the plumes a silvery appearance. When picked newly opened, the flowers are excellent dried. Best grown in large containers. When placed in a pond, the angle of the leaves and decorative flowers make a good contrast to other aquatic plants. Often planted to prevent soil bank erosion, but care should be taken, since the plant is so invasive that it can smother native plants and choke waterways. Found in up to 6½ ft (2 m) of still water in swamps and on lakesides throughout temperate to subtropical climates. ‡ 4½–10 ft (1.4– 3 m). Z3–11 H11–1. **'Variegatus'** Smaller, with finer foliage, the leaves have yellow edges and thin yellow and green stripes that become paler in the summer; smaller purple-silver flowers. ‡ 4½ ft (1.4 m).

PHUOPSIS
RUBIACEAE

Delicate yet vigorous low-growing carpeter with aromatic foliage and a profusion of pretty summer flowers.

A single, deciduous species found on rocky slopes and sand dunes in the Caucasus and northern Iran. Although introduced early in the 19th century, this mat-forming plant is not common, perhaps due to its unusual, pungent scent. It colonizes bare ground by using its yellowish, wiry roots to form patches of finely textured foliage on lax stems, from the tips of which are borne upright heads of tiny, starlike, pink flowers.

CULTIVATION Easy to grow in sun or bright shade, preferably in well-drained soil.

PROPAGATION By division or semiripe cuttings, or from seed.

PROBLEMS Usually trouble-free.

P. stylosa syn. *Crucianella stylosa* (Caucasian crosswort) Quick growth soon creates a tangle of sprawling, bristly, square-edged stems, covered in rufflike clusters of slender, pointed, fresh-green leaves, up to ⅝ in (1.5 cm) long. From early to late summer, spherical flowerheads bob above the foliage, each about 1 in (2.5 cm) across and crowded with spicy-scented, light pink flowers, their five pointed petals joined behind into a short tube. Long, slim styles darting out from the flowers have inspired the image of a pincushion stuck with pins. Makes good ground cover for banks, the front of open borders, or path edges and mingles into neighboring plants. Attracts butterflies and bees. ‡ 8–12 in (20–30 cm). Z5–8 H8–5. **'Purpurea'** Flowers a deeper purple-pink.

PHYSALIS
Ground cherry
SOLANACEAE

Hardy deciduous plants whose orange-red fall lanterns light up the late season garden.

About 80 species of deciduous perennials and annuals found in open and sunny or shaded places worldwide, but especially the Americas. The leaves are simple or deeply cut; the tiny bell-shaped flowers are inconspicuous but the berries that follow are enclosed in very showy, orange or red, papery lanternlike capsules. In some species the berries are edible. Ornamental species are grown for their decorative lanterns, which come

into their own in fall. For mixed borders or more natural areas, such as the edge of a woodland garden. One species, *P. edulis,* is grown specifically for its edible fruits.

CULTIVATION Grows well in any well-drained soil, and full sun or part-shade.

PROPAGATION By division in spring. From seeds in spring, for species only, at 59°F (15°C).

PROBLEMS Usually trouble-free.

P. alkekengi (Chinese lantern) A vigorous plant spreading by rhizomes; the somewhat triangular, mid-green leaves, about 4¾ in (12 cm) long, are rather uninspiring. Small, cream flowers appear in midsummer but are followed by ⅝-in (1.7-cm) red or scarlet berries enclosed in orange-red lanterns about 2 in (5 cm) across. Ideal, where space permits, for providing fall interest, but where border space is limited, grow the plant in a more natural part of the garden where it has room to spread. All parts of *P. alkekengi,* except for the ripe berries, are toxic, and contact with the foliage may cause a skin allergy. From central and southern Europe, and western Asia to Japan. ‡ 24–30 in (60–75 cm). Z3–9 H8–1. ⚠ **var.** *franchetii* Larger than species, with more pointed lanterns. ‡ 36 in (90 cm). **var.** *franchetii* **‘Gigantea’** Much larger berries and lanterns. **var.** *franchetii* **‘Variegata’** Yellow and cream variegated foliage.

PHYSOSTEGIA
Obedient plant
LAMIACEAE

Intriguing and colorful plants—individual flowers can be pushed in any direction and will stay there. About 12 upright perennial species

from moist woods and grasslands in North America, only one of which is commonly grown. Square, upright, unbranched stems carry alternating pairs of toothed, lance-shaped leaves that have a distinctive small bristle on each tooth tip. The two-lipped, pink, purple or white flowers are held in upright, usually branched, spikes on very short stalks. Much loved by flower arrangers because the individual flowers can be pushed to the visible side of the stem and will remain in place, so enhancing the display—and hence the common name.

CULTIVATION Moist but not-too-fertile soil, in full sun or part-shade.

PROPAGATION From seed sown in fall, or by division in early spring as growth starts.

PROBLEMS Crown rot, rust.

P. virginiana (Obedient plant, false dragonhead) Vigorous plants, spreading by underground runners, rapidly forming a large clump; upright stems, which may require support if grown in fertile soil, are clothed with pairs of more or less lance-shaped, sharply toothed leaves, to 4¾ in (12.5 cm) , set at right angles to each other up the stem. The rose pink to purple flowers are closely packed in spikes, up to 10 in (25 cm), that arise at the top of the shoots and from the upper leaf-bases, to give a very full head of blooms from late summer onward. It needs frequent division to keep it within bounds. Variegated cultivars tend to produce green shoots, which should be dug out. eastern and central North America. ‡ 4 ft (1.2 m). Z2–8 H8–1. **‘Alba’** White flowers, slightly earlier than other cultivars, followed by bright green seed pods. ‡ 36 in (90 cm) **‘Crown of Snow’** (Schneekrone)

White, but less invasive and slightly smaller than ‘Alba’. Seed-raised forms of ‘Alba’ are sometimes sold under this name. ‡ 32 in (80 cm). **‘Miss Manners’** Pure white, but with good manners (not invasive). The stems form secondary branches to improve the display. Introduced by Massachusetts horticulturist Darrell Probst. ‡ 24 in (60 cm). **‘Olympic Gold’** Gold-edged leaves that fade to cream and light green as they age. Pale pink flowers. ‡ 20 in (50 cm). **‘Red Beauty’** Dark pink, not really red. ‡ 30 in (75 cm). **‘Rosea’** syn. ‘Rose Crown’, ‘Rose Queen’ Bright pink, larger than usual flowers. ‡ 3¼ ft (1 m). **Schneekrone** *see* ‘Crown of Snow’. **‘Summer Snow’** Pure white with dark green foliage. Slightly shorter than ‘Alba’. ‡ 32 in (80 cm). **‘Summer Spire’** Slender, tapering, rosy pink spikes. ‡ 32 in (80 cm). **‘Vivid’** Very bright magenta-pink flowers on a dense plant. ‡ 24 in (60 cm). **var.** *speciosa* Larger, more coarsely toothed leaves. Not all botanists recognize the validity of this variety. **var.** *speciosa* **‘Bouquet Rose’** Lilac-pink flowers. ‡ 4 ft (1.2 m). **var.** *speciosa* **‘Pink Bouquet’** Bright pink; flops badly. ‡ 4 ft (1.2 m). **var.** *speciosa* **‘Variegata’** Grayish green foliage irregularly edged with cream. Pale pink flowers. ‡ 24–36 in (60–90 cm).

PILOSELLA
Mouse-ear hawkweed
ASTERACEAE

These are useful colonizers, forming carpets of leafy rosettes with orange or yellow, dandelion-like flowers.

About eighteen perennial species are native to short grasslands, dunes, rocky places, and open, dry habitats across Europe, Asia, and North Africa. Forms spreading colonies of leaf rosettes that arise from ground-level

ABOVE 1 *Physalis alkekengi*
2 *Physostegia virginiana* ‘Vivid’
3 *Pilosella aurantiaca*

shoots (stolons), the hairy leaves are narrowly elliptic to inversely egg-shaped and typically untoothed. The orange or yellow flowerheads, consisting solely of ray florets, are borne singly or in dense clusters on top of the mostly leafless stems. The plant differs from the similar *Hieracium* in small details of fruit and in the presence of stolons.

CULTIVATION Thrives in any well-drained site in full sun. Tolerant of drought and poor soil.

PROPAGATION By division at almost any time of year, or from seed.

PROBLEMS Usually trouble-free.

P. aurantiaca syn. *Hieracium aurantiacum* (Fox and cubs, Orange hawkweed, Grim the collier) Evergreen perennial with leafy stolons giving rise to spreading colonies of leaf rosettes. The grayish green, hairy, lance-shaped to elliptic leaves to 8 in (20 cm) long are held in basal rosettes and are sometimes finely toothed. From these arise erect, wiry, leafless stems bearing dense, terminal clusters of up to 12 or more vivid orange flowerheads from early summer to early fall. These are set off against conspicuous, bristly, black hairs on the stem and bracts. It is a vigorous plant, but ideal for establishing in short, rough grasslands or for ground cover on wild banks, road shoulders, or tops of walls. Naturalized in North America, but native to mountain grasslands and rocky slopes in northern and central Europe. It is classified as a noxious weed in 5 states. ‡ 20–40cm (8–16in). Z5–9 H9–5

PIMPINELLA
APIACEAE

A delicate and attractive pink-flowered form is one of the most attractive of the whole family.

Of the 150 species of annuals, biennials, and perennials distributed widely across Eurasia and into North Africa, most are unremarkable and are not grown in gardens. Only one is an especially fine perennial and is generally grown. The basal foliage is variable and may be undivided or split into opposite pairs or into threes, although the stem leaves are usually twice split into opposite pairs. The flowerheads are made up of a number of umbels, with white, yellow, pink, or purple florets; each of the five petals is turned down at the tip.

CULTIVATION Best in full sun, in moist soil.

PROPAGATION From seed or by division.

PROBLEMS Usually trouble-free.

P. major (Greater burnet saxifrage) A noticeably variable species, the lower leaves are once divided into three to nine, coarsely toothed segments; the upper leaves are smaller and reduced and at their base sheathe the flowering stem. Flowers vary from white to pink and are produced in summer in umbels of 10–25 rays, 1½–3 in (4–8 cm) across, on tall, wiry stems. An effective plant for meadow plantings, flowering later than many other members of the family, but rarely seen in gardens in its more common wild white form. Best in moist soil, where it self-seeds readily. From rough grasslands and woodland margins in much of Europe, except the far north, and into the Middle East and the Caucasus. ‡4 ft (1.2 m). Z5–7 H7–5. **‘Rosea’** Good, deep pink flowers fading to a softer pink with age. By far the most widely grown form.

PLANTAGO
Plantain
PLANTAGINACEAE

Intriguing, if not beautiful plants; some members providing interest and a conversation piece for the front of beds and borders.

Of cosmopolitan distribution, there are at least 250 species of annuals and perennials, plus a few small, woody-based perennials. Most have basal rosettes of oval to lance-shaped, untoothed leaves; in some, the leaves are narrowly strap-shaped, deeply dissected, or both. Dense spikes of tiny, almost petal-less flowers have relatively large, mobile stamens, which in some species are conspicuous, and packed together, often in a cylindrical flowerhead, at the top of leafless flowering stalks. Familiar as garden and farm weeds, a few useful garden forms do exist.

CULTIVATION Thrives in all garden soils, ideally plant in sunny spot, though part-shade is tolerated.

PROPAGATION By division when dormant or from seed, although cultivars may not come true.

PROBLEMS Powdery mildew.

P. asiatica Rosettes of long-stalked, deciduous, broadly oval, 4–6 in (10–15 cm) long, spreading leaves with distinctively parallel veining. From early summer to fall, erect, leafless, flowering stems occur, each packed at the top with many tiny green and white florets bearing long-stalked, white stamens. Widespread throughout Asia east to Malaysia. ‡12–14 in (30–35 cm). Z3–11 H11–1. **‘Variegata’** Foliage patterned with creamy white.

P. lanceolata (Ribwort plantain) A familiar plant of waste places in grassland, and everywhere as a weed of gardens and farmland; two ornamental forms are grown. Mature plants form dense clumps of more or less erect, strongly ribbed, lance-shaped leaves to 12 in (30 cm) long. Wiry, leafless, furrowed stems above the leaves in summer, bearing very congested, ovoid to cylindrical spikes of tiny brown flowers with yellow stamens. Originally native to Europe and Asia, but now a cosmopolitan weed. ‡16–24 in (40–60 cm). Z3–11 H11–1. **‘Golden Spears’** Foliage suffused with yellow. **‘Streaker’** Leaves with white streaks.

P. major (Greater plantain) Common weed in farms, gardens, and neglected lawns. Although variable, it generally develops clumps of spreading rosettes formed of long-stalked, broadly oval, prominently ribbed leaves to 8 in (20 cm). In summer, the slender, totally green flower spikes stand high above the foliage, with the small, dull purple stamens making little, if any, decorative impact. Cosmopolitan. ‡8–16 in (20–40 cm). Z3–11 H11–1. **‘Rosularis’** (Rose plantain) An intriguing mutation in which the foreshortened flower spikes bear dense rosettes of small leaves fancifully likened to green roses. ‘Frills’,

ABOVE 1 *Plantago asiatica* ‘Variegata’ **2** *P. major* ‘Rubrifolia’ **3** *Platycodon grandiflorus*

‘Rosea’ and ‘Rosulata’ are almost, if not fully, identical. **‘Rubrifolia’** Leaves purplish maroon. Prone to mildew.

P. media (Hoary plantain) Softly downy, elliptical to oval, 1½–2½-in (4–6-cm) leaves, which are sometimes slightly toothed, form single or small clusters of rosettes with a generally grayish cast. Upright stems are topped with conspicuous flower spikes with large, showy white or mauve-tinted stamens. A sweet scent is a bonus. One of the most decorative of the plantain species. Native to Europe and Asia in alkaline soil. ‡8–12 in (20–30 cm). Z3–11 H11–1

PLATYCODON
Balloon flower
CAMPANULACEAE

Bell-like flowers open from inflated buds that give the plants their common name.

A single species that is native to grassy meadows in Asia is grown as a border perennial, potted plant, and cut flower. The alternate-leaved, hairless stems grow from basal rosettes of more or less oval, slightly bluish leaves and bear blue, pink, or white, bell-like, five-petaled flowers in summer, which open from distinctive inflated, balloonlike buds. Balloon flowers are good for the front of well-drained borders; children like to pop the intriguing unopened flowers.

CULTIVATION Grow in a deep, well-drained soil either in sun or dappled shade. Best left to mature into good-sized clumps.

PROPAGATION From seed, or by basal cuttings that should be taken with a piece of the crown attached. Although large clumps can be divided, the success rate is low.

LEFT *Pimpinella major*

PROBLEMS Slugs and snails.

P. grandiflorus Slow to emerge in spring and easy to damage during spring cultivation, the new growth is a tight cone of pale green that opens to show light, sometimes bluish green leaves with toothed edges. They darken as they unfurl and become a shiny mid-green. The flowers open to form broad bells, to 2 in (5 cm) across, with five-pointed petals with darker veins and edges that roll back. They appear in few-flowered clusters on the top of the stems in summer and make a good cut flower if the end of the stem is seared, as is done for poppies. Plants increase slowly and are best left undisturbed for several years. Mark the location with care to avoid accidental damage. Cultivars are all intended to be raised from seed, so may be variable. From China, Manchuria, and Japan. ‡ 24 in (60 cm). Z4–9– H9–1. **'Albus'** White with yellow veins. **'Apoyama'** Dwarf blue. ‡ 10 in (25 cm). **'Fairy Snow'** White flowers with purple veins. ‡ 10 in (25 cm). **Astra Series** Single and semidouble flowers in blue, pink, and white that will bloom the first year from seed. ‡ 6 in (15 cm). **Fuji Series** Blue, pink, or white. A Japanese series intended for cut-flower production, but good in the garden. **Hakone Series** Blue or white, single- and double-flowering plants from seed, but not blooming until the second year. **'Mariesii'** Dwarf blue. Pink and white varieties of this are sometimes listed but are probably misnamed. ‡ 18 in (45 cm). **'Perlmutterschale'** (**Mother of Pearl**) Light pink. **var**. *pumilus* Dwarf blue, perhaps the parent of 'Apoyama'. ‡ 10 in (25 cm). **'Sentimental Blue'** Paler blue, most flowers have only four petals. Flowers in its second year from seed. ‡ 12 in (30 cm). **'Shell Pink'** Slightly darker pink flowers than 'Perlmutterschale'.

POA
POACEAE

Best known for its use as a lawn grass, and as a weed, there are also some very attractive forms for the garden.

Some 500 perennial and annual species are found in cool temperate regions from the Arctic to tropical mountain tops in Africa, usually growing in meadowland from sea level to high elevations. Dense root systems spring from crowded evergreen clumps, from which grow flat, but sometimes very thin, leaves with slightly rounded points shaped like the keel of a boat. The flower stems are usually held above the foliage and carry a plume of flowerheads, sometimes compact but more often loose and delicate. With blue foliage that stays attractive through the winter if grown in the sun in well-drained soil, some of the larger species make graceful specimen plants. Some species are known to survive in highly polluted soils and they are often the first to colonize bleak landscapes.

CULTIVATION Grow in fertile, medium to light, moisture-retentive but well-drained soil; give the clumps a light trim in the spring and comb out any dead foliage.

PROPAGATION From seed or by division in spring. Divide cultivars and varieties.

PROBLEMS Rust.

P. chaixii (Broad-leaved meadow grass) Slowly spreading tufts of bright green, wide, flat leaves, 18 in (45 cm) long and ¼–½ in (5–10 mm) wide, with prominent veins and a rounded point, grow out from a wide, somewhat flattened, pale colored base. The leaves fade back in the winter and can look ratty. In late spring to midsummer, the straight, tall flower stems carry airy pyramid-shaped plumes of greenish purple flowers. Makes a delicate addition to late spring bulbs, or grow in wildflower lawns and meadows. Found in open forests and mountain woods, throughout central and southern Europe to the Caucasus. Inflorescenes 12–18 in (30–45 cm). ‡ 24–36 in (60–90 cm). Z4–8 H8–1.

P. colensoi (Evergreen tussock grass, Blue tussock grass) Densely packed, erect tussocks of very fine, inrolled leaves, 12 in (30 cm) long and 1/16 in (0.5 mm) wide, are intense blue-green to pale green in color and have a curious rubbery texture. Lax, greenish flower stems carry sparse plumes of green to blue-brown flowers, fading to brown, which nod among the foliage in early to late summer. Looks very similar to some of the blue fescues, but differs in keeping its intense color all through the year. It is also deep-rooted and drought-tolerant. Native to tussock grasslands, often on rocks from lowlands to mountainous areas of New Zealand. ‡ 12 in (30 cm). Z7–8 H8–7

P. curvula see *Eragrostis curvula*

P. labillardierei (Silver tussock grass, Common tussock grass) Dense clumps of blue-gray to bright green, long, thin leaves up to 26 in (65 cm) long and ⅛ in (3 mm) wide, which spray upward

LEFT *Poa labillardierei*

and outward in a fountain of graceful foliage. In early summer to midsummer, erect flower stems carry sparse flowerheads just above the leaves with pale green to purple-gray flowers held at the tips of the stems, spreading over the top of the leaves in an airy mist. Needs plenty of sun and moisture-retentive, but very well-drained, soil. Plants from New Zealand tend to be hardier than those from Australia. A native of subalpine tussock grasslands, often on volcanic soil, in New Zealand, and moist river flats and open forests in Australia. ‡ 24–48 in (60–120 cm). Z7–8 H8–7

P. trichodes see *Eragrostis trichodes*

PODOPHYLLUM
Custard apple, May apple
BERBERIDACEAE

Providing some of the most colorful and highly textural leaves of any woodland perennial.

About 14 species, mostly from Asia, are enjoying a surge of popularity following the introduction of several new species. A scaly rhizome with round scars on the upper surface is fat and tight in the Asiatic species but more slender and extensive in the American species. Stems carry two, occasionally one or three, leaves whose blades can be broad and rounded or star-shaped and up to 24 in (60 cm) across, in tones of glossy green or suffused with sensational tones of burgundy and black. As they emerge, they resemble folded umbrellas. In mid-spring, flowers are usually carried at the point where the stem divides to carry the two leaves, or beneath the largest of the two leaves on each stem, and can possess a disagreeable odor. Most need pollinating by a different individual in order to produce the fruit, which ripens in mid- to late summer. Fruits of the Asian species are used in traditional medicine.

For many years only the American *P. peltatum* and, to a lesser degree, the Himalayan *P. hexandrum* were seen, but many of the new species introduced from Asia are rewriting the perceptions of podophyllums. ⚠

CULTIVATION Easily grown in a wide range of climates, although those from lower altitudes, such as *P. difforme*, are adapted only to mild, summer-warm climates. They appreciate woodland shade to part-shade in cool, humus-rich soil with even moisture.

PROPAGATION By division in early spring, as growth resumes, for those with more extensive root systems; by root cuttings for more compact species. Seed, sown fresh, will germinate the following spring.

ABOVE *Podophyllum pleianthum*

PROBLEMS Usually trouble-free, although seedlings seem very susceptible to bacterial leaf spot when overcrowded.

P. delavayi This sensational woodland plant features broad, rounded, 12-in (30-cm) foliage with five to eight deep lobes in tones of burgundy, green, and black with a satinlike finish. The flowers with their six, sometimes more, reddish pink 2-in (5-cm) petals, come in clusters of up to six and are the most dramatic of all the species; they are produced below the foliage and possess a mildly unpleasant smell of rotting meat. They are carried on pendulous stalks at the joint of the leaf stems and are pollinated by flies. The 1½-in (3.5-cm) fruits are dark red. Considered by many to be among the most beautiful foliage plants recently introduced into western cultivation. From dense forests in western China. ‡ 8 in (20 cm). Z6–9 H9–6

P. difforme Irregularly hexagonal leaves, up to 7 in (18 cm) across at most, are richly mottled and marked in a wide spectrum of colors. In the wild, the clusters of up to three flowers are held immediately under the topmost leaf, while in gardens, strangely, they are usually carried at the joint of the two leaf stems. Each of the six petals is about 1 in (2.5 cm) long, in salmon pink to reddish purple followed by a ¾-in (2-cm), yellowish green berry. Since plants tend to start into growth in late fall and remain evergreen during winter, they are best suited to areas that are warm in winter. From dense forest in southern China. ‡ 12 in (30 cm). Z6–9 H9–6

P. emodi see *P. hexandrum*

P. hexandrum syn. *P. emodi* A distinctive species in that its broad-petaled, rose red flowers, with petals up to 1¼ in (3 cm) long, are held above the foliage as leaves and stems emerge from the ground. Variable in its foliage; generally pairs of rounded and jagged leaves, to 6 in (15 cm) across or more and with up to five lobes, are borne on tall stems. Their initial handsome mottled tones of purple and bronze ultimately fade to green. The flowers are followed by brilliant red, egg-sized fruits, up to 2½ in (6 cm) long, held beneath the foliage. Compact in growth. From mountain slopes and woods in the western Himalaya. ↕24 in (60 cm). Z5–8 H8–4. **'Chinense'**, **'Majus'** Both are supposedly larger in all aspects with more brilliant leaf mottling, but are seed-raised and insufficiently distinct for these names to be valid.

P. 'Kaleiodoscope' Dramatic hexagonal foliage is bright green with more or less symmetrical markings in bronze and silver. Mature plants carry up to 20 burgundy-colored flowers, each with 2 in (5 cm) long petals. Said to be a hybrid between *P. delavayi* and *P. difforme*, introduced by Terra Nova Nurseries in Oregon. ↕12 in (30 cm). Z6–9 H9–6

P. peltatum (May apple) Quickly forms expansive colonies; its pairs of rounded leaves, with five to eight deep lobes and up to 12 in (30 cm) across, are joined at their centers, or at one side, to upright stems. The first leaf is larger than the second and has more lobes. Nodding, solitary, white or occasionally cream or pink flowers, with petals up to 1¼ in (3 cm) long, are produced in spring, hidden beneath the foliage where the stems divide, and are unexpectedly and agreeably fragrant. The 2-in (5-cm) fruits ripen to yellow in midsummer, by which time they are edible; they cause intestinal upset if eaten before ripening. Forms with apricot, pale pink, and maroon fruits have been recorded. Though useful in the wild woodland garden, it can be too aggressive. From woods in the eastern US. ↕15 in (38 cm). Z3–9 H8–2

P. pleianthum Spreading steadily, this fine garden plant features pairs of large, glossy green, slightly lobed leaves to 18 in (45 cm) across on especially tall stems. In early summer, clusters of ¾ in (2 cm) wide, blood red, balloon-shaped flowers appear at, or slightly above, the juncture of the two leaves and emit an odor of questionable appeal although of short duration. Egg-shaped, 1¼-in (3-cm) fruits ripen to greenish yellow in late summer. More vigorous than many, but not aggressive. From Taiwan and southern China. ↕24 in (60 cm). Z6–9 H9–6

P. versipelle The tallest and most robust species, its deeply lobed, umbrella-shaped leaves, to 24 in (60 cm) across, create a bold impression. The clusters of up to 19 balloon-shaped, burgundy-red flowers, which have a disagreeable musty odor, emerge from the stem just below the leaf blade and are often visible above the foliage as the stems appear in spring. The 1¼-in (3-cm) fruits are yellowish green. From southern China and Vietnam. ↕4 ft (1.2 m). Z6–9 H9–6

POLEMONIUM
Jacob's ladder, Sky pilot
POLEMONIACEAE

Attractive spring and early summer bloomers, with long, leaves often neatly divided to form a primitive ladder.

Twenty-five species of annuals and perennials from rocky alpine regions or damp meadows in the Northern Hemisphere and South America. They form clumps, with sometimes evergreen basal rosettes of leaves, typically with numerous leaflets in pairs that are slightly offset, plus a leaflet at the tip. The flower stems are also leafy; the leaflets may be neatly spaced or tightly gathered. The ¼–1¼-in (5–30-mm), bell- to saucer-shaped flowers have five equal-sized petals, forming a tube at the base, and may be blue, white, or pink, or occasionally purple or yellow. Many striking new cultivars have been grown in recent years, for both their flowers and foliage. In particular, many prolific sterile hybrids of *P. carneum* x *P. caerulea* have been introduced. Many plants in nurseries are incorrectly named.

CULTIVATION Grow in fertile, well-drained soil in sun or part-shade. Shade is essential where summers are hot, and even so, plants are often short-lived. Some species are very fussy and not covered here.

PROPAGATION Species from seed, cultivars by division.

PROBLEMS Powdery mildew.

P. archibaldiae A confusing, bushy, mid-sized plant with leaves crowded with 21–31, lance-shaped leaflets and a long season of deep lavender-blue flowers in short spikes from late spring to early fall or even mid-fall. Sets very few seeds and is not invasive. Sometimes considered to be a form of *P. foliosissimum*; however, a fertile, gardenia-scented, white-flowered plant is sometimes sold under this name. Native to the Rocky Mountains. ↕32 in (80 cm). Z4–8 H8–1

P. boreale (Northern Jacob's ladder) Erect plants form a basal clump of leaves with six to eleven pairs of oval to elliptical leaflets that are slightly downy at first and from which grows an upright flowering stem carrying six to eight large, pale blue flowers with a distinct yellow eye in midsummer. Plants have a unpleasant odor, and are often short-lived, but easy to grow from seed. Unfortunately sold under a range of incorrect names. Native to the northern parts of Europe, Asia, and North America. ↕12–18 in (30–45 cm). Z4–8 H8–1. **'Heavenly Habit'** Violet

to blue flowers in clusters above the foliage and will usually rebloom if deadheaded.

P. brandegeei Sticky basal leaves up to 4 in (10 cm) long have their oval to oblong leaflets arranged in opposite pairs at the base but appearing more clustered toward the tip. The clusters of yellow to golden, rarely white, trumpet-shaped flowers are held well above the foliage in early summer. Appreciates good drainage in part-shade where summers are hot and humid. If growing well, it will self-seed freely. From the Rocky Mountains. ↕8 in (20 cm). Z4–8 H8–1

P. Bressingham Purple ('Polbress') An eye-catching plant with dark purple foliage, divided into the usual opposite pairs of leaflets, at its richest in spring then greening as the season progresses. The clustered, slightly fragrant, blue to pale lavender flowers are held well above the leaves. Selected from hundreds of seedlings by Adrian Bloom of England. ↕24–30 in (60–75 cm). Z4–8 H8–1

P. caeruleum (Jacob's ladder, Greek valerian) A very variable species, the basal leaves are up to 16 in (40 cm) long and have 19–27, lance-shaped or elliptical leaflets reducing in size toward the tip of the leaf. Sprays of soft blue, ½–1-in (10–25-mm) flowers with bright yellow stamens appear in early summer. It seeds freely and can become a nuisance. From northern Europe and Asia. ↕36 in (90 cm). Z4–9 H9–1. **'Album'** *see* subsp. *caeruleum* f. *album*. **'Bambino Blue'** Paler and later cup-shaped flowers on shorter plants. ↕18 in (45 cm). **Brise d'Anjou** ('Blanjou') Each leaflet is edged in a creamy yellow, the intensity of the color becoming closer to white in deep shade. Not robust,

COMPLETING THE PICTURE

THE NEATLY DIVIDED foliage of *Polemonium caeruleum*, while making a wonderful foil for its upright stems carrying perky blue flowers, can be rather sparse at the base, and so a low complementary plant is needed—one that will organize itself naturally to peep through the gaps left in the rich green foliage. *Anthemis punctata* subsp. *cupaniana*, with its pretty silver foliage, carries its sparkling white daisies on stems that are long enough to find their way to the light, but not as long that the flowers weigh them down. This invaluable sun-loving little daisy also has the enormously valuable feature of flowering in almost every month of the year.

often short-lived. Remove the unremarkable flowers to encourage good foliage (*see* Variegated Polemoniums). ↕24 in (60 cm). **subsp. *caeruleum* f. *album*** syn. 'Album' White flowers. **'Idylle'** Large, pale blue flowers on upright stems. Introduced from Belgium in 1993. ↕18–24 in (45–60 cm). **'Larch Cottage'** Golden variegated foliage, especially brilliant in spring, and pale blue flowers. ↕24 in (60 cm). **var. *nipponicum*** Larger, later flowers from midsummer onward. From Japan to Siberia. **'Snow and Sapphires'** Leaflets edged in white, and blue flowers in late spring (*see* Variegated Polemoniums). Z4–8 H8–1

P. carneum (Salmon Jacob's ladder) Forms a spreading clump with rosettes of basal leaves, each leaf is up to 8 in (20 cm) long with 13–21, oval to elliptical leaflets and shorter leaflets on the flowering stem. Small clusters of saucer-shaped, pale pink to salmon flowers, which darken with age, appear in summer. Less easy to grow than most, best in constant moisture but with good drainage and a little shade. Self-seeds freely when growing well. Native to the foothills of the Cascade Mountains. ↕16 in (40 cm). Z4–8 H8–1. **'Apricot Delight'** Darker pink flowers with apricot centers, in early summer, above bronze-colored foliage. ↕18 in (45 cm).

P. cashmerianum A range of different species and cultivars are offered under this invalid name. Best avoided.

***P.* 'Churchills'** Lilac buds open to give small, ½-in (1-cm) mauve flowers from late spring to early fall. A sterile hybrid between *P. carneum* and *P. caerulea*. ↕32 in (80 cm). Z4–8 H8–1

***P.* 'Elworthy Amethyst'** Pink flowers with apricot centers. Does best in full sun where summers are not too hot. A sterile hybrid between *P. carneum* and *P. caerulea*, which is like a robust, non-seeding version of *P. carneum* 'Apricot Delight'. ↕16 in (40 cm). Z4–8 H8–1

P. foliosissimum (Leafy Jacob's ladder) A variable, long-flowering species with 1¼–6-in (3–15-cm) basal leaves with 9–31 oblong or elliptical leaflets and a noticeably large, single leaflet at the tip. The upright stems have foliage that, unlike other species, is roughly the same size as the basal leaves and is topped with dense heads of generally bright violet-blue, occasionally cream or white, flowers for most of the summer. Native to Colorado, Utah, Wyoming, New Mexico, and Arizona. ↕36 in (90 cm). Z4–8 H8–1

***P.* 'Glebe Cottage Lilac'** Lilac flowers on upright stems in summer. Best in a sunny location. A sterile hybrid between *P. carneum* and *P. caerulea* introduced by Carol Klein of Glebe Cottage Plants in Devon, England. ↕36 in (90 cm). Z4–8 H8–1

***P.* 'Hannah Billcliffe'** Vigorous and early flowering, the white flowers turn lilac as they age. A sterile hybrid between *P. carneum* and *P. caerulea*. ↕36 in (90 cm). Z4–8 H8–1

***P.* 'Hopleys'** Fragrant, pale lilac flowers in summer and early fall. Tolerant of most conditions except dry shade, but prone to mildew. A sterile hybrid of *P. carneum* and *P. caerulea*. Introduced by Hopleys Plants in Hertfordshire, England. ↕30 in (75 cm). Z4–8 H8–1

***P.* 'Lambrook Mauve'** Mounds of almost evergreen foliage support branched stems bearing masses of bell-shaped, pale mauve flowers with yellow centers in late spring and early summer. Grows equally well in shade or sun. Since it is sterile, it is never a nuisance. A hybrid of *P. reptans* and *P. carneum*. ↕18 in (45 cm). Z4–8 H8–1

***P.* 'Northern Lights'** Compact, with large, pale blue, fragrant flowers from early summer to fall. Sterile, so never a nuisance; probably a hybrid of *P. boreale*. ↕12–16 in (30–40 cm). Z4–8 H8–1

P. pauciflorum Sparse basal foliage with elliptical to lance-shaped leaves to 6 in (15 cm) long, mainly on the stems and sticky at the top. Trumpet-shaped, 1¼–1½ in (3–4 cm) long flowers, pale yellow inside, soft apricot outside, and may be tinged in blue, carried slightly nodding or horizontally in small heads for most of the summer. Needs shade from hot sun, moisture. From mountain streamsides in the southwestern US. ↕12–20 in (30–50 cm). Z7–9 H9–7. **subsp. *hinckleyi*** Flowers yellow with red markings, early summer to early fall. From Arizona and Texas. **subsp. *pauciflorum*** Leaves covered with silver hairs. From Mexico. **'Sulphur Trumpets'** Silver foliage, yellow flowers.

***P.* 'Pink Beauty'** Compact mounds of foliage with pale mauve, bell-shaped flowers on branched stems. A hybrid between *P. reptans* and *P. carneum* and, in effect, a dwarf version of 'Lambrook Mauve'. Not pink. ↕10–12 in (25–30 cm). Z4–8 H8–1

RIGHT 1 *Polemonium caeruleum*
2 *P. carneum* 'Apricot Delight'
3 *P.* 'Lambrook Mauve'

P. reptans A low mound of bright green foliage, attractive all summer and divided into seven to nineteen, oppositely arranged, oblong to elliptical leaflets, spreads slowly from underground stems, and may also self-sow. Clusters of light blue to white, ⅝–¾-in (1.5–2-cm), drooping flowers open in spring. A lovely woodland garden plant. Native to damp woodlands in eastern North America. ↕12–28 in (30–70 cm). Z4–8 H8–1. **'Blue Pearl'** Clusters of nodding, light blue flowers on arching stems. Perhaps a hybrid with the rarely seen *P. pulcherrimum*. ↕4–8 in (10–20 cm). **'Pink Dawn'** Compact, with bronzed foliage and lilac flowers with a pink tinge. Sometimes listed as *P. reptans* 'Pink Beauty' and not the same as the 'Pink Beauty' listed above. ↕12 in (30 cm). **'Stairway to Heaven'** Foliage irregularly edged in white, tinged pink. Dramatic and dependable. Selected at the New England Wildflower Society's Garden in the Woods in Massachusetts (*see* Variegated Polemoniums). **'Virginia White'** White flowers.

***P.* 'Sapphire'** Small, light blue flowers in arching sprays in late spring over dark green foliage that shows off the flowers well. A sterile hybrid of *P. reptans*. ↕18 in (45 cm). Z4–8 H8–1

***P.* 'Sonia's Bluebell'** Bushy, purplish stems topped with clusters of scented, pale blue, flared flowers with white anthers in early summer. The plant smells of new-mown hay. A sterile hybrid from Carol Klein of Glebe Cottage Plants in Devon, England. ↕24 in (60 cm). Z4–8 H8–1

P. yezoense Bushy plants, spreading slowly by rhizomes, feature mostly basal leaves, 5–6 in (13–16 cm) long and on 1½-in (3.5-cm) stalks, with up to 21

VARIEGATED POLEMONIUMS

There is no doubt that all variegated polemoniums look very dramatic, but they vary in their vigor and their cultural needs. Although known occasionally from previous centuries, the first modern variegated form was the rarely seen *P. caeruleum* 'Larch Cottage', introduced in 1991. Found at Larch Cottage Nurseries in Cumbria, England, the golden variegated leaves are especially effective early in the season.

The first of these variegated forms to achieve widespread popularity was *P. caeruleum* Brise d'Anjou. Discovered by Rene and Maurice Prouteau in Anjou, France, and introduced by Blooms of Bressingham in 1994, the leaves are neatly edged in cream, but the flowers are small, and it proved to be a rather weak, short-lived plant. Growing in containers with regular watering and fertilizing certainly helps develop an impressive plant, as does removing the flowering stems as they develop.

In 2002, *P. caeruleum* 'Snow and Sapphires' was introduced by Terra Nova Nurseries in Portland, Oregon, having been discovered by Floyd McDonald of Morning Glory Farms in Tennessee. The leaves are edged in white, rather than cream, and the flowers are larger, making a bolder combination of flower and foliage. The plant is also more robust, longer-lived, and more tolerant of summer heat.

The most recent is *P.* 'Stairway to Heaven'. In 1999, nursery manager William Cullina noticed a plant with variegated leaves in batch of seedlings of *P. reptans* grown at the New England Wildflower Society's Garden in the Woods in Massachusetts. Once the pink and white variegation proved stable, it was introduced and has proved to be perhaps the best of them all, although definitely a shade-lover. Other, rarely encountered, variegated forms include 'Pam' and 'Woodpeckers'.

LEFT 1 *Polygonatum* x *hybridum*
2 *P. odoratum* **3** *P. verticillatum*

oval to lance-shaped leaflets. Large, fragrant, ¾–1¼-in (2–3-cm), slate blue flowers, each with a distinctive central ring of bright purple, open on long stalks in mid- to late summer. From Japan. ↕ 16 in (40 cm). Z4–8 H8–1. **'Purple Rain'** Foliage dark purple and taller, darker flower stems. Propagate by division; seedlings will vary in the color of the leaves. ↕ 24–32 in (60–80 cm).

POLYGONATUM
Solomon's seal
CONVALLARIACEAE

A varied range of attractive and elegant woodlanders grown as specimen clumps or ground cover.

About sixty species are from Asia, Europe, and the US; most are herbaceous perennials spreading by stolons (creeping stems at the soil surface) and, in some cases, may be too vigorous for the well-ordered garden. They range from tall, swarthy clumps of gracefully nodding stems to tiny but vigorous, ground-covering colonies; a few rare species are epiphytic. The leaves, usually lance-shaped, are carried alternately or in clusters (whorls) along the stems. Small, bell-shaped, pendulous flowers, often white but sometimes pink, red, or yellow, or tipped in green, are produced in clusters below the leaves in the leaf joints along the stem, followed by crops of black, blue, or red fruit.

Although possessing some charm in floral and foliage effects, most are used because of their stature, texture, and utility in shaded conditions. Included are both classics for shaded borders and dramatic species that are too rarely grown in gardens but slowly becoming appreciated more widely. The naming of the species with tendrils is confused and currently being studied. ⚠

CULTIVATION Undemanding plants presenting few challenges. Most respond well to lightly shaded situations in cool, humus-rich soil with even moisture, although will

tolerate full sun in summer–cool climates. The taller, tendril-leaved species are best grown at the base of a shrub or small tree and allowed to twine through the lower branches. Species that spread vigorously by stolons can be restricted by reducing the perimeter of the colony in early spring. Easily adapted to container culture, which can more effectively display the flowers.

PROPAGATION Divide in early spring before growth emerges; each piece should have a healthy terminal bud. Sow fresh seed, without the flesh, in late summer or fall. Germination will normally occur the following spring, but plants take three to five years to flower.

PROBLEMS Slugs, deer, and rabbits are troublesome, and few species produce a second flush of growth; Solomon's seal sawfly is another pest. (see Solomon's Seal Sawfly).

P. biflorum Upright or arching stems carry alternately arranged, lance-shaped or elliptical, 1½–7-in (4–18-cm) leaves, with no hairs on the undersides. Up to four white, green-tipped flowers ¾ in (2 cm) long are produced in clusters at the leaf joints in mid-spring. Similar to *P. pubescens* but has hairs on the veins on the leaf undersides. Variable in height. From the eastern US. ↕ 36 in to 7 ft (90 cm to 2.2 m). Z3–7 H9–1.

P. cirrhifolium Climbing by tendrils at the foliage tips, slender, 4-in (10-cm), lance-shaped leaves are carried in whorls of three to six on weak stems. Small, 1-in (2.5-cm), bell-shaped, white, green, or purple flowers are produced in the leaf joints in early summer, followed by crops of bright red fruits, ripening to black. A highly textural species worthy of cultivation as a climbing plant through moderate-sized shrubs or trees. Often confused with other species having tendrils. From the Himalaya. ↕ 5 ft (1.5 m). Z5–8 H8–1.

P. curvistylum A charming, dwarf species with dark purple stems offering

whorls of very narrow, slightly hook-tipped leaves, which are often blushed with purple when first emerging. The pendulous clusters of two or more 1-in (2.5-cm) flowers, white or pink with purple spotting and flaring mouths, are followed by crops of translucent, red fruit. Often confused with the much taller *P. cirrhifolium*. From China. ↕ 15 in (38 cm). Z5–8 H8–1.

P. falcatum A tall, dramatic species with narrow, lance-shaped or sickle-shaped, alternately arranged leaves to 10 in (25 cm) long. Clusters of two to five, large white, ¾-in (2-cm), bell-shaped flowers are produced along the stem in early summer, followed by blue-black fruit. Particularly susceptible to slug damage when emerging in spring. *P. odoratum* is often incorrectly offered under this name. From Japan. ↕ 5 ft (1.5 m). Z4–9 H9–1. **'Variegatum'** see *P. odoratum* var. *pluriflorum* 'Variegatum'.

P. graminifolium Delicate-looking plant that forms substantial colonies of stems with whorls of three very narrow, bright leaves up to 2 in (5 cm) in length. The solitary, relatively large, 1-in (2.5-cm) pink bell-shaped flowers, vanilla-scented, are produced in the leaf joints in midsummer, occasionally in pairs, although they may be hidden within the dense foliage. From the Himalaya. ↕ 18 in (45 cm). Z3–7 H9–1.

P. hirtum A splendid though variable species, too infrequently grown, with strongly arching stems carrying alternately arranged, deep and glossy green, 2¾–6-in (7–15-cm), lance-shaped or oval leaves. Appearing in mid-spring, the clusters of up to five white, green-tipped, ¾-in (2-cm) flowers, followed by bluish black fruits, are produced in the leaf joints but are often hidden by the foliage. Moderately aggressive if grown under fertile conditions, but effective in containers. From Europe, Russia, and Turkey. ↕ 8–36 in (20–90 cm). Z5–8 H8–1.

P. humile A very vigorous and effective dwarf, upright species providing a lovely weed smothering, decidedly

textural ground cover. Broadly lance-shaped, 2¾-in (7-cm) foliage is arranged alternately with charming, green-tipped, white, ½-in (1-cm) bells, usually produced singly or occasionally in pairs in the leaf joints. They are followed by blue-black fruits. Variegated forms are grown in Japan. Thrives in shaded sites, tolerating dry shade when firmly established. From Japan, Korea, northern China, and Siberia. ↕ 2 in (5 cm). Z5–8 H8–4.

P. x hybridum By far the most widely cultivated species, vigorously spreading colonies of thick rhizomes give rise to erect and sturdy stems, which nod gracefully at the apex. They carry alternate, broadly lance-shaped leaves to 8 in (20 cm) with up to five white, green-tipped bells produced along the stems at the leaf joints in early summer, resulting in crops of blue fruit. Hybrid between *P. multiflorum* and *P. odoratum*. ↕ 4 ft (1.2 m). Z6–9 H9–6. **'Betburg'** Rich purple-brown foliage when first emerging, best grown in full sun for the best effect. A splendid German selection. **'Striatum'** Vigorous and sprightly with large leaves streaked with creamy white.

P. multiflorum Arching rounded stems, forming substantial clumps, carry alternate, 2–6-in (5–15-cm) long, elliptical to oval leaves, which tend to clasp the stem at the base. Two to four unscented, white, ¾-in (2-cm) flowers with green tips, flaring at the mouth, are carried in stalked clusters in the leaf joints. Tolerates more sun than many species if given adequate summer moisture. Like *P. odoratum* but rounded, not angled, stems. From Europe and Asia. ↕ 3¼ ft (1 m). Z4–8 H8–1.

P. odoratum Decidedly angled stems carry alternately arranged, lance-shaped to oval leaves to 5½ in (14 cm) long. In the leaf joints, small clusters of one to four but occasionally more, moderately fragrant, ½–¾ in (1–2 cm) white, green-tipped, cylindrical or bell-shaped flowers are produced in late spring. They are followed by blue-black berries. Widely distributed species from Europe to East Asia. ‡ 3¼ ft (1 m). Z3–8 H9–1. **'Flore Pleno'** Less than imposing, fully double flowers. **var. pluriflorum** Differs in botanical details and often has striking red stems. From Japan. **var. pluriflorum 'Variegatum'** Leaves edged in creamy white. Tall and vigorous. Often sold as *P. falcatum* 'Variegatum'. **'Silver Wings'** Bluish green foliage along compact stems and with relatively large flowers. Not variegated. ‡ 15 in (38 cm).

P. sibiricum Climbing; elegant whorls of four to six narrow, lance-shaped, 6-in (15-cm) leaves, with a tendril at the tip, on floppy stems. Clusters of up to 30 ½-in (1-cm) white or pinkish bells are followed by red berries, which turn black as they mature in late summer. Widely distributed, sometimes confusing species whose name is sometimes used to cover all the species with tendrils at the tips of the leaves. From China, Mongolia, and Siberia. ‡ 4 ft (1.2 m). Z5–8 H8–5

P. verticillatum An excellent garden plant forming robust, dense mounds of slender yet erect stems, which carry whorls of three to seven, very narrow almost linear, 2¾–6-in (7–15-cm) leaves, each with a long pointed tip. The ½-in (1-cm) flowers are mostly white, though may possess purple to pink speckling, or purple, and later give rise to colorful crops of red fruit. Though the stems may be freestanding if grown in border setting, the plant is better grown near a shrub or small tree in which it will support itself. A widely distributed and noticeably variable species. From Europe and Asia. ‡ 3¼ ft (1 m). Z5–8 H8–5. **'Himalayan Giant'** Taller, more robust. ‡ 6½ ft (2 m). **'Rubrum'** Foliage and stems emerge with a reddish blush; reddish purple flowers. Usually raised from seed and variable in its coloring. **'Serbian Dwarf'** Short with fat stems and reliably producing copious crops of red fruit. ‡ 24 in (60 cm).

POLYGONUM
Knotweed
POLYGONACEAE

Interesting stems, not the tiny, late summer flowers, are one of the primary attractions of this easygoing, sun-loving plant.

Growing in various open habitats in some of the temperate regions of the Northern Hemisphere, there are now only a handful of perennial species in this once large and diverse group of perennials, annuals, and climbing plants. Most have been moved to *Persicaria* or *Fallopia*, and synonyms of the most familiar are

given here. The simple leaves come in a range of shapes and the tiny flowers, generally white or pink, usually appear late in the summer on stems that appear jointed.

CULTIVATION Thrives in a sunny position with moist, yet well-drained, soil.

PROPAGATION By division in spring.

PROBLEMS Usually trouble-free.

P. amplexicaule see *Persicaria amplexicaulis*

P. bistorta see *Persicaria bistorta*

P. campanulatum see *Persicaria campanulata*

P. equisetiforme see *P. scoparium*

P. scoparium syn. *P. equisetiforme* This odd but intriguing deciduous plant looks like a horsetail (*Equisetum*) with its dense clumps of wiry, apparently leafless, green stems. The narrow, ⅝-in (1.5-cm) long leaves fall early, leaving the stems bare, when they carry a myriad of tiny, white, fragrant flowers from mid- or late summer. A difficult plant to use in the garden but makes an interesting specimen in a border, particularly in a Mediterranean or gravel garden. It also looks good in association with paving. Tolerates dry soil and needs a warm, sheltered spot. From Corsica and Sardinia. ‡ 20–48 in (50–120 cm). Z8–10 H10–1

POLYPODIUM
Polypody
POLYPODIACEAE

Attractive and resilient low ferns that are sadly discredited by the confusion surrounding their names.

Perhaps 150 species of evergreen ferns with creeping rhizomes are found worldwide. Many species previously included in *Polypodium* are now assigned elsewhere, leaving a group of similar plants, all with fronds produced at short intervals from a stout rhizome usually about ¼ in (5 mm) in diameter. The fronds are divided once with a row of oblong segments along each side of the midrib. The naked sporing structures are round, arranged in a single row along either side of the midrib of each segment on the underside of the frond. These distinctive, but generally similar ferns, have been troubled by much confusion in their naming, although pteridologists (that is, fern experts) are working to clarify the situation.

CULTIVATION Grow in well-drained soil in full or dappled shade; not tolerant of waterlogging and good in wall crevices. Beware of infestation by small, creeping weeds.

PROPAGATION Species by division or from spores; most cultivars by division.

PROBLEMS Blotching on leaves has been attributed to nematode, but the case is not yet proven. The blotching is usually worst in poorly drained sites in heavy clay.

P. australe see *P. cambricum*

P. cambricum syn. *P. australe* (Southern Polypody) Forms a mat of erect, light green, triangular or broadly oval fronds to 6 in (15 cm) across, with the second pair of segments from the base the longest, and the segments slightly toothed. Fronds appear in late summer or fall and remain fresh and green until early or mid-spring, giving added value during the off-season of most other herbaceous plants. No fronds visible from late spring to midsummer. Prefers well-drained, alkaline soil; thrives in sun or shade. Found in limestone rocks and soil; where these are absent, it may be found on old limestone walls, in southern and western Europe and western Asia. ‡ 8–12 in (20–30 cm). Z6–8 H8–6. **Cambricum Group** (Welsh polypody) Fronds sterile, thin and papery; the leaf segments are deeply lacerated; the lacerations from one segment to the next overlapping each other. First found near Cardiff in 1668, and possibly the first fern cultivar ever described. **Cambricum Group 'Whilharris'** Fronds lance-shaped; stiff segments all deeply lacerated. **'Grandiceps Fox'** Narrow fronds with large crests at the tips of the segments and a crest at the tip as wide as, or wider than the frond. **'Omnilacerum'** Frond narrowly triangular, most segments irregularly lacerated. The name means "fully lacerated" but fronds lacerated for their entire length are unusual. Fertile, comes true from spores. ‡ 20 in (50 cm). **'Whilharris'** *see* Cambricum Group 'Whilharris'.

P. glycyrrhiza (Licorice fern) Evergreen fern with lance-shaped, dark green fronds opening in spring, the segments slightly wavy, narrower than in the other species, and sharply pointed at tip. The rhizome tastes strongly of licorice, and was used as a food sweetener by

native Americans. Sporing structures smaller and neater than other species. Grows on rocks and trees in the northwestern US and western Canada. ‡ 16 in (40 cm). Z4–9 H9–1. **'Longicaudatum'** Fronds fully divided only toward base, the upper part tapering to a long, slender point. The conspicuous frond tips are very striking in a large colony.

P. interjectum (Intermediate polypody) Fronds opening in early summer, bluish green, leathery in texture, narrowly egg-shaped with the longest segments near the middle of the frond. Easy to grow, with a slight preference for slightly alkaline soil. Found on walls, rocks, and fencerows in much of Europe. ‡ 12 in (30 cm). Z5–9 H8–1. **'Cornubiense'** Fronds of two types, some twice-divided, others as above. An occasional frond may be half-and-half. Coarse, but robust and spreading quickly in a dryish border or rockery. Possible form of *P. x mantoniae*, the hybrid between *P. interjectum* and *P. vulgare*. ‡ 12 in (30 cm).

P. vulgare (Common polypody) Fronds, produced in spring, are oblong; most segments are the same length, and papery. Very similar to *P. interjectum* and can only be separated with experience. Best grown in dappled shade. Native mainly to acidic rocks and soil, and on trees in much of Europe, western Asia, and the US. ‡ 12 in (30 cm). Z6–8 H8–6. **'Bifidomultifidum'** syn. 'Bifido-grandiceps', 'Bifido-cristatum' Fronds long and narrow, rarely more than 2 in (5 cm) wide, with a flat, fan-shaped crest, and the leaf segments forked or with small crests. ‡ 16 in (40 cm).

POLYSTICHUM
Shield ferns
DRYOPTERIDACEAE

Among the most handsome of hardy ferns, the shield ferns give all-season interest in the garden.

Probably 200 to 300 species are found throughout all temperate and tropical regions. Short rhizomes bear rosettes of fronds, which may be once, twice, or many times divided. The smallest divisions of the frond commonly have a characteristic shape with a single prominent thumblike lobe on one side at the base, and their margins usually have bristly-pointed teeth. The spore-bearing organs on the underside of the frond are covered by a round, shield-shaped structure attached in the center, hence the common name of shield fern. In many species and cultivars, the young growth in spring is very conspicuous and attractive from its covering of silvery or gingery scales. All of those described here are evergreen unless stated otherwise. These ferns combine dependability and elegance and also include some of the hardiest of all ferns.

LEFT *Polypodium vulgare*

CULTIVATION Grow in moist, well-drained soil in an airy situation with some shade. With old plants, the crown of new fronds can slowly grow above ground level with the risk of the roots drying out as they pass down the side of this "trunk." A simple mulch around the crown will solve this, or the plant can be lifted and replanted lower in the ground.

PROPAGATION By division of mature plants, and from spores or bulbils. Several species tend to remain as a single crown, and must be propagated from spores (*see* Propagating Shield Ferns, *p.383*).

PROBLEMS Generally trouble-free, but dense plantings may be afflicted by the fungus *Taphrina wettsteiniana*, and in very humid conditions botrytis can be troublesome (*see* Diseases of Shield Ferns).

P. acrostichoides (Christmas fern.) Tufted fern with a branching rhizome forming a clump of leathery, dark green, narrowly oblong fronds divided into many pairs of narrow leaflets. Spores are borne on much shorter leaflets in the upper part of some fronds, resulting in a characteristic abrupt narrowing of the top third of the frond, distinguishing it from *P. munitum*. Formerly used for Christmas greenery in North America; in the wild, fronds emerge green after many months under the snow. Native to damp woodlands in eastern North America. ‡ 24 in (60 cm). Z3–8 H8–1

P. aculeatum (Hard shield fern) Tufted fern with short-stalked, leathery, lance-shaped fronds that narrow toward the base. They are divided into many pairs of dark green leaflets, which are further divided into small segments that are wedge-shaped at the base and rarely

stalked. It seldom produces side crowns, so is propagated from spores. The evergreen fronds arch very elegantly from the crown, making it one of the most attractive European ferns. Grows in woods, fencerows, and streamsides in much of Europe. ‡ 16–24 in (40–60 cm). Z4–8 H8–1

P. braunii Compact, tufted fern with lance-shaped, slightly glossy fronds, twice-divided, the bristles on the fronds are more conspicuous than on most other species. Very similar to *P. setiferum*, which has less bristly fronds and smaller ultimate segments, and generally a fern of primary interest to the specialist. From cool, moist forests in central Europe, North America, and East Asia. ‡ 16 in (40 cm). Z3–8 H8–1

P. munitum (Sword fern) Upright to arching, narrowly lance-shaped, dark green fronds to 5 ft (1.5 m) long, are divided into many pairs of narrow, tapering, bristly-toothed segments. One of the largest species of *Polystichum* and very handsome, it makes an excellent garden plant. With adequate moisture, can do well in full sun. Unlike many shield ferns, tends to produce plenty of side-crowns, allowing division, although a saw may be needed to cut them off. Grows abundantly in moist woodlands in western North America. ‡ 3¼–5 ft (1–1.5 m). Z3–8 H8–1

P. polyblepharum (Japanese tassel fern) Robust fern; arching, very glossy, deep green fronds to 28 in (70 cm) long, with many narrow divisions, each further divided into oblong leaflets. Spectacular in spring, when the tassel-like, uncurling fronds are densely covered with ginger-brown scales. Native to open forests and damp grasslands in Japan, South Korea, and eastern China. ‡ 20 in (50 cm). Z6–8 H8–5

P. proliferum (Mother shield fern) Slightly tender, semi-evergreen fern with a rhizome developing into a short trunk. The spreading, lance-shaped, glossy, dark green fronds are twice divided and bear a bulbil on the midrib

LEFT 1 *Polystichum polyblepharum*
2 *P. setiferum* Divisilobum Group
3 *P. setiferum* Plumoso-divisilobum Group **4** *P. tussimense*

DISEASES OF SHIELD FERNS

The fungus *Taphrina wettsteiniana* can attack almost any species of *Polystichum*, but is usually only a problem where many polystichums are grown close to one another—for example, in a nursery or in a collection. The symptoms are small, yellowish brown blotches scattered over the leaf, usually more plentiful near the base, in wet summers. In wet weather, the lesions produce a somewhat translucent film of spores on the underside of the frond—the spores are spread by splash, so individual plants that are well spaced— for example, 10 ft (3 m) apart—are unlikely to cross-infect. The genus *Taphrina* also includes peach leaf curl, a very difficult disease to eradicate.

It is best to remove diseased fronds and burn them as soon as they are recognized and soak the crown of the fern with a systemic fungicide, spraying the underside of the fronds at the same time. If the disease persists, repeat the treatment. If the fern is special, it might be worth transferring it to a greenhouse and thenceforth avoid wetting the fronds. If the fern is not special, the infected plant can be destroyed. It is worth reiterating that, even though this is a serious disease, it is unlikely to occur outside of large collections of polystichums, although it can be present on ferns bought from nurseries.

In species with densely overlapping fronds, high humidity near the crown of the plant can also invite infection by *Botrytis*. This is also controlled with a systemic fungicide but is much less damaging. It is, however, more common. The symptom is a general blackening of the infected areas. In an open situation in the garden, *Botrytis* is unlikely to appear.

BRIGHT SPARKS AMONG FERNY FOLIAGE

ALLOWING INTERESTING FOLIAGE to intermingle creates quietly effective plant pictures for a very long season and can be even more effective when enlivened with leaves that carry brighter sparks of color. Here there are two ferns. The stalwart *Polystichum setiferum*, grows well in dry conditions, but here luxuriating with more moisture yet retaining its compact crown, is matched with the Japanese silver painted fern, *Athyrium niponicum* var. *pictum,* with prettily silvered foliage and a little more of a tendency to creep. Between the two, *Houttuynia cordata* 'Chameleon', with its flashes of red and yellow, enlivens the scene.

near the tip of the frond. A recent and beautiful addition to northern temperate gardens. Needs a moist, well-drained, shady site in a sheltered garden and particularly well suited to an urban or coastal garden. From cool forests at low altitudes and rocky places in the hills in southeastern Australia. ‡ 30 in (75 cm). Z5–9 H9–5

P. rigens Tufted fern with a short, erect rhizome bearing several spreading, very leathery and rigid fronds. Yellow-green when young, the fronds mature to mid-green, and are twice-divided, the smallest divisions oval and almost prickly to the touch. Grows wild in sparse upland forests in China and Japan. ‡ 16 in (40 cm). Z6–9 H9–6

P. setiferum (Soft shield fern) An upright rhizome eventually branches to form several crowns of spreading, mid-green fronds to 3¼ ft (1 m) long, whose stalks are quite long. Fronds oblong and scarcely narrowed at the base, twice-divided, the smallest divisions blunt at their base with a distinct stalk. The fronds are soft to the touch, and the segments are tipped with a soft bristle. Increase from spores or by division; some cultivars by bulbils. Similar to *P. aculeatum* but easily distinguished from it by its long-stalked fronds. The uncertain naming of some

cultivars and groups is currently being clarified. Native to damp woodlands and shady hedges in much of Europe. ‡ 16–24 in (40–60 cm). Z6–9 H9–6. **Acutilobum Group** Fronds lance-shaped, slightly leathery, the smallest divisions with an acute tip and base. Plants in the Divisilobum Group have been confused with this group, but are quite distinct. **'Bevis'** syn. 'Plumosum Bevis', 'Pulcherrimum Bevis' Fronds dark green with smallest segments narrowed, the upper divisions sickle-shaped and sweeping toward the tip of the frond, somewhat resembling braiding. A splendid cultivar that virtually never produces spores and

has therefore been propagated only by division, making it somewhat uncommon. Recently, it has been tissue-cultured and is now more widely available. **Congestum Group** Both frond and side divisions shortened and thickened, causing leafy parts to overlap. Fronds somewhat brittle. **Cristatum Group** Crests at the tips of fronds and segments. **Decompositum Group 'Dahlem'** Fronds notably erect, more densely leafy toward base, the secondary divisions at the base of the frond are sickle-shaped. **Divisilobum Group** Frond stiffer, more or less horizontal, and two to three times divided with narrow ultimate divisions.

Bulbils often produced along the frond midrib. **Divisilobum Group 'Dahlem'** *see* Decompositum Group 'Dahlem'. **Divisilobum Group 'Divisilobum Densum'** syn. 'Plumoso-multilobum' Frond often horizontal, up to four times divided with leafy parts overlapping densely in the lower half of the frond. Ultimate segments tiny but not narrowed, retaining the same general shape of the species. Easily propagated from bulbils, but particularly susceptible to fungal diseases and best grown in a sheltered but airy site. **Divisilobum Group 'Iveryanum'** Spreading, triangular to lance-shaped, leathery, dark green fronds, three times divided and crested at the tip of the frond and its segments. Often produces bulbils. **Divisilobum Group 'Divisilobum Wollaston'** Frond broad at base, almost triangular, with bulbils: some frond parts aborted near base of frond. **Multilobum Group** Frond stiffer and divided two or three times but not narrowed as they are in the similar Divisilobum Group. Often produces bulbils. **Plumoso-divisilobum Group** Frond up to four times divided, very lacy, with narrow ultimate divisions and occasional bulbils. Very beautiful, but rare. **'Plumosum Bevis'** *see* 'Bevis'. **Plumosum Group** Frond two to three times divided, the ultimate segments are papery with toothed margins. Spores are almost never produced, so this group is rare. **'Pulcherrimum Bevis'** *see* 'Bevis'.

P. tsussimense Small with lance-shaped, light to mid-green fronds, which are neatly twice-divided into narrow, finely pointed segments. A delightful fern for the front of a border or trough. Often sold as a house plant but very hardy. From rocky forests and streamsides in East Asia from Thailand to Japan. ‡ 8–12 in (20–30 cm). Z6–9 H9–5

POTENTILLA
Cinquefoil
ROSACEAE

Dependable plants producing some of the most brilliant colors in the border.

About 500 shrubby, annual, biennial, and perennial species are found widely throughout the Northern Hemisphere from mountains to meadows, usually in alkaline soil; many of the most gardenworthy originate in Asia, in particular the Himalaya. The perennial species are clump-forming plants, developing from fibrous roots. The alternately arranged leaves may be divided into pairs of opposite lobes or split into three to seven fingers, often strongly veined and toothed. The leaves are largest at the base, reduce in size up the stems, and may be hairy with silvery undersides. The simple, usually five-petaled flowers are arranged in open sprays, each saucer-shaped, or sometimes cup-shaped or starry, and usually open over an extended period from spring to fall. Closely related to the strawberries, *Fragaria*

PROPAGATING SHIELD FERNS

A few *Polystichum* species produce a solitary bulbil near the tip of the frond, and this can be used for propagation. Ideally, leave the frond on the plant but weighed down so the base of the bulbil is in contact with the soil. By the following season, it should have roots and can be potted up to grow on. If the bulbil is removed, plant it firmly in a low-nutrient mix so that the bulbil is level with the soil in the pot, not buried. Water and place in a plastic bag on a shady windowsill. It should develop roots within a few months.

Some cultivars of *P. setiferum* produce several small bulbils along the midrib. Weigh the frond down in fall and transplant rooted plantlets the following summer. Alternatively, detach a frond with the largest bulbils, lay it in a container of low-nutrient mix and carefully weigh the frond down with grit, pegs, or stones so that the bulbil-bearing midrib is in firm contact with the soil. Water, then place in a closed plastic bag on a shady windowsill. By the following spring, at least some of the bulbils should have rooted.

(*see* Hybrids and a Name Change, *p.201*), many of the most widely grown perennial potentillas are hybrids derived from *P. atrosanguinea* and/or *P. nepalensis*; many are similar to each other except for their flower colors.

CULTIVATION Generally easy to grow, the garden hybrids thrive in a well-drained, moderately fertile, moist, open border in full sun, although plants do best and flower for longer in a cool location. Staking is rarely needed. Once the blooms have faded, remove the flower stems at ground level. By contrast, the low-growing species from higher altitudes need gritty, very well-drained, fairly poor soil. Some of the European species with invasive habits are best in rough, grassy, wilder areas.

PROPAGATION Species may be raised easily from seed sown in fall or in early spring, but cultivars and hybrids will not come true. Clump-forming plants may be split in spring; those spreading by runners may grow on from rooted plantlets.

PROBLEMS Usually trouble-free.

P. alba A low-growing, clump-forming plant with refined appearance, the five-lobed leaves, up to 2½ in (6 cm) across, are dark green above and silvery beneath; each ¾–1½-in (2–4-cm) lobe is reverse egg-shaped or lance-shaped. Small, white, 1-in (2-cm) flowers in small clusters in late spring and early summer on spreading stems. Best in well-drained soil and an open sunny position. From central and southern Europe. ‡3 in (8 cm). Z5–8 H8–3

P. anseriana (Silverweed) Low-growing, with soft, feathery, silver leaves up to 8 in (20 cm) long, and the small yellow flowers appear in summer. Usually regarded as an invasive weed rather than a garden plant because it spreads quickly by runners, it is, however, attractive in rough grass in full sun, and the variegated form has its proponents. Common throughout Europe. ‡3 in (8 cm). Z3–8 H8–1. **'Golden Treasure'** Delicate, variegated selection with leaves splashed with gold. Requires full sun and a well-drained soil for optimum growth.

P. 'Arc-en-ciel' Large, double, yellow-orange, 1½-in (4-cm) flowers are held on arching stems for a long season, the first blooms opening in mid-spring and continuing well into late summer. ‡12 in (30 cm). Z4–8 H8–1

P. argentea (Silvery cinquefoil) Small, dark green, toothed, hand-shaped leaves, silvery beneath and 1 in (2.5 cm) across, are held on spreading rather than upright stems. Small, yellow flowers held in clusters appear in early summer. Somewhat weedy, but attractive in wilder parts of the garden. Grows in sun in dry fields and roadsides in Europe and Asia. ‡20 in (50 cm). Z3–8 H8–1

P. atrosanguinea Soft, dark green, toothed leaves are split into three leaflets with hairy, silvery undersides and held on long leaf stalks. In summer, erect, slender stems carry small clusters of deep red, sometimes orange-red, 1¼-in (3-cm) flowers. Best in a cool, bright position. From high altitude scrub between Sikkim and Afghanistan. ‡18–36 in (45–90 cm). Z5–8 H8–5. **var. argyrophylla** Orange-yellow flowers. From the eastern Himalaya.

P. 'Blazeaway' Large, yellow-orange flowers, flecked and suffused with orange-red, on slender stems during summer above slightly silvery foliage. An excellent border plant, introduced by English nurseryman Alan Bloom in 1971. Not 'Blaze Away' as sometimes seen. ‡12 in (30 cm). Z5–8 H8–5

P. calabra Spreading stems carry leaves that are divided into two or three leaflets, gray-green or silver above and silver below. Clusters of small, yellow flowers open in early summer. Needs sun and well-drained soil. Similar to *P. argentea* but with smaller, narrower, silver leaves. From Sicily. ‡12 in (30 cm). Z5–8 H8–5

P. 'Emilie' Double, dark, maroon-red, 1¼ in (3 cm) long, cup-shaped flowers, edged and flecked with yellow, are carried on branched stems above typical lobed, strawberry-like foliage for a long summer season. ‡16 in (40 cm). Z5–8 H8–5

P. erecta Low rosettes are made up of dark green leaves with silver undersides divided into three or four leaflets, about 1 in (2 cm) long. The slender flowering stems bear small, four-petaled, yellow flowers about ½ in (1 cm) across during summer. Not showy, but useful with other wild flowers in less formal gardens. From Europe. ‡20 in (50 cm). Z3–7 H7–1

P. 'Etna' Silvery foliage shows off semidouble, 1¼-in (3-cm), rich crimson flowers, edged with yellow in summer. Thrives in a sunny border with moist soil. A hybrid of *P. atrosanguinea* and *P. nepalensis*. ‡2 in (5 cm). Z5–9 H9–5

P. 'Flambeau' Clouds of double, dark red flowers held on tall, slender stems for an especially long season from spring until late summer. A fine border perennial. A hybrid of *P. atrosanguinea*. ‡36 in (90 cm). Z5–8 H8–5

P. 'Flamenco' Clump-forming plant with lobed, green foliage and single, rich red, 1¼-in (3-cm) flowers from spring into summer. A hybrid of *P. atrosanguinea* and *P. nepalensis* found as a self-sown seedling by Alan Bloom of England and introduced in 1973. ‡18 in (45 cm). Z5–8 H8–5

P. 'Gibson's Scarlet' A neat, clump-forming plant, the 1¼-in (3-cm),

RIGHT **1** *Potentilla* 'Gibson's Scarlet' **2** *P. nepalensis* 'Miss Willmott' **3** *P. recta* 'Warrenii' **4** *P.* 'William Rollison'

cup-shaped, semidouble flowers in the brightest scarlet with a darker eye are held above soft lobed leaves for a long season from early summer. One of the best red-flowered perennials. A hybrid of *P. atrosanguinea* and *P. nepalensis*. ‡18 in (45 cm). Z5–8 H8–5

P. 'Gloire de Nancy' Clusters of slightly limp, semidouble, 1¼-in (3-cm), red and orange flowers, which appear throughout summer. Best in a sunny border. A hybrid of *P. atrosanguinea* and *P. nepalensis*. ‡18 in (45 cm). Z5–8 H8–5

P. 'Helen Jane' Raspberry pink flowers, 1¼ in (3 cm) across, with darker cherry red centers, are held on sturdy stems above large, hairy leaves. A hybrid of *P. nepalensis* often raised from seed, so may be variable. Introduced by Thompson & Morgan Seeds. ‡18 in (45 cm). Z5–8 H8–5

P. x hopwoodiana Rich green leaves are divided into five leaflets; the flowers are pink, darker, and almost red at the base, and with white edges. A gorgeous hybrid between *P. nepalensis* and *P. recta*. Said to have been introduced in 1829. ‡16 in (40 cm). Z5–8 H8–5

P. 'Jean Jabber' Gray, strawberry-like foliage, covered in fine, silver hairs, sets off open sprays of yellowish orange flowers with red centers. Sometimes listed as *P. x hybrida* 'Jean Jabber'. ‡24 in (45–60 cm). Z5–8 H8–5

P. megalantha Green, 3-in (8-cm) basal leaves, which are hairy below, are split into three, reverse egg-shaped, toothed leaflets. Clusters of saucer-shaped, 1½-in (4-cm), bright yellow flowers appear during summer on neat, compact plants. From Japan. ‡12 in (30 cm). Z5–8 H8–5

P. 'Melton Fire' Compact and particularly long-flowering. The first reddish pink blooms, which are splashed creamy yellow with a darker eye, open in late spring and continue until fall. A chance seedling at a Thompson and Morgan Seeds trials site. ‡12 in (30 cm). Z5–8 H8–5

P. 'Monsieur Rouillard' Clusters of double or semidouble, rich red, 1¼-in (3-cm) flowers, splashed with yellow markings, are produced throughout summer. ‡16 in (40 cm). Z5–8 H8–5

P. nepalensis Hairy, 4-in (10-cm), basal leaves are divided into five oval leaflets with toothed edges and in summer wiry, branched, red-tinged stems bear saucer-shaped, red, pink, or orange flowers about ¾ in (2 cm) across. The cultivars have all been raised from seed and may be variable. From alpine meadows in the western Himalaya. ‡36 in (90 cm). Z4–7 H9–4. **'Miss Willmott'** syn. *P. willmottiae* Compact with dark-eyed, cherry pink flowers. Introduced about 1920; a number of different plants may be found under this name. ‡16 in (40 cm). **'Ron McBeath'** Very compact with dark-centered, carmine-rose flowers borne

freely all summer. Introduced from Himachel Pradesh in 1998. ‡12 in (30 cm). **'Roxana'** Distinctive, copper-pink flowers with red centers. **'Shogran'** Very compact, with dark-eyed, pink flowers all summer. Discovered on Mount Shogran in Pakistan and introduced in 2000.

P. recta Forms clumps of hairy, fingered, 4-in (10-cm) leaves divided into five or seven toothed leaflets; during summer, upright stems carry many pale yellow flowers, 1 in (2.5 cm) across. Widespread in Europe and Asia. ‡20 in. (50 cm). Z4–8 H8–1. **'Alba'** White flowers. **var. sulphurea** Very pale yellow, sometimes cream, flowers. **'Warrenii'** Brighter, golden yellow flowers.

P. rupestris Airy, double-toothed, slightly downy leaves are divided into five to nine leaflets arranged in opposite pairs. Delightful, pure white flowers with yellow centers appear in late spring. An easily grown species, given a sunny, well-drained site. Widely distributed in mountainous regions on rocky slopes in full sun from Britain east to Turkey and Siberia. ‡16 in (40 cm). Z5–8 H8–5

P. thurberi Forms a tight clump of deeply lobed foliage cut into five to seven fingers, which are broader at the tips; the stems carry open, lax heads of cup-shaped, dark red, ¾-in (2-cm) flowers with a darker eye. Excellent in moist, well-drained borders. From coniferous forests, moist grasslands, and alongside streams, in sun or semi-shade in Mexico and the southern US. ‡20 in (50 cm). Z5–8 H8–5. **'Monarch's Velvet'** Sumptuous, almost velvety, raspberry red flowers, with a dark red eye, for a long summer season. Reliable, prolific, one of the finest herbaceous potentillas. ‡24–30 in (60–75 cm).

P. x tonguei Superb, clump-forming perennial with low spreading stems, the soft, divided, rich green foliage is split into three to five reverse egg-shaped leaflets and clusters of bowl-shaped, soft apricot flowers with dark red centers, creating a dramatic bicolored effect all summer. Can be overvigorous. A hybrid of *P. anglica* and *P. nepalensis*. ‡6 in (15 cm). Z5–10 H8–3

P. 'Volcan' Deep red, cup-shaped, 1¼–1½-in (3–4-cm), semidouble flowers with darker red centers appear in summer and early fall above mid-green, lobed leaves. Best in fertile, well-drained soil. A hybrid of *P. atrosanguinea*. ‡12 in (30 cm). Z5–8 H8–5

P. 'White Queen' Unusual in producing large, pure white, 2–2½-in (5–6-cm) flowers, dotted with a yellow eye, above strawberry-like foliage in spring and early summer. For sunny, well-drained borders. A hybrid of *P. recta*. Often raised from seed; may be variable. ‡20 in (50 cm). Z5–8 H8–5

P. 'William Rollison' Clusters of the usual strawberry-like foliage throw up sprays of semidouble, brick orange,

1¼-in (3-cm) flowers, variously flushed with yellow, and with yellow backs to the sometimes slightly twisted petals. May be listed incorrectly as 'William Robinson'. ‡18 in (45 cm). Z4–7 H7–1

P. willmottiae see *P. nepalensis* 'Miss Willmott'

P. 'Yellow Queen' Well-branched plants carry clusters of double, bright yellow flowers over a long summer season. The best yellow-flowered cultivar. ‡18 in (45 cm). Z5–8 H8–5

PRIMULA
Primrose
PRIMULACEAE

Versatile and varied, with colorful flowers in a wide range of colors, and popular for more than five centuries.

More than 430 species are native throughout mostly moist, temperate or alpine areas of the Northern Hemisphere, with just two species south of the equator. More than 250 species have been cultivated, perhaps 130 today, but only about 30 (and their hybrids) are important in the garden. Only those generally considered perennials, rather than alpines or requiring frost protection, are considered here. Ranging in height, when in flower, from about an inch (a few centimeters) to more than 20 inches (half a meter), all produce a basal rosette of entire to lobed, often hairy leaves. The usually relatively large and showy regular flowers, with five lobes fused into a tube, are either borne individually on the stems arising from the base,

or in one or more clusters (whorls) on a leafless stem, which may have small, sometimes leaflike, bracts. In most species, in order to promote cross-fertilization, different types of flowers are produced on different plants: some are "pin"-eyed and some are "thrum"-eyed (*see* Pin and Thrum Primulas). Many species produce a meal (farina), a harmless crystalline pigment, on the buds, below the leaves, or in the flowerhead. Some species can produce a protein, primine, which is allergenic to a small number of people, although others can become sensitized after long exposure.

This large genus has been split into nearly forty sections (*see* Primula Classifications, *p.386*), not all of which are covered here, grouping together those with botanical similarities and often with similar cultural preferences in the garden. The section name is given in brackets after each entry. ⚠

CULTIVATION Most prefer well-drained but moisture-retentive soil, so plentiful organic matter, such as well-rotted leaf mold and/or compost with added grit or pulverized bark, is indicated; the larger species in particular are heavy feeders that appreciate well-rotted manure buried beneath. Cool, humid conditions are preferred in summer, and the soil should never dry out. Some thrive in wet, boggy conditions. Alkalinity is tolerated by most species, but very alkaline soil is unlikely to have the right physical characteristics. Dappled shade in summer is often helpful, particularly in areas with hot summers.

PIN AND THRUM PRIMULAS

In all but about 10 percent of *Primula* species, two types of flowers are produced on separate plants—the so-called pin-eyed and thrum-eyed plants occur in equal numbers. In pin-eyed plants, the stigma (the female organ that receives pollen) lies at the mouth of the flower and resembles the head of a pin, while the anthers (which produce pollen) are sunk lower down in the tube. In thrum-eyed plants, the arrangement is reversed and the anthers lie at the mouth of the flower while the stigma is sunk in the tube. This arrangement helps to ensure that plants are fertilized by pollen from a different plant and rarely self-pollinate. In a few species, including *P. japonica* and most *P. chungensis* and *P. prolifera*, the anthers and stigmas lie together in the mouth of the flower and plants are naturally self-fertile.

THRUM-EYED

Anthers

Protruding stigma

PIN-EYED

LEFT 1 *Primula alpicola*
2 *P. auricula* 'Matthew Yates'
3 *P. bulleyana* subsp. *beesiana*

PROPAGATION Most primulas are best raised from seed; indeed, for some, like *P. prolifera*, it is much preferred. Mature plants become very susceptible to viruses, which are easily transmitted to healthy stock by aphids or handling, and also spread through division or cuttings, but viruses are not carried in the seeds. However some, like double primroses, will not set seed, and many popular plants are unsuitable for seed-raising because they will not come true. Even those like the Barnhaven selections, which were originally raised from seed, will rarely come true in a garden setting. These include 'Inverewe', 'Johanna', and nearly all primrose-form and polyanthus hybrids (*see* Primula Classifications) such as 'Guinevere' and 'Wanda'. They are, after all, specifically adapted for cross-pollination (*see* Pin and Thrum Primulas, *p.385*). These must be divided and, as with most other primulas, the division can be done in fall or after flowering. Be aware, however, that, although they may show no symptoms of viral infection, they are almost sure to be carriers. Here, those that should be divided and not raised from seed, or which can be divided, are marked Division. Those which can, or should, be raised from seed are marked Seed.

PROBLEMS Virus infection, usually by cucumber mosaic virus, is the most dangerous disease. Transmitted by aphids, on hand tools, and when dividing plants, it can be recognized by weak, stunted, and distorted growth, thin flower color, and increased toothing and/or pale mottling of foliage. Many old cultivars have probably disappeared at least partly as result of weak growth resulting from viral infection.

In addition to virus diseases, aphids, cutworms, woodlice, earwigs, slugs, and snails, most primulas are also susceptible to vine weevil. The main symptom is sudden collapse while in growth; lifting the plant reveals comma-shaped, cream maggots with orange heads, and a detached or nonexistent root system. Search for the adult weevils at night with a flashlight (particularly if done in midsummer), and use either biological control or a specific systemic control.

P. 'Alan Robb' (Primula/dPrim) Vigorous, pale apricot orange, double flowered primrose with bronzed foliage. A seedling selected from the Barnhaven double primroses (*see* The Barnhaven Story, *p.392*). Division. ↕6 in (15 cm). Z4–8 H8–1

P. alpicola (Sikkimenses) Deciduous, oval leaves, up to 16 in (40 cm) but often shorter, with a rounded base,

PRIMULA CLASSIFICATIONS

This is such a large genus that it is divided into 38 sections of botanically similar species, and these are often given in nursery catalogs. The border perennial primulas covered here include representatives of only ten sections, and the names appear alongside each entry. Their main features are outlined below. Primula enthusiasts will have become familiar with the section names in use since the 1940s. However, recent research has resulted in some changes; the new names are used here, with the previous names given in brackets.

Auricula (Auricula) Often small, spring-flowering mountain plants from Europe with somewhat leathery leaves, which are sometimes mealy and emerge rolled inward along their length (*see* Auriculas, *p.387*).

Capitatae (Capitatae) Disklike heads of flowers with the central flowers not developing. Similar to Denticulatae in effect, but later-flowering, and shorter-lived. From the Himalaya.

Cortusoides (Cortusoides) Woodland primulas, mostly from eastern Asia, with often rounded, lobed, hairy leaf blades, narrow leaf stalks and mostly pink flowers, usually in a single cluster.

Crystallophlomis (Nivales). Bog plants with smooth, fleshy, mealy leaves and one or more tiers of flowers on mealy stems. From mountains in Asia.

Denticulatae (Denticulata) "Drumstick" primulas with a tight spherical head of lilac, purple, or red flowers on a mealy stalk in spring. From the Himalaya.

Muscarioides (Muscarioides) Short-lived, often biennial Chinese species with soft hairy leaves and many small flowers arranged in a spike.

Oreophlomis (Farinosae, in part). Pink-flowered, dwarf, spring flowers for boggy places. From Central Asia.

Primula (Vernales) Plants with familiar soft, hairy leaves, resembling those of the primrose, and including such harbingers of spring as the primrose (*P. vulgaris*), cowslip (*P. veris*), oxlip (*P. elatior*) and their hybrids. The type of flower is indicated as follows:

  Poly Polyanthus form, with the flowers gathered together at the top of a distinct stem.

  dPoly Polyanthus form but with double flowers.

  Prim Primrose form, with the flowers held singly on individual stalks.

  dPrim Primrose form, but with double flowers.

Proliferae (Candelabra) Tall spires of colorful flowers in tiers arise in early summer. Easy, often naturalizing in wet positions. From China.

Sikkimenses (Sikkimensis) Moisture-loving, and similar to the Proliferae, but usually with a single cluster of mealy faced, drooping flowers in midsummer. Mostly from the Himalaya.

---

appear in late spring on narrow, whitish stalks and often have an olive cast and a very distinctive, closely wrinkled surface. In early summer, three to fifteen, fragrant, pale primrose yellow flowers with a mealy face and said to be "the shape of a Chinese coolie hat" nod from upright stems, usually in a single cluster. Best in cool, moist soil in sheltered positions; good between rhododendrons. Best replaced every 3–4 years. Division or seed. From wet river marshes and alpine meadows in southeastern Tibet. ↕8–12 in (20–30 cm). Z4–8 H8–1. **var. alba** Flowers ivory white. **var. luna** The incorrect name for the usual form of *P. alpicola*. **var. violacea** Flowers dark purple to midnight blue.

P. anisodora see *P. wilsonii* var. *anisodora*

P. auricula (Auricula) Spreading rosettes of smooth, rounded, evergreen, often mealy leaves to 5 in (12 cm) but often less, are carried on somewhat woody stems. The leaf edges may be smooth, toothed, white-mealy, or green but hairy. In mid- and late spring, two to twenty funnel-shaped, golden to pale yellow flowers, usually with a clearly defined mealy white eye, are carried on stout, green to white stems. Plants with flowers of other colors, as well as some yellows, are hybrids with *P. hirsuta* and are technically forms of *P. x pubescens* (*see* Auriculas, *p.387*). Best in heavy soil, but grows poorly in both waterlogged soil and in drought, and prefers midday shade in the south. Divide or raise from seed; propagate prized cultivars (*see also* Auriculas,

p.387) by division only, after flowering, or by rooting rosettes as cuttings. Some are very long-lived and not apparently prone to virus, but others succumb readily. From limestone crevices in cliffs and boulders, mostly above 4,900 ft (1,500 m). From the Alps, Jura, Appenines, and Carpathians, Europe. ↕4–8 in (10–20 cm). Z3–8 H8–1. **'Blue Velvet'** Large flowers of a vivid blue-purple with a small, white eye and slightly mealy foliage. The nearest to a pure blue. Good in the open ground. **'Broadwell Gold'** Large, bright yellow flowers with a white eye and mealy leaves. **'Crimson Velvet'** Rounded heads of deep crimson flowers with a creamy eye. **'Dales Red'** Dark red flowers, flushed violet, with a broad cream center. Vigorous. **'Dusty Miller'** Foliage, stems, and calyces heavily covered with creamy meal; flowers dull violet with a large white eye. *See also* 'Old Red Dusty Miller' and 'Old Yellow Dusty Miller'. **'MacWatt's Blue'** Sweetly scented, deep royal blue flowers. Both eye and leaves are mealy white. Somewhat floppy. **'Matthew Yates'** Double flowers of a very dark burgundy, appearing black in some lights. Vigorous. **'Old Red Dusty Miller'** Deep dull chestnut red flowers with a white mealy eye and with very mealy foliage. A number of forms are grown under this name. **'Old Yellow Dusty Miller'** Bronzy yellow with a white mealy eye and with very mealy foliage. A number of forms are grown under this name. **'Osbourne Green'** An old variety with purple, green-edged flowers with a large white center and with mealy leaves. Found in a garden at Avoca, Co. Wicklow, Ireland. **'Red Gauntlet'** Quite vigorous with single flowers in a good cherry red to scarlet. One of the best. **'Trouble'** Double flowers of a light café-au-lait color and with slightly mealy foliage.

P. **'Barbara Midwinter'** (Sredinskya x Primula) Clusters of pink, pin-eyed flowers on 4-in (10-cm) long stems with small, rounded, evergreen leaf blades on long, narrow, pink stalks. A hybrid of *P.* 'John Fielding' and *P. juliae* raised by John Fielding of England. Requires moist, sheltered and shaded conditions. Division. ↕4¾ in (12 cm). Z7–9 H9–7

P. **Barnhaven Blues Group** (Primula/Prim) Vigorous primroses with dusky leaf tones and giving a range of blue shades in the yellow-eyed flowers. For any cool, damp spot in part-shade. From Barnhaven (*see p.392*). Division. ↕6 in (15 cm). Z4–8 H8–1

P. beesiana see *P. bulleyana* subsp. *beesiana*

P. **'Blue Riband'** (Primula/Prim) Dwarf primrose, with thrum-eyed flowers in mid-blue with a central red ring around the throat and red flower stems. Thrives in any cool, damp spot with good soil and part-shade. Division. ↕4 in (10 cm). Z4–8 H8–1

P. **'Blue Sapphire'** (Primula/dPrim) Pale blue, double-flowered primrose; ideal for cool, damp spots in good soil and part-shade. Division. ↕6 in (15 cm). Z4–8 H8–1

P. x *bulleesiana* (Proliferae) Hybrids between yellow *P. bulleyana* and its purple subsp. *beesiana* produce a rainbow continuum of colors through orange, salmon, pink, carmine, and purple but do not otherwise differ from their parents. Very similar swarms of plants commonly occur in the wild. Plants in this color range are often sold as 'Harlow Carr', 'Hidcote', or 'Inshriach' and if fertile have only involved these parents. Similar hybrids that also involve *P. pulverulenta*, such as 'Rowallane Rose', some of which have a dark rather than yellow eye to the flower, are more commonly sterile and

must be propagated by division. ↕8–16 in (20–40 cm). Z4–8 H8–1

P. bulleyana (Proliferae) Appearing in late spring, deciduous, spreading, grass-green, finely wrinkled leaves with small teeth have a pinkish red midrib and are narrowed to the base and rounded at the end. In early summer, later than in other species of this type, flowers are borne on a somewhat stout, mealy stem in two to five clusters, each of three to six flowers, the red buds opening to ¾-in (2-cm), yellow-eyed flowers, varying in color from yellow to purple, but typically golden orange. Grow in open or part-shaded, humus-rich, sheltered sites that never dry out, ideally by ponds or streams. Division or seed: easy from seed, and will self-sow and naturalize. Divide large clumps at any time they are in growth, except in hot weather. From wet meadows around 1,000 ft (300 m) in northwest Yunnan province extending to southwest Sichuan province, China. ↕8–16 in (20–40 cm). Z5–8 H8–5. **subsp. beesiana** syn. *P. beesiana* Flowers purple with a yellow eye. Sometimes treated as a separate species, *P. beesiana*.

P. burmanica (Proliferae) Deciduous perennial, with leaves appearing in late spring and flowering in early summer, the spreading, dark green, finely wrinkled leaves with small teeth have a pinkish red midrib and are narrowed to the base and rounded at the end. Flowers are borne on stout stems with no mealy coating in two to five clusters, each of three to six purple flowers with a greeny orange eye. Grow in open or part-shaded, humus-rich, sheltered sites that never dry out, ideally by ponds or streams. Best raised from seed if groups are isolated from related species; otherwise, some offspring will be hybrid (but still good). Plants propagated by division may be virused. From wet meadows and forest clearings at about 9,800 ft (3,000 m) on both sides of the frontier between Burma and Yunnan province, China. ↕8–16 in (20–40 cm). Z5–8 H8–5

P. **Candelabra hybrids** (Proliferae) A loosely applied name covering hybrids between all species within the section Proliferae, including *P. bulleyana*,

AN UNEXPECTED SETTING

YOU EXPECT to find wild primroses in the woods or fencerows, but sometimes plants can surprise you. Here, in a sunny and moist border, clumps of the British native primrose are surrounded in spring by the emerging foliage of the variegated form of another British native, the yellow flag iris, *Iris pseudacorus*. The yellow stripes match the primrose flowers prettily, and at this early stage, when the iris leaves are only starting to develop, the primroses remain in view. Later, the iris foliage will make a denser cover with more dramatic striping as well as buttery flowers—but will also cast the shade that the primroses appreciate in summer.

P. cockburniana, P. japonica, and *P. pulverulenta* but most usually *P.* x *bulleesiana*. Plants come in a wide and unpredictable range of flower colors. ↕8–16 in (20–40 cm). Z4–8 H8–1

P. capitata (Capitatae) A very variable, short-lived, sometimes biennial, evergreen with prostrate or slightly rising, oblong, mid-green leaves with a strongly wrinkled surface and small and irregular but densely set sharp teeth and sometimes strongly mealy below. The sometimes mealy stems bear a very compact, single head of small, stalkless, violet flowers, which may or may not also be mealy; the central flowers are sterile, smaller, and do not open, making the shape of the flowerhead flattened rather than rounded. Flowering can be at any time from late spring to early fall. Easy in cool, well-lit conditions with reasonably well-drained soil that does not dry out. Best treated as a biennial and raised from winter-sown seed each year. From well-drained, but moist and open habitats, usually above the tree line in the Himalaya and China, from

eastern Nepal to southern Sichuan. ↕4–10 in (10–25 cm) Z4–8 H8–1. **subsp. mooreana** Robust, with some meal and a ruff of large bracts below the head. Very late-flowering, usually in early fall.

P. **'Captain Blood'** (Primula/dPrim) Vigorous, blood red, double-flowered primrose selected from the Barnhaven double primroses. For any cool, damp spot in part-shade. Division. ↕6 in (15 cm). Z4–8 H8–1

P. **Chartreuse Group** (Primula/Poly) Robust polyanthus with cream flowers, shaded green in the center, and iced pale green or white, and with mid-green leaves. Thrives in any good soil that does not dry out. From Barnhaven (*see* panel, *p.392*). Division. ↕8 in (20 cm). Z4–8 H8–1

P. chionantha (Crystallophlomis) A stout stock carries erect, deciduous, spear-shaped, smooth and fleshy leaves, lacking teeth and covered with white or yellow meal, especially on the undersides. In mid- and late spring, upright stems carry one to three clusters of three to five, ¾-in (2-cm), flat-faced, white flowers, sometimes with a darker tube, on a stout, mealy stem. The only one of more than 30 species in this section (*Crystallophlomis*) that is fairly easy to grow and thrives in fertile, cool, humus-rich sites that remain very moist but do not become waterlogged. Division or seed: long-lived, it self-sows when grown in groups. From wet meadows and streamsides mostly above the tree line in western China. ↕6–12 in (15–30 cm). Z4–8 H8–1. **subsp. sinopurpurea** Purple-flowered. In the garden, these two plants are often mixed, and both colors frequently come from the same seed batch.

P. chungensis (Proliferae) Short-lived with spreading, deciduous, pale, slightly yellowish green leaves, narrowed to the base and with a whitish green midrib that is pink at the base, are rounded at the end, finely wrinkled, and with small teeth. In late spring, upright, slender, mealy stems carry three to six clusters of two to five, ⅝–¾-in (1.5–2-cm), flat-faced flowers in golden orange, opening from scarlet buds. Often confused with *P. bulleyana*, but flowers earlier, has a more delicate structure, and the leaves lack the pink midribs of *P. bulleyana*. Requires more shelter and part-shade than other candelabra relatives, but will naturalize in suitable conditions with humus-rich soil that remains very moist but is not waterlogged. Propagate from seed; usually self-fertile, but more vigorous if grown in groups, even self-sowing when thriving. Native to clearings in wet, coniferous forest in southeastern Tibet (Xijang), as well as the borders with India (Arunchal Pradesh), Burma, and Sichuan and Yunnan provinces, China. ↕12–18 in (30–45 cm). Z5–8 H8–5.

P. cockburniana (Proliferae) Delicate, deciduous, short-lived perennial, or biennial, the usually prostrate leaves are oblong, pale green with a white midrib and stalk, and finely wrinkled with small teeth. The flat-faced, ⅝–¾-in (1.5–2-cm) flowers, in early summer, are borne in one to three clusters of two to five flowers on a slender, silver, mealy stem, and are fiery orange-scarlet. Each flower is set in a short, cup-shaped, silver calyx, creating an attractive silver and red combination. A yellow-flowered form has occasionally been seen. It thrives in any cool, perpetually moist site with reasonable light, but small and easily overwhelmed by other plants. Seed: invariably self-fertile, but best grown in groups to allow cross-pollination; raise afresh each year. From wet meadows in southwest Sichuan, western China. ↕8–16 in (20–40 cm). Z5–8 H8–5.

P. 'Corporal Baxter' (Primula/dPrim) Scarlet-flowered, double primrose, not very vigorous but with flowers of a piercing color. A seedling selected from the Barnhaven double primroses. For any cool damp spot in part-shade and good soil. Division. ↕6 in (15 cm). Z4–8 H8–1

P. cortusoides (Cortusoides) Soft, mid-green, deciduous leaves have a shallowly lobed, narrowly oval blade equaling the narrow, hairy stalk. In late spring, shortly after growth starts, stems bear one, sometimes up to three, clusters of five to eight ¾-in (1.8-cm), funnel-shaped, pinkish purple flowers sometimes with an orange eye. Similar to *P. polyneura* but the leaf blade is triangular, rather than oval. Fairly long-lived in a humus-rich, "woodsy" soil in part-shade. Seed; not easy to divide. From shaded cliffs and gaps in coniferous woodlands from the European side of the Urals east to northern China, Manchuria, and North Korea. ↕8–12 in (20–30 cm). Z3–8 H8–1

P. 'Cowichan Series' (Primula/Poly) Beautiful polyanthus with large, flat-faced flowers, which lack an eye, and have strong, uniform colors to give effects of purity and serenity. Most have bronze-tinted leaves. Developed by Florence Bellis (*see* The Barnhaven Story, *p.392*), flower colors typically vary to some extent within the many groups. Thrives in any good soil that does not dry out, though best in part-shade. Division. ↕8 in (20 cm). Z4–8 H8–1. **Amethyst Group** Mainly violet-blues with dark, leaden foliage. **Garnet Group** Mainly ruby reds, foliage with a brownish hue. **Venetian Group** Mainly pinkish red, often with a black center.

P. 'David Valentine' (Primula/Poly) One-sided clusters of drooping, slightly funnel-shaped, sterile, purple, ¾-in (2-cm), single flowers on upright stems. Somewhat like a more vigorous version of *P. elatior* subsp. *amoena*. Raised by the eponymous professor of botany at Durham University, England, from intentional crosses of *P. juliae* on to *P. elatior* in about 1968. Thrives in any cool damp spot in part-shade. Division. ↕6 in (15 cm). Z4–8 H8–1

P. 'Dawn Ansell' (Primula/dPrim) Double white, jack-in-the-green primrose with neat flowers set against an enlarged, green calyx. Raised by a well-known breeder of doubles, Dr. Cecil Jones of Llanelli, Wales. Thrives in a cool damp spot in part-shade. Division. ↕6 in (15 cm). Z3–8 H8–1

P. denticulata (Denticulatae) (Drumstick primula) Deciduous, rough, leathery leaves are dark green above, paler below, and broadly strap-shaped with regular short teeth. The stalkless flowers, opening in early spring as growth begins, are usually lilac-blue and carried in a tight, globular head initially nestling in the developing rosette and then rising on a stout, mealy stem. Very easy and often invasive in cooler, more humid areas, but thriving in any heavy, moist soil. Division or seed: beware inferior self-sown seedlings, and divide

RIGHT 1 *Primula* Cowichan Series
2 *P. denticulata* var. *alba*
3 *P. florindae* **4** *P.* 'Guinevere'
5 *P.* Gold-laced Group

good forms. Many cultivars are raised from seed and so may vary in their coloring. From damp meadows throughout the Himalaya and western China. ‡12–16 in (30–40 cm). Z2–8 H8–1. **var. alba** syn. 'Snowball' White flowers. **'Glenroy Crimson'** Deep red flowers. **'Karryann'** Violet flowers, the leaves edged in cream. Division only. **'Robinson's Red'** Brilliant red, perhaps the best of the reds but rarely seen. Dwarf. ‡8 in (20 cm). **'Rubinball'** Flowers pink to red. **'Rubin'** Red flowers, sometimes ruby red. **'Rubin Selection'** Carmine red flowers, often in tight heads. **'Snowball'** see var. alba.

P. **'Duckyls Red'** (Primula/Poly) A vegetatively propagated polyanthus with velvety, deep red, eyeless flowers and bronzy leaves. Selected from the Garnet Group of Barnhaven Cowichans at the garden at Duckyls, East Sussex, England. For any cool spot in good soil. Division. ‡8 in (20 cm). Z4–8 H8–1

P. **elatior** (Primula) (Oxlip) Evergreen, or sometimes summer-dormant perennial, the whole plant is covered with soft, short hairs. The wrinkled, reverse egg-shaped, slightly grayish green leaves are primroselike but with a more slender stalk, narrowing noticeably at the base and almost without teeth. The stem bears one-sided clusters of somewhat drooping, slightly funnel-shaped, ¾-in (2-cm) flowers of a luminous, clear pale yellow, rarely purple, in early and mid-spring. The seedpods are noticeably long. Usually easy in most open garden settings, sometimes self-sowing and naturalizing. Division or seed: divide good plants, or grow in groups to encourage self-sowing but beware of hybrids. From dense, wet woods in southern, western, and central Europe. ‡6–10 in (15–25 cm). Z4–8 H8–1. **subsp. amoena** syn. subsp. *meyeri* Beautiful purple flowers. From the Caucasus and northeastern Turkey.

P. **'Elizabeth Killelay'** (Primula/dPoly) An exquisite double-flowered, gold-laced polyanthus with nearly fully double, maroon flowers with a silvery edge and a yellow eye. Grows well in any cool damp spot in part-shade in good soil. Division. ‡6–10 in (15–25 cm). Z4–8 H8–1

P. **'Eugenie'** (Primula/dPrim) A blue-flowered, double primrose with dark green foliage, selected from the Barnhaven double primroses. For any cool, damp spot in part-shade in a good soil. Division. ‡6 in (15 cm). Z4–8 H8–1

P. **florindae** (Sikkimenses) (Himalayan cowslip) The largest of all species, this deciduous, long-lived, sometimes over-vigorous perennial has relatively upright, dull green, leathery, short-toothed leaves with rounded blades to 8 in (20 cm), which are heart-shaped at the base and held on even longer, narrow, reddish stalks. Mealy stems carry a single cluster of up to 80 nodding, pale yellow flowers with

mealy stalks from early to late summer. Orange, red, and purple-flowered forms grown under this name are hybrids. Vigorous and persistent in any fertile soil that does not dry out and tolerant of considerable flooding, especially in winter. Seed: easy to raise, and seed remains viable for several years. Often self-sows invasively and needs to be meticulously deadheaded. A number of forms are available, simply named by color. Native to a few wet river flood-plains high in relatively dry parts of southeastern Tibet (Xijang). ‡14–40 in (35–100 cm). Z3–8 H8–1. **hybrids** Orange and scarlet flowers. Originally arose from hybridization with *P. alpicola* var. *violacea*, and possibly *P. waltonii* and *P. ioessa*, but are now indistinguishable from *P. florindae* except in flower color. **'Ray's Ruby'** Deep ruby red, but less commonly deep pink to purple.

P. **'Freckles'** (Primula/dPrim) Dark red, double primrose with white spots, over dark green foliage. Selected from plants from American doubles breeder Rosetta Jones. For any cool, damp spot in part-shade and good soil. Division. ‡6 in (15 cm). Z4–8 H8–1

P. **'Garryarde Guinevere'** see *P.* 'Guinevere'

P. **'Gigha'**. syn. *P.* 'Winter White' (Primula/Prim) Very early flowering primrose with gold-centered white flowers and pale green leaves. Probably derived from an eastern Mediterranean form of *P. vulgaris* subsp. *sibthorpii* but said to have been found on Gigha, an island in the Inner Hebrides, Scotland. Best in a sheltered spot, in part-shade and a humus-rich soil. Sometimes damaged by hard weather. Division. ‡6 in (15 cm). Z4–8 H8–1

P. **Gold-laced Group** (Primula/Poly) Relatively small-flowered and long-stalked polyanthus with dark red to deep chocolate flowers and each petal edged in gold. Primrose forms are also occasionally seen. For any cool, damp spot, better in part-shade and good soil. Division: seedlings rarely come true unless hand-pollinated. ‡10 in (25 cm). Z5–8 H8–4. **Barnhaven** Most modern, gold-laced polyanthus originate from Barnhaven. **Beeches strain** Vigorous, with good flower form and rich colors. **Victoriana Series** Gold-laced forms in three shades of red plus a silver-laced crimson.

P. **'Guinevere'** syn. *P.* 'Garryarde Guinevere' (Primula/Poly) Classic polyanthus, often listed as 'Garryarde Guinevere', with deep bronzy purple foliage and pale mauve flowers in a delightful and original combination. One of several hybrids originally raised at Garryard, Co. Tipperary, Ireland, that may include *P. juliae* in their parentage. For any cool, damp spot in part-shade. Division: has been thus propagated for nearly a century and has stayed unexpectedly healthy. ‡6 in (15 cm). Z4–8 H8–1.

P. **Harlow Carr hybrids** (Proliferae) Candelabra-style plants in a wide range

of colors, usually focused on *P.* x *bulleesiana*, and originating at the RHS garden at Harlow Carr, Yorkshire, England. Division or seed. ‡8–16 in (20–40 cm). Z4–8 H8–1

P. **Harvest Yellows Group** (Primula/ Poly) Robust, highly scented polyanthus with flowers in ivory to yellow to orange shades; robust mid-green foliage. Developed from Gertrude Jekyll's Munstead strain. Thrives in any good soil that is kept moist. From Barnhaven (*see panel, p.392*). Division ‡8 in (20 cm). Z4–8 H8–1

P. **Hose-in-hose** (Primula) Originally a yellow primrose with the calyx transformed into the same shape and color as the petals, resulting in the appearance of one flower sitting inside the other. The name is applied to this one character and can refer to a wide range of forms of *P. vulgaris* and now also occasionally in *P.* x *polyanthus*, *P.* x *pruhonicana* and other hybrids and in additional colors (*see* Unusual Primula Forms, *p.390*, and *P.* You and Me Series, *p.395*). For any good soil kept moist; better in part-shade. Division, after flowering: will not come true from seed. ‡6 in (15 cm). Z4–8 H8–1

P. **Inshriach hybrids** (Proliferae) Candelabra-style plants in a wide range of colors, usually focused on *P.* x *bulleesiana*, and originating at the famous Inshriach Nursery, Aviemore, Scotland. Division or seed. ‡8–16 in (20–40 cm). Z4–8 H8–1

P. **'Inverewe'** syn. *P.* 'Ravenglass Vermilion' (Proliferae) Deciduous, candelabra-style plant flowering in early summer and best known for its relatively large, sterile flowers, to 1 in (2.5 cm), in a very intense scarlet-orange and set in three to six clusters against silver-mealy stems. Flowers are the same color as *P. cockburniana*, but 'Inverewe' is a much bigger and more robust plant. Probably a cross between *P.* x *bulleesiana* and *P. cockburniana*. Vigorous in a cool, damp, fertile place that never dries out. Completely sterile, but multiplies well and is best divided after flowering. Seems not to be virused. Division. ‡12–16 in (30–40 cm). Z4–8 H8–1

P. **ioessa** (Sikkimenses) Deciduous, somewhat smooth, spreading foliage is oblong, gradually narrowing to a winged stalk and a dull, slightly bluish green with a markedly wide white midrib and regular, round teeth. In early summer, stems bear a single, one-sided head of four to twelve, drooping, cowbell-shaped flowers, which have a mealy face and are lilac-blue, pink or occasionally creamy white. Seed; not long-lived, rarely persisting for more than two flowering seasons, so division is not an option, but easy to raise from seed. Enjoys cool, moist but well-drained, fertile soil and sheltered positions. Dormant until late spring so its position should be carefully marked.

The species name is pronounced "yo-essa." From wet alpine meadows in southeastern Tibet, Bhutan, and eastern Nepal. ‡8–12 in (20–30 cm). Z5–8 H8–5

P. **'Iris Mainwaring'** (Primula/Prim) A miniature primrose with a blue, single flower, tinged red. Very neat. For any good soil in part-shade that is kept moist, but readily smothered by more vigorous neighbors. Division, after flowering. ‡4 in (10 cm). Z4–8 H8–1

P. **Jack-in-the-Green** (Primula) Originally a yellow primrose with an enlarged, leafy, green calyx. The name is applied to this one character and can refer to a wide range of forms of *P. vulgaris* and now also occasionally in *P.* x *polyanthus*, *P.* x *pruhonicana*, and other hybrids (*see* Unusual Primula Forms, *p.390*, and *P.* 'Dawn Awsell', *p.388*). For any good soil that is kept moist, better in part-shade. Division. ‡6 in (15 cm). Z4–8 H8–1

P. **japonica** (Proliferae) Deciduous, with no mealy coatings; jaggedly toothed, wrinkled, egg-shaped leaves are semiprostrate and a sickly pale yellowish green with a reddish stalk. In late spring, tall, upright stems bear three to six clusters of four to six, flat-faced flowers about ¾ in (2 cm) in diameter, in white, pink, or red, sometimes with an orange eye. Most other pink- or red-flowered candelabra primulas with wrinkled leaves have a mealy coating. Easy in any moist, fertile soil and can be invasive but not usually long-lived. Seed from plants grown in groups tends to give rise to more vigorous stock than seed from isolated plants. If

RIGHT *Primula* 'Inverewe'

ABOVE *Primula japonica* 'Miller's Crimson'

pure colors are required, keep different forms apart. Often self-sows and sometimes naturalizes. Seed: flowers in its first year, and best replaced after two or three years' flowering. From boggy places by mountain streams in all four main islands in Japan. ‡6–16 in (15–40 cm). Z4–8 H8–1. **'Alba'** White buds and flowers. **'Apple Blossom'** Pale foliage and pink buds, which open to a crinkled white flower. **'Carminea'** Dark reddish flowers with a darker eye and pale foliage. **'Miller's Crimson'** Pinkish crimson flowers with a darker eye; leaves dark olive green. **'Postford White'** Crinkled, white flowers with an orange eye, usually on dark stems, and with dark olive green foliage. Often very robust, the best white candelabra for most gardens.

P. **'Jay Jay'** (Primula/Poly) A miniature polyanthus with small, dark red, jack-in-the-green flowers from the noted American hybridizer Peter Klein and raised from his hand-crossed seed after his death. For any cool, damp spot in part-shade and good soil. Division. ‡4¾ in (12 cm). Z4–8 H8–1

P. **'Johanna'** (Oreophlomis) Deciduous, semiprostrate, smooth, pale green, oval leaves have a short, reddish stalk but no hairs or meal. In mid-spring, dark stems bear a head of four to twelve, spreading, sterile, pinkish flowers with a yellow eye, each petal lobe deeply notched. A cross between *P. clarkei* and *P. warshenewskiana* by Henrik Zetterlund of Gothenburg in 1980 and named after his daughter. Enjoys a moist, well-drained situation away from the hottest sun, where it will increase modestly. Not a large plant and easily overwhelmed. Propagate by division as it comes into growth. Benefits

from regular division every two to three years. ‡4¾–6 in (12–16 cm). Z4–8 H8–1

P. **'John Fielding'** (Sredinskya x Primula) Semi-evergreen, with oval, entire, hairy leaf blades on narrow, pinkish leaf stalks and, in early spring, 4-in (10-cm) stems bear an open head of large, flat-faced flowers of a rich pure pink, the lobes shallowly notched. Raised by the eponymous photographer and horticulturist by crossing *P. juliae* on to *P. megaseifolia*. Best when given shelter, shade, and humidity in "woodsy" soil. Persists best in very mild regions. Division. ‡4¾–6 in (12–15 cm). Z4–8 H8–1

P. juliae (Primula) A creeping, mat-forming plant, lacking meal or hairs, the deciduous, semiprostrate, fairly waxy and shiny, dark green, toothed leaves are thin in texture, the blade kidney-shaped and wider than long with a narrow pinkish stalk. In early spring, yellow-eyed, vivid purple, 1¼-in (3-cm) flowers are borne individually on wiry, red stalks, in clusters alongside the rosettes of leaves. Plants with other flower colors, including white, are mostly hybrids and often known as Juliana primroses. Enjoys moist, shaded sites with high humidity, although if grown in too much shade, flowers less freely. This dwarf, mat-forming subject is easily swamped by other plants. Divide as it comes into growth. Naturalized near Glasgow, Scotland. Quite widespread in woods near streams in the eastern half of the Caucasus. ‡2½–3 in (6–8 cm). Z3–8 H8–1

P. **'Ken Dearman'** (Primula/dPrim) A double-flowered primrose with flowers splashed with yellow, orange, and copper. Selected from the

Barnhaven double primroses. For any good soil which is kept moist, in part-shade; divide after flowering. Division. ‡6 in (15 cm). Z4–8 H8–1

P. **'Kinlough Beauty'** (Primula/Poly) A dwarf polyanthus with salmon pink flowers, each petal with a central pale stripe. A hybrid of *P. juliae* found in a garden at Kinlough, Co. Antrim, Northern Ireland. Sometimes sold as 'E. R. Janes', unstriped plants are sometimes incorrectly sold as 'Kinlough Beauty'. For any good soil in part-shade that is kept moist, but readily smothered by more vigorous neighbors. Division, after flowering. ‡6 in (15 cm). Z4–8 H8–1

P. kisoana (Cortusoides) Spreading, deciduous leaves have blades scarcely longer than broad, angled and slightly lobed, thick and softly hairy, on narrow and thickly hairy stalks. In mid-spring, upright stems bear one, or sometimes two, heads of three to five, rose or white, flat-faced, yellow-eyed, 1-in (2.5-cm) flowers. Needs a humus-rich site that never dries out in part-shade, creeping slowly when well-suited. Division, as it comes into growth. From Japan, where it is very rare. ‡4–6 in (10-15 cm). Z5–8 H8–5. **var.** *alba* Flowers white.

P. **'Lady Greer'** (Primula/Poly) A dwarf semi-creeping, miniature polyanthus with fragrant, funnel-shaped, cream flowers with a cold, slightly greenish tone borne on short stems. Thought to have originated in Ireland. The parentage may include *P. juliae, P. elatior,* and possibly *P. x polyantha*. Fairly vigorous in sheltered sites in part-shade. Division. ‡4–6 in (10–15 cm). Z3–8 H8–1

P. **'Lilian Harvey'** (Primula/dPrim).

Cerise pink, double-flowered; mid-green foliage from the Barnhaven double primroses. Dwarf but vigorous in sheltered sites in part-shade. Division. ‡6 in (15 cm). Z4–8 H8–1

P. **'Lois Lutz'** (Primula/Poly) Polyanthus with vivid purple flowers and a small, yellow eye set against dark green, mat-forming foliage. For any cool, damp spot in part-shade and good soil. From the garden of the eponymous Pennsylvania primula enthusiast. Division. ‡8 in (20 cm). Z4–8 H8–1

P. **'MacWatt's Cream'** (Primula/Poly) A dwarf, semi-creeping, miniature polyanthus with funnel-shaped, cream flowers that become tinged with pink as they age. Very similar to *P.* 'Lady Greer' but with a warmer coloring. Raised by Dr. John MacWatt, a well-known grower of primulas in Scotland, early in the 20th century. Fairly vigorous in sheltered sites in part-shade. Division. ‡4–6 in (10–15 cm). Z4–9 H8–1

P. **'Marianne Davey'** (Primula/dPrim) Cream-flowered double primrose with mid-green foliage, probably selected from the Barnhaven double primroses. For sheltered sites in part-shade in a good soil, divide while in growth. Division. ‡6 in (15 cm). Z4–9 H8–1

P. **'Marie Crousse'** (Primula/dPrim) A double flowered primrose with mauve flowers splashed with white. Introduced from France in about 1880, a number of similar plants, including a lilac-pink double, have been grown under this name. For sheltered sites in part-shade in good soil; divide while in growth. Division. ‡6 in (15 cm). Z4–9 H8–1

P. **'Miss Indigo'** (Primula/dPrim)

UNUSUAL PRIMULA FORMS

For hundreds of years, unusual forms of the wild primrose and its relatives have fascinated primula enthusiasts. Two are illustrated in *Hortus Floridis* of 1614, while John Parkinson's *Paradisus Terrestris* of 1629 illustrated over 20 unusual forms, most with abnormal flower structures. Referred to as anomalous or more appealingly as Elizabethan primroses, these strange forms occur occasionally in the wild in primroses and cowslips as well as in garden hybrids. They are grown for their curiosity value but also, in many cases, because they are undeniably attractive. Those with an enlarged calyx and single or double flowers are known as "jack-in-the-green" or, when the calyx is especially enormous and perhaps distorted, "gallygaskins." "Feathers" have a finely cut calyx and petals. Forms with one flower sitting inside the other are known as "hose-in-hose," while those with an enlarged calyx striped in the same color as the petals are known as "jackanapes." The combination of hose-in-hose and jackanapes is known as the "pantaloon."

Hose-in-hose

Jack-in-the-green

Jackanapes

Feathers

Dark violet, double-flowered primrose, the petal edges frosted in silver and with dark green leaves. One of the most popular and prolific double primroses, selected from the Barnhaven double primroses. Fairly vigorous in sheltered sites in part-shade. Division. ‡6 in (15 cm). Z4–9 H8–1

P. 'Old Port' (Primula/Poly) Very dark bronzy leaves show off blackish purple flowers. A sister seedling to 'Tawny Port' and possibly the same as 'Garryard Crimson', a name no longer seen. Sometimes said to be a primrose, not a polyanthus, so there may be more than one plant carrying this name. Fairly vigorous in sheltered sites in part-shade. Division. ‡8 in (20 cm). Z4–8 H8–1

P. Paris '90 Group (Primula/Poly) Robust polyanthus; large white or cream flowers have a blue picotee edge and/or are blue on their backs. For any good soil that is kept moist. From Barnhaven (*see* panel, *p. 392*). Division. ‡8 in (20 cm). Z4–8 H8–1

P. 'Peter Klein' (Oreophlomis) Deciduous perennial, creeping when it is growing well; lacks both meal and hairs. At flowering, the small, rounded, smooth, olive green leaves have a narrow, pinkish stalk but, in summer, new leaves are oblong and stalkless, like a small *P. rosea*. Pink flowers with a whitish center and a yellow eye, and lobes deeply forked, borne in a single cluster of six to twelve on a short stem. Similar to 'Johanna' but flower stems are paler. A hybrid of *P. rosea* and *P. clarkei* from the eponymous Peter Klein of Tacoma, WA, from about 1966. Thrives in a moist, well-drained situation away from hot sun; increases modestly but is easily overwhelmed. Sterile, so propagate by division as it comes into growth; it benefits from regular division every 2–3 years. ‡4¾– 6 in (12–15 cm). Z4–8 H8–1

P. poissonii (Proliferae) More or less

evergreen, lacking meal or hairs, the leaves are erect, smooth, dark green, narrowly oblong, finely toothed, and narrowing almost imperceptibly to a stalk. In early summer, a stout, green stem bears one to three tiers of yellow-eyed, reddish purple, ⅝-in (1.5-cm) flowers. The calyx is uniformly dark, unlike that of *P. secundiflora,* which is striped in silver. Most of the other candelabra species have wrinkled leaves. Until recently, plants often proved less vigorous and striking than other candelabra species, and rarely self-sowed. However, recent collections from the wild have introduced vigorous, large-flowered plants of a vibrant red, and these persist well in a fertile, humus-rich bed in a cool place and have become excellent garden plants. Division or seed. Often abundant in wet meadows in Yunnan and Sichuan provinces, China. ‡14–18 in (35– 45 cm). Z4–8 H8–1

P. x *polyantha* (Primula/Poly) (Polyanthus) Evergreen, sometimes losing the foliage in summer, and flowering in winter and spring, the spreading, reverse egg-shaped, wrinkled leaves are olive green in color, gradually narrowed to an often reddish stalk, and hairy especially on the veins below. Flowers sometimes borne at the base first, but then on a fairly stout, hairy stalk in a single head of four to twelve, flat-faced flowers up to 1½-in (4-cm) or more in diameter. This name is used to cover hybrids between the primrose, *P. vulgaris,* and the cowslip, *P. veris;* these occur in the wild and have been cultivated for more than 500 years. Colors apart from yellow derive from pink or purple eastern forms of the primrose (subsp. *sibthorpii* and subsp. *heterochroma*) and were already in cultivation by the early 16th century. It is not always easy to distinguish between derivatives of the primrose, derivatives of *P.* x *polyantha,* and those in which at least one other species has

also been involved in hybridization, e.g., *P.* x *pruhoniciana*. Cultivars, therefore, are listed here simply under their cultivar name. Grow in any fertile soil in moderately good light; they also make useful house, greenhouse, or conservatory plants for winter color in a cool position, and also make spectacular winter and spring bedding displays. All can be divided, but many are usually raised from seed sown in the spring and planted out in the fall to flower through winter and spring. Modern series intended for bedding may be much less hardy. ‡6–8 in (15– 20 cm). Z5–7 H7–5

P. polyneura (Cortusoides) Deciduous mid-green leaves are softly hairy with a shallowly lobed, rounded-triangular blade (narrowly oval in the otherwise similar *P. cortusoides*) equal in length to the narrow, hairy stalk. Flowering in late spring, shortly after growth starts, stems bear usually one, but sometimes two or three, clusters of five to eight flat-faced, pinkish purple, ¾-in (2.2-cm) flowers with or without an

ABOVE 1 *Primula* 'Miss Indigo' **2** *P. poissonii* **3** *P. polyneura*

orange eye. Straightforward in a woodland bed in a high-humus, moisture-retentive, but well-drained soil, with at least part-shade, good shelter, and humidity. Can survive for a number of seasons; divide after flowering, but best grown from seed. Widespread in mountain woods in western China. ‡8–16 in (20–40 cm). Z3–8 H8–1

P. prolifera (Proliferae) Fresh green, wrinkled, narrowly egg-shaped, evergreen leaves without meal, narrow to a green, winged stalk; and green stems, sometimes mealy at the top, bear two to five tiers of three to six bright golden yellow, fairly wavy flowers, about ¾ in (2 cm) across, in late spring or early summer. Other yellow candelabra primulas are deciduous and have reddish buds and pink leaf stalks. Very vigorous in boggy ground and on streamsides. The evergreen

GROWING FROM SEED

While many popular cultivars must be propagated vegetatively, usually by division, many successful collections are dominated by young, seed-grown stock.

Because most seed is set, and seedlings are stronger, as a result of crosses between pin-eyed and thrum-eyed plants (*see* Pin and Thrum Primulas, *p.385*), it is always a good idea to collect seed from plants growing in groups, so that pins and thrums grow together.

Seed is usually ripe when the seedpod browns and starts to split at the apex. Store dry seed in paper packets in the refrigerator at 39°F (4°C) until ready to sow in early winter or midwinter. Sow thinly on the surface of a seed-starting mix with added

drainage (gritty sand); cover with sand and stand outside, open to all weathers, until germination takes place, usually in mid-spring. Pot on the seedlings while they are small and have just one true leaf; keep moist and sheltered and use a dilute liquid fertilzer every two weeks. Young plants can be planted out any time they are in growth, as long as they are kept watered, but the summer of their first year or the spring of the following year are preferable.

Young plants do not overwinter well outside in pots or trays, but do much better in cold frames. Until they come into growth, they will need periodic inspection to make sure they are not too dry. Most are easier to manage in the open ground, where they should be replaced once early vigor is lost.

leaves suffer in the winter. Seed is best saved from plants in groups that give rise to the most vigorous seedlings. Long-lived when growing well and can be divided as it comes into growth. From wet places in mountain woods from Indonesia to India. ‡10–24 in (25–60 cm). Z4–8 H8–1

P. x *pruhoniciana* (Primula/dPrim) Evergreen, usually somewhat creeping plants, lacking meal or more than scattered hairs, the oval leaves are usually bronze-green with a red to purple midrib, narrowed at the base and arising from pointed, reddish crowns. The roots are also often reddish. From midwinter to mid-spring, and sometimes in fall, flowers are borne singly or in a single cluster on a short, usually reddish stem, and are white to purple, usually somewhat funnel-shaped, and with a yellow or orange eye. The use of this name is restricted to hybrids between *P. juliae* and *P. vulgaris* 'Coerulea' but is often used more loosely to cover hybrids with *P. juliae* involving any form of *P. vulgaris* and even those involving *P. veris*. Most cultivars, therefore, are listed here simply under their cultivar name. This broader group is often known as Julianas or Julian primroses. Vigorous in cool, moist, fertile soil in part-shade, but requiring regular division and replanting after flowering and some weaken as a result. Some cultivars are intended to be raised from seed; others are mostly sterile and should be divided. ‡4–10 in (10–25 cm). Z4–8 H8–1

P. x *pubescens* (Auricula) Spreading rosettes of fleshy, smooth, rounded, evergreen, often, but not necessarily, mealy leaves to 4¾ in (12 cm) but often less, are carried on woody stems. In mid- and late spring, two to twenty funnel-shaped flowers, in a wide range of colors, usually with a clearly defined mealy, white eye, are carried on short, stout, green to white stems. A long-established hybrid between *P. auricula* and *P. hirsuta* and similar to *P. auricula,* which has yellow flowers. There is some disagreement about which cultivars belong under *P. auricula,* and which belong here. Best in full light or slight shade in an exposed site with good drainage; in these conditions, some are long-lived, especially in areas with cooler summers. Most cultivars are intended for vegetative propagation and are sterile, therefore divide or root them from cuttings taken with a long stem and kept in a cool humid place. ‡3–7 in (8–18 cm). Z4–8 H8–1. **'Boothman's Variety'** Dark purple flowers with a small white eye. Vigorous. **'Harlow Carr'** Cream-flowered, with a hint of pink on aging, and typically with a small, extra petal. Easily grown. **'Mrs. J. H. Wilson'** A rich, luminous purple with a slightly star-shaped, white eye. A very reliable old cultivar. **'The General'** Somewhat temperamental, but a magnificent bright military red.

LEFT 1 *Primula prolifera*
2 *P. pulverulenta* Bartley Group **3** *P. rosea*

THE BARNHAVEN STORY

There has long been a demand for primroses and polyanthus in unusual colors, and while some of the more recent introductions are not only uncomfortably gaudy but not entirely hardy, the cultivars from Barnhaven are different.

Barnhaven was the name of the barn and acre of streamside land in Oregon to which Florence Bellis moved with her first trays of primrose seedlings in 1937. The next year, every one of the 1,231 seedlings she planted bloomed and she sent out hand-painted flyers to attract customers. They came, bought her plants of 'Munstead Strain', 'Sutton's Brilliance', and 'Crimson King', and her business began.

She began to create her own selections, the first of which was 'Kwan Yin' in flashing Chinese red. Her famous Barnhaven Cowichans were developed after crossing 'Kwan Yin' with the original Cowichan, said to have been found in a garden in British Columbia. The first was "garnet to almost black, oxblood ruby… on dark wiry stems" and with almost no eye.

Her business developed and Florence became an authority on primroses and polyanthus. When she retired in 1965, the stock passed to England, to Jared and Sylvia Sinclair in the Lake District, who continued her work, making many more fine introductions.

When they made the decision to retire, there was much consternation at the thought that the Barnhaven introductions might disappear, but they were taken over by Angela Bradford in France, and more recently they passed to David and Lynne Lawson, who now send seed to all parts of the world from Barnhaven's current home in Brittany, France.

The Barnhaven strains have long been characterized by their extraordinary colors and their toughness. All Barnhaven seeds are produced by painstaking hand-pollination, and over Barnhaven's long history it is only fair to say that at times the quality has been known to falter. But with rigorous attention to careful hand-pollination and the choice of only the best parent plants, the toughness and unique colors of the Barnhaven primroses and polyanthus can live on.

Barnhaven primroses and polyanthus are originally made available as seed, or as plants raised from seed, but good forms are often selected and propagated by division; garden plants rarely come true from seed. Only the more widely grown forms are described here: there are many more.

P. pulverulenta (Proliferae) Deciduous, slightly grayish green, finely wrinkled, arching leaves, to 12 in (30 cm) long and with small teeth, are narrowed to the base with a whitish midrib and rounded at the end. The 1-in (2.5-cm) tubular flowers borne, in late spring and early summer, on a stout mealy stem in two to five tiers of three to eight flowers, are typically carmine red with a darker or yellow eye. The flower stems, bracts, and calyx are mealy. Very vigorous in wet conditions, forming large clumps when established and, after *P. bulleyana,* the easiest species of candelabra primula and usually the tallest. Will self-sow and naturalize, producing a mass of color in favored situations. Large, long-lived clumps can be dug up and divided any time they are in growth, though not in hot weather. From streamsides and other wet places in forests above 6,500 ft (2,000 m) in Sichuan, western China. ‡12–40 in (30–100 cm). Z4–8 H8–1. **Bartley Group** syn. 'Bartley Strain' Flowers are very pale pastel shell pink with a darker eye. **'Bartley Pink'** Rose pink, paler at the edges, with a dark red eye.

P. **'Quaker's Bonnet'** see *P. vulgaris* 'Lilacina Plena'

P. **'Ravenglass Vermilion'** see *P.* 'Inverewe'

P. **'Red Velvet'** (Primula/dPrim) Double, red-flowered primrose; the dark leaves feature a red edge. For sheltered sites in part-shade in a good soil. Division. ‡6 in (15 cm). Z4–8 H8–1

P. rosea (Oreophlomis) Finely toothed, deciduous leaves are smooth, bright green, lacking meal or hairs, oblong with no obvious stalk, and small at flowering but then becoming longer. With leaves emerging and flowers opening together early in the season, the flowers are almost stemless at first; the green stem elongates in fruit to 8 in (20 cm), and the flowers are pink to crimson with a yellow eye, about 1¼ in (3 cm) across, and carried in a single head. Best grown in very wet ground that is subject to periodic irrigation—for example, the edges of lakes and streams—but not tolerant of prolonged submergence in winter. Propagate from seed, or by division after flowering; sometimes naturalizes and individual plants can be long-lived. From wet alpine meadows and boggy places up to 14,000 ft (4,300 m) in the northwestern Himalaya. ‡8 in (20 cm). Z3–8 H8–1. **'Grandiflora'** Large, mid-pink flowers. Division. **'Gigas'** Carmine-pink flowers. **'Micia Visser de Geer'** Brilliant, penetrating crimson. Outstanding if it is not infected by viruses. Division.

P. **'Rose O'Day'** (Primula/dPrim) Pale rose red, double-flowered primrose with pale green leaves. For sheltered sites in part-shade in a good soil. Division. ‡6 in (15 cm). Z4–8 H8–1

P. **'Rowallane Rose'** (Proliferae). A tall, vigorous plant with pale green, toothed leaves, no meal, and pale crimson flowers with a dark center. A sterile hybrid between *P. japonica* and *P. pulverulenta* from Rowallane Garden near Belfast, Northern

Ireland. Division. ↕14 in (35 cm).
Z4–8 H8–1

P. 'Roy Cope' (Primula/dPrim)
A vigorous, red, double-flowered; dark
bronzy leaves. Selected from Barnhaven
double primroses. For sheltered sites in
part-shade in fertile soil. Division. ↕6 in
(15 cm). Z4–8 H8–1

P. 'Schneekissen' (Snow Cushion)
(Primula/Prim) An attractive, dwarf,
generally vigorous primrose with pure
white flowers on pink stems and small,
shiny, dark green, rounded leaves
forming a small mat. Raised by Georg
Arends in 1931. For sheltered sites in
part-shade in good soil. Division. ↕4 in
(10 cm). Z4–8 H8–1

P. secundiflora (Proliferae) Semievergreen, arching, spear-shaped leaves,
lacking meal or hairs, are smooth,
bright, and pale green with small
rounded teeth and a whitish winged
stalk. The mealy stems bear one (rarely
more) clusters of drooping, red-purple,
bell-shaped flowers, each backed by a
very distinctive black and silver striped
calyx, in midsummer. Not long-lived,
tending to rot at the base during very
cold and hot spells; new batches are
best raised from seed regularly.
Sometimes self-sows and naturalizes,
especially in damp paved areas. Best
in rich, moist to fairly wet sites, and
appreciates top-dressing in summer
with well-rotted compost or manure.
A beautiful plant that should be grown
more widely. From wet slopes and
streamsides above about 9,800 ft
(3,000 m) in western China. ↕16–32 in
(40–80 cm). Z4–8 H8–1

P. sieboldii (Cortusoides) (Sakurasoh)
Deciduous, creeping perennial, both
flowers and leaves appearing in late
spring and often disappearing by late
summer; the pale green, hairy leaves,
lack meal and are corrugated, with a
narrowly oval, lobed blade and a long
narrow stalk. The white to purple
flowers are borne in a single loose head
of five to eight on a green, hairy stem,
each flat-faced flower, up to 1½ in
(3.5 cm) across, has a narrow tube and
petal lobes, which are slightly notched
to deeply frilled and lacy. Easy and
long-lived in sheltered, humus-rich
conditions that do not dry out until at
least midsummer. Propagate by division
as it comes into growth, or from seed.
Select cultivars were originally
propagated by division for showing,
especially in Japan, where at least 700
cultivars were developed. Now,
competitive plants are usually seed-
propagated, but the best forms are easy
to divide. Expect more good forms to
become more widely available as
interest in the West grows. From damp
places near rivers and clearings in scrub
and woodlands from eastern Siberia to
Japan. ↕6–12 in (15–30 cm). Z4–8
H8–1. **'Carefree'** Large and substantial
deep pink flowers, not heavily dissected.
'Dancing Ladies' A mixture
containing white with the reverse of
petals pink plus various pink and rose
shades; petals both fringed and
unfringed. **'Geisha Girl'** Large, pink,

narrowly dissected flowers. **f. lactiflora**
White flowers in a range of forms.
'Lilac Sunbonnet' A bluish, broad-
based, slightly cone-shaped flower.
'Snowflake' Aptly named, the highly
dissected filigree white petals really do
look like a magnified snowflake.
A good garden plant. **'Winter Dreams'**
White, with slightly dissected flowers
but not as much so as 'Snowflake'.

P. sikkimensis (Sikkimenses) Deciduous
clump-former; the wrinkled, arching
leaves are narrowly oblong, gently
narrowing to a winged stalk, rounded
at the tip and with small, rounded
teeth. The mealy stems bear a single
head of ten to forty drooping, fragrant,
mealy faced, yellow flowers about
1¼ in (3 cm) across in midsummer.
Differs from *P. florindae* and yellow
forms of *P. alpicola* principally in its very
different leaf shape. Straightforward in
rich, damp, moisture-retentive sites and
appreciates heavy feeding with well-
rotted manure; long-lived when suited.
Best from seed gathered from garden
groups and will self-sow and naturalize
but less invasive than *P. florindae*. Can
also be divided as it comes into growth.
Widespread in alpine meadows, streams,
and lakesides in the Himalaya, mostly
above 9,800 ft (3,000 m). ↕24–36 in
(60–90 cm). Z4–8 H8–1

P. Silver Dollar (Primula/Poly)
Robust, large-flowered polyanthus in a
wide mixture of bold flower colors
with often pronounced, yellow eyes,
borne on quite tall stems. The name
given to the original Barnhaven
polyanthus developed by Florence
Bellis, now used both for her original
ten color groups, and also for more
recent additions to the range making
over twenty different color groups in
all. From Barnhaven (*see panel, p.392*).
Division. ↕8 in (20 cm). Z4–8 H8–1

P. Silver-laced Group (Primula/Poly)
Relatively small-flowered and long-
stalked polyanthus with dark red to
deep chocolate or sometimes deep blue
flowers and each petal edged in white.
Primrose forms are also occasionally
seen. For any cool damp spot, better in
part-shade and good soil. Best divided:
seedlings rarely come true unless they
have been hand-pollinated. ↕8 in
(20 cm). Z4–8 H8–1

P. Snow Cushion see *P.* 'Schneekissen'

P. Spice Shades Group (Primula/Poly)
Large flowered polyanthus in a wide
mixture of muted flower colors
including chocolate, coffee, ginger, and
other brownish shades with yellow eyes,
borne on quite tall stems. For any good
soil that does not dry out. From
Barnhaven (*see panel, p.392*). Division.
↕8 in (20 cm). Z4–8 H8–1

P. Striped Victorians Group (Primula/
Poly) Silkily sheened polyanthus with
large flowers in blue, violet, pink or
cream, always distinctly veined and
striped like Japanese irises. For any
good soil that does not dry out. From
Barnhaven (*see panel, p.392*). Division.
↕8 in (20 cm). Z4–8 H8–1

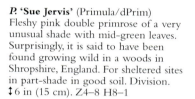

P. 'Sue Jervis' (Primula/dPrim)
Fleshy pink double primrose of a very
unusual shade with mid-green leaves.
Surprisingly, it is said to have been
found growing wild in a woods in
Shropshire, England. For sheltered sites
in part-shade in good soil. Division.
↕6 in (15 cm). Z4–8 H8–1

P. 'Sunshine Susie' (Primula/dPrim)
Bright gold, overpowering, double-
flowered primrose with mid-green
leaves selected from the Barnhaven
double primroses. For sheltered sites in
part-shade in good soil. Division. ↕6 in
(15 cm). Z4–8 H8–1

P. 'Tawny Port' (Primula/Poly)
Polyanthus with bronzed leaves and
ruby red flowers, a sister seedling of the
darker 'Old Port'. Fairly vigorous in
sheltered sites in part-shade. Division.
↕8 in (20 cm). Z4–8 H8–1

P. 'Tie Dye' (Primula/Prim) Very
unusual, but fairly weak primrose
originating in New Zealand with sky
blue flowers, flecked white, looking like
washed denim, and with a large yellow
eye. For sheltered sites in part-shade in
a good soil. Division. ↕6 in (15 cm).
Z4–8 H8–1

P. 'Val Horncastle' (Primula/dPrim)
Pale, double primrose in the color of
the wild primrose; slightly bronzed
foliage. Selected from the Barnhaven
double primroses. For sheltered sites in
part-shade in good soil. Division. ↕6 in
(15 cm). Z4–8 H8–1

P. veris (Primula) (Cowslip) Evergreen,
though sometimes summer-dormant,
the slightly gray-green, wrinkled,
ascending leaves are shortly hairy,
rounded at the tip and more or less
abruptly contracted into a narrowly
winged stalk. The green, shortly hairy
stem bears, in mid-spring, a single head
of four to twenty, somewhat drooping,
cup-shaped, golden yellow flowers,
½–¾ in (1–2 cm) in diameter, each
petal lobe with a ruby red mark at its

base, and emerging from a loose, baggy,
pale green calyx. Easy and sometimes
vigorous in any fertile, well-drained soil
in good light. Most often used for
naturalizing in rough grass or meadows.
Raise from seed, or divide at any time
when in growth. From well-drained
neutral to alkaline grasslands and scrub
in the British Isles, from Norway to
Spain, Turkey, and eastern Siberia.
↕6–10 in (15–25 cm). Z3–8 H8–1.
'Katy McSparron' Fully double-
flowered, with deep yellow flowers
and an expanded, grayish calyx.
Division only. **'Sunset Shades'** A
mixture of red and orange flowers.
Red-flowered cowslips have derived
from backcrossing to *P.* x *polyantha*
and are sometimes informally called
Canadian cowslip.

P. vialii (Muscarioides) (Red-hot poker
primula) Deciduous, relatively short-
lived perennial, the erect, softly hairy,
spear-shaped leaves are pale green and
have inrolled margins. The green stems,
lacking hairs but mealy toward the top,
bear compact spikes of 30–120, small,
lilac flowers in midsummer; each calyx
is brilliant red, so that the unopened
buds give the flowering spike a red tip.
Best planted in groups in fertile,
moisture-retentive, sheltered sites in the
open or in part-shade. Emerges very
late, so the place should be marked.
Good seed is usually set when grown
in groups, and this is the only feasible
means of propagation. Often treated
as a biennial in warm, dry areas,
but when suited in cool, humid
conditions can be relatively long-
lived, flowering for 10 years or more.
A quite extraordinary plant and worth
any trouble to maintain. Becoming rare
in meadows, pasture, and scrub in
western China. ↕12–18 in (30–45 cm).
Z5–8 H8–5

P. Victorians Series (Primula) Large
flowered, usually ruffled polyanthus, the

flowers have a silky or velvet texture, yellow eyes of varying sizes, and green leaves. Various groups of colors are available: **Carnation Victorians Group** Carmine, cerise, and hydrangea pinks; **Fuchsia Victorians Group** Reds, pinks, and purples, some with a silver edge on the petal; **Mauve Victorians Group** Purple and mauve shades; **Muted Victorians Group** Relatively tall, smoke gray or frosted sepia tones; **Old Rose Victorians Group** Rose pink shades; **Striped Victorians Group** see P. Striped Victorians Group; **Valentine Victorians Group** Pinks with a white center, dwarf; **Violet Victorians Group** Shades of violet, plum, or damson. For any good soil that does not dry out. Not to be confused with the Victoriana Series of Gold-laced Polyanthus. From Barnhaven (see panel, p.392). Division. ‡8 in (20 cm). Z4–8 H8–1

P. vulgaris (Primula) (Primrose) Early spring flowering evergreen, sometimes dormant in summer, the low, arching, wrinkled, mid-green, oblong foliage is rounded at the tip and gently narrowed to the stalk. The upward facing, flat-faced flowers, 1–1½ in (2.5–4 cm) across, are borne independently on shaggily hairy stalks and may be yellow, pink, or white, usually with a yellow eye. Best in heavy soil and dislikes exposure, sun-baked sites, waterlogging, or sandy or very acidic soil. When growing well, will seed around and even become invasive; good for naturalizing in woodlands or shaded grasslands. When conditions are hot and dry in summer, can disappear for up to six months, apparently without harm. Best from seed, which can be saved, but can be quickly distributed by ants. Can be divided after flowering, but often becomes infected with viruses. From deciduous woodlands, banks, and shaded grassland in Britain, southern Norway, and northern Spain to northern Africa, Lebanon, Iran, and the Caucasus. ‡6 in (15 cm). Z4–8 H8–1. **var. *alba*** White flowers. Most white flowered primroses are subsp. *sibthorpii*. **'Alba Plena'** Double white flowers; an ancient name, though the plants grown may be of more recent origin. Division only. **Hose-in-hose Group** see P. hose-in-hose.

Jack-in-the-Green Group *see* P. Jack-in-the-Green. **'Lilacina Plena'** syn. 'Quaker's Bonnet' A beautiful old variety with tightly double, pinkish lilac flowers; still vigorous. Division only. **subsp. *sibthorpii*** Flowers pink or occasionally white. From eastern Mediterranean to the Caucasus. **'Viridis'** Flower a dirty green. An old, unusual, but weak form. Division only.

P. **'Wanda'** (Primula/Prim) Prolific, with golden-centered, vivid purple flowers and purple-flushed leaves. Well known, popular, and generally resilient, but not always as vigorous as formerly. Best in full light and thrives in most sites with good soil that does not dry out. Division. ‡4–6 in (10–15 cm). Z3–8 H8–1

P. **'Wanda Hose-in-Hose'** (Primula/Prim) A hose-in-hose version of 'Wanda' with the calyx transformed into petals, resulting in one vivid purple flower presented inside the other. Best in full light and grows well in most sites with a good soil that does not dry out. Division. ‡4–6 in (10–15 cm). Z4–8 H8–1

P. **'Wanda Jack-in-the-Green'** (Primula/Prim) A Jack-in-the-green version of 'Wanda', with an enlarged purplish green calyx surrounding the vivid purple flower. Best in full light and thrives in most sites in good soil that does not dry out. Division. ‡4–6 in (10–15 cm). Z3–8 H8–1

P. **Wanda Group**, *P.* **Wanda hybrids**, *P.* **Wanda Series** (Primula/Prim) Plants offered under these names are now usually Wanda Supreme Series, or plants derived from them, and have little or no connection with *P.* 'Wanda'.

P. **Wanda Supreme Series** (Primula/Prim) Compact, large-flowered primroses, some with neat, rounded flowers and some with notched petals, in eighteen separate colors and a mixture, most with dark green or

RIGHT 1 *Primula viallii* **2** *P. vulgaris* **3** *P. vulgaris* 'Alba Plena' **4** *P. vulgaris* subsp. *sibthorpii*

DOUBLES—GONE AND BACK AGAIN

Double primroses have always turned up occasionally in the wild; they are recorded in the earliest literature and have always had a special place in the hearts of gardeners. In the nineteenth century, named doubles began to appear in France and Ireland; 'Marie Crousse', introduced in about 1880, is one of the best known. Doubles became more widely available when Florence Bellis used pollen from 'Marie Crousse' to pollinate selected single-flowered plants, and when she retired, she had 340 doubles in flower, primrose and polyanthus types.

The old doubles tended to decline because they were overpropagated and also became infected with virus, which reduced their vigor. But seed-raised doubles were further developed by Jared and Sylvia Sinclair and it is from these plants that many of today's best known doubles like 'Captain Blood' and 'Sunshine Susie' were selected. Apart from their inherent beauty, the other feature that caused these particular forms to be selected was their suitability for propagation in the laboratory by tissue culture. As part of this procedure, the debilitating virus is eliminated. The result is that the few cultivars, now so widely available that they can sometimes be seen in home improvement stores and mass markets, start their life in the garden with increased vigor, but may eventually become infected.

bronzed foliage. Bred for hardiness as an overwintered bedding plant by the British bedding plant breeder Floranova. Division. ‡6 in (15 cm). Z5–8 H8–5

P. wilsonii (Proliferae) Aromatic, evergreen perennial with smooth, shiny, dark green, arching, oblong leaves with small, blunt teeth. Green stems, lacking hairs or meal, bear two to five clusters of small, cup-shaped, dark red to blackish, golden-eyed flowers on short stalks in midsummer. Requires fertile, moist soil in a sheltered position and dislikes being too waterlogged in winter; can be killed by freeze-thaw cycles. Not easy or vigorous, so not often seen in gardens, but can be lovely when well grown. Usually short-lived and propagated mainly from seed. From wet meadows above 8,100 ft (2,500 m) in western China. ‡20–36 in (50–90 cm). Z5–8 H8–5. **var. anisodora** syn. *P. anisodora* Flowers blackish, slender, greenish ring around the center.

P. 'Winter White' see *P.* 'Gigha'. Not to be confused with Barnhaven's Winter White Group.

P. **You and Me Series** (Primula) Hose-in-hose polyanthus in five colors (white, cream, yellow, rose pink with a faint white edge, and red with a bright white edge). Offered as seed or seed-raised plants, but good forms can be divided. For any good soil that does not dry out. Division. ‡6 in (15 cm). Z3–8 H8–1

PROSARTES *see* DISPORUM

PRUNELLA
Self-heal
LAMIACEAE

Adaptable and vigorous low ground cover with decorative flowers loved by bees over a long period in summer.

About 7 species of semi-evergreen plants from Africa, Asia, Europe, and North America, the two European species are found in grassy places, woodland clearings, and wasteland and are commonly cultivated, though one, *P. vulgaris*, mostly as a medicinal herb (and lawn weed). With short rhizomes and prostrate stems that often root at intervals along their length, self-heals soon form spreading mats of small, oval leaves. Leafy, square-edged stems rise above the basal foliage, holding aloft short, stout flower spikes with clusters of sagelike, two-lipped flowers projecting beyond a dense core of calyces and broad, rounded bracts, which are both often tinged maroon. Species grown together may hybridize.

CULTIVATION Thrives in moist soil in sun or light shade; they dislike summer drought.

PROPAGATION Generally by division.

PROBLEMS Usually trouble-free.

P. grandiflora Forms dense, creeping patches of dark green, narrowly oval leaves up to 3½ in (9 cm) long and 1½ in (4 cm) wide, with edges smooth or scalloped. In bloom from early to late summer, the upright, oblong spikes are crowded with rich purple-lipped flowers, 1–1¼ in (2.5–3 cm) long. Distinguished from the similar but smaller-leaved *P. vulgaris* by the absence of leaves attached immediately below the flower spikes. Remove spent flowers to prevent prolific self-seeding. Cultivars have more luxuriant growth and flowers in a range of shades. Found usually in dryish, alkaline soil in continental Europe northward to southern Sweden and central Russia. ‡6–12 in (15–30 cm). Z5–7 H8–5. **'Alba'** Creamy white flowers. **'Blue Loveliness'** Purple-blue flowers. **'Loveliness'** Pale lilac flowers. **'Pagoda'** Mixture in purples, pinks and whites; will flower in the first year from seed **'Pink Loveliness'** Soft pink flowers. **'Rosea'** Pink flowers. **'White Loveliness'** White flowers.

PSEUDOTRILLIUM *see* TRILLIUM

PTEROCEPHALUS
DIPSACACEAE

Flowers and foliage combine to create a delightful color combination in a single plant.

Approximately 25 species of annuals, perennials, and shrubs from the Mediterranean region to eastern Asia, only one of which is widely grown. Their opposite pairs of leaves may be simple or variously toothed or lobed. Flowerheads, much like those of the closely related *Scabiosa*, are displayed well above the foliage.

CULTIVATION Grows well in all free-draining soils in sunny situations.

PROPAGATION From seed or cuttings.

PROBLEMS Usually trouble-free.

P. parnassii see *P. perennis*

P. perennis syn. *P. parnassii* A cushion-forming perennial making 12-in- (30-cm-) wide cushions of 1¼–2-in (3–5-cm), oval, densely borne, gray-hairy leaves with rounded, shallow teeth and often short, lateral lobes. Pink to rose-purple flowerheads, up to 1½ in (4 cm) across, freely spangle the foliage in summer. From Greece and Albania. ‡4–6 in (10–15 cm). Z5–7 H7–5

PULMONARIA
Lungwort
BORAGINACEAE

Popular ground-cover plants, often with striking foliage and flowers in a range of colors.

Between 10 and 18 species, according to different estimates, of semi-evergreen or deciduous perennial plants, widely distributed in mainly shady places in woodlands and mountains in Europe and western Asia. These are hairy plants, forming clumps or rosettes, and sometimes bearing glands that make them sticky to touch.

Relatively slowly creeping, compact rhizomes support basal leaves arranged in rosettes, the leaf blades are usually large, from narrowly lance-shaped to oval, with the base shape ranging from heart-shaped to very gradually narrowing; they can have a sharply pointed or blunt tip. The margin is never divided or toothed, but may be wavy, the stalks can be short or longer than the leaf blade. The stem leaves are smaller and often relatively narrow compared with the basal leaves, and are unstalked or clasping the stem. All leaves are rough and covered with hairs that are usually bristly but sometimes soft. The leaves are often covered in prominent spots, which can be the main decorative feature of these plants,

most frequently in silvery white, or sometimes in pale green. In some cultivars the silver marking is so strong that it covers most or all of the leaf. The basal leaves often enlarge in summer, after flowering.

The flowering stems are upright or somewhat sprawling, unbranched, rough, covered with bristly hairs, and usually not exceeding 10–12 in (25–30 cm). The flowers are carried in short, somewhat leafy terminal clusters, which elongate a little when in fruit. The main flowering time is spring, although some begin flowering in late winter, and a few forms occasionally continue into early summer. The funnel-shaped flower consists of a long, cylindrical, bell-shaped tube-opening with five shallow lobes, the tube partly concealed by a hairy calyx.

There are two distinct forms of flower (*see* Pin and Thrum in Pulmonarias, *p.398*): those with short stamens and long styles ("pin" flowers), and those with long stamens and short styles ("thrum" flowers), the former usually being larger and more showy. Flower colors range from purple, violet, or blue to shades of pink and red, or sometimes white. The buds are usually pink, the color changing as the flowers open and mature. These color transformations are thought to give a cue to pollinating insects, and the flowers offer a valuable nectar source for early-flying bumblebees. Hummingbirds may also visit.

Many new introductions have arisen as self-sown seedlings and been spotted by sharp-eyed gardeners and nurserymen. More recently, Dan Heims at Terra Nova Nurseries in Oregon, in particular, has run a thoughtful breeding program with mildew-resistance as an important goal.

Most pulmonarias are very hardy,

BELOW 1 *Prunella grandiflora*
2 *Pterocephalus perennis*

especially under snow cover. Semi-evergreen species and cultivars may lose their leaves in harsh weather but should recover in spring. In warmer areas or very dry conditions, most pulmonarias suffer.

CULTIVATION The great majority of pulmonarias are very shade-tolerant, and some will even grow in heavy shade, though the flower display is likely to be reduced. A few are reasonably tolerant of full sun, including P. 'Blue Ensign', P. 'Glacier', P. 'Mary Mottram', P. officinalis Cambridge Blue Group, P. longifolia, and P. mollis.

They are tolerant of most soils, except those that are continuously wet, and are especially useful in heavy clay, though their preference is for reasonably fertile, humus-rich soil that is not too dry. Most tolerate an alkaline soil. Good soil preparation prior to planting is wise; regular thorough watering during the first season will aid good establishment. Apply an annual mulch of leaf mold, composted bark, or other organic material. All make excellent ground cover in dappled shade under trees and shrubs, forming noninvasive, neat clumps of handsome leaves.

Vigorous pulmonarias, such as P. 'Barfield Regalia' and P. rubra, should be divided every four to five years, but others do not need to be split and replanted as often.

PROPAGATION Pulmonarias can be propagated from seed, or by division, and root cuttings. No Pulmonaria cultivar will ever come true from seed, so this propagation method is only used for species grown in isolation. Self-sown seedlings often turn up but they will be variable.

Division is the easiest method: clumps are divided after flowering or in fall. Some can be divided into many pieces, while others increase much more slowly. Small divisions are best potted and kept shaded for fall planting; larger divisions can be planted straight into the ground. Pulmonarias originating from P. longifolia and P. saccharata can also be propagated by root cuttings in fall. Cut strong-looking young roots into sections about 2 in (5 cm) long, insert in deep trays or pots of free-draining potting mix, and overwinter in a cool frost-free place.

PROBLEMS Powdery mildew. Can also be affected by viruses, aphids, caterpillars, sawflies, slugs, and snails.

P. angustifolia There is much confusion regarding the identity of this plant, since the plant widely grown as P. angustifolia is almost certainly not the true species. The familiar plant is a more or less deciduous, sparsely hairy

LEFT 1 Pulmonaria angustifolia subsp. azurea **2** P. 'Barfield Regalia' **3** P. 'Cotton Cool'

POWDERY MILDEW

The most widespread problem with pulmonarias is powdery mildew. A powdery white growth coats the leaf surfaces, beginning with isolated patches, which eventually merge, and may also rise on to the stems, stem leaves, and even into the flowerheads. Although it is rare for plants to be killed, they can be disfigured and cease to be attractive in the garden, and may also be weakened so that growth and flowering is restricted.

Powdery mildew is especially prevalent in hot, dry conditions—the combination of high temperatures, low soil moisture, and low humidity quickly encourages infection. Planting in shade and keeping the soil moist can be good preventatives. Fungicides often have little impact, partly because the rough surface of the leaves prevents even distribution of the spray. Many gardeners simply cut off the infected leaves, or even remove the foliage entirely—but this must be followed by thorough watering and plenty of liquid fertilizer. Some cultivars, especially some new American introductions, are said to be resistant and these include 'Apple Frost', 'Cotton Cool', 'Excalibur', P. longifolia subsp. cevennensis, 'Margery Fish', 'Milky Way', 'Moonshine', and 'Victorian Brooch'.

plant, forming many small clumps of elliptical to lance-shaped to narrowly oval, plain green leaves. The ¾-in (1.8-cm), bright blue flowers are produced from early to mid-spring. Prefers light shade and moist, well-drained soil from acidic to neutral; in alkaline soil, may suffer from chlorosis. Easily divided. The true species is more extensively softly hairy, with narrow, lance-shaped leaves and narrower flowers produced from mid-spring into summer and is very rare in gardens. The origin of this impostor is unclear. ↕10–12 in (25–30 cm). Z2–7 H7–1. **subsp. azurea** Dark green, unspotted, leaves and bright blue flowers opening from pink buds. ↕10–12 in (25–30 cm). **'Blaues Meer'** Long, unspotted, 12-in (30-cm), dark green leaves and large, bright blue flowers, freely produced. From German breeder Ernst Pagels. ↕12 in (30 cm). **'Munstead Blue'** Smallish leaves, lighter than other cultivars; earlier, clear blue flowers. From Gertrude Jekyll. ↕6 in (15 cm).

P. 'Apple Frost' Semi-evergreen, fresh green leaves are heavy mottled in silver; rose pink flowers in spring. Said to be resistant to mildew. Introduced by Oregon's Terra Nova Nurseries in 1997. ↕10–12 in (25–30 cm). Z4–8 H8–1

P. 'Barfield Regalia' Vigorous semi-evergreen plant, with narrow leaves to 18 in (45 cm) long on 8-in (20-cm) stalks, each leaf with a small number of more or less regularly spaced, pale green spots, or may be almost unspotted. Flowers "pin," large, violet-blue to dark blue, borne in branched clusters on upright stems in early

spring. A very distinct plant that is probably one of the best purple-blue-flowered cultivars. Named by English plantsman Richard Nutt, who originally obtained it from the garden of Margery Fish. ↕12–18 in (30–45 cm). Z4–8 H8–1

P. 'Beth's Blue' syn. *P.* 'Cedric Morris' Distinct, compact, semi-evergreen with dark green, 13-x-4¾-in (32-x-12-cm) leaves sparsely spotted with pale green. Flowers "pin," in rich blue with no hint of pink, carried in tight clusters on upright stems. Perhaps a hybrid between *P. longifolia* and *P. affinis,* from Beth Chatto's garden in Essex, England. ↕12 in (30 cm). Z4–8 H8–1

P. 'Beth's Pink' syn. *P.* 'Beth Chatto's Red' Semievergreen; oval, 10-x-4-in (25-x-10-cm) leaves narrow abruptly into stalks and heavily spotted with whitish or very pale green. Flowers "pin," coral red, acquiring a slight tinge of violet as they age, borne in mid- to late spring. Possibly a *P. affinis* hybrid, from Beth Chatto's garden in England. ↕10 in (25 cm). Z5–8 H8–5

P. 'Blauer Hugel' Compact semi-evergreen with long, narrow leaves bearing a few evenly spaced spots. Flowers clear blue, freely produced in spring. Similar to *P.* 'Little Star'. From Ernst Pagels in Germany. ↕12 in (30 cm). Z4–8 H8–1

P. 'Blue Crown' Vigorous, semi-evergreen with narrow, dark green leaves, with a few bold, large spots. Flowers are dark blue or violet-blue, and freely produced in spring. Does not flower well in deep shade. Can be susceptible to mildew. A tough and long-lived hybrid of *P. longifolia* from Dutch breeder Piet Oudolf. ↕10–12 in (25–30 cm). Z4–8 H8–1

P. 'Blue Ensign' Vigorous, deciduous plant with broad, very dark green, unspotted leaves to 10 in (25 cm) long. Flowers are "pin," large, rich blue or blue-violet, in compact clusters on more or less upright stems in spring. One of the showiest cultivars, and one of the best deep-blue-flowered forms. Like *Ranunculus ficaria* 'Ken Aslet Double', found in Bowles' Corner of the Royal Horticultural Society Garden Wisley, England. Tolerant of sun, but can be susceptible to mildew. ↕10–12 in (25–30 cm). Z5–8 H8–5

P. 'Blue Moon' see *P. officinalis* 'Blue Mist'

P. 'Blue Pearl' Deciduous with rounded, unspotted leaves, the "thrum" flowers are pure blue, a little lighter than in the similar *P.* 'Mawson's Blue' with which it may be confused. One of the older cultivars and probably a hybrid of *P. angustifolia*. ↕8–12 in (20–30 cm). Z4–8 H8–1

P. 'Cedric Morris' see *P.* 'Beth's Blue'

P. 'Chintz' Unusual, with mid-green leaves that have sparse or moderate pale green spotting. The "thrum" flowers are

SURPRISES IN THE SHADE

TO GARDENERS INTERESTED in perennials for the first time, pulmonarias simply have spotted leaves and celandines are infuriating weeds. Here we prove that this is by no means always the case. The clean, fresh, plain green foliage of *Pulmonaria angustifolia* is never spotted and makes a bright background for the sparkling blue spring flowers. Growing alongside is *Ranunculus ficaria* 'Brazen Hussy', a form of celandine rarely seen in the wild area or as a weed among the roses. This was the first of the celandines with attractive foliage, its deep bronze leaves setting off the sunny, brassy yellow flowers wonderfully. Although without the infuriating weediness of its wild cousins, 'Brazen Hussy' does self-sow, and the foliage of its seedlings may be greener and less effective.

carried in tight clusters on short stems; each is bicolored with five, broad, pink stripes, one on each lobe against a white background, that turn purple and finally blue. Usually there is a white vein in the center of the stripe, dividing it in two. Found in Jennifer Hewitt's garden in Shropshire, England, as a seedling of *P. officinalis* and introduced by Elizabeth Strangman at Washfield Nursery, Kent, England. ↕6–10 in (15–25 cm). Z4–8 H8–1

P. 'Cotton Cool' Semievergreen with long, narrow, tapered leaves held more or less upright and completely silver, sometimes with a dark green margin. The flowers are blue and pink, carried in dense clusters. Tolerant of drought. A good long-lived plant, one of the best for foliage, and a hybrid of *P. longifolia* raised by *Hosta* and *Hemerocallis* expert Diana Grenfell of Hampshire, England. ↕8–12 in (20–30 cm). Z4–8 H8–1

P. 'De Vroomen's Pride' Leaves near-white with a narrow green edge; the

flowers blue fading to pink. Similar to a number of other cultivars and perhaps the same as 'Reginald Kaye'. ↕10–16 in (25–40 cm). Z4–8 H8–1

P. 'Diana Clare' Decorative semi-evergreen with long, pointed, silver-green leaves and large, violet-blue flowers that have a longitidinal purple stripe between the lobes. Bob Brown at Cotswold Garden Flowers, Worcestershire, England, raised and introduced this hybrid of *P. longifolia*, and named for his wife. ↕8–12 in (20–30 cm). Z4–8 H8–1

P. 'Dora Bielefeld' Bright green leaves are lightly spotted in pale silvery green, and the large, clear pink, "pin" flowers open from coral pink buds. This may be the best pink-flowered cultivar among the older cultivars, but it is often incorrectly listed as a form of *P. saccharata*. ↕10–12 in (25–30 cm). Z4–8 H8–1

P. 'Excalibur' Vigorous, with silver

leaves having a narrow, dark green margin: the flowers, freely produced in spring, open from coral pink buds, becoming light blue. Can scorch in full sun and does not tolerate drying out, so requires shade and continuously moist soil. A seedling of 'Margery Fish' from Terra Nova Nurseries, OR. ↕8–12 in (20–30 cm). Z4–8 H8–1

P. 'Glacier' An attractive semi-evergreen, the 6-x-3-in (15-x-8-cm) leaves are lightly spotted in pale yellowish green, widen abruptly at base, with stalks about twice as long as leaves. Flowers are "pin," large, and borne on spreading stems in spring; they open from pink buds and turn a very pale blue, sometimes also palest pink or white on the same plant. Found in a garden in Surrey, England. Can tolerate sun if the soil is moist. ↕8–12 in (20–30 cm). Z4–8 H8–1

P. 'Highdown' see *P.* 'Lewis Palmer'

P. 'Lewis Palmer' syn. *P.* 'Highdown'

Vigorous, with long, narrow, dark green leaves that are about twice as long as their stalks. They are strongly spotted and blotched with conspicuous, greenish white spots over up to half the leaf surface. Flowers are large, rich violet-blue, facing mostly upward and outward, in spring. Perhaps a hybrid of *P. longifolia*, named for a famous English horticulturist. ↕12–14 in (30–35 cm). Z5–8 H8–5

P. 'Little Star' Compact, with narrowly lance-shaped, short leaves with a few small, silvery spots. The flowers change from dusky pink in bud to cobalt blue, freely produced on short stems over a long period in spring. A seedling of *P. longifolia* 'Bertram Anderson', from Oregon's Terra Nova Nurseries. ↕6–8 in (15–20 cm). Z4–8 H8–1

P. longifolia Attractive, semi-evergreen, clump-forming, slightly bristly plant, with narrowly lance-shaped, usually conspicuously white-spotted leaves, reaching up to 16 in (40 cm) or even 24 in (60 cm) in length. The flowers are funnel shaped, ⅜–⅝ in (8–12 mm) long, turning from pink to violet or bright blue, and borne in dense clusters in spring. Tolerates full sun better than most, and will not grow well in heavy shade. Prefers moisture-retentive soil, but can tolerate some drought. From western Europe. ↕8–16 in (20–40 cm). Z3–8 H8–4. **'Ankum'** syn. 'Coen Jansen' Compact plant, forming a good mound of narrow, wavy-margined, very silvery leaves to 12 in (30 cm) long. The small flowers are bright violet-blue. From Dutch breeder Coen Jansen. ↕12–13 in (30–34 cm). **'Bertram Anderson'** Long, narrow, dark green leaves are spotted silver, the flowers small, but vivid blue. Named for the Gloucestershire, England, horticulturist

PIN AND THRUM IN PULMONARIAS

Pulmonarias are like primulas: the flowers contain both male and female parts but come arranged in two different ways. In the flowers on some plants you will see that the stigma (the female part) is prominent; this is because the style that supports it is long. These flowers are termed "pin," since the stigma looks like a pinhead. In the flowers on other plants, the style is shorter, so the stigma is more hidden behind a ring of anthers (male parts) in the throat of the flower. These flowers are described as "thrum."

This arrangement has three horticultural consequences. First, in general, plants with "pin" flowers tend to have larger and more showy flowers. Second, this arrangement facilitates cross-pollination rather than self-pollination, so self-sown seedlings around the garden are likely to be hybrids between two different plants and thus variable. Third, the nature of the flower can help identify otherwise similar cultivars: 'Barfield Ruby' is a pin, while the otherwise very similar 'Redstart' is a thrum.

RIGHT 1 *Pulmonaria* 'Glacier'
2 *P.* 'Lewis Palmer' **3** *P. mollis*

E. B. Anderson. ↕10–12 in (25–30 cm). **subsp. cevennensis** Very long, heavily silvered leaves reach almost 24 in (60 cm). From Cevennes, France. ↕12 in (30 cm). **'Coen Jansen'** see 'Ankum'. **'Dordogne'** Larger, lance-shaped leaves are well-spotted in silver-white with blue flowers borne on upright stems. Originally wild-collected in France, introduced by Kent's Washfield Nurseries, England. ↕12–18 in (30–45 cm).

P. 'Majesté' Leaves are shiny and almost completely silver with a fine green margin; the flowers are pink, then turning blue. Does best in shade, but will withstand more sun with ample moisture. Can be difficult to grow on drier soil. One of the earlier silvery-leaved pulmonarias, from La Ferme Fleurie Nursery in France. ↕8–12 in (20–30 cm). Z4–8 H8–1

P. 'Margery Fish' Long, narrow leaves are spotted to almost completely silver, the flowers opening from pink buds and turning blue in early spring. Mildew-resistant; the parent of many recent American introductions. Originated with Margery Fish, often listed as a form of *P. vallarsae*, but more likely to be a hybrid of *P. saccharata*. ↕12 in (30 cm). Z4–8 H8–1

P. 'Mary Mottram' syn. *P.* 'Wendy Perry' Large, 12 x 4 in (30 x 10 cm) leaves on stalks up to 9 in (22 cm) long are almost completely covered in silver at the base, apart from a narrow green margin, and the stem leaves are densely spotted. The large, "pin" flowers are violet-blue, with brown calyces, produced early. The very similar 'Wendy Perry' is sometimes listed separately and is said to be a more vigorous and floriferous. Tolerant of full sun. Grown by Mary Mottram in her Devon Nursery in England. ↕12 in (30 cm). Z4–8 H8–1

P. 'Mawson's Blue' syn. *P.* 'Mawson's Variety' Deciduous, with plain dark green, unspotted leaves; the rich dark blue "thrum" flowers appear fairly late. It appears that the original 'Mawson's Blue' cultivar, which first appeared in a Cumbria, England, nursery during the 1930s, was a different plant from the one now grown under this name—it was probably a hybrid of *P. angustifolia*. ↕8–12 in (20–30 cm). Z4–8 H8–1

P. 'Merlin' Neat, compact, semi-evergreen; with lance-shaped leaves that are variably spotted bright silvery green, sometimes almost completely covered. Flowers "pin," pale pink to pale blue. A hybrid of *P. longifolia,* from the garden of horticulturist Valerie Finnis, founder, the Merlin Trust, in Northamptonshire, England. ↕8–12 in (20–30 cm). Z4–8 H8–1

P. 'Milchstrasse' (**Milky Way**) Large, lance-shaped leaves are heavily spotted

with silver. Blue flowers open from wine red buds and later fade to pink. A hybrid of 'Margery Fish' from Oregon's Terra Nova Nurseries. ↕12 in (30 cm). Z4–8 H8–1

P. Milky Way see *P.* 'Milchstrasse'

P. **mollis** Impressive, deciduous, clump-forming plant with very long, plain dark green, softly hairy leaves to 24 in (60 cm), oval to more or less lance-shaped and held upright at first. Large, funnel-shaped flowers are rich blue, often fading to purplish pink, produced in spring; sticky with glandular hairs. Grows best in light to moderate shade. Prefers moist soil, but tolerates drying out better than other pulmonarias. The largest of all pulmonarias; excellent ground cover although needs plenty of space. From central and southeastern Europe, Central Asia, Siberia, Mongolia, and China. ↕18–24 in (45–60 cm). Z6–8 H8–6

P. **'Moonshine'** Leaves are rounded, silvery white with thin dark green margins and the smallish flowers are pale blue. From Oregon's Terra Nova Nurseries. ↕8 in (20 cm). Z4–8 H8–1

P. **'Moonstone'** Semi-evergreen, with decorative, heavily spotted leaves and white flowers becoming very pale blue-gray. Introduced by Carol Klein of Devon's Glebe Cottage Plants, England. ↕12 in (30 cm). Z4–8 H8–1

P. **'Mrs. Kittle'** Neat and upright in habit. Narrow leaves, to about 6 in (15 cm) long, long-stalked, spotted and blotched in silvery white. The "pin" flowers are very pale pink, opening from pink buds and gradually turning pale lavender. Found at a small nursery at Kittle in Wales and popularized by Dutch horticulturist Coen Jansen. ↕9–12 in (22–30 cm). Z4–8 H8–1

P. **officinalis** (Lungwort) Clump-forming, semi-evergreen with roughly hairy, variably white-spotted, oval to heart-shaped leaves. Bright rose pink flowers, turning to purple and blue, are borne in clusters in spring. The oldest species in cultivation, known in gardens since the 16th century, when it was grown as a medicinal herb. Found in much of Europe. ↕6–8 in (15–20 cm). Z6–8 H8–6. **'Blue Mist'** syn. *P. officinalis* 'Bowles' Blue', *P.* 'Blue Moon' Leaves spotted whitish green with large, very pale, clear blue "pin" flowers opening from lavender-tinged buds. Originally from Amy Doncaster, introduced by Elizabeth Strangman of Washfield Nurseries, England. There may be more than one plant sold under this name. **Cambridge Blue Group** Heart-shaped, spotted leaves with very freely produced pale blue "thrum" flowers, pink-tinged in bud. Tolerant of sun as long as the soil is kept moist. A number of similar plants are offered as 'Cambridge Blue', so they are all best classified as Cambridge Blue Group. Another originally from Amy Doncaster via Kent's Washfield Nurseries. ↕10–14 in (25–35 cm). **'White Wings'** Silver-spotted leaves

RIGHT 1 *Pulmonaria* Opal **2** *P.* 'Roy Davidson' **3** *P. rubra* 'David Ward' **4** *P. rubra* 'Redstart'

with late, white "pin" flowers, each with a distinct pink eye. Sometimes confused with *P.* 'Sissinghurst White' but distinct in its pink eye, pinker calyces, and more compact habit; it is also less susceptible to mildew. ↕10–12 in (25–30 cm).

P. **Opal** ('Ocupol') Excellent semi-evergreen with narrow, well-spotted leaves, the flowers open from palest pink buds, turning to luminous pale blue. Possibly a *P. saccharata* hybrid. ↕10 in (25 cm). Z4–8 H8–1

P. **'Paul Aden'** see *P.* 'Reginald Kaye'

P. **'Polar Splash'** Rounded, dark green leaves have bright silver spots and may be tinged purple in winter. Blue flowers fade to pink. From Oregon's Terra Nova Nurseries ↕8–9 in (20–23 cm). Z4–8 H8–1

P. **'Raspberry Splash'** Upright, pointed, dark green leaves with distinct silver spots are held upright, the flowers dark pink, freely produced. A hybrid of *P. longifolia* from Terra Nova Nurseries. ↕12 in (30 cm). Z4–8 H8–1

P. **'Reginald Kaye'** Semi-evergreen; the large, rounded leaves, with larger silver spots in the center and smaller spots at the edge, are very decorative during the summer. The flowers open pink, turning light blue, and are borne in dense clusters. More than one plant may be sold under this name and a number of other very similar plants— 'De Vroomen's Pride', 'Paul Aden', and 'Silver Mist'—should probably be included here. Originated as a seedling from Reginald Kaye's nursery in Lancashire, England, and introduced by Beth Chatto. Often listed as *P. saccharata*, but closer to *P. officinalis*. ↕8–12 in (20–30 cm). Z4–8 H8–1

P. **'Roy Davidson'** Excellent, popular, semievergreen with narrow leaves, lightly spotted in silver. The "pin" flowers, in a distinct pale to mid-blue, fading to pink, are borne in dense clusters. A seedling of *P. longifolia* 'Bertram Anderson' selected by American horticulturist Roy Davidson. ↕12 in (30 cm). Z4–8 H8–1

P. **rubra** (Red lungwort) Semi-evergreen, tufted plant with rosettes of distinctively light green, softly hairy, more or less oval leaves to 6 in (15 cm) long. Coral red flowers are borne in late winter and spring. Needs a moist, shady spot and does not tolerate drying out. From the Balkans, Bulgaria, Romania, the Carpathians, and the Middle East. ↕8–20 in (20–50 cm). Z5–8 H8–3. **var. albocorollata** White flowers, with pale apple green leaves. Cultivated plants are all "thrum," so seedlings are hybrids—and turn out red-flowered. **'Ann'** The leaves have light green spotting; the bright pink-

red, "pin" flowers have white margins and white veins. Vigorous and free-flowering. Selected by John Metcalf of Four Seasons Nursery, Norfolk, England. **'Barfield Pink'** Unspotted, soft green leaves; the "thrum" flowers are bright red, with white margins and white veins. Similar to 'Ann', but less vigorous and prolific. **'Bowles' Red'** Leaves faintly spotted pale green with coral-red flowers. From English horticulturist E. A. Bowles. ↕12 in (30 cm). **'David Ward'** Long, pale green leaves with white margins, the "thrum" flowers are coral-red. Requires a shaded, moist situation. Not easy to grow: less vigorous, the leaves can scorch in sun or wind and plants are susceptible to slug and snail damage. A spontaneous mutation of 'Redstart' originating in Beth Chatto's Essex, England, nursery around 1986, and named after the nursery's propagator. The first of the variegated *Pulmonaria* cultivars to be introduced. ↕12 in (30 cm). **'Rachel Vernie'** Basal leaves soft gray-green with darker green streaks and margins, and some white edges; the stem leaves have a white margin. The "pin" flowers are coral red. More vigorous than the similar 'David Ward' and the leaves do not scorch in full sun. Originated with Shropshire horticulturist Jennifer Hewitt and named for her younger daughter. ↕12 in (30 cm). **'Redstart'** Vigorous and compact with plain, fresh green leaves and large, coral red flowers. Probably not distinct from the species. ↕12–18 in (30–45 cm).

P. saccharata (Bethlehem Sage) Handsome semi-evergreen forming dense clumps of elliptical leaves, to 11 in (27 cm) long, that are strikingly spotted or mottled in silvery white. The ⅝ in (1.8 cm) long flowers open from

BELOW 1 *Pulmonaria saccharata* 'Mrs. Moon' **2** *P.* 'Sissinghurst White'

pink or reddish purple buds and gradually change to sky blue in early and midspring. Easily propagated by root cuttings. Many cultivars are available, but some listed under *P. saccharata* are better placed under *P. officinalis*, or may be hybrids. From southeastern France and northern Italy. ↕12–18 in (30–45 cm). Z4–8 H8–1. **Argentea Group** At their best, leaves become completely silver-gray in late summer; the flowers are pink at first, turning violet-blue. Slightly variable, but always good. Originally from Margery Fish of East Lambrook Manor, Somerset, England. ↕10–12 in (25–30 cm). **'Dora Bielefield'** see *P.* 'Dora Bielefield'. **'Frühlingshimmel'** (**Spring Sky**) Silver-spotted leaves on plants with a slightly running habit, the flowers open wide from pale pink buds into clear blue; the calyx is reddish brown. Perhaps more closely related to *P. officinalis* than *P. saccharata*. Very similar to 'Blauhimmel', if not the same plant, but said to differ by its slightly deeper-colored flowers. ↕8–10 in (20–25 cm). **'Glebe Cottage Blue'** syn. 'Glebe Blue' Well-spotted leaves and blue flowers borne in dense clusters. From Carol Klein at Glebe Cottage Plants, Devon. **'Leopard'** Leaves regularly spotted in silver-white, the flowers reddish pink fading to lavender. Very similar to 'Beth's Pink', 'Diana Chappell', and 'Nürnberg'. Found in the garden of horticulturist and writer Graham Stuart Thomas around 1970. ↕8–12 in (20–30 cm). **'Mrs. Moon'** Silver-spotted leaves that are prone to mildew, but a range of plants are now grown under this name with flowers variously described as "lilac tinted red," "magenta buds with flowers turning blue," and "pink to violet"; they are probably seedlings. It is not clear if the true plant, known since at least the 1930s, is still grown. **'Reginald Kaye'** see *P.* 'Reginald Kaye' **'Silverado'** Leaves oval, silvery gray with a narrow border of dark green. The flowers are

blue, pink, and white. Said to be rust-resistant—though rust is not a widespread problem. ↕14 in (35 cm). **Spring Sky** see 'Frühlingshimmel'.

P. **'Silver Mist'** see *P.* 'Reginald Kaye'

P. **'Silver Shimmers'** Semi-evergreen with large, long, wavy-edged, silver leaves and large, steely blue flowers. ↕8 in (20 cm). Z4–8 H8–1

P. **'Silver Streamers'** Lance-shaped leaves with wavy margins are silver, almost white. Violet-blue flowers open from pink buds; each have a dark calyx. From Oregon's Terra Nova Nurseries. ↕8–10 in (20–25 cm). Z4–8 H8–1

P. **'Sissinghurst White'** Evergreen; silver-spotted leaves and early, pure white flowers. Susceptible to mildew. Sometimes confused with *P. officinalis* 'White Wings', but more vigorous and lacks the pink eye. Probably a hybrid of *P. officinalis*. Distributed by the garden at Sissinghurst Castle, Kent, England, but did not originate there. ↕12 in (30 cm). Z4–8 H8–1

P. **'Smoky Blue'** Vigorous and healthy, the dark green, purple-tinged leaves have light silver spotting. The flowers are an uninteresting, soft dusky pink. Probably a hybrid of *P. officinalis*. ↕10–12 in (25–30 cm). Z4–8 H8–1

P. **'Spilled Milk'** Compact, with mostly silver, mildew-resistant leaves with green margins and few green blotches. Flowers open blue and fade to pink. Another from Terra Nova Nurseries, OR. ↕8–12 in (20–30 cm). Z4–8 H8–1

P. **'Trevi Fountain'** Semievergreen with long, silver-spotted leaves, and large, cobalt blue flowers. From Terra Nova Nurseries, OR. ↕12 in (30 cm). Z4–8 H8–1

P. **'Victorian Brooch'** Unusual, almost

round leaves have large silver spots, the outward facing, magenta-rose pink flowers, set in a dark red calyx, carried on upright stems. From Terra Nova Nurseries. ↕12 in (30 cm). Z4–8 H8–1

P. **'Weetwood Blue'** Long, narrow leaves, with stalks shorter than the blades, are deep green and unspotted or with a few pale green or white spots. The smallish "pin" flowers, borne on upright or spreading stems, open from dark purplish pink buds into intense clear blue. From the Devon, England, garden of Harold and Joan Bawden, probably a hybrid of *P. longifolia*. ↕8 in (20 cm). Z4–8 H8–1

P. **'Wendy Perry'** see *P.* 'Mary Mottram'

PULSATILLA
RANUNCULACEAE

Showy flowers, ferny foliage, and silvery seed heads make a great combination for a sunny border.

Thirty species of deciduous plants growing in grasslands and rocky slopes in the mountains of Europe, North America, and Asia, one of which is widely grown in gardens. Compact clumps of dissected, often hairy leaves arise from a woody rootstock. In spring and early summer, large bell-shaped or starry flowers, with a bold yellow center, open well above the leaves. By summer, these give way to equally attractive, feathery seed heads.

CULTIVATION Grows best in very well-drained, fertile soil in full sun. Dislikes being transplanted and winter dampness.

PROPAGATION From seed sown as soon as ripe; cultivars by basal or root cuttings, but difficult.

PROBLEMS Usually trouble-free.

P. vulgaris (Pasque flower) Compact rootstock produces a tuft of finely dissected, fernlike 1¼–3-in (3–8-cm) leaves, silky when young, and repeatedly split into opposite pairs of slender leaflets. In mid- and late spring, erect stems appear, each bearing a single nodding, bell-shaped, purple flower, 2½–3 in (6–8 cm) across, with long silky hairs on the outsides of the petals and with a bold boss of yellow stamens in the center. As the flowers fade, the stems extend to as much as double the height of the plant and carry attractive, silky seed heads. From short grasslands and mountain meadows in Europe, from eastern England to the Ukraine. ↕6–8 in (15–20 cm). Z5–7 H7–5. **'Alba'** Flowers white. **'Barton's Pink'** Clear pink flowers and light green leaves. **'Blaue Glocke'** Lilac-blue flowers. **'Eva Constance'** Compact, with deep red flowers in late spring and early summer. ↕4–6 in (10–15 cm). subsp. *grandis* **'Papageno'** Leaves more finely dissected and silkier, developing after the flowers; flowers to 3½ in (9 cm)

LEFT **1** *Pulsatilla vulgaris*
2 *P. vulgaris* 'Alba'

across, with a variable number of extra petals, ranging from violet-blue to reddish and white. ↕ 8 in (20 cm). **'Röde Klokke'** Flowers deep red. **var. rubra** Flowers from rusty red to purplish red. **'Weisser Schwan'** White flowers, selected form of 'Alba'.

PUYA
BROMELIACEAE

Evergreen, unusually tough bromeliads grown for their exotic, architectural qualities and often spectacular flower spikes.

About 170 species grow on rocky hillsides or scree slopes in dry terrain in the Andes, between northern Chile and Colombia. Some are giants, 30 ft (10 m) high when in flower; others rarely exceed 12 in (30 cm). They form clumps of rosettes of tough, long, narrow, often viciously barbed or toothed leaves, usually blue-green above and silvery underneath; individual rosettes die after flowering.

The flowers, usually carried in branched flowerheads from the center of the rosettes, may be huge, towering structures. Individual bell-shaped blooms have three petals, usually white, green, or violet, and may be followed by green seed capsules. In the wild, plants are often pollinated by hummingbirds.

Growing at higher levels than other bromeliads, many are cold-tolerant, and some will grow outside in frost-prone areas, especially if some winter protection is provided. Few species are widely cultivated, but increasing interest in the genus and demand for bold, architectural, spiky plants such as these, especially when they display a degree of drought-tolerance—is gradually

allowing more to be introduced.

CULTIVATION Excellent drainage and full sun in an open site helps plants overwinter, especially in marginal areas. Grows well on slopes, as it is found in the wild, and is also suitable for gravel gardens in sheltered sites in any type of well-drained soil. They also do well in maritime areas. However, because of their barbed foliage, these bromeliads are best planted well away from path edges. They can also be grown in pots, but ensure adequate drainage; in addition, the pot should be moved to a frost-free place in winter.

PROPAGATION Sow ripe seed at 68°F (20°C). Can take years to flower.

PROBLEMS Usually trouble-free.

P. alpestris Clump-forming rosettes, up to 3¼ ft (1 m) in width, are made up of narrow, gently arching, gray-green leaves, silver-white beneath, up to 24 in (60 cm) long and about ¾ in (2 cm) wide. The leaf edges are lined with sharp, hooked teeth. Mature plants throw up columns of flowers on bold, reddish stems; the individual flowers are bell-shaped and an incredible metallic sapphire blue color, overlaid with a greenish shine. Relatively hardy and easy to grow in a sunny border, but also does well in a container. From arid, high altitude areas, often in coastal regions, of Chile. ↕ 5 ft (1.5 m). Z9–11 H11–9

P. chilensis Forms a tough woody base

to the clumps of large rosettes, which are composed of tough, long, straight, pointed, green leaves that reach 3¼ ft (1 m) in length and 2½ in (6 cm) across and are edged with sharp spines. The soaring flower spikes appear in summer; the 2 in (5 cm) long individual flowers are bell-shaped and a startling greenish yellow in color. The plants are self-sterile. This is one of the larger species that can be considered as reasonably hardy in temperate regions. From central Chile. ↕ 12 ft (4 m). Z9–11 H11–1

P. coerulea A variable species but generally developing clumps of rosettes up to 6½ ft (2 m) across, each rosette supported on a stout stem. The grayish green leaves, which are paler beneath, are up to 24 in (60 cm) long and are edged with reddish, hooked barbs. The upright, tubular flowers are shiny, dark blue, and produced in branched heads. From Chile. ↕ 6½ ft (2 m). Z9–11 H11–9

P. mirabilis Rosettes of long and narrow, almost grassy, silvery green leaves, to 24 in (60 cm) long and ¾ in (2 cm) wide, edged with fine spines that are less sharp than in some other species. In summer, fairly slender stems carry large, nodding and tubular flowers in a pale silvery green with protruding yellow-tipped stamens and a dark calyx. The spike is one-sided and blooms are produced more sparsely than in many species, giving it a more graceful look. Adapts well to large containers. One of the smaller ones of this group, and more manageable than many of the others. From high altitude regions of Argentina and Bolivia. ↕ 3–5 ft (1–1.5 m). Z9–11 H11–7

PYRETHROPSIS *see* RHODANTHEMUM
PYRETHRUM *see* TANACETUM

RIGHT 1 *Puya chilensis* **2** *P. mirabilis*

R

RANUNCULUS
Buttercup
RANUNCULACEAE

Varied, easy spring and summer flowers for moist sites, in white and lemon as well as classic buttercup-yellow.

This large, botanically complex genus of around 400 species of annuals and perennials has an almost worldwide distribution, but is concentrated mainly in northern temperate regions. The name *Ranunculus,* meaning "little frog," is an allusion to the damp habitats of many species. Only some 30 species are grown in gardens; mainly deciduous, they vary from undemanding border or rock garden plants to alpine house treasures, and also include some aquatics, meadow wildflowers, a few common weeds, and the half-hardy former florists' flower *R. asiaticus.*

Plants generally grow from fibrous rootstocks, though some have bulblike bases or tubers. Most form a basal clump of stalked leaves, often toothed and divided into lobes or cut more deeply into segments, although some species have simpler, heart-shaped or strap-like foliage. Separate flowering stems, usually bearing smaller leaves, are topped, either singly or in loose clusters, by open, symmetrical, cup-shaped flowers with a glossy sheen to their petals and a central boss of many short stamens.

The flowers are usually yellow or white, more rarely orange, green, red, or purple, and are normally composed of five petals, each with a nectar-secreting pit at the base. Double or pale-flowered cultivars have appeared in several species.

All *Ranunculus* are more or less poisonous. ⚠

CULTIVATION Requirements vary widely, but species for the open garden generally enjoy moisture-retentive soil in sun to part-shade. Some become dormant after flowering.

PROPAGATION By division.

PROBLEMS Usually trouble-free.

R. acontifolius (Fair maids of France) Forms a mound of dark green foliage from fibrous roots, its jaggedly toothed leaves dividing into three to five roughly oval leaflets that join each other at angles around the leaf stalk, like fingers on a hand (or like aconite leaves, as the name suggests). In spring to early summer, the leaves are hidden under a profusion of ½–¾-in (1–2-cm), white, yellow-centered flowers, held in loose sprays on upright, branching

stems with narrow, stalkless leaflets. Best in fertile, moisture-retentive to damp soil, in sun or shade. Dies away after flowering. Grown since the late 16th century, but rarely seen in gardens except in its exquisite double form, 'Flore Pleno'. From alpine meadows, woods, and streamsides in central Europe. ‡6–36 in (15–90 cm). Z5–9 H9–5 **'Flore Pleno'** Masses of long-lasting, tightly double buttons float on wide-branching stems. A shade-tolerant gem highly prized for woodland plantings. ‡24–36 in (60–90 cm).

R. acris (Meadow buttercup) A short rhizome and fibrous roots support a clump of long-stalked, often hairy, basal leaves cut into three to seven stalkless segments, which are each finely lobed and toothed. Bears loose clusters of ½–1-in (1.5-2.5-cm), bright yellow flowers in late spring to early summer, on upright, branching stems with smaller leaves. Could be confused with *R. bulbosus,* but lacks a cormlike swollen base, and with *R. repens,* but lacks runners. Apart from its place in wildflower meadows, *R. acris* is usually grown in its double-flowered version. Easy to grow, it prefers moist conditions in sun and thrives in bog gardens or as a water marginal. Weed out bright yellow plants self-sown from pale-flowered cultivars. A variable species, it is widely distributed in Europe and Asia, often in damp meadows and woodland clearings. ‡6–40 in (15–100 cm). Z4–8 H8–1. **'Citrinus'** Subtle lemon-yellow flowers, golden at the center. ‡24–30 in (60–75 cm). **'Flore Pleno'** Neat mats of dissected foliage smothered in long-lasting, densely double, brilliant yellow pompons on wiry, almost leafless stems. ‡24–36 in (60–90 cm). **'Stevenii'** Large, generally with creeping rhizomes, although plants offered under this name are variable, sometimes having semidouble flowers. ‡4 ft (1.2 m). **'Sulphureus'** Pale yellow flowers with deeper yellow stamens. ‡24–30 in (60–75 cm).

R. amplexicaulis (White buttercup) Forms a low clump of narrowly oval, gray-green, smooth, unlobed foliage arising from noninvasive fibrous roots, with separate flowering stems bearing narrower leaves that clasp the stem at their base. Shallowly cupped, ¾–1-in (2–2.5-cm) flowers, white with yellow centers, appear in early summer and are held above the foliage, either singly or in sparse clusters. Petals are often tinged pink on the reverse, and flowers sometimes have more than five petals. For an open position in humus-rich soil in sun or semi-shade; needs moisture in summer but dislikes winter wet. May self-seed; divide in spring as it starts into growth. From alpine meadows in the Pyrenees and northern Spain. ‡2–12 in (5–30 cm). Z4–8 H8–1

RIGHT 1 *Ranunculus acontifolius* 'Flore Pleno' **2** *R. acris* 'Citrinus' **3** *R. acris* 'Flore Pleno'

R. bulbosus (Bulbous buttercup) A compact, fibrous root system supports long-stalked, hairy basal leaves, divided into three main segments, each lobed and toothed with the middle segment usually clearly stalked. Bright yellow, ½–1¼-in (1.5–3-cm) flowers are held above the foliage, singly or in sparse clusters, during spring and early summer. Dies down in midsummer, remaining dormant until fall. Easy to grow in most soils, thriving in well-drained conditions in sun and good among grasses. Not generally considered a garden plant, except for use in wild areas and buttercup lawns in preference to the rampant *R. repens*. Similar to *R. acris* but with a cormlike swelling at the base of the plant. From meadows, hedgerows, fixed dunes, and streambanks in Europe, North Africa, and the Caucasus. ‡6–20 in (15–50 cm). Z7–9 H9–7. **'F. M. Burton'** A little-known treasure with lemon-yellow flowers. ‡12 in (30 cm).

R. constantinopolitanus Clump-forming, with softly hairy, rounded leaves, 1¼–4 in (3–10 cm) across, deeply dissected into three toothed segments that range from broad and overlapping to narrowly wedge-shaped. Plants are topped in early summer by yellow flowers to 1¼ in (3 cm) across, held singly or in loose clusters on upright stems. Prefers moist, humus-rich soil in sun. An extremely variable species rarely seen in cultivation, except in its double form. Dwarf forms are found at high altitudes. From marshy meadows and similar habitats in the Mediterranean and Caucasus. ‡8–30 in

(20–75 cm). Z7–9 H9–7. **'Plenus'** Carries tight, double, bright yellow rosette flowers with a central green eye. Can be slow to establish after spring division. Grown since the 18th century. ‡12–18 in (30–45 cm).

R. ficaria (Lesser celandine) Fibrous roots and characteristic, club-shaped tubers support a low mound of rather fleshy, hairless, dark green, rounded to narrowly heart-shaped leaves, about 1¾ in (4 cm) across, usually with angled or scalloped edges, often glossy and mottled above in silver or purple.

Flowers are held on separate stems, singly or in sparse clusters, appearing from early to late spring, after which the plant lies dormant until the following midwinter. The star- or shallowly cup-shaped flowers, up to 1¾ in (4 cm) wide, usually have 7–13 petals that bleach to white with age; they tend to close in cloudy weather. Easy to grow, preferring damp, fertile soil in sun or shade. Good under deciduous shrubs with early-flowering perennials. Prevent self-seeding of fertile cultivars by deadheading or risk losing the original plant in a mass of

LEFT *Ranunculus constantinopolitanus* 'Plenus'

less desirable seedlings. Sterile cultivars need less attention. Propagate cultivars by division in fall. From damp grassy places, ditches, and woods in Europe, northwestern Africa and southwestern Asia; naturalized and invasive in North America (*see* The Lesser Celandine, *p.404*). ‡2–6 in (5–15 cm). Z4–8 H8–1. **var. albus** A name used for plants with pale cream to white flowers; some distinct white-flowered clones have been given cultivar names. **'Anemone Centred'** *see* 'Collarette'. **var. aurantiacus** syn. 'Cupreus' Vivid copper-orange petals with chestnut backs. Flowers fade as they age, leaving an orange eye at the center. Silver marbled leaves with dark veining. **'Beamish's Double'** *see* 'Collarette'. **'Brambling'** Distinctive triangular, dark bronze leaves etched heavily in lichen-green. Discovered in a Surrey, England fencerow in 1993. **'Brazen Hussy'** Highly glossy, deep purple-brown leaves. Introduced by Christopher Lloyd from a plant found in a wood near his garden in Sussex, England. Most self-sown seedlings are inferior. **'Chrysanthemum'** *see* 'Double Bronze'. **subsp. chrysocephalus** syn. 'Major' Huge, robust plants, more than double the usual size, with long-stalked leaves up to 2¾ in (7 cm) across and 2-in (5-cm) flowers. No bulbils. From the eastern Mediterranean. ‡16 in (40 cm). **'Collarette'** syn. 'Anemone Centred', 'E. A. Bowles', 'Beamish's Double') Double yellow flowers with a

RANUNCULUS FICARIA GALLERY

R. ficaria var. *aurantiacus*

R. ficaria 'Brazen Hussy'

R. ficaria 'Double Bronze'

R. ficaria 'Double Mud'

R. ficaria Flore Pleno Group

R. ficaria 'Green Petal'

R. ficaria 'Salmon's White'

R. ficaria 'Yaffle'

single outer ring of spreading, round-tipped petals surrounding a central ruff densely packed with much smaller, darker yellow petals. Flowers have a green eye when fresh, turning yellow with age. Dark veining on leaves. Infertile. **'Coppernob'** Wonderful combination of dark purple leaves and orange flowers. The first successful deliberate hybrid, from a cross between 'Brazen Hussy' and var. *aurantiacus*, made in 1990 by horticulturist Wendy Perry of Cornwall, England. **'Cupreus'** see var. *aurantiacus*. **'Double Bronze'** syn. 'Chrysanthemum', 'Wisley Double Yellow' Open, daisylike double flowers with several overlapping rings of large, blunt-tipped petals and a central frill of yellow stamens. The bright yellow petals are given a rich tone by bronzing on the backs. Scant dark feathering in the center of the leaves. Fertile, but sets

LEFT *Ranunculus gramineus*

little seed. **'Double Mud'** Double, creamy-white flowers with a pale yellow center. Petal backs are brown-gray aging to a deeper gray. Leaves sparsely marbled with light green. Fertile. **'Dusky Maiden'** Foliage with a central zone of red-brown bordered in dark green. **'E. A. Bowles'** see 'Collarette'. **Flore Pleno Group** A range of plants with fully double, pompon-style flowers in golden to acid yellow, sometimes with a central eyelike boss of small petal-like structures. Infertile. **'Green Petal'** Strange double mops formed of irregularly bunched green petals with a fine yellow stripe. No stamens. Late-flowering. **'Ingwersen'** see 'Primrose'. **'Ken Aslet Double'** syn. 'Starry White' Beautifully formed, small flowers with white outer petals giving way to inner layers of yellow petals, then green at the center. Turns translucent white with age. One of the best double whites, found in Bowles' Corner at the RHS Garden in Surrey, England in 1993. Fertile, but produces little seed. **'Leo'** Early-flowering double, with the edges of the petals rolled in and the tip rolled back. Collected by Alan Leslie, former RHS botanist, from a streamside in Bulgaria in 1994 and named for the flower's resemblance to a lion's mane. **'Major'** see subsp. *chrysocephalus*. **'Picton's Double'** Fully double, acid-yellow, pompon flowers have a central green boss and bronze tinting on the back of the blunt-tipped petals. Sparsely marbled leaves. Infertile. Plants of this type are much confused. Obtained by Percy Picton of Old Court Nurseries, Worcestershire, England from a local garden. **'Primrose'** syn. 'Ingwersen' Pale lemon-yellow flowers, the backs aging from pale green to gray, with a slight silvering on the leaves. Plants of this type occur often in the wild, so similar and identical forms have many

names. **'Randall's White'** Pale cream flowers developing slatey backs, with rounded petals; large, silvered leaves with a central dark stripe. Discovered by Allan Robinson, former Rock Garden Superintendent at the RHS Garden at Wisley, and named in honor of his cat. **'Salmon's White'** Flowers open almost white, with green reverses turning indigo-blue. Leaves have some silvering on their edges. **'Starry White'** see 'Ken Aslet Double'. **'Tortoiseshell'** Superb, with large, bronze leaves speckled in green and red, in patterns that vary between plants. **'Wisley Double Yellow'** see 'Double Bronze'. **'Yaffle'** After a first flush of yellow flowers, produces gold-streaked green petals that are small, rounded, and sometimes bent backward. Vigorous, with slight silvering and dark veining on the leaves. Named for its resemblance to the coloring of the bird better known as the green woodpecker.

R. gramineus Remarkable among buttercups for its slender, grasslike leaves, which are distinctly blue-green and marked with parallel veins, forming low, neat tufts above fibrous roots. A haze of bright yellow flowers appears just above the foliage from April to July with slim, upright stems each bearing one or a few upward-facing, ¾–1¼-in (2–3-cm) cups. After flowering, the leaves wither. A tough, reliable plant for borders, best in full sun and free-draining, but not poor, soil. Will tolerate part-shade. May self-seed, producing somewhat variable offspring. Divide in spring, when the plant has begun to grow. From dry grasslands and open woods in southern Europe and North Africa. ‡6–14 in (15–35 cm). Z6–8 H8–6

R. montanus Clump-forming with a compact rootstock, producing geranium-like basal leaves deeply divided into three to five egg-shaped segments, with either toothed or smooth edges. Separate stems with

THE LESSER CELANDINE

The lesser celandine, *Ranunculus ficaria*, is notorious as a potential spreader in the garden. It has a fearsome reputation as a garden weed and can be hard to eradicate when established, but its short growing season is some compensation: it disappears below ground by late spring. As one of the earliest spring wildflowers, it brightens areas where it may safely be allowed to naturalize and form extensive colonies.

In Britain, more than 100 cultivars of this very variable species have been named and introduced since the 1950s, nearly all discovered in wild-growing populations. Many owe their selection to commendably alert, botanically minded gardeners who spotted them in the wild. They differ (in some cases only slightly) in flower color, flower form, and leaf markings, with an array of singles in shades of cream, pale yellow, orange, and green, as well as a range of doubles. Horticulturist Walter Ingwersen introduced 'Green Petal', 'Primrose',

and var. *aurantiacus*, while several cultivars are associated with, but probably none named by, horticulturist E. A. Bowles. The selection is not nearly as large in North America.

Correct identification of cultivars can be difficult, particularly with the doubles, because duplicate names exist for identical or very similar forms; also, there is a lack of published descriptions by which to match plants with their names. The NCCPG National Collection at Rowden Gardens in Devon, England, is helping untangle the confusion.

In North America, *R. ficaria* was first introduced from western Europe as a medicinal herb. But, as it does in Europe, it can spread rapidly and is now a nuisance in the northeast and northwest, especially alongside rivers and streams. Interestingly, here too there are signs of variation but in North America the focus is more on preventing it from smothering the native flora than looking for garden-worthy forms.

ALMOST WILD

NATURALISTIC PLANTINGS featuring combinations of wild flowers work well together whatever the colors; here, these two bright shades create a lovely, relaxed planting. Backed by fresh ferns, the European columbine *A. vulgaris*, with its familiar rich blue bonnets, self-seeds enthusiastically. It will, however, hybridize with garden columbines to produce other, less suitable shades that would not look as effective with the yellow buttercups. This double form of the wild meadow buttercup, *R. acris* 'Flore Pleno', flowers much longer than the familiar single-flowered form, which quickly drops its petals.

narrowly lobed leaves extend above the foliage to bear yellow buttercups from late spring to midsummer. The shallowly cupped flowers, a few to each stem, are ¾–1½ in (2–4 cm) across. A variable species, one of several similar European mountain buttercups and usually represented by the cultivar 'Molten Gold'. From meadows, open woods, screes, and snow patches in the Alps, Jura, and Black Forest areas of Europe. ↕2–10 in (5–25 cm). Z5–8 H8–1. **'Molten Gold'** A dwarf selection with a mat of dainty, glossy leaves and brilliant yellow flowers on short stalks. May need dividing every few years, in spring, to keep it flowering profusely. Prone to damage by slugs. ↕4 in (10 cm).

R. repens **'Flore Pleno'** syn. *R. repens* var. *pleniflorus* An alarmingly invasive weed in its wild, single-flowered state, but attractive and useful in this double form, it throws out long, overground runners that send down fibrous roots at intervals to support new rosettes of basal leaves. The leaves are up to 3½ in (9 cm) across, divided into three broadly oval leaflets, with the central leaflet projecting beyond the others on a long stalk, and all three cut further into tooth-edged segments. In summer, yellow, ¾–1¼–in (2–3-cm) pompon flowers, tightly packed with numerous petals, are carried singly or in loose clusters on upright stems with few leaves. Allow to naturalize freely in moist soil, or curtail its spread by planting in a container placed on a hard surface. For sun or part-shade. This name covers a range of very similar double forms. Intriguingly, the wild species is pollinated by rain. From grassland and other generally damp habitats in Europe and Asia; widely naturalized elsewhere. ↕6–12 in (15–30 cm). Z3–8 H8–1

REHMANNIA
SCROPHULARIACEAE

Exotic-looking, foxglovelike plants for warm and sheltered borders or a cool greenhouse.

There are nine species of perennials from China, sometimes treated as biennials, only two of which are generally grown. They form basal rosettes of large, hairy, veined, lobed or toothed leaves, from which spring hairy, wiry stems carrying open heads of alternate leaves, like the rosette foliage only smaller, and flamboyant foxglove- or mimulus-like, two-lipped flowers with spotting in the throat.

CULTIVATION Grow in light shade in free-draining soil, enriched with humus, or in full sun in cool areas. In mild areas, they will survive the winter, but where frost is expected, overwinter in frost-free greenhouse conditions or treat as biennials.

PROPAGATION From seed, or cuttings taken in spring.

PROBLEMS Slugs and snails.

R. angulata see *R. elata*

R. elata syn. *R. angulata* (Chinese foxglove) Rosettes of 8–10-in (20–25-cm), reverse-egg-shaped, lobed or toothed, mid-green leaves support branched, wiry stems bearing smaller leaves. Nodding, tubular, bright purplish pink 2¾–4-in (7–10-cm) flowers, with a paler throat and reddish spotting, appear in summer and fall. From China. ↕5 ft (1.5 m). Z14–15 H12–10. **'Popstar'** Compact, with pink flowers. Raise from seed. ↕24 in (60 cm).

R. glutinosa Small compact rosettes, spreading by slender runners, are composed of 4-in (10-cm), hairy,

scalloped leaves with purple undersides. Multi-branched stems carry sparse, nodding, tubular 2-in (5-cm) flowers, reddish-brown-veined with deep purple that coalesces into the throat, fading to yellowish brown at the end of the petals. From northern China. ↕6–12 in (15–30 cm). Z9–11 H12–9

REINECKEA
CONVALLARIACEAE

Tough, mat-forming plant with leathery foliage, making useful ground cover for shady places.

From open woodlands in Japan and China, the single species of spreading evergreen stems produce tufts of narrow leaves, and short spikes of pink flowers are borne in early summer, sometimes followed by small, glossy red berries. An easy-growing plant for carpeting under shrubs, but not free-flowering in cooler regions.

CULTIVATION Thrives in light shade in a woodland or under shrubs; dislikes alkaline soil.

PROPAGATION By division in spring, or from seed.

PROBLEMS Slugs and snails.

R. carnea Steadily creeping plant, spreading to form a mat of evergreen foliage. The tufts of arching sword-shaped leaves are arranged in two ranks. In late spring or early summer, short spikes of small, starry, pale pink flowers

LEFT *Rehmannia elata*

ABOVE 1 *Rheum* 'Ace of Hearts'
2 *R. palmatum* 'Atrosanguineum'

appear, to be followed, in warm areas, by glossy red berries. Makes good evergreen ground cover in full shade, if the soil is not dry, but will rarely flower. Needs warm summers to flower and fruit freely and to increase well. Larger-flowered forms have recently been introduced from China. From woodlands in southern Japan and China. ↕8 in (20 cm). Z7–9 H9–7

RHAZYA *see* AMSONIA

RHEUM
Ornamental rhubarb
POLYGONACEAE

Robust perennials, mostly making handsome specimen plants for island beds or the back of the border.

About 50 species of the fleshy-rooted, clump-forming perennials with woody crowns come mainly from temperate and subtropical Asia, with a few in eastern Europe. In the wild, they mainly inhabit mountain slopes, in the open or among shrubs, sometimes in very wet situations. The foliage is mainly large and heart-shaped to rounded, often lobed and somewhat corrugated, and sometimes boldly veined and showing striking dark reddish tones as it first unfolds from conspicuous red buds. Although the individual, star-shaped flowers are small, insignificant, and without petals, the often stout, hollow stems carry them densely in bold, branching spikes, sometimes sheltered by striking leaflike bracts. They are followed by conspicuous winged seeds. The edible rhubarb, *R. x hybridum*, is a hybrid between two rarely grown species, *R. rhabarbarum* and *R. rhaponticum*.

CULTIVATION Most fertile soils are suitable; those that are moisture-retentive are best. Thrives in sun or part-shade.

PROPAGATION By division or from seed in spring.

PROBLEMS Usually trouble-free.

R. 'Ace of Hearts' syn. *R.* 'Ace of Spades' A comparatively recent garden hybrid, with 10–14in (25–35cm) long, boldly veined, heart-shaped leaves, red-purple flushed beneath, deep green and red-veined above. Numerous white to palest pink flowers are carried in large airy clusters from mid- to late summer. ‡3¼–5 ft (1–1.5 m). Z3–9 H9–5

R. alexandrae Compact clumps of deep green, oval to heart-shaped, 8in- (20cm) long leaves make a satisfying base for the bold flower spikes. These are formed of tiny, yellow-green flowers partially and attractively hidden by a conspicuous column of 2¾–4¾in (7–12cm) long, oval, greenish yellow bracts. This rarely seen plant deserves to be grown more often, but requires a cool, moist climate to do well. Native to open mountainsides of western China and Tibet. ‡3¼–4 ft (1–1.2 m). Z6–8 H8–6

R. australe syn. *R. emodi* Not unlike culinary rhubarb in overall appearance, the stout roots carry oval leaves, to 24 in (60 cm) long with hairy undersides, on reddish stalks that are

almost as long. Deep purplish red flowers are borne densely in large, vertically branched clusters during summer. A sun-loving plant from open Himalayan mountain slopes. ‡5–8¼ ft (1.5–2.5 m). Z5–8 H8–5

R. emodi see *R. australe*

R. kialense Attractively bronze-green, oval, papery leaves, usually no more than three to five and carried on stalks up to twice as long as the leaf blade, rarely exceed 6 in (15 cm) long and form basal tufts. They make a pleasing foil for the clusters of rose-red, sometimes greenish white, flowers that emerge in early summer on slender unbranched stems carrying one or two smaller leaves. The smallest and one of the most recent ornamental rhubarbs to be introduced, from the mountains of China. ‡16–20 in (40–50 cm). Z5–8 H8–5

R. palmatum The tallest and most imposing of all the ornamental rhubarbs, especially in its colored-leaved forms. Stout roots support distinctive, 20–36in (50–90cm) long, rounded leaves, deeply lobed and sharply toothed, supported on robust stalks about as long as the leaf blade. Erect flowering stems bear long, well-spaced branches crowded with greenish white to cream flowers in summer. An accent plant *par excellence*. From China. ‡8¼ ft (2.5 m) or more. Z5–9 H9–1. **'Atrosanguineum'** syn. 'Atropurpureum' Young leaves entirely a rich purplish red aging to deep green above. Flowers deep reddish pink. **'Bowles' Crimson'** Flowers dark red, darker than those of 'Atrosanguineum', the mature leaves remaining red beneath. **var. rubrum** Flowers flushed red. **var. tanguticum** Shorter, with more deeply lobed red-flushed leaves and

compact clusters of white, pink, or crimson flowers. Sometimes treated as a separate species. ‡5–6½ ft (1.5–2 m).

RHODANTHEMUM
ASTERACEAE

Compact, sunny, sun-seeking daisies with silver leaves.

About 15 species of herbaceous perennials, some woody at the base, come from the Mediterranean and North Africa. Only one species is regularly grown in cultivation, but it features an unusually varied range of synonyms. The leaves are typically narrowly lobed and silver-gray, with fine, dense hairs on all surfaces, and make an ideal background for classic daisylike flowerheads with white outer ray florets and yellow inner disk florets.

CULTIVATION Must have well-drained soil and a sunny, sheltered position.

PROPAGATION From cuttings or seed.

PROBLEMS Usually trouble-free.

R. hosmariense syn. *Chrysanthemopsis hosmariense*, *Chrysanthemum mariesii* var. *hosmariense*, *Chrysanthemum hosmariense*, *Leucanthemum hosmariense*, *Leucanthemopsis hosmariense*, *Pyrethropsis hosmariense* (Moroccan daisy) A bushy, woody-based plant spreading tightly by rhizomes, with lobed, silver-gray leaves. A succession of daisylike, 1½-in (3.5-cm) flowerheads are held individually on stems 8–10 in (20–25 cm) tall. These long-lasting flowers appear from late spring to midsummer, or in warm areas almost year-round. Prefers sunny, warm, dry situations and hates winter rain with a vengeance. From Morocco. ‡12–16 in (30–40 cm). Z9–11 H12–7

RHODIOLA
CRASSULACEAE

Impressively hardy and rather succulent plants for the front of sunny borders.

There are about 50 very varied perennials from Asia, North America, and Europe, only one of which is widely grown. The thick, fleshy rhizomes have brown scale-like basal leaves and erect, unbranched or occasionally branched aerial stems bearing fleshy, alternate, egg-shaped, triangular, or lance-shaped grayish green leaves, with entire or toothed edges. In the summer they produce tight clusters of star-shaped flowers, with white, pink, red, orange, or green petals. Closely related to *Sedum*, distinct in having leaves on the rhizome and flower stems emerging from the leaf joints. Excellent at the front of the herbaceous border.

CULTIVATION Needs full sunshine and well-drained, moderately fertile soil.

PROPAGATION From seed, or by division or leaf cuttings.

PROBLEMS Slugs, aphids.

R. rosea (Roseroot) Clump-forming, with thick, branching rhizomes and stout, erect flowering stems. The basal leaves are triangular and scalelike, while those on the aerial stems are alternate, fleshy, blue-green, broadly or narrowly egg-shaped, becoming larger toward the top of the stem; they have entire or toothed margins. In the early summer,

BELOW 1 *Rhodanthemum hosmariense*
2 *Rhodiola rosea*

terminal clusters of 30–70 pink buds open to reveal bright yellow-green flowers. From rocky mountainous places across the Northern Hemisphere. ↕12 in (30 cm). Z4–8 H8–1

RODGERSIA
SAXIFRAGACEAE

Statuesque, moisture-loving, summer-flowering plants that are valued mainly for their bold, handsome foliage.

Seven species of large, deciduous plants grow in damp woodlands and by streamsides in eastern Asia from the Himalaya to China, Korea, and Japan. Several of them are deservedly popular for their imposing stature and, given adequate moisture, they will grow well in a more open garden situation. All grow from a stout, branching, creeping root, from which arise large, long-stalked leaves, variously divided into several leaflets and often attractively tinged with bronze or purple, especially in early summer and again in fall. Branched clusters of tiny, creamy white or pink flowers are borne on leafy stems in summer. These remain attractive and colorful as they go to seed in fall and usually persist well into winter. Hybrids and selections are now appearing, improving the range of foliage and flower color.

CULTIVATION Grow in fertile, moist, humus-rich soil in sun or part-shade. In conditions that are too dry, the foliage will scorch: regular mulching with composted bark, leaf mold or good garden compost will help retain moisture. The fresh young foliage may be damaged by late frosts. Cut away foliage damaged by drought or frost to improve the look of plants.

PROPAGATION By division in early spring or fall, or from seed.

PROBLEMS Usually trouble-free.

R. aesculifolia Vigorous plant with long-stalked, crinkly leaves 12 in (30 cm) across, divided into about seven oblong, toothed, usually noticeably veined, usually bronze-tinged leaflets rather like a horse-chestnut leaf (hence the name: horse chestnut is in the genus *Aesculus*). In midsummer, large clusters of small pale pink or white flowers open on tall leafy stems that overtop the leaves. From moist woods in northern China. ↕5–6½ ft (1.5–2 m). Z5–8 H8–1. **var. henrici** see *R. henrici*.

R. henrici syn. *R. aesculifolia* var. *henrici* Forming a large clump, and generally similar to *R. aesculifolia,* but distinct in its pink flowers, which deepen in color with age, and in several other small botanical features. From western China. ↕5 ft (1.5 m). Z5–8 H8–5

R. 'Herkules' Compact, clump-forming plant with bronze-tinged

leaves and small light pink flowers in branched clusters in early summer and midsummer. Makes a superb specimen, especially near water. A hybrid of *R. pinnata*, or perhaps a selection of it. ↕3¼ ft (1 m). Z5–7 H7–5

R. 'Irish Bronze' A hybrid, or perhaps a selection, of *R. aesculifolia* with bronze stems and leaves. Pale pink flowers fade to near-white. ↕6½ ft (2 m). Z5–8 H8–5

R. 'Parasol' Clumps of long-stalked leaves, composed of narrow, light green leaflets, the starry, creamy-white flowers are carried in branched clusters on green stems. A hybrid of *R. aesculifolia* and *R. podophylla*. ↕5 ft (1.5 m). Z5–8 H8–5

R. pinnata Robust plant making a clump of red-stalked leaves, each comprising two groups of three glossy, bronze-tinged leaflets separated by a short stalk and therefore, despite the name, not pinnate in the usual botanical sense (that is, like a rose leaf). Small, starry flowers, which may be white, or pale or deep salmon-pink, are borne in large, branched clusters, in early summer or midsummer. Although originally describing individual plants, the cultivar names found under this species are now often applied rather loosely to a range of plants with similar general characteristics. From western China. ↕3¼–4 ft (1–1.2 m). Z5–7 H7–5. **'Elegans'** Pale pink buds opening to creamy-white flowers, in a more slender cluster. **'Superba'** Large leaves that are a deep purplish bronze in spring, then a greenish bronze in summer, with deep rose-pink flowers becoming a striking red-bronze in fall and winter, borne on dark red stems.

R. podophylla Robust plant forming a spreading clump of handsome foliage. Long-stalked leaves to 36 in (90 cm) across are composed of five broad leaflets, each jaggedly toothed and lobed toward the tip. The leaves open a deep bronze-purple, usually becoming green by midsummer, but taking on deep reddish tints in fall. Small creamy-white flowers are borne in large branched clusters in mid- or late summer. From moist woodlands and shaded streamsides in Japan. ↕3¼–5 ft (1–1.5 m). Z5–8 H8–5. **'Rotlaub'** Good deep bronze young foliage, often retaining the color through the summer. **'Smaragd'** Leaves green; free-flowering.

R. purdomii Name usually, but wrongly, used for a pink-flowered variant of *R. aesculifolia* with bronze young leaves. This name has no status and should not be used.

R. sambucifolia Large clumps of mid-green leaves composed of two to four pairs of oblong leaflets, with a single

RIGHT **1** *Rodgersia aesculifolia*
2 *R.* 'Irish Bronze' **3** *R. pinnata*
'Superba' **4** *R. podophylla*

HARMONY IN A DAMP BORDER

CREATING A DENSE BUT sympathetic intermingling of perennials in a damp border works as well as elsewhere, especially since there should always be moisture for these plants whose roots are in competition all season. Here rodgersia, astilbe, cimicifuga, and hosta lean out over a gravel path in an intriguing blend of foliage—from the broad hosta leaves to the prettily dissected astilbes—and with flowers in plumes, spikes, and bells.

terminal one. Flowering stems may be green or brownish, and carry arching, conical, branched clusters of starry white or pale pink flowers in early summer or midsummer. From moist woodlands in western China. ‡32–48 in (80–120 cm). Z5–8 H8–5

R. tabularis see *Astilboides tabularis*

ROMNEYA
California tree poppy
PAPAVERACEAE

Imposing plants with gray foliage and sumptuous flowers that are among the largest in the poppy family.

The one species is restricted to southwestern North America, where it is found in sunny, rocky areas. A suckering plant, and woody at the base, it has upright stems with a gray-blue bloom. Its gray-blue

leaves are irregularly divided, usually with two or three pairs of lobes at the base and a lobe at the tip. Dramatic, fragrant, white flowers, with the crumpled-silk look of poppies, are carried singly at the tips of the shoots in summer and fall.

Sometimes classed as a shrub, this handsome plant is usually treated as a herbaceous perennial in gardens. Although established plants may be cut to the ground by frost in severe winters, they will sprout again from below ground once spring arrives; young plants may not be so lucky.

CULTIVATION Best in sunny, warm, sheltered positions, especially close to warm walls and fences, or in open, well-drained soil. Plants respond well to mulches of compost or well-rotted manure. Established plants greatly resent disturbance.

PROPAGATION By root cuttings.

PROBLEMS Botrytis.

R. coulteri A suckering, woody-based plant with erect, sometimes branched stems bearing leathery, gray-green, oval to lance-shaped, sharply lobed or toothed leaves, 2¾–4¾ in (7–12 cm) long. The large, solitary, bowl-shaped flowers, 4–5 in (10–13 cm) across and produced from midsummer to early fall, are pure white with five or more, usually six, overlapping petals contrasting with a large boss of golden stamens in the center of each sweetly scented bloom. Restricted to a limited area of southern California, especially the mountains southeast of Los Angeles. ‡10 ft (3 m). Z8–10 H9–2. **subsp. trichocalyx** Slimmer plant with more finely cut foliage and several flowers in a cluster, rather than solitary flowers. Also more invasive. From southwestern California and northwestern Mexico, from San Diego southward into Baja California. ‡3¼–6½ ft (1–2 m). ‘**White Cloud**’ syn. *R. x hybrida*. Fine large-flowered form.

R. x *hybrida* see *R. coulteri* ‘White Cloud’

ROSCOEA
ZINGIBERACEAE

Unusual orchidlike plants that add a touch of distinction to a choice site.

About 17 species of fleshy-rooted, deciduous perennials come from forests, scrub, and open slopes along the Himalayan chain and into China. Foliage varies from lance-to strap-shaped, and is usually only partially developed at flowering time. Carried either in stalkless clusters or in short spikes, each flower has a long curved tube and three petals, the upper one forming a hood, the lower one a lip; there are also some smaller, petal-like stamens.

CULTIVATION Moist but well-drained, neutral to acidic soil is preferred; although usually best in part-shade, if the soil is moist they do well in more open sites. Young growth is late in appearing, often not until spring is well advanced.

PROPAGATION By division or from seed, ideally sown as soon as ripe.

PROBLEMS Usually trouble-free.

R. alpina Narrowly elliptical to lance-shaped leaves elongate to 4–6 in (10–15 cm), and pink to purple, occasionally white 1¼–1½-in (3–4-cm) flowers open one at a time from the immature leaf tuft. At flowering time in early summer, plants are only 4–6 in (10–15 cm) tall, but exceed this at maturity. The only alpine species, from

RIGHT **1** *Romneya coulteri* ‘White Cloud’ **2** *Roscoea cautleyoides* **3** *R. humeana*

forests and open sites in southwestern China to Pakistan. ‡6–12 in (15–30 cm). Z6–9 H9–6

R. auriculata Small, clump-forming plant, the foliage up to 10 in (25 cm) long and varying from narrowly strap-shaped to broadly lance-shaped. From summer to early fall, 2–2½in- (5–6cm) long, bright purple, occasionally white, flowers with white, petal-like stamens open in succession. From Sikkim and Nepal. ‡ 10–20 in (25–50 cm). Z6–9 H9–6

R. australis Tufts of glossy, 4–6-in (10–15-cm), slightly sickle-shaped leaves with, in early summer, 1¼–2½-in (3–6cm) white-tubed, purple flowers with a prominent lip-petal. A pure white form is also known. Resembles *R. tibetica* in overall appearance but always with a white tube to the flower. Isolated from all other known species in the wild—and native not to Australia, but Burma. ‡6–12 in (15–30 cm). Z7–9 H9–7

R. 'Beesiana' Clumping plant with rather narrow leaves, the bases curling round the stems. Yellow flowers, often with purple streaks; pale- and white-flowered forms are also seen. Nicely blends the characters of *R. auriculata* and *R. cautleyoides*, of which it is presumed to be a hybrid. ‡ 14–18 in (35–45 cm). Z6–9 H9–6

R. cautleyoides Slim stems bear foliage varying from narrowly strap-shaped to lance-shaped, the lightish green leaves sparsely borne and often not fully developed at flowering time. Pale yellow, 2-in (5cm) long flowers in late spring and early summer. From western China. ‡12–20 in (30–50 cm). Z6–9 H9–6. **'Kew Beauty'** Deep green leaves and darker, finer flowers. **'Jeffrey Thomas'** Distinctive straw-yellow flowers.

R. humeana The most robust species, with rich green, oblong to oval leaves, 8–10 in (20–25 cm) long. Blooms when the leaves are part grown: the rich purple flowers are 1½–2½ in (4–6 cm) long, appearing from late spring into summer. Pink, white, and yellow forms are also known in the wild. From the mountains of southwestern China. ‡12–14 in (30–35 cm). Z7–9 H9–7

R. purpurea syn. *R. procera* Lance-shaped to oval leaves, 6–10 in (15–25 cm) long, and pale purple, white, or purple- and white- striped, 2in (5cm) long flowers in summer, sometimes into fall. The purple- and white-flowered form was formerly known as *R. procera*. Rather like a less robust *R. humeana*. From the Himalaya. ‡8–12 in (20–30 cm). Z6–9 H9–6

R. scillifolia A slender, small-growing species, having narrowly strap-shaped leaves to 4¾ in (12 cm) in length and pink or dark purple flowers, ¾–1 in (2–2.5 cm) long, opening one at a time in summer. From damp, open upland pastures in southwestern China ‡6–10 in (15–25 cm). Z8–9 H9–8

R. tibetica Rarely more than 6 in (15 cm) tall at flowering, but eventually taller; the basal tufts of lance-shaped, narrowly oval to oblong leaves reach 6–8 in (15–20 cm) in length. From early to late summer, 1¼–2½in (3–6cm) long flowers range from white or rose through shades of mauve, violet, and purple to almost blue, but not all of these color forms are yet found in gardens. From western China, Tibet to Bhutan, and Burma. ‡6–12 in (15–30 cm). Z7–9 H9–7

RUDBECKIA
Coneflower
ASTERACEAE

Showy yellow daisies valued for their generous production of cone-centered flowerheads late in the season.

Sixteen species are native to habitats ranging from damp woodlands to dry prairies of North America. Mostly perennial, they are either clump-forming or spread by rhizomes, with erect stems bearing alternate, undivided to deeply lobed leaves. Each stem bears one to several long-stalked, upward-facing, daisylike flowerheads consisting of a prominent, dark, conical or columnar disk surrounded by horizontal to drooping ray florets in various shades of yellow. Deviations include some cultivars of *R. laciniata* that are fully double, with all disk florets transformed into ray florets, and two species where ray florets are lacking. All are useful as cut flowers.

R. hirta (Black-eyed Susan) is usually grown as an annual and many seed-raised cultivars in various shades of yellow to reddish brown are offered, including some large-flowered doubles. Distinguished by individual florets in the cones, having styles that protrude, creating a noticeably fuzzy appearance.

CULTIVATION All need full sun and prefer fertile, moisture-retentive soil. They flag at the first sign of drought. Divide every four or five years in spring to maintain vigor. The taller species, especially *R. laciniata*, can benefit from staking.

PROPAGATION In spring, from seed sown, or by division or basal cuttings, preferably taken with roots attached.

PROBLEMS May be troubled by aphids. Prone to powdery mildew, especially in dry soil.

R. californica (California coneflower) Clump-forming deciduous perennial with broadly lance-shaped, untoothed to deeply toothed leaves, to 10-in (25-cm). Flowerheads to 5 in (13 cm) across, consisting of a greenish yellow, conical to columnar disk and spreading yellow ray florets, are borne solitarily on unbranched stems from July to

RIGHT 1 *Rudbeckia fulgida* var. *deamii*
2 *R. fulgida* var. *sullivantii*
3 *R. laciniata* 'Goldquelle'

August. Native to moist meadows in the mountains of California. ↕5–6½ ft (1.5–2 m). Z4–9 H9–1

R. fulgida (Orange coneflower) Deciduous and slowly spreading by rhizomes. The lower leaves are lance-shaped to egg-shaped, their shape, color, hairiness, and toothing varying according to the subspecies. The closely spaced, leafy stems branch at the apex and, between late summer and mid-fall, bear several long-stalked, yellow, daisylike flowerheads, to 4 in (10 cm) across, with conical, purplish brown to black centers. The floriferousness and precise flower timing depends on the

subspecies, but all are prolific and reliable. Native to a wide range of open and shaded and dry or damp habitats in the southern and eastern US. ↕16–39 in (40–100 cm). Z4–9 H9–1. **var. deamii** (Deam's coneflower) Basal leaves egg-shaped, coarsely toothed. From Ohio, Indiana, and Illinois. ↕24 in (60 cm). **var. fulgida** Basal leaves lance-shaped to narrowly oval, grayish green, densely hairy with scattered marginal teeth. From the eastern United States. ↕16–39 in (40–100 m). **var. speciosa** (Orange coneflower) Basal leaves egg-shaped, their margins shallow-toothed or scalloped. From the eastern United States. 24–39 in (60–100 cm). **var.**

speciosa **Viette's Little Suzy** ('Blovi') Dwarf. ↕12–14 in (30–35 cm). **var. sullivantii** (Sullivant's coneflower) Leaves are egg-shaped, coarsely toothed, upper surface dark green, hairless. From the northeastern U.S. ↕24–39 in (60–100 cm). **var. sullivantii** 'Goldsturm' Deep yellow, flowering from July to October. Raised from seed, so may be variable. First noticed in a Czechoslovakian nursery in 1937 by Heinrich Hagemann, at the time an employee of the German horticulturist Karl Foerster. ↕28–36 in (70–90 cm). 1999 Perennial Plant of the Year.

R. laciniata (Cutleaf coneflower) Virtually hairless, deciduous plant, spreading by rhizomes, with lower leaves to 12 in (30 cm) long, either deeply lobed or divided into leaflets. Erect leafy stems with smaller leaves, progressively less divided toward the apex, bear long-stalked, 6-in (15-cm) flowerheads from midsummer to early fall. The prominent, elongated central cones are greenish brown to greenish yellow and the broad, drooping ray florets are yellow. Native to streambanks and damp habitats in central and eastern North America. ↕5–8 ft (1.5–2.5 m). Z3–9 H9–1. **'Goldkugel'** Fully double, neater flowerheads than those of 'Goldquelle' and 'Hortensia', 2½ in (6 cm) across. ↕6½ ft (2 m). **'Goldquelle'** Flowerheads fully double, messier than those of 'Goldkugel', 3½ in (9 cm) across. Raised by Benary in 1948. ↕3¼–4 ft (1–1.2 m). **'Herbstsonne'** Very tall, flowering late summer to early fall. Introduced in 1906. ↕6½–8¼ ft (2–2.5 m). **'Hortensia'** (Golden Glow) Flowerheads fully double, messier than those of 'Goldkugel', 3½ in (9 cm) across. Dates from 1894. ↕5 ft (1.5 m). **'Juligold'** Similar to

ABOVE 1 *Rudbeckia laciniata* 'Herbstsonne' **2** *R. occidentalis* 'Black Beauty'

'Herbstsonne' but flowering mid- to late summer. ↕8¼ ft (2.5 m).

R. maxima (Great coneflower) Clump-forming, deciduous perennial with broadly elliptic, hairless, waxy blue-green leaves to 24 in (60 cm). The paddle-shaped basal leaves are long-stalked and form a loose, cabbagelike rosette; those on the stem are stalkless and stem-clasping. Flowerheads with an elongated 2¾-in (7-cm) dark brown cone fringed with drooping yellow ray florets to 2¾ in (7 cm) are borne on tall stems from midsummer to early fall. One of the more unusual coneflowers and tolerant of damp soils. Native to open habitats in the south-central United States. ↕8¼ ft (2.5 m). Z4–8 H8–1

R. occidentalis (Western coneflower) Deciduous perennial with short rhizomes and elliptic to broadly egg-shaped leaves to 12 in (30 cm). Sparsely branched, leafy stems bear, in midsummer, curious flowerheads consisting of a columnar black disk, to 2 in (5 cm) long, lacking ray florets but surrounded at the base by green bracts. Native to mountain slopes and damp woods in western North America. ↕20–54 in (50–200 cm). Z3–10 H9–1. **'Black Beauty'** Seemingly indistinguishable from 'Green Wizard' but propagated vegetatively, not from seed. ↕3¼–5 ft (1–1.5 m). **'Green Wizard'** More restricted height range than the species. From seed. ↕3¼–5 ft (1–1.5 m).

R. subtomentosa (Sweet coneflower) Deciduous perennial with short

RUDBECKIA FLOWER STRUCTURE

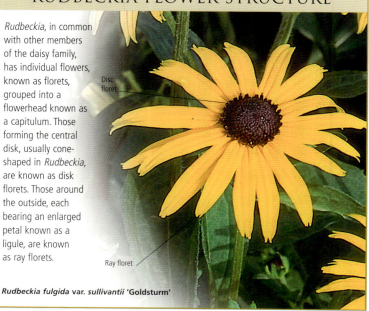

Rudbeckia, in common with other members of the daisy family, has individual flowers, known as florets, grouped into a flowerhead known as a capitulum. Those forming the central disk, usually cone-shaped in *Rudbeckia*, are known as disk florets. Those around the outside, each bearing an enlarged petal known as a ligule, are known as ray florets.

Disc floret

Ray floret

Rudbeckia fulgida var. sullivantii 'Goldsturm'

A GOLDEN PRAIRIE

WHERE SPACE ALLOWS, broad sweeps of perennials in prairie-style plantings look spectacular. Here, a familiar and award-winning border perennial, *Rudbeckia fulgida* var. *deamii*, is allowed to make a bold impact in an expansive sunny summer planting. It is punctuated occasionally by other perennials—achilleas, verbascums, and kniphofia—in a very similar bright yellow coloring but with different flower shapes. Movement, softness, and harmonious coloring are introduced by the backing of calamagrostis and other grasses. It is clear that the rudbeckia and the grasses have the upper hand here, and intervention may occasionally be needed to allow the other perennials to develop.

rhizomes and softly hairy, grayish green, lance-shaped to egg-shaped leaves to 6 in (15 cm). The lower leaves are usually three-lobed. The stems branch at the apex and bear, from late summer to early fall, 3-in (8-cm) flowerheads with a purplish brown disk and yellow 1½-in (4-cm) ray florets. The flowerhead is said to have a licorice-like aroma. Native to prairies and lowlands of central and eastern North America. ↕4 ft (1.2 m). Z4–7 H7–1.

R. triloba (Brown-eyed Susan) Clump-forming, deciduous, short-lived perennial with egg-shaped leaves, the lower often deeply three-lobed. The branched stems bear numerous short-stalked 2¾-in (7-cm) flowerheads, with a hemispheric purplish black disk and yellow 1-in (2.5-cm) ray florets. Very floriferous, from midsummer to mid-

fall, but individual plants usually live for no more than three years, so best raised regularly from seed. Native to damp prairies and open woods in the central and eastern United States. ↕20–60 in (50–150 cm). Z3–11 H11–1. **'Takao'** Robust, with strong stems. ↕2¼ ft (70 cm). Z3–10 H11–1.

RUMEX
Dock
POLYGONACEAE

Most may be weeds and some are unremarkable, but a few docks are handsome and valuable foliage plants for the wild garden.

About 200 annual, biennial, or deciduous perennial plants grow in grassy places, wet meadows, and mountains throughout the cooler

parts of the world, especially in the Northern Hemisphere. From a taproot or a slender rhizome, leafy stems arise, bearing broad leaves and loose or dense clusters of tiny greenish or reddish flowers in a terminal spray in summer. The small, often winged seeds are decorative in some species.

CULTIVATION Grows well in any soil in sun or part-shade.

PROPAGATION From seed or by division.

PROBLEMS Usually trouble-free.

R. flexuosus Clump-forming plant with slender, branched and wavy stems bearing narrow, reddish brown leaves to 4 in (10 cm) long, with crisped margins and pale veins. Open sprays of tiny greenish to reddish flowers appear in mid- and late summer. A novelty plant, rather than a great beauty, but useful for its distinctive foliage color. From damp grasslands in New Zealand. ↕8–16 in (20–40 cm). Z5–9 H9–5

R. hydrolapathum (Great water dock) Handsome plant forming sheaves of erect, lance-shaped, bright green leaves to 3¼ ft (1 m) long. From midsummer to early fall, tall stems bear dense clusters of tiny greenish flowers, but these are best removed to prevent excessive seeding. Needs moist soil all year and makes an excellent plant for the margin of a large pond. From riverbanks and canal-sides throughout Europe, including Britain. ↕3¼–6½ ft (1–2 m). Z5–9 H9–5

R. sanguineus var. *sanguineus* (Bloody dock, Red-veined dock) Upright, often purple stems bear oval green leaves to 6 in (15 cm) long, each veined with reddish purple. Tiny green, later reddish, flowers form a loose spray at the top of the stems from early to late summer, becoming brown as the seeds ripen. Grown for its strikingly colored leaves. Probably a garden selection, but sometimes found in the wild in the British Isles. ↕12 in (30 cm). Z6–8 H8–6. **var. *viridis*** The usual wild form, lacking the dramatic purple veining, and with little garden value. From grassy places and woodlands in Europe, North Africa, and western Asia.

R. scutatus (French sorrel) Sprawling plant with a tough rootstock bearing gray-green, arrow-shaped or oblong leaves that are slightly fleshy. Greenish red flowers turn purple as the ¼ in (6mm) wide seed-heads develop. The leaves have a pleasant acidic flavor and may be added to salads. Grows in rocky areas of southern Europe, North Africa and western Asia. ↕6–12 in (15–30 cm). Z5–9 H9–5. **'Silver Shield'** Young leaves silvery-green. Best cut back once or twice in the summer to maintain good foliage color.

RIGHT 1 *Rumex flexuosus*
2 *R. sanguineus* var. *sanguineus*
3 *R. scutatus* 'Silver Shield'

S

SALVIA
Sage
LAMIACEAE

Long-lived, sun-loving, summer- and fall-flowering plants for both cold and milder gardens.

More than 900 species are widely distributed across North and South America, Africa, Europe, and Asia, mostly growing in grasslands or on rocky exposed hillsides with a few in deciduous or mixed woodlands. They may be shrubs, perennials (some woody at the base), or annuals; some are as tall as 10 ft (3 m) or more. The majority form spreading clumps of upright, square-angled stems bearing stalked or unstalked leaves that are often small, thick, gray or green, and occasionally lobed or dissected. They are topped with spikes of flowers, sometimes branched, on which the individual flowers are sometimes held on very short flower stalks. They are grouped in clusters (whorls) of two to thirty flowers; these clusters may be tightly packed one above the other, or more openly arranged, and may be interspersed with leafy bracts. The showy, tubular flowers have an upper and lower lip, and each flower sits within a two-lipped calyx (*see* Salvia Flower Structure). At the base of the tube are found four hard, oblong or rounded seeds arranged in a square. There is sometimes a fine line between shrubby and herbaceous perennial species (some become woodier in milder climates), but the woodier species have been excluded.

Salvias can be distinguished from each other by differences in flower and leaf, the folds within the flower tube, the placement of the stamens, either within the tube or extended from it, the hairiness of the style, and by many other characters such as hair type that require close scrutiny. Sometimes even botanists find it tricky.

This is a huge and diverse group that, as well as a wide range of very hardy to rather tender perennials, includes culinary herbs and flamboyant summer bedding plants. More are being introduced and named, and the classification and naming of these invaluable plants is currently being refined and clarified as British botanist James Compton, in particular, studies salvias around the world, in the wild as well as in gardens.

CULTIVATION Most are sun-lovers, grows well in a wide range of soil types, although a well-drained soil is preferred, with the addition of a light mulch of manure or other organic matter during winter.

PROPAGATION Salvias are among the easiest of plants to propagate by soft cuttings, taken at any time of the year as long as suitable growth is available. These can root within two weeks and often more quickly. They are also easily raised from seed or by division of established clumps.

PROBLEMS White fly, red spider mite, aphids, some fungal diseases.

S. ambigens see *S. guaranitica* 'Blue Enigma'

S. amplexicaulis Clump-forming plant with many erect stems, covered in stiff hairs, that carry unstalked, green, oblong leaves, untoothed and with a noticeably pointed apex. The blue or violet-blue flowers are small but plentiful and produced in clusters of six to eight on upright spikes from among green leafy bracts during early summer and midsummer. Very closely related to *S. nemorosa*, but in the taller and hairier *S. amplexicaulis*, the leaves lack leaf stalks and there are more flowers in each flower cluster. For well-prepared soil in full sun. Divide or raise from seed. From the eastern Mediterranean. ‡ 32–36 in (80–90 cm). Z4–8 H8–4

S. angustifolia see *S. reptans*

S. arizonica (Arizona sage) Short, with a ground-covering, although not invasive, habit and stems that branch and run underground. These support upright stems carrying smooth leaves, more or less triangular in outline, with saw-shaped margins and somewhat shiny above. Deep blue flowers in loose clusters of six from midsummer to early fall. A well-grown mature clump can measure more than 3¼ ft (1 m) across. Best in a sunny, well-drained position in the front of the border or openings between paving stones. Divide or raise from seed. From meadows and rocky slopes in the US and northern Mexico. ‡ 12 in (30 cm). Z7–9 H9–7

S. atrocyanea One of the tallest perennials; thick stems emerge from large, white, swollen tubers and carry large, green, heart-shaped leaves up to 6 in (15 cm) or more long, the undersides covered in soft hairs. The deep blue flowers can reach ¾ in (2 cm) in length and are borne between larger soft green, leaflike bracts on spikes over 12 in (30 cm) long in late summer and fall. These spikes are frequently carried horizontally on the main stem, creating a graceful, arching effect. The new shoots are prone to early frost damage if unprotected but will regrow quickly. For open, sunny positions with protection from spring frosts. Divide, take cuttings, or raise from seed. From South America. ‡ 6–10 ft (2½–3 m). Z8–11 H11–7

S. azurea A shortly running root system carries lax arching stems, often branched toward the tips, with long

ABOVE 1 *Salvia cacaliifolia*
2 *S. confertiflora*

and narrow, 4 x ½ in (10 x 1 cm) leaves with slight toothing along the margins. Each branched flower stem carries a lax profusion of many attractive and showy, azure blue flowers in loose clusters of four to six from late summer to mid-fall. Each displays a broad, downward-facing lower lip. For open, sunny positions in well-drained soil. Divide, or raise from seed. From the US south to Mexico. ‡ 32–36 in (80–90 cm). Z5–9 H9–5. **var. *grandiflora*** syn. *S. pitcheri, S. azurea* subsp. *pitcheri* Flowers have longer tubes and broader lower lips. From Mexico.

S. blepharophylla (Eyelash-leaved sage) A running root system supports a mounded clump of short stems carrying egg-shaped or triangular, green, 2-in (5-cm) leaves with long hairs all along the margins, giving the species its common name, on short stalks. Each stem elongates into an open spike carrying loose clusters of two to six vibrant scarlet flowers, the lower lip slightly longer than the upper, emerging from a purplish calyx from midsummer to early fall, sometimes later. For open, sunny positions in well-drained soil at the front of borders. Divide, take cuttings, or raise from seed. From central Mexico. ‡ 18–24 in (45–60 cm). Z8–10 H10–8

S. buchananii (Buchanan's sage) A multibranched perennial, woody at the base but with new shoots emerging from below ground; the ½–2¾ in (1–7 cm), dark shiny green, slightly succulent leaves are narrowly egg- or spear-shaped. Atypically, many, new leaves may develop in existing leaf joints. From early summer to early fall, stems extend to carry large magenta-purple flowers covered in purple hairs. For open sunny positions in well-drained soil at the front of borders, or against a protective sunny wall.

SALVIA FLOWER STRUCTURE

The upright flowering stem of *Salvia patens* 'Chilcombe' shows the large two-lipped flowers, in this species carried in pairs up the stem. The male anthers and the female style are enclosed within the hooded upper lip. When the flower drops, four seeds will be seen arranged in a square inside the base of the calyx. These unusually large flowers show clearly how the flower is structured; in many species the flowers are much smaller and much more tightly packed on the spike, often in whorls (tiers of clustered flowers).

Bract

Upper lip

Floral tube

Lower lip

Calyx (plural calyces)

Salvia patens 'Chilcombe'

Propagate from cuttings. Known only from material once found in a garden located in Mexico City. ↕25 in (62 cm). Z9–10 H10–9

S. bulleyana see *S. flava* var. *megalantha*

S. cacaliifolia The many erect stems carry pointed-tipped, triangular, 2–4 in (5–10 cm) leaves, heart-shaped at the base, on stalks almost as long. These are topped with 10 in (25 cm) branched spikes carrying widely spaced pairs of gentian-blue, ½ in (1 cm) flowers that, although unexpectedly small, appear in large numbers from early summer repeatedly until mid-fall. For open, sunny, protected positions in well-drained soil, usually needing winter protection, too. Take cuttings or divide large plants. From the mountains of southern Mexico and Central America ↕36–40 in (90–100 cm). Z9–10 H9–1

S. caerulea see *S. guaranitica* 'Blue Enigma'

S. chamaedryoides (Germander sage) Several creeping woody branches make sizable ground-covering clumps clothed in small, egg-shaped, gray or ash-colored leaves, which are evergreen in mild climates. From early summer to early fall, short flowering stems produce many deep blue flowers, the lower lip broad and cleft in the middle, which are beautifully set off against the pale gray leaves. Surprisingly hardy in very well-drained soil in sun; a well-grown mature clump can measure more than 6 ft (2 m) in diameter. Divide or take cuttings. From the southern US and northern Mexico, on rocky slopes. ↕24 in (60 cm). Z7–11 H11–7

S. concolor One of the tallest perennial salvias, though woody at the base, and capable of reaching an astonishing 20 ft (6 m)—though usually much less. Vigorous stems emerge each spring from large swollen tubers, the new shoots often tinted strongly in blue. The large, green, more or less egg-shaped, coarsely toothed leaves can reach 6 in (12 cm) or more in length and are covered on both surfaces in soft hairs. The deep blue flowers, up to 1¼ in (3 cm) long, are borne in clusters of six to ten in 12 in (30 cm) spikes, emerging from a blue-tinted calyx in late summer and fall. For open, sunny positions; the new shoots need protection from spring frosts. Divide, take cuttings, or raise from seed. *S. guaranitica* is sometimes sold under this name. From Mexico. ↕7–9 ft (2.2–3 m). Z8–11 H11–7

S. confertiflora One of the taller and more dramatic species, with thick stems clothed in dark reddish brown hairs. The leaves are large, heart-shaped, densely felted on both surfaces, green above and yellowish tawny below, and in fall the stems terminate in a display of long, thin, flower spikes that tower above the foliage. The hairy, tubular flowers are not showy, being barely ¼ in (5 mm) long, but are borne in such profusion—up to 15 per cluster—and possess such curious orange-red

floral tubes with pale throats, that the overall effect is stunning. For open, sunny positions at the center or back of a border, with protection from spring frosts. Divide, take cuttings, or raise from seed. From South America (Brazil). ↕6½–10 ft (2–3 m). Z9–10 H9–9

S. darcyi A robust species bearing brittle, semiwoody stems and angular heart-shaped leaves, the stems emerging each spring from thin, white, swollen tubers. The green leaves, to 2¼ in (6 cm) long, are very sticky because they are covered on both sides in soft hairs with sticky glands at the tips. The deep scarlet, ¾ in (2 cm) flowers are borne in 6–12 in (15–30 cm) spikes from summer into fall. Resents excess water surrounding the dormant root system during winter, and its brittle stems are prone to damage by strong winds, so provide a sheltered, well-drained, sunny site. The new shoots are prone to frost damage if unprotected. Divide, take cuttings, or raise from seed. Discovered by Carl Schoenfeld and John Fairey of Yucca Do Nursery, TX, in 1988. From the mountains of Nuevo Leon in Mexico. 3¼–5 ft (1–1.5 m). Z8–11 H11–7

S. dolichantha Tuberous-rooted; the stems are covered in fine, dark brown hairs and carry broadly egg-shaped or broadly spear-shaped, irregularly saw-edged leaves that have hairs only along the veins and sometimes produce a point at each sawtooth tip. From midsummer until early fall the stems bear several smooth, dark purple, 2 in (5 cm) flowers. Easily distinguished from similar species by the long, straight, dark purple flowers, whose lower lips extend farther than the upper ones, and its distinctive foliage. For open, sunny positions in well-drained soil in the front of borders; does not grow well in waterlogged soil. Propagate from seed. From mountain meadows in Sichuan province, China. ↕20–30 in (50–75 cm). Z8–11 H11–7

S. farinacea (Mealy sage) Slender, branched upright stems with a dense coating of very fine blue or white hairs rise from slender tubers and carry long, dark green, smooth and slightly shiny 4 x 1 in (10 x 2.5 cm) untoothed leaves. Each stem is topped by a dense spike of attractive and showy intense dark blue flowers from midsummer to mid-fall. Each flower has a broad, downward-facing lower lip; blue-flowered plants tend to have blue hairs; white-flowered cultivars tend to have white hairs. One of the most attractive summer bedding plants, fitting well into perennial and mixed borders and unexpectedly hardy. There are a number of attractive seed-raised cultivars intended for summer bedding. For open, sunny positions in well-drained soil. Usually raised from seed, but division is also possible. From the southern US to Mexico. ↕32 in (80 cm). Z8–11 H11–1

S. flava var. ***megalantha*** Tuberous roots support upright or rather arching stems carrying, mostly toward the base, broadly egg-shaped or more triangular

LIGHTENING THE DARKNESS

BUILDING ON THE rich purple flowers of *S.* x *sylvestris* 'Mainacht' can take you in one of two directions. You can add to the sultry sumptuousness with the dark foliage of heucheras and wine-leaved weigelas, and with more dark flowers. Alternatively, you can add lighter touches, as here. The silver foliage of *Artemisia* 'Powis Castle' and the silver helichrysum in the front make long-season foliage companions, while the pink diascia spikes reflect the salvia shape, but in a paler color. The sharply cut foliage of *Geranium sanguineum* nestles around the base of the salvia, its pink bowls providing a contrasting shape and lighter tone.

leaves, hairy only along the undersides of the veins. In succession during mid- and late summer, several smooth, distinctively upward-curving, yellow, 1 in (2.5 cm) flowers appear, each with a brown or purple mark in the center of the lower lip. Closely related to the purple-flowered *S. bulleyana*, under which name it is often offered. Grows well in open, sunny positions in well-drained soil in the front of borders. Raise from seed. From mountains in Yunnan province, China. ↕10–26 in (24–65 cm). Z8–11 H11–7

S. forsskaolii Several erect branches carry large, light green, lyre-shaped or egg-shaped leaves reaching 6 in (15 cm) or more in length, with irregular lobing along the margins. From early summer into midsummer, the straight stems carry clusters of showy, violet-blue flowers whose upper lips arch in a sickle shape over the lower lip, which is streaked or blotched in white or yellow. Grows well in most soils in a part-shaded site. Divide or raise from seed.

From the Balkans and northern Turkey. ↕18–40 in (45–100 cm). Z6–8 H8–6

S. glutinosa From a slowly spreading underground rootstock, erect, very sticky branches emerge to carry large, sticky leaves that are light green, spear-shaped or egg-shaped, reaching 5 in (13 cm) or more long and with toothed margins. The 1¼–1¾ in (3–4 cm), sticky yellow flowers have spreading lower lips that are speckled or streaked with brown markings and appear from early summer into mid- or late summer. Grows well in most soils in a part-shaded site. Very sticky, as you will have gathered, and also surprisingly tolerant of dry shady conditions. Divide or raise from seed. From woodlands from France to Russia. ↕18–36 in (45–90 cm). Z7–9 H9–7

S. guaranitica A running rootstock produces frost-tender shoots in spring that develop to carry heart-shaped or egg-shaped, 1½–4¾ in (4–12 cm) leaves that may be pale green to dark green,

and smooth or softly hairy; the degree of hairiness varies with the cultivar. The stalked, blue, 1–2 in (2.5–5 cm) flowers are held in either a green or black calyx according to the cultivar and are borne in spikes over 12 in (30 cm) long in late summer and fall. For open, sunny places in the back of the border with protection from spring frosts. Taller cultivars with the largest flowers and hairiest leaves are the least tender, and are capable of withstanding only a few degrees of frost. Best propagated by cuttings or division. From woodland margins in subtropical regions of South America inhabited by the Guarani people, from Paraguay to Brazil. ‡ 4–9 ft (1.2–2.7 m). Z7–10 H11–8. **'Argentine Skies'** Pale slatey blue flowers. Raised by horticulturist-gardener Charles O. Cresson of Pennsylvania. **'Black and Blue'** Tall, vigorous, and tender, with very hairy leaves and dark blue flowers beautifully offset by a black calyx. ‡ 9–12 ft (2.7–4 m). **'Blue Enigma'** syn. *S. ambigens*, *S. caerulea* Pale green, almost hairless, rather shiny leaves with dark blue flowers set in a green calyx.

S. hians (Wide-mouthed sage) Tuberous roots support mainly basal, more or less egg-shaped or heart-shaped, hairy toothed leaves to 10 in (25 cm) long, with stalks about as long, and white with hairs below. The sticky and heavily fragrant stems bear several hairy, widely flaring, blue or violet-blue flowers, each 1–1¾ in (2.5–4 cm) in length, during early summer and midsummer; the throat of the tube is often white with blue speckling or streaking. For open, sunny positions in well-drained soil at the front of borders; it hates poorly drained soil and resents being moved. Raise from seed. *S. forsskaolii* is sometimes mistakenly sold under this name. From high mountain meadows in Himalayan India. ‡ 10–26 in (24–65 cm). Z6–9 H9–6

S. 'Indigo Spires' Strong upright stems carry green, egg-shaped leaves up to 4 in (10 cm) long, tapering to a graceful tip. Long spikes carry many short, dark blue flowers in succession from early summer until late fall. For open, sunny positions in well-drained soil in the middle or rear of borders. Divide or take cuttings. A vigorous hybrid between *S. longispicata* and *S. farinacea* from the Huntington Botanic Garden in California. ‡ 4 ft (1.2 m). Z8–11 H11–7

S. involucrata (Bracted sage, Roseleaf sage) A sprawling plant, the many arching stems bearing egg-shaped or heart-shaped, aromatic leaves up to 4 in (10 cm) long, green above and below, some with a pinkish hue on the leaf midribs and stems. From midsummer to mid- or late fall, expanding spikes of showy, vibrant, rose red, 2 in (5 cm) long smooth flowers with inflated tubes and rather short lips emerge from long or rounded bracts that are frequently

rose-tinged and curl back at the apex. Bracts are an integral part of the plant's overall display. Best in a sheltered but sunny position with protection against spring frosts. Take cuttings or divide large plants. From central Mexico. ‡ 4–5 ft (1.2–1.5 m). Z10–11 H11–10. **'Bethellii'** Erect, with smooth heart-shaped leaves and compact, rounded flower clusters elongate gradually to reveal rose red flowers among rounded rose red bracts. ‡ 4 ft (1.2 m). **'Boutin'** Smaller, erect, with narrower dark rose bracts, darker rose red flowers, and smooth, egg-shaped leaves. ‡ 36 in (90 cm). **'Hadspen'** Vigorous and lax, the coarsely hairy, aromatic leaves heart-shaped with narrow pointed tips and pink midveins, while the long arching stems carry rose red flowers and long white bracts tinged pink and curling at the apex. ‡ 4 ft (1.2 m).

S. jurisicii Lax, much-branched stems are densely covered in long hairs, the dark grayish green leaves reaching 3 in (8 cm) in length and each divided into four to six pairs of narrow linear segments; the whole leaf is covered in long hairs. From early summer into midsummer, clusters of four to six small, usually pale or darker blue or occasionally violet, pink, or white flowers appear, less than ½ in (1 cm) across and covered in very long hairs; the upper lip is slightly longer than the smooth, wider lower lip. The flowers slowly turn upside-down as they mature so that the lower part of the flowering stem is covered in flowers whose hairy upper lips face downward while the smooth lower ones are above them. Ideal in hot dry places in well-drained soil. Divide, take cuttings, or raise from seed. From Macedonia. ‡ 12–24 in (30–60 cm). Z4–8 H8–1

S. leptophylla see *S. reptans*

S. leucantha (Mexican bush sage) Erect white stems, with a dense covering of fine white hairs, produce many lateral branches and carry narrowly lance-shaped, aromatic leaves, reaching 2–4 in (5–10 cm) long. From late summer to mid- or late fall, stems and side branches are tipped with finely hairy spikes of narrow tubular flowers that are densely covered in fine hairs and held in a hairy, white or colored calyx. The 1½ in (3.5 cm) long flowers have straight tubes that curve upward toward the short lips and are densely hairy outside. They vary from white or pale pink to deep violet-purple and often contrast with white or purple calyces. Best in a sheltered, sunny position; will grow to maturity very rapidly if protected from spring frosts. Best from cuttings, or divide large plants. An increasing range of cultivars, mainly from the US and South Africa, is becoming popular. From subtropical forests in Mexico and Central America. ‡ 4 ft (1.2 m). Z9–11 H11–4. **'All Purple'** see 'Midnight'. **'Danielle's Dream'** Erect, with a soft pale pink, densely hairy flower in a white calyx. From South Africa. **'Midnight'** syn. 'All Purple' Flowers and calyx both purple. **'Purple Velvet'** Erect, with deep

purple hairy flowers emerging from a purple calyx. **'Santa Barbara'** Purple flowers have paler purple lips and purple calyx. Very dwarf with a wider spread. ‡ 24 in (60 cm). **'White Mischief'** Compact, with narrower, lance-shaped leaves, white flowers blushing slightly with age, from a white calyx. Mature flowers fade with the palest tinge of pink. From South African garden designer Vicki Ferreira. ‡ 36 in (90 cm).

S. lyrata (Cancer weed, Lyre-leaf sage) Short-lived; produces taprooted rosette of ground-hugging, dark green leaves that may have a reddish midvein. The leaves are lyre-shaped or occasionally segmented, reaching 3 in (8 cm) in length. The straight stems carry clusters of three to ten, pale to dark lavender-blue, rarely pinkish to purple, 1 in (2.5 cm) flowers whose lower lips are broadly spreading and which open in early summer and continue until late summer or later. Grows well in lighter, well-drained, sandy soil and part-shade. Grow from seed, but select seedlings carefully to match the appropriate cultivar. From the eastern US. ‡ 12–24 in (30–60 cm). Z5–10 H10–4. **'Burgundy Bliss'** syn. 'Purple Volcano' Deep burgundy-red foliage and pale lavender flowers. An improved form of a plant found at the North Carolina Botanic Garden. **'Purple Knockout'** Purple-red leaves, purple-red stems, and paler pinkish purple flowers. **'Purple Volcano'** see 'Burgundy Bliss'.

S. madrensis One of the tallest, most striking salvias: thick, strong, erect stems are curiously angular and feature large, soft-textured, heart-shaped green leaves, to 6 in (15 cm) long, covered on both surfaces in soft hairs. From early to mid-fall, the stems elongate and break into lateral branches tipped with 12 in (30 cm) spikes of deep golden yellow flowers, up to 1¼ in (3 cm) long. The pale yellow floral tube is straight but slightly inflated, and the upper lip is densely covered in deep golden hairs. Best in an open, sunny position against a wall, with protection from spring frosts. Divide, take cuttings, or raise from seed. From subtropical lowland forest margins in western Mexico. ‡ 7–9 ft (2.2–2.7 m). Z7–11 H11–7. **'Red Neck Girl'** Earlier-flowering, with red stems. From Tony Avent's Plant Delights Nursery in North Carolina.

S. merjamie A short-lived species, the erect, glandular, sticky and rather aromatic stems frequently branched from about half-way. The mint-scented, 6 in (15 cm) leaves are oblong, rather coarse, and waved and toothed along the edges. Each branched flowering stem carries many attractive and showy lavender or sky blue flowers in erect profusion during early summer and midsummer; each flower has a strongly sickle-shaped upper lip. For an open, sunny position in well-drained soil. Grow from seed. From the highlands of central and eastern Africa, and Yemen. ‡ 12–24 in (30–60 cm). Z8–11 H11–7. **'Mint-sauce'** Mid-blue flowers and typically aromatic leaves.

LEFT 1 *Salvia guaranitica* 'Black and Blue' **2** *S. guaranitica* 'Blue Enigma' **3** *S. involucrata* 'Bethellii'

S. mexicana (Mexican sage) Tall, erect, multi-stemmed species; the rhomboid or egg-shaped green leaves, to 6 in (15 cm) long, are usually smooth above and vary from smooth to softly hairy below. The blue flowers, held in either a green- or dark-bluish black-stained calyx, are borne in 6 in (15 cm) spikes from early to late fall. The smooth upper lip of the calyx, with only three veins on it, is a distinguishing feature of this species. The ½–1 in (1–2.5 cm) floral tube is usually dark blue, sometimes paler or, rarely, white. Selections are being made that vary in

NORTH AND SOUTH

Salvias vary in their tolerance of cold and damp. Some, like *Salvia pratensis*, *S. nemorosa*, and their allies, are very tough; hardy down to zone 5, they are utterly dependable. But this genus is widely distributed, not only around the world but in various climatic zones; they grow wild in northern Europe and in South America, and those from the balmy south are far less hardy than those from the colder north. In zones 7–10, the less hardy *S. guaranitica*, *S. involucrata*, and *S. leucantha* are often grown in the same borders as the far tougher *S. x sylvestris*.

Even less hardy, the slightly tuberous *S. farinacea* and *S. patens*, which are often grown from seed as summer bedding and container plants, can be brought through the winter in the warmest parts of zone 8, and in sheltered and well-drained corners of other gardens. The comfort of a warm wall, good drainage, absence of leaky gutters, and shelter from icy winds and early spring frosts, plus a winter mulch of coarse bark chips, will all help coax the more tender species through the winter. But beware: many of these tender species flower so late in the season that, in areas subject to early frosts, flowering can be cut short.

height, leaf size, and shape, and flower size and color. Best in an open, sunny place at the back of a border with protection from spring frosts. Divide, take cuttings, or raise from seed. Often found as a roadside plant in huge numbers in central and southern Mexico. ↕ 36 in to 9 ft (90 cm to 2.7 m). Z8–11 H11–7

S. napifolia (Turnip-leaved sage) Slowly spreading underground rootstock from which emerge several erect but arching stems. The hairy and rather sticky leaves are light green, lyre-shaped, frequently with one or two pairs of small, triangular or egg-shaped segments at their base, and may reach 5 in (13 cm) in length. The small, ⅝ in (1.5 cm) long, violet-blue flowers are borne in clusters of 6–12 from early summer into mid- or late summer. Very closely related to *S. verticillata*, from which it differs in having fewer flowers per cluster and in other technical floral details. Surprisingly tolerant of a wide range of soils and of full sun or part-shade. Divide, or raise from seed. From Turkey. ↕ 36 in (90 cm). Z8–11 H11–7

S. nemorosa (Woodland sage) A confusing species, the ground-hugging rosette made up of coarse, green, heart-shaped to oblong leaves, scalloped along the margins and reaching 7 in (18 cm) in length. The flowers are carried tightly along the spikes, making an impressive show; each cluster is made up of two to six flowers that are initially hidden by overlapping green, or more often purple, leaflike bracts, which then spread open to reveal the maturing flowers. The individual flowers, opening from early to late summer, are small, ⅜–⅝ in (8 mm to 1.4 cm) long, and may be blue, violet blue, pink, or white. Cultivars formerly placed here are now considered hybrids and will be found under *S. x sylvestris* (see Solving Salvia Confusions, p.417). Grows well in most soils in full sun. Divide, or raise from seed. From

Europe to Russia. ↕ 12–24 in (30–60 cm). Z5–9 H9–5. **subsp. *tesquicola*** Calyx covered in long hairs and with longer floral tubes. From eastern Europe to Russia.

S. nipponica A slowly spreading underground rootstock supports several strong, erect branches emerging from a bushy mass of light green, spear-shaped leaves with pointed tips and reaching 2–4 in (5–10 cm) in length. The 1 in (2.5 cm) long, pale cream or yellow flowers have spreading lower lips and appear from late summer to mid-fall. Tolerant of shady conditions or full sun, and most soils. Divide or raise from seed. From woodlands in Japan. ↕ 16 in (40 cm). Z6–9 H9–6. **'Fuji Snow'** Dramatic, white-edged leaves. Introduced from Japan by Japanese plant expert Barry Yinger.

S. patens (Gentian sage) Some of largest flowers of all salvias. From a white-fleshed tuber several branches emerge from a few stems carrying mid-green, five-angled or spear-shaped 2–3 in (5–8 cm) leaves with pronounced lobing and sometimes with darker blotching. Each branch terminates in an open spike of spectacular, paired gentian blue flowers, 2–3 in (5–8 cm) long. Best in open, sunny positions in well-drained soil; mulch to help tubers overwinter, or lift and store them like dahlias. Often used as seasonal bedding or container plant. Take cuttings, or raise from seed. From the mountain forests of central Mexico. ↕ 24–60 in (60–150 cm). Z8–9 H9–8. **'Blue Angel'** Deep Oxford blue flowers and slightly soft hairy leaves. Grown for many years simply as *S. patens*. ↕ 18–24 in (45–60 cm). **'Cambridge Blue'** Pale blue flowers and slightly soft hairy leaves. ↕ 18–24 in (45–60 cm). **'Chilcombe'** Dusky lilac flowers with slightly soft hairy leaves. Found in John Hubbard's Dorset, England, garden of the same name. ↕ 18–24 in (45–60 cm). **'Guanajuato'** Robust plant with

ABOVE 1 *Salvia leucantha*
2 *S. patens* 'Cambridge Blue'
3 *S. pratensis* Haematodes Group

relatively hairless, stiffly angled leaves and much larger and more pendulous, deep blue, 3 in (8 cm) flowers. Found by James Compton, John d'Arcy, and Martyn Rix in the Guanajuato mountains of central Mexico. ↕ 5 ft (1.5 m). **'Oxford Blue'** No different from the species. **'Royal Blue'** No different from the species. **'White Trophy'** White flowers, fading with a hint of gray. Originated with Christopher Lloyd at Great Dixter, East Sussex, England. ↕ 18–24 in (45–60 cm).

S. pitcheri see *S. azurea* var. *grandiflora*

S. pratensis (Meadow clary) Very variable in height and color, the ground-hugging rosette consists of coarse, egg- or heart-shaped, green leaves, up to 7 in (18 cm) in length, that may be hairless or sparsely hairy. From early to late summer, clusters of four to six flowers are carried loosely along upright flowering stems, the green bracts much shorter than the relatively large, ⅝ in (1.5 cm), blue, violet-blue, pink, or white flowers. Tolerant of a wide range of soil conditions, but prefers full sun. Divide, especially for cultivars, or raise from seed. Related to *S. nemorosa*, from which it differs in its taller stature, larger, more sickle-shaped flowers, and much shorter bracts. A parent of the garden hybrids known as *S. x sylvestris*. From Europe to Russia. ↕ 36 in (90 cm). Z3–9 H9–1. **'Albiflora'** White flowers. ↕ 30 in (75 cm). **Haematodes Group** Seed-raised plants with pale but intense blue flowers. ↕ 4 ft (1.2 m). **'Rosea'** Rose pink flowers. ↕ 30 in (75 cm).

S. przewalskii Tuberous with triangular, spear- or lance-shaped leaves, 2–4½ in (5–11 cm) long, have densely white-hairy undersides. The much-branched

LEFT *Salvia* 'Purple Majesty'

flowering stems are covered in fine white hairs and, from early summer until early fall, bear several finely hairy, gradually flaring, purple, reddish brown, or rarely white, ¾–1¾ in (2–4 cm) flowers with upper and lower lips of equal length. For open sunny positions in very well-drained soil at the front of borders. Grow from seed. From forest margins and meadows in western China. ↕ 24 in (60 cm). Z8–11 H11–7

S. 'Purple Majesty' Stiff, erect stems bear green, egg-shaped leaves up to 3 in (8 cm) long, and are tipped, from late summer until mid-fall, with 12 in (30 cm) spikes carrying several violet purple flowers, each 1 in (2.5 cm) long and entirely smooth. For an open, sunny position in well-drained soil in

SALVIA HYBRIDS

It is perhaps not surprising that the clearly similar *Salvia pratensis* and *S. nemorosa* hybridize with each other, but there is also a range of hybrids featuring other species, with more emerging. One of the more surprising is the 1995 introduction *Salvia* 'Mulberry Jam'. This appears to be a hybrid between the tall perennial *S. involucrata* and the twiggy shrub *S. microphylla*. It arose in the California garden of *Salvia* author Betsy Clebsch, although the surprise is mitigated by recognition that these two species are among the more promiscuous of all salvias and, therefore, the most likely to hybridize. Another perennial/shrub cross is 'Cherry Queen', *S. blepharophylla* x *S. greggii*, raised in North Carolina by Richard Dufresne.

'Mulberry Jam' is only slowly becoming available, but 'Indigo Spires' is already widely grown. This vigorous hybrid between the rarely grown tall, blue-flowered species *S. longispicata* and the short mealy sage, *S. farinacea*, arose by chance at the Huntington Botanical

Garden in California and was introduced in 1979.

'Purple Majesty' is a hybrid between the tall, orange-red-flowered cultivar *S. gesneriiflora* 'Tequila' from Mexico, which has black calyces, and the South American deep-blue flowered *S. guaranitica*. Also from California's Huntington Botanical Garden, this is the result of a deliberate cross made in 1979 by Fred Boutin, for whom a cultivar of *S. involucrata* is named.

These are exciting times for salvias, with a wider range of species being grown and more hybrids undoubtedly to be introduced. But a word of warning is also needed. The long bed in which the Royal Horticultural Society's trial of salvias was grown from 1995 to 1997 demonstrated how freely some species can self-sow. So with the tendency of some to hybridize and of cultivars not to come true, raising perennial salvias from seed is perhaps unwise—and, for most, unnecessary when they are so easy to raise from cuttings.

the middle or at the rear of borders. Divide, or take cuttings. A hybrid between S. *gesneriiflora* 'Tequila' and S. *guaranitica* from California's Huntington Botanic Garden. ↕ 36 in (90 cm). Z7–10 H10–7

S. recognita Somewhat shrubby and covered in sticky, glandular, aromatic hairs; the leaves are light greenish gray above and gray-hairy beneath, and consist of one to two pairs of egg-shaped leaflets and one larger egg-shaped or oblong segment at the tip. In early summer to midsummer, the shoots terminate in a much-branched flowering stem bearing several showy, lilac-pink, 1½–1¾ in (3.5–4 cm) long flowers with a widening tube and straight upper lip; the lower lip faces downward. Short-lived but prolific and extremely showy; grows best in an open, sunny position in very well-drained soil. Raise from seed, or take cuttings. From the mountains of central Turkey. ↕ 3¼ ft (1 m). Z8–11 H11–7

S. repens (African creeping sage) A short-stemmed, vigorous, creeping species, the scented leaves narrowly oblong and rather coarse, reaching 3 in (8 cm) in length, with sawtoothed margins. The erect, aromatic stems are often branched in pairs from the middle, and in early summer to midsummer carry a profusion of showy purple, lavender, blue, or white flowers, each usually less than ½ in (1 cm) long. In many forms, the upper lip is a different color from the extended lower lip. Best in an open, sunny position in well-drained soil, but can creep too vigorously. Divide, or raise from seed. From eastern South Africa. ↕ 12–24 in (30–60 cm). Z8–11 H11–7

S. reptans syn. *S. angustifolia*, *S. leptophylla* (Jacquin's sage) Running

roots support rather lax, branched stems carrying extremely narrow, almost threadlike leaves, often less than ¼ in (5 mm) wide with lightly toothed edges. Each branched flower stem carries many attractive and showy azure to mid-blue flowers in lax profusion from late summer to mid-fall, each flower displaying a broad downward-facing lower lip. For an open, sunny position in well-drained soil. Divide, or raise from seed. Very closely related to S. *azurea*, but shorter and with much more slender leaves. From the US and Mexico. ↕ 12 in (30 cm). Z8–11 H11–7

S. roemeriana Low-growing, with multibranched stems covered in white flattened hairs, leaves pale green above, gray-hairy below, the lowest sometimes with small lateral kidney-shaped leaflets and a larger terminal kidney-shaped segment, up to 1 in (2.5 cm) long. Leaf margins waved and toothed or notched. From early summer into late summer, upright, branched stems are lined with clusters of two to four large, 1–1½ in (2.5–3.5 cm), bright scarlet flowers; the tube of each flower is gradually downward-curving, the upper lip slightly longer than the wider, notched lower lip, which narrows before it joins the tube. Ideal in hot, dry raised borders, but short-lived, surviving mainly via its copious quantities of freely germinating seed. From the southern US and northern Mexico. ↕ 12–18 in (30–45 cm). Z8–11 H11–7

S. scabra Erect, rather woody stems carry rough-textured, lyre-shaped green leaves, 1 in (2.5 cm) long, often with a pair of lateral segments at the base and scalloped and waved margins. The flowers, carried on purple-tinged stems and emerging from a purple calyx, are lilac to pink, ½ in (1.3 cm) long, and have straight floral tubes; the lower lip is cleft. Easy in open, sunny places, in light soil on a slope or in a raised bed. Grow from seed, which is produced generously. From sandy flats and rocky hillsides in South Africa. ↕ 28 in (70 cm). Z8–11 H11–7

S. sinaloensis Slowly spreading to make a tight, bushy clump wider than it is tall. Upright stems carry oblong or lance-shaped leaves, to 1 in (2.5 cm) long, with pointed tips and saw-shaped margins and slightly hairy on both surfaces. Both stems and leaves deep purple-red in chilly conditions. Small, deep blue flowers, in clusters of four to six, are up to ½ in (1.3 cm) long; their lower lip has a pronounced white streak. Avoid alkaline soils; grows best in very well-drained sandy soil in a sunny spot in the front of a border, or in gaps between paving stones. Divide, take cuttings, or raise from seed. From rocky slopes in western Mexico. ↕ 12 in (30 cm). Z8–11 H11–7

S. spathacea (Pitcher sage) Robust species with a lax bushy habit, slowly spreading by rhizomes to form large leafy clumps up to 6 ft (1.8 m) across. The sprawling stems and calyces are sticky with clammy aromatic oils; leaves are spear-shaped or oblong leaves to

8 in (20 cm) long, green and slightly hairy above and softly green or white-hairy below, with notched or scalloped margins. Dusky, dark wine red flowers on dark purple-red stems in tightly packed clusters of up to 20 among green to purple, 1¾ in (4 cm) bracts. Each flower is more than 1 in (2.5 cm) long, extending from a calyx almost as long. Best in fertile but well-drained soil in sunny border positions. Divide, take cuttings, or raise from seed. From woodlands and scrub in California. ↕ 30 in (75 cm). Z8–11 H11–7

S. x superba Prolific upright stems, woody at the base and much-branched, carry oblong to lance-shaped leaves with scalloped margins. Long, tightly crowded, red-purple flowering spikes bear deep blue sterile flowers set in clusters of six among purple bracts. A hybrid between *S. pratensis* and *S. amplexicaulis*, generally resembling a larger version of *S. nemorosa*. Cultivars formerly included here are now considered better placed under *S. x sylvestris*. For a sunny mid-border position in most reasonable soils. Take cuttings, or divide. ↕ 30 in (75 cm). Z5–9 H9–5

S. x sylvestris Upright stems carry more or less lance-shaped, rather rough, 2¾ in (7 cm) leaves, with scalloped edges, that may be rounded to heart-shaped at the base. Flowers vary from white through pink to a range of dark blue and violet shades. These are hybrids between *S. nemorosa* and *S. pratensis*: such crosses occur where the two species grow together in the wild and also in cultivation. Cultivars fall into two groups that differ in the general style of their flowering spikes. Most cultivars are more akin to *S. nemorosa*, with their flower clusters tightly grouped on the stems; some, in the style of *S. pratensis*, have larger flowers in more widely spaced clusters. For sunny front or mid-border positions in any reasonable soil. Take cuttings, or divide. ↕ 12–30 in (30–75 cm). Z5–9 H9–4. **'Amethyst'** Upright, with tightly packed violet flowers, a purple calyx, and amethyst-purple bracts. ↕ 24 in (60 cm). **'Blauhügel'** (Blue Hill) Short and erect with purple stems tightly packed with clusters of mid-blue flowers and small purple bracts. ↕ 18 in (45 cm). **'Blaukönigin'** (Blue Queen) Short, erect blue stems tinged with purple are tightly packed with clusters of deep blue flowers and small blue-purple bracts. ↕ 18 in (45 cm). **'Caradonna'** Very dwarf, the dark, almost blackish purple stems are tightly packed with dark purple bracts and calyces, and vivid violet-blue flowers. Derived from 'Wesuwe'. ↕ 12 in (30 cm). **'Dear Anja'** Green stems are tightly packed with blue flowers whose lower lips are edged with white. Selected by Dutch horticulturist Piet Oudolf and named for his wife. ↕ 36 in (90 cm). **'Forncett Dawn'** Tall, with grayish green leaves and upright purple-pink stems crowded with pink flowers. From John Metcalf, Four Seasons Nursery, Norfolk, England. ↕ 26 in (65 cm). **'Indigo'**

Branching purple-blue stems carry well-spaced clusters of lavender-blue flowers with arching upper lips. ↕ 24 in (60 cm). **'Lapis Lazuli'** Lax, reddish pink stems bear well-spaced clusters of reddish pink calyces and rose-colored flowers with arching upper lips. ↕ 28 in (70 cm). **'Lubecca'** Upright stems are tightly clustered with pinkish purple bracts and calyces, and deep blue flowers. ↕ 24 in (60 cm). **'Mainacht'** ('May Night') Short and tightly clump-forming, erect, deep pinkish purple stems are tightly packed with bracts in the same shade and with deep blue flowers. Perennial Plant of the Year in 1997. ↕ 18 in (45 cm). **Marcus** (**'Haeumanarc'**) Very short with tightly packed deep blue flowers and almost green bracts. A dwarf selection of 'Mainacht', not a spontaneous mutation of 'Ostfriesland' as sometimes thought; named for Marcus Häusermann, Stuttgart, Germany. ↕ 12 in (30 cm). **'Ostfriesland'** (**East Friesland**) Robust, with purple stems crowded with pinkish purple bracts and violet flowers. Sometimes raised from seed, so could be variable. ↕ 18 in (45 cm). **'Plumosa'** see 'Pusztaflamme'. **'Porzellan'** Robust, with green stems packed with green bracts and white flowers that fade with a hint of blue. ↕ 18 in (45 cm). **'Pusztaflamme'** syn. 'Plumosa'. Green stems are tightly packed with clusters of highly doubled flowers consisting of many petal-like violet purple segments. **'Rosenwein'** Rather lax, with tightly packed reddish calyces and bracts and soft pink flowers. ↕ 18 in (45 cm). **'Rose Queen'** Lax, pinkish purple-tinged stems carry well-spaced clusters of pink flowers whose upper lips arch downward. ↕ 24 in (60 cm). **'Rubin'** Short and erect, with reddish purple stems crowded with reddish purple bracts and flowers. ↕ 18 in (45 cm). **'Rügen'** Very short, with well-spaced mid-blue flowers with arching upper lips on green stems. ↕ 12 in (30 cm). **'Schneehügel'** (**Snow Hill**) Short and erect, the stems tightly packed with clusters of white flowers with small green bracts. ↕ 18 in (45 cm). **'Tänzerin'** Erect, with tightly packed spikes of violet-blue flowers with reddish purple bracts and calyces. ↕ 24 in (60 cm). **'Viola Klose'** syn. 'Violet Queen' Short, with branching, dark violet-blue stems carrying well-spaced clusters of dark violet-blue flowers that have arching upper lips. ↕ 18 in (45 cm). **'Wesuwe'** Erect, with dark purple stems crowded with dark purple calyces and deep blue-violet flowers. ↕ 24 in (60 cm).

S. taraxacifolia Short-lived, low-growing species; multibranched stems covered in fine hairs emerge from a basal rosette. The lyre-shaped leaves are gray above, gray to white with hairs below, the lowest leaves with small, lateral, egg-shaped leaflets and the terminal segment much larger, reaching 1 in (2.5 cm) in length. The leaf margins are wavy and toothed or notched. The upright stems are covered in white or pale pink, 1–1½ in (2.5–3.5 cm) flowers in well-separated clusters of 5–10 from early summer into midsummer. The straight tube emerges from a spiny-toothed calyx, the upper lip equal in length to the wider, lower lip, which is often flecked with yellow, brown, or purple. Ideal for hot, dry places at the front of borders or in raised beds, in well-drained soil. Usually self-sows generously. From the Atlas mountains of Morocco. ↕ 12–18 in (30–45 cm). Z8–11 H11–7

S. transsylvanica A flat rosette of large, 7–10 in (18–24 cm), coarse, egg- or heart-shaped leaves, green above and with dense white hairs underneath. Tall, well-branched stems carry clusters of large, ¾ in (2 cm), dark blue or violet-blue flowers of four to six from early to late summer. Tolerates a wide range of soil conditions but prefers full sun. Divide, or raise from seed. Taller than *S. pratensis* and with bushier growth and larger leaves. From Romania. ↕ 36 in (90 cm). Z6–8 H8–6. **'Blue Cloud'** Blue flowers. ↕ 30 in (75 cm).

S. uliginosa (Marsh sage) Thick, white underground stems form sizable clumps.

SOLVING SALVIA CONFUSIONS

Stand in front of a border and look at plants of *Salvia amplexicaulis*, *S. nemorosa*, *S.* x *superba*, and *S.* x *sylvestris* and, frankly, you might think they were all the same species, and indeed, the wild species are parents of the hybrids. Research is currently under way involving, among other things, the analysis of DNA evidence, and this may prove that *S. amplexicaulis* is indeed merely an eastern form of *S. nemorosa* with hairier stems and leaves.

The situation is complicated by the fact that these species hybridize with each other. *S.* x *superba* is a sterile hybrid between *S. pratensis* and *S. amplexicaulis* that arose at the Royal Botanic Garden, Kew, England, and has also been thought to be a cross between *S.* x *sylvestris* and *S. amplexicaulis*. *Salvia* x *sylvestris* was once thought to be a wild species in its own right, but has now been proved to be a hybrid between *S. nemorosa* and *S. pratensis*.

Such is the similarity of these plants that botanists still struggle to place cultivars under the appropriate species, and in the past, cultivars have been placed under *S. nemorosa*, *S. pratensis*, *S.* x *superba*, and *S.* x *sylvestris*. But now, apart from a limited number of cultivars that are clearly forms of *S. pratensis*, they are all considered hybrids and placed under *S.* x *sylvestris*, where they fall into two groups: one with flower spikes tending toward the tightly packed display of *S. nemorosa* in form, and one with the more widely spaced spikes of *S. pratensis*. Expect further clarification of the situation in coming years.

Tall, erect stems with narrowly lance-shaped green leaves, to 4 in (10 cm), often smooth above and vary from smooth to sparsely hairy below, with margins almost untoothed or gently sawtoothed. From late summer to late fall, flowers in a pale but intense blue emerge from a green calyx on long, straight stems that extend as they age. The tube is usually white, ⅜ in (8 mm) in length; the pale blue lower lip has a white blotch. For open, sunny places in positions at the back of a border, with protection from spring frosts. A winter mulch is advisable in cold areas. Divide, or take cuttings. From damp watercourses in Argentina, Brazil, and Uruguay. ↕3–7 ft (1–2 m). Z6–9 H9–6. **'African Skies'** A spurious cultivar, not different from the species.

S. verbenaca Rosette-forming plant with extremely variable foliage, the leaves frequently deeply and broadly lobed, sometimes with wavy or scalloped margins. Straight or branching flower stems carry short green bracts and small blue, lilac, or violet flowers ¼–⅝ in (0.6–1.5 cm) in length. Distinguished from *S. nemorosa* by its short, green bracts and from *S. pratensis* by much smaller flowers. For full sun in most soils. Divide, or raise from seed. From Europe to Russia. ↕12–28 in (30–70 cm). Z8–11 H11–7

S. verticillata A spreading, many-stemmed plant, the leaves frequently lyre-shaped with one or two pairs of small lateral segments, and softly hairy on both surfaces. Straight flower stems carry clusters of 10–30 lilac blue or white flowers. Similar to *S. napifolia* but with two to three times as many flowers per cluster. Easy in full sun and most soil types, but can self-sow too enthusiastically in lighter soil. Divide, or raise from seed. From Europe to Russia. ↕12–32 in (30–80 cm). Z6–8

H8–6. **'Alba'** syn. 'White Rain' Pale green leaves and white flowers. **'Purple Rain'** Dark green leaves and reddish purple stems, calyx, and flowers. Selected by Dutch horticulturist Piet Oudolf. **'Smouldering Torches'** Leaves suffused with purple. A selection from 'Purple Rain' raised by Piet Oudolf. **'White Rain'** see 'Alba'.

SANGUINARIA
Bloodroot
PAPAVERACEAE

Exquisite spring woodland species with both decorative flowers and foliage.

Just one species of patch-forming woodlander; it is found in the northeastern US and Canada and is one of the most unusual members of the poppy family. A stout rhizome carries bold, rounded, grayish leaves, preceded by delightful pure white flowers. Although the flowers of the wild species are fleeting, the handsome foliage that follows adds interest over many months. Primarily valuable in humus-rich shade gardens, especially in woodlands; plants form slow-spreading clumps and, once established in the garden, greatly resent disturbance. The common names relates to the fact that most parts of the plant ooze an orange-red juice when cut.

CULTIVATION Thrives best in moist humus-rich soil; grows poorly in summer drought or full sun.

PROPAGATION By division.

PROBLEMS Slugs, vine weevil.

S. canadensis A stocky plant; thick, branching rhizomes are horizontal and

lie close to the soil surface. The leaves, which are folded down the center at first, emerge at the same time or just after the flowers. They are eventually more or less heart-shaped, to 8 in (20 cm) across with a shallowly lobed and scalloped margin, bluish green above but paler beneath. The solitary, anemone-like flowers, each 1½–1¾ in (3.5–4 cm) across and with eight or twelve oblong pure white petals, are borne on a slender, fleshy stalk among the expanding leaves, in mid- and late spring. Pink-flowered forms with pink-flushed young leaves, carrying names such as 'Amy', 'Peter Harrison', and 'Rosea', are occasionally seen. From woodlands and in rocky places in the northeastern US and eastern Canada. ↕8–12 in (20–30 cm). Z3–9 H9–1. **f. multiplex** Fully double, far longer-lasting flowers. Almost certainly the same as 'Plena' which apparently has smaller flowers, but long-established clumps of f. *multiplex* generally produce small flowers. **'Plena'** see f. *multiplex*.

SANGUISORBA
ROSACEAE

Graceful, vigorous, and quietly stylish perennials for subtle late summer color, most of them moisture-loving.

About ten species of these mainly deciduous plants are found in the temperate Northern Hemisphere, often in mountains and usually in moist habitats such as meadows, streamsides, and bogs. Some species were previously classified as *Poterium*, and research is still needed to clarify the situation. Most are grown in gardens and are fairly large in stature, their robust rootstocks producing a generous clump of decorative foliage above which sway tall, wiry, branched stems, often

flushed with red, bearing dense flower spikes in white, pink, or red. The leaves are divided into opposite pairs of round-tipped, oval to oblong leaflets with toothed edges, up to 2¾–3 in (7–8 cm) long in most species, and generally increasing in size toward the tip of the leaf. Foliage is generally fresh green, varying to blue-green or grayish, and may in spring be pink-flushed, followed by vivid fall tints.

From midsummer to early fall many tiny flowers appear, variously clustered into sumptuous, drooping tassels, upright plumes, or rounded buttons. The flowers have colorful sepals rather than true petals, and long, showy stamens that give the spikes a shaggy or fluffy texture that is often likened to a bottle brush. The flowers may open in succession, either from the top of the spike downward, or upward from the base.

Where species have been introduced from different wild sources, there is some variation in stock available from nurseries, and inadvertent hybridization among seed-raised plants may be the cause of some confusion. The number of cultivars is increasing as plant breeders explore their potential for hybridization and demand grows for their use in naturalistic planting schemes. These perennials are also ideal in meadows.

CULTIVATION Grows well in any good garden soil with moisture in sun or part-shade; some are adapted to drier conditions. May need deadheading to prevent abundant self-seeding.

PROPAGATION By division or from seed (germination may be erratic). Seed collected from gardens where several species grow together is likely to produce varied hybrid offspring. Division is highly recommended.

PROBLEMS Usually trouble-free.

S. albiflora Most probably a dwarf, white-flowering form of *S. obtusa*.

S. armena Substantial clumps comprise striking silvery blue leaves, each holding 15–19 narrowly oval leaflets with heart-shaped bases. Pinkish to maroon flowers are held in nodding or upright oblong spikes to 2¼ in (5.5 cm) long, but the flowers of garden plants are often grayish white. Difficult to distinguish from plants offered as *S. caucasica*, which is not a valid name. Less reliant on moist soil than most; not often seen but prized among those who grow it. From the mountains of northeastern Turkey, particularly Erzurum, in land historically part of Armenia (hence the species name). ↕36–60 in (90–150 cm). Z4–9 H8–1

S. canadensis (Canadian burnet) A stately species and one of the tallest, its slender white flower spikes also outdo the other species in size, reaching a length of up to 5½ in (14 cm) and standing upright like candles on the top of towering stalks. They open upward from the base. Each leaf is composed of around 13 leaflets, heart-shaped at the base and rounded at the tip. Found in eastern North America. ↕4–6½ ft (1.2–2 m). Z3–8 H8–1

S. caucasica see *S. armena*

S. hakusanensis Large, gray-green leaves can reach 20 in (50 cm) in length and are split into about 13 leaflets, which are broadly rounded at the tip and heart-shaped at the base. The vivid pinkish purple, nodding flower spikes are supremely fluffy (due to a large number of stamens). Often confused with *S. obtusa*, but its flower spikes are much fluffier. One of the finest sanguisorbas, the species name referring to Hakusan, one of the three most sacred mountains in its native Japan; found also in Korea. ↕16–36 in (40–90 cm). Z6–9 H9–6

S. magnifica see *S. obtusa*

S. menziesii Handsome species whose upright, egg-shaped flowerheads in deep purple-red begin opening in late spring, earlier than many sanguisorbas. The ⅝–2¾ in (1.5–7 cm) spikes remain brilliantly colored when in seed. Blue-green, oval to oblong leaflets number nine to fifteen per leaf. Resembling *S. officinalis*, but with slightly longer flowerheads softened in outline by haze of long, reddish stamens, this plant possibly originated as a hybrid between *S. officinalis* and *S. stipulata*. Named in honor of Scottish botanist and naval surgeon Archibald Menzies. Native to Alaska southward to Washington. ↕12–32 in (30–80 cm). Z4–8 H8–1

S. obtusa syn. *S. magnifica* Valued for its subtle combination of gray-green foliage and soft pink bottle brushes, its large leaves, up to 20 in (50 cm) long, are divided into roughly 13 leaflets, crowded closely together along the stem, and are heart-shaped at the base while very broadly rounded at the tip. Fluffy and nodding, the flower spikes, 2–3½ in (5–9 cm) long, open from the top downward. White-flowered forms are sometimes listed as *S. albiflora*; the lower-growing, grayer-leaved, pink form recently introduced from eastern Russia as *S. magnifica* probably also belongs here. One of the showiest and most widely grown species. From Japan and Russia. ↕24–48 in (60–120 cm). Z4–9 H8–1. **'Lemon Splash'** see *S. officinalis* 'Lemon Splash'.

S. officinalis (Great burnet) The leaves are made up of 7 to 15 leaflets that vary from oval to narrowly oblong. The larger leaflets, at the leaf tips, reach 1½–2¾ in (4–7 cm) in length. Swarming above the foliage from midsummer, the many tight, dark red, egg-shaped flowerheads are typically ½–2 in (1.5–5 cm) long and open

from the top down. Formerly used in medicine; the resemblance of the flowerheads to blood clots was thought to signify the plant's ability to staunch bleeding (and from this use comes the name *Sanguisorba*, which means "blood-absorbing"). Widely distributed in the Northern Hemisphere. ↕24–48 in (60–120 cm). Z3–8 H8–1. **'Arnhem'** Maroon flowers. Tall, and may therefore need support with stakes or from other tall perennials. ↕6½ ft (2 m). **'Lemon Splash'** Yellow-flecked foliage and burgundy flowers. Discovered in Japan by Dan Hinkley of Heronswood Nursery, WA. This cultivar may be listed under *S. obtusa*. ↕24 in (60 cm). **'Pink Tanna'** Dark pink flowerheads with a halo of pale pink stamens. ↕20–36 in (50–90 cm). **'Tanna'** see *S.* 'Tanna'.

S. sitchensis see *S. stipulata*

S. stipulata syn. *S. sitchensis* (Sitka burnet) Narrow, tapering plumes of greenish white to cream flowers, 1¼–3 in (3–8 cm) long, open from the base upward and stand upright above the foliage. The leaves, heart-shaped at the base and rounded at the tip, are composed of nine to fifteen leaflets. Earlier-flowering than many species; purple-tinged forms also exist. A little-known but attractive species that is similar to the taller *S. canadensis*, but with broader leaves. Found in western North America, from Alaska to Oregon; also China, Japan, Korea, and Russia. 12–36 in (30–90 cm). Z4–9 H8–1

S. 'Tanna' Neat, dwarf mounds of blue-green foliage are dotted in summer with an abundance of small, wine red balls. From Japan; often listed as a cultivar of *S. officinalis*. Tolerates drier conditions than most. ↕12–20 in (30–50 cm). Z4–9 H8–1

S. tenuifolia (Oriental burnet) A tall, elegant species with distinctively slender leaflets and slim, catkinlike spikes of white to red flowers quivering at the tip of willowy stems. The leaves are composed of 15–19 leaflets, edged with neatly pointed teeth and typically 2–2¾ in (5–7 cm) long by ⅝–¾ in (1.5–1.7 cm) wide. The ¾–2¾ in (2–7 cm) flower spikes, which taper toward the tip, are usually nodding and open from the top downward. From China, Japan, Korea, Mongolia, and Russia. ↕36–60 in (90–150 cm). Z9–7 H7–1. **'Alba'** Beautiful white tassels, with long stamens tipped in contrasting black anthers. ↕5–6½ ft (1.5–2 m). **var. parviflora** White flowers, but smaller in stature and flower size than 'Alba'. **'Pink Elephant'** A recent introduction with long, pinkish red spikes on tall stems. ↕6 ft (1.8 m). **'Purpurea'** Deep red-purple flowers. Plants offered under this name vary, some having drooping spikes, others with tighter, upright heads resembling those of *S. officinalis*.

RIGHT **1** *Sanguisorba canadensis*
2 *S. menziesii* **3** *S. officinalis*
4 *S. tenuifolia* 'Alba'

SAPONARIA
Soapwort
CARYOPHYLLACEAE

Hardy and robust sun-lovers for a long period of summer color. About 20 species of annuals and sometimes rather woody, deciduous or evergreen perennials come from rocky places and alpine meadows in the mountains of Europe (especially southern Europe) and southwestern Asia. Both the mat-forming and taller clump-forming plants sometimes spread vigorously, with small, narrow, egg- to lance-shaped leaves. Five-petaled, flat, rounded flowers, mainly in shades of pink, almost cover the plants in summer or stand up in slightly ragged spikes. The smaller species are ideal for rock gardens and gravel gardens, and in gaps in paved areas. Taller species can be planted in mixed or herbaceous borders.

CULTIVATION Grow in a sunny position with well-drained soil.

PROPAGATION By division or soft stem-top cuttings in spring or from seed sown in spring

PROBLEMS Slugs and snails.

S. x *lempergii* **'Max Frei'** A restrained, evergreen mat-forming plant: against a background of mid-green, lance-shaped foliage, loose heads of pale pink, ½ in (1 cm) wide flowers delight the eye over a very long period, from early summer onward. For the front of a mixed border or overhanging a wall. An unexpectedly robust hybrid of *S. cypria* and *S. sicula*. ↕12–16 in (30–40 cm). Z5–8 H8–4

S. officinalis (Soapwort) A deciduous, upright perennial, spreading rapidly by rhizomes. Narrow, egg-shaped, mid-green leaves with a rough surface grow

to 1½–2¾ in (4–7 cm) long, and in late summer and early fall the stems are topped with heads of pink, red, or white ¾ in (2 cm) wide flowers. Long cultivated as a source of soap, and has escaped and naturalized in many areas where it is not truly native. For a mixed or herbaceous border, and vigorous enough for wilder places. From Europe. ↕24 in (60 cm). Z3–9 H9–1. **'Alba Plena'** Double white flowers from pink buds. **'Dazzler'** syn. 'Variegata' Leaves heavily variegated with cream, and with pink flowers; more restrained in habit. **'Rosea Plena'** Double, soft pink flowers. **'Rubra Plena'** Double red flowers turning pink with age; spreads rapidly. **'Variegata'** *see* 'Dazzler'.

SARRACENIA
Pitcher plant
SARRACENIACEAE

Beauty and terror combine in these colorful, beguiling denizens of mysterious bogs.

Eight species and many hybrids grow in nitrogen-impoverished, acidic bogs and savannas in North America. Most are cultivated but none is widely grown, largely because of their rather specific cultural requirements.

Sarracenias grow from thick, creeping rhizomes with wiry roots that probe deeply for water and anchor the top-heavy plants. The leaves have two forms. Most conspicuously, they are modified into "pitchers": cylindrical vessels, usually covered by a hood, that trap and digest insects, thereby helping these plants thrive in nutrient-poor habitats. The pitchers are brightly colored and lure prey with sweet secretions. Once the prey enters the pitcher, it slips on waxy cells and falls into the pit. Once inside, stiff, downward-pointing hairs prevent its escape. The insect drowns and its body is digested by enzymes and absorbed by the plant to fuel its growth. The pitchers of most species are deciduous, though a few are persistent. In addition to pitchers, plants produce modified leaves with flattened blades (phyllodes) that are sometimes formed late in the season and persist over winter, allowing the plants to photosynthesize until the

new pitchers are formed in spring.

Each outward-facing to nodding flower is borne singly and consists of five thick, colorful sepals above a buttonlike structure at the center, on the reverse side of which the sexual organs are found. Five floppy, paddle-shaped petals hang between the lobes of the inflated button, which from the side looks a little like an umbrella with five points. The ovary develops with the button attached after the petals fall. Some flowers are sweetly fragrant, others smell musty.

Many hybrids occur in the wild where different species grow together, and many more have been produced in cultivation. Many are unexpectedly beautiful and some excellent named cultivars are occasionally, but increasingly, available. One focus of hybridization that gardeners will appreciate is on creating forms that are less demanding in their cultural requirements.

CULTIVATION Pitcher plants thrive with consistent moisture, and when grown outside are best in an artificial bog created in a plastic- or rubber-lined pocket of milled sphagnum, or in a 30:70 washed sand and sphagnum peat mixture. Water only with acidic rain or well water, distilled water, or ionized water with a pH value below 6. Do not fertilize the plants. This is a highly specialized form of bog gardening and it pays to seek additional, detailed advice.

PROPAGATION Divide congested crowns in spring or summer, cutting the sections apart with a sharp knife.

PROBLEMS Usually trouble-free.

S. alata Robust, with slightly curved, ascending, slender, olive to chartreuse pitchers, usually veined in red, that flare just below a wide hood. Some plants have red pigments in the upper third of the pitcher. The inside of the hoods may be deep red, lending an attractive bicolored effect. New pitchers are produced after flowering. Flowers with large, bright yellow sepals and pale, nearly white petals are borne on compact stems, giving the plants a squat

RIGHT 1 *Sarracenia flava* **2** *S. purpurea* **3** *S. rubra*

look when in flower. They open in early and mid-spring and reach half the height of mature pitchers. Best in full sun. Superficially reminiscent of the more familiar *S. rubra*, but larger and stockier. From savannas and bogs in Alabama, Louisiana, and Texas.
‡12–36 in (30–90 cm). Z4–9 H8–1

S. 'Doodle Bug' see *S*. Little Bug Series

S. flava (Yellow pitcher plant) The most dramatic, if a rather variable, species, with erect pitchers flaring toward the top and capped by a flat hood. Plants vary in the amount of red tinting to the green pitcher: some have red just at the neck or throat of the hood, some have rusty hoods, while others are deep red throughout. The huge, showy yellow flowers, up to 4 in (10 cm) wide, emerge in early spring; mature clumps may sport dozens of stems. The 12–24 in (30–60 cm) leaves persist through the winter and accompany the flowers, followed by fresh pitchers that emerge as the flowers fade. Best in full sun. Once common in savannas, bogs, and seeps, but now rare, from Virginia to Georgia and Florida. ‡24–48 in (60–120 cm). Z7–10 H10–7

S. leucophylla A showy species; ruffled, flaring hoods standing erect above the gaping mouths of the tall, elegant pitchers in late summer and early fall; the upper 6 in (15 cm) of the pitcher tube, as well as the hood, is glowing white between green or red veins. Variants with intense red veins make the white seem more pronounced, while those with no pigment appear ghostly. Phyllodes overwinter and often carry the plant into summer, with a few pitchers produced after flowering. The rich red flowers face outward on tall stems. Needs more water than other species and is intolerant of summer drought. Increasingly popular as a cut flower. From savannas and bogs in southern Georgia and Florida, west into Mississippi. ‡36–48 in (90–120 cm). Z5–9 H9–1

S. 'Lady Bug' see *S*. Little Bug Series

S. Little Bug Series Series of prolific, dwarf, and relatively easy to grow hybrids, making clumps about 8–10 in (20–25 cm) across, raised by Rob Gardner and Larry Mellichamp of the University of North Carolina. ‡8 in (20 cm). Z5–9 H9–1. **'Doodle Bug'** Green, upright pitchers patterned in red and white at the top. A hybrid of *S. alabamensis* and *S. psittacina*. **'Lady Bug'** Stout red pitchers, green at the base, spotted with white. A hybrid involving *S. minor*, *S. psittacina*, and *S. purpurea*. **'Love Bug'** Narrow, deep red pitchers. A hybrid involving *S. jonesii*, *S. leucophylla*, *S. minor*, *S. psittacina*, and *S. purpurea*. **'Red Bug'** Narrow, erect red pitchers, green at the base. A hybrid of *S. rubra* and *S. wherryi*.

S. 'Love Bug' see *S*. Little Bug Series

S. purpurea Thick rhizomes carry, at the

RIGHT *Sauromatum venosum*

tip, inflated pitchers that turn up from short, more or less horizontal stems and are green with purple veins, sometimes completely purple, with an upright green hood richly veined in purple that, uniquely, leaves the pitcher uncovered. The mid-spring flowers are deep blood red. A lovely, variable, and very hardy species, more tolerant of alkalinine soil than others, and an important parent in many hybrids. Long naturalized in Cumbria and Ireland (*see* Sarracenia in History) but native to North American bogs and coastal plains from Newfoundland south to Georgia. ‡12–24 in (30–60 cm). Z2–9 H9–1

S. 'Red Bug' see *S*. Little Bug Series

S. rubra Varying noticeably in coloration and stature, this most delicate pitcher plant has thin, ascending pitchers topped by small, overhanging hoods. The pitchers, green to olive and veined with red, vary widely in girth and degree of coloration, some forms being extremely rare and localized. New pitchers are produced in early summer. The red, or sometimes green, 1 in (2.5 cm) flowers appear in mid- and late spring and often exude a sweet, roselike fragrance. Easy in light soil in full sun and tolerates shade better than many. From coastal savannas and bogs to mountainous seeps scattered through North Carolina to Alabama. ‡12–24 in (30–60 cm). Z7–10 H10–7

SATUREJA see CALAMINTHA

SAUROMATUM
ARACEAE

Summer-flowering plants with bizarre flowers and especially striking foliage.

Two species of tuberous-rooted plants are native to the Himalaya, southern India, and East and West Africa, but only one is commonly grown for the unusual and attractive lobed leaves that open after the flowers on strikingly purple-spotted stems. The characteristic hooded flowering spikes give off a powerful stench of rotting meat, which attracts flies in great numbers—and the flies pollinate the flowers.

CULTIVATION Grows well in a well-drained, fertile soil either in sun or in part-shade.

PROPAGATION By removing offsets from the tuber.

PROBLEMS Usually trouble-free.

S. guttatum see *S. venosum*

S. venosum syn. *S. guttatum* (Monarch of the East, Voodoo lily) Fast-growing plant usually sold as flowering-sized

tubers. Each tuber produces a single flower spike to 10 in (25 cm) tall, in early summer or midsummer. The dull green hood of the flower spike is heavily blotched with deep purple within, purplish green outside, and soon curls back to reveal the long, slender, blackish purple spadix (*see* The Arum Family, *p. 74*). As the flower spike dies down, a boldly purple-spotted stem bears a single leaf, divided into several narrow, radiating lobes, that expands to about 16 in (40 cm) across. Sometimes grown from a dry tuber in a saucer on a windowsill. Hardy and provides a focal point for a border outdoors. From the Himalaya and southern India. ‡30 in (75 cm). Z7–10 H11–10. **'Indian Giant'** Leaves to 30 in (75 cm) across; less heavily spotted stems. ‡36 in (90 cm). Z6–10 H10–6

SAXIFRAGA
Saxifrage
SAXIFRAGACEAE

Shade- and moisture-loving treasures flowering early or late and in an increasing range of attractive foliage forms.

About 400 species of hardy evergreen, partially evergreen, or deciduous plants grow mainly in mountainous parts of Europe, Asia, and North America. Many are alpines, some quite demanding, but shade-loving kinds from relatively moist conditions, including forest areas, and the so-called "mossy" cushion- or mat-forming types are more suitable for general plantings, including woodland gardens and shrub borders. Leaves vary greatly from large and kidney-shaped to mosslike. Flowers are generally five-petaled and star- or cup-shaped.

CULTIVATION Mossy saxifrages and several others thrive in light shade or some sun with moist yet well-drained, neutral to alkaline soil.

Others, including *S. fortunei*, are best in part-shade, moist yet well-drained acidic soil with abundant humus.

PROPAGATION By division in spring. Detach rooted rosettes of mat- and cushion-forming types, or use unrooted rosettes as cuttings. From seed for species only, sown in fall in an open cold frame.

PROBLEMS Aphids, slugs, and vine weevil grubs.

S. 'Apple Blossom' Forms a mat of evergreen gray-green foliage spangled with cup-shaped pink flowers in late spring and early summer. An ideal mossy saxifrage for a well-drained bed. ‡4¾ in (12 cm). Z5–7 H7–5

S. x arendsii Fairly thick, pale green, deeply cut leaves to 2 in (5 cm) long are produced in dense tufts; small, cup-shaped, purple to rose flowers appear in late spring and early summer. Prefers good drainage. This name has been used to cover mossy hybrids between a number of species, including *S. cespitosa*, *S. granulata*, *S. hypnoides*, *S. moschata*, and *S. rosacea*. Most are now classified independently and are listed here simply under their cultivar names. The *S. x arendsii* of nurseries is described here. ‡8 in (20 cm). Z5–7 H7–5. **'Triumph'** Crimson flowers.

S. 'Black Beauty' Evergreen, mossy saxifrage for a well-drained bed with rosettes of dark green leaves, above which deep red, cup-shaped flowers appear in late spring and early summer. ‡8 in (20 cm). Z5–7 H7–5

S. 'Bob Hawkins' A mossy, evergreen mat-former, ideal for a shady, well-drained situation. Large, soft rosettes of deeply cut, white and green variegated leaves, to ¾ in (2 cm) long and green-white, cup-shaped, ¾-in (2-cm) flowers appear in late spring and early summer. ‡6 in (15 cm). Z5–7 H7–5

S. cortusifolia var. fortunei see
S. fortunei

S. cuneifolia syn. *S. dahurica* Easy
woodlander; rosettes of wedge-shaped
or roundish, leathery green leaves, with
purple undersides, up to 1 in (2.5 cm)
long. Sprays of tiny, starry white flowers
spotted with yellow or red in late
spring and early summer. Thrives in
moist yet well-drained, humus-rich soil
and part-shade. From Europe, from the
Carpathians to the Pyrenees. ‡ 8 in
(20 cm). Z5–7 H7–5. **'Variegata'** Leaves
variegated creamy white and green.

S. dahurica see *S. cuneifolia*

S. 'Dartington Double' Mossy
saxifrage, forming a hummock of soft
evergreen foliage topped with double
white flowers in late spring and early
summer. ‡ 6 in (15 cm). Z5–7 H7–5

S. 'Dubarry' An old but gardenworthy
mossy saxifrage; large evergreen
hummock of green foliage above
which rich crimson cup-shaped flowers
appear in late spring and early summer.
‡ 4–4¾ in (10–12 cm). Z5–7 H7–5

S. 'Elf' An evergreen, dwarf, mossy
saxifrage, for a shady, well-drained spot,
with green foliage and cup-shaped,
carmine flowers in late spring and early
summer. ‡ 4 in (10 cm). Z5–7 H7–5

S. exarata Compact, evergreen, mossy
cushion; green lobed leaves to ¾ in
(2 cm) long, and white or green-yellow
flowers, sometimes tinted with red,
which appear from late spring to early
fall. Best in humus-rich, moist yet well-
drained, neutral to alkaline soil and
light shade. From mountains of central
and southern Europe, the Caucasus,
and northwestern Iran. ‡ 4 in (10 cm).
Z5–7 H7–5. **subsp. moschata** Flowers
yellow, often tinged with red; foliage
hairy. One of the main parents of the
many mossy hybrids. **subsp. moschata**
'Cloth of Gold' Golden foliage.

S. 'Findling' Mossy saxifrage forming
a hummock of soft evergreen foliage.

SAXIFRAGA FORTUNEI AND ITS CULTIVARS

Saxifraga fortunei is a delightful woodland
perennial. Its distinctive flowers, which have
one or two long lower petals and three or
four shorter upper ones, are invaluable
because they follow long after almost all
other woodlanders, bringing color, interest,
and a hint of Asia to shady plantings as late
as mid-fall.

This species would be an essential shade
perennial for its flowering habit alone, but
from Japan, where they have long treasured
this plant, have come a succession of striking
foliage forms. For many years the dark-
leaved 'Wada', which was previously known
as 'Wada's Variety', was the only form of this
species that we saw. However, Japanese
gardeners have selected forms not only for
their rich, dark foliage but also for variegated
leaves, and in more recent years more of
these forms have arrived in the gardens of
the western world. North American plant
breeders, including Don Heim, Dan Hinkley,
Francis Cabot, Siskiyou Nursery, and others,
have used these imports in developing
new cultivars for the shade garden. Visitors
to Japan are continuing to bring back
new forms.

Saxifraga fortunei

'Black Ruby'

'Blackberry and Apple Pie'

'Cherry Pie'

'Mount Nachi'

'Rokujô'

White, cup-shaped flowers appear in
late spring and early summer. ‡ 6 in
(15 cm). Z5–7 H7–5

S. 'Flowers of Sulphur' see
S. 'Schwefelblüte'

S. fortunei syn. *S. cortusifolia* var. *fortunei*
Deciduous or partially evergreen
clump-former, ideal for a woodland
garden or shrub border. Fleshy, lobed,
rounded or kidney-shaped leaves with
toothed edges, up to 4 in (10 cm)
across, green but reddish purple below
and often becoming flushed with
purple as they mature. Galaxies of ½ in
(1 cm) starry white flowers with two
long lower petals appear from late

summer through to mid-fall or later.
Avoid planting in frost pockets, since
fall frosts can ruin the flowers. Slugs are
a major problem. From Japan. ‡ 12 in
(30 cm). Z6–8 H8–6. **'Black Ruby'**
Glossy, almost black leaves; reddish pink
flowers. ‡ 8 in (20 cm). **'Blackberry**
and Apple Pie' Green leaves stained
with red, edges scalloped; buff-colored
flowers. **'Cheap Confections'** Green
leaves with scalloped edges; bright pink
flowers. ‡ 8 in (20 cm). **'Cherry Pie'**
Green glossy foliage; deep pink flowers.
'Cotton Crochet' Glossy green leaves;
double flowers. **'Crystal Pink'** Leaves
variegated cream, green, and pink.
‡ 7 in (18 cm). **'Five Color'** Leaves
variegated green, white, pink, yellow,

and red. **'Mount Nachi'** Leaves marked
with red and covered in red bristles.
‡ 10 in (25 cm). **var. obtusocuneata**
Deeply cut hairy leaves. ‡ 10 in (25 cm).
'Purpurea' *see* 'Rubrifolia'. **'Rokujô'**
Red-bristled leaves marked with red.
‡ 10 in (25 cm). **'Rubrifolia'** syn.
'Purpurea' Leaves strongly flushed red,
red stems. ‡ 8 in (20 cm). **'Sugar Plum**
Fairy' Large, pale green scalloped
leaves; pale pink flowers. **'Wada'** Large
shiny green leaves, purple-red below.
‡ 20 in (50 cm).

BELOW 1 *Saxifraga cuneifolia*
2 *S.* 'Dartington Double'
3 *S. x geum* **4** *S. hirsuta*

S. × geum An evergreen mat-former making good ground cover with rosettes of 3 in (8 cm), spoon-shaped green leaves with scalloped edges. Clouds of tiny, star-shaped, white flowers spotted with red appear in early summer or midsummer. Rather like *Saxifraga × urbium* (see London's Pride?, *p.424*). For the border or woodland garden. A natural hybrid of *S. hirsuta* and *S. umbrosa*. From the Pyrenees. ‡8 in (20 cm). Z6–8 H8–6. **Dixter form** Originated at Great Dixter, Christopher Lloyd's East Sussex garden, in England, and distributed by Beth Chatto, but not different from the usual form. See also *Adiantum pedatum* 'Miss Sharples,' *p.42*).

S. 'Golden Falls' A very bright evergreen, mossy saxifrage whose green foliage is tinted with yellow. Red-pink, cup-shaped flowers appear in late spring and early summer. ‡3 in (8 cm). Z5–7 H7–5

S. granulata Evergreen clump-former with bulbils on stems and roots. Green, kidney-shaped leaves with toothed or scalloped edges, 1¼ in (3 cm) long, are produced in loose rosettes. Clusters of rounded white flowers ⅝ in (1.5 cm) across appear on upright stems in late spring. The plant dies down and rests in summer. Thrives in moist but well-drained, humus-rich, neutral to alkaline soil and light shade, but will take full sun if the soil remains moist. Looks best in a meadow. Bulbils can be "sown" in early spring at 50°F (10°C). From Europe and North Africa. ‡8–14 in (20–35 cm). Z7–8 H8–7. **'Flore Pleno'** syn. 'Plena' Double flowers.

S. 'Hi-Ace' Forms a hummock of soft evergreen foliage, the leaves variegated green and white; rose pink, cup-shaped flowers appear in late spring and early summer. ‡6 in (15 cm). Z5–7 H7–5

S. hirsuta A prostrate grower of sprawling habit for a shrub border or woodland garden. Hairy, kidney-shaped or rounded leaves, to 1½ in (4 cm) long, with scalloped edges, are bright green with purple-red undersides. Tiny white flowers, usually with a yellow patch at the base of the petals and light pink spots, appear from late spring to midsummer. Best in moist soil with light shade. From southwestern Europe and Ireland. ‡4¾–12 in (12–30 cm). Z5–7 H7–5 **S. 'Knapton Pink'** A mossy saxifrage with a rather open habit of growth and hairy rosettes of leaves that provide dull green yet attractive foliage for winter. Large, cup-shaped, soft pink flowers appear in late spring and early summer. ‡4 in (10 cm). **S. 'Pearly King'** Delightful dwarf evergreen mossy saxifrage forming a hummock of green foliage, with white cup-shaped flowers in late spring and early summer. ‡4 in (10 cm).

S. 'Peter Pan' Compact in habit and ideal for rock gardens, this evergreen mossy saxifrage forms dark green cushions studded with red, cup-shaped flowers in late spring and early summer. ‡4 in (10 cm). Z5–7 H7–5

S. 'Pixie' Mossy type forming a hummock of soft evergreen foliage covered with cream and pink, cup-shaped flowers in late spring and early summer. ‡6 in (15 cm). Z6–9 H9–5

S. 'Pixie Alba' see *S.* 'White Pixie'

S. sarmentosa see *S. stolonifera*

S. 'Schwefelblüte' syn. *S.* 'Flowers of Sulphur' Mossy plant forming a tight hummock of bright green evergreen foliage. Pale yellow, cup-shaped flowers appear in late spring and early summer. ‡4 in (10 cm). Z5–7 H7–5

S. 'Silver Cushion' syn. *S.* 'Silver Mound' A distinctive mossy saxifrage forming a compact evergreen hummock of silver-gray and green variegated leaves that contrast beautifully with the pale pink flowers that appear in late spring and early summer. ‡4¾ in (12 cm). Z5–7 H7–5

S. 'Silver Mound' see *S.* 'Silver Cushion'

S. spathularis (St. Patrick's cabbage) Evergreen; rosettes of spoon-shaped green leaves, which are very distinctive, being deeply cut at the edges. Sprays of ½ in (1 cm) wide, crimson-spotted, white flowers, with yellow spots at the base of the petals, are carried on leafless, reddish stalks from early to late summer. Good ground cover, best in part-shade with moist yet well-drained soil containing abundant humus. From Ireland and southern Europe. ‡8 in (20 cm). Z5–8 H8–5

S. stolonifera syn. *S. sarmentosa* (Mother of thousands) Rosette- or tuft-forming evergreen or deciduous woodland plant with round, lobed, bristly mid-green leaves with silvery veins, red-flushed below, up to 3½ in (9 cm) wide. Loose, airy heads of tiny white flowers spotted with red or yellow are carried on thin stems in late summer and early fall. Produces plantlets at the ends of long, thin red stolons (trailing above-ground stems) and these can be rooted in pots while still attached to the parent to produce new plants. Ideal for ground cover in a shady border or woodland garden. From China and Japan. ‡12 in (30 cm). Z7–9 H9–5. **'Cuscutiformis'** White flowers, no spots. **'Harvest Moon'** White flowers, yellow foliage. **'Maroon Beauty'** White flowers and maroon leaves with silver-gray veins and red hairs.

S. umbrosa Evergreen ground cover forming loose cushions of rosettes made up of generally spoon-shaped, medium green, 1¼ in (3 cm) leaves, reddish below, with scalloped edges. They make a good background for the dainty sprays of tiny, star-shaped white flowers spotted with crimson that appear on thin reddish stems from early summer onward. Ideal for a woodland

RIGHT **1** *Saxifraga* 'Peter Pan'
2 *S.* 'Silver Cushion' **3** *S. stolonifera*
4 *S. umbrosa* 'Primuloides'

ABOVE 1 *Saxifraga* x *urbium*
2 *S.* 'White Pixie'

garden, shrub border, rock garden, or border shaded by buildings. Best in part-shade, but performs well in complete shade. From the Pyrenees. ‡12 in (30 cm). Z5–8 H8–5. **'Clarence Elliott'** More compact with minute rose pink flowers. ‡6 in (15 cm). **'Primuloides'** Primroselike leaves; rose pink flowers. ‡6 in (15 cm).

S. x *urbium* (London's pride) Vigorously spreading evergreen ground cover forming large rosettes of spoon-shaped, toothed, leathery, mid-green leaves up to 1½ in (4 cm) across. Airy sprays of tiny white star-shaped flowers, tinted or spotted with red-pink, are produced on thin stems from early summer onward. Best in part-shade, but does well in complete shade and also in poor soil. A garden hybrid of *S. spathularis* and *S. umbrosa* (see London's Pride?). ‡12 in (30 cm). Z6–7 H7–6. **'Aureopunctata'** Green leaves spotted with yellow. **'Miss Chambers'** syn. 'Chambers' Pink Pride' Pink flowers. **'Variegata'** Leaves variegated yellow and green.

LONDON'S PRIDE?

There has been much confusion over the classification of this plant and its correct common name. Known since the 17th century, *Saxifraga* x *urbium* is garden hybrid between *Saxifraga spathularis* and *S. umbrosa*. Although naturalized in Great Britain, and in a few places in Europe, the two parent species do not naturally grow together, so natural origin seems unlikely. Oddly, it rarely sets seed. It was long grown as *S. umbrosa*, but *S.* x *urbium* is distinct in its longer, less hairy leaf stalks and more boldly toothed leaves. Why the common name "London pride"? John Parkinson, in his

Paradisus Terrestris of 1629, used "London pride" for a form of sweet William (*Dianthus barbatus*). Later, however, it seems likely that *S.* x *urbium* was introduced to cultivation by the horticulturist and garden designer George London (1681–1714), who laid out the gardens at Hampton Court. So it should probably be more correctly known as London's pride. To confound the situation further, evidence also exists that the bright red *Lychnis chalcedonica*, often known as Maltese cross, bore the common name of London Pride in early 19th-century New England.

S. 'White Pixie' syn. *S.* 'Pixie Alba' Ideal for a rock garden; mossy saxifrage forming a hummock of soft evergreen foliage. White-flowered version of *S.* 'Pixie', the cup-shaped blooms appearing in late spring and early summer. ‡6 in (15 cm). Z5–7 H7–5

SCABIOSA
Pincushion flower, Scabious
DIPSACACEAE

Friendly, long-blooming perennials with pincushion flowerheads that are good in the garden and good for cutting.

About 80 species of annuals, biennials, and perennials come mainly from dry, sunny places in the Mediterranean region, but also from Asia and Africa. The slightly hairy leaves are sited mostly at the base and range from simple to much dissected, depending on the species. The domed flowerheads, sometimes reminiscent of those in the daisy family, come in shades of blue, pink, cream, white, or purple, at the top of long, slender stems. Each head is made up of small individual florets:

the central ones are small, but those around the outside are larger and more showy. Unopened flowerheads show the buds in a distinctive spiral arrangement. The flowers are a good source of nectar and are enjoyed by butterflies and bees, making this a good subject for a wild or wildlife garden. They grow best where summers are cool, and grow poorly in hot, humid climates.

CULTIVATION Best in a well-drained, alkaline soil in full sun. Should be divided every three or four years to remain vigorous.

PROPAGATION Species from seed sown in spring; hybrids by basal cuttings in spring or by division in spring or fall.

PROBLEMS Almost trouble-free; one type of rose chafer and leafhopper occasionally cause problems.

S. arvensis see *Knautia arvensis*

S. atropurpurea (Sweet scabious) Short-lived perennial, sometimes behaving as an annual or biennial. The basal leaves are a narrow spoon shape and are entire or toothed, while those on the stems are deeply toothed or lobed. The fragrant, purple to crimson, 2 in (5 cm) flowerheads held on wiry stems are excellent for cutting and plants will bloom for most of the summer if deadheaded. Propagate regularly; the following cultivars are raised from seed, so may vary. Spellings of "Chile" and "Chili" in the cultivar names often vary. From southern Europe. ‡36 in (90 cm). Z4–11 H8–3. **'Ace of Spades'** Double, almost black flowers. Comes true from seed. ‡24 in (60 cm). **'Chile Black'** Deep purple flowers. ‡18 in (45 cm). **'Chili Pepper'** Rose red. ‡24 in (60 cm). **'Chili Sauce'** Dark pink. ‡24 in (60 cm). **'Peter Ray'** Maroon-black flowers, larger than those of 'Chile Black' but equally dark. ‡24 in (60 cm).

S. 'Butterfly Blue' Low-growing, with gray-green leaves and an impressively continuous display of small, lavender-blue flowers from early summer well into early fall. Good for the front of a border and particularly effective when mass-planted. Perennial Plant of the Year in 2001. Sometimes, incorrectly, sold as 'Irish Perpetual Flowering' or as a form of *S. columbaria*. ‡12–18 in (30–45 cm). Z3–8 H8–1

S. caucasica Lance-shaped basal leaves are covered with a white bloom, making them appear gray-green; the stem leaves are divided into narrow segments and are less grayed. Large, pale blue florets with showy petals surround a central disk of smaller, white to cream florets with very rudimentary petals. Flowering in mid- and late summer, it is particularly valuable to give blue and pink shades to balance the predominantly yellow flowers of this season. It is also a good cut flower, but should be cut before the central flower buds open for longest vase life. Native to the Caucasus, northeastern Turkey,

and northern Iran. ‡24 in (60 cm). Z4–9 H9–1. **var. alba** White flowers, comes true from seed. **'Blausiegel'** (**Blue Seal**) Sky blue with very large outer florets. More vigorous than 'Clive Greaves'. **'Clive Greaves'** Soft lavender-blue and very free-flowering. It was named for a nursery salesman who met James House (the son of Isaac—see House's hybrids, below) at a flower show in the 1920s and persuaded him to name one of his scabious seedlings after him. **'Fama'** Large, lavender-blue flowers. ‡18 in (45 cm). **'Goldingensis'** Dark lavender. ‡18 in (45 cm). **House's hybrids** A mix of lavender through sky blue to white. Developed by a market gardener, Isaac House, in Bristol, England, to meet the demand for these cut flowers in a range of colors. A few have been selected and named. **'Kompliment'** Dark lavender-blue. **'Miss Willmott'** Pure white; creamy white central disk. One of the House selections, named for the well-known English gardener. **Perfecta Series** Ranges from lavender to white, grown from seed. **'Stäfa'** Rich blue outer flowers, pale blue central ones.

S. columbaria (Small scabious) Well-branched, giving a greater quantity of smaller flowers; both stems and foliage are covered in small hairs, more so on some plants than on others. Basal leaves are spear-shaped with untoothed edges, while those on the stems become progressively more dissected as the stems grow. The 1½ in (4 cm) blue flowers appear in summer and can continue into fall if plants are deadheaded. Plants often grow wider than they are tall. Naturalized in eastern North America; native to Europe, western Asia, and into northern Africa. ‡28 in (70 cm). Z3–8 H8–1. **'Butterfly Blue'** see *S.* 'Butterfly Blue'. **'Misty Butterflies'** Blend of soft pink to lavender-blue shades. ‡10 in (25 cm). **'Nana'** Blue. ‡4–16 in (15–40 cm). **'Pink Mist'** see *S.* 'Pink Mist'. **subsp. ochroleuca** syn. *S. ochroleuca* Cream to yellow flowers. ‡24 in (60 cm).

S. drakensbergensis Stout stems carrying very few stem leaves emerge from a relatively fleshy rosette to carry heads of white flowers over a long period, from early summer to mid-fall if deadheaded. A high-altitude plant that does not do well where summers are hot and humid, from the Drakensberg Mountains in South Africa. ‡3¼–4 ft (1–1.2 m). Z4–7 H8–1

S. farinosa A rather woody crown, not dying down to the ground in winter, carries spoon-shaped leaves with scalloped edges and wiry stems topped with mauve flowers in early summer. From northern Africa. ‡12–18 in (30–45 cm). Z9–11 H11–9

S. gigantea see *Cephalaria gigantea*

S. graminifolia (Grass-leaved scabious) Clumps of green, grasslike, evergreen leaves, silvered with hairs, with solitary, spherical, 2 in (5 cm) pale pink flowers produced on wiry stems over several weeks in midsummer. A good edging

LEFT 1 *Scabiosa atropurpurea* 'Chile Black' **2** S. 'Butterfly Blue' **3** *S. caucasica* 'Clive Greaves' **4** *S. caucasica* 'Miss Willmott' **5** *S. lucida*

plant for the front of a border; more heat-tolerant than other commonly grown species. From southern Europe. ‡12 in (30 cm). Z5–7 H7–5

S. 'Helen Dillon' Neat, evergreen clumps of rather shiny green foliage with lavender flowers over a long period from late spring to early fall. ‡8 in (20 cm). Z5–7 H7–5

S. lucida Clumps of lance-shaped, silvery green, toothed leaves support unbranched stems with a few more boldly silvered, divided stem leaves and solitary rosy lilac flowers for most of the summer. From central Europe. ‡24 in (60 cm). Z4–9 H9–1

S. 'Miss Havisham' Distinctive; lime green and buff-colored buds open to light pink flowers all summer. Named for Miss Havisham of *Great Expectations*, and sometimes misspelled "Miss Haversham." There is also a rarely seen *David Copperfield*-inspired 'Betsy Trotwood'. ‡24 in (60 cm). Z5–7 H7–5

S. ochroleuca see *S. columbaria* subsp. *ochroleuca*

S. 'Pink Buttons' Clumps of deeply cut, gray-green leaves and a long season of pink flowers on branched, wiry stems. A darker pink, and taller, than the more frequently seen 'Pink Mist'. ‡30 in (75 cm). Z4–8 H8–1

S. 'Pink Mist' Gray-green, deeply cut leaves set off pink flowers, paler in the center, in a continuous display from early summer to early fall. Like a pink version of 'Butterfly Blue', often listed under *S. columbaria*, and paler and shorter than 'Pink Buttons'. ‡18 in (45 cm). Z3–8 H8–1

S. rumelica see *Knautia macedonica*

S. succisa see *Succisa pratensis*

SCHIZACHYRIUM
POACEAE

Graceful grass tolerant of dry conditions and turning delicate pastel shades in the fall.

Some 60 annual and perennial species are found throughout the tropics on savanna and prairie grasslands, and sandy beaches. Slowly spreading with clumps of basal leaves, the often slender, leafy branching stems turn delicate pastel shades of blue and pale orange in the fall. In late summer to fall, flower spikes squeeze out from the angles between the leaves and branches, usually in the form of compact elongated lances, sharply pointed and growing throughout the foliage. The main distinguishing feature of *Schizachyrium* is a tiny ring of hairs at the point where the flowers grow out from the leaves, although this can only be seen when magnified. A tough grass: some species are important pasture grasses, all are drought-resistant, and some surprisingly hardy. It is best grown in drifts in a natural setting, much as it would grow in the wild.

CULTIVATION Grow in very well-drained, light but moderately fertile soil, in full sun.

PROPAGATION From seed or by division.

PROBLEMS Usually trouble-free.

S. scoparium (Little blue stem) Arching clumps of slender branching stems slowly spread, carrying fine-textured, pointed leaves 20 in (50 cm) long and ¼ in (7 mm) wide. Gray-blue in spring, through summer the color becomes more intense, then turns to pastel shades of pink, blue, red, and pale salmon on mauve pink stems. In late summer to mid-fall, the leafy stems bear wispy flower spikes, with small spiraling bent bristles, up to 2 in (5 cm) long, which squeeze from the angles of the leaves and stems like long, fat needles. At first they are glistening blue-green; as they mature, the bristles become fluffy and the needles turn pink or russet-red. Tolerant of drought and a range of soil conditions. Characteristic grass of the American tallgrass prairie. **'The Blues'** Better blue foliage than the species. Selected by Kurt Bluemel, VA, from a portion of seeds given to him by Dr. Richard Lightly, DE. ‡4 ft (1.2 m). Z2–7 H7–1

BELOW *Schizachyrium scoparium*

SCHIZOSTYLIS
IRIDACEAE

Late-flowering perennials that bring elegance and color to both garden and home.

One species is found wild in mountainous areas of Africa, where it grows in moist places, often on riverbanks. Spreading slowly into clumps, more or less evergreen, narrow, upright leaves sheathe flowering stems carrying flat, bright red flowers composed of six petals with pointed or rounded tips, in fall and early winter.

CULTIVATION Grow in a sunny spot in moist soil that does not dry out in summer or fall. Plants will grow poorly if they are allowed to dry out.

PROPAGATION By division.

PROBLEMS Leaf spot in wet fall weather.

S. coccinea Thongy rhizomes slowly build into dense clumps; shoots may arise more widely spaced when plants are thriving. Narrow, upright, keeled, bright green, slenderly sword-shaped foliage, up to 24 in (60 cm) high and 2 in (5 cm) wide, is arranged in opposite rows. Flowering stems, which start to appear in late summer, carry spikes of 6 to 14 bright red, ¾–1½ in (2–4 cm) flowers with a satiny sheen, which open upward from the base in succession, also in opposite rows, over several weeks. They last well when cut for the house. In cooler areas, because of the late flowering season, which can extend into winter, late flowers are best cut and protected from heavy rain and frost indoors. In permanently moist soil this is a superb plant; it does not grow

well in drought. Mulch after flowering; divide and replant in improved soil every two years. From moist, open places in central Africa and eastern Cape Province. ↕24 in (60 cm). Z7–9 H9–7. **f.** *alba* White flowers with narrow, pointed petals. **'Ballyrogan Giant'** Large pink flowers on tall plants. ↕32 in (80 cm). **'Fenland Daybreak'** Narrow petals but large flowers in rich pink with red veins near the center. **'Hilary Gould'** Large, pale rose pink, goblet-shaped flowers. **'Jennifer'** Strong-growing, the large flowers with broad, round-tipped petals are paler in the center. **'Maiden's Blush'** Round-tipped pink petals form a rather cup-shaped flower. **'Major'** Large, bright red flowers with broad petals. **'Mollie Gould'** Very long flowering season, starting early, with pale pink flowers flecked with red. ↕32 in (80 cm). **'Mrs. Hegarty'** An old Irish cultivar with small pink flowers with narrow petals. **'November Cheer'** Pink flowers with red veins. A spontaneous mutation of 'Major', selected by English plantsman Alan Bloom. **'Pallida'** Pale shell pink. **'Pink Princess'** Vigorous, the large pale pink flowers with a yellow center. **'Professor Barnard'** Deep pink flowers of moderate size with dark anthers. **'Red Dragon'** Vigorous; large, bright red flowers. **'Snow Maiden'** Large white flowers; broad, rounded petals. The best white. Plants with smaller, grayish white flowers are sometimes sold under this name. **'Sunrise'** syn. 'Sunset' Large salmon pink flowers with broad, rounded petals. Rather lax habit. One of the best pinks. **'Sunset'** *see* 'Sunrise'. **'Tambara'** Large, reddish pink flowers; often the first to flower, as early as late summer. A wild selection. **'Viscountess Byng'** Small, pale pink flowers with narrow petals. Late-flowering; especially intolerant of dry soil. **'Zeal Salmon'** Large, spectacular, salmon pink flowers. ↕32 in (80 cm).

SCHOENOPLECTUS
Bull rush, Club rush
CYPERACEAE

Moisture-loving clumps of often tall, erect, architectural stems growing from vigorous root systems.

Some 80 annuals and perennials are found throughout the world's temperate regions in lakes, at pond margins, and in marshes or boggy infertile soil. Slowly spreading clumps, often growing from large, invasive root systems, of dense clusters of slightly ridged, cylindrical to sharply angled solid green stems, which usually turn orange-brown and die back in fall. The flowerheads appear throughout summer, spraying out from the tops of the stems or bursting out from the sides, with clusters or loose umbrellas of small, cone-shaped, brown to green flowers. Many used as accent plants for large water gardens when grown in drifts at the water's edge or in shallow water but they can be very invasive. In smaller ponds and bog gardens, restrict them in strong containers in heavy clay loam. Variegated forms tend to be smaller and less invasive than the species. Many have leaves and stems tough enough to be used for making paper and matting.

CULTIVATION Grow in tubs of heavy clay loam topped with grit, in up to 4¾ in (12 cm) of water, or in drier, infertile, neutral to acidic soil for smaller plants, although they will still need to be kept under control.

PROPAGATION From seed or, for cultivars, by division.

RIGHT *Schoenoplectus lacustris* subsp. *tabernaemontani* 'Zebrinus'

ABOVE 1 *Schizostylis coccinea* 'Major' **2** *S. coccinea* 'Sunrise' **3** *S. coccinea* 'Viscountess Byng'

PROBLEMS Usually trouble-free.

S. lacustris subsp. *tabernaemontani* **'Albescens'** (Candy rush, White rush) Erect, rounded, slightly angled stems grow from a strong, invasive root system into graceful clumps. The slender stems are vertically striped white and pale peppermint-green, especially on the new growth, then become greener through the summer. The clusters of white to pale brown, cone-shaped flower spikes, not always produced, appear at the very tops of

the stems in early summer to early fall. Best grown in containers or tubs in shallow water where the vertical emphasis of the stems is particularly effective. First found growing in shallow, brackish water and boggy ground in Japan. ‡4–5 ft (1.2–1.5 m). Z5–9 H9–5. **'Zebrinus'** Stems with horizontal bands of dark green and yellowy white. Brown flower clusters.

SCHOENUS
CYPERACEAE

Clump-forming, rushlike bog plants, many featuring stems in unusual color combinations.

Some 60 perennial species are found from sea level to low mountains in open, moist, and boggy areas, mainly in New Zealand and Australia, with a few found in temperate regions of Malaysia and the Northern Hemisphere. The root system can be invasive, but usually forms clumps of stout, erect, rushlike stems or sparse tufts of very narrow foliage. The flowerheads, at the tops of the stems, are usually small and rather inconspicuous, either compact and rounded or forming looser umbrellas of brown or greenish flowers. The small seeds can be brightly colored.

Many species from New Zealand have unusual coloration, often in bands and blotches up the stems, with reds and oranges becoming most noticeable in fall and winter.

CULTIVATION Grow in moist but well-drained soil, in full sun—for example, in an open bog garden—for best stem color.

PROPAGATION From seed or by division.

PROBLEMS Usually trouble-free.

S. pauciflorus (Bog rush) Spreads slowly on short, stout roots from which grow dense tufts of very slender, deeply grooved stems in deep brown to maroon and chestnut brown, green to purple-red and almost black at base. In the winter the foliage becomes flecked and banded with bright orange. In late spring to midsummer, small, inconspicuous round flowerheads appear at tops of stems, the pale green to dark red-purple flowers opening into loose, sparse clusters that mature into polished pale reddish brown seeds. Tolerates most soils but best in moisture-retentive but well-drained ground in full sun. From lakesides and boggy areas on mountainsides in New Zealand. ‡32 in (80 cm). Z7–10 H10–7

SCROPHULARIA
Figwort
SCROPHULARIACEAE

Medicinal herb grown in its sparkling variegated form.

About 200 species of often coarse biennials and perennials, some woody-based, from wet habitats in northern the temperate regions of the world. Only one cultivar is widely grown. All have square stems, bearing leaves that may be opposite or alternate, entire or toothed, simple or lobed, and terminal, open spikes of two-lipped flowers in red, purple, or greenish yellow. Many are unpleasantly scented; most are pollinated by wasps.

CULTIVATION Grow in well-drained but moist, humus-rich soil and part-shade.

PROPAGATION From seed or by division.

PROBLEMS Slugs and snails.

S. auriculata (Water figwort) Erect, hairless or occasionally slightly downy herbaceous perennial with square, four-winged stems and dark green, rather wrinkled, egg-shaped, toothed, 2–10 in (5–25 cm) leaves. The flowers are green, with a purple-brown upper lip, and produced in spikes held well clear of the leaves from early summer to early fall. Best in permanently moist but well-drained soil and part-shade. The species is rarely grown. From watersides and moist woodlands in Europe and North Africa. ‡3¼ ft (1 m). Z5–9 H9–5. **'Variegata'** Leaves boldly and irregularly edged with cream. Remove flowers to encourage better foliage.

SCUTELLARIA
Skullcap
LAMIACEAE

Summer-flowering relatives of *Salvia* boasting distinctive, tubular flowers.

Three hundred or more sometimes shrubby perennials and a few annuals, relatively few of which are grown in gardens, are found in most parts of the world, except for the coldest regions. Usually spreading by rhizomes, they grow in a range of habitats in the wild, but generally resent shade and waterlogged soil. All have square stems and may be open and sprawling or bold and upright in habit. The leaves are opposite and usually toothed and hairy. The pretty, tubular, two-lipped, salvia-like summer blooms may be blue, violet, pinkish, yellow, or white, and curve upward and flare toward the tip. Sometimes borne singly or in pairs, they are more usually carried along one side of a spike.

CULTIVATION Best in a bright spot in fairly rich, well-drained soil that does not dry out in summer.

PROPAGATION Divide clumps in fall or spring, or take basal cuttings in late spring or early summer. Sow seed in a cold frame in fall.

PROBLEMS Aphids.

S. altissima Bushy and upright deciduous perennial with branched or unbranched stems. The large, egg-shaped, toothed or scalloped, almost hairless leaves are carried on long stalks. The pretty ¾ in (2 cm) flowers vary in color but are usually bluish purple with a much paler lower lip, and are carried on lax, one-sided spikes from early summer to early fall. A woodland plant, it will tolerate some shade, and enjoys fertile soil. Naturalized through western Europe, including parts of southern England, but native to Italy and the Balkans eastward to Turkey and the Caucasus. ‡24–40 in (60–100 cm). Z5–9 H9–5

S. baicalensis A variable deciduous plant, becoming more erect as the season progresses. The stems, often purple-tinged, sometimes branch at the base. The almost stemless, 1½ in (4 cm) leaves are narrowly egg-shaped and quite hairless except for a fringe around the margins. In mid- and late summer, the hairy, blue-purple, 1 in (2.5 cm) flowers are carried on dense, occasionally branched spikes. Enjoys good drainage. From rocky places with some shade in Siberia and parts of Mongolia, China, and Japan. ‡12–16 in (30–40 cm). Z5–8 H8–5

ABOVE *Scutellaria incana*

S. galericulata A leafy, deciduous plant, rapidly spreading on purple-tinged stems from a spreading rootstock. The short-stalked, 2¾ in (7 cm) leaves, egg-shaped or narrow and oblong, are usually scalloped and either hairless or have a short, downy covering. The ¾ in (2 cm) curving flowers vary from blue to pink, often marked white inside and at the base; the lower lip is paler. They appear from early summer to early fall in pairs, spaced out on one side of the spike. For moist soil. Widespread in damp places in temperate Asia, Europe, and North America. ‡ 12–28 in (30–70 cm). Z5–8 H8–5

S. hastifolia A leafy, rapidly spreading plant: the upright, branched or unbranched, purple-tinged stems have short, oblong to egg-shaped, 1 in (2.5 cm) leaves, each with two pointed lobes at the base, and carry strongly curved, blue-violet flowers from early summer to early fall. Similar to *S. galericulata* but shorter and with smaller leaves. For moist conditions and dappled shade. From damp grassland from northwestern Spain through Asia Minor and the Caucasus as far north as Sweden and Finland. ‡ 6–16 in (15–40 cm). Z5–8 H8–5

S. incana A hairy, upright, deciduous perennial with attractive, showy flowers. The 4 in (10 cm) leaves are large and egg-shaped or diamond-shaped, with scalloped margins and very hairy white undersides. Branching flowerheads carry, from early summer to early fall, many tubular, blue, 1 in (2.5 cm) flowers that are hairy on the outside. For a well-drained, sunny spot. From dry sites in the eastern US from New

York to Virginia. ‡ 16–48 in (40–120 cm). Z5–8 H8–5

S. indica A creeping perennial, spreading on slender rhizomes but rarely becoming invasive. Hairy, white, egg-shaped or triangular, 1 in (2.5 cm) leaves heart-shaped at the base and scalloped on the edges. Densely hairy flowerhead carries, from early to late summer, blue or pale purple, ¾ in (2 cm) flowers, the lower lip obviously broad. Best in good drainage and full sun. From mountains in Mongolia, China, and Japan ‡ 8–16 in (20–40 cm). Z3–9 H9–1. **var. parvifolia** Smaller, thicker, ¾ in (2 cm) leaves and lilac blue flowers. ‡ 8 in (20 cm). **var. parvifolia 'Alba'** Flowers white.

S. lateriflora Erect, deciduous perennial with thin, stalked, usually hairless, roughly toothed, egg-shaped, 2¾ in (7 cm) leaves that may be quite narrow. From early summer to early fall, upright or spreading flower spikes carry tiny flowers that are usually pinkish white but occasionally blue and may be lost among the foliage. For moist situations; widespread in swampy habitats in North America. ‡ to 32 in (80 cm). Z3–8 H8–1

S. scordiifolia Low-growing, deciduous and spreading by rhizomes, the stems branching at the base and carrying short-stalked, wrinkly, oblong or lance-shaped, 1½ in (3.5 cm) leaves with few teeth and little hair. The ¾ in (2 cm) flowers are violet blue and hairy, and carried in loose, one-sided spikes from early to late summer. Best in sun and well-drained soil. From exposed sites in Siberia, Japan, Mongolia, and China. ‡ 4–12 in (10–30 cm). Z5–8 H8–5. **'Seoul Sapphire'** Flowers blue.

SECURIGERA *see* CORONILLA

SEDUM
Stonecrop
CRASSULACEAE

Most appreciated for its undemanding, succulent-leaved, border perennials noted for their late summer flower color.

The majority of the 500 or so mostly succulent plants, ranging from annuals to evergreen or deciduous perennials, subshrubs, and shrubs, inhabit dry or rocky areas, particularly in mountainous regions, but some are found in lowland, wetland, coastal, or epiphytic habitats. They are widely distributed throughout northern temperate regions, with a few in the Southern Hemisphere and tropical mountains. Their stems may be erect or trailing, the latter often rooting and forming dense mats. They bear alternate, opposite or whorled, succulent leaves in a wide variety of shapes,

RIGHT **1** *Sedum aizoon* 'Euphorbioides'
2 *S.* 'Bertram Anderson'
3 *S.* 'Carl' **4** *S. cauticola*

the most obvious distinction being between cylindrical and flattened leaves. The flowers are four- to nine-petaled (mostly five-petaled), star-shaped, and held in terminal clusters. Those of *S. spectabile* and a number of hybrids produce copious nectar that is a great attractor of butterflies, moths, and bees.

The identification of many species and cultivars depends on differences in the size and color of the flower parts in the individual florets in the flowerhead. The dark-leaved forms in particular are often confused, and details of flower structure and leaf shape may need to be examined closely.

Many species, particularly the Mexican ones, are tender and more often seen as houseplants. The hardy species and cultivars come in a wide range of sizes and habits. The smaller subjects are suitable for rock gardens, scree beds, or walls. The vigorous, mat-forming types make effective ground cover and the robust, erect herbaceous perennials can be grown in mixed or herbaceous borders.

CULTIVATION Virtually all sedums require a well-drained site in full sun. Soil of low to moderate fertility is preferable, since excess nutrients will encourage soft, leafy stems that are likely to flop and not flower well. The larger herbaceous types can be divided every three to four years to maintain vigor and an upright habit, but most will perform well for many years if left alone.

PROPAGATION From seed or by division in spring, or by leaf and stem cuttings in spring and early summer. Many regenerate from single leaves or portions of stem.

PROBLEMS Slugs, snails, and aphids. Mildew can sometimes affect the larger herbaceous types and seems to be encouraged by rich, moist soil; rust can also be a problem. Damp winters or poorly drained soil can encourage crown and root rots.

S. **'Abbeydore'** syn. *Hylotelephium* 'Abbeydore' Clump-forming deciduous perennial with erect stems and leaves that are oblong to wedge-shaped, to 4 in (10 cm) long, blue-green at first but assuming a purple tinge as the season progresses. In mid- and late summer, the flowerheads are made up of small domed clusters, the individual flowers having pale pink petals contrasting with purplish pink carpels (*see* Taxonomic Tangle) and purplish pink filaments. Unusually in this group of sedums, the carpels fade to a paler rather than a darker color on aging. A hybrid between *S. spectabile* and *S. telephium* from Abbeydore garden in Devon, England, introduced in about 1990. ‡18 in (45 cm). Z3–9 H8–1

S. **aizoon** Deciduous perennial with stout, unbranched stems arising from a fleshy rootstock and clad in egg-shaped to lance-shaped, alternate, toothed leaves to 3 in (8 cm) long that often become orange-flushed in fall. Flat-topped clusters, about 1½ in (4 cm) across, of rich yellow flowers, each ⅝ in (1.5 cm) across, are borne from early to late summer. Native to grassy slopes, scrub, and rocky streamsides in Siberia, Japan, and China. ‡12–16 in (30–40 cm). Z3–8 H8–1.
'Euphorbioides' Darker red stems, darker green leaves and orange-yellow, ⅝ in (1.7 cm) flowers. ‡10 in (25 cm).

S. **alboroseum** see *S. erythrostictum*

S. **Autumn Joy** see *S.* 'Herbstfreude'

S. **'Bertram Anderson'** syn. *Hylotelephium* 'Bertram Anderson' Deciduous, sprawling stems, about 12 in (30 cm) long. Egg-shaped to circular, toothed gray-green leaves, to 2 in (5 cm) long and flushed dusky purple. Hemispherical flowerheads, to 4 in (10 cm) across, produced from late summer to early fall: the individual flowers, to ⅝ in (1.5 cm) across, emerge from purplish pink and green buds to reveal purple-pink petals and carpels. A hybrid of *S. cauticola* named for the horticulturist E. B. (Bertram) Anderson. ‡8 in (20 cm). Z5–9 H9–5

S. **'Carl'** syn. *Hylotelephium* 'Carl' Clump-forming deciduous perennial with erect stems bearing inversely egg-shaped, flat, pale gray-green leaves that are retained on the lower reaches of stem, in contrast to other similar cultivars. Dense, slightly domed flowerheads of bright pink flowers are produced in late summer to early fall, the petals, carpels, and filaments all the same color and the petals equal to the filaments in length. A hybrid of *S. spectabile* and *S. telephium* named by Monksilver Nursery, Cambridgeshire, England, for former employee Carl West. ‡18 in (45 cm). Z4–8 H8–1

S. **cauticola** syn. *Hylotelephium cauticola* Deciduous perennial spreading by rhizomes, with trailing to slightly ascending stems to 6 in (15 cm), and blunt-toothed, rounded to spoon-shaped leaves to ¾ in (2 cm) long,

---

mainly opposite but sometimes scattered, and gray-green in color, often speckled with deep red. Rounded flowerheads, to 4 in (10 cm) across, bear pinkish red flowers, to ½ in (1 cm) across, from late summer to early fall. The buds are green and pink, the petals pale pink, and the carpels dark pink, with contrasting dark brown anthers. Differs from *S. ewersii* in its toothed leaves, usually showing red speckling. From Japan. ‡6 in (15 cm). Z5–9 H9–1.
'Lidakense' Smaller, more circular, less prominently toothed leaves; more effective as ground cover.

S. **erythrostictum** syn. *S. alboroseum*, *Hylotelephium erythrostictum* Clump-forming, deciduous perennial with erect, unbranced stems bearing opposite, egg-shaped, toothed, pale gray-green leaves, to 4 in (10 cm) long. Dense, slightly domed flowerheads, to 6 in (15 cm) across with prominent leafy bracts, are produced in late summer and early fall, and consist of bicolored flowers with white petals and pink carpels, and stamens that are the same length as the petals. Differs from *S. spectabile* in being taller and more slender, possessing leafy bracts in the flowerheads that half-enclose it before flowering, and having white rather than pink petals. Native to China and Japan, where it inhabits rocky slopes. ‡12–24 in (30–60 cm). Z6–9 H9–6.
'Frosty Morn' Narrower leaves with upturned edges and white margins about ¼ in (5 mm) wide; the variegation extends into the flowerheads. Tends to revert and can splay in rich soil. ‡18 in (45 cm).
'Mediovariegatum' Leaf yellowish green with a conspicuous central splotch of creamy yellow. Tends to revert. **'Pink Chablis'** Shorter form of 'Frosty Morn'. ‡12 in (30 cm).

S. **ewersii** syn. *Hylotelephium ewersii* Deciduous; twiggy base from which arise sprawling, reddish brown stems. Opposite, grayish green leaves, to ¾ in (2 cm), broadly egg-shaped to circular, untoothed and unstalked, and with heart-shaped bases. The dome-shaped flowerheads, to 4 in (10 cm) across, are

---

ABOVE *Sedum erythrostictum* 'Frosty Morn'

borne on ascending stems from late summer to early fall; individual, ½ in (1 cm) flowers have purplish pink petals and dark pink carpels. Differs from *S. cauticola* in that its leaves lack red speckling. From rocky slopes in Central Asia, the western Himalaya, Mongolia, and China. ‡6 in (15 cm). Z5–9 H9–5

S. **'Green Expectations'** syn. *Hylotelephium* 'Green Expectations' Deciduous, clump-forming perennial with erect, deep red stems and grayish green leaves, to 4 in (10 cm), narrowly egg-shaped, shallowly toothed, often turning maroon at the edges. Broadly conical flowerheads, to 6 in (15 cm) across, produced in early fall; individual flowers have green buds with a hint of red flushing on opening to greenish white petals and carpels, the latter aging to green. A hybrid of *S. telephium*. ‡24 in (60 cm). Z4–8 H8–1

S. **'Herbstfreude'** (**Autumn Joy**) syn. *S.* 'Indian Chief', *Hylotelephium* 'Herbstfreude' Deciduous, clump-forming perennial with erect stems bearing gray-green, elliptic to inversely egg-shaped, sharp-toothed leaves, to 3½ in (9 cm) long. Broad, flat-topped, deep pink flowerheads in late summer and early fall, to 8 in (20 cm) wide, take on rich brownish hues as the flowers die. Buds are greenish white; ¼ in (5 mm) flowers consisting of pale pink petals and dark pink carpels. Carpels, which provide most of the flower color, are longer than the petals, which are longer than the rudimentary stamens. A hybrid of *S. spectabile* and *S. telephium* raised by Georg Arends (*see panel, p. 87*) and released in 1955. ‡18–24 in (45–60 cm). Z3–10 H10–1

S. **hidakanum** Deciduous, mat-forming perennial with trailing stems bearing opposite, almost circular, slightly

ABOVE 1 *Sedum* 'Herbstfreude'
2 *S. kamtschaticum* 'Variegatum'
3 *S.* 'Ruby Glow'

toothed, purplish gray leaves to ¾ in (2 cm) long. Flowers, to ½ in (1 cm), consisting of pale pink petals and dark pink carpels, are carried from midsummer to early fall in rounded flowerheads ¾–1¼ in (2–3 cm) in diameter. Native to rocky slopes in Japan. ↕4 in (10 cm). Z4–8 H8–1

S. 'Indian Chief' see *S.* 'Herbstfreude'

S. 'Joyce Henderson' syn. *Hylotelephium* 'Joyce Henderson' Clump-forming deciduous with erect maroon stems. Broadly elliptic, toothed leaves, to 5 in (13 cm), often flushed or mottled with purple, especially toward the end of the season. Flat-topped flowerheads, to 6 in (15 cm) across, are produced from late summer to early fall, the flowers with pale pink petals, pale pink filaments, and pale pink carpels that fade to reddish brown. A hybrid of *S. spectabile* and *S. telephium* subsp. *maximum* 'Atropurpureum'. ↕30–34 in (75–85 cm). Z4–8 H8–1

S. kamtschaticum (Kamchatka stonecrop) Evergreen or semi-evergreen, with a woody rootstock from which arise ascending stems bearing opposite or alternate, narrowly wedge-shaped, irregularly toothed, dark green leaves, to 2 in (5 cm) long. Leafy, sparse, flat-topped flowerheads, to 2 in (5 cm) across, are produced from late summer to early fall; the star-shaped ⅝–¾ in (1.5–2 cm) flowers have five orange-yellow petals with orange carpels that age to dark orange or red, contrasting strikingly with the petals. Found on rocky slopes in northeastern Asia. ↕4–12 in (10–30 cm). Z3–8 H8–1. **var. *ellacombeanum*** Leaves opposite, broader, paler green. From Japan. **var. *floriferum* 'Weihenstephaner Gold'** More prolific, with flowers arising from both leaf joints and shoot tips. Leaves more bronze in color and flowers, ½–⅝ in (1.2–1.5 cm) across, are a paler yellow, with yellow carpels aging to pink. There are two flowering periods: from late spring to early summer and late summer to early fall. Originated at Sichtungsgarten Weihenstephan, in Germany, in about 1958. ↕10 in (25 cm). **var. *kamtschaticum* 'Variegatum'** Slower-growing; untoothed cream-edged leaves with, in full sun, a thin margin of orange or pink. Petals are a paler yellow; carpels pinkish orange.

S. 'Matrona' syn. *Hylotelephium* 'Matrona' Clump-forming, deciduous, with sturdy, erect, maroon stems. The olive-green, 5 in (13 cm) leaves are broadly elliptic, toothed, with a maroon midrib and sometimes entirely flushed in purple, especially at the end of the season. Flat-topped flowerheads, 6 in (15 cm) across, are produced from late summer to early fall; white buds open to pale pink petals, slightly darker at tip, that are the same length as the pale pink filaments; the pale pink carpels fade to reddish brown and green. Arose as a seedling hybrid of *S. spectabile* and *S. telephium* subsp. *maximum* 'Atropurpureum' in about 1986 at the nursery of Ewald Hugin in Freiburg im Bresgau, southern Germany. ↕24–30 in (60–75 cm). Z3–8 H9–1

S. middendorffianum Evergreen or semi-evergreen, with ascending stems arising from a woody rootstock and bearing opposite or alternate, dark green, linear, toothed leaves to 1½ in (4 cm) long. Leafy, sparse, flat-topped flowerheads, to 2 in (5 cm) across, are produced from early summer to midsummer. The star-shaped, ⅝ in (1.5 cm) flowers have pale yellow petals and greenish yellow carpels. Found in rocky sites, often among trees, in northeastern Asia. ↕4–8 in (10–20 cm). Z6–9 H9–6

S. pluricaule syn. *Hylotelephium pluricaule* Deciduous, and spreading with rhizomes: the creeping, branched stems, to 4 in (10 cm), carry alternate or opposite gray-green leaves to 1 in (2.5 cm) long, untoothed and oblong to circular. Flowerheads borne from late summer to early fall consist of purplish pink, ½–⅝ in (1–1.3 cm) flowers. In the true species, the new shoots do not emerge until early summer; plants sold under this name are often *S. ewersii* var. *homophyllum*. Native to mountain slopes, cliffs, and sea cliffs in eastern Siberia, Sachalin, and Japan. ↕6 in (15 cm). Z4–8 H8–1

S. populifolium syn. *Hylotelephium populifolium* Deciduous, branched subshrub, somewhat sprawling in habit but forming a slowly spreading colony. The stems bear bright green, alternate, triangular to egg-shaped, long-stalked, deeply and irregularly toothed leaves. The flowerheads appear in late summer and consist of a dense, slightly domed cluster to about 4 in (10 cm) across. The individual flowers, each about ½ in (1 cm) across, have white petals (sometimes with a faint pink tinge), yellowish white carpels, and a hawthorn scent. Native to open, rocky areas in western Siberia. ↕10–16 in (25–40 cm). Z6–9 H9–6

S. reflexum see *S. rupestre*

S. rosea see *Rhodiola rosea*

S. 'Ruby Glow' syn. *Hylotelephium* 'Ruby Glow' Deciduous perennial with numerous prostrate, unbranched, red stems, 16–20 in (40–50 cm) long, radiating from a central rootstock and carrying opposite, oval, shallowly toothed leaves, to 2¾ in (7 cm) long, grayish green flushed purple, markedly so in full sun. Loose flowerheads, to 2½ in (6 cm) across, appear from late summer to early fall at upturned tips of sprawling stems. Grayish pink buds open to ¼ in (7 mm) flowers with pinkish red petals and deeper red carpels. A hybrid of *S. cauticola* and *S. telephium* raised by Georg Arends (*see panel, p.87*) and released in 1960. ↕6–8 in (15–20 cm). Z5–9 H9–1

S. rupestre syn. *S. reflexum* (Reflexed stonecrop) Evergreen, mat-forming, with stems up to 14 in (35 cm) long; the nonflowering shoots sprawl acrosss the soil and root. The grayish green, sharply pointed, linear, cylindrical, ½–¾ in (1.2–2 cm) long leaves are arranged spirally around the shoots. When flowering in midsummer, stems ascend weakly and produce a domed or rounded flowerhead. The six- or seven-petaled flowers, ½–¾ in (1.3–1.8 cm) across, have bright yellow petals and yellow carpels. Found on walls, rocks, and rocky banks in western and central Europe, southern Scandinavia, and western Ukraine. ↕6–12 in (15–30 cm). Z6–9 H9–6. **'Angelina'** syn. 'Gold Mound' Bright yellow foliage in spring, fades to greenish yellow in summer and takes on orange tints in fall. Rarely flowers. Found by Austrian Christian Kress in a garden in Croatia.

S. spectabile syn. *Hylotelephium spectabile* (Ice plant, Butterfly stonecrop) Clump-forming, deciduous plant with erect stems carrying unstalked, egg-shaped, shallowly toothed and very pale grayish green leaves, to 4 in (10 cm) long, oppositely arranged or in clusters around the stems. Broad, flat-topped, 6–8 in (15–20 cm) flowerheads are produced from midsummer to early fall: the ⅜–½ in (0.9–1.2 cm), five-petaled flowers have pink petals and darker pink carpels, and the stamens, being longer than the petals, protrude prominently from the flower. Usually shorter than *S. telephium*, it differs in having opposite leaves and in the stamens being longer than the petals. Also similar to *S. erythrostictum*. ↕12–16 in (30–45 cm). Z4–9 H9–1. **'Brilliant'** Flowers ½ in (1.2 cm) across, the petals, stamens, and carpels bright carmine-pink, aging to greenish, then brown. ↕18 in (45 cm). **'Iceberg'** Leaves very pale grayish green, petals white, carpels white with pink tips. Flowers sometimes revert to pink. ↕ 14 in (35 cm). **'Meteor'** Leaves very pale grayish green, petals and carpels vivid pink. ↕ 16 in (40 cm). **'Septemberglut'** Flowers small, only ⅜ in (9 mm) across, but the rich purplish pink flowers ensure it is one of the darkest. ↕ 18 in (45 cm). **'Stardust'** Leaves very pale grayish green, the flowerheads all white or a mixture of pink and white on the same plant.

S. spurium (Caucasian stonecrop) Evergreen or semi-evergreen mat-former; branching, prostrate rooting stems. The leaves, to 1 in (2.5 cm), are opposite, inversely egg-shaped, bluntly toothed toward the apex, dark green but often red-flushed, long, and mostly clustered toward the stem tips. The ascending flowering stems bear flat-topped flowerheads, to 2½ in (6 cm) across, from mid- to late summer and consist of five-petaled flowers, to ¾ in (2 cm), with pale pink petals and slightly darker carpels. Tolerant of part-shade. From damp, mountainous habitats in the Caucasus, northern Iran, Armenia, and Kurdistan. ↕ 4 in (10 cm). Z4–9 H9–1. **'Coccineum'** syn. 'Splendens' Leaves heavily flushed red, flowers crimson. **'Erdblut'** Leaves flushed purple, flowers purple. **'Fuldaglut'** Leaves dark purplish red, flowers carmine-pink. Raised by Heinz Klose of Germany in 1974. **'Green Mantle'** Larger, consistently green leaves. Flowers white fading to very pale pink. **'Purpurteppich'** Leaves purplish red but paler than 'Fuldaglut', flowers carmine pink. Raised by German Ernst Benary in 1933. **'Schorbuser Blut'** Slow-growing; the

leaves are first green, edged with red, but turn darker by fall. Flowers dark purplish pink. Variable. **'Splendens'** *see* 'Coccineum'. **'Variegatum'** syn. 'Tricolor' Leaves narrow, green edged with white, red-flushed in sun. May revert.

S. 'Stewed Rhubarb Mountain' syn. *Hylotelephium* 'Stewed Rhubarb Mountain' Deciduous clump-former with arching pink stems bearing alternate, egg-shaped, gray-green leaves to 3 in (8 cm), with purple margins and midrib. From late summer to early fall the domed flowerheads, to 4 in (10 cm) across, exhibit a simultaneous mixture of pale green, pale pink, and dark pink. Pink buds open to flowers about ½ in (1 cm) across with white petals with purplish pink tips, white stamens, and pale green carpels, all aging to dark pink. A hybrid of *S. telephioides* and *S. telephium* raised by Bob Brown of Cotswold Garden Flowers, Worcestershire, England, in 1993. ↕ 12 in (30 cm). Z3–9 H9–1

S. 'Strawberries and Cream' syn. *Hylotelephium* 'Strawberries and Cream' Deciduous clump-former with erect, reddish purple stems carrying broadly elliptic leaves, to 2¾ in (7 cm), in green flushed purple and sharply toothed. Domed flowerheads to 4 in (10 cm) across, some flowers also clustered at the leaf joints, from late summer to early fall, show a mixture of dark pink and white. The flowers, up to ½ in (1 cm), emerge from deep pink buds and consist of pale pink petals, green carpels with pink tips, and white stamens that are longer than the petals. A hybrid of *S. spectabile* and

RIGHT 1 *Sedum spurium* 'Schorbuser Blut' **2** *S.* 'Stewed Rhubarb Mountain' **3** *S.* 'Strawberries and Cream'

S. telephium subsp. *maximum* 'Atropurpureum'. ↕ 24 in (60 cm). Z4–8 H8–1

S. 'Sunset Cloud' syn. *Hylotelephium* 'Sunset Cloud' Clump-forming deciduous plant with trailing to slightly ascending purple stems, to 16 in (40 cm), that splay out from the center and carry mainly opposite, rounded to spoon-shaped, toothed, blue-green leaves, to 2 in (5 cm). The flowerheads, to 2½ in (6 cm) across, are borne from late summer to early fall and consist of ½ in (1 cm) flowers with short white petals that do not contribute to the color, and dark reddish pink carpels. Raised by Jim Archibald at The Plantsman Nursery in Dorset, England, in about 1972, and derived from *S. cauticola*—possibly with the same parentage as *S.* 'Vera Jameson'. ↕ 12 in (30 cm). Z4–8 H8–1

S. telephium syn. *Hylotelephium telephium* (Orpine) Deciduous clump-former with erect stems; the usually unstalked, toothed, bluish green, oblong to egg-shaped leaves, to 4 in (10 cm), are mostly alternate. Broadly conical flowerheads, to 4¾ in (12 cm) across, are produced from late summer to mid-fall, with some flower clusters at the leaf joints. The five-petaled, ½ in (1 cm) flowers have reddish purple petals and carpels with stamens that are shorter than, or no longer than, the petals. A variable species with a number of subspecies and varieties, the distinguishing features of which are not always clear, especially in cultivated plants. Differs from *S. spectabile* in the mostly alternate leaves and stamen length. Found in woods, banks, and rocky places from Europe through Russia and China to Japan. ↕ 8–28 in (20–70 cm). Z4–9 H9–1. **'Arthur Branch'** Red stems, deep purple shiny leaves, reddish purple flowers. A hybrid of *S. telephium* subsp. *maximum* 'Atropurpureum'. **var. borderei** Leaves narrowly elliptic with a wedge-shaped base, and deeply toothed. Flowerheads made up of rounded clusters of purplish pink, ¼ in (7 mm) flowers are produced from mid- to late summer. ↕ 10–16 in (25–40 cm). **'Lynda et Rodney'** Purplish red stems and very dark brownish purple, narrowly elliptic to wedge-shaped leaves. The domed, 6 in (15 cm) flowerheads, with secondary flower clusters on the upper quarter of the stems, are produced from late summer to early fall. The relatively small, ¼ in (5 mm) flowers consist of pale pinkish purple petals and red carpels, both darkening with age. Found in the wild in northwestern France and named for Lynda Windsor and Rodney Davey of RD Plants, Devon, England. ↕ 32 in (80 cm). **'Lynda Windsor'** Purple stems with very dark purple, 2½ in (6 cm) leaves, the main flowerhead made up of smaller clusters with many subsidiary clusters arising from leaf joints below.

SEDUM SPECTABILE

Sedum spectabile

S. spectabile 'Brilliant'

S. spectabile 'Meteor'

S. spectabile 'Stardust'

Individual flowers small, ¼ in (5 mm), the buds, petals, and carpels deep reddish purple, filaments paler purple. Raised by RD Plants, Devon. ‡ 36 in (90 cm). **subsp. maximum** Leaves well-spaced and sparse, broadly egg-shaped, stalkless, stem-clasping, and often opposite or in clusters around the stem. Buds pale green, petals greenish white, carpels white with a pink flush fading to greenish brown. ‡ 16–32 in (40–80 cm). **subsp. maximum 'Atropurpureum'** Red stems, deep purplish brown leaves, and pink flowers in widely branching, diffuse flowerheads of small clusters. With a loose habit, it may require support, and is slow to increase and variable. A parent of many purple-leaved cultivars. ‡ 28 in (70 cm). **subsp. maximum 'Gooseberry Fool'** Gray-green leaves with upturned margins are slightly red-flushed, especially on the midribs. Broad flowerheads, to 8 in (20 cm) across, of ½ in (1 cm) flowers with greenish white petals, white filaments slightly longer than the petals, and green carpels, becoming pink-flushed with age. Arose as a seedling in the garden of Englishman Graham Stuart Thomas. ‡ 18–24 in (45–60 cm). **'Mohrchen'** Purplish red stems and dark brownish purple leaves; 6 in (15 cm) flowerheads, supplemented by flower clusters on the upper quarter of the stems, consist of relatively small, ½ in (5 mm) flowers with pale pinkish purple petals and red carpels, both darkening with age. Similar to 'Lynda Windsor' but shorter. Raised by P. and B. zur Linden at their nursery in Germany. ‡ 12–18 in (30–45 cm). **'Munstead Red'** Bright red stems and green, 2½ in (6 cm) leaves, slightly flushed purple. Loose heads of hemispherical flower clusters, each flower with pinkish purple petals and deep purplish red carpels that fade reddish brown. ‡ 12–18 in (30–45 cm). **'Purple Emperor'** Red stems carry broadly elliptic leaves of a dark, deep purple. The flowerheads, to 8 in (20 cm) across, consist of smaller rounded clusters of greenish pink flower buds opening to pale purplish pink petals, with carpels of a darker

CLASSIC PLANTING IDEAS

TWO CLASSIC ELEMENTS of planting design are illustrated here. The vertical spikes of *Kniphofia* 'Little Maid' at the very front are bold and distinctive but do not make such a dense group that they obscure the plants behind—indeed, the fact that you can see through them is part of their charm. And revealed behind are the almost flat heads of *Sedum spectabile* 'Brilliant', making a striking contrast. Additional contrast in shape is provided by the softer spikes of the caryopteris at the back and, arching in from the side in an altogether more relaxed style, the fine foliage of the miscanthus, which will soon be enhanced by its soft, elegant flowering plumes.

pink aging to maroon and brown. A hybrid of *S. telephium* subsp. *maximum* 'Atropurpureum' with *S. telephium* subsp. *ruprechtii*, selected by Graham

Gough from his mother's garden in Newhaven, Sussex, England, and introduced by Washfield Nursery, Kent, in the 1990s. ‡ 20 in (50 cm). **'Roseovariegatum'** Not variegated, but the young, pale pink spring shoots eventually mature to green. ‡ 14 in (35 cm). **subsp. ruprechtii** Stems ascending from a prostrate position but with a tendency to flop. The leaves, to 3 in (8 cm), are opposite, broadly egg-shaped to almost circular, stem-clasping, and grayish green with some pink flushing. Flowerheads with an overall pale yellow effect consist of white buds, white petals with some pink edging, and pale green carpels fading to brownish red. ‡ 14–16 in (35–40 cm). **subsp. ruprechtii 'Hab Gray'** Slightly more compact and with pink-flushed flower buds. ‡ 12 in (30 cm).

S. 'Vera Jameson' syn. *Hylotelephium*

LEFT 1 *Sedum telephium* subsp. *maximum* **2** *S. telephium* 'Purple Emperor'

'Vera Jameson' Clump-forming and deciduous. Purple stems to 16 in (40 cm); rounded, toothed, gray-green leaves, to ¾ in (2 cm), that are strongly flushed purple in full sun. Flowerheads, to 2½ in (6 cm) across, are produced from early to mid-fall and consist of ⅜ in (9 mm) flowers with pale pink petals and pinkish red carpels. A hybrid of *S.* 'Ruby Glow' and *S. telephium* subsp. *maximum* 'Atropurpureum', introduced by Joe Elliott in Worcestershire, England, in 1970 and named for the owner of the garden in which it arose. ‡ 10 in (25 cm). Z4–9 H9–1

SELINUM
APIACEAE

One of the most beautiful of the carrot family, dubbed the "Queen of Umbellifers" by E. A. Bowles.

Six tap-rooted perennial species come from meadows and scrub in mountainous areas of Europe to Central Asia; only one is seen in gardens. Upright, sometimes red-

ABOVE 1 *Selinum wallichianum*
2 *Semiaquilegia ecalcarata*

tinted stems carry foliage divided into opposite pairs of bright green leaflets, split once or twice more into further pairs. Each segment may be slender and almost hairlike, elliptical, or lance-shaped. Large, broad, relatively sparse umbels of white, sometimes purple-tinted flowers at the top in summer. Once valued as lawn specimens, they are now grown in mixed and perennial borders but are best not crowded so that their stature can be admired.

CULTIVATION Adaptable, but best in well-drained but reasonably moist, fertile soil, in sun or light shade.

PROPAGATION From seed, or by careful division in spring.

PROBLEMS Slugs; powdery mildew.

S. tenuifolium see *S. wallichianum*

S. wallichianum syn. *S. tenuifolium* A charming plant, for both its very finely divided, fresh green ferny leaves with their tiny elliptical leaflets, and its flat-topped heads, or umbels, of pure white flowers, as delicate as lace, which are borne from mid- or late summer. The flowers are held in large umbels, to 8 in (20 cm) across, surrounded by quite prominent greeny white bracts. Several forms, not yet distinguished by names, are grown: one, with deep reddish purple stems, is particularly attractive. From light scrub and damp mountain meadows on the Himalayan foothills from Kashmir east to Bhutan. ‡ 5 ft (1.5 m). Z4–7 H7–4

SEMIAQUILEGIA
RANUNCULACEAE

Dainty and delicate relatives of the familiar columbine (*Aquilegia*) for the rock garden and sheltered situations.

Seven species of these small, and sometimes short-lived perennials are found in mountain areas in Asia; only one is usually grown. A basal rosette of leaves, each split into three leaflets and then again into threes once or twice more, supports slender stems and open heads of nodding, bell-shaped, spurless flowers. The plants now treated as *Semiaquilegia* have an unfortunate history of being moved into, and out of, *Aquilegia* or *Isopyrum*, under which names they may still sometimes be listed.

CULTIVATION Best in a sheltered spot, out of cold or strong winds but with protection from drying sun. Moist, humus-rich, neutral or acidic soil is necessary.

PROPAGATION From seed sown fresh.

PROBLEMS Slugs and snails.

S. ecalcarata syn. *Aquilegia ecalcarata* Finely divided, bright green, 12 in (30 cm) leaves tinged with purple are twice split into threes, each leaflet in turn having two or three lobes. The nodding, deep purple or sometimes deep pink or occasionally white, ⅝ in (1.5 cm), spurless flowers are produced in airy sprays on purple wiry stems, each flower with an upper row of flaring petals and a lower row that forms a bell shape. From western China. ‡ 12–18 in (30–45 cm). Z6–8 H8–6. **'Flore Pleno'** Double flowers.

SENECIO
ASTERACEAE

Unexpectedly attractive and noninvasive relations of familiar garden weeds.

This large, highly variable, cosmopolitan group of about 1,000 species includes annuals, biennials, herbaceous perennials, succulents, climbers, shrubs, and even a few small trees. They occupy a wide range of habitats, including waste ground, marshlands, grasslands, mountainous areas, seashores, and woodland clearings. The leaves may be entire or lobed, and the majority have clusters of flowers, with a few having flowers carried singly. The flowers may be daisylike with both ray florets and disk florets, or the ray florets may be missing. They have little in common of interest to the gardener. This extraordinary assemblage of species includes both garden weeds like groundsel (*S. vulgaris*) and agricultural weeds like ragwort (*S. jacobaea*), which is highly toxic to grazing animals, as well as some attractive ornamentals.

CULTIVATION Needs vary widely.

PROPAGATION By division in spring, or from cuttings.

PROBLEMS Usually trouble-free.

S. polyodon Vigorous, carpet-forming, deciduous; rosette of basal leaves and erect, slender, branched stems that are covered with sticky hairs. Stem leaves are narrow and toothed, and clasp the stem. In late spring to early fall, it produces fuchsia-purple, magenta, or violet daisylike flowers with yellow disks. Best in sun and well-drained soil, where it may self-sow. From the grasslands in South Africa. ‡ 12 in (30 cm). Z4–9 H9–4

S. pulcher Erect, deciduous or evergreen perennial with leathery green leaves. The stems may be unbranched or branch toward the tips and are woolly-hairy when young, then becoming hairless. The basal leaves are elliptical, tapering toward the base, and have scalloped margins, while the stem leaves are lance-shaped with a toothed margin. In summer and fall, it produces daisylike flowers with long purple ray florets and a yellow disk, sometimes singly but more often in small clusters.

Best in a sheltered spot: the partially evergreen foliage tends to become damaged in winter. From Argentina, Brazil, and Uruguay. ‡ 24 in (60 cm). Z10–11 H11–6

S. smithii Vigorous and clump-forming, with robust, erect stems and leathery, glossy, toothed, dark green foliage: the stalked lower leaves are oblong to egg-shaped, with a truncated base, and woolly-hairy beneath, while the stem leaves are triangular to egg-shaped and without a stalk. In early summer to midsummer, it produces large clusters of 2 in (5 cm), daisylike flowers, with white ray florets and a yellow disk. Ideal in wet soil in full sun or part-shade. From marshes and streamsides in Argentina, Chile, and the Falkland Islands. ‡ 4 ft (1.2 m). Z6–8 H8–6

SERIPHIDIUM *see* ARTEMISIA

SESELI
APIACEAE

Striking plants combining pretty, often finely cut, sometimes bluish foliage and attractive heads of flowers.

Some 65 biennials and perennials come from dry rough grassland, scrub, or rocky situations, usually in alkaline soil, throughout Europe into Central Asia. Very few are seen in gardens, although many are interesting and ornamental plants. They have either tap or fibrous roots; the leaves are split, sometimes repeatedly, into pairs or trios of leaflets, each leaflet slender and hairlike or broader and sharply toothed. The flowerheads are made up of a number of umbels, the individual florets being white, or sometimes yellow or pink. Some mountain species from southern Europe are undeservedly neglected and should be more widely grown for their finely divided bluish or grayish foliage.

RIGHT 1 *Senecio pulcher* **2** *S. smithii*

ABOVE **1** *Seseli gummiferum* **2** *Sesleria caerulea*

CULTIVATION Best in well-drained, alkaline soil, in full sun.

PROPAGATION From seed.

PROBLEMS Usually trouble-free.

S. gummiferum A stout and rigid, upright, almost succulent, short-lived perennial or biennial clothed with finely cut, intensely blue-gray leathery leaves. After two or three years, pink flowers, turning white as they mature, are produced on branched stems at the top of the plant. These are held in unusually tight compact heads with between 20 and 60 florets per umbel, giving a striking appearance. Plants die after flowering. Best in a very well-drained spot with a sunny exposure, where it will form an eyecatching, quite unique specimen. From the Crimea and southern Aegean. ‡ 3¼ ft (1 m). Z6–9 H9–6

SESLERIA
Moor grass
POACEAE

Tough, long-lived grasses with colorful two-toned foliage: often the first grasses to flower in spring.

In the wild, the 27 species are found mainly on mountain rocks in the Balkans and into Asia. Densely tufted evergreen grasses, their slowly creeping root systems form low-growing, loose mats of wide, keeled leaves with blunt points, often in different shades on the upper and lower surfaces. Many have attractive flowers, some flowering in early spring. The flower stems are usually straight and slender. Flowerheads rounded and compact but may be cylindrical, and are silvery green to purple-black and hung with prominent yellow stamens. These very tough little grasses make

excellent and colorful ground cover for use on path edges and they are most attractive planted with small spring bulbs.

CULTIVATION Well-drained, fertile, neutral to alkaline soil in full sun. Divide early-flowering species after flowering in mid-spring; otherwise, divide earlier in the year.

PROPAGATION By division. Plants tend to hybridize readily, sometimes even with other genera, so avoid raising from seed.

PROBLEMS Usually trouble-free.

S. albicans see *S. caerulea*

S. autumnalis (Fall moor grass) An atypical species with dense clumps of slender, slightly arching, blue-green leaves, ¼ in (7 mm) wide, turning almost lime green in the fall. From early summer to mid-fall, tall, chunky stems carry flower spikes up to 5 in (12 cm) long, purple-black at first turning silver-green to violet, and hung with white stamens. A cool-season grass, its foliage dies back in summer, with new growth in fall and spring. Found in alkaline soil in northern Italy through to Albania and into the Middle East. ‡ 4 ft (1.2 m). Z5–8 H8–5

S. caerulea syn. *S. albicans* (Blue moor grass) Dense, low-growing tufts on short, slender, creeping roots; the bicolored leaves, ¹⁄₁₆–¼ in (2–6 mm) wide, bluntly pointed, the top surface smooth glossy green and the underside matte blue-gray. The way the leaves lie allows both green and blue sides to be seen in the same clump. The flower stems appear very early in the year, from early spring through to early summer, carrying compact, egg-shaped flowerheads, at first dark purple and then silvery green fading to buff. Slowly spreads to make ground cover in damper places. From damp pastures and mountain grasslands on limestone throughout central Europe, and north to Iceland. ‡ 18 in (45 cm). Z5–8 H8–5

S. glauca see *S. nitida*

S. heufleriana (Blue-green moor grass) Slowly spreading upright clumps of two-toned, ⅛ in (3 mm) leaves, blue-green on the top surface, becoming greener through the summer, and with a silvery bloom on the underside; both surfaces are visible. Flower stems appear early in the spring, from early to mid-spring, growing high above the foliage, carrying compact, 1¼ in (3 cm) pencils of dark green flowers that appear almost black when just opened and are covered with pale yellow stamens. Good in drifts among spring flowers and bulbs. Native to limestone in woods, on rocks, and on rocky slopes in central and eastern Europe and in the Caucasus. ‡ 30 in (75 cm). Z5–8 H8–5

S. nitida syn. *S. glauca* (Gray moor grass) Large, dense, slowly spreading clumps of more or less upright leaves build to a mound up to 12 in (30 cm) high. The ¼ in (6 mm) leaves are two-toned but as they lie flat the foliage appears blue-gray, the color of the upper surface of the leaf. Slender flower stems appear in mid- to late spring, carrying nearly black, oval flowerheads that gradually turn silvery green and are hung with yellow stamens. Appears as a prominent blue fountain of foliage in the spring landscape but, being a cool-season grass, tends to die back in the summer during hot weather. Grow with bulbs such as dwarf irises and other plants that grow best in free-draining soils. Native to alkaline soil in mountains in central and southern Italy and Sicily. ‡ 30 in (75 cm). Z5–8 H8–5

SIDALCEA
Prairie mallow
MALVACEAE

Neat, bushy plants with delicate, fingered foliage and spikes of small, hollyhock-like flowers for many midsummer weeks.

About 20 species of annuals or short-lived perennials grow in central

and western North America, usually on well-drained, nonalkaline soil. Although very variable in the wild, and puzzling to botanists, all are upright and bushy, forming dense clumps, with usually glossy green, rounded lower leaves and divided foliage on the flowering stems. The branched stems carry flowers in crowded spikes, the blooms usually 2–2¼ in (5–6 cm) across with five petals and a central cluster of stamens. The flowers are produced from early summer and usually last through mid- and late summer as secondary spikes open later below the main, terminal flower spikes. Flowers come in shades of crimson, pink, and white, and the petals usually have an attractive silky sheen that adds to their beauty. The old flowers drop as they fade, giving the plants a clean, neat appearance.

The hybrids, mainly involving *S. candida* and *S. malviflora*, are generally rather similar except in their flower color and height.

CULTIVATION Best in full sun in moist, well-drained soil that is not wet in winter. Plants can be short-lived, especially in heavy soil. Taller cultivars may need staking in exposed situations but most are self-supporting. Cut back after flowering to encourage fresh foliage and promote a long flowering season.

PROPAGATION From seed (for species and some seed strains) or by division in spring.

PROBLEMS Usually trouble-free, though hollyhock rust may be a problem in warm, moist weather. Slugs and snails attack young plants.

S. 'Brilliant' Dense spikes of deep, carmine rose pink flowers like small hollyhocks on upright stems in mid- and late summer. Attractive to butterflies. ‡ 30 in (75 cm). Z5–9 H9–5

S. candida (White checkermallow) Slightly variable; deep green, more or less heart-shaped, lobed or scalloped basal leaves to 8 in (20 cm), may redden in full sun, and smaller, finely five-fingered stem leaves; small, pure white flowers with blue anthers in early and mid-summer. Flowers 2¾–4 in (7–10 cm) across; petals vary from narrow, resulting in open flowers, to rounder and fuller. Some plants have dark stems and some flowers have pink anthers. A parent of many cultivars, from the Southwest US. ‡ 24–36 in (60–90 cm). Z5–8 H8–5. **'Bianca'** Taller, with pure white flowers. ‡ 3¼ ft (1 m).

S. 'Croftway Red' Prolific, deep reddish pink flowers that bloom in mid- and late summer. Raised and introduced by Croftway Nursery, Sussex, England. ‡ 32 in (80 cm). Z5–9 H9–5

S. 'Elsie Heugh' Distinctive in the fringed tips to the large, pale pink, silky petals. Still the most popular cultivar, though introduced in 1936. ‡ 36 in (90 cm). Z5–9 H9–5

S. 'Little Princess' Bushy and free-flowering. Pale pink flowers fade as they age; pink anthers. Shortest and most compact cultivar, more so than 'Puck'. ‡ 16 in (40 cm). Z5–9 H9–5

S. 'Loveliness' Shell pink flowers on bushy, self-supporting plants. ‡ 30 in (75 cm). Z5–9 H9–5

S. malviflora Woody-based, spreads slowly by rhizomes. Hairy stems and rounded or kidney-shaped, toothed or lobed foliage, larger at the base and progressively smaller up the stems, where the leaves become five-fingered, and heads of white-veined, pink or purple, 2 in (5 cm) flowers. The parent, with S. candida, of most cultivars. From dry places in forest and scrub in the western US. ‡ 3¼ ft (1 m). Z5–7 H8–2

S. 'Mr. Lindbergh' Bluish green leaves and deep, rosy red flowers, earlier than most, in early summer and midsummer. Said to come true from seed, but this seems unlikely. ‡ 28–48 in (70–120 cm). Z5–9 H9–5

S. 'Mrs. Borrodaile' Darker than most cultivars, with deep, dusky rose-magenta flowers. ‡ 3¼ ft (1 m). Z5–9 H9–5

S. 'Oberon' Neat, compact, and self-supporting, with soft rose pink flowers. Raised by English plantsman Alan Bloom and introduced in 1963. ‡ 28 in (70 cm). Z6–8 H8–6

S. oregana A woody taproot supports mostly basal, glossy green, 6 in (15 cm) lobed foliage; stems with coarse hairs and smaller, divided stem leaves topped with rose pink flowers, each petal notched at the tip. Native to open, wet places in western North America. ‡ 28–40 in (70–100 cm). Z5–9 H9–5

S. 'Party Girl' Bright pink flowers with white centers and stamens. From seed, so may be variable. ‡ 30 in (75 cm). Z6–8 H8–5

S. 'Puck' Clear pink flowers above bushy, compact growth. Until the recent introduction of 'Little Princess', the shortest, most compact, and most dependably self-supporting cultivar. Raised by Alan Bloom and introduced in 1963. ‡ 24 in (60 cm). Z5–9 H9–5

S. 'Purpetta' Purple-pink flowers with a white center. From seed; reputed to come true ‡ 3½ ft (1.1 m). Z5–9 H9–5

S. 'Reverend Page Roberts' Dark buds and flower stems and pale silvery pink flowers. One of the tallest and oldest cultivars, named for a noted horticultural cleric from Norfolk, England. ‡ 4¼ ft (1.3 m). Z5–9 H9–5

S. 'Rosaly' Pale pink flowers and slender leaves. From seed, so may be variable. ‡ 4¼ ft (1.3 m). Z5–9 H9–5

S. 'Rosanna' Deep rose pink flowers. From seed, so may be variable. ‡ 3¼ ft (1 m). Z5–9 H9–5

S. 'Rose Queen' Robust, well-branched, self-supporting stems; dark rose pink flowers in early summer and midsummer. ‡ 3¼ ft (1 m). Z5–9 H9–5

S. 'Sussex Beauty' Glowing, satin pink flowers on robust plants. Once thought lost but, thankfully, still with us. ‡ 36 in (90 cm). Z5–9 H9–5

S. 'William Smith' Rich, salmon pink flowers in dense spikes. ‡ 3¼ ft (1 m). Z5–9 H9–5

SILENE
Campion, Catchfly
CARYOPHYLLACEAE

Hardy spring- and summer-flowering sun- or shade-lovers, adding a refreshingly natural touch.
About 500 species of annuals, biennials, and deciduous or evergreen perennials, some with

GOING WILD IN THE WILD

GARDENERS WHO PREFER PASTELS should look away now, as two California natives come together in a startling grouping. In this dry, poor soil, *Sidalcea malviflora* develops relatively few spikes and opens just a few flowers on each spike at a time. But the color is so intense that the impact is still dramatic. Around and among it, the brilliant orange of the annual California poppy, *Eschscholzia californica*, is a natural partner. Gardeners who prefer softer colors could replicate this in a quieter way, since *S. malviflora* is the parent of many cultivars in pastels colors, and California poppies also come in more subdued shades. But it wouldn't be the same.

woody bases, come from a range of habitats including meadows, open woodlands, mountains, coastal cliffs, and gravel beaches throughout the Northern Hemisphere. Varying from mat-forming to upright in habit. The variable leaves are often lance-shaped to egg-shaped. The flowers, about 1 in (2.5 cm) across, have five petals, and each petal often has a notched or split tip. The calyx is often inflated like a balloon. Silenes have a range of uses, including in mixed or perennial borders and meadow or prairie-style plantings.

CULTIVATION Most grow well in any well-drained, reasonably fertile, neutral to slightly alkaline soil, although some do best in very well-drained conditions. For full sun or light, dappled shade.

PROPAGATION By division after flowering or cuttings in spring. Species can be raised from seed. May self-seed freely.

PROBLEMS Slugs, snails, and powdery mildew.

S. asterias Clump-forming; provides intense color over a long period. The mound of dark green foliage is a good background for flat, dense heads of tiny, intense red, sweetly scented flowers that are carried on strong stems from late spring onward. Best in a mixed or herbaceous border in full sun with well-drained soil. From southeastern Europe. ↕ 24 in (60 cm). Z6–9 H9–6

S. dioica syn. *Melandrium rubrum*, *S. rubra* (Red campion) Partially evergreen, clump-forming plant; the pointed, oval, deep green leaves grow to 3½ in (9 cm) long, and clusters of red flowers with notched petals provide continuous color from late spring to midsummer. Ideal for natural planting schemes, including woodland gardens; the cultivars are more suited to mixed and herbaceous borders. Best in moist yet well-drained soil with light, dappled shade. From Europe. ↕ 32 in (80 cm). Z6–9 H9–6. **'Clifford Moor'** Dark green leaves edged creamy yellow; pink flowers. ↕ 12 in (30 cm). **'Compacta'** *see* 'Minikin'. **'Flore Pleno'** syn. 'Rubra Plena' Double red flowers. ↕ 24 in (60 cm). **'Graham's Delight'** syn. 'Variegata' Cream and green variegated leaves, red flowers. ↕ 36 in (90 cm). **'Inane'** Dark purple leaves and pink flowers. **'Minikin'** syn. 'Compacta' Bright dusky pink flowers. ↕ 12–16 in (30–40 cm). **'Richmond'** Double, deep rose pink flowers. **'Rosea Plena'** Double, dusky pink flowers. ↕ 24 in (60 cm). **'Rubra Plena'** *see* 'Flore Pleno'. **'Thelma Kay'** Leaves variegated cream and green, double pink flowers. ↕ 12 in (30 cm). **'Variegata'** *see* 'Graham's Delight'.

S. fimbriata syn. *S. multifida* Hairy, clump-forming, deciduous plant with upright, leafy stems, the 4 in (10 cm) dark green leaves somewhat egg-shaped, and loose heads of white flowers, up to 1½ in (4 cm) across with deeply cut petals and balloonlike calyces, produced from late spring to midsummer. Cut back after flowering to encourage more flowers. Suitable for dry soil in part-shade in borders or naturalistic planting schemes. From the Caucasus. ↕ 24 in (60 cm). Z6–9 H9–6

S. maritima see *S. uniflora*

S. multifida see *S. fimbriata*

S. nutans (Nottingham catchfly) Hairy, deciduous plant, the lower leaves spoon-shaped with long stalks. The loose heads of scented, white flowers, ¾ in (2 cm) across and with deeply split petals, open in the evening from early summer onward; they are often tinged greenish yellow and pink. For borders and naturalistic planting schemes in full sun and well-drained soil; good in seaside gardens. From most of Europe, northern Asia, North Africa, and the Caucasus. ↕ 20 in (50 cm). Z3–7 H7–1

S. rubra see *S. dioica*

S. schafta Clump-forming, partially evergreen hairy plant with bright green, ¾ in (2 cm), lance-shaped leaves and sprays of long-tubed, ¾ in (2 cm) wide, deep magenta flowers with notched petals produced in abundance during late summer and early fall. Best in well-drained soil and full sun. From the Caucasus. ↕ 10 in (25 cm). Z4–8 H9–3. **'Shell Pink'** Pale pink flowers.

S. uniflora syn. *S. maritima*, *S. vulgaris* subsp. *maritima* (Sea campion) Woody based, semi-evergreen, mat-forming plant with ¾ in (2 cm), gray-green, lance-shaped, fleshy leaves. The showy white, 1 in (2.5 cm) flowers, with their deeply notched petals and balloonlike calyces, perform from early summer onward. Good at the front of sunny, well-drained borders, in gravel gardens, and also in containers; thrives in seaside gardens. From the Atlantic coasts of Europe, including the British Isles. ↕ 8 in (20 cm). Z3–7 H7–1. **'Alba Plena'** *see* 'Robin Whitebreast'. **'Compacta'** Short, with white or pink flowers. ↕ 4 in (10 cm). **'Druett's Variegated'** syn. 'Variegata' Cream and green variegated leaves; white flowers. ↕ 4 in (10 cm). **'Robin Whitebreast' (Weisskehlchen)** syn. 'Alba Plena', 'Flore Pleno' Double white flowers. ↕ 6 in (15 cm). **'Rosea'** Pale pink flowers. **'Variegata'** *see* 'Druett's Variegated'. **'White Bells'** Short, with large, clear white flowers. ↕ 4 in (10 cm).

S. vulgaris subsp. *maritima* see *S. uniflora*

SILPHIUM
ASTERACEAE

Imposing herbaceous plants that have the same look and appeal as perennial sunflowers.

At least 20 deciduous species come from **prairies** and woodland clearings in eastern North America. Densely clump-forming, their strong, tall stems bear lance-shaped to oval leaves, which may be toothed or lobed; they may be arranged in opposite pairs or alternately, or in clusters, or sometimes are all gathered at the base. Topping the stems are loose clusters of yellow or rarely white daisylike flowers.

Big and chunky rather than stylish and elegant, they make impressive specimens at the back of a large border or in a wild situation.

CULTIVATION Thrives in a sunny site in ordinary soil; part-shade is acceptable, though support may then be needed.

PROPAGATION By division or from seed.

PROBLEMS Usually trouble-free.

S. laciniatum (Compass plant) The 8–16 in (20–40 cm) long, deeply lobed, raspy basal leaves tend to stand in a vertical plane, the blades aligned north and south—hence the common name. Smaller leaves to 4 in (10 cm) are carried alternately up the bristly stems. Notch-tipped, golden ray florets form sunflower-style heads 3½–4¾ in (9–12 cm) across, opening from the uppermost leaf joints during late summer and fall. ↕ 6–10 ft (1.8–3 m). Z5–9 H9–5

S. perfoliatum (Indian cup) Sturdy, four-angled, smooth stems bear

BELOW *Silphium perfoliatum*

8–12 in (20–30 cm) long, toothed oval leaves in stalkless pairs. The blades of each pair unite around the stem forming a shallow cup—hence the common name. In late summer, the stem tips branch to form a loose cluster of bright yellow sunflowers, 2¼–3½ in (6–9 cm) across. ↕ 3–8 ft (1.8–2.5 m). Z5–9 H9–5

SISYRINCHIUM
IRIDACEAE

Grassy plants with small, starry flowers for edging, gravel, and borders in sun or part-shade.

This rather confused group of about 100 species, mainly perennials but including a few annuals, comes from well-drained soil to moist meadows, usually in sunny locations. Most are found in South America, some in North America, and one, rather surprisingly, in Ireland. They are grown for their pretty, starry flowers: the blue-flowered species are often known as blue-eyed grass.

Plants form clumps, often spreading by short rhizomes, with fans of long, narrow, more or less sword-shaped foliage; they range in habit from dwarf mats of upright foliage to rather sprawling clumps. Most are semi-evergreen, overwintering as small fans of foliage, and flower in early summer; although the flowers are individually short-lived, they open over several weeks. The starry, ½–¾ in (1–2 cm) flowers, usually in shades of blue or yellow, are carried in small clusters of up to eight on flattened, often branched stems, each cluster sheathed by a small leafy bract. They usually open flat in bright sunlight, and have a prominent pointed tip and a yellow base; the three outer petals are broader than the three inner ones. The flowers are followed by round seed capsules, although some cultivars seem sterile. The fans of foliage may die after flowering but the dead fans usually only need removing from larger species such as S. striatum.

Sisyrinchiums are not well understood: many species are very similar and therefore difficult to distinguish, and their classification is confusing. Some have been called Phaiophleps and Bermudiana and there are many synonyms. Now that they are becoming more popular, further research should clarify the situation.

CULTIVATION Plant in sun in well-drained, moist soil. Wet winters, poorly drained soil, and excess cold are the chief dangers, though many are short-lived and should be propagated regularly. Clear away unsightly old, blackened foliage of larger species when the fans die after flowering.

PROPAGATION Easily grown from seed, although some may self-sow and become a nuisance when conditions are favorable. Cultivars should be divided in spring.

PROBLEMS Usually trouble-free.

S. angustifolium syn. *S. bermudianum* (Narrow-leaved blue-eyed grass) Among slender, ¹⁄₁₆–⅛ in (1–3 mm) wide foliage, the stems break into two or three branches and these branches carry two or three flowers from each bract in early summer. Each flower is pale blue with a dark edge around the yellow eye that extends as three lines into the ⅜–½ in (8–12 mm) petals; these petals have prominent thin points. The flowers are followed by spherical seeds. Native to moist meadows, stream banks, and damp, open patches at woodland edges in most parts of the eastern US; the plants that are found in Ireland are now also considered native. ↕ 8 in (20 cm). Z3–8 H8–1. **'Lucerne'** Larger, ¾ in (2 cm) flowers. Found in a garden in Switzerland.

S. **'Ball's Mauve'** see *S.* 'E. K. Balls'

S. bellum see *S. idahoense* var. *bellum*

RIGHT 1 *Sisyrinchium* 'Biscutella'
2 *S.* 'Californian Skies' **3** *S. californicum* Brachypus Group **4** *S.* 'E.K. Balls'

S. bermudianum see *S. angustifolium*

S. **'Biscutella'** Small, brown and cream flowers are held on slender stems above narrow foliage, each petal shaded and veined with coppery brown on cream with a yellow eye. Although the individual flowers are not showy, they are produced in large numbers and make an interesting summer display. ↕ 12 in (30 cm). Z7–8 H8–7

S. **'Blue Ice'** Large, ¾ in (2 cm), dark-veined, pale blue flowers have broad petals and yellow eyes. Neat and free-flowering. ↕ 6 in (15 cm). Z7–8 H8–7

S. **'Californian Skies'** Bright, deep blue flowers with yellow eyes and an inky blue rim, and three dark veins running through the petals. Neat, free-flowering. ↕ 6 in (15 cm). Z5–8 H8–5

SIMPLE PLEASURES

ONE OF THE basic principles of grouping plants is to bring together species that are similar in some ways, yet different in others. This is an example. In the background, *Sisyrinchium striatum* has upright stems and slender foliage growing from a compact rootstock, as does the *Iris sibirica* in front. Both are in the iris family. But while the sisyrinchium has clusters of rather small flowers all the way up the stems, the iris has just a few, much larger flowers gathered at the top. The flowers are connected in color, however, as the honey throat of this iris, 'Gatineau', picks up a similar color in the buds of the sisyrinchium.

S. californicum (Golden-eyed grass) The flat, winged stems emerge above slender, grayish green, ¼ in (5 mm) wide foliage, carrying yellow flowers, ⅝–¾ in (1.5–2 cm) across, and marked with brown veins; although starry, they do not have obviously pointed petal tips. It has a long flowering season in spring and early summer. Grows wild in moist soil near the Pacific coast in California, Oregon, and Washington. ↕18 in (45 cm). Z8–9 H9–7. **Brachypus Group** Shorter. ↕5–6 in (12–15 cm).

***S.* 'Devon Skies'** This superb dwarf cultivar has large, pale blue flowers with broad petals, each with a deeper zone around the yellow eye. The outer petals are especially wide and have five instead of three dark veins. ↕6 in (15 cm). Z7–8 H8–7

***S.* 'Dragon's Eye'** A compact and free-flowering cultivar, with pale blue, starry flowers with yellow eyes held above fans of short foliage in summer. ↕6 in (15 cm). Z7–8 H8–7

***S.* 'E. K. Balls'** syn. *S.* 'Ball's Mauve' Requiring well-drained soil and full sun, this is a dwarf plant with a long flowering season. The large, ¾ in (2 cm) blooms are purple with a yellow eye and deeper veins. Does not self-seed. ↕8 in (20 cm). Z7–8 H8–7

S. graminoides Sparsely branched stems have two or three flowers emerging from behind each bract, blue flowers with yellow eyes and distinctive pointed petal tips. Closely related to—and perhaps even the same as—*S. angustifolium*. Native to the Southeast US. ↕8 in (20 cm). Z5–8 H8–5. **'Album'** White flowers.

***S.* 'Iceberg'** Small, white flowers produced for a very long period from early summer to fall above the grassy foliage. ↕8 in (20 cm). Z7–8 H8–7

S. idahoense Pale-leaved plant with slim, ¹⁄₁₆–⅛ in (1–3 mm) wide leaves, the winged, unbranched stems carrying ¾ in (2 cm) wide, violet flowers with yellow eyes in summer. Each flower has elliptical petals, a darker purple zone around the yellow eye, and three dark veins through each petal, and is followed by spherical seeds. Prefers moist soil and may self-seed freely. Native to Washington, Oregon, northern California, Idaho, Utah, and Colorado. ↕12–16 in (30–40 cm). Z7–8 H8–7. **'Album'** White flowers. **var. *bellum*** syn. *S. bellum* Purple flowers with wedge-shaped petals, usually on shorter stems. **var. *bellum* 'Rocky Point'** Large, yellow-eyed, purple flowers. Very short. From California and Oregon, and Mexico. ↕6 in (15 cm). **var. *macounii*** syn. *S. macounii* Larger, ¾–1 in (2–2.5 cm) flowers. From the San Juan islands in British Columbia, Canada. ↕16 in (40 cm).

S. macrocarpon Bluish green foliage sets off large, 1 in (2.5 cm), bright yellow or slightly ocherish yellow flowers with a hexagonal brown ring around the eye for a long summer season. The flowers are carried in small clusters on flattened stems with one or two bracts. From Argentina. ↕12 in (30 cm). Z7–8 H8–7

S. macounii see. *S. idahoense* var. *macounii*

***S.* 'Marion'** Clumps of narrow, grassy foliage with ¾ in (2 cm) flowers, purple with darker veins, throughout summer. ↕4 in (10 cm). Z7–8 H8–7

***S.* 'Mrs. Spivey'** syn. *S.* 'Mrs. Spinvey' Masses of small, white, starry flowers with narrow petals and yellow eyes held above neat, grassy foliage. ↕8 in (20 cm). Z7–8 H8–7

S. palmifolium Upright, with narrow, blue-green leaves; the branching stems carry large clusters of bright yellow flowers that open in the late afternoon. Only recently introduced, this is one of the showiest and most prolific species and is sometimes placed in the separate genus *Eleutherine* because of its nocturnal flowers. From Brazil, Peru, Uruguay, and Argentina. ↕18 in (45 cm). Z7–9 H9–7

S. patagonicum A slender, grassy plant, the narrow, ¹⁄₁₆ in (1 mm) wide foliage overtopped by unbranched, leafless, flattened, ¹⁄₁₆ in (1 mm) wide stems carrying clusters of two or three starry, golden yellow, brown-veined flowers. From Patagonia. ↕12 in (30 cm). Z4–8 H7–1

***S.* 'Pole Star'** Free-flowering and showy with large, white, 1¼ in (3 cm) flowers in midsummer on compact plants. ↕6 in (15 cm). Z7–8 H8–7

***S.* 'Quaint and Queer'** Features the usual slender foliage but is unusual in its three broad, cream outer petals alternating with the browner, narrower inner petals. All petals have three brown veins and there is a yellow eye in the center. Superficially similar to 'Biscutella' in general coloring, but distinct in its alternately colored petals. ↕12 in (30 cm). Z6–8 H8–6

S. striatum syn. *Phaiophleps nigricans* Robust species forming clumps of fans of grayish green, ¾-in- (2-cm-) wide leaves. It produces stiffly upright stems packed with slightly cup-shaped, cream or pale yellow flowers along their length in midsummer. Each petal is striped in brown. Best in full sun in well-drained soil. Plants vary noticeably in height according to soil conditions and moisture. An excellent front-of-the-border plant or in gravel. From Chile and Argentina. ↕32 in (80 cm). Z7–8 H8–7 **'Aunt May'** Leaves striped in cream. Less vigorous, but still flowers freely. ↕20 in (50 cm).

SMILACINA *see* MAIANTHEMUM

BELOW 1 *Sisyrinchium* 'Quaint and Queer' **2** *S. striatum* 'Aunt May'

SOLIDAGO

Goldenrod

ASTERACEAE

Large clusters of flowerheads provide a brief, late-summer punch of bright yellow, usually for the back of the border.

About 150 deciduous perennials grow on prairies, waysides, river banks, and mountain slopes. Most are native to North America but a few occur in South America and Eurasia. Some North American species are naturalized in Europe, giving them an unfortunate association with wastelands. They may be clump-forming or spread by rhizomes; the alternate leaves extend all the way up the erect stems and are mostly lance-shaped or elliptical, and toothed. The individual yellow, rarely white, flowers are seldom more than ¼ in (5 mm) across but are held in dense sprays that themselves make up loose or dense, cylindrical, conical, or pyramidal flowerheads. The majority of species are large and robust and make spreading clumps with a rather short flowering period, so they need to be carefully sited. A few are very short and suited to the front of the border. The hybrid cultivars tend to be intermediate in height with slightly longer flowering periods. All attract a wide range of insects and make good cut flowers.

In North America, goldenrods are often thought to provoke an allergic reaction. In fact, the unobtrusive ragweed *Ambrosia*, which often grows alongside goldenrod and flowers at the same time, causes the problem—but the showier neighbor gets the blame.

CULTIVATION Tolerate a wide range of poor soils but prefer moisture-retentive, moderately fertile conditions in full sun. The taller, more vigorous types need plenty of space and are suitable for naturalizing, or for the back of a border where the often mildewy foliage can be masked. Regular division should not be seen as a priority, but if undertaken every three or four years will help maintain vigor and floriferousness, and reduce mildew infection.

PROPAGATION By division or basal cuttings in spring, or from seed.

PROBLEMS Powdery mildew.

S. caesia (Wreath goldenrod) Clump-forming, with hairless, purple stems covered with a white bloom. Lance-shaped, grayish green, toothed leaves to 4¾ in (12 cm) are borne all the way up the stem, although absent from the base at flowering time. Unusually for a goldenrod, the dark yellow florets are grouped in small clusters in leaf joints and held close to stem for most of its length. Clusters may elongate slightly at the stem tip, producing horizontal branches with a similar arrangement of

CUT FLOWERS

Although *Solidago* was popular as cut flowers a century ago, until a decade or two ago you could not buy goldenrod as a cut flower—because it had gone out of fashion and no one sold it anymore. No one sold it because no one wanted to buy it. Then, slowly, the unusual shape of its flower sprays, its bright color, and its long vase life, along with the ease with which it can be grown, combined to return it to its former popularity in mixed bouquets and then be sold in its own right. Goldenrod is now recognized as a very useful cut flower.

The modern hybrids are the best for cutting—for example, 'Crown of Rays', 'Goldkind', and 'Gardone'. Cut them when between a quarter and half of the individual florets are open and immediately plunge them into water with flower preservative added; preservative has an especially beneficial effect on goldenrods and should also be used in vase water when the stems are arranged. Keep the flowers as cool as possible until they can be arranged.

Goldenrods are also easily dried, by placing them in an empty vase in a warm dry place, then stripping off the dried leaves before use.

flower clusters. Flowers from early to mid-fall. More shade-tolerant than most species. Native to woods and clearings in central and eastern North America. ‡3¼ ft (1 m). Z4–8 H8–1

S. canadensis (Canada goldenrod) Creeping rhizomes carry erect stems, hairy toward the apex, that bear lance-shaped, toothed leaves to 6 in (15 cm), which are absent from the base at flowering; each leaf has three veins. A large, broadly conical flowering spray consisting of many florets clustered densely on horizontal branches is produced from early to mid-fall. Widely naturalized on wastelands in Britain and Europe, a situation that demonstrates its resilience but has tarnished its garden credentials. Found in prairies, open woods, meadows, and roadsides throughout North America. ‡5–8 ft (1.5–2.5 m). Z3–9 H9–1

S. 'Cloth of Gold' Compact, with deep yellow florets carried in horizontal, conical, radiating sprays from late summer to early fall. ‡12–18 in (30–45 cm). Z5–9 H9–5

S. 'Crown of Rays' (**Strahlenkrone**) Erect, with bright yellow florets in a flat-topped display of dense, conical sprays from late summer to early fall. Perhaps derived from *S. juncea*. ‡16–24 in (40–60 cm). Z5–9 H9–5

S. cutleri (Cutler's alpine goldenrod) Clump-forming, with compact mounds of green, spoon-shaped to elliptic leaves to 1¾ in (4 cm). The yellow florets are grouped in dense cylindrical clusters making tight displays: plant is covered in flowers late summer to early fall. Native to mountain grasslands in the

north-eastern US. ‡12–20 in (30–50 cm). Z5–9 H9–5

S. flexicaulis (Zigzag goldenrod) Spreads by rhizomes, the ribbed, wiry, zigzag stems bear egg-shaped, sharply toothed leaves to 6 in (15 cm) long. Pale yellow florets are borne in spikes or small clusters at the top of the stems from mid- to late summer. Thankfully, mildew-resistant. From woods and thickets in eastern North America. ‡4 ft (1.2 m). **'Variegata'** Yellow specks and streaks on the leaves, most apparent in spring but barely noticeable at flowering time in late summer to early fall. ‡24 in (60 cm). Z3–9 H9–1

S. 'Gardone' Clump-forming, producing a large display of horizontal, conical sprays, the bright yellow florets are enhanced by yellow buds and flower stalks. Flowers from midsummer to early fall and relatively mildew-resistant. ‡3¼ ft (1 m). Z4–8 H8–1.

S. Golden Baby see *S.* 'Goldkind'

S. 'Goldenmosa' Erect, red-flushed stems bear large, conical flowerheads composed of pale yellow florets on yellow flower stalks, from late summer to early fall. An older cultivar dating from 1949, perhaps derived from *S. caesia*. ‡30 in (75 cm). Z5–9 H9–5

S. 'Golden Thumb' see *S.* 'Queenie'

S. 'Golden Wings' Vigorous, clump-former with broad, tiered displays of horizontal, spreading branches of deep yellow florets from early to mid-fall. ‡6–6½ ft (1.8–2 m). Z5–9 H9–5

S. 'Goldkind' (**Golden Baby**) Clump-former with upright stems bearing compact displays of dense, broadly conical sprays of deep yellow florets from mid- to late summer. Raised by German seed company Benary and comes fairly true from seed in isolation. ‡24 in (60 cm). Z5–9 H9–5

S. 'Laurin' Compact, with large sprays composed of deep yellow florets from late summer to early fall. ‡12–16 in (30–40 cm). Z5–8 H8–5

S. 'Queenie' syn. *S.* 'Golden Thumb' Very short, with yellow foliage and conical displays of yellow florets from late summer to early fall. ‡12 in (30 cm). Z5–8 H8–5

S. rigida syn. *Oligoneuron rigidum* (Stiff goldenrod) Clump-forming; stiff stems bearing elliptic, grayish hairy, normally untoothed leaves to 10 in (25 cm), the lower ones long-stalked and paddlelike, the upper ones stalkless. Large, deep yellow florets to ½ in (1 cm) across in dense, flat-topped clusters from late summer to mid-fall. Favored for its rigid stance and handsome foliage. Native to dry prairies and open woods in central and eastern North America. ‡30–60 in (75–150 cm). Z3–9 H9–1

S. rugosa (Wrinkleleaf goldenrod) Spreads by rhizomes, with erect, roughly hairy stems carrying elliptical

to lance-shaped leaves to 5 in (13 cm) long, with deeply impressed veins, attached to the midrib in opposite pairs. Its broad, loose, conical display is formed by long, arching wands that bear the pale yellow florets from late summer to mid-fall. Native to damp woods and meadows of eastern North America. ‡3¼–7 ft (1–2.5 m). Z3–9 H9–1. **'Fireworks'** Reputedly this cultivar is less spreading than the species, with darker stems and longer, more slender branches making up the airy display. Discovered by Ken Moore at North Carolina Botanic Garden, and introduced in 1993. ‡3¼ ft (1 m).

S. sphacelata (Fall goldenrod) Spreads by rhizomes to form a mat of semi-evergreen, heart-shaped, toothed leaves to 4¾ in (12 cm), from early to mid-fall; its leafy stems bear dense, arching, narrow, wandlike spikes of yellow florets. Native to open woods and rocky places in the eastern US. ‡18–48 in (45–120 cm). Z5–9 H9–1. **'Golden Fleece'** More prolific in flower and reputedly less invasive than

ABOVE 1 *Solidago* 'Goldenmosa'
2 *S.* 'Goldkind' **3** *S. rugosa* 'Fireworks'

the species. Introduced by Mt. Cuba Center in Delaware. ‡18 in (45 cm).

S. Strahlenkrone see *S.* 'Crown of Rays'

S. 'Tom Thumb' Very short and compact; tight, conical plumes of yellow florets open from late summer to early fall. Short enough for the very front of the border. ‡12 in (30 cm). Z5–9 H9–5

S. virgaurea (Goldenrod) Clump-forming, with erect stems bearing toothed leaves, to 4¾ in (12 cm) long, generally spoon-shaped at the base of the plant and lance-shaped farther up the stem. The relatively large yellow florets, to ½ in (1 cm) across, are held in a cylindrical or narrowly conical display from midsummer to early fall. Relatively mildew-resistant. Found in a wide variety of habitats, from open woodlands to grasslands, rocky places, and cliffs in Europe, North Africa, and Asia. ↕12–40 in (30–100 cm). Z5–9 H9–5. **'Variegata'** Foliage splashed and speckled in yellow, more noticeably on young foliage. Flowers in late summer and early fall. ↕28 in (70 cm).

x SOLIDASTER
ASTERACEAE

A subtle and attractive goldenrod hybrid for borders, attracting insects and cutting.

Garden hybrids between *Aster* and *Solidago*, these clump-forming, deciduous perennials have erect stems, lance-shaped leaves, and crowded sprays of fertile, yellow flowers. The daisylike flowerheads are usually slightly larger than those of *Solidago* but with paler yellow ray florets, especially on fading. They attract a wide range of insects and are excellent as cut flowers.

x *Solidaster luteus* was the first to arise, just prior to 1910 in the nursery of Leonard Lille in Lyon, France. Other forms of the hybrid involving different *Solidago* parents have subsequently been observed in the wild in North America. All crosses noted so far have *Aster ptarmicoides*, an aster with white disk and ray florets that resembles a *Solidago*, as the aster parent.

CULTIVATION Thrive in any fertile, well-drained soil, in sun or light shade. Less vigorous than *Solidago*, they need a position near the front of a border.

PROPAGATION By division or basal cuttings. Seedlings will show a great deal of variation.

BELOW x *Solidaster luteus* 'Lemore'

PROBLEMS Powdery mildew, rust.

x *S. hybridus* see x *S. luteus*

x *S. luteus* syn. x *S. hybridus* Clump-forming deciduous perennial with lance-shaped, roughly hairy leaves to 4¾ in (12 cm) long. The densely branched, broadly conical flowerheads, borne from mid- to late summer, occupy about half the total height of the plant, and consist of individual ¼–⅜ in (5–8 mm) flowers with a whorl (cluster) of ⅛–¼ in (3–5 mm) bracts, deep yellow disk florets, and 12 to 25 pale yellow ray florets. Young plants are prone to flopping and need support. A hybrid between *Aster ptarmicoides* and *Solidago canadensis*. ↕24–32 in (60–80 cm). Z5–8 H8–5. **'Lemore'** Smaller flowerheads, ¼–⅜ in (5–7 mm) across, about 25 ray florets, the whorl of bracts ⅛ in (3 mm) long. **'Super'** Smaller flowerheads, ⅛–¼ in (4–5 mm) across, and taller habit. ↕3¼–4¼ ft (1–1.3 m).

SPARTINA
POACEAE

Tall, vigorous, but handsome arching wetland grasses from saltwater and freshwater marshes.

Some 15 perennial species are found growing in fresh and salt water on intertidal mudflats, coastal dunes, and freshwater swamps on both coasts of North America, and the Atlantic coasts of Europe and Africa, as well as on dry prairies inland in North America. Large colonies of robust root systems support long, wide, glossy, pointed leaves growing from clawlike points on the roots, and have the ability to extract salt from water, secreting it as salt crystals on the leaf surface. The tall, arching, leafy flower stems carry graceful one-sided plumes of ropelike flowerheads. Short bristles mature into seeds that can attach themselves to fur and clothing.

A very tough grass that has long been used for thatching, packing, bedding, and hay, some species can become serious weeds, blocking waterways and swamping other marsh plants. Fortunately, it grows well in drier conditions, where it will grow into a smaller, less invasive plant, but is no less handsome, especially in fall when the foliage and flowers turn to gold.

CULTIVATION Best in moisture-retentive, not-too-fertile soil, in sun to part-shade. Can be grown, and restricted, in containers in pond margins, but will need some support and frequent division in spring.

PROPAGATION By division in spring.

PROBLEMS Usually trouble-free.

S. pectinata (Prairie or Freshwater cord grass) Large swaths of foliage spread on vigorous rhizomes with pink claws from which grow shiny green, ribbonlike arching leaves, ⅜ in (1.5 cm)

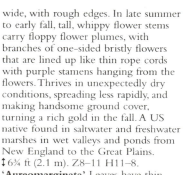

wide, with rough edges. In late summer to early fall, tall, whippy flower stems carry floppy flower plumes, with branches of one-sided bristly flowers that are lined up like thin rope cords with purple stamens hanging from the flowers. Thrives in unexpectedly dry conditions, spreading less rapidly, and making handsome ground cover, turning a rich gold in the fall. A US native found in saltwater and freshwater marshes in wet valleys and ponds from New England to the Great Plains. ↕6¾ ft (2.1 m). Z8–11 H11–8. **'Aureomarginata'** Leaves have thin yellow margins and fainter, narrow, pale yellow stripes.

SPEIRANTHA
CONVALLARIACEAE

An unassuming yet elegant spring-flowering shade-lover that makes pleasing ground cover.

One evergreen species from moist shady places, including forests, is found in China. Spreading steadily by thick rhizomes, its rosettes of unstalked leaves provide the setting for a galaxy of dainty, white, starry lily-of-the-valley-like flowers in spring. Makes excellent ground cover in woodland gardens or shrub borders.

CULTIVATION Best in a sheltered position in part- or full shade, and moist yet well-drained leafy soil.

PROPAGATION By division.

PROBLEMS Usually trouble-free.

S. convallarioides syn. *S. gardenii* Basal rosettes of somewhat egg-shaped, 6 in (15 cm), dark green leaves with pointed tips clasp upright flower stems that

ABOVE 1 *Spartina pectinata* 'Aureomarginata' **2** *Speirantha convallarioides*

support loose heads of white, scented, starry flowers in mid- and late spring. Spreads well to make effective ground cover. From China. ↕6–8 in (15–20 cm). Z7–10 H10–7

S. gardenii see *S. convallarioides*

SPHAERALCEA
Globe mallow
MALVACEAE

Attractive smaller-flowered hollyhock relations for sunny, well-drained banks and raised beds.

About 60 species of small shrubs, often slightly woody perennials, and annuals grow mostly in mountainous dry areas, mainly in North America. They are often short-lived. Most have grayish leaves, often attractively crinkled, arranged spirally on stems that may be upright, or lie flat on the ground with turned-up tips. The leaves vary greatly in shape from long and narrow to lance-shaped, and may be undivided, toothed, lobed, or split into fingers. The saucer-shaped flowers, resembling those of hollyhocks and carried over a long season, have five reverse-egg-shaped petals in red, orange, yellow, white, pink, or lavender, often with a contrasting zone at the base, and are carried either singly, in clusters coming out of the leaf joints, or in open heads.

CULTIVATION Best in well-drained soil and full sun, these plants are well suited to gravel gardens, and in cooler areas they are valuable for large summer container plantings. Good winter hardiness depends on excellent winter drainage; the plants will be much less hardy in wetter winter soil. Cut any remaining top-growth back hard in spring.

PROPAGATION Preferably by cuttings.

PROBLEMS Hollyhock rust.

S. fendleri An upright, woody-based perennial, with branching stems carrying 1–2½ in (2.5–6 cm) leaves that are green above and paler or silvery below, and boldly split into three lobes. The ½ in (1 cm) flowers, in shades of pink, orange, or even violet, crowd the upper stems during the late summer. From dry climates in the southern US. ‡ 4 ft (1.2 m). Z5–9 H9–5

S. 'Hopleys Lavender' Upright, with gray leaves; the lavender flowers opening from midsummer until fall. Introduced by Hopleys Plants of Hertfordshire, England. ‡ 36 in (90 cm). Z5–9 H9–5

S. munroana A lax plant building into a wide mound of gray stems carrying deeply cut, ¾–2¼ in (2–6 cm), egg-shaped gray leaves gently lobed into three or five segments with scalloped edges. The 1¼–1¾ in (3–4 cm), pale orange to apricot-pink flowers line the stems throughout summer. From Utah, Wyoming, and Nevada. ‡ 24 in (60 cm). Z4–10 H11–8. **'Manor Nursery'** Low-growing with cerise flowers, the leaves edged in cream. ‡ 10 in (25 cm). **Pale pink** Paler-flowered form without a proper cultivar name.

BELOW 1 *Sphaeralcea fendleri*
2 *Spiranthes cernua* var. *odorata*

S. 'Newleaze Coral' Coral orange flowers with red spots in the center and deeply cut gray foliage. ‡ 24 in (60 cm). Z5–9 H9–5

SPIRANTHES
Spiral flower
ORCHIDACEAE

Braids of glistening, hooded, little creamy white blooms on stalwart, smartly contrasting dark green stems bid the garden farewell in fall.

Two-thirds of these 30-some species of tuberous, terrestrial orchids are native to North America, the others to both tropical and temperate regions spanning Europe and Asia. They are named "spiral flower" for the tall stem's typical spiral-staircase arrangement of small, bell-shaped, crystalline flowers, the gradual to tight coils formed by naturally uneven cell growth.

CULTIVATION Plant either in fall or in early spring, in shade to full sun in good garden soil. A broad pH range is tolerated; semiaquatic species prefer wet soil but also grow well in moist soil. Mulch in winter in coldest zones to protect from soil frost heave. May flower without leaves, especially in drought; foliage climbs higher on the stem in standing water. Easily forms clumps from the root tips, particularly if not crowded by other plants. Good at pond edges and in wet meadows and moist woodlands, but very adaptable.

PROPAGATION Will often self-sow, blooming in their second season from seed. Divide underground stems in spring.

PROBLEMS Slugs, but otherwise it is usually trouble-free unless a virused plant is obtained.

S. cernua var. *odorata* syn. f. *odorata*, *S. odorata* (Fragrant nodding lady's tresses, Coastal fragrant lady's tresses, Fall lady's tresses) The more southerly, taller variety of *S. cernua* (or a separate species, depending on the taxonomist delving into this somewhat confusing complex) blooms from late summer to first frost in northern areas, but through to early spring in warm climates. Three to six thin, shiny, evergreen grasslike leaves to 8 in (20 cm) long form a ground-hugging rosette, with some leaves on the single stem that arises to create a spiral pigtail of dense, sweetly scented, waxy white, ⅜ in (1.4 cm) flowers, arranged in several tiers separated by turns. Bee-pollinated, the flower's lip is as long as other parts of the nodding bloom. Glistening texture is astonishing under a hand lens. Native to ditches and wet spots in coastal areas of southeastern US, from New Jersey into Texas. ‡ 12–20 in (30–50 cm). Z4–9 H9–1. **'Chadds Ford'** Notably the best cultivar, more vigorous and taller with larger and more fragrant flowers smelling of vanilla-jasmine, carrying up to 50 blooms per graceful, 24 in (60 cm) stem, and standing up well to rain and wind. Discovered in a Delaware ditch by Dick Ryan in 1960s, but named for the Pennsylvania hometown of Merlin Brubaker, who in 1973 won the first award for growing the plant ‡ 18–24 in (45–60 cm).

S. odorata see *S. cernua*

SPODIOPOGON
POACEAE

Gray-hairy flowers top grassy foliage that turns coppery gold in the fall.

Nine perennial species are found on grassy hillsides in subtropical Asia, from Turkey and India to Japan and Thailand; only one is generally grown. Thick, lush, upright clumps of quite wide-bladed leaves spread on slowly creeping roots, some species having what appear to be short stalks attaching the leaves to the stems. The leaves turn attractive shades of orange, dark red, and copper in fall. The flower stems carry loose or compact plumes of spiky flowers, covered with soft white hairs and ending in a longer bristle. Grow in herbaceous borders with fall flowers that will be complemented by the rich foliage.

CULTIVATION Thrives in moisture-retentive soil, but tolerates well-drained soil, in sun to light shade.

PROPAGATION From seed or by division.

PROBLEMS Usually trouble-free.

S. sibiricus (Gray beard) Lush, erect, slowly spreading clumps with straight stems carry quite wide, glossy green,

¾ in (2 cm) leaves with a prominent white stripe in the middle. The leaves grow almost horizontally from the stem and turn rich reds and oranges in the fall before fading to dull bronze. In late summer to early fall, the leafy stems carry, just above the foliage, pyramidal upright plumes of reddish spikes with white hairs that shimmer in the late summer sun. Looks best grown in drifts with other fall grasses and flowers, in full sun. Native to grassy banks, open forest glades, and thickets in moist soil in Japan, Korea, Manchuria, and eastern Siberia. ‡ 4 ft (1.2 m). Z4–8 H8–1

SPOROBOLUS
Dropseed grass
POACEAE

Warm season grasses, mainly from the tropics, with shiny flowers and round seeds.

Some 160 annual and perennial species are found in tropical and subtropical regions of the world in a variety of habitats, most commonly on open savannas on dry and rocky, grazed and trampled soil, though some species grow on heavy clay and even in mangrove swamps. Most are tightly clump-forming, growing into fountains of narrow, arching leaves, some turning spectacular colors in fall before dying back in winter. Tall, leafless flower stems carry loose or more compact to almost cylindrical heads of shiny clusters of flowers, ripening to smooth, round to oval seeds that swell in wet weather before dropping to the ground. Seeds of some species are, or have been, an important food source for native peoples living on the North

BELOW *Sporobolus heterolepis*

American prairies and African savannas. Only one species is usually grown in gardens, and is most effective planted in drifts in an informal setting, or in gravel gardens and herbaceous borders where the fall color can be appreciated.

CULTIVATION Grow in well-drained but fertile soil in full sun; tends to flop and flower poorly in shade.

PROPAGATION From seed; division is possible but can be hard work. A warm-season grass, so division should be left until late spring.

PROBLEMS Usually trouble-free.

S. heterolepis (Prairie or Northern dropseed) One of the most elegant of the so called "bunch grasses" growing on the North American prairies. Dense clumps, dying back over winter, are made up of threadlike ⅛ in (2–3 mm) leaves that are bright glossy green in the summer, turning yellow orange in the fall before fading to copper. In late summer to early fall, slender stems carry lose, airy pyramids of tiny dark green to purple flowers borne on hairlike stalks and with, unusually, a pungent scent similar to crushed coriander. In cool, wet summers the flowers may be shy to open properly. Slow-growing, it grows best in open, light fertile soil with plenty of moisture, but tolerates most soils and very dry conditions. Native to dry open ground from Quebec to Texas and Colorado. ↕ 24–48 in (60–120 cm). Z3–8 H10–2

STACHYS
Woundwort
LAMIACEAE

Mostly spreading perennials making colorful and valuable ground cover in a range of situations.

Most of the 300 or so species are evergreen or deciduous, sometimes woody-based perennials, but include a few annuals, biennials, and shrubs. Found in a wide range of habitats from marshes, woodlands, and open sites throughout temperate and subtropical zones in both Northern and Southern hemispheres.

The perennials may be clump-forming but more usually spread by rhizomes, and many release a fetid aroma when crushed. Leaves are opposite and held on square-sectioned stems; basal leaves have stalks while those on the aerial stems may be stalked or unstalked. Leaf margins are usually scallop-toothed. The flowers are held in clusters, either spaced out along the stem and accompanied by small pairs of leaves, or condensed into terminal spikes (though even these usually have a few clusters below the main spike). Each tubular flower is two–lipped, normally in shades of reddish purple or pink with subtle markings in the throat and on the lower lip.

CULTIVATION Those with silver-hairy leaves tolerate poor soil and need good drainage with full sun. Others are shade-tolerant or thrive in waterlogged positions.

PROPAGATION Divide in spring. Some can be grown from cuttings and most from seed.

PROBLEMS Slugs and snails may attack early-season growth.

S. affinis syn. *S. sieboldii* (Chinese artichoke) Deciduous, growing from small, yellowish white, elongated tubers resembling segmented caterpillars tapered at each end. The roughly hairy leaves, to 1¼–4¾ in (3–12 cm) long, are narrowly egg-shaped, scallop-toothed, and stalked. Erect or leaning stems bear, in mid- or late summer, widely spaced clusters of about six flowers, each about ½ in (1.3 cm) long and reddish purple with darker spotting on the lower lip. The tubers are edible; they are harvested after the foliage has died back and are eaten raw or boiled for 5–10 minutes. It needs fertile, permanently damp soil in full sun or part-shade. Most cultivated forms seem reluctant to flower in cool temperate gardens and in such situations are only worth growing as a curious vegetable. Native to damp slopes and wet areas in China. ↕ 12–48 in (30–120 cm). Z5–9 H9–5

S. albotomentosa Upright or sometimes rather sprawling evergreen with a fruity aroma, densely covered in white hairs. The egg-shaped leaves, 1¾–3½ in (4–9 cm) long, gray-hairy above and densely white-hairy below, are usually heart-shaped at the base and have deeply impressed veins and scalloped margins. The flower stems, produced from early summer to mid-fall, bear widely spaced clusters of orange-pink, 1 in (2.5 cm) flowers. First named in 1983; differs from *S. coccinea* in its dense white hairs. Native to rocky places in Mexico, it needs a sharply drained site in full sun. ↕ 16–39 cm (40–100 cm). Z5–9 H9–5

S. betonica see *S. officinalis*

S. byzantina syn. *S. lanata*, *S. olympica* (Lamb's ear) Mat-forming evergreen. Stout rhizomes bear rosettes of thick, silver-felted, narrowly spoon-shaped leaves, to 4 in (10 cm) long, with fine scallop-toothed margins. Between early summer and early fall, erect stems bear clusters of up to 20 flowers, closely spaced at the tip of the stem, forming a spike, but more widely spaced below. The pink or purple flowers can be up to 1 in (2.5 cm) long but are usually shorter, barely protruding from the dense white wool of the flower clusters. Needs a well-drained position in full sun and poor soil; it may be affected by powdery mildew. In addition to its soft, velvety, tactile leaves, this is one of the best silver-leaved plants for dense

RIGHT 1 *Stachys byzantina* 'Big Ears'
2 *S. byzantina* 'Primrose Heron'
3 *S. byzantina* 'Silver Carpet'
4 *S. macrantha* 'Superba' **5** *S. officinalis*

ground cover, either for large areas or for edging. It will creep over paving with the most minimal rooting opportunities. Native to dry, rocky slopes, scrub, and waste ground in southwestern Asia. ‡12–40 in (30–100 cm). Z4–8 H8–1. **'Big Ears'** syn. 'Countess Helene von Stein' Large, oval, gray-felted leaves to 10 in (25 cm); flowers purple. ‡32–40 in (80–100 cm). **'Cotton Boll'** syn. 'Sheila McQueen' Flower spike resembles a knobby club and consists of dense, irregular, congested clusters superimposed on each other and almost hiding the flowers. Dries well. Named by Beth Chatto. ‡16–24 in (40–60 cm). **'Countess Helene von Stein'** see 'Big Ears'. **'Primrose Heron'** Leaves emerge pale yellow and mature to yellowish gray-green, the edges of the leaves upturned giving a slightly cupped effect. ‡16 in (40 cm). **'Sheila McQueen'** see 'Cotton Boll'. **'Silver Carpet'** Forms a dense carpet and rarely, if ever, flowers. ‡6 in (15 cm). **'Striped Phantom'** syn. 'Variegata' Leaves variegated with cream streaks and splashes, flowering stems shorter than usual. Pinch out any plain green shoots. Raised from seed, so variable. ‡10 in (25 cm). **'Variegata'** see 'Striped Phantom'.

S. citrina Woody-based perennial with basal rosettes of densely white-hairy, egg-shaped or oblong, 2 in (5 cm) leaves with shallowly scalloped margins and erect, unbranched stems carrying shorter-stalked ¾ in (2 cm) leaves with untoothed edges. Clusters of pale yellow, 1 in (2.5 cm) flowers appear in late spring or early summer and are mostly grouped into terminal heads. Native to dry, rocky sites in Turkey and requiring full sun. ‡10–14 in (25–35 cm). Z5–7 H7–5

S. coccinea (Scarlet hedgenettle) Semi-shrubby evergreen perennial with ascending but broadly spreading stems bearing softly hairy, narrowly egg-shaped 3 in (8 cm) leaves with scalloped margins. Widely spaced whorls of scarlet ¾ in (2 cm) flowers are produced from early spring to mid-fall. Best in a well-drained site, though found by streams and in canyons in the southern US and Mexico. ‡8–24 in (20–60 cm). Z4–8 H8–1

S. discolor syn. S. nivea Woody-based, densely hairy perennial with basal rosettes of 4¾ in (12 cm), lance-shaped leaves with deeply scalloped margins and erect, unbranched stems carrying shorter and narrower leaves. Tiered clusters of yellow, 1 in (2.5 cm) flowers grouped in terminal heads are produced in early summer and midsummer. Thrives in full sun in moderately fertile soil. A white-flowered variant of S. officinalis with dark green leaves is incorrectly sold under this name. Native to grassy and rocky places in the Caucasus. ‡8–12 in (20–30 cm). Z5–9 H9–5

S. grandiflora see S. macrantha

S. lanata see S. byzantina

S. macrantha syn. S. grandiflora (Big-sage) Forms slowly spreading clumps or rosettes of broadly egg-shaped, dark green, wrinkled, hairy, scallop-edged, 4 in (10 cm) leaves. Erect, unbranched stems bear clusters of flowers in dense spikes from late spring to late summer. Unusually prominent, trumpet-shaped, 1½ in (3.5 cm) flowers are long compared to those of other species and usually purplish pink. Thrives in fertile soil in full sun but tolerant of shade. Plants sold as S. macrantha 'Alba' or 'Nivea' are usually white forms of S. officinalis. Native to rocky slopes, grassy places, and scrub in Turkey, the Caucasus, and northwestern Iran. ‡14–24 in (35–60 cm). Z7–9 H9–7. **'Robusta'** Flowers purplish mauve. ‡22–24 in (55–60 cm). **'Rosea'** Flowers rose pink. **'Superba'** Flowers deep pinkish purple; from seed, so variable. **'Violacea'** Flowers violet-purple.

S. mexicana see S. thunbergii

S. monieri see S. officinalis

S. nivea see S. discolor

S. officinalis syn. S. betonica, Betonica officinalis (Betony) Dense, sometimes evergreen colonies of rosettes of stalked, oblong to egg-shaped, somewhat hairy, 4¾ in (12 cm) leaves with scalloped margins. Erect, unbranched stems bear two to four pairs of smaller, shorter-stalked leaves and, from early summer to early fall, tiers of ¾ in (1.8 cm), normally deep reddish purple flowers, clustered into dense terminal spikes. Pink-flowered cultivars tend to fade to white, giving flowerheads a bicolored appearance. Needs light soil in sun or part-shade. In the past, a number of cultivars have been attributed to the rarely seen S. monieri, from which this differs with its distinctively taller growth and shorter flowers. Found in fencerows, heaths, and grassy places in Europe, North Africa, and southwestern Asia. ‡8–40 in (20–100 cm). Z5–8 H8–4. **'Alba'** Corolla white. Plants sold under this name vary in height and have leaf color ranging from pale to dark green. They may also be sold as S. discolor, S. macrantha 'Alba', and S. macrantha 'Nivea'. ‡12–28 in (30–70 cm). **'Hummelo'** Flowers deep purplish pink. ‡20 in (50 cm). **'Rosea'** Leaves dark green, flowers pink, flowerheads tight. ‡8–16 in (20–40 cm). **'Rosea Superba'** Leaves mid-green, flowers pink, in flowerheads looser than those of 'Rosea'. ‡16–40 in (40–100 cm). **'Saharan Pink'** Compact, with pink corollas. ‡6–8 in (15–20 cm). **'Wisley White'** Flowers white, compact habit. Introduced by Washfield Nursery, England; however, the connection with Wisley is not clear. ‡12 in (30 cm).

S. olympica see S. byzantina

S. sieboldii see S. affinis

S. sylvatica (Hedge woundwort) Pungently aromatic, roughly hairy perennial spread by rhizomes, the erect stems carrying stalked, egg-shaped,

5½ in (14 cm) leaves, heart-shaped at the base and with scalloped edges. Tiers of dark reddish purple flowers are clustered into loose terminal spikes, from early summer to early fall. Thrives in most soils, very tolerant of dry shade. Found in woods, hedgerows, and rough ground throughout temperate Europe and Asia, and naturalized in eastern North America. ‡12–32 in (30–80 cm). Z5–8 H8–5. **'Huskers'** Leaves irregularly variegated cream and white.

S. thunbergii syn. S. mexicana Clump-forming; sprawling, non-rooting stems bearing egg-shaped, finely toothed, dark green shiny leaves, to 4 in (10 cm) long. Tiered, deep reddish purple flowers held in loose terminal spikes from midsummer to early fall. Needs full sun and well-drained soil, where it can provide useful ground cover. Native to forest margins and scrub in southern Africa. ‡8–16 in (20–40 cm). Z5–9 H9–5. **'Danielle'** Yellowish green leaves. Originated as a spontaneous mutation in a Dutch nursery.

STEMMACANTHA see CENTAUREA

STIPA
POACEAE

Clump-forming grasses from arid areas with elegant, sometimes tactile, airy plumes

Over 300 mainly perennial species grow in temperate and warm regions on steppes, prairies, and tundra on rocky, exposed slopes. Clump-forming, their thin, often inrolled, tough, harsh-textured leaves, hairy underneath, are used to make paper and matting. The airy flowerheads are made up of tiny flowers, usually spindle-shaped or cylindrical with conspicuous hairs, often very long, in the form of soft feathers or stiffer needles. Once the seeds are ripe, the hairs help disperse the seeds by propelling them over the ground and then screwing the seeds into cracks in the hard soil.

Grasses for very dry open situations, they are best grown in drifts for spectacular light and wind effects, especially if backlit by the sun. Some also make very beautiful

LOW LIGHT IN THE FALL

AS THE SUN steadily shines lower in the sky, the soft light picks up every detail in the tawny seed heads of *Stipa gigantea* as they lean from their clumps of slender leaves. The light also brings a sparkle to the fat orange heads of *Kniphofia uvaria* 'Nobilis'. As the fading flowers turn yellow, they pick up the color in the big stipa, and also where the sun hits the clumps of smaller grasses in the front. The broad green *Bergenia cordifolia* by the lawn edge provides a solid contrast to all this fiery light and slender leafage.

LEFT 1 *Stipa barbata* **2** *S. calamagrostis*
3 *S. capillata* **4** *S. gigantea*

potted plants where the flowers can be touched as well as seen. They can also be used effectively to soften hard landscaping or as a contrast to more vertical plantings.

Although outwardly some of the species seem very different, on closer examination the similarities are more obvious, and suggestions for dividing *Stipa* into different genera have not been taken up by most botanists—but have led to some confusion with names. Only the familiar *S. arundinacea* has been moved, with general agreement, into the genus *Anemanthele*.

CULTIVATION Grow in well-drained, light soil in an open, sunny position. The roots tend to be rather shallow and they dislike being divided; therefore, if old plants start to die out in the center, grow new plants from seed. Most species are cool-season grasses, dying back in the summer: once the seeds have been shed, they can become rather scruffy, since new growth does not start again until the winter.

PROPAGATION From freshly gathered seed. Some species self-sow but others may not produce viable seed in cool gardens. Propagate cultivars by division but do not make divisions too small. Short cuttings comprising a single leaf joint will sometimes root in early fall.

PROBLEMS Plant bases tend to rot in congested wet conditions.

S. arundinacea see *Anemanthele lessoniana*

S. barbata (Silver feather grass) Tidy clumps are made up of very thin, inrolled, blue-green, 1/16 in (2 mm) wide leaves. In mid- to late summer, long, slender flower stems fly magnificent flower plumes, each with tiny polished flowers from which waft soft white hairs up to 10 in (25 cm) long. On first opening, they look like sleek feathers with angular twists, then disappear with the ripe seeds. Looks most spectacular grown in drifts where the light catches the airy plumes, but once flowering is over, the whole plant looks scruffy, so cut it back or hide it with other plants. Can be short-lived and does not like cold, wet winters, so collect and sow fresh seed for planting out the following spring—just in case. Native to dry open hills and grasslands in Spain, Sicily, Italy, the Caucasus, North Africa, and Turkey. ‡ 16 in (40 cm). Z7–10 H10–1. **'Silver Feather'** ('Ecume d'Argent') Gray-green leaves, flower hairs pale silvery gold. ‡ 32 in (80 cm).

S. brachytricha see *Calamagrostis bracytricha*

S. calamagrostis syn. *S. lasiagrostis*, *Achnatherum calamagrostis, Lasiagrostis calamagrostis, Calamagrostis argentea* Dense, arching clumps of flat, finely pointed, 1/4 in (5 mm), green leaves die back in the winter. From early summer to mid-fall, arching flower stems carry shimmering, airy, one-sided plumes, up to 12 in (30 cm) long, of greenish white, feathery flowers with short hairs that fade to pale yellow and keep their graceful appearance through the winter. Best in a sheltered but open position in large drifts where the mix of seed heads and new flowers can be admired. An unfortunate victim of disagreement among botanists, hence the many synonyms. From alkaline, rocky ground, mostly on exposed mountains, in southern and central Europe. ‡ 4 ft (1.2 m). Z7–10 H10–1

S. capillata Dense, insignificant clumps of very fine, inrolled, light green leaves, 1/16 in (1 mm) wide, dying back in the winter. In mid- and late summer and sometimes through to late fall, a mass of slender, tall stems bear the spiky, silver flowerheads. Each flower has needlelike hairs, up to 8 in (20 cm) long, which, when backlit by the sun, look like fine shards of splintered glass. Grow in drifts in an open position in very well-drained soil, where the sun and wind can move through the flowers. In very wet and cold summers the flowers occasionally become self-pollinating and do not open completely. From dry, exposed places in southern Europe to Mongolia and the western Himalaya. ‡ 3 1/4 ft (1 m). Z7–10 H10–1. **'Brautschleier'** (**Bridal Veil**) Fine white needles. ‡ 4 ft (1.2 m).

S. extremiorientalis syn. *S. pekinensis Achnatherum pekinense*, Stiff, open clumps of erect, pale yellowy green 3/8 in (1.5 cm) wide leaves turn a soft yellow in the fall before dying back over winter. In late summer and early fall, tall stems carry shiny green heads of oatlike flowers with bent needles up to 10 in (25 cm) long. After the seeds have dispersed, the remains of the flowerheads turn black, making an interesting contrast with other beige winter foliage. Takes a little more shade than other species and makes an elegant contrast to late summer flowers in borders and gravel gardens, especially if left with other fall seedheads. Found on grassy slopes and forest margins on mountains in Japan and China and on the Russian Pacific coast. ‡ 4 1/4 ft (1.3 m). Z6–9 H9–6

S. gigantea (Giant feather grass, Golden oats) Large, dense, evergreen clumps. Fine, gray-green inrolled leaves, 1/4 in (6 mm) wide. From late spring to midsummer, slender stems tower over foliage, carrying loose, fluttering plumes of golden, oatlike flowers with stiff, 2 3/4–4 3/4 in (7–12 cm) hairs and hung with yellow stamens that catch the light and shimmer in the wind, eventually ripening to a pale straw yellow and persisting through the winter. One of the most elegant ornamental grasses. Although often grown as a specimen plant, it is attractive, in large drifts, as in the wild, either in gravel gardens or

CONFUSING NAMES

Not only has there been disagreement about whether certain species rightfully belong in other genera, but three of the *Stipa* species have such similar names that they are often confused—even in otherwise authoritative sources. *Stipa tenacissima, S. tenuifolia,* and *S. tenuissima* almost look like variations on the spelling of the same name; not so. These are three distinct grasses, originating in different parts of the world, that have become confused in gardens.

Stipa tenacissima, from Europe and North Africa, is a coarse, robust deciduous plant, tough enough to make rope, with 1/8 in (3 mm) wide inrolled leaves and flowers with short bristles.

Stipa tenuifolia, from Australia, is a deciduous, arching plant with 1/16 in (2 mm) wide leaves and silky flowers with long hairs.

Stipa tenuissima, from the Americas and the most widely grown, is a noticably erect evergreen (but tending to flop on overly fertile soil), with 1/16 in (1 mm) wide inrolled leaves and flowers with long hairs; it self-sows prolifically.

Stipa tenacissima

Stipa tenuifolia

Stipa tenuissima

against walls and buildings where it has some protection from cold, wet winters. Native to Spain, Portugal, and Morocco. ↕ 6½ ft (2 m). Z8–11 H11–1. **'Gold Fontaene'** Larger, showier flowerheads. Introduced by German plantsman Ernst Pagels. ↕ 8 ft (2.5 m).

S. grandis Basal clumps, dying back over winter, comprise very narrow, inrolled, gray-green, 1/16-in (1-mm) leaves, with hairy edges on the underside. In misummer, the slender flower stems carry purplish flowers, each with stiff whiskers up to 1¾ in (4.5 cm) long, fading to buff later in the summer. Grow in drifts in open, dry positions where the sun will catch the stiff, wispy hairs. Found on steppes and mountain slopes in Siberia, China, and Mongolia. ↕ 3¾ ft (1 m). Z7–10 H10–1

S. lasiagrostis see *S. calamagrostis*

S. lessingiana syn. *Anemanthele lessingiana* Compact, upright clumps, dying back over winter, are made up of thread-thin, inrolled leaves, 1/32 in (0.5 mm) wide and up to 16 in (40 cm) long. In early summer, stems twice as high as the foliage carry delicate 4–8 in (10–20 cm) plumes, each flower having stiff, angled hairs, 4¾–8 in (12–20 cm) long, with feathery, softer tips. Grow this grass in drifts in informal settings in exposed sites. Not to be confused with *Anemanthele lessoniana*. Found on open, dry hillsides in eastern Iran, western Siberia, and Central Asia. ↕ 30 in (75 cm). Z7–10 H10–1

S. pekinensis see *S. extremiorientalis*

S. pennata (Feather grass) Small, tight clumps of slightly arching, stiff, 1/16–¼ in (1–6 mm) wide, very pointed leaves, green with a bluish bloom on the undersides and dying back over winter. Many slender stems appear in early to late summer, waving their extraordinary flowerheads above the foliage, each flower carrying a curving hairy tail up to 12 in (30 cm) long: the effect is of thin, white fluffy feathers streaming out in the wind. Grown in the US since the 1800s. It needs a warm sunny position where the sun can light up the flower plumes and without too much competition from other plants. Found in central and southern Europe to Asia and the Himalaya. ↕ 36 in (90 cm). Z5–8 H8–5

S. pulcherrima (European feather grass) Neat, tight clumps, with very thin 1/16-in (1.5-mm) leaves, die back over winter. In mid- and late summer, long slender stems support delicate flower plumes that look very similar to those of *S. pennata*, but with even longer feathery hairs growing into curling fluffy tails up to 20 in (50 cm) long. Most spectacular in large groups, but will not always survive cold, wet conditions and needs dry, very well-drained soil, against a wall or in a raised bed. Native to steppes and rocky ground in central and southern Europe through to Iran and Siberia ↕ 3¼ ft (1 m). Z5–8 H8–5. **'Windfeder'** Taller, with even longer curling hairs, in early summer to midsummer. ↕ 4 ft (1.2 m).

S. splendens syn. *Achnatherum splendens, Lasiagrostis splendens* Mounds of slender dark green, flat to inrolled, ½ in (1 cm) wide leaves, feeling very rough and rigid, form large, robust, evergreen clumps. From late spring to midsummer, tall, erect, rather wiry stems carry large, airy pink-red flower plumes, each tiny individual flower spike with a 4 in (10 cm) long hair. Grown since 1836, when it was probably used as a specimen plant, but looks even better grown in drifts and especially useful by salt-treated paths and drives. The seeds are not always viable and plants are best divided, the clumps being more robust than those of other species. Found on semidesert, gravel, rocky slopes, and saline meadows from the Caucasus and Kazakhstan to China and Mongolia. ↕ 5–8 ft (1.5–2.5 m). Z7–10 H10–7

S. tenacissima (Esparto grass) A coarse, rather rough grass, which should not be confused with the more delicate *S. tenuissima* (*see* Confusing Names) forming dense tussocks, with tough, inrolled ⅛ in (3 mm) wide leaves that die back over winter. In mid- and late summer, tall stems carry dense, narrow stubby flower spikes with short bristles. Long used to make mats, rope, and paper, it is one of the less decorative grasses and, if it is grown, is best confined to more informal parts of the garden. Native to open, dry areas in southern Spain and North Africa. ↕ 24–40 in (60–100 cm). Z6–8 H8–6

S. tenuifolia Arching clumps, dying back in the winter, of bright green leaves up to 1/16 in (2 mm) wide. In mid- to late summer, slender stems carry clouds of airy plumes up to 12 in (30 cm) long, each little flower having a soft, elbowed, 2¾ in (7 cm) long hair. Best grown in drifts by pathways where the flowers can be touched. Similar to, and often confused with, *S. tenuissima* (*see* Confusing Names). A native of dry, open grassland in Australia. ↕ 24–36 in (60–90 cm). Z7–10 H10–1

S. tenuissima syn. *Nassella tenuissima* (Pony tails) Dense, erect, evergreen clumps of inrolled bright green leaves up to 1/16 in (1 mm) wide. Wiry stems appear from late spring to late summer carrying ethereal, shiny pale green plumes fading to beige, the tiny flowers having angled soft hairs 1¼–4 in (3–10 cm) long. The overall effect is of large shaving brushes, and the flowerheads stay attractive after the flowers and seed heads have disappeared, their ends becoming white and wispy. Best in poor sandy soil in full sun, otherwise it tends to flop over from the center. Looks best grown in long drifts where the effects of light and wind can be seen running through the flowers and foliage. It is also a very attractive potted plant, placed where it can be touched. Self-seeds in great masses around the parent plant, which tends to be rather short-lived and dislikes being divided. A native of dry rocky slopes and exposed grasslands in New Mexico, Texas, Mexico, and Argentina. ↕ 24 in (60 cm). Z7–11 H11–7. **'Pony Tails'** The common name, sometimes incorrectly used as a cultivar name.

S. turkestanica Small evergreen tufts of green, inrolled leaves, just 1/32 in (0.5 mm) wide with, in mid- to late summer, slender wiry stems carrying elegant, narrow pale green flowerheads, hung with tiny oatlike flowers from which grow long, twice-bent needles 3–8 in (8–20 cm) long. Grow as a substitute for *S. gigantea* in smaller gardens, where it will make an equally showy specimen, or in drifts in gravel gardens, by paths, and other well-drained areas. Found on rocky slopes, scree, rocks, and on mountains in Iran to Pakistan and Tadzhikistan. ↕ 16 in (40 cm). Z7–10 H10–1

STOKESIA

Stokes' aster

ASTERACEAE

Colorful giant cornflowers over a long summer season for a sunny, well-drained situation.

Just one perennial species from North America forms a basal rosette of strap-shaped evergreen leaves that persists over winter, helping to shelter the fleshy rootstock. Then, in summer, the relatively large, daisylike flowerheads are carried over a long season. Bold but not garish, *Stokesia* makes a great front-of-the-border plant and also a good cut flower.

CULTIVATION Best given sun and shelter; also needs well-drained soil, especially to ensure survival over the winter. In colder climates, the rootstock will benefit from a protective mulch over the winter.

PROPAGATION By division in spring or root cuttings in late winter.

STOKESIA LAEVIS CULTIVARS

S. laevis 'Alba'

S. laevis 'Blue Star'

S. laevis 'Klaus Jelitto'

S. laevis 'Purple Parasols'

Where variation is not a problem, seed can also be sown in fall, but seedlings will rarely come true.

PROBLEMS Winter rain can cause rot.

S. cyanea see *S. laevis*

S. laevis syn. *S. cyanea* Elliptical to lance-shaped leaves up to 8 in (20 cm) long make a basal rosette, from which emerge upright stems carrying shorter stem-clasping leaves. The ray florets of the 4 in (10 cm) flowerheads are finely divided and usually in shades of blue, although white, pink, and purple are also seen; the disk florets are somewhat larger than is typical for daisy flowers and so produce the cornflower-like effect. Flowers are produced from early summer to early fall, but the season can be prolonged by regular deadheading. From North Carolina southwest to Louisiana. ‡12–18 in (30–45 cm). Z5–9 H9–5. **'Alba'** White flowers. **'Blue Star'** Lavender-blue flowers. This name is sometimes used for the species itself. From seed, may be variable. **'Colorwheel'** White flowers aging through lavender to dark blue-purple. From Georgia's Itsaul Plants. **'Honeysong Purple'** Large, vibrant, dark purple flowers with a reddish pink center. From Alex Summers, founder of the American Hosta Society. **'Klaus Jelitto'** Large blue flowers early in the season. **'Mary Gregory'** Soft creamy yellow flowers. **'Omega Skyrocket'** syn. 'Skyrocket' Tall plants carry theoretically lilac flowers, which in fact fall anywhere between white and blue. ‡36–48 in (90–120 cm). **'Peachie's Pick'** Dense and compact with large blue flowers. From Mississippi gardener Peachie Saxon. **'Purple Parasols'** Powder blue flowers changing as they age to dark blue, indigo, purple, and finally magenta. **'Silver Moon'** Creamy white flowers. **'Skyrocket'** see 'Omega Skyrocket'. **'Träumerei'** White flowers with a faint pink center. From seed, so may be variable.

STROBILANTHES
ACANTHACEAE

Increasingly popular, sometimes unexpectedly hardy and prolific shade-lovers.

Over 250 species of sometimes woody-based perennials come from Asia and Madagascar; relatively few are regularly cultivated, and most of those mainly as greenhouse or conservatory plants, or in summer seasonal plantings. Erect or spreading branches carry oppositely arranged, egg-shaped, lance-shaped, or elliptical leaves, often with one leaf of a pair larger than the other. The tubular to funnel-shaped flowers, often two-lipped and hooded, have five lobes and may be blue, purple, white, or occasionally yellow. They are carried in cone-shaped loose or compact heads, or in spikes, at the shoot tips and from the upper leaf joints. The majority are tropical in origin and not hardy in temperate gardens, and the few hardy species are not yet well known, although experience of them is increasing.

CULTIVATION Grow in well-prepared free-draining soil in light shade. Some also perform well in the sun if the soil remains moist. In colder areas, protect with a deep winter mulch.

PROPAGATION Sow seed in spring or take basal cuttings in spring or early summer.

PROBLEMS Red spider mite.

S. atropurpurea see *S. attenuata*

S. attenuata syn. *S. atropurpurea* Woody-based perennial with unequal pairs of lance-shaped, soft-hairy, dark green leaves up to 4 in (10 cm) long, with prominent veins. In late summer, many erect, branching stems with purplish tints produce dense spikes of 1¾-in (4-cm) curved, tubular flowers in indigo or purple with white throats. From northern India. ‡4 ft (1.2 m). Z9–11 H11–1. **subsp.** *nepalensis* Flowers purple, on creeping plants. ‡12 in (30 cm).

S. nutans Forms a dense, vigorous, creeping, weed-smothering clump. Hanging clusters of pure white flowers appear in late summer. An epiphyte in the wild, growing on tree trunks, but good in shade under large shrubs. From Nepal. ‡8 in (20 cm). Z9–11 H11–1

S. wallichii Upright, branching perennial; oval or elliptical, toothed pale green leaves, the lower ones with stalks and the upper ones without. Prolific, loose, sometimes zigzagged, one-sided spikes of violet-blue to purple, 1¼ in (3 cm) flowers appear in late summer and fall. A low, 12 in (30 cm), pale-flowered form is the one usually seen. Requires part-shade and well-drained soil. From Sri Lanka. ‡15–24 in (38–60 cm). Z9–11 H11–1

STYLOPHORUM
PAPAVERACEAE

Discreet patch-forming woodlanders for shade and woodland gardens, where they will sometimes self-sow.

Two of the three species of evergreen perennials or biennials, from shaded woodland habitats in eastern North America and China, are grown in gardens. These relatively fast-growing, easy, hardy, and dependable plants have mostly soft, divided foliage in basal rosettes and stiff, ascending stems topped with yellow or orange, slightly crinkled flowers. Although the individual flowers are short-lived, they are produced in succession.

RIGHT 1 *Strobilanthes wallichii*
2 *Stylophorum diphyllum*
3 *Succisa pratensis*

CULTIVATION Thrives best in dappled shade in humus-rich, moisture-retentive soil.

PROPAGATION From seed.

PROBLEMS Slugs.

S. diphyllum (Celandine poppy) Tufted perennial with downy stems and foliage, the long-stemmed, 8–12 in (20–30 cm), lobed, bluish green leaves having five to seven oblong, bluntly toothed leaflets. The basal long-stalked leaves form a loose rosette, the smaller stem leaves have shorter stalks. Bright yellow, bowl-shaped, 1¼–2 in (3–5 cm), poppylike flowers, generally with four petals, are borne in small clusters at the stem tips from late spring to midsummer, one flower opening at a time. Native to the eastern woodlands of North America. ‡12–16 in (30–40 cm). Z4–8 H8–1

S. lasiocarpum Short-lived perennial or biennial forming flattish, pale green, rather brittle, congested leaf rosettes. These have four to seven roughly opposite, jaggedly toothed lobes and may reach 18 in (45 cm), the end leaflet much larger than the others. They generally have a whitish bloom beneath and ooze a reddish sap when cut. The lemon yellow flowers are shallowly cupped, 1¼–1¾ in (3–4 cm) across, and borne in succession above the foliage from late spring to early fall. A very worthwhile plant, yet surprisingly little-known. Native to central and eastern China. ‡18 in (45 cm). Z4–8 H8–1

SUCCISA
DIPSACACEAE

Demure but attractive bee and butterfly plants for damp meadows or wild gardens.

One species of perennial is native to wet meadows in Europe, western Asia, and North Africa. Long, oval leaves are mainly in a basal rosette; the upright, slightly hairy stems are branched toward the top to carry scabious-like heads of violet to mauve, sometimes pink or white, flowers from midsummer onward.

CULTIVATION Best in a moist location that does not dry out in summer, in sun or part-shade.

PROPAGATION From seed or cuttings.

PROBLEMS Usually trouble-free.

S. pratensis syn. *Scabiosa succisa* (Devil's bit scabious) Long, stout roots support a rosette of 2–12 in (5–30 cm), usually undivided, lance-shaped to elliptical, thinly hairy leaves narrowed into a short stalk. Slender, upright stems carry shorter, narrower, eventually paired leaves. The ¾–1 in (2–2.5 cm) flowerheads, held on thin stems at the tip of the shoot and in the upper leaf joints, are freely produced over a long period. Usually mauve to dark bluish purple; when grown from seed, pink

or white flowers may appear. Popular with bees and butterflies. Found in Europe and North Africa. ‡6–24 in (15–60 cm). Z4–7 H7–1

SYMPHYANDRA see CAMPANULA
SYMPHYOTRICHUM see ASTER

SYMPHYTUM
Comfrey
BORAGINACEAE

Rather coarse but often handsome plants invaluable for ground cover in difficult situations.

About 35 species of bristly perennials, spreading widely by rhizomes, are native to various damp habitats, including woodlands, scrub, streamsides, and roadsides in Europe and western Asia. The stems are usually upright at first, and then often become sprawling; their leaves are often rough to touch, hairy, oval or elliptical in shape, with a heart- or wedge-shaped base. The basal leaves are long-stalked, the stem leaves short-stalked or stalkless. Nodding bell- or funnel-shaped flowers have five short lobes, and are

RIGHT *Symphytum caucasicum*

borne in dense, coiled clusters in spring and summer. They come in a wide range of colors, from blue and purple to pink, pale yellow, or white.

Valuable ground covers, especially in their variegated forms, they must be sited carefully because of their invasive habit. Deep roots allow regrowth even after plants have supposedly been entirely dug up. The common comfrey, *S. officinale*, is often grown for use as a nutrient-rich fertilizer (*see* Comfrey as an Organic Fertilizer) and is one of the oldest medicinal herbs known to humans, cultivated since about 400 BCE. Plants of all symphytums contain a toxic alkaloid. ⚠

CULTIVATION Generally adaptable, most comfreys prefer dappled shade but will also grow in full sun or even deep shade. Ideally, the soil should be moist, fertile, and deep, though they will survive in most soils, including heavy clay.

PROPAGATION By division, ideally in spring or fall, or root cuttings in

early to mid-winter, although this method is not suitable for variegated cultivars because the resulting plants will have plain green leaves.

IN FRIENDLY COMPETITION

THREE TOUGH, resilient, and in two cases rather aggressive plants here settle into happy equilibrium in a part-shaded border. Arching from tight, woody clumps, the flowers of this delicately picoteed form of *Helleborus* x *hybridus* age well without becoming too dull and green and lean into the light over the blue spikes of *Ajuga reptans*. The color of the bright spring spikes of this creeping shade-lover is picked up in the tints of the symphytum, whose coral buds reflect the coloring in the hellebore flowers. This too can be vigorous: while the hellebore can hold its own, the bugle may continue to peep through or may need rescuing in a few years.

PROBLEMS Usually trouble-free, except occasional rust and their own invasiveness.

S. asperum (Rough comfrey) Roughly hairy plant. Branched stems covered in short, stout, hooked bristles, the leaves very rough to touch, oval or elliptical with a heart-shaped or rounded base, and up to 7½ in (19 cm) long. Carries branching clusters of 10–20 nodding, tubular, rich blue flowers, up to ⅝ in (1.7 cm) long, opening from pink-red buds in spring and summer. Classified as a noxious weed in California. From the Caucasus, northeast Turkey, and northern Iran, and naturalized in Europe and the US. ↕36–60 in (90–150 cm). Z3–9 H9–1

S. caucasicum Attractive but very invasive clump-forming plant, the hairy, basal leaves oblong to oval, to 8 in (20 cm) long, narrowing to winged stalks, while the stem leaves are oval to lance-shaped and tapered at the base. Drooping clusters of blue, tubular flowers, to ⅝ in (1.7 cm) long, open in spring from red-purple buds. Great ground cover for wilder places. From the Caucasus and Iran. ↕16–24 in (40–60 cm). Z3–9 H9–1. **'Norwich Sky'** Pretty azure blue flowers, but very invasive. ↕18 in (45 cm).

S. 'Goldsmith' A low-growing evergreen, the heart-shaped, dark green hairy leaves, to 8 in (25 cm) long, with broad creamy yellow edges. The ⅝-in (1.5-cm) tubular flowers are pink, blue, and white and open in spring and early summer. Rather shallow-rooted, and thus much easier to control than many other comfreys. A hybrid of *S. ibericum* introduced by Dorset, England, plant breeder Eric Smith. ↕6–12 in (15–30 cm). Z5–9 H9–5

S. grandiflorum see *S. ibericum*

S. 'Hidcote Blue' Spreads strongly; more or less upright stems carry rough, oval to elliptical leaves to 8 in (25 cm)

long. Pale blue flowers, ⅝ in (1.5 cm) long, open in mid- to late spring from pink-red buds, and gradually fading. ↕20 in (50 cm). Z4–7 H7–1

S. 'Hidcote Pink' syn. *S. 'Roseum'* A vigorous spreader. Upright stems carry rough, oval to elliptical, 8 in (25 cm) leaves and ⅝ in (1.5 cm) flowers in pink and white, fading with age. The connection with Hidcote Manor garden is not fully established. ↕18 in (45 cm). Z5–9 H9–5

S. ibericum Hairy, creeping plant, producing sprawling sterile stems in the first year, followed by upright fertile stems in the second, from spreading, branched rhizomes. The leaves are broadly oval, sharply pointed, to 10 in (25 cm) long, with a heart-shaped base and long, winged stalks. The flowers have a reddish hue in bud, becoming pale yellow, ⅝–¾ in (1.4–2 cm) long, produced in dense clusters of about 20. This plant is often offered as the much less common *S. grandiflorum*, which is distinguished mainly by its larger flowers. Spreads rapidly and makes excellent ground cover under trees and shrubs. From the Caucasus and northeastern Turkey, naturalized in Britain. ↕12–16 in (30–40 cm). Z3–9 H9–1. **'All Gold'** Leaves rich golden yellow in spring, turning green in summer; flowers pink-mauve. Although usually listed as a form of *S. ibericum*, this plant appears unrelated to it. ↕30 in (75 cm). **'Blaueglocken'** Flowers light blue opening from coral red buds. Probably a hybrid between *S. ibericum* and *S. x uplandicum*. ↕15 in (38 cm). **'Gold in Spring'** Slower-growing, the new leaves golden, the flowers pink and cream. ↕8–12 in (20–30 cm). **'Wisley Blue'** Blue flowers.

S. 'Langthorns Pink' Vigorous; clusters of pink flowers in early summer. May

RIGHT 1 *Symphytum* 'Hidcote Blue'
2 *S.* 'Hidcote Pink'
3 *S. ibericum* 'All Gold'

COMFREY AS AN ORGANIC FERTILIZER

Comfrey has been found to have a high level of nitrogen, phosphorus, and potassium nutrients in the foliage. Organic gardeners have known this for a long time and have used comfrey in the following ways.

Freshly cut comfrey leaves (not the flowering stems) may be used as fertilizer when planting. Simply place the leaves in the bottom of the planting hole, where they will break down rapidly and provide nutrients to the roots.

Alternatively, a liquid fertilizer of comfrey may be created by brewing comfrey tea. Fill a container half full with fresh comfrey leaves, add water, cover the container, and allow the mixture to steep for 3 to 6 weeks. Please note that the fermenting brew has a foul smell and, therefore, the container should be placed outside and at a considerable distance from sensitive noses! The comfrey tea brew may be used full

strength or half strength (the color of weak tea). Use the tea each time plants are watered. It is an excellent organic source of nutrients.

A comfrey liquid fertilizer concentrate may also be made by placing fresh comfrey leaves in an old bucket and weighing the leaves down with a rock. Place a cover on the bucket and allow the leaves to decompose for several weeks. The leaves decompose into a smelly but excellent black nutrient-filled goo. Dilute the concentrated goo about 15 to 1 with water, and use as you would use the comfrey tea. Extra concentrate can be stored in a plastic container until it is needed.

Finally, comfrey leaves make a good mulch around vegetables and flowers. Comfrey leaves don't use as much nitrogen during composting as do high-carbon mulchs like straw or leaves and are therefore preferred.

ABOVE 1 *Symphytum ibericum* 'Wisley Blue' **2** *S.* x *uplandicum* 'Variegatum'

flower a second time if flowered stems are cut down. Probably a hybrid of *S.* 'Rubrum' and *S.* x *uplandicum*. ‡3¼–4 ft (1–1.2 m). Z5–9 H9–5

S. orientale Short-lived, softly hairy perennial with branched stems, the leaves oval or oblong, usually with a heart-shaped or rounded base, and up to 5½ in (14 cm) long, with the stalk narrowly winged on top. The smaller upper leaves are short-stalked or stalkless. The tubular, funnel-shaped, flowers are pure white, ⅝–¾ in (1.4–2 cm) long, and produced in late spring and early summer. Less invasive than some other comfreys and suitable for a mixed border. From Turkey and Ukraine; naturalized in Britain, France, and Italy. ‡24 in (60 cm). Z6–9 H9–5

S. peregrinum see *S.* x *uplandicum*

***S.* 'Roseum'** see *S.* 'Hidcote Pink'

***S.* 'Rubrum'** Deep crimson-red tubular flowers are set against hairy, dark green leaves from late spring into summer. Less invasive than most. Perhaps a hybrid between a form of *S. officinale* and *S. grandiflorum*. ‡18 in (45 cm). Z4–8 H8–1

S.* x *uplandicum syn. *S. peregrinum* (Russian comfrey) A robust, bristly plant with branching stems, the oval to lance-shaped, stalked basal leaves 14 in (35 cm) long, the shorter stem leaves stalkless. The flowers are tubular, ½–¾ in (1.2–1.8 cm) long, pinkish in bud, opening to blue or sometimes purple or violet, and carried in drooping clusters in spring and summer. A decorative but invasive hybrid of *S. asperum* and *S. officinale*, now naturalized widely in Europe. ‡16–60 in (40–150 cm). Z3–9 H9–1. **'Axminster Gold'** Foliage with broad,

bright yellow margins; blue flowers from pink buds in summer. ‡4 ft (1.2 m). **'Mereworth'** Large leaves, to 20 in (50 cm) long, irregularly variegated, either spotted and splashed in yellow or with a pale green central splash. Flowers purple in summer. ‡4 ft (1.2 m). **'Variegatum'** Evergreen, grayish green leaves are broadly margined with cream. Pale mauve or blue flowers open from lilac buds in late spring and early summer. ‡24–36 in (60–90 cm).

SYNEILESIS
ASTERACEAE

Intriguing shade-tolerant plants grown mainly for their striking and elegant young leaves.

BELOW 1 *Syneilesis aconitifolia* **2** *Synthyris missurica* var. *stellata*

About five deciduous species grow in woodlands in China, Japan, and Taiwan; two are increasingly grown in gardens. From their short rhizomes, the deeply divided leaves arise in spring, gradually enlarging until, in summer, they are joined by tall, branched sprays of rather insignificant pinkish flowerheads. The young leaves are umbrella-like, with drooping, fingerlike lobes loosely covered with silky hairs. As they grow, they gradually they lose the hairs and the leaf divisions become more spreading.

CULTIVATION Thrives in moist shade, but tolerant of drier conditions once established.

PROPAGATION By division or from seed.

PROBLEMS Slugs and snails.

S. aconitifolia Slowly forming a spreading clump, the rounded leaves, to 12 in (30 cm) across, are split almost to the base into narrow, forked, and toothed lobes; when they are young they are covered with long silky hairs. In late summer or early fall, the tiny reddish pink flowerheads, ¼ in (5 mm) across, open in flat-topped sprays. The flowers, which are held well above the handsome leaves, are unexciting, and may be removed in order to show off the foliage. From woods in low mountains in northern China, Korea, and western Japan. ‡28–48 in (70–120 cm). Z5–9 H9–5

S. palmata Slowly colonizing plant with long-stalked, rounded leaves, 6–12 in (15–30 cm) across, which are divided to the base into sharply toothed and lobed leaflets. The young leaves are attractively covered with shaggy white hairs. The small purplish pink flowerheads, which are just ¼ in (6 mm) across, open in loose conical sprays from midsummer to early fall or later. The foliage effect is similar to that

of *S. aconitifolia*, but the flowers are more attractive. From moist woods in Korea and southern Japan. ‡3¼ ft (1 m). Z4–8 H8–1

SYNTHYRIS
SCROPHULARIACEAE

Hardy spring-flowering shade-lovers whose bold foliage and flower spikes create delicate woodland impact.

About 14 species of deciduous and evergreen plants for woodland gardens or shrub borders come from woodlands in western and central North America. Low-growing, tufted plants, generally spreading by rhizomes, they feature usually heart- or kidney-shaped leaves, and spikes of tube- or bell-shaped flowers in spring, mainly blue to violet, but sometimes in white or pink.

CULTIVATION Thrives in moist yet well-drained, reasonably fertile soil that contains abundant humus. Will not tolerate wet conditions in winter. Need part- or deep shade.

PROPAGATION By division in early spring or from seed sown in fall.

PROBLEMS Relished by slugs and snails.

S. missurica Clump-forming, deciduous plant. The rounded, heart- or kidney-shaped, long-stalked leaves, which have bluntly toothed edges, are about 2 in (5 cm) across, and are deep green with a leathery texture. From early to late spring, the abundant, dense spikes of tubular, bell-shaped, dark lavender-blue flowers, approximately ¾ in (2 cm) long, thrust their way through the clumped foliage. From Arctic Canada to the western and central US. ‡10 in (25 cm). Z2–6 H6–1. **var. *stellata*** Jaggedly toothed leaves and bell-shaped violet-blue flowers. From Washington and Oregon. ‡6 in (15 cm).

T

TANACETUM
Tansy
ASTERACEAE

Attractive aromatic plants, usually with finely dissected leaves and prolific daisy- or buttonlike flowers in white, yellow, or pink.

About 150 species of predominantly perennial plants, some woody-based, but also including a few annuals, growing in a wide variety of open situations, from cliffs and alpine slopes to grassy meadows and streamsides. The majority are native to Eurasia, with a few outliers in North Africa and North America. A varied group, some species of which have at times been placed in other genera. The alpine species are low-growing and often mound-forming with densely white, hairy leaves, whereas the larger species are generally clump-forming. The aromatic, alternate, basal leaves are usually deeply divided and fernlike, although a few species have undivided leaves. Erect or sprawling stems, sometimes with leaves, bear terminal flowerheads either singly or in clusters. The flowerheads are either daisylike ray florets of white, yellow, or pink, or buttonlike and lacking ray florets. Contact with foliage can cause dermatitis or an allergic response in susceptible individuals. ⚠

CULTIVATION Requirements vary. Some are best in light soil in full sun, others are less demanding or prefer richer soil and tolerate part-shade.

PROPAGATION Divide or sow seed in spring. Cuttings from the woody-based species can be taken in spring or late summer.

PROBLEMS Usually trouble-free.

T. balsamita syn. *Balsamita major, Chrysanthemum balsamita* (Alecost, Costmary) Aromatic and spreading by rhizomes, the erect stems bear oblong to elliptical leaves with heart-shaped bases; the basal leaves are stalked and may reach 12 in (30 cm), while those on the stem are shorter, to 8 in (20 cm), and may be lobed toward the base and unstalked. The numerous, small, ½–¾ in (1–2 cm) flowerheads, with yellow disk florets and, if present, short, white ray florets, are held in tight terminal clusters from late summer to mid-fall. Needs a sunny site; sometimes grown in herb gardens and among otherwise unscented plantings for its camphor-scented leaves, which were used to flavor ale before the use of hops. Native to grassy places and meadows from Europe to southwestern Asia. ↕12–48 in (30–120 cm). Z6–9

GROWING PYRETHRUMS

The cultivars of *Tanacetum coccineum*, formerly included in *Pyrethrum* and *Chrysanthemum*, are easy and prolific. They are best suited to a border in full sun in light, well-drained, nutrient-poor soil and are short-lived in heavy soil. Vigor is maintained by cutting back hard after flowering, which encourages fresh new foliage and sometimes a second flowering, and dividing every three years. The double-flowered and white-flowered cultivars tend to be the least vigorous. Twiggy supports and close planting help to produce the best display.

Plants can be divided in midsummer, if watered well afterward, and this avoids disruption to flowering and ensures that plants are well-established for flowering the next year. Only replant the youngest shoots with fibrous roots. For the most prolific display, especially in heavy soil, plant the young pieces in pots, or in good soil in a cold frame, and grow them on. Replace them in the garden with late-sown annuals, then plant them out the following spring.

Some cultivars are customarily raised from seed—'Robinson's Giant', 'Robinson's Pink', 'Robinson's Red', 'Duro', and 'Super Duplex'—and may be a little variable. Others are intended to be propagated by division or cuttings, but most of these have been raised from seed at times, so they too may prove unexpectedly variable.

H9–6. **subsp. *balsamita*** Flowerheads without ray florets. **subsp. *balsamitoides*** Flowerheads with ray florets.

T. coccineum syn. *Chrysanthemum coccineum, Pyrethrum coccineum* (Pyrethrum, Painted daisy) Clump-forming, with mainly basal foliage, the 4¾ in (12 cm), elliptical to oblong leaves are once divided into six to ten pairs of sharply toothed linear lobes, giving a fernlike appearance. The long flower stems, bearing smaller leaves, are usually unbranched and carry solitary, yellow-centered, daisylike flowerheads, to 2¾ in (7 cm) across, between early summer and midsummer. In the wild species, the ray florets are an unremarkable pale pink, but in cultivars they are shades of deeper pink or white, and the flowerheads can be semidouble or double. The doubles are best described as anemone-flowered because the center of the flowerhead develops into a dome of colored florets, distinct in shape from the ray florets, but the same color. Most are good cut flowers. They prefer full sun and light, well-drained, nutrient-poor soil, but are short-lived in heavy soil and can be affected by slugs, snails, and powdery mildew. Native to mountain meadows in the Caucasus and southwestern Asia. ↕12–32 in (30–80 cm). Z5–9 H9–5. **'Aphrodite'** Double; florets white. ↕24–30 in (60–75 cm). **'Beauty of Stapleford'** Single; ray florets mid-pink; prolific. ↕24–30 in (60–75 cm). **'Brenda'** Single; ray florets deep pink. ↕24–30 in (60–75 cm). **'Duro'** Single large flowers have purple-red rays on long stems. Seed-raised mixture. ↕32 in (80 cm). **'Eileen May Robinson'** Single; ray florets pink. ↕24–32 in (60–75 cm). **'Evenglow'** Single; ray florets salmon red. ↕24–30 in (60–75 cm). **'H. M. Pike'** Single; ray florets bright red. ↕24–30 in (60–75 cm). **'James Kelway'** Single; ray florets deep scarlet. ↕24–30 in (60–75 cm). **'Madeleine'** Double; small, pale rosy pink pompons. ↕20–30 in (50–75 cm). **'Robinson's Giant'** Single; seed-raised mixture with ray florets in pink or red shades. ↕36 in (90 cm). **'Robinson's Pink'** Single; ray florets pink. ↕24–30 in (60–75 cm). **'Robinson's Red'** Single; ray florets red. ↕24–30 in (60–75 cm). **'Super Duplex'** Single and semidouble;

FEVERFEW AND MORE

GOLDEN FEVERFEW, *Tanacetum parthenium* 'Aureum', is a fine plant around which to base a summery association, although, since it is relatively short-lived, it pays to build a planting around it that is made up of similarly short-term plants. Then you can make a fresh start with a new grouping when it all starts to deteriorate.

The salmon-flowered bedding salvia makes a surprisingly good companion, and wild herb Robert, *Geranium robertianum*, has prettily laced foliage, which makes a good early-season partner, followed by these dainty pink starlike flowers. And, in contrast, there is an occasional blue campanula peeping through.

ABOVE **1** *Tanacetum balsamita*
2 *T. coccineum* 'Eileen May Robinson'
3 *T. parthenium* 'Aureum'
4 *T. vulgare* 'Silver Lace'

seed-raised mixture with rays white and various pink and red shades. ‡32 in (80 cm). **'Snow Cloud'** Single; ray florets white. ‡24–30 in (60–75 cm). **'Vanessa'** Double; ray florets carmine-rose tinted orange in the center. The only one to survive of seven raised and introduced by Alan Bloom in 1961. ‡24–30 in (60–75 cm).

T. macrophyllum (Rayed tansy) Erect, unbranched stems, spreading by compact rhizomes, carry egg-shaped to elliptical leaves to 8 in (20 cm) long, downy and glandular beneath and deeply divided into five to six pairs of lance-shaped, saw-toothed lobes; they are carried up the stems. The numerous small, ½ in (13 mm) flowerheads, with yellow disk florets and dingy white ray florets, are held in flat-topped clusters of 40–100. Thrives in sun or shade and any soil. Sometimes misidentified as *Achillea grandifolia,* which has scales between the ray florets; these are absent in *Tanacetum*. Native to woodlands and tall herb communities in southeastern Europe, the Caucasus, and southwestern Asia. ‡3¼–5 ft (1–1.5 m). Z4–9 H9–1.

T. niveum syn. *Pyrethrum niveum* (Silver tansy) Clump-forming perennial, or biennial, forming a hemispherical mound of grayish foliage covered with small, white, daisylike flowerheads. The egg-shaped to elliptical, grayish green 2 in (5 cm) leaves are deeply divided into three to five pairs of lance-shaped, saw-toothed lobes. From midsummer to early fall, it is covered in yellow-centered, white-rayed flowerheads to 1 in (2.5 cm) across. Being short-lived, it is often treated as a bedding or container subject. Cut back after flowering to prolong its life. Sow seed in late winter for flowers in first year. Native to open, rocky areas in western Asia and the Caucasus. ‡20–36 in (50–90 cm). Z4–9 H9–1. **'Jackpot'**

Most cultivated plants are offered under this name; it is not clear if this cultivar is, in fact, distinct from the species.

T. parthenium syn. *Chrysanthemum parthenium, Matricaria parthenium, Pyrethrum parthenium* (Feverfew) Pleasantly aromatic, evergreen, generally short-lived, woody-based perennial with erect, branched stems. The egg-shaped, yellowish green, 3 in (8 cm) leaves are once or twice divided into three to five pairs of linear to wedge-shaped lobes with untoothed or scalloped margins. Daisylike, ⅝–1 in (1.5–2.5 cm) flowerheads, with yellow centers and white ray florets, are borne in dense clusters of up to 30 from midsummer to mid-fall. Suitable for the front of a border but tolerant of part-shade. Young plants from a fall sowing are winter-green. Various double-flowered forms are in cultivation, often of a rather ragged appearance—the two named doubles below have better-presented flowerheads consisting of a domed center surrounded by a neat row of ray florets. All are raised from seed and may prove variable. Native to a wide range of open habitats from southeastern Europe to the Caucasus. ‡12–36 in (30–90 cm). Z4–9 H9–1. **'Aureum'** Leaves yellowish green for a long season, flowerheads single, and ray florets slightly yellow-tinged. Young plants can be used for edging or carpet-bedding and clipped to shape. ‡12 in (30 cm). **'Rowallane'** Double, pure white flowerheads with white centers. Stems dark brown, taller than most types. First noticed in Rowallane garden, Northern Ireland. ‡36 in (90 cm). **'White Bonnet'** Double flowerheads, sometimes regarded as less of a pure white than 'Rowallane'. Stems green. Discovered by Graham Stuart Thomas in a garden in Reading, England. ‡24 in (60 cm).

T. serotinum see *Leucanthemella serotina*

T. vulgare syn. *Chrysanthemum vulgare* (Tansy) Vigorous, aromatic, deciduous perennial, with strongly spreading rhizomes. The stiff, erect stems carry

oblong, deep green, fernlike leaves, to 6 in (15 cm) long, divided into seven to ten pairs of linear, sharply toothed lobes. Yellow, buttonlike flowerheads to ½ in (1 cm) across, lacking ray florets, are held in dense, flat-topped clusters of up to 70 from midsummer to early fall. A vigorous patch-forming plant that will compete well with vigorous grasses in wilder areas of the garden. The colored-leaved cultivars can be cut back in midsummer to obtain fresh growth if flowers are not required. Prone to blackfly. Inhabits grassy places and riverbanks throughout Europe, North Africa, and temperate Asia. ‡3¼–5 ft (1–1.5 m). Z4–8 H8–1. **var. crispum** Larger, more finely divided leaves giving a curled, parsleylike appearance. Reluctant to flower in cooler summers. **'Isla Gold'** Leaves yellow, the color lasting throughout the summer. Originated at Isla Nursery, Cambridgeshire, England. **'Silver Lace'** Leaves variegated with white flecks in spring, the markings fading with onset of summer.

TELEKIA
Yellow oxeye
ASTERACEAE

Coarse, but dramatic, yellow daisies with large, bold leaves, and at its best an imposing and impressive plant.

Two deciduous, perennial species found in moist woodlands, streamsides, and alpine zones from central Europe to the Caucasus, only one of which is grown. Clump-forming perennials with alternate, egg-shaped to heart-shaped leaves, stalked below and stem-clasping above; the large, yellow daisylike flowerheads consist of yellow disk florets and narrow, yellow ray florets. They are borne solitarily or in clusters at the apex of either a solitary or a branched stem. If left undivided, it will form

a large and impressive clump, ideal as a seasonal, structural feature in wilder areas of the garden. Distinguished from the similar *Inula* by the presence of scales between the disk florets.

CULTIVATION Prefers deep, moisture-retentive soil in dappled sun or part-shade. Provide shelter from wind and intense sunlight, both of which may disfigure the leaves.

PROPAGATION By division or from seed.

PROBLEMS Slugs and snails.

T. speciosa syn. *Buphthalmum speciosum* (Yellow oxeye) Deciduous, aromatic perennial with short rhizomes and erect, hairy stems that are branched toward the apex. The large basal leaves,

RIGHT *Telekia speciosa*

to 12 in (30 cm), are stalked, heart-shaped, coarsely toothed, and softly hairy beneath; the upper leaves are unstalked. From early to late summer, the branched stems bear 2–3 in (5–8 cm) flowerheads with brownish yellow disk florets and deep yellow ray florets ½–1 in (1–2.5 cm) long. Effective for naturalizing in wild parts of the garden, or as an isolated subject in rough grass or next to water, provided shelter is given. Native to damp woodlands and streamsides from central and southeastern Europe to Turkey and the Caucasus. ↕5–6½ ft (1.5–2 m). Z5–8 H8–5

TELLIMA
Fringe cups
SAXIFRAGACEAE

Pretty, easy to grow, drought-tolerant, spring- and summer-flowering shade-lover.

One fully hardy, semievergreen species growing in cool, moist woodland in western North America. A steadily creeping, rosette-forming plant with mainly basal leaves of variable shape, and tiny, pale green flowers carried on upright stems. The plant comes in several attractive and distinctive foliage forms. Ideal for ground cover in a woodland garden or shrub border.

CULTIVATION Thrives in part-shade with moist, humus-rich soil, but often performs creditably in dry shade.

PROPAGATION By division in spring, or from seed of species, not cultivars, sown as soon as ripe in a cold frame.

PROBLEMS Slugs may be a problem.

T. grandiflora Rather variable, 2–4 in

BELOW *Tellima grandiflora*

(5–10 cm) long, hairy leaves may be heart-or kidney-shaped or triangular, with five to seven lobes and toothed or scalloped edges. The ½ in (8 mm) long, five-petaled, bell-shaped, fringed flowers are carried on the upper half of upright, hairy stems from late spring to midsummer. They are white, tinged with green, but the overall appearance is pale green. Being drought-tolerant, the species and its forms will also take full sun and dry soil. Remove any green shoots on variegated plants. Sometimes self-seeds so freely as to be a nuisance. ↕32 in (80 cm). Z4–8 H8–1. **'Delphine'** Cream and light green variegated foliage, red-ringed green flowers. ↕12 in (30 cm). **'Forest Frost'** Silvery leaves with red tints in winter, green and pink flowers. ↕24 in (60 cm). **Odorata Group** Red-flushed leaves, scented green flowers. Rather variable. ↕20 in (50 cm). **'Purpurea'** *see* Rubra Group. **'Purpurteppich'** Leaves washed with burgundy in summer, green flowers fringed with pink. ↕24 in (60 cm). **Rubra Group** syn. 'Purpurea' Deep green leaves tinted with bronze, green flowers fringed with pink. Rather variable. ↕24 in (60 cm).

TELEXONIX *see* BOYKINIA
TETRAGONOLOBUS *see* LOTUS

THALICTRUM
Meadow rue
RANUNCULACEAE

Elegant ferny foliage and prolific fluffy flowers are combined with both subtlety and impact.

About 130 species from moist, shady places, meadows, and watersides in both the Old World and the New World. With many good candidates for the garden, they vary from border stalwarts to huge, 12 ft (4 m) specimens to diminutive, spreading ground covers less than 6 in (15 cm) tall.

Fibrous or tuberous roots, or rhizomes, support slender, willowy stems that carry foliage often similar in appearance to that of *Aquilegia*, being split into three, or twice divided into opposite pairs, the leaflets themselves lobed or toothed, and with an overall bluish cast. The floral effects of most species are delivered by dense clusters of stamens with individual flowers lacking petals. In many species, the parts of the calyx are enlarged and very showy, replacing the missing petals, and are commonly referred to as petals. In some species, individual plants are either male or female, or some fully fertile plants may also be produced. The flower color ranges from pure white through yellow, pink, mauve, and purple, and flowers may appear from mid-spring to early fall.

In recent years, expeditions to China and Korea in particular have led to an increase in the number of species grown, and the variability of some species is also now being appreciated. The collections of

Daniel Hinkley, from Washington State, and Bleddyn and Sue Wynn-Jones, from Wales, have been especially interesting and these new forms are beginning to be made available.

CULTIVATION All are easy and present few challenges. The taller garden species and hybrids are best sited in the middle or back of the border in full sun and may need staking in rich conditions. They should not be cut to the ground after flowering as new growth will not appear until late the following spring. Spent flowers should be removed to prevent an overabundance of self-sown seedlings.

PROPAGATION Easily produced from seed sown in fall, which germinates the following spring but usually produces a rather variable batch of plants. The rootstock of the taller species can be quite woody and does not allow for easy division, but the smaller species, with their more spreading root systems, are easily divided as growth resumes.

PROBLEMS Usually trouble-free.

T. aquilegiifolium Leafy mounds of bluish leaves, twice or three times split into three-toothed leaflets, are topped, from late spring to midsummer, with a dense, frothy mass of pink to lavender flowers from which the petals quickly drop, leaving the stamens to provide the color. The plant is popular, easy, and long-lived in full sun or a part-shaded border. From Europe across to China, Japan, and Korea. ↕4 ft (1.2 m). Z5–9 H9–5. **var. album** Lovely pure white, with flower buds that are slightly blushed before they open. **'Purpureum'** Flowers deep rose pink; from seed, so variable. **'Thundercloud'** Rich lilac purple flowers. ↕ 3.5 ft (1.1 m).

THALICTRUM FLOWERS

In thalictrum flowers, the color is not provided by the petals as is the case in so many plants. In fact, to be technically accurate, the flowers have no petals. However, as for many members of the buttercup family, the colored sepals have become modified to look like petals. In some species, another relatively uncommon factor is that plants are either male or female and carry either stamens or pistils. In both cases these too provide color and in this species, *T. aquilegiifolium*, are the main contributors as the sepals drop off as the flowers open.

Sepals

Stamens

Bud

Thalictrum aquilegiifolium

T. decorum see *T. delavayi* var. *decorum*

T. delavayi Variable species with 16 in (40 cm) leaves repeatedly split into opposite pairs of rounded leaflets, the relatively large, 1¼ in (3 cm), bicolored flowers with lavender petals and yellow stamens are offered in elegant loose sprays, sometimes carried on dark stems, from midsummer to early fall. A number of botanical variants have been described but are rarely seen. A superb late-blossoming species and one of the most desirable mid- to late summer perennials for sunny borders. Often offered, incorrectly, as *T. dipterocarpum*, which is a different plant. From western China. ↕5 ft (1.5 m). Z4–7 H7–1. **'Album'** pure white flowers and lime green foliage. **var. decorum** syn. *T. decorum* Very large flowers on vigorous, erect stems clad with handsome bluish green foliage. Deserving of wider use. From Yunnan province, southwestern China. **'Hewitt's Double'** Sensational sterile double with very finely textured leaves and a hazy display of tiny lavender, roselike flowers for a tremendously long period in midsummer to fall. Slow to establish but worth the wait.

T. diffusiflorum One of the largest-flowering of all species, the wiry, often well-branched stems carry 6 in (15 cm), bluish green leaves repeatedly divided into opposite pairs. The bicolored lavender and yellow flowers, 1½ in (4 cm) wide, are held in sometimes rather sparse sprays. It is difficult to establish but worth coddling in part-shaded sites in evenly moist, well-drained soil. Staking is advised. From Tibet. ↕30 in (75 cm). Z5–9 H9–5

T. dipterocarpum see *T. delavayi*

T. 'Elin' Handsome, powdery blue foliage is carried along unusually tall, yet stout and sturdy, stems capped in mid- to late summer with a haze of

LEFT 1 *Thalictrum aquilegiifolium*
2 *T. delavayi* 'Hewitt's Double'
3 *T. flavum* subsp. *glaucum*

soft yellow and lavender flowers. Does not need staking. A superb hybrid between *T. flavum* subsp. *glaucum* and *T. rochebrunianum* selected in Sweden and introduced through Coen Jansen in Holland. ‡ 8 ft (2.5 m). Z5–9 H9–5

T. flavum Spreading rhizomes support robust stems, sometimes sprouting roots at the base, clad with bluish green leaves split two or three times into opposite pairs of more or less oblong leaflets. Fragrant, pastel yellow flowers come in dense clusters in early summer and midsummer. ‡ 6 ft (1.8 m). Z3–10 H10–9. **subsp. glaucum** Handsome, powdery blue foliage and soft yellow flowers. Variable. **'Illuminator'** Foliage emerges bright chartreuse-gold fading to bluish green. Handsome when emerging with spring bulbs.

T. isopyroides A dwarf species for full sun with distinctive and highly ornamental, repeatedly divided, 1¾ in (4.5 cm), finely textured, powdery blue foliage and rather insignificant greenish brown flowers. It is worth growing for its foliage alone. Best in full sun and sharply drained soil. From central and southwestern Asia. ‡ 15 in (38 cm). Z5–9 H9–5

T. kiusianum Dwarf, ground-covering species forming a dense mat of rosettes of pretty textural leaves, like those of a maidenhair fern, through which rise wiry stems carrying clouds of tiny lavender-pink flowers from late spring through summer. Spreads steadily in cool, moist, well-drained conditions. From moist, vertical, moss-covered surfaces in Japan and Korea. ‡ 6 in (16 cm). Z4–8 H8–1

T. lucidum Rather tufted plant, the leaves repeatedly split into opposite pairs of slender, glossy, deep green, sometimes bluish foliage for which this plant is worth growing. But there are also dense heads of creamy white flowers in midsummer. For evenly moist conditions in full sun. From central and eastern Europe, and Turkey. ‡ 4 ft (1.2 m). Z5–8 H8–5

T. minus A variable species, with a compact or spreading root system carrying leaves repeatedly split into three, and sometimes green, sometimes prettily blued. The small flowers can be green, yellowish, or purple-tinted and are carried in heads that may be dense or open, usually nodding at first then turning upward. Best in a moist meadow garden or a wild border. From Europe and Asia. ‡ 36 in (90 cm). Z6–9 H9–6. **'Adiantifolium'** Especially finely divided, bluish leaves and yellow flowers, but raised from seed, so variable and not always distinct.

RIGHT 1 *Thelypteris palustris*
2 *Thermopsis lanceolata*

T. polygamum see *T. pubescens*

T. pubescens syn. *T. polygamum* Sturdy, upright stems carry repeatedly and variably divided, pale or dark green leaves and flowers with white or sometimes purplish petals and stamens, opening from yellow buds in early summer and midsummer. Variable—many botanical variants have been named but are not now considered consistent and distinct. For full sun and moderately moist soil, best in the meadow or wildflower border. From the eastern US and Canada. ‡ 4 ft (1.2 m). Z4–8 H8–1

T. rochebruneanum A very robust species and perhaps the tallest of all, with large, mid-green leaves, divided repeatedly into threes with individual leaflets ¾–1¼ in (2–3 cm) long. The stems are topped by a haze of bicolor lavender and yellow flowers similar to those of *T. delavayi* but smaller. Dramatic and impressive, but will require staking in rich soil. From Japan. ‡ 5–12 ft (1.5–4 m). Z5–9 H9–5

T. thalictroides see *Anemonella thalictroides*

T. tuberosum A lovely dwarf, tuberous-rooted, broadly rounded plant offering mostly basal leaves split two or three times into opposite pairs, and upright stems carrying relatively large 1¼ in (3 cm) flowers with broad, creamy white petals in early summer. For full sun or light shade at the front of the border. From Spain and southwestern France. ‡ 24 in (60 cm). Z5–9 H9–5

THELYPTERIS
THELYPTERIDACEAE

A vigorous fern frequently used to colonize a boggy area or pond margin.

About 17 deciduous species, mostly tropical in origin, with twice-divided fronds, arising from slender, creeping rhizomes. The segments are oblong and bluntly pointed, and the spore heaps soon lose their kidney-shaped, membranous covers, appearing naked. Until recently, *Thelypteris* was considered to be a very large, diverse genus, but it has recently been split into many much smaller genera, including *Phegopteris*.

CULTIVATION Grow in permanently moist, humus-rich soil in sun or dappled shade.

PROPAGATION By division; from spores.

PROBLEMS Usually trouble-free.

T. decursive-pinnata see *Phegopteris decursivepinnata*

T. palustris (Marsh fern) A deciduous fern with a long, creeping rhizome bearing well-separated, upright, lance-shaped fronds that are twice-divided. The fertile fronds are taller, with narrower segments, and the spore-bearing structures are scattered on the undersides. Surprisingly, it does quite well in a shady border, given good organic soil, but it does not grow so tall or spread so rapidly as in wetter conditions. Grows in marshes and fens in Europe, including the British Isles, North Africa, Asia, and eastern North America. ‡ 3¼ ft (1 m). Z5–8 H8–5

T. phegopteris see *Phegopteris connectilis*

THERMOPSIS
FABACEAE

Bold and impressive late-spring-flowering perennials with lupinelike flowers in slender spikes.

About 20 species of deciduous perennials with fleshy, sometimes invasive roots native to North and South America, Asia, Siberia, and India.

The leaves have three widespread, more or less lance-shaped leaflets, very similar to those of *Baptisia*, to which it is closely related. However, here the leaves are green, rather than blue-green, and the seedpods are flattened, not inflated. Some of the more vigorous species are more suitable for the wild garden, where they attract bees and butterflies.

CULTIVATION Grow in well-drained soil in sun.

PROPAGATION From seed. Established plants resent the disturbance of division.

PROBLEMS Powdery mildew, leaf spot.

T. caroliniana see *T. villosa*

T. fabacea see *T. lupinoides*

T. lanceolata Erect, usually unbranched stems carry narrow, stalked leaves that are divided into three, oval leaflets to 2¾ in (7 cm) long, each ending in a point. The 1 in (2.5 cm) yellow flowers are held well above the foliage in crowded spikes in late spring. The plant is often confused in catalogs with the much shorter *T. lupinoides*. Native to northern Japan, Korea, and Siberia. ↕ 3¼ ft (1 m). Z2–7 H8–1

T. lupinoides syn. *T. fabacea* Erect, usually unbranched stems carry unstalked, delicate foliage, broader than that of the taller *T. lanceolata* and with leaflets to only 1½ in (4 cm) long; some botanists have merged the two species. Soft lemon yellow, 2 in (5 cm) blooms in early summer. From Alaska and Siberia, it is equally hardy. ↕ 12–18 in (30–45 cm). Z2–7 H8–1

ORIGINS

Modern tiarellas come from two sources. A number of good forms were found in the wild, including 'Glossy'; some others, now seen less frequently, like 'Slick Rock 'and 'Running Tapestry', were introduced by Jim Plyler at Natural Landscapes Nursery, West Grove, Pennsylvania.

The varied assemblage of new hybrids began in the late 1980s with crosses by Charles Oliver at The Primrose Path nursery in Pennsylvania between selected forms of the eastern types to produce the vigorous 'Tiger Stripe'. This was then crossed with an individual of *T. trifoliata* var. *laciniata* with unusually well-cut foliage. Descendants of this pairing included 'Martha Oliver' and 'Elizabeth Oliver,' which are ancestors of all of the cut-leaf forms on the market today. *Tiarella* breeding was taken up by Terra Nova Nurseries in Oregon in the 1990s, and they produced many of those grown today.

However, many of the cultivars currently on the market are very similar to one another and differ mainly in leaf outline and amount of maroon blotching. Even enthusiasts may not find it necessary to grow them all.

T. montana see *T. rhombifolia* var. *montana*

T. rhombifolia var. montana syn. *T. montana* Spreads slowly by underground stems, which support upright shoots carrying stalked leaves with ¾–3 in (2–8 cm), oval leaflets. Showy, upright spikes of 1 in (2.5 cm), bright yellow flowers in spring and early summer. Can become invasive in rich soil, but a good plant for the wild garden. From the mountains of Colorado and New Mexico. ↕ 36 in (90 cm). Z4–8 H9–1

T. villosa syn. *T. caroliniana* An almost unbranched clump with slightly hairy stems and pale green leaves, each leaf having three more or less elliptical leaflets to 3½ in (9 cm) long, that are silky on the underside. Tall spikes of ¾ in (2 cm) yellow flowers open in late spring. A good garden plant that does not spread. Native to the US from North Carolina to Georgia. ↕ 36 in (90 cm). Z4–8 H9–1

TIARELLA
Foamflower
SAXIFRAGACEAE

Elegant woodlanders much improved as garden plants by recent American breeding.

Three to five species of noticeably variable, small evergreen plants native to the woodlands of North America and East Asia. Heart-shaped, slightly hairy leaves, 1¼–4¾ in (3–12 cm) across, make neat and attractive clumps or spread more widely to form a ground-covering mat. In spring and early summer there are 12–20 in (30–50 cm) tall, slender, upright stems carrying spikes of small, starry white or pink flowers, usually opening from darker buds, which sometimes have a spicy fragrance.

In eastern North America, all are currently classified as *T. cordifolia*, but for horticultural purposes, running types are referred to as *T. cordifolia* and clumping as *T. wherryi*. The leaves are often heavily patterned with maroon, either as a central blotch or as striping and mottling along the veins, and may be deeply, sometimes dramatically, lobed. The appearance of the maroon leaf blotching is seasonally variable, with buds formed in fall opening into the most intensely marked leaves; summer foliage may be much lighter than foliage that appears in the spring. The flowers vary greatly in abundance, density, and substance.

On the Pacific coast of North America, all forms are included under the rarely grown *T. trifoliata*, and have small, white flowers in loose, branched sprays, blooming in the summer. All of the traits of these three North American species have

RIGHT 1 *Tiarella cordifolia*
2 *T.* 'Pink Brushes' **3** *T.* 'Pink Pearls'
4 *T. wherryi*

been combined and recombined to produce the new garden hybrids, mainly from The Primrose Path nursery and from Terra Nova Nurseries (*see Origins, p. 454*).

All mound sizes are given as width first, height second. Heights refer to flower stems.

CULTIVATION Best in moist, humus-rich soil in shade. Running types can be used as an exceptionally beautiful, if sometimes rather thin, ground cover, the clumping forms in drifts along woodland paths. All make good cut flowers.

PROPAGATION By division.

PROBLEMS Black vine weevil (*see The Problem with Vine Weevils, p. 255*), and sometimes foliar nematodes, an unsightly problem controlled by removal of affected foliage.

T. '**Black Snowflake**' Seven narrow, almost separate, glossy leaflets, heavily marked with maroon, are about 3 in (8 cm) across and form a 12 x 8 in (30 x 20 cm) clump with pink flowers in tight spikes. From Terra Nova Nurseries. ↕ 12 in (30 cm). Z3–8 H8–1

T. '**Black Velvet**' Deeply cut into wide lobes, heavily marked with maroon and with a velvety surface, the 4 in (10 cm) leaves form a 14 x 10 in (35 x 25 cm) clump with long spikes of white flowers. From Terra Nova Nurseries. ↕ 18 in (45 cm). Z3–8 H8–1

T. '**Butterfly Wings**' Seven separate leaflets, heavily marked with maroon and held in two different planes, make leaves about 2¾ in (7 cm) wide that form a 12 x 6 in (30 x 15 cm) clump; pale pink flowers. From Primrose Path nursery. ↕ 14 in (35 cm). Z3–8 H8–1

T. cordifolia Running evergreen with heart-shaped, 2½–3 in (6–8 cm), fresh green leaves, each with three to five shallow lobes, and faintly to boldly streaked, striped, or mottled in scarlet to maroon, or sometimes plain green. In favorable garden conditions may spread to form an even cover several yards across and 4–6 in (10–15 cm) high. White to pale pink flowers are carried in erect spikes in spring. Grow in moist shade. Easily propagated by removing rooted plantlets from runners in late summer. From rich woodlands, and even wet streamsides, of eastern North America, Quebec to southern Appalachians. ↕ 8 in (20 cm). Z3–8 H8–1. **var. collina** see *T. wherryi*. '**Glossy**' Bold, glossy, plain green leaves and white flowers.

T. '**Cygnet**' Leaves about 2¾ in (7 cm) across, marked centrally with maroon, are deeply cut into narrow, unlobed segments, with the middle segment elongated and supposedly resembling the outstretched neck of a flying swan. Light pink flowers above a 12 x 6 in (30 x 15 cm) mound. Very similar to 'Ninja', but with slimmer, unlobed segments. From Terra Nova Nurseries. ↕ 16 in (40 cm). Z3–8 H8–1

T. '**Elizabeth Oliver**' Deeply lobed, somewhat frilly leaves, about 2¾ in (7 cm) across, marked centrally with maroon. Pink, fragrant flowers stand above a 16 x 6 in (40 x 15 cm) patch, which expands by 3–4¾ in (8–12 cm) runners. From Primrose Path. ↕ 16 in (40 cm). Z3–8 H8–1

T. '**Inkblot**' Undivided, heart-shaped leaves about 3 in (8 cm) across, with a large, diffuse, central maroon blotch make a 12 x 8 in (30 x 20 cm) mound, above which stand pink flowers. Similar to 'Tiger Stripe', but the maroon coloration is more central and less crisp. From Terra Nova Nurseries. ↕ 16 in (40 cm). Z3–8 H8–1

T. '**Iron Butterfly**' The leaves, about 2¾ in (7 cm) across, are heavily marked with maroon and are deeply cut into narrow segments that make a 12 x 6 in (30 x 15 cm) clump below spikes of pale pink flowers. It is similar in leaf shape to 'Cygnet' and 'Ninja,' but the maroon coloration is more extensive. From Terra Nova Nurseries. ↕ 16 in (40 cm). Z3–8 H8–1

T. '**Jeepers Creepers**' The deeply lobed leaves are about 3 in (8 cm) across, the lobes, wide and touching, are heavily striped with maroon along the veins below the white flowers held in long spikes. A running form making 8 in (20 cm) tall ground cover. From Terra Nova Nurseries. ↕ 16 in (40 cm). Z3–8 H8–1

T. '**Martha Oliver**' Deeply lobed leaves about 3 in (8 cm) across, each lobe lightly marked with maroon along the main vein; hairier than most, they make a clump about 12 x 6 in (30 x 15 cm) below long spikes of white flowers. The earliest of the hybrids with *T. trifoliata* and largely eclipsed by its later, more contrastingly colored descendants. Especially good, dark red, fall foliage color. From Primrose Path nursery. ↕ 16 in (40 cm). Z3–8 H8–1

T. '**Mint Chocolate**' Leaves about 2¾ in (7 cm) across, deeply lobed into narrow fingers, the middle one elongated, and each with a central maroon stripe, make a 12 x 6 in (30 x 15 cm) mound below spikes of cream flowers. The leaf outline is more regular and less deeply cut than the similar 'Cygnet' and 'Iron Butterfly.' From Terra Nova Nurseries. ↕ 14 in (35 cm). Z3–8 H8–1

T. '**Neon Lights**' Leaves about 4 in (10 cm) across, deeply cut into wide, irregular lobes, with a central maroon blotch taking up most of the leaf surface, make a 16 x 8 in (40 x 20 cm) mound. White flowers in long spikes. From Terra Nova Nurseries. ↕ 16 in (40 cm). Z3–8 H8–1

T. '**Ninja**' Mounds about 12 x 6 in (30 x 15 cm) are made up of leaves 2¾ in (7 cm) across, marked centrally with maroon, and deeply cut into narrow segments, with the middle lobe elongated and itself lobed below long spikes of pale pink flowers. The leaf

supposedly resembles a leaping human figure. Very similar to 'Cygnet' but with slightly broader, slightly lobed segments. From Terra Nova Nurseries. ↕ 16 in (40 cm). Z3–8 H8–1

T. '**Pink Bouquet**' The leaves are about 2¾ in (7 cm) across, marked centrally with maroon, and deeply lobed into narrow fingers, the middle one elongated, make a neat 10 x 6 in (25 x 15 cm) clump below short, pink flower spikes. Resembles 'Mint Chocolate' but with leaves less heavily marked with maroon and with pink flowers. From Terra Nova Nurseries. ↕ 12 in (30 cm). Z3–8 H8–1

T. '**Pink Brushes**' Lobed, maplelike leaves about 4 in (10 cm) across, matte with a quilted surface and with central maroon blotching, make a 14 x 8 in (35 x 20 cm) mound below long-lasting pink flowers in dense spikes. Very vigorous. From Primrose Path nursery. ↕ 16 in (40 cm). Z3–8 H8–1

T. '**Pink Pearls**' Angular, but unlobed and unpatterned green leaves, about 4 in (10 cm) across, make a 14 x 8 in (35 x 20 cm) clump. Spreading stems carry white flowers that open from pink buds later than other cultivars, from late spring into summer. A hybrid between *T. wherryi* and *T. trifoliata* var. *unifoliata* from Primrose Path nursery. ↕ 16 in (40 cm). Z3–8 H8–1

T. '**Pinwheel**' Leaves about 2¾ in (7 cm) across, deeply cut into wide, irregular lobes, each marked with a central maroon stripe, make a 10 x 6 in (25 x 15 cm) mound below white flowers on short spikes. Very similar to other cultivars with wide-lobed leaves and being supplanted by more heavily patterned cultivars, such as 'Sea Foam'. From Terra Nova Nurseries. ↕ 12 in (30 cm). Z3–8 H8–1

T. polyphylla Clump-forming, the hairy foliage makes a mound about 10 x 6 in (25 x 15 cm) with rounded, heart-shaped, lobed, occasionally slightly toothed, plain, green leaves, about 2¾ in (7 cm) across, below the spikes of pink flowers. Grow in moist shade and propagate from fresh seed or by division. Native to moist deciduous forests of eastern Asia. ↕ 12 in (30 cm). Z5–8 H8–5

T. '**Spanish Cross**' Leaves about 2¾ in (7 cm) across, deeply cut into irregular lobes heavily marked with maroon at the base, make 12 x 8 in (30 x 20 cm) mounds below short spikes of light pink flowers. The leaf lobes are wider than those of 'Ninja' and 'Iron Butterfly' but narrower than those of 'Neon Lights,' 'Pinwheel', and 'Sea Foam'. From Terra Nova Nurseries. ↕ 12 in (30 cm). Z3–8 H8–1

T. '**Spring Symphony**' Lobed, maplelike leaves, about 3 in (8 cm) across and with a small amount of basal maroon, form a 10 x 6 in (25 x 15 cm) clump below pink flowers on very short stems. Generally similar to 'Pink Brushes,' but smaller and with looser

flower spikes. From Terra Nova Nurseries. ↕ 10 in (25 cm). Z3–8 H8–1

T. '**Tiger Stripe**' Unlobed leaves up to about 4 in (10 cm) across, extensively striped with maroon in spring, make a 14 x 8 in (35 x 20 cm) mound below light pink flowers. From Primrose Path. ↕ 16 in (40 cm). Z3–8 H8–1

T. wherryi syn. *T. cordifolia* subsp. *collina* Forms a neat, 12 x 8 in (30 x 20 cm) clump of heart-shaped leaves to about 3 in (8 cm) across, which are often patterned with maroon, and sometimes deeply lobed. White to pink flowers are carried in erect spikes in spring. Grows best in light shade but tolerates part-sun and is easily divided. From rich deciduous woodlands, in the uplands of the southeastern US. ↕ 14–18 in (35–45 cm). Z3–7 H7–1. *T.* '**Bronze Beauty**' New foliage lobed, bronze, turning bronze-green; white flowers from pink buds. '**Heronswood Mist**' Green foliage freckled with white markings; white flowers. Similar to 'Skid's Variegated'. '**Oakleaf**' Leaves with five deep lobes turning reddish in fall; pink flowers. Selected at the University of Delaware. '**Skid's Variegated**' Green foliage freckled with white markings; white flowers. Similar to 'Heronswood Mist'.

TOLMIEA
Piggyback plant
SAXIFRAGACEAE

Hardy, low-growing, but vigorously spreading shade-lover much appreciated for its attractive foliage.

One species of evergreen or semi-evergreen plant related to *Heuchera* and *Tiarella* and growing

BELOW *Tolmiea menziesii* 'Taff's Gold'

in moist conifer forests in western North America. Spreading quickly by rhizomes, and making good ground cover for woodland gardens and shrub borders, the soft, hairy leaves bear plantlets where the leaf blade and stalk meet. The spikes of small flowers, produced in late spring and summer, are not showy, and the plant is grown mainly for its pleasing foliage.

CULTIVATION Thrives in cool conditions with part- or full shade, and moist soil containing abundant humus. Foliage will be scorched in full sun, so deep shade is preferable in warm climates. In very cold climates, grow as a house or greenhouse plant.

PROPAGATION By division in spring, plantlets at any time. Hold the leaves down onto to the soil with rocks; then, after several months, cut the leaf stalks, dig up the rooted plantlets, and plant elsewhere.

PROBLEMS Usually trouble-free.

T. menziesii A hairy, clump-forming plant quickly making effective ground cover. Long-stalked, rounded, five- to seven-lobed leaves, to 4¾ in (12 cm) long, have toothed edges and are pale to lime green. Spikes of small, cup-shaped, ½ in (1 cm) long, green and purple-brown flowers rise well above the foliage in late spring and early summer. From western North America. ‡12–24 in (30–60 cm). Z6–9 H9–6. **'Taff's Gold'** syn. 'Goldsplash', 'Maculata', 'Variegata' Light green leaves mottled and spotted with pale gold and cream. Cut out any green leaves that appear.

TOVARA see PERSICARIA

TRACHYSTEMON
BORAGINACEAE

Coarse but effective ground-covering plants for large, shady spaces.

One or two species of tough, stout, hairy perennials, native to a variety of shady habitats in the Caucasus, Turkey, Greece, and Bulgaria. Far-reaching creeping rhizomes support large, oval, dark, long-stalked basal leaves and smaller, oval to lance-shaped, stalkless stem leaves. Sparsely branched stems bear leafy clusters of purple-blue star-shaped flowers that resemble those of borage. Needs space and can be invasive.

CULTIVATION Easy to grow in sun or shade on almost any soil except waterlogged soil. Suitable for ground cover in dry shade, where it will spread faster than most other plants.

LEFT 1 *Trachystemon orientalis*
Tradescantia Andersoniana Group:
2 'Concorde Grape' **3** 'Isis'

PROPAGATION By division.

PROBLEMS Usually trouble-free.

T. orientalis (Abraham, Isaac, and Jacob) Impressive, fast-spreading, roughly hairy, deciduous perennial whose fat rhizomes, up to 2 in (5 cm) thick, support oval to heart-shaped 4–20 in (10–50 cm) leaves on stalks 4–10 in (10–25 cm) long, and also stalkless, clasping stem leaves. Branched clusters of five to fifteen star-shaped, purplish blue flowers, resembling those of borage, are produced in spring. Excellent ground cover, tolerant of almost any conditions. Native to the Caucasus, Turkey, and Bulgaria. ‡8–24 in (20–60 cm). Z6–8 H8–6

TRADESCANTIA
Spiderwort
COMMELINACEAE

Distinctive summer and fall perennials related to some of our most popular house plants.

Around 65 species of perennial plants from North and South America and named for John Tradescant, the 17th-century naturalist and gardener. Many are frost-tender, but the hardier species and hybrids, derived from species such as *T. virginiana*, from the eastern US, where they grow in woods, scrubland, and meadows, are usually grown for their distinctive three-petaled flowers. Often seen in cottage gardens, where they make effective and undemanding flowering plants.

The clump-forming plants are composed of tufts of quite succulent, upright stems growing from a fleshy rootstock. The lance-shaped or oval leaves are borne alternately and are usually mid-green but are sometimes golden or bluish. The short-lived flowers are composed of three petals enclosed in paired, boat-shaped bracts and held in clusters that usually appear at the end of the stems.

Plants now collected together as *T.* Andersoniana Group are perhaps the most commonly cultivated and are of complex hybrid origin. Most are generally of similar appearance, differing mainly in flower color, although recently more compact or colored foliage selections have been introduced, improving them as garden plants. They are self-sterile (an individual plant will produce no seed) but when several are grown together, plants seed freely—sometimes rather too freely. These are not in the top tier of perennial plants, and can look untidy at times, but they have a distinctive look, bloom at a convenient height, and have a long flowering season, lasting until the first frost.

CULTIVATION Generally easy to grow and thrives in a moist soil, and often thriving best with some shade unless constant moisture can be provided, they are good plants for streamside

ABOVE *Tradescantia* Andersoniana Group: **1** 'Karminglut' **2** 'Osprey'

plantings, or even the bog garden. Deadheading is not required, but the taller selections may need some staking. If several named cultivars are grown, take care to prevent inferior seedlings from overrunning clumps.

PROPAGATION Divide in fall after flowering or in spring.

PROBLEMS Slugs and snails, and rust.

T. Andersoniana Group Clump-forming plants develop upright, branching stems with long, lance-shaped, usually mid-green leaves. The three-petaled purple—or sometimes blue, pink, or white—flowers, up to 1½ in (4 cm) across with prominent stamens, appear in clusters at the end of shoots during summer and into fall, opening in early morning, often to close by mid-afternoon. Best grown in sun, and in moist, rich soil in herbaceous borders. This name is given to hybrid plants derived from *T. virginiana* and various other species originating from the prairies and moist meadows of the central and eastern US. ‡16 in (40 cm). Z5–9 H9–5. **'Bilberry Ice'** From purplish buds, white flowers emerge that are tinged blue, each petal with a purplish stripe down the center to eye-catching effect. Compact, rounded habit. Z3–9 H9–3. **'Blue and Gold'** syn. 'Sweet Kate' Dramatic, bright, golden yellow foliage that creates an effective contrast with its rich blue flowers. Needs particularly good moist, fertile conditions. ‡14 in (35 cm). **'Blue Stone'** Strong, vigorous, and prolific with 1¼ in (3 cm), lavender-blue flowers over long periods in summer. ‡24 in (60 cm). **'Charlotte'** Reddish purple summer flowers; tall. ‡24 in (60 cm). **'Chedglow'** Golden foliage, usually a greenish gold rather than bright yellow, with rich purple flowers in summer. Discovered by Martin Cragg-Barber and introduced by Hopleys Plants, Hertfordshire, England. **'Concorde Grape'** Dwarf, with bright purple flowers and

distinctive purplish blue foliage. ‡14 in (35 cm). **'Danielle'** Especially large, pure white 2 in (5 cm) flowers. ‡18 in (45 cm). **'Innocence'** White flowers with yellowish centers over long periods in summer. ‡20 in (50 cm). **'Iris Prichard'** Distinctive, white flowers with pale blue shading, held above green foliage. **'Isis'** Prolific, with large, dark blue 1½ in (4 cm) flowers from late spring until early fall. One of the best and most reliable. **'J. C. Weguelin'** Delightful, large, 1½ in (4 cm) flowers of delicate palest blue. **'Karminglut'** (**Carmine Glow**) Purplish red flowers. ‡24 in (60 cm). **'Leonora'** Golden green foliage with purple flowers in summer. **'Little Doll'** Dwarf and prolific; in summer, light blue flowers are held above grassy green foliage. ‡10 in (25 cm). **'Little White Doll'** Dwarf and prolific, with white summer flowers held above grassy green foliage. ‡10 in (25 cm). **'Osprey'** Prolific, with large numbers of large, white flowers with attractive blue stamens, from late spring until fall. ‡20 in (50 cm). **'Pauline'** Large, bright, rich velvety purple 1 in (2.5 cm) flowers. **'Purewell Giant'** Fine, purplish red flowers above bright green foliage on large, rounded plants. ‡18 in (45 cm). **'Purple Dome'** Large, rich purple flowers produced from early summer until fall. **'Red Grape'** Distinctive, bright crimson red flowers all summer and into fall, above grassy gray-green foliage. ‡18 in (45 cm). **'Rubra'** Darkish, reddish tinged, grassy foliage topped by large, red, 1½ in (4 cm) flowers in summer and into fall. **'Sweet Kate'** *see* 'Blue and Gold'. **'Sylvana'** Compact, with bright red flowers from spring through to late summer. **'Zwanenburg Blue'** Very large, rich blue, 2 in (5 cm) flowers. ‡20 in (50 cm).

T. brevicaulis see *T. virginiana* 'Brevicaulis'

T. virginiana Upright, branched, fleshy stems carry spirally arranged, long, narrow, sharply pointed, slightly fleshy

RIGHT *Tricyrtis formosana*

green foliage to 14 in (35 cm) long and 1 in (2.5 cm) wide. Clusters of lilac, blue, or purple ¾ in (2 cm) flowers, occasionally pink or white, are borne during the summer. Increasingly lanky as the season progresses. One of the parents of the Andersoniana Group. From eastern US. ‡20 in (50 cm). Z3–9 H9–3. **'Brevicaulis'** syn. *T. brevicaulis* Long, green, grassy foliage with masses of bright pink-purple flowers. Sometimes treated as a species. **'Caerulea Plena'** Clusters of double, dark mauve-blue flowers.

TRICYRTIS
Toad lily
UVULARIACEAE

Choice shade-lovers with the special quality of flowering during the fall.

About 20 species of woodlanders from Asia grown for their colorful and prettily patterned flowers, as

well as for their handsome foliage. They have been long cultivated in Japan, where they are known as *hototogisu* or "cuckoo." Steadily spreading, sometimes vigorous, clumps of fat, upright or arching stems carry alternate oval or lance-shaped leaves, often clasping the stem at the base. Elegant orchidlike flowers, in open heads above leafy mounds of foliage, or sometimes from the leaf joints, have six petals and, in the center, a noticeable fused column of reproductive parts (stamens and pistils) that extends significantly outward. Flowers range from pure white and butter yellow through pink, lavender, and deep purple, and are often intricately spotted and marked inside. With a few exceptions, *Tricyrtis* flower in late summer through fall with some not opening until the middle of fall. As such, they are invaluable wood-land plants, bringing color and fascinating flowers when most other

woodland flowers are finished. There is an increasing range of hybrids and selections, including variegated forms, arriving in western gardens from Japan. Some are expensive at first, but most are well worth growing. The names, however, may be slightly muddled. Some—'Tojen', for example—are also proving to be excellent and long-lasting cut flowers.

CULTIVATION Best in evenly moist, humus-rich soil in light to full shade. Drying of the soil during the summer will lead to stress and desiccation of the foliage, which will detract from the floral display later. Mulching will cool the soil and diminish the need for continual water during the growing season. Several species grow naturally alongside waterfalls and could be employed near water features in the garden, if the soil remains moist. Several can spread aggressively.

PROPAGATION From cuttings taken in summer before flowering begins, or divide in early spring just as growth resumes. Fresh seed germinates well.

PROBLEMS Slugs. Virus diseases are also common and are easily transmitted from plant to plant by insects, especially aphids. The symptoms are dark purple blotches on the petals; there is no cure, so infected plants should be burned.

T. 'Adbane' Clumps of glossy, green foliage spread strongly and are capped, in late summer and early fall, by open heads of starry, lavender flowers with dark purple spotting. A Japanese hybrid. ‡ 30 in (75 cm). Z5–9 H9–5

T. affinis Arching stems covered in stiff hairs carry oval, sharply pointed, hairy, silvery green, or spotted leaves to 4 in (10 cm) with small clusters of upward-facing, 1 in (2.5 cm), white flowers spotted with purple carried in the leaf joints in late late summer and early fall. From Japan. ‡ 3¼ ft (1 m). Z5–9 H9–5. **'Key Lime Pie'** Foliage with a green central stripe. Selected by Massachusetts horticulturist Darrell Probst.

T. bakeri see *T. latifolia*

T. dilitata see *T. macropoda*

T. 'Empress' Extra-large white flowers with narrow petals heavily spotted with purple are held in terminal clusters in early and mid-fall. Spreads strongly. A hybrid of *T. formosana*. ‡ 3¼ ft (1 m). Z5–9 H9–5

T. flava subsp. **ohsumiensis** see *T. ohsumiensis*

T. formosana Spreading strongly, the erect stems are brownish at the base, fading to green at the top, and slightly hairy. They carry glossy, green, heart-shaped leaves to 2 in (5 cm) long that clasp the stem, especially high on the plant, and usually lavender, purple-spotted flowers in terminal clusters late in the season. This is a very variable plant in its flower coloring. Only flowers dependably in mild climates with a long, frost-free fall. From Taiwan. ‡ 3¼ ft (1 m). Z6–9 H9–6. **'Dark Beauty'** Deep purple flowers and dark green foliage. **'Gilt Edge'** Leaves edged in gold and with slightly earlier, white-spotted, purple flowers. Selected in Japan. ‡ 12 in (30 cm). **'Gilty Pleasure'** Golden foliage. A spontaneous mutation of 'Gilt Edge' with lavender- and purple-spotted flowers in early fall. **'Samurai'** Leaves with an irregular, creamy white edge and purple, plum-spotted flowers in early fall. ‡ 16 ft (5.5 m). **'Shelley's'** Pure white flowers, boldly spotted in dark purple. **Stolonifera Group** Aggressively spreading, the purple-pink, plum-spotted flowers open from midsummer to early fall, so they avoid most early frosts. Probably a hybrid between *T. hirta* and *T. formosana*. ‡ 3.5 ft (1.1 m). **'Variegata'** Leaves narrowly rimmed in yellow; purple-pink flowers.

T. hirta A compact rootstock supports densely hairy stems bearing dark green, heart-shaped, hairy, ¾–2 in (2–5 cm) leaves, clasping the stems. The upward-facing white flowers are spotted purple and appear both at the tips of the shoots and from the upper leaf joints in late summer. *T. macropoda* is sometimes sold under this name. From Japan.

‡ 36 in (88 cm). Z4–9 H9–8. **'Alba'** Pure white flowers from late summer to mid-fall on somewhat arching stems. **'Albomarginata'** Leaves with a narrow, creamy white margin; the white flowers are spotted deep purple. **'Golden Gleam'** Golden foliage in spring, white flowers speckled in lavender. **'Miyazaki'** Develops into colonies of somewhat arching stems with a profuse display of light lavender-pink flowers. Tolerates more sun than most. ‡ 30 in (75 cm). **'Variegata'** Leaves edged with a narrow, white band; pretty mauve, purple-spotted flowers open in late summer.

T. 'Hototogisu' Dense, low-growing, and vigorously spreading plant with arching stems and uniquely colored lavender-blue flowers, the color intensifying in cooler temperatures in late summer and early fall. Oddly, *hototogisu* is the Japanese common name for all *Tricyrtis*. Probably a hybrid of *T. hirta*. From Japan. ‡ 24 in (60 cm). Z5–9 H9–5

T. ishiiana Spreading boldly, the densely produced stems carry broad, dark green foliage to 4 in (10 cm) and relatively large, butter yellow, almost tubular flowers, rustily spotted within, produced at the tip of the shoots and in the leaf joints during late summer and early fall. Very distinctive but needing full shade, and rich, acidic, moist but well-drained soil. Especially prone to slug damage. From Japan. ‡ 24 in (60 cm). Z4–8 H8–4

T. 'Kohaku' White and yellow-suffused flowers with bold burgundy spotting are carried in clusters in the leaf joints from midsummer to early fall. Spreads steadily. A lovely recent Japanese hybrid. ‡ 30 in (75 cm). Z5–8 H8–5

T. latifolia syn. *T. bakeri* The earliest, easiest, and most easily recognizable of all species, the erect, hairy stems carry broadly oval, 3 in (8 cm) foliage, heart-shaped at the base and clasping the stems. It is topped by upward facing, mustard-yellow, brown-spotted flowers in clusters from early to late summer. From Japan and China, ‡ 30 in (75 cm). Z5–9 H9–5

ABOVE 1 *Tricyrtis formosana* 'Variegata'
2 *T. hirta* 'Variegata' **3** *T.* 'Kohaku'
4 *T.* 'Tojen'

T. 'Lemon Lime' Lovely golden foliage, lightly spotted with green contrasts the heavy, deep purple spotting on the clusters of lavender flowers. ‡ 24 in (60 cm). Z5–9 H9–5

T. 'Lightning Strike' Large, green, oval leaves streaked in yellow; the lavender flowers, spotted with purple, appear in midsummer to mid-fall. Spreads steadily. Very effective in deeply shaded sites in evenly moist soil. From Japan. ‡ 30 in (75 cm). Z4–8 H8–4

T. 'Lilac Towers' Stiffly upright, slightly downy stems carry hairy, lightly spotted leaves and clusters of white, purple-spotted flowers at the shoot tips and in the leaf joints at midsummer. Often sold as a cultivar of *T. hirta*; may be a hybrid between *T. hirta* and *T. affinis*. ‡ 3¼ ft (1 m). Z5–8 H8–5

T. macrantha A distinctive species with arching stems, sometimes touching the ground, and covered with rough brown hairs; the clasping leaves are oval to lance-shaped or linear and dark glossy green. Very large, 1¼–1½ in (3–4 cm), tubular, yellow flowers, spotted brown inside, are carried in the leaf joints from late summer to mid-fall. From wet areas in southern Japan. ‡ 36 in (90 cm). Z8–9 H9–8. **subsp. macranthopsis** Smooth stems and leaves more deeply cut at the base. The yellow, tubular flowers are spotted purple-brown. **subsp. macranthopsis 'Juro'** Fully double, lemon yellow flowers.

T. macropoda syn. *T. dilitata* Hardy and pretty, the oval, bright green, waxy textured, oval foliage, 4–4¾ in (10–12 cm) long, is held along upright slender stems, which carry creamy-white, ⅜–¾ in (1.5–2 cm) flowers, spotted with purple, in the upper leaf joints from midsummer to early fall. This name has been mistakenly applied to a number of different plants, so beware. From Japan and Korea. ‡ 36 in (90 cm). Z5–8 H8–5

T. 'Moonlight Treasure' Large, buttery yellow flowers in clusters of two to five at almost every leaf joint in late summer and early fall are set off by tough, leathery, silvered and spotted foliage. Better than most in dry conditions. Perhaps a form of *T. ishiiana*. ‡10 in (25 cm). Z4–8 H8–4

T. ohsumiensis syn. *T. flava* subsp. *ohsumiensis* A distinctive and demure species forming many-stemmed clumps of stiffly upright stems carrying broad, 2–8 in (5–20 cm), elliptical to oblong leaves, clasping the stem at the base, and large, 1¼ in (3 cm), butter-yellow, upright-facing flowers in late summer and fall. It is especially susceptible to slug damage when emerging in early spring. From southern Japan. ‡24 in (10 cm). Z4–7 H7–4

T. 'Shimone' Upright, spreading stems topped with clusters of very fragrant, white flowers, intensely spotted with rich reddish purple, in late summer to mid-fall at the leaf joints and stem tips. This may be the same as 'Sinonome'. Perhaps a hybrid of *T. hirta*, selected in Japan. ‡36 in (90 cm). Z5–8 H8–5

T. 'Tojen' Elegantly arching stems carry large, glossy, dark green leaves with yellow-throated, clear lavender-purple, orchidlike flowers fading to white in late summer and early fall. A vigorous, popular, and widely available hybrid and a good cut flower. ‡30 in (75 cm). Z5–8 H8–5

T. 'White Towers' Short, upright, rather slow plant with hairy stems and leaves and a pretty display of white flowers with purple anthers held tightly in the leaf joints. Similar in general appearance to 'Lilac Towers' and perhaps a hybrid between *T. hirta* and *T. affinis*. Confused with *T. latifolia* 'Alba', which flowers earlier with the flowers in clusters at the branch tips. ‡12–18 in (30–45 cm). Z5–9 H9–5

TRIFOLIUM
Clover
PAPILIONACEAE

Unexpectedly colorful clovers for the herbaceous border or naturalized planting.

Over 200 of annual, biennial, or perennial species are from most temperate and subtropical regions of the world, with the notable exception of Australasia. Upright to sprawling stems carry the typical clover leaves made up of three leaflets, although four, five, and seven leaflets are known in some cultivars; they are always held alternately on the stem. The flowerheads can be at the ends of the branches, or in the leaf joints. The individual flowers are pealike but much reduced in size, and are usually crowded together in large numbers. Many species are considered weedy and invasive; however, some are suitable for growing as ornamentals and have become popular in recent years for either flowering or foliage effect.

They look particularly effective when grown in longer grasslands and wildflower meadows and are a source of nectar for bees and other insects.

CULTIVATION Sun is required and fertile, moist but well-drained, soil preferred.

PROPAGATION By division or from seed.

PROBLEMS Pea and bean weevil

T. ochroleucum (Sulfur clover) Upright and hairy, with each leaf split into three more or less lance-shaped leaflets up to 1¼ in (3 cm) long and about a third as wide. Pale whitish yellow flowers are gathered in spherical or rather oblong heads, with short stalks or sometimes none, at the tips of the shoots. Care should be taken in siting as it can become invasive. From shady or damp places in Europe and Asia. ‡12–20 in (30–50 cm). Z6–9 H9–6

T. pannonicum (Hungarian clover) Bushy, upright perennial, about as wide as it is high. Each branch has reverse egg-shaped leaflets toward the base changing to more or less lance-shaped leaflets toward the top. The stems are topped with large heads, up to 4 in (10 cm) in length, of attractive creamy yellow flowers. Due to its height, it might require some support. Makes a good cut flower. From meadows and open scrub in southeastern Europe. ‡3¼ ft (1 m). Z6–9 H9–6

T. pratense (Red clover) Upright or spreading perennial with reverse, egg-shaped to almost round leaves that are hairy on the undersides. Flowerheads about ¾ in (2 cm) in diameter, and usually stalkless, are crowded with tiny pink, white, or cream in flowers. Prefers neutral, slightly moist soil, but will grow adequately in others. Can be grown as a green manure and is particularly beneficial to the soil due to the nitrogen-fixing capabilities of bacteria in its roots. Native to most of Europe and naturalized in North America. ‡8–24 in (20–60 cm). Z6–9 H9–6. **'Dolly North'** *see* 'Susan Smith'. **'Gold Net'** *see* 'Susan Smith'. **'Nina'** Yellow leaves; rather weak. **'Susan Smith'** Variegated, the green leaves have their veins marked with yellow.

T. repens (White clover) Creeping stems, 8–20 in (20–50 cm) long, which root from the leaf joints, carry leaves usually with three leaflets, each reverse egg-shaped or reverse heart-shaped, often with an angled, whitish band toward the base. Clusters of small white flowers, sometimes tinged with red, are held at the leaf joints during the spring, summer, and into the fall on short stalks. Only cultivars are usually grown, some of which are by-products of a commercial breeding program aimed at improving clover as an agricultural crop. Prefers well-drained, alkaline soil conditions and can be grown as a green manure, although it can become invasive. Many look good weaving around heucheras, but the effect can be

ruined by weevils. Naturalized in North America but native to Europe. ‡8–24 in (20–60 cm). Z3–11 H11–3. **'Atropurpureum'** *see* 'Purpurascens'. **'Dragon's Blood'** White and green variegated leaves with red splashes. **'Good Luck'** Leaves with four or more leaflets, each blotched at the base with dark red. **'Green Ice'** syn. 'Ice Cool' Each leaflet has a silver center. **'Harlequin'** Each leaflet is silver, with a triangular, green mark at the base, at the tip of which is a little red feathering. The effect is to give the whole leaf a bold, triangular center. **'Pentaphyllum'** *see* 'Quinquefolium'. **'Purpurascens'** syn. 'Atropurpureum' Purple-bronze leaves with a green margin. **'Purpurascens Quadrifolium'** syn. 'Tetraphyllum Purpureum' Purple-bronze leaves with four leaflets; flowers white. **'Quinquefolium'** syn. 'Pentaphyllum' Purple-bronze leaves with five leaflets; flowers yellow. **'Tetraphyllum Purpureum'** *see* 'Purpurascens Quadrifolium'. **'Wheatfen'** Purple leaves and deep red flowers. **'William'** Green leaflets with the outer half to two-thirds of each tinged with pink to magenta. Found by William Lyall of Manor Nursery in Essex, England, in his lawn.

T. rubens A very ornamental bushy, upright, perennial with blue green, more or less lance-shaped leaflets with tiny teeth and silvery hairs giving them a velvety texture. The pointed flower clusters, up to 3 x 1 in (8 x 2.5 cm), are silvery at first, then the deep red flowers open from the bottom up, creating impressive, silver-tipped, crimson cones. They are held singly, or sometimes in pairs, at the stem tips. Can be grown as a green manure; the flowers are also good for cutting. Native to central and eastern Europe. ‡12–24 in (30–60 cm). Z5–9 H9–5. **'Peach Pink'** Flowers pale pink.

TRILLIUM
TRILLIACEAE

Captivating spring woodlanders; they excite passion and dedicated cultivation.

Extremely popular temperate-zone woodland or shade garden plants, with almost fifty species native to eastern and western North America, and eastern Asia—from the Himalayan Mountains to Japan and the Kamtchatka Peninsula.

Trilliums are deciduous, long-lived, spring flowering, herbaceous perennials, consisting of a horizontal or somewhat bulblike, semi-upright underground stem, the rhizome, which is covered with dry scales that represent the true leaves. A large, single, terminal bud gives rise to all above-ground growth, including the one or two, or rarely three, stems.

In most species, the other end of the rhizome appears "cut off" by

RIGHT **1** *Trifolium pratense* 'Susan Smith' **2** *T. repens* **3** *T. rubens*

a controlled deterioration of the rhizome from the previous year. Along the rhizome, under the dry scales, lie dormant buds that may or may not give rise to new plantlets, according to species and the growing conditions for each individual plant.

When growth begins, the terminal bud gives rise to a specialized flowering branch that is loosely termed the stem but more correctly called the scape or peduncle. At the top, all adult trilliums normally produce three approximately equal-sized, roughly rhombic, egg-shaped or oval leaves with pointed tips. Unlike the closely related members of the lily family, the leaves are net-veined.

The flowers consist of three petals and three alternating sepals. The plants fall into two groups: in some species, each flower is carried on a short stalk (pedicel) above uniformly green leaves; these are termed the pedicellate trilliums, each flower being held on a pedicel. In the other, sessile group, the flower sits directly on the leaves (sessile: without a pedicel) and the leaves are patterned with sparse to widespread, pale to intensely darker green and bronze mottling. In the latter group, the petals tend to stand more or less erect and are closely clustered, while in the former group, they are more flared.

The petal colors range from white to deep maroon red or purple-brown and may be solid-colored or with markings of another color. The maroon-red or purple-toned species produce mutants in which the red colors are deleted and underlying yellow or green colors remain. Fruits consist of a fleshy, berrylike capsule containing seeds with an oily area that is attractive to ants that carry them off. All parts of the plant are toxic to humans. Deer, however, can eat them with impunity.

PARTNERS IN THE SHADE

THIS IS GOOD EXAMPLE of an upright, clump-forming plant effectively fronted by a smaller, more delicate plant, which creeps between and around its stems. *Trillium chloropetalum* is one of the more robust trilliums and makes impressive spring clumps when not caught by late frosts.

In front, the elegant, creeping *Tiarella cordifolia*—here, the rarely seen 'Slick Rock'—intermingles with the trillium stems, its graceful foliage and foamy white spikes providing a pretty contrast to the broader trillium leaves. If it strays too far, pieces of the tiarella can easily be removed.

LEFT *Trillium chloropetalum*

Not all species are equally gardenworthy. Some, especially among the sessile species, are too similar to each other. The pedicellate species are generally more colorful, in some cases more conspicuous, and more widely grown. However, in recent years, trilliums have inspired devoted study and the accumulation of significant collections featuring many rare variants. Far more species than are covered here are grown in specialist collections, but many are only occasionally available from nurseries or are difficult to grow.

CULTIVATION Most trillium species enjoy the shade of deciduous trees but will also tolerate nearly full light in a garden setting. They prefer ordinary garden soil that is slightly acidic, neutral, or slightly alkaline. Well-rotted leaf mold benefits most species, but avoid peat, which may encourage the rhizomes to rot. Fertilize lightly before the leaves appear. Most tolerate considerable summer drought and are very hardy, but can be damaged by late frosts.

PROPAGATION By division or from seed. Seed propagation is a very slow process, seedlings flowering after four to seven years. Division of the rhizome after flowering is more practical (*see* Dividing Trilliums, *p. 461*).

PROBLEMS Aphids, slugs, and deer. In the wild, the overpopulation of deer has caused trillium decimation equaled only by the bulldozer.

T. albidum (Sessile) (White toadshade) A robust, easily clump-forming species; the large egg-shaped to rhombic overlapping leaves, to 8 x 6 in (20 x 15 cm), are strongly to weakly mottled with dark spots, which often fade late in the season. The large, showy, diamond-shaped petals, to 3 x 1¼ in (7.8 x 3 cm), are white, cream, or slightly pink at the base and flare slightly as they rise brightly from the trio of leaves. One of the showiest and most adaptable species; thrives in any rich, more or less neutral soil. Native to coastal forests, meadows, and thickets, from California north to Oregon. ‡9–24 in (22–60 cm). Z6–9 H9–6

T. catesbaei (Pedicellate) Slender plant

with flowers nodding below and sometimes obscured by the elliptical to egg-shaped leaves, to 6 x 3 in (15 x 8 cm), although in most plants the narrow leaves lift enough to make the plants and flowers fairly showy. The green sepals are noticeably recurved, and the leaves enlarge after flowering. The wide petals, to 2 x ¾ in (5 x 2 cm), are strongly recurved, wavy toward the tip, and may be white, pink, or deep rose, deepening in color with age; they have contrasting bright yellow anthers. Best in acidic soil in light shade; can be tricky and does not form large clumps. Grows in acidic soil under evergreen shrubs. From the southeastern US. ‡8–16 in (20–40 cm). Z7–9 H8–1

T. chloropetalum (Sessile) (Giant trillium) A large, robust, and highly variable species with weakly to strongly mottled, broadly egg-shaped leaves, about 2¾–6½ in (7–17 cm) long and as wide, and somewhat rounded at the tip. The flowers are altogether variable. From 1¾–3½ in (4.5–9 cm) long and ⅜–1 in (1.5–2.5 cm) wide, the petal shape is rather variable with a wedge-shaped base and the tip more or less rounded or with a weakly pointed tip or even appearing cut off. The color may be cream, white, yellowish,

ABOVE **1** *Trillium erectum*
2 *T. grandiflorum*

greenish, dark red-maroon, purple, or brown. Much confused with *T. sessile* but larger and far more showy. From California. ‡ 8–24 in (20–60 cm). Z6–9 H9–6. **var. *chloropetalum*** The petals are never white and always have an underlying yellow pigment often obscured by the red-purple or brown overtones. ‡ 8–16 in (20–40 cm). **var. *giganteum*** Petals range from white to deep garnet purple, no underlying yellow. ‡ 16–24 in (40–60 cm).

T. cuneatum (Sessile) (Whippoorwill flower) Making good-sized, vigorous, imposing clumps, the egg-shaped leaves, to 7 x 5 in (18 x 13 cm), are strongly mottled at flowering, the mottling fading later in the season. Petals typically up to 2½ x 1¼ in (6 x 3 cm) dark maroon, brown-purple—rarely green, yellow, or bicolored—and darkest at the base. Less easy to grow in mild regions than *T. chloropetalum* since it requires a steady winter cold spell. Best in an alkaline soil but also tolerates acidic conditions. From the southeastern US. ‡ 6–18 in (16–45 cm). Z6–9 H9–6

T. erectum (Pedicellate) (Red trilllium) Early-flowering, clump-forming species, the leaves are rhombic in shape, widest near the middle, 2–8 in (5–20 cm) long and wide, and with a long-pointed tip. Typically, the flowers open dark maroon-red, fading to dull purple, but may also be cream, yellow, white, or pink. The petals are lance-shaped, to 2 x 1¼ in (5 x 3 cm), with a slender point, or egg-shaped. In some plants, the flowers are held erect on their stalks; in some they dangle above or even under the leaves. Easy to grow in moist, well-drained, weakly acidic to neutral woodland soil, resistant to frost damage, and relatively easy to divide. Hybridizes with a number of other species in the wild. From deciduous woods in eastern Canada, south to the southeastern US. ‡ 4–24 in (10–60 cm). Z4–7 H7–3. **f. *albiflorum*** White flowers. **'Beige'** Beige flowers. **f. *luteum*** Yellow flowers, sometimes with dark veins.

T. flexipes (Pedicellate) (Bent trillium) Tall, showy, robust though rather variable plant; the rhombic leaves are 2¾–10 in (7–25 cm) long and as wide, and almost overlapping in many forms. The flower stalk (pedicel) varies from stiffly erect in the best garden forms to leaning or drooping. The tip of the

pedicel, just behind the flower, is flexed like a bent knee so the flowers are displayed facing outward. The flowers are unusually heavy-textured and long-lasting, occasionally fragrant, with petals egg-shaped or reverse egg-shaped, white or creamy white, to 2 x 1½ in (5 x 4 cm), and followed by large fruits like crab apples. Sometimes produces lovely hybrids with *T. erectum*. The plant prefers neutral soil, but will tolerate any but strongly acidic soil. From the eastern US. ‡ 8–20 in (20–50 cm). Z4–7 H7–3

T. grandiflorum (Pedicellate) (Wake robin) One of the showiest and largest-flowered white trilliums, and often a

natural clump-former, the dark green leaves, to 8 x 6 in (20 x 15 cm), are more or less egg-shaped, sometimes with dark wine-maroon undertones when young. The large, funnel-shaped flowers are pure white, fading to dull purple with age, with overlapping, thin-textured petals, to 3 x 1½ in (7.5 x 4 cm). A wonderful shade plant in the eastern US, but the similar *T. ovatum* may be easier to cultivate in other areas. Grow in more or less neutral to slightly acidic soil, enriched with woodland leaf mold. More susceptible to botrytis than most species. From Quebec, Canada, south to the eastern US. ‡ 4–12 in (10–30 cm). Z4–7 H7–3. **'Flore Pleno'** Double

DIVIDING TRILLIUMS

Most trilliums increase slowly, yet because they take so long to flower from seed, it is tempting to divide the plants. Clump-forming species are more effective in the garden if left to increase undisturbed, but if they must be split, do it carefully. After flowering, dig up the plant and cut off the terminal bud and about one inch of rhizome. The terminal bud produces a hormone that inhibits the growth of the buds behind it on the rhizome. When the cut surface is dry, treat each surface with sulfur or other fungicide.

Plant the terminal bud section as insurance for the future; it may even flower the following season. The remainder of the rhizome should be promptly replanted and, freed from the inhibiting effects of the terminal bud, one or more of the dormant buds should form small offset plantlets the following year. These new shoots can be left to develop into a multi-stemmed clump, or they can be removed when dormant and planted separately. The offsets will flower faster than the seedlings.

TRILLIUM FLOWERS

Trilliums are divided into two groups according to how the flowers are held above the three leaves. Flowers of pedicellate species, such as those of *T. ovatum*, are held on stalks (pedicels) ½–2½ in (1–6 cm) long, and their petals tend to flare widely. Those of sessile species, such as *T. chloropetalum*, are held directly above the leaves without a stalk (sessile) and the petals tend to be held more or less erect.

Trillium chloropetalum

Trillium ovatum

flowers. Various double-flowered forms are found in the wild and in gardens.

f. roseum Pink, the exact shade depending on soil and climate.

'Snowbunting' Perfect, double white, gardenia-like flowers. Found in Erin, New York, by the local postmaster in 1924 and eventually passed to Montreal Botanic Gardens, from where it was more widely distributed.

T. kurabayashii (Sessile) Large, vigorous clump-former, the egg-shaped leaves, to 9 x 6½ in (22 x 17 cm), are green, without the slight bluish tones seen in the similar *T. cuneatum*, highly to weakly mottled, and rather drooping. The upright, flaring petals, to 4 x 14 in (10 x 35 cm), are reverse-spear-shaped and very dark maroon or red-purple, rarely clear or muddy pale yellow or greenish. Sometimes, incorrectly, grown as *T. sessile californicum* and was previously considered a form of *T. chloropetalum*. Enjoys rich loamy soil and responds to fertilizers, becoming large and vigorous, but susceptible to frost damage in some areas. Local in coastal northern California and in the Northern Sierras. ‡8–24 in (20–60 cm). Z6–9 H9–6

T. luteum (Sessile) (Yellow trillium) Robust plant, sometimes but not always forming clumps, bearing heavily mottled, egg-shaped to almost round leaves, to 6½ x 4 in (17 x 10 cm). The very long-lasting, strongly lemon-scented flowers have spear-shaped petals, to 2½ x ¾ in (6 x 2 cm), in a strong to weak lemon yellow color or, occasionally, in greenish yellow. Easy in more or less neutral to slightly alkaline soil, but intolerant of highly organic or acidic soil and excellent both in eastern North America and Europe, though sometimes susceptible to botrytis. From the eastern US. Very abundant near the

Great Smoky Mountains National Park. ‡4–16 in (10–40 cm). Z5–7 H7–4

T. ovatum (Pedicellate) (Western white trillium) Like a smaller version of the more familiar *T. grandiflorum*, from which it can be difficult to distinguish: the egg-shaped to rhombic leaves, to 8 x 4¾ in (20 x 12 cm), with prominent main veins, are medium to dark green, some individuals showing a dark maroon undertone when young. The white petals, to 2¾ x 1½ in (7 x 4 cm), fading with age to rose pink, often have darker tones near the main petal veins, rarely overlap each other, and are usually narrower and less wavy than those of *T. grandiflorum*. Generally easy to cultivate, but susceptible to damage from late frosts. Grows from California north to British Columbia, Canada, and in the western US, but there are also isolated populations in southern Colorado and northern Wyoming. ‡6–28 in (15–70 cm). Z5–8 H8–5.

f. hibbersonii Dwarf, often pale pink. Found only on Vancouver Island and in British Columbia, Canada. ‡2–10 in (5–25 cm).

T. recurvatum (Sessile) (Prairie trillium) Tall, distinctive, but hardly beautiful, with brittle rhizomes, not much thicker than a heavy pencil, at the soil surface. Egg-shaped, elliptical, or spear-shaped leaves, to 7 x 2½ in (18 x 6 cm), have strong dark mottling and, unusually, they have noticeable stalks. The sepals reflex down and back distinctively against the stem and the egg-shaped, pointed, erect, dark purple-maroon petals, to 2 x ¾ in (5 x 2 cm), exaggerate the tallness. Very easy in a fairly heavy clay loam and thrives in most except acidic peaty soil. Responds well to a general fertilizer. From the eastern US. ‡6–20 in (15–50 cm). Z5–8 H8–3

T. rivale syn. *Pseudotrillium rivale* (Pedicellate) (Brook wake robin) A small plant, 1¼–2 in (3–5 cm) tall at blooming, and often forming clumps; the plant continues to expand during and, for a while, after flowering. The glossy green leaves, to 3 x 2½ in (8 x 6 cm), have a slight bluish cast and may be uniformly colored, or the principal veins may be of a lighter silverish green that makes the plant even more attractive. They are held on ½–1¼ in (1–3 cm) stalks. The egg-shaped or almost round, white petals, to 1¼ x 1 in (3 x 2.5 cm), abruptly taper to a short, nipplelike tip and usually have a few to many moderate to strong red—mostly basal flecks—some plants are so heavily flecked they appear almost solid purple. After pollination, the erect flowers bend beneath the leaves to develop their seeds. Small, but one of the finest and most charming of all species, and well worth a good spot high in acidic humus. Plant deeply in cold areas. Sometimes now placed in its own genus, *Pseudotrillium*. From northern California and Oregon. ‡4–6 in (10–15 cm). Z5–8 H8–5

T. sessile (Sessile) (Sessile trillium) A less showy species, the leaves are rather broadly attached at the base and oval or almost round, to 4 x 3 in (10 x 8 cm), weakly to strongly mottled, the mottling fading after flowering. The petals are elliptical to spear-shaped, to 14 x ¾ in (35 x 2 cm), usually maroon-red with brownish undertones, becoming browner and less attractive with age. Yellow-petaled forms are often only dry-straw-colored, or muddy. Early-blooming and long-lasting, less flamboyant than many but interesting in massed plantings. It is often confused with other species, especially the dark forms of *T. chloropetalum* and *T. cuneatum*,

which have been supplied in its place. Widespread across the eastern US. ‡3–10 in (8–25 cm). Z4–8 H8–1

T. sulcatum (Pedicellate) Very large, splendid plant with overlapping, rhombic to reverse egg-shaped leaves, to 8 x 9 in (20 x 22 cm). The flowers, borne on 2½–4½ in (6–11 cm), stiffly erect stalks, flexed at the top, display the large, dark red-maroon, broadly egg-shaped petals, to 2 x 1¼ in (5 x 3 cm), to great advantage. Flowers may also be white, creamy, grizzled tan, rose, picoteed, clear strong yellow, or bicolored, though these may be hybrids. Petal carriage varies from being held forward, like a candle snuffer, to somewhat recurved, giving the flower a flat, gaping look. Similar to *T. erectum* but more showy and with kinked flower stalks. From the eastern US. ‡12–28 in (30–70 cm). Z6–8 H8–6

T. undulatum (Pedicellate) (Painted trillium) Distinctive and colorful plants, the stem emerges from the ground with the flower bud already partially unfurled and petal colors showing. As it expands, entire plant is a dark greenish maroon or wine color; the dark coloring persists until full blooming, when it begins to fade to dark green. The egg-shaped leaves, to 11 x 4½ in (28 x 11 cm), have a definite stalk; the petals, to 2 x ¾ in (5 x 2 cm), spread widely to create a flattish bloom, and the outer half of each petal is wavy. Each petal is white with, at the base, an inverted V-shaped, dark red mark with a few dark red veins radiating from it. When pollinated, the petals fade in a few hours to a translucent white. The round, bright scarlet fruit is impressive but it is quickly eaten by

BELOW 1 *Trillium luteum* **2** *T. sessile*

PHYTOPLASMA INFECTIONS

In wild populations of *Trillium grandiflorum*, petals with green stripes, picotees, and petal enlargement may occur. Some plants completely change character, producing tufts of leaves or unusually long flower stalks. This condition has been shown to be caused by infection from phytoplasma, organisms not unlike viruses, which creates these sometimes rather attractive results. The condition may stabilize and plants may bloom with the same deformities for years, or the plants may deteriorate rapidly and die.

The infected plants can be very attractive, but there is not yet full agreement on the extent to which infection harms the plant: some enthusiasts promptly destroy any plant that shows the signs of infection, since there is no effective treatment. Other enthusiasts treat them as valuable members of their collection. Although many of the green striped or patterned forms are undeniably enticing and were given names by early botanists, the former course seems wiser.

The organism is believed to be spread by leafhoppers or other sucking insects and has also appeared in *T. erectum* and *T. undulatum*. The same type of organism causes the distortions seen in parrot tulips, aster yellows disease, and green petal disease of strawberries.

birds. It is difficult to grow outside its native regions, but it does grow well in deep, humus-rich, acidic, cool soil. From Quebec and the Canadian Maritime provinces to the eastern US. ‡8–24 in (20–60 cm). Z4–8 H8–1

T. vaseyi (Pedicellate) (Sweet beth) A grand plant, the largest in its group and with the largest flower, the rhombic leaves, 4–8 in (10–20 cm) long and as wide, cover the bloom like an umbrella. However, the flower stalk is 1½–3 in (4–8 cm) long and the bloom is not obscured; indeed, on vigorous plants, the size of the flower displayed below the leaves is startling; the petals are a deep crimson, maroon red, or a brownish red and up to 2¾ x 2½ in (7 x 6 cm). The plant benefits from rich leaf mold in the soil, at least part-shade, and protection from wind. From lower slopes and valley floors of the mountains in the southeastern US. ‡12–24 in (30–60 cm). Z6–8 H8–6

TRITONIA *see* CROCOSMIA

TROLLIUS
Globe flower
RANUNCULACEAE

Hardy and coolly elegant moisture-loving plants for a damp border or sunny pond margin.

About 30 species of deciduous perennials growing in wet meadows, streamsides, and mountain gullies in Europe, northern Asia, and North America. Compact clumps of leaves, attractively lobed or fingered and each division again divided or toothed, throw up erect stems, each bearing similar and alternately arranged leaves; topped in early summer by a solitary bowl- or cup-shaped flower. These have up to 15 showy, outer petal-like sepals, and about the same number of narrow inner petals, and are followed by clusters of seedpods. Supreme bog garden plants, and always well-behaved.

CULTIVATION Grow in full sun or part-shade, in moist soil on a pond or stream bank, or in a border if the soil is constantly moist.

PROPAGATION By division or from seed.

PROBLEMS Powdery mildew.

T. chinensis Compact, clump-forming, plant, the dark green, 2½–4¾ in (6–12 cm) basal leaves are deeply divided into five lance-shaped lobes, themselves lobed and toothed. Erect, leafy stems bear three to seven smaller versions of the basal leaves and are topped by solitary, shallowly bowl-shaped, yellow flowers with erect, orange-yellow, spiky inner petals. From damp grasslands in northeastern China. ‡24–36 in (60–90 cm). Z4–8 H8–1. **‘Golden Queen’** Forms a compact clump of dark green, deeply cut basal leaves. In late spring and early summer, bowl-shaped, rich orange, 2 in (5 cm) flowers, with prominent inner petals, are carried well above the foliage. ‡24 in (60 cm). Z3–7 H7–1

T. x *cultorum* Clump-forming, with attractively divided, dark green leaves and many solitary, globular or cup-shaped flowers, 1½–2¾ in (4–7 cm) across, in shades of yellow. Complex garden hybrids probably involving *T. europaeus*, *T. chinensis*, and the rarely seen *T. asiaticus*. There are many cultivars, mostly compact plants flowering in late spring and early summer. Easily grown in moist soil in a sunny position. ‡24–36 in (60–90 cm). Z3–7 H7–1. **‘Alabaster’** Globe-shaped, pale creamy yellow flowers in late spring and early summer. Not very vigorous. ‡24 in (60 cm). **‘Canary Bird’** Rounded, clear lemon-yellow flowers. ‡30 in (75 cm). **‘Cheddar’** Cupped, semidouble, creamy yellow, 2 in (5 cm) flowers. ‡18–24 in (45–60 cm). **‘Earliest of All’** Light yellow flowers in mid- and late spring. ‡20 in (50 cm). **‘Etna’** Flowers deep orange. **‘Feuertroll’** Deep orange-yellow flowers with darker orange inner petals. ‡26 in (65 cm). **‘Goldquelle’** Bright yellow, 2¾ in (7 cm) flowers in early summer. ‡30 in (75 cm). **‘Lemon Queen’** Pale lemon-yellow, 2¾ in (7 cm) flowers in late spring and early summer. ‡24 in (60 cm). **‘Orange**

RIGHT 1 *Trollius chinensis* ‘Golden Queen’ **2** *T.* x *cultorum* ‘Alabaster’ **3** *T.* x *cultorum* ‘Earliest of All’

LEFT 1 *Trollius* x *cultorum* 'Lemon Queen' **2** *T.* x *cultorum* 'Orange Princess' **3** *T. pumilus* **4** *T. stenopetalus*

Globe' Globe-shaped, golden orange flowers. ‡ 24 in (60 cm). **'Orange Princess'** Strong growing with deep orange-yellow flowers. ‡ 36 in (90 cm). **'Prichard's Giant'** Tall, with rich orange-yellow flowers. ‡ 36 in (90 cm). **'Superbus'** Golden yellow flowers from late spring to midsummer and a few later. ‡ 20 in (50 cm).

T. europaeus (Globe flower) A variable plant, the compact clumps are formed of mid-green leaves to 4¾ in (12 cm) wide, deeply divided into three to five lobes, each wedge-shaped segment often again lobed and toothed. The erect stems carry reduced versions of the basal leaves and, from late spring or early to late summer, are topped with spherical, clear lemon yellow, 1¼–2 in (3–5 cm) flowers with incurved, petal-like sepals. From damp grassy meadows in lowlands and mountains of Europe, North America, and western Asia. ‡ 24–32 in (60–80 cm). Z5–8 H8–5

T. hondoensis Slender plant forming a compact clump of divided basal leaves to 4¾ in (12 cm) wide. Each erect stems bears a few smaller leaves and a single, buttercup-like flower 1¼–1½ in (3–4 cm) across. The petal-like sepals are deep yellow and form a spreading collar below the crown of narrow inner petals. From stream banks and wet mountain meadows in central Japan. ‡ 16–32 in (40–80 cm). Z5–8 H8–5

T. papavereus see *T. stenopetalus*

T. pumilus Slow-growing, with glossy, five-lobed leaves, 1½–2½ in (4–6 cm) wide, forming a neat tuft. In late spring and early summer, the bright yellow, wide-open flowers like large buttercups, 1–1½ in (2.5–3.5 cm) across and purple on the sepal backs, are produced on erect stems that are usually without leaves. From alpine meadows in Western China, Tibet, and the eastern Himalaya. ‡ 8–12 in (20–30 cm). Z4–6 H8–5

T. stenopetalus syn. *T. papavereus* Long-stalked leaves up to 3 in (8 cm) wide are split into three lobes, and the outer two are often again lobed. The upright stems bear a few smaller leaves and end with a bowl-shaped, yellow flower to 1½ in (4 cm) across opening in late spring and early summer. Like a taller version of *T. pumilus*. From the mountains of northern Burma and western China. ‡ 10–16 in (25–40 cm). Z5–8 H8–5

T. yunnanensis Forms a neat clump of glossy, deeply lobed, rather variable leaves, to 4 in (10 cm) wide, split into three or five more or less egg-shaped lobes, each lobe itself lobed. In early summer and midsummer, the sparsely leafy, erect stems bear a solitary, bowl-shaped, orange-yellow, ¾–1½ in (2–4 cm) flower. From grassy mountain meadows in western China. ‡ 20–28 in (50–70 cm). Z5–8 H8–5

TROPAEOLUM
TROPAEOLACEAE

Attractive climbing versions of the familiar nasturtium—all with a great deal more finesse.

Eighty to ninety climbing or trailing annuals or perennials, many with tuberous roots, from Central and South America. A few perennial species are grown outside in gardens. Alternate leaves are more or less rounded in outline, and may be lobed or toothed; their long leaf stalks often twist around twigs or other structures for support. The loosely funnel-shaped, spurred, usually long-stalked, orange, red or yellow (sometimes blue or purple) flowers are produced individually from the leaf joints and usually have five petals, sometimes fewer, sometimes fringed or more boldly lobed; the upper two petals are distinct from, and often smaller than, the lower three. The distance between the leaves, and hence the flowers, tends to shorten significantly toward the tip of the stems, creating a crowd of flowers.

CULTIVATION Most like moist, well drained, fertile soil in full sun or part-shade. Supports are needed for climbing types. Water and fertilize freely.

PROPAGATION By division of tubers; some will root from spring cuttings.

PROBLEMS Caterpillars, flea beetles, slugs, and black fly.

T. pentaphyllum A delicate but rampant tuberous climbing species with purple stems and leaf stalks; the 1½ in (4 cm) leaves are deeply cut in to five divisions. Soft red flowers, ¾–1¼ in (2–3 cm), with long pink spurs and green interiors spotted in red, are followed by large bunches of dark blue-black berries. Tends to flower in late spring and early summer and then become dormant. Best in a sunny site and well-drained soil. In cold areas, mulch the roots before winter or lift the tubers and store in a frost-free place. From Chile. ‡ 10 ft (3 m). Z8–11 H11–8

T. polyphyllum Spectacular, scrambling, and trailing rather than climbing species making a mat up to 3¼ ft (1 m) across. From a long, slender, very deeply growing tuber emerge usually prostrate stems radiating across the soil. Attractive, long-stalked, silvery gray, deeply lobed foliage, to 3 in (8 cm) long, itself attractive, is a fine background for masses of deep yellow, occasionally orange or ocher, long-spurred, 1½ in (4 cm) flowers, freely produced in summer. Tends to be hardy due to the depth of the rhizomes. Best left undisturbed in a well-drained, sunny place. Difficult to divide as rhizomes may be up to 3¼ ft (1 m) deep. From Chile. ‡ 4 in (10 cm). Z8–11 H11–8

T. speciosum (Scottish flame flower) Delicate, climber for cool climates.

1

2

3

LEFT 1 *Tropaeolum polyphyllum*
2 *T. speciosum* **3** *T. tuberosum* var.
lineamaculatum 'Ken Aslet'

Deep-rooting, thin, white rhizomes
produce slender stems with green, hairy
1½ in (4 cm) leaves, each with up to
seven notched, wedge-shaped lobes.
Long-spurred, 1¼ in (3 cm) flowers are
bright scarlet followed by blue-black
round fruits. Prefers cool, moist but
well drained soil in shade for its roots,
but where its shoots can grow into the
sun—such as under a *Rhododendron*.
Sometimes planted to scramble up yew
hedges, which it does very well. From
Chile. ↕ 12 ft (4 m). Z8–11 H11–8

T. tuberosum Red or purple-tinted
stems grow from large purple-marked,
yellow tubers that are potato-like and
edible. Three to six-lobed, bluish green
leaves, whose long stalks clasp their
supports, carry from their leaf joints
1¼–1½ in (3–4 cm), showy scarlet and
yellow, cup-shaped flowers with scarlet
spurs on slender, red-tinted stalks from
late summer to frost. The tubers are
frost-tender and must be lifted and
stored in frost-free conditions in cold
areas. Cultivated for the tubers in South
America as mashua; a huge range of
local selections have been made but are
rarely grown elsewhere. From Columbia,
Ecuador, Peru, and Bolivia. ↕ 4–6 ft
(1.2–1.8 m). Z8–11 H11–8. **var.
lineamaculatum 'Ken Aslet'** Pretty
two-tone orange and red-tinted flowers
produced earlier than the species on
deep red stalks. Handsome rounded
blue-green foliage. Named for the
former head of the rock garden at the
RHS Garden at Wisley, England. ↕ 25 ft
(8 m). **var. *piliferum* 'Sidney'** Orange
flowers from very slender tubers.

TULBAGHIA
ALLIACEAE

Long-flowering perennials with
narrow, onion-scented foliage and
clusters of starry flowers in summer.
   About 25 species, all native to
central and southern Africa. Only a
few are grown in temperate gardens.
From corms or rhizomes spring
dense clumps of narrow, evergreen
or semi-evergreen, onion-scented,
hairless, green or grayish foliage.
Clusters of about ten starry flowers,
usually in shades of pink, lilac, or
white, are produced throughout
summer on upright stems. Blooms
each have a narrow tube and six
lobes, sometimes with hooked tips,
opening at 90 degrees to the tube,
making a flat-faced flower. Flowers
are sometimes fragrant, especially at
night, and are notable for small
protrusions at the base of each lobe,
the corona, which can look like the
trumpet of a *Narcissus*, but are
usually present in much-reduced
form, as a series of small teeth.

CULTIVATION Best in full sun and in
well-drained soil, and suitable for
gravel gardens, in paving, and at the
base of sunny walls. In cold areas,
grow in pots and overwinter in
frost-free conditions.

PROPAGATION By division or from
seed; seedlings flower in their
second or third year.

PROBLEMS Aphids.

T. 'Fairy Star' Clusters of about ten
pale pink flowers, each of which has a
darker eye. Blooms freely throughout
the summer and early fall. Short. A
hybrid of *T. violacea* and the rarely
seen *T. cominsii,* raised by Bob Brown
of Cotswold Garden Flowers,
Worcestershire, England. ↕ 12 in
(30 cm). Z7–10 H10–7

T. 'John May's Special' Large, purple
flowers with rounded lobe tips; the
inner three lobes are paler at the
base; the corona is white. Best of
the hardier cultivars. ↕ 32 in (80 cm).
Z7–10 H10–7

T. violacea Forms dense clumps of
narrow, grayish green foliage up to
12 in (30 cm) long and ½ in (1 cm)
wide. Leafless, flat, purplish stems are
topped with starry, lightly fragrant, ¾ in
(2 cm), lilac flowers in summer, with
about 10–15 flowers per cluster. Each
lobe has a darker stripe along its center.
Ideal in pots of loam-based potting
mix on a sunny patio or in sheltered,
sunny borders; admired for its long
season of flowers. The rare var. *robustior*
is the parent of the best cultivars due to
its greater vigor and size. From South
Africa. ↕ 18 in (45 cm). Z7–10 H10–7.
'Alba' White flowers opening from
pale pink buds. **'Pallida'** White flowers,
from pink buds with pink corona
segments. **'Silver Lace'** (syn. 'Variegata')
Slightly larger flowers and gray-green
leaves with white stripes. Valuable as a
foliage plant when not in bloom.

TUNICA *see* PETRORHAGIA

RIGHT *Tulbaghia violacea* 'Silver Lace'

U

UNCINIA
Hook sedge
CYPERACEAE

Sedges with colorful foliage and polished seeds, each ending in a distinctive little hook.

About 35 perennial species are found in cool, moist, exposed places from Australia and New Zealand to New Guinea, and in the Americas from Mexico and the West Indies. Loose evergreen tufts, with fibrous roots or sometimes spreading on short runners, have quite narrow, flat leaves keeled at the base and feeling rough along the edges. The Australian and New Zealand species, in particular, often have colorful red to mahogany foliage. The slender, straight flower stems are usually three-sided, and carry rather insignificant, cylindrical flower spikes with the male flowers at the top. The lower female flowers ripen to shiny three-sided nutlets, each with a little hook at the end that attaches itself to fur and fabric and so disperses the seeds.

A cool-season plant that dies back in hot weather, its foliage becomes most colorful from fall to early spring. It looks spectacular when grown in drifts with other cool-season, moisture-loving grasses and sedges and plants with contrasting colors. There is some confusion over the naming of the New Zealand sedges; even botanists sometimes find it difficult to distinguish between the different species.

CULTIVATION Needs well-drained, moisture-retentive soil in full sun. The roots must be kept cool, so cover with pebbles, stones, or a mulch that will contrast with the leaf color. Best in a little shade in areas with hot summers.

PROPAGATION From seed or by division.

PROBLEMS Usually trouble-free.

U. egmontiana (Orange hook sedge) Dense, translucent tufts comprise flat, narrow, ⅛-in (1.5-mm) leaves that are dull red to green with orange streaks and tints, increasing in the fall and through the winter. Slender stems carry thin flower spikes, up to 3½ in (9 cm) long, of reddish green flowers that ripen to shiny black nutlets. Best in groups in a sheltered position by damp path edges or boggy areas. From mountainous regions on tussock grasslands, scrub, and bogs in New Zealand. ‡ 16 in (40 cm). Z8–11 H11–8

U. rubra (see also *U. uncinata rubra*) (Red hook sedge) Loose tufts, spreading in swaths on short runners, comprise very thin, flat, dark red to bronze-green leaves. Long stems carry the narrow, rigid flower spikes, up to 2½ in (6 cm) long, with red to red-brown flowers ripening to a little yellow-brown nutlet with a hook twice its size. Allow it to creep over damp parts of the garden, growing it with contrasting blue and variegated sedges, or keep moist in interesting pots that can be brought inside over winter if necessary. Mostly from mountains and damp peaty places in New Zealand. ‡ 12 in (30 cm). Z8–11 H11–8

U. uncinata (Hook sedge) Dense evergreen tufts of slightly arching, glossy leaves, 1½–2 in (4–5 mm) wide, are variable in color but usually dark green to reddish brown. Slender flower stems appear in July to August, slightly hairy below the very narrow, compressed flower spikes, which are up to 8 in (20 cm) long with yellow to light brown flowers maturing to polished yellow-brown nutlets. It thrives in drier conditions than its native habitat indicates and best in sun or part-shade. Grows from sea level to low mountains in wet crevices, forests, and scrub in New Zealand. ‡ 18 in (45 cm) Z8–11 H11–8. *rubra* A name sometimes used for *U. rubra* and sometimes for particularly well-colored forms of *U. uncinata;* the confusion is exacerbated by the fact that leaf coloration can vary with weather and environment.

UNIOLA *see* CHASMANTHIUM

UROSPERMUM
ASTERACEAE

Resembling a large, hairy but extremely elegant pale-flowered dandelion.

Two Mediterranean species, one annual and one perennial, grow in dryish cultivated places; only the perennial is usually seen in gardens. The foliage may be oblong to lyre-shaped, divided or undivided, and is carried alternately on the stems and, in the perennial species, in a basal rosette. The whole plant exudes a milky sap. The upright stems carry one or a few yellow flowers which, like dandelions, are composed entirely of ray florets, though they may have a dark center. They are followed by fluffy seed-heads, each seed carried on the wind by a tuft of feathery bristles.

A fine plant for the Mediterranean garden and the front of sunny borders, it is also sometimes used as a cut flower.

CULTIVATION Grow in any good, well-drained soil in a sunny position.

PROPAGATION From seed, or by division in spring.

PROBLEMS Usually trouble-free, though not long-lived.

U. dalechampii A rosette of hairy, jaggedly divided, more or less reverse-egg-shaped leaves, 2–7½ in (5–19 cm) long, each lobe turned to point toward the base, supports upright stems clad with smaller, less noticeably divided, alternately arranged versions of the basal leaves. The 2-in (5-cm) flowers are carried singly, or two or three on a stem, and are usually pale yellow, sometimes painted in red, pale purple, or brown on the backs of the outer petals. The tip of each petal is split into five, the margins of each tooth with a fine dark rim. Each flower is followed by an attractive head of fluffy wind-blown seeds. The plant is sometimes short-lived, occasionally biennial. From fields and olive groves from Spain east to the former Yugoslavia. ‡ 16 in (40 cm). Z6–9 H9–6

UVULARIA
Bellwort, Merrybells
CONVALLARIACEAE

Valuable elegant yet tough woodland plants that add distinction to a shady site and make impressive specimens in rich soil.

BELOW **1** *Uncinia uncinata* **2** *U. rubra* **3** *Urospermum dalechampii*

There are five species of herbaceous perennials from the forests of eastern North America. Creeping rhizomes form clumps or small colonies of wiry, erect stems arching at the tips and sometimes branching toward the top. Smooth-edged, stalkless, more or less elliptical leaves are arranged alternately in two ranks along the stem, and may encircle it. Nodding, six-petaled, slender bell-shaped, yellow flowers, up to 2 in (5 cm) long, arise from the uppermost leaf joints.

CULTIVATION Moist but well-drained soil in part-shade, ideally enriched with humus.

PROPAGATION By division or from seed.

PROBLEMS Slugs and snails.

U. grandiflora The largest-flowered species, slowly forming colonies with fleshy roots. The stems, usually with just one branch, carry 2½–5in (6–13cm) long, oval to lance-shaped, downy leaves with white hairs beneath, the bases of the upper ones encircling the stems. In late spring, each stem carries up to four rich yellow flowers to 2 in (5 cm) long. Tolerates alkalinity in humus-rich soil. From most of the

RIGHT 1 *Uvularia grandiflora*
2 *U. grandiflora* var. *pallida*
3 *U. perfoliata* **4** *U. sessilifolia*

eastern U.S., but endangered in some areas. ↕12–26 in (30–65 cm). Z3–8 H7–1. **var. *pallida*** Pale yellow flowers.

U. perfoliata Fleshy-rooted plants making tight colonies; the more or less oval leaves, 1½–4¼ in (4–11 cm) long, have a slightly grayish cast and their bases clasp the stem. The pale yellow flowers, just one per stem, rarely exceed 1¼-in (3-cm) in length. Similar to *U. grandiflora* but less colorful as a garden plant. Does best in acidic soil. From the eastern and southern U.S., but endangered in some states. ↕10–20 in (25–50 cm). Z3–9 H8–1.

U. sessilifolia syn. *Oaksiella sessilifolia* The smallest species, with 2¾–3½ in (7–9 cm) long, oblong to lance-shaped leaves, bright green above and grayish beneath. Pale yellow or straw-colored, ⅝–1-in (1.5–2.5-cm) flowers open singly on slender, usually branched stems from late spring to early summer. From the eastern U.S. into southern Florida. ↕14 in (20–35 cm). Z3–9 H8–1.

SHADES OF YELLOW

THE SLENDER, DAFFODIL YELLOW FLOWERS of *Uvularia grandiflora* stand out brightly among the fresh green foliage as the clump slowly expands. Behind, in this moist border, *Trollius europaeus* carries its bright globes in a very similar shade. This, too, is a clump-former, and both plants will grow side by side, year after year, steadily building into ever more impressive specimens if provided with a rich mulch every spring. The last daffodils of the season, *Narcissus poeticus* var. *recurvus*, with their red-rimmed yellow eyes, provide an attractive accompaniment.

V

VALERIANA
Valerian
VALERIANACEAE

Attractive foliage and airy flowerheads impart a delightfully naturalistic effect in many parts of the garden.

There are up to 200 species of deciduous, sometimes woody-based perennials, shrubs, and annuals from moist grassy places and woods to mountains throughout the world except Australia. Spreading by rhizomes, or with taproots, the oppositely arranged leaves vary in shape, the perennials most often with a basal rosette and with stem leaves divided into opposite pairs of leaflets. They are often aromatic, not always pleasantly so. Wide, flat-topped or domed airy heads of small, narrowly tubular, lobed flowers top the stems in summer in shades of pink, white, or yellow.

Grow valerian for both flowers and foliage in mixed or herbaceous borders, naturalistic planting schemes, and informal cottage-style gardens.

CULTIVATION Thrives in any moisture-retentive soil with full sun or dappled shade, although mountain species prefer a sunny spot with well-drained soil. Tall kinds may need supports, such as twiggy birch branches.

BELOW 1 *Valeriana officinalis*
2 *V. phu* 'Aurea' **3** *Vancouveria hexandra*

PROPAGATION In spring, by division or from seeds or basal stem cuttings.

PROBLEMS Usually trouble-free.

V. officinalis (Common valerian) Clump-forming, hairy or smooth deciduous plant with fleshy, branching stems. The 8 in (20 cm) long, aromatic leaves are composed of up to 25 bright green, lance-shaped leaflets. Branching, rounded, slightly domed heads of ¼-in-(5-mm-) long, tubular, pink or white flowers create a delightfully airy effect between early and late summer. An herb with medicinal and economic uses, it is included in some perfumes and used for flavoring foods and drinks. From Europe, including the British Isles, and western Asia. ‡ 4–6½ ft (1.2–2 m). Z4–9 H9–1. **subsp.** *sambucifolia* Particularly attractive foliage, with up to nine toothed-edged leaflets.

V. phu 'Aurea' Clump-forming deciduous plant spreading by rhizomes, grown in mixed or herbaceous borders for its attractive aromatic foliage, soft yellow in its spring rosette and turning lime- to mid-green by summer. Lower leaves are simple or deeply lobed, somewhat elliptical and about 8 in (20 cm) long. Flat-topped heads of white, tubular flowers about ¼ in (4 mm) long appear in early summer. The wild species is not grown. ‡ 5 ft (1.5 m). Z5–9 H9–5

V. pyrenaica A stately clump-forming deciduous plant, producing large, egg-shaped to almost circular, deep green leaves, to 8 in (20 cm) long, with deeply toothed edges. Slightly domed heads of light pink flowers, ¼ in (5–6 mm) in length, appear on maroon-flushed stems in late spring and early summer. From the Pyrenees, but naturalized in Britain since at least 1782, mainly in lowland Scotland. ‡ 36 in (90 cm). Z5–9 H9–5

VANCOUVERIA
Inside-out flower
BERBERIDACEAE

Charming American woodlanders with more dainty delicacy than powerful punchiness.

There are three similar species of evergreen and deciduous plants from the forests of California, Oregon, and Washington. They spread slowly to form loose colonies with slender, wiry stems clad in leaves formed of three to nine separate, slightly waved leaflets, often with three lobes. In early summer, the foliage is overtopped by airy clusters of small, white or yellow, pendulous flowers formed of six, reflexed, petal-like sepals. The genus is the American counterpart of the Asian *Epimedium*, differing in having six petals; epimediums have four.

CULTIVATION Thrives in moist but well-drained soil in part-shade.

PROPAGATION From seed or by division.

PROBLEMS Usually trouble-free.

V. chrysantha Slowly expanding colonies composed of leathery leaflets that are oval or broader than long, up to 1½ x 1½ in (4 x 4 cm), dark green above and grayish with hairs beneath. Yellow, ½-in (1–1.3-cm) flowers in loose heads of up to 15 open in early summer. Generally similar to *V. hexandra* but evergreen and with yellow flowers. Best in soil enriched with humus. From Oregon. ‡ 8–12 in (20–30 cm). Z6–8 H8–6

V. hexandra Forms small, slowly spreading colonies; the deciduous leaves are white with hairs on first opening, developing thin-textured, oval leaflets 2–3 in (5–8 cm) long, bright green above, grayish beneath. From late spring into summer, ½ in (10–13 mm) wide, white flowers dangle from threadlike stalks in airy sprays of up to 45 blooms. The most commonly cultivated species. From Washington to California. ‡ 8–14 in (20–35 cm). Z5–8 H8–5

VERATRUM
MELANTHIACEAE

Hardy shade-lovers with distinctively pleated leaves and the bonus of quietly elegant summer flowers.

About 20 species of deciduous plants grow in moist meadows and open woodlands throughout the Northern Hemisphere, spreading by thick, black rhizomes. The large, alternately arranged, pleated and veined, mid- or deep green, egg-shaped or elliptical leaves make a bold statement. In summer, sturdy, hollow, leafy, vertical stems bear numerous spikes of tiny, star-shaped green, white, red-brown, or almost black flowers followed by attractive heads of seed capsules up to 1 in (2.5 cm) across.

Early-flowering species go dormant in summer after setting seeds. Veratrums are ideal for woodland gardens or other natural parts of the garden, such as long-grass areas, or for planting among shrubs and similar perennials in a more formal border. All parts are very toxic if eaten; foliage and sap may cause a skin allergy. ⚠

CULTIVATION Thrives in part-shade in moist yet well-drained fertile soil rich in humus; full sun is acceptable provided the soil does not become

dry. Protect from cold drying winds.

PROPAGATION By division in early spring or fall or from seed.

PROBLEMS Slugs and snails.

V. album A tall, imposing, and variable clump-forming species with downy stems carrying ten to twelve elliptical or oblong leaves, 12 in (30 cm) long and 6 in (15 cm) wide, toward the base. In early summer and midsummer, ⅜–¾-in- (1.5–2-cm-) wide green-white or white flowers are freely and densely produced on slightly downy, sometimes branched stems. From Europe, North Africa, and northern Asia. ‡ 6½ ft (2 m). Z12–15 H12–10

V. nigrum (black fake hellabore) Compact and clump-forming with large, broadly elliptical leaves, 14 in (35 cm) long and 8 in (20 cm) wide, becoming smaller high up the stem. The ⅜-in (1.5-cm), red-brown to almost black flowers, striped green on the undersides, are freely produced, in mid- and late summer, on branched stems, but have an unpleasant scent. From southern Europe, Asia, and Siberia. ‡ 24–48 in (60–120 cm). Z6–9 H9–6

V. viride Compact, forming clumps of oval or elliptical leaves, 12 in (30 cm) long and 6 in (15 cm) wide, becoming smaller near the top of the stem. Green to yellow-green flowers, ¾ in (2 cm) across, appear on repeatedly branched stems in early summer and midsummer. Tolerates wet soil. From North America. ‡ 6½ ft (2 m). Z3–8 H8–1

VERBASCUM
Mullein
SCROPHULARIACEAE

Colorful, and increasingly popular, spires of flowers in a widening range of colors.

ABOVE 1 *Veratrum album* **2** *V. nigrum*

About 300 species grow mainly in Europe and Turkey on poor dry soil or disturbed ground, often in situations where there is little competition from other plants. They are mostly biennials but include several short-lived perennials, annuals, and a few low shrubs.

The plants vary from 8 in (20 cm) to 6½ ft (2 m) in height, with usually soft and often densely woolly, alternate leaves, most often gathered in a basal rosette that can be an attractive feature in itself. They may be undivided to deeply lobed, with smooth or toothed margins. The five-petaled flowers are usually yellow, but sometimes white, purple, or in reddish shades, and are borne in erect, branched or unbranched spikes. The flowers are followed by a spherical capsule, like that of a foxglove, containing many very long-lived seeds. More than half the species are extremely rare in the wild. Several of the cultivated species are grown under invalid or incorrect names and may actually be hybrids.

Verbascums have long been put to practical use, albeit not in recent times. The spikes were dipped in tallow and used as candles; the woolly leaves were used as warm liners for shoes; and the seed was employed to drug fish and make them easier to scoop up.

In recent years, many (some say too many) new hybrids, in an increasingly wide range of colors, have been introduced. However, while they make good plants for the herbaceous border, few of them are long-term perennials, and since many fail even to reappear in their second spring, their reputation has become tainted. Some come in new shades that are difficult to describe,

blending pinks and purples and golds and tans, and nurseries resort to evocative yet not altogether informative descriptions, such as "Like the balmy sun falling behind the Sierra Mountains." Many of the older hybrids have been lost, either because they have been superseded by better plants or because the necessary repeated propagation has been neglected. Their lack of longevity has, of course, contributed to their disappearance. Strict biennials such as *V. bombyciferum* and *V. densiflorum* have been excluded from this coverage.

CULTIVATION Best in well-drained soil in sunny situations. Ideal for hot climates, although the flowers of some may be damaged by strong sunshine. Their limited life is further shortened when grown in wet winter soil. Ideal in perennial or mixed borders, and especially in dry and gravel gardens, but ensure that they are not crowded by their neighbors. Remove the old flower spikes as the last flowers fade to stimulate the development of fresh ones, although not all will respond. At the end of the year, remove dead flower spikes and any trash that has collected in the leaf rosette. Mulleins will often self-seed if conditions are suitable, and need plenty of space. They are not suitable for small containers and will stop growing when their roots have colonized all of the available soil.

PROPAGATION Species are best grown from seed. Some cultivars are also intended to be raised from seed, but seed from home-saved plants may well have crossed with other cultivars to produce unpredictable hybrids. Many cultivars can be

propagated by root cuttings or very careful division.

PROBLEMS Mullein moth (*see* Mullein Moth, *p.471*), red spider mite, and powdery mildew.

V. **'Annie May'** (Breckland Verbascum) Deep, damson-pink flowers that hardly fade from late spring to early fall; the foliage and stems also show purple tints. ‡ 36 in (90 cm). Z5–9 H9–5

V. **'Apricot Sunset'** (Breckland Verbascum) Apricot flowers fade to dusky pink, having opened from darker buds. ‡ 3¼ ft (1 m). Z5–9 H9–5

V. **'Banana Custard'** see *V.* x *hybridum* 'Banana Custard'

V. **'Blushing Bride'** Lavender and pink flowers, darkening with age, on slender stems. Sterile, so keeps on flowering. A good cut flower. From Terra Nova Nurseries. ‡ 18 in (45 cm). Z5–9 H9–5

V. **Breckland Verbascums** A growing series raised by Patricia Cooper of Magpies Nursery in the Breckland area of Norfolk, England. All are sterile and thus have a long flowering season, and all have a slight but noticeable scent early in the morning. See 'Annie May', 'Apricot Sunset', and 'Norfolk Dawn'.

V. **'Caribbean Crush'** Flowers in tones of apricot, gold, yellow, peach, pink, and copper are all carried on the same spike. ‡ 4 ft (1.2 m). Z5–9 H9–5

V. chaixii (Nettle-leaved mullein) A vigorous, short-lived perennial or biennial with a large basal rosette. Egg-shaped to oblong, grayish green leaves, 5½–12 in (14–30 cm) long, are densely covered in gray felt and have rounded teeth and a rounded or abruptly

VERBASCUM FLOWERS

Mulleins have a fairly conventional floral structure. The five petals are more or less equal in size and shape, and there are also five widely spreading male organs, the stamens, each made up of a stalk (the filament) supporting the anther, which produces the pollen. The filaments may be clothed in long yellow, white, or violet hairs that give the impression of the flower having a colored eye. In the center is the female organ, composed of the ovary, style, and stigma. The style, topped by the stigma, receives the pollen, and the ovary matures into a capsule filled with tiny seeds. Unlike most members of the foxglove family, the flowers are symmetrical.

Verbascum 'Caribbean Crush'

RECENT INTRODUCTIONS

In recent years, a great many new verbascums have been introduced, beginning with 'Helen Johnson'; some arose as chance seedlings in the borders of observant gardeners, while others are the result of careful plant-breeding programs. There has been such a rush of newcomers that some have said we are now seeing too many.

However, some are significant improvements on older cultivars, in terms of improved longevity and a greater range of flower colors, and others are sterile, which prolongs the flowering season and does away with the nuisance of self-sown seedlings.

New introductions have come from four main sources in Britain and the US. Thompson & Morgan Seeds have introduced a number developed at their research facility in Suffolk, England, which are intended to be raised from seed. These include 'Banana Custard', 'Copper Rose', and 'Snow Maiden'.

Patricia Cooper of Magpies Nursery, in an unusually sandy area of Norfolk, England, known as the Breckland, has introduced the Breckland Verbascums. All are sterile and long-flowering, and have a noticeable early-morning scent; they include 'Annie May', 'Apricot Sunset', and 'Norfolk Dawn'.

Alongside Hampshire's Test River, National Council for the Conservation of Plants and Gardens (NCCPG) National Collection holders Vic Johnstone and Claire Wilson have developed the Riverside Group, which are now becoming available. Look out for 'Aurora', 'Aztec Gold', 'Charlotte', 'Cherokee', 'Clementine', 'High Noon', 'Kalypso', 'Moonshadow', and 'Virginia'. Some report these as long-lived, others are greatly disappointed.

In Oregon, Terra Nova Nurseries, better known for their *Heuchera* breeding, have also been developing new introductions that are sterile and prolific, and are also good perennials. Some of these include 'Blushing Bride', 'Dark Eyes', 'Honey Dijon', 'Lavender Lass', 'Moonlight', 'Plum Smokey', 'Sierra Sunset', 'Sugar Plum', and 'Sunshine Spires'.

It is not easy to select the best of all from this rush of newcomers, and some of them are certainly short-lived; but most deserve a trial in the garden.

truncated base; their stalks are ¼–1 in (5–25 mm) long. Pale yellow or white flowers, ¼–1 in (5–25 mm) wide, are born in long spikes on branched stems; stamens are covered with purple hairs. Best in dry, well-drained soil, where it should be reliably perennial. Grow from seed or take root cuttings. One of the most widely grown species, it readily hybridizes with *V. phoeniceum* to produce perennials with pastel-colored flowers. A number of hybrid cultivars are incorrectly sold under this name,

and are listed separately. From southern and central Europe, and Russia. ‡3¼ ft (1 m). Z5–9 H9–5. **'Album'** Slightly smaller with pretty white flowers with contrasting, purple stamens. Usually comes true from seed. ‡36 in (90 cm). **'Sixteen Candles'** Unusually well-branched yellow spikes.

V. **'Cherry Helen'** The silvered buds open to dusky, cherry-colored flowers from midsummer to early fall. ‡4 ft (1.2 m). Z5–9 H9–5

V. **'Cotswold Beauty'** (Cotswold Group) Pale bronze-colored flowers, with a purple center, open from dark bronze buds, from early summer, to midsummer above gray-green leaves. Similar to 'Helen Johnson', but a little paler and with a purple center. Sometimes incorrectly listed under *V. chaixii*. ‡4 ft (1.2 m). Z5–9 H9–5

V. **Cotswold Group** 'Cotswold Beauty', 'Cotswold Queen', 'Gainsborough, 'Mont Blanc', 'Pink Domino', and 'Royal Highland' but not 'Cotswold King' (see The Cotswold Group, p. 472).

V. **'Cotswold Queen'** (Cotswold Group) Biscuit-yellow flowers, stained purple at the base of the petals with purple stamens, appear from early to late summer. ‡4 ft (1.2 m). Z5–9 H9–5

V. **'Cotswold King'** Large yellow and cream, slightly scented flowers with a neat red marking in the center. Said to come true from seed if grown in isolation. Probably a robust form of *V. creticum*. ‡5 ft (1.5 m). Z5–9 H9–5

V. **'Dark Eyes'** Surprisingly compact, broad gray leaves send up short pyramids of large, peachy-gold flowers with deep red eyes and purple stamens. Good in containers. From Terra Nova Nurseries. ‡12 in (30 cm). Z5–9 H9–5

V. **'Domino'** see *V.* 'Pink Domino'

V. epixanthinum A short-lived perennial, sometimes biennial, densely covered with wool and grown for both leaves and flowers, The basal leaves are rather variable in shape—from oblong to egg-shaped with untoothed or toothed margins—and are densely yellow or white woolly on both sides, or green above and woolly beneath, with a ¾–4¾-in- (2–12-cm-) long stalk. The unstalked stem leaves are similarly shaped. The 1–1½-in (2.5–3.5 cm) flowers are yellow with violet stamens and are held on lax, unbranched or slightly branched stems from early to late summer. Almost a monster Mediterranean alpine rather than a border perennial. Introduced in 1999 from the mountains of Greece. ‡10–60 in (25–150 cm).

V. **'Gainsborough'** (Cotswold Group) Large sulfur yellow flowers and grayish green foliage. A good perennial and without doubt one of the best hybrid mulleins. Sterile, so only needs dead-heading for appearance's sake. ‡5 ft (1.5 m). Z5–9 H9–3

V. **'Helen Johnson'** A very attractive, sadly short-lived perennial with grayish green leaves and caramel-pink flowers, but often dying after flowering. Similar, but inferior, small-flowered plants are sometimes seen under this name. A chance seedling found at the Royal Botanic Gardens Kew, England. The plant is possibly a hybrid between *V. bombyciferum* and *V. phoeniceum*. ‡36 in (90 cm). Z5–9 H9–5

V. **'Honey Dijon'** Slightly cup shaped, with rich peachy gold flowers and a plum-colored eye over felted foliage. From Terra Nova Nurseries. ‡18 in (45 cm). Z5–9 H9–5

V. × *hybridum* This is a loosely used name that should correctly be applied

BELOW 1 *Verbascum chaixii* 'Album'
2 *V.* 'Cotswold Queen'
3 *V.* 'Gainsborough'

only to hybrids of *V. pulverulentum* and *V. sinuatum* (rarely seen) but it is more often used as a catch-all name for any hybrid mullein. All three cultivars included here are to be raised from seed and were developed and introduced by Thompson and Morgan Seedsmen, Inc., NJ; they might be better treated individually. ‡4–6 ft (1.2–1.8 m). Z5–9 H9–5. **'Banana Custard'** Unusually large and dramatic flowers in two-tone yellow densely packed on tall spikes. ‡5–6 ft (1.5–1.8 m). **'Copper Rose'** Flowers in a range of pastel colors including copper, tan, pink, and apricot. A sterile F1 hybrid. ‡5 ft (1.5 m). **'Snow Maiden'** Vigorous, with branched spikes of pure white flowers and grayish green leaves. ‡4–5 ft (1.2–1.5 m).

V. **'Jackie'** A short-lived perennial or biennial with a rosette of dark green leaves and short spikes of peachy pink flowers. Demands a sunny position and very well-drained soil, and may be killed by winter rain in colder countries. A compact hybrid of *V. dumulosum* and *V. phoeniceum* often treated almost as a bedding plant and good in containers. ‡24 in (60 cm). Z5–9 H9–5

V. **'Jackie in Pink'** Like a pure pink version of 'Jackie', this short-lived plant has short, well-branched spikes of soft pink flowers with a plummy center above green rosettes. Deadhead for maximum flower power. ‡18 in (45 cm). Z5–9 H9–5

V. **'Jolly Eyes'** The white flowers are faintly blushed in pink and open from darker blushed buds and have a dark center of purple stamens. ‡24–36 in (60–90 cm). Z5–9 H9–5

V. **'Lavender Lass'** Ruffled foliage throws up a forest of slender spikes of two-tone lavender flowers. Sterile, and, therefore, has a long season. From Terra Nova Nurseries. ‡24 in (60 cm). Z5–9 H9–5

V. **'Megan's Mauve'** Grayish green leaves set off deep mauve-purple flowers in early summer and midsummer. The color fades in bright sunshine, so plant in a little shade. A spontaneous mutation of 'Helen Johnson'. ‡4 ft (1.2 m). Z5–9 H9–5

V. **'Monster'** Vigorous, with mid-green leaves up to 24 in (60 cm) long; it has multibranched stems carrying pale yellow flowers with red stamens. Raised by Norfolk, England's, Pat Cooper and originally called 'Primrose Skies'. ‡8 ft (2.4 m). Z5–9 H9–5

V. **'Mont Blanc'** (Cotswold Group) Pure white flowers with grayish green, evergreen foliage. Can be distinguished from most hybrid mulleins by its lighter center. ‡36–42 in (90–110 cm). Z5–9 H9–5

V. **'Moonlight'** Large flowers in the palest yellow have lavender stamens and are carried on well-branched plants. From Terra Nova Nurseries. ‡18 in (45 cm). Z5–9 H9–5

MULLEIN MOTH

The mullein moth (*Cucullia verbasci*) is viewed both as a pest and as a solution to a pest problem. In Britain, its most colorful of caterpillars—verbascums are almost worth growing in order to attract them—can devastate garden verbascums, large numbers of them munching through flower buds and destroying foliage.

Occasionally also found on buddleias, these 2-in (5-cm) grayish caterpillars with colorful black and yellow spots eat round holes in the leaves and also feed on the flower buds; they can defoliate a plant very quickly. They feed from late spring to midsummer, then pupate in the soil and hatch into rather dowdy brown adults the following spring.

In North America, the biennial *Verbascum thapsus* has been introduced from Europe and is spreading in meadows and forest openings at a rate that has caused some alarm, especially as it is such a prolific seeder and its seeds last so long in the soil. Mullein moth has been introduced in an attempt to control its spread. This would be troubling were it not for the fact that of the 14 *Verbascum* species found in North America, not one is native. However, this moth has only proven partially successful in controlling *V. thapsus*; a European weevil has also been introduced for the purpose and has proved to be more successful, eating about half the developing seeds.

V. **'Norfolk Dawn'** (Breckland Verbascum) Large flowers in buff and biscuit shades open in successive flushes up the stem rather than opening steadily from base to top. It is the most vigorous and dramatic of the Breckland Verbascums. ‡32–60 in (80–150 cm). Z5–9 H9–5

V. nigrum (Dark mullein) Very vigorous, soundly perennial, forming a large basal rosette of egg-shaped to oblong, stalked and slightly toothed, variably downy leaves with a rounded base. In mid- and late summer, the slightly downy stems carry smaller, unstalked, egg-shaped leaves and long spikes of dark yellow, ¾–1-in (18–25-mm) flowers with violet stamens. Easy to grow, and raise from seed, but needs plenty of space. From Scandinavia, to Spain, northern Italy, and east as far as Siberia. ‡4 ft (1.2 m). Z3–8 H8–1. **var. *album*** White flowers with purple stamens.

V. olympicum (Olympic mullein) A stately, short-lived perennial or biennial forming a basal rosette, to 3¼ ft (1 m) across, of grayish white, woolly, lance-shaped, 6–28-in (15–70-cm) leaves with noticeably pointed tips. Woolly stem branches form a bold candelabra carrying spikes of bright golden yellow flowers, ¾–1¼ in (2–3 cm) wide, with white or whitish yellow stamens. Good in hot climates, but in cooler areas it often dies after flowering. Needs plenty of space, and best in groups of four or five; ensure it does not have to compete

COLOR CONNECTIONS

THE OLD MOSS ROSE 'William Lobb', with its slightly gray-tinted purple flowers, paling in the center, has a rather weak habit and tends to arch; its stems are best supported. By bold contrast, the gleaming upright spikes of *Verbascum chaixii* var. *album* are pure white and determinedly upright. The two plants go well together as the white verbascum petals pick up the pale coloring in the heart of the rose, while their dark eyes connect with the dusky coloring in 'William Lobb'.

with other species. Cut back after flowering to promote a fall flush. Other species may be sold under this name. Often much taller in gardens than in the wild, where it may only reach 3¼–5 ft (1–1.5 m). From Greece and Turkey. ‡6–8 ft (1.8–2.4 m). Z5–9 H9–5

V. **'Patricia'** Blended buff and pink in each flower. ‡3¼ ft (1 m). Z5–9 H9–5

V. phoeniceum (Purple mullein) A short-lived perennial or biennial plant with a rosette of dark green, egg-shaped or oblong, hairless or slightly downy leaves, often with a slightly wavy edge. From late spring to late summer, it produces branched spikes of purple flowers; in gardens, violet or red flowers—and more rarely white, pink, or lilac flowers—are also seen. It readily self-seeds and will hybridize with other nearby mulleins,

so has been much used in breeding. Seems unusually vulnerable to red spider mite. From southern Europe and north Asia. ‡36–48 in (90–120 cm). Z4–8 H8–1. **'Album'** White flowers. **'Flush of White'** A compact, seed-raised plant with large white flowers. ‡30 in (75 cm). **hybrids** This name usually covers plants with pastel-colored flowers resulting from hybridization with other species. **'Violetta'** Tapering spikes of dark purple-violet flowers from late spring to late summer, often with a second crop if deadheaded. A seed-raised cultivar from Jelitto Staudensamen. ‡36 in (90 cm). Z4–8 H8–1

V. **'Pink Domino'** syn. *V.* Domino (Cotswold Group) The ruffled, raspberry-pink flowers have a darker center and are held on slender spikes from early summer to midsummer. ‡4 ft (1.2 m). Z5–9 H9–5

THE COTSWOLD GROUP

The Cotswold Group, sometimes known as the Cotswold Hybrids, includes many well-known plants, some with the Cotswold prefix, such as 'Cotswold Queen', and others without, such as 'Gainsborough'. Originally introduced in the 1920s, their origins are not clear, and neither their raiser nor their parentage is known. Indeed, the plants now usually placed in this group seem to be an odd mix of cultivars not necessarily related.

In general, they are vigorous plants in a wide range of colors: white and yellow are most common, but various brown, pink, and peach shades are also found. Some of the original plants of this type have been lost, but a number of them still persist and are regaining popularity.

The Cotswold Group has been studied at Britain's National Council for the Conservation of Plants and Gardens (NCCPG) National Collection of *Verbascum*. 'Cotswold Beauty' and the rarely seen 'Cotswold Gem' are certainly related, 'Gainsborough' and 'Mont Blanc' are also a pair, as are 'Pink Domino' and 'White Domino'. But none of these pairs seems related to each other in terms of possible parents or to 'Cotswold Queen'—and certainly not to the much more recent 'Cotswold King'. Perhaps they have only their place of origin in common.

V. **'Pink Petticoats'** Prettily rippled pink flowers are attractively tinted in peachy shades; free-flowering. ↕ 4 ft (1.2 m). Z5–9 H9–5

V. **'Plum Smokey'** Silvered green rosettes grow from a crowded mass of slender spikes, carrying large, smoky-purple flowers for many months. From Terra Nova Nurseries. ↕ 18 in (45 cm). Z5–9 H9–5

V. **'Primrose Skies'** see 'Monster'.

V. **'Raspberry Ripple'** Creamy pink flowers tend toward raspberry pink at the center; deadhead for a second flush. ↕ 24 in (60 cm). Z5–9 H9–5

V. **Riverside hybrids** An exciting range of new hybrids raised by Vic Johnstone and Claire Wilson, holders of an NCCPG National Plant Collection of *Verbascum* in England. They are said to be reliably perennial (though not all gardeners report this experience), with branched stems and bright colors (*see* Recent Introductions, *p.470*).

V. **'Royal Highland'** (Cotswold Group) Apricot-yellow flowers. First exhibited at the Royal Highland Show in Scotland in the 1960s. ↕ 4 ft (1.2 m). Z5–9 H9–5

V. **'Sierra Sunset'** Large ruffled flowers in shades of orange and melon are set off by deep red eyes over velvety green foliage. From Terra Nova Nurseries. ↕ 18 in (45 cm). Z5–9 H9–5

V. **'Southern Charm'** Modestly sized, 1-in (2.5-cm) flowers in a range of rich pastel shades—from cream to pale pink, pale lavender, and buff—with purple stamens from early summer to early fall. Flowers in its first year from seed if sown early. Raised by Thompson & Morgan Seeds by crossing *V. chaixii* with *V. phoenecium*, but sometimes listed under *V. x hybridum*. ↕ 24–48 in (60–120 cm). Z5–9 H9–5

V. **'Sugar Plum'** Clear, plum-colored flowers with creamy stamens are held on crowded spikes on dwarf plants for many months. From Terra Nova Nurseries. ↕ 18 in (45 cm). Z5–9 H9–5

V. **'Summer Sorbet'** Dark magenta-purple flowers have a darker center. ↕ 4 ft (1.2 m). Z5–9 H9–5

V. **'Sunshine Spires'** Large ruffled flowers in shades of gold and yellow, each with a purple eye, are carried on branched spikes over gray felted foliage. From Terra Nova Nurseries. ↕ 5 ft (1.5 m). Z5–9 H9–5

VERBENA

Vervain

VERBENACEAE

Stylish but usually more demure perennial relations of the container-garden favorites.

Two hundred and fifty annuals and perennials, some woody-based, are native to tropical and subtropical America. They vary from spreading or loosely dangling to bolt upright. Mostly oppositely arranged leaves may be long and slender, or much neater, and are almost always lobed, toothed, dissected, or divided in some way. Flowerheads are carried at the tips of the shoots, sometimes at the leaf joints, and come in tight clusters that vary from tall and slender to broadly flat-topped. Each small individual flower has a long tube and then flares at the tip into five lobes; each plant usually carries many clusters that can be increased by pinching to encourage branching. They are popular with butterflies. Reliable bloomers from late spring onward, verbenas are often the last to hold out, even after many frosts. The foliage is apt to remain green through much of winter.

Some species—for example, *V. rigida*—are widely used as bedding plants but they will overwinter, particularly in milder areas and when they are well mulched. Some highly bred bedding cultivars may also overwinter in zone 9 and above.

CULTIVATION Best in full sun with good drainage.

PROPAGATION From seed or by cuttings.

PROBLEMS Powdery mildew.

V. bonariensis Tall, slender, and rigidly straight, the slim but strong four-sided stems carry widely spaced pairs of more or less lance-shaped, unstalked, 5-in (13-cm) leaves that are toothed toward the tips. From midsummer to the first frost, large heads of tiny, ¼-in (6-mm), star-like blooms in lilac-purple are carried in domed clusters up to 2 in (5 cm) across on open branched heads. The overall effect is colorful, but this is the archetypal see-through plant, since the sparsely leaved stems do not block the view of plants behind. Does not need staking. May be hardier than indicated with a good snow cover, and usually self-seeds freely, so reappears even if killed. Extremely easy to grow with full sun, and a reliable lure for butterflies. Named for the city of Buenos Aires, where it was first collected. Native to South America. ↕ 36–78 in (90–200 cm). Z7–11 H11–7

V. corymbosa Spreading plant densely clad in handsome, velvety, toothed, more or less egg-shaped 1–2½-in (2.5–6-cm) leaves that, although green, look slightly frosted with silver. All summer, it bears a profusion of star-shaped, richly lilac-colored, ½-in (1-cm) flowers jutting from dark purple bracts. Easily grown, quick to flower, and more self-branching than most verbenas and perhaps less prone to powdery mildew than other species. From South America, mostly southern Chile and Argentina. ↕ 36–60 in (90–150 cm). Z9–11 H11–9

V. hastata (Blue vervain) Stiffly upright, branched or unbranched plant with long, slender, lance-shaped leaves, 6 in (15 cm) long and 1½ in (4 cm) across; young seedlings are difficult to distinguish from *V. bonariensis* but on maturity prove twice as wide and with shorter stalks. The flowers open relatively few at a time, their opening progressing to the tips of long, candle-like spires. They are usually vivid violet, and striking even from a distance, but can be more watery in color. Avoid wet soil in winter. Native to North America. ↕ 5 ft (1.5 m). Z3–9 H9–1. **'Alba'** Pure white. **'Rosea'** Vivid pink.

V. macdougalii (Spike verbena) Upright, rather sparsely branched stems carry pairs of very small, broadly lance-shaped, deeply textured, apple green leaves, ½ in (10 mm) long and ⅛ in (4 mm) wide and coarsely toothed. A plump spike, up to 10 in (25 cm) long, sometimes with a few secondary spikes, is encircled by pale lavender-colored flowers. Tends to be a thirsty plant. The

BELOW 1 *Verbena bonariensis*
2 *V. hastata* 'Rosea'

leaves can cause dermatitis. From high, dry grasslands in the southwestern US. ↕24–36 in (60–90 cm). Z3–9 H9–1 ⚠

V. peruviana Mat-forming, covering the soil with slender stems carrying ¾-in (2-cm), broadly lance-shaped, notched, deep green, felted leaves. Striking white-centered, cherry-red blossoms are held in tight clusters above the green mat from midsummer to early fall. Refreshingly different from most verbenas; thrives in dry conditions and tolerates wetter situations. Native to Argentina and southern Brazil. ↕2 in (5 cm). Z9–11 H12–9

V. rigida Small tubers support a stiff, more or less upright, slightly hairy plant carrying pairs of stalkless, 3-in (7.5-cm), oblong, deep green, very coarse, toothed leaves rather like those of *V. bonariensis*, tending to clasp the stem. The stems are topped with usually three dense clusters of purple flowers. Can self-seed irritatingly in damp climates. Mulch in marginal areas to increase winter hardiness. Naturalized in the southeastern US, but native to southern Brazil and Argentina. ↕12–24 in (30–60 cm). Z8–11 H11–1. **'Polaris'** Exquisite silvery blue flowers.

VERNONIA
Ironweed
ASTERACEAE

Showy perennials bringing sunset-purple color to the summer and fall border.

A large and very varied group of 500 to 1,000 species of annuals, perennials, climbers, subshrubs, shrubs, and trees from the Americas, Asia, Africa, and Australia. Only a few perennials are grown in gardens. Growing from woody, fibrous-rooted crowns, most cultivated species have many tall, stiff stems clothed in deep green, lance-shaped leaves. These are topped by flat heads of tubular flowers in pink, purple, or occasionally white. The name "ironweed" presumably arises from the rust red hairs that are prominent in the spent flowerheads and on the fruits.

The broad violet-colored flower clusters of ironweeds demand attention in the summer and fall garden. Place them at the middle or rear of the border with late-season perennials, or in naturalistic gardens and meadows.

CULTIVATION Easy to grow and will thrive under most garden situations, but best in rich, evenly moist soil in full sun or light shade. The clumps get very large in time, but seldom need division.

PROPAGATION By cuttings or from seed; self-sown seedlings will usually appear if plants are not deadheaded.

PROBLEMS Leaf miner.

V. arkansana syn *V. crinita* Large, coarse-textured with stout, waxy stems densely clothed in wide, 7–8-in- (18–20-cm-) long, oval leaves with white undersides. Quite variable in size, more likely in response to environmental conditions rather than genetic variability. The tight clusters of small, violet flowerheads open in late summer. More drought-tolerant than most species. Native to North America, from Quebec and Ontario south to Arkansas and Oklahoma. ↕36 in–9½ ft (90 cm–2.4 m). Z3–7 H7–1. **'Mammuth'** Dense clusters of large flowers on stout, self-supporting stems. From Piet Oudolf in Holland. ↕6 ft (1.8 m).

V. crinita see *V. arkansana*

V. fasciculata Smooth, upright stems have evenly spaced, 6-in (15-cm), lance-shaped, deep green toothed leaves and tight, upright clusters of red-violet flowers in mid- to late summer with fewer flowers in the head than seen in other species. Native to wet prairies, marshes, and ditches in North America, from Ohio and Saskatchewan south to Missouri and Oklahoma ↕36–48 in (90–120 cm). Z4–8 H8–3

V. noveboracensis (New York ironweed) Stiff, tall stems carry 6–8-in (15–20-cm), mostly toothless, lance-shaped leaves topped with broad, showy clusters of 1-in (2.5-cm), red-violet, occasionally white, flowers. The flowerheads on mature plants can be 2 ft (60 cm) across with hundreds of flowers. Best in rich, evenly moist soil in full sun or light shade. Established plants are moderately drought-tolerant. From low meadows, floodplains, pond margins, and seeps from Massachusetts and Ohio south to Florida and Mississippi. ↕to 6 ft (1.9 m). Z4–8 H8–3

VERONICA
Speedwell
SCROPHULARIACEAE

Easy-to-grow sun-lovers whose neat foliage combines with slender spikes for borders or cutting.

About 250 annuals and perennials, some rather woody at the base, grow in a wide range of habitats from boggy lakesides to mountain screes, mainly in Europe but also in other temperate areas of the Northern Hemisphere. The basal leaves are opposite, while those on the flowering stems are usually alternately arranged; they vary in shape from broadly lance-shaped to almost round and may be smooth-edged or toothed, stalked, or unstalked. The flowers are carried in spikes, sometimes short and loose, sometimes taller and more densely packed; each four- or five-petaled flower is made up of a short tube flaring into lobes that are often of unequal sizes.

This is a varied group, including high and demanding alpines as well as marginal aquatics and easy-to-grow perennials. The taller perennials, such as the *V. spicata* 'Sightseeing' mix, are increasingly used as cut flowers; they should be cut when a

RIGHT 1 *Veronica austriaca* subsp. *teucrium* 'Crater Lake Blue' **2** *V. gentianoides*

third to a half of the spike is open and plunged immediately into water containing a flower preservative.

CULTIVATION Most prefer a sunny position and well-drained soil, but a few need aquatic habitats and are not covered here. The erect species, such as *V. longifolia*, should be trimmed back to ground level in the fall and the mat-forming species deadheaded. Most lose their foliage during the latter part of the summer and tend to look rather untidy. Cut back to the base at this stage. •

PROPAGATION Grow species from seed and named cultivars by division or cuttings in the spring or fall.

PROBLEMS Powdery and downy mildews.

V. austriaca Clump-forming with erect stems and lance-shaped or rounded leaves, deeply divided once or twice into long lobes. Bright blue, ½-in (10–13-mm) flowers are held in paired spikes in the leaf joints. Wonderful for the front of the herbaceous border needing full sunshine and well-drained soil. From pine forest, scrub, and rocky slopes, from central to eastern Europe, Turkey, and the Caucasus. ↕20 in (50 cm). Z4–8 H8–3. **'Ionian Skies'** Sky blue flowers. ↕12 in (30 cm). **subsp. *teucrium*** Taller, with deeply toothed, egg-shaped or oblong, hairy, grayish green leaves; produces spikes of bright blue flowers during summer. More adaptable. ↕36 in (90 cm). **subsp. *teucrium* 'Crater Lake Blue'** Compact, with short spikes of intense gentian blue flowers. ↕12 in (30 cm). Z4–8 H8–3. **subsp. *teucrium* 'Kapitän'** Gentian blue flowers. **subsp. *teucrium* 'Royal Blue'** Deep blue flowers. ↕12 in (30 cm). **'Shirley Blue'** see *V.* 'Shirley Blue'.

V. chamaedrys (Bird's-eye speedwell, Germander speedwell) Makes a vigorous, ground-hugging mat of sprawling stems with two lines of long hairs along their length. They carry unstalked, slightly hairy, lance- or egg-shaped, toothed, bright green, 1½-in (4-cm) leaves. Bright blue flowers with white eyes are held in the leaf joints in paired 3–6-in (8–15-cm) spikes. Ideal for a flower meadow or woodland garden but can be invasive. Easy in full sun or part-shade; cut back in late summer to keep it tidy. Variegated forms are less vigorous. Naturalized in North America and a common grassland native in Western Europe. ↕10 in (25 cm). Z3–7 H7–1. **'Pam'** Blue flowers with white center and creamy white leaves with green central markings. Constantly reverts. ↕8 in (20 cm). Z3–7 H7–1

'Darwin's Blue' Clump-forming plant with dark green, toothed, lance-shaped foliage and prolific vertical spikes carrying densely packed, rich violet

flowers well above the foliage. ↕16 in (40 cm). Z3–8 H8–1

V. **'Eveline'** Forms a tight clump of unusually dark green, lance-shaped, 4½-in (11-cm) leaves supporting a prolific array of vertical spikes crowded with small, purplish red flowers from early to late summer. A hybrid of *V. longifolia*. ↕20 in (50 cm). Z4–8 H8–3

V. gentianoides A mat- or clump-forming perennial, individual plants producing rosettes of glossy elliptical or lance-shaped leaves that often coalesce to form a low, rounded hummock. Erect stems are produced in the early summer, topped by spikes of pale blue, white, or, more rarely, deep blue, cup-shaped, ⅝-in (1.6-cm), slightly blue-veined flowers. Best in moist, well-drained soil that does not dry out in the summer. Divide named cultivars in the spring or fall. From moist grassland and open woodland in the Caucasus, Ukraine, and Turkey. ↕18 in (45 cm). Z4–7 H7–1. **'Alba'** Slightly larger, very pale blue flowers. **'Barbara Sherwood'** More vigorous, with deeper blue flowers and more distinct veins on the petals. ↕16 in (40 cm). **'Pallida'** Extremely pale blue flowers. ↕18 in (45 cm). **'Robusta'** Vigorous robust form, with long spikes of light blue flowers. ↕24 in (60 cm). **'Tissington White'** White flowers delicately lined in pale blue; less vigorous. ↕12 in (30 cm). **'Variegata'** Less vigorous, with cream and green variegated leaves and pale blue flowers. ↕20 in (50 cm).

V. 'Goodness Grows' Bushy, compact, making a low, matlike clump of lance-shaped to linear, hairy, 2 in (5 cm) long leaves. The upright, 6 in (15 cm) high spikes of deep blue flowers open from late spring to midsummer and again if dead-headed. A hybrid of *V. alpina* 'Alba' and *V. spicata* from Goodness Grows nursery in Lexington, GA. ↕12–16 in (30–40 cm). Z3–8 H8–1.

V. grandis More or less erect stems carry pairs of oppositely arranged, more or less oblong leaves with toothed margins. From early summer to early fall, 6-in (15-cm) spikes carry china-blue flowers. Similar to *V. longifolia* but with smaller leaves and more heart-shaped at the base. Best in very well-drained soil. From Siberia. ↕36 in (90 cm). Z4–8 H8–3.

V. longifolia (Long-leafed speedwell) A variable plant, the erect stems carrying pairs, or sometimes clusters, of lance-shaped or parallel-sided, toothed, mid-green, 4¾-in (12-cm) leaves with long-pointed tips. Stems are topped by spikes to 10 in (25 cm) long, sometimes with one or two secondary spikes, crowded with masses of lilac-blue flowers from early summer or midsummer until early fall. Ideal in the middle of the herbaceous border, though established plants may be as much as 4 ft (1.2 m) across. Usually needs support. From riverbanks and damp places in Europe and Asia, naturalized in the northeastern US. ↕36 in (90 cm). Z4–8 H8–1. **'Alba'** Narrow, tapering spikes of white flowers. **'Blauer Sommer'** Bright blue flowers. ↕32 in (80 cm). **'Blauriesin'** (**Blue Giantress**) syn. 'Forester's Blue' Long spikes of deep lavender-blue flowers, good for cutting. ↕24 in (60 cm). **'Joseph's Coat'** Leaves patterned in cream, green, and gold with pale blue flowers in mid- and late summer. **'Lilac Fantasy'** Pale blue flowers with darker stamens. **'Rose Tone'** Pale rose pink flowers, comes true from seed. ↕32 in (80 cm). **'Rosea'** Rose pink flowers, with branched

stems. **'Schneeriesin'** Narrow spikes of pure white flowers.

V. montana 'Corinne Tremaine' Mat-forming, with softly hairy, egg-shaped, toothed leaves that have creamy-green edges aging to white, held on long stalks. From the end of spring to summer, it bears short spikes of pale lilac-blue flowers with darker veins, although it is rather shy-flowering. Needs full sun and well-drained soil. Take cuttings in the late spring or early summer. The plain green-leaved species, from woodlands in the Caucasus, Europe, and North Africa, is rarely grown. ↕12 in (30 cm). Z3–8 H8–1

V. pectinata Mat-forming, woody at the base, with deeply toothed or divided, lance-shaped, evergreen, 1-in (2.5-cm) leaves, that have a dense covering of white hairs. The spikes of white-eyed, saucer-shaped, violet-blue or blue flowers are held in the leaf joints in summer. Ideal for sunny, dry situations in the garden. From dry, rocky places, oak forests and olive groves in the east Balkans and Turkey. ↕4 in (10 cm). Z2–7 H7–1. **'Rosea'** Rose pink flowers, much more widely grown.

V. peduncularis Mat-forming with branched rhizomes, the prostrate stems turn up at the tips and carry glossy, lance-shaped, egg-shaped or round leaves up to 1 in (2.5 cm) long. The foliage is green or bronzy green, deeply toothed and slightly downy or hairless and shiny. In late spring and early summer, 3-in (7.5-cm) spikes of deep blue, white-eyed flowers, occasionally pink or lilac, are produced at the leaf joints and continue to flower into the summer. Needs full sun and well-drained soil. From alpine meadows, grassland, scrub, and rocky places, in the Caucasus, Turkey, and Ukraine. ↕4 in (10 cm). Z6–8 H8–6. **'Alba'** White flowers. **'Georgia Blue'** syn. 'Oxford Blue' Free-flowering bushy plant, with flushed-purple young foliage and deep blue, white-eyed flowers. Introduced by horticulturist Roy Lancaster and sometimes said to be a form of the rarely seen *V. umbrosa*. ↕12 in (30 cm).

V. 'Pink Damask' Upright, clump-forming plant with toothed, 2½–3-in (6–7.5-cm), lance-shaped leaves in opposite pairs at the base and gathered in clusters higher up the stem. Long, densely packed spikes of pastel pink flowers open over a long season from midsummer onward. Best in a sunny position, in moist but well-drained soil; may need staking in exposed situations. A good cut flower. Deadhead after flowering. ↕24 in (60 cm). Z4–8 H8–1.

V. prostrata syn. *V. rupestris* (Prostrate speedwell). Vigorous mat-forming, with prostrate stems sometimes turning up at the tips, and carrying dark green, hairy, narrowly oblong or egg-shaped, ½–1-in (12–25-mm) leaves, sometimes with toothed margins. Short, 1½-in (4-cm) spikes of flowers in various blue shades open in early summer. Plant in full sun or part-shade, in moist, well-drained soil. Good in gravel and between

LAVENDER PINKS IN PERFECT HARMONY

THIS COULD SO EASILY have gone wrong. The veronica and viola are so similar in shade that, with their different habits of growth, they create a delightful association—the lax viola relaxing around the base of the neatly upright veronica. But so many veronicas exhibit bluer tints, or indeed are blue, that exactly the right shade of 'Heidekind' was needed to go with *Viola* 'Nellie Britton'; the wrong color would not have worked as effectively. Alongside, the stretching stems of *Ajania pacifica*, each leaf edged in silver hairs, work their way into the spaces.

paving stones but can be invasive. From Europe. ‡6 in (15 cm). Z5–8 H8–5. **'Aztec Gold'** syn. 'Buttercup' Golden yellow foliage and lavender-blue flowers; the leaves retain their color for most of the season but turn greenish in part-shade. **'Blue Sheen'** Wisteria blue flowers. **'Buttercup'** *see* 'Aztec Gold'. **'Golden Halo'** Bright green leaves irregularly but boldly splashed with golden yellow and clear blue flowers. **'Loddon Blue'** Bright blue flowers. **'Mrs. Holt'** Less vigorous, with soft pink flowers. **'Nana'** Dwarf, with blue flowers. ‡3 in (8 cm). **'Spode Blue'** Royal-blue flowers. **'Trehane'** Free-flowering, with bright blue flowers and yellow-green foliage. Sometimes reblooms. ‡8 in (20 cm).

V. repens Vigorous mat-forming, rooting with tiny, ⅛–⅜-in (4–8-mm), egg-shaped, elliptic or rounded bright green leaves. Flowers in short spikes of up to six from the leaf joints and are usually pink, rarely white or pale blue. The area around the flowers is slightly downy, but the rest of the plant is hairless. Best grown in full sun and moist but well-drained soil; makes good ground cover under dwarf bulbs. From damp areas in Spain and the Corsican mountains. ‡4 in (10 cm). Z4–8 H8–1. **'Sunshine'** syn. 'Pine Knot Sunshine' Golden yellow foliage and clusters of bright blue flowers. Discovered by Judith Tyler of Pine Knot Farms, VA.

V. rupestris see *V. prostrata*

V. **'Shirley Blue'** Erect, 2½–4-in (6–10-cm) spikes of intense blue flowers open from dark buds, from early to late summer, set off by good mounds of deeply toothed, pale grayish green

leaves. Often considered the best of the shorter-flowering speedwells, but has been raised from seed so can be variable. ‡8–16 in (20–40 cm). Z4–8 H8–1.

V. spicata Clump-forming, with masses of short stems rooting as they go, clothed in 3 in (8 cm), toothed, lance-shaped leaves, which are silvery downy, especially below. Dense, tapering spikes of small, clear blue flowers in a prolific summer season. Superb for the front of the border. Needs full sunshine; plants should be deadheaded after flowering. From dry grassland and rocky places in Europe, Turkey, and Central and East Asia. ‡24 in (60 cm). Z3–8 H8–1. **'Alba'** Grayish green leaves and white flowers. ‡18 in (45 cm). **'Blaufuchs'** syn. 'Blue Fox' Lavender-blue flowers. **'Erika'** Dwarf, with pink flowers. 12 in (30 cm). **'Glory'** syn. 'Royal Candles' Tapering spikes of deep violet-blue flowers. A hybrid of *V.* 'Sunny Border Blue.' ‡12 in (30 cm). Z4–8 H8–1. **'Heidekind'** Deep pink flowers and gray leaves. ‡10 in (25 cm). Z3–8 H8–1. **'Icicle'** syn. 'White Icicle' Grayish green foliage and white flowers over a long period. **subsp.** *incana* Entirely covered with silvery gray hairs setting off purplish blue, star-shaped flowers. Avoid wet soil. From eastern and central Europe. Z3–8 H8–1. **subsp.** *incana* **'Silver Carpet'** Silvery green leaves and dark blue flowers. **'Nana Blauteppich'** Very dwarf, with bright blue flowers. ‡2 in (5 cm). **'Noah Williams'** Creamy white flowers and white-edged leaves. **'Romiley Purple'** Unusually bushy with dark violet-blue flowers. **'Rosenrot'** Long tapering spikes of rose pink flowers. **'Rotfuchs'** syn. 'Red Fox'. Deep rose red flowers and glossy dark green leaves. ‡12 in

(30 cm). **'Royal Candles'** *see* 'Glory'. **'Sightseeing'** Vigorous seed-raised plants with rich pink, white, and blue flowers. ‡18 in (45 cm).

V. **'Sunny Border Blue'** Vigorous, with dark violet-blue flowers over rich green leaves from early summer to the first frost; especially if dead-headed. Probably a hybrid of *V. longifolia* and *V. spicata*. Perennial Plant of the Year in 1993. Introduced in 1946 by Connecticut's Sunny Border Nurseries. ‡24 in (60 cm). Z3–8 H8–1.

V. **'White Icicle'** see *V. spicata* 'Icicle'

V. **'White Jolanda'** Vigorous, clump-forming plant with toothed green leaves and dense spikes of white flowers with secondary spikes from the leaf joints below the main spike. ‡18–24 in (45–60 cm). Z4–8 H8–1

VERONICASTRUM
Culver's root
SCROPHULARIACEAE

Tall wands of dense flowers add lift, elegance, and distinctiveness to the summer garden's profile.

About 20 species grow in North America and Eurasia; only a few are generally cultivated. Dense, fibrous-rooted crowns, sometimes spreading by rhizomes, support usually erect stems, though in some the stems arch and root at the tips. Toothed, lance-shaped leaves alternate up the stems, or are gathered in tiered clusters (whorls) of up to seven. The small, flattish, four-lobed flowers, in white, pink, or purplish tones, are packed into dense spikes at the tips

ABOVE 1 *Veronica prostrata* 'Trehane'
2 *V. spicata* 'Romiley Purple'
3 *V. spicata* 'Rotfuchs' **4** *Veronicastrum virginicum* f. *roseum* 'Pink Glow'

of the shoots, sometimes also in the upper leaf joints, giving the appearance of a candelabra. These are mainly tall and elegant plants for the back of the summer border. Some botanists amalgamate the many variants into just two species.

CULTIVATION Best in rich, moist soil in full sun or light shade. Staking may be necessary in shaded sites, as tall species lean to the light.

PROPAGATION Easily divided, but best left to form impressive clumps.

PROBLEMS Powdery mildew.

V. sibiricum A hairless or slightly hairy plant with a tight rootstock, rhizomes spreading slowly, erect stems carry tiers of 4–6 lance-shaped or oblong, finely toothed leaves to 6 x 2 in (15 x 4.5 cm). Stems are topped by long, slender, compact, erect or slightly goosenecked spikes of purple or blue fragrant flowers, sometimes with reddish overtones. Good for cutting and easy from seed. From Russia, China, Japan, and Korea. ‡4–6 ft (1.2–1.8 m). Z4–8 H8–3.

V. villosulum (Trailing veronicastrum) An atypical species that is a climbing or sprawling plant, the lax stems rooting at the tips when they touch the ground and bearing jagged, 4–6 in (10–15 cm) long, broadly lance-shaped leaves. Densely packed clusters of blue flowers

are carried in the leaf joints in summer. More curious than beautiful, but gaining in popularity. From forests and thickets in Japan and China. ‡30–72 in (90–80 cm). Z4–8 H8–3.

V. virginicum (Culver's root) Stout, leafy stems carry lance-shaped, 6–8-in (15–20-cm) leaves arrayed up the stem in clusters (whorls) of three to six until just below the branched flowerheads. A single, erect, creamy white spike opens first but is followed by secondary spikes, creating a compound cluster with two to three tiered whorls of spikes surrounding a larger, central spike. The strong vertical form adds lift and excitement to the middle or rear of beds and borders in late summer and early fall. The dried seed heads are attractive in the garden or in arrangements, and if left standing for winter interest, self-sown seedlings may be plentiful. From open woods, low meadows, and prairies from Ontario and Manitoba south to Georgia and Louisiana. ‡36–72 in (90–180 cm). Z4–8 H8–3. **'Alboroseum'** Pale pink. **'Album'** A dubious name for any white-flowered plants—which is most of them. **'Apollo'** Upright lilac-blue flowers. **'Diane'** Robust, white-flowered form. **'Fascination'** Upright to drooping, lilac-blue spikes. **'Lavendelturm'** Branched, lavender spikes. **f. roseum** Pink flowers. **f. roseum 'Pink Glow'** Compact plant with pale pink flowers. ‡5 ft (1.5 m). **'Spring Dew'** An excellent pure white. **'Temptation'** Purple-blue, flowering in early summer and midsummer.

VINCA
Periwinkle
APOCYNACEAE

Attractive, spring-flowering ground cover plants for sun or light shade, with a wide range of good foliage forms.

Seven species of evergreen and deciduous plants, mostly mat-forming, grow in woodlands in much of Europe, Central Asia, and North Africa. Three of these are commonly cultivated. Clumps or rooting mats of slender stems carry pairs of the neat oval leaves; the characteristic starlike, blue, purple, or white flowers with their five lopsided petals are borne singly just above the foliage in winter, spring, or summer. Most vincas are very tolerant of shade, but they flower more freely with some sun. Some species, especially *V. minor*, are proving invasive, making broad carpets in natural woodlands and tending to smother the indigenous flora. Do not discard garden plants by simply dumping them in wild places.

CULTIVATION Grow in any soil that is not too dry, in sun or shade.

PROPAGATION By division, or by removing rooted pieces.

PROBLEMS Usually trouble-free.

V. difformis Spreading evergreen plant with glossy, dark green, lance-shaped leaves. Typical 1¼–1½-in (3–4-cm) flowers in an unusual shade of milky pale blue open on erect, leafy shoots from early to late spring. Less hardy than other species. From North Africa and southwestern Europe. ‡12–18 in (30–45 cm). Z8–9 H9–8. **Greystone form** Large white flowers above dark foliage. **'Jenny Pym'** Rose pink flowers, fading to white in the center.

V. major (Greater periwinkle) Vigorous evergreen plant forming a clump of erect leafy shoots bearing broad-petaled, violet-blue 2-in (5-cm) flowers in early spring, often continuing intermittently through the summer. Long, trailing shoots develop in summer, with oval, dark green leaves. These shoots root at the joints to form new clumps; if necessary, the shoots can be trimmed off in winter or early spring to keep the plant within bounds, otherwise it will spread indefinitely. Widely naturalized, but native to open scrub in the western and central Mediterranean region. ‡18 in (45 cm) Z7–9 H9–7. **'Maculata'** syn. 'Aureomaculata' Leaves with a central greenish yellow blotch, brightest when grown in good light. **var. oxyloba** Flowers deep purple, with very narrow petals. **'Reticulata'** Leaves marked with creamy yellow veins. **'Variegata'** syn. 'Elegantissima' Leaves boldly margined with creamy white. **'Wojo's Jem'** Dark green leaves with a bold central splash of bright creamy yellow speckled with green.

V. minor (Periwinkle) Prostrate evergreen plant making a mat of long, rooting stems bearing neat, often dark green, oval leaves. In mid- and late spring, sometimes into summer, solitary, violet-purple flowers, 1 in (2.5 cm) across, are borne on short, upright shoots. Very shade-tolerant, but flowers most freely in sun. There has been some confusion regarding the cultivars listed below, and it is not uncommon for the wrong plant to be offered. From woodlands in most of central and eastern Europe and Central Asia. ‡6–8 in (15–20 cm). Z4–9 H9–1. **f. alba** White flowers opening from pink or white buds. **f. alba 'Gertrude Jekyll'** Compact plant with small, dark green leaves and pure white flowers. ‡4 in (10 cm). **'Alba Variegata'** White flowers, with leaves at first narrowly margined with yellow, soon fading to cream. **'Argenteovariegata'** Light violet-blue flowers above narrowly cream-edged leaves. **'Atropurpurea'** Flowers deep reddish purple. **'Aureovariegata'** Young leaves with bright yellow margins, becoming paler in summer. **'Azurea Flore Pleno'** syn. 'Caerulea Plena' Light violet-blue, double flowers. **'Blue and Gold'** Leaves narrowly margined with bright yellow; flowers violet-blue. **'Blue Drift'** Pale violet-blue flowers above dark green leaves. **'Bowles Blue'** *see* 'La

Grave'. **'Bowles Variety'** see 'La Grave'.
'Burgundy' Flowers deep wine red;
not very distinct from 'Atropurpurea'.
'Caerulea Plena' see 'Azurea Flore
Pleno'. **'Dartington Star'** see *V. major*
var. *oxyloba*. **'Double Burgundy'** see
'Multiplex'. **'Illumination'** Deep green
leaves with a large dramatic central
splash of creamy yellow; flowers violet-
blue. **'La Grave'** Large, broad-petaled
reddish purple flowers. **'Maculata'**
Dark green leaves with greenish yellow
central blotch. **'Multiplex'** Reddish
purple, irregularly double flowers.
'Purpurea' see 'Atropurpurea'. **'Ralph
Shugert'** Leaves finely edged with
creamy white; flowers purplish blue.
'Rubra' see 'Atropurpurea'. **'Sabinka'**
Compact and low-growing, with
smaller leaves and violet-blue flowers.
↕ 4–6 in (10–15 cm). **'Silver Service'**
Flowers double, violet-blue, above
white-margined leaves. **'Sterling
Silver'** Light blue-violet flowers
above narrowly white-edged leaves.
'Variegata' see 'Aureovariegata'.
'Variegata Aurea' see 'Aureovariegata'.
'White Gold' Leaves splashed with
yellow, flowers violet-blue.

VIOLA
Pansy, Viola, Violet
VIOLACEAE

Indispensable small plants offering
a wide range of flower colors and
patterns, diverse foliage, and year-
round interest.

About 500 species of deciduous
and evergreen perennials and
annuals, occasionally woody at the
base, are found in mainly cool to
warm-temperate climates worldwide.
They grow from sea level to high
altitudes, with a few native to Arctic
and tropical areas, plus a few small
Hawaiian shrubs. Although they
constitute a diverse group, all are

CATEGORIES OF VIOLA

Most species and cultivars of *Viola* can
be grouped into three main categories,
each with a number of subdivisions.

Violet Includes sweet violets (*V.
odorata* and its hybrids with *V. suavis* and other
species) and Parma violets. (For more on
Parma violets, see Parma Violets, *p.482*.)
  VT Single-flowered forms and hybrids
of *V. odorata*.
  DVt Double-flowered forms; hybrids
of *V. odorata*, often with many petals.
  PVt Single-flowered Parma violets.
  dPVt Double-flowered Parma violets,
often with innumerable petals.

Pansy Includes all forms of *V. x
wittrockiana* (hybrids of *V. tricolor*,
V. lutea, *V. altaica*, and other species).
Mostly annuals and biennials grown
from seed.
  SP & FP Show pansy and fancy
pansy—types of exhibition pansies.
Flowers conforming to exhibition rules,
not suitable for borders and not
included here.
  BP Bedding pansy. More floriferous
and often more robust than exhibition

types, flowering from fall to early
summer; suitable for bedding and
containers but not included here.
  T Tricolor pansy. Smaller flowers,
more like wild *V. tricolor*, suitable for
bedding and containers.

Viola Includes all forms of *V. x
williamsii* (hybrids of *V. cornuta* with cultivated
pansies) and other plants derived from
V. cornuta. Mostly perennials grown
from cuttings. All except ExVa are
suitable for bedding, rock gardens,
sunny well-drained borders,
and containers.
  ExVa Exhibition viola. Flowers
conforming to exhibition rules, not
suitable for borders and are not
included here.
  Va Bedding viola. Compact, flowering
freely for many months in summer.
Many cultivars are scented.
  Vtta Violetta. Refined bedding violas,
more compact and with rayless flowers
  C *V. cornuta* cultivars and hybrids.
Seedling selections and hybrids with
flower shape, foliage, and habit similar
to *V. cornuta*.

VIOLA STRUCTURE

The *Viola* flower stem carries
a pair of small bracts, and bends
over at the top. The bend is partly
hidden by the appendages of
the five sepals; the latter are
usually shorter than the five
petals. The lowest petal
extends backward into
a spur, which contains
the nectaries.

Petal

Five sepals, each
with appendage

Stipules

Viola lutea

Spur of
lower petal

Stem turned
over at top

Two bracts

instantly recognizable by their flowers.
Their habitats include woodlands,
meadow, scree, bog, stabilized sand
dunes, and semidesert. They have
been used for medicinal purposes
since medieval times.

Growing from fibrous or fleshy
roots, or rhizomes, the stemmed or
stemless flowers come in two forms.
The normal, showy, springtime
flowers have five petals, the lower
one with a spur; these often fail to
set seed naturally. In summer, most
also produce petal-less, self-fertile
flowers whose buds never open
but which give plentiful seeds that
always come true to type. These
are referred to as cleistogamous,
from the Greek *kleistos* meaning
closed. Pansies, violas, and violettas
produce only petaled flowers, which
easily cross-pollinate, producing
variable offspring (see Categories
of Viola).

Violet leaves are heart-shaped,
elongated, or divided, in many cases
enlarging once the showy spring
flowering has finished. Pansy leaves
are oval and do not enlarge in the
same way. The leaves of all species
have at their base a pair of
rudimentary leaves (stipules), which
are small and toothed in violets,
divided and more prominent in
pansies and their allies. The
distinctive three-lobed seed capsules
of violets either rest on the soil and
open gently, the seeds sometimes
being dispersed by ants or, as in all
pansies, stand on erect stalks and
pop their seeds out as they dry.

Development of the various
groups has taken place all over the
world. Britain, France, and a few
other countries played leading roles
in 200 years of selection and
hybridization of the sweet violet,
V. odorata, with similar species
such as the rarely seen *V. suavis*,
giving rise to hundreds of cultivars.
Sweet and Parma violets were
widely grown on a commercial
scale for cut flowers and essential
oils until the first half of the 20th
century, especially in England,
France, Italy, and the US; now a
much smaller industry. By crossing
pansies with multistemmed
perennial species, especially
V. cornuta, tufted pansies were
created—usually called violas. These
are compact, tufted perennials that
have abundant, often scented flowers
smaller than those of pansies.

Refinement produced violettas,
with smaller flowers lacking rays
(the dark lines radiating from the
throat), a more compact habit and,
typically, good scent. British breeder
Richard Cawthorne, well known
for his displays at the Chelsea
Flower Show, introduced some
excellent modern cultivars. Breeding
seed-raised violas and pansies
for seasonal displays is now an
important multinational business.
These are not covered here.

RIGHT 1 *Viola alba* **2** *V.* 'Bowles' Black'

CULTIVATION Most species grow
well in fertile, neutral to slightly
alkaline soil including organic
matter, but allowance should be
made for the wide range of native
soils, habitats, and climates in which
Viola species grow. Soils rich in
nitrogen encourage excessive foliage
and poor flowering. Woodland
species tolerate shade in summer;
otherwise, good light is preferred,
and established violas, violettas, and
some species can take full sun.
They are best planted when small.
Deadheading violas promotes a
longer flowering season; it is less
effective on violets.

Violas, violettas and many violets
may be left in place for at least two
or three years, so long as they do
not become undernourished,
diseased, or congested. They vary
greatly in their hardiness, from Z1
to Z9, while the few tropical or
subtropical species, such as those
from the Hawaiian Islands and
Southeast Asia (not covered here),
may be Z11.

PROPAGATION Seed, cuttings, division
and layering are all useful for
different types of *Viola* at different
times (see Propagation, *p.480*).

PROBLEMS Spider mites (see Spider
Mites, *p.483*), aphids (including

SNEAKING IN AT THE FRONT

SO OFTEN, MEMBERS of the parsley family, *Apiaceae*, lose their lower leaves by flowering time. The result is that the stems at the base are revealed, and this detracts from the remaining foliage and, of course, the flowers. The answer is to choose a low plant to set in front that will weave its shoots in and among the stems, both to hide them and to provide appropriate foliage and flowers—for this position, violas are ideal. Here, *Meum athamanticum*, which should be more widely grown, is fronted by the dainty little *Viola* 'Belmont Blue', which fills this territory well and sneaks a few long stems up among the delicate, flat, white heads.

violet aphid), slugs, snails, violet gall midge, gray mold, powdery mildew, downy mildew, black root rot, leaf spots, rusts, and pansy sickness. Looking at that list of potential problems, you'd never believe they are easy to grow—but they are. Violet root rot, a noted disease of kniphofias and other plants, is named for its color, not the plant.

V. alba An evergreen rosette of heart-shaped leaves appears in early spring and increases in size from spring to summer, reaching 6 in (15 cm) in width, and puts out runners that bear the fragrant flowers at the same time. The blooms, to ¾ in (2 cm) wide, are, despite the name, just as likely to be violet-blue as white. Similar to *V. odorata* except that in *V. odorata* the runners root more readily and produce flowers from the rosettes, including those at the end of previous years' runners, rather than from the new runners. One of the subspecies may be an ancestor of the Parma violet. Grow in well-drained, fertile soil including humus, in good light or light shade. From central, eastern, and southern Europe. ↕6 in (15 cm). Z5–8 H8–1

V. 'Alice Witter' see *V. sororia* 'Alice Witter'

V. 'Ardross Gem' (Va) Long-stemmed, dark blue flowers, up to 1¼ in (3 cm) across, with a splash of gold on the lower petal, opening from late spring until well into fall. Compact in growth, prolific, and very resilient in adverse weather. A real charmer. ↕2 in (5 cm). Z5–8 H8–5

V. arenaria see *V. rupestris*

V. 'Aspasia' (Va) Strongly scented flowers ¾ in (2 cm) across, grading from cream on the upper petals to yellow on the lower ones; makes a large, free-flowering mound. Benefits from division every few years. Raised by Richard Cawthorne of England. ↕6 in (15 cm). Z5–8 H8–5

V. banksii see *V. hederacea*

V. 'Belmont Blue' (C) syn. *V.* 'Boughton Blue' Pale sky blue flowers, 1 in (2.5 cm) across, with a hint of lilac and a yellow eye, from late spring to late summer. ↕4 in (10 cm). Z5–8 H8–5

V. 'Beshlie' (Va) Pale yellow, highly fragrant, long-stemmed flowers, 1 in (2.5 cm) across, are produced in abundance. May develop blue shades on upper petals in cooler areas. Raised by Richard Cawthorne and named for author and illustrator Beshlie Heron. ↕8 in (20 cm). Z5–8 H8–5

V. biflora (Twin-flowered violet) A deciduous mountain violet with slender creeping rhizomes that put out a few stems and kidney-shaped leaves up to 1½ in (4 cm) long in spring. From late spring to early summer, by unscented yellow flowers ⅜ in (1.5 cm) across with brownish rays. The flowers are not produced in pairs, although superficially they appear to be paired. Prefers damp soil and can tolerate a little shade. From Japan, the Himalaya, Alps, Pyrenees, and Scandinavia; rare in North America. ↕3–6 in (8–15 cm). Z4–8 H8–1

V. 'Blue Moonlight' (C) The pale creamy yellow flowers are 1¼ in (3 cm) across and the upper petals have a pale blue flush. Larger and fuller-flowered than typical *V. cornuta* but retains a vigorous perennial habit. ↕4¾ in (12 cm). Z5–8 H8–5

V. 'Boughton Blue' see *V.* 'Belmont Blue'

V. 'Bowles' Black' (T) Almost black flowers with a small yellow center. A short-lived perennial of loose habit reflecting its *V. tricolor* parentage (*see* Black Pansies). Propagate the darkest forms from cuttings; often comes almost true from seed, but the color can drift toward purple. Obtained from horticulturist E.A. Bowles and named after him by Perry's Hardy Plant Farm, Middlesex. ↕4 in (10 cm). Z5–8 H8–1

V. 'Buttercup' (Vtta) Deep yellow flowers that are highly scented, 1 in (2.5 cm) across, are produced freely

above neat, compact foliage. Originally called 'Rock Orange' when introduced by D. B. Crane in the 1890s. ↕6 in (15 cm). Z5–8 H8–5

V. 'Clementina' (Va) Large, long-stemmed, rich purple flowers, 2 in (5 cm) across, make a large, showy clump. ↕8 in (20 cm). Z5–8 H8–5

V. 'Clive Groves' (VT) Vigorous, with large, very fragrant, reddish purple flowers from winter to early spring. A chance seedling, and probably a hybrid, found near *V.* 'The Czar' in Clive Groves's Dorset, England nursery in 1980. ↕8 in (20 cm). Z5–8 H8–5

V. 'Coeur d'Alsace' (VT) Rosy salmon flowers, from winter to early spring. Raised by Armand Millet in France in 1916 but originally it was described as a more rose-purple color. ↕8 in (20 cm). Z5–8 H8–5

V. 'Columbine' (Va) Rounded, 1¼ in (3 cm) wide, white or pale lilac flowers, splashed with violet and with a yellow eye, are held clear of the compact foliage from mid-spring to early fall. Vigorous, but not scented. Similar to 'Elaine Quin' but paler. Not to be confused with the sweet violet of the same name. ↕6 in (15 cm). Z4–9 H7–1

V. coreana syn. *V. grypoceras*

V. cornuta (Horned violet) A spreading evergreen pansy with 2-in (5-cm), egg-shaped leaves and notched rather than divided stipules. Its multiple stems form compact mounds when given good light, but are able to reach up between and into other plants if given competition. Abundant, slightly fragrant, violet to lilac-blue flowers, 1 in (2.5 cm) across, are produced from late spring to mid-fall, their long, slender, hornlike spur giving the plant its name. Being a good long-flowering perennial, and producing many shoots from the network of roots, it has been used extensively in breeding, giving rise to many, often scented cultivars. Grow in good light to keep plants compact, in soil with plenty of humus. The plant makes good ground cover in light shade and tolerates warmer and drier conditions than pansies. Propagate by cuttings or division in early spring; seedlings of cultivars rarely come true. From the Pyrenees. ↕6 in (15 cm). Z6–9 H9–6. **Alba Group** White flowers opening in late spring to late summer, will spread and self-seed even if grown in the shade. Vigorous. **(Alba Group) 'Alba Minor'** White flowers, more compact. ↕4 in (10 cm). **Lilacina Group** Lilac flowers. **'Minor'** Compact, with slightly smaller, ¾ in (2 cm) wide pale mauve flowers. ↕4 in (10 cm). **Purpurea Group** Dark purple-blue to violet flowers. **'Victoria's Blush'** Pale pink flowers, with magenta rays and central flush, and pale magenta around the outer edges.

V. corsica (Corsican pansy, Corsican violet) Narrow-leaved wild pansy with unscented, elongated violet flowers, up

BLACK PANSIES

Black pansies have an allure that tempts many gardeners, and over the years a number have been introduced. Many of these, such as 'Turbo Black', 'Springtime Black', 'Black Princess', 'Black Angel', and 'Blackjack', are intended for bedding and are naturally very short-lived. However, there are some that persist a little better. The best-known of these are 'Molly Sanderson' and 'Bowles Black', but 'Raven' and 'Roscastle Black' are also well worth considering.

'Molly Sanderson' is generally thought to be the darkest, and the petals have a matte surface that seems to enhance the richness of the color. 'Bowles Black' is also very black at its best, but so many unselected seedlings are sold, or turn up self-sown in gardens, that its color cannot be depended upon; it is also short-lived and a taller, more straggly, small-flowered tricolor type. 'Blackjack' is basically a more bushy and dependably well-colored version of 'Bowles Black'.

'Roscastle Black' is probably the most prolific and the most reliable, but the color is less good than that of 'Molly Sanderson', while 'Raven' has a rather different low, spreading habit. None of them has any scent.

Whichever cultivar you choose, it pays to see plants in flower and to pick ones that are a good color. Then you can propagate from cuttings and deadhead regularly to prevent poorly colored self-sown seedlings from diluting the richness of your stock.

to 1½ in (3.5 cm) across, which may have a yellow or white throat and dark rays on the lower petal. This species is produced in good numbers from early spring to late fall. Grows well in many well-drained soils, given good light; takes a lot of heat and will perform in hanging baskets. From Corsica, Sardinia, and Elba. ↕ 8 in (20 cm). Z4–9 H7–1

V. cucullata syn. *V. obliqua* (Marsh blue violet) Creeping deciduous plant, the rhizome produces kidney- to heart-shaped leaves up to 3½ in (9 cm) long in spring. These are soon followed by unscented violet flowers, ¾ in (2 cm) across, from mid-spring to early summer, held well above the foliage. Similar to *V. sororia* but the flowers are often held farther above the leaves and the cleistogamous (produced by self-pollination) seedpods are held well above the soil. Several cultivars have been ascribed to *V. cucullata*, often incorrectly, through confusion with *V. sororia*. Adaptable and tolerates cold wet conditions, in the open or in light shade. Sometimes grown for cut flowers because of the long stems. From North America. ↕ 10 in (25 cm). Z3–8 H7–1.
'Alba' syn. f. *albiflora* White flowers with a creamy green throat with dark lines in the throat on the lower petal. Sometimes sold as *V. cucullata striata alba* or *V. sororia* 'Albiflora', the latter being a different plant.

RIGHT 1 *Viola cornuta* **2** *V. corsica* **3** *V.* 'Elaine Quin' **4** *V. elatior* **5** *V.* 'Etain'

V. **'Dancing Geisha'** (VT) Slender, creeping, deciduous rhizomes produce clumps of crinkled and deeply cut foliage, marked in silvery gray along the veins, followed by broad-petaled, fragrant, lilac or white flowers above the foliage from early to late spring. Best in rich, moist, humus-rich soil in a cool place with light shade. A hybrid of uncertain parents, but showing a Japanese influence, from Terra Nova Nurseries. ↕ 6 in (15 cm). Z5–9 H8–1

V. **'Dawn'** (Vtta) Prolific, scented, pale lemon, slightly frilled flowers, 1–1½ in (2.5–3.5 cm) across, the lower petal a little darker, appear from mid-spring to midsummer. Divide regularly to help overcome a tendency toward woodiness. ↕ 6 in (15 cm). Z5–8 H8–5

V. **'Delphine'** (Va) Unusual elongated lavender petals, veined with violet and, rarely, with turquoise. Somewhat trailing in habit; good in containers and the edges of raised beds. ↕ 8 in (20 cm).

V. **'Eastgrove Blue Scented'** (C) Long-stemmed, well-scented mid-blue flowers, 1½ in (4 cm) across, with short dark rays and a yellow eye on vigorous, spreading plants. From Eastgrove Cottage Nursery, Warwickshire, England. ↕ 4¾ in (12 cm). Z5–8 H8–5

V. **'Elaine Quin'** (Va) Rosy-mauve flowers, 1¼ in (3 cm) across, are streaked with white; a compact, strong grower but unscented. 'Columbine' is similar, but paler. From Bouts Cottage Nurseries, Worcestershire, England. ↕ 4¾ in (12 cm). Z5–8 H8–5

V. elatior syn. *V. erecta* A very distinctive, upright, stiffly branched, deciduous violet, with lance-shaped, toothed leaves up to 3½ in (9 cm) long and bearing pale lavender-blue flowers, 1 in (2.5 cm) across, with a white throat and spurs up to ⅛ in (4 mm) long in late spring and early summer. Prefers moist soil in light shade, but tolerates much drier conditions, including alkaline soils. Benefits from shelter or basal support from low neighbors to keep the stems upright. From central Europe to Siberia and China. ↕ 12–20 in (30–50 cm). Z5–8 H8–5

V. erecta see *V. elatior*

V. **'Etain'** (Va) Strongly scented, yellow flowers with an orange eye, up to 1¾ in (4.5 cm) across, shade out to a lavender-violet border and are held on strong, upright stems. Some plants under this name are the otherwise rarely seen 'Elizabeth' (white petals flushed with lavender-blue). Similar to 'Helen Dillon', but darker. Grows and propagates better in warmer climates. ↕ 6 in (15 cm). Z4–8 H8–4

V. **'Fiona'** (Va) White, long-stemmed, highly fragrant flowers, 1½ in (4 cm) across, are slightly suffused with pale

mauve. Vigorous and popular. ↕8 in (20 cm). Z5–8 H8–5

V. 'Foxbrook Cream' (C) Lemon-cream flowers, 1–1½ in (2.5–4 cm) across, turn lilac as they age. Vigorous. ↕4 in (10 cm). Z5–8 H8–5

V. 'Governor Herrick' (VT) A branching rhizome carries large, shiny, evergreen, heart-shaped leaves and deep bluish purple flowers to 1½ in (3.5 cm) across, on stiff stems, from mid-fall to early spring. Longer lasting as cut flowers than scented, single, sweet violets, but tends to lose its scent soon after picking. Prefers fertile, well-drained soil in good light to slight shade, but tolerant of poor, chalky soil. Divide roots or runners in late spring or early summer. Resistant to spider mite. Probably a hybrid of *V. odorata* and *V. sororia*, introduced in 1908. Named for a governor of Ohio. ↕8 in (20 cm). Z5–8 H8–5

V. gracilis syn. *V. velutina* A mat-forming, evergreen wild pansy with erect or ascending stems bearing elongated leaves up to 1¼ in (3 cm) long and stipules with four to eight segments. Violet or yellow flowers, 1¼ in (3 cm) across, with a slender, ¼-in (6–7-mm) spur, bloom from early to late summer. Best in poor, well-drained soil. Used in hybridizing with *V. cornuta* and violas. From western Turkey, northern Greece, Bulgaria, and Albania. ↕6 in (15 cm). Z5–8 H8–5

V. 'Green Goddess' Somewhere between a pansy and a viola. Olive-green flowers, 1½ in (4 cm) across, with a large yellow center rayed in black, appear from mid-spring to late summer. Takes full sun but retains its color best in shade. Short-lived. Raised by Thompson & Morgan Seedsmen, Inc., NJ. ↕8–16 in (20–40 cm). Z5–8 H8–5

V. 'Grey Owl' (Va) The mauve-gray flowers, 1¼ in (3 cm) across, graduate to yellow on the lower petal. Gorgeous, but not easy to grow well. ↕4¾ in (12 cm). Z5–8 H8–5

RIGHT 1 *Viola hederacea*
2 *V.* 'Huntercombe Purple'
3 *V.* 'Jackanapes'

V. grypoceras syn. *V. coreana* A violet with a short rhizome. A few stems carry smooth heart- to kidney-shaped leaves, up to 1¼ in (3 cm) across, with slightly toothed edges. Pale purple, scentless flowers, ¾ in (2 cm) across with a narrow ¼–⅜-in (6–8-mm) spur, from mid- to late spring. *V. grypoceras* var. *exilis* and *V. grypoceras* f. *variegata*, are sometimes listed, but the majority of such plants prove to be *V. variegata*, which is more strongly variegated, unbranched, and has rounder leaves. Prefers light shade and fertile, well-drained soil with good humus content. From China, Japan, Korea, Russian Asia, and Taiwan. ↕6 in (15 cm). Z5–8 H8–5

V. 'Haslemere' (Va) see *V.* 'Nellie Britton'

V. hederacea From a small rosette, long thin runners root readily at the leaf nodes to form a carpet. The leaves are round or kidney-shaped and the purple and white flowers are produced on stems held above the foliage in summer. Research has revealed that the varied plants commonly known as *V. hederacea* represent several related species, and it seems likely that the plant most commonly sold as *V. hederacea* is, in fact, *V. banksii*. The smaller cultivars, some of which have blue petals, may also represent other species. Grow in moist humus-rich soil in light shade, in pots or hanging baskets. Easily divided by removing rooted runners. From Australia. ↕4 in (10 cm). Z5–8 H8–5

V. 'Huntercombe Purple' (Va) Masses of sumptuous purple-violet, slightly elongated flowers, 1¼–1½ in (3–4 cm) across with a white eye, continue well into fall on compact plants. ↕6 in (15 cm). Z5–8 H8–5

V. 'Inverurie Beauty' (Va) A profusion of mauve-violet, well-scented flowers, 1¼ in (3 cm) across with a pale orange

1

2

3

PROPAGATION

Seed, stem cuttings, root cuttings, and division can all be used to propagate *Viola* species and cultivars, but not all methods are suitable for all plants. The seed of many violet species needs winter chilling to break dormancy; sow in fall or early winter. The seed of violas can be sown at any time of year, but sowing in late summer allows seedlings to establish before the winter. For all *Viola*, the seeds should be covered with no more than ⅛ in (4 mm) of fine soil. Germination may take from two weeks (violas) to several months (violets), during which time it is best to exclude light. Light and fresh air should be admitted as soon as germination occurs.

Viola cultivars may be propagated by division in spring, or by cuttings. Cuttings should be taken from stems that are not hollow, either from early

to late summer (for fall planting), or from late summer to early fall (for spring planting). The cuttings often have roots before being severed from the parent, or can be encouraged to produce them by late summer pruning-back and dressing with compost.

The runners of sweet violets and related species may be layered, then severed a few weeks later. Stemless violets with fleshy roots may be increased by root cuttings or by division if multiple crowns have formed. Rhizomes may be cut or broken into pieces, preferably with roots attached and preferably in late winter, when they have no leaves and before new root growth starts. Stem cuttings may be used for branched violets, while species with rhizomes or multiple stems can be divided successfully in either spring or fall.

eye, are carried on long stems suitable for cutting. ‡8 in (20 cm). Z5–8 H8–5

V. 'Irish Molly' (Va) Unusual flowers, 1½ in (4 cm) across, from mid-spring to early fall; upper petals are maroon-brown, lower petals khaki-yellow-green with a rayed dark blotch, and yellow in the eye and middle of the lower petal. Popular for its unusual coloring, and a parent of many unusually colored, seed-raised bedding violas. Hints of pansy parentage are shown by the small dark blotch on the petals and its tendency to fade away in late summer; take cuttings in spring. ‡8 in (20 cm). Z5–8 H8–5

V. 'Ivory Queen' (Va) The abundant, scented, elongated, creamy lemon flowers, 1½ in (4 cm) across, with the lower petals pale lemon colored, are held on long stems from late spring to mid-fall. Very vigorous. ‡8 in (20 cm). Z5–8 H8–5

V. 'Jackanapes' (Va) Eye-catching, scentless flowers, 1¼–1½ in (3–3.5 cm) across, with crimson-brown upper petals and yellow lower petals with dark rays near the throat, appear from mid-spring to early fall. Vigorous but short-lived, suggesting some *V. tricolor* in its ancestry. Selected by Gertrude Jekyll and said to have been named after her pet monkey, whose cheeky face she thought it resembled. ‡6 in (15 cm). Z7–9 H7–1

V. 'Jeannie Bellew' (Va) Prolific, scented, cream flowers, 1 in (2.5 cm) across, are tinged with lavender on the edges until later in the season. It is named for its raiser, a member of the Jameson Irish whiskey family. ‡6 in (15 cm). Z5–8 H8–5

V. 'Julian' (Va) Prolific, sturdy, short-stemmed, mid-blue flowers, 1¼ in (3 cm) across, darker and slightly frilly toward the edges, with a yellow eye, are carried over neat compact foliage. Flowers almost endlessly. Raised at Kaye's Nursery, Silverdale, Lancashire, England. ‡6 in (15 cm). Z5–8 H8–5

V. 'Königin Charlotte' (**Queen Charlotte, Reine Charlotte**) (VT) Produces very fragrant blue flowers freely from late summer to mid-spring; they are unusual in being turned upward. Introduced in Germany in 1900 and probably a hybrid of *V. odorata*. ‡8 in (20 cm). Z6–8 H8–6

V. koreana see *V. variegata*

V. labradorica (Labrador violet) Deciduous violet with a woody rootstock, the stems and heart-shaped leaves are soon followed in mid- and late spring by scentless, violet-blue flowers, ¾ in (2 cm) across. The true *V. labradorica* is rarely grown; the plants commonly found under that name, sometimes with a *purpurea* suffix, are *V. riviniana* Purpurea Group. From Greenland and northeastern North America. ‡6 in (15 cm). Z3–8 H8–3

V. 'Letitia' (Va) Dusky pink flowers, 1–1¼ in (2.5–3 cm) across, with

maroon-purple rays and a yellow-orange eye, appear from mid-spring to early fall. 'Vita' is similar but has larger flowers of a deeper pink. From Richard Cawthorne. ‡8 in (20 cm). Z5–8 H8–5

V. 'Little David' (Vtta) Slightly frilled, cream flowers, 1 in (2.5 cm) across, with a hint of blue on the upper two petals and purple edging, are held well above the foliage. Vigorous, compact, long-lived, and said by some to have the rich fragrance of freesias. ‡6 in (15 cm). Z5–8 H8–5

V. lutea (Mountain pansy) A creeping, fibrous root system produces many, largely unbranched stems to create the tufted habit that made it so important in the development of bedding violas. The stems bear evergreen, oval leaves, divided stipules with a broader lobe at the end, and scentless, yellow or violet flowers ¾–1¼ in (2–3 cm) across with ⅛–¼-in (3–6-mm) spurs, from late spring to late summer, sometimes later. One of the parents of the garden pansy, it is distinct from *V. tricolor* primarily in the latter's being annual or biennial, and single-stemmed. Prefers fertile soil in cool climates. Copes with high rainfall if well-drained. Good ground cover. From the uplands of western and central Europe. ‡6 in (15 cm). Z5–9 H9–5

V. 'Maggie Mott' (Va) Strongly scented, silvery-mauve flowers, 2 in (5 cm) across, from mid-spring to midsummer, become paler toward the bottom petal and have a yellow eye. An old-fashioned favorite named for the daughter of Mr. Albert Mott of Sunningdale, Berkshire, England, in whose garden it was raised in the late 1860s. ‡4¾ in (12 cm). Z5–9 H9–5

V. 'Magic' (Va) Early and late flowers, 1 in (2.5 cm) across, are pale violet; the main flush is white with slightly violet rays. Several plants are grown under this name, with slightly different color changes. ‡6 in (15 cm). Z5–8 H8–5

V. mandshurica (Manchurian violet) Building into clumps of foliage over a few years, narrow, deciduous leaves emerge before the purple, scentless flowers, 1¼ in (3 cm) across, appear in spring and early summer. White, pink, and double-flowered plus brown-leaved forms are occasionally seen. Best in moist soil in good light or light shade. From China, Japan, Korea, Russian Asia, and Taiwan. ‡8 in (20 cm). Z6–9 H9–6. **'Fuji Dawn'** Irregularly marbled leaves in ivory, pink, and green turn plainer green during summer. From Ray Brown at Plantworld, Devon, England.

V. 'Mars' (Va) Plain, rich violet flowers, 1¼ in (3 cm) across, have a pale eye. Confused with the hybrid violet of the same name. Raised by Richard Cawthorne and a hybrid of two Greek species. ‡8 in (20 cm). Z5–9 H9–5

V. 'Mars' (VT) A creeping rhizome gives rise to tufts of heart-shaped leaves, 1½ in (4 cm) across, with purplish centers spreading out along the veins,

giving the plant its main feature. Lavender-blue flowers produced reluctantly in mid-spring. Confused with the viola of the same name. Grow in fertile humus-rich soil in light shade. A Japanese hybrid of the rarely seen *V. hirtipes* f. *rhodovenia* and *V. japonica*, introduced by Terra Nova Nurseries, Oregon. ‡7 in (18 cm). Z5–8 H8–5

V. 'Martin' (Va) Abundant, long-stemmed, violet-blue flowers, 1¼ in (3 cm) across with a yellow eye, appear early and continue over a long period. Compact. ‡6 in (15 cm). Z5–8 H8–5

V. 'Molly Sanderson' (Va) Compact, with matte black, yellow-eyed flowers, 1¼ in (3 cm) across (*see* Black Pansies, *p.479*). Grow in light shade to prevent flagging. From the eponymous Irish gardener. ‡6 in (15 cm). Z5–9 H9–5

V. 'Moonlight' (Va) Scented creamy yellow flowers, 1 in (2.5 cm) across, with slight rays, appear on long stems. Reliable. ‡8 in (20 cm). Z5–8 H8–5

V. 'Mrs. Lancaster' (Va) Strongly scented, pure white, slightly rayed flowers, 1¼ in (3 cm), across on compact

ABOVE 1 *Viola lutea* **2** *V. mandshurica* **3** *V. 'Nellie Britton'*

plant. Shade-tolerant but avoid dry conditions. ‡6 in (15 cm). Z5–8 H8–5

V. 'Myfawnny' (Va) Strongly scented, delicately marbled, mauve and lilac flowers, 1¼ in (3 cm) across, have darker rays and appear from mid-spring to early fall. Very free-flowering, compact, and robust. ‡4¾ in (12 cm). Z5–8 H8–5

V. 'Nellie Britton' (syn. *V. 'Haslemere'*) (Va) Soft lavender-pink, slightly purple-rayed flowers, ¾ in (2 cm) across, late spring to late summer. Raised by Thompson & Morgan in 1923 as 'Haslemere', it was almost forgotten until saved and distributed by Nellie Britton, Devon, England, horticulturist. ‡4¾ in (12 cm). Z5–7 H7–1

V. obliqua see *V. cucullata*

V. odorata (Sweet violet) Semievergreen; a short rhizome with fibrous roots bears a rosette of rounded to heart-shaped leaves producing slender rooting runners and scented flowers up to 1 in

ABOVE 1 *Viola odorata* **2** *V. palustris* **3** *V. pedata* **4** *V. riviniana* **5** *V. rupestris*

(2.5 cm) across from late winter to early spring. Flowers are usually violet or white, but cultivars exist with intermediate colors as well as pink and yellow-buff. All have a blunt, purple, ¼-in (6-mm) spur. The world's best-known violet, with many cultivars, some, collectively called semperflorens or quatre saisons types, start flowering as early as late summer. For yellow-flowered variants, see *V.* 'Sulfurea'. It is not always clear if sweet violets are cultivars of *V. odorata* or hybrids. Best in fertile, well-drained soil including humus, with good light to slight shade; well suited to naturalizing in an open woodland setting. Self-seeds readily (seed from cleistogamous flowers is much more likely to come true). From Europe, African Atlantic islands, Mediterranean islands and margins, and western Asia. ‡8 in (20 cm). Z6–8 H8–6. **'Alba'** This name is used for a range of white-flowered plants; many have distinct names. **Rosea Group** This name is used for several pink-flowered forms that are difficult to distinguish but may have distinct names.

V. palustris (Marsh violet, Bog violet) Deciduous violet, the rootstock sends out slender creeping roots and runners. Smooth, kidney-shaped leaves followed by pale lilac, sometimes almost white, scentless flowers, up to ⅝ in (1.5 cm) across, with ¹⁄₁₆-in (2-mm) spurs from mid-spring to midsummer. Grow in wet, peaty soil, through hills of moss, or in damp lawns, in good light to slight shade; prefers a cool situation. Europe, northern US, Canada, and northern Asia. ‡6 in (15 cm). Z5–8 H8–5

V. papilionacea see *V. sororia*

V. **'Pat Kavanagh'** (C) Yellow flowers, 1¼–1½ in (3–4 cm) across with faint dark rays, gain a lilac tinge at the edges as they fade. ‡4 in (10 cm). Z5–8 H8–5

V. pedata (Bird's-foot violet) Stemless, clump-forming, semievergreen violet, with a short, stout rhizome producing lateral roots giving rise to new crowns. Leaves are divided almost to the base into five or more segments. Unscented flowers, 1¼ in (3 cm) across, open from mid-spring to early summer or later, and are usually pale violet with noticable orange stamens in the center. The many variants, include forms with the upper two petals deep purple, all the petals white, or leaves more finely divided. Does not produce cleistogamous flowers, unlike the somewhat similar *V. pedatifida*, which also has less prominent stamens. Needs good light and acidic, moist, well-drained, gritty, and peaty soil that is not waterlogged in winter. From eastern North America. ‡6 in (15 cm). Z4–8 H8–1

V. pedatifida (Larkspur violet) Clump-forming, semievergreen or deciduous violet with leaves divided into 5–11 segments and further divided at the tips. The scentless, violet-blue flowers, ¾ in (2 cm) across, have dense white beards on the three lower petals and open from mid-spring to early summer. Adaptable and will tolerate damp conditions. Self-seeds freely. Similar to *V. pedata* but even hardier and produces cleistogamous flowers. From North America. ‡4¾ in (12 cm). Z2–8 H8–1

V. priceana see *V. sororia* f. *priceana*

V. **'Princesse de Galles'** (**Princess of Wales**) (VT) Large lilac-blue flowers in winter. The most widely grown scented sweet violet. Other sweet violet cultivars are often sold under this name. Raised by Armand Millet in France in 1889 and probably a hybrid of *V. odorata*. ‡12 in (30 cm). Z5–8 H8–5

V. **Queen Charlotte** see *V.* 'Königin Charlotte'

V. **'Raven'** (Va) Velvety deep purple flowers, 1 in (2.5 cm) across, have a yellow eye (see Black Pansies, *p. 479*). Divide every few years to retain vigor. ‡6 in (15 cm). Z5–8 H8–5

V. **'Rebecca'** (Vtta) Highly scented flowers of palest cream, the edges slightly frilled and irregularly splashed with purple, appear from mid-spring to early fall. ‡6 in (15 cm). Z5–8 H8–5

V. **Reine Charlotte** see *V.* 'Königin Charlotte'

V. riviniana (Common dog violet, Wood violet) Semievergreen violet

with fibrous roots. A rosette of leaves produces low branches and scentless violet-blue or occasionally white flowers up to 1 in (2.5 cm) across with a pale blunt spur ¼ in (5 mm) long, usually notched at the end, in mid- and late spring. May produce new shoots from the roots, unlike similar species. Thrives in fertile soil containing humus in good light to light shade, but it can take deeper shade in summer. Good for naturalizing in woods or short turf, but grows well in borders. Self-seeds readily. From Europe, African Atlantic islands, some Mediterranean islands, and central and north European Russia. ‡8 in (20 cm) Z5–8 H8–5 **'Ed's Variegated'** Heavily cream-speckled leaves. Introduced by Bob Brown of Cotswold Garden Flowers in Worcestershire, England and named for his son, Edmund. **Purpurea Group** Purple-leaved, the color stronger when grown in a sunny position. Sometimes sold as *V. labradorica* and *V. labradorica purpurea*. **f. *rosea*** Pink flowers. Often sold as *V. rupestris rosea* or *V. arenaria rosea*.

V. **'Roscastle Black'** (Va) Velvety purplish black flowers, 1¼ in (3 cm) across, are held well above the foliage from mid-spring to midsummer or later. Sturdy and reliable, making a large clump (see Black Pansies *p. 479*). ‡8 in (20 cm). Z5–8 H8–5

V. rupestris syn. *V. arenaria* (Teesdale violet) Semievergreen violet, with a rosette of leaves. Low branches and scentless, violet-blue flowers up up ⅝ in (1.5 cm) across, with a short un-notched spur, in spring and early summer. Similar to *V. riviniana* but with stems of leaves and flowers covered in short hair,

and less pointed summer leaves. Grows well in many soils, in light shade to full sun. From western central and northern Europe through Asia as far as Siberia and China. ↕4 in (10 cm). Z5–8 H8–5. *rosea* see *V. riviniana* f. *rosea*.

V. **'Saint Helena'** (VT) Pale lavender-blue flowers from late winter to spring. Less vigorous than most, but one of the strongest-scented garden violets, with a very sweet fragrance. Probably a hybrid of *V. odorata*. ↕6 in (15 cm). Z5–8 H8–5

V. selkirkii (Great spurred violet) A slender rhizome with small, deciduous, toothed, heart-shaped leaves. From early to late spring, scentless flowers appear, ¾ in (2 cm) across with narrow or broad petals, in pale violet or rarely white with a white throat and a prominent, blunt, ⅛–⅜-in (4–8-mm) spur. Often short-lived, but it may maintain itself by self-seeding. Adaptable and hardy, but prefers cold, damp soil rich in humus, in an open position or otherwise in light shade. Daniel Defoe based his sailor character Robinson Crusoe on the real-life Alexander Selkirk, for whom this violet was named around 1820. From Greenland, Scandinavia, northern Asia, Japan, Canada, and the northern US. ↕4 in (10 cm). Z3–7 H7–1. **f. *variegata*** Daintier, with prominent silvery variegation following the leaf veins. Distinguished from *V. variegata* by having pointed leaves. Comes true from seed. ↕2¾ in (7 cm).

V. septentrionalis see *V. soraria*

V. soraria syn. *V. papilionacea*, *V. septentrionalis* (Sister violet) Greenish rhizomes creep along the surface, sometimes branching, putting up deciduous heart-shaped leaves up to 4 in (10 cm) long, and short-spurred, scentless, violet-blue flowers ¾ in (2 cm) across from early to late spring. Similar to *V. cucullata* but with cleistogamous seedpods held close to the ground or sometimes in the soil. Many color variants, some with variegated leaves or flowers. Not fussy about soils, as long as there is some humus; tolerates damp and good light to light shade. Self-seeds freely and may spread rapidly. From eastern North America. ↕6 in (15 cm). Z3–9 H9–1. **'Albiflora'** White flowers. Sometimes sold as *V. cucullata* 'Alba', or *V. cucullata* 'Albiflora'—a different plant. Other names including 'Snow Princess', 'White Sails', 'Immaculata,' and 'White Ladies' may often, but not always, prove to be this plant. **'Alice Witter'** White flowers with a pink to purplish red flush around the throat. The amount of darker coloration varies from plant to plant, from a hint to a large splash. **'Freckles'** White flowers speckled with violet. The less often seen 'Speckles' and 'Dark Freckles' have slightly different speckling patterns. **f. *priceana*** syn. *V. priceana* (Confederate violet) White

LEFT 1 *Viola selkirkii* **2** *V. soraria* 'Freckles' **3** *V. soraria* f. *priceana* **4** *V. variegata*

flowers with a blue-gray flush toward the center. The amount of darker color varies from plant to plant. **'Red Giant'** Reddish purple flowers. ↕8 in (20 cm). **'Speckles'** see 'Freckles'.

V. **'Sulfurea'** (VT) Variable; some plants have creamy flowers with an apricot throat, some a slightly buff color, others slightly lemon. Most are unscented and flower from late winter to early spring. Found by a mailman on the edge of a woods in Indre, France, around 1896. ↕8 in (20 cm). Z5–8 H8–5

V. **'Sylettas'** (VT) see *V. variegata* 'Sylettas'

V. **'The Czar'** (VT) Strongly scented, deep purple flowers on long stems are produced freely in spring. Stems long enough for cutting. Many impostors are sold under this name. Probably a hybrid of *V. odorata* and of historic significance, having given rise to many fine cultivars. Raised by F. J. Graham of Cranford, Middlesex, and introduced by Thomas Softly of Ware, Middlesex in 1863. ↕12 in (30 cm). Z4–8 H8–1

V. **'Tiger Eye'** (Va) Striking, scented, deep golden yellow flowers, 1 in (2.5 cm) across. Black veins radiate from a small central patch along the veins to the edge. One of the Angel Series of seed-raised bedding violas developed by Floranova, Norfolk, England. Introduced in 2001, but not reliably perennial. Sometimes misspelled 'Tiger Eyes'. A successor to the rare sterile 'Eye of the Tiger', with narrower flowers. ↕6 in (15 cm). Z7–9 H9–7

V. **'Tony Venison'** (C) Yellow and green, striped foliage fades slightly in summer below pale blue flowers 1 in (2.5 cm) across. A spontaneous mutation in the garden of veteran garden writer Tony Venison, introduced by Hopleys Plants, Hertfordshire, England, in 1983. ↕4 in (10 cm). Z5–8 H8–5

V. variegata (Cyclamen-leaved violet) A short, slender rhizome produces a small clump of deciduous, somewhat rounded, more or less heart-shaped leaves, purplish on the underside, each up to 2 in (5 cm) across with light variegation along the veins. The unscented flowers are usually a reddish purple, ¾ in (2 cm) across with a prominent spur, and open in mid- and late spring. Worth growing just for its foliage, though not long-lived, and best in gritty, humus-rich soil in light shade. Self-sows reliably, and comes true from cleistogamous flowers. Similar to *V. selkirkii* f. *variegata*, but with less pointed leaves. Often listed for sale incorrectly as *V. grypoceras* f. *variegata*, *V. grypoceras* var. *exilis*, *V. koreana*, or *V. coreana*. From Korea, Japan, China, and Russia. ↕¾ in (2 cm). Z5–8 H8–5. **'Sylettas'** Free-flowering. Introduced by Thompson & Morgan Seedsmen, Inc., NJ, in 1997.

V. velutina see *V. gracilis*

V. **'Victoria Cawthorne'** (C) Profuse, somewhat star-shaped, magenta-pink flowers, 1¼ in (3 cm) across, with rays

on the lower three petals, are held well above the foliage. Tough and popular. ↕4 in (10 cm). Z5–8 H8–5

V. **'Vita'** (Va) Dusky pink, yellow-eyed flowers, 1 in (2.5 cm) across. From Sissinghurst Castle, Kent, England, former home of gardener Vita Sackville-West. ↕8 in (20 cm). Z5–8 H8–5

V. **'White Pearl'** (Va) Strongly scented, pearly white flowers, 1 in (2.5 cm) across, have a yellow-orange eye. Vigorous. ↕8 in (20 cm). Z5–8 H8–5

V. x *williamsii* The collective name for the highly variable group of hybrids of *V. cornuta* and the cultivated pansies, *V.* x *wittrockiana*. Name rarely used by gardeners but may be seen in literature.

V. **'Winona Cawthorne'** (C) Lilac flowers, 1½ in (3.5 cm) across, with lemon-white on the lower petal and a yellow eye. From Richard Cawthorne. ↕4 in (10 cm). Z5–8 H8–5

V. x *wittrockiana* The collective name for the mostly seed-raised garden pansy, the highly variable group of hybrids of *V. tricolor*, *V. lutea*, *V. altaica*, and other species. Name rarely used by gardeners but often seen in catalogs and literature.

V. **'Woodlands Cream'** (Va) Cream flowers, 1½ in (4 cm) across, streak pale blue as they age, and have an orange eye. ↕8 in (20 cm). Z9–11 H9–1

VISCARIA *see* LYCHNIS

SPIDER MITES

Spider mites can be destructive pests, especially on sweet violets grown under cover, but also sometimes on plants grown in the open garden.

Despite being barely visible to the naked eye, spider mites can multiply rapidly and cause significant damage, typically speckled yellowish leaves and webbing like that made by spiders. Many plants, in addition to violets and pansies, are susceptible, especially in greenhouses or under cold frames. The best pesticides are based on vegetable oils, but they need careful, thorough application, since they are not systemic. Parasitic mites give good control, *Phytosieulus persimilis* being recommended against the common two-spotted spider mite, *Tetranychus urticae*, but they must be reintroduced each year and are not effective in the open garden.

Two-spotted and other pest mites are hardier than their parasite, over-wintering in soil and leaf litter, so removing dead leaves is wise. At any time of year, it may even be necessary to remove live foliage from badly infested plants. All affected material should be destroyed, including entire plants if weakened beyond recovery. The risk of infestation may be reduced by maintaining a cool, humid atmosphere and avoiding planting in dry, sunny places, where most plants are unlikely to thrive even without mite attack.

WXY

WAHLENBERGIA
CAMPANULACEAE

Hardy dwarf campanula look-alikes, for milder climates, that flower profusely in summer.

About 150 diverse species of annuals and generally short-lived deciduous perennials, mainly from the mountains of Europe, South Africa, and Australasia. The leaves are usually alternate, variable in shape but generally lance-shaped or elliptical, and the blue, violet, or white flowers are starry, bell-like, or saucer-shaped and appear in abundance during summer on long stems or in open clusters. Similar to *Campanula*, but differing in the way the seeds are shed from the seed capsules. Ideal for growing in gaps in paving.

CULTIVATION Best in light, sandy, well-drained soil that contains plenty of humus, in part-shade with shelter from cold, drying winds.

PROPAGATION By division, from seed or basal stem cuttings in spring.

PROBLEMS Slugs and snails.

W. albomarginata Short-lived tufted plant spreading by rhizomes making rosettes of ¾in- (2cm) long, elliptical, lance-shaped or somewhat spoon-shaped, leathery, hairy, medium green leaves, often purplish beneath. They make a good background for the pale blue or white bell-shaped flowers, about 1 in (2.5 cm) across, that peer

BELOW 1 *Wahlenbergia albomarginata*
2 *W. gloriosa*

toward the sky from early summer onward. From New Zealand. ↕2–8 in (5–20 cm). Z6–7 H7–6

W. gloriosa Tufted plant spreading by rhizomes, whose thick, lance-shaped, deep green leaves, ¾–1¼ in (2–3 cm) long, have wavy, toothed edges. The ¾in- (2cm) wide star-shaped flowers, facing upward, are dark violet-blue and freely produced from early summer onward. From Australia. ↕2 in (5 cm). Z8–10 H10–8

W. undulata Tufted, upright plant with mid-green foliage that makes a good background for the abundance of large, light blue, open bell-shaped flowers that appear on long, thin stems from early

summer onward. From the Drakensberg Mountains, South Africa. ↕12–24 in (30–60 cm). Z8–10 H10–8. **'Melton Bluebird'** Flowers open rich sky-blue and pale with age. ↕14 in (35 cm).

WALDSTEINIA
Barren Strawberry
ROSACEAE

Versatile, low-growing ground cover, valuable for dry shade, with neat foliage and abundant spring flowers.

Six species of semi-evergreen plants native to mountain woods and clearings have a wide distribution in the north temperate zone.

ABOVE 1 *Waldsteinia geoides*
2 *W. ternata*

Named for the Austrian botanist of the late 18th century, Count Franz Adam Waldstein-Wartenburg, the three species usually seen in cultivation are strawberry-like in habit and look fairly similar, differing mainly in flower size and leaf structure. Underground rhizomes enable them to spread, forming mounded mats of shiny, toothed, deeply lobed or divided leaves, which may take on purplish tints in winter. From mid-spring to early summer, the foliage is sprinkled with bright yellow, saucer-shaped

flowers, in sparse sprays held above the leaves on separate stems. The plants produce inedible, nutlike fruit quite unlike a strawberry and, in fact, are more closely allied to another relative, *Geum*.

CULTIVATION Will grow in sun or light shade in most soils, preferably well-drained, and is drought-tolerant when shaded. Good planted in groups; will carpet slopes, naturalize under shrubs, or edge dry, north-facing borders.

PROPAGATION By division or from seed.

PROBLEMS Usually trouble-free.

W. fragarioides Colonizing the ground by runners as well as rhizomes, the dense covering of foliage is composed of leaves divided into three wedge-shaped, stalkless leaflets, up to 2 in (5 cm) long. Above these appear yellow, ⅜–¾-in (1.5–2-cm) flowers, their petals varying from oval to rounded. A little-known American equivalent to the more familiar European *W. ternata*, but with larger leaflets. From eastern North America, particularly the Appalachian mountains, and a threatened species in six states. ↕4–8 in (10–20 cm). Z3–8 H8–1

W. geoides Forming clumps that spread gradually from short rhizomes, this compact species has basal leaves that are roughly heart-shaped in outline, with five to seven coarsely toothed lobes. The flower stems carry leafy bracts and are topped with lax clusters of small ½–⅝-in (1–1.5-cm) yellow flowers with reverse egg-shaped petals, held on long stalks. From east-central Europe west to Ukraine. ↕6–10 in (15–25 cm). Z4–7 H7–1

W. ternata syn. *W. trifolia*, *W. sibirica* A vigorous carpeter, spreading by both rhizomes and rooting runners, the three wedge-shaped, stalkless leaflets that

make up the leaves reach 1¼-in (3-cm) in length. Loose clusters of flowers, each ⅝–¾ in (1.5–2 cm) across with rounded petals, are held over the foliage. By far the most widely grown of the species and occasionally available in flat modules like squares of sod to cover large areas. From east-central and southern Europe and also much farther east, in Siberia and Japan. ↕4–6 in (10–15 cm). Z3–8 H8–1. 'Mozaick' Leaves flecked in yellow.

W. trifolia see *W. ternata*

W. sibirica see *W. ternata*

WOODSIA
WOODSIACEAE

Small, pretty ferns, easy to grow and valued for their tolerance of open positions.

About 25 species of small, mostly rock-dwelling, generally deciduous ferns are widely distributed in the Northern Hemisphere and South America, with two species in southern Africa. A short rhizome supports a tuft of oblong or lance-shaped fronds divided into many pairs of leaflets, which may be simple or further divided into small oblong segments. The spore clusters on the undersides of the fronds are protected by a characteristic cup of hairs or scales. Do not allow plants to be smothered by larger neighbors. The new fronds open earlier in spring than most ferns and, in most species, the frond stalk is jointed near the base, so the old fronds simply fall off in late fall.

CULTIVATION Grow in moist, humus-rich but well-drained soil in an open, partly sunny position.

PROPAGATION From spores.

PROBLEMS Usually trouble free

W. obtusa (Cliff fern) Tufted, clump-forming, deciduous fern with narrow, lance-shaped, light gray-green fronds 4–14 in (10–35 cm) long, composed of pairs of triangular leaflets each divided into toothed, oblong segments. Easily grown fern, perhaps most effective when several are planted together. Grows in rock crevices and on shaded stone walls in eastern North America, from Canada to Georgia and Texas. ↕4–12 in (10–30 cm). Z3–10 H10–3

W. polystichoides Plant forming a compact clump of many light green, narrowly oblong fronds, 4–10 in (10–25 cm) long, divided into pairs of narrow, slightly sickle-shaped leaflets, each with a small lobe at the base. The fronds are finely hairy, giving a soft, grayish green appearance. As the name suggests, the fronds resemble those of some of the smaller species of *Polystichum*. A most attractive small fern with plenty of character, it deserves to be more commonly grown. Grows on boulders and cliffs in full sun or light shade. Native to northeastern Asia, from Manchuria to China, Japan, and Taiwan. ↕2–6 in (5–15 cm). Z4–8 H8–1

WOODWARDIA
Chain ferns
BLECHNACEAE

Bold, and sometimes dramatic, evergreen and deciduous ferns with delicately patterned fronds.

About 14 species grow in damp woodlands in Europe, Asia, and North America. Large ferns with fronds twice to three times divided, the spore-bearing structures are arranged in a "chain" of dashes along each side of the ultimate segments, hence the common name. Several species produce bulbils near the frond tip or all over the upper surface of the frond—as in the tender *W. orientalis*. The bulbil-producing species have arching fronds, the others are more erect in growth.

CULTIVATION Grow in acidic soil with plentiful moisture, but not stagnant.

PROPAGATION From spores of bulbils.

PROBLEMS Usually trouble-free.

W. fimbriata Tall evergreen fern with erect, lance-shaped, dark green fronds that are twice divided but do not produce bulbils. Thrives in a sheltered, moist site and neutral to acidic soil. A rare example of a tall evergreen plant suitable for wetter places. From Mexico, the western United States, and southwestern Canada. ↕3¼ ft (1 m), up to ↕6 ft (1.8 m) in the wild. Z8–9 H9–8

W. radicans Evergreen fern with arching, lance-shaped, mid-green fronds to 5 ft (1.5 m) long; the fronds are twice divided and bear one or more large buds or bulbils on the underside, near the tip. The bulbils root where they touch the ground, eventually forming a colony. This chain fern thrives in moist or wet soil in semi-shade in sheltered city or coastal gardens; not reliably hardy elsewhere. Found in damp shade in southwest Europe and the Atlantic Islands. ↕28 in (70 cm). Z8–9 H9–8

W. unigemmata Wide-arching fronds, to 6½ ft (2 m) long, are lance-shaped and twice divided, and the young foliage is a striking deep red as it emerges, eventually turning green and producing bulbils. Throughout the season there are usually some red fronds. Similar to the less hardy *W. radicans* but distinct in the red coloring of its young fronds. Grow in a moist, sheltered site. Widespread in Asia from the Himalayas to the Philippines, China, and Japan, and common in Taiwan. ↕28 in (70 cm). Z8–9 H9–8

BELOW 1 *Woodwardia fimbriata*
2 *W. radicans* **3** *W. unigemmata*

Z

ZALUZIANSKYA
SCROPHULARIACEAE

Intriguing, very distinctive, long-flowering and fragrant sun-lovers for mild regions or small containers.

About 35 species of sticky annuals, evergreen perennials, and woody-based perennials from rocky places and meadows in southern and eastern Africa. The longish leaves, arranged oppositely low on the plant and alternately higher up, often have toothed edges, and the white, red-backed flowers are distinctive, with five widely spreading, horizontal petals, in some species the tips being deeply split. They are fragrant in the evening.

CULTIVATION Thrives in moist, well-drained soil that contains plenty of humus, and a position in full sun. Cut the plants hard back promptly after flowering to keep them bushy.

PROPAGATION Plants are short lived, so propagate regularly by cuttings in summer or from seed in spring.

PROBLEMS Aphids.

Z. ovata Clump-forming evergreen with sticky gray-green egg-shaped leaves, about 1½ in (4 cm) long, with toothed edges. The white, crimson-backed, scented flowers are ¾–1 in (2–2.5 cm) across, deeply cleft at the tips, and open over a long period, from early summer onward. From South Africa. ↕ 10 in (25 cm). Z9–10 H10–9

Z. 'Semonkong' Mats of deep green leaves about 1½ in (4 cm) long with jagged edges, more lax than those of Z. ovata, make a good background for the strongly scented, white, crimson-backed flowers, ¾–1 in (2–2.5 cm)

BELOW *Zaluzianskya ovata*

across, with deeply cleft petal tips, produced over a very long period from early summer onward. ↕ 10 in (25 cm). Z9–10 H10–9

ZANTEDESCHIA
Arum Lily, Calla, Calla Lily
ARACEAE

Tuberous perennial grown for elegant, often spectacular flowers in damp or semiaquatic sites.

Eight species of medium to large perennials with branching, fat and fleshy rhizomes found in swamps and lakesides in South Africa. Plants have large, bold, elegant, evergreen or deciduous, green and sometimes spotted foliage, which may be triangular or heart-shaped in some or narrow lance-shaped in others. The flowers often overtop the foliage; the spathe color may be white, yellow, or various pink and purple shades, and is at its peak in midsummer. These classically formed flowers have been developed into many variously colored cultivars, which are continuously being introduced. Although many are relatively untried as garden perennials, some are used as potted plants (both indoors and out) and most make excellent cut flowers, lasting for an extended period. All parts of the plant are poisonous, and the sap may cause skin irritation. ⚠

CULTIVATION All species require humus-rich soil and ample moisture and grow well in fertile soils or generous containers. Heavy feeders, they benefit from organic fertilizer. Best in full sun, but can tolerate light shade.

PROPAGATION Divide in spring before new growth emerges.

PROBLEMS Aphids, leaf spot.

Z. aethiopica (Arum Lily, Calla Lily) One of the largest, and evergreen in mild climates, its bright green arrow-shaped to triangular leaves may reach 18 in (45 cm) long by 8 in (20 cm) wide and are held on longer stems. The 10-in (25-cm) pure white spathes, produced in summer, are tinged green on the outside of the tip, and the 3½-in (9-cm) pale yellow spadix develops orange berries. May be grown in shallow water or wet sites and looks stylish in large containers. Widely naturalized in suitable climates. From South Africa. ↕ 16 in (40 cm). Z8–10 H10–4. **'Apple Court Babe'** Shorter, more compact. ↕ 24 in (60 cm). **'Crowborough'** Larger spathes, hardier and more tolerant of dry conditions. Found by Graham Stuart Thomas in a garden in Sussex England. **'Green Goddess'** Spathes streaked in green and white, said to be hardier. **'Mr. Martin'** Very large white spathes,

RIGHT 1 *Zantedeschia* 'Black Eyed Beauty' **2** *Z.* 'Cameo' **3** *Z. elliottiana* **4** *Z.* 'Mango' **5** *Z.* 'Pink Persuasion'

larger than 'Crowborough'. Tough and adaptable. Originally a seed strain from the garden of the retired vet in Worcestershire, England. **'Pershore Fantasia'** Leaves splashed in creamy-yellow. **'White Sail'** Neat, 4-in (10-cm), pure white spathes.

Z. albomaculata Narrow, deciduous, spear-shaped, green leaves, to 16 in (40 cm) long by 8 in (20 cm) wide, usually marked with translucent white spots as the name suggests, are held on long stems that are sometimes spotted in purple. The flowers are held above the foliage, with white, cream, pale yellow, or occasionally pink spathes up to 5 in (13 cm) long. From South Africa and tropical East Africa. ↕18 in (45 cm). Z10–11 H11–7

Z. **'Black Eyed Beauty'** Leaves heavily spotted in white, the spathe is pale yellow-cream with a prominent black blotch in the throat. A hybrid of *Z. elliottiana.* Z8–10 H10–1

Z. **'Cameo'** Heavily mottled foliage with a pale creamy-peach spathe, turning a rich orange over a long blooming period in summer. The near-black throat contrasts strikingly. Z8–10 H10–1

Z. elliottiana (Yellow Calla) Deciduous, rounded leaves, heart-shaped at the base, about 11 in (28 cm) long by 10 in (25 cm) wide, are green and heavily marked with translucent spots and held on stems longer than the leaf blades. The yellow 6-in (15-cm) spathe encircles a 2¾-in (7-cm) yellow spadix. Generally similar to *Z. albomaculata,* but with more rounded leaves and bright gold-yellow spathes. Not known in the wild and possibly a hybrid. Z8–10 H10–1

Z. **'Kiwi Blush'** White, with a pale pink throat that becomes richer as the flower ages. ↕30 in (75 cm). Z8–10 H10–1

Z. **'Mango'** The spathes are lush mango to orange, deepening to scarlet; the foliage is speckled with silver-white. Z8–10 H10–1

Z. **'Pink Persuasion'** Spathe opens rich pink with apricot shades, becoming deeper pink with age; lightly spotted foliage. Z8–10 H10–1

Z. rehmannii Narrow, unspotted leaves, 6–16 in (15–40 cm) long by ¾–2¾ in (2–7 cm) wide, are held on stems to 8 in (20 cm), and in late spring to summer the 4¾-in (12-cm) spathes appear and vary from white to pink to pinkish purple, all with a dark blotch in the throat. Attractive in its own right, but much used to create hybrids. From South Africa and Swaziland. ↕24–36 in (60–90 cm). Z8–10 H10–1

Zauschneria
Hummingbird Trumpet, Wild Fuchsia
ONAGRACEAE

Hummingbird favorites in the wild, and gardeners' favorites for their flamboyant flowers.

Four species of woody-based perennials from dry open areas in western North America. Often developing into dense colonies, upright to sprawling stems radiate from a dense, suckering crown and are clothed with semievergreen, lance-shaped to narrowly oval foliage, which is softly hairy to woolly. The brilliant scarlet, tubular flowers have flat faces with four notched petals and protruding stamens; an inflated four-lobed sheath covers the tube, giving the impression of eight petals. Flowering begins in high summer and continues until hard frost, and the flowers are attractive to hummingbirds, which pollinate the flowers as they feed on their nectar. When grown in areas without hummingbirds, no seed is set. The seeds are surrounded by silky hairs. Though native to arid regions, they often grow best along streams where the roots seek available water. They can also be used on walls, and in dry gardens and gravel beds to add months of carefree color. Plants are very drought-tolerant once established, though bloom more reliably and fully with even moisture, and may be overly aggressive when growing well.

The genus *Zauschneria* has been included by some botanists in *Epilobium*, under which name they may be found in catalogs. They are retained separately here due to their different flower structure and tendency to develop a woody base.

CULTIVATION Set out young, well-rooted plants in average to rich, well-drained soil in full sun or light shade.

PROPAGATION From seed or from cuttings. Alternatively, remove runners and treat as cuttings.

PROBLEMS None

Z. arizonica see *Z. californica* subsp. *cana*

Z. californica syn. *Epilobium canum* (California Fuchsia) Spreading outward by runners, softly hairy, semievergreen, lance-shaped to oblong, 1-in (2.5-cm) leaves clothe the reclining stems of this woody-based plant, the shoots topped with a ceaseless summer display of 1–1½-in (2.5–4-cm) scarlet flowers. The most familiar and widely cultivated species and easy to grow in average to rich, well-drained soil in full sun or light shade, although lean soil helps curb its expansion. From open ground, scrub, and along rocky streams in California and Baja, Mexico. ↕24–36 in (60–90 cm). Z8–11 H11–8. **'Albiflora'** White flowers. **subsp.** *cana* syn. *Epilobium canum* subsp. *canum* Woolly leaves on compact stems; extremely drought-tolerant. ↕24 in (60 cm). **subsp.** *cana* **'Sir Cedric Morris'** Woolly foliage on 18-in (45-cm) mounds. **'Dublin'** syn. 'Glasnevin' Prolific and compact with orangey-scarlet flowers and green foliage on horizontal stems. Originated at the Glasnevin Botanic Garden, Dublin. ↕10 in (25 cm). **subsp.** *latifolia* syn.

Epilobium canum subsp. *latifolium* The showiest form, without a woody base, with wider green leaves, robust growth, and larger flowers on compact plants. Native to moister areas and at higher elevations. ↕12–24 in (30–60 cm). **'Olbrich Silver'** Scarlet flowers and woolly silver foliage. ↕15–20 in (38–50 cm) **'Sierra Salmon'** Uniquely colored salmon-pink flowers. **'Solidarity Pink'** Soft-shell-pink. **'Western Hills'** Reddish orange flowers with gray-green leaves. From Western Hills garden in northern California. ↕15 in (38 cm).

Zingiber
Ginger
ZINGIBERACEAE

Curious but increasingly popular relations of the culinary ginger with colorful conelike flower clusters.

About 100 perennial species from forests in the Indomalayan region to East Asia and tropical Australia with branching, aromatic rhizomes, best known for the culinary spice derived from the roots of *Z. officinale.* Narrow, often aromatic, lance-shaped leaves are borne on either side of thin, reedlike stems. Individual flowers are often insignificant, but are produced in brilliantly colored, waxy bracts that provide the ornamental value. Flowers develop on stems that appear direct from the ground and do not carry normal leaves; in some species these look like brightly colored clublike cones, and have increasingly been grown as cut flowers in recent years. The individual flowers are fleeting, but the overall flower spike is long-lived. Generally easy to grow, and also vigorous, in the right climate.

CULTIVATION Best in moist and fertile organic soil in full sun to part-shade. In borderline areas, protect with a heavy mulch in winter or move to a frost-free place.

ABOVE 1 *Zauschneria californica* 'Dublin' **2** *Zingiber zerumbet*

PROPAGATION By division.

PROBLEMS Usually trouble-free.

Z. clarkei Tall, leafy stems carry large leaves up to 16 in (40 cm) long and 3½ in (9 cm) wide and, unusually, the orange-yellow flushed brownish red flowers are borne at the top of the leafy shoots, emerging two or three at a time from green bracts. In temperate areas, it is best grown in a container, in which it will reach about half its normal height, and should be moved inside in winter. From subtropical forests of Bhutan and northeastern India. ↕6½ ft (2 m). Z7–10 H10–1

Z. mioga (Japanese ginger) Relatively hardy species growing from yellowish rhizomes that support stems carrying narrow green leaves up to 12 in (30 cm) long. The sulfur-yellow flowers, produced continuously from midsummer to early fall, may extend to 4-in (10-cm) and emerge from the green conelike bracts arising directly from the rhizomes and sitting right on the soil surface. Best in a sunny situation. The flowers are edible and used in tempura, a traditional deep-fried Japanese dish. The new shoots are also used as a garnish. From Japan. ↕24 in (60 cm). Z7–10 H10–1. **'Variegata'** syn. 'Dancing Crane' Strong white variegation on narrow pointed leaves.

Z. zerumbet A tall plant, its long narrow leaves, up to 14 in (35 cm) long, are arranged oppositely along the stem and have hairy undersides. In mid- to late summer, separate 2-in (5-cm) stalks grow out of the ground carrying green cone-shaped bracts that resemble pinecones. The green cone turns red over a couple of weeks, and then small creamy-yellow flowers appear on the cone. They make excellent cut flowers. Naturalized in some areas, but native to Southeast Asia. ↕6½ ft (2 m). Z7–11 H11–1. **'Darceyi'** Foliage striped in cream. ↕4 ft (1.2 m).

INDEX OF COMMON NAMES

Common names have many regional variations, and are therefore imprecise as a means of plant identification. A single plant may have several common names, and one common name may refer to a number of plants – for example, "mallow" may describe *Lavatera* or *Malva*, while the "marsh mallow", *Althaea officinalis*, is different again. What follows is a comprehensive list of the common names used in this book, in alphabetical order according to the first word of each name.

A

Abraham, Isaac, and Jacob see *Trachystemon orientalis*
Abyssinian banana see *Ensete ventricosum*
African creeping sage see *Salvia repens*
African lily see *Agapanthus*
African love grass see *Eragrostis curvula*
Agrimony see *Agrimonia*
Alaska lupin see *Lupinus nootkatensis*
Alecost see *Tanacetum balsamita*
Aleutian maidenhair see *Adiantum aleuticum*
Alkanet see *Anchusa*
Allegheny spurge see *Pachysandra procumbens*
Alpine cattail see *Alopecurus alpinus*
Alpine foxtail see *Alopecurus alpinus*
Alum root see *Heuchera, H. americana*
American cowslip see *Dodecatheon*
American galingale see *Cyperus eragrostis*
American ipecac see *Gillenia stipulata*
American red baneberry see *Actaea rubra*
American spikenard see *Aralia racemosa*
Amur silver grass see *Miscanthus sacchiflorus*
Andrews' lady's slipper see *Cypripedium x andrewsii*
Angel's fishing rod see *Dierama*
Anise hyssop see *Agastache foeniculum*
Apple mint see *Mentha suaveolens*
Arizona sage see *Salvia arizonica*
Arkwright's catchfly see *Lychnis x arkwrightii*
Armenian poppy see *Papaver lateritium*
Aromatic aster see *Aster oblongifolius*
Arum lily see *Zantedeschia*
Asphodel see *Asphodelus*
Atlas daisy see *Anacyclus*
Atlas festuca see *Festuca mairei*
Auricula see *Primula auricula*
Autumn fern see *Dryopteris erythrosora*
Autumn goldenrod see *Solidago sphacelata*
Autumn lady's tresses see *Spiranthes cernua* var. *odorata*
Autumn moor grass see *Sesleria autumnalis*
Avens see *Geum*

B

Baby's breath see *Gypsophila*
Back-bent calanthe see *Calanthe reflexa*
Balloon flower see *Platycodon*
Balsam see *Impatiens*
Banana see *Musa*
Baneberry see *Actaea*
Barren strawberry see *Waldsteinia*
Barrenwort see *Epimedium*
Bastard balm see *Melittis*
Basuto torch lily see *Kniphofia caulescens*

Bats-in-the-belfry see *Campanula trachelium*
Beach aster see *Erigeron glaucus*
Beach wormwood see *Artemisia stelleriana*
Beard grass see *Andropogon*
Beardlip penstemon see *Penstemon barbatus*
Bear's breeches see *Acanthus*
Bear-skin grass see *Festuca eskia*
Beebalm see *Monarda*
Beech fern see *Phegopteris connectilis*
Beetleweed see *Galax*
Bee-weed see *Aster cordifolius*
Bellbine see *Calystegia*
Bellflower see *Campanula*
Bellwort see *Uvularia*
Bergamot see *Monarda*
Bethlehem sage see *Pulmonaria saccharata*
Betony see *Stachys officinalis*
Big blue stem see *Andropogon gerardii*
Bindweed see *Calystegia*
Bird's-eye speedwell see *Veronica chamaedrys*
Bird's foot trefoil see *Lotus corniculatus*
Bird's-foot violet see *Viola pedata*
Birthwort see *Aristolochia clematitis*
Bishopweed see *Aegopodium podagraria*
Bistort see *Persicaria*
Black arum see *Arum pictum*
Black baneberry see *Actaea spicata*
Black cohosh see *Actaea racemosa*
Black horehound see *Ballota nigra*
Black pea see *Lathyrus niger*
Black sedge see *Carex nigra*
Blanket flower see *Gaillardia*
Blazing star see *Liatris spicata*
Bleeding heart see *Dicentra, D. spectabilis*
Bloodroot see *Sanguinaria*
Bloody cranesbill see *Geranium sanguineum*
Bloody dock see *Rumex sanguineus* var. *sanguineus*
Bluebead see *Clintonia*
Bluebell see *Campanula rotundifolia, Mertensia*
Blue bugle see *Ajuga genevensis*
Blue bunch grass see *Festuca idahoensis*
Blue buttons see *Knautia arvensis*
Blue cardinal flower see *Lobelia siphilitica*
Blue cohosh see *Caulophyllum thalictroides*
Blue cupidone see *Catananche*
Blue eryngo see *Eryngium planum*
Blue-eyed Mary see *Omphalodes verna*
Blue false indigo see *Baptisia australis*
Blue fescue see *Festuca glauca*
Blue flax see *Linum perenne*
Blue giant hyssop see *Agastache foeniculum*
Blue globe thistle see *Echinops bannaticus*
Blue grama see *Bouteloua gracilis*
Blue-green moor grass see *Sesleria heufleriana*
Blue gromwell see *Buglossoides purpurocaerulea*

Blue moor grass see *Sesleria caerulea*
Blue oat grass see *Helictotrichon sempervirens*
Blue phlox see *Phlox divaricata*
Blue-pod lupin see *Lupinus polyphyllus*
Blue star see *Amsonia*
Blue tussock grass see *Poa colensoi*
Blue vervain see *Verbena hastata*
Blue wheatgrass see *Elymus magellanicus*
Blue wild rye see *Leymus arenarius*
Blue wood aster see *Aster cordifolius*
Bluff lupin see *Lupinus variicolor*
Boer love grass see *Eragrostis chloromelas*
Bog rush see *Schoenus pauciflorus*
Bog violet see *Viola palustris*
Borage see *Borago*
Border phlox see *Phlox paniculata*
Bottle brush grass see *Hystrix, H. patula*
Bowles's mint see *Mentha x villosa* var. *alopecuroides*
Bowman's root see *Gillenia trifoliata*
Bracted sage see *Salvia involucrata*
Brazilian giant rhubarb see *Gunnera manicata*
Bridal wreath see *Francoa*
Bristle-leaved hawkbit see *Leontodon rigens*
Broad buckler fern see *Dryopteris dilatata*
Broad-leaved meadow grass see *Poa chaixii*
Broad-leaved penstemon see *Penstemon ovatus*
Broad-leaved poker see *Kniphofia northiae*
Brook wakerobin see *Trillium rivale*
Brown-eyed Susan see *Rudbeckia triloba*
Brown knapweed see *Centaurea jacea*
Buchanan's sage see *Salvia buchananii*
Buchanan's sedge see *Carex buchananii*
Buckler fern see *Dryopteris*
Buffalo rose see *Callirhoe involucrata*
Bugbane see *Actaea*
Bugle, bugleweed see *Ajuga, A. reptans*
Bulbous buttercup see *Ranunculus bulbosus*
Bull rush see *Schoenoplectus*
Burning bush see *Dictamnus*
Bush's coneflower see *Echinacea paradoxa*
Butter and eggs see *Linaria vulgaris*
Butterbur see *Petasites*
Buttercup see *Ranunculus*
Butterfly flower see *Hedychium*
Butterfly milkweed see *Asclepias tuberosa*
Butterfly stonecrop see *Sedum spectabile*
Button eryngo see *Eryngium yuccifolium*
Byzantine peony see *Paeonia peregrina*

C

Calamint see *Calamintha*
Calico aster see *Aster lateriflorus*
California coneflower see *Rudbeckia californica*
California fuchsia see *Zauschneria californica*

Californa spikenard see *Aralia californica*
California tree poppy see *Romneya*
Calla, calla lily see *Zantedeschia, Z. aethiopica*
Campion see *Lychnis, Silene*
Canada goldenrod see *Solidago canadensis*
Canadian burnet see *Sanguisorba canadensis*
Cancer weed see *Salvia lyrata*
Candy rush see *Schoenoplectus lacustris* subsp. *tabernaemontani* 'Albescens'
Cardinal flower see *Lobelia cardinalis*
Cardoon see *Cynara cardunculus*
Carnation see *Dianthus*
Carnation sedge see *Carex panicea*
Carolina phlox see *Phlox carolina*
Catchfly see *Lychnis, Silene*
Catmint see *Nepeta*
Catnip see *Nepeta cataria*
Caucasian crosswort see *Phuopsis*
Caucasian stonecrop see *Sedum spurium*
Celandine poppy see *Stylophorum diphyllum*
Chain fern see *Woodwardia*
Chamisso arnica see *Arnica chamissonis*
Chamomile see *Chamaemelum*
Chatham Islands forget-me-not see *Myosotidium*
Chatterbox orchid see *Epipactis gigantea*
Cheddar pink see *Dianthus gratianopolitanus*
Chervil see *Chaerophyllum*
Chicory see *Cichorium*
Chilean evening primrose see *Oenothera stricta*
Chilean giant rhubarb see *Gunnera tinctoria*
Chilean quaking grass see *Briza subaristata*
Chinese artichoke see *Stachys affinis*
Chinese chives see *Allium tuberosum*
Chinese foxglove see *Rehmannia elata*
Chinese lantern see *Physalis alkekengi*
Chinese silver grass see *Miscanthus sinensis*
Chinese yellow banana see *Musa lasiocarpa*
Chives see *Allium schoenoprasum*
Chocolate cosmos see *Cosmos atrosanguineus*
Christmas fern see *Polystichum acrostichoides*
Christmas rose see *Helleborus niger*
Cinnamon fern see *Osmunda cinnamomea*
Cinquefoil see *Potentilla*
Cliff fern see *Woodsia obtusa*
Clinton's wood fern see *Dryopteris clintoniana*
Clover see *Trifolium*
Club rush see *Schoenoplectus*
Clustered bell flower see *Campanula glomerata*
Clustered poppy mallow see *Callirhoe triangulata*
Coastal fragrant lady's tresses see *Spiranthes cernua* var. *odorata*
Cobra lily see *Arisaema*
Cocksfoot see *Dactylis*
Coco yam see *Colocasia esculenta*
Cohosh see *Caulophyllum*
Columbine see *Aquilegia*
Comfrey see *Symphytum*
Common bistort see *Persicaria bistorta*
Common daisy see *Bellis perennis*

Common dog violet see *Viola riviniana*
Common foxtail see *Alopecurus pratensis*
Common horehound see *Marrubium vulgare*
Common marsh poker see *Kniphofia linearifolia*
Common monkshood see *Aconitum napellus*
Common polypody see *Polypodium vulgare*
Common quaking grass see *Briza media*
Common reed grass see *Phragmites australis*
Common sedge see *Carex nigra*
Common sneezeweed see *Helenium autumnale*
Common spotted orchid see *Dactylorhiza fuchsii*
Common St John's wort see *Hypericum perforatum*
Common toadflax see *Linaria vulgaris*
Common tussock grass see *Poa labillardierei*
Common valerian see *Valeriana officinalis*
Common wormwood see *Artemisia vulgaris*
Compass plant see *Silphium laciniatum*
Coneflower see *Echinacea, Rudbeckia*
Confederate violet see *Viola sororia* f. *priceana*
Coral bells see *Heuchera, H. sanguinea*
Coral spurge see *Euphorbia corralloides*
Corsican hellebore see *Helleborus argutifolius*
Corsican pansy see *Viola corsica*
Corsican violet see *Viola corsica*
Costmary see *Tanacetum balsamita*
Cowslip see *Primula veris*
Cranesbill see *Geranium*
Creeping gunnera see *Gunnera prorepens*
Creeping Jenny see *Lysimachia nummularia*
Creeping phlox see *Phlox stolonifera*
Crested buckler fern see *Dryopteris cristata*
Crimson-seeded sedge see *Carex baccans*
Crinkleroot see *Cardamine diphylla*
Crown vetch see *Coronilla*
Cuckoo flower see *Cardamine pratensis, Lychnis flos-cuculi*
Cuckoo pint see *Arum maculatum*
Culver's root see *Veronicastrum virginicum*
Cupid's dart see *Catananche*
Curling thread rush see *Juncus filiformis* 'Spiralis'
Custard apple see *Podophyllum*
Cutleaf coneflower see *Rudbeckia laciniata*
Cutler's alpine goldenrod see *Solidago cutleri*
Cyclamen-leaved violet see *Viola variegata*
Cyperus sedge see *Carex pseudocyperus*
Cypress spurge see *Euphorbia cyparissias*

D

Dahurian bugbane see *Actaea dahurica*
Daisy *see Bellis*
Dalmatian toadflax see *Linaria dalmatica*

Dame's violet see *Hesperis matronalis*
Dark brown New Zealand sedge see *Carex petriei*
Dark mullein see *Verbascum nigrum*
Dark sedge see *Carex atrata*
Darnel fly grass see *Eragrostis airoides*
Day flower see *Commelina*
Daylily see *Hemerocallis*
Dead nettle see *Lamium*
Deerfoot see *Achlys, A. triphylla*
Deer grass see *Muhlenbergia rigens*
Deer tongue grass see *Panicum clandestinum*
Desert candle see *Eremurus*
Devil's bit scabious see *Succisa pratensis*
Dittany see *Dictamnus*
Dock see *Rumex*
Dog fennel see *Eupatorium capillifolium*
Doll's daisy see *Boltonia*
Doll's eyes see *Actaea pachypoda*
Dotted horsemint see *Monarda punctata*
Dragon arum see *Dracunculus*
Dragon's head see *Dracocephalum*
Drop-seed grass see *Sporobolus*
Dropwort see *Filipendula vulgaris*
Druce's cranesbill see *Geranium* x *oxonianum*
Drumstick primula see *Primula denticulata*
Dusky cranesbill see *Geranium phaeum*
Dusty miller see *Lychnis coronaria*
Dutch rush see *Equisetum hyemale*
Dwarf borage see *Borago pygmaea*
Dwarf sweet flag see *Acorus gramineus*
Dyer's chamomile see *Anthemis tinctoria*
Dyer's woodruff see *Asperula tinctoria*

E

Eared lady fern see *Athyrium otophorum*
Early phlox see *Phlox maculata*
Eastern maidenhair see *Adiantum pedatum*
Eastern skunk cabbage see *Lysichiton camtschatcensis*
Ebine see *Calanthe discolor*
Elecampane see *Inula, I. helenium*
Elephant yam see *Amorphophallus paeoniifolius*
Elephant's ears see *Bergenia*
Elk clover see *Aralia californica*
Eryngo see *Eryngium*
Esparto grass see *Stipa tenacissima*
Ethiopian banana see *Ensete ventricosum*
Ethiopian grass see *Pennisetum villosum*
European dune grass see *Leymus arenarius*
European feather grass see *Stipa pulcherrima*
Evening primrose see *Oenothera*
Evergreen tussock grass see *Poa colensoi*
Everlasting flower see *Helichrysum*
Everlasting pea see *Lathyrus grandiflorus*
Eyelash-leaved sage see *Salvia blepharophylla*

F

Fair maids of France see *Ranunculus aconitifolius*
Fairy bells see *Disporum*

False banana see *Ensete*
False chamomile see *Boltonia*
False dragonhead see *Physostegia virginiana*
False indigo see *Baptisia*
Feather grass see *Pennisetum villosum, Stipa pennata*
Feather reed grass see *Calamagrostis epigejos*
Feather top see *Pennisetum villosum*
Female peony see *Paeonia officinalis*
Fennel see *Ferrula, Foeniculum, F. vulgare*
Fern-leaf peony see *Paeonia tenuifolia*
Fescue see *Festuca*
Feverfew see *Tanacetum parthenium*
Field eryngo see *Eryngium campestre*
Figwort see *Scrophularia*
Fishbone water fern see *Blechnum nudum*
Five-nerve helianthella see *Helianthella quinquenervis*
Flame grass see *Miscanthus* 'Purpurascens'
Flat-topped white aster see *Aster umbellatus*
Flax see *Linum*
Flax lily see *Dianella*
Fleabane see *Erigeron, Inula*
Flowering fern see *Osmunda, O. regalis*
Fly grass see *Eragrostis airoides*
Foamflower see *Tiarella*
Foamybells see x *Heucherella*
Foothill penstemon see *Penstemon heterophyllus*
Forget-me-not see *Myosotis*
Fountain grass see *Pennisetum, P. alopecuroides*
Four o'clock plant see *Mirabilis jalapa*
Fox and cubs see *Pilosella aurantica*
Foxglove see *Digitalis*
Foxglove beardtongue see *Penstemon digitalis*
Foxtail grass see *Alopecurus*
Foxtail lily see *Eremurus*
Fragrant evening primrose see *Oenothera stricta*
Fragrant nodding lady's tresses see *Spiranthes cernua* var. *odorata*
French honeysuckle see *Hedysarum coronarium*
French lilac see *Galega officinalis*
French sorrel see *Rumex scutatus*
Freshwater cord grass see *Spartina pectinata*
Fringe cups see *Tellima*
Frog-spawn bush see *Euphorbia characias*

G

Galaxy see *Galax*
Gas plant see *Dictamnus*
Gayfeather see *Liatris*
Gentian see *Gentiana*
Gentian sage see *Salvia patens*
German catchfly see *Lychnis viscaria*
Germander sage see *Salvia chamaedryoides*
Germander speedwell see *Veronica chamaedrys*
Giant feather grass see *Stipa gigantea*
Giant catmint see *Nepeta grandiflora*
Giant dead nettle see *Lamium orvala*
Giant fennel see *Ferula communis*
Giant forget-me-not see *Myosotidium*
Giant helleborine see *Epipactis gigantea*

Giant hyssop see *Agastache*
Giant scabious see *Cephalaria gigantea*
Ginger see *Zingiber*
Ginger mint see *Mentha* x *gracilis* 'Variegata'
Goatsbeard see *Aruncus*
Goat's rue see *Galega*
Globe artichoke see *Cynara cardunculus* Scolymus Group
Globe flower see *Trollius, T. europaeus*
Globe mallow see *Sphaeralcea*
Globe thistle see *Echinops*
Golden-eyed grass see *Sisyrinchium californicum*
Golden flax see *Linum flavum*
Golden fountains see *Carex dolichostachya* 'Kaga-nishiki'
Golden hawk's beard see *Crepis aurea*
Golden knee see *Chrysogonum*
Golden male fern see *Dryopteris affinis*
Golden marguerite see *Anthemis tinctoria*
Golden oats see *Stipa gigantea*
Goldenrod see *Solidago, S. virgaurea*
Golden seal see *Hydrastis, H. canadensis*
Golden star see *Chrysogonum*
Goldie's wood fern see *Dryopteris goldieana*
Goutweed see *Aegopodium podagraria*
Grama grass see *Bouteloua*
Grass-leaved scabious see *Scabiosa graminifolia*
Gray's sedge see *Carex grayi*
Great burnet see *Sanguisorba officinalis*
Great coneflower see *Rudbeckia maxima*
Greater burnet saxifrage see *Pimpinella major*
Greater celandine see *Chelidonium, C. majus*
Greater knapweed see *Centaurea scabiosa*
Greater periwinkle see *Vinca major*
Greater plantain see *Plantago major*
Greater pond sedge see *Carex riparia*
Great globe thistle see *Echinops sphaerocephalus*
Great leopard's bane see *Doronicum pardalianches*
Great lobelia see *Lobelia siphilitica*
Great spurred violet see *Viola selkirkii*
Great water dock see *Rumex hydrolapathum*
Great woodrush see *Luzula sylvatica*
Great yellow gentian see *Gentiana lutea*
Greek Jerusalem sage see *Phlomis samia*
Greek valerian see *Polemonium caeruleum*
Green alkanet see *Pentaglottis*
Green dragon see *Arisaema dracontium*
Greeneyes see *Berlandiera*
Green-leaved tussock grass see *Chinochloa flavicans*
Grey beard see *Spodiopogon sibiricus*
Grey fescue see *Festuca glauca*
Grey hair grass see *Corynephorus canescens*
Grey moor grass see *Sesleria nitida*
Grim the collier see *Pilosella aurantica*
Gromwell see *Buglossoides*
Ground cherry see *Physalis*
Ground clematis see *Clematis recta*
Ground elder see *Aegopodium, A. podagraria*

H

Hair fescue see *Festuca amethystina*
Hair grass see *Corynephorus, Deschampsia, Koeleria*

FURTHER INFORMATION

The information in this book is derived, primarily, from the experience and expertise of our contributors. I, and they, have relied upon the *RHS Plant Finder*, internationally recognized as the ultimate authority on the names of garden plants, and on the expert botanists of the RHS as well as other specialists thanked below.

For serious further enquiry I would especially recommend these websites:

www.rhs.org.uk – Royal Horticultural Society
plants.usda.gov – Plants Database from the United States Department of Agriculture
www.efloras.org – Flora of North America, and Flora of China
www.bsbi.org.uk – Botanical Society of the British Isles

Many of the plants in this book are easy to find in garden centers, but some are rarely seen, and usually are only found in specialist nurseries. The organizations below may provide a starting point in finding some of the more unusual plants.

American Horticultural Society (AHS)
7931 East Boulevard Drive
Alexandria, Virginia 22308
http://www.ahs.org

Horticopia On-line Plant Information
http://www.horticopia.com

The Perennial Plant Association (PPA)
3383 Schirtzinger Rd
Hilliard, Ohio 43026
http://ppa@perennialplants.org

American Fern Society
http://www.amerfernsoc.org

American Hemerocallis Society
http://www.daylillies.org

American Hosta Society
http://www.hostacociety.org

North American Native Plant Society
http://www.naps.org

The New York Botanical Garden
Vascular Plant Types Catalog
http://sciweb.nybg.org/science2/hcol/vasc/index.asp

Chicago Botanic Garden
Research and Collection of Perennials
http://www.chicagobotanic.org

Missouri Botanical Garden
Kemper Center for Home Gardening
http://www.mobot.org/gardeninghelp/plantinfo.shtml

POTENTIALLY HARMFUL PERENNIALS

All the plants listed below are safe to include in your garden, provided that you treat them with respect and grow them only for their ornamental value. There are three areas of potential risk: external contact with parts of these plants may cause skin reactions, eye irritiations, or both; internal contact may result in poisoning. You should note that some "poisonous" plants are more hazardous than others: when taken internally several of these plants cause mild illnesses, but a few may have very severe effects. Therefore do not eat or otherwise ingest any plant described as poisonous, and position them well out of the way of young children and family pets.

Aconitum	poisonous; skin irritant
Actaea	poisonous; skin irritant
Alstroemeria	skin irritant
Anchusa	poisonous
Arisaema	poisonous; skin and eye irritant
Arnica	poisonous; skin irritant
Arum	poisonous; skin and eye irritant
Asclepias	skin irritant
Caltha	poisonous
Caulophyllum	poisonous
Chamaemelum	skin irritant
Chelidonium majus	poisonous; skin and eye irritant
Chelone	skin irritant
Chrysanthemum	skin irritant
Cichorium	skin irritant
Colocasia esculenta	poisonous; skin and eye irritant
Convallaria majalis	poisonous
Cryptotaenia	skin irritant
Cypripedium	poisonous
Delphinium	poisonous
Dicentra	poisonous
Dictamnus	skin irritant
Digitalis	poisonous
Dracunculus	poisonous; skin and eye irritant
Euphorbia	poisonous; skin and eye irritant
Gillenia	poisonous
Helenium	poisonous; skin irritant
Helianthus	skin irritant
Helleborus	poisonous; skin irritant
Hypericum perforatum	poisonous
Iris	poisonous; skin irritant
Lobelia	poisonous; skin and eye irritant
Lupinus	poisonous
Lysichiton	poisonous; skin and eye irritant
Mirabilis	poisonous; skin and eye irritant
Persicaria	skin irritant
Physalis alkekengi	poisonous; skin irritant
Podophyllum	poisonous
Polygonatum	poisonous
Primula	skin and eye irritant
Ranunculus	poisonous
Symphytum	poisonous
Tanacetum	skin irritant
Veratrum	poisonous
Verbena macdougalii	poisonous; skin irritant
Zantedeschia	poisonous; skin and eye irritant

PUBLISHER'S ACKNOWLEDGMENTS

Dorling Kindersley would like to thank all the staff at the Royal Horticultural Society, especially Susannah Charlton and Simon Maughan. In addition, thanks go to Cooling Brown Book Publishing for development work undertaken in the early stages of this project. The publishers would also like to thank the following private individuals and staff at the locations and organizations listed below for their help with the photography for this encyclopedia. All are located in the UK.

Birmingham Botanical Gardens and Greenhouses Ltd.; Blackmore and Langdon; The Botanic Nursery; Bowden Hostas; Bridgemere Nurseries; Chris Searle; Claire Austin Hardy Plants; Claire Wilson and Vic Johnstone; The Crown Estate (Saville Garden); Duffryn Garden (Cardiff City Council); Hart Canna; Hillview Hardy Plants; Kingston Maurward College; Knoll Gardens; Leeds City Council; Long Acre Plants; New World Plants; Osborne House; Park Green Nursery; Pershore College; The Plantsman's Preference; Pollie's Perennials and Daylily Nursery; Rickards' Hardy Ferns; Royal Botanic Garden, Kew; Royal Horticultural Society; University of Cambridge Botanic Garden; Ventor Botanic Garden; Water Meadow Nursery; Winchester Bulb Growers.

DK Publishing, Inc., would like to thank Katy Moss Warner, President of the American Horticultural Association, for her steadfast enthusiasm for the project, and David Ellis, Director of Communications, for his stewardship of the project from start to finish.

We are greatly indebted to the Perennial Plant Association (PPA) for assistance with the compilation and editing of this encyclopedia. In particular, PPA members Kurt Bluemel, Dr. Steven Still, Dr. Denise Adams, and Dr. Laura Deeter reviewed the entire book and contributed their expertise on the use of perennials in American gardens. Based in Hilliard, Ohio, the PPA is dedicated to improving the perennial plant industry through educational programs and promotion of the use of perennial plants in the landscape. Members of the PPA include horticulture and nursery industry professionals, educators, and garden writers. For more information about the PPA, visit www.perennialplant.org.

Thanks to Nicole Gibson and Elaine Lee of the AHS for help on the hardiness and heat zones.

For editorial support and assistance on this edition, many thanks to Christine Heilman, Jenny Siklós, Jane Perlmutter, Jennifer Williams, Katie Dock, Stephanie McCain, and Nicola Nieburg.

PHOTOGRAPHIC CREDITS

Dorling Kindersley would like to thank the following for their kind permission to reproduce their photographs:

(Key: a-above; b-below/bottom; c-center; f-far; l-left; r-right; t-top)

1 Andrew Lawson; 2 Marianne Majerus Photography: Designer: Piet Oudolf; 3 Picturesmiths Ltd: Roger Smith/ Killerton; 4–5 Andrew Lawson: Hadspen Gardens, Somerset; 6–7 John Glover; 8–9 Marianne Majerus Photography: Cherry Tree Lodge Nursery, Lancs.; 10–11 Andrew Lawson: Pensthorpe Waterfowl Park, Norfolk; 12–13 Jonathan Buckley: Designer: Christopher Lloyd, Great Dixter; 13 Bloompictures: (tl), Garden World Images: G Harland (t), judywhite/ GardenPhotos.com (tc); 14 Picturesmiths Ltd: Roger Smith/ Manor Farm Cottage (bl) Science Photo Library: Annie Haycock (tr); 14–15 Bloompictures; 15 Andrew Lawson: (tr) (br), Marianne Majerus Photography: (cr); 16 FLPA: (t); 16–17 naturepl.com: Georgette Douwma; 17 Alamy Images: Konrad Zelazowski (tc), Graham Rice/ GardenPhotos.com (tr); 18–19 Bloompictures; 19 Jonathan Buckley: Designers: Alan Gray and Graham Robeson, East Ruston Old Vicarage, Norfolk (br), GAP Photos Ltd: John Glover (tl); 20 Courtesy of Arley Hall, Cheshire: (b); John Glover: East Lambrook Manor, Somerset (tr), The Manor House, Upton Grey, Hampshire (tc); 21 Charles Mann: Dianne and Berry Cash (b), Diane L. Mattis: Designer: David Culp (t); 22 Jonathan Buckley: Designer: Christopher Lloyd, Great Dixter (l); 22–23 Andrew Lawson: Designer: Piet Oudolf, RHS Garden Wisley (b); 23 Jonathan Buckley: Designer: Maurice Green, Landor Road, Warwickshire (t); 26 Chris F. Burrows: (cl) (bl), The Garden Collection: Jonathan Buckley/ Waterperry Gardens, Oxon (cr), Marianne Majerus Photography: Tanglefoot, Hampshire (tr); 27 GAP Photos Ltd: John Glover (b); 28 Marianne Majerus Photography: Designer: Piet Oudolf; 29 Alamy Images: Ron Sutherland/GPL; 30–31 Marianne Majerus Photography: Hermannshof; 32 John Fielding: (bl); 33 Andrew Lawson: (bl); 34 Picturesmiths Ltd: Roger Smith/ Cotswold Wildlife Park & Gardens (br); 36 DK Images: Roger Smith (br); 37 Garden World Images: P. Lane (br); 41 Garden World Images: G. Harland (bl); 43 Picturesmiths Ltd: Roger Smith/ Hazel Court (cl), Roger Smith/ Pine Cottage Plants (cr) (br); 44 Picturesmiths Ltd: Roger Smith/ Holbrook Garden (tl), Roger Smith/ Pine Cottage Plants (bl), Roger Smith/ Bicton College (cl); 45 Garden Picture Library: J S Sira (tr), Picturesmiths Ltd: Roger Smith/ Manor Farm Cottage (tl); 48 Garden World Images: W.Halliday (tr); 49 Garden World

Images: (bl); 51 Garden World Images: (bc), R. Coates (ftr) (tr) (fcr), Garden Picture Library: Sunniva Harte (br), Howard Rice (cr), J S Sira (fcl) (ftl) (tl), Science Photo Library: Adrian Thomas (cl); 52 Picturesmiths Ltd: Roger Smith/Cotswold Wildlife Park & Gardens (tl); 53 Garden World Images: D. Gould (b); 54 David Constantine/ www.kobakoba.co.uk: (bl); 57 Chris F. Burrows: (t); 60 Garden World Images: E. Gabriel (c), P. Harcourt-Davies (tc), P. Harcourt-Davies (cr); 61 Picturesmiths Ltd: Roger Smith/ Manor Farm Cottage (br); 62 Graham Rice/GardenPhotos.com: (bl); 64 Garden World Images: A. Baggett (cl) (c), L. Cole (tl); 65 Clive Nichols: Hadspen Gardens, Somerset (tl); 66 Garden World Images: G. Harper (tl); 67 GAP Photos Ltd: Visions (br), Garden World Images: (bc); 69 Garden Picture Library: John Glover; 73 Garden World Images: D. Sams (cl); 74 Garden World Images: G. Harland (bl), Garden and Wildlife Matters: Steffie Shields (br); 78 Andrew Lawson: Waterperry Gardens, Oxon (br); 79 Garden World Images: (t); 85 Picturesmiths Ltd: Roger Smith/ Marwood Hill Gardens (tl), Roger Smith/ Rushfields of Ledbury (tr); 86 Graham Rice/GardenPhotos.com: (br); 88 Harpur Garden Library/Marcus Harpur: Designers: Piet Oudolf and Arne Maynard, RHS Chelsea 2000 (br); 89 DK Images: Roger Smith (tr) (cl) (bl), Photos Horticultural: (tl); 90 DK Images: Roger Smith (tl) (cl); 91 Seven Publishing Ltd: Sarah Cuttle (tr); 94 Graham Rice/GardenPhotos. com: (tl); 95 Picturesmiths Ltd: Roger Smith/Cotswold Garden Flowers (br); 99 Garden World Images: (tl); judywhite/GardenPhotos.com: (br); 100 Andrew Lawson: Hadspen Gardens, Somerset (tl); 103 Garden World Images: (c), F. Davis (b), Garden and Wildlife Matters: John Feltwell (tl); 104 Garden World Images: (bl), Harpur Garden Library: (fbr), Marianne Majerus Photography: (br); 105 Harpur Garden Library/Marcus Harpur (tl), Andrew Lawson: (tr); 106 Picturesmiths Ltd: Roger Smith/ Warren Hills Cottage (cl); 110 DK Images: Roger Smith (tr) (cr); 112 DK Images: Roger Smith (tl); 113 James Young: (c); 114 John Glover: (bl); 115 Jonathan Buckley: (tr), Science Photo Library: Adrian Thomas (cr); 118 Picturesmiths Ltd: Roger Smith/ Tinpenny Farm (bl); 124 GAP Photos Ltd: Richard Bloom (tr), Garden World Images: (cla) (cb) (b), G Harper (cra), T. Jennings (tc); 125 Eric Crichton Photos: (tr); 127 Harpur Garden Library/Jerry Harpur (tl), Photos Horticultural: (br); 128 Picturesmiths Ltd: Roger Smith/ White Windows (cr); 130 Andrew Lawson: (tr); 131 John Fielding: Blackthorn Nursery (tr), Harpur Garden Library/Jerry Harpur: Designer: Tom Hobbs (br), Plant Images/C. Grey-Wilson (bl); 132 Garden World Images: (bl); 133 Andrew Lawson: (tr); 134 GAP Photos Ltd: Richard Bloom (cr),

Garden World Images: (bl), Garden Picture Library: Linda Burgess (t), Andrew Lawson: (br); 135 Garden World Images: A. Baggett (bl); 136 Harpur Garden Library/Jerry Harpur: Designer: Linda Cochran, USA (tr), RHS Hyde Hall, Essex UK (br); 137 John Glover: RHS Wisley, Surrey (bl); 138 Photos Horticultural: (bl); 139 Garden World Images: (tl), Andrew Lawson/ Torie Chugg (c), Picturesmiths Ltd: Roger Smith/ Tinpenny Farm (cl); 140 Garden World Images: (tl), Picturesmiths Ltd: Roger Smith/ Ivycroft Plants (br); 142 Andrew Lawson: Bosvigo House, Cornwall (tl); 143 Picturesmiths Ltd: Roger Smith/ Ivycroft Plants (bl), Roger Smith/ Killerton (br); 144 GAP Photos Ltd: Neil Holmes (c), Garden World Images: L. Thomas (br); 146 Garden World Images: K. Howchin (cl); 148 Picturesmiths Ltd: Roger Smith/ Cotswold Garden Flowers (tl), Roger Smith/ Kestrel Cottage (tc); 149 Justyn Willsmore: (bl) (tr); 150 Dr David W. Bassett: (b); 152 John Glover: Great Dixter (br); 154 Dr David W Bassett; 156 Jerry Pavia Photography Inc: (tl); 158 DK Images: Roger Smith (br); 159 DK Images: Roger Smith (cr); 160 Andrew Lawson: (bl); 161 DK Images: Roger Smith (bl) (br) (tr), Picturesmiths Ltd: Roger Smith/ Penhow Nurseries (ca); 162 DK Images: Roger Smith (bl); 163 Garden World Images: D Gould (cb); 164 Andrew Lawson: (br); 169 Clive Nichols: Hadspen Garden, Somerset (l), Picturesmiths Ltd: Roger Smith/ Tinpenny Farm (tr); 170 Picturesmiths Ltd: Roger Smith/ Tinpenny Farm (bl); 171 Picturesmiths Ltd: Roger Smith/ Warren Hills Cottage (br); 174 Harpur Garden Library/Marcus Harpur: Harvey's Garden Plants, Bradfield, Suffolk (bl); 179 Andrew Lawson: (br); 180 Garden World Images: R Ditchfield (tr), G Harland (tl), G Harper (cl), A Shilling (br), C Wheeler (cr); 182 Garden World Images: (tl); 183 Garden World Images: Dr Alan Beaumont (tl); 184 John Glover: (bl), Andrew Lawson: (cl) (br); 187 Andrew Lawson: (br); 190 Andrew Lawson: Designer Piet Oudolf, Humme (br); 191 Timothy Walker: (b); 192 Garden World Images: R Coates (bl); 194 DK Images: John Fielding (cl), Andrew Lawson (tr); 195 Andrew Lawson: (b); Garden World Images: D. Gould (bl); 197 Garden Picture Library: J S Sira (ca); 198 Picturesmiths Ltd: Roger Smith/ Rushfields of Ledbury (br); 199 DK Images: Roger Smith (cl) (cr) (b); 200 DK Images: Roger Smith (tr), Andrew Lawson: Hadspen Garden, Somerset (bc); 201 DK Images: Deni Bown (bc), Andrew Lawson (tr), Roger Smith (br); 203 DK Images: Roger Smith (bc); 204 DK Images: Roger Smith (br), Kim Taylor & Jane Burton (t); 205 Jerry Pavia Photography Inc: (cr); 206 DK Images: Roger Smith (br), GAP Photos Ltd: Richard Bloom (bl) (tr); 207 DK Images: Roger Smith (br); 208 DK Images: Roger Smith (bl) (bc); 209 Photos Horticultural: (tr);

210 DK Images: Roger Smith (bl), **GAP Photos Ltd:** Visions (bc); **212 Eric Crichton Photos:** (tl); **213 DK Images:** Roger Smith (tl) (crb) (br), **Garden Picture Library:** Howard Rice (cl), **Andrew Lawson**/ Torie Chugg (bl), **Science Photo Library:** Anthony Sweeting (cr); **214 DK Images:** Roger Smith (tr); **215 DK Images:** Roger Smith (bl); **216 DK Images:** Roger Smith (bl) (bc) (br), **Garden World Images:** Jacqui Dracup (tc) (cra), L. Thomas (tr), John Swithinbank (cla); **218 DK Images:** Roger Smith (bc), **Garden World Images:** B Stojanovic (tr); **220 DK Images:** Roger Smith (tl) (tl); **221 DK Images:** Roger Smith (bc) (br); **222 DK Images:** Roger Smith (bl), **Garden Picture Library:** Chris Burrows (br), **Garden World Images:** D. Gould (b); **223 Garden World Images:** G Harper (tl), L. Thomas (tc); **224 Garden World Images:** (tr), **Harpur Garden Library**/Marcus Harpur: Harvey's Garden Plants, Bradfield, Suffolk (bl), **Andrew Lawson:** (br), **Clive Nichols:** (tl); **225 John Glover:** (b); **228 DK Images:** Roger Smith (b); **229 Garden World Images:** A. Baggett (br); **230 DK Images:** Roger Smith (tc) (tr), **judywhite/GardenPhotos.com:** (bl); **231 DK Images:** Roger Smith (tr); **233 Andrew Lawson:** (b); **234 DK Images:** Roger Smith (tr), **Mike Grant:** (cr); **235 DK Images:** Roger Smith (tr); **236 Graham Rice/GardenPhotos.com:** (cb) (cr) (cl) (bl) (br); **237 DK Images:** Roger Smith (tc); **238 Graham Rice/GardenPhotos.com:** (t) (b) (ca) (cb); **239 Graham Rice/GardenPhotos.com:** (ca); **240 Graham Rice/GardenPhotos.com:** (bl); **241 John P Peat:** (cra), **Ted Petit:** (tr); **242 DK Images:** Roger Smith (cl) (bl); **243 DK Images:** Roger Smith (br), **Photos Horticultural:** Glen Chantry Garden (t); **244 DK Images:** Roger Smith (tc) (cl); **245 DK Images:** Roger Smith; **247 DK Images:** Roger Smith (tc) (cr); **248 DK Images:** Roger Smith (br); **251 DK Images:** Roger Smith (br), **Charles Oliver:** (clb) (bl) (bc) (br); **252 Charles Oliver:** (tl) (cl); **253 Eric Crichton Photos:** (b), **Charles Oliver:** (tr); **254 Charles Oliver:** (tl) (cl) (bl) (br); **255 Charles Oliver:** (tr) (c); **256 DK Images:** Roger Smith (br); **259 Garden World Images:** G. Kidd (b); **260 DK Images:** Roger Smith (tr); **261 DK Images:** Roger Smith (cra); **262 Jerry Pavia Photography Inc:** (tl); **265 DK Images:** Roger Smith (clb); **266 DK Images:** Roger Smith (br); **268 DK Images:** Roger Smith (tl); **269 DK Images:** Roger Smith (br); **270 Andrew Lawson:** (b); **271 Chris F. Burrows:** (tr), **Picturesmiths Ltd:** Roger Smith/ Manor Farm Cottage (br), **Plant Images/C. Grey-Wilson:** (tl); **274 DK Images:** Roger Smith (b), **GAP Photos Ltd:** Richard Bloom (tc); **276 Claire Austin:** (bl) (br) (clb), **GAP Photos Ltd:** Richard Bloom (crb), Neil Holmes (tl) (cla), D. Gould (tr); **277 DK Images:** Roger Smith (c) (b), **GAP Photos Ltd:** Neil Homes (t); **278 Garden World Images:** Jackie

Knight (tl); **280 Claire Austin:** (br), **Picturesmiths Ltd:** Roger Smith/ Rushfields of Ledbury (cr); **281 DK Images:** Roger Smith (t) (b); **282 Andrew Lawson:** Designer Tim Reese (tl); **283 Claire Austin:** (br), **DK Images:** Roger Smith (tl) (tr); **284 Picturesmiths Ltd:** Roger Smith/ Manor Farm Cottage (tr), Roger Smith/ Tinpenny Farm (tl); **285 Picturesmiths Ltd:** Roger Smith/ Manor Farm Cottage (bc); **286 Picturesmiths Ltd:** Roger Smith/ Tinpenny Farm (tl); **287 Claire Austin:** (cr), **DK Images:** Roger Smith (cl) (bl) (br), **Picturesmiths Ltd:** Roger Smith/ Tinpenny Farm (tr), Roger Smith/ RNRS (tl); **288 DK Images:** Roger Smith (tl), **Picturesmiths Ltd:** Roger Smith/ Manor Farm Cottage (tr); **290 Garden World Images:** (cr), **Garden and Wildlife Matters:** Martin P. Land (tr), **John Glover** (bl); **291 Garden World Images:** F. Davis (cr), **Garden Picture Library:** Lynn Keddie (cra), **Holt Studios International:** M. Szadzuik/R. Zink/ FLPA (cl); **292 Science Photo Library:** Adrian Thomas (tc); **293 Garden World Images:** K. Howchin (t), L. Thomas (b); **295 Harpur Garden Library**/Jerry Harpur: Great Dixter (br); **297 Holt Studios International:** Peter Wilson/ FLPA (br); **299 Andrew Lawson:** (tl); **302 The Garden Collection:** Liz Eddison (c) (br), **Picturesmiths Ltd:** Roger Smith/ Manor Farm Cottage (cr); **304 Clive Nichols:** Butterstream, Eire (br); **306 DK Images:** Deni Bown (tr); **308 Picturesmiths Ltd:** Roger Smith/ Cotswold Garden Flowers (tl); **310 GAP Photos Ltd:** John Glover (bl), **Andrew Lawson:** (tr); **311 DK Images:** Bob Rundle (tc), **Andrew Lawson:** (r); **314 Andrew Lawson:** Sticky Wicket, Dorset (bl); **315 Garden World Images:** (cl) (c) (bl) (bc) (br), A. Graham (cr), C. Hawes (ftl) (tc); **316 DK Images:** Jerry Harpur (tl), **Andrew Lawson** (tr), **Picturesmiths Ltd:** Roger Smith (br); **320 Jerry Pavia Photography Inc:** (tc); **321 Picturesmiths Ltd:** Roger Smith/ Manor Farm Cottage (br), Roger Smith/ Tinpenny Farm (clb); **322 GAP Photos Ltd:** Visions (fbl) (bl), **Picturesmiths Ltd:** Roger Smith/ Manor Farm Cottage (crb); **323 Garden World Images:** Tony Cooper (tr); **325 Graham Rice/GardenPhotos.com:** (tr) (cr), **Plant Images/C. Grey-Wilson:** (cl); **326 Andrew Lawson:** (c), **Marianne Majerus Photography:** (r); **327 Garden World Images:** L. Cole (c); **328 Garden World Images:** (br); **329 Chris F. Burrows:** (br), **GAP Photos Ltd:** Neil Holmes (c), **Garden World Images:** Dr A. Beaumont (bc), L. Cole (tr); **331 Graham Rice/GardenPhotos.com:** (tl); **332 DK Images:** Roger Smith (bl), **Garden Picture Library:** Sunniva Harte (bc); **333 DK Images:** Roger Smith (cr); **334 Garden World Images:** R. Coates (br), D. Warner (bc); **335 Andrew Lawson:** Hadspen Garden, Somerset (tr); **336 DK Images:** Roger Smith (bl); **337 Garden World Images:** (tc); **338 Derek St Romaine:** (tl); **339 GAP Photos Ltd:** John Glover (bl); **341 DK Images:** Picturesmiths Ltd:

Harlow Carr (tl), Roger Smith (tr); **343 John Fielding:** (br); **345 judywhite/GardenPhotos.com:** (tr); **347 Garden World Images:** (tl) (bc); **350 DK Images:** Roger Smith (cl); **351 DK Images:** Roger Smith (clb), **Garden World Images:** G. Thompson (bc); **352 Clive Nichols:** Mottisfont Abbey, Hampshire (bl); **354 Jerry Pavia Photography Inc:** (tl); **355 DK Images:** Roger Smith (cla) (clb) (crb) (bl) (br); **356 DK Images:** Roger Smith (bl); **357 Garden World Images:** G. Harland (tc); **358 Garden World Images:** C. Hawes (bl), **Jerry Pavia Photography Inc:** (tr); **361 DK Images:** Roger Smith (clb); **362 DK Images:** Roger Smith (tr); **363 Andrew Lawson:** Eastgrove Cottage, Hereford (br); **367 Andrew Lawson:** (tc) (tr); **368 Photos Horticultural:** (bc); **371 Andrew Lawson:** (br); **372 DK Images:** Roger Smith (tr); **373 Garden World Images:** G. Kidd (bc), L. Thomas (br); **375 Mike Grant:** (tr); **377 Ray Cox:** (tr); **378 Andrew Lawson:** (br); **379 DK Images:** Roger Smith (cr), **Picturesmiths Ltd:** Roger Smith/ Brook Cottage Garden (br); **382 DK Images:** Roger Smith (cr); **383 Andrew Lawson:** Designer: Wendy Lauderdale (tl); **386 DK Images:** Roger Smith (cl); **387 Andrew Lawson:** RHS Rosemoor, Devon (tr); **388 GAP Photos Ltd:** Visions (bc); **390 Bob Brown/ Cotswold Garden Flowers:** (br), **GAP Photos Ltd:** John Glover (c), **Garden Picture Library:** Juliette Wade (bc), **Graham Rice/GardenPhotos.com:** cr); **391 DK Images:** Roger Smith (tc); **397 Andrew Lawson:** (tr); **398 Graham Rice/GardenPhotos.com: (**br); **400 DK Images:** Roger Smith (bl); **402 Chris F. Burrows:** (c); **403 Garden Picture Library:** Sunniva Harte (bl), Howard Rice/Monksilver Nursery (cr) (fcr) (fbr); **404 Clive Nichols:** Designer: Mark Brown (br); **408 Photos Horticultural: (**tl); **410 judywhite/ GardenPhotos.com:** (tr); **411 Garden Picture Library:** Didier Willery (br), **Andrew Lawson:** (tr), Lady Farm, Somerset (br); **413 judywhite/ GardenPhotos.com:** (tr); **417 Garden World Images:** B Stojanovic (bl); **419 Garden World Images:** D. Gould (b); **420 Garden World Images:** B.Mathews (b), G.Stokoe (cr); **422 GAP Photos Ltd:** Richard Bloom (c), John Glover (cr), Neil Holmes (tc), **Garden World Images:** L. Thomas (tr), S. Pearson (cl); **423 Garden World Images:** (t) (cr) (b), L. Thomas (cl); **424 Garden World Images:** L. Thomas (tc), **Picturesmiths Ltd:** Roger Smith/ Manor Farm Cottage (tl); **425 Garden World Images:** (br); **427 Garden World Images:** D. Gould (tl); **428 GAP Photos Ltd:** Richard Bloom (tl), Marcus Harpur (cr), Neil Holmes (br), **Garden World Images:** R. Coates (tr); **431 GAP Photos Ltd:** Richard Bloom (bl), Visions (bc) (cr) (br); **432 Garden World Images:** Tyrone (bc), **Harpur Garden Library**/Jerry Harpur: Beth Chatto (tr); **434 Clive Nichols:** Strybing Arboretum, California (bl); **435 Andrew Lawson:** (br); **436 GAP Photos Ltd:** Marcus

Harpur (bl), Neil Holmes (br), **Picturesmiths Ltd:** Roger Smith/ Tinpenny Farm (tl); **437 GAP Photos Ltd:** Jerry Harpur (ca), **Garden World Images:** (cb) (br), **Picturesmiths Ltd:** Roger Smith/ Manor Farm Cottage (bl); **438 Garden World Images:** (bl); **439 Picturesmiths Ltd:** Roger Smith/ Tinpenny Farm (cr); **440 Garden World Images:** B.Mathews (tr); **441 GAP Photos Ltd:** Neil Holmes (bc), **Photos Horticultural:** (bl); **443 Clive Nichols:** Cotswold Wildlife Park, Oxfordshire (br); **444 Garden World Images:** C. Fairweather (bl), Clive Nichols: (tr), Designer: Jenny Jowett (br), Designers: Pam Schwert/ S.Kreutzberger (tl); **445 Garden World Images:** (cl), John Glover: Los Gatos, California. Designer: Chris Jacobsen (tl), Clive Nichols: Designer: Mark Laurence (tr); **446 Chris F. Burrows:** (br), **Garden World Images:** (tc) (tr),V. Ingr (tl), L. Thomas (cl), **Picturesmiths Ltd:** Roger Smith/Cotswold Garden Flowers (cb), **Plant Images/C. Grey-Wilson:** (cr); **447 Andrew Lawson:** (b); **448 GAP Photos Ltd:** Neil Holmes (t), **Garden World Images:** R. Coates (b), G. Kidd (c); **449 GAP Photos Ltd:** Neil Holmes (bc),Visions (tl), **Garden World Images:** Dr A. Beaumont (br); **450 John Fielding:** (bl); **453 Martin Rickard:** (bc); **454 Charles Oliver:** (cl) (cr); **456 Garden World Images:** T. Sims (t); **458 Carole Drake:** (tr) (cra), **GAP Photos Ltd:** Visions (ftl), **Photos Horticultural:** (tl); **459 Garden World Images:** L. Cole (c), **Andrew Lawson:** (t) (b); **460 Graham Rice/ GardenPhotos.com:** (tr), **Andrew Lawson:** (bl); **461 Garden World Images:** L. Cole (bc); **464 Garden World Images:** L. Thomas (c), **Harpur Garden Library**/Marcus Harpur (bc); **465 Picturesmiths Ltd:** Roger Smith/ Cotswold Garden Flowers (br); **466 Garden World Images:** A. Baggett (br), **Photos Horticultural:** (bl); **467 Eric Crichton Photos:** (cr), **Garden Picture Library:** John Glover (tc), Sunniva Harte (br), **Andrew Lawson:** (bl), **Derek St Romaine:** (tr); **471 Eric Crichton Photos:** (tr); **474 Andrew Lawson:** Sticky Wicket, Dorset (bl); **477 Mike Hardman:** (tr) (cr) (tl); **478 Andrew Lawson:** (tl); **479 Garden World Images:** (b), **Mike Hardman:** (tr) (c) (cr); **480 Mike Hardman:** (t) (tc) (tr); **481 Mike Hardman:** (t) (cl) (bl) (bc); **483 Mike Hardman:** (t) (clb) (b); **484 GAP Photos Ltd:** Friedrich Strauss (tl), **Rob Suisted/Nature's Pic Images:** (bl); **485 GAP Photos Ltd:** A. Jones (bc), **Garden World Images:** C. Hawes (bl), **Jerry Pavia Photography Inc:** (br); **486 GAP Photos Ltd:** Visions (tr) (br), **Garden Picture Library:** John Glover (cr), **Andrew Lawson:** (bl); **487 Garden Picture Library:** (tr)

All other images © DK Images. For further information see: **www.dkimages.com**

Editor-in-Chief's Acknowledgments

First, I would like to thank all my contributors for their determination to make this book as accurate and as interesting as possible; many have also provided valuable advice in relation to plants on which they did not contribute text, and this also has been of great benefit. Linda Jones and her dedicated team at the Wisley Trials Office have been a regular and significant help to many involved with this book, as have the staff of the libraries at the RHS and at the Royal Botanic Gardens, Kew. The thoughtful judgment of members of the RHS Herbaceous Plant Committee, past and present, and especially those involved in judging trials of perennials, has been a constant source of wisdom over the years. The book has also benefited from the reservoir of knowledge among members and National Plant Collection® holders of the National Council for the Conservation of Plants and Gardens, and members of the Hardy Plant Society.

In addition, many individuals have been of help both to myself and to contributors: James Armitage, Claire Austin, Judy Barker, Paul Beardsley, Toby Bradshaw, Chris Brickell, Gene Bush, John Carter, Nathalie Casbas, Alan Cook, Roy Coombs, Tom Cope, Pat Edwards, Fergus Garrett, Liz Gilbert, Clive Groves, Russell Graham, Keith Hammett, Ian Hodgson, Masashi Igari, Vic Johnston, Paddy Kitchen, Christopher Lloyd, John Metcalf, Clare Morton, Andrew Norton, Rob Peace, Mark Roberts, Keith Sangster, Joe Sharman, John Snocken, Jane Sterndale-Bennett, Elizabeth Strangman, David Ward, Claire Wilson, and Trevor Wood.

I would also especially like to thank contributor Peter Barnes for his invaluable help on a number of botanical, horticultural, and editorial issues. The scientific staff at the RHS have provided help on a wide range of issues, and I particularly appreciate the advice of past and present members of the RHS Advisory Panel on Nomenclature and Taxonomy (APONAT) under the chairmanship of Alan Leslie, who individually and collectively have clarified many tricky issues to the great benefit of this book. Tony Lord, Consultant Editor of the *RHS Plant Finder*, and everyone on the *Plant Finder* team, deserve the gratitude of all home gardeners and professionals for, every year, producing the standard reference on the names of garden plants.

Many thanks to my friends at DK, and those who have moved on, for bringing this complicated book from an idea to what you hold in your hand: David Lamb, Mary-Clare Jerram, Anna Kruger, Linda Martin, and the teams of hard-working editors, designers, photographers, and picture researchers. Pam Brown and then Pippa Rubinstein, Jo Doran, and Katie Dock have managed the day-to-day progress of producing the book with professionalism and good humor; without them the book would have been much the poorer—and probably still wouldn't be finished. I would also like to thank Julie Goldsmith, Susannah Charlton, and Simon Maughan of RHS Publications for their help and support.

As ever, my agent Vivien Green handled business matters with her usual cheerful efficiency.

I'd also like to thank all my horticultural friends, on both sides of the Atlantic, for sharing their experiences and insights so freely. In particular I'd like to thank Brian Halliwell and Alan Cook for, in their very different ways, encouraging my earliest interest in perennials at Kew, and then Elizabeth Strangman, Graham Gough, and Christopher Lloyd for proving that dedicated plantsmanship can be such fun.

Finally I'd like to thank my wife Judy for so many things that I could not fit them all in, even into a book of this size.

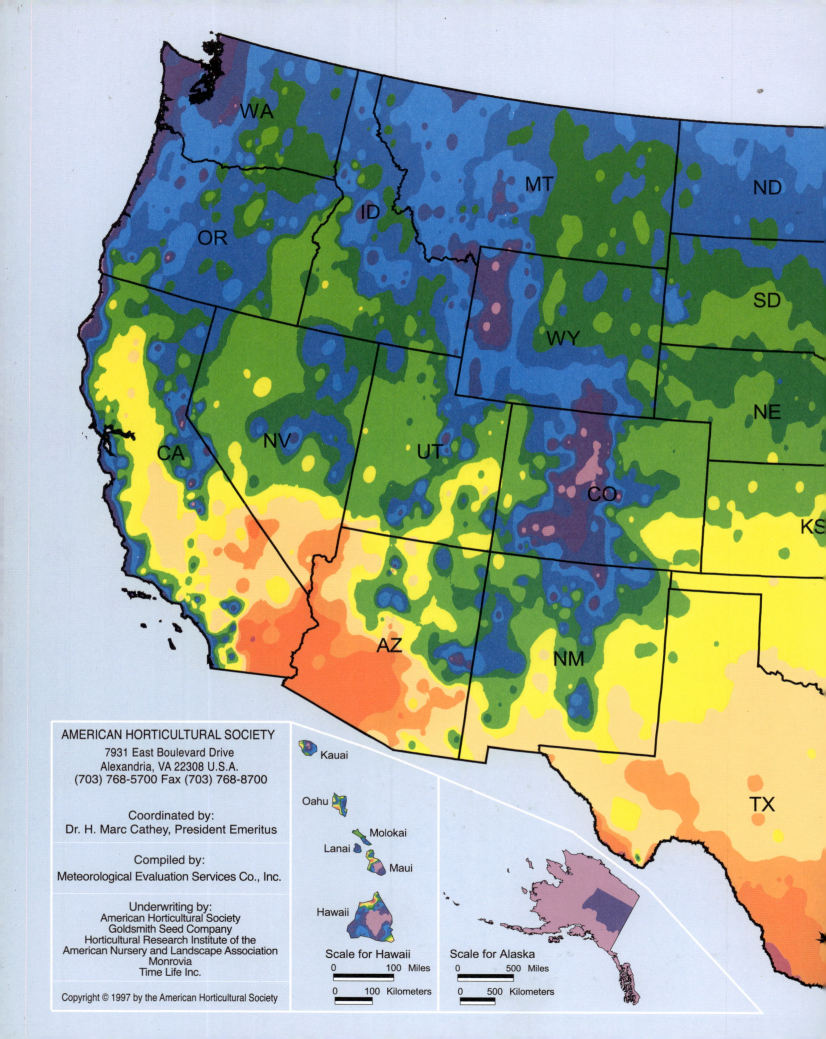

WA

OR

ID

MT

ND

SD

WY

NE

NV

CA

UT

CO

KS

AZ

NM

TX

Kauai

Oahu

Molokai

Lanai

Maui

Hawaii

AMERICAN HORTICULTURAL SOCIETY

7931 East Boulevard Drive
Alexandria, VA 22308 U.S.A.
(703) 768-5700 Fax (703) 768-8700

Coordinated by:
Dr. H. Marc Cathey, President Emeritus

Compiled by:
Meteorological Evaluation Services Co., Inc.

Underwriting by:
American Horticultural Society
Goldsmith Seed Company
Horticultural Research Institute of the
American Nursery and Landscape Association
Monrovia
Time Life Inc.

Scale for Hawaii

0   100   Miles

0   100   Kilometers

Scale for Alaska

0   500   Miles

0   500   Kilometers